ETHICS APPLIED

Editor
Michael L. Richardson
with
Karen K. White
St. Petersburg Junior College

McGraw-Hill, Inc.
College Custom Series

*New York St. Louis San Francisco Auckland Bogotá
Caracas Lisbon London Madrid Mexico Milan Montreal
New Delhi Paris San Juan Singapore Sydney Tokyo Toronto*

ETHICS APPLIED, Editor Michael L. Richardson with Karen K. White

ETHICS APPLIED

Copyright © 1995, 1993 by St. Petersburg Junior College, 8580 66th Stet North, Pinellas Park, Florida 34665. Copyright under International, Pan American, and Univerl Copyright Conventions. All rights reserved. No part of this book may be reproduced in any form witho permission in writing from the copyright holder. An exception is permitted for excerpts of 1,000 word r less used in a review, or, if copyright holder is properly credited, for up to two pages used in academ instruction.

4 5 6 7 8 9 0 DOC DOC 9 0 9 8 7

ISBN 07-055008-5

Library of Congress Cataloging-in-Publication Data

Ethics Applied/Editor Michael L. Richardson, 1944, with Karen K. White
ISBN No. 0-07-055008-5

     1.Ethics.   2.Ethics-History   3.Business Ethics
     4.Professional Ethics   5.Science and Ethics.   6.Social Ethics

McGraw-Hill's College Custom Series consists of products that are produced from canera-ready copy. Peer review, class testing, and accuracy are primarily the responsibility of the author(s).

Editor: Judy T. Ice
Cover Art: Jack Barrett
Cover Design: Diogenes Ruiz
Cartoons: Don Addis
Printer/Binder: R.R. Donnelley & Sons Company
Manufactured in the United States of America
First Edition, Second Printing, Summer 1994

Dedication

**To the students, faculty, trustees,
alumni and staff of St. Petersburg Junior College**

ACKNOWLEDGMENTS

In the fall of 1982 Paul Ylvisaker, then dean of the Harvard School of Business, addressed the Association of Governing Boards of Colleges and Universities. He challenged postsecondary education to do more in the study of ethics. In the audience was Thomas H. Gregory, former chairman of the Florida Commission on Ethics who subsequently became chairman of the District Board of Trustees of St. Petersburg Junior College. Gregory accepted the challenge. The college's president shared it with the college faculty. By early 1985, after careful planning, the college established a required course in Applied Ethics for Associate in Arts degree students. The college is indebted to the memory of Dr. Ylvisaker, now deceased, for his inspiration and guidance. Without his encouragement this textbook would not have been attempted.

Among the many who played vital roles in the book's creation are Dr. Emily Baker, Instructor-in-Charge of the Applied Ethics Department at the college; Dr. Carl M. Kuttler, Jr., SPJC president, whose vision and commitment made the project possible; trustees including Chairman Joseph H. Lang, Robert C. Young, Stanley A. Brandimore, Pamela Jo Davis, Demos A. Megaloudis – and Mac J. Williams, chairman, who died in the spring of 1993 as the book was being completed; Dr. Karen K. White, who guided the establishment of the department and the course, served as textbook project manager, and brought invaluable classroom expertise to assisting the editor in the book's creation.

The college also wishes to acknowledge the professional services of publisher's editor Judy Ice of McGraw-Hill, as well as these individuals who assisted in various ways from simple encouragement to detailed editing: Jim Moorhead, Robert Sullins, William Buck, James Olliver, David Henniger, Jonathan Isaacs, Shirley Crane, Jo Smith, Kim Corry, Charles McCoy, Gloria Bowens, Kathy Smolen, Tim Brock, Lynn Hammond, Shirley Hunter, Virginia Chilcote, Diogenes Ruiz, Will Ragsdale, William Martin, Edward Gebhard, Margaret Richardson and Bob White.

Especially the college appreciates the outstanding contributions of the authors, for their expertise, cooperation and enthusiasm.

PERMISSIONS

Society of Professional Journalists, "Code Of Ethics" (Adopted 1926; revised 1973, 1984, 1987). Reprinted with permission.

Reprinted with permission from Code for Nurses with Interpretive Statements, (c) 1985, American Nurses Association, Washington, DC.

Paul J. Friedman, Professor of Radiology and Dean for Academic Affairs, School of Medicine, University of California, San Diego. Reprinted with the permission of the author.

Aristotle, from "Nicomachean Ethics," edited by Terence Irwin 1985. Reprinted with the permission of Hackett Publishing Company, Inc., Indianapolis, IN and Cambridge, MA.

Joseph Butler, from Five Sermons, pp.48-49, edited by Stephen Darwall, 1983. Reprinted with the permission of Hackett Publishing Company, Inc., Indianapolis, IN and Cambridge, MA.

For permission to photocopy this selection, please contact Harvard University Press. Reprinted by permission of the publishers from FEDERAL CONFLICT OF INTEREST LAW by Bayless Manning, Cambridge, Mass.: Harvard University Press, Copyright (c) 1964 by the President and Fellows of Harvard College.

For permission to photocopy this selection, please contact Harvard University Press. Reprinted by permission of the publishers from IN A DIFFERENT VOICE by Carol Gilligan, Cambridge, Mass.: Harvard University Press, Copyright (c) 1982 by Carol Gilligan.

For permission to photocopy this selection, please contact Harvard University Press. Reprinted by permission of the publishers from MORALITY OF ABORTION: LEGAL AND HISTORICAL PERSPECTIVES by John T. Noonan, Cambridge, Mass.: Harvard University Press, Copyright (c) 1970 by the President and Fellows of Harvard College.

"Customer Service: The Last Word" April 1991; "The Mystery-Shopper Questionnaire" April 1992; "Paul Hawken Replies" July 1992. Reprinted with permission, Inc. Magazine, April 1991. Copyright (1991) by Goldhirsh Group, Inc., 38 Commercial Wharf, Boston, MA 02110.

Johnson & Johnson, "Our Credo." Reprinted with the permission of the company.

Bernard Williams, "A Critique of Utilitarianism" from Utilitarianism For and Against. Reprinted with the permission of Cambridge University Press.

Thomas Widner, "Ethics and the Investment Industry," America Magazine, December 12, 1987. Reprinted by permission of America Press, Inc.

"Copyright 1992, Josephson Institute." Reprinted by permission.

FOREWORD

American society, at least, has functioned in large measure for 200 years on a glorious assumption: Basic moral and ethical values would be inculcated by the institutions of family, community and religious organizations. That assumption, though increasingly tenuous, has worked. Public education, for the most part, has operated on the same assumption and added another: The *study* of those values occurs primarily in postgraduate education in the humanities and in liberal arts curricula. But the marketplace has been telling us for some time that many workers are not prepared for the *application* of these values in their daily jobs. Regularly, the news media parade before us an array of ethical failures in all walks of life. St. Petersburg Junior College was certainly among the first to require for graduation a course in applied ethics to address this marketplace need, and now, due to the college faculty's experience, the college has contributed a textbook on the subject.

It is a bold initiative, deep into the practical application of ethics to life's decisions, and wide in the range of issues it analyzes. It is a noble beginning: first, because there simply are few textbooks in *applied* ethics and secondly, because as a public institution-sponsored text, it may be unique. By bringing together authors from across the nation and from the appropriate disciplines and professions, it is a pioneering effort.

I strongly commend it to those institutions who are wrestling with the issue of values education. It is well past time higher education recognized that, in the world of work, at least, there, indeed, are some practices that are right and some that are wrong. The book, of course, skillfully avoids indoctrination, but it provides readers with a veritable banquet for ethical thought as well as appropriate instruction in how to apply one's beliefs to daily decisions.

America's community, junior and technical colleges, particularly responsive to their communities' needs, now have an advanced tool to stimulate teaching in critical thinking and ethical decision-making. They will find in *Ethics Applied* an instrument that will serve as a catalyst to begin their own efforts in this increasingly important field. It goes without saying that no college should tackle ethics instruction without this volume in its possession.

Let me be the first to congratulate the college's trustees, faculty, and its president, Dr. Carl M. Kuttler, Jr., for this significant undertaking in ethics education .

Dale Parnell
Professor, Oregon State University
Past President and Chief Executive Officer
American Association of Community Colleges

INTRODUCTION

Perhaps, in this instance, you *can* tell a book by its cover. Artist Jack Barrett, whose work has graced galleries in the U.S. and Canada, captures in a glance the theme of this text with his portrayal of a stoplight emphasizing the yellow light. Those who conceived the textbook and those who commissioned and produced it have no desire to tell anyone which direction to turn. Their objective is to cause a thoughtful pause that will lead readers to look and listen with heightened awareness of the risks and rewards of ethical decisions made in life. Look more closely at the St. Petersburg, Fla. artist's work and notice this is an *urban* stoplight hanging above a four-way intersection, reflecting the worldwide population shift from rural to urban life where a person encounters many mixed signals in the modern world. The bright yellow could be suggesting that when decisions are made, when ethics are applied, it happens best in the bright light of openness (this from the Sunshine State, whose "government in the sunshine" open-meetings and open-records laws have become models for ethical public decision-making).

Ethics is a discipline related to what is good and bad including moral duty and obligation, values and beliefs used in critical thinking about human problems. In *Ethics Applied*, the emphasis is on *applying* that thinking to daily decisions. The textbook was spawned by the vision and concern of the Applied Ethics faculty of St. Petersburg Junior College. Since the spring of 1985 this faculty has been teaching a course in Applied Ethics required for its Associate in Arts degree students. The concept of the course, as has been noted in the Acknowledgments, was inspired by Dr. Paul Ylvisaker, former dean of the Harvard School of Education, who in 1982 urged colleges and universities to require courses in ethics to meet an emerging societal need. The course was based, in part, on the work of the Hastings Center Institute for Society, Ethics and the Life Sciences, which directed a two-year study on "The Teaching of Ethics in Higher Education."

As faculty members pioneered the teaching of the course, they identified the need for a textbook and contributed heavily to the content and design of this one (three SPJC faculty are among the authors). The goal is to provide a text that has great breadth and balance, is written with clarity by an amalgam of academicians and practicing professionals for the postsecondary student experiencing a first taste of ethics study, and emphasizes actual application of ethics to daily decision-making. Considerable effort has been made to avoid indoctrination. Eight philosophical life-views are presented as exemplars (see Chapter 3) with the stipulation that the philosophies are only guideposts to assist students in recognizing and applying their own moral and ethical lights.

In 1959 the Ford Foundation and Carnegie Corporation jointly sponsored a study entitled "The Education of American Businessmen" (the sexism of that era is not unnoticed today). The study urged training for managers to develop "a personal philosophy or ethical foundation." American society has been rocked on its heels many times before and since due to moral failure and ethical scandal. The need for ethics in the marketplace has never been more pronounced; so it is that approximately 40 % of this text is devoted to marketplace ethics, but not to the exclusion of the classical ethical concerns of life-and-death decisions and social justice.

The book is divided into five parts. *Part I: The Dilemma Of Applied Ethics* is a wake-up call to the array of conflicts of interest that pose ethical challenges in every walk of life. It meets students where they are, with no assumption that they have given much thought to the issues of ethics. It relies heavily on actual news stories of recent vintage that depict the ethical traps into which many have fallen, from Ivan Boesky to Janet Cooke. It also explores the ethical implications of such apparently mundane transactions as paying for roof repairs.

Part II: The Examined Life takes up Socrates' warning of the dangers of an unexamined life and begins the examination process. Carefully, slowly, in an explanatory style, authors show students how to develop critical-thinking skills, to recognize behavior and to understand eight different moral philosophies, introduced as exemplars – moral theories and the accounts and stories from which they are drawn. In fact, Chapter 3 is the fulcrum of the book as to philosophical instruction, and it is expected that students will want to read it more than once. Moral development itself is explained so that students can recognize stages of moral awareness in decision-making. Finally, readers are outfitted with an understanding of patterns of moral reasoning, logic and syllogisms, making complete their equipment for ethical reasoning.

Part III: The Individual And Ethical Issues is subdivided into chapters dealing with issues in the family, societal and global contexts. It features chapters on abortion, death and dying, bioethics, sexual ethics, pornography, punishment, the environment, war and economic justice. These are often heavily devoted to information peculiar to each subject. In this way the book practices what it has instructed in earlier chapters – that, often, the key to ethical decision-making is a complete examination of the details and implications of an issue. Students are challenged to apply general moral principles to the problems inherent in these issues and to reach conclusions about them.

Part IV: "The Business Of America ..." – Ethics In The Marketplace is a five-chapter section full of information about the ethical implications of actions on the job – ranging from insider trading to sexual harassment to the actual communications of commerce. Here the student finds the grist of the business world – corporate culture, discrimination in the workplace, employee rights, the corporate social audit, unscrupulous advertising, employer and employee obligations, and more. Case studies include accounts of firms that have been successful in bringing ethical sensitivity into the workplace.

Part V: Institutional Responses To Ethical Conflicts includes two chapters special to the book. "Ethical Decision-Making In Public Office" at first may seem to be an oxymoron. It is offered as a challenge to students to see the potential of ethical public service as well as to assist in assessing the ethics of government decisions affecting us everyday. The final chapter is an examination of codes of ethics as they have evolved in the past two decades. It offers analytical tools for students who are likely to find themselves one day in a job that has a code of ethics attempting to regulate their behavior.

Chapters include selections from other authors and readings to add balance to the discussion of issues. A concluding guide, "For Further Inquiry," establishes a baseline for student learning activity but, of course, is not intended to supplant the instructor's primary role in teaching and learning.

An *Appendix, Comprehensive Glossary* and *Index* complete the text. These instruments are offered to assist instructor and student as they pursue the application of their own ethical standards in daily choices.

Perhaps uniquely, the text is illustrated with cartoons. The intent here obviously is not to suggest that the issues of life are frivolous but that a sense of humor goes a long way in promoting understanding and endurance.

It is important that students remember the purpose of the text is to equip them to recognize and use their own moral compasses – not to persuade them of any particular philosophical life-view. The authors recognize that both faculty and students have rights in the classroom which may be invoked if they are subjected to ridicule or harassment for their beliefs, and that these grievances may be appealed to faculty and administration or to local, state and federal human relations agencies and to state and federal courts.

A final note: A writer is often asked to describe in a few words the purpose of a book. "If you could sum up what this book is about," authors are asked, "what would you say?" We would be remiss if we did not attempt an answer, and it goes like this: "There are general moral principles in life. And there are human problems. A person can build self-confidence in taking control of problems by understanding and applying general moral principles, making ethical judgments and reaching conclusions about the most appropriate action to take in the various situations of life. When you do that, you have practiced applied ethics." To that end, the book is dedicated.

– The Editor

THE AUTHORS

(In order of their appearance in the textbook with chapter titles following.)

Roy Peter Clark, B.A. and M.A. Providence College, Ph.D. State University of New York at Stony Brook, is dean of the faculty at The Poynter Institute for Media Studies in St. Petersburg, which has centers on ethics, writing, graphics and broadcasting. The Long Island native teaches writing and has established a national newspaper writing center at Poynter to hold seminars and workshops for editors, reporters, students, and teachers from around the world. Among his publications is *Coaching Writers: Editors and Reporters Working Together*.

– Conflict Of Interest

Paul de Vries, M.A. and Ph.D. University of Virginia, holds the Endowed Chair in Ethics and the Marketplace at King's College, New York, and is president of the International Research Institute on Values Changes, based in New York, Beijing and Moscow. He is co-author of two recent books, *Ambitious Dreams*, and *The Taming of the Shrewd*

– The Ethics Construct, Dimensions Of Moral Development

David I. Seiple, Ph.D. Columbia University, M.T.S. Drew University Theological School, is director of research, Workplace Literacy Foundation and Adjunct Assistant Professor of Humanities at New York University, S.C.E. His publications include *John Dewey and the Aesthetics of Moral Intelligence* (forthcoming).

– Exemplars In The History Of Moral Theory, Punishment, War

Allen F. Plunkett Jr., B.A. and M.R.E. Providence College, is Associate Professor of Ethics at St. Petersburg Junior College where he teaches Applied Ethics, Logic and Philosophy and is sponsor of the Phi Theta Kappa Chapter at the Tarpon Springs Center. He is ethics consultant to Mease Hospital in Dunedin, Fla..

– Patterns Of Moral Reasoning

Nancy S. Jecker, M.A. Philosophy, Stanford University, M.A. and Ph.D. University of Washington, is associate professor at the University of Washington School of Medicine, Department of Medical History and Ethics. She is 1993 visiting fellow at the DeCamp Program in Ethics and the Life Sciences, Princeton University, and winner of the American Journal of Nursing 1992 Book of the Year as editor of *Aging and Ethics: Philosophical Problems in Gerontology*.

– Abortion

Robert Marlin Veatch, B.S. Purdue, M.S. California at San Francisco, B.D., M.A. and Ph.D. Harvard University, is director of the Kennedy Institute of Ethics at Georgetown University, Washington, D.C. He was a teaching fellow at Harvard and served as associate for medical ethics at The Hastings Center, Hastings-On-Hudson, N.Y., before he became professor of medical ethics at Georgetown. He is author of *Value-Freedom in Science and Technology; Death, Dying and the Biological Revolution; A Theory of Medical Ethics;* and *Case Studies in Medical Ethics.* He is the senior editor of the *Kennedy Institute of Ethics Journal* and has served on the editorial boards of the *Journal of the American Medical Association,* the *Journal of Medicine and Philosophy* and the *Encyclopedia of Bioethics.*

— **Death And Dying, Bioethics**

Susan Neiburg Terkel, B.S. Cornell University, is author of 12 books on social and medical issues, including *Abortion: Facing The Issues, Should Drugs Be Legalized?, Understanding Child Custody,* and *Ethics.* She was founder and director of Temple Beth Shalom School, Hudson, Ohio, and is on the faculty of the Earth Art School in the Cuyahoga Valley National Recreation Area. She has appeared on network radio and television to discuss ethics and moral education.

— **Sexual Ethics**

Emily Baker, M.S. Criminal Justice, University of Southern Mississippi, and J.D. Mississippi College School of Law, is instructor-in-charge of the St. Petersburg Junior College Ethics Department and instructor of Applied Ethics. For 16 years she presided as County Court Judge in Jackson County, Miss. She also has served as a consultant to the National Resource Center on Child Sex Abuse and as a trustee for the National Council of Juvenile and Family Court Judges.

— **Pornography**

Dorothy Kay Hall, Ph.D. Physical Geography, University of Maryland, is a scientist in the Laboratory for Hydrospheric Sciences at NASA/Goddard Space Flight Center. She has been involved in numerous field expeditions in the Arctic, and is the author of more than 100 technical publications, including a book dealing with remote sensing of the Arctic for global-environmental change studies.

— **The Environment**

Russell G. Wright, B.S. and Ed.D. Science Education, University of Maryland, is director of the Event-based Science Project of the Montgomery County Schools, Rockville, Md. In 1992 he received a $1.03-million National Science Foundation grant to develop an earth science curriculum and is the writer of 35 publications.

— **The Environment**

Ric S. Machuga, M.A. Philosophy, University of Oregon, M.A. History, California State University, is tenured professor of philosophy, ethics, and history at Butte College in Oroville, Calif. He was a Regents Fellow in Philosophy at the University of California. His publications include numerous critical essays in *Magill's Literary Annual* and elsewhere.

— **Economic Justice**

William Fred Edmonson, M.B.A. University of Southern Mississippi, Ed.D. University of Mississippi, former dean of instructional affairs at Itawamba Community College in Fulton, Miss., is president of Panola College in Carthage, Texas. He was selected "Outstanding Educator in America" while at North Florida Junior College (1971). His recent publications include *A Code of Ethics: Do Corporate Executives and Employees Need One?* and *A Content Analysis of Codes of Ethics and Related Documents from 100 of America's Largest Community, Junior and Technical Colleges.*

– Business And Professional Responsibility, Social Implications In Business, Employee Issues And Obligations

Joanna DiCarlo Wragg, B.A. Florida State University, a Pulitzer Prize-winning editorial writer and former associate editor of the *Miami Herald,* is vice president of Wragg & Casas Public Relations, a communications and public relations firm in Miami. Past president of the National Conference of Editorial Writers, where she also served as chair of the Professional Standards Committee, she is completing her master's in philosophy at the University of Miami. Formerly editorial director of WPLG-TV (ABC) Miami, she is a member of the Miami-Dade Community College Committee of 100 and a non-lawyer member of a Florida Bar Grievance Committee. **– Communications In Commerce**

Garland Thompson, J.D. Temple University School of Law, is a member of the Editorial Board of the *Baltimore Sun,* executive editor of *The Crisis,* official publication of the National Association for the Advancement of Colored People, and a Freedom Forum Fellow teaching at the University of Kansas. His interest and research contributed to a landmark Equal Employment Opportunity Commission case.

– Discrimination In The Workplace

Donald Pride, former press secretary for two-term Florida Governor and U.S. Senate candidate Reubin Askew, is director of investigations for the Chief Inspector General, Office of the Governor, State of Florida. Former editor of a New England daily newspaper, editorial writer and political writer for the *St. Petersburg Times* and columnist for the *Tampa Tribune,* he was a candidate for Florida Secretary of State.

– Ethical Decision-Making In Public Office

Michael Richardson, award-winning editor of editorials of the *St. Petersburg Evening Independent* and former member of the editorial board of the *St. Petersburg Times,* is executive assistant to the president of St. Petersburg Junior College. Author of a human rights documentary, *After Amin – The Bloody Pearl,* he is a past chairman of the professional standards committee of the National Conference of Editorial Writers (NCEW) and former president of the NCEW Foundation.

– Ethical Decision-Making In Public Office

Keith Goree, B.A. Harding University, M.A. Abilene Christian University, is associate professor of Applied Ethics and Honors Applied Ethics at St. Petersburg Junior College. He is currently writing an applied ethics text for secondary students. **– Codes Of Ethics**

Don Addis, B.A. University of Florida, is an editorial cartoonist for the *St. Petersburg Times,* and renown for his "Bent Offerings" distributed by Creators Syndicate Inc. His pungent wit has appeared in national publications for more than three decades. The prize-winning artist is the 1993 recipient of the first-place award for newspaper panel cartoons by the National Cartoonists Society. **– Cartoons**

CONTENTS

PART IV: 'THE BUSINESS OF AMERICA ...'

Part I

The Dilemma Of Applied Ethics

FREEDOM IS:

— CREATIVITY'S BATTERY MATE

Share it with someone you love.

What freedom means to me is... my business!

THE PROMISE OF FREEDOM is NOBLE, BUT GET IT IN WRITING.

— Choosing.

— TELLING THE GOV'T. WHERE TO GET OFF

— having a party, not obeying one.

— Telling a cop you disagree with him

— Visiting Georgia without a visa.

— walking in the halls without a permission slip —what John Wayne's

— A ROUND-TRIP TICKET TO SIBERIA

— The substance eagles breathe at 4,000 feet.

— coming home and finding it there. —what doesn't separate the rich from the poor.

— The most desirable form of turmoil.

— staying up with the grown-ups?

— LEGALIZED HUMAN DIGNITY

— THE RIGHT to HATE APPLE PIE IF YOU WANT TO.

— intellectual elbow room — anarchy with a brain.

— NEVER HAVING TO SAY "YOUR MAJESTY"

— THE ANTIDOTE FOR FEAR.

— Responsible Disorder.

— JUST ACROSS THE YARD AND OVER THE WALL

— FREEDOM IS ALIVE & WELL ABOARD THE CONSTITUTION

— a jealous lover

— COMMON SENSE

— it's own reward.

FREEDUM iz SPELLED auk Darn wae i want to

freedom is feeling the tug, ignoring the tug. Ask your pillow.

FREEDOM WORK BETTER IF YOU THINK OF IT AS OURS, NOT YOURS.

Freedom is tax exemption for the National Atheist Foundation.

Freedom is having the Power to do harm... and not using it.

absolute freedom is absolutely expensive

Like a Garden, it has to be cultivated.

FREEDOM? I'M INSANE TO IT!

Freedom's understated want to nothing. But it's too...

Keep your freedom out of my freedom

Is freedom ready for self government?

Freedom is HABIT-FORMING

FREEDOM MAKES YOUR POOR OPINION AS GOOD AS MY INSPIRED WISDOM

freedom is wearing a comb-kin cap while all around you are in hard hats.

LET FREEDOM ZING!

FREEDOM iz COMPLAINING about Not having enough freedom

freedom is being at Liberty to say

Freedom is only for those with the guts to live with it.

FREEDOM IS EASIER SAID THAN DONE

freedom is a communicable condition

Freedom is not a product, but a tool.

FREEDOM is MORE IMPORTANT THAN ORDER!

frees a crowd.

Chapter 1

Roy Peter Clark

CONFLICT OF INTEREST

"Justice, I think, is the tolerable accommodation of the conflicting interests of society, and I don't believe there is any royal road to attain such accommodations concretely."
— Learned Hand, former Chief Justice of the United States

"Once you give up integrity, the rest is a piece of cake."
— J.R. Ewing, of television's *Dallas* bragging on his ethics.

"For this is the journey that people make: To find themselves. If they fail in this, it doesn't matter much what else they find."
— adapted from James A. Michener, *The Fires of Spring*

After a big storm, you discover that the roof of your house leaks. You are concerned because times are tough. You don't want to deplete your savings by having to pay for costly roof repairs. Someone recommends Acme roofers to you: "Good work at a fair price."

Mr. Johnson of Acme inspects your roof. "You've got some pretty extensive damage," he says. "It'll take three days to fix it."

"How much?" you ask.

"Well, we'd usually get about $3,000 for this. But I'd be willing to do it for $1,500 – if you pay me in cash."

Roy Peter Clark, B.A. and M.A.,Providence College, Ph.D. State University of New York at Stony Brook, is dean of the faculty at the Poynter Institute for Media Studies, which has centers on ethics, writing, graphics and broadcasting.

You are surprised, and then relieved. What a good price! Much less than you expected. But suddenly you get a funny feeling in the pit of your stomach. "I wonder why he wants to be paid in cash?"

Welcome to the world of ethics! Even if you have integrity, doing the right thing may not be a piece of cake.

Doing The 'Right Thing'

Your roofer is a member, in good standing, of the underground economy. He lowers his price in exchange for cash payments. His goal is to avoid paying taxes. He is breaking the law, but he, and others like him, have been at this a long time, and there is little chance he will be caught. People don't turn him in for one simple reason: Self interest. He does provide good service at the best price in town. Americans appreciate a bargain, don't they?

Imagine that your roofer has offered you his best deal. Now consider these questions:

1. Is it wrong for you to pay him in cash?
2. Is it wrong for you to act in your family's self-interest? After all, times are hard.
3. What do you need to know about your roofer, his business, and his motives in order to make a good decision? How would you find out?
4. Is Mr. Johnson really doing any harm? Isn't he helping people by offering a low price?
5. Why is your stomach still hurting?

Your 'Gut Instinct'

We have several names for that pain in your stomach. Some call it your conscience. Some call it your sense of right and wrong. Others call it your gut reaction. Whatever it is, maybe it resides in another part of your body. Perhaps you hear a "warning bell" or see a "flashing light." We say that something "smells fishy." We look at a person in conflict and wonder, "What's eating him?"

Our body wisdom sends us signals about what is right and wrong. We may read volumes of philosophy or sit at the feet of a wise and ancient holy man. We may be young or old. Rich or poor. But for many of us, an ethical decision may begin not with an idea, but with a feeling in the gut. Ethics cannot end there, however. It must move from the gut to the heart, mind, and soul. We grow as ethical people by moving from our instinct to rules and guidelines that light the way.

Let's return to the tough decision we need to make about the repairs on our roof. We're suspicious of the roofer's motives, but what next? Maybe there are some "rules" that would help. Is there a law against paying Mr. Johnson in cash? Probably not, but there are laws against evading your taxes. Am I, in some way, helping him break the law? Am I his accomplice? Aren't there some "rules" that say "a person should not lie or steal," or "people should respect the legitimate authority of government," that is, they should pay their taxes?

The world of law is smaller than the world of ethics. You can follow the law and still do something wrong. Perhaps you have every legal right to pay in cash and take the lower price. You may have heard someone say this before: "Just because it's legal, doesn't make it right."

When we talk about ethics, we say that acts have consequences. You go out drinking, you get behind the wheel of a car, you hit someone, she dies, her children are left without a mother, their lives are changed forever, and so is yours.

There's a problem: You can't always see how things will turn out. Sometimes good comes out of bad. Terry Anderson, an American reporter taken hostage for almost seven years in Lebanon, often talks passionately about the good things that have happened to him as a result of his painful captivity. He would not have chosen that path or wished it on others, but fate, destiny, providence, whatever name we give those mysterious forces that shape our lives have unforeseen consequences. Good comes out of bad. Or in the words of an old religious saying: "God writes straight with crooked lines."

When some people talk about ethics, about what is right and wrong, they want to go beyond their gut instinct and even beyond the rules that they know. They want to follow a process of moral reasoning – moving from general moral principles to the facts of the matter – that ultimately leads them to a good conclusion. Learning to apply this process is central to the purpose of this book (and Chapters 2 and 5 amplify these processes). Such thinking often progresses through a series of questions. A news reporter, for example, working on a sensitive story may ask this series of questions:

1. What good will be accomplished by publishing this story?
2. How can I best fulfill my duty to inform citizens about this important issue?
3. Will anyone be hurt if I publish this?
4. Are there ways I can minimize that harm?

These questions often are best answered through consultation with others. The reporter who talks with editors, with sources, with other reporters, and with independent experts will benefit from the conversation. Good talk, especially with good people, often leads to good decisions.

In the Charles Schulz comic strip Lucy Makes A Pitch

Peanuts, a meeting occurs on the pitcher's mound:

> *Linus*: "If you strike out this last guy, Charlie Brown, you're going to make him very, very unhappy ... "
> *Lucy*: "That's right. Are you sure you want to bring unexpected grief into that poor kid's life?"
> *Charlie Brown*: "Just what I need ... ninth-inning ethics."

Ethics Sources

Our sense of right and wrong comes from many places. We may learn our sense of fairness, how to share, from growing up with brothers and sisters. We may go to church or synagogue and learn the Ten Commandments or the Sermon on the Mount. Years of schooling can teach us values such as hard work, honesty, and tolerance. Films and literature also are among those influences that help to form us with their powerful messages.

Advancement within our profession may lead us to embrace a special set of values and duties, which is sometimes call the "ethos" of that profession. The word "ethics" comes from that Greek word "ethos." It refers to "the guiding beliefs, standards, or ideals" that define a group or set it apart.

But the forces that shape us, and the institutions that nurture us, are complex and contradictory. An abusive family warps the child into a life of abuse. The church may teach us intolerance for the beliefs of others. Schools may teach us narrow-mindedness and pressure us to cheat in our classes. Not all literature or film, of course, appeals to our better instincts. And the only thing some people learn about ethics in their profession is how to avoid them.

The Root Of Our Children's Lack Of Morals

WASHINGTON – It all started in the late 1960s, says William Kilpatrick of Boston College, when we stripped education of its moral component.

The "it," of course, is the despicable behavior of our children. They are self-centered, self-indulgent and short-sighted. They are loyal to nothing, feel entitled to everything and are forever crying about what someone – a teacher, a group or "the system" – has done to them. Their moral standards, if one dares call them that, are of the most elastic sort.

How could such wonderful parents as ourselves have produced such awful offspring?

Kilpatrick, a professor of education, tries to tell us in his new book, *Why Johnny Can't Tell Right From Wrong: Moral Illiteracy and the Case for Character Education.*

He said the idea for the book came to him when the subject of the Ten Commandments came up in class and he decided to have his students recite them so he could list them on the board. They couldn't.

"It wasn't that *individuals* couldn't think of them all," he told a reporter for the *Boston Globe*. "The whole class working together to come up with the complete list couldn't do it."

He saw that episode as proof of what he came to call "moral illiteracy" – the failure of schools to teach, and of students to learn, the eternal verities. I see it in simpler terms: The Commandments are such a mixture of ethics and overlapping religious proscriptions that it's hard to remember them all – even while violating them.

My guess is that professor Kilpatrick and the *Globe* reporter couldn't have named all 10 before they got embarrassed and went and looked them up – and that you can't either. Try it, and you'll see what I mean.

But what of Kilpatrick's central point: That the cause of our downhill slide is the neglect of moral teachings in our schoolrooms?

The schools are as likely a culprit as any. I don't doubt that it was a serious mistake to abandon moral and ethical instruction (as opposed to instruction *about* morals and ethics). But it's not our only mistake, and a case could be made for any of a number of starting points for our – that is, our *children's* – awfulness. It all started (we could argue) with Reagan conservatives and their condonation of the economics of greed. How can our children be modest and compassionate when they have been taught by their national leadership that rich is good and poverty the just reward of sloth?

It all started with the liberal idea that how we feel is more important than what we do. Feeling is inherently individual, and to focus on how we feel is to free ourselves of concern for others (except insofar as looking after others makes us feel good about ourselves). The path from feeling to self-indulgence is short and smooth. You can get there – our children got there – without even thinking about it.

It all started with co-ed dorms. In the old days (our days) we were not left to our own impulsive devices. There were rules and structures and expectations that kept us from doing what everybody knew we were dying to do. The rules and expectations have changed utterly (can you imagine members of your high school class being urged by teachers and public officials to practice "safe sex"?). And the structures that used to save us the necessity of the hard choice (I'd love to, Bob, but where?) have been replaced by co-ed dorms.

It all started with right-on-red. The rules used to have clear and consistent meaning. Things were good or bad, right or wrong. Green meant "go," red meant "stop." Now everything is confused and conditional. Red means "stop, but if the street is relatively clear, or if you have confidence in your car's acceleration, go ahead and turn right."

The upshot is just what you'd expect. More and more people are merely almost stopping on red, and frightening numbers are going straight through on red. And the practice is not limited to driving. For growing numbers of people, ALL rules are marked with asterisks that tempt us (tempt our children) to stretch the limits to the breaking point.

It all started with the notion (first recorded in the Garden of Eden) that anything forbidden is, on that account, more desirable. But don't blame poor Adam and Eve.

It all started with Satan.

St. Petersburg Times, January 12, 1993
William Raspberry
Washington Post Writers Group

ETHICS IN THE CLASSROOM

To make this more practical, let's talk about something you already know a lot about: The ethics of the classroom. Do you know someone who has:

1. Looked on another student's test paper during an exam?
2. Copied a term paper word for word from another source, an act we call "plagiarism"?
3. Bought a term paper from a service and handed it in as his or her own?
4. Ripped a page out of a research journal, depriving others of that information?

These acts would violate most people's gut feelings of right and wrong. They probably go against the rules of the college. And it would be hard to imagine a process of reasoning that would justify them. Yet these are common acts, done out of laziness, carelessness, panic, frustration, or jealousy.

Ideally, a person who studies ethics would become a better person, but "doing" ethics and "being" ethical are not the same thing. You can master the knowledge in this book – and then steal the book! You can learn a process of moral reasoning that should lead to a good choice – and then make a bad one. Making real-life decisions will be difficult, even if you can make an A in your college ethics course.

Guilt-Free Lying Scares Teacher

Americans are so accustomed to being lied to by everyone, especially the government, that it's not surprising that school children have no shame in cheating and lying, according to Pasadena high school teacher Jonathan Schorr. A 1986 study found that 73 % of California high schoolers admitted to cheating at least once on a test, and a majority had done so more than a few times. – *L.A. Times* (LAT), 3/1/92

Ethics: Easier Said Than Done
Copyright 1992, Issue 17
The Joseph and Edna Josephson Institute of Ethics

ETHICS NEARER HOME

Some decisions in the classroom are harder than the ones listed above:

1. You know a student in first period has taken a test you will take at the end of the day. Should you talk with him about it?
2. The lady who lives next door is a teacher. She volunteers to "help" you with your term paper. What amount of help would be right to accept?
3. Should you bring your ethics teacher gifts to help you do well in the course?

And what about the ethical responsibilities of the teacher? Your instructor may receive a copy of this book for free, in the hope he may adopt it for his course. Is it right for him to sell it to a used book dealer? Instructors often make friends with some students. Is this a good thing to do? Perhaps an instructor asks a student out for a date. They are both adults and single. How do you feel about that? It is permissible by law (as of this writing), but is it ethically wise?

Ethics Program Developed

She was a high school math teacher, 24 years old, who was suffering emotionally because of her husband's accidental death. She really didn't have any close friends. Teaching took most of her time. When John was a sophomore, he was a student in her homeroom. When he was a junior, John was her algebra student. She did not teach John his senior year.

However when John, now 19 and a senior, began having trouble with calculus, he turned to her for tutoring. It wasn't long before the teacher realized she looked forward to the tutoring sessions. After a while, the relationship progressed. By the time John was in the last few months of his senior year, their relationship had developed into a sexual one.

When school officials discovered the relationship, the teacher was reported to the state Department of Education. Her job and her license to teach were in jeopardy. The teacher thought she had done nothing wrong. After all, she reasoned, John was 19. And his parents approved of their relationship, often inviting her over for meals and including her on family outings.

The 25 members of the state's Florida Education Standards Commission had a different reaction when they discussed this case and others at a recent meeting in Orlando where they previewed a new ethics course for educators. "It's purely a case of a teacher taking advantage of a situation," said Harold Parten, a commission member from Brevard County.

St. Petersburg Times, December 21, 1992
by Amelia Davis

We have a sense that professors have a duty to their students and to their profession. Professors need to work hard, keep up to date in their field of study, prepare classes well, be open to opinions other than their own, treat students fairly, not exploit their power and authority over students, and not play favorites, especially when it comes to evaluation and grading. You probably have never seen any of this written down before, but any violation of these principles is likely to make your stomach hurt.

Welcome to the world of ethics – even in your own classroom.

As The Stoplight Turns ...

When people first study ethics, they sometimes come into the class with this idea: There are so many gray areas in life, and so many different opinions, that decisions can only be made on a case-by-case basis. In the face of what is called "situational ethics," frustrated students throw up their hands and reject the hard work necessary to reach a good moral judgment.

It is true, there are few moral principles that apply without exception. Even the rule, "Thou shalt not kill," is not absolutely and universally enforced. We kill in self-defense. We kill in war. We electrocute heinous murderers. And many people think abortion, permitted by law, is the killing of a human being.

Many dilemmas are difficult to resolve because they involve the conflict of two competing good goals.

- It is good to deter people from murder.
- It is good not to kill.
- Capital punishment suggests it is difficult to do both.

- It is good for a journalist to inform the public about important social issues.
- It is good not to invade a person's privacy.
- In some cases it may be impossible for the journalist to carry out his public duty without harming others.

Consider the case of tennis star and social activist Arthur Ashe. He contracted the HIV virus through a blood transfusion during surgery. Years later, *USA Today* received a tip that Ashe had AIDS. Although the tip was reliable, the paper has a policy of not using unnamed sources, especially in important stories. A reporter went to Ashe about the story. Although Ashe wanted to retain his privacy, he announced in a news conference that he had AIDS and criticized the press for its pursuit of this story.

When they heard about this story, many people, including many journalists, had a gut reaction that something was wrong, that a good man, fighting a fatal illness, was harmed unnecessarily by an insensitive press. *USA Today* had its defenders. The argument went like this:

• Even a public figure like Ashe should be able to keep things to himself to protect his family.
• But Ashe built his reputation as an athlete and a social activist through publicity. He's a role model. The public cares about what happens to him.
• Yes, but shouldn't he have the right to decide the time and place to reveal his condition?
• Listen, AIDS is one of the great public health menaces of our lifetime. The press needs to help make people care about those with AIDS.
• Like it or not, there's still a stigma in our society about having the disease.
• We help remove the stigma by reporting fully on the nature of the illness, and we humanize its effects by showing lots of different kinds of people can get it.
• But you are hurting a person without good reason, just to sell newspapers. If you had ethics, you'd consider the consequences of your actions.
• You're wrong about us, and about the reaction. Most of the things that resulted from this report were good: People were informed that anyone can get the disease; Ashe was surrounded by sympathetic admirers; his role as a social activist was enhanced not weakened. He was even selected Sportsman of the Year by *Sports Illustrated.* The story about his award was titled, "The Eternal Example: Arthur Ashe epitomizes good works, devotion to family and unwavering grace under pressure." Ashe died early in 1993, and was widely eulogized as a great humanitarian and athlete.

Love 'Em And Leave 'Em

The message is simple: "You love us as athletes, but you are indifferent about us academically. You are more than willing to provide academic counselors and tutors to help several dozen athletes stay eligible, but you're not willing to take more black non-athletes, who will be better prepared than the athletes and have a better chance of graduating." – Arthur Ashe criticizing colleges for not providing many of their black athletes and non-athletes with a quality education.

Ethics: Easier Said Than Done, Issue 17

Think about the issues in this case, and discuss them in your class. If you were the reporter who got the tip, how would you have relieved that pain in your stomach?

In considering this case, think of ethics in two ways: red light and green light.

Ashe defenders are holding up a red light to the press. Stop pursuing this exploitative story lest you do unnecessary harm. Hold back. Restrain yourself.

Defenders of the newspaper believe that the purpose of the press is to publish – including, at times, painful and private things people want to hide. The green light shines for them. Inform the public. Tell difficult truths.

The language we use often reflects whether we are taking a red light or green light point of view:

Red light: Thou shalt not kill.
Green light: Love thy neighbor.

Red light: Don't miss Mass on Sunday.
Green light: Love God and worship him.

Red light: Don't cheat on your exams.

Green light: Be an honest, hard-working student.

And the *yellow light* that often flickers caution as we approach decisions, if we honor it, can cause us to pause and ponder the implications, to weigh the conflicting interests, to start a process of moral reasoning that leads to a decision we can feel is rational and defensible.

SELF-INTEREST: NOW OR LATER?

Our society honors those who act against their obvious self-interest. We admire those who reject the easy road, who make difficult sacrifices for the cause of justice. Mother Teresa and her followers reject material comforts and devote their lives to the service of the poor and dying in Calcutta, India. The struggle for racial justice led the Rev. Martin Luther King Jr. to the jails of Birmingham, and finally to his death by an assassin's bullet.

We can trace the values of selflessness far back into our culture, to the story of Socrates, the Greek philosopher, who submitted to execution by drinking hemlock rather than compromise his principles; and to the story of Jesus, who Christians believe suffered and died by crucifixion so that humankind might find eternal life.

Dr. Stockmann, the hero of Henrik Ibsen's play, "An Enemy of the People," risks his personal fortune, his reputation in the community, his family, and his personal safety in an effort to tell the citizens of his community one unpopular and agonizing truth: That the waters of the town's therapeutic warm springs are poisoned. No matter that the town's tourist economy is in jeopardy. The doctor yells out the truth, even in the face of ostracism and death: "The children are poisoned! The people are poisoned!"

WHEN MORAL LIGHTS GO OUT

The news of the day too often reveals a gloomier picture of human conduct, one in which the forces of self-interest or special interest subvert values such as altruism and sacrifice. The consequences of moral blindness can be devastating. If only Dr. Stockmann had been living in France in 1985.

In France, 1,200 hemophiliacs received blood transfusions that senior French health officials knew were contaminated with the HIV virus, which causes AIDS. More than 250 of these patients have died, and by 1992 others were continuing to die at the rate of one per week. As the Associated Press reported, prosecutors accused health officials of having "delayed buying U.S. equipment to test blood for HIV and decontaminate infected blood in order to give French researchers more time to develop their own methods."

The prosecutors described one health official as "a cold bully who refused to dispose of ... blood stocks, worth $40-million, even though they were contaminated." Greed, fear, blind adherence to bureaucracy, an unwillingness to challenge authority, and unethical definitions of acceptable risk – all conspired to create one of the great atrocities of the late 20th century.

One of the great moral outrages of all time occurred in France in 1992. A single outraged health official, enflamed with moral vision and willing to risk his own position for the greater good, might have saved more than 1,000 lives. Ethics is not a theoretical academic exercise. Ethics can save lives!

Think about this case, and imagine yourself as a French health official who has heard rumors about the existence of contaminated blood.

    1. Will you "blow the whistle" on the situation? How and under what circumstances?

    2. Who are the people who have a stake in your decisions?

    3. What are you willing to risk in making this decision: Your job? your friendships? your career? your personal safety?

Here are cases where exposing wrongdoing was vindicated:

Whistle-blowers Backed Up

Sometimes those who act by the courage of their convictions have power allies:

• The Labor Department has upheld the claim of Charles D. Varnadore, a technician at the Oak Ridge National Nuclear Laboratory in Tennessee, who said that after he complained about safety, plant managers retaliated by ordering him to do useless work in a room filled with toxic and radioactive chemicals. – *N.Y.Times* (NYT), 2/5/92

• The dismissal of veteran Pentagon scientist Aldric Saucier, who blew the whistle on abuses in the "Star Wars" program, was blocked by the Army Secretary and a review of the decision was ordered. – LAT, 2/23/92

Ethics: Easier Said Than Done, Issue 17

A 'KILLING' AT ANY COST?

The 1980s will become known as a period of great expansion for parts of the American economy. The value of stocks climbed and climbed. Huge corporations merged. Powerful investors acquired great companies through complicated financial maneuvers. The 1980s created many millionaires.

The desire to "make a killing" in the financial world also created, in the minds of many, a moral bankruptcy, the consequences of which have seeped into the 1990s. Our nation's high degree of indebtedness, some say, has threatened our children's financial future. As a result of poor management, government policy, bad loans, and corrupt practices, many savings and loans went broke. Some people lost their life's savings. The American taxpayer will have to pay the price, at a cost of hundreds of billions of dollars.

In the 1946 movie, "It's a Wonderful Life," Jimmy Stewart interrupts his honeymoon (with Donna Reed!) to face a crisis at the savings and loan owned by his family. Folks have heard rumors of financial problems and stage a run on the S&L, all determined to withdraw their money. Stewart pleads with them to keep confidence in their institution, and offers to pay them the best he can – with his wedding money!

This image of the honest, small-town businessman, has been replaced in America by the corrupt financial wizard and the acquisitive corporate raider, such as the one portrayed by Richard Gere in the 1990 film "Pretty Woman." Gere regains his moral compass with the help of a young streetwalker, played by Julia Roberts, who reveals to Gere that they are really in the same business: Prostituting themselves for money.

Some famous financial giants of the 1980s began the 1990s in prison as a result of ethical scandals and financial crimes such as "insider trading" and "influence peddling." The financial markets are at times so unstable, and so important to the nation's economic health, that laws have been established to protect their integrity. It is illegal, for example, to use special inside information of a company's plans in order to invest in that company and profit from a stock deal.

Conflicts Of Interest

When a person faces conflicting loyalties, such as those cited above – between public safety and the profit of one's company, between public health and one's professional standing, between personal profit and the integrity of the company – it is called a "conflict of interest," a very important idea in the study of ethics.

To take the concept from the theoretical to the practical, let's consider some rulings of the Florida Commission on Ethics, which renders advisory opinions to public officials concerned about ethical conflicts of interest, among other issues:

Florida Commission On Ethics, Advisory Opinions, Summary Excerpts Of Actual Cases

CEO 89-24. (June 14, 1989)

CONFLICT OF INTEREST: A certified public accountant who serves on the State Board of Independent Colleges and Universities would violate Section 112.313(7)(a), Florida Statutes, were his firm to provide accounting services to colleges and universities under the regulation of the Board. Section 112.313(6), Florida Statutes, could be violated if he were to use his position as Board member in an attempt to solicit business from entities under the Board's regulation. CEO 86-37 and 85-14 are referenced.

CEO 90-35. (April 26, 1990)

CONFLICT OF INTEREST: A prohibited conflict of interest would be created under Section 112.313(7), Florida Statutes, were a city public works director, whose department is responsible for the erection and maintenance of street signs, to own 80% of the stock of a corporation which sells street signs to developers for use within the city. The public works director has regulatory powers over developments within the city which would conflict with his private interests in selling signs to the developers of these projects.

CEO 90-54. (July 27, 1990)

CONFLICT OF INTEREST: Sections 112.313(3), and 112.313(7), Florida Statutes, prohibit a city council member, who is also the President and majority stockholder of a solid waste disposal company, from purchasing waste disposal services from his company for the city. Section 112.313(12), Florida Statutes, provides exceptions to this situation. Additionally, the council member is prohibited from voting on any proposed purchase of solid waste disposal services from his company because such a measure would inure to the council member's special private gain.

CEO 90-62. (September 7, 1990)

ANTI-NEPOTISM: Section 112.313(5), Florida Statutes, prohibits a city police chief from appointing, employing, promoting, or advancing his father to a position in the city police department. However, when the father was employed with the police department prior to the time that the police chief assumed his position, the father's employment would be grandfathered in. So long as the father were not promoted or advanced subsequently, the anti-nepotism law does not preclude the police chief from supervising his father. As favoritism in the terms or conditions of the father's employment may violate Section 112.313(6), Florida Statutes, the police chief should be cautioned against misuse of his official position to benefit his father.

CEO 91-40. (July 19, 1991)

CONFLICT OF INTEREST: A prohibited conflict of interest is created where a city police officer installs home burglar alarm systems during his off-duty hours for a home burglar alarm business which he co-owns. Under Section 112.313(7)(a), Florida Statutes, a temptation to dishonor is present due to the tension between the officer's interest in promoting and protecting his products, services, and customers and the performance of his public duties in enforcing a burglar alarm ordinance. CEO 91-22, CEO 85-22, CEO 82-23, CEO 81-76, and CEO 81-67 are referenced.

CEO 91-65. (December 6, 1991)

CONFLICT OF INTEREST: A prohibited conflict of interest exists under Section 112.313(7)(a), Florida Statutes, when a school psychologist engages in a private practice in which he gives counseling, therapy, consultation, and psychoeducational evaluations to students of the school district which employs him and to their parents. The Commission has advised in prior opinions that qualified D.H.R.S. and Department of Corrections personnel were not prohibited from engaging in private psychiatric or psychological practices where the personnel did not accept as clients or patients those persons eligible for services through these Departments, and referrals were not accepted from Department personnel. The same would apply to school psychologists; however, here the interests of the school psychologists and the nature of their private responsibilities coincide with their public duties and responsibilities to "tempt dishonor," thereby resulting in their possible disregard of their public duties and the public interest.

A *St. Petersburg Times* editorial (January 9, 1993) discusses how easily unethical practices can lead down a slippery slope into a swamp of fraud and institutional decay:

Michael Milken, the junk bond genius behind Wall Street's biggest, boldest securities fraud ever, is out of jail after just 22 months .... On March 2, he will be free to return home, with only community service to stand between him and full enjoyment of his estimated $500-million fortune.

In retrospect, Milken seems the archetype of a 1980s villain – brilliant, ruthless and impeccably self-interested. The high-risk bond market he created was a significant factor in weakening the savings and loan system.

Milken 'earned' $550-million in 1987 with his bond schemes, a feat that inspired a kind of suicidal emulation, not the suspicion it deserved. The sobering fact is that his actions were not judged according to an ethical standard at the time ....

By 1990, Milken had admitted to six felonies, and hundreds of financial institutions were in crisis. Trickle-down economics was revealed to be a joke, and not a very funny one at that.

While many small investors will never recover from the madness of the '80s, Milken made a fortune .... Looked at another way, Milken got to keep more than $700,000 for each day he spent behind bars.

Milken can never return to work in the securities industry, but there are no restrictions on how he can invest his money. A friend has been quoted as saying that the reformed financier is planning to donate heavily to education, or perhaps to the riot-damaged sections of Los Angeles.

Those are two good causes for a citizen of the 1990s. Time will tell if Michael Milken is truly such a man.

A breach of ethics can occur on a very personal level, between you and your roofer. Corrupt practices can also distort an entire economy and threaten the standard of living of a whole society. Another demonstration of such conflicts occurred in America's savings and loan industry:

KEATING FIVE

Life In An Ethical Vacuum

"There's nothing left for me of things that used to be. Government is supposed to serve and protect, but who? Those who can gather the most savings from retired people? It takes billions to fill the pockets of 'spendocrats.'" – suicide note of Anthony Elliot.

Anthony Elliot had intended to leave his money to an organization that serves abused children. Instead, the 89-year-old retired accountant slit his wrists and forearms Nov. 26 in Burbank, Calif., having seen his savings junk-bonded into oblivion by Lincoln Savings and Loan Association, under the direction of owner Charles Keating. Elliot lost $200,000 and in his suicide note blamed federal regulators for his loss.

But the blame goes not to a single source. Certainly blame for Lincoln's failure must be put on Keating, whose questionable business practices, regulators say, included an accounting scam to send big but unearned dividends to an associated company and "file-stuffing" to correct the paper trail.

And blame goes, as well, to the federal bank regulators, who did not act more quickly against Lincoln before seizing it in April 1989.

But the blame must rest, too, with the so-called "Keating Five." As the hearings in the Senate Ethics Committee continue to show, pressure was put on bank regulators not to do their jobs by U.S. senators intervening on the behalf of Keating, a big-time contributor to their campaigns and causes.

Tallahassee Democrat
December 6, 1990

Some of that excess was explained by a prominent American business leader, R. J. Haayen, Chairman and CEO, Allstate Insurance Company, in a 1988 speech:

"If the Seventies were the 'Me Decade,' then some say the Eighties, and perhaps the Nineties, should be called the 'Mine Decade.' Greed is in, we are told. Everyone wants to be what one writer calls 'the honcho with the condo and the limo ... and lots of dough.' And they don't much care how they get it.

"Well, I think that particular media portrait is a little overdrawn. If everyone is so greedy and unprincipled today, why has the percentage of charitable giving by individuals and businesses increased dramatically during this decade? And why, in a recent poll, did nearly half of those interviewed say they were *personally* involved in charity or volunteer work?

"And what about the hundreds of Wall Street whiz kids who *weren't* arrested?

"But if the doings of Ivan Boesky and his ilk are relatively rare, they nevertheless have focused our national attention on what is and isn't acceptable business behavior. So this is an excellent time to be discussing the question of corporate ethics in America."

Consider another commentary and examples of this trend:

Milken's After-Prison Profit

Jailed financier Michael Milken and his former firm, Drexel Burnham Lambert Inc., settled more than 150 lawsuits for a total of $1.3-billion, including fines already paid. After paying a total of $900-million in fines, Milken is left with an estimated personal fortune of $125-million and a family fortune of about $500-million. The Federal Deposit Insurance Corp. and the Resolution Trust Corp. will split about $500-million of the proceeds. They had sued Milken and many of his former Drexel colleagues because many of the failed S&L's taken over by federal regulators had invested heavily in junk bonds peddled by Milken. – *L.A.Times*, 3/10/92, 2/28/92; *Wall Street Journal* (WSJ) 1/22/92; NYT, 3/6/92, 1/27/92, 1/28/92

Ethics: Easier Said Than Done, Issue 17

YOUR INTEREST, MY INTEREST

You may never become a billionaire or influence the future of great financial institutions, but, chances are, early in your professional life, you will confront one of the most common, and most serious, of ethical dilemmas: Conflict of interest.

Remember this important term. If you work in journalism, in criminal justice, in medicine, in business, in government, in almost any job, you will encounter a conflict of interest. Most people fail to see these conflicts. Instead, they trip over them, bruising their reputations and damaging the integrity and credibility of their professions.

It is easier to illustrate examples of conflict of interest than to define it:

A JOURNALIST'S SCENARIO

Imagine that you are a journalist writing an opinion column about a new city park that will be built either in the East End or the West End of town. The park will raise property values wherever it is built. You write passionately about the need to build the park in the often neglected West End as a source of civic pride and a safe place for folks to gather.

There is only one problem: YOU live in the West End. That means YOU have a conflict of interest. Such a conflict comes from what ethicist Bob Steele describes as "competing loyalties." You should be loyal, as a journalist, to fair and even-handed reporting and analysis, for the public good. You are also loyal to your neighborhood, to your friends who live there, and to your family's standard of living.

In cases of conflict of interest, we often learn that "appearances" are as important as "reality."

Imagine that you are a reader from the East End. You want a park in your neighborhood, too, but now the newspaper is arguing to put it across town. Then you hear a rumor: "Oh, that columnist from the *Tribune*. He's a West Ender! The fix is in. We never got a fair shot. I've heard that the publisher lives on the West End, too! Those guys are just in it for themselves."

Even if the columnist has taken his own biases into account and researched with care and written with the intention to be fair, he cannot avoid the appearance of conflict.

Put yourself in the place of the editor of this columnist. Having read this book(!) you recognize the conflict of interest. Imagine a conversation with the columnist in which you look for escape routes to avoid the traps of conflict of interest. You have the best intentions. You want to express a strong opinion on an important public issue. You want to avoid conflict of interest, and even the appearance of conflict.

> **Consider and discuss these solutions:**
>
> 1. **Disclose, in the newspaper, the nature of the columnist's conflict. He should acknowledge early that he is a West Ender, and use his knowledge of the area to build his case. He should also invite responses from the East Enders.**
> 2. **If he is unwilling to reveal his conflict, see if you can find an alternate writer, who is not a stakeholder in the outcome of the issue.**
> 3. **Better yet, see if you can find a writer who lives on the East End, who is willing to make the case for the West End. No one speaks in a more powerful voice than when speaking against obvious self-interest. "I've lived my whole life on the East End, but I know in my heart that this city needs to invest its resources on the West End."**

You don't need to be Gandhi or Jesus Christ or Martin Luther King Jr. to act powerfully against immediate self-interest for the larger good. Real-life illustrations appear with the next edition of your newspaper:

News/Business Wall Crumbles

The wall that has traditionally separated the news and business sides of newspapers continues to come down brick by brick. The recession has taken a serious toll on businesses and has had a peripheral effect on newspapers – in order to keep advertisers, newspapers are increasingly catering to them by toning down or not running critical articles. A forthcoming report by the nonprofit Center for the Study of Commercialism that examined more than 50 cases of stories allegedly being killed or downplayed by the news media to appease advertisers concludes that advertiser favoritism is widespread and that the problem has been worsened by the recession. – WSJ, 2/6/92; *Editor and Publisher* (E&P), 1/18/92

Ethics: Easier Said Than Done, Issue 17

Columnist Admits His Failings

I was arrested for (driving under the influence) ... at a police roadblock. Blew a .21 (blood alcohol test), more than twice the state's measure of conclusive intoxication. I am free on bond awaiting trial. Although I didn't injure anyone, I realize more with each passing hour how many people I hurt – my friends, my children ... . – Tom Opdyke, a traffic columnist for the *Atlanta Journal and Constitution (AJ/AC)* whose confession was a positive sign of accountability. – AJ/AC, 3/1/92

Ethics: Easier Said Than Done, Issue 17

Plagiarism Plagues Texas Daily

The cost of exposed plagiarism can be steep because it erodes a paper's stock in trade – credibility. Just ask James Walker, who resigned after 13 years at The Fort Worth *Star-Telegram* after lifting quotes from a TV report and another newspaper article without attribution. On the other side of the same newsroom, editorialist Bill Youngblood was suspended for one week after he wrote an unsigned editorial that borrowed an unattributed passage from a New York *Times* opinion piece. – E&P, 1/18/92

Ethics: Easier Said Than Done, Issue 17

The Cost Of Freebies

The editor of the *Newport* (R.I.) *Daily News*, a past ethics chairman of the Society of Professional Journalists, took the high ground in refusing a trip paid for by the Walt Disney Co. to cover the anniversary of Disney World. Unfortunately, two days after he explained his decision in a column, his paper trumpeted the success of the Newport County Convention and Visitor's Bureau in enticing New York travel writers to the area with free lunches, gifts, and expense-paid visits. – CJR, Jan./Feb. 1992

Ethics: Easier Said Than Done, Issue 17

A MATTER OF TRUST

You have studied hard in college and worked hard in your career and risen to a position of influence in your community as a successful corporate attorney. You enjoy donating your time and energy to non-profit and charitable organizations, one of which is the local community college.

You have accepted a position as a member of the Board of Trustees, and you influence the President of the college, the other board members, and the direction of the entire institution. As a successful corporate lawyer, you have many important clients. A large construction company has retained your services for 10 years. You represent this company in many important business deals, and their success has contributed to your success.

The community college is about to undertake a 10-year project to expand the campus, a project that, when completed, will require the construction of three classroom buildings, a library expansion, and a student union. The construction company you work for plans to compete for this job. It will offer, along with six other contractors, a bid to do the work. You have a conflict of interest. Do you see it?

Consider and discuss the following alternatives:

> 1. Resign immediately from the Board of Trustees.
> 2. Tell your construction client you can no longer represent them.
> 3. Don't bother to reveal the nature of your conflict. You know you are an honorable person, and you are experienced enough to choose what is right.
> 4. Disclose the nature of your conflict as quickly and as widely as possible.
> 5. Consult state law and the state bar association to find guidelines governing such conflicts.
> 6. Choose not to vote on any question in which you face a conflict.

Now imagine yourself as the president of the construction company. Consider and discuss the implications of these choices:

> 1. Fire your attorney.
> 2. Ask him to resign from the Board of Trustees.
> 3. Ask him to lobby hard so that your company can gain the contract.
> 4. Ask him to feed you information so that you can offer a bid that is lower than the rest, but high enough to maximize profits.
> 5. Ask for a meeting with the Board to discuss the potential conflicts.
> 6. Consult experts on business ethics.

In pondering your decisions, consider the following thoughts about the ethics of college trustees, from the summer 1989 edition of the *Trustee Quarterly of the Association of Community College Trustees*. Read them as a guide to solving the problems in the above case studies. Do they shed any light?

THE LEGAL PROFESSION

Lawyers encounter conflicts of interest every day, some subtle, some blatant:

Should Lawyers Snitch On Clients?

In what may be a watershed for the privileged relationship between lawyers and their clients, the Manhattan law firm of Kaye, Scholer, Fierman, Hays & Handler paid $41-million to settle a $275-million Federal lawsuit that charged the giant firm and three of its partners with deceiving regulators by withholding harmful information about their client Charles H. Keating and his defunct Lincoln Savings & Loan. For the first time, the Government used racketeering statutes to freeze the assets of a law firm, essentially threatening the firm with bankruptcy until it would settle. Critics saw the Federal use of RICO laws as akin to extortion and a dangerous attack on attorney-client privilege. A *New York Times* editorial questioned why the government "treated the firm like a potential fugitive." But the government argued that a lawyer's ethical obligation to expose its client's lies also applies during the regulatory process and that when a client is supported by the taxpayers, as Keating's bank was, the lawyer's obligation is to the public as well as his client. – *Newsweek* (N), 3/23/92; NYT, 3/3, 3/5, 3/10, 3/13/92

Ethics: Easier Said Than Done, Issue 17

PHYSICIAN, HEAL THYSELF

In thinking about conflict of interest, you've played the role of journalist, lawyer, and business person. Now you have a chance to be a physician. You are the best and most successful "knee doctor" in the city, a specialist in athletic injuries. You have built such a large practice that you can afford to invest in a new business venture. You form a business partnership with an old friend who is a physical therapist. Together you construct "Sports Health," a place where people can work out, stay fit, or undergo physical therapy after an accident or injury.

If you can already see the vague outline of a conflict of interest, you are, indeed, learning about ethics. Let's give our knee doctor the benefit of the doubt. Imagine him as a person who has the concern of his patients foremost in his mind. He has found a way, he thinks, to invest in better care for his patients. Let's read his mind:

"I've invested in this 'Sports Health' because I wanted to create a place where my patients could get the best possible physical therapy at a fair price. We only buy the best equipment, and we only hire the most experienced therapists. Sure, I'll make a profit, but it's a fair one. I've seen other facilities. I know that 'Sports Health' offers my patients the best chance for rehabilitation. I should get praise for investing in my community this way. I shouldn't be condemned as some self-serving ethical criminal."

Now, let's consider this case. Imagine you are a patient of this doctor. He wants to refer you to "Sports Health."

1. What information would you need from him in determining whether to take his advice?
2. Do you think states should make such self-referrals illegal?
3. Conduct a debate in which you defend this doctor against a legislator who wants to ban such practices?
4. Can you think of analogous examples of self-referral in other businesses or professions?

Here are some other cases:

Taking Care Of Business

Prompting charges of conflict of interest, self-dealing and fraud from regulators and from within the profession itself, many doctors are placing in jeopardy their duties of loyalty and independent judgment by referring patients to facilities in which they have a (usually undisclosed) part ownership. There is growing evidence that doctor-owned clinics generally charge more and perform more unnecessary procedures per patient than facilities without doctors as investors. The Center for Health Policy Studies estimates that these kinds of services are adding half a billion dollars to health care costs every year in Florida alone. – Newsday, 3/30/92

Ethics: Easier Said Than Done, Issue 17

Patients' Records A Gold Mine

Doctors and pharmacists routinely open their confidential patient records to data-collectors that sell them to pharmaceutical companies anxious to know exactly how their products are selling. Even though patients' names are supposedly deleted, critics say that those entrusted with medical records have no right to hand them over, without patients' knowledge or consent, to an unregulated industry. – WSJ, 2/27/92

Ethics: Easier Said Than Done, Issue 17

In The 'Public Interest'

Lawmakers and other governmental employees have special ethical concerns because citizens expect them to act in the public interest. Money and power can help build schools, shelter the homeless, and cure disease, but money and power are also corrupting influences that, at times, test the moral stamina of the most upright governmental official.

Here's an example:

Regulators Like To Go First Class

Dallas city council members and members of the Dallas/Fort Worth International Airport Board frequently received free seating upgrades from the airlines from coach to first class – until the city attorney's office pointed out that they risked breaking conflict of interest laws. – *Dallas Morning News* (DMN), 2/24/92

Ethics: Easier Said Than Done, Issue 17

The television news program *60 Minutes* (Jan. 17, 1993) told the sad story of an FBI sting operation involving the state legislature of South Carolina. Reporter Mike Wallace explains: "It is not a happy thought, perhaps in this very political week before the inaugural, but it's a fact of life nonetheless, that politicians, generally speaking, are held in low esteem by the American electorate; perceived, too many of them, as having a hand in the till, as more interested in the corrupt money that will help elect and re-elect them, than in giving value received to the voters who put them in office."

That pessimistic perception was reinforced when 17 South Carolina legislators, one-tenth of the Legislature, were charged with taking money bribes in exchange for their votes. Sixteen were convicted. Such gross violation of the public trust is overshadowed by the more common patterns of influence and conflict of interest:

A. Legislators need money to run their campaigns and stay in public office.
B. People called "lobbyists," representing a variety of special interests, try to influence the legislators.
C. Lobbyists use many forms of influence, including promises to deliver blocks of voters who stand behind their cause.
D. The lobbyists work for political action committees, or PACS. These groups often make campaign contributions to people running for office.

These are legal activities and not "bribes for votes." But it is easy to imagine the traps of conflict of interest.

Now you get to be a state senator. You face a vote on whether certain high-powered automatic weapons, sometimes called "assault rifles," should be banned. These weapons are not commonly used for hunting or for home protection. They are more often used by violent gangs engaged in drug wars, or, in some dramatic cases, in massacres committed by disturbed individuals. Your mail runs about 60/40 in favor of banning the weapons.

There is a powerful lobbying group in your state, Guns-R-Us, that represents the interests of gun owners. This group routinely fights efforts to ban categories of firearms. It believes that the right to bear arms is protected by the Constitution, and should not be limited.

A lobbyist offers you this deal: Vote against the ban. If you do, Guns-R-Us will support you in your upcoming primary campaign. Guns-R-Us will contribute money to your "war chest," and encourage its members to support you.

You stand up to this pressure. You tell Guns that you will vote your conscience and what you believe is the will of the people. You vote for the ban, but the bill loses. The lobbyist returns to your office.

She has a check for $1,000. She tells you that, in spite of your vote, Guns considers you an important and influential senator.

"But you know how I feel," you tell her. "This isn't going to get me to change my mind."

"We understand that," she said. "We're not trying to buy your vote. We just want you to listen to our side when certain issues come up."

In the past, you've had to dig deeply into your personal finances to pay your campaign expenses. Every penny counts. But you worry about the abuses of this process of influence.

Answer these questions and explain your reasoning:

> 1. Would you take the money?
> 2. Where might you look for guidance and advice in reaching a good decision?
> 3. What steps could you take to protect yourself from falling into traps of conflict of interest?

A further elaboration and study of official conflicts of interest, lobbying, campaign finance dangers and governmental employee whistleblowing can be found in Chapter 20.

CONFLICT OF INTEREST: LEGAL HISTORY, GUIDELINES

Although they were not called "conflicts of interest," controversial activities by high government officials were condemned from the earliest days of the republic. People with government authority inevitably have opportunities to increase their personal wealth. That temptation toward corruption led, from as early as 1789, to some spot restrictions on those in government.

The century from 1860 to 1960 increased those restrictions significantly, but in sporadic ways, and with lots of exemptions. The problem for government is always to attract talented people to public service. Such people often are drawn from business or other professions, and opportunities for conflict of interest are inevitable.

Before 1960 confusing and incoherent regulations, filled with loopholes, attempted to control government officials in such activities as "assisting outsiders in governmental dealings, self-dealing, outside compensation, and restrictions on post-employment activities." It was like trying to lasso a stallion with dental floss.

During the early 1960s, under the leadership of President John F. Kennedy, modern conflict of interest rules for government officials were created. A seminal report by the New York City Bar Association titled *Conflict of Interest and Federal Service* and an Advisory Panel on Ethics and Conflict of Interest in Government, created by the president, made recommendations which, in 1963, became law.

Bayless Manning, a professor at Yale Law School and a key scholar of conflict of interest rules, wrote *Federal Conflict of Interest Law* (Harvard University Press, 1964). Quoting extensively from the earlier Bar Association report, Manning attempts to draw a narrow definition of conflict of interest in government:

> (*For permission to photocopy this selection, please contact Harvard University Press. Reprinted by permission of the publishers from FEDERAL CONFLICT OF INTEREST LAW by Bayless Manning, Cambridge, Mass.: Harvard University Press, Copyright © 1964 by the President and Fellows of Harvard College.)

"The term 'conflict of interest,' with related terms, has a limited meaning in this study. Any interest of an individual may conflict at times with any other of his interests. This book, however, is concerned with only two interests: One is the interest of the government official (and of the public) in the proper administration of his office; the other is the official's interest in his private economic affairs. A conflict of interest exists whenever these two interests clash, or appear to clash.

"A conflict of interest does not necessarily presuppose that action by the official favoring one of these interests will be prejudicial to the other, nor that the official will in fact resolve the conflict to his own personal advantage rather than the government's. If a man is in a position of conflicting interests, he is subject to temptation however he resolves the issue. Regulation of conflicts of interest seeks to prevent situations of temptation from arising. An Internal Revenue agent auditing his own tax return would offer a simple illustration of such a conflict of interest. Perhaps the agent's personal interest in the matter would not affect his discharge of his official duty; but the experience of centuries indicates that the contrary is more likely, and that affairs should be so arranged as to prevent a man from being put in such an equivocal position." (Bar pp. 3-4)

"But conflict of interest is a special concern, different from theft, bribery, or fraud, and the difference requires special attention and regulation.

"The mint worker who takes home part of the daily product is an example. In a rather elemental way he is involved in a conflict of interest, but we call him a thief, not an offender against conflict of interest principles. His offense is an act of commission. Its criminal character depends entirely on what he does, not who he is. And his act – the taking of the money – is itself the evil consequence that the law seeks to prevent.

"Similarly, the government contracting officer who accepts money from a contractor in exchange for granting him a contract puts himself in an extreme position of conflict between his official duty and personal economic interest. Again we have a specialized name for this offense ... bribery. Unlike theft, it must involve an official. Its essential element is a payment to influence official action. It assumes a quid for a quo; the official is to do something in his official character in return for payment.

"But now assume that the same contracting officer simply receives a large gift from the contractor. There is no agreement or discussion about any contract, and the officer in fact does not give the contract to the donor. If this act is to be forbidden, it cannot be on a theory of theft or bribery. It must be on the theory that the conflict of interest set up by the gift is LIKELY to lead to a warping of the official's judgment, or is likely to create the appearance of improper influence. If the official were not an official, the gift would be unexceptionable under federal law. The wrong arises entirely out of the undesirably inconsistent position of the official, first in his relationship to the outside party, and second in his relationship to his federal employer ...

"Regulation of conflicts of interest is regulation of evil before the event; it is regulation against potential harm. These regulations are in essence derived, or secondary – one remove away from the ultimate misconduct feared. The bribe is forbidden because it subverts the official's judgment; the gift is forbidden because it may have this effect. This potential or projective quality of conflict of interest rules is peculiar and important. We are not accustomed to dealing with law of this kind. It is as though we were to try to prevent people from acting in a manner that may lead them to rob a bank, or in a manner that looks to others like bank robbery." (Bar pp. 18-20)

Although these reports limited themselves to the executive branch of government, the experts who drafted them knew that rules controlling the actions of Congress would become necessary. They could almost foresee, three decades into the future, the explosion of special interests, armies of professional lobbyists, and the corrupting influence of PAC money. Their early efforts at defining the problem of conflict of interest and drafting legislation to control it set the legal and ethical groundwork for all those who have concerned themselves with conflict of interest in government – at any level.

Because of the dangers of undue influence and conflict of interest, states now have laws that create standards of conduct for public officers and others employed by the state. For example, Florida law states: "No public officer, employee of an agency, or candidate for nomination or election shall solicit or accept anything of value to the recipient, including a gift, loan, reward, promise of future employment, favor, or service, based upon any understanding that the vote, official action, or judgment of the public officer, employee, or candidate would be influenced thereby." (Florida Statutes 112.313)

Many gray areas remain, and many opportunities for temptation. For example, the same law which prohibits "gifts" permits "Contributions or expenditures ... campaign-related personal services provided without compensation by individuals volunteering their time, or any other contribution or expenditure by a political party."

BEST ANTIDOTE TO CONFLICT

One strategy, above all others, armors the professional against the most painful consequences of conflict of interest. The strategy? Disclosure. In many conflict of interest cases, disclosure of the conflict is the antidote: The reporter tells her editor, and then the public, that he lives on the West End. The doctor discloses his personal interest in the therapy center, and offers you a list of other therapists, as well. The attorney immediately informs her fellow board members that she represents the construction company, and asks for their advice.

Disclosure works in personal, everyday cases as well: "I'd be happy to give you a job recommendation for Angela, but you should know, she's my godchild."

Inevitably, *secrecy makes conflicts of interest seem worse*. To the common observer, your failure to disclose your conflict creates the suspicion that you have something to hide. Disclosure is the sunshine that slays that dragon and preserves credibility. It has one other beneficial effect. Disclosure inspires conversation, and begins the process of moral reasoning in a social setting that best insures a good resolution.

NATIONAL AND GLOBAL INTERESTS

The word "incest" describes one of our most powerful taboos – the legal ban against sex among close relatives. By analogy, the word "incestuous" is often used to describe ethical conflicts that extend into the highest reaches of our government and influence global and international issues.

It works this way: For the past eight years you have worked in a high government position in the Department of Commerce. You were appointed by the President of the United States. You are an expert on international trade, and you have worked closely with the Congress, and have made many contacts in business and in government.

A new administration has been elected, and it is time for you to leave government service and take the next step in your career. What will you do? You are approached by a U.S. law firm that represents the interests of Japan on issues of international trade. You are offered $500,000 a year to use your knowledge of the system and your numerous personal contacts to lobby Congress on behalf of Japanese business interests.

Perhaps you see why people call such a system "incestuous." Working for the government one day, then lobbying the government the next, seems an unhealthy form of "influence peddling" filled with all sorts of opportunities for conflict of interest.

In November of 1992, Bill Clinton was elected President of the United States, running on a platform of change. A month after the election, the office of the president-elect issued this statement about ethics in government:

"Last month, the American people voted for change. They made it clear that they want to take their government back, and that they want to end business as usual in Washington. In recent years, too many former top officials began to sell their access and influence almost the day after they left office. That saps public confidence in our political process.

"During his Presidential campaign, Governor Clinton promised the American people that he would seek to 'stop the revolving door' by requiring his top appointees to refrain from lobbying their agencies for five years. Today, we are announcing rules that keep that promise to the American people. Top officials will be required to sign a pledge agreeing to these new standards. These rules seek to change the climate in Washington, and usher in a new era of public service."

Political commentators Jack Germond and Jules Witcover described the most significant of these new ethical standards: "The Clinton code prohibits 1,100 appointees from lobbying their former agencies for five years and from lobbying for foreign governments at any time. That should put a damper on those ex-officials profiting from retainers of $500,000 a year or more from big interests, domestic or foreign, from the day they leave the government."

From the first days of the Clinton administration, these new rules became easier to promulgate than to enforce. A *New York Times* editorial declared 12 days before Clinton's Jan. 20,1993 inauguration that anyone might be able to predict the fact of his promise to free American government from the grip of special interests: "Broken from Day One."

The irony was this: The new ethical rules shone a bright light on the possible conflicts of the president-elect's own appointees, some who seemed unwilling to play by the new rules. As the *Times* concluded: "Bill Clinton needs to give new instructions to his Cabinet appointees before these (confirmation) hearings continue. If necessary, he should find new appointees to replace those who demonstrate greater allegiance to their private trades than to the president-elect's promise to the people."

It didn't take long before criticism mounted:

Ethics Code Won't Alter Political Realities

WASHINGTON – President-elect Bill Clinton's tough new ethics code is a welcome recognition that too many ranking government officials have been trading on their public service to enrich themselves in private life. But it won't repeal the basic laws of politics.

The Clinton code prohibits 1,100 appointees from lobbying their former agencies for five years and from lobbying for foreign governments at any time. That should put a damper on those ex-officials profiting from retainers of $500,000 a year or more from big interests, domestic or foreign, from the day they leave the government.

The fact that Bill Clinton can't stop influence-peddling is not a valid reason for sneering at his code of ethics. It is important for any president to set a tone for his administration. The voters have made it all too obvious that they are fed up with business-as-usual in Washington.

But it would be asking too much to expect any president to repeal the fundamental laws of politics.

Jack W. Germond and Jules Witcover
Tribune Media Services, Inc.

Federal employees received formal guidelines about ethical behavior in 1986:

How To Stay Out Of Trouble;
Ethical Conduct For Federal Employees In Brief

What are the general standards of conduct (for federal employees)?
An employee must avoid any action that might result in or create the appearance of:
• Using public office for private gain;
• Giving preferential treatment to anyone;
• Impeding Government efficiency or economy;
• Losing complete independence or impartiality;
• Making a Government decision outside official channels; or
• Affecting adversely the confidence of the public in the integrity of the Government.

Employees must be particularly careful that private interests and activities do not impact adversely on or conflict with their public duties. The following sections address specific questions that you may have.

ARE YOU ALLOWED TO USE GOVERNMENT PROPERTY FOR PERSONAL REASONS?

No. You have a positive duty to protect and conserve Federal property and to obey all rules and regulations regarding its use. You cannot directly or indirectly use or allow the use of Government property for other than officially approved activities. This includes property leased to the Government. (5 C.F.R. 735.205) A few examples of the improper use of Government property include:

• Using Government envelopes to send payroll checks to the bank or for other personal matters;
• Using Government photocopy equipment for personal matters;
• Using a Government-owned, leased, or rented vehicle or aircraft for non-official purposes;
• Using Government telephones to make personal telephone calls. (This includes local and long distance calls over both commercial facilities and the Federal Telecommunications System);
• Selling commercial products in a Government building;
• Using Government computers and word processors for personal matters;

Office of Government Ethics
Public Service-Public Trust, January 1986

Ethical problems are not restricted to American government:

Truckloads Of Scandal

In the fourth major scandal to hit Japan in the last three years, a trucking company called Tokyo Sagawa Kyubin allegedly made payoffs amounting to $80 million to politicians and Yakuza to help it get access to new routes and service areas. The scandal is unusual in that it has illuminated the back alleys of the Japanese system, showing how huge sums of money flowed from legitimate financial institutions through a major trucking company and into the hands of politicians and organized crime. – NYT, 3/1/92; LAT 2/24/92

Ethics: Easier Said Than Done, Issue 17

Corruption Spreads In Russia

It seems that Russian officials have become even greedier under the newly semi-democratic system than they were under Communism. State officials are grabbing former state property as they build their private portfolios. Bribery has become the cost of doing business, and more than ever, part of every day life as people struggle to find food and grease the wheels of the Kafkaesque bureaucracy. – NYT, 3/14/92; LAT 3/1/92

Ethics: Easier Said Than Done, Issue 17

IS THERE AN ETHICAL DECLINE?

On September 19, 1992 the *St. Petersburg Times* conducted a survey on the hotly debated issue of "family values." One question asked, "Would you say the nation is undergoing a period of moral improvement or a period of moral decline?" Three out of every four respondents thought their country was in a period of moral decline.

No question on the survey, which covered areas such as abortion, pre-marital sex, obscenity, and sex-education, received such a one-sided response. It could be argued that Americans, given their Puritan heritage, have always seen their country in this way. But the voices proclaiming moral outrage seem a bit louder and more diverse in the America of the 1990s. They come from those who condemn the "secular humanism" in our society and want to see prayer in public schools, but not sex education. They come from those who think pornography and other media images of women inspire violence against women.

Some blame urban crime, gang violence, and drug dependency on the breakdown of the traditional family structure. Others say that crimes of affluence, committed by "white collar" criminals, have ruined our economy and destroyed our trust in America. Argument, compromise, and sound moral reasoning have been replaced by shouting and sloganeering:

Right to life!
Freedom of choice!

Affirmative action!
Reverse discrimination!

Ban handguns and assault rifles!
Guns don't kill people, people do!

Ban those lyrics!
Freedom of expression!

SEEKING COMMON GROUND

These conflicts tear at the fabric of what we call community. People define themselves in terms of their most narrow self-interest. Rather than seek common ground, they retreat to islands of self-centeredness. They become alienated from the institutions that seek to bond them to a common moral purpose. Or as one "citizen" was heard to say: "The people shouldn't pay for the Savings & Loan mess. The government should."

WHERE WE ARE

It is difficult for individuals to form a moral compass without the help of the sustaining institutions that form our society. At the heart of the "good society" is the family, but no family can do its job of raising children alone. Parents need the support of neighborhoods, religious institutions, schools, businesses, labor unions, the media, and government at every level. Yet many people consider all these institutions to be in serious decay. As a result they feel adrift, heartsick, drawn back to self-interest and self-reliance as the only means of survival.

"If the well-being of its children is the proper measure of the health of a civilization," wrote *Fortune* magazine in 1992, "the United States is in grave danger. Of the 65 million Americans under 18, fully 20% live in poverty, 22% live in single-parent homes, and almost 3% live with no parent at all. Violence among the young is so rampant that the American Academy of Pediatrics calls it a public health emergency.

"The loss of childhood innocence is a recent phenomenon, affecting all income levels and all ethnic groups. Playground fights that formerly ended in bloody noses now end in death. Saturday-night cruising can end in drive-by shootings. Schools that once considered talking in class a capital offense are routinely frisking kids for weapons, questioning them about drugs. AIDS has turned youthful experimentation with sex into Russian roulette. And good public education, safe streets, and family dinners – with both mother and father present – seem like quaint memories of a far distant past. The bipartisan National Commission on Children wrote in *Beyond Rhetoric*, its 1991 report, that addressing the unmet needs of American youngsters 'is a national imperative as compelling as an armed attack or a natural disaster.'"

> Cain, having killed his brother Abel, asks God, "Am I my brother's keeper?"
>
> The Golden Rule tells us: "Do unto others, as you would have others do unto you."
>
> Thomas Kochman, a scholar of cultural diversity, prefers: "Do unto others, as they would do unto themselves."

All such imperatives derive from an ethic of connectedness and community. It is not only that we have individual rights but also that we have collective responsibilities. The study of ethics can lead us to an understanding of what those are.

We began this chapter with the case of you and your roofer. Would you pay him in cash for a lower price, knowing that he was trying to avoid paying taxes? Try to remember your first reactions, your gut instincts, when you read that case. Think about it again, in the light of these other cases, and any classroom discussions you have had in trying to figure out the right thing to do. Add the following story into your thinking.

In August of 1992, Hurricane Andrew hit the southeast coast of Florida. One of the most powerful storms on record became one of America's most terrible disasters. Thousands of homes were destroyed, resulting in billions of dollars' worth of damage.

A storm need not have ethics, but the people who build houses do. An investigation of the storm damage revealed that the damage to houses was, in many cases, greater than it need have been. The problem, said investigators, was sub-standard construction. In some cases, flimsy staples, instead of sturdier nails, were used to attach roofs to houses.

Perhaps nothing in America symbolizes community more powerfully than a row of sturdy houses filled with families and surrounded by helpful neighbors. That image might be little more than Norman Rockwell mythology. But the people devastated by Hurricane Andrew believed that their homes would be constructed up to legal standards. So think, once more, about your deal with ACME roofers. Is your immediate self-interest identical to your long-term interests? How far are you willing to put your trust in someone who engages in shady business practices? And, when the next storm hits, will you be left without a roof over your head, in the literal and ethical sense?

CONCLUSION

When decisions are difficult, when pursuing the subtle keys to positive outcomes seems hard, it is easy simply to back away from the struggle. But that itself becomes a decision, and often it is one that leads to the perception by someone, perhaps someone we value or someone in authority, that our behavior is unethical. Yet tough decisions can be made. Juries do it every day. Judges do it with human lives on the line. Newspaper editors make those hard ethical choices that float among personal, professional, corporate and societal interests. A doctor decides to operate. A lawyer decides to sue. A nation chooses to go to war. If we don't face the struggle of choice as it is presented to us, SOMEONE ELSE will make the decision for us. Choosing to be sensitive to conflicts of interest can sharpen one's decision-making skills. That gnawing in the stomach can be converted into critical thinking that produces ethical decisions. Persisting in the struggle for ethical decisions helps produce ethical lives; it may even be the foundation to a sound society. To close, consider these words from former Chief Justice Learned Hand, in a speech to the Board of Regents, University of the State of New York, October 24, 1952: "The mutual confidence on which all else depends can be maintained only by an open mind and brave reliance upon free discussion."

FOR FURTHER INQUIRY

CASE STUDIES

The following cases are compiled from the records of the Florida Commission on Ethics. They provide insight into the situations of conflict of interest that can arise. View them not just from the perspective of the public official involved but also from the view of affected businesses and citizens.

CEO 90-14–March 8, 1990

COUNTY SUPERVISOR OF ELECTIONS ASSIGNING COPYRIGHT OF COUNTY-OWNED COMPUTER SOFTWARE TO FORMER COUNTY EMPLOYEE

Question: Would a prohibited conflict of interest be created were you, a Supervisor of Elections, to assign to a former county employee the rights to use a county-owned computer software program which is unavailable to the general public, when the county employee intends to use the program for his personal benefit? Your question is answered in the affirmative.

In your letter of inquiry, you advise that you are the Supervisor of Elections in Collier County. You further advise that the county owns several computer programs which are derivatives of a program to which a former employee claims ownership. This employee has resigned from his position with the county, and now is requesting that you, as Supervisor of Elections, turn over to him the program which you represent the county owns. You wish to know whether you will violate any provision of the Code of Ethics if you do so.

In regard to your question, Section 112.313(8), Florida Statutes, provides:

> Disclosure or Use of Certain Information. – No public officer or employee of an agency shall disclose or use information not available to members of the general public and gained by reason of his official position for his personal gain or benefit or for the personal gain or benefit of any other person or business entity.

This provision prohibits you from disclosing information which is unavailable to the general public and gained through use of your official position in order to benefit yourself or someone else. If the computer program is owned by the county and is not available for use by the general public, you would be prohibited by Section 112.313(8) from giving it to an individual who intends to use it for personal gain. See CEO 89-26.

The penalties for violations of the Code of Ethics are contained in Section 112.317, Florida Statutes. In cases where we determine that an elected county official has violated the Code, we may recommend any of the penalties set forth in that statute to the Governor. The Governor would have the discretion to decide whether to impose any penalty and, if so, what penalty should be applied.

You also have asked several questions regarding the application of the Code of Ethics to the former county employee. Pursuant to Section 112.322(3), Florida Statutes, only this employee or a person who has the authority to hire or fire him can request an opinion regarding his conduct. As we have been informed that you lacked the authority to hire or fire him and that he was not an employee of the Supervisor of Elections, we cannot address those questions here.

Accordingly, we find that Section 112.313(8), Florida Statutes, would be violated were you to provide a county-owned computer program to a private individual who intends to use the program for his personal gain.

Summary: Section 112.313(8), Florida Statutes, prohibits a Supervisor of Elections from allowing a former county employee to use county-owned software programs for his personal benefit, when use of the software is unavailable to the general public. CEO 89-26 is referenced.

CEO 90-25–March 8, 1990

Conflict Of Interest

CITY COMMISSION MEMBER OWNING BILLBOARDS VOTING ON PROPOSED BILLBOARD ORDINANCE

Question: Is a City Commission member prohibited by Section 112.3143, Florida Statutes, from voting on a proposed billboard ordinance where the commission member owns several billboards within the city?

Your question is answered in the affirmative.

In your letter of inquiry, you advise that ... is a City Commissioner in the City of Lakeland. You advise that the City is considering revising its sign ordinance regulating off-premises advertising (billboards), on premises advertising and identification signs, and temporary point of purchase (portable and trailer) signs. As part of this process, the City Commission enacted a moratorium on the issuance of permits for new billboards. During this moratorium, the Mayor has appointed three Commission members to serve on a committee to propose revisions to the existing ordinance. The initial proposal by the committee consists of a total ban on new billboards and elimination of existing billboards on a seven year schedule. The subject Commission member, who does not serve on the sign ordinance committee, owns five billboards, which constitute less than four % of the approximately 138 billboards within the City. Including permits for new billboards issued immediately prior to the enactment of the moratorium, the Commission member's percentage of ownership of the outstanding permits is less than three %. The large majority of existing billboards are owned by a national company and several local companies whose primary business is outdoor advertising. You inquire whether this Commission member may participate in deliberations and votes regarding revisions to the billboard ordinance.

The Code of Ethics for Public Officers and Employees provides in relevant part:

> No county, municipal, or other local public officer shall vote in his official capacity upon any measure which insures to his special private gain or shall knowingly vote in his official capacity upon any measure which insures to the special gain of any principal, other than an agency as defined in s. 112.312(2), by whom he is retained. Such public officer shall, prior to the vote being taken, publicly state to the assembly the nature of his interest in the matter from which he is abstaining from voting and, within 15 days after the vote occurs, disclose the nature of his interest as a public record in a memorandum filed with the person responsible for recording the minutes of the meeting, who shall incorporate the memorandum in the minutes. However, a commissioner of a community redevelopment agency created or designated pursuant to s. 163.356 or s. 163.357 or an officer of an independent special tax district elected on a one-acre, one-vote basis is not prohibited from voting. (Section 112.3143(3), Florida Statutes.)

Under this provision, a local official is prohibited from voting on any measure which would inure to his "special private gain." Whether a gain is "special" will depend in part on the size of the class to be affected by the vote. See CEO 87-24 and CEO 77-129. You note that the current proposal is for a ban on billboards which are owned by a small class of businesses in the community. However, you are uncertain at this time exactly what form the final proposal to the Commission will take.

Were the vote to concern a ban on billboards, as is currently proposed, we find that the subject Commissioner would be prohibited from voting on an ordinance revision due to his ownership of billboards within the City. The class of persons is small enough that the proposal would constitute special private gain to the Commissioner. Though his interest is a small portion of the total market, this is not determinative of the issue. "Conflict" is defined at Section 112.312(6), Florida Statutes, as a "situation in which regard for a private interest tends to lead to disregard of a public duty or interest." In this situation, the fact that other members of the affected class hold far larger interests does not change the fact that the measure will have a direct financial effect on the Commissioner as a member of a small group of billboard owners.

In your letter of inquiry you have cited CEO 86-59, but we do not find it analogous to this situation. In that opinion, no voting conflict was found where city council members voted on a sign ordinance and were involved in businesses which had some relationship to the sign industry. This was based on the council members being part of a large class of persons affected indirectly by the ordinance rather than being members of the smaller class of persons directly affected. There, the directly-affected class consisted of sign owners, lessors, and other users. The indirectly-affected class, in addition to being much larger, had a more speculative and remote interest from which we could not conclude that the measure would inure to their "special gain." However, in this case, the subject Commissioner is a member of the directly-affected class, the class size is small, and the effect of billboard restrictions on his financial interests is clear.

Under these circumstances, a voting conflict would be created, and Section 112.3143(3) would require the Commissioner to publicly state the nature of his interest prior to the vote, abstain from voting, and file a memorandum of voting conflict within 15 days after the vote occurs with the person responsible for recording the minutes of the meeting. Commission Form 8B has been provided for purposes of making the required disclosure.

However, were the proposal to the Commission to be more expansive, including various types of signs and other matters, or differ in its effect on billboards, it is possible that the class size would be larger or the effect may differ regarding the subject Commissioner. If this situation occurs, you may wish to provide us with more specific information and request additional guidance.

With regard to participation in deliberations on the issue of the sign ordinance, Section 112.3143(3) requires only abstention from voting as noted above. While appointed public officers are precluded from participating in any matter which inures to their special private gain before disclosing the nature of their interest under Section 112.3143(2)(b), Florida Statutes, elected local officials need only abstain from voting on such matters. However, we note the following provision of the Code of Ethics:

> Misuse of Public Position. – No public officer or employee of an agency shall corruptly use or attempt to use his official position or any property or resource which may be within his trust, or perform his official duties, to secure a special privilege, benefit, or exemption for himself or others. This section shall not be construed to conflict with s. 104.31.

We would caution the subject Commissioner to avoid even the appearance of using his official position to favor his private interests.

Accordingly, we find that Section 112.3143(3), Florida Statutes, prohibits the subject City Commissioner from voting on an ordinance restricting billboards where he owns billboards within the City.

Summary: A City Commission member is prohibited by Section 112.3143, Florida Statutes, from voting on a proposed ordinance prohibiting billboards, where the commission member owns several billboards within the city. Under the circumstances presented, the measure would inure to the Commissioner's special private gain, and he would be required to disclose the nature of his interest, abstain from voting, and file a voting conflict memorandum.

BIBLIOGRAPHY

• Beachamp, Tom L., and Terry P. Pinkard. *Ethics and Public Policy: An Introduction to Ethics.* Englewood Cliffs, N.J.: Prentice-Hall, 1983.
• Bellah, Robert N. *The Good Society.* New York, N.Y.: Knopf, 1991.
• ————. *Habits of the Heart: Individualism and Commitment in American Life.* New York: Harper & Row, 1986.
• Bok, Sissela. *Lying: Moral Choice in Public and Private Life.* New York: Vintage Books, 1979.
• ————. *Secrets: On the Ethics of Concealment and Revelation.* New York: Vintage Books, 1983.
• *Conflict of Interest and Federal Service.* A Report of the Special Committee on the Federal Conflict of Interest Laws. New York: The Association of the Bar of the City of New York, 1960.
• *Ethics: Easier Said Than Done.* Edited by Michael Josephson. Marina del Rey, Cal.: The Joseph and Edna Josephson Institute of Ethics, Issue 17, 1992.
• Fulghum, Robert. *All I Really Need to Know I Learned in Kindergarten.* New York: Ivy Books, 1988.

• Gilligan, Carol. *In A Different Voice: Psychological Theory and Women's Development.* Cambridge, Mass.: Harvard University Press, 1982.
• Haayen, R.J. (CEO, Allstate Insurance Company). Speech on business ethics. Reprinted in *Illinois State Business Week,* September 28, 1988.
• *How to Keep Out of Trouble: Ethical Conduct for Federal Employees, In Brief.* Washington, D.C.: Office of Government Ethics, 1988.
• Ibsen, Henrik. *An Enemy of the People.* Adapted by Arthur Miller. New York: Penguin Books, 1979.
• Lambeth, Edmund B. *Committed Journalism: An Ethic for the Profession* . Bloomington, Ind.: Indiana University Press, 1986.
• MacIntyre, Alasdair. *After Virtue.* South Bend, Ind.: Notre Dame University Press, 1981.
• Manning, Bayless. *Federal Conflict of Interest Law.* Cambridge, Mass.: Harvard University Press, 1964.
• Pojman, Louis P. *Ethics: Discovering Right and Wrong.* Belmont, Cal.: Wadsworth Publishing, 1990.

Part II

The Examined Life

THE ENFORCERS

Chapter 2

Paul de Vries

THE ETHICS CONSTRUCT

"Many more people see than weigh."
  – The Earl of Chesterfield, Philip Dormer Stanhope, *Letters 1748*

"In everything one must consider the end."
                  – Jean De La Fontaine, *Fables Book III*

Are we all asleep? Two mayors of this city have been convicted and put in jail in the past 20 years, and quite a few of our other "public servants" should see what they were doing. And everyone pays for it with higher taxes and stupid decisions. Why do the voters put up with it? We have had the best politicians money could buy – if you know what I mean. So many sweetheart arrangements with contractors and developers – anyone could have been locked in the slammer, too.

This is not fair! Can you believe it? I do everything that Professor Brown asked the class to do, and I get a "C" – just a measly "C"! Cute little Terry turns papers in late, they look sloppy, and they're on the wrong topics, but they come back with an "A" or an "A-" on them. What's going on? I sure deserve something better. Does the great Professor Brown even read what I write?

No one seems to care! As you can see, I am a handicapped person, and I have the legal handicapped sticker on my car. But what good does that do? I still have to drive my wheelchair all the way across the parking lot, rain or shine. The cars in the handicapped zone do not have the proper stickers. I wonder why? Do they have any idea the pain they cause me? Can they imagine how frustrated and angry this makes me? I am so mad!

These people act like they are not accountable to anyone! Nothing seems to matter to them. At my job last summer, some of the employees spent more than half of their "working" time, their office time,

Paul de Vries, M.A. and PhD. University of Virginia, holds the Endowed Chair in Ethics and the Marketplace at King's College, New York, and is president of the International Research Institute on Values Changes, based in New York, Beijing and Moscow.

on the phone with their family and friends – even their "long distance" friends. The telephone lines were filled with gossip, not business. It is so amazing that the corporation is still in business. No wonder its prices are so high! I predict that someday the whole company will collapse, and those busy little gossipers will have to use their own phones on their own time – between visits to the unemployment office, of course. Whom will they exploit then?

WHAT DO WE VALUE?

What do we think is important to talk about? What conversation gets our attention? What are our most crucial thoughts? What makes us sincerely concerned, or angry?

Your answers to these questions may be a little different from what other people say, and your response today may be different from what you said yesterday and what you will say tomorrow. Nevertheless, the ever-present, familiar gap between the way we hope things might be and the way they are – this chronic gap accounts for a tremendous amount of our daily conversation, conceptualization, and concerns.

> You think or dream about what could be,
> you recognize how things really are, and
> you know the difference – you see the gap.

From this gap comes our interest in the news media, history and even gossip. Also this gap provides both the motivation and the material for our favorite music and movies, as well as great world literature and philosophy. Moreover, we have all been aware of this gap for years – ever since our first childhood disappointments.

This gap has a simple name: *Human problems.*

Do you remember the first time you complained that another child was given more milk, or a bigger cookie, than you were given? Probably not, that was so long ago. You were too young to remember. However, most of us have been complaining almost as long as we could talk. "It is not fair," "It's not right," "Someone ought to do something" – so we have often claimed and argued, ever since we were very small children. And what concerns have been more important to us? Not many. What issues provide better material for novels, movies, or television programs?

Moreover, you probably do not remember the first time you felt ignored, the first time you saw that others were uncaring, or the first time you knew that someone got away with "murder." We make these observations daily – in the experiences of our own lives, and when we are reading newspapers or fiction, watching movies or television programs. Is it possible for us even to imagine what the world would be like without this chronic gap we call human problems? How would our lives be? Would we be happy? Would we be bored?

Just think of the variety included in the wide range of questions we call human problems. Think, for example, of all the problems that were raised in Chapter 1. Here, for good measure, are some more:

- Whom should I trust?

- When, if ever, is violence justified?

- Should I do what I want, even if he (or she) is disappointed?

- It is so easy to cheat – why is it wrong?

- Has this product been tested enough to sell it to customers?

- Why should I treat people equally if they do not seem equal?

- Really, is there anything wrong with greed?

- Should I tell the truth even if it hurts someone else?

- Is there any cause worth living for – or dying for?

- Is it a good thing to disobey an unjust law?

- Should I put my seat belt on even for short trips?

- Should I report it when my boss breaks the law?

- Can anyone really love me?

- How do you recognize a love that will last until death?

So, Where Is The Answer Book?

Not only do we humans cope with these and other problems, but we face four additional difficulties in dealing with them. Frankly, our human problems are often quite difficult to talk and think about – because of these four hurdles.

First, these human problems are *concerned with us,* not another species, and so there is always some personal risk involved. Even if we are talking about someone else's wrong decisions or hurtful behavior, we always run the risk that we ourselves could be criticized for the same mistakes. The fact is, the faults we can easily point out in others are often similar to the faults other people just as easily see in us. It is quite wise sometimes not to criticize – in order to avoid the pain of having our own faults brought up.

Moreover, it can be almost as dangerous to praise someone. When we point out good character in another person, we run another kind of risk – the risk that someone will ask why our own character does not match up so well, or ask when we plan to learn from such a good example. The point is, when we praise fair or caring decisions, others may wonder why we ourselves are not more fair or caring. Simply put, when we praise something good, it raises a standard for our own behavior. That could be costly! Could it be worth the price?

Second, our language is equipped with *words that help hide* or neutralize human problems. For example, we describe or refer to different "lifestyles" and say there are "different strokes for different folks" – strongly suggesting that the answers to some major human problems do not make any real difference anyway. If these are only questions of style – or lifestyle -- then they are not really problems; they are merely occasions for us to express our choices of taste. In the lifestyle language there are no objective guidelines, goals, or standards. But is this a true picture of our needs? Human rights, basic fairness, caring about ourselves and others, personal and group responsibility – are these concerns merely stylish concepts, merely matters of taste? Some human problems may in fact be mere matters of personal preference, but we should be careful not to let the common lifestyle language paint over substantial human concerns.

A third difficulty is that some people try to avoid talking about human problems with any depth – with anything more than superficial comments or complaints – because they consider these to be strictly personal or private concerns. Some people think that these problems are not supposed to be matters of public discussion, comparison, or criticism. Even though their decisions and behavior will affect you – especially if you become their employee, employer, friend, lover, spouse – they get touchy about questions probing their values. To take an extreme case, if you believe that theft or murder is justified, I have a personal interest in knowing. Of course, since people's values are eventually shown in their behavior, what is the point? *Values are never ultimately private.* What are people's actual purposes, then, in hiding their values under some "privacy" claim?

There is perhaps a fourth complication, and one that is related to these others. In modern times some people have blindly taken it as a matter of fact that "*all truth is scientific.*" That is, if a concern or claim cannot be strictly scientifically tested or demonstrated, many people consider it to be not even a matter of truth – whether it is literature, art, common sense, religion, or ethics. All these areas are treated as merely matters of personal taste. And notice this: What is especially humorous about this belief is that the very doctrine that "all truth is scientific" is not itself scientifically testable, so it cannot be considered true.[1] As a result, this common doctrine can be "only a matter of taste" itself! By its own assertion, it can carry no authority or conviction. Why believe it, if it denies its own truth?

It may turn out that some human problems are matters of taste, but we should not be blind to sources of truth and enduring guidance when they help us cope with human problems.

PROBLEMS, PROBLEMS, PROBLEMS

So the human problems remain. They may be difficult to talk about, but there is no defensible escape from our responsibilities to try to solve them. And whenever we thoughtfully join the effort, we are doing ethics, for *ethics involves critical thinking about human problems.* We call it "critical thinking" [2] because it is thinking that makes a difference: It has a critical edge and a critical mass. It includes the best imagination, analysis, synthesis, logic, comparison, knowledge, wisdom, deliberation and resolution applied to specific problems. It is "critical thinking" because it is not mere personal reflection or day-dreaming but rather the finest of our thinking for the purpose of solving problems.

When we do it well, "critical thinking" is also self-critical and self-adjusting. Reflective experience helps improve the critical thinking process, and critical thinking itself helps the person who uses it to be a better person. Of course, critical thinking involves logic, but it is more than logic. It includes effective uses of stories, common sense, and perception as well. Critical thinking brings together our best skills and achievements. Ethics, utilizing critical thinking, brings the optimum resources each of us can bring to resolve human problems. Simply put, ethics is being smart about our problems.

SOURCES, TYPES OF PROBLEMS

Literature, movies, and television shows – as well as the news media – thrive on both the uses and abuses of sex and violence. These two dimensions of news, art and entertainment draw our interest, attract our money, and keep our attention. Often the sex represented is perverted, degrading and unrealistic, and the violence seems excessively gross, vulgar, and exaggerated. As a result, even the reader and observer are degraded and demeaned. Why do sex and violence remain unmistakably powerful dimensions of our lives, thoughts, and imaginations? News reporters, advertisers, novelists and story writers, as well as Hollywood and television producers, know this fact well. As a result they use or exploit sex and violence in a multitude of ways for their own fame and fortunes.

Think about it. What does our high interest in sex and violence say about us? What does it show us about who we are and what we seem to want? Why does it always tug at our attention? These questions do not have simple answers, because everyone's interests and motives are a little different. We can repeatedly discover two common themes, nevertheless.

Violence usually occurs in individual fights or in battles – in a conflict between good and evil forces, or at least where courage, valor, and skill are necessary to win. This violence is especially satisfying to the reader or observer when a particularly powerful and skillful evil force is crushed. In the safety of our homes, and for the 30 minutes of the program, the three hours of the movie, or perhaps the three days we take reading the novel, we can begin to imagine ourselves devoted to a cause like that, one for which it is truly worth living – even one for which fighting or dying might make sense. And even this imaginative (vicarious) commitment to a purpose can satisfy a profound longing in our souls. That is, the vivid and violent story can awaken in us – if only for a short time period and in our imagination – a sense of deep purpose and meaning for which we may often hunger, but from which our modern "comfortable numbness" usually insulates us.[3]

Of course, when the terrible fight is over, we can close the book and go to sleep, push the remote control button to turn off the television, or relax in the comfortable theater seats while the credits run. There is no real blood to wipe up, and there are no wounds to heal, but our souls might still be energized. After all, we have glimpsed the vision that a costly struggle for justice can be worthwhile, and that the problems that hinder the rule of justice can be conquered. This is the first theme that gives some explanation for our interest in violence in media, literature, and entertainment.

Sex is of interest to almost any red-blooded man or woman. No deep explanation is necessary here. The so-called sexual revolution has created a glut of explicit sexual literature and entertainment – though rarely being at all explicit about devoted, faithful, fulfilling love in a marriage. Also, these public depictions of sex, because they are so drained of personal intimacy, tend to depict perverted and exploited sex. At best, they may satisfy some odd curiosity. However, they also can arouse our desire for something better than we have or than what is depicted in the movie or literature – our desire for a real and vital love affair, for a person with whom we could be totally intimate, for a passion that will not quit, for a sincere and devoted relationship. In short, we may be momentarily reminded of our human aspirations for enduring love, intimacy, and faithfulness, as well as the obstacles of mind and heart in pursuing them. This is the second theme that gives some explanation for our interest in sex in media, literature, and entertainment.

So violence and sex in media, literature, and entertainment can make us more conscious of the justice and love in which we sincerely seek to participate. In addition, the plot of any news story, work of literature, movie, or television show always focuses on some human problem, or even some set of human problems. The story line explores the different ways various characters deal with these problems – foolishly, or intelligently, or something in between. As a result, our lives are surrounded by a full range of real and imaginary cases of human problems, and examples of both careless as well as critical-thinking approaches to resolving them. Of course, it is the critical-thinking approaches that an ethical person examines and exemplifies.

STEP BY STEP

Ethics, critical thinking about human problems, involves four crucial steps. These are just the four steps of any critical thinking process. The four steps are not always equally important, not all of them need to be emphasized specifically in each situation in which a human problem is resolved, and they are not always sequential. Nevertheless, each of the four steps is necessary, or else our critical thinking is incomplete.

---

1. Recognizing a problem

      Key Question: What is truly going on?

2. Engaging all available information

      Key Question: Is your information factual and fair?

3. Deciding what to do and doing it

      Key Question: What do you really care to achieve?

4. Being able to explain the decision to yourself and others

      Key Question: To whom, for what, are you accountable?

We will now examine each of these steps one at a time and consider some examples and explanations. We will also look for a standard of excellence for each step, a pattern that epitomizes our best hopes and efforts for that step. Finally, we will look at the difference between ethics and other problems.

First of all, however, we may want to review whether a problem even has moral dimensions. It may simply be *non-moral,* having no particular ethical value at all, beyond the place of moral consideration. For example, is it a moral matter whether I choose the right fork to eat my salad? Not at all! (It could become one, however, if I hear my mother's voice ordering me to use a certain fork and then I choose not to use that one!) A non-moral, or amoral, matter is simply devoid of moral account; a potted plant cannot be a prostitute. By contrast, *moral* matters – while not relying exclusively on some authority or tradition – nonetheless do address issues of conduct and societal import while offering some sense of being impartial. (Meanwhile, *immoral* conduct is that which flaunts its way past any of those standards and does as it pleases.) See "moral" on p. 737.

STEP ONE: RECOGNIZE THE PROBLEM

Literature, news, history, movies, religion – these can all be resources for helping us recognize problems around us. However, more easily than we realize, people can become complacent, and become accustomed to very wrong, unjust, and uncaring practices and policies as if that were just the way life should be. Without some vision or concept of what life could be, and without thoughtfully observing what is going on, even intelligent and educated people can blindly resign themselves to morally bankrupt policies, disgusting decisions and corrupt circumstances.

Prophets and seers in history – such as the biblical prophets, as well as Socrates, Confucius, Gandhi, and even Thomas Jefferson and Martin Luther King Jr. – often contributed the most by clearly

---

pointing out to people the facts that should have been quite obvious for everyone to see. These prophets – literally, people who speak out – described what should have been self-evident truths, such as: The people were playing games with their religion, the poor were unfairly treated, the rulers had no concept of justice, the leaders can earn true respect and trust only through developing good character, violence breeds violence, all people have some inalienable rights, and racial bigotry degrades both the hater and the hated. What could be more apparent and indisputable for everyone to see? Nevertheless, seeing the obvious may not be very simple to achieve, and talking about what is self-evident often takes courage in the face of substantial danger. Many of the prophets have sacrificed their lives for making such self-evident claims.

Comedians, artists, fiction writers, political commentators – like prophets and seers, these often play the role of "speaking out" about the unmistakable truths that most others have not recognized. They help jar us from the comfortable complacency and conformity that can numb our minds and hearts. The incessant "Why?" question of young people, children, teachers, and philosophers can help produce the same result.

Consider the pattern: In Hans Christian Andersen's famous story, only the little child could recognize that the emperor had no clothes. Apparently few Germans during World War II asked themselves why multitudes of Jews were continually herded into cramped prison camps, with precious few of them occasionally leaving. The Massachusetts Bay Colony forced Roger Williams to leave because he insisted that American Indians were human beings with rights. The former Soviet Union and other communist regimes were cruel and corrupt, but when Ronald Reagan said the obvious, calling the Soviet Union an "evil empire," he altered the world's perception – he made people look again.

Recognizing a problem – research has shown how difficult and important this step is. People can learn moral principles and study the cases in which they apply. They can write wonderful essays about these principles, engage in thoughtful discussion about them, and apply these principles within prepared cases and other assignments for college ethics classes. They can even earn an "A" in their ethics classes – but the ethical quality of their lives may still not be improved or affected. Even when they face real life cases very much like the ones they studied in their ethics course, they often miss the similarity and do not even see a problem. Precious few will recognize the simple fact that the principles they have studied might actually apply in their own daily lives. How can this be?

People can go to church or synagogue or temple week after week. They can even listen carefully to the lessons and participate in thoughtful discussion. Right and wrong can be utterly clear. But the very next week the same people might cheat on their spouses or lie to the Internal Revenue Service – and never recognize that there was a problem. How can this be?

A great story was told, by Jesus, about two people who went up to the Jerusalem Temple to pray. The tax collector beat on his own chest, saying "God have pity on me, a sinner." At the same time another man, who was overt about his religious devotion, stood by himself praying, "Thank you God that I am not greedy and dishonest or like that tax collector over there." In interpreting the story, Jesus praised only the tax collector's approach. Unfortunately, the most natural response when we hear this story is to think, "I am sure glad I'm not like that awful man who thought he was so much better than the tax collector." The hard part is to recognize that this very reaction demonstrates how similar we can be to the "devout" one who thought he was so superior. How morally blind can we be? The answer: We can be far more blind than we realize.

Years ago, Professor Will Herberg told the story about a conference of intelligent and responsible people who met to discuss ideas on how to become involved in reducing crime and violence in our society. These valuable deliberations were interrupted only by the desperate cries for help from a young woman. She was being beaten for several minutes right under the windows of their meeting room. *The conferees watched from the windows, but not one person moved to help the victim.* This true story is a sad parable of much of life. Was this the conduct these conference thinkers really wanted? Were they even aware of the huge gap between their aspirations and their actions? Did they see that their behavior belied their beliefs? Did their ethical deliberations make any difference for their actions?

RECOGNIZING THE PROBLEMS OF RECOGNIZING THE PROBLEM

Recognition of facts depends on more than just being awake and having our eyes and ears open. What we see depends on so much more. In examining the history of science, Thomas S. Kuhn[4] has observed that two people can look at the same phenomenon and examine the same data, and yet see quite different things – even if they are both highly intelligent and have trained minds. For example, a seasoned scientist may continue to apply an old and deeply flawed theory while, at the same time, a young scientist interprets the same phenomena and data according to a new theory. The new concepts allow the younger scientist to recognize facts that the older scientist might not even consider – let alone see.

In one case, two historic chemists, Joseph Priestly (1733-1804) and Antoine Lavoisier (1743-1794), both studied combustion quite thoroughly. On the one hand, Priestly used a number of ideas but never considered the role of oxygen in the combustion process – mainly because his theory did not even include the concept of oxygen at all. On the other hand, Lavoisier observed that oxygen played a major role in combustion. The big difference was that Lavoisier was using a new theory in which the concept of oxygen was introduced for the first time – a theory that *he* had developed. In a similar example, a science teacher, seasoned in the discipline, may immediately see the trajectories of subatomic particles in a cloud chamber. While the students see only the droplets, the trained eye of the teacher will recognize the equally obvious but more significant structures.

Two additional common examples might help us see more clearly both the difficulties and resources involved in "recognizing a problem." First, you spend months at your school without actually noticing a particular person until you see him or her across the table at lunch or in the library. You start talking a little and some interest develops between the two of you. Although you had never noticed that person before, you now seem to run into him or her constantly. That very special face stands out even in a crowd, and you recognize who it is immediately. What made the difference? Two things had changed. You became informed about that person and you have developed some interest in him or her.

Our second common example is quite different, but the general pattern is similar. Before you learned your first language, printed words looked to you like only marks on paper. To you these shapes had no meaning, no significance. None of them stood out. In the process of learning the language you began by learning the shapes, sounds, and names of all the letters. Then you sounded out or spelled out printed words as you began the elementary steps of reading. Now you read words, phrases, and even whole lines at a glance, without even thinking about the specific letters or their shapes. Think about it as you read this page. In the process of learning language your perception of the printed page has dramatically changed. What is important stands out. You hardly even notice the shapes of letters and words. A related process occurs when additional languages are mastered, although there are some differences, and a similar process occurs as we learn to understand oral language.

How can we learn to recognize words and meanings immediately, without consciously sorting through a multitude of sounds and shapes? Obviously our minds have the awesome capability of learning and even inventing languages. And this learning process is enhanced by two factors. First, repeated use and familiarity makes even complicated steps of recognition occur automatically and immediately. Second, you have an interest in communicating whether as a child, or perhaps as an adult student of another language. In fact, we learn a language the fastest if we go to a place where people are using it constantly around us – contributing to the language's familiarity – and when we have to use the language to cope with problems, get around, eat, and find the bathroom – contributing to our interest in the language.

So is it possible to cultivate and expand our abilities to recognize human problems? Yes, and the two most important ingredients for enhancing our capacities to recognize a problem are these:

1. Familiarity with the problem's patterns.
2. Personal interest in addressing the problem.

General familiarity with the complexities of life – acquired through thoughtful experience, the study of history and literature, the examination of religious traditions, an awareness of the checks and balances of our political and business structures, and so on – can help a person be alert to problems. Personal interest in our own improvement must also be cultivated. Because we are often far more interested in improving others than improving ourselves, it is easier to see the speck of a problem in someone else's eye than to recognize the telephone pole of a problem sticking out of our own eye.

We should never forget the famous story of the "Good Samaritan." It took an outsider, a veritable reject in the community, to recognize the problem and provide the help that was obviously needed. The people who were supposed to be community examples and religious leaders bypassed the wounded crime victim. They had spent much of their lives thinking about righteous actions, but they neither truly recognized nor understood the problem lying right in front of them. Perhaps they were blind because they had neither studied nor experienced the ravages of crime, and remained unfamiliar with its real costs. Perhaps, also, they could not imagine being in the same need as the crime victim on the side of the road – so they lacked the interest to help such a needy person. Moreover, they were probably blind to many other obvious problems and needs around them as well. In contrast, the Samaritan, as an outcast, had personally experienced at least some of the violence of society against himself. Whether or not he had been a victim of the same crimes, he had personally identified with the needy, seen such disaster before, and could easily imagine similar attacks against himself. Consequently, he could see what the others missed. Whom do we each resemble, the "moral leaders" or the Samaritan?

STEP TWO: ENGAGING ALL AVAILABLE INFORMATION

Ethical decisions are informed decisions; critical thinking about human problems requires knowledge. We need information about the problem, its history, possible solutions, and the consequences of various decisions. Rarely do we have time to acquire that amount of knowledge on the spot within the time we have to make a wise decision. Instead, our primary sources are the knowledge, experience, and understanding we can acquire over a period of time as we become intelligent, mature, caring people. Then, occasionally additional facts of a new human problem are added to our veritable library of (1) knowledge, (2) experience, and (3) understanding that we carry around within us in our hearts and minds.

First, *knowledge* is essential. How else can we make decisions – for our lives, our time, our bodies, our families, our relationships, our careers, our governments, our places of worship – unless we know about purposes and possibilities, facts and fashions? This is, of course, one of the main reasons why you are in college, and this is one reason why some of the courses are mandated for graduation or for completion of a major.

Can you imagine trying to sort through a problem in racial understanding if you had no knowledge of prejudice, diversity of culture, human rights, the value of all human beings, and the personal and social effects of discrimination? One could get lost in a hurry. And the pressures to engage in non-marital sex could be overwhelming if you had no knowledge of the meaning of marriage, the biology of sex, of diseases transmitted through sex, the sometimes dubious protection provided by "safer" sex, and the benefits of commitment and faithful love. Access to knowledge often enhances behavior.

Second, *experience* prepares us to cope with human problems as well – especially experience that is not passive but dynamic and responsive. We are all shaped by the interaction we have with our families, friends, religious authorities, teachers, bosses, employees, and neighbors, as well as natural objects. A passive experience is almost an oxymoron – a contradiction in terms. Anyone we call "experienced" has also reflected upon and learned from life's experiences. Experienced people act and then digest the results of their actions in order to act more effectively and skillfully in the future. Such savvy people frequently re-evaluate both the intentions and consequences of their actions in order to make even more wise decisions.

The process of gaining experience is itself a circular spiral – like a helix. Experienced people are usually more open to new and surprising experiences, building upon the confidence that experience brings, sustaining the openness encouraged by experience itself. The benefits of this practiced openness – or teachability – to critical thinking are then evident to anyone who is thoughtful and sensitive.

The basic structure of experience is shaped like the form of a spiral spring we call a helix. It revolves round and around, each time coming back to a different place and on another level. At each turn there are new requirements and rewards. Experienced people actively expand their knowledge in order to extend their effective mastery of their living, working, and playing environment. The circularity of experience both demands and honors engaged thought.

Experience also helps us to interpret, modify and use the theories we learn in study – theories of management, education, personality, religion, and ethics. Theories are abstractions, so they never fully represent reality. Nevertheless, experienced people can continue to make use of theoretical structures, because they understand both the limits and strengths of these tools. Our awareness of their limits forces us to use theories more cautiously and humbly. Our best theories are still only tools in our own hands, to be used by us, and interpreted or modified by our own perceptive experience.

Third, *understanding* is another essential resource for engaging all available information when coping with human problems. As with experience, the process of understanding follows helictical patterns. We cannot understand a part of a situation unless we have some understanding of the larger picture, and we cannot understand the larger picture unless we understand many of the parts. For example, as Gadamer points out, we cannot understand a problem apart from understanding the larger situation, culture or history in which it plays a role. However, we cannot understand that larger picture unless we understand some of the particular problems within it.

Is this a frustrating vicious cycle, since we cannot understand either the problem or its greater context without some understanding of both? If we need to understand the problem in order to understand the context, and understand the context in order to understand the problem, where can we start? The answer is simple: *We start where we are, and with the understanding that we have.* We already have some understanding of the particular problem and the context in which we find it. Probing the problem more enriches our understanding of the larger picture, which in turn helps us to frame the problem better. The very interdependence of the problem and its context gives us resources of understanding. If we had only isolated problems, we would be lost.

For example, imagine that you are trying to help a friend, Ken, who is suicidal. He sees no more reason to live, and he has lost the desire to overcome the disappointments he finds now in his path. If this were all you understood, it would be difficult to know where to begin. But you have known Ken for six months. You have had some good times together; you know a few of his interests and frustrations; you are able to get him talking, reflecting, thinking, maybe even hoping. At the same time, his present suicidal attitude gives another dimension to your six months of friendship, and that extended friendship with Ken provides you with some resources to understand what you should do now.

Consider another example. You work as one of the student managers of the college's Sports Center, and you have keys to the pool area and other sections. Nice. But you have promised the Sports Center Director to unlock the doors to the pool only during specific hours. A friend, Julie, has come up with plans for a "private" pool party with a few other acquaintances – at 1 a.m. Saturday – after another party that is scheduled in the Student Lounge right after the school game. The proposed private pool party would definitely not be during regular pool hours. She promises to keep it all a secret, and you are invited to join in the fun with only a few other men and women. She offers even to pay you something for your trouble as well.

However, you were not born yesterday. You were trusted with the pool keys because people can count on your character; you have been responsible when under pressure before. Besides, you know that people who are already breaking regulations are less likely to keep their promises to keep it a secret. The thought of such a party has already crossed your mind before – you have a good imagination, too – and you have already resisted the idea. All of this larger background places Julie's attractive suggestion in a meaningful context, so that you understand what is going on. At the same time, your present conversation with Julie gives new meaning to the dimensions of trust, character, promise, imagination, and temptation that are always part of the larger picture. Only with some awareness of these broader issues do you understand the particular problem you face, but the broader issues have meaning for you only because of problems like this one that Julie has thrown you. It is all connected.

AND IT'S GOLDEN

The *Golden Rule* is an excellent model for this kind of helictical experience and understanding: "Do for others what you would want them to do for you." This ancient rule highlights two central features of our second step of ethics: Engaging all available information. First, information is crucial. The assumption of this rule is that the other people involved in the problem are at least a little bit different than you are, and you need to understand their perceptions, hopes and ideals – from their point of view. Listening and observing, as well as drawing from your own resources of experience and understanding, will make all the difference.

Second, the processes of engaging information are generally helictical, involving the larger picture of your own thoughts and values each step of the way – and the *Golden Rule* embodies this pattern. You are probably part of a larger corporation, college, church, synagogue, or other community organization that has ethical policies you are expected to apply. Even then, you can think through the loop of the *Golden Rule* to evaluate both those policies and your own decisions. Because of this rule, nothing is merely a duty or a policy, and we cannot blame or blindly follow someone else's standards.

As a result, this ancient standard of fairness, or justice, establishes the epitome of the second step of ethics. We engage all available information by bringing our knowledge, experience, and understanding into the problem-solving situation. And we do this in a way that the others involved in the problem should recognize as fair, because it is the approach we would want them to take if our roles were reversed. The standard is not what others want us to do, *but what we would want them to do if they were us.* And our primary resource for applying a standard such as the *Golden Rule* is the accumulated knowledge, experience, and understanding that we bring with us into every situation and problem.

JUST SAY 'YES'

Getting To Yes (1981) by Roger Fisher and William Ury is a very useful resource, demonstrating how we can expand the information we need. This book, subtitled *Negotiating Agreement Without Giving In*, has a marvelous example of how moral imagination assists in understanding the views of others. An example the authors used shows how a tenant and a landlady might have different perceptions of a rent increase. Compare the two perceptions below, factor by factor.

Putting ourselves in another's shoes is not a panacea, but it does allow us to take a more objective perspective and to make fairer decisions. Moreover, the *Golden Rule* usually uses the resources of knowledge, experience, and understanding that we already have – that we carry in our hearts and minds. However, sometimes we have to supplement this with new information.

CASE: ROOM TO SPARE

First we have to recognize the problems, then engage the available information. In the following scenario, are these two steps evident in Michelle's and Tom's thinking? What do you think?

"Tom, dinner was great. It sure beats the lunches we've shared at the college cafeteria. Meals like this help detoxify my system! And what atmosphere! This hotel dining room is exquisite. And being with you – just the two of us – was very special. If it won't shock you too much, I'll take you to my favorite restaurant in a couple weeks. You'll love it. Of course, I'll pay the tab then."

"What are you saying, Michelle? We've been friends for a long time now, and you know how I feel about you. I really want to go upstairs. I've reserved a room. We could watch a movie together and see what happens. No one else needs to know. We're far enough away from our families and the college. Please, let's just see."

"Tom, you're wonderful. And I take your 'suggestions' for the rest of the evening as a compliment. Really. But to actually do what you are suggesting would require me to give up something I'm not prepared to give up."

"What?! Are you a virgin or something?

"Well yes, kind of."

"You're so sexy. I never would've guessed it! You – a puritan? Really? What is the point?" (Tom is getting a little excited, although he keeps his voice low. Then he starts sounding like a familiar radio announcer.) "Welcome to the 20th century. We have technology to take care of your worries. One little cap of protection for him, no pregnancy or disease for her. Live safe with science, and your problems disappear. Just say 'Yes,' and the best things in life are free!"

"Wonderful performance, Tom (clapping). But the answer is still no – although I would love to do it. Really. But your science and technology are not good enough. Good condoms can stop sperm, but AIDS viruses are a lot smaller, and they can get through. Pills and patches don't help either. But more important than those worries, I have my own plans. This is my body, and I plan to give it only when the time is super right. We *are* friends, but I am not making that decision now."

(Silence. Tom has not heard these lines before.)

"C'mon, Tom, let's go for a walk. The evening is wonderful!!"

Now let's discuss these questions:

1. Does Tom see any problem here? Please explain.

2. Does Michelle see any problems? Please explain.

3. Are Tom and Michelle working with different assumptions, different knowledge, different experience, different understanding? How does each difference affect their decisions?

4. What did Michelle mean when she said she is "kind of" a virgin? Is she really a virgin? Or has she decided to live like a virgin again, on the basis of previous experience or some new information? Does it really matter?

STEP THREE: MAKING A DECISION AND DOING IT

Our critical thinking about human problems necessarily includes our decisions, our problem-resolutions. "Thinking" that does not lead to a decision, that does not make a difference, is not "critical thinking," because it is not really engaged in life in the first place. Unlike abstract thought, critical thinking must make some impact, or it is no longer "critical," no longer significant. Critical thought reaches beyond the comfortable ranges of mental imagination and into our flesh-and-blood behavior, decisions, risks.

Story problems, or word problems, are necessary for learning mathematics, and a science course is never complete without some laboratory work. We say people understand mathematics, not when they can explain mental steps, but only when they can use the tools of mathematics in solving concrete problems. How very easy it is to feel that we have understood a method or rule before we have fruitfully used it. Our understanding of even a simple rule or method is often very different once we have mastered its use in actual practice! Real know-how makes all the difference. A similar point can be made about ethics, except that the stories and problems of ethics are often more complicated, and we cannot simply wrap it all up with a lab report.

"That is the story of my life," we often say – especially when we are faced with major frustrations. Our diaries may not make good novels or movies, yet all of our lives are stories, stories of problems and decisions. Our lives are sequences of events with apparent story lines and ongoing motifs, crises, obstacles. We start new chapters of our lives with major decisions or changes. Patterns established in early chapters are often repeated later in more complex variations.

We perpetually "read" the tales of our lives as we seek to understand what is going on in each other's lives; we continually "write" them through the ongoing themes, character development, and general story-lines of our decisions and plans. Our responses, actions, and attitudes are some of the main methods by which we continue to write our flesh-and-blood autobiographies.

It is here in the real story – where the "rubber meets the road," where what we eat and do affects our own health, where our present choices determine a future we will live with – that critical thinking about human problems must be tested. Does it produce the best in relationships, opportunities, and character? Only our decisions and actions show what we truly believe, what we really desire, value, and care about. Our actual decisions and their consequences both concretely and measurably expose the quality of that critical thinking. Far more effectively and powerfully than public statements and corporate policy pronouncements, our choices and behavior express our actual thoughts and preferences and impact others' thoughts and actions. Our decisions convey what we truly care about most.

DECISIONS, DECISIONS, DECISIONS

The critical-thinking tools of decision making enable us to resolve the human problems we face. Our problems may not be neatly "solved" like textbook cases or TV detective stories, but some resolution is necessary in order for us to go on – with our lives, relationships, education, career, family.

Even the "decision" not to decide is, of course, a decision. "Not choosing" now is still a choice, a conclusion of thought, an attempt to resolve the problem for now. Giving someone else the responsibility, putting off a decision, passing the buck – these are all possible choices, and they are paragraphs in our personal stories that will continue to live with us. How exactly do we want our story lines to go?

These stories are the primary environment of all our thought, decisions, and behavior. Even when we are thinking abstractly, that is an event in our personal stories. There are boring chapters dealing with time wasted and well spent. More interesting are the paragraphs about how we acted in a crisis, under pressure, and when the temptations were huge. And even though few of our biographies will be published, our lives are there for others to see and "read" any time.

It is no coincidence that every major religious leader was a skillful story-teller – both in the Judeo-Christian tradition and elsewhere. The Talmud, Koran and Bible are chock-full of stories – stories that reveal the deepest patterns of our lives, our sins, our hopes, as well as the sweeping patterns of what adherents see as God's story. Religious literature is usually concrete and vivid – actual accounts of events, not abstract theory. The chronicles of Moses' life, for example, report actual history through stories; the accounts of Jesus' life contain narratives of His telling parables – so this story includes stories about stories. And most of what we teach, from business management to physics, is some form of story: Divulging successful growth strategies and recounting fascinating phenomena.

WHO CARES?

Augustine (A.D. 354-430) was the first person to write and publish an autobiography, and his dramatic and revealing story is still considered valuable literature, penetrating in its psychological and spiritual insights. His thinking will be examined among others in Chapter 3. He saw in his own life the way his own decisions revealed both his temporary wants and his long-term priorities and motivations. Augustine also wrote extensively – from a historical and theological perspective – about the frightening collapse of the Roman Empire that he observed occurring right before his eyes. The Vandals entered and plundered his city in northern Africa as he lay on his own deathbed.

On the basis of his discerning and sagacious observations of both individuals and empires, Augustine repeated one particular theme in dozens of his books: The most important attribute of persons or organizations is what they care about the most. That is, what people and organizations love most will always be shown in the patterns of their lives and history, even if these cares and priorities are not evident in every individual decision. What we truly care about will keep cropping up and be utterly evident over a period of time.

For example, when students cheat on a paper or a test, it is evident that they care more for the appearance of knowledge and skill than actually having knowledge and skill. Similarly, when people are unfaithful in marriage, it is evident that they care more for the pleasure or excitement of the affair than working toward a stable and happy marriage. Claims that either incident of cheating was just a fleeting mistake – having nothing to do with the cheater's real character – would fall on deaf ears for Augustine and almost anyone else. Sometimes we come to know our own actual cares best by reflecting our own decisions and behavior. Of course, any changes in our cares will be shown in our choices and conduct.

EXEMPLARS AS THINKING MATERIAL

Stories of other people's problems and decisions are tremendous materials to help us make wise decisions in our own lives – whether those stories depict good or bad decisions. History, literature, case studies, the news, religious books, movies, anecdotes – what rich resources we have for stories! Even the living, personal examples of people we admire are stories we "read" by observation and from which we can learn. Stories that might help show us what can be done or what should be avoided we will call *exemplars or approaches to moral reasoning* – patterns of ethical behavior as demonstrated in time-tested stories of concrete problems and resolutions and the summation of the values in them. Central to understanding an exemplar is recognizing its duality as both the embodiment of and the *illustration* of that approach.

Exemplars include a large variety of case studies, anecdotes, and even fables and myths that are used in various types of meetings and training seminars within college classes and clubs, business corporations, government offices. Courses in business, sociology, political science, and other subjects include some of these case studies. To the extent that we learn from watching the actions of others, ongoing corporate and organizational decisions and actual leadership behavior can also function as exemplars. Every family and religious group uses sets of exemplars serving a similar function. Each of these different kinds of exemplars fulfill slightly different purposes in the various environments of critical ethical thought. Nevertheless, four major contributions to critical thinking are common to the various kinds of exemplars. We will examine the contributions of these tools later.

Exemplars used in critical ethical thought can depict either admirable or objectionable concrete puzzle resolutions for human problems. In fact, exemplars often include in their rich texture a whole range of qualities of critical thought. However, they are never merely the run-of-the-mill, moderately good stories of concrete problem-resolution. Instead, they stand out as especially good or bad examples – or both instructively good and bad examples – of critical thinking about human problems. They become exemplary models or paradigms of what a person should do or avoid. They open windows of understanding to possible decisions and experiences.

Simple explanations of the widespread use of exemplars in critical ethical thought are certainly not correct. For example, it would be a gross mistake to think that exemplars are plentiful in actual critical thought as a condescension to immature popular minds, to some presumed limited capacity of the minds of students and business leaders and the rest of us who frequently use exemplars. That "explanation" could betray intellectual arrogance. Exemplars are illustrations of ethical principles – but not merely that. Exemplars are essential to our very understanding of decisions and their role in critical thinking about human problems. What is more natural or useful than comparing one story or experience with another?

FIRST CONTRIBUTION: AGREEMENT

There are at least five contributions that exemplars make as tools for mature critical thinking about human problems. First, exemplars facilitate *agreement*, even where agreement on detailed moral rules or general moral policy eludes us. People only rarely share particular, detailed rules for ethical decisions, even within communities and corporations. Yet shared exemplars pervade internal community and corporate discussions. And even highly regulated industries and organizations have detailed rules only where there are special problems or particular legal regulations. Nevertheless, we generally work under conditions of broad agreement between people on numerous particular stories and cases.

In fact, even when there is a general unity of conviction that a mistake was made in a particular case, it is nearly impossible to come up with a useful detailed rule on which everyone can agree. For example, we can all agree, with our 20/20 hindsight, that Ford Motor Company was wrong to fail to include an $11 design improvement or a $5 rubber bladder that would have made the Pinto fuel tank much less explosive. There is no agreement, however, on what price would have been too much for such a safety device. No car is completely safe; nor do we for a minute expect any auto maker to design and produce a perfectly safe car. Some potential safety features are just not worth their cost. But what is the breaking point? What is the functional limit of reasonable cost? What is a sensible price to pay for our lives and safety? Consensus on these points is hard to find – very hard to find.

Consider a different example: For fire protection most of us have installed one or more smoke detectors in our apartments or houses. However, very few have invested in an internal sprinkler system, though it would provide additional fire protection for us and our families. Is this wise? At what point are additional safety precautions no longer worth their price? Explicit guiding rules elude us in most topics like this in practical decision-making. Nevertheless, we will generally agree on specific examples of safety precautions.

SECOND CONTRIBUTION: IMPARTIALITY

Of course, we not only want to come to agreement, we want those agreements to be *impartial*. Here exemplars are a great asset as well. It is not easy to rise above both personal wants and the desires of one's particular group. It takes effort, courage, and character to rise to the level of moral impartiality. It may be the greatest challenge of moral behavior. For example, applying the *Golden Rule* is difficult when we cannot imagine ourselves in someone else's shoes – for example, someone quite a bit older, of the opposite sex, with different cultural values, with marked differences of family obligation. How can I really know what it is "I would have them do for me" were I so different? It seems unrealistic actually to "walk a mile" in another's shoes. How can I forget who I am?

Harvard professor John Rawls tries to imagine that we can step behind a hypothetical *"veil of ignorance"* to resolve human problems with objectivity, unadulterated by personal preferences. How could we remember the relevance of the pressing human problems we need to help resolve if we at the same time forget our places in life, and forget what we know? How can I cut off the vital human cares that so energize our individual and group endeavors – and still understand the problems? (And you can wrestle with Rawls in Chapters 3 and 14.)

Clearly, impartial ethics needs the aid of moral imagination, not ignorance. Impartiality calls us to step imaginatively beyond the factual limits of our own particular lives – but on the basis of knowledge about ourselves and others, and as much knowledge as we can get, not on the basis of ignorance. After all, unaided imagination is generally unrealistic.

Here is where exemplars are essential in facilitating impartial moral agreement. Concrete problems and resolutions uniquely cultivate and guide ethical imagination. A well-stated case study enables us to examine thoroughly another's decision as if it were ours to make. A vivid anecdote empowers and equips us mentally to "put on the shoes" of a different personality and see a problem from another's perspective.

Just as importantly, case studies, anecdotes, outstanding people, fables, and parables can ingeniously take us "off guard." High-quality, time-tested exemplars can free us from blinding personal preferences and the rigid expectations of our roles. As a result of this liberating impact of exemplar-guided moral imagination, we are able to discover together the impartial moral agreements we desire. This effect of stories has been understood by the astute since ancient times, and good leaders and effective critical thinkers have used this tool for fair moral accord.

An ancient classic example of this effective application of exemplars comes from Jewish tradition. It is the account of Nathan's use of the Sheep Owner Parable to bring King David to his moral senses. David, king of Israel, lusted after Bathsheba, a beautiful woman who was married to a soldier in David's army. After "sleeping" with her, she became pregnant. David, anxious not to have his own sin revealed, devised plans to escape blame. When these did not work, he finally gave military orders that placed Bathsheba's husband in serious danger. This last plan worked: Her husband was killed. David was then able to marry the widow Bathsheba.

Nathan went to David to confront him about these evil choices. Moreover, Nathan was clever: He told a profound, time-tested story (an exemplar), with the implication that he was asking for advice. The story dealt with a man who had only one sheep but whose sheep was taken away and eaten by a rich man. David became angry at such behavior and decreed that the rich man in Nathan's story must pay four times over. Nathan's simple response was: "You are the man." King David had jumped to the right moral judgment in the parable before he recognized how the story was an obvious analogy of his own evil decisions. Needless to say, as a powerful king, David might not have been so quick to recognize his own moral error if Nathan had tried to work out some agreement with David on a detailed moral rule or on some application of one of the great moral principles. King David's power and his "righteous" self-image might have blinded him.

In short, exemplars help us to become impartial through expanding our moral imagination and knowledge, and through catching us off guard to see parallel problems and solutions where our prejudices are not quite as strong as in questions of our own personal decisions.

THIRD CONTRIBUTION: INTEGRATION OF DIVERSE VALUES

The third contribution of exemplars for critical ethical thought is that exemplars uniquely *integrate* and *balance* diverse sets of values. All of us have multiple priorities and values, all of which are important to us. For example, we want to be respected, loved, and trusted; we want to succeed, be comfortable or even rich; we want to have some enduring meaning and purpose. In fact it is futile to try to list all our values. It would be even more difficult to create formulas for proportioning, balancing, or integrating them. And every human problem involves a number of things we care about.

For example, how would you rate the value of honesty in comparison with the value of helping someone feel good? In some circumstances these two values are almost entirely contradictory. And how should a business rate the values of service to customers, quality of product, commitment to integrity, monetary profit, personal growth of employees, and so forth? This is a complicated mix. Individual moral principles state important truths, but in a form that keeps them isolated from the competing principles. Autobiographies of great people, management stories of excellent corporations, religious narratives and parables, heroic family stories – these bring together multiple values in balanced, integrated, even interwoven fabric. What are some of the stories your family, business, community organization or religious group tells?

FOURTH CONTRIBUTION: PERSONAL JUDGMENT

The fourth contribution of exemplars in pursuing critical ethical thought is that they appropriately cultivate mature *personal judgment*, making detailed moral rules useful in exceptional cases only. There is a place for detailed rules only when exemplars seem too ambiguous or too weak. For example, in society at large, we legislate laws only when personal examples and tacit cultural patterns, regularly expressed in stories – such as religious traditions and case law – prove inadequate in important cases of personal judgment.

In a similar way, in the excellent companies that Peters and Waterman researched they found that the stronger the culture – the richer the repertoire of exemplars – the less need there was "for policy manuals, organization charts, or detailed procedures and rules." [5] Large organizations are much too complex to be run by detailed rule books. Instead, they need people who can make wise moral judgments that are consistent with the culture and purposes of the organization. Dee Hock of VISA correctly points out, "substituting rules for judgment starts a self-defeating cycle, since judgment can only be developed by using it." [6] This is so obvious that it has to be stated. Like a muscle that needs exercise, personal judgment develops through use; otherwise it will atrophy. The only way to develop it is to use it. Good exemplars give us veritable ethical laboratories for exercising and cultivating moral judgment – especially when it comes to history, literature, and case studies. Conversely, the experience of watching television and movies is so passive that we rarely have the opportunity to reap any benefits of practiced moral judgments.

FIFTH CONTRIBUTION: FLEXIBILITY

Our fifth and last contribution of exemplars is this: Exemplars equip us with the irreplaceable *flexibility* necessary to make responsible decisions within the environment of continual change. The goal is to resolve concrete human problems and conflicts maturely. However, considerations weigh differently in each particular case, as we all know. Thus, even the best detailed moral rules will become quite arbitrary in a new situation. Freshly applying general moral principles in each new case is too complicated and too risky. By assigning exemplars an essential place in our toolbox for critical thinking about human problems, we can have both a community of deeply shared values on the one hand, and on the other the attention to detail that also demands individual, creative, critical ethical thought.

In summary, exemplars should be recognized as essential tools for responsible decisions, and for critical ethical thought in general, for these contributions that they make. To review:

> 1. Quality exemplars enable us to create moral agreement where such consensus otherwise eludes us.

2. Creative exemplars aid us tremendously in achieving impartial decisions.

3. Frequent use of exemplars uniquely facilitates the balanced integration of diverse personal and organizational values.

4. Using and rethinking exemplars helps cultivate personal moral judgment by exercising critical thinking about human problems.

5. Exemplars provide an irreplaceable resource for the flexibility so valuable for mature ethical decisions.

Exemplars contribute these essential resources for good, critical, ethical thought – as well they should. They can vividly and usefully depict what we care about – both what is important and who is important.

STEP FOUR: ABILITY
TO EXPLAIN THE DECISION

Once you have recognized a human problem, engaged information, and made your decision, is everything wrapped up? Not quite. What else is there? There is one more step, the follow through step, that brings the process full circle. This is the step that continues to help hone our attention on the other steps. Simply this, we must be able to explain our decision to ourselves and others – our God or higher power, teachers, bosses, IRS agents, family, friends and neighbors as well as, perhaps, the prying media.

Of course, most of the time, no one directly asks us for an explanation. But the possibility that they might ask – and the honesty of our own conscience asking us anyway – helps make the other steps more serious. We are more likely to give them the critical attention they deserve instead of letting them slide. In a way, it is similar to target shooting. The whole process is silly if no one checks how close your aim was to the center of the target.

> READY – Recognize the problem.
> AIM – Engage all available information.
> FIRE – Make a decision and do it.
> CHECK – Be able to explain your decision.

There are many other good analogies and examples for this fourth step. Here are five more. What examples could you add to this list?

> • tape-recording a song or speech to see how well it
> really sounds.
> • completing regular sales and accounting reports to measure
> how well the business is actually doing.
> • checking the results of an experiment to be sure it really
> did come out as it should.
> • knowing that you will get a grade for an assignment, and
> thus trying to follow the teacher's instructions.
> • the team watching the video of last night's football game
> to see what really happened – the good and the bad.

Critical thinking involves being accountable for the quality of our thinking and decision-making. The crucial value here is *accountability*. Unlike digestion and blood circulation, we have considerable personal control over the character of our thought – both our general habits of thought and our particular problem-resolutions. Animal and plant behavior we explain primarily in terms of genetic background and environmental influences. While genetics and environment deeply affect us humans as well, we are also capable of evaluating, learning, choosing, and changing our behavior.

Our evaluation of our own and others' ethics – critical thought about human problems – involves two simple assumptions. First, human thought is not infallible. That is the understatement of this chapter! Even our most instantaneous thinking processes are open to error and can be corrected. Careful, ponderous thought also can go wrong in a variety of ways. Even seasoned critical thinkers can continue to make mistakes. Our thinking is exposed to the power of prejudice, limited by inexperience, blinded by self-conceit, and open to careless mistakes of many other sorts as well.

Second, we have reliable standards for evaluating whether ethical decisions match up. The vast majority of so-called ethical dilemmas – real ones, not the fictitious ones created in late-night bull sessions or by philosophers trying to demonstrate irresolvable conundrums – can be solved through the use of critical thinking, a sort of rigorous common sense. We have already noticed four general criteria for appraising our own (and others') critical thinking about human problems – each associated with one of the four steps of ethics. Am I truly aware of what is going on, of what is needed? Are my information and decisions fair to all concerned? Does this decision show what and who I genuinely believe are worth caring about? Can I actually defend this decision before my conscience, my family, my God, my friends and others?

FOUR STEPS OF THE ETHICS CONSTRUCT: CRITICAL THINKING ABOUT HUMAN PROBLEMS

1. Recognizing a problem
Key Question: What is truly going on?
Working Value: Awareness – being awake, smart, vigilant, alert
2. Engaging all available information
Key Question: Is your information factual and fair?
Working Value: Fairness, justice
3. Deciding what to do and doing it
Key Question: What do you really care to achieve?
Working Value: Care, community
4. Being able to explain the decision to yourself and others
Key Question: To whom, and for what, are you accountable?
Working Value: Accountability

An additional general standard for ethics is consistency: Applying the same values to ourselves as we seek in others. We cannot arbitrarily change values. Confucius said it well: "The faults I find in others I correct in myself." [7] King David of Israel demonstrated this wisdom when Nathan confronted him, as we say above. David recognized that the principle by which he convicted the rich man in Nathan's story applied to himself as well, and he had the courage and integrity to follow its implications. [8]

A clever example of this standard of consistency is used in some business partnership agreements. When one partner wants to buy out the other partner, the first partner names the price for the second partner's shares. The second partner then has the option of turning down that purchase price and buying out the first partner instead for the same price per share. The incentive is on the first partner to name a fair, or even generous price, because the alternative – too low a valuation – could result in the second partner exercising the buy-out option on him. The simple standard of consistency is so profound. Can you give other examples of this power of consistency?

Consistency, of course, can never be our highest standard of critical thinking. The famous American philosopher Ralph Waldo Emerson wisely warned against elevating consistency as an ultimate virtue. "Foolish consistency is the hobgoblin of small minds," he said. First, foolish consistency would inhibit us from making reasonable exceptions to general rules and policies, even if these exceptions would be completely fair. Should you always tell the truth, even to the hateful henchmen of a racist government? Must you come to a full stop at every stop sign, even if you are rushing a dying person to the hospital?

Second, foolish consistency would limit our growth, improvement, maturing process – as individuals and as a society. The ability to learn from experience, and the skills of improving our relationships, behavior, character, and society – these are even more precious than consistency. With mere consistency we could all behave like children, slavery would be permitted, and racial and sexual discrimination could never be overcome.

THE POWER WHY?

World-renowned psychologist Viktor Frankl used to ask patients preparing to leave the psychiatric hospital two questions. "Will you take your own life?" Invariably the answer was "No." "Why not?" he would immediately ask. If patients hesitated or could not come up with a convincing reason, he concluded that they were not yet ready for normal human freedom. We all need reasons to live, in order to keep on living. So Frankl believes.

We also need reasons to do what is right. The multiple checks and balances of accountability force each of us to come up with reasons for doing the right thing. And if we do not have good reasons for our decisions, they are probably not ethical. The stronger our reasons for doing what is right, the more likely we will do it even when it seems that no one else is watching. It has been well said that the true character of people is revealed by what they are willing to do in the dark when there are no human observers. [9]

WHAT KIND OF ACCOUNTABILITY?

Historically, accountability for our decisions has embraced a whole range of different types of reasons – character, goals, results, traditions, duties, human rights, promises, commandments, and so forth. However, in modern times there has been a major split between two camps of intellectuals with mutually incompatible definitions of accountability. But it really is not necessary to take sides. We can choose to use several kinds of accountability if we wish. (And even more on this subject occurs in Chapters 3 and 4.)

The prime conflict is between two camps of ethical theorists – let's call them the "duty-devoteds" or deontologists and "outcome-obsessed" or consequentialists. Both sides claim the implied endorsement of great thinkers of the past – such as Socrates, Plato, Aristotle, Augustine, and Aquinas – but there is some question how many of these more modern assumptions they would be willing to swallow.

The great economist Adam Smith commented about 200 years ago, as the modern period for ethics was just beginning, that modern ethical theories are nearly worthless. He maintained these theories make futile distinctions, and they provide no positive benefit to character and conduct. In the *Wealth of Nations,* Smith surveyed different periods of thought, evaluating their contributions to critical thinking about human problems. Smith's most devastating criticism falls on modern intellectual thought, and it is only modern ethics that Smith calls "debased." Smith himself wrote on ethics, too, but his ideas rose well above such controversies as between the "duty-devoted" and the "outcome-obsessed."

DUTY ONLY

Smith's own teacher, Hutcheson, was a member of the "duty-devoted." This camp claims that results, effects, and consequences are irrelevant when we evaluate people's choices and conduct. We only need to examine people's intentions or aims, they allege.

As a "duty-devoted," Hutcheson tried to convince Smith and other people that the intention to do good is praiseworthy even when there are no deemably good results. He went so far as to claim that praise is out of place if good results are produced without the explicit aim of producing them. But Smith disagreed with his teacher, insisting that Hutcheson's distinction was false. How could one talk only of "good intentions" without insisting on results? How could you ignore the humanitarian results of well-disciplined self-interest in the free market? How could you disregard the essential win-win agreements produced in business and other productive human relationships?

One of the greatest heroes of the "duty-devoted" camp is Immanuel Kant. Kant developed this statement of general duty, which he believed was a principle of reason applicable to all human choices: "Act only on that maxim through which you can at the same time will that it should become a universal law." By concentrating only on the maxims of our actions, Kant taught that we should consider the consequences and results of our behavior morally irrelevant. Kant also saw people as self legislators. This is an unusual role in which people create their own duties. In Kant's general vision, people are responsible to no one but themselves, i.e., everyone is only self-accountable, with rational consistency and the Categorical Imperative as their main standards of duty.

While he recognized a duty for individuals rationally to analyze each choice for it to be considered morally good, he completely rejected an obligation to consider consequences. The actual results of choices do not matter. If my will is good, I am okay. Applying this approach, Kant advised that moral people should tell the truth to soldiers of even unjust governments in locating innocent fugitives – because moral people should will that the truth will be told. If innocent blood is spilled as a result, the blood "guilt" is not on those good people who cooperate, but only on the unjust political leaders. Isn't that convenient? What do you think of that reasoning? Are pure ethical *intentions* our only responsibility?

WHEN ONLY 'THE END' IS IN SIGHT

On the other side of the fight over modern ethics are the people who say that intentions matter not at all. To this second camp, all that counts are consequences, results, and effects. These thinkers are being called the "outcome-obsessed" because of their emphasis on ends or purposes. A variety of seemingly worthy goals has been selected by various sub-camps of the "outcome-obsessed" as the primary values for measuring results, and happiness and pleasure have been most frequently selected by leading "outcome-obsessives."

Jeremy Bentham is perhaps the pre-eminent spokesman for this hedonist-consequentialist camp (for more on these terms, see Chapter 3). He rallied followers with the claim that the only thing that mattered in anyone's life was the quantity of pain and pleasure that was experienced. Nothing else moves us, he argued, nothing else makes any difference. So a decision is to be deemed morally good or bad depending only on its impact for pleasure or pain. Bentham's quantitative evaluation of a choice took account of many aspects of pleasure and pain in deciding how right the choice was. The crucial feature is a narrow sense of "utility": How useful is this decision for increasing pleasure and decreasing pain?

Bentham's evaluation process included measurements of the intensity of the pleasure – its duration, its certainty, its purity, its remoteness, its tendency to create other pleasures, and such – for each person involved in the decision. Any painful results are measured in a similar way, using all these dimensions. Then all the pleasures of all the interested parties are added together, and all their pains are subtracted, to calculate the "net benefit" – or utility – the single evaluation of the decision.

This theory tends to ignore most human rights, duties, promises, and intentions. For its advocates, promises and rights seem important only to the extent that violating them would cause pain – or possible pleasure. Where are the general human rights or basic human duties within Bentham's camp? Intentions contribute nothing either. Bentham himself went so far as to claim that love was the same as lust and that there is no important difference between the attitudes and values associated with each of these. The only difference, he suggested, is after the fact – the actual impact of a decision on all that are concerned. We use the term "love" for the relationships that after some time give more pleasure than pain, and "lust" for the relationships that after some time give more pain than pleasure. How long we should wait to take an inventory of the results is unclear – one month? five years? fifty years? We will not know whether a decision was good or bad until such an inventory is taken. Otherwise we are only guessing.

What would be the results of following this method of accountability? For example, even after publicly promising "for better, for worse, for richer, for poorer, in sickness and in health – to love and to cherish," people from Bentham's philosophical camp believe that these promises mean nothing. All that matters are results. And when there are more sicknesses than health, or less riches than wanted, one is obligated to call the relationship bad and promptly change it, with no regard to promises.

COST-BENEFIT ANALYSIS

Cost-benefit analysis in business and government – as well as in personal decisions – is a distant cousin of Bentham's approach. Business persons will likely find many justifications for corporate actions/policies using this method.

Fair and honest predictions of costs and benefits are an essential ingredient to almost any responsible choice – whether these are off-the-cuff projections for minor decisions, or carefully prepared cost-and-benefit forecasts for major decisions. No rational person would make a decision without some such predictions; everyone would consider them important information when evaluating a decision later. The only question is, how well are the cost-benefit analyses conducted? Two main criteria must be met.

First, the best net needs to be cast – and cast broadly enough – to collect all the relevant dimensions of cost and benefit. There are many kinds of potential failure here, too numerous to list. For decisions in which we already have a strong interest, for example, it is very easy to underestimate costs and overrate benefits. It is also tempting to choose programs whose costs are borne by others, with or without their consent.

Second, promises and basic human rights, as well as the inherent value of all human beings, should not be ignored, even when normal cost-benefit nets miss them. Cost-benefit analysis helps us understand one particular dimension of any decision, and it is a significant area for rational accountability – especially in government and business. However, human dignity and integrity are critical dimensions for every decision as well. Cost-benefit analysis cannot override human dignity and integrity – nor can any rational person ignore costs and benefits. But a tunnel vision that attempts to restrict accountability to one of these dimensions is the most dangerous policy.

ACCOUNTABILITY CHAUVINISM

One caution: In moments of weakness, chiefs on each side of this philosophical battle over modern ethics have conceded some truth to the other side. But these qualifications are rarely heard by their camps-men and camps-women. Are the primitive perspectives of "duty-devoted" and "outcome-obsessed" so important to defend? Are people so frightened by the full-blooded complexities of our lives?

Is it any better to allow for the full range of explanations for our choices and behavior, as long as they are based on *true awareness, actual fairness, authentic caring, and honest accountability*? A model for such human breadth is Dr. Martin Luther King Jr. He had a clear sense of human duty defined by what he understood as the biblical standard of fairness. To him, responsibility to God's laws and a commitment to his vision of justice established a duty no one should compromise.

At the same time, results were essential for Dr. King. It is important to contribute to real progress toward a more loving and fair community, and that progress is assured if our own behavior is guided by love – even love for those who hate us. Dr. King believed that Aristotle was right to say that our goals should define our means, and then those means are measured by the end result. Loving behavior will help produce a loving society. As he said to his audience in his first major speech at age 26:

"If you will protest courageously, and yet with dignity and Christian love, when the history books are written in future generations, the historians will have to pause and say, 'There lived a great people – a black people – who injected new meaning and dignity into the veins of civilization.' This is our challenge and our overwhelming responsibility. "

Both duties and outcomes do matter, of course. Sometimes it makes sense to concentrate more on one than the other, but it is always a mistake to ignore either one.

HUMAN PROBLEMS AND LEGAL CONCERNS

"There ought to be a law!" people have often said, and then sometimes someone has gone on to write a law on the subject. The motivation is similar to ethics; laws have been written in an effort to solve human problems. And, like moral decisions, laws sometimes have the unfortunate effect of increasing or complicating human problems. Kings, queens, presidents, judges, and legislators have often been greedy, prejudiced, misinformed, and foolish, and so the laws they create and enforce can actually do more harm than good. In any case, like moral decisions, laws and those who write and enforce them can be evaluated in terms of how aware, fair, caring, and accountable they are. This is appropriate because these laws affect our problems, our lives, our hopes, and our futures.

Moreover, ethics includes the ways we use laws, too. For example, legal regulations can be used to deceive and exploit others, and they can be used to help give people respect, protection, and liberty. Moreover, whenever we try to solve one of our human problems, existing laws can function as part of the problem, or part of the solution, or both. In the civil rights cause, for example, the segregation laws were part of the problem, while civil rights laws helped to address the problem. How would people have behaved without the segregation laws in the first place? That is hard to say, but the segregation laws did add muscle to the terrors of racism.

When people think about the purposes of governments and their laws, they usually appeal to ethical intentions or goals – for the benefit of the rulers, citizens, or both. Plato (c. 427-347 B.C.), for example, claimed that all laws of society are rough approximations of an eternal standard of justice, although some laws are far closer to that standard than others. Paul (c. A.D. 5-67) stated that government is established by God in order to approve what is good and to punish those who do evil. Thomas Jefferson (1743-1826), the main author of the Declaration of Independence, asserted that governments derive "their just powers from the consent of the governed" for the purpose of producing "safety and Happiness" for the citizens. Similar perspectives have been held by other people as well. Seeking justice, approving the good, punishing evil, creating safety and happiness – these are all explicitly ethical goals that help to solve human problems. In contrast, when personal power is the goal, governments and laws will take on selfish and egocentric methods and ambitions. In such cases human problems are multiplied and our fellow citizens are not served.

LAW IS LAW

Nevertheless, a legal responsibility is not the same as a moral responsibility. Once a law is adopted by a government, that law has some authority over us, but the power behind the idea is no longer merely its moral quality. From then on, the substantial power of government and its enforcement tools are there to "persuade" people to behave according to the law. As a result, even when a person thinks that the law is bad, he or she still has some reason to live up to it.

People's obedience to the law – or their appearance of obeying the law – often follows without people even thinking about its moral value. Their main motivation is to avoid confrontations with any of the various courts or law enforcement agencies. Who wants the expense, hassle, and bad publicity this might involve? Is this why much of what corporate America does in the name of ethics seems so illusory? In many cases, the ethics department of a corporation employs a battery of lawyers merely to help it avoid or solve legal problems. The broader ethical issues are often completely missed or ignored, because in most cases the corporations and their lawyers are not even considering or asking those questions. What difference do they make? (See more on this in Chapters 15 and 21.)

Let us draw some lines. *Can a law be immoral?* Of course, that is our primary motivation for reforming laws. *Can a law's enforcement be immoral?* Yes, that is why we have limited terms of office, political campaigns, investigative reporting, police review boards, and such like. Informed people assume that the laws they have and the people who enforce them will often fail to solve the problems they were supposed to solve – whether from weakness, ignorance, exploitation, or some other source.

Can a moral responsibility be illegal? Sometimes. Some of our greatest heroes engaged in "civil disobedience." The founders of the United States believed, on the basis of certain moral concerns, that they had a responsibility to rebel against the authority of England. This, of course, violated the English law that they were under – to say the least. In 1955, Ms. Rosa Parks believed she had a moral responsibility to defy the Montgomery laws that would take away her seat on the bus just because a white man wanted to sit on the same row of seats. She had already engaged in some serious critical thinking about discrimination in bus seating, and she broke the law for the sake of her own dignity, the self-respect of her children, and the dignity of many other people as well. The rest is history. Of course, many expressions of civil disobedience have been less successful than the protest of Ms. Parks and the American War of Independence.

Can laws be amoral – neither especially good or bad solutions to human problems? Yes, in a way of speaking. There is no profound ethical reason why "stop" signs have to be red. They could just as well be green or pink – although red seems to catch our attention more than these colors. Would not "hot pink" stop signs catch our attention a little more, though? Also, there is often no major moral significance to the specific content of zoning laws. Nevertheless, zoning decisions can still be fair or unfair, and without zoning laws society itself would be much less fair, caring, and accountable. In any case, it is necessary to solve problems, like traffic safety and community planning, in ways that are at least not unfair or uncaring, and in ways that are consistent and accountable.

Can laws be a poor replacement for ethics? Yes, and far more often than we usually realize. Too often both corporations and private citizens are more concerned for what they can get away with – without peer rejection or punishment of the authorities – rather than for what is moral. And even when there is an appearance of legality, the moral problems the laws were written to solve do not really get solved. For example, there are many ways people discriminate on the basis of race. Legislators, law enforcement and the courts may not be capable of keeping up or finding sufficient evidence for all of them. In general, it often seems as if the introduction of laws to help solve human problems does not even increase our opportunities, nor decrease our responsibilities, for solving them.

AS A RULE, IT'S NOT THE RULE

Not only do laws not replace the opportunities and responsibilities of ethics, but much of ethics has very little to do with rules at all. We discovered this in our discussion of exemplars earlier in the chapter. Perhaps when we were children our most memorable encounters with ethics were the rules of our parents, teachers, or religion. However, as we grow up we find many other sources for wisdom and guidance – common sense, independent thinking, the examples of people we know, the stories we read and hear, team or group decision-making, and such like. We will see more about these different tools of ethics in Chapter 5 of this book.

History is rich with criticism of rule-based ethics – especially in the Taoist and Christian traditions. Taoists considered the rules taught by Confucianists and other moralists to be positively harmful to personal and public morality. The specific contents of the rules were not the problem; they thought the net effect of any moral rules to be negative. Similarly, Jesus criticized the religious leaders of his time for the way their rigid rules had blinded them and their followers. These moralists were well-practiced in applying the rules, but blind to the value of people and to people's needs.

What are the hazards of rule-based ethics? First, rules can merely cover up rather than solve our human problems. For example, you should not have to tell people how to respect their own parents. If they have so denied their natural impulses that they have no idea how they should honor their parents, the mere appearance of honor taught by the rules would be a farce. If we are really so lost, so morally degenerate, the Band-Aids of formal rules will neither cover nor heal our "values pathology." What is needed is the restoration of the person.

Second, moral discipline often backfires. The very behavior that the rules are supposed to reduce may become even more likely because of the rules. Do you remember when you were a child and your mother asked you not to eat the cookies? For a moment, think very seriously about this rule: "DO NOT THINK ABOUT MONKEYS." Chances are that you are now thinking of monkeys because the rule said not to. It's a joke. Without the rule you probably would not have thought about monkeys all day. The T-shirt saying "DON'T THINK ABOUT GOD" causes people to think about God. One of the best ways to get people to read a book is to censor it, because forbidden fruit tastes the sweetest.

Speaking against a movie can quadruple the ticket sales. Detailed statements forbidding immoral business behavior can serve as an idea bank for the less creative, greedy mind.

Third, lists of detailed rules can be used to condemn the behavior of others, a problem that is related to the one above. With any substantial list, careful examination of another person's behavior will always uncover some flaw, some breaking of the code. No one can follow a detailed code with perfect consistency, especially in the ambiguous world in which we live. Disciplined rules are too often used as ammunition for attacking, condemning, ostracizing, rejecting, or firing people whom we do not like. What may be only a cultural difference, or a matter of choice, is then tragically used to abuse other people and to divide the human race. Even if this were not the original intent of the moral rules, it can be their net effect.

So rules can sometimes be harmful: (1) They can cover up problems rather than solve them. (2) They can backfire, since telling us not to do something often increases our interest in doing it. And (3) they can be used to hurt others rather than improve our selves and society. Rules can be useful, of course, but as with anything powerful they have to be used with caution.

BENEFITS OF MORAL CHOICES

Ethics, critical thinking about human problems, provides numerous benefits to each of us – and to society. Frankly, these advantages are more numerous and intricate than we can explain here. But let us stretch our imaginations anyway.

First, "not to decide is to decide." When faced with human problems we can put off decisions, but that itself is a decision. We can also react badly, without using the critical thinking skills of perception, information, stories, and reasoning. But then we still are responsible – we will still live, or die, with the consequences of our choices. Why not use our abilities to make our decisions well?

Second, we are more than rabbits and tomato plants. We are not limited to hormones and photosynthesis to guide us. In fact, our decisions help make us who we become. Even the simple decisions that each one of us makes help form our character and reputation. Is anything more important than character in our lives, families, and careers?

Third, our communities and commitments make a difference. What would the world be like without ethics? Ancient Chinese thinker Hsuntzu (298-238 B.C.) pointed out that the necessity for ethics is obvious to the most elementary human intelligence. Here is his simple argument: We humans need to have guidelines that will help us work together. On the one hand, for us to work together successfully, our community's guidelines must be recognized as fair – at least to some measure of fairness. On the other hand, if we do not work together, our lives are destined for poverty and failure. We will be poor because as individuals we can do so little on our own.

> A single individual needs the support of the accomplishments of hundreds of workmen. Yet an able man cannot be skilled in more than one line, and one cannot hold two offices simultaneously. If people live all alone and do not serve one another, there will be poverty.

Also, we will even fail to harness natural resources for good:

> Man's strength is not equal to that of an ox; his running is not equal to that of a horse; and yet ox and horse are used by him. How is this? I say that it is because men are able to form social organizations whereas others are unable ... When united, men have greater strength; having greater strength, they become more powerful; being more powerful, they can overcome other creatures.

That is, without some minimal level of fairness in society, all of us, and the human race in general, are in jeopardy. Our projects and our lives will fail. Moral community is our chief source of strength in a hazardous world. To Hsuntzu, this should be obvious to any human of minimal intelligence. Is this why even some of the worst communities and governments have at least some fairness? Is there honor among thieves?

Finally, there are levels of personal spiritual development that are possible only as we use some of the disciplines of ethics, critical thinking about human problems. The process of becoming a whole person seems to require cultivating certain personal skills. We will understand more about that in Chapters 4 and 5 of this book. Can you think of any other benefits to ethical thought?

SUMMARY

In this chapter we have uncovered the essential steps of ethical thinking – critical thinking about human problems – and we have compared ethics with some other types of thought, and looked at some benefits. In today's problems and choices, and in today's decisions, can you recognize the four steps and the four values of the ethics construct?

FOR FURTHER INQUIRY

EXERCISES

Please examine the story below. As you consider each part of this case study, try walking through the four steps of critical-ethical thought. Do all four steps for practice, and see what difference it makes.

PAPER JUSTICE – PART I

Click.

The nearly silent turnstile of the college library registered one more body. Kyle, a little bemused, glanced back at the "No Exit" sign now immediately behind him. The exit was a few feet away, next to the book check-out counter. It's good to know where the exit is, he thought with a chuckle.

Well, in Kyle's experience of two semesters, the library was not one of the more familiar parts of the college. He had been here a few times before, but only for a quiet place to study, or rest. This time he had to find a book, or even a few books. Kyle's research paper for ethics class was due the next Friday. It was certainly time to get started.

"Hey, hunk, you're right on time," Tricia whispered. She was in the same class. Tricia had agreed to help him use the computerized book search. "These computers will find what you're looking for in a minute. So, what topic did you choose for your paper?"

Kyle stroked his chin. "That's my first problem. You know I can do pretty well memorizing class notes for the tests, but this research stuff is something else. It's so new. My high school didn't prepare me for this at all. Would you believe, I've never written a research paper in my life."

"Oh, it's not so hard, Kyle," Tricia teased as she nudged her hand against his biceps. "I've written dozens of them."

"SSHHH!" Kyle warned firmly, and then started whispering again. "This is the library, Trish. I only told you one of my problems. Even if I knew how to do it, I really don't have any time. Chemistry reports, a project for management class, a big test in accounting – and I have to wait on tables at the restaurant every night. It's too much."

For several seconds they both silently stared at the blank computer screen in front of them.

"I have an idea," Tricia broke the silence with a very low voice, causing Kyle to lean a little closer to hear her better. "I have found so much material for my research I could easily write two papers. Really. Writing is such a breeze anyway. Then, when the restaurant closes Thursday night you can come over, look at what I've written for you, we could make some changes on my computer, and – *voila!* – your paper will be done. It's no problem." She grabbed his arm in a reassuring gesture.

QUESTIONS FOR THOUGHT AND DISCUSSION
1. Is there a problem here?
2. Does Kyle know what he is doing? Does Tricia know what she is doing? Is either one really alert to the real and potential problems involved?
3. Could Kyle have avoided his present crisis? Explain.

PAPER JUSTICE – PART II

"Tricia, you're too nice." Kyle was calling several hours later. Tricia had written down her phone number for him. "You are so sweet to offer to help. Frankly, I was getting depressed about all this work. You cannot imagine. Tricia, you're saving my life. But what can I do for you?"

"Don't worry about it, hunk. Something will come up. Maybe my car will break down again."

"How about chemistry? I'm getting mostly "A's" there. I could show you my lab reports. It would definitely make your reports easier."

"Thanks but no thanks," Tricia said cautiously. "I'd rather struggle through it myself. If I'm going to make it in nursing, I'd better start thinking like a chemist now or I'll be really lost later on. But my car has some kind of terminal disease. Maybe you could come over and look at it Saturday when all your other work is out of the way. That's what I need."

Kyle didn't respond right away. After 10 seconds of silence, he started talking again slowly: "Hmmm. You know you're right. I wasn't thinking before. Now I don't know what to do."

"What do you mean? What's the problem?" Tricia was confused.

"You don't want me to help you with chemistry because you need to learn it. That makes sense. Shouldn't I do my own ethics paper for the same reason? I have to learn how to write a paper sometime. And, actually, Prof. Wier said each one of us should do our own research and writing. I'd better think about this again."

"Don't be silly, Kyle." Tricia was confident. "It's not at all like chemistry. Get real. You're not going to have to do ethics again once this course is out of the way, but chemistry is part of the lifeblood of my nursing career. I have to know what I'm doing there."

QUESTIONS FOR THOUGHT AND DISCUSSION
1. Is ethics at all like chemistry or not? Will "ethics" come up again in Tricia's and Kyle's lives? How?
2. Will Kyle face an ethical problem of cheating when he gets in business? Will Tricia face an ethical problem of cheating in nursing? How will they decide then? Will it make a difference to anyone?
3. What have you learned in ethics class – and in this chapter – that Kyle and Tricia seem to be forgetting?

PAPER JUSTICE – PART III

It was 11:30 Thursday night. For the past 20 minutes Kyle had, for the first time, been reading "his" research paper that Tricia had written for him for ethics class: "A Comparison of Plato and Rawls on the Standard of Justice in Society." It was kind of interesting; the style was smooth; it was long enough; and there were five books in the bibliography. Kyle made six or seven minor changes to make the paper fit more his own personal style, and ran it out of Tricia's printer.

"What a nice girl," he thought to himself, though he knew that "girl" is not quite the right word to use. How glad he was that they had talked after class a few days ago. There was no way he could have done a paper like this in the time he had. His life was so busy. Now he had a great paper to turn in.

Kyle half hugged Tricia while they both watched the printer finish the last page. "You're Wonder Woman. Let's take a look at your dying car this Saturday after lunch. I have to work the tables Saturday evening."

QUESTIONS FOR THOUGHT AND DISCUSSION

1. If he hands this paper in to Prof. Weir at the ethics class on Friday, what would, if anything, this say about Kyle's priorities?
2. What would it take for Kyle to change his mind about turning in this paper Tricia wrote? Could he ask Prof. Weir for an extension, and next week turn in something he would actually write himself?
3. Does Kyle respect Tricia? Does Tricia respect Kyle? What concept do they have of each other? How do they view themselves?

PAPER JUSTICE – PART IV

There it was again: "A Comparison of Plato and Rawls on the Standard of Justice in Society." Kyle silently re-read the title. Prof. Weir had just handed it back to him.

He quickly flipped past all of Tricia's work and the good professor's remarks. There on the last page was a "B+." Hmmm, not bad considering the amount of work I put into it," he mused to himself.

However, something else immediately caught his eye. Next to the "B+" Prof. Weir had attached a short note: "Kyle, this is a creative paper – good research and thoughtful comparisons. Nice job. I have a question for you about one of your points. If we can clarify it, your grade might go up, but we should talk about your ideas in any case. Please make an appointment soon."

QUESTIONS FOR THOUGHT AND DISCUSSION

1. Should Kyle make an appointment with Prof. Weir? Could he bluff knowledge of the subject of "his" paper? Should he try to bluff it?
2. Is Prof. Weir suspicious about whether Kyle really wrote the paper? What clues might he be going on?
3. What might Prof. Weir do if Kyle does not make the appointment to talk with him?

READING

More Effective Thinking
Dr. Edward de Bono

Should we condemn our traditional thinking methods, which were set in place by the last Renaissance? Surely they have served us well in science, in technology, in democracy and in the development of civilization itself?

There is no doubt that our existing thinking culture has taken us very far. It is pointless to speculate that a different thinking culture might have taken us even further – especially in human affairs – because such speculation can never be tested. We can be duly appreciative of our traditional thinking culture and also realize that it is inadequate. It may have been adequate for the period in which it was developed (ancient Greece and medieval Europe), but at that time there were stable societies, agreed perceptions and limited technical change. Today there are problems caused by rapidly accelerating change and the uneven nature of that change. In part these things are caused by the "cleverness" of our traditional thinking systems and a lack of "wisdom." The inadequacy of our traditional thinking culture may be pinpointed as follows:

• We need to shift from a destructive type of thinking to a much more constructive type.
• We need to change from argument to genuine exploration of a subject .
• We need to lessen the esteem in which we hold critical thinking and to place it below constructive thinking.
• We need to match skills of analysis with an equal emphasis on skills of design.
• We need to do as much idea-work as we do information-work. We need to realize that the analysis of data is not enough.
• We need to shift from an obsession with history to a concern for the future.
• We need to emphasize "operacy" as much as knowledge. The skills of doing are as important as the skills of knowing.
• We need, for the first time, to realize that creative thinking is a serious and essential part of the thinking process.
• We need to move from our exclusive concern with the logic of processing to the logic of perception.

ENDNOTES

1. Because it directly undermines any claim to its own truth, the doctrine that "all truth is scientific" is considered self-referentially absurd.
2. The concept of critical thinking that is developed here is a selection of the major points made by several authors. Among them are the following:
3. See Paul de Vries, "The Original Sin," *Christianity Today*, May 15, 1987.
4. See Thomas S. Kuhn, *The Structure of Scientific Revolutions*.
5. Thomas Peters and Robert Waterman, *In Search of Excellence* (New York: Harper and Row, 1982) p. 75.
6. Peters and Waterman, p. 278.
7. Confucius, *Analects*.
8. II Samuel 11 and 12, *The Holy Bible*.
9. See the story of Gyges' Ring in Plato's *Republic*, Book II. A ring that would make us invisible would be almost too powerful for humans to handle, because the temptations for crime and evil would be so great. In *The Hobbit* and other novels, J.R.R. Tolkien (1892-1973) developed the same idea. Nevertheless, we can achieve mature character where our internal motivations are strong enough to resist temptation, without external pressure of other people and without the threat of being caught. We will return to this idea in Chapter 4.

Chapter 3

David Seiple

EXEMPLARS IN THE HISTORY
OF MORAL THEORY

"My definition of a philosopher is of a man up in a balloon, with his family and friends holding the ropes which confine him to earth and trying to haul him down."

– Louisa May Alcott, *Thoreau's Flute*

"Without civic morality communities perish; without personal morality their survival has no value."

– Bertrand Russell

"Reason is a light that God hath kindled in the soul."

– Aristotle

One way to approach the study of applied ethics is through the historical development of ethical theory. The story of that development is an account of a number of well-known *exemplars* – approaches to moral reasoning that have been tested against the implications, advantages and shortcomings of rival points of view. These may or may not be accompanied by time-tested stories, legends, myths and factual accounts, as we learned in Chapter 2.

We might at first wonder how the study of past theories has much relevance to our own situation here and now. For it is true, of course, that the specific circumstances that attracted the moral concern of, say, a medieval monk or a 19th-century social reformer are not precisely our own. But does that mean that the *general process* of moral deliberation conveyed in each of those historical examples is irrelevant to us?

To see the relevancy of this process, perhaps we need to remind ourselves at this point just what a study of ethics is supposed to provide. It certainly won't give us all the answers we'd like to have concerning the moral choices we face from day to day. Nor should it. Each individual situation has to be patiently

David I. Seiple, Ph.D. Columbia University, M.T.S. Drew University Theological School, is director of research, Workplace Literacy Foundation and Adjunct Assistant Professor of Humanities at New York University, S.C.E.

assessed on its own terms. But to do that, we need to have a model that sets forth, in a general way, the sorts of factors we need to consider. (Otherwise, where do we begin? How would we proceed?) And why suppose that those models need to be exactly similar to our own case? All we can (or should) hope for is that accounts of past moral thinkers connect just enough to our own lives, so that we detect some moral options we might not have thought of, or some limitations to a particular approach that we might otherwise have missed. After that, we still need to develop our own approach for ourselves – but then, by that point, we should be in a much better position to do it. (And remember: The author's purpose is to acquaint you with these exemplars, to explain and analyze them, not to persuade you of any of them.)

So here, in the waning years of the 20th century, we find ourselves beneficiaries of a number of historically distinct approaches to morality, to which we give convenient labels. We shall see, for example, that Aristotle's theory is commonly called an ethic of "self-realization," while St. Thomas Aquinas is a proponent of "natural law." But let's not feel too constrained by those separate labels, as if our choice of approach had to be entirely dependent upon one or another of the exemplars we will consider. For many of these different theories are not logically distinct from one another. It is possible to combine various theories: Aquinas, for one, does so. You should feel free to do the same.

PRE-MODERN ETHICAL THEORY

Moral philosophy as we know it in the West arose in Ancient Greece, out of the social dislocations surrounding the Peloponnesian War (431-404 B.C.). As Americans learned during the 1960s, war often undercuts the very values that seem most secure, and for this reason the Athenian experience during this period is closer to our own than we might at first suppose. Today, so many different people have so many different intuitions on moral matters – on sexual ethics and abortion, for example, or on euthanasia – that it's tempting to wonder if there really *are* any solid answers to those issues. But might this not really be a great opportunity for us, just as it was for the Ancient Greeks, to think through these moral issues free from the restraints of dogmatically held beliefs? The philosopher Aristotle famously said that philosophy begins in wonder, but he might have added that it begins in confusion as well.

Moral philosophy in Greece centered on the notion of moral virtue. For generations prior to this period, the closest equivalents to our English term "virtue" were Greek words that referred to the kingly and warriorly traits lionized in Homeric poetry. But as the old social arrangements began to disintegrate in the face of the disruptions of war, so did the accompanying cultural assumptions. So a few bold people began asking many hard questions about moral "virtue." What is virtue, really? Is it anything more than social custom? How do we learn about it? And what difference does it make if we don't bother asking all these questions?

The standard historical account of the origin of Western philosophy gives special credit to a man named Socrates (469-399 B.C.). However, some real credit needs to be awarded as well to a group of Socrates' contemporaries known as the Sophists, who may have been the first to anticipate what has become (as we'll see later on) a modern philosophical preoccupation: Concern over the complexities of everyday language. These Sophists made their living as what we would call consultants, teaching the young male elite how to use words in any way necessary to win them popular acclaim – a bit like public relations experts these days. Sophists were able to trade on their understanding of the seductiveness and versatility of well-crafted rhetoric, and this was a skill they were very willing to pass on to others – for the right price, that is.

Sophism did not evolve into anything like a unified philosophical position, and it was not even clear who was and who was not a Sophist. Socrates, who despised the Sophists' tendency toward self-promotion and cynicism, was brought to trial by Athenians who couldn't tell the difference between Socratic and Sophistic morality (and so branded Socrates himself a Sophist). Thus it is useful for us to draw the distinction rather clearly, and we will begin to do so by introducing two moral exemplars – one more typical of some of the Sophists, the other fully developed by the followers of Socrates (especially Plato and Aristotle).

> **EXEMPLAR: The Theory of Egoism. The Egoist is someone who has the aim of always acting for perceived self-interest, usually in the long term, even at the expense of the well-being of others.**

It is very natural to be preoccupied with one's own self-interest. Consider the question of whether or not to obey some particular law – to stop at a red light on the highway, for example. Let's say you are in a great hurry to make an appointment, you are sure there are no other cars at the intersection, and there are no police anywhere in view. Should you really bother obeying the law (just this once ...)? There are a number of reasons you might imagine in favor of obeying. For example, what if everyone decided to disobey any law that seemed personally inconvenient? But there are very tempting considerations that might outweigh them all: You are in danger of missing a contact you absolutely cannot afford to miss, every single moment counts, no one is watching, and you simply don't need this red light right now.

However, this only begins to get to the point. An Ethical Egoist is not just someone who acts out of self-interest. No sane person is indifferent to her own interests. But what happens when those interests appear to conflict with the interests of others? The law against embezzlement is intended to protect the interests of investors, but let's say you are a bank officer who has devised a fool-proof scheme for making off with the contents of somebody's safe deposit box. You know you won't ever get caught. So why not? Or let's say you are an entrepreneur who can make a fortune by building a business that would (legally) pollute an underdeveloped neighborhood. Why bother with *their* interests? (Would they bother with *yours*, after all?)

The status of law was very much a concern to Sophists during Socrates' own day. Many Sophists believed that all morality is like law, in that both are devised purely as a social convenience to enhance the chances of human advancement. Protagoras, the earliest Sophist (490-421 B.C.), is reported to have held that legal and moral prescriptions are a way of ensuring social cooperation,[1] and it is easy to see how that would be in everybody's self-interest. This points out the fact that many people have thought that a society of ethical egoists would actually be the best arrangement for all concerned. Thomas Hobbes (1588-1679) seems to have believed that following moral prescriptions (be kind to others, be honest, *et cetera*) is the best way of attaining what each of us most wants – peaceful coexistence in an otherwise hostile social environment.[2] Adam Smith (1723-1790) laid the basis for free enterprise economics by insisting that if people are allowed to use their money in whatever way their economic self-interest dictates, the common good will automatically be enhanced, as if by the workings of some "invisible hand."

Thus there are many different versions of ethical egoism, some of which (like Adam Smith's version) raise serious questions of fact. Is it really true, for example, that the good of all is actually promoted if everyone follows his own perceived self-interest? One recent test case might be American society during the Reagan years, where government regulations on business were minimized so that investors and managers could have maximum freedom to enhance their profit margins. Think, for example, about the deregulation of the airline industry or the savings-and-loan institutions. What you think about the results of that experiment might reflect your views about ethical egoism in general.

Socrates' disciple Plato, at any rate, did not think much of Sophism. Ethical egoism, which only takes one's own personal concerns as the standard of conduct, is frequently linked with a doctrine known as *hedonism*, the theory that defines those concerns in terms of one's own personal gratification. Put simply, this would mean that I am morally obliged to do only what I think will give me pleasure. This view Plato places vividly in the mouth of Callicles,[3] a character in the *Gorgias* (a dialogue named after one of the prominent Sophists). Here Callicles is portrayed in conversation with Socrates:

> CALLICLES: ... How can a man be happy if he's a slave to anything? No, my friend; what is beautiful and just by nature I shall now explain to you without reserve. A man who is going to live a full life must allow his desires to become as mighty as may be and never repress them. When his passions have come to full maturity, he must be able to serve them through his courage and intelligence and gratify every fleeting desire as it comes into his heart. This, I fancy, is impossible for the mob. That is why they censure the rest of us, because they are ashamed of themselves and want to conceal their own incapacity. And, of course, they maintain that licentiousness is disgraceful, as I said before, since they are trying to enslave men of a better nature. Because they can't accomplish the fulfillment of their own desires, they sing the praises of temperance and justice out of the depths of their own cowardice. But take men who have come of princely stock, men whose nature can attain some commanding position, a tyranny, absolute power; what could be lower and baser than temperance and justice for such men who, when they might enjoy the good things of life without hindrance, of their own accord drag in a master to subdue them: The law, the language, and the censure of the vulgar? .... The truth, which you claim to pursue, Socrates, is really this: Luxury, license, and liberty, when they have the upper hand, are really virtue, and happiness as well; everything else is a set of fine terms, man-made conventions, warped against nature, a pack of stuff and nonsense!

> *Gorgias*, Part III.
> From *The Dialogues of Plato* (Bantam, 1986)

This is not a view that Plato's Socrates finds at all congenial. The notion that one could act purely out of untrammeled desire and still attain genuine happiness, strikes him as patently absurd. People who do that, Socrates thinks, are themselves like slaves trying to carry water to a perforated jar with a leaky sieve! They are captive to their own passions, battered back and forth as the wayward mood strikes, and never fully satisfied; each spent passion yields to yet another, with no end in sight.

Socrates would say that morality itself is incompatible with this view of life. Do you see why he would say that? For what do we really mean when we use notions such as "good" and "virtuous," if it's not to draw a contrast between moral conduct and behavior of this wretched sort? Callicles would obliterate the distinction.

To mark that distinction between real virtue and its opposite, let's begin by introducing another moral exemplar, which will designate a competing tradition initiated by Socrates and elaborated by Plato and Aristotle:

> **EXEMPLAR: The Theory of Self-Realization. The Self-Realization theorist is one whose aim is to act in whatever way will actualize self-potential.**

At first glance, Self-Realization Theory may not seem to be too different from Ethical Egoism. The two views actually coincide in the case of recent pop psychology, where the aim of life is taken to be "doing one's own thing" – and where one's "thing" turns out to be just whatever one wants very much to do. But this misses the interesting contrast between a thinker like Plato and someone like Callicles.

Plato. Plato (430-347 B.C.) has the idea that our desires should not rule our conduct, and that (at least some) people have instead an inherent capacity to govern their lives in accordance with "Reason." Through Reason we come to understand the truth about human nature – about the store of talents, interests, and abilities that define a person's "true" self, and that await just the right conditions for coming into actual being.

What would this mean, in practical terms? We would need to become much clearer than we often are about the traits of the "true self." This is another way of saying that we need to understand what the moral virtues are, as distinct from the vices. Socrates would probably insist that Callicles confuses these categories at almost every turn. In fact, we might say that the willingness to inquire seriously into these kinds of questions is itself one of the moral virtues necessary for self-realization.

From the accounts we have of him, Socrates himself seems to provide us with an exemplar of this preliminary virtue. He left no actual writings, so we must piece together our picture of him through the accounts given by others, including Xenophon and Aristophanes. But Socrates' own pupil Plato presents the most vivid of these portrayals. They are often constructed in the form of a dialogue between Socrates and some unsuspecting other party who complacently thinks he knows more than he really does (Callicles, for example). Through it all, Socrates is disarmingly self-effacing, and only by listening to his ironic banter and relentless interrogation does it begin to dawn upon us what Socrates is really up to. We eventually see that Socrates is very much aware of the power and complexity of perplexing issues that most of his contemporaries simply took for granted.

For the most part, these issues involve the traits of character (the virtues) that mature human beings possess. And for the most part, these are generally familiar notions: They are usually the object of much settled opinion in society at large. (Even today, almost everybody, if asked, would say that people should be trustworthy, courteous, sympathetic to others, and so on.) But it is obviously not enough simply to have opinion on these matters and be able to mouth hallowed phrases in conversation. What's really at stake is the way people actually conduct their lives, not just the stories they like to tell about themselves. And this is what most interested Socrates, as we can see from reading excerpts from the dialogue of Plato called the *Euthyphro*.

First, however, some background to the story. Socrates chances upon an acquaintance named Euthyphro, who is currently the object of some scandal because he has decided to bring his own father to trial for (what we would call) negligent homicide in the death of a slave. Euthyphro thinks he is doing the virtuous thing, based on the fact that in Socrates' day, people generally thought it appropriate to be "pious" ("holy") – to act in a manner approved by the recognized gods, whose stories were recounted in the poetry and drama that formed the exemplars of that era's cultural life. Though most of his contemporaries were shocked at the idea of a son prosecuting his own father, Euthyphro is confident that he can rather easily justify his conduct when Socrates asks him to do so.

SOCRATES. So now in Zeus's name, tell me what you confidently claimed just now that you knew: What sort of thing do you say the pious and impious are, both with respect to murder and other things as well? Or is not the holy ... the same in every action? And the unholy, in turn, the opposite of all the holy – is it not like itself, and does not everything which is to be unholy have a certain single character with respect to unholiness?

EUTHYPHRO. No doubt, Socrates.

SOCRATES. Then tell me, what do you say the holy is? And what is the unholy?

EUTHYPHRO. Well, I say the holy is just what I am doing now, prosecuting murder and temple theft and everything of the sort, whether it is a father or mother or anyone else who is guilty of it. And not prosecuting is unholy. Now, Socrates, examine the proof I shall give you that is a dictate of divine law. I have offered it before to other people, to show that it is established right not to let off someone guilty of impiety, no matter who he happens to be. For these same people worship Zeus as the best and most righteous of the gods. And they agree that he put his own father in bonds for swallowing his children unjustly; yet, and that that father had in his turn castrated his father, for similar reasons. Yet they are angry at me for indicting my father for his injustice. So they contradict themselves: They say one thing about the gods and another about me ...

SOCRATES. But in the name of Zeus, the God of Friendship, tell me: Do you truly believe that these things happened so? ...

EUTHYPHRO. Not only those, Socrates. As I just said, I shall explain many other things about religion to you if you wish, and you may rest assured that what you hear will amaze you.

SOCRATES. I should not be surprised. But explain them another time at your leisure; right now, try to answer more clearly the question I just asked. For, my friend, you did not sufficiently teach me before, when I asked you what the holy is: You said that the thing your are doing now is holy, prosecuting your father for murder.

EUTHYPHRO. Yes, and I told the truth, Socrates.

SOCRATES. Perhaps. But, Euthyphro, are there not many other things you say are holy too?

EUTHYPHRO. Of course there are.

SOCRATES. Do you not recall that I did not ask you to teach me about some one or two of the many things which are holy, but about that characteristic itself by which all holy things are holy? For you agreed, I think, that it is by one character that unholy things are unholy and holy things holy. Or do you not recall?

EUTHYPHRO. I do.

SOCRATES. Then teach me what this same character is, so that I may look to it and use it as a standard, which, should those things which you or someone else may do be of that sort, I may affirm that they are holy, but should they not be of that sort, deny it ...

EUTHYPHRO. Some other time, Socrates. Right now I must hurry somewhere and I am already late.

From Dialogues of Plato, Vol, translated by R.E. Allen

If we take Euthyphro as typical, we would say that the virtue of "piety" for the Greeks was a universally acknowledged but poorly understood cultural norm. In conducting his life along the perfunctory lines dictated by culturally embedded ideals, the average Athenian was not able to give any clear, rational account of what he was doing—he simply followed the common practice and hoped for the best.

And this is where the need to be clear about virtue comes in. Popular opinion shifts as easily as sand in a hurricane, and we can't really be certain that what is generally accepted as right at one moment will still be accepted later on. So what people really need, according to the Socratic tradition in philosophy, is the ability to think rationally about their conduct, and this means the capacity to know what the human virtues *really* are – quite apart from the contradictions and vagueness that plague naive common sense. We need to know what the ideal of human excellence is if we are ever to bring our own conduct into accordance with it; indeed, Socrates is said to have held that whatever he believed firmly to be "fair and good" he would *necessarily* do. Such for him was the power of clear thinking: There is a necessary connection between knowledge and virtue.

But so far, this really tells us more about what virtue is not, than about what it is. Socrates himself was a trailblazer, and from our most reliable accounts, we can say that Socrates himself probably gave very few positive answers to philosophical questions such as this. It was left to his disciples to fill in those details. The first influential disciple was Plato.

Though a follower of Socrates, Plato is justly famous in his own right because he is more than just a conduit for his teacher's ethical views. His positive view about virtue is that *virtue is a quality of soul that makes happiness possible.* That quality is *internal harmony*, in which our inner drives, so often the prelude to frustration and predicament, are placed under the authority of our rational side. Reason has the power to eliminate contradictions, and frustration is the result of a contradiction between one's desires and one's capacities. So a life guided by Reason is presumably a life that escapes the tensions of contradiction.

Unfortunately, however, Plato's discussions about the virtues lacks the concreteness we would hope for in a *moral* theory. More and more as he matured, Plato applied Socrates' analytical style of questioning in a very different direction, to a range of issues that had not interested Socrates in the least – especially abstract metaphysical speculations about some separate realm of existence underlying the everyday world. This is the famous Platonic doctrine of the Forms – which Plato organized under a value-concept he called "the Good" – and philosophers since then have pointed out that, just from knowledge of the Good, it is unclear how we are supposed to answer some of those pesky Socratic questions about "virtue."

Plato's mature work was easily adapted to Christian theology, especially by St. Augustine (354-430), for whom "the Good" came to be seen as God Himself. But even here Platonic ethics could not stand on its own, just because the main thrust of Plato's most mature work does tend toward such absorption in the otherwordly vision of the Good itself, rather than the earthly condition of mortal beings. *Morality* is very much about the mundane choices we are forced to confront in everyday life, and Plato himself never carried this part of his ethical program through. As a result many commentators since have denied that Plato even had an ethical theory, and St. Augustine himself had to supplement Plato's vision with the moral directives contained in the Christian scriptures.

Aristotle. In the pre-Christian era, it was left to Plato's own pupil Aristotle (384-322 B.C.) to bring those moral issues to the fore, and here the Self-Realization Theory takes on considerably more detail.

Aristotle defines "good" in terms of a goal, purpose, or end-state toward which something develops. A person who attains such a purpose or goal is self-realized. Here, as we have already seen, Plato's general idea had actually been quite similar, in that Plato viewed the Form of the Good as the object of a person's highest aspirations. For the Platonist, a person is self-realized to the extent that he gains a clear vision of the Good – rather like the Hindu who gains a meditative experience of Brahman, or the Buddhist who attains Nirvana.

But for Plato (as for many East Asian religious philosophies) the line between "higher" and "lower" aspirations reflected his own distrust of embodied existence. Aristotle, on the other hand, widens this purposive (goal-oriented) framework to include even the purely physical events that comprise the situations of everyday life. We might wonder here whether Aristotle did not go too far in that direction: For him, even an inanimate stone falls to earth as a result of the "purpose" it has in returning to its natural place of rest! Still, modern biology has readapted this in the form of what are called "functional explanations." The function of the lungs, for example, is to bring air into the bloodstream.

Aristotle actually thought that each human being as a whole has a goal or function, which he called "eudaimonia" – traditionally translated as "happiness" (which some modern philosophers now call "flourishing") – and when he elaborates finally on that, he sounds once again rather like the otherwordly disciple of Socrates. But unlike Plato, Aristotle does not ignore the purposes that pertain to our physical and cultural existence, and in Aristotle we find strong hints of an ethical view that speaks much more directly to the moral urgencies people typically experience than anything we find in Plato. For one thing, Aristotle (unlike Plato) acknowledges a variety of "goods." This is at least suggested by the opening sentence of the *Nicomachean Ethics* which states that "*Every* craft and *every* inquiry, and similarly *every* action and project, seems to aim at some good." And this brings out the intimate relation between being a "good" and being the object of desire. When we are fully engaged in any activity, we are directed toward a purpose that seems truly desirable, worth pursuing. So the particular "good" for, say, a student might be the knowledge to be gained from doing careful homework (*et cetera*).

But do you see how "good" in this sense is really a morally neutral term as it stands? Is simply being the object of desire sufficient to lend moral approval to it? What about a murderer who sees the death of his victim as a "good" in this sense?! Within an Aristotelian framework, what adds the evaluative dimension is an account of the *function* of the human being – his or her *natural* good – and any desire that impedes the attainment of that cannot, in the *moral* sense, be considered "good."

"*Eudaimonia*" is the term Aristotle uses to designate this supreme moral good, but the term alone (or any English equivalent) fails to give us much specific information. Aristotle himself thinks that identifying it further is a relatively simple matter once some general characteristics have been noticed (though ever since then, others have not been so sure of this). He considers it obvious, for example, that happiness is the *final* goal of a person's life – not something he aims for as a means to anything else. For this reason wealth cannot be that goal, because money is merely a means for conducting other pursuits. He also remarks that happiness is not any kind of momentary state, but can be ascribed only to the entire life of a person; and this means that happiness depends on a pattern of conduct, sustained over time by stable traits of a person's character. Those traits of character that support a happy life are the virtues, so that "happiness" – the good toward which humans naturally aim – is defined in terms of activity conducted in accordance with virtue.

But this does not of course go very far in clarifying what Aristotle means by "*eudaimonia*"; it only transfers the nub of the question back upon the notion of "virtue" itself. And here again Aristotle is an ethical pluralist. There are many specific virtues, says Aristotle, and there is even more than one general kind of virtue. There are the intellectual virtues, and then there are the moral virtues proper. Unfortunately, the connection between them is none too clear. On the one hand, the "moral virtues" are those we would probably need in order to conduct well the normal affairs of daily life in the upper echelons of Athenian society – such as self-control, courage, gentleness, even wittiness – and these turn out to exclude a range of virtues that other societies have highly valued (such as the Christian virtue of loving one's enemies).

The "intellectual virtues," on the other hand, are supposed to reflect what is unique and important about human nature across the board – namely, human rationality. And this makes Aristotle only a *half-hearted* pluralist. For here, in his sweeping vision of human nature, we find the key to "happiness" for Aristotle, and perhaps the most powerful indication of his deep debt to Plato. For despite Aristotle's departure from his teacher's asceticism, their intuitions about what finally makes human life most worthwhile do not greatly diverge. Aristotle notices that humans share much in common with the lower animals; what makes humans distinct is their power of reason. From this Aristotle concludes that their peculiar *function* is to exercise that power. Because Aristotle thinks of philosophical truth as fixed and immutable, happiness becomes characterized as a life of rational contemplation of eternal truths.

So what do we make of all this? The picture Aristotle gives here, of human life at its most fruitful, certainly has its attractions. This is not a bad existence for a person of leisure whose daily obligations do not intrude into his life's main preoccupation. But on what basis are we to accept the view that this is the *highest* human calling? Aristotle was, of course, a philosopher, and those who have become philosophers would long ago have found another line of work had they not become entranced with the joy of playing with abstract ideas. But why others not so socially blessed as he, should be deemed incapable of a truly happy life is not so clear. And this raises a puzzle that has only become more pronounced through the subsequent history of ethics: *To what extent should the satisfactions of one's own peculiar circumstance serve as a comment upon the affairs of others?*

That is not a question we can consider here, but it is one worth keeping in mind. For it represents one of the persistent pitfalls of moral evaluation – the danger of generalizing inappropriately, from our own situation onto others that don't really match it. Aristotle might have succumbed to this occupational hazard here, in a big way.

But at the same time, even if he had done so, does it really compromise the interest and originality of his work as a whole? Should we be too critical of Aristotle for failing to accommodate essentially different forms of thinking that Aristotle could not have known anything about? Certainly what we have in Aristotle is *a model for aiming at self-realization*, through the process of *asking certain sorts of questions about virtue, with an eye toward discovering the sort of human being we should be if we, as rational beings, are to reach our full potential for living a satisfying life.* And insofar as living a satisfying life is important to you, Aristotle might be worth keeping in mind.

As you gain more familiarity with the range of available moral exemplars, you will probably begin to see how these represent various styles of approach to morality that have made their mark on our culture through the historical influence of individual philosophers. You may also begin to see that it is possible to mix and match among these various exemplary styles, so that a style suitable to your own moral sensibilities begins to emerge.

We have just seen how, for example, if we stay within an Aristotelian framework, we evaluate character traits and conduct by attending to the *function* of the human being – which is to aim at his or her *natural* good. Any desire or mood that impedes the attainment of that cannot, in the moral sense, be considered "good." But what does this mean for the actual conduct of life? Everyday life consists of actions we perform, and if our conduct is not to be based just on our arbitrary moods, we need some additional basis for deciding what we should do. One way to do this is to refer to some notion of "lawfulness" – a notion that some philosophers have wanted to combine with the Aristotelian idea of "naturalness." This presents us with a third moral exemplar:

> **EXEMPLAR: The Theory of Natural Law. A Natural Law Theorist is one who bases conduct upon the order inherent in the universe.**

Aristotle believed that everything in the universe has its natural place and function, and some of his successors, known as the *Stoics*,[4] drew the conclusion that this natural order of things is regulated by some "cosmic law." Human beings, unlike the lower creatures, are rational beings who can understand all this. And there is an affinity between human reason and the "reason" that governs the cosmos: If a person can grasp the orderliness of all things, that vision would be so strikingly powerful that the Platonic ideal of inner harmony (peace of mind) could be immediately accomplished. That is because we ourselves, being a part of that order, have the principles of natural law somewhere embedded in our inner being. The emotions that cause us discomfort need only be submitted to the control of the inner law in order for our desires to be reconciled with our life's circumstances. And that would bring us the only kind of true happiness humans can really expect to have in this life.

But is this life the only life bequeathed to us? This is one of the questions raised by the advent of Christianity, and it is primarily through Christianity that Natural Law Theory still exercises influence upon contemporary culture.

In the midst of the disintegration of the Classical (Greek and Roman) World – which began to occur around the end of the fourth century A.D. – Christianity was the most prominent new cultural form to appear on the scene in Europe and the Mideast. The blending of various moral exemplars adopted from Aristotelian and Christian perspectives is illustrated in the way that Christians often adopted two of the key elements of Aristotle's conceptual framework.

The first of these, as we have already mentioned, is Aristotle's functional (goal-oriented) view of human nature, as the basis for his ethic of self-realization. Ordinarily, to say that I have a "goal" is only to say that I intend to bring something about – a passing exam grade, a completed shopping task, a successful social encounter. But, as we have seen, Aristotle means more than this. He means to say two things about all of us *as human beings*: First, that we all have an essential human nature, which is innate at birth; and secondly, that our nature is only a potentiality until it develops through the unfolding of our personal history. Just as an acorn contains the potential of full growth as an oak, so the human contains the potential of self-realization as a fully rational being.

But rationality is not the only basic fact about human existence. The second of these conceptual elements retained from Aristotle was *communitarianism* – the assumption that the essentials of human identity are bound up in social interaction. It is not insignificant that Aristotle's major work in moral philosophy (the *Nicomachean Ethics*) claimed to be about politics, nor that his major work in social philosophy (the *Politics*) was billed as a companion to the *Ethics*. This interpenetration of two arenas of concern reflects the cultural distance between Aristotle's time and our own – and not just in terms of the particulars of language and custom. Today some say we live in an era of "individualism," where it feels natural for us to prioritize our own perceived needs over and above the good of the society at large, and where it is not unusual for people to take no interest at all in the daily political life of their communities. But Aristotle conducted his political associations in the context of rather tiny city-states where all participants knew each other pretty well, and where the sheer complexity of our modern political system, with its competing interest-groups and social urgencies, would have been unimaginable. In such a setting it was nearly just as unimaginable for any male citizen to shun participation in the political life of his community.

These two received elements – the Greek notions of self-realization and communitarianism – took root in what might at first seem to be a rather inhospitable conceptual setting. For Christianity began as a sect of Judaism, with views of the world very different from the Greek. And there is no more striking contrast between the Greek and Hebraic view of things than in their respective ideas about God. Aristotle conceived of God as the Unmoved Mover, who sets in motion (but does not actually create) the stuff of the universe, and then simply retires from the scene. The Hebraic notion of God is very different. God not only creates the world out of nothing, He plays the crucial role in world history. Not only does He create man and woman "in His own image" – He delivers up His chosen people from bondage in Egypt, demands their obedience, judges their conduct, and metes out appropriate punishment or reward. The Hebraic God is anything but removed.

From the records we have, it seems certain that Jesus of Nazareth, himself a Jewish rabbi, preferred the image of God-as-Father to God-as-Judge. The active role of the Hebraic Deity is preserved in Christianity where the very appearance of Christ on Earth was ascribed in early renderings to the activity of Divine Incarnation. The Divine and the human being, in this view, have an irrevocable relationship, which is estranged but not abrogated by the willful disobedience of humankind.

St. Thomas Aquinas. However, despite the obvious tension between the Greek and Judeo-Christian sensibility, one of the remarkable cultural events of the West was the attempt on the part of theologians and philosophers, during a period of more than a thousand years, to reconcile the two. Though the attention of most cultural historians is no longer riveted on that effort, it remains very much alive in Roman Catholicism, whose major philosophical figure is the 13th Century's St. Thomas Aquinas (1225-1274).

Despite its debt to the Christian Scriptures, Thomistic ethics relies heavily on the pre-Christian assumptions of the Greeks, and especially Aristotle. Aquinas in fact believes that his own Christian commentary on the *Nicomachean Ethics* discloses that work's true meaning – despite the fact, of course, that Aristotle wrote it several centuries before the birth of Jesus. This indicates once again the dramatic cultural gap between our own historically conscious era and the pre-modern. For the medieval mind, though truths make their full historical appearance only at the pregnant moment ordained by God, they are eternally constituted and in no way dependent for their content upon the historical process itself.

Fortunately for those who never heard of Christ, however, the God of Aquinas (we are told) has made human nature capable of understanding His Will on its own. So it is that even pagans, according (originally) to St. Paul's letter to the Romans (Ch. 1:10), are "without excuse" for their wickedness, because Divine Truth is "present for the mind to see in the things He has created." One has simply to use the "natural light" of reason itself, and the same truths we learn more explicitly from Scripture are independently available to us.

And this points to a crucial and influential component of Thomistic thought. We are capable of being guided by reason because our "souls" are fundamentally rational. God is fully rational as well, and because the world operates according to His law, reliable moral decision-making really depends upon whether or not we are at home with our own natural inclinations. There is, in other words, a *natural law* for humankind to follow, and insofar as we adhere to that, we are bringing into being the rich potential that is inherent in the deepest part of ourselves. Here then is Aristotle in Christian dress: An ethic of self-realization that defines human potential in terms of man's innate capacity to act in whatever way God intends – which is further defined in terms of Natural Law Theory. (There are, on the other hand, many Natural Law Theorists who would not count themselves religious.)

Some later philosophers, such as John Locke (1632-1704), made use of the notion of natural law in a rather different way – to expand on the notion of *natural rights*. As we shall see later on, morality has a very specific connection with the notice of obligation. We say, for example, that we have a moral obligation (or duty) to help others in need or to keep our promises. But it is possible to think of this the other way around as well: Others have a right to receive our assistance under certain circumstances, or to expect us to do what we promise. Locke thought that this was a feature of nature itself, in that human beings, every bit as much as any other part of nature, have an essential makeup. Today we might paraphrase it this way: Just as water is naturally and fundamentally hydrogen and oxygen, a human being is naturally and fundamentally a bearer of rights that must not be violated. These, Locke thought, conform to the laws of God – and, at least in this reference to the laws of God, Locke agrees with Aquinas.

But you may have noticed, in our discussion of Aquinas so far, that there is more here than simply an ethic of Self-Realization, or even a theory of Natural Law.

Some versions of Natural Law Theory – early Stoicism, for example – are actually incomplete by themselves, in that they do not fully deal with the idea of *moral obligation*. Let's say that you have thought long and hard about the world around you, and you have reached some conclusions about the way things work. Maybe it seems natural to you that parents and children treat each other respectfully, or that people at a certain stage in life get married and raise a family. But what is "natural" is not always what in fact happens. Plenty of family members hate each other, and they scarcely give each other the time of day. Plenty of people never get married, and many people refuse to raise children, either by ignoring them after they are born or else by aborting them before they can be. That might not be "natural" – but so what? Why do we have to do what is "natural"?

Christianity and other world religions have a ready answer to this kind of question, which provides us with a fourth moral exemplar:

> **EXEMPLAR: The Theory of Divine Command. A Divine Command Theorist is one who bases conduct on what is understood to be the Will of God.**

A Divine Command Theorist is able to answer the question "Why be moral?" with a straightforward response: "Because God demands it of us." Demands typically carry both obligation and consequence, and both these elements have been a major concern to Christian ethics from the outset. We see this once again in Aquinas, and we see it as well in later Protestant thinkers – especially among such groups as Baptists, Calvinists and Lutherans. And today, Christians who consider themselves fundamentalists or evangelicals or born-again typically make use of the Divine Command exemplar. So have many Jewish and Moslem thinkers.

Aquinas, like Aristotle, is a eudaimonist. Of the many distinct "goods" a person can pursue, Aquinas insists, happiness is man's natural "end" – a way of speaking which, conveniently in the English, conveys both the Greek and the Christian influence. On the one hand, as Aristotle said, happiness is what we naturally pursue as life's *goal*. Jesus of Nazareth spoke of having "life and having it more abundantly," presumably in the present as well as the future. But ultimate end is also where the faithful, through the fulfillment of God's promise to man, are supposed to *end up* after death – as resurrected souls bathed in the eternal illumination that emanates from the Deity. This is the consequence of tending seriously to one's moral obligations to God and man. For some, these obligations emphasize works: The beatific vision is awarded only to those whose earthly existence has reflected purity of heart, through a life of virtuous deeds – deeds, of course, that coincide with God's commands. For others, the obligations emphasize faith: Only by faith in the "grace of God" – unmerited favor – will they enjoy fulfillment on earth and a heavenly home.

But how are we poor souls to know the Will of the Divine? The search for God's Will can include human reason. It can rely on conscience. It can make use of prayer – of any word or thought addressed to God or gods for such purposes as petition, adoration, confession or thanksgiving. To pursue the Will of God, the monotheistic religions – Judaism, Christianity, Islam and their variants – all turn to certain "sacred scriptures" for their journeys. The most widely published book in history is the *Holy Bible*, containing as it does the primary scriptures both for Judaism and for Christianity, itself an offshoot of Judaism. Its adherents claim it as a guide for faith and practice. Its detractors discredit its religious authority but some accord it literary value. As H.L. Mencken, American critic and atheist, wrote:

> "It is full of lush and lovely poetry. The Bible is unquestionably the most beautiful book in the world. Allow everything you please for the barbaric history in the Old Testament and the silly Little Bethel theology in the New, and there remains a series of poems so overwhelmingly voluptuous and disarming that no other literature, old or new, can offer a match for it .... No other religion is so beautiful in its very substance – none other can show anything to match the great strophes of flaming poetry which enter into every Christian gesture of ceremon(y) and give an august inner dignity to Christian sacred music. Nor does any other, not even the parent Judaism, rest upon so noble a mythology. The story of Jesus ... is, indeed, the most lovely story that the human fancy has ever devised ... Moreover, it has the power, like all truly great myths, of throwing off lesser ones, apparently in an endless stream."
>
> – H.L. Mencken
> "The Poetry of Christianity," *The World's Best*
> (New York, The Dial Press, 1950), pp. 148-150)

The actual content of God's Will for mankind, as Thomistically rendered, comprises a blend of Greek and Christian sources. The seven virtues enunciated by St. Thomas are four derived from Hellenic tradition (Prudence, Temperance, Fortitude, and Justice) and three derived from St. Paul (Faith, Hope, and Love). But this causes some difficulties, doesn't it? For example: Does simply naming the virtues tell us specifically what to do in actual circumstances? Exactly *which* possible action is the prudent one, or the loving one? Don't we need further guidance?

Aquinas thought that human law can be one of our sources for that guidance. Ideally, the law not only gives us specific directives as to how to behave justly; it also provides us with strong deterrence when temptation strikes. And this communitarian preoccupation reveals once again the Aristotelian roots of Thomistic thought. Though Aquinas does not counsel blind adherence to the codes of one's community (in fact he explicitly denies that any legal prescription that violates natural law can be valid), he does believe that the legal system ought to serve a moral function, which is to orient us appropriately toward life in our own community. That communal context is deemed necessary to the fulfillment of our own full potential as humans. So here, as with Aristotle, the ethic of self-realization coincides with the social conscience of communitarianism.

The communitarian side of Thomism is emblematic of a crucial development in the history of Christianity. In the decades following the life of Jesus, Christians assumed that the world was about to end in apocalyptic fire and judgment, to be followed by the Second Coming of Christ and the establishment of God's Kingdom. But history did not end as the early Christians understood it would, and attention gradually turned toward the task of conducting social life, as far as possible, along the moral lines ordained by Scripture.

And this (some people think) presents us with yet a further difficulty. For what does an ethic based upon a medieval view of man and society say to us in the modern world? We in the late 20th century share a form of life that is very different from the medieval; in one way at least, moral matters seem more perplexing for us than they were to believers in the 13th century. Not that folks back then were really any better, morally speaking, than we are. "Temptation" and "sin" must have been as familiar to them as greed and narcissism are to us. The difference perhaps is that, by and large, they *knew* they were "sinning," whereas for many in the modern world, with all its opinionated diversity, the category itself seems to have lost some of its clarity and power.

Today, for example, even many Catholic school children eventually discover that distinguishing our "natural" from our "perverse" inclinations may not be as simple as we would wish. The difference is certainly not apparent simply from the qualities of the inclinations themselves – just from how they actually feel to us, in other words. For example, many otherwise faithful and practicing Catholics no longer adopt the Church's stand on birth control, abortion, or on premarital or same-sex relations. One can't help but wonder why, if the natural light were as powerful as Aquinas believed, it would leave so many well-intentioned believers in such a quandary. Or is it a case of our own natural inclinations being so stubborn as to deny or ignore that light? This debate seems unending.

But does this really weigh heavily against the basic Christian position? That a unified Christian world-view no longer seems to dominate American cultural life, or that there are doubts and disagreements within the Christian community – these are primarily sociological observations that may say nothing whatsoever about the actual merit of the Christian ethic. In response, a Christian might well want to argue that the problem is not with natural reason itself, but with our corrupted human capacity to make use of it. In other words, the fact that people have trouble distinguishing right from wrong does not mean that there is no way to do so. Perhaps we all could make use of natural reason if we were in a less imperfect spiritual state. And this raises issues well beyond the scope of this discussion. How we ought to account for human imperfection is a notoriously troublesome theological question. (One solution, the Doctrine of Original Sin, developed in its classic expression in the writings of St. Augustine [354-430], describes an inherited taint we all allegedly possess as a result of the sin of Adam and Eve.)

One point we need to stress, however, is that the actual *content* of the Christian ethic is less important, from the standpoint of our philosophical discussion here, than the general *form* that a Christian's moral deliberation might take. That form is expressed in the Divine Command Theory – which directs us to determine what "God's Will" is. And if you are not a Christian – if you are a Jew, or a Buddhist,[5] or a Hindu, or a Muslim – you also can make use of this general approach. You will consult different scripture, you will invoke different spiritual guides, and you will rely on different religious formulas than we have cited here. But you will still be striving to determine, as best you can, what the spiritual authority you rely on demands of you, in the kind of moral circumstance you find yourself faced with. Consider, for example, these sayings from the Muslim's *Koran*:

In the alternation of day and night, in the rains from heaven that come to quicken the parched
earth, in the shifting winds, and in the clouds pressed into service between heaven and earth,
there are signs enough of Allah's (God's) rule for people who have understanding.
Allah (God) loves all those who do good.
Allah is with those who patiently endure.
Wrong not and you will not be wronged.
If you do good, you do good for your own soul; if you
do evil, you do it to yourselves.

And notice a similar concern over Divine Command in the Egyptian Book of the Dead:

I have done what people speak of,
What the gods are pleased with,
I have contented a god with what he wishes.
I have given bread to the hungry,
Water to the thirsty,
Clothes to the naked,
A ferryboat to the boatless.
I have given divine offerings to the gods,
Invocation-offerings to the dead.
Rescue me, protect me,
Do not accuse me before the great god!

from Miriam Lichtheim, *Ancient Egyptian Literature,*
Volume II: The New Kingdom (University of California Press, 1976)

Christians as well as followers of many other faiths believe that God created human nature complete
with an innate sense of right and wrong, called "conscience." And conscience might be thought of in
terms of each of the exemplars we have been discussing so far. You might, for example, regard
following your conscience as a way to secure your own place in heaven (that would be an egoistic
concern). Or maybe you think of following your conscience as the best way to develop your full
potential as a self-realized human being. Or again, following your conscience might mean identifying
the laws of your own nature. And many people think of conscience as an internal set of rules that will
tell us exactly what God commands us to do.

Some people, however, have found this last notion of conscience – as a rendering of Divine Command
– very problematic. In its simplistic form (they would point out) the Divine Command Theory is an
example of a general position called *moral legalism*, which is the view that morality consists simply
of following prescribed rules. And there are a number of problems with this sort of view. Notice two
of these. (1) First, it is not clear that every conceivable situation even has a governing rule! In simple
cases, such as murder, the moral rule certainly seems clear enough. But should I kill another human
being if his actions are threatening the life of some third person? And what if that third party has just
threatened the well-being of his would-be assailant? You see the point: The more details we add, the
harder it is to discover a simple rule to decide the case for us. (2) And secondly, many (especially
modern) ethicists favor the idea of *moral autonomy*. This too is a complicated notion, but its main
point is that "I am autonomous" in a particular activity if *I myself* am the source of the motive behind

doing it. For example, students who pursue pre-med studies in college only to please their parents, and not because that career squares with their own self-ascertained goals, are not being autonomous. This illustrates what some perceive as difficulty for Divine Command Theorists. If God merely commands our assent to His moral commands and we comply irrespective of our own preferences, what does that do to the concept of human autonomy?

On the other hand, suppose you are a Christian or a Jew or a Muslim who wants to preserve the idea of moral conscience without sacrificing moral autonomy. You might want to regard conscience as an active faculty within us – created by God as a very part of our "soul" – autonomously directing our thought and feelings. This would mean that the Will of God is "written on the heart" in a way that empowers the believer to use his or her own natural capacities for deliberation and action. It would preserve human freewill and, in some sense, moral autonomy.

Joseph Butler. Something like this modern notion of moral autonomy may underlie the moral theory of Joseph Butler (1692-1752), for whom conscience is the inner faculty that clarifies and directs not only our self-interested conduct but also our genuinely benevolent acts (kindness toward others). And here Butler's ethical views are aimed against some very different assumptions about human nature made famous by the ethical egoist Thomas Hobbes (1588-1679). According to Hobbes, a human being is nothing but a machine whose operating system is designed to promote its own survival and to enhance the pleasure and diminish the pain of human existence. Actions that appear to be altruistic are really undertaken "for gain or for glory" – nothing but veiled attempts to further one's own interests. And this often involves shrewd calculation, even to the point of giving up some immediate advantage to oneself. According to this theory, humans engage in organized social cooperation or tolerate governmental constraints only because the contrary would be so much worse; because people are selfish by nature (Hobbes says), collective existence devoid of social regulation would be a "war of all against all" – rather like the popular conception of prehistoric cavemen. So Hobbes is very much an anti-communitarian: He sees humans as being naturally selfish, and directed in all their conduct toward (what they take to be) their own personal well-being. So if I am helpful toward others only because I want God to guarantee my access to Life Eternal, I am being a Hobbesian egoist.

Here Hobbes sounds something like a modern version of Callicles, whereas Butler, like Socrates in the *Gorgias*, wants to preserve a notion of virtue that does not collapse into pure egoism. Butler does recognize that humans are motivated in part by what he calls "self-love" – which is the concern we all have for our own happiness. That's only a natural interest in survival and prosperity, and there is nothing wrong with it. But that (he says) is not all there is to human conduct. Butler argues that it's normally quite wrong to speak of our own happiness as actually the *goal* of the specific actions we take. The goal itself is the particular object we have in our mind's eye when we undertake it, and "happiness" is the satisfaction we receive from obtaining some of those goals.

Let's see what this would mean. A Hobbesian would insist that we ought to calculate shrewdly just which activities might be to our own overall self-interest. (Maybe I really should help the elderly cross the street, but my reason for doing it is going to involve, say, the esteem I'd be acquiring in the eyes of others.) So, as Hobbes tells it, the aim is to cultivate in ourselves a savvy alertness toward the ways we can manipulate situations on our own behalf. And to this, Butler provides the communitarian's response against such an all-consuming engagement with our own "private and contracted affection":

> *Disengagement* is absolutely necessary to enjoyment; and a person may have so steady and fixed an eye upon his own interest, whatever he places it in, as may hinder him from *attending* to many gratifications within his reach, which others have their minds free and open to ... Immoderate self-love does very ill consult its own interest; and how much soever a paradox it may appear, it is certainly true that even from self-love we should endeavor to get over all inordinate regard to and consideration of ourselves.

> – Joseph Butler, *Five Sermons*
> (Indianapolis: Hackett Publishing Company, Inc., 1983), pp 48-49.

The point of this rather quaintly written passage is that, for Butler, our social impulses are no less natural than our self-interested ones. Benevolence is as much a part of human nature as self-love. Butler thus stands squarely within the Socratic theory of virtue, which could take seriously an entire range of character traits – courtesy, generosity, compassion, and so forth – that Hobbes and the Sophists before him either ignored altogether, or else reduced to strategies of egoistic concern. And the crucial point Butler insists on is that *those strategies are self-defeating in the end*, and this is due to the nature of "happiness." For *real human happiness cannot be gained by aiming directly at it*. Take here the case of friendship. If I hold my friend in esteem only because of what his presence in my life will do for me, then I am not being a real friend to him, and I will surely miss out on the satisfactions of genuine friendship.

Butler's overall response to Hobbes has seemed correct to a great many ethicists ever since. Yet some aspects of Butler's thinking strike many modern philosophers as anachronistic and uninspiring. It is not hard to see why. For one thing, Butler actually assumes that all of our moral duties cooperate nicely together, so that a person's life doesn't really present any irreconcilable conflicts of interest! These days, that does not seem at all to be the experience of many of us. If you are a physician faced with a decision over whether or not to end life-support to an incapacitated patient, you are likely to feel very acutely the pressures from various sides of the question – your own oath as a physician to preserve life weighs against the interests of the family, who have already born quite enough emotional and financial pain. It may not be at all apparent how these competing interests nicely coincide.

Butler would acknowledge the *appearance* of conflict here. But he would also point out that our vantage point is extremely limited. And this is where "conscience" comes in: God gives us the ability to follow inner directives, so that even if we can't see how all things work together for good, from God's point of view they really do, just as long as we do His Will.

For many moral philosophers nowadays (though by no means all) this seems to be a highly questionable assumption. The reason for contemporary skepticism on this is not just that Butler rejects any idea of deep moral conflict. The real sticking point for modern moral philosophy is Butler's religious orientation, which is no longer taken for granted by all philosophers. Butler appeared on the scene (early 1700s) just after the advent of the Scientific Age in Europe, when many of the curiosities of the material world were beginning to disclose themselves to the methodical inquiries of physicists, chemists, and biologists. Gradually, the world was becoming "secularized," so that today (many people think) we no longer *need* to refer to God in order just to explain many of the physical occurrences of daily life. Accordingly, many modern ethical writers are less content to rely on theologically inspired answers to philosophically motivated questions. In that case, the appearance of moral conflict does not seem so easily smoothed away even by the assurance of religious faith.

Nowadays, in confronting philosophical problems, not everyone *assumes* (as one apparently could in the Middle Ages, and even to some extent during Butler's own lifetime) that the shape of a satisfactory answer is bound to have an explicitly theological contour. For many philosophers in our "modern" world, for better or worse, theology is likely to raise more questions than it answers.

Modern Ethical Theory

In periodizing history, anyone's judgment about where exactly the term "modern" should be used is bound to be somewhat arbitrary. For the history of ethics, some have used "modern" to refer to Butler; others have not wanted to use it before the appearance of G.E. Moore's *Principia Ethica* in 1903. (We'll see why later on.) But by any account, certainly a number of defining traits can be formulated to set modern ethics apart from its premodern roots. One of these traits, as we have just noted, is secularization. Another of these, as we shall see again later on, is an increased sensitivity to the subtleties of the words people use. Especially in the 20th century, philosophers have become aware of the complex distinctions we can forge by means of our language, and the need to take account of this when asking questions about our moral beliefs. At this point, however, let's concentrate for a moment on one other trait of modern ethical thinking, and that is the fact that *the style of reasoning we use in moral matters reflects the style of reasoning we use in a court of law.* And this is related to the idea of *conflict of interest.*

To see this, consider what happens in a legal proceeding. There is a defendant accused of a crime, and the court is charged with the task of assessing responsibility. The crime is an infraction of a rule – against stealing, say, or against taking the life of another human being – and of course one of the requirements is to determine the bare facts of the case. (Did someone's property really disappear? When? Is the missing person really dead? Did he die of unnatural causes?) But one of the complications here is that the task does not end with an assessment of these sorts of facts. The real onus placed upon judge and jury has to do with ascribing the degree of blameworthiness. For even if everybody involved can be made to agree on many of the most basic facts of a case, there is very often pretty substantial disagreement as to what and where the blame is. This parallel with law here is very strong. Even if one person admits to killing another, for example, it may still be unclear as to whether the event was spontaneous or premeditated, and that makes all the difference as to what kind of punishment will be meted out.

To reflect this, let's make use of the notion of *defeasibility*. "Defeasibility" is a term legal scholars use, and it is a term that some ethicists have borrowed for similar purpose. In practice, as we noticed in our discussion of Butler, rules are never as simple as, say, the Ten Commandments might lead us to suppose. Of course, "Thou shalt not steal" is a rule that applies in society, as a kind of social "given." But we commonly say that its applicability is only *prima facie* (literally: "At first sight"), and this implies not only that the rule carries the force of a command, but also that a trial may reveal extenuating circumstances and that the charge of stealing brought against a defendant might be mitigated. In Victor Hugo's famous novel *Les Miserables*, for example, after the starving hero Jean Valjean steals a loaf of bread, his nemesis Inspector Javert pursues him relentlessly, on the grounds that the letter of the law must be maintained at all costs. Because most readers of the book find themselves in sympathy with the thief, it's a good bet that a jury selected from among Hugo's readers would exonerate Jean Valjean. In other words, the charge of thievery (or perhaps the penalty imposed after conviction) is *defeasible*: Generally speaking, stealing is socially unacceptable, but there can be excusing conditions (extreme personal hardship, in this case) which would ease the censure. We tend to say that even though what such a person did was wrong, he's not completely to blame. Similarly, though everyone agrees that John Hinckley tried to assassinate Ronald Reagan, the *prima facie* charge of attempted murder was lessened, by reason of the defendant's mental disability which rendered his blame defeasible, or annullable.

Ethical rules, like points of law, seem to share this trait of defeasibility. Any one of us as a moral agent is held responsible for conduct befitting his or her state as a member of society. Similarly, as members of society we are bound by law. Yet most of us would agree that the responsibility is not absolute. Consider the case of truth-telling. Is it wrong to utter an untruth? Well, yes and no. "Always tell the truth" is only a very rudimentary rule of thumb, as we can readily see by asking ourselves the question: Would we be held morally liable if, for example, we did not know that our utterance was untrue? Of course not. Ignorance tends to constitute a pretty solid excuse for not uttering the truth, and that seems quite clear to anybody nowadays.[6]

For us this issue of exoneration, which is so closely related to the defeasibililty of moral obligation, gets very complicated. Though ignorance is generally considered a good excuse, someone may have a false belief that she could have and should have known to be false: A driver speeding down a dark, rainy road may believe there is no pedestrian at the crosswalk because she is not taking appropriate care to look closely enough. And suppose you are a physician whose patient has just been diagnosed with a terminal disease. In that event, do you tell the truth, the whole truth? That would depend, once again, on what you decide the defeasibility conditions are, and this is where conflict of interest enters in. For might it not be true that such hard news actually harms the patient's mental stability and adds to the burden of illness? The patient, in other words, has a legitimate interest in preserving the emotional energy needed for physical recovery – though also an interest in knowing the truth about her situation. So you might decide to withhold the very facts which, under ordinary circumstances, a patient has a clear right to know.

In other words, "defeasibility" refers to the fact that moral prescriptions have the force of obligation, but can also be overridden if other commanding considerations intersect. Unfortunately, however, there seem to be no clear-cut procedures for deciding what all those considerations are and just how much weight to put on them. The best anyone can do is to rely on a moral sensitivity developed only from patient, attentive practice at thinking through these kinds of real-life examples. And this case of the physician illustrates just why we need to develop that kind of moral awareness. For imagine a doctor who has not become clear about this matter. He might end up concealing information for the wrong reason – let's say he simply didn't want to deal with the discomfort of discussing it. As any mature adult knows, if we operate generally out of that kind of habit, we are headed for disaster because important decisions often demand that we handle discomfort appropriately. One way of reading the history of ethics, in fact ,would be in terms of its increasing concern for *accentuating and clarifying the place of moral rules and principles, as a hedge against arbitrariness during the important moments of daily life.*

So we can usually imagine cases where, like the physician, we might actually be inclined on *moral* grounds to break the rule. And in morality just as in law, the exact criteria for defeasibility have been controversial. Much of the history of modern ethics has also to do with specifying more precisely just what those criteria are. To see this, we need to introduce two pairs of concepts.

The Right vs. the Good. Modern philosophers have typically distinguished between two kinds of moral judgments that ancient philosophers never even noticed – moral judgments based on criteria for "right" action, and those based on what is supposed to make states of affairs "good." Most modern philosophers have insisted that much rests on this distinction. As we are about to see, in fact, much of the history of modern moral philosophy can be seen as a series of disputes about which of these two general conceptions is more fundamental.

The difference between them is not at all hard to understand. In ethics, the word "right" usually refers to a class of actions – what people *do*. When people keep their promises, love their neighbor as themselves, honor their father and mother, return lost property if they know the owner, or help those in need – we commonly say that they are doing the "right" thing; and other actions, more or less opposed to these, we of course call "wrong." On the other hand, there is a moral category that does not consist of actions at all, but rather of those *states of affairs* that might be the *consequences* of actions. The telltale difference here is grammatical: Whereas actions of course are named by verbs, states of affairs are typically designated by nouns. World peace, personal satisfaction, a restored ozone layer, a healthy body – these are examples of "goods."

Consequentialism vs. Deontologism. But though the difference between these two notions of "good" and "right" may be more or less clear, you might not see right away just why the distinction is interesting or important. We are not dealing with a mere trivial technicality. In fact, we are still dealing with the issue of defeasibility, which is treated differently by the various major figures in the history of modern ethics. And this is going to require the introduction of a second pair of concepts – *consequentialism* and *deontologism* – each of which correspond to one more moral exemplar.

Let's say you are a physician faced with a question of whether of not to tell your patient some very bad diagnostic news. You might feel strongly here that it is your duty, pure and simple, to tell the truth regardless of the results. You might decide that in moral matters such as this one, moral responsibility really stops at the boundaries of one's own conduct, and that further results should be left to take care of themselves. (Is it really your responsibility how someone else deals with the truth?) This would mean that your moral thinking reflects a fifth exemplar:

> **EXEMPLAR: The Theory of Deontology. A Deontologist is someone who bases conduct on an innate sense of moral duty.**

Someone who is well disposed toward the Divine Command Theory is likely to be friendly to deontologism. Both views place heavy importance upon fulfilling moral obligations. It is even possible to think of the Divine Command Theory as a type of deontologism. But "deontologism" is a wider category, based on the way one goes about discovering what those rules are. It stems from the Greek word *deon,* which means duty. Simply put, whereas the Divine Command Theory relies on scriptural revelation, or the teaching of Church tradition, or even direct illumination from God, the deontologist does not need to mention God.

Immanuel Kant. The most extreme (and famous) deontological theory is that of Immanuel Kant (1724-1804), who for example claims that it is never, under any circumstance at all, morally permissible to lie. In other words, there are not (in Kant's view) any conditions of defeasibility when it comes to the rule against lying, and this he thinks holds for any of our other duties as well. This is because Kant regards what is morally "good" as entirely dependent upon what is morally "right." (We'll see shortly that a consequentialist would put it the other way around, claiming that what we ought to do depends upon what we want to cause to happen.)

Kant rejects the idea that the *moral* good is in any sense dependent upon what we desire. The moral good consists only in the virtue of acting from our sense of duty, regardless of any other inclinations we may have. And this means that we need to act regardless of the inclinations that Christianity has traditionally favored: For example, Kant would insist that acting with benevolence towards others, even if we are doing what the moral rule requires, is not enough. We need to act from a willingness to perform our duty, and for the sake of duty alone.

But how do we know what our duty in any given situation is? Kant's idea here is that we can test any course of action by asking whether or not it satisfies a principle he calls the "Categorical Imperative," which he formulates as the requirement to act only in a way that we could consistently intend for everybody else to act as well. This is the basis for his insistence on the inviolability of the rule against lying. Kant thinks that anybody who uses his categorical test will see that the successful lie requires a trusting public. If lying were the rule rather than the exception, no one would be believed, and the lie would fail. And that is the problem that the liar who is subject to the Categorical Imperative must face: it is logically inconsistent to intend that nobody believe anyone, and at the same time that others believe the liar.

The case of the liar brings out other aspects of the Kantian theory as well. A liar for example might want to be considered an exceptional case: My lie (he might say) can have its intended effect if I alone am permitted to lie when it seems convenient, while others are not. Wishing for that kind of world is not wishing for the logically impossible. But it is wishing for a situation that, Kant would insist, undermines the very basis of morality. In this regard the Categorical Imperative has had lasting influence in modern ethics: It gives us a picture of morality that is not a matter of special pleading, but a code of conduct that applies impartially to all. Morality, according to the prevailing modern view, has to be *universalizable*.

Yet Kant's test alone does not actually provide our moral convictions with any real content. It simply relies on our intuitions to generate candidates for us to test out, so at best Kant's theory remains incomplete. And Kant's psychological theory, which supposes that humans can be motivated by some rational power independent of desires, fears, *et cetera*, has failed to convince the many who have wondered what, then, is left to serve as a motive for conduct!

On the other hand, if a deontologist decides to abandon Kant's grand program, he is left with some version of ethical *intuitionism*, which is the theory that we know moral rules only by a direct act of "intuition" rather than by logical argumentation. But you might want to ask some questions at this point. How do we know that our bare intuitions about moral rules amount to much more than ingrained prejudice? For example: Not too long ago in the United States it was thought, that the races should be strictly segregated, with separate public facilities, entrance ways, and seating arrangements; and this was commonly held by many whites (and even some blacks) to enjoy the status of moral law. Nowadays, of course, most of us would not admit to such beliefs (at least not in public). But if we think a little further, we might find ourselves wondering whether the moral rules we currently profess might not strike our future descendants as outmoded also. In other words, if all we have to go on are our moral intuitions, how do we know they are reliable?

This kind of consideration has led some philosophers to search for a more objective grounding for those beliefs, one that could assure us that we are not just being duped by our accidental place in ever-changing cultural history.

Consequentialism is a theory about moral deliberation that claims to correct that defect of deontologism, and it does this by encompassing a broader range of factors than the typical deontologist would want to consider. For the central feature underlying consequentialism is the idea that we are responsible not just for our actions, but for their foreseeable consequences as well.

> **EXEMPLAR: The Theory of Consequentialism. A Consequentialist is one who determines conduct by assessing the moral quality of the results likely to follow from various possible courses of actions.**

Consequentialism requires careful calculation as to which possible course of conduct will produce more or better good than its alternatives. This general approach to ethical reasoning (sometimes referred to as *teleologism*) treats moral conduct as a means to some desired end: The "right," in other words, is defined in terms of the "good." This stems from the Greek word *telos,* meaning goal, end or purpose. We can imagine that the physician who decides whether to tell the truth to a patient on the basis of the emotional harm the news is likely to cause, might be a good example of a consequentialist – one who might consider truth-telling to be a duty under ordinary conditions but defeasible in the face of the harmful consequences that seem likely in any given case.

THE UTILITARIANS: JEREMY BENTHAM AND JOHN STUART MILL

Ethical consequentialism is not a new theory: Joseph Butler in fact was a consequentialist himself. But since the early part of the last century, *utilitarianism* has been the standard version of the consequentialist position, and its guiding principle (the Principle of Utility) can be roughly stated as: *Always act in order to promote the greatest amount of satisfaction (pleasure or happiness) for the greatest number of people*. Utilitarianism, in other words, has written into it more than just a formulation of the typical consequentialist insistence that to judge an act's moral worth, we have to estimate an act's effects: It contains as well a general stipulation as to just what those effects should look like.

Jeremy Bentham. There were a number of different interpretations of the Utility Principle, especially regarding that vague word "satisfaction." What, shall we say, constitutes being "satisfied"? Jeremy Bentham (1748-1832), who invented the word "utilitarianism" and became its first influential proponent, took the view that "satisfaction" is nothing but pleasure. (You may remember we first met Bentham in Chapter 2.) And in this regard, says Bentham, there is no reason to suppose that the pleasures experienced by animals are any different in kind from the human pleasures. Perhaps humans simply have the capacity for more intense pleasures and more varied pleasurable activities.

Bentham's view does have the obvious advantage of offering us just what a consequentialist would want: An *empirical basis* for objectively deciding when a moral rule should be applied. To say that a belief is based "empirically" is to say that it is accepted because we have concrete evidence from our experience in favor of it. Take Kant's example of lying, where we can easily imagine a conflict of interest between the obligation to tell the truth and the obligation to protect a person's well-being. Bentham's most famous disciple, John Stuart Mill (1806-1873), treats the lying case as an opportunity for "weighing these conflicting utilities against one another, and marking out the region within which one or the other preponderates."[7] This would be an empirical test. In other words, what we need to do in such a situation is to anticipate and mathematically calculate the amount of satisfaction which, from past experience, we have learned is likely to result from each of our various options (from telling the whole truth, from withholding some information, from telling a white lie, *et cetera*). The greater the estimated sum, the more justified we are in acting in that particular manner.

But some even among Bentham's own followers – Mill in particular – found some aspects of this procedure peculiarly shallow. Bentham makes no significant mention of "the deeper feelings" that have traditionally been associated with the notion of human dignity and spirituality. There is little in Bentham to suggest, for example, that the appreciation of beauty is to be preferred to an equally intense satiation of a glutton's appetite. Mill, then, amends Bentham's Utility Principle to include the notion that what is to be maximized in moral conduct is "happiness" – taken in a *qualitatively* distinct way from mere "pleasure."

Yet you might well wonder if Mill's revision doesn't present us with problems of its own, especially if we wish to retain the main framework of Bentham's program in order to sustain the advantage of empirical testability. For notice what happens when we accept Mill's suggestion: The objective criterion we thought we had – that is, measurable amounts of satisfaction – now gets clouded by the addition of this qualitative dimension. We know fairly well how to measure quantity. But how do we *measure* the qualitative difference between dignified and crass pleasure-experiences? How in fact do we even empirically define the distinction between the two? Mill's answer to this last question is, like Aristotle, to rely on the convictions of the most cultured in our social group. But then, does this not return us directly to the very problem utilitarianism was designed to avert —the reliance on the mere intuition behind those convictions?

One of the main difficulties with consequentialism is its reliance on uncertain probability assessment. For how do we know just what results of some act are likely to be? Butler was himself a consequentialist, but he was very aware of this, warning us that our estimations of the greater good might very well lead us into "the most shocking instances of injustice, adultery, murder, perjury, and even of persecution."[8] You might firmly believe, for example, that adultery is *prima facie* wrong; but suppose your marriage seems hopelessly disintegrating, and you happen to meet someone attractive, who very much seems to need the affection you very much want to give. At the time it probably seems as if what's to be gained from breaking the marriage vow far outweighs what might be lost. And yet, it may be just as conceivable that your original rule-governed instinct might be reliable after all: Maybe the guilt created on both sides would end up poisoning the entire affair, and destroying any hope for marital reconciliation.

The point here is that it's very tough to tell in these matters. We simply cannot predict reliably, in a great many cases, just what the outcome of a course of action is likely to be. Here is where it is tempting to bring back the moral rules a deontologist so depends on.

Rule-Utilitarianism vs. Act-Utilitarianism. At first glance it might seem as if consequentialism involves a significant demotion for the status of moral rules. But there is one roundabout way of maintaining the importance of rules within the utilitarian-consequentialist framework, and that is the position known as *Rule-Utilitarianism*. A Rule-Utilitarian is one who thinks that what is important is not the happiness produced in any one specific case – say, of adultery. What is important for the Rule-Utilitarian is the sum total of happiness produced by abiding by a moral rule overall. In other words: What would happen if the rule were *generally* disregarded? Even if we cannot know the likely outcome in some specific case, that does not mean we have no idea about the likely result if a particular kind of action were taken by a great many people. This is a position taken by some social conservatives on matters having to do with family values. (What would happen to society if adultery became common practice? What if the homosexual lifestyle became the norm rather than the exception?) But one does not have to be this sort of conservative to see the appeal of Rule-Utilitarianism. For suppose you are a clerk in a bank whose child is in need of expensive medical attention that your insurance won't cover. Let's say you have a chance to "borrow" the needed funds without your employer's knowledge. You might find yourself asking: What if everybody decided to use their jobs to appropriate funds that are not theirs to use?

So the advantage of the rule-utilitarian approach is not hard to see: It appears to handle troublesome cases where ignorance of specific consequences seems to thwart decision-making. But many utilitarians themselves have had serious doubts about this approach all the same. For we are still left with unappealing dilemmas. The case of the tempted bank clerk is an example, for she might also find herself asking: What if all of us chose not to help our children when they are faced with a life-or-death situation? What kind of society would that produce? Here, once again, we are faced with the problem of moral conflict of interest: Two conflicting loyalties appear to pull us in incompatible directions. So it would seem as if, once again, we are drawn back to considering the very particular circumstances of the individual case before us. And even without these extreme cases of conflict, it seems clear that this is what Rule-Utilitarians themselves have to do in practice. Their approach is based on considering what the adherence or rejection of some rule is likely to produce in *specific* cases, and the more we know about each specific case, the better we are able to come up with a usable answer to the quandary.

Considerations such as this have suggested to many utilitarians that the only viable form for their theory is *Act-Utilitarianism* – which is the view that any act should be assessed based upon the total happiness produced in its own actual context, rather than upon the results of general adherence to the rule. And, from the utilitarian perspective, this makes all the sense in the world just as long as we have enough information to guide us reliably. In the case of the bank clerk once again: Maybe she knows for sure that the bank would not be hurt by her use of spare funds; maybe she knows of a way to avoid detection, so her own life would not be ruined as a result (or, on the other hand, maybe she has determined that the welfare of her child is more important than her own future); and maybe she has exhausted all other possibilities open to her. In that case (an Act-Utilitarian *might* conclude), it could conceivably make sense to take the money.

Cases such as this bring out once again the importance of individual moral development and training. When faced with such crucial life-issues, one can't very well count on simply stopping one's other affairs and signing up for a course on moral reasoning at one's local college! We need to be prepared as we go.

Indeed, these are very troublesome issues even when the information we need to assess consequences is available to us. So, back to the question of committing adultery due to unusually dire marital circumstances. This is a case where we simply may not have all the information we need. We may not have any idea at all about how we are likely to feel after the affair is under way. So the considerations that even act-utilitarianism recommends may not help us much. How should we proceed in that kind of case?

Indirect Consequentialism. One response to this kind of perplexity makes use once again of moral rules, and it's not a solution that Jeremy Bentham himself would have recommended. Bentham had faith in the eventual triumph of scientific reasoning, and constructed his theory accordingly; so a strict Benthamite would say that – even when we turn out to be in error – our actual deliberations ought to reflect the utilitarian ideal. This would mean that we should always act on the best information we do have, so that our motives should be utilitarian-approved even if the consequences sometimes are not. But others, including Mill (and Butler as well), held a different view of the matter that came to be known as *indirect consequentialism*. This view holds that in unclear cases it is acceptable for a person to use the moral rule just as a deontologist would – as a firm guide for conduct, quite apart from explicit consideration of the consequences. After all, in these sorts of instances there *is* no way to proceed from standard utilitarian motives, precisely because we lack information about consequences. On this account, we can be very glad that following the moral rules simply seems to work out for the best.

But upon reflection, this kind of approach is likely to leave us troubled once again. For what then becomes of the very basis for utilitarianism? It was supposed to give us some way out of relying purely on moral rules, by providing us with an empirical test for their application. But here we have a situation where the hoped-for outcome – that is, where following the rule would turn out to promote the greatest good for the greatest number of persons – is simply assumed, in advance, and that simply begs the question. It assumes the very thing we would like to have empirically demonstrated. So, for example, when consequentialists such as Butler hold that following the rule actually does happen to produce the greatest happiness overall (we simply can't see that it does, from where we mortals stand), we can admit that this would be fortunate indeed. We would very much welcome the happy coincidence of social custom with concrete consequences, because that would solve some of the major conundrums in ethics. But that hasn't been shown to be so, and (according to the indirect view) it cannot be shown. So we have to wonder here: Is Butler's kind of confidence really anything more than wishful thinking?

So where does this leave us? We have seen that utilitarianism, like consequentialism in general, invites the agent to contemplate more than just the restricted context of his or her own singular acts. Bentham, in fact, was not really interested in individual conduct at all, except as viewed from a larger social framework and as sanctioned through enlightened legislation based on the Principle of Utility. Utilitarians generally tend to be politically minded in just this way: The moral force of individual acts is always constituted by their impact on the greater social unit. And this is both a strength and a weakness of the theory. It represents a considerable strength in relation to the problem presented by deontologism. For rather than risking slavish adherence to traditional prejudices (which, from deontological considerations alone, we can never be certain are not secretly invading our moral intuitions), utilitarianism proposes putting even our firmest moral beliefs to the test of actual practice in concrete contexts. The defeasibility conditions for a moral rule, then, turn out to be spelled out in the most general way by the Principle of Utility. (So if lying in a particular instance contributes to the greater well-being, then so be it.)

Utilitarianism and the rights of persons. A major problem still confronts the utilitarian, however. Does utilitarianism respect the rights of persons? If the controlling consideration in our moral deliberations is restricted to the greater social good, might this not lead us to commit actions that no moral being could tolerate? Here, it would seem as if the ideal of "obligation" is conceptually paired not only with "moral responsibility" but also with "rights": We are responsible to others (who, because they occupy the same social context, have prima facie claims upon us, just as we do on them). A deontologist would want to point out that the danger of utilitarianism is always that the rights of the individual might get lost in subservience to the "greater good." Consider this example from the contemporary philosopher Bernard Williams:

> Jim finds himself in the central square of a small South American town. Tied up against the wall are a row of twenty Indians, most terrified, a few defiant; in front of them several armed men in uniform. A heavy man in a sweat-stained khaki shirt turns out to be the captain in charge and, after a good deal of questioning of Jim which establishes that he got there by accident while on a botanical expedition, explains that the Indians are a random group of the inhabitants who, after recent acts of protest against

the government, are just about to be killed to remind other possible protestors of the advantages of not protesting. However, because Jim is an honored visitor from another land, the captain is happy to offer him a guest's privilege of killing one of the Indians himself. If Jim accepts, then as a special mark of the occasion, the other Indians will be let off. Of course, if Jim refuses, then there is no special occasion, and Pedro here will do what he was about to do when Jim arrived, and kill them all. Jim, with some desperate recollection of schoolboy fiction, wonders whether if he got hold of a gun, he could hold the captain, Pedro and the rest of the soldiers to threat, but it is quite clear from the setup that nothing of that kind is going to work: Any attempt at that sort of thing will mean that all the Indians will be killed, and himself. The men against the wall, and the other villagers, understand the situation, and are obviously begging him to accept. What should he do?

> Bernard Williams, *A Critique of Utilitarianism,* in J.J.C. Smart and Bernard Williams, Utilitarianism For and Against (New York: Cambridge University Press, 1973), pp. 98-99.

Here, many of us would probably find our deepest moral instincts rebelling against the direction the Principle of Utility would carry us – which would be to accept the captain's offer. In other words, many of us if faced with this case might instinctively feel more comfortable operating from such deontological principles as: "Never intentionally take the life of another human being." And at this point we have to decide: Do we listen to those instincts, or do we acquiesce to Benthan's reformist program – a program that has more than just large-scale political ramifications? For if Bentham is right, our own moral sentiments need to undergo a cleansing and reordering that will leave human conscience radically altered.

Here it is worth noting that many philosophers have concluded that, even so, pure consequentialism would be an unsatisfactory theory. In its classical form at least, the Principle of Utility is not even a *purely consequentiali*st notion. For there remains the issue of fairness. Bentham's own view was that each individual should count as one, and no more than that, in the final calculation; which means that we ought to be concerned not just with the sum of pleasures that an act produces, but also with its fair distribution. And that does not seem to be a consequentialist consideration at all, because the greatest good for the greatest number might still mean a very poor situation for the underprivileged few, and this was something even Bentham did not wish to sanction. The idea that everyone has a right to "life, liberty, and property" (as John Locke claimed) or a "fair" share in the allotment of social goods (as contemporary social philosophers on the political Left have insisted) is a deontological constraint, reminiscent of the impartiality restriction implicit in Kant's Categorical Imperative.

Contractarianism. If we take the position of Locke, we would say that everybody has an inviolable right to survival, freedom, and material possessions – rights which the government is bound to protect (even if doing s*o might v*iolate the Utility Principle!) But some have thought that this cannot possibly be correct because in itself it does so little to remove economic and political barriers to enhancing the qualify of life for economically disadvantaged people. In other words, it might be argued that liberty and property, if not the preservation of life itself, require a competitive access to society's material and cultural resources. In this spirit, the social philosopher John Rawls (1921 -) has insisted that in determining general rules of association, a society should assume that the well-being of the least well off is the basic test of moral rules. We do this by imagining ourselves in an "original position" of ignorance about the particulars of our own situation, so that whatever rules we adopt will derive from considerations other than narrow self-interest based on social standing, race, ethnicity, et cetera. Here the result for Rawls is that, as with Locke, the rules governing society resemble a contract undertaken by its members, with the understanding that its provisions are more likely than any others to yield a satisfactory context for mutual cooperation and personal fulfillment.

But think for a moment. Is this proposal free from difficulty? While Rawls' theory is addressed to the inadequacies of utilitarianism, does it really resolve all of them? A proposal such as Rawls' provides an abstract ideal for social organization and private conduct. When we think about applying it, we have to wonder what kinds of concrete systems such thin creatures, veiled from all personal history and prejudice, could invent from that cultural vacuum surrounding the "original position." (For more on Rawls, see Chapter 14.)

And by this point, we may find ourselves wondering if *either* deontologism or consequentialism can be patched up well enough to provide a satisfactory, unified theory of ethics. This reemphasizes what we said earlier: Moral deliberations may require a mixing and matching of a number of exemplars. This is not to say, however, that moral deliberations reduce to *crude rationalization*. Just because I may not have a single theory to handle every moral case, this does not mean that I am exempt from the serious business of carefully assessing my own inclinations and behavior. There is still a big difference between asking serious moral questions and looking for ways to excuse behavior that simply feels convenient.

RECENT TRENDS IN MODERN ETHICS

Metaethics. Given the difficulties that seem to plague both deontologism and consequentialism, some recent philosophers have turned away from applied ethics altogether. This has been one of the main trends in 20th-century ethics, at least in Britain and North America, and it goes under the name of *metaethics*. We cannot pretend to have considered the historical development of ethics without treating this development as well.

Earlier in this discussion, sensitivity to the details of linguistic usage was cited as a characteristic of sophisticated study of ethics. Our everyday moral instincts are the starting point for all moral reflection, and we are fully aware of those instincts only as we articulate them. But notice: Is our ordinary language reliably transparent or unambiguous in its meaning? For example, Christ's description of the supremely ethical life was "to love your God with all your heart, all your mind, all your soul and all your strength and your neighbor as yourself." Yet in deciding how to "love" our neighbor we'd clearly better be very careful how we choose to interpret that prescription! This drives home the point that we can answer questions about morality only if we can first answer some questions about language.

"Metaethics" is an ethical view that makes these linguistic concerns paramount. The contrast here is with "normative ethics," which (as we have been seeing here so far) attempts to identify and, where possible, justify the moral norms we ought to follow. (Applied ethics is a branch of normative ethics.) Metaethics *per se*, on the other hand, is concerned *only* with the way our moral language operates. Metaethical inquiry targets not what we should do morally; it targets what we are doing linguistically when we take a moral stance. It asks not whether or when I should lie; it asks what I mean if I say, "Lying is wrong." Metaethics thus aims at moral neutrality, in the interests of simply describing the linguistic usage that pervades our moral conversations.

Metaethics received its first substantive expression in the early part of this century, in the *Principia Ethica* of G.E. Moore (1873-1958). It is apparent from reading Moore that an interest in metaethics does not necessarily preclude normative concerns, for Moore himself had strong intuitions about what is good and what is right, and these form a major part of his discussion. But he presents his normative views as the logical result of his metaethical arguments: He says, for example, that the word "good" stands for a moral quality that can only be intuited (not conceptually defined). This he thinks must be so because the only alternatives he can think of are unacceptable. So his main strategy is metaethical: It is based on clarifying the way he thinks we have to use our moral language if we are not to slide into incoherence. But he also thinks that attending to the way we properly use our moral language can direct our attention to the kinds of "goods" that ought to direct our moral conduct. So for Moore metaethical inquiry has normative implications.

Thus there were two sides to Moore's ethical work. His treatment of normative issues gave rise to that form of deontologism known as *intuitionism*, whose main proponents were H. A. Pritchard (1871-1947), W. D. Ross (1877-1971) and, toward the end of his career, Moore himself. The other, metaethical side of Moore's work eventually evolved (in the hands of others) into various forms of *noncognitivism*. A noncognitivist in ethics (which Moore himself was not) is one who denies that any of our moral claims are really true, in the sense they would have to be if those claims constituted genuine knowledge. This presents a new wrinkle in modern moral discussion. Utilitarians and Kantians had both assumed that we can, at least in principle, *know* that an act is right (though, as we have seen, they disagreed on the basis for its being so). And Moore himself thought he *knew* certain things in the world are good – "personal affection and the appreciation of what is beautiful in Art or Nature," for example. Before this point, modern moral theories had purported to describe some range of "moral facts." But in the philosophical generation following Moore, some theorists – notably A.J. Ayer (1910-1989), Charles L. Stevenson (1908-1979), and R. M. Hare (1919-) – denied, on metaethical grounds, that moral claims are knowledge-claims at all because (they claimed) moral language is not really descriptive.

Whenever I use my words to describe something, I have to assume that there is a relation between my utterance and something outside it which makes that utterance true (or, if I am wrong, makes it false). This simply means that if, for example, I sincerely say that "it's snowing outside," there must really be snow out there, or else I'm in error. But the best-known varieties of noncognitivism regard our moral utterances as nothing more than expressions – of feelings or of commands, depending on which form this general theory takes. The *emotivist* (Ayer) claims that an utterance such as "Murder is wrong" is really the outward manifestation of a feeling or attitude of disapproval ("Murder – boo!"). On the other hand, the *prescriptivist* (Hare) claims that the same moral utterance is an imperative ("Don't kill any human being!").

The difference between these two expressionist theories may seem too subtle to trouble us, but there is indeed an important distinction here, and that concerns the possibility of basing one's moral preferences on genuine rational argument. Of the two, only the prescriptivist leaves that possibility open. This is because imperatives can stand in the kind of relation to one another that allows rational argument: If someone asks me why I told him to close the door, my rational response can be: "Don't make me freeze!"

Emotivism vs. Critics. Now critics have attacked emotivism on the ground that this kind of rational relation cannot hold among subjective attitudes. Emotivism regards all the reasons we might give for our moral beliefs as nothing more than rhetoric, whose function is to cause our listener to acquiesce to our own point of view. In that case, "good" reasons are simply those appeals that happen to work, and if this sounds familiar from the early part of this discussion, it should. For now we have come full circle. The early Sophists had pretty much this same notion about the function of moral discourse – one engages in moral discussion not to determine the "truth" about norms and virtues, but simply to convince others to see things one's own way. For them, there was no "truth" to moral claims, beyond the subjective conviction an individual imports into the situation.

The most convincing retort to this subjectivist view may still be the Socratic response. Socrates famously said that "the unexamined life is not worth living," and what he meant was that human dignity or happiness depends upon our ability to take stock of ourselves and, if necessary, amend not only our conduct but the character from which that conduct derives. That is a tough task under any circumstances, because habits are notoriously resistant to change. But it is an impossible task without a store of moral concepts that do more than just reflect one's own subjective prejudices. Emotivism, because it regards all moral language as strategically directed toward convincing others, leaves no room for moral *self*-evaluation.

Prescriptivism, on the other hand, at least provides some basis for this kind of self-reflection, in that it locates the moral point of view outside a purely egoistic frame of reference. In this, prescriptivism is really a noncognitivist version of Kantianism: It stipulates that (despite the fact our moral rules and principles are neither true nor false) they are universalizable. Like Kant, the prescriptivist insists that a moral agent decides ethical matters based on considerations of impartiality, which do not allow special exceptions favorable to oneself or one's friends. Thus for example the imperative "Don't make me freeze!" functions as a moral directive only when it derives from some impartial considerations, such as: "Don't fail to assist another human being in distress!" Insofar as it is simply the utterance of a personal preference (for example: "Don't fail to help *me* whenever I think I need it!"), it lacks moral standing.

But is the universality requirement enough? A considerable amount of recent discussion has been spent on whether or not prescriptivism, given its position as a noncognitivist theory, can successfully accommodate the rational side of our moral practices. Doubts about its ability to do so rest in part upon doubts about the basis of noncognitivism itself, especially as this basis took modern shape through Moore's discussion in *Principia Ethica*.

Ethical Naturalism. Moore's ethical work is undoubtedly best known for his "refutation" of ethical *naturalism*. "Naturalism" in ethics is the view that there are no moral facts over and above what we describe when we give a complete inventory of the natural world. This would exclude from morality a range of considerations that often play a commanding role in many people's moral thinking – the Will of God, for example (unless we identify God *with* the world, as pantheists have). For the ethical naturalist, all value is actually embedded in nature, and proper moral discourse implicitly reflects that. And here, Moore thought, is where the problem with naturalism lies. Moore, in an argument reminiscent of the philosopher David Hume (1711-1776), denied that our moral language could function as the naturalist thinks, owing to an irrevocable logical gap between the facts of nature and the values of morality. To miss this gap, Moore claimed, is to slide into "the naturalistic fallacy."

According to Moore, the naturalistic fallacy originates with an illicit statement of identity. Consider again the utilitarian[9] approach to the issue of lying. Should a physician lie to a patient who would suffer from learning the likely prognosis of his disease? Recall how the utilitarian might begin reasoning this way: Telling the whole truth will probably inhibit the patient's recovery; therefore I ought not to tell him the whole truth. But notice the logic of this reasoning. We have here a *factual* premise (which concerns the probable development of certain physical events), and from that this utilitarian would derive an *ought*-statement (which here concerns a physician's duty to a patient). Now clearly this is not a valid argument as it stands, because nothing explicitly stated in the premise warrants the introduction of any "ought." To correct this, part of what's needed is the introduction of an identity statement, which would bridge that gap. Here the utilitarian's strategy is to apply his brand of consequentialism based on the Utility Principle: What I ought to do is to produce the greatest possible amount of good for all concerned, and *the situation that contains the greatest measure of pleasure (or happiness) has to contain the greatest amount of good.* But what is the basis for this latter statement? According to the classical utilitarian view, it is true because "good" just *is* "pleasure" (or "happiness"). If that is so, then (depending upon the other circumstances of the case) it might indeed follow that the physician should lie to protect the patient's health (and therefore, of course, his happiness).

But is there really an identity between "good" and any such natural state (such as pleasure or happiness)? Moore did not see how there could be. He thought that such an identity had to entail what is called an "analytic" connection between the words themselves – between the word "good" and some natural descriptive term such as "pleasant." For any such logical connection to hold (Moore thought), the relation of entailment between them would have to be self-evident, beyond the possibility of doubt. But clearly that is not the case, for it still seems worth asking whether or not the "good" really *is* "pleasure," and so on – which is of course one reason theoretical debates in ethics have such a long and contentious history!

Many consider this discussion of Moore's, along with its subsequent treatment at the hands of his critics and supporters, the pivotal debate in 20th-century ethics. It supplies the shared ground for the various forms of noncognitivism, in that if Moore is wrong in his rejection of naturalism, then the debates between, say, emotivism and prescriptivism would not much matter – because either one is true only if naturalism is false.

Now because noncognitivism shares Moore's anti-naturalistic bias, many have thought that the unacceptable consequences deriving from noncognitivism mean that Moore has to be wrong. In the case of prescriptivism, for example, Hare himself has admitted that a Nazi could be a prescriptivist, just as long as the Nazi himself would be willing to suffer extermination if he unexpectedly discovered he were a Jew (through the retrieval of a long-lost birth certificate perhaps). Here Hare is forced to move away from Kant and toward a kind of radical existentialism reminiscent of Jean-Paul Sartre (1905-1980). Hare has to concede that prescriptivism provides no basis for deciding among basic moral assumptions, and that each person must "make up his own mind which way he ought to live; for in the end everything rests upon such a decision of principle." And this would seem to suggest that the moral life is at bottom an *irrational* project – which would mean that the Sophists were basically right all along.

Modern theories of virtue. We have seen how the preoccupation with the precision and function of language has been one of the marks of modern ethics, and how the metaethical program takes this concern to its limits. In the case of noncognitivism, normative ethics virtually disappears from the purview of philosophy, and recently many philosophers have reacted against this displacement of more traditional moral concerns. Those concerns encompassed not only normative ethics (which provides recommendations as to what I should *do*), but also theories of virtue (which gives guidance as to what kind of person I should *be*). In other words, one prominent trend in recent moral philosophy has been to return to Greek and Judeo-Christian moral topics. This move is associated with the contemporary revival of ethical naturalism, in the work of writers such as Elizabeth Anscombe, Philippa Foot, and Alasdair MacIntyre.

The overt appeal of this revival of virtue ethics is in the way it addresses some obvious flaws in the other modern theories, especially deontologism. For against a Kantian, the virtue-theorist denies that the value of morality lies only in the accomplishment of duty or in the formation of a duty-bound character. What is lacking in the Kantian picture is sensitivity to the concerns that traditionally have captured the attention of the most religiously minded persons, whose main interest is in the care of the "soul."

It is worth noting that whether one believes literally in a soul (as distinct from the body) is not really the point here; for we could regard religious language in its broadest function, as symbolic of the personal human traits we most value in those we meet – traits of honesty, benevolence, and so forth. And the religious life has usually emphasized the need not only to cultivate those individual traits of character, but also to integrate those traits into a harmonious interplay where one reinforces the other (and this returns us to Plato's version of the Self-Realization Theory). As any monk knows, this is not easily accomplished, and it is impossible if one attends only to what's required for the overt performance of duties. On this view the moral life is one of continual self-reflection, tempered by a recognition of the real limits (as well as the necessity) of moral deliberation. The modest aim is just to do the best one can, and let God handle the rest. In Joseph Butler we noticed this same confidence in the providential workings of our own limited deliberations. And whether or not that same kind of moral optimism can find a permanent home in our secular world is an interesting question.

But some virtue-theorists, notably Alasdair MacIntyre, have suggested that secularism undercuts not virtue-theory, but its modern competitors. For as the horizons of culture expand in the modern world, the horizons of imagination expand as well, and the moral choices that were once culturally fixed become increasingly discretionary. The claim here is that without the theological foundation provided, for example, by medieval Christianity, there is no authority (other than arbitrary personal choice) supporting the selection of either duties to perform or goods to pursue. We saw this already in the case of prescriptivism, and MacIntyre now extends that same critique to both deontologism and utilitarianism. The legal model upon which modern moral theory depends, with its notion of law and defeasibility, turns out to be peculiarly unsuited to a secular cultural setting; for moral practice, like legal practice, is vacuous without some duly constituted authority that rescues it from capriciousness.

Virtue-theory then seeks to reestablish a source for morality that is broader than individual autonomy, and for this it appeals to the general communitarian orientation that we already met in Aristotle. Most of the virtues we regard so highly, after all, are other-directed: Generally speaking, we are courteous or generous or kindly or honest towards others besides ourselves. And at this point in the discussion, ethical naturalism reenters, in a way that makes clear why recent virtue-theorists have typically been ethical naturalists as well.

Recall Moore's original criticism of ethical naturalism, which was that no factual statement can logically lead to a value statement, except through an illicit identification. Is this really true? Suppose I know that one person (Jim) has made a brutal remark to another (Jane), and suppose I know that there is no obvious explanation for this in anything that Jane had done. It was simply a gratuitous insult. Those, let us say, are facts. Yet if true, they surely justify my saying that Jim was being rude, and "rude" is a value-term. It applies to people who lack the virtue of courtesy, and it does so because of the linguistic practices that have taken root in our English-speaking community (which precedes any individual member's standing as autonomous moral agent). That is the first complaint against Moore's argument.

The second complaint concerns the famous linguistic point in Moore's argument, where he simply assumed that no identity statement that is not analytic can warrant an inference from fact to value. That was the force behind his observation that we can always ask whether or not the "good" really is pleasure (or happiness). Because we can always sensibly ask that, it is clear that the relation between "good" and a naturalist term such as "happiness" is not analytic, which is to say that our idea of happiness is not self-evidently "contained" in our idea of the good. (If it were, our question "Is happiness really the good?" would strike us as not even worth asking, the same way the question "Is happiness really happiness?" does.) But is this the only kind of identity there is? Clearly not. Even granting Moore's notion of analyticity, identities can be learned as well as intuited. We learn that water is H_2O, we learn that Venus is the morning star, and perhaps we even learn, over the course of much spiritual struggle, that happiness consists in living a certain kind of virtuous life. In that case, we would have to say that one of the seminal discussions of modern philosophy has left us in a blind alley.

Virtue-theory's critics. Despite its appeal, however, virtue ethics is not without its obvious difficulties. For one thing, there may be no simple list of virtues that remain constant from one culture to the next. (Christian humility, for example, was unknown to Aristotle.) Is a virtue-theorist then faced with a dilemma – must we either abandon all hope of objectivity (so that we admit fostering certain virtues only due to an accident of cultural history), or else hunker down into ethnocentric favoritism?

Moreover, it is fine to say, as virtue-theorists do, that moral deliberation should not be reduced to some hair-splitting enterprise that aims at always doing just the right thing regardless of the implications for one's own character. But how exactly should that deliberation proceed? Simply by "getting in touch" with one's own virtues? The problem here is that virtues are notoriously silent on concrete details: The fact that I may have a kindly disposition toward others would not alone tell me exactly how I should behave toward any specific person. (Should I just give him money the next time I see him?) And what do I do in the case of moral conflict? Remember that physician who had trouble reconciling her kindliness toward her patients with her honesty. Here conflict among moral rules gets recapitulated at the level of the virtues.

And this reasonably portrays where things now stand. For although there is general agreement in contemporary ethical discussion that the virtues have been handled inadequately so far in the modern debate, how exactly to correct this remains controversial. But we can speculate as to where the debate may turn next. For example: One way to address the problem of moral conflict and still remain within the tradition of virtue-theory may be to take up the suggestion of the American philosopher John Dewey (1859-1952), who in effect transformed the Aristotelian notion of "practical wisdom" into the master virtue of "intelligence," a virtue capable of discerning the moral quality of each unique situation, in a way that directs conduct. The skeptic however will wonder how such a notion of moral discernment differs from the old cognitivist intuition, which stood so vulnerable to easy infection from unfounded prejudice. Reading Dewey, one can glean a sketchy answer to this sort of objection, but Dewey never worked this out in any detail, and a final verdict rests with those currently reviving and assessing Dewey's program.

One thing is clear, however, and that is the fact that moral decision-making cannot reliably proceed unless moral agents have been educated appropriately, so that they are deeply sensitive to the appeal of the range of normative moral arguments we have been presenting in this discussion. That of course is the rationale for a course in applied ethics. It is also one reason for the abiding interest in the philosophy of Dewey, who has been the single most influential philosopher of education in American history. And it is the reason we need to spend some time considering the question of moral development – as we shall in the following chapter.

READINGS

From *Nicomachean Ethics*

Aristotle

The Proper Aim of Ethical Theory

Since these, then, are the sorts of things we argue from and about, it will be satisfactory if we can indicate the truth roughly in outline; since (that is to say) we argue from and about what holds good usually (but not universally), it will be satisfactory if we can draw conclusions of the same sort.

How to judge an ethical theory

Each of our claims, then, ought to be accepted in the same way (as claiming to hold good usually), since the educated person seeks exactness in each area to the extent that the nature of the subject allows; for apparently it is just as mistaken to demand demonstrations from a rhetorician as to accept (merely) persuasive arguments from a mathematician.

Further, each person judges well what he knows, and is a good judge about that; hence the good judge in a particular area is the person educated in that area, and the unconditionally good judge is the person educated in every area.

Qualifications of the student of ethics

This is why a youth is not a suitable student of political science; for he lacks experience of the actions in life which political science argues from and about.

Moreover, since he tends to be guided by his feeling, his study will be futile and useless; for its end is action, not knowledge. And here it does not matter whether he is young in years or immature in character, since the deficiency does not depend on age, but results from being guided in his life and in each of his pursuits by his feelings; for an immature person, such as an incontinent person, gets no benefit from his knowledge.

If, however, we are guided by reason in forming our desires and in acting, then this knowledge will be of great benefit....

(The excerpt above was taken from Chapter 2)

... A clearer account of the good: The human soul's activity expressing virtue

But presumably the remark that the best good is happiness is apparently something (generally) agreed, and what we miss is a clearer statement of what the best good is.

(1) If something has a function, its good depends on its function

Well, perhaps we shall find the best good if we first find the function of a human being. For just as the good, i.e. (doing) well for a flautist, a sculptor, and every craftsman, and, in general for whatever has a function and (characteristic) action, seems to depend on its function, the same seems to be true for a human being, if a human being has some function.

(2) What sorts of things have functions?

Then do the carpenter and the leatherworker have their functions and actions, while a human being has none, and is by nature idle, without any function? Or, just as eye, hand, foot and, in general, every (bodily) part apparently has its functions, may we likewise ascribe to a human being some function besides all theirs?

(3) The human function

What, then, could this be? For living is apparently shared with plants, but what we are looking for is the special function of a human being; hence we should set aside the life of nutrition and growth. The life next in order is some sort of life of sense-perception; but this too is apparently shared with horse, ox and every animal. The remaining possibility, then is some sort of life of action of the (part of the soul) that has reason. Clarification of 'has reason' and 'life'

Now this (part has two parts, which have reason in different ways), one as obeying the reason (in the other part) the other as itself having reason and thinking. (We intend both.) Moreover, life is also spoken of in two ways (as capacity and as activity), and we must take (a human being's special function to be) life as activity, since this seems to be called life to a fuller extent.

(4) The human good is activity expressing virtue

(a) We have found, then, that the human function is the soul's activity that expresses reason (as itself having reason) or requires reason (as obeying reason). (b) Now the function of F, e.g., of a harpist, is the same in kind, so we say, as the function of an excellent F, e.g., an excellent harpist.(c) The same is true unconditionally in every case, when we add to the function the superior achievement that expresses the virtue; for a harpist's function, e.g., is to play the harp, and a good harpist's is to do it well. (d) Now we take the human function to be a certain kind of life, and take this life to be the soul's activity and actions that express reason. (e) (Hence by (c) and (d) the excellent man's function is to do this finely and well. (f) Each function is completed well when its completion expresses the proper virtue. (g) Therefore (by (d), (e) and (f) the human good turns out to be the soul's activity that expresses virtue.

(5) The good must also be complete

And if there are more virtues than one, the good will express the best and most complete virtue. Moreover, it will be in a complete life. For one swallow does not make a spring, nor does one day; nor similarly, does one day or a short time make us blessed and happy. (Excerpted from *Nicomachean Ethics*, translated by Terence Irwin, Hackett Publishing Company, P.O. Box 44937, Indianapolis, Ind. 46204)

METAPHYSICAL FOUNDATIONS OF MORALS
First Section
Transition from the Common Rational Knowledge of Morality
Immanuel Kant

Nothing can possibly be conceived in the world, or even out of it, which can be called good without qualification, except a GOOD WILL. Intelligence, wit, judgment, and the other *talents* of the mind, however they may be named, or courage, resolution, perseverance, as qualities of temperament, are undoubtedly good and desirable in many respects. But these gifts of nature may also become extremely bad and mischievous if the will which to make use of these gifts, and which therefore constitutes what is called *character,* is not good. It is the same with the *gifts of fortune.* Power, riches, honor, even health, and the general well-being and contentment with one's condition which is called *happiness,* all inspire pride and often presumption if there is not a good will to correct the influence of these on the mind, and with this to rectify also the whole principle of acting and adapt it to its end. The sight of a being, not adorned with a single feature of a pure and good will, enjoying unbroken prosperity can never give pleasure to an impartial rational spectator. Thus a good will appears to constitute the indispensable condition for being even worthy of happiness.

Indeed, quite a few qualities are of service to this good will itself and may facilitate its action, yet have no intrinsic, unconditional value, but are always presupposing a good will; this qualifies the esteem that we justly have for these qualities and does not permit us to regard them as absolutely good. Moderation in the affections and passions, self-control and calm deliberation are not only good in many respects, but even seem to constitute part of the intrinsic worth of a person; but they are far from deserving to be called good without qualification, although they have been so unconditionally praised by the ancients. For without the principles of a good will, these qualities may become extremely bad. The coolness of a villain not only makes him far more dangerous, but also immediately makes him more abominable in our eyes than he would have been without it.

A good will is good not because of what it performs or effects, nor by its aptness for attaining some proposed end, but simply by virtue of the volition; that is, it is good in itself and when considered by itself is to be esteemed much higher than all that it can bring about in pursuing any inclination, nay even in pursuing the sum total of all inclination. It might happen that, owing to special misfortune, or to the niggardly provision of a step-motherly nature, this will should wholly lack power to accomplish its purpose. If with its greatest efforts this will would yet achieve nothing and there should remain only good will (to be sure, not a mere wish but the summoning of all means in our power), then, like a jewel, good will would still shine by its own light as a thing having its whole value in itself. Its usefulness or fruitlessness can neither add to nor detract anything from this value. It would be, as it were, only the setting to enable us to handle it the more conveniently in common commerce and to attract to it the attention of those who are not yet experts, but not recommend it to true experts or to determine its value.

However, there is something so strange in this idea of the absolute value of the mere will in which no account is taken of its utility, that notwithstanding the thorough assent of even common reason, a suspicion lingers that this idea may perhaps really be the product of a mere high-flown fancy, and that we may have misunderstood the purpose of nature in assigning reason as the governor of the will. Therefore, we will examine this idea from this point of view:

We assume, as a fundamental principle, that no organ (designed) for any purpose will be found in the physical constitution of an organized being, except one which is also the fittest and best adapted for that purpose. Now if the proper object of nature for a being with reason and a will was its *preservation,* its *welfare,* in a word its happiness, then nature would have hit upon a very bad arrangement when it selected the reason of the creature to carry out this function. For all the actions which the creature has to perform with a view to this purpose, and the whole rule of its conduct would be far more surely prescribed by (its own) instinct, and that end (happiness) would have been attained by instinct far more certainly than it ever can be by reason.

Should reason have been attributed to this favored creature over and above (such instinct), reason would only have served this creature for contemplating the happy constitution of its nature, for admiring it, and congratulating itself thereon, and for feeling thankful for it to the beneficent cause. But (certainly nature would not have arranged it so that) such a creature should subject its desires to that weak and deceptive guidance, and meddle with nature's intent. In a word, nature would have taken care that reason should not turn into *practical* exercise, nor have the presumption, with its feeble insight, to figure out for itself a plan of happiness and the means for attaining it. In fact, we find that the more a cultivated reason applies itself with deliberate purpose to enjoying life and happiness, so much more does the man lack true satisfaction.

From this circumstance there arises in many men, if they are candid enough to confess it, a certain degree of *misology;* that is, hatred of reason, especially in the case of those who are most experienced in the use of reason. For, after calculating all the advantages they derive, not only from the invention of all the arts of common luxury, but even from the sciences (which then seem to them only a luxury of the intellect after all) they find that they have actually only brought more trouble on themselves, rather than gained in happiness. They end by envying, rather than despising, the common run of men who keep closer to the guidance of mere instinct and who do not allow their reason to have much influence on their conduct. We must admit this much; that the judgment of those, who would diminish very much the lofty eulogies on the advantages which reason gives us in regard to the happiness and satisfaction of life, or would even deny these advantages altogether, is by no means morose or ungrateful for the goodness with which the world is governed. At the root of these judgments lies the idea that the existence of world order has a different and far nobler end for which, rather than happiness, reason is properly intended. Therefore this end must be regarded as the supreme condition to which the private ends of man must yield for the most part.

Thus reason is not competent enough to guide the will with certainty in regard to its objects and the satisfaction of all our wants which it even multiplies to some extent; this purpose is one to which an implanted instinct would have led with much greater certainty. Nevertheless, reason is imparted to us as a practical faculty; that is, as one which is to have influence on the *will.* Therefore, if we admit that nature generally in the distribution of natural propensities has adapted the means to the end, nature's true intention must be to produce a *will,* which is not merely good as a *means* to something else but *good in itself.* Reason is absolutely necessary for this sort of will. Then this will, though indeed not the sole and complete good, must be the supreme good and the condition of every other good, even of the desire for happiness.

Under these circumstances, there is nothing inconsistent with the wisdom of nature in the fact that the cultivation of the reason which is requisite for the first and unconditional purpose, does in many ways interfere, at least in this life, with the attainment of the second purpose: Happiness, which is always relative. Nay, it may even reduce happiness to nothing without nature failing thereby in her purpose. For reason recognizes the establishment of a good will as its highest practical destination, and is capable of only satisfying its own proper kind in attaining this purpose.: The attainment may involve many a disappointment over otherwise desirable purposes.

Therefore we must develop the notion of a will which deserves to be highly esteemed for itself and is good without a specific objective, a notion which is implied by sound natural common sense. This notion needs to be clarified rather than expounded. In evaluating our actions this notion always takes first place and constitutes the condition of all the rest. In order to do this we will take the notion of duty which includes that of a good will, although implying certain subjective restrictions and hindrances.. However, these hindrances, far from concealing it or rendering it unrecognizable, rather emphasize a good will by contrast and make it shine forth so much the brighter.

I omit here all actions which are already recognized as inconsistent with duty, although they may be useful for this or that purpose. The question whether these actions are done *from duty* cannot arise at all since they conflict with it. I also leave aside those actions which really conform to duty but to which men have *no* direct *inclination,* performing them because they are impelled to do so by some other inclination. For in this case we can readily distinguish whether the action which agrees with duty is done *out of duty* or from a selfish point of view. It is much harder to make this distinction when the action accords with duty and when besides the subject has a *direct* inclination toward it. For example, it is indeed a matter of duty that a dealer should not overcharge an inexperienced purchaser, and wherever there is much commerce the prudent tradesman does not overcharge, but keeps a fixed price for everyone, so that a child buys of him as well as any other. More are thus *honestly* served; but this is not enough to make us believe that the tradesman has so acted from duty and from principles of honesty; his own advantage required it. It is out of the question in this case to suppose that he might have besides a direct inclination in favor of the buyers, so that out of love, as it were, he should give advantage to one over another. Hence the action was done neither out of duty nor because of inclination but merely with a selfish view.

On the other hand, it is a duty to maintain one's life; in addition everyone also has a direct inclination to do so. But on this account the often anxious care which most men take of their lives has no intrinsic worth and their maxim has no moral import. No doubt they preserve their life *as duty requires,* but not *because duty requires.* The case is different, when adversity and hopeless sorrow have completely taken away the relish for life; if the unfortunate one, strong in mind, indignant at his fate rather than despondent or dejected, longs for death and yet preserves his life without loving it. (If he does this) not from inclination or fear but from duty, then his maxim has a moral worth.

To be beneficent when we can is a duty; besides this, there are many minds so sympathetically constituted that without any other motive of vanity or self-interest, they find a pleasure in spreading joy (about them) and can take delight in the satisfaction of others so far as it is their own work. But I maintain that in such a case, however proper, however amiable an action of this kind may be, it nevertheless has no true moral worth, but is on a level with other inclinations; e. g. the inclination to honor which, if it is happily directed to that which is actually of public utility and accordant with duty and consequently honorable, deserves praise and encouragement but not respect. For the maxim lacks the moral ingredient that such actions be done *out of duty,* not from inclination. Put the case (another way and suppose) that the mind of that philanthropist were clouded by sorrow of his own, extinguishing all sympathy with the lot of others, and that while he still has the power to benefit others in distress he is not touched by their trouble because he is absorbed with his own; suppose that he tears not himself out of this deadening insensibility, and performs the action without any inclination for it, but simply from duty; only then has his action genuine moral worth. Furthermore, if nature has put little sympathy into the heart of this or that man, if a supposedly upright man is by temperament cold and indifferent to the sufferings of others, perhaps because in respect of his own sufferings he is provided with the special gift of patience and fortitude so that he supposes or even requires that others should have the same, such a man would certainly not be the meanest product of nature. But if nature had not specially shaped him to be a philanthropist, would he not find cause in himself for attributing to himself a value far higher than the value of a good-natured temperament could be? Unquestionably. It is just in this that there is brought out the moral worth of the character which is incomparably the highest of all; namely, that he is beneficent, not from inclination, but from duty.

To secure one's own happiness is a duty, at least indirectly; for discontent with one's condition under pressure of many anxieties and amidst unsatisfied wants might easily become a great *temptation to transgression from duty.* But here again, without reference to duty, all men already have the strongest and most intense inclination to happiness, because it is just in this idea that all inclinations are combined in one total. But the precept for happiness is often of such a sort that it greatly interferes with some inclinations. Yet a man cannot form any definite and certain conception of the sum of satisfying all of these inclinations, which is called happiness. It is not then to be wondered at that a single inclination, definite both as to what it promises and as to the time within which it can be gratified, is often able to overcome such a fluctuating idea (as the precept for happiness). For instance, a gouty patient can choose to enjoy what he likes and to suffer what he may, since according to his calculation, at least on this occasion he has not sacrificed the enjoyment of the present moment for a possibly mistaken expectation of happiness supposedly found in health. But, if the general desire for happiness does not influence his will, and even supposing that in his particular case health was not a necessary element in his calculation, there yet remains a law even in this case, as in all other cases; that is, he should promote his happiness not from inclination but from duty. Only in following duty would his conduct acquire true moral worth.

Undoubtedly, it is in this manner that we are to understand those passages of the Scripture in which we are commanded to love our neighbor, even our enemy. For love, as an affection, cannot be commanded, but beneficence for duty's sake can be, even though we are not impelled to such kindness by any inclination, and may even be repelled by a natural and unconquerable aversion. This is *practical* love and not *psychological.* It is a love originating in the will

and not in the inclination of sentiment, in principles of action, not of sentimental sympathy.

The second proposition is: That an action done from duty derives its moral worth, *not from the purpose* which is to be attained by it, but from the maxim by which it is determined. Therefore, the action does not depend on the realization of its objective, but merely on the *principle* of volition by which the action has taken place, without regard to any object of desire. It is clear from what precedes that the purposes which we may have in view for our actions, or their effects as regarded as ends and impulsions of the will, cannot give to actions any unconditional or moral worth. Then in what can their worth consist if it does not consist in the will as it is related to its expected effect? It cannot consist in anything but the *principle of the will,* with no regard to the ends which can be attained by the action. For the will stands between its *a priori* principle which is formal, and its *a posteriori* impulse which is material, as between two roads. As it must be determined by something, it follows that the will must be determined by the formal principle of volition, as when an action is done from duty, in which case every material impulse has been withdrawn from it.

The third proposition, which is a consequence of the preceding two, I would express thus: *Duty is the necessity of an action, resulting from respect for the law.* I may have an *inclination* for an object as the effect of my proposed action, but I cannot have *respect* for an object just for this reason: That it is merely an effect and not an action of will. Similarly, I cannot have respect for an inclination, whether my own or another's; I can at most, if it is my own, approve it; if it is another's I can sometimes even cherish it; that is, look on it as favorable to my own interest. Only the law itself which is connected with my will by no means as an effect but as a principle which does not serve my inclination but outweighs it, or at least in case of choice excludes my inclination from its calculation; only such a law can be an object of respect and hence a command. Now an action done from duty must wholly exclude the influence of inclination, and with it every object of the will, so that nothing remains which can determine the will objectively except the *law,* and (determine the will) subjectively except *pure respect* for this practical law, and hence (pure respect) for the maxim to follow this law even to the thwarting of all my inclinations.

Thus the moral worth of an action does not consist of the effect expected from it, nor from any principle of action which needs to borrow its motive from this expected effect. For, all these effects, agreeableness of one's condition and even the promotion of the happiness of others, all this could have also been brought about by other causes so that for this there would have been no need of the will of a rational being. However, in this will alone can the supreme and unconditional good be found. Therefore the pre-eminent good which we call moral can consist in nothing other than the *concept of law* in itself, *which is certainly only possible in a rational being,* in so far as this conception, and not the expected effect, determines the will. This is a good which is already present in the person acting according to it, and we do not have to wait for good to appear in the result.

But what sort of law can it be the conception of which must determine the will, even without our paying attention to the effect expected from it, in order that this will may be called good absolutely and without qualification? As I have stripped the will of every impulse which could arise for it from obedience to any law, there remains nothing but the general conformity of the will's actions to law in general. Only this conformity to law is to serve the will as a principle; that is, I am never to act in any way other than *so I want my maxim also to become a general law.* It is the simple conformity to law in general, without assuming any particular law applicable to certain actions, that serves the will as its principle, and must so serve it if duty is not to be a vain delusion and a chimerical notion. The common reason of men in their practical judgments agrees perfectly with this and always has in view the principle suggested here. For example, let the question be: When in distress may I make a promise with the intention of not keeping it? I readily distinguish here between the two meanings which the question may have: Whether it is prudent, or whether it is in accordance with duty, to make a false promise. The former undoubtedly may often be the case. I (may) see clearly that it is not enough to extricate myself from a present difficulty by means of this subterfuge, but that it must be carefully considered whether there may not result from such a lie a much greater inconvenience than that from which I am now freeing myself. But, since

in spite of all my supposed *cunning* the consequences cannot be foreseen easily; the loss of credit may be much more injurious to me than any mischief which I seek to avoid at present.

That being the case, one might consider whether it would not be more *prudent* to act according to a general maxim, and make it a habit to give no promise except with the intention of keeping it. But, it is soon clear that such a maxim is still only based on the fear of consequences. It is a wholly different thing to be truthful from a sense of duty, than to be so from apprehension of injurious consequences. In the first case, the very conceiving of the action already implies a law for me; in the second, I must first look about elsewhere to see what results may be associated with it which would affect me. For it is beyond all doubt wicked to deviate from the principle of duty; but to be unfaithful to my maxim of prudence may often be very advantageous to me, although it is certainly wiser to abide by it. However, the shortest way, and an unerring one, to discover the answer to this question of whether a lying promise is consistent with duty is to ask myself, "Would I be content if this maxim of extricating myself from difficulty by a false promise held good as a general law for others as well as for myself?" Would I care to say to myself, "Everyone may make a deceitful promise when he finds himself in a difficulty from which he cannot extricate himself otherwise"? Then I would presently become aware that while I can decide in favor of the lie, I can by no means decide that lying should be a general law. For under such a law there would be no promises at all, since I would state my intentions in vain in regard to my future actions to those who would not believe my allegation, or, if they did so too hastily, they would pay me back in my own coin. Hence, as soon as such a maxim was made a universal law, it would necessarily destroy itself.

Therefore, I do not need any sharp acumen to discern what I have to do in order that my will may be morally good. (As I am) inexperienced in the course of the world and incapable of being prepared for all its contingencies, I can only ask myself: "Can you will that your maxim should also be a general law?" If not, then my maxim must be rejected, not because of any disadvantage in it for myself or even for others, but because my maxim cannot fit as a principle into a possible universal legislation, and reason demands immediate respect from me for such legislation ... Indeed, I do not *discern* as yet on what this respect is based; into this question the philosopher may inquire. But at least I understand this much: That this respect is an evaluation of the worth that far outweighs all that is recommended by inclination. The necessity of acting from *pure* respect for the practical law (of right action) is what constitutes duty, to which every other motive must yield, because it is the condition of a will being good *in itself,* and the value of such a will exceeds everything.

Thus we have arrived at the principle of moral knowledge of common human reason. Although common men no doubt do not conceive this principle in such an abstract and universal form, yet they really always have it before their eyes and use it as the standard for their decision. It would be easy to show here how, with this compass in hand, men are well able to distinguish, in every case that occurs, what is good, bad, conformable to duty or inconsistent with it. Without teaching them anything at all new, we are only, like Socrates, directing their attention to the principle they employ themselves and (showing) that we therefore do not need science and philosophy to know what we should do to be honest and good and even wise and virtuous. Indeed, we might well have understood before that the knowledge of what every man ought to do, and hence also (what he ought) to know is within the reach of every man, even the commonest. We cannot help admiring what a great advantage practical judgment has over theoretical judgment in men's common sense. If, in theoretical judgments, common reason ventures to depart from the laws of experience and from the perceptions of the senses, it plunges into many inconceivabilities and self-contradictions, (or) at any rate into a chaos of uncertainty, obscurity and instability. But in the practical sphere (of just action) it is right that, when one excludes all sense impulses from (determining) practical laws, the power of judgment of common sense begins to show itself to special advantage. It then even becomes a subtle matter as to whether common sense provides tricky excuses for conscience in relation to other claims regarding what is to be called right, or whether, for its own guidance, common sense seeks to determine honestly the values of (particular) actions.

In the latter case, common sense has as good a hope of hitting the mark as any philosopher can promise himself. A common man is almost more sure of doing so, because the philosopher cannot have any other (better) principle and may easily perplex his judgment by a multitude of considerations foreign to the matter in hand, and so he may turn from the right way. Therefore would it not be wiser in moral matters to acquiesce in the judgment of common reason, or at most to call in philosophy only for rendering the system of morals more complete and intelligible and its rules more convenient for use, especially for disputation, but not to deflect common sense from its happy simplicity, or to lead it through philosophy into a new path of inquiry and instruction?

Innocence is indeed a glorious thing, only it is a pity that it cannot maintain itself well and is easily seduced. On this account even wisdom, which otherwise consists more in conduct than in knowledge, yet has need of science, not in order to learn from it, but to secure for its own precepts acceptance and permanence. In opposition to all the commands of duty that reason represents to man as so greatly deserving respect, man feels within himself a powerful counterpoise in his wants and inclinations, the entire satisfaction of which he sums up under the name of happiness. Reason issues its commands unyieldingly, without promising anything to the inclinations and with disregard and contempt, as it were, for these demands which are so impetuous and at the same time so plausible and which will not allow themselves to be suppressed by any command. Hence there arises the *dialectic;* that is, a disposition to argue against these strict laws of duty and to question their validity, or at least to question their purity and strictness. (There is also a disposition) to make them more accordant, if possible, with our wishes and inclinations; that is to say, to corrupt them at their very source and to destroy their value entirely, an act that even common practical reason cannot ultimately approve.

Thus the *common reason of man* is compelled to leave its proper sphere and to take a step into the field of a *practical philosophy,* but not for satisfying any desire to speculate, which never occurs to it as long as it is content to be mere sound reason. But the purpose is to secure on practical grounds information and clear instruction respecting the source of the principle (of common sense) and the correct definition of this principle as contrasted with the maxims which are based on wants and inclinations, so that common sense may escape from the perplexity of opposing claims, and not run the risk of losing all genuine moral principles through the equivocation into which it easily falls. Thus when practical, common reason cultivates itself, there arises insensibly in it a dialectic forcing it to seek aid in philosophy, just like what happens to practical reason in its theoretic use. Therefore in this case as well as in the other (common sense) will find no rest but in a thorough critical examination of our reason.

(Excerpted from *Metaphysical Foundations of Morals*, The Modern Library, Random House Publishing, New York, 1949.)

FOR FURTHER INQUIRY

Suggested Readings

• A very serviceable account of the development of ethics since the Greeks can be found in Alasdair MacIntyre, *A Short History of Ethics* (Macmillan, 1966), which contains an especially good survey of Aristotle. However, probably the best single treatment of the history of Western ethics is still the 19th-century work by Henry Sidgwick, *Outlines of the History of Ethics* (Beacon Press); the work passed through half a dozen editions, until the sixth (1931) was enlarged after Sidgwick's death to include a section on the early 20th-century. As a companion piece to Sidgwick, the clearest and most comprehensive account of modern Anglo-American moral philosophy, from Moore through the revival of naturalism, is probably W. D. Hudson's *Modern Moral Philosophy* (Doubleday, 1970). For an excellent general topical introduction, see Louis P. Pojman, *Ethics: Discovering Right and Wrong* (Wadsworth, 1990).

• For a history of ethics from a Thomistic perspective, see Vernon Bourke (Doubleday, 1968), and for the standard topical treatment of Christian ethics, see Paul Ramsey, *Basic Christian Ethics* (University of Chicago, 1977). For a specific defense of the Divine Command Theory, see Carl F. H. Henry, *Christian Personal Ethics* (Eerdmans, 1957), Robert M. Adams, "A Modified Divine Command Theory of Ethics" in

Gene Outka, *Religion and Morality: A Collection of Critical Essays* (Anchor, 1973), and Philip Quinn, *Divine Commands and Moral Requirements* (Oxford, 1978).

• For a picture of how things now stand for the consequentialist-deontologist controversy, see J.J.C. Smart and Bernard Williams, *Utilitarianism For and Against* (Cambridge, 1973); there, Smart gives a defense of act- (as opposed to rule-) utilitarianism, while Williams argues the anti-utilitarian position. For a broader picture of current trends, including a defense of moral pluralism, see Charles Larmore, *Patterns of Moral Complexity* (Cambridge, 1987).

• A brief but excellent survey of the reemergence of virtue theory is given in the introduction to Robert B. Kruschwitz and Robert C. Roberts *The Virtues: Contemporary Essays on Moral Character* (Wadsworth, 1987). This volume anthologizes a number of representative articles, though it lacks the famous watershed piece by Elizabeth Anscombe ("Modern Moral Philosophy," *Philosophy* 33 [1958]). A history of the earlier demise of the idea of virtue is given in Alaisdair MacIntyre, *After Virtue* (Notre Dame, 1981), and for other references on the topic, see the very comprehensive bibliography in Kruschwitz and Roberts.

ENDNOTES

1. This concern over exoneration in the cases of *prima facie* blame is one of the major characteristics of moral discussion, and the recognition of its importance might be taken as a defining moment in the historical appearance of what we call "ethics." The ancient Greek poet Homer apparently knew nothing about it. In the *Odyssey*, as Alasdair MacIntyre points out, Odysseus returns home at long last from Troy and finds that his house has become a den of suitors intent on carrying off the woman they had very naturally assumed was his widow. But their ignorance is no haven against the husband's righteous anger. He blames them simply for having a false belief and deals with them in typically gruesome, warriorly fashion. We on the other hand are likely to assume that false beliefs, and the utterances that proceed from them, do not automatically constitute grounds for blame.

2. John Stuart Mill, *Utilitarianism*, (New York: Penguin, 1962), Ch. 11, p. 275.

3. Joseph Butler, "A Dissertation Upon the Nature of Virtue" in Stephen L. Darwall, ed., *Five Sermons* (Indianapolis, 1983), p. 74.

4. It is of historical interest that Moore himself, when he wrote the *Principia*, regarded himself as a "utilitarian." But in this, Moore differed significantly from those (like Bentham and Mill) who commonly attract the label, and I have altogether ignored this part of his theory.

5. Plato, *Protagoras*, 322c-328d.

6. There are conflicting interpretations of Hobbes, however. See Jean Hampton's discussion on Hobbes in Lawrence C. Becker, ed., *Encyclopedia of Ethics* (Garland, 1992).

7. The extreme view uttered by Callicles is not reflected in any other Sophistic texts, and Callicles himself is cited only in Plato's writing, so he may have been a purely Platonic invention rather than an historical person. But if so, Plato's intention seems to be to show where some of the Sophists' teachings (notably Gorgias') are likely to lead.

8. The best known of the Stoics were Cicero (106-43 B.C.), Epictetus (55-135), and the Roman Emperor Marcus Aurelius (121-180).

9. It is sometimes said that Buddhism is more a philosophy of life than a religion. This is because, especially in its earlier form (kept alive today throughout Southeast Asia in the Theravadin tradition), Buddhism does not appeal to a Deity. But its ethical precepts are revealed in scripture, just as in Islam or Christianity, and in this sense the fundamental idea behind "Divine Command" is capture by the notion of Scriptural Revelation.

10. See Note 1.

11. John Stuart Mill, *Utilitarianism*, (New York: Penguin, 1962), Ch. 11, p. 275.

12. Joseph Butler, "A Dissertation Upon the Nature of Virtue" in Stephen L. Darwall, ed., *Five Sermons* (Indianapolis, 1983), p. 74.

13. It is of historical interest that Moore himself, when he wrote the *Principia*, regarded himself as a "utilitarian." But in this Moore differed significantly from those (like Bentham and Mill) who commonly attract the label, and I have altogether ignored this part of his theory.

THE STORY OF MAN

© 1992 Creators Syndicate, Inc.

8-17

Chapter 4

Paul de Vries

DIMENSIONS OF MORAL DEVELOPMENT

"If a man will begin with certainties, he shall end in doubts; but if he will be content to begin with doubts, he shall end in certainties."

— **Francis Bacon**

"Equality – I spoke the word, as if a wedding vow. Ah, but I was so much older then; I'm younger than that now."

— **Bob Dylan**

"Science without religion is lame; religion without science is blind."

— **Albert Einstein**

Thinking is a great exercise! It is an asset we humans have that gives us an edge in coping with nature and in working with each other. To make a decision – and even to decide not to decide – requires thought. When we do not like the situation we are in, and when we dream of a better day, we are thinking. Ethics, as critical thinking about human problems, always involves thought.

Nevertheless, we often do one more thing as well. We think about thinking; we reflect on our own thinking processes. Perhaps nothing is more natural, although we do not do it as young children. Gradually, however, as we grow up and become young adults, we develop the ability to think about our thinking. And right now we are thinking about thinking about thinking. You see, it is not so hard, even if it sounds complicated.

Years ago some scholars were concerned to establish a way to talk about language. They wanted to analyze the ways in which we use words to describe facts, express emotions and feelings, make commitments, convince other people to do things, and such like. And they wanted to express and

Paul De Vries, M.A. and Ph.D. University of Virginia, holds the Endowed Chair in Ethics and the Marketplace at King's College, New York, and is president of the International Research Institute on Values Changes, based in New York, Beijing and Moscow.

analyze all these functions in ways that were not complicated by the ambiguities, prejudices, and connotations of the various "natural languages"– such as English, Spanish, Swahili. They sought to create a "meta-language" above ordinary language through which we could then analyze and critique ordinary language.

What they produced was, of course, another language – or perhaps a dialect of a "natural" language, especially English. They usually used English to introduce the other language and to define some of its terms. Of course, English could be critiqued in the new meta-language, but they found they could also critique the new meta-language in ordinary English. That is, English, or another "natural" language, could be a "meta-language" to the meta-language. This discovery reduced some of the attractiveness of an artificial meta-language. Why not just use English to analyze and critique English? English could be its own meta-language! In the process we create new words within English to make it more powerful and useful as a language and as its own meta-language, but that is to be expected. After all, English and all other living languages are self-adjusting, developing languages.

The pattern is the same in ethics and critical thought. We as individuals, and in groups, adjust our ways of talking and thinking in order to solve our problems with greater sensitivity, fairness, care, and accountability. Let's look at four people's statements and evaluate them for those factors.

JOSE AND THE GUYS

Jose : "Look, guys. This is kind of complicated, but I think we have a little problem. The six of us get together all the time because we like each other – or at least we like to "tolerate" each other. Fine. But we also are the only friendly guys our age on the block. So, in a way, we're stuck with each other. But it isn't so bad.

"It used to be a lot rougher. You can't play our kind of basketball without a referee and not have some real disagreements, some big differences. An instant replay camera might've helped sometimes, but we figured ways of working things out without killing each other – often just doing the play over. I know I'm talking too much, but this is my point. Tom here doesn't mind playing basketball, but he's not our strongest player. Now don't laugh. He didn't ask to be 5'3" either. And I think he's serious about our coming to his house to play 'Monopoly' – whatever that is.

"We always go with the majority – five to one – and play basketball here at the park. That's fair; that's democracy; that's what they taught us in school since the beginning of time. But maybe once in a while we should do what Tom wants – not even one sixth of the time, really, but once in a while. That's fair, too, isn't it? He should get something for putting up with us and our comments about his size. I know this sounds crazy coming from me, but let's find out what his 'Monopoly' is, and maybe next time it rains we won't have to watch TV – or hear our mothers yell at us to read a book."

Jose knows that the group of guys had worked through problems of fairness in their games together – even using democracy with some good results. Now he thinks that is not yet fair enough for one member of the group. Could there be other issues of fairness he has not yet thought about in the way this neighborhood bunch works and plays together?

SHEILA AND JERMAINE

Sheila: "Hey! I wasn't born yesterday! I know what's going on in most men's heads when they see a slender woman like me in a skirt like this. Believe me. I can see it in their eyes – I can feel it sometimes even without looking. And I've read all the stories about date rape. Yeah, yeah, yeah. Terrible stuff.

"Most guys are stronger than women, and those hormones can have strange and regrettable effects. Okay. But Jermaine is different; he's a gentleman, a real guy. He treats me nice and says the sweetest things. I feel important – and safe – when he's around. Besides, if he tries anything, I'm prepared. That self-defense class at the college taught me a few things. A woman doesn't have to be stronger – just smarter and quicker!

"If Jermaine steps out of line, he'll regret it faster than he'll know what hit him. And if any one else looks at my legs too much, Jermaine can handle it. Besides, a little jealousy is good. So don't worry. We'll have a great time at the dance tonight."

Sheila has become sensitive to some of the temptations and dangers she and others face. Is she aware enough?

VICTOR AND HIS FATHER

Victor : "You know, I miss my father a lot – so very much! Not that we always got along; not that I always wanted to see him. I know he wanted to see me finish college. But he has been dead for a while, and my life goes on. You know, he was so smart.

"When I was a kid he would always come into the room just when I was about to do something wrong. It was like he could see through walls. And he knew what was going on inside my head. Perhaps he had been through the same temptations. And when I messed up, I got punished – how well I remember!

"But here is the funny thing: I cannot get him out of my mind. Don't misunderstand me, I have dealt with the grief process – my personal loss was resolved months ago. But I think about him every day. I know he is not really checking on me, and I do not fear him any more. I'm not worried that he will punish me if I mess up.

"Still, when I have a decision to make, I often ask myself what he would do. I don't always do what he would do, and I don't think I have to, but I ask myself, anyway. In a sense, I want to honor his memory. Does this sound crazy? I am still devoted to him – perhaps now more than ever when he was alive.

"I am my own self, but I do respect his memory; I want to honor his name. And perhaps, in some sense, he knows."

Victor grew up with his father demanding accountability to certain standards and expectations. Of course, Victor had gotten away with some "misdemeanors" when his father was not looking. Now Victor is a young adult and his father is gone. Should he still feel accountable even if his father is not there?

CHRISSA AND THE WORLD

Chrissa: "Don't ask. My head is still spinning. You know how guilty I felt for being such a selfish American teenager. Not that I'm rich or privileged or anything, but so many others in the world have far less than I have. You know – all those pictures of starving children and mothers. So I raised the money and gave my whole vacation to the great cause – Save the World Foundation. 'Go to a Third World country and make a difference.'

"Ah, yes. Their slogans are great, but the organization stinks. It is so hard to explain. I knew that living conditions would be rough, with no running water or electricity. And with my long hair, what a pain! And I grumbled, of course, but the living conditions were okay. Really. And I didn't mind cleaning people's dirty, stinking bodies at the clinic. I had nightmares about that before I left, but I was prepared to give a lot. I had decided to reach beyond myself.

"But here's my point: Why the indignity? Why did the site director keep yelling at me? Why did he look at me as if I was dirt? Why did he keep haranguing about 'selfish Americans like you'? He never gave one compliment, not one word of encouragement the whole time. No warmth. And he treated the patients at the clinic even worse. He never looked into their eyes. He never really listened.

"Hundreds of times the words formed in my head: 'Hey, Mr. Big Guy, these people are important, and I'm important, too. It's not just the work we do that counts. It's dignity; it's human relationships.' But I never said those words. He knew I was angry and hurt – that's why he kept calling me selfish. No wonder that country's so depressed, with people like him 'helping.'"

Chrissa understands that she can be selfish and that she can provide help and care for others – including those who cannot help her or pay her back in some material way. But she still wants others to care about her, even if she does not want them to take care of her or coddle her. Is it okay for her to be angry if others do not treat her as an important person? Should she worry whether she is being selfish again?

In each of these examples, the personal patterns of awareness, justice, care, and accountability are changing and developing. Jose, Sheila, Victor and Chrissa, are alive, learning, and growing – and engaged in a process that may continue the rest of their lives. And their personal development is not limited to just one dimension.

For example, we heard about Sheila's changing awareness of problems, but her own understandings of justice, care, and accountability are probably developing at the same time. Those changes could be either quite rapid or so slow that they are barely noticeable to her.

Similarly, Victor understands a new level of accountability, but his ability to recognize problems and his comprehension of justice and care may or may not be shifting.

The changes Sheila, Jose, Chrissa, and Victor are "enduring" – and even choosing – are sometimes puzzling, surprising, exciting, fulfilling, or even painful and disorienting. Nevertheless, changes like these are normal for young people and adults. Wherever we came from, and however mature we are physically, it still takes years of experience, reflection, pain, and accomplishment before we begin to fulfill our moral potential.

MORAL DEVELOPMENT'S GROWING PAINS

As we develop in our awareness of problems or our comprehension and application of justice, care and accountability, we can think about our own thinking and behavior. We can recognize and sometimes choose those changes that happen to us. Certainly, these changes are consequential to us as well as to the people with whom we live and work. Is there anything more important to people around you than the development of your moral character and the patterns of your responses to problems around you?

We have a definite stake in our own development and in the growth of others around us. We can expect changes and recognize them when they come. When we understand these changes, we are less surprised or resistant, and we can even experience the pleasure of watching our own character grow and become more mature. While there may be few things we can do to actually hasten our own character development, we can at least avoid stunting it. By expecting certain positive changes toward maturity, we can nourish these developments when they begin.

However, there is a double role for pain in this maturing process. The changes, when they occur, take us out of established patterns of thought and behavior in which we have become comfortable. Personal stagnation may be boring, but it can be cozy.

Character building is rewarding, but it may require costly adjustments. Do you remember when you tried to get into last-year's snow boots or swim suit, after you had grown a size? If you have grown in a way that your family and friends have not, your relationships will "fit" a little differently.

Pain frequently plays another role as well. It is the most frequent and powerful stimulus for personal moral growth in any of the four dimensions of ethics. Of course, personal disappointment and failure can come our way with no positive effect; we can be numb to any benefit.

But when disappointment leads us to reflect on our lives and to consider changes in our own attitudes – or when tragedy leads us to take a new perspective on others' suffering – our own behavior may well become more sensitive, fair, caring, or accountable. Pain and difficulty make us wonder:

- Would we be genuinely aware of what is happening around us if there were no problems to solve?
- Could justice be an issue if there were unlimited resources available to all?
- Would we learn to be caring in a world without pain?
- Could accountability make sense in a world without temptations to evil?
- Are any of these reasons why we have pain?

Of course, success and accomplishment can help us grow as well. Pain is not the only stimulus for personal development. Moreover, simply by our being around other people and repeatedly solving little problems, our comprehension of these aspects of ethics can increase, even with very little pain. Our personal growth depends more on an openness to learn and on an eagerness to get our lives right than it does on the surrounding circumstances.

In any case, whether we are self-conscious of it or not, moral development occurs, and people can recognize themselves at different stages of that development. Humans, by definition, are neither born mature nor do they automatically grow into maturity. By our decisions and our reactions to experiences and problems, we take a hand in developing our own moral character. We influence the character development of others, and we often affect the moral character of our families, schools, businesses, communities, churches and synagogues, governments, and the world.

Look at it this way. You probably find that people around you often come up with answers to the problems of life that are quite different from your own answers. You may have found something your boyfriend or girlfriend did to be shocking or puzzling. In the past you may have considered these only varieties of opinion or part of the differences between men and women, older and younger, of different ethnic backgrounds.

But these divergent responses to life situations could also be caused by disparities in people's moral development stages as well. With this awareness in our backgrounds, we should be more tolerant of children as well as of less-mature adults. We will also have an initial vision and understanding of what the more-mature adults around us are thinking and feeling.

MORAL DEVELOPMENTS OF THE AGES

Personal moral development has been a preeminent concern to some of the greatest intellects throughout the centuries – from Plato (427 – 347 B.C.) to Carol Gilligan in our own time. Psychologists and philosophers especially have given considerable thought to the way we think about our own thought and behavior. These scholars have developed numerous divergent theories about moral development – theories that often compete and conflict with one another. Unfortunately, intellectuals generally select one particular dimension of moral development – such as justice or accountability – and build a theory that gives attention almost exclusively to that dimension. They may be selecting the dimension that they consider to be the most important for problem-solving, and they may not have seriously considered or thought about the other dimensions. In fact, their own ideas may have seemed so powerful that their full attention was given to development and application of one basic theme. As ordinary mortals, however, we can read and integrate even these diverse theories within our own lives.

When these intellectuals describe the kind of people they consider mature, it is usually a given fact that children are a far cry from the ideal of maturity. Intellectuals then try to create theories about how people can be nurtured step by step into this preferred ideal. Obviously, when these ideal patterns differ from one another, the maturing processes and stages vary as well.

The goal makes all the difference. As a result, exemplary behavior on one scale may be considered immature on another. For example, if the ideal person is one who makes detached, impartial decisions of justice, then the "baggage" of emotional involvement and personal commitment will be treated as symptoms of an immature level. However, if caring for yourself and others is the ideal pattern for human life, then detached, impartial decisions are understood as immature, if not positively pathological. It will be our task to see through these incompatible intellectual theories, and to discover even deeper congruences that each of them does not have.

SEQUENTIAL AND CUMULATIVE

Now, just before we look at different theoretical developmental scales, there are two very important general observations for you to consider. First, where development comes in a sequence of stages, it is possible for a person to make progress as well as to retreat. There is no "locked in" security in the success of a higher level. A person can achieve very mature thought and behavior, and yet prefer the "benefits" of less mature patterns, simpler choices, more selfish results, and such like. People can withdraw to less mature levels – immediately or later –

EARLY SIGNS OF MORAL DECLINE

DELIVERIES

PLEASE DO NOT TAKE THESE BOXES ↓

because they feel more comfortable there, because they can achieve their personal goals better there, it takes less thought and information there, or for some other reason. In fact, for most of these theories, the higher levels involve mental and emotional concentration and difficult balances to maintain. Consistent upper-level behavior is almost impossible.

Second, in spite of what some of the theorists argue, the stages of moral development appear to be generally cumulative.[1] Ability to function on a higher level does not surgically remove one's ability to also function on lower levels – because we choose to or because we feel tired, threatened, angry, or whatever. We have achieved a higher level when we have acquired the ability to perform on that level, while the total collection of our present motives and our methods of thought and action may be quite a "mixed bag." Even the best saints and heroes can be quite self-centered and selfish at times.

In fact, people often are moved by a mixture of motives for the very same decision and action. For example, Chrissa (in a scenario opening this chapter) may have volunteered her vacation time to work in a Third World country because she truly cares about the health and happiness of fellow human beings. Fine. She may also have seen this as an opportunity to get some sun and surf, to get away from an unwanted "boyfriend" for a while, or to be able to say she had "seen the world." Does this take away from her genuine care for the people she wanted to serve?

Jose thinks that he and his buddies should be more fair to Tom and do what Tom wants for a change – play a game of Monopoly. Perhaps, however, Jose is interested in learning Monopoly for other reasons, too. What if his father has urged him to start getting into games that stretch his mind? What if an attractive and bright young woman he has been trying to get close to has a reputation for playing and enjoying Monopoly? Would these other motives diminish Jose's concern for fairness to Tom?

MIXED MOTIVES

This term is used in our language to describe insincere behavior. Do Chrissa and Jose have mixed motives? They probably do. Does the mixture of their motives take away from their genuine commitment to care or fairness? Do we have to assume that there is only one real reason for their behavior? That would be unfair to almost any human choice. If our care for others and our concerns for fairness to them is mixed with some self-centered motives, should we assume that the care and justice motives are only pretenses? Are the "real" motives always selfish? Not really. Of course, there is the old joke: *For everything we do there are two motives: a good motive ... and the real motive.*

But is that joke true to life? It certainly is cynical. In fact, the good motives are often the real motives. Moreover, clusters of diverse good motives often work together – including motives of concern for oneself and others.

Here is a classic problem: Religiously aware people generally believe that they should be fair, caring, and accountable in their behavior, because this is how God asks them to believe and behave. The same ones are convinced that God rewards people whose consciousness and conduct demonstrate devotion to fairness, care, and accountability – with happiness and other benefits in this life and in life after death. Now, if they are "good," is it because they are just seeking these great rewards, or because they want to honor and obey God? What is the real reason? Can it not be both? In fact, what kind of world would it be if good behavior were not rewarded?

In a similar way, politicians can even have good motives. They propose and vote for good programs because they want to get re-elected. Nevertheless, their commitment to the good programs may be genuine, and their desire to be re-elected may be quite good and appropriate as well. Of course, there are also some hypocritical believers and manipulative politicians who have mixtures of dangerous and deceitful motives. But we should not attribute those to everyone.

For the same reason that interests, memories, and habits from our childhood and youth stay with us throughout our lives, some of our motivations and behavior patterns are cumulative as well. It would be frightening to meet people who had totally "outgrown" childhood. Are they human? Are they for real? When no one else is watching could they be a little selfish or a little playful? Who needs plastic saints?

The point is that the higher stages of personal development enable you to recognize more accurately what is going on, to engage broader information, to act with more conscious and consistent care, and to explain your behavior with greater reliability. The menu gets longer, but adults can still pick from the "children's selections" once in a while – for better or for worse.

DEVELOPING ROOM

Just think about how different the world appears to you now than it did when you were a child! Then words were indistinct sounds or markings on paper – without clear meaning. Now you converse with others with little effort, and you read whole phrases at a glance, immediately recognizing the meaning. Then, as a child, computers seemed to be weird boxes with TV screens. Now you recognize computers in a variety of uses at home, work, and school. Then, years ago, you may have even thought of matches, the kitchen stove, and household cleaning chemicals as toys for your amusement – or at least you were quite curious about them. Now you see them in terms of their risks, dangers, and positive uses.

Moreover, as a child you probably thought the world revolved around you. Objects were there for you to use; people were there to meet your needs. Now, hopefully, you have matured beyond that egocentric view of the world. There are other "selves" in addition to yourself, and these others have legitimate claims upon you for fair treatment, caring action, and accountability, while they are also responsible for you. The world indeed seems very different than it did to you as a child.

Of course, there are some people who really never do grow up. Some remain illiterate, computer naive, firebugs, or egocentric. When an adult is stuck in a child-like state we consider it abnormal, pathological, or criminal. An adult firebug is a pyromaniac or an arsonist. An adult who has no sense of moral responsibility to others – no conscience – is a sociopath, suffering from an anti-social, personality disorder. Even if a few sociopaths have managed to become kings, queens, senators, dictators, corporate bosses, police officers, or some of your neighbors, we can still recognize that the lack of a moral conscience is a tragic defect in personality.

STAGES OF AWARENESS

The first and often the most difficult developmental dimension is the ability to recognize the moral human problems around us. This is a challenge for child-raising, but it is also an enduring hurdle for adults in their own continuing development. For example, children usually need to be taught to share their own toys and to respect other people's property, including their toys. Being able to recognize and restrain their own possessiveness takes time and training for children to develop.

Adults may have difficulty recognizing the obvious as well. For example, some major corporations have had difficulty convincing their male managers to stop sexually harassing female employees. One corporation made tremendous progress when it created a video vignette and required all managers to watch it. In the vignette a female manager pressures one of her male employees for a "date," and the relationship is clearly as manipulative, degrading, and unprofessional as it is in the more common situation – where a male manager propositions a female employee. By turning the tables, the video aids male managers' imaginations, helps them to recognize how manipulative and degrading sexual harassment is. As a result, they are far more likely to recognize and avoid any sexual harassment of their employees in the future.

Acquiring the ability to recognize a kind of problem or a range of problems can sometimes have the form of a religious conversion. Suddenly you see clearly what is totally obvious to you now – and yet other people may remain insensitive or blind to it. For example, in the early history of the Massachusetts Colony, Roger Williams became convinced that American Indians were just as human as he or other white people. It was wrong to treat them differently, or to take their land without fair compensation. When he defended his perspective, he was forced by the authorities to leave Massachusetts, and so he founded Rhode Island with a deeper commitment to human rights. In a similar way, when Abraham Lincoln actually watched a slave auction, he became far more deeply convinced of the gross unfairness and the human degradation of slavery. Perhaps you have experienced a similar moral conversion on some other issue.

Whether in dramatic or in subtle ways, we can grow in our ability to recognize problems. The range of problems we are able to recognize, and the accuracy with which we identify them, varies from person to person on a broad continuum. Even our greatest saints and heroes who were intensely accurate in their perceptions of some major problems have sometimes been nearly blind on other weighty matters. For example, Thomas Jefferson recognized with great acuity the injustices of England's government in its dealings with the American Colonists. In our Declaration of Independence he was able to proclaim with brilliance and courage that

"We hold these truths to be self-evident, that all men are created equal, that they are endowed by their Creator with certain inalienable Rights, that among these are Life, Liberty and the pursuit of Happiness ... "

Nevertheless, for a variety of possible reasons, Jefferson continued to hold slaves. Were these persons not human? Were they not equal? Was not their right to liberty inalienable? Even if we allow that Jefferson was probably a nicer-than-average slaveholder, or that he was protecting his slaves from even worse conditions elsewhere, the apparent inconsistency is definitely hard to explain. Nevertheless, we all know that no one is perfectly perceptive about everything. What kinds of moral blindness do you see in people around you? Are there areas of moral blindness you have uncovered in your own life? Can you explain them to others?

What is crucial is that our minds and imaginations have been stretched to include some concept for the problem before us, or we may not ever notice the problem. And how are our minds and imaginations stretched? There are at least five instruments for doing this, as we will see shortly. Each instrument can help open up our moral and intellectual pores. Without some such instruments our minds tend to trust completely the established patterns, continuing to overlook just the kinds of problems we have already recognized.

We almost always *assimilate* new experiences into established categories of our thought and perception. This is the initial stage in any growth in awareness. Change in our perception occurs only as we are puzzled, stretched, or *awakened* by a new experience. We may stay in this middle stage briefly until we find or create improved categories. If we cannot find or create a sufficient change, we may simply return to the first stage of assimilation. This middle stage of awakening, however, may lead us successfully to *accommodate* our perception and thought by adding or creating some new categories of active awareness. [2]

For example, Sheila in a monologue at the beginning of this chapter is aware of at least some of the problems of lust. Earlier in her life she did not recognize these dangers and just loved the attention she received. But something awakened her to the problems of lust – the pointed advice of a friend, a story in literature or in the newspaper, a hurtful experience – and now she recognizes clearly what she had been blind to before. She was able to accommodate her thought and perception to these newly discovered dimensions of reality. Will she be awakened to additional hazards of lust or to other problems in life? Most certainly she will, or else she will be very easily hurt. And can she accommodate her perception and thought to recognize those additional problems? Yes, as long as she is alive.

Jose, in the first monologue, is also becoming more aware of problems around him. Perhaps for months, or even years, he thought that problems of group cooperation could all be resolved in a simple democratic procedure. He knew that Tom was unhappy that his own requests for the group to play Monopoly were never fulfilled. Nevertheless, Jose was partly or completely blind to this as a problem to be solved. What awakened Jose? Perhaps he was in a discussion or read an article about ways to protect minority rights and interests, perhaps other people helped him notice how unhappy Tom was, or perhaps Jose is an ignored minority in another group and he was awakened to this particular pattern of a problem there. Now, having accommodated his thought to recognize this type of problem, he will be more likely to see examples of it elsewhere. Will Jose recognize additional dilemmas in democracy and further problems in other areas of life? Probably so – as long as his brain functions.

Instruments Of Awareness Development

What instruments help awaken us to additional problems around us? There are numerous tools that lead us to accommodate out thought and perception, but here is a brief list of five:

The first instrument is our own personal stake. We are far more alert to injustices and the lack of care or accountability when we are the real or potential victims. For example, products that manufacturers consider "good enough" are less likely to be deemed good enough by alert customers or consumer advocates. Similarly, women are more sensitive to patterns of sexual harassment and alert to recognize it because they are more likely than men to be its victims. In the previous example, Jose may be more sensitive to minority interests if he himself is in an ignored minority.

The second instrument we bring to bear is a substantial knowledge of various literatures and stories. Good literature draws us into other people's perspectives and experiences – thereby stretching our own repertoires of concepts. For example, we do not have to live in a crime-ridden neighborhood – or be the victim of unsafe products, or have AIDS – to recognize the many problems associated with these situations. There are plenty of news reports and sensitive stories that help us perceive the issues more clearly.

Fiction can be tremendously valuable in this effort. Nathan's story about the sheep owner used in Chapter 2 of this book is a fine example. Science fiction novels and movies – including even *Star Trek* episodes – can also help sensitize us to partly hidden problems before us here and now, not just in the distant future. An even more potent source is history, where we can investigate the actual results of people's decisions – not just the imagined consequences created by story-writers. Of course, reading itself is not essential; stories and episodes of history do not have to be read or even seen on videos. Illiterate peoples usually have huge repertoires of stories that help stretch their moral imaginations.

The third instrument is the awareness of potential solutions. Most of us tend to minimize problems that we think are unsolvable. But when there is a way to make a positive difference we are less pained giving full attention to the problems. A farmer is less apt to complain about plowing around rocks in the field if he thinks the rocks are very deep. When it is discovered that these big rocks are only two inches thick, the farmer is more apt to see them as a problem to be solved. Huge pot holes irritate us more than large rainstorms, and we are more likely to focus on others' bad habits than their permanent handicaps. The sweltering heat in some factories was not seen as much of a problem until air conditioning was available. In general, the problems that can be solved draw our attention more. Studies have shown that mere abstract or theoretical knowledge of how to handle problems does not increase awareness – but concrete hope for specific problems does.

The fourth instrument is perceived frequency. On the one hand, when spouse abuse, child abuse, and date rape were seen as rare, they received little attention. Few people discussed them, and victims were left largely on their own in dealing with these problems. Most people were not alert to watch for them. However, when we understand their frequency and danger, we are more alert to recognize symptoms of their presence. On the other hand, when some problems become overwhelmingly frequent, people can become numb to them as well; their hope that there will be a solution is diminished.

The fifth instrument is personal sensitivity and eagerness to learn from experience. We are created with a feedback system that allows us to learn from our own experience. Did I learn anything from those successes? Did I grow from those failures? As we said earlier, we can think about our thinking. We can see our blindness to problems as itself a problem, and then take steps to become more sensitive.

These five instruments can aid our awareness of human problems – our personal stake, stories, potential solutions, frequency, and personal openness to learn from experience. Are there any other instruments to make us morally aware that you can think of?

STAGES OF JUSTICE

Several scholars have given significant attention to the development of our ability to reason ethically. They have studied ways that children, youth, and adults engage information and recommend or resolve decisions. They have noticed that the very structures of thought change as we mature. Also, they have observed that when presented with a complicated story with a moral dilemma, people at different stages of development select out of the available information distinct sets of facts as relevant data for a good solution to the dilemma. These studies have concentrated especially on the second step of problem-solving outlined in Chapter 2 of this book – engaging information and reasoning. Not surprisingly, therefore, they have focused primarily on issues of justice and fairness in both patterns of thought and in sifting through information. After all, justice is the key value for the second stage of problem-solving.

Jean Piaget was the first to provide such a study.[3] He noticed that children faced with the same problems approach them differently as they mature. Their very perceptions of reality change, and this evolution moves in stages from less complex to more complex perceptions. In each successive stage, the child accommodates greater and greater complexity of reality in his or her experiences. For example, gradually as children approach adulthood they shift from responding primarily to rules or duties that are imposed by others – or assumed to be fixed – to understanding moral guidance based on cooperative arrangements and win-win agreements that are freely selected. The more mature children engage in "autonomous" thinking, deciding, and problem-solving.

KOHLBERG'S THEORY

Lawrence Kohlberg became so impressed with Piaget's ground-breaking work that he devoted a lifetime of writing and research to this subject. In the process, he developed a theory much more detailed and complex than Piaget's view. In fact, he discovered *six stages in our development of moral judgment,* as well as fairly thorough means of recognizing whether a person is in one stage or another.

Kohlberg's vision is useful and profound; it has captured the imagination of many writers, and spawned a wealth of literature. In short, he sees our development in making fair moral decisions progressing through three levels: Pre-conventional (egocentric), conventional (social), and post-conventional (principled). Also, each of the three levels of development for Kohlberg is divided into two stages, so that there are six stages in all. Each stage represents a different approach to justice and fairness.

Primarily, Kohlberg theorized that persons move sequentially through the stages with no guarantee they will reach the higher stages. As one progresses, there may be some overlap among stages (and one may regress temporarily). Second, Kohlberg stated that our moral thinking at each stage is dominated by these structures of that stage. To him, each stage is a complete, holistic unit. Let's look more closely at the stages.

At the first level, *pre-conventional (egocentric) people* make their decisions on personal bases – either in terms of obedience to a power figure or in terms of personal agreements with other individuals. On this level, the social structure is not really utilized. Straight obedience to some authority to avoid punishment or negative physical consequences is the main feature of *Stage 1*; pursuing self-interest and the satisfaction of others only for personal gain governs *Stage 2*.

At the second level, *conventional (social) people* make decisions on the basis of social patterns and rules – whether these patterns are informal or are explicitly stated. On this level, people use and fit the social and moral structure. This social structure is defined in terms of stable friendships and harmony in personal roles in *Stage 3*; more explicit legal and moral conventions for the good of society dominate *Stage 4*.

At the third level, *post-conventional (principled) people* seek to follow timeless principles – whether or not these principles will be articulated within the conventional structures. On this level, people see some of the limitations of the social structures, and they try to fix them or rise above them. In *Stage 5*, for example, various procedures are developed for the goal of protecting everyone's basic rights and improving the social conventions. In *Stage 6,* decisions are made on the basis of impartial, ideal, eternal principles that perfectly protect everyone's claim to fairness – regardless of the influence of social and moral conventions.

In short, people can have three attitudes to conventional social and ethical structures around them: They can act apart from them, in conformity to them, or in a role of mastery over them. Another way to make these developments clear is to compare the primary guidelines on each level and stage.

Level One: Pre-Conventional (Egocentric)
Stage 1: Do what you are told in order to avoid punishment or other negative physical consequences.
Stage 2: Seek your interests and the interests of others if meeting theirs will benefit you.

Level Two: Conventional (Social)

Stage 3: Develop lasting friendships that seek to understand and satisfy each person's interests.

Stage 4: Live up to the explicit agreements, laws, duties, and expectations that help define the groups in which you participate and allow them to function in harmonious order.

Level Three: Post-Conventional (Principled)

Stage 5: Develop fair ways of bringing the agreements, laws, duties, and expectations of your groups into *closer* harmony with broader basic human rights.

Stage 6: Follow and seek to advance the basic principles of human fairness and justice – regardless of your personal circumstances.

Please note that while people's *motives* may change, their actual *behavior* may not as they mature through the six stages. For example, students may abstain from cheating and plagiarism for various reasons – they are afraid of being caught, they see that everyone's real interests are served this way, they respect the rules, or they are devoted to the ultimate standards of fairness. They may move from one stage to another, while their behavior stays the same. What changes between stages is not necessarily the behavior but rather the motives and rationale that people use to define their problems and interpret their decisions. Of course people do change their behavior, too, but they can stay on the same stage and do that. *For Kohlberg, it is not what people do but* why *they do it that defines their stage of moral development at a given time.*

Let us look again at the examples of Jose and Chrissa that we examined earlier in the chapter. How would their stage of development in making fair decisions affect their approaches to their particular problems? Consider what they might say.

Jose and his group of friends face their problem through the six stages from Jose's point of view:

Level One: Pre-Conventional (Egocentric)

Stage 1: Let's do what Tom says. He may not be the best ball player out here, but he's too handy with a knife to suit me. Let's just do what he says we should do or else we may have a rumble.

Stage 2: Look guys, I really want to be able to count on playing basketball regularly this spring. Tom promises not ever to say or even to think the word "Monopoly" again for two months – if we will just try the game once this afternoon. And he'll keep playing so we can have three on three (that's my favorite). I think we should try it.

Level Two: Conventional (Social)

Stage 3: Tom is our friend, and he plays hard as a member of our group when we are together. Let's at least try playing his game of "Monopoly." At least we can try this game for friendship's sake. I like Tom and I want him to think I'm a good friend.

Stage 4: Look, we agreed we'd go by majority rule out here. Four guys already have said we'd play Monopoly. So let's get on with it. Besides Tom would be happy about it and it will make things go easier all spring.

Level Three: Post-Conventional (Principled)

Stage 5: Look guys, in the past we have gone with strict democracy: Every time we vote five to one to play basketball. But we could also vote for another method of choosing. Maybe, for example, it would be more fair for each of us to pick our group activity one day a week. We could then try Tom's suggestion. Actually, others of us in our group probably have some creative ideas, too, besides basketball all the time.

Stage 6: Whatever we do, guys, respecting and appreciating each other is what is important. We don't need a rule that we will do what Tom wants once a week or once in two months. It's a matter of justice; let's try to be fair about it. If we try Tom's game of "Monopoly," then we will have a pattern for making future decisions – just like some rational guys who respect everyone.

Chrissa looks at her problem from the perspective of each of the six stages:

Level One: Pre-Conventional (Egocentric)
Stage 1: Oh well. To keep out of trouble with the site director, I'll do what he says.
Stage 2: Perhaps I should talk with the site director. Maybe if I butter up the jerk, I'll get a better report. At least, I'll have more peace and quiet around here.

Level Two: Conventional (Social)
Stage 3: You know, I should really try to see things from the site director's perspective. Maybe he'll like me and see I'm a good person. He has so much to take care of, he does not have the time or energy to really care for people. I can be more patient with him – and maybe we can even become friends.
Stage 4: I should use my job description and the public literature and purpose statement of Save the World Foundation to improve our communication. If I work within the structures and guidelines of the organization I can help the level of cooperation and service. Those guidelines are there for that purpose.

Level Three: Post-Conventional (Principled)
Stage 5: However the organization is structured, something is missing, something is not working. There is no reason why people should feel so bad about doing good! Truly, the organization stinks. I'll fulfill my obligation to Save the World Foundation and to the people I promised to help during my vacation. But I'm also looking for a way to help this organization see what it is doing – and change so it will fulfill its mission.
Stage 6: Yes, Save the World Foundation needs restructuring, and working with its representatives has been difficult. I'll try to help them wake up and change, because theirs is a worthwhile cause even if they're a little weary now. Every human being has infinite and eternal value, and together what the organization and I do will help disadvantaged people see and feel their worth.

To summarize, Kohlberg's focus is on *why* people do things. His six stages have been described in brief with various terms. For easy reference, they may be restated this way:

> # WHY PEOPLE ACT
> ## (Kohlberg's Six Stages)
>
> **Stage 1: Obedience/Punishment**
>
> **Stage 2: Instrument and Relativity**
>
> **Stage 3: Interpersonal Concordance**
>
> **Stage 4: Law and Social Order**
>
> **Stage 5: Social Contract**
>
> **Stage 6: Universal Ethical Principles**

Let us now explore in some depth the six stages that Kohlberg has written so much about. His primary explanations revolve around a dilemma that a man named Heinz faces in the following story. Kohlberg and his colleagues might ask people how Heinz should approach his problem, and their answers help reveal the stage on which they are thinking. Think about what Heinz should do in this dilemma, a human problem that is used constantly in the literature of moral development, and a story that is not difficult to imagine.

> In Europe, a woman was near death from a very bad disease, a special kind of cancer. There was one drug that the doctors thought might save her. It was a form of radium that a druggist in the same town had recently discovered. The drug was expensive to make, but the druggist was charging 10 times what the drug cost him to make. He paid $200 for the radium and charged $2,000 for a small dose of the drug. The sick woman's husband, Heinz, went to everyone he knew to borrow the money, but he could get together only about $1,000, which was half of what it cost. He told the druggist that his wife was dying, and asked him to sell it cheaper or let him pay later. But the druggist said, "No, I discovered the drug and I'm going to make money from it." Heinz got desperate and broke into the man's store to steal the drug for his wife. [4]

After reading or hearing this story, people are asked: "Should Heinz have done that? Was it wrong or right? Why?" At each stage children, youth, and adults can say that Heinz was right or wrong (Kohlberg says that). What differentiates the stages is more the answer to the "Why?" question.

PRE-CONVENTIONAL (EGOCENTRIC) PEOPLE

On the first stage people respond in terms of the superior power of authorities who provide fixed rules of behavior, or the threat of punishment. Morality, then, is a matter of obedience to explicit rules which others have passed on to us and enforced in some way. People on this stage are likely to say that Heinz is wrong because he stole something, and is likely to be punished for stealing by the law. This first stage involves an unquestioning acceptance of the power of law and authority – only because of the punishment and negative consequences it can inflict, without considering any other human interests or purposes that may be at the basis of the laws involved. On this stage the traditional *Golden Rule* might not apply, but the older Chinese tradition's version might: "Do not do unto others as you would not have them do unto you."

So, any time we slow down and drive within the speed limit only because a police officer is watching and we don't want to get fined – not at all because of the inherent safety benefits to ourselves and others – we are functioning on this stage. Moreover, any time we directly obey the leaders of a political group or party, corporate bosses, moral or religious authorities, without consciously considering the purposes of their rules or directives, we are thinking in this initial stage. Of course, our involvement in this stage can be very effective so long as the authorities providing the rules and meting the punishment are trustworthy.

Those in the second stage – still at the pre-conventional level – think in terms of the interests that each person brings to the problem, and they will try to "make a deal" to seek some level of cooperation or exchange for their own personal benefit. In a sense, each person is seen as an egocentric negotiator, not bound by others' rules or social commitments. Your own needs and interests are paramount, and the needs and interests of others are of concern only to the extent that meeting them helps you. Here the *Golden Rule* must be diminished to apply: Seek to fulfill others' interests and needs only when doing so helps to fulfill yours. The fear of negative consequences in Stage 1 is replaced here by a desire for personal reward.

In the Heinz story, then, both Heinz and the druggist have the right to do what they want to do – and take the risks and rewards that may follow. Obeying the law or not obeying the law is merely a matter of prudence. There is no deep desire to obey if detection and punishment are unlikely. As a result, Stage 2 people are concerned about obedience to authority if it somehow benefits them.

CONVENTIONAL (SOCIAL) PEOPLE

The third stage of Kohlberg's theory initiates the conventional (social) level. Here public roles, expectations, personal relationships and observations are crucial. Now shared feelings and interests are more important than the individual interests that dominated Stage 2. From this personal knowledge, you can imagine putting yourself in other people's shoes. On this third stage the *Golden Rule* is based upon concrete knowledge of other people's feelings and expectations: Do for others what you would want them to do for you, based upon your personal knowledge and relationships with them.

The driving force is one's self-image and peer-image as a "good person"; you want to be a good person in your own eyes and in the opinions of others. Essential is doing the right thing, having good motives, and maintaining concern for others, through trust, loyalty, respect, and gratitude. People in Stage 3 are additionally aware that they and their associates are actively looking out for each other within enduring friendships. While in Stage 2 they bargained for each favor, in Stage 3 they know each other – including the "inner selves" – well enough to accommodate needs and desires.

Moreover, the inner quality of being "a good person" is understood on this stage to be more important than particular acts of rule-obedience to avoid punishment that Stage 1 had portrayed. As a result, Stage 3 provides a level of stability and cooperation unachieved in Stages 1 and 2.

In Heinz's story, then, the most crucial factors in Stage 3 are Heinz's relationships – with his wife and with the druggist. His commitment to his wife is probably the deeper and more dear relationship, and it is her appraisal of him as a "good person" that will count the most. Nevertheless, Heinz still has some desire to be considered a "good person" by the druggist as well, and would relish receiving his approval, too, if possible.

Stage 3, however, fails to define morality outside the personal contacts with friends, relatives, or others in one's group. Fortunately, Stage 4 seeks to remedy that lack by institutionalizing expectations and services through a system of general laws and trained moral conscience. It is not interpersonal agreement and understanding that guides now, but the social system that defines both our roles and rules of behavior. The more personal touch of justice in Stages 1, 2 and 3 is now replaced by a matrix of fair laws, and our primary moral responsibility is to society and its institutions, rather than merely to the flesh-and-blood people we know. The *Golden Rule* is here stabilized and institutionalized: Fulfill your legal responsibilities to society while you expect that others will fulfill their legal responsibilities to society as well. As a result, Stage 4 seeks even more stability than was achieved in Stage 3, along with a broader knowledge and greater consistency of moral responsibility.

In Stage 4, therefore, justice is defined by general rules and shared expectations that are binding on everyone. This institution of law protects us from chaos and gives meaning to human life. No one is personally privileged or above the law; therefore, no one should make an exception of his or her own case. Because sets of social laws usually prohibit stealing but do not require saving lives, Heinz's theft is more likely to be criticized in Stage 4. If Heinz asked, "What if everybody did it?" he would realize that society would suffer if everyone committed theft. As a consequence, Heinz should realize that according to Stage 4, it would be wrong for him to steal regardless of punishment or reward, regardless of how others feel about him, but rather because it would be best for society.

POST-CONVENTIONAL (PRINCIPLED) PEOPLE

A higher level of stability, generality, and abstraction is reached in the fifth stage of Kohlberg's theory. Here existing legal structures are not as important as methods for selecting and improving systems of laws. The standard here is not concrete rules but rather individuals as equal contractors within the larger social system. These rational contractors select what is the most fair to all, and also what promotes the greatest good for the greatest number. The assumption of Stage 5 is that our own societies and their laws can gradually be reformed to live up to mutually agreed-upon standards. Informed citizens should then agree to abide by these rational dictates as a matter of contract they freely endorse–because that society continues to be subject to rational self-improvement.

What actually unites people is this law-making process, not the laws themselves that had provided the social glue in Stage 4. The *Golden Rule* for the fifth stage is then: With their cooperation, seek to create for others and for yourself the rational and impartial society you would want them to create.

In short, the central feature of Stage 5 is a consensus-building procedure – whether or not that procedure is some version of democracy. Above the specific self-rewarding bargains of Stage 2, beyond the more stable personal relationships of Stage 3 – and even above the consistent legal structures and consciences of Stage 4 – Stage 5 hangs on people's general commitments to create and obey rational laws for the benefit and for the rights of every person. The procedure is the defining standard. What if the right procedure is followed, but you still disagree with the particular laws and rights that were established through that rational procedure? You are then obligated to try to change the laws, obeying them while you seek reform; otherwise the laws and rights would be a farce. They would not be laws and rights at all if people were always allowed to selectively obey them.

In the story, one could conclude in stage five that Heinz may or may not obey the laws against theft, depending on whether he viewed the purpose of the law as promoting justice for society. An escape loophole exists in Stage 5. Heinz could still justify his breaking the law if he is firmly convinced that the society's laws are not rational enough – if it does not build in sufficient safeguards, for example, for protecting human lives. Your "contract" with society certainly does not include standing by and watching your spouse die unnecessarily! Should the laws or courts justify or excuse such a theft to protect a live? If Heinz honestly thinks such a justification of theft is a rational standard, he can morally excuse his theft, even if he is still punished by the society. Stage 5's standard of rationality provides, then, some protection for human rights. As a result, Stage 5 provides principles for fair social cooperation, without violating the individual rights that should be rationally defended.

At Stage 6, according to Kohlberg, the ultimate stage in the development of moral reasoning and in the refining of the concepts of justice, we find another level of protection of individuals' rights. Stage 6 people seek to define not only the due processes for deriving people's obligations and rights within a society, but general positive principles for society as well. We should ask not only what procedures would rational people follow, but what great principles of general cooperation would they use to select or reject proposed social laws and human rights.

These general principles for Stage 6 may include standards of equality for human rights and the respect for the dignity and value of every human being. The general principle one selects must be consistently applied regardless of personal taste. The *Golden Rule* for Stage 6 is: Do for others what you would have them do for you – totally apart from any prejudice, inequality, or personal feelings, and independent of established punishments, mutual agreements, personal knowledge, structures of law, and so forth. Unlike the qualified versions we saw on other stages, this is the purest and simplest form of the Golden Rule. It is what Jesus and Confucius saw as the basis of all other obligations. [5]

In the story, Heinz could appeal to universal respect for life. He could claim that the protection of human life is always more important than the protection of property. Of course, then Heinz would have to excuse another person's theft of property from him, if that would help save a life as well. With Heinz's now-established devotion to the protection of life, he would probably be willing to negotiate a gift or a loan to protect a life, rather than forcing the desperate people involved to steal from him. He must see every life as sacred, not only his or his wife's life.

His wife's fate would not merely be determined by due process, as in Stage 5, or by law, as in Stage 4, or by his personal commitment to her, as in Stage 3, or on the basis of a mutually beneficial agreement, as in Stage 2, or even on some other person's command that he should always protect his wife's life, as in Stage 1. Stage 6 recognizes the protection of life as a possible universal principle of justice whether or not it was created by due process, an established law, an implicit expectation in Heinz's marital relationship, a bargain he struck with her, or some authority's rule.

The chief advantage of the higher stages in the development of moral reasoning is the internalization of fair thought processes. Also, when the thought processes are more internalized they are more stable. On one extreme, in Stage 1, a person relies on others to provide rules and punishments to guide behavior. When authorities change their opinions, or new authorities come along, people in Stage 1 change without taking any responsibility. On the other extreme, in Stage 6, every law, human right, moral incentive, and punishment is subjected to the scrutiny of a universal criterion for rationality, impartiality, and equality. The word of no authority goes without challenge. Even the Golden Rule itself, which some might regard as a classic definition of justice, and which has its clearest formulation in Stage 6, must be scrutinized by itself: Apply the *Golden Rule* to others and yourself as you would have others apply it.

Apart from the internalization and stability that developed moral reasoning supplies, our talk of moral virtue will be superficial or hypocritical. In contrast, some of our greatest moral heroes, such as Socrates and Martin Luther King Jr., addressed the problems of their time in Stages 5 and 6. And Kohlberg himself, in later years, confessed he had stopped trying to differentiate between Stages 5 and 6. Here is a selection from Lawrence Kohlberg's *Education for Justice: A Modern Statement of the Socratic View.*

KOHLBERG ON KOHLBERG

The fact that there are no traits of character corresponding to the virtues and vices of conventional language should comfort us. Those who try to achieve the bag of virtues prescribed by the culture find themselves in the plight described by the theme song of the show, *You're a Good Man, Charlie Brown.*

You're a good man, Charlie Brown. You have humility, nobility and a sense of honor that is very rare indeed. You are kind to all the animals and every little bird. With a heart of gold, you believe what you're told, every single solitary word. You bravely face adversity; you're cheerful through the day; you're thoughtful, brave and courteous. You're a good man, Charlie Brown. You're a prince; could be a king.

With a heart such as yours you could open any door if only you weren't so wishy-washy.

If we, like Charlie Brown, define our moral aims in terms of virtues and vices, we are defining them in terms of the praise and blame of others and are caught in the pull of being all things to all people and end up being wishy-washy. The attraction of the bag of virtues approach to moral education is that it encourages the assumption that everyone can be a moral educator. It assumes that any adult of middle-class respectability or virtue knows what virtue is and is qualified to teach it by dint of being adult and respectable. We must all make these assumptions as parents, but perhaps they are not sound. Socrates asked "whether good men have known how to hand on to someone else the goodness that was in themselves" and went on to cite one virtuous Greek leader after another who had nonvirtuous sons."

The delicate balance between social reform and moral education is clarified by the example of Martin Luther King. King was a moral leader, a moral educator of adults, not because he was a spokesperson for the welfare of blacks, not because he was against violence, not because he was a minister of religion, but because, as he himself said, he was a drum major for justice. His words and deeds were primarily designed to induce America to respond to racial problems in terms of a sense of justice, and any particular action he took had value for this reason, not just because of the concrete political end it might achieve.

I have used King as an example of a moral educator to indicate that the difference between the political reformer and the moral educator is not a difference in the content of their concern. Civil rights is as much a matter of morality as is honesty in financial matters. The distinctive feature of moral education as against ordinary political action is in the relation of means and ends. Black power politicians using unjust means in the name of civil rights are clearly not in the enterprise of teaching justice, any more than are policemen in the enterprise of teaching honesty when they shoot down rioters. King's acts of civil disobedience, however, flowed directly from a sense of principles of justice and thus were moral leadership, not just propaganda or protest.

Let me recapitulate my argument so far. I have criticized the "bag of virtues" concept of moral education on the grounds, first, that there are no such things and, second, if there were, they couldn't be taught or at least I don't know how or who could teach them. Like Socrates, I have claimed that ordinary people certainly don't know how to do it, and yet there are no expert teachers of virtue as there are for the other arts. Rather than turning to nihilism, I have pointed to an example of an effective moral educator at the adult social level, Martin Luther King. Since I cannot define moral virtue at the individual level, I tried it at the social and found it to be justice, and claimed that the central moral value of the school, like that of the society, was justice. Justice, in turn, is a matter of equal and universal human rights. I pointed

to the cloud of virtue labels attributed to King and pointed out that only one meant anything. Justice was not just one more fine-sounding word in a eulogy; it was the essence of King's moral leadership.

My hope is to have stirred some feelings about the seriousness and the reality of that big word, that Platonic form, *justice*, because people like King were willing to die for it. I suppose there may have been people willing to die for honesty, responsibility, and the rest of the bag of virtues, but if so, I have no empathy with them. I am going to argue now, like Plato, that virtue is not many, but one, and its name is *justice*. Let me point out first that justice is not a character trait in the usual sense. You cannot make up behavior tests of justice, as Hartshore and May (1928-1930) did for honesty, service, and self-control. One cannot conceive of a little set of behavior tests that would indicate that Martin Luther King and Socrates were high on a trait of justice. The reason for this is that justice is not a concrete rule of action such as lies behind virtues like honesty.

To be honest means "Don't cheat, don't steal, don't lie." But justice is not a rule or a set of rules, it is a moral principle. By a moral principle, I mean a mode of choosing that is universal, a rule of choosing that we want all people to adopt always in all situations. We know it is all right to be dishonest and steal to save a life because it is just, because one person's right to life comes before another person's right to property. We know it is sometimes right to kill, because it is sometimes just. The Germans who tried to kill Hitler were doing right because respect for the equal values of lives demands that we kill someone who is murdering others, in order to save lives. There are exceptions to rules, then, but no exception to principles. A moral obligation is an obligation to respect the right of claim of another person. A moral principle is a principle for resolving competing claims: You versus me, you versus a third person. There is only one principled basis for resolving claims: Justice or equality. Treat every person's claim impartially regardless of the person. A moral principle is not only a rule of action but a reason for action. As a reason for action, justice is called *respect for* people.

Because morally mature people are governed by the principle of justice rather than by a set of rules, there are not many moral virtues, but one. Let me restate the argument in Plato's terms. Plato's argument is that what makes a virtuous action virtuous is that it is guided by knowledge of the good. A courageous action based on ignorance of danger is not courageous; a just act based on ignorance of justice is not just; and so on. If virtuous action is action based on knowledge of the good, then virtue is one, because knowledge of the good is one. I have already claimed that knowledge of the good is one because the good is justice. Let me briefly document these lofty claims by some lowly research findings. Using hypothetical moral situations, I and my colleagues have interviewed children and adults about right and wrong in the United States, Britain, Turkey, Taiwan, and Yucatan. In all cultures, we find the same forms of moral thinking. There are six forms of moral thought, and they constitute an invariant sequence of stages in each culture. These stages are summarized in the Appendix.

Why do I say that existence of culturally universal stages means that knowledge of the good is one? First, because it implies that concepts of the good are culturally universal. Second, because people at a given level are pretty much the same in their thinking regardless of the situation they are presented with and regardless of the particular aspect of morality being tapped. There is a general factor of maturity of moral judgment much like the general factor of intelligence in cognitive tasks. If they know one aspect of the good at a certain level, they know other aspects of the good at that level. Third, because at each stage there is a single principle of the good, which only approaches a moral principle at the higher levels, for instance, there is some reason for regard for the law and some reason for regard for rights. Only at the highest stage, however, is regard for universal human rights. At this point, both regard for law and regard for human rights are grounded on a clear criterion of justice that was present in confused and obscure form at earlier stages.

Let me describe the stages in terms of the civil disobedience issue in a way that may clarify the argument I have just made. Before the Civil War, we had laws that allowed slavery. According to the law, escaped slaves had to be returned to owners like runaway horses. Some people who didn't believe in slavery disobeyed the law, hid the runaway slaves, and helped to escape. Were they doing right or wrong?

A bright, middle-class boy, Johnny, answers the question this way when he is 10: "They were doing wrong because the slave ran away himself. They're being just like slaves themselves trying to keep 'em away." Asked, "Is slavery right or wrong?" he answered, "Some wrong, but servants aren't so bad because they don't do all that heavy work."

Johnny's response is Stage 1, *punishment and obedience orientation.* Breaking the law makes it wrong; indeed, the badness of being slaves washes off on their rescuers.

Three years later, Johnny is asked the same question. His answer is mainly Stage 2 *instrumental relativism.* He says "They would help them escape because they were all against slavery. The South was for slavery because they had big plantations and the North was against it because they had big factories and they needed people to work and they'd pay. So the Northerners would think it was right but the Southerners wouldn't."

So early comes Marxist relativism. He goes on: "If a person is against slavery and maybe likes the slave or maybe dislikes the owner, it's OK for him to break the law if he likes, provided he doesn't get caught. If the slaves were in misery and one was a friend he'd do it. It would probably be right if it was someone you really loved."

At the end, his orientation to sympathy and love indicates the same Stage 3, *orientation to approval, affection and helpfulness,* better suggested by Charlie Brown.

At age 19, in college, Johnny is Stage 4, *orientation to maintaining a social order of rules and rights.* He says, "They were right, in my point of view. I hate the actual aspect of slavery, the imprisonment of one man ruling over another. They drive them too hard and they don't get anything in return. It's not right to disobey the law, no. Laws are made by the people But you might do it because you feel it's wrong. If 50,000 people break the law, can you put them all in jail. Can 50,000 people be wrong?"

Johnny here is oriented to the rightness and wrongness of slavery itself and of obedience to law. He doesn't see the wrongness of slavery in terms of equal human rights but in terms of an unfair economic relation, working hard and getting nothing in return.

The same view of rights in terms of getting what you worked for leads Johnny to say about school integration, "A lot of colored people are now just living off of civil rights. You only get education as far as you want to learn, as far as you work for it, not being placed with someone else, you don't get it from someone else."

Johnny illustrates for us the distinction between virtue as the development of principles of justice and virtue as being unprejudiced. In one sense, Johnny's development has involved increased recognition to the fellow-humanness of the slaves. From thinking of slaves as inferior and bad at age 10, he thinks of them as having some sort of rights at age 19. He is still not just, however, because his only notions of right are that you should get what you earn, a conception easily used to justify a segregated society. In spite of a high school and college education, he has no real grasp of the conceptions of rights underlying the Constitution or the Supreme Court decisions involved. Johnny's lack of virtue is not that he doesn't want to associate with blacks, it is that he is not capable of being a participating citizen of our society because he does not understand the principles on which our society is based. His failure to understand these principles cuts both ways. Not only does he fail to ground the rights of blacks on principles, but he also fails to ground respect for law on this base. Respect for law is respect for the majority. But if 50,000 people break the law, can 50,000 be wrong? Whether the 50,000 people are breaking the law in the name of rights or of the Ku Klux Klan makes no difference in this line of thought.

It is to be hoped that Johnny may reach our next stage, Stage 5, *social contract orientation*, by his mid-twenties, because some of our subjects continue to develop up until this time. Instead of taking one of our research subjects, however, let us take some statements by Socrates as an example of Stage 5. Socrates is explaining to Crito why he refuses to save his life by taking advantage of the escape arrangements Crito has made:

"Ought one to fulfill all one's agreements?" Socrates asks. "Then consider the consequences. Suppose the laws and constitution of Athens were to confront us and ask, 'Socrates, can you deny that by this act you intend, so far as you have power, to destroy us? Do you imagine that a city can continue to exist if the legal judgments which are pronounced by it are nullified and destroyed by private persons? At an earlier time, you made a noble show of indifference to the possibility of dying. Now you show no respect for your earlier professions and no regard for us, the laws, trying to run away in spite of the contracts by which you agreed to live as a member of our state. Are we not speaking the truth when we say that you have undertaken in deed, if not in word, to live your life as a citizen in obedience to us? It is a fact, then, that you are breaking covenants made with us under no compulsion or misunderstanding. You had seventy years in which you could have left the country if you were not satisfied with us or felt that the agreements were unfair.'"

As an example of Stage 6, *orientation to universal moral principles,* let me cite *Martin Luther King's "Letter from Birmingham Jail" (1965):*

"There is a type of constructive nonviolent tension which is necessary for growth. Just as Socrates felt it was necessary to create a tension in the mind so that individuals could rise from the bondage of half-truths, so must we see the need for nonviolent gadflies to create the kind of tension in society that will help men rise from the dark depths of prejudice and racism.

"One may well ask, 'How can you advocate breaking some laws and obeying others?' The answer lies in the fact that there are two types of laws, just and unjust. One has not only a legal but a moral responsibility to obey just laws. One has a moral responsibility to disobey unjust laws. An unjust law is a human law that is not rooted in eternal law and natural law. Any law that uplifts human personality is just, any law that degrades human personality is unjust. An unjust law is code that a numerical or power majority group compels a minority group to obey but does not make binding on itself. This is difference made legal.

"I do not advocate evading or defying the law, as would the rabid segregationist. That would lead to anarchy. One who breaks an unjust law must do so openly, lovingly, and with a willingness to accept the penalty. An individual who breaks a law that conscience tells him is unjust, and willingly accepts the penalty of imprisonment in order to arouse the conscience of the community over its injustice, is in reality expressing the highest respect for law."

King makes it clear that moral disobedience of the law must spring from the same root as moral obedience to law, out of respect for justice. We respect the law because it is based on rights both in the sense that the law is designed to protect the rights of all and because the law is made by the principle of equal political rights. If civil disobedience is to be Stage 6, it must recognize the contractual respect for law of Stage 5, even to accepting imprisonment. That is why Stage 5 is a way of thinking about the laws that are imposed on all, while a morality of justice that claims to judge the law can never be anything but a free, personal ideal.

PROBLEMS AT THE PEAK STAGE

As we observed before, Stage 6 makes the most sweeping claims for pursuing universal justice and engaging the broadest information – beyond even the proper processes of Stage 5. However, very rarely are people motivated by the concerns of Stage 6 alone. It takes a significant level of mental concentration and ability to abstract away the concerns for punishment, beneficial exchange, personal relationships, and stable society. Besides, what general principle or principles should rule Stage 6? The answer for Kohlberg is justice.

In addition, there may be very few humans in this world that are sufficiently rational and detached in their observations and decisions to maintain Stage 6 thought very long. Moreover, much that is attractive about the other stages is missing in Stage 6 – such as attention to personal interests and loyalties to lasting relationships. Someone totally oriented to such consistent universal justice may be our complete ideal – such as Socrates, Jesus, Gandhi, Lincoln, King, or any person whose life and values were so consistently lived for the highest and best for all that we would want to emulate him or her.

Would such a heightened sense of justice compromise or jeopardize some of the dimensions of the values we treasure within families and friendships?

BALANCING 'JUSTICE' AND 'CARE'

Moral reasoning and justice are intensely important, just as are moral human decisions, relationships, and care. They are poor substitutes for each other. Care always connotes closeness – shown especially in a hug, one of the most delightful expressions of care! Here personal interests and relationships play a big role. We seek to be near the people we care about. The Good Samaritan parable became the good "neighbor" first of all because he got close to the person in need. Caring about people who share no physical contact with us is more difficult. We care for the victims of a flood by sending resources and gifts. We care about customers through special attention to safety and quality – perhaps even going beyond what the industry standards require. The image of "arms length" perceptions and attitudes are grossly out of place when it comes to genuine care.

In a similar way, we often think about decisions of what is fair coming from diligent, detached analysis of information. The higher stages of justice prize abstract, impartial, and impersonal reasoning. Personal, emotional considerations are not the primary focus. Meanwhile, actions that arise from care generally spring from some kind of attachment to people or to specific results. We care about how decisions affect others' welfare as well as our own. When others are hurt, we are hurt. When they are benefited, we feel good.

The highest levels of thinking about justice are impersonal; a just decision involves a careful and fair resolution of a problem, undistracted by – but not unconcerned with – any personal feelings or commitments. In contrast, a caring decision expresses personal feeling, concern, or commitment to other people involved. We also require just decisions to be impartial – without respect for elevated social positions or privilege. No favoritism is allowed. In contrast, one way of saying that we care for someone is to say that we are "partial to" that person.

Furthermore, justice is disinterested. We consider it immoral for a legislator or judge to make a decision on a matter in which he or she has a personal interest. We suspect that a decision would not be fair or just when the people in power have personal interest in the results of the decision. In contrast, a truly caring person takes an intense interest in both the content and the effects of the decisions he or she makes. Of course, people can be intensely "interested" in the sense of truly caring about the people and about good results, but still make an unbiased, disinterested decision – all at the same time.

Finally, justice is blind. Our vivid symbol for justice is a blindfolded woman holding an analytical balance. This blindness is crucial to implementing the impartial and detached aspects of justice. Meanwhile, care requires an eagerness to learn more about the other. In care, the eyes are wide open! We sometimes say that love is blind, but what we mean is that care – or love – is willing to make allowances for weakness. These and other points of contrast between common symbols of justice and care are displayed in the following chart. Notice the impact of the terms we use to describe such basic concepts as "justice" and "care" on our understanding of personal moral development.[6]

A Comparison

JUSTICE	CARE
Impersonal analysis	Personal decision
Impartial to	Partial to (be fond of)
Detached	Attached
Disinterested	Interested
Arm's Length	Hug
Blind	Eyes wide open

Another Voice

The requirements of justice by themselves, especially in Stages 5 and 6 of the development of reasoning, may seem to drain us of much of what is important to us as humans. We may be capable of thinking in these levels of abstraction, and can also imaginatively detach ourselves from our interests and relationships for brief periods of time. Our lives and friendship are too important to distort in reality.

Carol Gilligan uncovered this problem in her studies of the development of young men and women. It seemed that women were less comfortable detaching themselves from their friendships and personal relationships than men were. A larger percentage of women seemed to remain at Stage 3 of Kohlberg's scale of stages. Combining this discovery with the fact that Kohlberg did his initial studies with young men only, Gilligan became suspicious that there was a sex-based bias against women in Kohlberg's theory.

For example, Carol Gilligan contrasts the responses of two 11-year-old, bright and articulate sixth graders – Jake and Amy. Contrary to popular stereotypes, Amy loves mathematics and is planning to become a scientist, while Jake's favorite subject is English. Nevertheless, Jake approaches the Heinz dilemma discussed earlier as if it were an abstract, self-contained problem of logic or mathematics. At the same time, Amy has more of a feeling for the various interests and relationships involved.

The following excerpt from *In a Different Voice* is typical of the way Professor Gilligan describes the contrast between Jake and Amy – and in general between the ways men and women tend to think: [7]

GILLIGAN'S EMPHASIS

The dilemma that these 11-year-olds were asked to resolve was one in the series devised by Kohlberg to measure moral development in adolescence by presenting a conflict between moral norms and exploring the logic of its resolution. In this particular dilemma, a man named Heinz considers whether or not to steal a drug which he cannot afford to buy in order to save the life of his wife. In the standard format of Kohlberg's interviewing procedure, the description of the dilemma itself – Heinz's predicament, the wife's disease, the druggist's refusal to lower his price – is followed by the question, "Should Heinz steal the drug?" The reasons for and against stealing are then explored through a series of questions that vary and extend the parameters of the dilemma in a way designed to reveal the underlying structure of moral thought.

Jake, at 11, is clear from the outset that Heinz should steal the drug. Constructing the dilemma, as Kohlberg did, as a conflict between the values of property and life, he discerns the logical priority of life and uses that logic to justify his choice:

For one thing, a human life is worth more than money, and if the druggist only makes $1,000, he is still going to live, but if Heinz doesn't steal the drug, his wife is going to die. (*Why is life worth more than money?*) Because the druggist can get a thousand dollars later from rich people with cancer, but Heinz can't get his wife again. (*Why not?*) Because people are all different and so you couldn't get Heinz's wife again.

Asked whether Heinz should steal the drug if he does not love his wife, Jake replied that he should, saying

that not only is there "a difference between hating and killing," but also, if Heinz were caught, "The judge would probably think it was the right thing to do." Asked about the fact that, in stealing, Heinz would be breaking the law, he says that "the laws have mistakes, and you can't go writing up a law for everything that you can imagine."

Thus, while taking the law into account and recognizing its function in maintaining social order (the judge, Jake says, "should give Heinz the lightest possible sentence"), he also sees the law as man-made and therefore subject to error and change. Yet his judgment that Heinz should steal the drug, like his view of the law as having mistakes, rests on the assumption of agreement, a societal consensus around moral values that allows one to know and expect others to recognize what is "the right thing to do."

Fascinated by the power of logic, this 11-year-old boy locates truth in math, which he says, is "the only thing that is totally logical." Considering the moral dilemma to be "sort of like a math problem with humans," he sets it up as an equation and proceeds to work out the solution. Since his solution is rationally derived, he assumes that anyone following reason would arrive at the same conclusion and thus that a judge would also consider stealing to be the right thing of Heinz to do. Yet he is also aware of the limits of logic. Asked whether there is a right answer to moral problems, Jake replies that "there can only be right and wrong in judgment," since the parameters of action are variable and complex. Illustrating how actions undertaken with the best of intentions can eventuate in the most disastrous of consequences, he says, "like if you give an old lady your seat on the trolley, if you are in a trolley crash and that seat goes through the window, it might be that reason that the old lady dies."

Theories of developmental psychology illuminate well the position of this child, standing at the juncture of childhood and adolescence; at what Piaget describes as the pinnacle of childhood intelligence, and beginning through thought to discover a wider universe of possibility. The moment of preadolescence is caught by the conjunction of formal operational thought with a description of self still anchored in the factual parameters of his childhood world – his age, his town, his father's occupation, the substance of his likes, dislikes, and beliefs. Yet as his self-description radiates the self-confidence of a child who has arrived, in Erikson's terms, at a favorable balance of industry over inferiority – competent, sure of himself, and knowing well the rules of the game – so his emergent capacity for formal thought, his ability to think about thinking and to reason things out in a logical way, frees him from dependence on authority and allows him to find solutions to problems by himself.

This emergent autonomy follows the trajectory that Kohlberg's six stages of moral development trace, a three-level progression from an egocentric understanding of fairness based on individual need (Stages 1 and 2), to a conception of fairness anchored in the shared conventions of societal agreement (Stage 3 and 4), and finally to a principled understanding of fairness that rests on the free-standing logic of equality and reciprocity (Stages 5 and 6). While this boy's judgments at 11 are scored as conventional on Kohlberg's scale, a mixture of Stages 3 and 4, his ability to bring deductive logic to bear on the solution of moral dilemmas, to differentiate morality from law, and to see how laws can be considered to have mistakes points toward a principle conception of justice that Kohlberg equates with moral maturity.

In contrast, Amy's response to the dilemma conveys a very different impression, an image of development stunted by a failure of logic, an inability to think for herself. Asked if Heinz should steal the drug, she replies in a way that seems evasive and unsure:

Well, I don't think so. I think there might be other ways besides stealing it, like he could borrow the money or make a loan or something, but he really shouldn't steal the drug – but his wife shouldn't die either.

Asked why he should not steal the drug, she considers neither property nor law but rather the effect that theft could have on the relationship between Heinz and his wife:

If he stole the drug, he might save his wife then, but if he did, he might have to go to jail, and then his wife might get sicker again, and he couldn't get more of the drug, and it might not be good. So, they should really just talk it out and find some other way to make the money.

Seeing the dilemma as not a math problem with humans but a narrative of relationships that extends over time, Amy envisions the wife's continuing need for her husband and the husband's continuing concern for his wife and seeks to respond to the druggist's need in a way that would sustain rather than sever connection. Just as she ties the wife's survival to the preservation of relationships, so she considers the value of the wife's life in a context of relationships, saying that it would be wrong to let her die because, "if she died, it hurts a lot of people and it hurts her." Since Amy's moral judgment is grounded in the belief that "if somebody has something that would keep somebody alive, then it's not right not to give it to them," she considers the problem in the dilemma to arise not from the druggist's assertion of rights but from his failure of response.

As the interviewer proceeds with the series of questions that follow from construction of the dilemma, Amy's answers remain essentially unchanged, the various probes serving neither to elucidate nor to modify her initial response. Whether or not Heinz loves his wife, he still shouldn't steal or let her die; if it were a stranger dying instead, Amy says that "if the stranger didn't have anybody near or anyone she knew," then Heinz should try to save her life, but should not steal the drug. But as the interviewer conveys through the repetition of questions that the answers she gave were not heard or not right, Amy's confidence begins to diminish, and her replies become more constrained and unsure. Asked again why

Heinz should not steal the drug, she simply repeats, "Because it's not right." Asked again to explain why, she states again that theft would not be a good solution, adding lamely, "If he took it, he might not know how to give it to his wife, and so his wife might still die." Failing to see the dilemma as a self-contained problem in moral logic, she does not discern the internal structure of its resolution; as she constructs the problem differently herself, Kohlberg's conception completely evades her.

Instead, seeing a world comprised of relationships rather than of people standing alone, a world that coheres through human connection rather than through systems of rules, she finds the puzzle in the dilemma to lie in the failure of the druggist to respond to the wife. Saying that "it is not right for someone to die when their life could be saved," she assumes that if the druggist were to see the consequences of his refusal to lower his price, he would realize that "he should just give it to the wife and then have the husband pay back the money later." Thus she considers the solution to the dilemma to lie in making the wife's condition more salient to the druggist or, that failing, in appealing to others who are in a position to help.

Just as Jake is confident the judge would agree that stealing is the right thing for Heinz to do, so Amy is confident that "if Heinz and the druggist had talked it out long enough, they could reach something besides stealing." As he considers the law to "have mistakes," so she see this drama as a mistake, believing that "the world should just share things more and then people wouldn't have to steal." Both children thus recognize the need for agreement but see it as mediated in different ways – he impersonally through systems of logic and law, she personally through communication in relationship. Just as he relies on the conventions of logic to deduce the solution to this dilemma, assuming these conventions to be shared, so she relies on a process of communication, assuming connection and believing that her voice will be heard.

An analysis research with 27-year-olds produced similar results for Gilligan. The women identified themselves primarily in terms of care, intimacy, attachments, and personal relationships; men emphasized more the categories of fairness, logic, and separation. Gilligan concludes that these women and men may have quite different concepts of adulthood

---

The participants in this study were an unequal number of men and women, representing the distribution of males and females in the class on moral and political choice. At age 27, the five women in the study all were actively pursuing careers – two in medicine, one in law, one in graduate study, and one as an organizer of labor unions. In the five years following their graduation from college, three had married and one had a child.

When they were asked at age 27, "How would you describe yourself to yourself?" one of the women refused to reply, but the other four gave as their responses to the interviewer's question:

"This sounds sort of strange, but I think maternal, with all its connotations. I see myself in a nurturing role, maybe not right now, but whenever that might be, as a physician, as a mother ... It's hard for me to think of myself without thinking about other people around me that I'm giving to." (Claire)

"I am fairly hard-working and fairly thorough and fairly responsible, and in terms of weakness, I am sometimes hesitant about making decisions and unsure of myself and afraid of doing things and taking responsibility, and I think maybe that is one of the biggest conflicts I have had ... The other very important aspect of my life is my husband and trying to make his life easier and trying to help him out."(Leslie)

"I am a hysteric. I am intense. I am warm. I am very smart about people ... I have a lot more soft feelings than hard feeling. I am a lot easier to get to be kind than to get mad. If I had to say one word, and to me it incorporates a lot, *adopted.*" (Erica)

"I have sort of changed a lot. At the point of the last interview (age 22) I felt like I was the kind of person who was interested in growth and trying hard, and it seems to me that the last couple of years, the not trying is someone who is not growing, and I think that is the thing that bothers me the most, the thing that I keep thinking about, that I am not growing. It's not true, I am, but what seems to be failure partially is the way that Tom and I broke up. The thing with Tom feels to me like I am not growing ... The thing I am running into lately is that the way I describe myself, my behavior doesn't sometimes come out that way. Like I hurt Tom a lot, and that bothers me. So I am thinking of myself as somebody who tried not to hurt people, but I ended up hurting him a lot, and so that is something that weighs on me, that I'm somebody who unintentionally hurts people. Or a feeling, lately, that it is simple to sit down and say what your principles are, what your values are, and what I think about myself, but the way it sort of works out in actuality is sometimes very different. You can say you try not to hurt people, but you might because of things about yourself, or you can say this is my principle, but when the situation come up, you don't really behave the way you would like ... So I consider myself contradictory and confused." (**Nan**)

The fusion of identity and intimacy, noted repeatedly in women's development, is perhaps nowhere more clearly articulated than in these self-descriptions. In response to the request to describe themselves, all of the women describe a relationship, depicting their identity *in* the connection of future mother, present wife, adopted child, or past lover. Similarly, the standard of moral judgment that informs their assessment of self is a standard of relationship, an ethic of nurturance, responsibility, and care. Measuring their strength in the activity of attachment ("giving to," "helping out," "being kind," "not hurting"), these highly successful and achieving women do not mention their academic and professional distinction in the context of describing themselves. If anything, they regard their professional activities as jeopardizing their own sense of themselves, and the conflict they encounter between achievement and care leaves them either divided in judgment or feeling betrayed. Nan explains:

"When I first applied to medical school, my feeling was that I was a person who was concerned with other people and being able to care for them in some way or another, and I was running into problems the last few years as far as my being able to give of myself, my time, and what I am doing to other people. And medicine, even though it seemed that profession is set up to do exactly that, seems to more or less interfere

with your doing it. To me it felt like I wasn't really growing, that I was just treading water, trying to cope with what I was doing that made me very angry in some ways because it wasn't the way that I wanted things to go."

Thus in all of the women's descriptions, identity is defined in a context of relationship and judged by a standard of responsibility and care. Similarly, morality is seen by these women as arising from the experience of connection and conceived as a problem of inclusion rather than one of balancing claims. The underlying assumption that morality stems from attachment is explicitly stated by Clair in her response to Heinz's dilemma of whether or not to steal an overpriced drug in order to save his wife.

Explaining why Heinz should steal, she elaborates the view ... on which her judgment is based:

"By yourself, there is little sense to things. It is like the sound of one hand clapping, the sound of one man or one woman; there is something lacking. It is the collective that is important to me, and that collective is based on certain guiding principles, one of which is that everybody belongs to it and that you all come from it. You have to love someone else, because while you may not like them, you are inseparable from them. In a way, it is like loving your right hand. *They are part of you;* that other person is part of that giant collection of people that you are connected to."

To this aspiring maternal physician, the sound of one hand clapping does not seem a miraculous transcendence but rather a human absurdity, the illusion of a person standing alone in a reality of interconnection.

For the men, the tone of identity is different, clearer, more direct, more distinct and sharp-edged. Even when disparaging the concept itself, they radiate the confidence of certain truth. Although the world of the self that men describe at times includes "people" and "deep attachments," no particular person or relationship is mentioned, nor is the activity of relationship portrayed in the context of self-description. Replacing the women's verbs of attachment are adjectives of separation "intelligent," "logical," "imaginative," "honest," sometimes even "arrogant" and "cocky." Thus the male "I" is defined in separation, although the men speak of having "real contacts" and "deep emotions" or otherwise wishing for them.

There seems at present to be only partial agreement between men and women about the adulthood they commonly share. In the absence of mutual understanding, relationships between the sexes continue in varying degrees of constraint, manifesting the "paradox of egocentrism" which Piaget describes, a mystical respect for rules combined with everyone playing more or less as he pleases and paying no attention to his neighbor. For a life-cycle understanding to address the development in adulthood of relationships characterized by cooperation, generosity, and care, that understanding must include the lives of women as well as men.

Among the most pressing items on the agenda for research on adult development is the need to delineate *in women's own terms* the experience of their adult life. My own work in that direction indicates that the inclusion of women's experience brings to developmental understanding a new perspective on relationships that changes the basic constructs of interpretation. The concept of identity expands to include the experience of interconnection. The moral domain is similarly enlarged by the inclusion of responsibility and care in relationships. And the underlying epistemology correspondingly shifts from the Greek ideal of knowledge as a correspondence between mind and form to the Biblical conception of knowing as a process of human relationship.

Given the evidence of different perspectives in the representation of adulthood by women and men, there is a need for research that elucidates the efforts of these differences in marriage, family, and work relationships.

My research suggests that men and women may speak different languages that they assume are the same, using similar words to encode disparate experiences of self and social relationships. Because these languages share an overlapping moral vocabulary, they contain a propensity for systematic mistranslation, creating misunderstandings which impede communication and limit the potential for cooperation and care in relationships. At the same time, however, these languages articulate with one another in critical ways. Just as the language of responsibility provides a web-like imagery of relationships to replace a hierarchical ordering that dissolves with the coming of equality, so the language of rights underlines the importance of including in the network of care not only the other but also the self.

As we have listened for centuries to the voices of men and the theories of development that their experience informs, so we have come more recently to notice not only the silence of women but the difficulty in hearing what they say when they speak. Yet in the different voice of women lies the truth of an ethic of care, the tie between relationship and responsibility, and the origins of aggression in the failure of connection. The failure to see the different reality of women's lives and to hear the differences in their voices stems in part from the assumption that there is a single mode of social experience and interpretation. By positing instead two different modes, we arrive at a more complex rendition of human experience which sees the truth of separation and attachment in the lives of women and men and recognizes how these truths are carried by different modes of language and thought.

To understand how the tension between responsibilities and rights sustains the dialectic of human development is to see the integrity of two disparate modes of experience that are in the end connected. While an ethic of justice proceeds from the premise of equality that everyone should be treated the same, an ethic of care rests on the premise of nonviolence that no one should be hurt. In the realization that just as inequality adversely affects both parties in an unequal relationship, so too violence is destructive for everyone involved. This dialogue between fairness and care not only provides a better understanding of relations between the sexes but also gives rise to a more comprehensive portrayal of adult work and family relationships.

As Freud and Piaget call our attention to the differences in children's feelings and thought, enabling us to respond to children with greater care and respect, so a recognition of the differences in women's experience and understanding expands our vision of maturity and points to the contextual nature of developmental truths. Through this expansion in perspective, we can begin to envision how marriage between adult development as it is currently portrayed and women's development as it begins to be seen could lead to a changed understanding of human development and a more generative view of human life.

MAN IS MAN? WOMAN IS WOMAN?

Carol Gilligan's interpretation of her research has raised a number of controversies that are beyond the purposes of this book. Did she study enough cases to make such general conclusions about men and women? In *Development in Judging Moral Issues*, James Rest reports on more than 20 extensive independent studies of men and women in which people were classified into Kohlberg's six stages of development of moral reasoning.[8] In each study, women's reasoning and justice concepts were rated, on an average, as high as or very slightly higher than men's.

However, even if Gilligan's conclusions had been broadly matched and accepted by others, would that mean that every man is more oriented to reasoning and fairness than women generally are? Of course not. Would it mean that every woman is more in tune with relationships and care than men generally are? Certainly not. No such stereotyping is ever either fair or caring to the individuals involved. Some women are far more skilled at detached impartial judgment than most men, and some men are more caring and sensitive to others than most women. In fact, the same person – man or woman – can score highly on both measures. Men and women can be very adept at reasoning and raising the justice issues from the perspective of Kohlberg's Stage 6 and still affirm their enduring relationships through caring decisions.

To demonstrate this claim of the real compatibility of reasoning and relationships, and of justice and care, we can look for people who did or do embody both. Mother Teresa is a great example of one whose high-level reasoning on justice issues is well known but who also embodies a deep sense of care as well. Moreover, the father of modern economics, Adam Smith, argued for three driving values in society and personal life – prudence, justice, and care (which he called benevolence). Smith considered care the greatest of these values.[9] In addition, Dr. Martin Luther King Jr. certainly had a well-developed ability to reason on justice issues. He is one of the few people Kohlberg himself clearly classified in Stage 6. Without contradiction, he lived and taught love and care at least as much as justice and rights.

Dr. King considered the self-giving love taught and lived by Jesus to be the most powerful instrument for change ("love your neighbor as yourself" and "love your enemies"). To this he added Augustine's advice to "love the sinner while you hate the sin" and Booker T. Washington's wisdom to "let no man pull you so low as to make you hate him." Only with such a relationship to others is a protest or an issue focused on what is just and fair, rather than on mere personal conflict. For Dr. King, the decision to love enhanced the cause of justice. Notice, for example, how Dr. King, as a young, unrenowned preacher in Montgomery, concluded his first public speech as a protest leader:

> "If you will protest courageously, and yet with dignity and Christian love, when the history books are written in future generations, the historians will have to pause and say, 'There lived a great people – a black people – who injected new meaning and dignity into the veins of civilization.' This is our challenge and our overwhelming responsibility." [10]

What other examples do you know about, of people who are intensely caring and who are also paragons of good reasoning and justice? Do you think of both men and women?

STEPS OF CARE

Whether or not women and men are statistically different in their maturity in justice and care – and whether or not any of us does very well with our lives without plenty of both detached reasoning and deep relationships – Carol Gilligan's most lasting contribution may be another dimension of her theory: *The steps of development she notices in people's understanding and expressions of care.* [11]

Perhaps understanding these steps will help people to be more understanding of changes in their own behavior, and more perceptive and tolerant of the shifts in others' conduct.

Briefly, Gilligan's theory describes three steps. The *first step* observes that people all seem to start out caring only for themselves. We seem to express selfish egoism quite easily. What motivates us in our decisions is our own desire for survival, at least, if not also greed and personal pride. Nevertheless, society often judges and restrains such behavior through peer pressure, laws, and psychological sanctions. The feeling of guilt for selfishness nudges many toward the second step.

Behavior on the *second step* is driven by responsibility to help others – especially our children and others who depend on us, but also others who seem to need special care. Both personal identity and survival are now understood in terms of the help we give to others, and how well they accept and benefit from that help. The need for other people's approval is a driving force for conduct on step two. Are we doing enough good to merit their acceptance?

Eventually people who remain on this second step are likely to encounter a number of problems. There are often completing claims for care, and our human needs for care are so insatiable – care for one's spouse, parents, children, neighbors, the disabled, the poorer children somewhere else in the city, the homeless, AIDS victims, orphans of war, the starving millions on another continent, and such like. The list could be endless, the burden of care overwhelming in size, and the opportunities to serve competing for our personal attention in innumerable directions. There is so much good that needs to be done for others! Can we give some attention to our own cares as well? These tensions of step two can be dissolved or ignored by retreating to step one, or maturely resolved in moving to step three.

On Gilligan's *third step* the former concern for producing large quantities of good for others is replaced by truth – honest awareness of our limits and the meaning of our mutual relationships. From step two to three there is also a shift in the source of approval. People on step three are not much affected by others' judgment – "You are selfish," "You are a great helper" – but have a more inner awareness and confidence in their goals and accomplishments.

On this step, according to Gilligan, we are also comfortable balancing and integrating our own interests with the interests of others. In the fourth short monologue at the beginning of this chapter, Chrissa is probably attempting to enter this third step. She seems honest about her own needs and the needs of others, but she remains disturbed by the accusations of her own "selfishness." Truth is the standard for this most mature step of care, but it is not truth in a wooden sense. Gilligan holds up as a good example the woman who comes before Solomon, the Jewish king, and seeks to save her child's life by denying being its mother. The point is that if she no longer claims to be the mother, Solomon will call off his bluffing threat to cut the baby in half and divide the corpse between the two women who claimed to be the baby's mother. Because the other woman tells Solomon to go ahead and kill the baby, Solomon recognizes who is the true mother. According to Gilligan, the mother "verifies her motherhood by relinquishing truth in order to save the life of her child." [12]

The driving vision of the third level is the universal, self-chosen injunction of care that embraces care for others and for oneself. Self-assertion then can have a place in structuring care for others and in helping us feel better about ourselves. Moreover, "once obligation extends to include the self as well as others, the disparity between selfishness and responsibility dissolves." [13] Consequently, the third step is a balanced and stable position.

How do these steps of care that Gilligan has uncovered match up with the stages of the development of justice? That is not totally clear. Is it possible to reach high levels of reasoning about justice while still caring only about yourself? Consider the member of Congress who argues eloquently and rationally for a very just cause, knowing it will get him re-elected. Also, people with a mature sense of care for oneself and others may have developed only to Stage 3 on the justice scale, depending essentially on interpersonal relations.

INDEPENDENT SCALES

The moral content of our behavior is supplied by our own reasoning and choices, especially as these are informed by justice and care. The particular blend of fairness and care depends on the individual person, that person's degree of development, and the particular challenges at hand.

The stages of development of justice and the steps of development of care are partly independent. Especially as we look at particular cases of problems and decisions, we can easily imagine approaches to problem-solving that exemplify, at the same time, a "high" degree of maturity on one scale and a "low" degree of maturity on another scale. The same person, of course, may be capable of functioning on a "high" level on both scales, but in the particular problem-solving case does not use all the acquired abilities. Alternatively, another person may have matured tremendously on one scale, with only limited growth on another scale, and so high-level functioning on both scales together would be beyond that person's ability.

Do examples bear this out? Can you think of people who can reason in terms of universal principles of justice and who are articulate about the need for dignity for all human beings – Stage 6 of Kohlberg's scale – and yet who, nevertheless, act with consistent selfishness – on Gilligan's Step 1?

To take some concrete cases, let us look again at the stories at the beginning of this chapter. None of these four short monologues from Jose, Sheila, Victor, and Chrissa gives us enough information for definitive classifications. However, we can make some instructive, tentative observations.

Jose's awareness of a problem is acute, and his concept of justice is reaching beyond the conventions of democracy that he has been taught. His concern for a more fair process for responding to Tom's requests – a process beyond conventional democracy – may evidence reasoning in Stage 4 or even 5. And what is Jose's level of care? He certainly has developed beyond thinking only of himself; he demonstrates genuine care for Tom and Tom's wishes, so he has achieved Step 2, at least. The fact that his justice development seems to be either in Stage 4 or 5, and his care development is either on step two or three, helps show at least partial independence of these dimensions of development.

Sheila is alert to some problems. However, in terms of reasoning and justice concepts, she seems preconventional – in Stage 1 and 2. She is relying on some level of punishment if Jermaine gets out of line, or some benefit securing his protection. Her level of care is unclear, although everything she says in this story revolves around herself. Her behavior here is still only in the first step of care.

What should we make of *Victor's* comments? His awareness of specific human problems around him is difficult to judge. However, he does have a pattern of moral reasoning that helps him figure out what is right – one that he may use along with other patterns of reasoning. This pattern was rooted in the punishment-and-reward system his father used when he was younger, and this relationship with his father may well have developed beyond Stage 2 into the friendship and personal loyalty of Stage 3. In fact, it is this deep loyalty along with his concern for honoring his father that come through especially strongly. In addition, the fact that he does not feel obligated to do what his father would want suggests some reasoning beyond Stage 3 as well. We would have to ask some questions of Victor before we would know how high his reasoning and his justice concept had developed. Moreover, on Gilligan's care development scale we know only that Victor has moved beyond selfishness in his relationship with his father. However, from what he says, he could still be selfish in most relationships, or he *may* have achieved the esteemed Step 3 of care. We can concretely imagine these different combinations of levels of maturity in Victor – and weave believable human stories to match. Does that demonstrate that these scales have some independence?

Chrissa is also quite alert to a human problem. While her personal ability to reason about justice is probably more advanced than this, her complaints about the site director focus on issues of Stage 3: The personal relationships and feelings of all those involved. Had she talked longer she may have made important observations on responsibilities to fulfill earlier fair agreements, or on how rational and impartial people would work together at the clinic – thus demonstrating some of her ability to reason in Stages 5 and 6. However, she might not use those abilities in solving every problem in which she finds herself. Finally, her sense of care is very advanced. Her concern for other people is genuine and strong, including physical and personal care for those who are neglected and ignored by nearly everyone else. Nevertheless, she is intensely aware and honest about her own need for care as well.

Chrissa honestly cares how the site director treats her – manipulating, exploiting – and it bothers her. However, the director's behavior does not at all detract from her mature "autonomy," including her own conviction of the value of her work and her personal dignity and worth. Of course, with more experience in life, she will probably be less angry when she again encounters people like the site director, but she may continue to care – honestly and deeply – about the ways others treat her. This sensitivity is completely consistent with the desire for truth and the care for self and others that characterizes step three.

DEVELOPMENT OF ACCOUNTABILITY

We have looked again at three of the aspects of ethics and critical thinking about human problems: Recognizing a problem, engaging all available information, and deciding what to do. We have also examined some of the personal development patterns associated with these steps – the development of awareness, fairness, and care. There is, however, one more step: Being able to explain the decision to yourself and others. As we saw in Chapter 2 of this book, the working value for this step is accountability.

Is there a developmental scale for accountability? Not exactly. After all, accountability depends not only on our own development, but also on the structures around us. A very immature person who is constantly followed by police, FBI, IRS agents, and the like, will probably be more "accountable"– at least in one common use of that word. But this aspect of accountability depends very little on personal development.

Notice there is an aspect of accountability that depends on personal development: Commitment. This is the subjective or personal aspect of accountability. To what extent and with what maturity are you committed to the other values you profess to believe? On the one hand, are those values – including justice and care – only attractive window dressing and wonderful talk? Do those values honestly explain your behavior? On the other hand, are they the standards you use if you honestly vindicate your decisions to yourself, your friends, your family or your God? Since this is so important, developmental positions of commitment have been analyzed and described by a number of important scholars. Here we will look briefly at the insights of Soren Kierkegaard, William Perry, and Donald Osgood on the development of commitment.

KIERKEGAARD'S CATEGORIES

Danish philosopher Soren Kierkegaard (1813-1855), the father of existentialism, described three main positions in life's development. He called them "stages of life," and they focused on one's definitive commitments. First, we all start out with no authentic or deep commitments. We do what feels good; we conform to peer pressure; we fit in to the roles and social patterns around us. In this position that Kierkegaard calls the "aesthetic stage," people never actually choose their roles or patterns of life. In fact, people in this position rarely even think of these as choices they could make.

On the one hand, he found that some in this position are "sexually active" because their hormones are strong or because they have developed highly successful methods of seducing others. Mimicking this point of view, for example, Kierkegaard wrote a fascinating pseudonymous work, "The Diary of the Seducer." In this "Diary" – a popular book in Kierkegaard's own time – "Johanes de Seducer" is almost carried away with the success of his clever methods. Even though he is a little bored, and he wonders if there is more meaning to life, he never ventures out of his comfort zone of erotic exploitation.

On the other hand, very responsible adults who are faithful to their spouses, devoted to their children, reliable on their jobs, and ardent members of their church or synagogue are generally still in this "aesthetic" position as well, according to Kierkegaard. They are faithful – or generally faithful – to their spouses because that is the simplest, more comfortable way to go. They are devoted to their children because this is the role society assigns to them, and they do not want to be criticized. Also, they are reliable on the job because they are paid, and they like having a job. Moreover, they are ardent about their religious practice because it feels good, going to church is a nice way to start the week, the sanctuary is beautiful, the songs and scripture readings are uplifting, and so forth. Again, commitment is based on good feeling and comfort, not explicit choice.

The people who have evaluated their lives, and made conscious choices about their life's directions, have already stepped into the second position of commitment – what Kierkegaard called the "ethical stage." Three attributes characterize people in this position. First, they have made an explicit choice and commitment to a set of values, quite conscious that they were thereby rejecting other sets of values. This commitment, therefore, requires some significant knowledge of alternative sets of values that were at least viable choices. According to Kierkegaard, one does not choose if there is only one believable choice. Second, the choice is always associated with a group. There is always a group of other people that provides mutual support and guidance for living out the chosen commitment. Third, the choices one makes on the basis of the commitment are always "rational" choices – choices that can be explained to others, especially those in the same "support" group.

Commitments in this second position can be very strong and meaningful. However, one's dependence on the "support" group for the definition of that moral commitment in the first place, and some continuing approval by the groups as well – these aspects can limit the depth of personal commitment. The third position allows us to go deeper and reduce these limitations. As in the second position, those in the third take responsibility for their choices, generally fit into a group, and are usually able rationally to explain their behavior to that group – but neither the group nor its approval is necessary for them. In fact, Kierkegaard thought that the group and its approval could well hinder sincere commitment.

What distinguishes the third position is the willingness to choose what you believe is right, even when there is no group that agrees with you, and no group to rationally understand and approve your choices. For Kierkegaard, this highest position of commitment is completely independent of peer pressure, herd instincts, and the comfort of others' praise. Our commitment is our choice alone – in total, unpretentious, naked honesty before our God. Because only we and God can be fully informed of our real thoughts and reasons – although we do deceive even ourselves sometimes – this level is far less open to hypocrisy and deceit than the "aesthetic" and "ethical" positions. Moreover, because this highest level of development forces the issue of "honest to God" sincerity, flexibility, and openness to keep learning, Kierkegaard chose to call it the "religious stage." Of course, by far most of what people in Kierkegaard's time, and our time, call "religion" merely feels right, on position one, or depends on the affirmation of the group, on position two. The sincerity, flexibility, and openness of this position of commitment are, in fact, the opposite of what many people mean by "religion." In Kierkegaard's vital sense of religion, it is the rare person whose moral commitments, standing by themselves, would endure the test of God's thorough inspection.

PERRY'S PICKS

Kierkegaard's three positions of commitment provide the simplest interpretation of our development in this dimension of ethics. William Perry observed nine positions in our development toward commitment. [14] He articulates these with considerable detail beyond for our purposes. Let us briefly explore the general trends he uncovers, nevertheless.

We start, according to Perry, with a "basic duality" of thought that characterizes position one. Without really questioning our patterns of life, and without seriously examining other choices, we assume that our patterns are right and alternatives are wrong. We trust and follow the people that we take to be our authorities, because our parents or our peer groups are guided by them.

Positions two, three, and four involve increasing comprehension of "multiplicity." Our own authorities do not give us all the answers to the problems we face. Is it because they want us to think for ourselves some? – or is it because they do not know the answers themselves? In addition, some other authorities – with whom we have been taught by parents or peer groups to disagree – may have some good advice. We are challenged to come up with reasons why we still stay with the authorities we use, and to understand why they give the advice and commands they give.

In positions five and six – for which Perry uses the term "relativity" – we begin to take significant responsibility for ourselves. We begin to be aware of the problems of commitment. We start to understand our particular situation, examine our theories, and think about our own processes of thought. In these positions, we come to realize that we must make our decisions in an uncertain world, a world in which alternative, contradictory choices can make some sense to us as well. These "relativity" positions are similar to Kierkegaard's "ethical stage" – except that Perry gives less emphasis on the role of group support.

Finally, positions seven, eight, and nine involve growing levels of "commitment." Logic and reasoning play some role, but on position nine, the highest level, there is an explicit awareness that logic is not enough. On this ninth position, there are some choices that we make, and that we choose to make wholeheartedly, even though logic is inadequate to explain these commitments. Moreover, even though our commitments are the deepest in Perry's ninth position, we remain ready to learn and to grow. Here we see much of the sincerity, flexibility, and openness of Kierkegaard's highest position.

Levels of deep commitment that match Perry's and Kierkegaard's highest positions are difficult to achieve and very rare to find. As a result, research based upon Perry's positions has usually stopped with some level of "relativity." Sadly, we do not have enough data on people with mature commitments; what we have is statistically insignificant. Kierkegaard would not have been surprised in the least. Why do you think this is the case?

OSGOOD'S GOOD CURVE

Donald Osgood, an American business management wizard, has uncovered a curve of personal development toward commitment. His discovery is based on decades of work with IBM and other Fortune 500 corporations, and apart from any knowledge of Soren Kierkegaard and William Perry. Nevertheless, progression along his curve is remarkably similar to development along Kierkegaard's and Perry's positions.

First on Osgood's curve, we start off "idealistic" – confident of our values and our ability to succeed. High expectations and goals dominate our thought, but our confidence is naive. This attitude always leads us to the second position, being "frustrated," because we experience the ubiquitous gap that we examined at the beginning of Chapter 2. Present circumstances are always a far cry from our goals and desires. Our initial reaction is usually dominated by fear, indecision, and anxiety. After all, the world is not so simple as we had believed or hoped.

The third attitude is "defiance." Fear and indecision are overcome as we realize that we have to take some responsibility in our own hands. This attitude could signal the beginning of Kierkegaard's "ethical stage" and Perry's "relativity" positions. However, defiance is usually negative and destructive, especially if it is covert, buried. Unfortunately, people can continue to "live" for years with covert resentments and defiance that pollute their relationships with parents, spouse, employer, society, country, and religious authorities. These people who harbor covert defiance slip into the fourth position, simply "resigned" to disappointment and aimlessness in their lives. In the words of the rock group Pink Floyd, they are "comfortably numb." [15]

Hope is found in position five, being "aware" of the problem. Our development toward commitment shares this essential step of any problem-solving activity. In Osgood's terms, at this point we become aware of some of the damage of our defiance and resignation, and we realize that we must change. Acting upon that realization draws us into the sixth attitude, "decisive." We consciously do something different, consciously take responsibility for our lives.

While we may be hesitant at first, our initial decisions for change make our lives more vital, meaningful, creative. As these decisions become stronger – much like the development of commitment in Perry's last three positions – we achieve the seventh and highest fulfillment on Osgood's attitude curve, "committed." In this position we do not expect perfection of ourselves, our plans, family, friends, job, school, community, society, nation. Nevertheless, we are committed to attempt our best ideals, with our best ability, while remaining realistic about our results and talent. This is not the fragile idealism that can be easily shattered, but purposeful and prudent devotion – sincere, flexible, and open to learn and grow further.

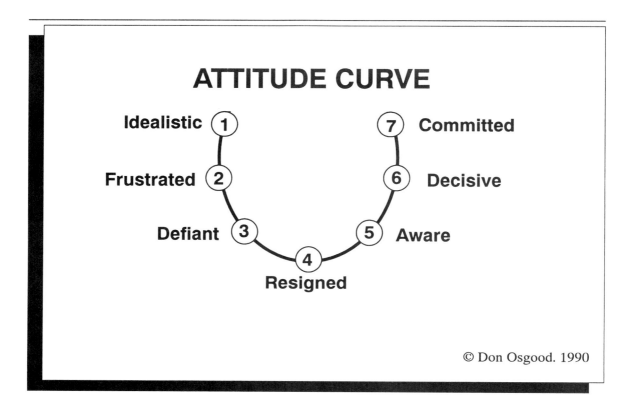

ATTITUDE CURVE

Idealistic (1)   (7) Committed

Frustrated (2)   (6) Decisive

Defiant (3)   (5) Aware

(4)
Resigned

© Don Osgood. 1990

These levels of commitment make us more accountable, whether others are watching and checking on us or not. The commitment that Kierkegaard, Perry, and Osgood describe so well in their highest positions of development is our deepest and strongest human quality of accountability – sincere, flexible and open.

ACCOUNTABLE FOR WHAT?

However important commitment and accountability are, they are parasitic values. They have no intrinsic worth. We are never merely "committed"; we have to be committed to some additional value. We are never merely "accountable"; we must be accountable for some standard, some goal. These standards and goals that we use are derived from the more or less mature stages of fairness and justice, and the more or less high steps of care that we achieve. Could a person be committed to a set of simplistic concepts of justice alone – mere punishment-and-reward systems? Yes, but you can also be committed in any of the other stages as well – including universal principles of justice. Can a person be committed only to selfish goals? Unfortunately yes, but many treasure far more the mature, honest care for self and others that Gilligan describes. Clearly, the developmental positions of accountability must be matched with development in these other dimensions as well, so that our accountability will have especially valuable content.

As you ponder these various approaches to moral development, keep in mind also the historical dimensions of ethical development and the exemplars of Chapter 3. Then anticipate that in Chapter 5 you will be able to add certain skills of expression and argumentation. Taken together, Chapters 2-5 can arm you to analyze your own life-views and express them in contrast with the views of others.

FOR FURTHER INQUIRY

DISCUSSION

Consider how Kohlberg would view the life of Marcus Junius Brutus (85-42 B.C.). Brutus was a noble Roman general, senator, and orator. He is especially well-known to us for having killed his best friend Julius Caesar in 44 B.C. Earlier, Caesar himself had pardoned Brutus from the accusation of treason – thereby saving his life. However, there was no win-win relationship between them, or even deep personal feeling. Instead of returning a favor, Brutus killed this friend in a futile effort to save the crumbling Roman Republic. He had become convinced that Caesar's power and ambition would transform the structure of Roman society. Considering this observed threat to be unjust and unfair, and a threat to the very values that make civility possible, Senator Brutus took his elevated concept of justice into his own hands and assassinated Caesar. For this extraordinary and devoted "justice" he is made into a kind of hero by Shakespeare and idealized by some as the last of the true Romans. Nevertheless, we all also stand warned against having friends like Brutus.

Even before this tragic incident with his friend Caesar, Senator Brutus was no stranger to placing justice above companionship and human kindness. It is reported that during an earlier period when he served as a judge, Brutus' own son was brought before him and accused of treason. Convinced of his own objective fairness, Brutus chose to try the case himself. Unfortunately, the information and evidence was convincing and convicting. Certainly not one to let personal feelings or care for others get in the way of justice, honorable Brutus condemned his own son to death! He received a pardon himself, from Caesar, from the accusation of treason, but he chose not to seek mercy for his own son.

QUESTIONS

1. In what stage would Kohlberg have placed Brutus's conception of justice? Why?
2. At what step would Gilligan have placed his level of caring? Why?
3. How would you characterize Brutus's level of accountability or commitment? Why?
4. What advice would you give Brutus during the trial of his son? Why?
5. What advice would you give him on the way to meeting Julius Caesar that fateful day? Why?

ENDNOTES

1. See James R.'s critique of other theorists, especially Lawrence Kohlberg, in *Development in Judging Moral Issues*, (Minneapolis: University of Minnesota Press), 1979, pages 48-74.

2. The terms "accommodate" and "assimilate" are borrowed from the description Jean Piaget (1896-1980) gave to perceptual change. Piaget referred to the middle stage as a "disequilibrium."

3. Piaget, *The Moral Judgment of the Child*, 1932.

4. Lawrence Kohlberg, *The Philosophy of Moral Development* (New York: Harper and Row) 1981.

5. See Jesus' comments in the Sermon on the Mount (St. Matthew, Chapters 5-7, especially 7:12) and Confucius' teaching in the *Analects*. Confucius uses the negative version: "Do not do to others what you would not want them do to you. "

6. From Paul de Vries and Barrey Gardner, *The Taming of the Shrewd* (Nashville: Thomas Nelson) 1992, p. 230.

7. Carol Gilligan, *In a Different Voice*, (Cambridge,

Massachusetts: Harvard University Press), 1982, pages 25-29.

8. James R. Rest, *Development in Judging Moral Issues*, (Minneapolis: University of Minnesota Press), 1979, pages 120-124.

9. See Adam Smith, *The Theory of Moral Sentiments*, and also an analysis of this book in Paul de Vries' article "Resource X: Sirkin and Smith on a Neglected Economic Staple," *Business and Professional Ethics Journal*, Fall, 1989.

10. Martin Luther King, Jr., *Testament of Hope*, (Harper: San Francisco), 1986, page 436.

11. See Gilligan, pages 64-105.

12. Gilligan, pages 104 and 105. This comment is based on the Biblical story in I Kings 3:16-28.

13. Gilligan, pages 93 and 94.

14. See William G. Perry, *Forms of Intellectual and Ethical Development in the College Years* (New York: Holt Rinehart and Winston), 1970.

15. See Pink Floyd, *The Wall*.

Persuasion

Chapter 5

Allen F. Plunkett Jr.

PATTERNS OF MORAL REASONING

"The knowledge of the world is only to be acquired in the world, and not in a closet."

– Earl of Chesterfield, *Letters, 1746*

"It appears to me that in Ethics, as in all other philosophical studies, the difficulties and disagreements, of which history is full, are mainly due to a very simple cause; namely to attempt to answer questions, without first discovering precisely *what* question it is which you desire to answer."

– George Edward Moore, *Principia Ethica*

"We make a ladder of our vices, if we trample those same vices underfoot."

– St. Augustine, *Sermons* 3

So there you were at lunch, merely expressing an opinion. It was no big deal, you thought. But it became one. In fact, it became an argument and it was embarrassing. No sooner had you said what you thought when someone objected: "That doesn't make sense!" Fighting humiliation, you tried again, restating your opinion. "You can't say that," someone else objected. "It's a free country," you argued. "Yes," they chorused, "but just because things are one way in one situation doesn't mean they'll be that way in another!"

"Yes, but . . ." you tried to counter.

The conversation ended as to your point.

You were a victim of how you said what you said – not the grammar of your discourse but the reasoning behind it. That particular exchange involved just one of many tenets and logical forms of reasoning (it was a "generalization," a term we will discuss later). You probably came away wondering, "How could I have expressed myself in a way that would have been more convincing?"

Allen F. Plunkett Jr., B.A. and M.R.E., Providence College, is Associate Professor of Ethics at St. Petersburg Junior College where he teaches Applied Ethics, Logic and Philosophy and is sponsor of the Phi Theta Kappa Chapter at the Tarpon Springs Center.

In part, this chapter will help you express your statements with an awareness of the patterns of *moral reasoning,* at least those in Western civilization. Perhaps it will help you win the next argument!

Throughout history, various civilizations and cultures have attempted, with varying degrees of success, to establish a rational and scientific system giving structure to the examination of various propositions and variables of human thought as expressed in language. Logic, for the record, can be seen as a discipline where mathematicians and philosophers got together and established some ground rules for examining the truthfulness or validity of what we say and how we say it. In much the same way, grammarians have developed a system of rules for language and sentence structure that is expressed, in part, by the diagramming of sentences. One of the rules is this: "A sentence must have a subject and a predicate." Similarly, mathematicians have created a system of notation and rules for the expression of concepts in mathematical terms.

Back to logic: In the evolution of recorded human thought, both Western and Eastern civilizations have contributed to systems by which propositions and variables may be stated and inferences and conclusions drawn. A *proposition* is a basic thought; e.g., "Humans eat food." A *variable* reflects modifications to that basic thought; e.g., "Some food is meat ... Some food is cold." *Inferences* are statements that can be drawn from the combining of propositions and variables; e.g., "Humans eat different kinds of food." *Conclusions* are statements that can be made as a result of reasoning the effects of propositions and variables and inferences upon each other (examining all the evidence as it were); e.g., "Not all the food humans eat is meat nor is it cold."

Chinese logic was very basic. It sought mainly to study the names of things and their relationship to each other. Indian logic ventured further, developing a system of categories, but it did not establish a system of variables. It succeeded in producing a five-member syllogism and an analysis of negation (the non-positive way of stating propositions; e.g., "No humans eat asteroids ... few eat rocks.")

Western thought leaped with Aristotle's formulation of predicate logic (which focused on noun expressions) and the Stoics advanced the logic of propositions. In the 17th century Leibniz advanced Western logic and Frege accelerated its development by the end of the 19th century. At the opening of the 20th century, the work of A.N. Whitehead and Bertrand Russell produced a masterpiece (*Principia Mathematica* 1910-1913), which brought logic to a still-higher level of mathematical and analytical sophistication.

The study of logic helps us understand that there are patterns of moral reasoning. It involves not only its history but also its philosophy, the notion of formal logic and the notion of applied logic. Philosophically, logic may be understood as a discipline that seeks to analyze truth in the expressions of language – just as physics studies truth in the physical realm. Logic may be understood two ways: (1) the study of truth solely based on the meanings of the terms in which they are expressed; or, more narrowly, (2) the study of truth that can be said to be valid if it meets the tests of the principle of predication and of certain specific terms known as logical constraints, including quantifiers, variables and connectives. Formal logic is a part of abstract discussion just as calculus is a part of mathematics – and might also be considered, comparably, to be on the same plane. Formal logic dissects propositions and their deductive arguments and studies the structures and logical forms found in them.

Applied logic is a discipline that not only deals with the basic forms of arguments but also adapts to daily life the abstract machinery and tools of pure logic to be used in examining down-to-earth issues of various subjects – that is, basic beliefs, commands and duties. Applied logic not only relates upward to the sciences and philosophy but also horizontally to everyday conversation, writings and public statements. It covers such concepts as these: The special relationships between two commands or between one question and another question; definitive forms of logic such as temporal logic or the logic of the parts and wholes; and other special forms such as, "I know ... ," "I believe ... ," "It is required ... ," "It is prohibited ...."

There also is a category called *informal logic*, which involves intuitive human processes of critical thinking. It includes the steps of observing, analyzing, developing potential solutions, verbalizing and evaluating, and is akin to the critical-thinking processes fully related in Chapter 2. Our purpose here is primarily restricted to making one aware that in the society in which we live and engage in discourse, we will find our statements subjected to the criticism of others who, knowingly or not, will be applying logic to test what we say and what we believe and what we do. Understanding these patterns of moral reasoning will help us think critically and avoid basic flaws in the way we present our thoughts to others.

STATEMENTS BUILT ON ROCK OR HOT AIR?

Often the way we state phrases can stifle conversation. Comments are made that are likely to be misinterpreted, distorted, or even understood but misapplied. Let's examine a point of view that starts out like this: "I'm in favor of limits on letting certain types of people into this country." This comment immediately evokes controversy, and lots of questions: What types of people? Poor? Non-English speaking? Those with large families? (Obviously, the operative word here – the pushed button – is "certain.") Once some elaboration has been elicited – say, "Those who are unskilled in a trade and who will not be able to carry their financial weight should be excluded from entering the country" – the next question is ... Why? And let's suppose the speaker responds thusly: "Because they will be a burden on the rest of us hard-working people because, let's face it, they are untrainable, uneducable, possibly unintelligent ... c'mon, most of them can't even speak our language."

Well, that's quite a mouthful and strongly put. But is it logical? Examined in terms of logic, does the argument stand up? Why, or why not? (Interestingly, if such an argument were to gain acceptance everywhere, would not every country then become isolated unto itself, at least in terms of human assimilation and acceptance? And would that be a good thing? Sometimes, the answer to an argument is simply to extend it onto a larger stage. At the very minimum, light is shed.)

What has been going on here is employment of one of the philosophical concepts drawn by John Rawls called the *"veil of ignorance."* This particular principle was discussed in Chapter 2 and is addressed later in Chapter 14. But by using the statement in a *reverse* manner, we can come to see the weakness of, "I'm in favor of limits on letting certain types of people into this country." Turn it around. Suppose, for instance, persons with a desire to learn high-tech medicine here in the U.S. can eventually practice back in their own countries, thus helping to control disease and increase quality of life in their homelands. In the long term this would reduce their dependence on First World countries. That way, everyone would gain.

A sound reasoning process in the presentation of any argument or discussion is essential to arriving at a reasonable and logical conclusion. Those questions mentioned previously may well be justified; maybe one doesn't understand how leading a person can elicit from them a wrong conclusion. Clarification of points leading to a conclusion may be necessary. It's possible that wrong assumptions are being made. Well-intentioned and well meaning persons at times have difficulty in trying to express their opinions. This can be caused by, among other things, ignorance, intimidation, language use, or at the very least being less informed on a topic than one should be to engage in a meaningful discussion.

Why do seemingly innocent discussions turn to arguments and why do arguments then progress (or regress) to outright confrontations and in some cases to hostile behavior? Often our arguments or decisions are based on just a few kinds of reasoning. People may make decisions because they believe it is a universal (or fundamental) law that must be followed. It can be reasonably assumed that students shouldn't cheat in a class, whether they are in St. Petersburg, Florida or St. Petersburg, Russia. There are some moral codes of reasoning that, for the great majority of people at least, appear inviolable.

The German philosopher Immanuel Kant, using *a priori* reasoning, concluded that universal moral laws do exist and proceeded to formulate his famous *categorical imperative,* which states that "one must will the maxim of his action to become universal law." Therefore, cheating or lying would be universally wrong if it were to become a norm of human behavior. Kant looked at what *ought* to be done, rather than what *is* being done (see Chapter 3).

But is it practical to assume that"right" behavior is that behavior which has been deemed correct in one's society? Various cultures have different codes or customs. In differing, cultures can become suspect in each other's eyes – questioned and deemed immoral by observers unfamiliar with those specific practices. For instance, suicide in some cultures is an expression of honor, whereas in some others it is illegal and/or wholly immoral. This is an example of *cultural relativism.* Businesses may find it difficult to compete in international markets when faced with paying bribes that in some countries are illegal while in others they are regarded simply as "a cost of doing business."

In the realm of cultural and social relativism, some practices may have been considered justifiable at some points in history while, in terms of modern values, they're judged now to have been wrong – and they certainly would be unacceptable in the 20th century; e.g. separate drinking facilities for minorities, denying women the right to vote or hold public office, which is still a practice in some nations.

Employing cultural relativism as the basis for reasoning can lead to several obvious problems. Can one culture dictate to another? Can persons in one culture, who find themselves immersed in another, ethically engage in the moral practices of that culture if they run contrary to their own? Case in point: In Saudi Arabia in 1991, during Operation Desert Storm, American servicewomen were utilized as truck drivers, a practice the Saudi society does not permit its women. Could the American women have reasonably defended their driving in a one-on-one scenario? Probably not to any effect, and they would have treaded on sensitivities besides. Some religions mandate that their followers work to convert others to their membership, while in some countries this practice of proselytizing is considered unethical and immoral under the penalty of death. What does good reasoning dictate in such a circumstance?

Another approach to reasoning is applying situational ethics, which involve *determining what is right for the moment.* For example, one might conclude that it is wrong to lie, but if a doctor surveys a situation whereby he or she must tell a patient some discouraging news, the physician may avoid doing so, believing that "now is not the right time," due to the possibility of increasing the traumatic condition of the patient. In a couple of days when the patient is better able to handle the situation, the doctor may then reveal the truth. But to delay telling the truth may not always be justifiable. For example, a restaurant operator has a restive employee whom he intends to fire – but suddenly a busy weekend is coming up and so he keeps her on board by telling her a promising future is at hand. His motive for hanging on to her applies only to the present situation. Does that justify his tactics for preventing her from leaving?

In this type of situation, a Kantian decision might better be called for, based upon what is in the best interests or well-being of the individual upon whom the action is being taken, and not by or for the interest of the doer. This is a major part of Kantian ethics and a measure of his formula in determining the Categorical Imperative – not using people as a means, but rather as an end.

Heretofore we have discussed single decisions made by an individual, usually toward another individual. Many various principles or philosophies can apply, as well as the thoughts of many philosophers. One that is certain to surface in the realm of a just decision, especially in regard to a society, would be that of John Rawls and his *veil of ignorance*. In this, Rawls states that when a decision is to be made, in order for it to be fair one must know the rules that will shape society and then consider the consequences of that rule – without knowing which side the rule-maker will fall on when the rule or decision is incorporated into that society. This, according to Rawls, is primary in the determination of a just society.

For example, let us suppose that a group of people is organizing a church and in the beginning it is necessary to use a space located in a small shopping mall. At the far end of the mall is a liquor store. The church begins to grow, and to occupy adjoining vacant storefronts. As it expands it draws closer and closer to the liquor store. Local law mandates that a liquor store may not operate within several hundred feet of a church. With church expansion, the law becomes violated. The church sues to have the liquor store removed based on the law. The law is a good law according to all involved, but when the judge rules, he upholds the law by ordering the *church* to move. This illustrates how the veil of ignorance might work.

The common problem with these approaches is that different conclusions are drawn form different backgrounds-which may include the categorical imperative, cultural relativism, situational ethics, veil of ignorance. As people of different cultural or social frames of reference meet to discuss issues – whether it be at a peace-negotiating table in some distant land, a group of disgruntled and racially mixed police officers in a large city, or a group of heterogeneous students in an academic setting – it is necessary to understand the nature of problems being discussed and the culture and moral norms of those involved in the discussion.

If we are to make our presence felt, if our ideas are to be given a fair hearing and if we expect to have a lasting influence on those interested in the discussion, it is essential that we present our thoughts, ideas and opinions in a factual, well-reasoned and well-organized manner.

This kind of presentation of our ideas may be termed *impact reasoning.* Among other things, it will be based on our value system, an understanding of the value systems of those around us, and the society into which we hope those thoughts and ideas will be inculcated. In sum, it is reasoning that, hopefully, will cause others to act according to our propositions.

But remember, social acceptance of a proposition does not make it moral (e.g., slavery in the United States before 1865). In the reasoning process, we hope to conclude with what we consider to be the right course of action, which may also be termed ethical behavior. But this then begs several questions: What is right? Who decides? What are the criteria used? Where do we begin?

THE PLACE TO START: ACQUIRE KNOWLEDGE

A Priori/A Posteriori Processes of Reasoning – Knowledge is acquired by two primary means called *a priori* and *a posteriori* reasoning. To begin with, in *a priori reasoning,* some knowledge can be claimed to be true or false universally. This type of knowledge is not dependent on any kinds of claims of empiricism (facts gained from experience). It does not, however, preclude that one learns a truth through a type of teaching process. For example, in the study of math, one needs to know that if a positive number is added to another positive number, the sum will increase. This is a universally accepted truth. If a statement is contradictory, then by definition it must be a false statement and its claim of being true can be universally disputed, i.e. a 12-year-old dog is not a puppy, by definition, even though its owner may say it acts like one.

A priori reasoning by all accounts then is knowledge learned through reason. If people are about to talk to a group and want to convince the audience that they should contribute to the cause of racial harmony, then the speakers should be aware of the type of audience they are addressing and take care not to offend with an alien style of discourse.

A posteriori reasoning is the use of knowledge gained through experience. The experience can be historical, anthropological, or may involve other kinds of data gained through human endeavor. For example, a certain battle may have occurred from which there are no survivors to relate the story of the events that took place. Historians in their attempt to discover the actual record of events may undertake to study the battle site, arrangements of artifacts, positions of those killed, types of armament, and from all of these pieces of evidence try to reconstruct some semblance of the battle. Various ideas and thoughts may emerge and as a result a close analysis may be made. There still may be certain bits of information that will be lacking and remain uknown to the historians, but the conclusion arrived at through their study and analysis would still have a great deal of credence.

May *a priori* and *a posteriori* reasoning cooperate in making arguments stronger? Yes. Let us consider the subject of mosquitoes. Using *a priori* reasoning we know that when certain elements are added together these factors create a larger total. This being the case, because it is known that mosquitoes breed in stagnant pools of water (*a posteriori* knowledge), to increase the number of opportunities to breed by creating additional open stagnant pools or marshes would add, of course, to the pestilence (*a priori* knowledge). Further studies might conclude that these breeding insects are causing encephalitis (this is done through testing thus is based on *a posteriori* reasoning). Reason, then, would dictate the removal from the area those elements contributing to the proliferation of mosquitoes.

Individual examples of *a priori* reasoning might further be demonstrated thusly:
1. No child is a senior citizen.
2. God cannot be omniscient and be contradictory.
3. A triangle has 180 degrees.

Examples of *a posteriori* reasoning might also include:
1. Earth is part of the galaxy known as the Milky Way.
2. During the week at Carova Beach, one encounters very few people.
3. Water freezes at 32 degrees Fahrenheit.

Applying these same techniques to moral reasoning, one can determine that it is wrong to lie by testing others (i.e., child lies to parent) and waiting for the consequences. Here one might have an observation of the conditions prior to the lie and the consequences may be minimal, if there are any at all. One could conclude it is all right to lie based solely on the consequences of this action; however, except for the recipient of the falsehood, those who know it is a lie know that an immoral or wrong action has been committed, *a priori*. This is why *a priori* claims are not dependent on circumstances but are known independently of the senses.

In summation then, we can state that there are two kinds of knowledge upon which philosophers agree: *A priori* reasoning, which is that knowledge based on the rational sense (reason) or gained prior to, or exclusive of, experience; and *a posteriori* reasoning, which is based on knowledge that has been acquired through sense experience. Most of our moral actions are based on *a posteriori* knowledge – on what has been deemed as good or bad, moral or immoral because of what we have learned.

Now, how shall we use these types of reasoning to make morally sound decisions? Once knowledge is attained and actions affecting that acquired knowledge are to be performed, it must then be determined who is to make the decision. A second step is to determine how the information affecting the action was obtained. The third step is determining whether a choice really exists.

Let's watch this process unfold in the following example of ethical reasoning (this example makes references to certain philosophers; other thinkers, great or small, might be used according to the preferences and values of the reasoner):

Who or what is the source of the knowledge? If an authority is cited (i.e. Bible [Old or New Testament], the Koran, the U.S. Constitution, or some element of society), is it legitimate and dependable? Are we truly free to choose, or has the choice been determined for us? If the choices are free, we can decide on our own authority. If the choice has been determined for us, then the decision is being based upon an outside lawgiver, which means individual or personal autonomy ceases to be a qualifier and authoritarian ethics takes hold and the decision maker is making a moral decision soley based upon an outside law-giver. For example, "Allah says, therefore Moslems do." Responsibility for the aforementioned choice is accorded the doer provided the doer was free to act. A difference between free will and freedom *of* will is the freedom to choose and the freedom to act. We all have the freedom to choose, but we do not always have the freedom to act. So in answering one question as to who is making the decision, although the action is being performed by an individual, is the person really free and fully informed enough to make the decision? Is it an act of an informed conscience? (According to John Stuart Mill this would be "educating the will by eradicating or weakening the desires that are likeliest to lead to evil.") If a person arrives at this point and sees that choices are available, then the responsibility for making one of the choices rests strictly with the decision maker.

PROCESSES OF ARGUMENTATION

At the outset of this chapter we were confronted by the problems of confusing and conflicting methods or statements in the presentation of arguments. Often discussions and conversations degenerate to arguments (sometimes pointless and needless) because of a statement that is misquoted, misapplied or simply misunderstood. Arguments, however, if constructed carefully, can be informative, educational, instructional and above all a means of constructing a positive course of action. Arguments through reason are very beneficial. Great philosophers, as we saw in Chapter 3, have contributed to great changes through inquiry and argumentation leading to rational discourse. Of course this last element, rational discourse, if it is the focus of any group, must be done with great care and planning. This is difficult when most comments are made from "how one feels" about a situation rather than "how one thinks" about it, or "how one knows" a point to be discussed. Points of view and opinions, as previously stated, are good starting points if they are based on rational thought. Otherwise, one unfounded point of view is as valid as another.

How do people know if they have constructed a good moral argument? There are two methods of identification to test the validity of an argument: (1) through the use of a negative method known as the detection of fallacies; or (2) through the use of formal analysis of the argument, which is logic, a positive method.

FAULTY REASONING

When a person reasons through a logical process, it is understood that he or she is reasoning through analysis –probing thought. If this type of reasoning is seen as flawed or fraught with error, one is then said to be guilty of fallacious reasoning.

FREQUENT FLAW: FALLACIOUS REASONING

Often people like to win arguments at any cost. They do this by using emotional appeals, by employing arguments that are totally erroneous and often illogical, or sometimes by exploiting situations that are advantageous to themselves. The purpose here is to win an argument using psychological means. It is very important to adherents of valid logic that this type of fallacious reasoning be avoided, and at the very least recognized by those who are being argued against. At least in this way, the person being argued against sees the invalidities for what they are.

Let us look at some of the types of fallacies that are used in everyday conversations. But first, be advised that the exact titles for these fallacies may appear slightly different than one source to another. Approximately 120 different fallacies have been identified. Some are similar to others. There is no national standard for the titles given these fallacies. The titles below are those chosen by the author and the fallacies described are most frequently titled as listed here.

COMMON FALLACIES
(from Latin *fallere* – to deceive)

An informal fallacy is an incorrect way of reasoning. It involves a manner of deception, intended or unintended. It is an attempt to persuade emotionally or psychologically, but not logically.

Informal fallacies are called such because of the *wording* of the argument, not the *form* in which the arguments are constructed.

Detection of fallacies is done through analysis of the content of the argument. The fallacies are mistakes that arise in ordinary conversation, rendering the argument(s) unsound.

1. AMBIGUITY— An argument is ambiguous if it shifts the meaning of a term or phrase in the middle of the argument. It occurs when we use a word or phrase in such a way that its meaning is not clear or can be taken in more than one way. Two ways in which an argument can be claimed to be ambiguous:

a) equivocation – A play on words by the arguer when the conclusion of the argument depends on one or more words being used, either explicitly or implicitly, in two different senses in the argument.

- I have a right to say what is necessary.
- What I am expressing I believe is right.
- Therefore, it is necessary that I express what I believe.

The problem here is in the use of the word "right" because (1) in the first premise, it indicates a freedom, whereas in (2) the second premise, the "right" is a moral belief. These uses of the term are not in the same context and therefore are in conflict.

b) amphiboly – The arguer misinterprets a statement that is ambiguous owing to some structural defect and *proceeds to draw a conclusion based on this faulty interpretation*. A grammarian might look upon this as a "dangling participle."

- The guide said standing in Tampa Bay, the Vinoy Hotel could be easily recognized.
- We can only conclude that the Vinoy Hotel must be in Tampa Bay.

The problem is that it is unclear whether the guide is standing in Tampa Bay or the Vinoy Hotel is standing in Tampa Bay. The statement is rendered confusing by inherent faulty word usage.

2. GENETIC FALLACY — This is an attempt to discredit a position by condemning its source, or beginning (genesis), or to establish a position by condemning the source of an opposed viewpoint. Two types of genetic fallacy are common:

a) *ad hominen* abusive (to the man) – This is an attempt to disparage the character of the person presenting the argument, to deny that person's intelligence, or to question his or her integrity, while not addressing the statements or arguments being presented. This is sometimes a "guilt by association" attack, and is also known as character assassination.

- Those who opposed the war were obviously wrong; they were just a bunch of cowardly, leftwing Libertarians.

b) *ad hominem* circumstantial – This begins the same way as "abusive," but instead of using verbal abuse in attacking the opponent, the person attempts to discredit the arguer's statements by alluding to certain circumstances that affect the opponent. This charges that the arguer is so prejudiced that he or she cannot be objective in his or her views.

- The Student Government is making bad policy for this college. But I suppose it should be expected because they're all members of the Young Turks political party.

3. FAULTY CAUSATION — This occurs whenever the connection between the premises and the conclusion depends on some imagined causal connection that more than likely does not exist. Sometimes in a causation argument, the cause can be valid, so examination of the facts is very important before "faulty" can be claimed. Three types of faulty causation are:

a) *Post Hoc* – (after the thing) – This states that because one event followed a previous event, the one following was caused by the first event and, therefore, similar events are likely to occur in the future.

- Allen had a beer and then got 100% on an Ethics exam.
- Therefore, Allen got 100% *because* he had a beer.

While the premise here may be true, it did not necessarily cause the conclusion.

b) *Slippery Slope* – This occurs when the conclusion of an argument depends upon the claim that a certain event will set off a chain reaction, leading in the end to some undesirable consequence – yet there is not sufficient logical reason why the chain reaction should take place.

- I certainly will not allow my daughter to go to the party down the street. I know that beer will be sneaked in and when that is gone, the party-goers will resort to smoking the weed, then they'll start smoking crack, lose their inhibitions and become sexually promiscuous, and she'll come home pregnant and I'm totally against her having an abortion, so she'll have to drop out of school. She's not going!!!

c) *Causal Inference From A Statistical Correlation* – This occurs when one states that because two phenomena are related statistically, they must be related causally. We can use statistics to help support an argument, but statistics only help; they do not of themselves prove anything.

- In 1985 the speed limit on the Penn turnpike was 55 m.p.h. and there were 25 fatalities. In 1986, the speed limit was raised to 65 m.p.h. and there were 50 fatalities. We can only conclude that whenever the speed limit on a highway is increased by 10 m.p.h. the fatality rate will double.

4. FALSE APPEAL TO AUTHORITY — This occurs when an alleged authority is not qualified or where there is reason to believe the authority is wrong, biased, or lying. One must be careful here, because there can be times when the "authority" or "group" may be in fact an acknowledged expert in the field in which the argument is being held. For example, the Surgeon General's report on cigarette smoking as being a hazard to one's health is a legitimate appeal to authority.

Example of fallacy: That great pianist Ray Charles says Pepsi is the best soft drink around. It must be, if Ray says so.

Or:

If, in an argument about creationism and religion, one appeals to Darwin, an expert in biology, the appeal would be fallacious.

5. ARGUMENT TO THE PEOPLE (*arguments ad popularum*) —This also is known as the "appeal to emotion." This fallacy is used to replace reason and rationality as the norm and is calculated to excite through enthusiasm, excitement, love or hate. Very often the advertising media use it to entice, employing such terminology as " the best," "the most nutritious," *et cetera.*

• Instead of arguing the facts of an issue, a writer might play upon the readers' negative response to such words as "communism" and "fascism" or their positive response to words and concepts like "God," "country," and "liberty." In the statement, "If you are a true American, you will vote against the referendum on busing," the writer avoids any discussion of the merits or weaknesses of the bill and merely substitutes an emotional appeal.

6. INVINCIBLE IGNORANCE — Despite facts to the contrary, the arguer insists on propounding the proposition or argument as legitimate.

- I really don't care where you got your map, I've traveled to Tallahassee many times and I know you must go through Fort Myers to get there.

7. ARGUMENT FROM IGNORANCE — The arguer insists that a statement is true until proved false or false until proved true. This fallacy happens in the developing sciences, psychic phenomena, and often in matters of religion.

- Scientists have been trying to prove for years that planet Earth was visted by alien beings eons ago. No proof exists. We can conclude that no alien being from outer space has ever visited planet Earth.

Note that the premises here are true. There is a strong inductive argument here, but an invalid deductive argument and conclusion.

8. INCONSISTENCY — This amounts to believing logically incompatible things at the same time. It is perhaps the most important fallacy! Consistency requires that we work out a harmony between our *ethical* beliefs and the way we live.

Inconsistency occurs when we contradict ourselves in word or action *without justification for the change.*

This fallacy is very common in parenting and politics and is often identified with the statement, "Do as I say, not as I do."

- On the first day a group is told, "I'll support stronger emission standards." Here the politician is talking to environmentalists. The next day he exclaims, "I'll do whatever I can to lower emission standards, if elected." On this day he is talking to industrialists.

9. STRAW MAN — This occurs when the arguer distorts the opponent's argument, attacks the weakend argument, and then concludes that the argument has been won. The term is derived from "setting up" an opponent as a straw man, or scarecrow, and then knocking him down.

- A candidate for town council suggests that an economy move for the town might be to eliminate using the lights at night on the Little League field. Her opponent picks up on this, claims that the youths will "suffer" in their program by having to cut their schedule, and then charges that the candidate doing the suggesting is obviously against youth programs in the town.

10. RED HERRING — This argument introduces an irrelevant point to divert the reader's attention from the main issue. This term originates from the tactic used by escaped prisoners of dragging a strong-smelling fish across their trail to confuse tracking dogs by making them follow the wrong scent. Example: Roommate A criticizes roommate B for his repeated failure to do the dishes when it was his turn. To escape the charges, B brings up instances in the past when A failed to repay money he borrowed. While A may indeed have a problem remembering his debt, that point isn't relevant to the original argument about sharing the responsibility for the dishes. (For this fallacy, the author drew from Jean Wyrick's book *Steps to Writing Well,* 4th ed. Holt, Rineheart and Winston, 1990, pp. 204, 223-225.)

11. EITHER-OR — The argument tries to suggest that there are only two sides to an issue – one right, one wrong.

- Example: "If you don't go to war against Iceland, you don't love your country." The statement is irrational because it fails to consider all reasonable possibilities, such as a patriotic people's right to oppose war as an expression of love for their country.

12. HASTY CONCLUSION (sometimes called Hasty Generalization) — This is caused by too much reliance upon inductive reasoning. Usually a hasty conclusion is reached concerning an entire group of things or individuals based on premises referencing a small sampling or an atypical sampling. Polls sometimes can be included in this fallacy, and stereotypes are typical of this fallacy. It is when one projects a general rule from a specific case.

- Example: This morning's paper had three stories about high school students from three sections of town who were involved in drug dealing. Therefore, young high school students in today's society are nothing but druggies and pushers.

After one is able to gather information, one must present that information in an acceptable manner. Let us now look at the types of arguments used and their construction or form. Arguments can be of two types: Deductive or inductive.

DEDUCTIVE AND INDUCTIVE REASONING

Deductive arguments are arguments that are so strong that the conclusion could not possibly be false if the premises are all true. In other words, in deductive arguments, the conclusion necessarily follows from the premises, or the premises, if true, prove the conclusion conclusively. Deductive arguments often can progress from a general first premise —if it is true—to a more specific conclusion. However, if the premise contains universal statements, then the conclusion must be universal.

Example: All citrus are fruit.

All oranges are citrus.

All oranges are fruit.

Inductive arguments are such that, the premises, if true, make the conclusion probable, or likely to be true, and which therefore make it reasonable to accept the conclusion. The conclusion, however, does not necessarily follow from the premises, even if the premises are true. The conclusion is essentially an "educated guess," based on reasonable probabilities. The rule of thumb here is that inductive arguments progress from a specific first premise to a more general conclusion with a qualifier such as "probably."

Example: All human beings have moral consciences.

The President of the United States is a human being.

The President of the United States probably has a moral conscience.

The preceding argument, of course, presents a fairly weak but valid, inductive conclusion. As more supporting examples are offered, the more probable and stronger the conclusion becomes.

Scientific or empirical method employs inductive reasoning. The theory of evolution, for example, is based on inductive reasoning; the conclusion that human beings are a product of an evolutionary process is an inductive conclusion. It may be a highly probable conclusion, but it is not absolutely provable, and thus is designated a "theory," not a proof.

Inductive reasoning is the type of reasoning that leads to advances in human knowledge, because it leads to conclusions not necessarily contained in the premises; one makes a leap into the probable. Deductive reasoning leads to more definite conclusions, but does not lead to knowledge break-throughs, because the conclusion is contained in the premises.

VALIDITY AND SOUNDNESS

In addition to understanding inductive and deductive reasoning, it is necessary to distinguish between soundness and validity in argumentation. A valid argument is simply an argument that is logically consistent; that is, an argument is valid if the given conclusion would necessarily follow from the given premises in that argument.

> Example: All human beings are purple.
>
> Jennifer is a human being.
>
> Jennifer is purple.

Notice that validity concerns only the form or structure of the argument and not the content of the argument; it has nothing to do with the argument's truth or falsity. A sound argument is a valid argument with only *true* premises. The above argument is therefore unsound, even though it is valid. A helpful way to remember these concepts is: validity=form; soundness=truth.

Soundness, then, concerns both form (or structure) and content. (See A. P. Martinich later in this chapter for further discussion.)

> Example: All human beings breathe oxygen.
>
> Karen is a human being.
>
> Karen breathes oxygen.

Because this is a valid argument containing only true premises, the argument is sound.

STANDARD ARGUMENT FORMS

The most common argument forms have been given standardized names. There are a few common standard argument forms, and if sound,they are all deductive and valid. In the following argument structures the symbols being used (P, Q) have only representational value. Other symbols (S,M,P, e.g.) may be used interchangeably. The first term of the equation (in our example, P) is known as the antecedent. *Ante* means "earlier" or "in front of," so the antecedent is the earlier part of the equation; the P is in front of the Q. The Q term represents the consequent. The consequent is the "result" or the consequent or consequence of an earlier action or event. (In the first example of the four standard argument forms, John is guilty of premeditated murder as a result (consequent) of the earlier (antecedent) condition of having intentionally killed Susan). Logical conclusions are reached either by affirming the antecedent or by denying the consequent.

A conditional syllogism simply traces a causally related series of events to their logical conclusion. In the game of dominoes, for example, if the dominoes are arranged so that knocking down the first one will cause the second one to fall, and the second one will cause the third to fall, and so on until the last domino falls, then logic tells us that knocking down the first domino will cause the last one to fall. Likewise, in any causally related series of events, then, it is logical for us to conclude that if a first event occurs, then the last one will also necessarily occur.

Lastly, a disjunction simply refers to events, things, or possibilities that are separated or that cannot be joined. Therefore, a disjunctive syllogism presents an "either-or" situation. Other types of argument forms can be proven true or false through "truth tables" discussed in courses in mathematics and formal logic. Some standard argument forms are presented below. Here are the meanings of the transactional symbols used: $\Rightarrow$ = then; $\therefore$ = therefore; $\sim$ = not; v = either-or.

1. **Modus Ponens (MP)**

   (affirming the antecedent)

   P = antecedent

   Q = consequent

	$P \Rightarrow Q$	If P, then Q
	$\underline{P}$	$\underline{\text{P (is affirmed)}}$
	$\therefore \quad Q$	Therefore Q

   Example: $P \Rightarrow Q$ If John intentionally killed Susan, then he is guilty of premeditated murder.

   $\underline{P}$ $\underline{\text{John intentionally killed Susan.}}$

   $\therefore \quad Q$ Therefore John is guilty of premeditated murder.

2. **Modus Tollens (MT)**

   (denying the consequent)

	$P \Rightarrow Q$	If P then Q
	$\underline{\sim \quad Q}$	$\underline{\text{Not Q}}$
	$\therefore \quad \sim P$	Therefore not P

   Example: $P \Rightarrow Q$ If John intentionally killed Susan, then he is guilty of premeditated murder.

   $\underline{\sim \quad Q}$ $\underline{\text{John is not guilty of premeditated murder.}}$

   $\therefore \quad \sim P$ Therefore John did not intentionally kill Susan.

3. **Disjunctive Syllogism (DS)**

   (denying either term of

   a disjunction)

	$P \text{ v } Q$	Either P or Q
	$\underline{\sim \quad P}$	$\underline{\text{Not P}}$
	$\therefore \quad Q$	Therefore not Q
	$P \text{ v } Q$	Either P or Q
	$\underline{\sim \quad Q}$	$\underline{\text{Not Q}}$
	$\therefore \quad P$	Therefore P

   Example: $P \text{ v } Q$ Either John killed Susan or he is not guilty of murder.

Example:	P v Q	Either John killed Susan or he is not guilty of murder.
	~ P	John did not kill Susan.
	∴ Q	Therefore he is not guilty of murder.

Example:	P v Q	Either John killed Susan or he is not guilty of murder.
	~ Q	John is guilty of murder.
	∴ P	Therefore John killed Susan.

This would be a good time to look at a few simple rules to keep in mind when formulating deductive arguments through the use of the categorical syllogism.

1) There must be two premises with two terms in each premise.

2) There must be a total of three terms in the two premises and conclusion.

3) Any syllogism that contains a premise beginning with "some," must have a conclusion proclaiming *some*. In other words, an argument with one premise beginning with "all" and another with "some" *must* have a conclusion beginning with some.

4) If both premises begin with "all," then the conclusion must end with *all*.

5) If one premise contains a negative such as, "Flamingos are not black," then the conclusion *must* contain a negative (no, are not).

6) If both premises contain negatives, then the argument is invalid.

Arguments are invalid if they violate any of these rules of deductive reasoning. The following figure summarizes common violations:

INVALID ARGUMENTS

1. An argument is invalid if it *attempts to affirm the consequent.*

2. An argument is invalid if it *denies the antecedent.*

3. An argument is invalid if it *denies either term of a disjunctive.*

4. An argument is invalid if a premise *contains a negative and the conclusion does not.*

Summary — Logical Applications

As we have noted, a deductive argument is a reasoning process that frequently can progress from a general first premise to a more specific conclusion, although this is not so in every case. The structure, then, of a typical deductive moral argument is as follows:

---

1. General moral principle

          2. Fact or non-moral premise

                    3. Specific moral judgment

An example of applying this would be as follows:

---

1. All killing is wrong.

        2. Capital punishment is killing.

                3. Capital punishment is wrong.

This argument (about capital punishment) begins with a *general* statement about killing being wrong, and concludes with a statement about a *specific* example of killing being wrong. Often when people make moral claims, they imply in those claims general moral principles. For example, if someone made the statement, "I believe abortion is wrong because it involves killing an innocent human being," they are implying that "it is wrong to kill an innocent human being." This is their *general moral principle*. Their *fact or non-moral premise* is "abortion involves killing an innocent human being." Their *specific moral judgment* (or conclusion) is, then, "abortion is wrong." It is helpful, in argumentation, to be able to dissect and separate the argument into (at least) these three distinct elements of it. In this way, the arguers can determine what general principles they are dealing with, and they can debate, initially, the merits of, and points of agreement concerning those general principles. Also, by introducing other issues that, if accepted, would seem to contradict those general moral principles, the arguers can determine whether or not the individual who makes a specific moral claim is consistent in opposing all (or other) specific examples that would violate their own implied general principle(s).

For example, in the above statement about abortion, an arguer who disagrees with this conclusion should cite other examples of killing that the individual opposing abortion may find morally justifiable. If the abortion opponent favors euthanasia, for example, this would seem to be a contradiction, and those arguing against the abortion opponent could note this and ask for clarification. This method of arguing helps keep arguments on a rational, rather than an emotional, plane.

© 1989 Creators Syndicate, Inc.

3-24

READINGS
LOGIC AND ARGUMENT FOR WRITING
A. P. Martinich

Reflection, would realize that *argument* is in fact equivocal; that is, has more than one sense or meaning. In one sense, *argument* is roughly synonymous with *quarrel*, and in another sense it is roughly synonymous with *reasoning*. In theory, philosophers engage only in the latter, although sometimes in the rush of disputation they stumble into the former. The philosophically relevant sense of *argument* has been made more precise by logicians who, in the course of 2,500 years, have discovered quite a bit – though far from everything – about arguments. Although this is not a logic text, a little logic is crucial for understanding the structure of a philosophical essay. (For a brief account, but one fuller than that given here, I recommend Wesley Salmon's *Logic*, second edition, Englewood Cliffs, NJ: Prentice Hall, 1981; for a full account, I recommend *Logic and Philosophy* by Howard Kahane, Belmont, Cal.: Wadsworth, 1984.)

WHAT IS A GOOD ARGUMENT

At the simplest level, there are two kinds of arguments: Good arguments and bad arguments. A good argument is one that does what it is supposed to do. A bad argument is one that does not. A good argument is one that shows a person a rational way to go from true premises to a true conclusion, as well as the subject allows. (Some subjects more easily or certainly show the way than others, say, mathematics more than aesthetics.) As explained here, a good argument is relative to a person. What might legitimately lead one person to a conclusion might not lead another person to the same conclusion, because so much depends upon the person's background beliefs. What a contemporary philosopher or physicist would recognize as a good argument is often not what an ancient Greek, even Plato, Aristotle, Ptolemy, or Euclid, would have recognized. Also, there may have been arguments that the ancient Greeks recognized as good arguments that we cannot.

The notion of a "good argument" is an intuitive one.

In this chapter I want to make this intuitive notion progressively more precise by considering the following definitions:

Df(1)An argument is a sequence of two or more propositions of which one is designated as the conclusion and all the others as premises.

Df(2)A sound argument is an argument that is valid and that contains only true premises.

Df(3)An argument is valid if and only if it is necessary that if all the premises are true then the conclusion is true.

Df(4)A cogent argument is a sound argument that is recognized to be such in virtue of the presentation of its structure and content.

Each of these definitions contains key technical terms and ideas that need to be explained, including *proposition* and *valid*. Let's begin by looking at Df(1), the definition of *argument*. Notice that an argument is characterized as a "sequence of propositions." Although *proposition* could be given a more technical formulation, for our purposes it is sufficient to understand this term as equivalent to a sentence that has a truth value' that is, it is a sentence that is either true or false. Propositions are sometimes contrasted with questions and commands, which cannot be true or false. *Proposition* is often used interchangeably with *statement* and *assertion* even though the meanings of these words can be different in important ways.

Returning to the definition of *argument*, we should notice that an argument is a *sequence* of propositions because the propositions are supposed to be related in some logically significant way. One of these propositions will be designated as the conclusion, that is, the proposition that is to be proved. Within the context of an essay as a whole, the conclusion is the thesis. Since subordinate propositions within the essay may have to be proved, these subordinate propositions may also be conclusions with their own sets of supporting premises. The premises are the propositions that lead to the conclusion. They provide the justification for the conclusion.

The above definition is abstract. Let's make it a bit less so by considering an extremely spare argument.

All humans are mortals. Socrates is a human.

Therefore, Socrates is mortal.

The first two sentences are premises. The third is the conclusion, as indicated by the word *therefore*. The premises are supposed to provide the rational force for accepting the conclusion. While this is a good argument, it is rhetorically lame. No one would seriously argue for such an obvious conclusion. It rarely happens that three simple sentences constitute a rationally persuasive argument, which typically requires elaboration and embellishment. Yet, at the beginning of our study, it is wise to keep the matter as simple as possible.

The definition of *argument* in Df(1) is neutral with respect to the issue of whether an argument is defective (bad) or not. Some arguments are defective and some are not. Our goal is to understand the nature of all arguments by concentrating on what constitutes a good one. We understand what a defective argument is by understanding how it fails to measure up to the criteria for good arguments. We do not understand a good argument by understanding how it fails to involve one or another mistake. As Parmenides said, "The ways of falsehood are infinite, while the way of truth is one."

To further refine the definition of a good argument, let's now consider the concept of a sound argument given in Df(2):

Df(2)A sound argument is an argument that is valid and that contains only true premises.

As this definition makes clear, there are two aspects to a sound argument: Validity and truth. An argument is unsound in either of two cases: If it is invalid or if one or more of its premises are false. Thus, to show that your argument is sound, you must show that the argument is valid and the premises are true. Since a sound argument is partially defined in terms of validity and since validity is a technical notion, we need a definition of it:

Df(3)An argument is valid if and only if it is necessary that if all the premises are true then the conclusion is true.

To put this in a slightly more colloquial form, the conclusion of a valid argument must be true whenever all its premises are true. The truth of the premises guarantees the truth of the conclusion.

In Df(3), validity is defined in terms of truth and necessity. Further, in Df(4) a cogent argument is partially defined in terms of a sound argument; and a sound argument is partially defined in Df(2) in terms of an argument; and an argument is partially defined in Df(1) as consisting of premises and a conclusion. This process of defining one thing in terms of other things cannot go on forever, no more than the stability of the Earth can be explained by saying that it sits on the back of an elephant that rests on the back of another elephant, that rests on the back of another elephant, ad infinitum. At some point, the process of

explanation must end. (Under all the elephants is a tortoise; and that is the end of it.)

As regards validity (and hence soundness and cogency), the process of explanation ends with truth and necessity. These two concepts are being taken as basic and will not be defined. I am relying upon our common understanding of the notions of truth and necessity to carry us. This is not to say that these notions are not problematic; it is just that one must stop somewhere. Cogency, soundness, and validity could have been defined using some other terms, and then some terms other than truth and necessity would have been basic and undefined.

There is nothing objectionable in leaving some terms undefined. Indeed, it is inescapable. In order to *say* anything, one must assume that the meanings of some words are understood. (This may form the foundation for a paradox involving how it is possible for people to learn a language if one must already know words before one can say anything; fortunately such a possible paradox is not our problem here.) In every enterprise, one eventually gets to a point at which something must be accepted without definition or argument. If the arguer and arguee cannot agree on any such point, there is a sense in which argument cannot get started. However, although neither *truth* nor *necessity* will be defined, a little more can and will be said about validity in Section 2 of this chapter.

A sound argument is a valid argument with true premises. Yet many sound arguments are unhelpful because they are not recognizable as such. They are not recognizable as good arguments. To incorporate the aspect of recognizability into our intuitive notion of a good argument, we must introduce the idea of a cogent argument, as spelled out in Df(4).

Df(4)A cogent argument is a sound argument that is recognized to be such by virtue of the presentation of its structure and content.

There are many reasons why a rational person might not recognize a good argument. If its logical form is too complex for any human being to recognize or the evidence needed to show that the premises are true is simply not available, a sound argument would necessarily fail to be cogent, because the condition of recognizability would be impossible to satisfy. However, many sound arguments are, as a matter of fact, not cogent because they are not properly formulated and/or adequate evidence is not adduced in support of key premises. Proper formulation of an argument involves its structure: The argument must be valid and the premises and conclusion must be set out in such a way that its validity is apparent. The matter of evidence, on the other hand, is related to an argument's content and involves once again the notion of truth. Each individual premise must be true, and the evidence presented must make the truth of each premise clear.

The intuitive notion of a good argument that we started with at the beginning of this chapter has evolved into the notion of a cogent argument. We can now summarize by saying that a good (i.e., cogent) argument involves three things: Formal validity (structure), true premises (content), and recognizability. This is what you should strive for in your writing. If any one of these elements is missing, your argument will not be cogent; if they are all present, it will be. (This is just a way of saying that these elements are individually necessary and jointly sufficient to produce a cogent argument.)

(Excerpted from *Philosophical Writing* by A.P.\Martinich, Prentice Hall, 1989.)

THE ALLEGORY OF THE CAVE
Plato

"Now, Glaucon," I said, "let me show in a figure how far our nature is enlightened. Behold, human beings living in an underground cave, which has a mouth open toward the light! Here they have been from their childhood, and are chained so that they can only see before them. Above and behind them a fire is blazing, and between the fire and these prisoners there is a raised way. You will see, if you look, a low wall like the screen which marionette players have in front of them, over which they throw their puppets."

"I see."

"And do you see men passing along the wall carrying all sorts of vessels and statues and figures of animals made of various materials, which appear over the wall? Some of them are talking, others silent."

"You have shown me a strange image, Socrates and they are strange prisoners."

"Like ourselves," I replied, "they see only their own shadows, or the shadows of one another, which the fire throws on the opposite wall of the cave."

"True," he said. "How could they see anything but shadows if they were never allowed to move their heads?"

"And of the objects which are being carried, in like manner they would see only the shadows. If they were able to converse with one another, would they not suppose that they were naming what was actually before them?"

"Very true."

"Suppose further that the prison had an echo which came from the other side. Would they not be sure to fancy, when one of the passers-by spoke, that the voice which they heard came from a passing shadow? To them the Truth would be literally nothing but the shadows of the images."

"That is certain."

"Look again! You see what will naturally follow if the prisoners are set free and so come to realize their error. At first when one of them is liberated and suddenly compelled to turn his neck round and look toward the light, he will suffer sharp pains. The glare will distress him. He will be unable to see the realities of which, in his former state, he saw only the shadows. Then conceive someone as saying to him that the shadows and images which he saw before were an illusion. But that now, when his is approaching nearer to Being and his eye is turned toward more real existence, he has a clearer vision. Will he not fancy that the shadows which he formerly saw are truer than the objects which are now shown to him?"

"Far truer, Socrates," he replied.

"He will be required to grow accustomed to the sight of the upper world. At first he will see the the shadows best. Last of all he will be able to see the sun, in its own proper place, and not mere reflections of it. He will then proceed to argue that this is what gives the seasons and in a certain way causes all things which he and his fellows have been accustomed to behold. When he remembers his old habitation and the wisdom of the cave and of his fellow prisoners, do you not suppose that he will pity them?"

"He most certainly will."

"If the inhabitants of the cave have been in the habit of conferring honors among themselves, he will no longer care for such honors or envy the possessors of them. Will he not endure anything rather than think as they do and live after their manner? If, however, such a one were suddenly to come out of the sun and be placed again in his old situation, he would be certain to have his eyes full of darkness. It would be very bad for him if there were a contest and he had to compete in measuring the shadows with the prisoners who had never moved out of the cave. In such an instance, the men of the cave would say of him that up he went and down he came without his eyes. They will maintain that it is better not even to think of ascending. Hence, if anyone tried to loose another from the cave and lead him up to the light, let them only catch the offender, and they would put him to death."

"No question, Socrates."

"This entire allegory you may now append, dear Glaucon, to the previous argument. The prison-house is the world of sight. The light of the fire is the sun. And the journey upward is the ascent of the soul into the intellectual world. Whether true or false, my opinion is that in the world of knowledge the Idea of Good appears last of all. It is the power upon which he would act rationally either in public or private life must fix his eyes. Moreover, you must not wonder that those who attain to this beatific vision are unwilling to descend to human affairs. Their souls are ever hastening into the upper world where they desire to dwell."

"Yes, this would be natural."

"And is there anything surprising, if one who passes from Divine contemplations to the evil state of man should be guilty of misbehaving? The bewilderments of the eyes arise from two causes – either coming out of the light, or going into the light. They are true of the mind's eye quite as much as of the bodily eye. He who remembers this when he sees anyone with perplexed and weak vision will not be too ready to laugh."

"Very true."

"Therefore, must there not be an art which will effect the conversion from Becoming to Being in the easiest and quickest manner?"

"Indeed there must, Socrates."

"By this conversion wisdom is rendered useful and profitable, or, on the other hand, hurtful and useless. Did you never observe the narrow intelligence flashing from the keen eye of a clever rogue? How eager he is. How clearly his paltry soul sees the clever way to his end! He is the reverse of the blind, but his keen eyesight is forced into the service of evil. And he is mischievous in proportion to his cleverness. But what if there had been a circumcision of such natures in the days of their youth? What if they had been severed then from their sensual pleasure? Then the very same faculty in them which is the cause of their evil would now see the Truth. This they would see as keenly as that to which their eyes are now turned."

"Very true," he replied.

"Then, " I said, "the business of us who are the founders of the state will be to compel the best minds to attain that knowledge which we have shown to be the greatest. They must continue to ascend until they arrive at the Good. When they have ascended and seen enough, however, we must now allow them to do as they now do. I mean that they must not be allowed to remain in the upper world, but must descend again among the prisoners in the cave and partake of their labors and honors, whether these are worth having or not."

"But is not this unjust? Ought we to give our best minds a worse life, when they might have a better?"

(from *PLATO'S COMPLETE WORKS* (abridged) by Henry Drake, Littlefield, Adams & Co. Paterson, New Jersey, 1959.)

THE FORMAL CAUSE OF EDUCATION
A. The First Essential Element For an Educated Man – Objective Truth

Robert J. Slavin

Thomistic education comprises two essential elements, the metaphysical and the psychological; or, in simpler language, education is concerned with objective truth and subjective development. Man in attaining this objective truth must be prepared not only for *learning* but also for *living*. The end of learning is the attainment of the intellectual habits or virtues; development for living demands the building in of the moral habits. The truly educated man will possess both objective truth and the twofold subjective development. To separate them, or to stress education for living while ignoring the intellectual virtues required for learning, has resulted in much of our present-day educational quackery. A mere knowledge of facts and things offers no genuine contribution to learning, to living, or to the attitude towards life as a whole which education should impart. Even vocational education, to be really considered education, should help integrate the student's life so as to enable him to see his work in relation to other types of work and to life. The more vicious error is that which insists on scholarship as an end in itself. Scholarship is good only for a mind that seeks to know totality of all things.

The horizon of education is limited only by the plasticity of the mind of man to attain being. If one would be a lover of wisdom, which is the end of education, the entire range of being is the field of his work. Moreover, since order is necessary for a proper knowledge of things, a hierarchy must be established which sets forth the relation of one known thing to another. Into this hierarchy must be incorporated scientific observations and individual facts. It is when facts become unified in a body of truth that they have significance in respect to the whole. The essential order demanded by wisdom is unity in multiplicity, for partial knowledge is not true knowledge either of the whole or of the part. For Thomas Aquinas certain definite truths, whose broad outlines embrace the totality of being, constitute the first essential element in the philosophy of education. These truths are:

I. *Objectivity of human thought.* The intelligible species, the subjective impressions and determinations of our intellect, are not the direct objects of thought. They are means by which the mind is led to a direct knowledge of objective reality. What we know first of all is the external object of which the species is a mental sign.[1] In the relation of the content of our act of thought in reality consists the truth of our knowledge. This character of truth does not presuppose a mechanical similarity between the manner of knowing and the manner of being of the object.[2] While knowledge is derived from experience, the intellect knows things according to its own nature.[3]

2. *The meaning of being.* That which our intellect attains primarily and into which it resolves all its concepts is being. It is necessary that we acquire all other concepts by addition to being. While knowledge is a science of things, intellectual knowledge penetrates the essence of things and implies a grasp of the very reason of being in things.[4] Being would not be attained by knowing if knowing did not already belong to being. Therefore the most perfect and intimate way of possessing a thing is by knowing it.[5]

3. *The Source of being.* Since created things partake of being they have their source in that Being whose essence is His existence.[6] Human thought is led as by a magnet toward Supreme Being, for God is the First Mover in the order of knowledge just as He is the First Cause in the order of being.[7] The object of knowledge is to arrange the parts of the world in perfect unity, estimate their relative values and unite them to Absolute Being. If there are things for the mind to know, it is in virtue of the conformity of beings with the Divine Intellect.[8] In other words, created truth is ordered towards Being, which is its End and Source, since by Being alone it exists and is perfected.

4. *The reality of supernatural truth.* Things are because God is. Knowing this from reason, there is yet a desire to penetrate into the inner life of God, and here philosophy is brought to a standstill. God's promise, however, is that our truth will be perfected by His Truth. In the philosophy of St. Thomas there is ample room left for the insertion of a divine gift which brings the intellect to the highest perfection of which it is capable.[9] Since the intellect is capable, in a finite way, of total intelligibility if God bestows this gift, Aquinas opens the door leading to the wide reaches of the supernatural. Curiosity and presumption are tempered by Revelation which likewise modifies the life of the educated man so that his mind will bring into focus the whole range of being.[10] Our extension in

being is measured not by the narrow limits of our person but by the vision of eternal truths. Whereas the intellect of God is a measure and not a thing measured, the human intellect is a thing measured, measured first of all by God who gives it the first principles of the speculative and practical order; and secondly by things, for the intellect does not give truth and goodness to things.[11]

5. *Self-evident first principles.* In the interpretation of life and the universe as a totality, in the harmonizing of individual facts, in the unification of knowledge, the process of education demands the constant application and flowering of metaphysical principles. These principles must not be known in a vague impractical way but must first be accepted and lived. There preexist in us certain seeds of knowledge, first principles, which one immediately knows, once the intellect contacts reality.[12] St. Thomas enumerates, besides the primary notion of being, the principles of contradiction, identity, sufficient reason and causality.

a) Intellectual grasp of being is included in every thought. From this grasp of being may be formulated the first indemonstrable principle, that one cannot at once both affirm and deny the same thing. This principle rests on the concept of being and non-being and metaphysically is the primary basis of all other principles .... [13]

b) Since, apart from being, nothing is knowable or intelligible, the first judgment in the ontological order must be an affirmation of the principle of identity. Because there cannot be an infinite regress in a series of concepts, therefore the first most simple and universal judgment must have being for its subject and that which primarily belongs to being for its predicate.[14] The principle of permanence or substance directly follows upon this prinicple of identity. Beneath all forms of change or movement there is a permanent and immobile element. It is this element which is being properly speaking because it *is*; for being is predicated of substance primarily and absolutely. From multiplicity the mind passes to unity; the changing and passing are only understood in terms of the permanent and lasting.

c) Everything must have a sufficient reason for its existence and essence either in itself or in another: In itself, if what belongs to it is of its own intrinsic constitution; in another, if what belongs to it does not pertain to its essential constitution; in another, if what belongs to it does not pertain to its essential constitution. Contingent, caused beings must then have sufficient reason of their being in something outside of themselves.[15]

d) This principle of sufficient reason is the basis for efficient and final causality. Efficient causality is directly perceived by the intelligence upon the presentation of an object. Since the end is the reason of being of the means, the principle of finality likewise has its basis in that of sufficient reason. That every agent acts for an end is shown by St. Thomas from his observation that otherwise one thing would not follow from the action of an agent more than another, unless it were by chance.[16]

The acceptance of these principles is a necessary condition for the discovery of truth. If they are ignored nothing can be known and the entire purpose of education is frustrated. In Thomistic pedagogy, knowledge is acquired when the mind is led from things to principles and back to things again.[17] These principles are not the homespun inventions of an armchair philosopher but postulates of reality formulated by the intellect because it is constituted to know reality. The human intellect must be measured by the standard of reality for it is not the source of truth. Only by rigid adherence to things as they are can the mind possess truth. In the integration of his knowledge, the philosopher, the wise man, obeys the demands of order. He perceives that the objective order imposed on man is in a general way the order of the nature of things with their respective laws, the order of truth, and the order of the supernatural life. This order flows from the Wisdom of the Maker of all things. It is proposed as a demand of his nature by being expressed in his reason. When objective truth brings the intellect of man to a contemplation of things in relation to the First Cause and Land End of all reality, then that man is being educated .... As Thomas Aquinas expressed it: Love of knowledge is the penetration of truth, not of any truth, but of that truth which is the Source of all truth, of that which relates to the First Being of all things; wherefore Its Truth is the First Principle of all truth, since the disposition of things is the same truth as in being.[18]

(Excerpted from *Essays in Thomism,* edited by Robert E. Brennan.)

FOR FURTHER INQUIRY

1) A local resident of a beach community has been told that certain types of unseemly behavior are occurring in remote areas on the beach. He decides, given the particulars, that this type of "ungodly" conduct must be stopped. He appoints himself as watchdog and begins to run people off the beach because of his disapproval of their behavior which he deems sexually immoral. Comment on this in relation to free will.

2) Al Parker works for a large company as supervisor. He oversees a portion of the company's business in locating new building sites. On a field assignment exploring for new sites, he comes across an exquisite piece of property that is environmentally sensitive. He is not attuned to the environment in this area as well as he perhaps should be. What are the evident problems here and how can they be reasoned? Can autonomy be employed ethically?

3) Kant's Categorical Imperative implies a sense of absolutism (the imperative itself is described as an absolute valid command). But autonomy is also a part of this imperative. If one's maxim is, "One ought not to kill," can that person justify war? Capital Punishment? Euthanasia? One's willingness to end one's own life?

4) A person is dying in a state that does not recognize right-to-die proclamations. The guardian of this person disagrees with the ideology of the state and strives to have the patient moved to a state that has legitimized right-to-die laws. The resident state disallows the transfer. Debate this issue.

5) A capital crime is committed in a country that espouses the death penalty. The murderer escapes to a country that finds the death penalty immoral. What obligations, if any, does the country to which the person fled have to the country seeking to execute the murderer? Cite the reasoning involved.

6) Identify any fallacies in the following:
   a) My brother who works for an American car manufacturer told me imports are greatly inferior to American cars, and as a supervisor for that manufacturer he ought to know.
   b) Three students passed his class by cheating. That teacher hasn't a clue as to what is going on in his class.
   c) Conservatives shouldn't trust liberals.
   d) The State of Florida rescinded the services tax on businesses. This caused a decline in revenues which led to less funding to education.
   e) Al: "You got a passing grade on that difficult exam?"
      Keith: "Sure did! Got a 'B.' A high 'B' at that."
      Al: "No one could possibly pass that test without cheating. How did you do it?"
      Keith: "I didn't cheat! I just studied the right material."
      Al: "How could you? You were absent from class for a couple of days. You must have cheated, even a little."
      Keith: "Sorry, but you're wrong. I studied."
      Al: "C'mon, prove you didn't cheat."
   f) While sitting, I thought the horse looked very large.
   g) My mother told me I couldn't go out because it is raining and I will catch a cold. I'll then have to stay home from school, miss my exam, have to take an 'F' and then repeat the course.

h) Hugh, a football purist, enjoys watching Dallas in the domed Texas Stadium on artificial turf.

i) I have always purchased my medication at that pharmacy, but I noticed that recently they have begun to sell beer and wine. Rather than support the decadence of drinking and insobriety, I will have to change my pharmacist.

j) Have you noticed that everytime the left fielder goes into his position, he begins by touching third base? I've noticed when he forgets that, on his next turn at bat he usually strikes out. When he plays at home his dugout is near the first base side and often he neglects to touch the base. That is the reason he has so many strikouts at home.

7. Are the following valid or invalid, and if invalid, why?

    a) No cheater will ever win.
        Al is not a cheater.
        Therefore, Al will win.

    b) All apples are fruit.
        Some apples are green.
        Therefore, some fruit is green.

    c) Some apples are green.
        Some fruit is green.
        Therefore, some apples are green fruit.

    d) All tigers are animals.
        All tigers and zebras have stripes.
        Therefore, some animals have stripes.

    e) All good things come to an end.
        This chapter has come to an end.
        Therefore, this chapter is good.

ENDNOTES

1. Summa Theologiae p. 1, q.85, a.2
2. ibid p. 1, q. 50, a.2; q. 84, a.1
3. ibid p. 1, q.84, aa 1-8
4. ibid p. 1 q. 79, a 3.
5. *Q.D. de Veritate:* q.10, a. 6, reply to obj. 2
6. *Summa Theologiae* p. 1, q. 3, a.4
7. *De Intellectu et Intelligibili* (Vives edition, opusculum xlix)
8. *S.T.* p.1, q.16, a.5, reply to obj 3.
9. *C.G.:*b.1,c.5
10. *C.G.:* b.1, c.5
11. *Q.D. de Veritate:* q.1, a.2, Also *Q.D. de Potentia:* q.7, a.10, reply to obj 5
12. *Q. D. de Veritate:* q.11,a . 1.
14. *In Metaphysicorum:* b. IV, 1. i
15. *S. T.* p.1, q. 3, a. 7
16. *S.T.* p. 1, q.44, a.4
17. *Q. D. de Veritate:* q.11, a. 1
18. *C. G. :* b. 1, c. 1

Part III

Ethics
Applied

McGraw-Hill

The Individual And Ethical Issues

THE POOR   THE INFIRM   THE ELDERLY

don
addis

Chapter 6

Nancy S. Jecker

ABORTION

"The pregnant woman cannot be isolated in her privacy. She carries an embryo and, later, a fetus ... it is reasonable and appropriate for a State to decide that at some point in time another interest ... becomes significantly involved. The woman's privacy is no longer sole and any right of privacy she possesses must be measured accordingly."
— Justice Harry A. Blackmun, *Roe vs. Wade*

"By restricting the right to terminate pregnancies, the State conscripts women's bodies into its service, forcing women to continue their pregnancies, suffer the pains of childbirth, and in most instances, provide years of maternal care. The State does not compensate women for their services; instead, it assumes that they owe this duty as a matter of course."
— Justices Anthony Kennedy, Sandra Day O'Connor,
David Souter, *Casey vs. Planned Parenthood*

The range of issues we will address in this chapter can be viewed usefully at four distinct levels. A first level concerns the *fetus's moral status as an individual being.* At this first level we will consider what qualities any being must possess for us to think of that being as having moral interests and rights of its own. While our chief concern will be the moral standing of human beings at the early stages of human development, the general questions the chapter poses are potentially relevant to human beings at other stages of life and to animals who belong to other species.

A second level broadens our initial focus on the individual and places *the fetus in the context of a unique relationship with another human being,* namely a pregnant woman. We will ask what ethical

Nancy S. Jecker, M.A. Philosophy, Stanford University, M.A. and Ph.D. University of Washington, is associate professor at the University of Washington School of Medicine, Department of Medical History and Ethics.

significance we should attribute to the fact that the fetus depends for its survival on inhabiting another human being's body. We will also consider how the fetus's moral status and rights may alter later in the course of fetal development as the fetus becomes viable and eventually could continue to survive on its own. An important question at this level of discussion will be the following: If we assume that a fetus has the same ethical rights and interests as a pregnant woman (obviously, a controversial assumption), how, ethically, should we resolve conflicts between the fetus and pregnant woman?

A third level of the abortion debate is broader still, and situates the predicament of *fetus and pregnant woman in the context of a family or future family*. A future family may include another parent and other offspring. One question the chapter will raise is: Does it make any ethical difference if a woman knows in advance that a particular fetus would be born with a serious genetic condition? A related question concerns the situation of a pregnant woman who already has a large family and cannot afford financially to support an additional child. What role, if any, should such considerations play in a decision about whether to bring a pregnancy to term?

A final level of debate situates the abortion debate *in the wider circle of the society and addresses law and social policies* regarding the practice of abortion. This section will review the 1973 U.S. Supreme Court decision, *Roe vs. Wade*, that decriminalized abortion, as well as several important legal decisions that occurred subsequent to Roe. Although many people who oppose abortion on ethical grounds also oppose legalizing abortion, it will be critical for us to distinguish between the ethical and legal permissibility of abortion decisions.

(Note: It is recognized that many Americans refer to the conception in the womb as a baby. Sadly, even the use of a single term – baby or fetus – occasionally has been viewed as taking sides in the abortion debate. Some even believe that *solely* using the word baby or *solely* the word fetus implies pejorative treatment of one side of the debate. No such use of the language is intended in this chapter. However, the least emotional contexts for discussion of the abortion issue are medical and legal, and because these professions rely on the term fetus, so will this chapter. Also, although various medical terms – zygote, conceptus, embryo and fetus – are used to refer to the developing human being in the womb, the author will use the term *fetus* globally to refer to all these stages.)

THE INDIVIDUAL:
WHAT IS THE ETHICAL STATUS OF THE FETUS?

A strange new world. Imagine that you are traveling to a distant planet in the solar system. The vessel on which you are traveling lands on a faraway planet. There you discover a new form of life that is nothing like life on earth. While observing these creatures and trying to understand their form of life, several colleagues on board your space craft report that this planet has abundant supplies of various natural resources that have become exceedingly scarce on earth. Your colleagues begin to discuss the potential for harvesting these vast resources and transporting them back to earth. Listening to the conversation, you begin to wonder what implications such a plan might carry for the new form of life that exists on this planet. You raise this concern with others. Together all of you begin to ask yourselves what is the right thing to do. You wonder, Do the strange creatures you have found here have any moral standing? In other words, should they be subjects of moral concern in their own right? Do these creatures possess moral rights? If so, do they have a right to life? One among you asks whether these strange forms of life have the same moral standing as adult human beings. Another person suggests that perhaps these alien creatures have greater moral importance than human beings and possess more significant moral interests. These are difficult questions. You and your shipmates are not altogether comfortable with them. Your discomfort only grows when you realize that if these creatures have moral claims against you, this may well conflict with your own interests in using the planet's resources to benefit yourselves and other people on Earth. The moral questions you have raised persist and continue to nag at your consciences.

Answers to such questions are not readily found. You and your companions settle upon the following procedure for framing the problem, and you agree among yourselves to use the following language to discuss it.

The Definition of "Person." You and your fellow travelers agree to use the term, "person," to refer to a being, potentially belonging to any species, who is a subject of moral concern and who possesses, in particular, a moral right to life. In your experiences, the most obvious examples of persons are normal adult human beings. But other examples might include certain non-human animals, such as dolphins or chimpanzees; God and angels, if they exist; and extraterrestrial beings, such as the ones you have discovered.

Next, you and your companions agree that you cannot dismiss the possibility that the form of life you have discovered is a person just because it is not human. Your reasoning here is that to assume that only instances of human life could count as persons would be similar to claiming that only members of favored racial groups possess certain rights or are full-fledged persons. The latter mistake is one you are (all too well) acquainted with: Racism. The former mistake, you suppose, might be dubbed, "speciesism."[1] Speciesism shows the folly of thinking that a being must look like a human being to be a person. Although having human facial features or human fingers and toes may elicit certain emotional responses in us, possessing such features is not necessary for being a moral person.

Finally, you and other members in the group set yourselves the explicit task of deciding what qualities a being must possess in order to qualify as a person. As you and the rest of the Earth crew are contemplating an excavation of the planet's natural resources, with potentially devastating consequences for the planet, you need to know not only whether this alien life form is a source of moral concern, but whether these creatures are *persons* with a right to life. If the sole moral claim these creatures had was not to be tortured or caused pain, you are confident that painless extinction would be feasible. Your concern, then, focuses on the question: Are these strange beings moral *persons*, possessing as all persons do a *right to life?*

Alternative Criteria for Personhood. Having framed the question in this manner, the debate soon heats up and reaches a boiling point. Among the initial criteria you debate as central to personhood are the following:

1. *Consciousness.* Consciousness is the capacity to have states of awareness, such as states of thinking or feeling. Someone suggests that consciousness is the key feature of personhood because it serves to distinguish beings that merit special treatment in their own right from mere objects that can be used as mere means to accomplish others' purposes. For example, flowers, rocks, and pieces of paper are not consciously aware of anything and so can serve simply as a means to serve the purposes of conscious beings.

2. *Self-consciousness.* Someone suggests that what matters is not just having a conscious flow of experiences but also having a concept of one's self, being aware of one's self as a separate being that exists over time. Self-consciousness presupposes not only consciousness, but also a conscious sense of one's self.

3. *Sentience.* Someone else offers the idea that the hallmark of personhood is sentience or the ability to have certain kinds of conscious experiences, such as pleasure and pain, enjoying

and suffering, forming wants and aims, having desires and tastes. More sophisticated forms of sentience would include more complex feelings, such as sympathy, honor, religious awe, love, or moral conscience. These capacities certainly make human beings morally special. So perhaps other creatures who have such capacities are special in the same way.

4. *The capacity to communicate.* Others propose that what makes someone a subject of a moral community is the capacity to communicate with at least one other being. Communication includes not just using words and language, but also entirely nonverbal modes of interacting. For example, nods or gestures or giggles can function as means of communicating feelings or plans or intentions. So too, loud noises can be used to convey thoughts without ever forming words.

5. *Reasoning.* Another possible criterion for personhood is the capacity to reason. The point here is not that individuals must be able to perform complex mathematical computations in order to merit moral consideration. Instead, reasoning may occur only at a very rudimentary level. A being reasons merely by formulating goals and identifying behaviors that are instrumental to achieving these goals. At a minimum, reasoning entails a conscience and deliberate thinking process. Reasoning may be evidenced, for example, by the capacity to solve novel puzzles, such as spell new words or find a new way of getting to a familiar location. Reasoning also may be apparent when someone engages in purposeful behaviors, such as using a tool.

6. *Social visibility.* Another shipmate advances the idea that someone qualifies as a person if that individual is part of a larger social group. This seems initially quite sensible because someone who existed on an island all alone could not be a subject of moral rights at all, because moral rights presuppose having certain claims against other people.

7. *The capacity for self-motivated activity.* Someone proposes that what makes a creature a person is that the creature is alive and capable of self-directed movement. For example, a rock is not a person because it is motionless. By contrast, creatures that can move at their own will sometimes qualify as persons.

8. *The capacity for moral agency.* Finally, someone suggests that a being should not be considered to be a full-fledged member of the moral community unless that being can potentially assume moral responsibilities toward others. The reasoning here is that a moral community will not survive long, or at all, if its members have rights and claims against others but no one has any duty to respect the rights or meet the claims of other people.

Everyone acknowledges that the various qualities under consideration could, in principle, be realized through a vast array of different physical materials. For example, reasoning might take place without a being possessing the gray brain matter we humans do. Likewise, consciousness could, in principle, exist in someone who did not possess a cerebral cortex of the sort with which we are familiar. Everyone also recognizes that the problem of how to treat the unfamiliar creatures on this planet is only the tip of the iceberg. It carries important implications for life forms generally, including human and non-human life forms on Earth.

Finally, everyone agrees that a systematic approach to evaluating standards for personhood is necessary. One approach would be to identify a single feature or set of features that a being *must* have in order to be a person. If it were possible to identify a necessary condition for personhood, it would be possible to *exclude* any creatures that lack that essential feature. For example, the group wonders whether any being that is permanently non-conscious could ever be a person. Perhaps, the capacity for consciousness is an absolute necessity for personhood.

Another approach would be to try to agree upon what quality or qualities are *sufficient* for personhood. A creature *need* not have this quality, but any creature that did would automatically qualify as a person. Whereas necessary conditions for personhood function as standards for excluding creatures from the category of personhood, sufficient conditions function as standards for *including* creatures. You wonder, for example, whether reasoning is sufficient to show personhood. Or are some other qualities also required to demonstrate personhood, such as the capacity to feel certain emotions?

PERSONHOOD: THREE POSITIONS

The above exercise shows that in order to understand more fully what moral personhood means, we need first to figure out what the necessary and sufficient conditions for personhood might include. This is a very large and difficult task. It is perhaps reassuring to know that you are not the first to embark on such an inquiry, at least with respect to the abortion question (aliens are another matter).

Generally speaking, there are three quite different positions people take with respect to when, in the course of development, a human being becomes a person. In order to give you a general sense of the personhood debate, this section describes each of the three views in a general way and then describes, in more detail, one particular version of each view.

A first position, often referred to as the conservative position on personhood, holds that a human being is a person from the moment of conception onward. The underlying criterion that supports this view does not refer to any of the eight criteria listed above. Instead, conservatives maintain that it is sufficient for personhood that a being has the *potential* or *likelihood* of developing the morally significant features that make a being a person. From the moment of conception, a healthy human being has the capacity, for example, to develop consciousness, reasoning, and sentience simply by virtue of having the complete set of human chromosomes. A well-known advocate of the conservative position, John Noonan, presents the following arguments in support of this position.[2]

An Argument Supporting the Conservative Position: Probability

1. It is seriously wrong to destroy any organism that has a significant probability of developing into a person.
2. If a spermatozoa is destroyed, one destroys an organism that has a chance of less than 1 in 200 million of developing into a person.
3. If an oocyte (egg) is destroyed, one destroys an organism that has a chance of less than 390 in 100,000 of developing into a person.
4. If a zygote (fertilized egg) is destroyed, one destroys a being that has an 80 per cent chance of developing into a person.
5. Therefore, it is seriously wrong to destroy a fetus (from zygote on), although it is not seriously wrong to destroy sperms and eggs.

An Argument Supporting the Conservative Position: Potentiality

1. Any organism that will, in the normal course of its development, come to have whatever property it is that endows a being with a right to life is itself a moral being with a right to life.
2. Beginning at conception, *homo sapiens* (who do not have gross abnormalities) will, in the normal course of development, come to have the properties that endow a being with a right to life.
3. Therefore, beginning at conception, *homo sapiens* (except those with gross abnormalities) have a right to life.

A second position, often referred to as the moderate position, holds that a human being becomes a person sometimes after conception but prior to birth. This position is held, for example, by the philosopher Wayne Sumner.[3] Sumner maintains that sentience is both a necessary and a sufficient condition for being a person. There is no doubt that a human being lacks sentience at the moment of conception; hence Sumner rejects the conservative position. Sumner instead locates the threshold of personhood during the second trimester of pregnancy. This is when the fetus's forebrain has developed, and in particular when the cerebral cortex, which is thought to be the seat of consciousness, and sentience has developed.

In the course of elaborating and defending what often is termed a moderate position, Sumner makes the following observations. He notes, first, that sentience admits of degrees. In its simplest form, sentience includes only the capacity to feel pain or pleasure. More complex forms of sentience include more subtle and complex emotions, such as feeling moral guilt or pride, feeling detachment or empathy toward others' suffering, feeling confidence or insecurity, feeling grief or joy. Because sentience admits of degree, using it as a standard for personhood enables us to think of moral standing as falling along a continuum, rather than being an all-or-nothing phenomenon. For example, we can think of creatures with the most basic kinds of sentience as having only a minimal right to life, and those with more complex capacities as having correspondingly greater moral standing.

One argument supporting this particular version of a moderate position is its explanatory power. That is, it has the apparent advantage of matching people's considered judgments about particular cases beyond the abortion question. Thus, if one believes that higher vertebrates, such as mammals, deserve greater moral protection of life than lower vertebrates, such as fish and reptiles, then this account of personhood can explain these beliefs. Sumner's position also can account for the belief that higher mammals, such as primates, are due greater protection of life than lower mammals, such as dogs and cats, because they have more sophisticated forms of sentience. By contrast, those positions that associate personhood with possessing certain all-or-nothing properties, such as potentiality, cannot explain such judgments. "Crude as this division may be," says Sumner, "it seems to accord reasonably well with most people's intuitions that in our moral reasoning paramecia and horseflies count for things, dogs and cats count for something, chimpanzees and dolphins count for more, and human beings count for most of all."[4]

A final position, usually referred to as the liberal position, locates personhood as occurring at birth or shortly thereafter. For example, Many Anne Warren maintains that the traits that are most central to being a person include qualities such as consciousness, reasoning, self-motivated activity, the capacity to communicate, and self-awareness.[5] She maintains further that it is not necessary to have all of these qualities to qualify as a person; however, any being that lacks all of these person-like features is not a person.

In support of a liberal position, Warren argues that the conservative position is deeply flawed on the following grounds:

An Argument Against the Conservative Position
1. Any being that has *none* of the qualities we associate with personhood (consciousness, reasoning, self-motivated activity, the capacity to communicate, self-awareness) cannot possibly be a person.
2. At the moment of conception, a human being does not have any of the qualities we associate with personhood.
3. Therefore a human being cannot possibly be a person at the moment of conception.

On this analysis, the potential to become a person by virtue of having the human genetic code does not confer personhood, as the conservatives suggest. For the human genetic code does not actually impart any of the qualities we associate with personhood. Thus, at the moment of conception a human being is still a tiny microscopic organism, and lacks the brain and other physical bases that humans require to support capacities such as consciousness and reasoning. Warren concludes that a human being who has the potential to develop into a person is a potential person. Such a being has potential and future, rather than actual, moral rights.

She goes on to point out that a small infant is not very much more person-like than a late stage fetus. A newborn infant, then, is not properly regarded as a person in its own right. However, Warren is also quick to note that there are many, many reasons why we should nonetheless protect the lives of newborn babies. Babies are valued by and give pleasure to other people. They cause parents delight and joy and are loved very much by their family members. Even strangers have strong responses to babies and would prefer, for example, paying taxes to care for infants who are not wanted, rather than allowing such infants to be killed or allowed to die. Warren draws the conclusion that so long as people feel this way about babies, killing babies is morally objectionable. It conflicts with the interests and rights of those who are persons.

THE MATERNAL-FETAL RELATIONSHIP: HOW SHOULD A CONFLICT OF INTEREST BE RESOLVED?

A Strange New World. Let us return briefly to the space story with which this chapter began. However, this time assume that you and your fellow spaceship travelers have reached some agreement about what the criteria for personhood are and have determined that the creatures in question are persons. Operating on these assumption, it is important to see that there are other vital ethical questions that your group must address before you can know how you ought to act toward the extra-terrestrial creatures. For example, even assuming that these creatures possess a moral right to life, this right may conflict with the rights and interests of other persons. One way this might occur is if the creatures in question require special chemicals to stay alive and these are in short supply on their planet. We might suppose that the chemicals these creatures need occur in abundance in the blood of human beings. What if the alien creatures figure this out and indicate their intention to keep you on the planet for nine months so that they can draw your blood and replenish their supply of the vital chemicals?

This may be inconvenient. Perhaps you and your shipmates had other plans and goals. Perhaps giving blood on a regular basis would make you feel weak and sick most of the time. It could even require long periods of bedrest or hospitalization. The amounts they require could even kill you. What's more, perhaps you have no desire whatsoever to be of service to these creatures. Although you believe that they are persons, perhaps you insist that you are a person too, and you possess moral rights and interests of your own that must be taken into account. Perhaps your space travel is part of an important scientific project and you are simply not free to put this project on hold and stay on the planet while these creatures harvest your blood. Or perhaps you are a mother or father and staying on this planet for nine months would irritate the babysitter, not to mention your spouse and children. Or perhaps you just started a new job. In short, you may begin to wonder why the interests and rights of extra-terrestrial life should automatically take precedence over your own rights.

Needless to say, in the actual world this kind of added moral complexity is present. Persons do not exist in isolation, but exist instead in the context of relationships and moral communities with other creatures. Persons depend on other persons in vital ways and require various things of each other. Although all persons by definition possess a right to life, this right is not always or necessarily absolute. It can conflict with the rights and interests of other persons and must be weighed against these in particular cases.

CONFLICTING INTERESTS

Returning to the abortion question, let us suppose for the purposes of argument that the fetus is indeed a person. Indeed, let us suppose that from the moment of conception onward all human beings are full-fledged persons. In other words, suppose that they are accorded the same moral standing that normal adult human beings are. The adventure of the spaceship travelers should make it abundantly clear that knowing that someone is a person hardly settles the question of how we are ethically required to treat that person. Thus, assuming that a fetus is a person does yet not decide the matter of whether or not abortion of the fetus is ever morally permissible. For the fetus exists in a moral community with other persons, and the fetus's rights and interests may be at odds with the moral rights and interests of others. These reflections suggest rather strongly that to know whether the fetus's assumed right to life overrides the rights and interests of others, we need to think more carefully about what implications upholding this right can have for the life and welfare of other persons.

It should be immediately clear that the fetus is in a special moral situation. Not only does the fetus exist in a community with other persons but the fetus also exists inside another person's body. Whereas the extra-terrestrial creatures described above needed other people's blood , the fetus needs to inhabit another person's physical being and grow inside it. This certainly involves a much more profound dependency between persons. When this relationship with another person is not wanted by the pregnant woman whose body is inhabited, she is likely to feel that a much more fundamental intrusion is occurring. Not only is another being drawing her blood, it is growing inside her and making use of her body for sustenance. Furthermore, whereas the extra-terrestrial creatures in the previous example wanted to treat people in ways that might make them weak or sick, supporting a fetus requires enduring various other burdens. Thus, during a normal pregnancy a woman not uncommonly experiences a range of uncomfortable symptoms, such as constipation, hemorrhoids, heartburn, pica (craving to eat substances other than foods, such as clay or coal), swollen ankles, varicose veins, leg cramps, backache, breathlessness, urinary tract infections, and lethargy. In addition, hormonal effects on the brain not uncommonly make pregnant women's moods more changeable, produce bouts of depression and crying, or cause them to be more easily angered or annoyed. Pregnant women are also at risk for various complications of pregnancy, some of which are life threatening.

It is important to remember that in most cases a pregnancy involves both a physical and an emotional bond between a pregnant woman and fetus; or, as some would say, between mother and her child. In the usual situation, then, the rights of the pregnant woman are not at odds with the rights of the fetus. Yet when conflict does arise, we need to ask how it can be ethically resolved. Assuming the fetus is a person, we need to ask what is most fair to the two persons who are most intimately involved in an abortion decision.

There are several kinds of conflicts that abortion can reflect and the differences here may prove ethically significant:

> **1. The fetus's assumed right to life conflicts with the pregnant woman's right to life**. In the most dramatic, and least common, example the fetus's continued development threatens the life of the pregnant woman. Here the fetus's right to life is in direct conflict with the same

right of the pregnant woman. For example, when a women has an ectopic pregnancy (a pregnancy that implants outside the uterus) her own life is threatened if the pregnancy is allowed to continue.

2. The fetus's assumed right to life conflicts with the pregnant woman's physical or emotional health. A somewhat different situation arises when the pregnant woman's physical or emotional health is placed in jeopardy by a continued pregnancy. For example, a woman who is known to have an underlying chronic condition, such as chronic hypertension (high blood pressure) or multiple sclerosis may wish to avoid pregnancy out of concern that it will adversely affect her health.

3. The fetus's assumed right to life conflicts with the pregnant woman's right to pursue important projects by imposing serious obstacles and hardships. In many cases harboring a fetus will not seriously harm a pregnant woman's life or health, but will impose other kinds of hardships. For example, continuing with a pregnancy may require dropping out of high school or college. Or when a pregnant woman decides to bring a fetus to term and then give the child up for adoption, the decision to sever relations permanently with one's child is an emotionally wrenching choice. By contrast, women who continue unwanted pregnancies and then go on to rear their children to maturity may face other hardships. For example, a single parent who lacks access to affordable child care may be forced to quit her job to care for her children. The result may be impoverishment and long-term dependence on public assistance. Generally speaking, pregnant women who lack adequate social and economic support following pregnancy encounter serious obstacles to pursuing whatever educational or career aspirations they envisioned for themselves.

4. The fetus's assumed right to life conflicts with a woman's right to decide. In virtually all situations in which a woman prefers an abortion, there exists a conflict between the fetus's right to life, on the one hand, and the pregnant woman's right to decide what will happen in and to her body, on the other hand.

In reviewing these potential conflicts between fetus and pregnant woman, it might at first glance be thought that only the first instance of conflict could conceivably be decided in favor of the pregnant woman. Thus, some might suppose that a person's right to life should always take precedence over other, less "vital," rights, – such as a right to have one's health, projects, or preferences protected.

In response to this suggestion, several objections can be made. First, in many other cases we do not think that a person's right to life takes precedence over interests and considerations that do not involve protection of life. For example, persons routinely refuse to take steps to protect the lives of other persons simply because taking these steps would be inconvenient. Thus, most individuals do not donate significant amounts of their income to charitable organizations that protect human life, such as famine relief organizations. Instead, most people spend their earnings on whatever they want, including non-essential items such as movies, alcohol, automobiles, or dinner out. Even though contributing money to charitable organizations could save lives, we usually think that people are justified in giving higher priority to pursuing their own interests.

The philosopher, Judith Jarvis Thomson, takes this point one step further.[6] Thomson argues that it is not only incorrect, but absurd, to suppose that rights to life have automatic priority over other rights. To show that this is so she first imagines a situation where she is "sick unto death, and the only thing that will save my life is the touch of Henry Fonda's cool hand on my fevered brow."[7] In such a situation, Thomson reasons:

I have no right to be given the touch of Henry Fonda's cool hand on my fevered brow. It would be frightfully nice of him to fly in from the West Coast to provide it. It would be less nice, though no doubt well meant, if my friends flew out to the West Coast and carried Henry Fonda back with them. But I have no right at all against anybody that he should do this for me.[8]

Next Thomson makes a similar point by imagining a situation where the Society of Music Lovers kidnaps someone and plugs that person into a famous violinist, who must remain plugged in to that person's body for nine months in order to remain alive. Thomson reasons that it is absurd to suppose that the famous violinist has a right to remain plugged in; instead the kidnapped party is ethically free to unplug this person. The suggestion is that the predicament of the kidnapped person is analogous to that of the pregnant woman who discovers that she is pregnant. Assuming the fetus is a person, even a famous violinist, Thomson reasons that the pregnant woman is ethically free to refuse to harbor the fetus.

Thomson's argument can be usefully summarized along the lines that follow. First, in the abortion case, Thomson considers the following proposal:

An Argument For Granting Priority To The Fetus's Right To Life
1. The fetus is a person with a right to life.
2. The pregnant woman has a right to decide what happens in and to her body.
3. Yet a person's right to life is always stronger than a person's right to decide what happens in and to her body.
4. Therefore, abortion is never permissible.

Thomson then proceeds to show the downfall of this initial argument by showing that the reasoning (in premise three) leads to absurd results.

Objection to the Argument
1. A violinist is a person with a right to life.
2. A person has a right to determine what happens in and to her body.
3. A violinist's right to life is always stronger than a person's right to decide what happens in and to her body.
4. Therefore, if the Society of Music Lovers kidnaps a person and plugs her into a famous violinist that needs to use her body for life support for nine months, it is not permissible to unplug the violinist.

In response to this argument it can be noted that there are several important differences between the initial argument and the analogy Thomson seeks to establish. First, the pregnant woman and her partner might be morally accountable for pregnancy occurring. For example, they may have omitted to take precautions, such as using contraceptive devices, to prevent pregnancy from occurring. Or even if precautions of this sort were taken and pregnancy occurred despite this, a pregnant woman and her partner might be considered responsible for bringing pregnancy about if they knew in advance of engaging in sexual intercourse that no method of birth control is 100% effective and that the risk of pregnancy occurring is therefore always present. Unlike the kidnapped person who was dragged unwillingly into a "plugged in" situation, when two people voluntarily engage in sexual behaviors that can lead to pregnancy they voluntarily undertake the risk of pregnancy.

Understood in this light, the violinist example is perhaps most analogous to a situation where a woman is raped and subsequently becomes pregnant. In this case, like the violinist case, a pregnant woman finds a fetus growing inside her that needs to rely on her body for nine months to survive. Like the person who is kidnapped and plugged into a violinist, a woman who is raped and subsequently becomes pregnant is forcibly put in a situation where a fetus is developing inside her.

In situations other than rape it might be useful to alter Thomson's original story. For example, in the case of failed contraception, a better analogy might be as follows.

The Revised Objection.
Imagine that you purchase tickets to see a concert performance put on by the Society of Music Lovers. You love this kind of performance and are very much looking forward to an entertaining evening. Before purchasing a ticket, you are informed that a certain percentage of ticket holders, say 5%, will be kidnapped by the Society of Music Lovers and plugged into famous violinists. The violinists will need to use the ticket holders' bodies for nine months. You decide to buy the ticket and go to the concert despite this risk, because you are so fond of the music and looking forward to the event. Suppose, however, that you are in the unlucky 5% of people who are kidnapped and plugged into a violinist. What are your obligations to the violinist?

In this case, unlike Thomson's original example, the kidnapped persons who attended the concert knew they were taking a risk and they freely decided to do so. This is analogous to the situation of a woman and man engaging in sexual relations and using contraception who are aware that contraception is not 100% effective. The couple chooses to assume the risk of an unwanted pregnancy and therefore are responsible for finding the woman "plugged in" to a fetus. What are the responsibilities of the couple to the fetus under these conditions? Assuming, as we are, that the fetus is a person, must a pregnant woman sacrifice her own interests to support the fetus? Must she sacrifice her health and welfare? Must she sacrifice her life?

One response to these questions holds that requiring pregnant women in this situation to continue with unwanted pregnancies is expecting too much. After all, we do not expect that men who father unwanted offspring will make similar kinds of sacrifices. For example:

> Men who engage in heterosexual intercourse do not lose (their) right (to defend their physical integrity). Nor should they. A father cannot legally be forced to donate a kidney, or even some easily replaceable blood, in order to save the life of his child. If men are not stripped of that right because of their sexual activity, then it is doubly unjust that women should be.[9]

Another response argues that a person who risks an unwanted pregnancy by having intercourse does incur certain obligations toward the fetus, but distinguishes between the minimal obligations a person is ethically *required* to meet and more generous acts of sacrifice and heroism that are *not* ethically mandatory. In making this distinction, this response invokes the parable of the Good Samaritan.

The Parable of the Good Samaritan
A man was going down from Jerusalem to Jericho, and fell among robbers who stripped him and beat him, and departed leaving him half dead. Now by chance a priest was going down the road, and when he saw him he passed by on the other side. So likewise a Levite, when he came to the place and saw him passed by on the other side. But a Samaritan, as he journeyed, came where he was; and when he saw him he had compassion. And went to him and bound up his wounds, pouring on oil and wine, and set him on his own beast and brought him to an

inn, and took care of him. And the next day he took out two denarii and gave them to the innkeeper saying, "Take care of him; and whatever more you spend, I will repay you when I come back."[10]

This parable brings into sharper focus the qualities or virtues associated with helping people in need.[11] The actual Samaritan in this parable has become paradigmatic of "the Good Samaritan," a type of person who will go to unusual lengths to help someone in need. We might contrast the Good Samaritan with a "Splendid Samaritan," a person who not only goes to unusual lengths for another person but also sacrifices his or her own welfare in the course of doing so. For example, we might regard the Samaritan in the parable as Splendid if the money he gave to the innkeeper was all the money he had at the time to feed and care for himself.

Both the Good Samaritan and the Splendid Samaritan stand in sharp contrast to what we might call the "Minimally Decent Samaritan," someone who meets minimal obligations but does nothing over and above this to help a person in need. Such a person lacks the heroic qualities that both the Good and Splendid Samaritans show. However, strictly speaking, a Minimally Decent Samaritan does not act wrongly or violate any moral obligations one is required to meet. In the parable, the Levite and priest were not even Minimally Decent Samaritans, because they failed to meet standards of minimally decent morality. Minimally Decent Samaritans in their situation may have called for someone else to help the injured man, and after help arrived gone on along their way.

What relevance do these distinctions bear on abortion situation? They suggest the usefulness of speaking not only in the vocabulary of rights or conflicts of rights, but also in the language of character and virtue. Assuming again that the fetus is a person, we might understand a woman's response to an unwanted pregnancy as falling along a continuum. At one end, perhaps, is a woman who cannot carry a fetus to term without placing her own life in peril. Here the sacrifice to help another is the ultimate sacrifice. A lesser, but still major, sacrifice involves a woman who places her own health at grave peril in order to sustain the life of the fetus. A still significant, but less grave, sacrifice might involve a woman who accepts serious and lasting hardships in order to sustain a fetus. These may be in the form of financial, educational, career or other interests. As noted above, every woman who continues an unwanted pregnancy to term makes a substantial sacrifice, because pregnancy always places physical limitations on what one is able to do; it involves significant discomfort for an extended period of time and culminates in painful labor.

In reflecting on the situation of a pregnant woman and fetus, Thomson concludes that "no person is morally required to make large sacrifices to sustain the life of another who has no right to demand them and this even where the sacrifices do not include life itself; we are not morally *required* to be good Samaritans."[12] In other words, according to Thomson, it is praiseworthy, even heroic, to sacrifice selflessly for others. However, no one is ethically required do this. Instead, people are ethically free to do less.

Although Thomson's analysis provides a general framework for weighing the interests of the woman and fetus, it does not yet settle the question of what responses specific situations merit. In other words, even assuming we accept the general distinctions between Splendid, Good, and Minimally Decent Samaritanism, we still need to determine what actions and situations fall under each of these headings. We also need to attend to the further question of what interests and responsibilities persons other than the fetus and pregnant woman have in abortion decisions.

THE FAMILY:
WHAT DO WE OWE FUTURE FAMILY MEMBERS?

Having explored both the moral status of the fetus as an individual, and the moral relationship between the fetus and pregnant woman, our discussion now moves to a new level. This third level locates the problem of abortion in the wider context of the future family that the woman and fetus may belong to and live within.

Abortion is frequently pictured as if it involved a woman and fetus exclusively. However, even those who think that an abortion decision should rest entirely with the pregnant woman, nonetheless admit that women often choose to include others in abortion decisions, and often consider the potential impact that their decisions have on family members. In a study of pregnant women contemplating abortion decisions, Carol Gilligan found that women tend to construct and resolve abortion decisions by thinking in terms of relationship and interconnection with others.[13] Thus, the women in Gilligan's study identified a responsibility to care for and avoid hurting others, and based their decisions about having an abortion on "a growing comprehension of the dynamics of social interaction ... and a central insight, that self and others are interdependent."[14] Rather than conceptualizing abortion as a conflict of individual rights, these women tended to see abortion as a problem of how best to care for and avoid harming people affected by their choices. Rather than thinking exclusively in terms of their own health or interests, these women revealed a concern for others and for safeguarding special relationships.

Considered in this light, it is important to think carefully about the consequences that having or aborting a fetus may produce, not only for the women and fetus, but for family relationships and other persons who are most intimately affected. Studies suggest that most women disclose an abortion decision to the fetus's biological father, and many women arrive at an abortion decision in tandem with the biological father.[15] Certainly, any decision to have or not to have a child has potentially important and longlasting effects on a couple's relationship. For example, an unmarried couple that brings a child into the world may decide to get married and rear the child together; the same couple may have postponed or avoided marriage altogether had the child been aborted. Any couple that has and raises a child (or an additional child) may find their relationship profoundly altered. Having and raising a child may bring a couple closer together, but it may also draw them apart by reducing the time and energy they have to devote exclusively to each other and to important goals and projects in their lives.

In addition to impacting a couple's relationship, abortion impacts the wider family circle. For example, a woman who has no children may consider whether she wants to have a family at all, or whether she is ready to begin a family now. Someone who already has children may think in other terms: Can she, or she and her partner, responsibly care for another child, or would an additional child spread family resources too thin? How large should the existing family become? In making a decision about whether to carry or abort a fetus, a woman's perception of family interests may loom especially large when the fetus's interests appear to be strongly at odds with the interests of other family members. Thus, a decision to abort a fetus with a serious genetic disease may rest largely on a woman's or a couple's perception of the financial and emotional stress a sick child would place on other family members. If Gilligan's description of the moral reasoning of women considering abortion is correct, then it is not abstract values, such as "life," that influence women's personal abortion choices. Instead, it is concrete persons and relationships that most affect her decision.

These reflections bring to light that abortion carries profound implications for other people. It also has the potential to alter the nature of relationships that have traditionally been central to women's lives. As others have noted, "When birth control and abortion provide women with effective means for controlling their fertility ... the relationships that have traditionally defined women's identities ... no longer flow inevitably from their reproductive capacity but become matters of decision."[16]

BIOLOGICAL FATHERS

Let us begin the ethical consideration of the family by thinking first about the interests and rights of the fetus's biological father. One basis for supporting a role for biological fathers in abortion decisions is the observation that during the latter half of the 20th century men have played an increasingly larger role in many aspects of pregnancy and child care. Thus, young men are much more likely than men of their fathers' generation to attend child birth classes; be present during labor and delivery; and participate in feeding, bathing, diapering and caring for offspring. It might be thought that men's involvement in these areas is a good thing; for example, such involvement enhances equality between the sexes. Further, it might be thought that a natural extension of men's heightened involvement in these areas should be to increase men's involvement in reproductive decisions generally, including decisions about having or aborting a fetus. According to this perspective, including men in reproductive decisions is part and parcel of fostering men's increased involvement in family life. Although only women can become pregnant, and only they can bear the burdens (as well as the pleasures) associated with pregnancy, there are many other aspects of child care where greater involvement and responsibility are possible for men.

From a quite different perspective, abortion opponents might also support greater involvement of boyfriends or spouses in abortion decisions (as well as greater involvement of parents and others). The reasoning here might be that all reasonable avenues for preventing abortion should be pursued. In many instances, including others in an abortion decision serves as an effective barrier to abortion. For instance, involving spouses or boyfriends invites the possibility that they may oppose, and try to stop, enactment of a women's decision to terminate her pregnancy.

The position that biological fathers should have a role in abortion decisions still leaves wide open the question of what, more specifically, their role should involve.

1. Informing the father. One position holds that the fetus's biological father should be involved in the decision at least to the point of being informed about the pregnancy and informed about a decision to terminate it. One consideration that lends support to such an approach is that both of the fetus's biological parents played a role in bringing the fetus into existence, so both have a right to be informed of the ultimate consequences that ensue from their procreative acts.

2. Finding out what the father's preferences are. A second view agrees with the first – that the fetus's biological father has a right to be told about the abortion decision. In addition, it states that the biological father's preferences must be solicited so that the pregnant woman is aware of what they are. Presumably a pregnant woman remains free to decide whether or not to consider her partner's preferences, and, if she does consider them, how much weight to assign to them. One basis for such a stance is that women contemplating abortion should consider the consequences of abortion for all parties affected by their decisions, and the biological father may be profoundly affected.

3. Regarding the father as having an equal voice in making an abortion decision. A still stronger view maintains that the biological father should have an equal voice with the biological mother in any decision to terminate a pregnancy. One reason that might justify this view is that even though he will not endure the consequences of nine months of pregnancy, the biological father will feel the long-term effects of having or losing a future child.

4. Regarding the father as having veto power over a woman's decision to have an abortion. A final account holds that the father should not only have an equal voice, but should have a potentially stronger voice by having the power to override a women's decision to have an abortion. The general idea is that an abortion should not take place if either partner objects, because both parties have a vital stake in the welfare of their future offspring.

To explore further how the interests of family members can impinge upon abortion decisions, let us focus in more detail on two distinct scenarios. A first scenario involves the decision to terminate a pregnancy when a fetus carries a genetic defect. A second scenario concerns a decision to terminate a pregnancy because a fetus is not of the desired sex.

FETUSES WITH SERIOUS GENETIC DEFECTS

There is a variety of tests that detect fetal abnormalities *in utero*. These include amniocentesis, ultrasound, alpha-fetoprotein screening, and chorionic villus sampling (CVS), among others. These tests can tell a pregnant woman whether her fetus has defects in body structure, such as missing limbs or heart malformations; genetic diseases, such as cystic fibrosis or Down's syndrome; or whether other risk factors are present, such as poor fetal development, heart rhythm disturbances, or abnormalities of the placenta.

Many pregnant women use prenatal testing for the explicit purpose of screening for fetal abnormalities. They intend to abort a fetus who has significant abnormalities. For example, women over 35 and women who have a family history of genetic disease are at greater risk of having a child with genetic abnormalities and frequently seek prenatal testing for this purpose. Other women pursue certain prenatal tests, such as ultrasound, as part of their routine prenatal health care. In this way, a woman may learn that a fetus has a certain defect or disease which was not anticipated.

Many people who personally oppose abortion identify certain exceptional circumstances as ethically warranting it, including the circumstance of a fetus with a genetic defect or other health problem. Thus some people hold that a prospective parent should not knowingly bring a child into the world who will suffer from a serious, painful and life shortening illness. Others hold that a pregnant women is justified in aborting a fetus who has a less serious, but still significant, abnormality. For example, a missing limb is a significant disability that will in the future impair the fetus's ability to walk and be viewed as physically unattractive, even though it will not shorten or otherwise threaten life. As suggested already, in evaluating the ethical aspects of such cases, it is often not just the effect that an impairment portends for the fetus, but also the impact that it will have on others. Prospective parents may be poorly equipped to cope with a seriously ill child, lacking the emotional maturity, economic resources, social support or desire to devote the added time and energy that this is likely to entail. In other cases, a more minor defect may simply be undesirable because it carries a stigma in the society. Any child with a physical disability is likely to have a harder time "fitting in," finding friends, getting a job, and pursuing other goals, because our society tends to discriminate against persons with disabilities.

The two cases described below represent different points along a continuum. In the first case, a couple has conceived a child with a serious genetic disease; in the second, a fetus has a comparatively minor structural abnormality.

Case 1: Maria is a 21-year-old woman who is pregnant with her second child. Her first child was born with cystic fibrosis (CF), a common life-shortening disorder. Persons with CF have a tendency to chronic lung infection and an inability to absorb fats and nutrients from foods.

As CF carriers, Maria and her husband, Ramon, have a one-in-four chance of having a child with CF with each pregnancy. They have decided they are not emotionally or financially able to care for a second child with CF and will abort an affected fetus.

They also want to find out as early as possible in Maria's pregnancy whether or not the fetus is affected with the disease. During her eighth week of pregnancy, Maria requests CVS to determine the fetus's health status. CVS involves removing a small piece of the chorionic villi (tissue pieces that attach the pregnancy sac to the wall of the uterus) from the pregnant woman. Because the genetic and biochemical makeup of these cells is identical to the genetic and biochemical makeup of the fetus's own cells, DNA tests can be applied to determine whether the fetus is affected with various genetic abnormalities, including cystic fibrosis. The test comes back positive and the couple feels distraught. Even though they had planned for this, they are devastated.

In thinking about abortion, Maria's physician informed her that although her first child has a severe case of CF, the disease is variably expressed, meaning that different people are affected differently. The physician encouraged Maria and Ramon to take some solace in the fact that although CF sufferers used to die in early childhood, the outlook has improved considerably. Most people with CF now survive into adult life. Still, CF remains a potentially serious and fatal disorder.

Case 2: Leah and Samuel are excitedly expecting their first child. During the course of her pregnancy, Leah has had several ultrasounds to check on fetal status. Ultrasound is a technique that emits sound waves and bounces them off the developing fetus. The waves are then converted into a picture on a TV monitor. During a routine ultrasound, Leah's physician notices a structural malformation in the fetus. Upon closer inspection, the physician determines that the fetus has a cleft palate.

Cleft palate is a gap in the roof of the mouth that runs from the behind the teeth to the nasal cavity. People affected with cleft palate sometimes have other birth defects, including partial deafness. Babies born with cleft palate must be bottle fed, and usually undergo surgery to repair the palate at about one year of age. Following surgery, further operations and speech therapy may be necessary.

Leah and her husband had imagined and hoped for a perfect baby. Because they are young and seem to be in excellent health, they are inclined to feel that the odds of having a healthy baby are in their favor. Although both of them feel attached to the fetus they have conceived, neither opposes abortion. They decide to have an abortion and try for a baby that does not have physical defects. Their reasoning is that a baby without cleft palate would probably be happier than a baby with this condition. As new parents, their job would be made easier if their child did not have to undergo surgeries and other therapies and suffer from ridicule and scorn from other children.

In thinking about these cases, you may wish to consider the following questions.

- What might it be like if you had CF or cleft palate when you were growing up?
- Do you think you would have the friends you have now?
- Do you think people would have treated you differently?
- What impact might having either one of these conditions have had on your parents?

If you had required surgery when you were very small, for example, would family members have to make certain sacrifices to care for you?

- What impact would the extra time and attention they might devote to you have on your siblings?
- In short, how would your family be different than it now is?
- On the other hand, what positive understandings or character traits do you imagine you and others might gain through dealing with these conditions?
- Do you think you would have become a more compassionate and caring person if you had received the special care and compassion of others?

Finally, what guidance is available to you by way of some of the exemplars discussed in Chapter 3? And, from Chapter 4, at what level of caring (Gilligan) or of moral development (Kohlberg) will your answers to the questions above place you?

SEX SELECTION

Having considered the problem of selective termination of pregnancy for the purpose of preventing birth defects, let us next turn to a different issue that also involves the selective termination of pregnancy. Sex selection refers to selective termination of pregnancies for the purpose of having a child of a particular sex, male or female. The sex of a human being is determined at conception when an ovum (egg) is fertilized by a male-producing or female-producing sperm. There are various techniques for detecting fetal sex *in utero*, including amniocentesis, ultrasonic scanning, and chorion biopsy. These techniques were not originally developed for the purpose of detecting sex, but rather for the purpose of detecting fetal abnormalities.

The desire to have a child of a certain sex may spring from a variety of reasons. In societies where women are abused and devalued, couples may prefer to have sons in order that their children have a better quality of life and are not subject to abuse and devaluation. Or prospective parents may prefer a son because men on average have higher incomes than women and so are better able to support their parents financially when they become old. Others prefer a child of a particular sex because they think (either consciously or unconsciously) that persons of that sex are more valuable. Concerns about the composition of a future family also play a central role in sex-selective abortions. Thus, many couples who use abortion as a means of selecting the sex of offspring have as their goal producing a family with a certain gender mix or balance. For example, a couple that already has one or more daughters may desire to have a son. Or a family that already includes two sons and one daughter may prefer a second daughter to a third son. Unlike most other abortion decisions, in sex-selective abortion a pregnant woman generally wants to become pregnant, but wants to continue with pregnancy only if the fetus that is conceived meets certain standards. Sex-selective abortion is in this respect analogous to abortions of fetuses with genetic or other defects. In both cases, a woman or couple desire to have a *child*, but want a certain *kind* of future child.

It is important to note that in most societies, prospective parents do have preferences about the sex of their future offspring, and they prefer having a son to having a daughter. Moreover, there exists a definite relationship between women's social, legal, and economic status and the tendency of both women and men to prefer sons. In general, son-preference increases as woman's social status declines.[17] Some argue that permitting sex selection only serves to perpetuate a sexist society in which women are devalued.[18] Others, however, claim that parents cannot be blamed for wanting the best for their future child.[19]

The two cases described below illustrate different circumstances in which parents desire to have an abortion because they prefer a child of a certain sex. In both cases, the personal situation of the couple is pivotal to the decision.

> **Case 1:** Cecile and Frank had never had a child but they had decided in advance that they wanted only boys. Frank felt that he would be a better parent to a son than a daughter. He had grown up with four brothers and had enjoyed the closeness that same-sex relationships had involved in his family of origin. He hoped to recreate these same strong bonds in his own family. Cecile had other reasons for preferring sons. As a child she had been molested by her father and she felt threatened by the prospect of a daughter being vulnerable to sexual abuse, either by Cecile's own father or by other men. Although she had been through counseling, Cecil continued to feel that she would be inclined to act in an over-protective way with a daughter and that her daughter would sense this and feel anxieties and fears.

Cecile and Frank clearly wanted to be the best parents they could be; both felt better equipped to parent boys than girls.

> • Although their intentions are well-meaning, should we as a society support sex selection?
> • Perhaps, if we do, other couples will abuse this option and selectively terminate fetuses for less laudable grounds. To what extent should a woman's or couple's personal reasons for wanting an abortion influence public policies?
> • In answering this question, consider the following further questions. If a woman is ethically entitled to have an abortion during the early stages of her pregnancy, do others have a right to determine what the reasons for that decision may be?
> • Alternatively, if we suppose that the right to choose abortion is not absolute and that only some reasons are sufficient to justify this choice, how do we implement a public policy that distinguishes "legitimate" from "illegitimate" reasons?
> • If there are as many reasons for abortion as there are women contemplating abortions, is it possible to define general categories of acceptable and unacceptable reasons?

But if we fail to even attempt to render such distinctions, perhaps many unethical choices will be allowed.

> **Case 2:** Stacey and Mohammed had four healthy girls. Now they wanted a boy. Although they were financially comfortable, they had decided that five children would have to be their limit. Thus, although they had taken "pot luck" so far, they did not want to continue in this manner. When Stacey became pregnant for the fifth time, the couple expressed their preferences for a son to Stacey's obstetrician and requested that the doctor perform ultrasonic scanning to determine the sex of the fetus. They indicated to the physician that they intended to abort a fetus of the "wrong" sex as early as possible in the course of pregnancy and then to try again.

Unlike the previous example, this example turns on a couple's desire to parent offspring of both sexes.

Whereas the previous couple feared they could not parent well, or as well, children who were female, this couple wants to experience the distinct pleasures of parenting boys as well as girls. In reflecting on this case, consider the following issues.

The effects of allowing this one couple to act on their preferences may not be terribly significant for the society. But the effects of a policy that permits such a practice on a larger scale could be quite significant.

- Should Stacey and Mohammed simply be grateful to have healthy children and forget about what sex the children are?
- Or should they be permitted to execute their preferences to have a son, as well as daughters?
- What are some advantages and disadvantages of such a policy?
- Do you think the ethical arguments for it are stronger or weaker than the ethical arguments against it?

Arguments For And Against 'Choosing Our Children.' Now that you have reflected independently about possible ethical bases for selective abortion, look briefly at some of the arguments that have been put forward by others. Summarized below are arguments frequently heard on both sides.

One argument against allowing abortion for purposes of sex selection or screening for genetic defects is based upon the implication this carries for how we may come to view our future children and our future families.[20]

First Argument Against Selecting the Sex or Health of the Fetus
1. Honoring parents' desires to have children of a particular kind leads to viewing children as products or commodities that can be ordered in accordance with parental specifications.
2. Viewing children in this manner devalues them. It is at odds with regarding children as beings who possess an inherent dignity and worth.
3. Therefore parents should not be permitted to pick the kind of children they want to have, including the sex or health of their child.

In response to this argument it can be noted that it is an empirical (factual) question whether or not the consequences the argument describes will occur. Until there is some evidence to support the claim that selective abortion will depersonalize our attitudes toward children and families, the argument's premises are more speculative than factually based.

Second Argument Against Selecting the Sex or Health of the Fetus
1. If parents are allowed to abort fetuses who are the "wrong sex" or have the "wrong" genetic features, this will lead society down a perilous slippery slope.
2. The next step along this slope will be that parents will want to abort fetuses who do not possess certain positive qualities, such as a certain hair or eye color, a high level of intelligence, or natural talents for music, mathematics or other areas.
3. Producing children according to parental specifications is unethical; it reinforces the tendency (noted above) to view children as objects to be produced.
4. Therefore, society should not allow the first step along this slippery slope to take place.

Once again, strengthening the argument would require showing that the consequences it predicts are likely to occur.

A final argument against choosing future children on the basis of their sexual or genetic qualities holds that such a practice necessarily involves wrongful discrimination. There are two versions this argument might take.

Third Argument Against Selecting the Sex or Health of the Fetus

Version One
1. Sexism is wrong.
2. It is inherently sexist to prefer one child over another child solely on the basis of that child's sex.
3. Selectively aborting fetuses of a certain sex is sexist in precisely this way.
4. Therefore, abortion for the purpose of sex selection is wrong.

Version Two:
1. Discrimination against handicapped individuals is wrong.
2. It is inherently discriminatory to prefer a healthy child over a handicapped child solely on the basis of the child's handicap.
3. Selectively aborting handicapped fetuses is discriminatory in precisely this way.
4. Therefore, abortion for the purpose of choosing healthy children over unhealthy children is wrong.

In addition to the above arguments, the following arguments might be advanced in support of *permitting* selective abortion. First, it might be argued that granting prospective parents this option increases their happiness.[21]

First Argument Supporting Selective Abortion

1. For many parents, the desire to have a child of a certain sex or a child who is healthy and free of handicaps is very strongly held.
2. Satisfying these preferences is therefore likely to increase parents' happiness significantly, whereas frustrating these preferences is likely to increase parents' misery.
3. Therefore selective abortion should be permitted.

As with the previous arguments that appealed to the negative consequences of allowing abortion, this argument turns on the strength of its empirical (factual) premise (premise two). We may discover that selective abortion for the purposes under consideration does not make parents happier, but only makes them guilty or miserable. Parents who select fetuses through aborting unwanted offspring may become miserable, for example, if they must make repeated efforts to become pregnant and go through repeated abortions when pregnancy does not bring the desired result.

A somewhat different basis for defending the right to abort a fetus in order to choose the sex or genetic health of a future child refers to the more general value of freedom of choice and action.[22,23]

Second Argument Supporting Selective Abortion

1. A democratic society, such as the United States, places a supreme value on freedom of conscience and action. In particular, we grant citizens basic liberties such as freedom of speech, assembly, and conscience.
2. Reproduction is as basic as these other freedoms and should therefore be included among them.
3. Then denying women the freedom to choose abortion is at odds with the basic ethical tenets of our society.

Against this argument it can be said that even basic liberties are not unlimited. Thus, freedom of speech is not absolute and can be limited when it incites people to violence. Freedom of religion is not tolerated indiscriminately or in ways that infringe upon the welfare of others. So too, it might be claimed that if the fetus is a person at some time prior to birth, then the liberties of the fetus's parents can be ethically constrained.

Clearly, none of the above arguments establishes conclusively that abortion for the purposes of sex selection or the avoidance of genetic defects is ethically permissible or impermissible. Yet, taken together, these arguments make evident the wide range of difficult issues that are at stake. Both the consequences of individual choices and public practices must be considered. In addition, certain non-consequentialist values, including liberty and respect for persons, are at issue. Any position regarding the permissibility of abortion must weigh carefully these and other ethical factors.

THE SOCIETY:
WHAT DO CURRENT LAWS AND POLICIES ALLOW?

Having discussed the ethical implications of abortion for the individual fetus, the pregnant woman, the biological parents, and the family, it is now time to cast our net still wider and view abortion from the perspective of the larger society, the context in which fetus, woman, and family are themselves situated. The purpose of this section is to review existing laws and regulations pertaining to abortion. Importantly, the emphasis here will not be on the ethical permissibility of abortion. Instead, the point of this section is to describe, in a summary fashion, the laws and policies that provide the framework within which personal ethical choices are currently made.

THE DECRIMINALIZATION OF ABORTION: *ROE VS. WADE*

Let us begin with the following case, which has played a pivotal role in shaping American abortion law.

> **The Case of Norma McCovery.** Norma McCovery was an unmarried pregnant women living in Dallas, Texas. She wanted an abortion but Texas law treated abortion as a criminal offense unless abortion was necessary in order to save the woman's life. Ms. McCovery had hoped to travel to California, because she had heard that abortion laws were less restrictive there and thought she could obtain an abortion. However, her poverty precluded her from raising the money she needed to pay for the trip. Her pregnancy continued and a baby was later born and put up for adoption.
>
> Some time after this occurred an attorney approached Ms. McCovery and asked her if she was willing to participate in a class-action suit (a law suit in which a group of people together make a common legal complaint against an opposing party) against the District Attorney of Dallas County. The suit would challenge the constitutionality of the Texas abortion law. Ms. McCovery agreed and the law suit proceeded, with the Federal Court ruling in Ms. McCovery's favor and declaring the Texas abortion law void.
>
> But the matter was hardly over. Instead, an appeal was made to the highest court in the land, the United States Supreme Court, which heard the case. To protect her identity, Ms. McCovery adopted the pseudonym, Roe, and the person against whom the case was brought, the District Attorney of Dallas County, was Mr. Henry Wade.

Norma McCovery's story became the well-known 1973 U.S. Supreme Court case, *Roe vs. Wade.*[24]

In a 7-2 decision, the Justices of the U.S. Supreme Court found the Texas law criminalizing abortion to be in violation of the United States Constitution. In doing so, the court rendered void laws in many other states that resembled Texas's law in making abortion a criminal offense. Before *Roe*, very few states had legalized abortion for any purpose other than to save the pregnant woman's life. After *Roe*, states were allowed to restrict abortion practices in some ways; however, they could no longer criminalize abortion as the Texas statute had done. Instead, *Roe* established that a woman's right to have an abortion was part of a fundamental "right of privacy."

The *Roe* decision, written by Justice Harry A. Blackmun, established a trimester approach (a "trimester" is a period of three months, or one-third of the length of a full-term pregnancy). This approach allows states to place increasing restrictions on abortion as the time period of pregnancy lengthens, so long as those restrictions reflect legitimate state interests. Specifically, the following restrictions are permitted under *Roe*.

Roe's Trimester Approach

> *First Trimester*. During the first 14 weeks of pregnancy, the abortion decision is treated as a private decision of the individual woman in consultation with her health care provider.

> *Second Trimester*. During the 15th through the 28th week of pregnancy, states may regulate abortion, but only for the purpose of promoting the health of the pregnant woman.

> *Third Trimester*. During the 29th through 42nd week of pregnancy, states may prohibit abortion to protect a viable fetus.

Although all states are required to follow these guidelines, they are also free to differ in ways not covered by these guidelines. Thus, abortion laws differ from one state to the next with respect to the use of state funds to fund abortion. Thirty states and the District of Columbia prohibit the use of state funds to pay for an abortion unless the woman's life is in danger; eight other states allow public funding to be used in limited circumstances, such as pregnancy resulting from rape or incest.

ABORTION LAW AFTER *ROE VS. WADE*

Subsequent to the *Roe vs. Wade* decision, the U.S. Supreme Court has ruled on several other abortion cases. Although the court's ruling in *Roe* has not been overturned, the effect of subsequent decisions has been to narrow and modify the abortion rights that *Roe* established.

In a 1989 decision, *Webster vs. Reproductive Health Services,* the U.S. Supreme Court upheld by a 5-4 vote a Missouri statue that placed various restrictions on abortion.[25] The *Webster* decision, written by Chief Justice William Rehnquist, allowed Missouri (and therefore other states) to favor childbirth over abortion and to prohibit state employees and facilities from assisting with abortion. In addition, the decision allowed states to impose regulations that require physicians to test for the viability of the fetus if they suspect that a fetus is at least 20 weeks old prior to performing an abortion. Despite these restrictions, a woman's constitutional right to have an abortion remained intact, and states were not allowed to prohibit abortions of nonviable fetuses.

By upholding Missouri's viability test requirement, the Supreme Court appeared to erode the trimester framework established in *Roe*. The *Roe* framework allowed state regulations during the second trimester only if they were for the purpose of protecting the health of the pregnant woman. However, the *Webster* decision allows state regulations during the second trimester that are not for the purpose of protecting the health of the pregnant woman. In *Webster,* the majority opinion (the opinion representing the vote of the majority of the nine Supreme Court Justices) criticized "the rigid trimester analysis of the course of a pregnancy enunciated in *Roe*" on the grounds that the court did "not see why the state's interest in protecting potential human life should come into existence only at the point of viability, and that there should therefore be a rigid line allowing state regulation after viability but prohibiting it before viability."[26] The viability tests that are currently available, such as ultrasound and amniocentesis, were not designed for the purpose of determining fetal viability and cannot pinpoint the exact age of the fetus. In addition, these tests add to the cost of abortion and therefore make it more difficult for many women to obtain an abortion.

Three years after Webster, in 1992, the U.S. Supreme Court ruled in another abortion case, *Planned Parenthood vs. Casey.* In Casey, the court reviewed and upheld certain portions of a Pennsylvania statue that placed restrictions on abortion.[27] Among the restrictions that the Pennsylvania statue imposed were the following:

Requirements of the Pennsylvania Statute

1. *Twenty-four hour waiting period.* A pregnant woman was required to give informed consent to an abortion. In addition, at least 24 hours must pass between her informed consent and the performance of an abortion. "Informed consent" was defined as including informing a pregnant woman about the nature and risks of the abortion procedure and its alternatives, the probable gestational age of the fetus, and the medical risks of carrying the fetus to term.

2. *Parental consent to abortion.* When the woman seeking an abortion was legally a minor Pennsylvania law required her either to obtain the consent of a parent or guardian, or to have a judge's certification that she was mature or that abortion was in her best interests.

3. *Spousal notification.* A married woman seeking an abortion was required to notify her husband of her intention. Exceptions to this requirement included situations in which a pregnant woman's husband was not the fetus's biological father, could not be located, or had criminally assaulted her or she feared that he would assault her if he were notified about her intention to have an abortion.

4. *Mandatory reporting.* Pennsylvania law also made it mandatory that health providers report to the Health Department after performing an abortion and include facts, such as the name of the physician performing the abortion, the woman's age, the county or state where she resided, the number of previous pregnancies and abortions she had had, and the probable gestational age and weight of the fetus.

In reviewing Pennsylvania's restrictions, the Supreme Court upheld, by a 5-4 vote, all restrictions except spousal notification. The majority opinion held that "a state may not give to a man the kind of dominion over his wife that parents exercise over their children ... Women do not lose their constitutionally protected liberty when they marry."[28] It is important to note that none of these restrictions challenges the basic idea established in *Roe*, that a woman has a constitutional right to have an abortion. Rather, the restrictions upheld in *Casey* chip away at aspects of this right and make it easier for states to impose restrictions on women seeking abortions.[29]

The Casey decision departed from *Roe* in two key respects. First, like *Webster*, the *Casey* decision rejected *Roe*'s trimester approach to regulating abortion. Second, *Casey* changed the standard applied to evaluate the constitutionality of state restrictions. Whereas *Roe* had held that the right to have an abortion was fundamental and could not be overridden unless a state had a *compelling interest*, *Casey* established that states could restrict abortion so long as restrictions do not impose an *undue burden* on women seeking abortions.

THE FUTURE OF ABORTION LAW

Future Supreme Court decisions will be profoundly affected by how the membership of the court changes in the years ahead, as several Justices are nearing retirement age. Some legal experts predict that efforts to overturn Roe are likely to continue.[30] Other scholars discern in the language of more recent abortion decisions a heightened appreciation of the "uniquely female burdens of unwanted pregnancy," and predict that the constitutional right to have an abortion is not itself in serious jeopardy.[31]

The entire debate about abortion will be profoundly altered in the event that RU 486, the so-called "abortion pill," becomes available in the United States. RU 486 induces abortion in early pregnancy by blocking the action of progesterone, a hormone that stimulates changes in the wall of the uterus necessary for implementation of a fertilized egg. The drug was developed by the French pharmaceutical company, Roussel Uclaf, and has been used in France since 1989. The drug is now undergoing government scrutiny and testing in America.

In the event RU 486 becomes available in the United States, state laws restricting abortion may pose less significant obstacles to woman seeking abortion. Because RU 486 acts before a fertilized egg becomes implanted in the uterus, it terminates pregnancy before a fetus proper has developed. Thus, state laws restricting abortion of viable fetuses would not apply to RU 486. Furthermore, certain ethical objections to abortion based on the status of the fetus would carry less weight when abortion is performed so early during the course of pregnancy.

OUTLOOK

Abortion is a complex problem for individuals, families, and the society. Even if we could reach an agreement about what ethical criteria should be applied to assess the fetus's moral status, this hardly settles the abortion controversy. Other considerations that must be addressed include the unique relationship of the fetus to another human being, the interests prospective parents may have in forming certain kinds of families, the interests of other family members, the welfare of the society in which abortion decisions occur, and the implications of abortion for other ethical choices, such as our treatment of human beings at the end of life and our treatment of non-human animals. The law governing abortion is in a period of transition; however, a woman's basic legal right to have an abortion remains intact. New technologies, such as RU 486, will have a profound impact on future ethical and legal debates.

READINGS
AN ALMOST ABSOLUTE VALUE IN HISTORY

The most fundamental question involved in the long history of thought on abortion is: How do you determine the humanity of a being? To phrase the question that way is to put in comprehensive humanistic terms what the theologians either dealt with as an explicitly theological question under the heading of "ensoulment" or dealt with implicitly in their treatment of abortion. The Christian position as it origi-

* For permission to photocopy this selection, please contact Harvard University Press. Reprinted by persmission of the publishers from MORALITY OF ABORTION: LEGAL AND HISTORICAL PERSPECTIVES by John T. Noonan, Cambridge, Mass.: Harvard University Press, Copyright © 1970 by the President and Fellows of Harvard College.

nated did not depend on a narrow theological or philosophical concept. It had no relation to theories of infant baptism. It appealed to no special theory on instantaneous ensoulment. It took the world's view on ensoulment as that view changed from Aristotle to Zacchia. There was, indeed, theological influence affecting the theory of ensoulment finally adopted, and, of course, ensoulment itself was a theological concept, so that the position was always explained in theological terms. But the theological notion of ensoulment could easily be translated into humanistic language by substituting "human" for "rational soul"; the problem of knowing when a man is a man is common to theology and humanism.

If one steps outside the specific categories used by the theologians, the answer they gave can be analyzed as a refusal to discriminate among human beings on the basis of their varying potentialities. Once conceived, the being was recognized as man because he had man's potential. The criterion for humanity, thus, was simple and all-embracing: If you are conceived by human parents, you are human.

The strength of this position may be tested by a review of some of the other distinctions offered in the contemporary controversy over legalizing abortion. Perhaps the most popular distinction is in terms of viability. Before an age of so many months, the fetus is not viable, that is, it cannot be removed from the mother's womb and live apart from her. To that extent, the life of the fetus is absolutely dependent on the life of the mother. This dependence is made the basis of denying recognition to its humanity.

There are difficulties with this distinction. One is that the perfection of artificial incubation may make the fetus viable at any time: It may be removed and artificially sustained. Experiments with animals already show that such a procedure is possible. This hypothetical extreme case relates to an actual difficulty: There is considerable elasticity to the idea of viability. Mere length of life is not an exact measure. The viability of the fetus depends on the extent of its anatomical and functional development. The weight and length of the fetus are better guides to the state of its development than age, but weight and length vary. Moreover, different racial groups have different ages at which their fetuses are viable. Some evidence, for example, suggests that Negro fetuses mature more quickly than white fetuses. If viability is the norm, the standard would vary with race and with many individual circumstances.

The most important objection to this approach is that dependence is not ended by viability. The fetus is still absolutely dependent on someone's care in order to continue existence; indeed a child of one or three or even five years of age is absolutely dependent on another's care for existence; uncared for, the older fetus or the younger child will die as surely as the early fetus detached from the mother. The unsubstantial lessening in dependence at viability does not seem to signify any special acquisition of humanity.

A second distinction has been attempted in terms of experience. A being who has had experience, has lived and suffered, who possesses memories, is more human than one who has not. Humanity depends on formation by experience. The fetus is thus "unformed" in the most basic human sense.

This distinction is not serviceable for the embryo which is already experiencing and reacting. The embryo is responsive to touch after eight weeks and at least at that point is experiencing. At an earlier stage the zygote is certainly alive and responding to its environment. The distinction may also be challenged by the rare case where aphasia has erased adult memory: Has it erased humanity? More fundamentally, this distinction leaves even the older fetus or the younger child to be treated as an unformed inhuman thing. Finally, it is not clear why experience as such confers humanity. It could be argued that certain central experiences such as loving or learning are necessary to make a man human. But then human beings who have failed to love or to learn might be excluded from the class called man.

A third distinction is made by appeal to the sentiments of adults. If a fetus dies, the grief of the parents is not the grief they would have for a living child. The fetus is an unnamed "it" till birth, and is not perceived as personality until at least the fourth month of existence, when movements in the womb manifest a vigorous presence demanding joyful recognition by the parents.

Yet feeling is notoriously an unsure guide to the humanity of others. Many groups of humans have had difficulty in feeling that persons of another tongue, color, religion, sex, are as human as they. Apart from reactions to alien groups, we mourn the loss of a ten-year-old boy more than the loss of his one-day-old brother or his 90-year-old grandfather. The difference felt and the grief expressed vary with the potentialities extinguished, or the experience wiped out; they do not seem to point to any substantial difference in the humanity of baby, boy, or grandfather.

Distinctions are also made in terms of sensation by the parents. The embryo is felt within the womb only after about the fourth month. The embryo is seen only at birth. What can be neither seen nor felt is different from what is tangible. If the fetus cannot be seen or touched at all, it cannot be perceived as man.

Yet experience shows that sight is even more untrustworthy than feeling in determining humanity. By sight, color became an appropriate index for saying who was a man, and the evil of racial discrimination was given foundation. Nor can touch provide the test; a being confined by sickness, "out of touch" with others, does not thereby seem to lose his humanity. To the extent that touch still has appeal as a criterion, it appears to be a survival of the old English idea of "quickening" — a possible mistranslation of the Latin *animatus* used in the canon law. To that extent, touch as a criterion seems to be dependent on the Aristotelian notion of ensoulment, and to fall when this notion is discarded.

Finally, a distinction is sought in social visibility. The fetus is not socially perceived as human. It cannot communicate with others. Thus, both subjectively and objectively, it is not a member of society. As moral rules are rules for the behavior of members of society to each other, they cannot be made for behavior toward what is not yet a member. Excluded from the society of men, the fetus is excluded from the humanity of men.

By force of the argument from the consequences, this distinction is to be rejected. It is more subtle than that founded on an appeal to physical sensation, but it is equally dangerous in its implications. If humanity depends on social recognition, individuals or whole groups may be dehumanized by being denied any status in their society. Such a fate is fictionally portrayed in *1984* and has actually been the lot of many men in many societies. In the Roman empire, for example, condemnation to slavery meant the practical denial of most human rights; in the Chinese Communist world, landlords have been classified as enemies of the people and so treated as nonpersons by the state. Humanity does not depend on social recognition, though often the failure of society to recognize the prisoner, the alien, the heterodox as human has led to the destruction of human beings. Anyone conceived by a man and a woman is human. Recognition of this condition by society follows a real event in the objective order, however imperfect and halting the recognition. Any attempt to limit humanity to exclude some group runs the risk of furnishing authority and precedent for excluding other groups in the name of the consciousness or perception of the controlling group in the society.

A philosopher may reject the appeal to the humanity of the fetus because he views "humanity" as a secular view of the soul and because he doubts the existence of anything real and objective which can be identified as humanity. One answer to such a philosopher is to ask how he reasons about moral questions without supposing that there is a sense in which he and the others of whom he speaks are human. Whatever group is taken as the society which determines who may be killed is thereby taken as human. A second answer is to ask if he does not believe that there is a right and wrong way of deciding moral questions. If there is such a difference, experience may be appealed to: To decide who is human on the basis of the sentiment of a given society has led to consequences which rational men would characterize as monstrous.

The rejection of the attempted distinctions based on viability and visibility, experience and feeling, may be buttressed by the following considerations: Moral judgments often rest on distinctions, but if the distinctions are not to appear arbitrary fiat, they should relate to some real difference in probabilities. There is a kind of continuity in all life, but the earlier stages of the elements of human life possess tiny probabilities of development. Consider, for example, the spermatozoa in any normal ejaculate: There are about 200,000,000 in any single ejaculate, of which one has a chance of developing into a zygote. Consider the oocytes which may become ova: There are 100,000 to 1,000,000 oocytes in a female infant, of which a maximum of 390 are ovulated. But once spermatozoon and ovum meet and the conceptus if formed, such studies as have been made show that roughly in only 20% of the cases will spontaneous

Part III: The Individual And Ethical Issues

abortion occur. In other words, the chances are about 4 out of 5 that this new being will develop. At this stage in the life of the being there is a sharp shift in probabilities, an immense jump in potentialities. To make a distinction between the rights of spermatozoa and the rights of the fertilized ovum is to respond to an enormous shift in possibilities. For about twenty days after conception, the egg may split to form twins or combine with another egg to form a chimera, but the probability of either event happening is very small.

It may be asked, What does a change in biological probabilities have to do with establishing humanity? The argument from probabilities is not aimed at establishing humanity but at establishing an objective discontinuity which may be taken into account in moral discourse. As life itself is a matter of probabilities, as most moral reasoning is an estimate of probabilities, so it seems in accord with the structure of reality and the nature of moral thought to found a moral judgment on the change in probabilities at conception. The appeal to probabilities is the most commonsensical of arguments; to a greater or smaller degree all of us base our actions on probabilities, and in morals, as in law, prudence and negligence are often measured by the account one has taken of the probabilities. If the chance is 200,000,000 to 1 that the movement in the bushes into which you shoot is a man's, I doubt if many persons would hold you careless in shooting; but if the chances are 4 out of 5 that the movement is a human being's, few would acquit you of blame. Would the argument be different if only one out of ten children conceived came to term? Of course this argument would be different. This argument is an appeal to probabilities that actually exist, not to any and all states of affairs which may be imagined.

The probabilities as they do exist do not show the humanity of the embryo in the sense of a demonstration in logic any more than the probabilities of the movement in the bush being a man demonstrate beyond all doubt that the being is a man. The appeal is a "buttressing" consideration, showing the plausibility of the standard adopted. The argument focuses on the decisional factor in any moral judgment and assumes that part of the business of a moralist is drawing lines. One evidence of the nonarbitrary character of the line drawn is the difference of probabilities on either side of it. If a spermatozoon is destroyed, one destroys a being which had a chance of far less than 1 in 200 million of developing into a reasonable being, possessed of the genetic code, a heart and other organs, and capable of pain. If a fetus is destroyed, one destroys a being already possessed of the genetic code, organs, and sensitivity to pain, and one which had an 80% chance of developing further into a baby, outside the womb, who, in time, would reason.

The positive argument for conception as the decisive moment of humanization is that at conception the new being receives the genetic code. It is this genetic information which determines his characteristics, which is the biological carrier of the possibility of human wisdom, which makes him a self-evolving being. A being with a human genetic code is man.

This review of current controversy over the humanity of the fetus emphasizes what a fundamental question the theologians resolved in asserting the inviolability of the fetus. To regard the fetus as possessed of equal rights with other humans was not, however, to decide every case where abortion might be employed. It did decide the case where the argument was that the fetus should be aborted for its own good. To say a being was human was to say it had a destiny to decide for itself which could not be taken from it by another man's decision. But human beings with equal rights often come in conflict with each other, and some decision must be made as to whose claims are to prevail. Cases of conflict involving the fetus are different only in two respects: The total inability of the fetus to speak for itself and the fact that the right of the fetus regularly at stake is the right to life itself.

The approach taken by the theologians to these conflicts was articulated in terms of "direct" and "indirect." Again, to look at what they were doing from outside their categories, they may be said to have been drawing lines or "balancing values." "Direct" and "indirect" are spatial metaphors: "Line-drawing" is another. "To weigh" or "to balance" values is a metaphor of a more complicated mathematical sort hinting at the process which goes on in moral judgments. All the metaphors suggest that, in the moral judgments made, comparisons were necessary, that no value completely controlled. The principle of double effect was no doctrine fallen from heaven, but a method of analysis appropriate where two relative values were being compared. In Catholic moral theology, as it developed, life even of the innocent was not taken as an absolute. Judgments on acts affecting life issued from a process of weighing. In the weighing, the fetus was always given a value greater than zero, always a value separate and independent from its parents. This valuation was crucial and fundamental in all Christian thought on the subject and marked it off from any approach which considered that only the parents' interests needed to be considered.

Even with the fetus weighed as human, one interest could be weighed as equal or superior: That of the mother in her own life. The casuists between 1450 and 1895 were willing to weigh this interest as superior. Since 1895, that interest was given decisive weight only in the two special cases of the cancerous uterus and the ectopic pregnancy. In both of these cases the fetus itself had little chance of survival even if the abortion were not performed. As the balance was once struck in favor of the mother whenever her life was endangered, it could be so struck again. The balance reached between 1895 and 1930 attempted prudentially and pastorally to forestall a multitude of exceptions for interests less than life.

The perception of the humanity of the fetus and the weighing of fetal rights against other human rights constituted the work of the moral analysts. But what spirit animated their abstract judgments? For the Christian community it was the injunction of Scripture to love your neighbor as yourself. The fetus as human was a neighbor; his life had parity with one's own. The commandment gave life to what otherwise would have been only rational calculation.

The commandment could be put in humanistic as well as theological terms: Do not injure your fellow man without reason. In these terms, once the humanity of the fetus is perceived, abortion is never right except in self-defense. When life must be taken to save life, reason alone cannot say that a mother must prefer a child's life to her own. With this exception, now of great rarity, abortion violates the rational humanist tenet of the equality of human lives.

For Christians the commandment to love had received a special imprint in that the exemplar proposed of love was the love of the Lord for his disciples. In the light given by this example, self-sacrifice carried to the point of death seemed in the extreme situations not without meaning. In the less extreme cases, preference for one's own interests to the life of another seemed to express cruelty or selfishness irreconcilable with the demands of love.

A DEFENSE OF ABORTION

Most opposition to abortion relies on the premise that the fetus is a human being, a person, from the moment of conception. The premise is argued for, but, as I think, not well. Take, for example, the most common argument. We are asked to notice that the development of a human being from conception through birth into childhood is continuous; then it is said that to draw a line, to choose a point in this development and say "before this point the thing is not a person, after this point it is a person" is to make an arbitrary choice, a choice for which in the nature of things no good reason can be given. It is concluded that the fetus is, or anyway that we had better say it is, a person from the moment of conception. But this conclusion does not follow. Similar things might be said about the development of an acorn into an oak tree, and it does not follow that acorns are oak trees, or that we had better say they are. Arguments of this form are sometimes called "slippery slope arguments" — the phrase is perhaps self-explanatory — and it is dismaying that opponents of abortion rely on them so heavily and uncritically.

I am inclined to agree, however, that the prospects for "drawing a line" in the development of the fetus look dim. I am inclined to think also that we shall probably have to agree that the fetus has already become a human person well before birth. Indeed, it comes as a surprise when one first learns how early in its life it begins to acquire human characteristics. By the tenth week, for example, it already has a face, arms and legs, fingers and toes; it has internal organs, and brain activity is detectable.1 On the other hand, I think that the premise is false, that the fetus is not a person from the moment of conception. A newly fertilized ovum, a newly implanted clump of cells, is no more a person than an acorn is an oak tree. But I shall not discuss any of this. For it seems to me to be of great interest to ask what happens if, for the sake of argument, we allow the premise. How, precisely, are we supposed to get from there to the conclusion that abortion is morally impermissible? Opponents of abortion commonly spend most of their time establishing that the fetus is a person, and hardly any time explaining the step from there to the impermissibility of abortion. Perhaps they think the step too simple and obvious to require much comment. Or perhaps instead they are simply being economical in argument. Many of those who defend abortion rely on the premise that the fetus is not a person, but only a bit of tissue that will become a person at birth; and why pay out more arguments than you have to? Whatever the explanation, I suggest that the step they take is neither easy nor obvious, that it calls for closer examination than it is commonly given, and that when we do give it this closer examination we shall feel inclined to reject it.

I propose, then, that we grant that the fetus is a person from the moment of conception. How does the argument go from here? Something like this, I take it. Every person has a right to life. So the fetus has a right to life. No doubt the mother has a right to decide what shall happen in and to her body; everyone would grant that. But surely a person's right to life is stronger and more stringent than the mother's right to decide what happens in and to her body, and so outweighs it. So the fetus may not be killed; an abortion may not be performed.

It sounds plausible. But now let me ask you to imagine this. You wake up in the morning and find yourself back to back in bed with an unconscious violinist. A famous unconscious violinist. He has been found to have a fatal kidney ailment, and the Society of Music Lovers has canvassed all the available medical records and found that you alone have the right blood type to help. They have therefore kidnapped you, and last night the violinist's circulatory system was plugged into yours, so that your kidneys can be used to extract poisons from his blood as well as your own. The director of the hospital now tells you, "Look, we're sorry the Society of Music Lovers did this to you — we would never have permitted it if we had known. But still, they did it, and the violinist now is plugged into you. To unplug you would be to kill him. But never mind, it's only for nine months. By then he will have recovered from his ailment, and can safely be unplugged from you." Is it morally incumbent on you to accede to this situation? No doubt it would be very nice of you if you did, a great kindness. But do you *have* to accede to it? What if it were not nine months, but nine years? Or longer still? What if the director of the hospital says, "Tough luck, I agree, but you've now got to stay in bed, with the violinist plugged into you, for the rest of your life. Because remember this. All persons have a right to life, and violinists are persons. Granted you have a right to decide what happens in and to your body, but a person's right to life outweighs your right to decide what happens in and to your body. So you cannot ever be unplugged from him." I imagine you would regard this as outrageous, which suggests that something really is wrong with that plausible-sounding argument I mentioned a moment ago.

In this case, of course, you were kidnapped; you didn't volunteer for the operation that plugged the violinist into your kidneys. Can those who oppose abortion on the ground I mentioned make an exception for a pregnancy due to rape? Certainly. They can say that persons have a right to life only if they didn't come into existence because of rape; or they can say that all persons have a right to life, but that some have less of a right to life than others, in particular, that those who came into existence because of rape have less. But these statements have a rather unpleasant sound. Surely the question of whether you have a right to life at all, or how much of it you have, shouldn't turn on the question of whether or not you are the product of a rape. And in fact the people who oppose abortion on the ground I mentioned do not make this distinction, and hence do not make an exception in the case of rape.

Nor do they make an exception for a case in which the mother has to spend the nine months of her pregnancy in bed. They would agree that would be a great pity, and hard on the mother; but all the same, all persons have a right to life, the fetus is a person, and so on. I suspect, in fact, that they would not make an exception for a case in which, miraculously enough, the pregnancy went on for nine years, or even the rest of the mother's life.

Some won't even make an exception for a case in which continuation of the pregnancy is likely to shorten the mother's life; they regard abortion as impermissible even to save the mother's life. Such cases are nowadays very rare, and many opponents of abortion do not accept this extreme view. All the same, it is a good place to begin: A number of points of interest come out in respect to it.

1. Let us call the view that abortion is impermissible even to save the mother's life "the extreme view." I want to suggest first that it does not issue from the argument I mentioned earlier without the addition of some fairly powerful premises. Suppose a woman has become pregnant, and now learns that she has a cardiac condition such that she will die if she carries the baby to term. What may be done for her? The fetus, being a person, has a right to life, but as the mother is a person too, so has she a right to life. Presumably they have an equal right to life. How is it supposed to come out that an abortion may not be performed? If mother and child have an equal right to life, shouldn't we perhaps flip a coin? Or should we add to the mother's right to life her right to decide what happens in and to her body, which everybody seems to be ready to grant — the sum of her rights now outweighing the fetus' right to life?

The most familiar argument here is the following. We are told that performing the abortion would be directly killing[2] the child, whereas doing nothing would not be killing the mother, but only letting her die. Moreover, in killing the child, one would be killing an innocent person, for the child has committed no crime and is not aiming at his mother's death. And then there are a variety of ways in which this might be continued. (1) But as directly killing an innocent person is always and absolutely impermissible, an abortion may not be performed.[3] Or, (2) as directly killing an innocent person is murder, and murder is always and absolutely impermissible, an abortion may not be performed. Or, (3) as one's duty to refrain from directly killing an innocent person is more stringent than one's duty to keep a person from dying, an abortion may not be performed. Or, (4) if one's only options are directly killing an innocent person or letting a person die, one must prefer letting

the person die, and thus an abortion may not be performed.[4]

Some people seem to have thought that these are not further premises which must be added if the conclusion is to be reached, but that they follow from the very fact that an innocent person has a right to life.[5] But this seems to me to be a mistake, and perhaps the simplest way to show this is to bring out that while we must certainly grant that innocent persons have a right to life, the theses in (1) through (4) are all false. Take (2), for example. If directly killing an innocent person is murder, and thus is impermissible, then the mother's directly killing the innocent person inside her is murder, and thus is impermissible. But it cannot seriously be thought to be murder if the mother performs an abortion on herself to save her life. It cannot seriously be said that she *must* refrain, that she *must* sit passively by and wait for her death. Let us look again at the case of you and the violinist. There you are, in bed with the violinist, and the director of the hospital says to you, "It's all most distressing, and I deeply sympathize, but you see this is putting an additional strain on your kidneys, and you'll be dead within the month. But you *have* to stay where you are all the same. Because unplugging you would be directly killing an innocent violinist, and that's murder, and that's impermissible." If anything in the world is true, it is that you do not commit murder, you do not do what is impermissible, if you reach around to your back and unplug yourself from that violinist to save your life.

The main focus of attention in writings on abortion has been on what a third party may or may not do in answer to a request from a woman for an abortion. This is in a way understandable. Things being as they are, there isn't much a woman can safely do to abort herself. So the question asked is what a third party may do, and what the mother may do, if it is mentioned at all, is deduced, almost as an afterthought, from what it is concluded that third parties may do. But it seems to me that to treat the matter in this way is to refuse to grant to the mother that very status of person which is so firmly insisted on for the fetus. For we cannot simply read off what a person may do from what a third party may do. Suppose you find yourself trapped in a tiny house with a growing child. I mean a very tiny house, and a rapidly growing child — you are already up against the wall of the house and in a few minutes you'll be crushed to death. The child on the other hand won't be crushed to death; if nothing is done to stop him from growing he'll be hurt, but in the end he'll simply burst open the house and walk out a free man. Now I could well understand it if a bystander were to say, "There's nothing we can do for you. We cannot choose between your life and his, we cannot be the ones to decide who is to live, we cannot intervene." But it cannot be concluded that you too can do nothing, that you cannot attack it to save your life. However innocent the child may be, you do not have to wait passively while it crushes you to death. Perhaps a pregnant woman is vaguely felt to have the status of house, to which we don't allow the right of self-defense. But if the woman houses the child, it should be remembered that she is a person who houses it.

I should perhaps stop to say explicitly that I am not claiming that people have a right to do anything whatever to save their lives. I think, rather, that there are drastic limits to the right of self-defense. If someone threatens you with death unless you torture someone else to death, I think you have not the right, even to save your life, to do so. But the case under consideration here is very different. In our case there are only two people involved, one whose life is threatened, and one who threatens it. Both are innocent: The one who is threatened is not threatened because of any fault, the one who threatens does not threaten because of any fault. For this reason we may feel that we bystanders cannot intervene. But the persons threatened can.

In sum, a woman surely can defend her life against the threat to it posed by the unborn child, even if doing so involves its death. And this shows not merely that the theses in (1) through (4) are false; it shows that the extreme view of abortion is false, and so we need not canvass any other possible ways of arriving at it from the argument I mentioned at the outset.

2. The extreme view could of course be weakened to say that while abortion is permissible to save the mother's life, it may not be performed by a third party, but only by the mother herself. But this cannot be right either. For what we have to keep in mind is that the mother and the unborn child are not like two tenants in a small house which has, by an unfortunate mistake, been rented to both: The mother *owns* the house. The fact that she does adds to the offensiveness of deducing that the mother can do nothing from the supposition that third parties can do nothing. But it does more than this: It casts a bright light on the supposition that third parties can do nothing. Certainly it lets us see that a third party who says "I cannot choose between you" is fooling himself if he thinks this is impartiality. If Jones has found and fastened on a certain coat, which he needs to keep him from freezing, but which Smith also needs to keep him from freezing, then it is not impartiality that says "I cannot choose between you" when Smith owns the coat. Women have said again and again "This body is *my* body!" and they have reason to feel angry, reason to feel that it has been like shouting into the wind. Smith, after all, is hardly likely to bless us if we say to him, "Of course it's your coat, anybody would grant that it is. But no one may choose between you and Jones who is to have it."

We should really ask what it is that says "no one may choose" in the face of the fact that the body that houses the child is the mother's body. It may be simply a failure to appreciate this fact. But it may be something more interesting, namely the sense that one has a right to refuse to lay hands on people, even where it would be just and fair to do so, even where justice seems to require that somebody do so. Thus justice might call for somebody to get Smith's coat back from Jones, and yet you have a right to refuse to be the one to lay hands on Jones, a right to refuse to do physical violence to him. This, I think, must be granted. But then what should be said is not "no one may choose," but only "*I* cannot choose," and indeed not even this, but "*I* will not *act*," leaving it open that somebody else can or should, and in particular that anyone in a position of authority, with the job of securing people's rights, both can and should. So this is no difficulty. I have not been arguing that any given third party must accede to the mother's request that he perform an abortion to save her life, but only that he may.

I suppose that in some views of human life the mother's body is only on loan to her, the loan not being one which gives her any prior claim to it. One who held this view might well think it impartiality to say "I cannot choose." But I shall simply ignore this possibility. My own view is that if a human being has any just, prior claim to anything at all, he has a just, prior claim to his own body. And perhaps this needn't be argued for here anyway, since, as I mentioned, the arguments against abortion we are looking at do grant that the woman has a right to decide what happens in and to her body.

But although they do grant it, I have tried to show that they do not take seriously what is done in granting it. I suggest the same thing will reappear even more clearly when we turn away from cases in which the mother's life is at stake, and attend, as I propose we now do, to the vastly more common cases in which a woman wants an abortion for some less weighty reason than preserving her own life.

3. Where the mother's life is not at stake, the argument I mentioned at the outset seems to have a much stronger pull. "Everyone has a right to life, so the unborn person has a right to life." And isn't the child's right to life weightier than anything other than the mother's own right to life, which she might put forward as ground for an abortion?

This argument treats the right to life as if it were unproblematic. It is not, and this seems to me to be precisely the source of the mistake.

For we should now, at long last, ask what it comes to, to have a right to life. In some views having a right to life includes having a right to be given at least the bare minimum one needs for continued life. But suppose that what in fact *is* the bare minimum a man needs for continued life is something he has no right at all to be given? If I am sick unto death, and the only thing that will save my life is the touch of Henry Fonda's cool hand on my fevered brow, then all the same, I have no right to be given the touch of Henry Fonda's cool hand on my fevered brow. It would be frightfully nice of him to fly in from the West Coast to provide it. It would be less nice, though no doubt well meant, if my friends flew out to the West Coast and carried Henry Fonda back with them. But I have no right at all against anybody that he should do this for me. Or again, to return to the story I told earlier, the fact that for continued life that violinist needs the continued use of your kidneys does not establish that he has a right to be given the continued use of your kidneys. He certainly has no right against you that *you* should give him continued use of your kidneys. For no body has any right to use your kidneys unless you give him such a right; and nobody has the right against you that you shall give him this right — if you do

allow him to go on using your kidneys, this is a kindness on your part, and not something he can claim from you as his due. Nor has he any right against anybody else that *they* should give him continued use of your kidneys. Certainly he had no right against the Society of Music Lovers that they should plug him into you in the first place. And if you now start to unplug yourself, having learned that you will otherwise have to spend nine years in bed with him, there is nobody in the world who must try to prevent you, in order to see to it that he is given something he has a right to be given.

Some people are rather stricter about the right to life. In their view, it does not include the right to be given anything, but amounts to, and only to, the right not to be killed by anybody. But here a related difficulty arises. If everybody is to refrain from killing that violinist, then everybody must refrain from doing a great many different sorts of things. Everybody must refrain from slitting his throat, everybody must refrain from shooting him — and everybody must refrain from unplugging you from him. But does he have a right against everybody that they shall refrain from unplugging you from him? To refrain from doing this is to allow him to continue to use your kidneys. It could be argued that he has a right against us that *we* should allow him to continue to use your kidneys. That is, while he had no right against us that we should give him the use of your kidneys, it might be argued that he anyway has a right against us that we shall not now intervene and deprive him of the use of your kidneys. I shall come back to third-party interventions later. But certainly the violinist has no right against you that *you* shall allow him to continue to use your kidneys. As I said, if you do allow him to use them, it is a kindness on your part, and not something you owe him.

The difficulty I point to here is not peculiar to the right of life. It reappears in connection with all the other natural rights; and it is something which an adequate account of rights must deal with. For present purposes it is enough just to draw attention to it. But I would stress that I am not arguing that people do not have a right to life — quite to the contrary, it seems to me that the primary control we must place on the acceptability of an account of rights is that it should turn out in that account to be a truth that all persons have a right to life. I am arguing only that having a right to life does not guarantee having either a right to be given the use of or a right to be allowed continued use of another person's body — even if one needs it for life itself. So the right to life will not serve the opponents of abortion in the very simple and clear way in which they seem to have thought it would.

4. There is another way to bring out the difficulty. In the most ordinary sort of case, to deprive someone of what he has a right to is to treat him unjustly. Suppose a boy and his small brother are jointly given a box of chocolates for Christmas. If the older boy takes the box and refuses to give his brother any of the chocolates, he is unjust to him, for the brother has been given a right to half of them. But suppose that, having learned that otherwise it means nine years in bed with that violinist, you unplug yourself from him. You surely are not being unjust to him, for you gave him no right to use your kidneys, and no one else can have given him any such right. But we have to notice that in unplugging yourself, you are killing him; and violinists, like everybody else, have a right to life, and thus in the view we were considering just now, the right not to be killed. So here you do what he supposedly has a right you shall not do, but you do not act unjustly to him in doing it.

The emendation which may be made at this point is this: The right to life consists not in the right not to be killed, but rather in the right not to be killed unjustly. This runs a risk of circularity, but never mind: It would enable us to square the fact that the violinist has a right to life with the fact that you do not act unjustly toward him in unplugging yourself, thereby killing him. For if you do not kill him unjustly, you do not violate his right to life, and so it is no wonder you do him no injustice.

But if this emendation is accepted, the gap in the argument against abortion stares us plainly in the face: It is by no means enough to show that the fetus is a person, and to remind us that all persons have a right to life — we need to be shown also that killing the fetus violates its right to life, i.e., that abortion is unjust killing. And is it?

I suppose we may take it as a datum that in the case of pregnancy due to rape the mother has not given the unborn person a right to the use of her body for food and shelter. Indeed, in what pregnancy should it be supposed that the mother has given the unborn persons such a right? It is not as if there were unborn persons drifting about the world, to whom a woman who wants a child says "I invite you in."

But it might be argued that there are other ways one can have acquired a right to the use of another person's body than by having been invited to use it by that person. Suppose a woman voluntarily indulges in intercourse, knowing of the chance it will issue in pregnancy, and then she does become pregnant; is she not in part responsible for the presence, in fact the very existence, of the unborn person inside? No doubt she did not invite it in. But doesn't her partial responsibility for its being there itself give it a right to the use of her body?6 If so, then her aborting it would be more like the boy's taking away the chocolates, and less like your unplugging yourself from the violinist — doing so would be depriving it of what it does have a right to, and thus would be doing it an injustice.

And then, too, it might be asked whether or not she can kill it even to save her own life: If she voluntarily called it into existence, how can she now kill it, even in self-defense?

The first thing to be said about this is that it is something new. Opponents of abortion have been so concerned to make out the independence of the fetus, in order to establish that it has a right to life, just as its mother does, that they have tended to overlook the possible support they might gain from making out that the fetus is *dependent* on the mother, in order to establish that she has a special kind of responsibility for it, a responsibility that gives it rights against her which are not possessed by any independent person — — such as an ailing violinist who is a stranger to her.

On the other hand, this argument would give the unborn person a right to its mother's body only if her pregnancy resulted from a voluntary act, undertaken in full knowledge of the chance a pregnancy might result from it. It would leave out entirely the unborn person whose existence is due to rape. Pending the availability of some further argument, then, we would be left with the conclusion that unborn persons whose existence is due to rape have no right to the use of their mothers' bodies, and thus that aborting them is not depriving them of anything they have a right to and hence is not unjust killing.

And we should also notice that it is not at all plain that this argument really does go even as far as it purports to. For there are cases and cases, and the details make a difference. If the room is stuffy, and I therefore open a window to air it, and a burglar climbs in, it would be absurd to say, "Ah, now he can stay, she's given him a right to the use of her house — for she is partially responsible for his presence there, having voluntarily done what enabled him to get in, in full knowledge that there are such things as burglars, and that burglars burgle." It would be still more absurd to say this if I had had bars installed outside my windows, precisely to prevent burglars from getting in, and a burglar got in only because of a defect in the bars. It remains equally absurd if we imagine it is not a burglar who climbs in, but an innocent person who blunders or falls in. Again, suppose it were like this: Peopleseeds drift about in the air like pollen, and if you open your windows, one may drift in and take root in your carpets or upholstery. You don't want children, so you fix up your windows with fine mesh screens, the very best you can buy. As can happen, however, and on very, very rare occasions does happen, one of the screens is defective; and a seed drifts in and takes root. Does the personplant who now develops have a right to the use of your house? Surely not — despite the fact that you voluntarily opened your windows, you knowingly kept carpets and upholstered furniture, and you knew that screens were sometimes defective. Someone may argue that you are responsible for its rooting, that it does have a right to your house, because after all you *could* have lived out your life with bare floors and furniture, or with sealed windows and doors. But this won't do − − for by the same token anyone can avoid a pregnancy due to rape by having a hysterectomy, or anyway by never leaving home without a (reliable!) army.

It seems to me that the argument we are looking at can establish at most that there are *some* cases in which the unborn person has a right to the use of its mother's body, and therefore *some* cases in which abortion is unjust killing. There is room for much discussion and argument as to precisely which, if any. But I think we should sidestep this issue and leave it open, for at any rate the argument certainly does not establish that all abortion is unjust killing.

5. There is room for yet another argument here, however. We surely must grant that there may be cases in which it would be morally indecent to detach a person from your body at the cost of his life. Suppose you learn that what the violinist needs is not nine years of your life, but only one hour: All you need do to save his life is spend one hour in that bed with him. Suppose also that letting him use your kidneys for that one hour would not affect your health in the slightest. Admittedly you were kidnapped. Admittedly you did not give anyone permission to plug him into you. Nevertheless it seems to me plain you *ought* to allow him to use your kidneys for that hour — it would be indecent to refuse.

Again, suppose pregnancy lasted only an hour, and constituted no threat to life or death (sic). And suppose that a woman becomes pregnant as a result of rape. Admittedly she did not voluntarily do anything to bring about the existence of a child. Admittedly she did nothing at all which would give the unborn person a right to the use of her body. All the same it might well be said, as in the newly emended violinist story, that she *ought* to allow it to remain for that hour — that it would be indecent in her to refuse.

Now some people are inclined to use the term "right" in such a way that it follows from the fact that you ought to allow a person to use your body for the hour he needs, that he has a right to use your body for the hour he needs, even though he has not been given that right by any person or act. They may say that it follows also that if you refuse, you act unjustly toward him. This use of the term is perhaps so common that it cannot be called wrong; nevertheless it seems to me to be an unfortunate loosening of what we would do better to keep a tight rein on. Suppose that box of chocolates I mentioned earlier had not been given to both boys jointly, but was given only to the older boy. There he sits, stolidly eating his way through the box, his small brother watching enviously. Here we are likely to say "You ought not to be so mean. You ought to give your brother some of those chocolates." My own view is that it just does not follow from the truth of this that the brother has any right to any of the chocolates. If the boy refuses to give his brother any, he is greedy, stingy, callous — but not unjust. I suppose that the people I have in mind will say it does follow that the brother has a right to some of the chocolates, and thus that the boy does act unjustly if he refuses to give his brother any. But the effect of saying this is to obscure what we should keep distinct, namely the difference between the boy's refusal in this case and the boy's refusal in the earlier case, in which the box was given to both boys jointly, and in which the small brother thus had what was from any point of view clear title to half.

A further objection to so using the term "right" that from the fact that A ought to do a thing for B, it follows that B has a right against A that A do it for him, is that it is going to make the question of whether or not a man has a right to a thing turn on how easy it is to provide him with it; and this seems not merely unfortunate, but morally unacceptable. Take the case of Henry Fonda again. I said earlier that I had no right to the touch of his cool hand on my fevered brow, even though I needed it to save my life. I said it would be frightfully nice of him to fly in from the West Coast to provide me with it, but that I had no right against him that he should do so. But suppose he isn't on the West Coast. Suppose he has only to walk across the room, place a hand briefly on my brow — and lo, my life is saved. Then surely he ought to do it, it would be indecent to refuse. Is it to be said, "Ah, well, it follows that in this case she has a right to the touch of his hand on her brow, and so it would be an unjustice in him to refuse"? So that I have a right to it when it is easy for him to provide it, though no right when it's hard? It's rather a shocking idea that anyone's rights should fade away and disappear as it gets harder and harder to accord them to him.

So my own view is that even though you ought to let the violinist use your kidneys for the one hour he needs, we should not conclude that he has a right to do so — we should say that if you refuse, you are, like the boy who owns all the chocolates and will give none away, self-centered and callous, indecent in fact, but not unjust. And similarly, that even supposing a case in which a woman pregnant due to rape ought to allow the unborn person to use her body for the hour he needs, we should not conclude that he has a right to do so; we should conclude that she is self-centered, callous, indecent, but not unjust, if she refuses. The complaints are no less grave; they are just different. However, there is no need to insist on this point. If anyone does wish to deduce "he has a right" from "you ought," then all the same he must surely grant that there are cases in which it is not morally required of you that you allow that violinist to use your kidneys, and in which he does not have a right to use them, and in which you do not do him an injustice if you refuse. And so also for mother and unborn child. Except in such cases as the unborn person has a right to demand it — and we were leaving open the possi-

bility that there may be such cases — nobody is morally *required* to make large sacrifices, of health, of all other interests and concerns, of all other duties and commitments, for nine years, or even for nine months, in order to keep another person alive.

6. We have in fact to distinguish between the two kinds of Samaritan: The Good Samaritan and what we might call the Minimally Decent Samaritan. The story of the Good Samaritan, you will remember, goes like this:

A certain man went down from Jerusalem to Jericho, and fell among thieves, which stripped him of his raiment, and wounded him, and departed, leaving him half dead.

And by chance there came down a certain priest that way; and when he saw him, he passed by on the other side.

And likewise a Levite, when he was at the place, came and looked on him, and passed by on the other side.

But a certain Samaritan, as he journeyed, came where he was; and when he saw him he had compassion on him.

And went to him, and bound up his wounds, pouring in oil and wine, and set him on his own beast, and brought him to an inn, and took care of him.

And on the morrow, when he departed, he took out two pence, and gave them to the host, and said unto him, "Take care of him; and whatsoever thou spendest more, when I come again, I will repay thee."

(Luke 10:30-35)

The Good Samaritan went out of his way, at some cost to himself, to help one in need of it. We are not told what the options were, that is, whether or not the priest and the Levite could have helped by doing less than the Good Samaritan did, but assuming they could have, then the fact they did nothing at all shows they were not even Minimally Decent Samaritans, not because they were not Samaritans, but because they were not even minimally decent.

These things are a matter of degree, of course, but there is a difference, and it comes out perhaps most clearly in the story of Kitty Genovese, who, as you will remember, was murdered while thirty-eight people watched or listened, and did nothing at all to help her. A Good Samaritan would have rushed out to give direct assistance against the murderer. Or perhaps we had better allow that it would have been a

Splendid Samaritan who did this, on the ground that it would have involved a risk of death for himself. But the thirty-eight not only did not do this, they did not even trouble to pick up a phone to call the police. Minimally Decent Samaritanism would call for doing at least that, and their not having done it was monstrous.

After telling the story of the Good Samaritan, Jesus said, "Go, and do thou likewise." Perhaps he meant that we are morally required to act as the Good Samaritan did. Perhaps he was urging people to do more than is morally required of them. At all events it seems plain that it was not morally required of any of the thirty-eight that he rush out to give direct assistance at the risk of his own life, and that it is not morally required of anyone that he give long stretches of his life — nine years or nine months — to sustaining the life of a person who has no special right (we were leaving open the possibility of this) to demand it.

Indeed, with one rather striking class of exceptions, no one in any country in the world is *legally* required to do anywhere near as much as this for anyone else. The class of exceptions is obvious. My main concern here is not the state of the law in respect to abortion, but it is worth drawing attention to the fact that in no state in this country is any man compelled by law to be even a Minimally Decent Samaritan to any person; there is no law under which charges could be brought against the thirty-eight who stood by while Kitty Genovese died. By contrast, in most states in this country women are compelled by law to be not merely Minimally Decent Samaritans, but Good Samaritans to unborn persons inside them. This doesn't by itself settle anything one way or the other, because it may well be argued that there should be laws in this country — as there are in many European countries — compelling at least Minimally Decent Samaritanism.7 But it does show that there is a gross injustice in the existing state of the law. And it shows also that the groups currently working against liberalization of abortion laws, in fact working toward having it declared unconstitutional for a state to permit abortion, had better start working for the adoption of Good Samaritan laws generally, or earn the charge that they are acting in bad faith.

I should think, myself, that Minimally Decent Samaritan laws would be one thing, Good Samaritan laws quite another, and in fact highly improper. But we are not here concerned with the law. What we should ask is not whether anybody should be compelled by law to be a Good Samaritan, but whether we must accede to a situation in which somebody is being compelled — by nature, perhaps — to be a Good Samaritan. We have, in other words, to look now at third-party interventions. I have been arguing that no person is morally required to make large sacrifices to sustain the life of another who has no right to demand them, and this even where the sacrifices do not include life itself; we are not morally required to be Good Samaritans or anyway Very Good Samaritans to one another. But what if a man cannot extricate himself from such a situation? What if he appeals to us to extricate him? It seems to me plain that there are cases in which we can, cases in which a Good Samaritan would extricate him. There you are, you were kidnapped, and nine years in bed with that violinist lie ahead of you. You have your own life to lead. You are sorry, but you simply cannot see giving up so much of your life to the sustaining of his. You cannot extricate yourself, and ask us to do so. I should have thought that — in light of his having no right to the use of your body — it was obvious that we do not have to accede to your being forced to give up so much. We can do what you ask. There is no injustice to the violinist in our doing so.

7. Following the lead of the opponents of abortion, I have throughout been speaking of the fetus merely as a person, and what I have been asking is whether or not the argument we began with, which proceeds only from the fetus' being a person, really does establish its conclusion. I have argued that it does not.

But of course there are arguments and arguments, and it may be said that I have simply fastened on the wrong one. It may be said that what is important is not merely the fact that the fetus is a person, but that it is a person for whom the woman has a special kind of responsibility issuing from the fact that she is its mother. And it might be argued that all my analogies are therefore irrelevant — for you do not have that special kind of responsibility for that violinist, Henry Fonda does not have that special kind of responsibility for me. And our attention might be drawn to the fact that men and women both *are* compelled by law to provide support for their children.

I have in effect dealt (briefly) with this argument in section 4 above; but a (still briefer) recapitulation now may be in order. Surely we do not have any such "special responsibility" for a person unless we have assumed it, explicitly or implicitly. If a set of parents do not try to prevent pregnancy, do not obtain an abortion, but rather take it home with them, then they have assumed responsibility for it, they have given it rights, and they cannot *now* withdraw support from it at the cost of its life because they now find it difficult to go on providing for it. But if they have taken all reasonable precautions against having a child, they do not simply by virtue of their biological relationship to the child who comes into existence have a special responsibility for it. They may wish to assume responsibility for it, or they may not wish to. And I am suggesting that if assuming responsibility for it would require large sacrifices, then they may refuse. A Good Samaritan would not refuse — or anyway, a Splendid Samaritan, if the sacrifices that had to be made were enormous. But then so would a Good Samaritan assume responsibility for that violinist; so would Henry Fonda, if he is a Good Samaritan, fly in from the West Coast and assume responsibility for me.

8. My argument will be found unsatisfactory on two counts by many of those who want to regard abortion as morally permissible. First, while I do argue that abortion is not impermissible, I do not argue that it is always permissible. There may well be cases in which carrying the child to term requires only Minimally Decent Samaritanism of the mother, and this is a standard we must not fall below. I am inclined to think it a merit of my account precisely that it does *not* give a general yes or a general no. It allows for and supports our sense that, for example, a sick and desperately frightened fourteen-year-old schoolgirl, pregnant due to rape, may of *course* choose abortion, and that any law which rules this out is an insane law. And it also allows for and supports our sense that in other cases resort to abortion is even positively indecent. It would be indecent in the woman to request an abortion, and indecent in a doctor to perform it, if she is in her seventh month, and wants the abortion just to avoid the nuisance of postponing a trip abroad. The very fact that the arguments I have been drawing attention to treat all cases of abortion, or even all cases of abortion in which the mother's life is not at stake, as morally on a par ought to have made them suspect at the outset.

Secondly, while I am arguing for the permissibility of abortion in some cases, I am not arguing for the right to secure the death of the unborn child. It is easy to confuse these two things in that up to a certain point in the life of the fetus it is not able to survive outside the mother's body; hence removing it from her body guarantees its death. But they are importantly different. I have argued that you are not morally required to spend nine months in bed, sustaining the life of that violinist; but to say this is by no means to say that if, when you unplug yourself, there is a miracle and he survives, you then have a right to turn around and slit his throat. You may detach yourself even if this costs him his life; you have no right to be guaranteed his death, by some other means, if unplugging yourself does not kill him. There are some people who will feel dissatisfied by this feature of my argument. A woman may be utterly devastated by the thought of a child, a bit of herself, put out for adoption and never seen or heard of again. She may therefore want not merely that the child be detached from her, but more, that it die. Some opponents of abortion are inclined to regard this as beneath contempt — thereby showing insensitivity to what is surely a powerful source of despair. All the same, I agree that the desire for the child's death is not one which anybody may gratify, should it turn out to be possible to detach the child alive.

At this place, however, it should be remembered that we have only been pretending throughout that the fetus is a human being from the moment of conception. A very early abortion is surely not the killing of a person, and so is not dealt with by anything I have said here.

Notes

1. Daniel Callahan, *Abortion: Law, Choice and Morality* (New York, 1970), p. 373. This book gives a fascinating survey of the available information on abortion. The Jewish tradition in David M. Feldman, *Birth Control in Jewish Law* (New York, 1963), part 5; the Catholic tradition in John T. Noonan, Jr., "An Almost Absolute Value in History," in *The Morality of Abortion*, ed. John T. Noonan, Jr. (Cambridge, Mass., 1970).

2. The term "direct" in the arguments I refer to is a technical one. Roughly, what is meant by "direct killing" is either killing as an end in itself, or killing as

a means to some end, for example, the end of saving someone else's life. See note 5 on this page, for an example of its use.

3. Cf. *Encyclical Letter of Pope Pius XI on Christian Marriage,* St. Paul Editions (Boston, n.d.), p. 32: "However much we may pity the mother whose health and even life is gravely imperiled in the performance of the duty allotted to her by nature, nevertheless what could ever be a sufficient reason for excusing in any way the direct murder of the innocent? This is precisely what we are dealing with here." Noonan *(The Morality of Abortion,* p. 43) reads this as follows: "What cause can ever avail to excuse in any way the direct killing of the innocent? For it is a question of that."

4. The thesis in (4) is an interesting way weaker than those in (1), (2), and (3): They rule out abortion even in cases in which both mother *and* child will die if the abortion is not performed. By contrast, one who held the view expressed in (4) could consistently say that one needn't prefer letting two persons die to killing one.

5. Cf. the following passage from Pius XII, *Address to the Italian Catholic Society of Midwives:* "The baby in the maternal breast has the right to life immediately from God. — Hence there is no man, no human authority, no science, no medical, eugenic, social, economic or moral 'indication' which can establish or grant a valid juridical ground for a direct deliberate disposition of an innocent human life, that is a which looks to its destruction either as an end or as a means to another end perhaps in itself not illicit. — The baby, still not born, is a man in the same degree and for the same reason as the mother" (quoted in Noonan, *The Morality of Abortion,* p. 45).

6. The need for a discussion of this argument was brought home to me by members of the Society for Ethical and Legal Philosophy, to whom this paper was originally presented.

7. For a discussion of the difficulties involved, and a survey of the European experience with such laws, see *The Good Samaritan and the Law,* ed. James M. Ratcliffe (New York, 1966).

ENDNOTES

1. Peter Singer, *Practical Ethics,* Cambridge University Press, New York, 1982, Chapter 3.
2. John Noonan, "An almost absolute value in history," In Noonan, *The Morality Of Abortion: Legal And Historical Perspectives*, Harvard University Press, Cambridge, MA, 1970: 51-59.
3. L.W. Sumner, "A third way," In *Abortion and Moral Theory*, Princeton University Press, Princeton, NJ, 1981, Chapter 4, pp. 124-160.
4. Sumner, "A third way," p. 84.
5. Mary Anne Warren, "On the moral and legal status of abortion," *The Monist 57*, 1973.
6. Judith Jarvis Thomson, "A defense of abortion," *Philos Public Aff, 1*, 1971. Reprinted in Joel Feinberg, ed., *The Problem of Abortion,* Wadsworth Publishing Company, Belmont, CA, 1984, pp. 173-187.
7. Thomson, "A defense of Abortion," p. 179.
8. Thomson, "A defense of Abortion," p. 179.
9. Mary Anne Warren, *Gendercide,* Rowman and Allanheld, Totowa, NJ, 1985, p. 89.
10. The Gospel of Luke 10:30-35.
11. Thomson, "A defense of abortion."
12. Thomson, "A defense of abortion," pp. 184 ff.
13. Carol Gilligan, *In A Different Voice,* Harvard University Press, Cambridge, MA, 1982.
14. Gilligan, *In A Different Voice,* p. 74.
15. Theodora Ooms, "A family perspective on abortion," In Sidney Callahan, Daniel Callahan, eds., *Abortion: Understanding Differences*, Plenum Press, New York, 1984, pp. 81-108, at p. 94.
16. Gilligan, *In A Different Voice,* p. 70.
17. Warren, Gendercide, p. 13.
18. Christine Overall, *Ethics and Human Reproduction*, Allen and Unwin, Boston, 1987, pp. 22 ff.
19. Warren, *Gendercide,* p. 105.
20. Maura A. Ryan, "The argument for unlimited procreative liberty: A feminist critique," *Hastings Cent Rep* 20, 1990: 6-12.
21. Warren, *Gendercide*, pp. 172-173.
22. Warren, *Gendercide*, pp. 179 ff.
23. Jean Bethke Elshtain, "Reflections on Abortion, Values and the Family," In Sidney Callahan, Daniel

Callahan, eds., *Abortion: Understanding Differences,* Plenum Press, New York, 1984, pp. 47-72.

24. *Roe vs. Wade,* 410 U.S. 113, 93 S. Ct. 705, January 22, 1973.

25. *Webster vs. Reproductive Health Services,* U.S. 109, S.Ct. 3040, 1989, reprinted in Ronald Munson, ed., *Intervention and Reflection: Basic Issues in Medical Ethics,* Fourth Ed., Wadsworth Publishing Company, Belmont, CA, 1992: pp. 92-94.

26. *Webster vs. Reproductive Health Services,* p. 94.

27. *Casey vs. Planned Parenthood of Southeastern Pennsylvania,* 112 S. Ct. 2791, 1992.

28. *Casey vs. Planned Parenthood of Southeastern Pennsylvania.*

29. John Robertson, "Casey and the Resuscitation of *Roe vs. Wade,*" *Hastings Cent Rep 22,* 1992: 24-28.

30. George J. Annas, "The Supreme Court, liberty, and abortion," *New Engl J Med 327,* 1992: 651-654.

31. Robertson, "Casey and the Resuscitation of *Roe vs. Wade.*"

Chapter 7

Robert M. Veatch

DEATH AND DYING

"Of all the wonders that I have yet heard, it seems to me most strange that men should fear seeing that death, a necessary end, will come when it will come."

– Shakespeare, *Julius Caesar*

"I know death hath ten thousand several doors for men to make their exit."

– John Webster, *Duchess of Malfi*

"It has been often said, that it is not death, but dying which is terrible."
– Henry Fielding

While death, like taxes, may still be one of the few certainties of life, the new technologies of the biological revolution have literally given humans the power to control the timing and conditions of their own deaths.[1] Unfortunately, sometimes we are able to keep patients alive, but not able to cure their diseases or restore them to normal health. Sometimes we can actually suspend patients in an ambiguous state in which we literally do not know whether they are alive or dead.

Nine-year-old Josef Camp was playing on the streets of inner-city Washington, D.C. one day when he bought a pickle from a street vendor. Soon after eating the pickle he went into convulsions and collapsed. The rescue squad brought him to the emergency room unconscious. His heart had stopped beating; he was not breathing. When they pumped his stomach they found traces of marijuana and PCP. Someone had apparently spiked the pickle as a practical joke.

The boy had been without oxygen so long that serious, irreversible brain damage had occurred leaving him permanently unconscious. In fact, some tests indicated that his brain had been without oxygen so long that it was destroyed. The physicians claimed there was nothing more they could do to restore

Robert Marlin Veatch, B.S. Purdue, M.S. California at San Francisco, B.D., M.A. and Ph.D. Harvard University, is director of the Kennedy Institute of Ethics at Georgetown University, Washington, D.C.

its function. He was left permanently unconscious, breathing on a ventilator, with organ functions maintained by aggressive support from a team of nurses and other care givers.

Some claimed he should be declared dead based on the evidence that his brain was dead. Others claimed he was still alive because his heart was still beating and he was breathing (albeit on a ventilator). They thought they should ask the parents for permission to withdraw the ventilator and let him die.

When the parents were asked, they turned to their religious tradition. They were Muslims and believed that Allah should be given a chance to intervene. They demanded that the physicians do everything possible to maintain Josef's life and give Allah a chance. The nurses were required to devote substantial attention to maintaining Josef while the parents' physicians, lawyers, and courts tried to sort out the case. The intensive life-support cost more than $1,000 per day until the boy died a hundred days later while decision-makers were still trying to sort out what to do.[2]

THE MAJOR DEFINITIONS OF DEATH

The first issue of debate in such cases is what it means for someone to be dead. Until the last part of the 20th century we all knew more or less what it meant to be dead. We would listen for a heartbeat, feel a pulse, or look for signs of breathing. But in the 1960s we began to question whether these were the only signs of death. With the invention of ventilators, we now had the capacity to maintain heartbeat and blood flow mechanically. If these are maintained, along with nutrition basics and blood pressure regulations, respiration will continue spontaneously – even if brain function was totally and permanently destroyed.

In the 1960s most Americans began to realize there could be great social benefits if these patients without brain function could be treated as dead. In some cases they were ideal sources of organs for transplant. It cannot be denied that some of those who began advocating a new, brain-based definition of death were also interested in procuring organs for transplant. Three major definitions of death have emerged from this controversy.

The Cardiac-Oriented Definition. Those who believe patients like Josef Camp are alive even if their brain function is permanently destroyed believe in the traditional definition of death. An individual is dead, according to this traditional view, when there is irreversible cessation of circulatory and respiratory function. This is often referred to as the "heart definition." When the heart is gone, the patient is gone. But at the University of Utah in December 1992, a critically ill patient named Barney Clark had his own heart removed because of irreversible heart disease. He was the first person ever placed on a mechanical artificial heart that was intended to be a permanent replacement for his heart. For 112 days the mechanical device continued to pump blood through his body with the regularity of a human heart. For much of that time Barney Clark was conscious, capable of carrying on conversations, and debating the wisdom of his new-found place in history.

Later, patients given artificial hearts were actually able to get up out of bed and leave the hospital, pushing their mechanical pumps around in a shopping cart-like basket. Surely, these people were still alive even though their hearts had long since stopped beating and had decayed into a formless mass. It is not the heart *per se* that the defenders of the traditional definition of death consider critical, but rather the bodily functions normally associated with the beating heart: circulation and respiration. Holders of this view – probably including Josef Camp's parents – believe one is dead when there is irreversible loss of these functions.

It is critical that the loss of function be irreversible. We do not believe someone really dies if the stoppage is only temporary and reversible. Thus someone who has a heart attack and is immediately rescued by someone competent in CPR, so that the heart begins functioning again, is not properly said ever to have "died." He had a cardiac arrest all right, – and would surely have died had not the heart stoppage been reversed in time, – but if we are careful with language, no one can suffer "clinical death" and recover. Deaths occur exactly one per person, at least in this world.

In the late 1960s some people began to criticize the cardiac-based definition of death. On a practical level, if these people with irreversible loss of brain function whose hearts continue to beat are considered alive, there would be terrible consequences – not only for potential transplant recipients, but also for many others who could benefit from other important uses for these arguably dead bodies. Critics of the heart-based definition claim these bodies are in reality nothing more than "respiring cadavers" (that is, dead bodies which continue to have heartbeats and respire because of ventilator support). They can be used by medical scientists not only for transplant, but also for research, teaching, and other therapeutic purposes. Great good is at stake in getting the definition of death right.

Still, even if these bodies are valuable, this alone cannot justify calling someone dead unless there are good reasons for doing so. Many people, however, have now accepted the belief that the essence of the human being is not mere flowing of blood and breath. They believe there is something more important, something more essential to being alive than just having a pump moving blood around the body. They see this view as too animalistic; unduly reducing the human too much to a mere biological organism.

The "Whole-Brain" Oriented Definition. In 1968 the Harvard Ad Hoc Committee on Definition of Death adopted a key report claiming that we should start treating people as dead when their brain function is totally and irreversibly lost.[3] The committee proposed a set of four criteria for measuring this irreversible loss of brain function: 1) unreceptivity and unresponsivity; 2) no movements or breathing; 3) no reflexes; 4) flat EEG.

It is widely accepted that once one meets these four criteria, one will lose heart and respiratory function soon, but that is not the basis for the new definition of death. In fact, someday scientists may be able to keep a heart beating in such patients indefinitely. The holders of this view believe that the essence of the human is its ability to integrate bodily functions so that one functions "as a whole." They believe, with good reason, that this integration is done by the brain so that when the brain irreversibly loses its capacity to function, then the individual as a whole is dead.

The first law establishing a brain-oriented basis for pronouncing death was passed in 1970 in Kansas. Now all U.S. jurisdictions have such a law and the prestigious U.S. President's Commission for the Study of Ethical Problems in Medicine and Biomedical and Behavioral Research has endorsed pronouncing death based on irreversible loss of all brain function.[4] Almost all countries throughout the world have such laws as well. Only Japan resists adopting a brain-based definition.[5] They do so in part based on traditional religious beliefs regarding the presence of a life force (a "soul") throughout the body.

Recently New Jersey has become the first state to modify its definition so that an individual has the right to present a document stating that on religious grounds he or she prefers the use of the traditional heart-based definition.[6] Not only Japanese, but some Orthodox Jews continue to insist that life is present as long as the heart beats. This "conscience clause" gives people the right to choose their own definitions of death. The reasoning offered for this discretion is that choosing a definition of death is essentially a matter of religious or philosophical or public policy choice. Deciding when to treat someone as dead is not something resolvable by medical science. People must choose based on their beliefs about when an individual ceases to be part of the human moral and political community. We generally agree that on such matters of religious and philosophical choice, individuals should be given maximum possible discretion. Hence New Jersey has chosen to give that discretion. Whether the people of that state were justified in giving it only on religious grounds rather than secular philosophical preferences is a matter of continuing controversy.

The "Higher-Brain" Definition. While a whole-brain definition of death is now widely accepted by the general public and the medical community, many philosophers are not yet satisfied. In particular, they have been questioning whether literally *all* of the brain must have ceased functioning in order for someone to be dead. We know that some parts of the brain perform rather elementary reflex functions. The cerebrum, the highest portion of the brain, is responsible for consciousness, thinking, feeling, memory, and voluntary muscle control, but the lower portions of the brain are responsible such functions as the cough reflex, eye blink, and control or respiration.

In 1971 J.B. Brierley published a report on two patients who had lost all cerebral function but continued to breathe on their own for several weeks because their lower brain tissues were still alive.[7] It is widely agreed that such patients can never again regain consciousness. They are in what is now called a permanent or persistent vegetative state. By the whole-brain definition of death they are clearly still alive because the lower brain (what is called the brain stem) is still functioning.

A number of philosophers have for several years been arguing that these people should no more be considered alive than those who have totally lost brain function.[8] They hold that what is really important for being considered alive and part of the human community is some capacity for consciousness or ability to interact socially with other humans. This is what some people have in mind when they refer to the human as a social animal. These critics believe that one is dead – that is, no longer part of the human community for social purposes – if one has irreversibly lost consciousness. They acknowledge that this would make Josef Camp, permanently vegetative patients, and others who are permanently unconscious dead by definition. They believe this is acceptable. That means their bodies must be treated with respect, but it also means we can treat them the way we treat other deceased people.

The defenders of the whole-brain-oriented position offer several criticisms of this position. They claim that it is a more radical break from tradition than the whole-brain position; that it relies on a concept of personhood about which there is no social agreement; and that treating people who have some purportedly unimportant brain functions remaining places us on a "slippery slope" that could lead to treating those with some limited remaining cerebral functions (such as the Alzheimer's patient or the severely retarded) as dead also. They ask, "Would you really bury someone who is still breathing?"

Defenders of the higher-brain position say that what is really the break from tradition came with the movement from a definition of death based on circulatory function to one based on neurological function. They believe the whole-brain defenders are just as guilty of risking a new definition as those defending the higher-brain position. They deny that their position is based on any view of personhood or personal identity, claiming that whatever personhood means it has nothing to do with the definition of death. They even deny that they are risking a slide down a slippery slope. They claim that the decisive difference between being alive and being dead is whether there is the presence of any mental function. (The Alzheimer's patient and the retarded clearly are alive by this criterion.) They even have accused the defenders of the whole-brain position of being on their own slippery slope because they try to draw a line between the top of the spinal cord and the base of the brain and there are no principled differences between the reflexes at the top of the spine and those at the base of the brain. They claim that there is a real qualitative difference between the presence and absence of any mental function that is much more significant.

Some defenders of the higher-brain position acknowledge that there are people who, for religious or other reasons, will not accept this position. They offer the proposal to extend the policy permitting conscientious choice among plausible alternatives, as people now have in New Jersey, but they would extend the range of choices for a definition to include complete loss of consciousness. They would propose that a society pick one of the three positions (based on circulatory, whole-brain, or higher-brain positions), whichever has the greatest support, as the default position and then let those who dissent opt for one of the other positions. If the whole-brain position were chosen, then some could exercise a choice in favor of the cardiac view and others could choose the higher-brain alternative.

MENTALLY COMPETENT PATIENTS

Josef Camp might already be dead, at least if the higher brain position were the default and perhaps if the whole-brain position were. However, if parents were also given the right to exercise conscientious dissent in favor of a reasonable alternative (at least if the patient had never been competent to express a position), then Josef's parents might have chosen to have Josef treated as alive until his heart stopped. What actually happened was that the neurologists could not agree that his brain was completely dead. Moreover, the District of Columbia at the time did not legally recognize a brain-based definition of death. Josef was legally alive. The real moral question was whether he had to be treated to be kept alive or whether the physicians could cease life support and let him die, even against his parents' wishes.

Often the definition of death gets undue attention when the real issue at stake, especially for patients who retain some brain function, is how they should be treated and what decisions are ethically acceptable.

Elizabeth Bouvia was born with severe cerebral palsy that left her a bedridden quadriplegic. She was totally dependent on others for her care. She suffered from continual painful arthritis for which she received morphine through a tube implanted in her chest. She suffered muscle contractures that left her unable to change her position. Still she was intelligent, having completed a master's degree in social work from San Diego State University. Her problems became so severe that her parents were no longer able to care for her. She was left without financial means.

In September of 1983 she reached the decision that she would refuse feeding while she starved herself to death. Because she needed the morphine infusion to control her pain, however, she asked to be cared for in Riverside General Hospital while she did this. When the physicians insisted that she would have to have a feeding tube if she stayed in the hospital, she sought a court order. A lower court ruled that she was mentally competent to refuse the feeding tube and had a legal right to do so, but appealed to concerns about the effect on other patients and the integrity of the physicians in ruling that, if she wanted to stay in the hospital, she would have to accept feeding. Others could not be forced to assist her in her plan to end her life.

Later at another hospital, physicians, relying on the earlier court decision, inserted a feeding tube. But the California Court of Appeals intervened, insisting that she had the right of self-determination to decline the treatment. The court ordered that the tube be removed.[9] In cases such as that of Elizabeth Bouvia, five major questions have been debated.

Suicide/Assisted Suicide/Homicide on Request. Many people, debating Elizabeth Bouvia's demand, claim that refusal of nutrition and hydration in her situation is tantamount to committing suicide. Others claim she is not committing suicide at all, but merely refusing life-sustaining medical treatment. The difference is controversial. Those who make the distinction focus on one of two dimensions: (1) her intention and (2) whether there is an active effort made to kill or simply an omission that allows the death to take place.

There is a strong tendency in contemporary discussion to call active interventions with the intention of producing death *killing*. Sometimes the term is extended to active efforts that accidentally cause death. Giving a patient a drug that unintentionally causes death would still be killing, according to this usage. Sometimes the term *killing* is extended to cover omissions that result in death, especially if death was the intention. The fight over whether the behavior is called killing is probably based on the widely held belief that killing is, by definition, morally wrong, while letting a patient die may not be in certain circumstances. If we could agree to make the moral assessment of each of these independent of whether we call it killing, the fight over the label would probably subside.

Let us first limit our attention to active interventions that intentionally result in death. If the individual who ends up dying is the one who acts – who points a gun to her own head or intentionally swallows a large dose of phenobarbital hoping to end her life – that we would call *suicide*. If someone assists by bringing the gun to the patient, helping her aim it or loading the gun for her, that would be called *assisted suicide* as long as the patient actually pulls the trigger. But what if the patient is too weak or otherwise incapable of pulling the trigger? If she begs someone else to shoot her or to administer the lethal drug, we could say that the person who does so is committing *homicide on request*.

In June of 1990, 54-year-old Portland, Oregon resident Janet Adkins had reached a decision that she should kill herself. She had been told she had the early stages of Alzheimer's disease. She feared that the disease, which leads to progressive loss of mental capacity, would take over. She wanted to act before she lost control of the decision.

She flew to Michigan to meet a pathologist named Jack Kevorkian, a physician committed to assisting people in ending their lives when they suffer form incurable diseases. After a dinner meeting, he took her to a van parked in a parking lot and attached her to a "suicide" machine he had invented. As originally attached an intravenous line permitted the flow of a harmless saline into her vein, but the machine was equipped with a valve that permitted her to switch the line to a lethal drug, which caused her death.

Since then, Dr. Kevorkian has assisted in a number of other deaths, using both the suicide machine and other methods of bringing about death. Since then, his license to practice medicine has been suspended both in Michigan and in California.

By our definition Jack Kevorkian has been engaging in assisting suicide. Were he to actually push the button that starts the lethal mixture flowing into the patient, he would then be committing homicide on request. Homicide on request is clearly illegal in all U.S. jurisdictions. The request on the part of a patient, even one who is suffering, does not make the killing legal. Assisting suicide is also illegal in most jurisdictions. When Kevorkian began his project, it was not illegal in Michigan, but the legislature rapidly enacted emergency legislation declaring it so. Suicide itself is generally not viewed as a criminal act in American law.

The question of ethics, however, is not whether any of these actions is legal, but rather whether one ought, morally, to engage in them. The classical ethical case against suicide is offered from within the Judeo-Christian tradition by the 13th century Catholic theologian, St. Thomas Aquinas.[10] He offered three arguments. First, insofar as the natural end of the human is to seek life, taking our lives thwarts that end and therefore violates the moral natural law. Second, insofar as our lives provide a service to the community, taking our lives deprives the community society of our services. And third, our lives belong to God and, therefore, taking our lives is taking something that does not properly belong to us.

David Hume responds point by point, claiming that suicide need not be a violation of our duty to ourselves, the community, or to God.[11] First, suicide for Hume can violate our duty to ourselves only if it violates our interests, and Hume believes that it is obvious when sickness or misfortune render our lives a burden, it is not contrary to our interest to end them. He claims some people are not useful to the community and their existence may actually be detrimental to it. Thus suicide is not always a violation of the community's interest. Finally, Hume addresses the claim that suicide is a transgression against God. He takes the natural law to refer to physical laws of nature, which cannot be violated, rather than moral laws, which morally ought not to be violated even though we are physically capable of doing so. Thus Hume, misunderstanding what Thomas means, argues that if humans are capable of committing suicide, it cannot be a violation of God's law.

Secular philosophers have divided over the ethics of suicide. Libertarians tend to side with Hume, claiming that our bodies belong to ourselves and that as long as we are substantially autonomous agents we can do what we want with them – including ending them.[12] Immanuel Kant, however, sides with Thomas, arguing that reason requires we must treat all persons as if they were ends in themselves. He believes that, logically, this means it is unethical to kill, and that this includes killing of the self.[13]

Whether suicide itself is considered unethical, assisting suicide and homicide upon request are more likely to be. This is because, in addition to the principled arguments against these involvements in the deaths of others, there are serious practical problems with any social policy that would accept assistance in suicide or homicide upon request. Because the one acted upon ends up dead (if the action is successful) it is difficult to make sure that the individual really was making the request and that he or she was mentally competent if there was one. Since the risk of abuse is grave, there is greater moral reservation against either assisting in suicide or in homicide upon request. At the very least, even if the principled objections to killing can be overcome, procedural safeguards would seem necessary. These might include having a public agency such as a court review the request to determine that it is authentic. Even then, most seem to believe the moral problems with such deaths are great.

However, even if suicide, assistance in suicide, and homicide on request are considered unethical, many would claim it is not obvious that Elizabeth Bouvia is really involved in any of these. Common usage reserves these terms to cases in which the patient is not terminally or critically ill. If the decision to actively end a life is motivated out of a desire to escape intractable suffering caused by an organic medical problem, we tend to label the intervention not as a suicide or homicide on request, but as a *mercy killing*.

Active Killing and Allowing to Die: Is There a Moral Difference? The second major question that confronts us when we debate how to treat terminally or critically ill patients who are still alive is whether there is any significant moral difference between actively killing them and simply allowing them to die by forgoing medical life support. Elizabeth Bouvia, whatever we think of her request, was clearly motivated by the apparently inescapable misery caused by her desperate medical condition.

Because she should clearly have understood that stopping her feeding would result in her death, would it not have been simpler and faster to simply kill her with an injection? Is there a difference morally between that and what she was demanding? The argument, sometimes called the *commission/omission distinction*, is one of the oldest and most heatedly debated in medical ethics.

SOME POOR ARGUMENTS FOR THE DIFFERENCES

Intuitively there is a difference. Some rather lame arguments have been given in support of the difference. One is that, intuitively, it feels as though there is a difference between injecting someone in order to kill them and simply withholding life support. It is probably true that most of us feel the intuitive difference, but that may simply be because we have always been taught there is such a difference. We cannot reasonably rely on our teachers' beliefs to prove that the difference is real. They may simply have been confused. The argument is circular.

Active killing is illegal. Another weak argument sometimes offered in favor of the difference, is that active killing is illegal in all jurisdictions, while forgoing medical treatment, even life-sustaining treatment, is generally legal. It is true that active killing even for mercy is illegal in all jurisdictions.

The Netherlands has recently been experimenting with an arrangement that makes active killing for mercy "quasi-legal" for patients who make a persistent and voluntary request to be killed after they are diagnosed as suffering from an incurable condition. Medical professionals and public officials have an agreement that medical professionals will not be prosecuted provided the mercy killing meets certain guidelines. These provide that the patient must, after careful consideration, make a voluntary request to be killed. The physician must inform the patient about his or her condition and about measures that could be taken to alleviate the suffering. At least one other physician must be consulted and there must be a written record of the proceedings. The euthanasia must be reported on the death certificate. Nevertheless, even in the Netherlands, mercy killing remains against the law.

In all other jurisdictions it is more straightforwardly illegal; mercy is not a defense against the crime and one who is proved to have killed for mercy will be convicted. Sometimes judges and juries will take the extenuating circumstances into account in sentencing, but there is no question that mercy killing is a crime whether committed by a physician or a lay person.

The fact that it is illegal does not however, settle the matter of whether it is ethical. It could be that our law is simply wrong here. Or it could be that even though it is ethical to kill for mercy, for practical reasons it should remain a crime in order to prevent abuses.

Physicians have reservations about mercy killing. A final poor argument for the difference is that physicians feel strong moral objections. In fact, the American Medical Association's Council on Ethical and Judicial Affairs declares that its members should not "intentionally cause death,"[14] but the fact that physician groups believe it is unethical for physicians to kill doesn't necessarily make it so. They cannot be the final authority for deciding what constitutes ethical for physicians. Moreover, even if the society believes that physician participation in killing for mercy is wrong, society could create a new role for doing the job. It could be performed by former licensed physicians like Jack Kevorkian or by others trained to do so. If there is really something morally different between active killing for mercy and forgoing medical treatment, there must be some better arguments.

SERIOUS ARGUMENTS ON THE DIFFERENCES

The consequences may really be different. Two arguments for retaining the distinction between active killing and forgoing treatment may be more plausible. The first, by appealing to the consequences, uses the same form of argument as those who would treat them as the same, but reaches the opposite conclusion. Whereas the defenders of the moral similarity of active killing and forgoing treatment believe that they are the same because the consequences are the same – either way, the person dies – some of the defenders of a moral difference claim they are not so sure the consequences are really the same.

Some years ago, a psychologist wanting to test the issue posted a notice to recruit American college students for what was supposed to be an experiment.[15] The notice claimed this was an experiment to study the best way to solve a future serious social problem of either overcrowding or genetic disease. The investigator presented the idea claiming that she simply wanted to understand which "final solution" to these problems would be the most humane. She made clear that the "final solution" would be to "humanely kill" the excess population or the genetically afflicted. What she did not make clear was that "final solution" was precisely the term used by the Nazis in their mass exterminations during World War II. She wanted to see how many people might be open to active killing not for the purpose of relieving suffering but to serve society's purposes. She found that 326 of 570 students more than 57% approved of the project. When the final solution was to be applied to minorities, the acceptance rate was even higher.

The implication was that if we were to legalize certain killings for mercy, we would be at risk of losing control of our social practices so that other killings would be more likely to occur. In the Netherlands, there are preliminary data suggesting that those who are worrying about the slippery slope have something to be concerned about. In the first study of physician-killings in the Netherlands, the investigators' best estimate was that about 2,300 patients were killed in accord with the agreement in a 12 month period, but an additional 1,030 were killed by physicians where there had not been such requests.[16] More information would be needed to conclude that tolerating active mercy killing after a persistent and voluntary request causes an increase in other killings, but the Netherlands data are a cause for concern. If tolerating active killing were to have worse consequences than simply permitting forgoing of treatment, that would be one reason to hold on to the difference.

Some hold that active killing is simply wrong. Even if it cannot be proved that the consequences of a rule permitting active killing are worse than one permitting forgoing treatment, some simply believe that active killing is immoral. Just as violating people's autonomy, lying to them, and breaking promises are believed by many to be inherently wrong-making characteristics of actions, so killing may be also, *even if there are no bad consequences*. People who believe some or all of these are wrong may believe they can produce rational arguments for their position. Immanuel Kant held that ethics requires that people be treated as ends in themselves and that one cannot simultaneously will that they be so treated and that they be killed. This applies even to killing oneself. Others hold that they know by intuition, revelation, or by moral traditions they take to be authoritative – that it is wrong to kill.

Autonomy requires forgoing life-support. A third and final argument for the moral difference between active killing and simply letting die is based on the moral principle of autonomy. At least as far as physicians, nurses, and other health professionals are concerned, the principle of autonomy requires that when a competent patient refuses to consent to treatment, the provider of health services cannot touch the patient. That means life-sustaining treatment must be omitted. But this patient autonomy can never authorize, justify, or require that the health provider actively kill; at most it could give permission. The health provider can be compelled to forgo; he or she cannot be obliged to kill. This, of course, does not establish that, for the patients themselves, there is a difference. If there is a difference for them, it must be for one of the other reasons.

Stopping Vs. Not Starting. The term, *forgoing* includes both decisions to withdraw treatment and to refrain from starting it in the first place. The third major question confronting someone who is attempting to decide about the morality of treatments for the terminally ill is whether the decision to *stop* a life-sustaining treatment is morally more like active killing or more like not starting it. Withdrawing a treatment is surely an active intervention. Psychologically, to a physician or a nurse, it must feel like injecting an air bubble or otherwise doing something that will kill the patient.

But the argument regarding patient autonomy is revealing. One reason why health care personnel cannot start treatment is if patients have not consented to it. The patient has the autonomy to refuse it. But just as she can exercise her autonomy by refusing to let it start, so she can exercise it by refusing to let it continue. Refusal to consent requires that the clinician refrain from treating. Rational patients would not give consent without restriction. If they think about it they would always limit consents with the phrase: "until I no longer agree that you can continue." Consents can be revoked, and when they are, the moral and legal requirements of autonomy demand that the clinician withdraw.

Another way of arguing that withdrawing is morally like withholding is to look at the intention of the one making the decision. While actions designed to kill necessarily involve the intention to kill, decisions not to treat may be rooted in the intention merely to avoid a treatment that is not going to serve a worthwhile purpose. Defenders of this view claim this may be true even if one knows full-well that the patient will die if the treatment is not provided. Likewise, the decision to withdraw consent may be based on the intention to avoid a treatment that is not serving any purpose any longer. These notions suggest two final distinctions that are relevant to deciding about treatments for terminally ill patients: deciding whether killing is direct or indirect, and whether the means provided are ordinary or extraordinary.

Direct Vs. Indirect Killing. If intention is morally important in deciding whether forgoing a treatment is ethical, then it will be necessary to understand the difference between direct and indirect effects that leave people dead. An effect is said to be direct if it results from a behavior (an action or omission) in which the intention of the perpetrator is the effect that is produced. If the effect is a death, then someone kills directly if one directly intends the death. For many of those who believe that killing is morally wrong, it is direct killing that they primarily have in mind.

For example, the Catholic Church has historically condemned all direct killing of innocent people. Its adherents make limited allowance for killing of aggressors and killing in wars they consider morally justified. They also make allowance for other killings – even active killings – in which the death is not intended. Anesthesia accidents and overdoses of pain-relieving narcotics kill and they do so by active intervention, but the deaths are not intended. Likewise, some omissions that lead to death may be chosen with only the direct intention of removing a burdensome treatment.

By contrast, some deaths are said to be "indirect effects" of morally justifiable actions. This gives rise to what is sometimes called the *principle of double effect* or *indirect effect*. An effect is indirect if it is not intended (and is not a means to a desired effect). Behaviors that produce evil indirect effects are considered ethical when four conditions are met: (1) The behavior itself must not be intrinsically immoral, (2) the evil effect must not be intended (even if one can foresee it will occur), (3) it must not be a means to the intended effect, and – critically – (4) the intended good effect must be proportional to the unintended evil effect; that is, the amount of good must exceed the amount of harm. Consider the following example.

Mrs. Jessica Martin was an 86-year-old woman who had lived a long, good life. Now, however, she was suffering from inoperable cancer of the pancreas. Her family had gathered around realizing that she had only days to live. Dr. Stuart Zelman, her physician, realized there was little that he could do now except keep her comfortable.

Cancer of the pancreas is one of the most painful diseases known to medicine. Dr. Zelman had been administering morphine sulfate, a potent narcotic, for relieving Mrs. Martin pain. Gradually, however, he had had to increase the dose in order to control her suffering. Narcotics exhibit what is called tolerance – the gradual lessening of effect as the body learns to adjust for the presence of the drug. Dosage must be increased little-by-little to produce the desired effect. But Dr. Zelman realized that as he increased the dose he was approaching the point at which he risked a serious side effect – depression of respiration. Too high a dose would completely block Mrs. Martin's ability to breathe. Dr. Zelman realized that classical medical ethics would not permit him to actively kill his patient even to relieve her intractable suffering, but does it count as killing if he administers a potentially fatal dose of narcotic when his real intention is to relieve her pain?

This is exactly the kind of case in which the difference between direct and indirect killing is important. If Dr. Zelman can honestly say that his intention is to relieve her pain – a goal that would reasonably be accomplished by increasing the morphine dose – then even if he unintentionally kills her, that outcome would not be unethical: not according to those who hold to the doctrine of indirect effect, provided the benefit of relieving her pain is deemed proportional to the harm of her death. While death might always be viewed as an unfortunate outcome, it is not, according to many, an ultimate evil. In this case she was inevitably going to die very soon no matter what Dr. Zelman did. While some, such as Orthodox Jews, could consider even the modest hastening of her death unacceptable, others, such as many Catholics, would not consider it an ultimate evil in these circumstances. Both U.S. law and the AMA, as well as many secular groups such as the President's Commission for the Study of Ethical Problems in Medicine and Biomedical and Behavioral Research, essentially adopt positions reflecting this notion of the potential licitness of such unintended or indirect killings. Whether these killings are acceptable depends on the final variable – proportionality – which is critical in understanding the ethics of decisions about the terminally ill.

Ordinary And Extraordinary Means Of Treatment

Deciding which treatments are morally required and which are expendable is one of the most controversial but important aspects of the ethics of caring for the terminally ill. Some older confusing language is now being replaced by new, clearer terms. We used to speak of treatments that were *ordinary* and those that were *extraordinary*. Ordinary treatments were morally required while extraordinary ones were not. While those terms are still used, they are often misleading.

Older, Largely Rejected Meanings. These terms were often taken by clinicians to carry their normal English language meanings. Ordinary treatments were thought to be common ones; extraordinary treatments, uncommon. That, however, is never what the theologians and philosophers meant by these words. It makes little sense to hold that just because a treatment is uncommon it is extraordinary. Someone with an unusual illness may get great benefit from some very unusual procedure. On the other hand some treatments that are used routinely, day-in and day-out, may still be doing no good. In fact they may be doing harm. Trying to figure out what is morally required by determining what is common makes no sense, and that is never what the terms "ordinary" and "extraordinary" meant.

Likewise, it not plausible to determine what is morally required and what is expendable by determining how *simple* or *complex* a procedure is. Some treatments that are very complex – high-technology gadgets, such as ventilators or kidney machines – may do great good for patients while some simple procedures such as IV fluids and antibiotics may do no good at all. Figuring out how common or how simple a treatment is does not help in determining whether it is morally imperative.

Current Meaning of the Terms. Today when we still use these terms, we use them only to convey a moral judgment about their importance. Ordinary simply means "morally required" (even if the treatment is very unusual and/or high-tech). Extraordinary simply means "morally expendable" (even if it is very common and/or technologically simple).

Criteria for Morally Expendable Treatment. That still leaves us with the question of what criteria should be used for determining that a treatment is morally optional. The classical answer generally has been based on the expected benefits and burdens of the proposed procedure. It is just common sense that medical treatments should not be provided if they are likely to do more harm than good for the patient (first tenet of the Hippocratic Oath: Do no harm). In fact, if the expected harms equal the expected benefits – if there is a tie, so to speak – there is still no reason to provide the treatment.

Catholic moral theologians have for centuries addressed the problem of the criteria for morally expendable treatments. Two criteria are usually mentioned. First, a treatment is expendable if it is *useless*. If it will do no good, then there is no reason for providing it. Second, even if it serves some useful purpose, such as prolonging life, it is still considered morally expendable if it is *gravely burdensome*. Pope Pius XII in 1957 said that treatments are extraordinary – that is expendable – if they "do not involve a grave burden for oneself or another."[17] Secular commentators have generally accepted these same criteria.

Proportionality. More recently there has been a movement to replace these older, more ambiguous terms with the term *proportionality*. It incorporates into one concept both the notions of uselessness and of grave burden. If a treatment is useless, it offers no benefit; the numerator of the fraction expressing the ratio of benefits to burdens would be zero. On the other hand if a treatment is gravely burdensome, that is a way of saying that the denominator of that fraction would be very large, implying a high likelihood that the burdens would be disproportional to the benefits.

Notice, however, that there are still some ambiguities. For example, Pius XII said that according to Catholic thought, a treatment must be *gravely* burdensome before it is expendable. Older Catholic thinking held that so-called extraordinary treatments are not morally required, but accepting them was nevertheless considered good or noble. These were of such a level of burden that we could not expect a human to endure them, but it would nevertheless be good if they were accepted. They would be "beyond the call of duty."

Recent secular thought and more recent Catholic thought seem to have abandoned this notion of burdensome life-prolonging treatments being noble even if they are not morally required. Secular thinkers might consider it rather foolish to accept a treatment that prolongs life, but prolongs it at a level of burden that exceeds the benefit. One area of lingering doubt is what should happen when the burdens are rather small, but are nevertheless greater than the benefits. Is such a treatment expendable as disproportionally burdensome, or is it still required because it imposes only a small burden?

The critical test case is the hypothetical situation of a treatment that offers no burdens but no benefits. A permanently unconscious patient such as Josef Camp (assuming he really is irreversibly unconscious) might be an example. Do we say of such a case that because the burden is not grave (there is actually no burden at all), the treatment is required if it will prolong his life? Or do we say that because the benefits are not greater than the burdens, there is no reason to provide such treatment? According to some uses of the concept of proportionality, a medical treatment is morally expendable if the expected benefits do not exceed the expected burdens.

The New-Found Subjectivity of the Judgment of Benefits and Burdens. A major new development in this discussion has been a new-found discovery that these judgments of benefit and harm are inherently grounded in something more than medical fact. The questions that are at stake are such issues as how valuable unconscious life is, how bad it is to be in pain, whether living extra days of bed-ridden life is worth it. Consider the various cases presented thus far in this chapter. In order to know whether the benefits of treatment outweigh the harms, Josef Camp's parents need to decide how valuable it is to give Allah a chance to intervene as well as whether there is value in unconscious life. Elizabeth Bouvia must decide whether it is better to die or live a painful life as a cerebral palsy victim unable to get out of bed. Jack Kevorkian and his patients must decide whether life is worth living as Alzheimer's disease and other critical conditions progress. Mrs. Martin has to decide whether the potential for relief of pain is worth the risk of respiratory depression and death. None of these is a question that medical science can answer.

Some might claim that these questions are nevertheless capable of some kind of objective answer. If there is an objective answer, however, it is objective in a different sense than questions of medical service are. It is objective only in the sense that basic religious or evaluative questions are objective. Some would claim that there are no objective answers to such evaluative questions; that they are nothing more than matters of personal preference or taste. Others hold to the view that God or reason or some other objective standard can provide truly objective answers. Either way, from the point of view of the finite human observer, these are questions totally beyond the capacity of medical science to answer. If physicians have no special expertise in answering them, we generally must rely on individuals – perhaps guided by the religious and philosophical sources – to provide answers.

This means that different patients with medically identical conditions are, based on their religious and philosophical convictions, going to give different answers to the question of what the benefits and the harms of various treatments are likely to be. Grave burden clearly involves these apparently subjective dimensions. The pain of cancer can be bad for one patient, but tolerable; while for a patient with an identical tumor and perhaps even the same objective level of pain, the burden can be intolerable.

Likewise, deciding whether a treatment is useless involves evaluative judgments. Consider, for example, a ventilator for a persistently vegetative patient. It is utterly useless for restoring consciousness. If that is the goal, it is useless. But it is very effective in some cases for keeping the unconscious patient's heart beating. If that is the goal, it is very useful.

Because these judgments of usefulness and burden involve these subjective dimensions, many people hold that the decisions about them should rest with the patient, if the patient is conscious and capable of communicating. Then the only way a physician can know how beneficial or burdensome a treatment is, to ask the patient (in fact, in some cases, even knowing whether the effect is a benefit or a burden will require asking the patient). That the treatment produces an effect is essentially a matter of medical science; that the effect is a benefit cannot be such a matter. If it is a "fact" at all it is a religious or "normative" fact.

Can simple, basic treatments be expendable? Throughout the 1970s the reasoning discussed here was applied to cases involving decisions to forgo ventilators, kidney machines, cancer surgery, and organ replacement – all major interventions that plausibly extend life, but that have also raised doubts about the benefits of the procedures. Generally, they were technologically complex – expensive procedures.

But once the reasoning based on proportionality was fully in place, people naturally began to apply it to other, more routine treatments. Elizabeth Bouvia's effort to refuse nutrition supplied through a nasogastric tube is an example of a procedure long considered "basic" or "fundamental" being eventually subjected to the proportionality reasoning. Other simple treatments that have been questioned on these grounds include supplying fluids through an IV line, doing cardio-pulmonary resuscitation, administering antibiotics for infection, and, in nursing, routine turning of the patient to prevent bed sores.

In nursing it is standard practice to turn a bed-ridden patient every two hours or so to prevent serious skin eruptions. These practices are governed by standard protocols that every nurse learns. For almost every patient, it is obviously in the patient's interest to follow such procedures.

But what of a patient with hours to live? Suppose such a patient has brittle bone disease, a condition that makes bones so brittle they might simply snap upon movement. If the patient has such a risk of broken bones and has hours to live, does the standard nursing protocol have to be followed?

One approach is to ask what the risks and benefits are. If the risks are great and the benefits negligible, then the proposed turning of the patient would fail the proportionality test. Because the only purpose of turning the patient is to prevent skin problems that will take days to develop, if the patient does not have days, then it seems reasonable to claim that there is no benefit. There clearly seems to be serious risk of pain. If that fact is combined with the lack of potential benefit, then many would conclude that turning the patient fails the proportionality test.

Likewise, some would argue there is little to be gained and a great deal of suffering to be risked if CPR is attempted on a patient who clearly is terminally ill. If the patient has made the assessment of the benefits and harms and finds CPR to come up wanting, then the patient might plausibly decide against resuscitation.

Similarly, if providing fluids will only prolong the agony of death, then medical hydration using an IV may offer greater risk of harm than benefit.

Three arguments have been put forward in defense of the traditional practice of providing food and fluids to all patients regardless of their condition. *First*, people such as Gilbert Meilaender, an ethicist from Oberlin College, have argued that supplying food and fluids are not medical tasks at all; they are not treatments, but simply basic care.[18] They being such, he has argued they should always be provided even if the patient is declining other life-prolonging treatments.

Critics of his position claim it really doesn't matter whether one calls these procedures medical or not. If the intervention does more harm than good, it should not be provided. To hold otherwise seems to commit one to the strange position that useless and burdensome medical procedures are morally expendable, but that useless and burdensome non medical procedures are imperative even if they do no good.

A second argument in favor of making nutrition and hydration mandatory are that they should always be provided as a symbol of our commitment to the hungry and thirsty.[19] Providing nutrition and hydration are therefore "symbolic acts" conveying our societal sense of the crucial importance of feeding the hungry and providing drink for the thirsty.

It is a matter of empirical fact whether these patients are actually hungry or thirsty.[20] For mentally competent patients, we can simply ask. Sometimes they say they are not hungry or thirsty; in fact, they claim that providing food or fluids makes them more uncomfortable. It would be odd to act symbolically in the name of the hungry and thirsty by forcing food and fluid on people for whom it simply makes them more uncomfortable. Many patients for whom nutrition and hydration are debated are actually unconscious. (We will take up their cases in the next section of this chapter.) It seems impossible, however, to say that unconscious patients are either hungry or thirsty. Hunger and thirst

'You think you're old? I've lived through six presidents, three wars and both health department inspections.'

are fundamentally psychological categories. Surely, we should do everything in our power to prevent the feelings of hunger and thirst. But unconscious people, by definition, do not have those feelings (because they do not have any feelings). The critics of the "symbolic acts" argument believe it would be odd to force food and fluids on people who are not hungry or thirsty in the name of symbolizing our commitment to make some other people more comfortable.

The final argument against permitting patients to refuse medically supplied nutrition and hydration is that doing so may make it more difficult to keep separate active mercy killing and decisions to forgo treatment. One of the practical arguments for a rule supporting the distinction was that it may be harder to prevent abuses if we accept the legitimacy of active killing for mercy. Everyone could end up dead if someone claimed that they would be better off killed. It would be difficult to document whether the patient actually requested the killing, especially if decisions were simply made in physician's offices rather than with formal due process judicial reviews. By contrast, permitting decisions to forgo treatment would result in death in only a relatively small number of people, those with certain medical conditions that will result in death if they are not treated.

This is part of the rule utilitarian argument for the sharp distinction between active killing and simply letting die. If withholding nutrition and hydration is included among the treatments that may be forgone, the practical calculations change considerably. Many more patients would be at risk for abusive decisions to forgo treatment. If oral feeding is included as well as nasogastric tubes and IVs, all of us could be made dead by someone's decision to let us die by forgoing intervention. If this practical consequentialist argument is the basis for distinguishing those things we can do to patients from those we cannot, then perhaps forgoing nutrition and hydration should be treated more like active killing. Of course, if one of the other arguments for the action/omission distinction is used, then this conclusion would not apply. For example, if there is something that is just intrinsically immoral about active killing that does not extend to letting nature take its course, then the fact that more people are at risk for being allowed to die than we first realized would not make a decisive difference. For those who reject the idea that there is a difference between active killing and letting die in the first place, none of this would be terribly important.

The conclusions about forgoing nutrition, hydration, CPR, medications, and protocols to turn patients are not yet clear. Some people hold that, because these are very simple, therefore they are required. Others hold that physicians can somehow know that they are objectively useless and therefore the physician can unilaterally omit them. Still others take a middle position: that their usefulness is a subjective matter, so the decision should rest with the patient or the patient's surrogate.

THE INCOMPETENT PATIENT

These choices are made by the patient himself or herself when the patient is mentally competent as were the patients in the cases in the previous section. But many of the most controversial cases involve patients who are not mentally competent. Josef Camp, the boy who ate the pickle, was 9 years old. He was never able to form a position while competent.

The controversies over decisions made on behalf of incompetent patients are heated, in part, because there are at least three different kinds of incompetent patients, and each of these involves different ethical principles and decision-making procedures. Some incompetent patients were formerly competent and formulated opinions about the kind of care they wanted to receive when they became terminally ill. Others have never been competent or, what amounts to the same thing, never left any record of their wishes. Among those who have never been competent, there is a further subdivision. Some have family or relatives who are able to participate as surrogates on behalf of the patient; others have no one who knew them while they were competent to be their agent for decision-making.

THE FORMERLY COMPETENT PATIENT
In 1979, Brother Joseph Fox, an 83-year-old member of the Catholic Order of the Society of Mary, underwent minor surgery. Something went wrong, and he suffered a cardiac arrest and was left in a permanent vegetative state.

Rev. Philip Eichner, S.M., the superior in his religious community and president of the Chaminade High School where Brother Fox had lived since his retirement, stepped forward to function as Brother Fox's surrogate. They had known each other for more than 25 years. Brother Fox's relatives, (several nieces and nephews,) agreed that Rev. Eichner was the appropriate agent for Brother Fox, but when he asked for the life-supporting ventilator to be disconnected the care givers at the hospital refused to comply.

Rev. Eichner sought judicial approval for the stopping of the ventilator based on the claim that it was Brother Fox's view that he would not want his life prolonged in that condition. Brother Fox had led discussions in the Chaminade community during the public controversy over the Karen Quinlan case and had reaffirmed his views two months prior to his surgery. He was quoted as saying, with regard to patients like Karen Quinlan, "Why don't they just let us go? I want to go."

After a lower court had authorized the withdrawal of the ventilator, the next higher court reversed the judgment before New York's highest court finally authorized the stopping in cases where the patient's previously expressed wishes are clearly known.[21] Brother Fox died while the court deliberations were still in progress.

The key to Brother Fox's case is that he left a clear record of his wishes expressed while he was competent. He not only led a discussion group on the issues surrounding the Karen Quinlan case, he also reaffirmed his position only two months before his surgery and unexpected, tragic accident. Moreover, he expressed views quite consistent with the religious tradition in which he was a life-long and deeply committed member.

He did not have a formal, written advance directive (or what is sometimes called a "living will"). That is not necessary. What is critical is that there is a clear expression of the patient's wishes, the authenticity of which was beyond dispute. Oral directives are plenty good enough as long as there is no controversy over what the person actually said. However, since one never knows how clearly one's words will be remembered, putting the advance directive in writing is generally best.

Type of Advance Directives. There are two major types of advance directives: *substantive* and *proxy*. *Substantive directives* specify a patient's substantive wishes. They tell what treatments the individual wants or does not want. In an earlier era they were used almost exclusively to specify refusals of treatment, but increasingly today it is becoming standard to assume patients do not want ventilators, CPR, and other life-prolonging technologies once they have become terminally ill and have lost mental competence. Now, as never before, it is crucial if one wants treatments to be continued that that fact be clearly specified in an advance directive.

Instead of trying to spell out exactly which treatments are desired, some people write a *proxy directive*, which names the individual whom the patient would like to serve as a surrogate decision-maker. The writer can name anyone – a spouse, other family member, or friend. The one named should normally be someone who knows the writer's wishes or at least understands his or her general values. It is especially critical to name someone if the next of kin is not the person the writer wants to make these decisions. It is also important if there is more than one person who is equally close. An elderly person may want to spare an infirm spouse the task, naming instead a son or daughter. Or a widow may have three children, one of whom she wants to name as her surrogate.

Ethical Principles Guiding Surrogate Decisions for Formerly Competent Patients. The task of making a life-and-death surrogacy decision is awesome. It is generally held that the first principle guiding such decisions is that the choice should be the one the patient would have made had he or she been competent to do so. Based on the advance directive or what is known about the individual's beliefs and values, the surrogate should choose what the individual would have chosen. Ethically, this notion is rooted in the moral principle of *autonomy*. Autonomy can still be morally relevant to a person who is not autonomous. It is what might be called *autonomy extended* – that is, extended into the period of incompetency.

Recently, some commentators have been arguing that there are cases in which the patient's formerly expressed beliefs and values should not prevail. They have in mind advanced Alzheimer's disease or severe head trauma, in which the individual appears to permanently and completely forget the former self. They claim that if the patient has so lost competence that there is a complete discontinuity of personal identity, then the "old person" who expressed wishes "in a former life" no longer should dictate to the "new person" who has no memory of the former individual. Lawyers Rebecca Dresser and John Robertson[22] and philosophers Allen Buchanan and Dan Brock[23] have all argued this position.

They have generated considerable controversy, however. Their critics doubt that the discontinuity between the old and new persons is as great as they imply. The critics believe there may be moral and social links remaining even if the "new" individual cannot express any memory of the old self. Most people seem to believe that they would want such decisions made on the basis of the views they held when they were competent. One who does not want his or her old views to dominate always has the right to designate some proxy and instruct the proxy to try to determine what would be best for the "new" person, but, barring such an instruction, the general pattern is that the decision should be guided by the last clear instruction of the competent individual. Legally, this is known as *substituted judgment*. The term is a bit confusing. It does not refer to substituting the beliefs and values of the surrogate. It is the patient's values that take precedence when substituted judgment is used. All states in the U.S. now have statutes or case law (judge-made law) authorizing the use of advanced directives under at least some circumstances.

Decisions Not Covered by Legal Statutes. The limits in the statutes governing advance directives can be quite severe. For example, most apply only when the patient is terminally ill. While this might seem to be the only time one would want a decision to forgo treatment made, the definition of terminal illness is usually quite narrow. It refers only to cases in which one is inevitably declining toward death in a relatively brief period of time regardless of medical interventions. Actually, if death is coming soon regardless, the decision to forgo may not be too critical. Other cases, not terminal under this definition, may be more the kinds of cases in which the individual wants to have treatment stopped: stable but persistent vegetative state (the state Karen Quinlan and Nancy Cruzan were in), advanced Alzheimer's disease, and other chronic, debilitating, but not terminal illnesses. Moreover, even if one has a certifiable terminal illness, some state statutes permit forgoing life support only when "death is imminent." That, of course, is when forgoing treatment becomes academic.

While all U.S. jurisdictions have some form of law granting the right to forgo treatment, other countries may not. Both these settings, as well as cases involving critical but nonterminal illness, press the question of what the legal and moral situation is when specific law does not apply.

In jurisdictions that have laws requiring informed consent for medical treatment (including all U.S. jurisdictions), more general common law would apply. It requires that a physician cannot treat without an adequately informed consent. As we have seen, if the treatment has begun, it cannot continue if consent is withdrawn. In the case of a competent patient, consent is grounded in the moral principle of autonomy. The patient cannot be touched without consent. To do so would constitute an assault (or in some situations medical negligence). The doctrine of informed consent is crucial in affirming the patient's right to refuse treatment, especially in cases such as nonterminal illness – a state to which "living will" statutes do not apply. Even then, the patient cannot be treated without adequately informed consent. In the case of the formerly competent patient, generally the wishes expressed while competent should prevail and a substituted judgment will be made by the patient's surrogate if the patient lapses into incompetency. Several different mechanisms are available for expressing one's wishes about terminal and critical care.

Advance Directives. The advance directives we have been examining are the most widely discussed mechanism. The group called the Euthanasia Educational Council in the 1970s introduced the most famous. Called the "Living Will," it permitted people to indicate they did not want "artificial" or "heroic" means, terms now largely abandoned because they lack precision. The group, now called Choice in Dying, still circulates copies of a revised form of its Living Will, which has been brought into the form called for by various state laws.

Several criticisms have been made of the original Living Will. For one thing, as originally written it merely gave permission to stop; it did not require it. Some patients have wanted to write such advance directives precisely because they feared that physicians would not stop treatment. Giving mere permission to stop would not provide adequate assurance. Most forms today do not merely give permission; they order that specified treatments be withheld or withdrawn.

Another significant problem with substantive advance directives is that they express wishes when one is mentally competent, perhaps many years from the time of crisis and when one's values may be quite different. Using a proxy directive helps alleviate some of these problems. The designated surrogate, guided by what he or she knows to be recently held views, can fine-tune the advance directive to the specifics of the patient's condition.

Another significant problem of the standard advance directive forms is that they appear to assume that all persons will have the same choices in mind. It is one-decision-fits-all. But in a world of great diversity and increasing medical complexity, there may be as many different views as there are people. Some may want to refuse medically supplied nutrition and hydration, others not; some may want to refuse only when permanently unconscious, others while still conscious and in pain. Some may want to refuse only high-tech machines, others simple devices as well. Most critically, some may want to use an advance directive to demand that certain life-supporting care continue. Clearly, no one standard form will work any longer.

Other groups have prepared sample forms that attempt to reflect the beliefs of their group. The U.S. Catholic Health Association has prepared a "Christian affirmation of Life" that uses the language of "no extraordinary means."[24] It excludes actions with the intention of causing death (although, as we have noted, that should not be taken as excluding all decisions in which death is foreseen but not directly intended).

The President's Commission for the Study of Ethical Problems in Medicine and Biomedical and Behavioral Research endorsed a combined substantive and proxy directive,[25] a proposal that has existed since the mid-1970s.[26]

Legislation. In addition to individually crafted advance directives, many jurisdictions have laws governing decisions about the care of the terminally ill. Several places have considered laws that would legalize active killing for mercy, beginning in 1937 in Great Britain and then in New York in 1947 and in other states in later years. None of these got very far until citizen initiatives got proposals – that would have legalized active killing upon the request of competent, terminally ill patients – placed on the ballots of the state of Washington in 1991 and California in 1992. Both received substantial minority votes, but neither passed.

Most legislation, beginning with the California Natural Death Act of 1976,[27] focused only on decisions to forgo life-prolonging interventions for the terminally ill.[28] The legislation varies from state to state, but generally permits forgoing treatment when the patient is terminally ill and death is imminent. Some state legislation prohibits refusal of nutrition and hydration under the statutory law. That, however, leaves open the possibility that one can still refuse under informed consent law. (Some states, including Maryland and Colorado, have either advisory opinions or case law that still permit forgoing nutrition and hydration, in spite of these limits, in cases in which an individual has a specific advance directive refusing these treatments.)

Issues To Be Addressed In An Advance Directive

Given the great variety of beliefs and values about terminal illness treatments, advance directives will come in many forms and styles. Among the issues that almost certainly should be included are these:

- What treatments are being refused
- What treatments are desired
- When the directive should take effect
- Whether a durable power of attorney (proxy) is to be appointed

Some advance directives will also include other more specific information that could be of concern to specific writers of such directives. This could include:

- What hospital (or jurisdiction) should be used.
- What physician should be consulted.
- What lawyer should be consulted.
- What ethics consultants or religious counselor should be involved.
- Whether refusal is under statutory or common law.

Never-Competent Patients Without Family Surrogates

Advance directives grounded in the moral principle of autonomy may be the answer for patients who were formerly competent patients and who have expressed their wishes while competent. But they are hardly helpful for the more tragic cases of infants and children or others who have never expressed their wishes while competent. For these patients someone else will have to decide. This group can be further divided into those who have family or others with whom they have a pre-existing relationship who can function as surrogates; and those who are utterly alone, without family to make the choices about medical care.

Sixty-seven-year-old Joseph Saikewicz was a resident of the Belchertown State School in Massachusetts, a facility that cared for the mentally retarded.[29] He had been their since the age of 5. He was described as having an IQ of 10 and a mental age of approximately 2 years and 8 months. He was not able to communicate verbally, resorting to grunts and gestures, but he was physically strong and generally was in good health until it was discovered that he was suffering from acute leukemia.

His physicians were considering chemotherapy and blood transfusions. The physicians had doubts about providing the treatment because it appeared that Mr. Saikewicz could not understand their purpose; i.e., he would perceive that his care givers were turning on him and hurting him for no understandable reason. It was agreed that with the treatment there would be a 30-50% chance of remission, but that the remission would probably last only 2-13 months. All agreed that they should do what was best for Mr. Saikewicz, but could not agree on what was best.

The only members of the family who could be located were two sisters who, when notified, said they would prefer not to become involved. All agreed that Mr. Saikewicz could make the choice himself, whether to receive the treatment and that no family were available to take on the decision-making role. The superintendent of the school was unclear whether the physician's opinion about what was in Mr. Saikewicz's best interest should prevail or whether they should err on the side of life – preferring to treat when the treatment can extend life, even though the life would involve the appearance of his care givers turning on him and inflicting suffering for reasons he could not understand.

Some might argue that patients like Joseph Saikewicz are not worth saving. That raises the terrible question of whether there are social and economic reasons why it might sometimes be acceptable to limit care to the terminally ill. The court, when it reviewed the case, however, rejected the idea that the decision should be based on which "significant others" would evaluate the quality of Mr. Saikewicz's life. While there may be cases in which societal judgments must intervene, before tackling that most difficult of ethical issues, it may be possible to make some choices in a more traditional ethical framework.

The Hippocratic ethic requires that the clinician work solely for the benefit of the patient. There has been significant doubt raised about some parts of the Hippocratic Oath. For example, the patient benefiting ethic that has sometimes been used to force benefits on patients against their will has now largely been replaced by an ethic focusing on the ethical principle of autonomy. As we saw earlier in this chapter, patients are expected to evaluate the evidence about the benefits and harms and choose a course that they believe fits their life plan, regardless of the clinician's personal opinion about whether it is the best plan.

But Joseph Saikewicz is unable to speak for himself. He left no clear record of his wishes about medical care. Someone must step into the role of decision-maker. He has no family or friends capable of playing that role. He is alone, dying, and out of control; among the most vulnerable of patients. And someone, in this case a physician, apparently believes he would be better off dead.

It is probably true that some patients who were mentally competent and in Mr. Saikewicz's position would forgo the treatment being offered. Some might even contemplate ending their lives. But in this case, if a decision is to be made to forgo treatment it will have to be made by a stranger.

THE PRINCIPLE FOR DECIDING: OBJECTIVE BENEFICENCE

Morally, if autonomy is ruled out, the decision-making principle, by default, must revert to the ethical principle of beneficence – the decision must be the one that will produce the most good. Before considering the possibility that the good of others should be factored into the decision, it is worth asking whether, as the physician apparently surmised, it could possibly be in Mr. Saikewicz's interest to have the treatment stopped.

Recalling that judgments of benefit and burden are necessarily subjective, it is crucial not to reduce the question to that of whether competent patients suffering from leukemia similar to Mr. Saikewicz's would accept the treatment. Mr. Saikewicz's situation is somewhat different. The chemotherapy and blood transfusion that would be understandable to competent patients appear to Mr. Saikewicz to be torture imposed by the people he has grown over many years to rely on for the basics of life. Arguably, the burden of these treatments will be much greater for him than for someone who could understand the reason for the apparently painful treatment.

We know that competent patients facing a choice about a burdensome treatment have sometimes concluded that, for their cases, forgoing treatment is justified when the benefits of treatment do not exceed the burdens. It is theoretically possible that a similar conclusion could be reached in the case of the patient who never expressed his wishes while competent.

But this is literally a life-and-death decision. We have seen that these judgments can be very subjective. A patient such as Mr. Saikewicz is in jeopardy of the whim, the idiosyncratic judgments, of the person who happens to assume the decision-making role. For this reason, we insist that the standard should be to do what is best, relying on the most objective assessment possible. The personal religious beliefs or preferences of the decision-maker cannot be imposed on the patient. There is no reason why a stranger's personal value system should be relevant. The legal standard in such cases is the *best interest standard*. The decision-maker must do what is best.

The Attending Physician As Decision-Maker. The key, then, is who should be the decision-maker. Historically that role has been assumed by the attending physician. In the day when the rule of thumb was to do everything possible, that was not terribly critical, but now that we are seriously entertaining the possibility that some life-prolonging treatments are not in the patient's interest, it can literally be a matter of life and death which physician happens to be on duty when the patient is brought to the hospital. It can make enormous difference which hospital is chosen by the emergency rescue squad. It seems odd that Mr. Saikewicz's life would be dependent on which physician he draws.

Hospital Ethics Committee As Decision-Maker. Some of the random variation could be eliminated if these key decisions to forgo treatment were referred to committees at the hospital made up of an interdisciplinary group of physicians, nurses, social workers, and chaplains, supplemented by a cross section of other perspectives such as those of philosophers, business people, lawyers, former patients, and families of patients. This committee would permit many different perspectives to be presented, neutralizing the individual biases of any one decision-maker.[30] Perhaps only with the approval of a hospital ethics committee could life-prolonging treatment be forgone for patients who were never able to express their own views while competent.

But there is a serious problem with this strategy. The hospital's ethics committee as a whole may have certain moral inclinations. We would expect a committee appointed by the administrators or trustees of a local hospital to reflect the value commitments of the institution. An orthodox Jewish hospital ought to have an ethics committee whose consensus opinions are different from those of a secular hospital or a Catholic hospital. Turning the decisions over to the ethics committee may simply be a way of making the decision based on the value system of the institution where the patient happened to reside. Unless the patient has chosen the hospital for its value system, that does not make much sense.

A Court-Appointed Guardian As Decision-Maker. The other alternative is to have some more public process for making this one special group of decisions. We have no idea what the wishes of these patients are. Without treatment they will die; with it they will live. Someone who is a stranger to the patient believes the patient would be better off dead. Because these patients are so vulnerable, some people believe it might be wise to bend over backward to protect their lives and permit withdrawal of treatment only after there has been a formal review with the protection of legal due process. If we are talking about a relatively small number of patients, perhaps the extra burden of review is worth it. Right now there is no clearly designated guardian for such patients. This limits not only decisions to forgo treatment, but decisions to authorize treatment as well. There is no one who can give consent to treatment in such cases anymore than there is someone who can authorize non treatment.

NEVER-COMPETENT PATIENTS WITH FAMILY SURROGATE

Fortunately, relatively few patients are in precisely this predicament. The more usual case of patients who have never been competent involves those who have family ready, wiling, and able to step into the surrogacy role. That was the position Josef Camp was in. It was also the situation of Karen Quinlan, Nancy Cruzan, and many other patients whose families have had to make the tragic choices for or against life support.

At 12:54 a.m. on the night of January 11, 1983, a call came to a Missouri police unit that there had been a single-car accident on a lonely road. When the rescue squad arrived six minutes later, they found Nancy Cruzan lying face down in a ditch 35 feet from her car without detectable signs of cardiac or respiratory function. They began resuscitation. By 1:12 a.m. spontaneous cardiac and respiratory function was restored, but there had been significant lack of oxygen to the brain. The incident left Nancy Cruzan with significant brain damage.

She lay in a coma for three weeks and, with the consent of her husband, a tube was implanted into her stomach so she could be fed directly through the tube. She was stabilized and remained hospitalized in this condition for years, not on a ventilator, oblivious to her environment except for reflexive responses to sound and perhaps painful stimuli. The cerebral cortical atrophy was irreversible, permanent, progressive, and ongoing. She remained a spastic quadriplegic with irreversible muscle contracture and tendon damage. She was in what is called a persistent vegetative state.

Her parents assumed the role of guardian and came to the conclusion that she would not want the life-support feedings to continue. They asked to have permission to terminate artificial hydration and nutrition.

The Missouri Supreme Court originally ruled that the state has an unqualified interest in life without regard to quality and that, therefore, her parents could not discontinue nutrition and hydration. The United States Supreme Court acknowledged that a state has the right to impose such limits; but, in the process, the court said that if the patient's own wishes were known, presumably they would have to prevail. Further court review in Missouri established that there was adequate evidence of her wishes that treatment could be stopped on that basis.

Cases such as Josef Camp's and Nancy Cruzan's raise the critical issue of whether family can ever make a choice to forgo life-prolonging interventions and, of so, on what basis. It is increasingly clear that the next of kin should be the presumed decision-maker in such cases. The current law in Florida, Iowa, Virginia, and other states specifically authorizes the next of kin to assume this role. Elsewhere, courts have generally accepted this procedure.[31] As long as they make uncontroversial choices, their role as surrogates has been accepted.

FAMILY CHOICES THAT ARE CONTROVERSIAL

What happens, however, when the choice is controversial? Nancy Cruzan's family made the controversial choice of deciding to forgo nutrition medically supplied through a gastrostomy. At the time, that was a particularly controversial choice, because, as we have seen, there has been great debate over whether medically supplied nutrition and hydration could ever be considered useless or burdensome. Clearly, in Nancy Cruzan's case the treatment was not burdensome. She was persistently vegetative, incapable of perceiving pain or discomfort. But it is still considered by some to be an offense to withhold nourishment from a human being even if there can be no awareness and even if the nourishment is merely prolonging vegetative life. Should Nancy Cruzan's family be permitted to make such a choice?

Likewise, Josef Camp's parents made a controversial choice, although theirs was problematic in insisting that life support continue. When there is disagreement about whether the next of kin has made the best choice, it is not yet clear what should be done.

Following the ethical framework developed for once-competent patients without familial surrogates, we generally insist that family members should try to do what they believe would be best for the patient. But what happens when there is dispute among the family, or when outside observers believe that the family has not made the best choice?

We could insist that they make the best possible choice regarding what is in their loved one's interest, but many are beginning to conclude we should not. That would, in effect, be telling them they are free to choose, but that they must make only the single best choice. Because deciding what is best is inherently subjective and controversial in such cases, we can assume there will sometimes be disagreements about what is best and no clear standards for making the choice.

An alternative that seems to be emerging is to instruct the family that they must do what they think is best, but then give them some limited range of discretion in picking among plausible options. It is often the case in medicine that there are many treatment options available and no clearly best choice. In such cases, it would be extremely difficult to insist that the family make only the one best choice. Instead they are increasingly being given discretion to choose among those options that are within what can be called the *limits of reasonable standard*.[32]

With this approach, several treatment options may be acceptable. Only in the extreme case would family choices be challenged. The family would be taken to court, much as is now done with Jehovah's Witness parents who try to refuse life-saving blood transfusions for their minor children. In those cases we know that the courts will temporarily take custody for purposes of consenting to treatment. We could in like manner seek court orders either to approve of treatment or get it stopped in other terminal illness treatment decisions.

We have not so far, had a case in which the courts took custody of a patient for purposes of overruling an unreasonable judgment of a family surrogate when the parental decision was to preserve the life. In theory that could happen. Someday there will be a patient who is so burdened by life-prolonging treatment; a case in which the prolongation will in any case be only temporary. If family members persist in inflicting severe pain or discomfort on such a patient in a fruitless effort to prolong life, some court may have to intervene and overrule.

In such a case as Josef Camp's, the court would face a difficult, perhaps insurmountable task, if it were to attempt to overrule the parents. Josef Camp, like Nancy Cruzan, was permanently unconscious. He could not feel pain. The chances of his parents being overruled on the grounds that they were inflicting burden on him were therefore remote.

The Search For Surrogate Principles. The moral principle permitting parents to have discretion in such cases is not yet fully established. Clearly, the surrogate must attempt to do what he or she thinks is best for the patient, but what of these special cases where the decision is controversial? It is becoming increasingly clear that doing what is literally best is not going to be what is required. If we are not going to insist that the family do what is the absolute best, then there must be some moral basis for familial discretion. We could call this the principle of *limited familial autonomy*. Under such a principle the family decision-makers would have the discretion to draw on family beliefs and values to exercise discretion as long as they did not exceed the limits of reasonableness. If they were to exceed what society can tolerate, then the state would have to step in and overrule. But it would do so, not when the family decision-makers made a modestly unexpected choice, but only when that choice was beyond reason.

SUMMARY AND OUTLOOK

If this is the direction the society is headed, Josef Camp's case will be instructive. We will not be able to resolve the problem his case presents simply by defining him as dead. He probably was not dead, at least by whole-brain criteria. Unless a state adopts a higher-brain definition of death, he will probably have to be treated as alive.

The clinicians cannot make a case in which they know, based on medical science, that the treatment is serving no useful purpose. Judgments of benefit and harm are essentially not matters of medical science. Once it is conceded that the ventilator will prolong the bodily functions, the key question is whether it serves any worthwhile purpose to do so. That is not a question medical science can answer. We could try to overrule his parents, claiming that the burdens of the treatment are too great. That probably would work in the case of some conscious, terminally ill patient, but not in the case of a permanently unconscious patient. If the treatment cannot be withdrawn on any of these grounds, there is only one other possibility. That would be to argue that it is the burden to the hospital staff, to patients, or to others in the society that justifies stopping treatment. That is a move that should be made only with fear and trembling. Up to now civilized society has been reluctant to do so. It may be the medical ethical question of the future. It also may be one that remains unresolved; one from which a society may draw greater light in the creative struggle over it than in mere line-drawing for solution's sake. Unfortunately, it is a question that is beyond the scope of this chapter to address.

READING
A RIGHT TO DIE:
MEDICAL, LEGAL AND MORAL ISSUES

Ethical issues weighed within Western tradition

The question of withholding or withdrawing life-sustaining medical treatment, and the related questions of suicide and euthanasia, are not just medical or legal issues — they are ethical ones as well. And the context in which these issues are considered and debated in Western intellectual tradition, which developed long before modern medical technology. Incorporating a variety of philosophical and religious perspectives, the Western tradition generally condemned suicide and murder, although killing was often deemed tragically necessary in self-defense, in just wars, and in carrying out certain official duties.

Over the centuries, Jewish scholars and Christian theologians, especially Roman Catholic ones, seriously considered whether there might be circumstances in which the deaths of individuals could be hastened in ways that were morally justified. Rabbinic scholars expressing Orthodox Judaism's view determined that such acts could never be justified. Catholic theologians, however, concluded that the prolongation of human life was not an absolute duty, and they developed certain distinctions and rules that 20th-century physicians and ethicists have found useful in grappling with the dilemmas posed by modern medicine.

The Catholic theologians still maintained that intentionally killing oneself or another was prohibited. But, beginning in the 16th century, they developed a distinction between *ordinary* and *extraordinary* means of prolonging life. Ordinary means, according to medical ethicist Gerald Kelly's 1951 interpretation, consist of medicines, treatments and operations that "offer a reasonable hope of benefit and [that] can be obtained and used without excessive expense, pain, or other inconvenience," while extraordinary means consist of those that cannot be so obtained or used, and that, if used, would not offer a reasonable hope of benefit. This distinction has been widely used to justify the withholding or withdrawing of life-sustaining treatments in certain circumstances. The patient in such cases is *allowed to die*, not *killed*.

Catholic theologians also developed the rule of "double effect." The rule's basic premises go back to St. Thomas Aquinas. He said that single acts can have two "effects," only one of which is intended. The morality of the act, he said, is determined by the intended effect, not the unintended one, even if the unintended one can be foreseen. Thus, a physician could morally give a dying person sedatives and analgesics to relieve his pain even though they might shorten his life.

The contemporary debate about withdrawing or withholding treatment from critically ill patients began in 1957. Dr. Bruno Haid, chief of anesthesia at the surgical clinic of the University of Innsbruck, Austria, was concerned about the new ability of anesthesiologists to prolong the lives of some patients incapable of spontaneous breathing, and so submitted several questions to Pope Pius XII regarding the morality of resuscitation. In response, the pope affirmed the ordinary/extraordinary distinction and said specifically that withholding or withdrawing mechanical ventilation did not constitute "direct disposal of the life of the patient, nor . . . euthanasia in any way."

The papal address marked not only a beginning, but an end. Until then, biomedical ethicist Robert F. Weir says, "serious reflection about the ethics of death and dying was largely the enterprise of Catholic moral theologians," who, for the most part, had "updated and revised the dominant views of the past." In the new era, such ethical questions would be taken up in a "wide-open, ongoing debate about the morality and legality of treatment abatement and the related issues of suicide and euthanasia in the light of new developments in medicine, law, and other spheres of life."

One of the most influential contributions to this new debate was a 1970 book, *The Patient as Person*, by Protestant ethicist Paul Ramsey. Borrowing from Catholic theologians, Ramsey set out three distinctions as fundamental to his own position on withdrawing or withholding medical treatment: ordinary/extraordinary, prolonging life/prolonging dying, and killing/allowing to die. "Taken together," Weir relates, "these distinctions led [Ramsey] to a further distinction between non-dying and dying patients: Non-dying patients should have their lives prolonged with medically indicated treatment, whereas dying patients require neither curing (because of its futility in such circumstances) nor killing (because direct killing is immoral), but ongoing care during the terminal phase of life."

Ramsey, of course, was not the only one to address such issues. Philosopher James Rachels, for instance, in a 1975 article in the *New England Journal of Medicine*, attacked the traditional distinction between killing someone and allowing him to die. The "bare difference" between the two, he said, "does not, in itself, make a moral difference. If a doctor lets a patient die, for humane reasons, he is in the same moral position as if he had given the patient a lethal injection for humane reasons. If his decision was wrong – if, for example, the patient's illness was in fact curable – the decision would be equally regrettable no matter which method was used to carry it out. And if the doctor's decision was the right one, the method used is not in itself important."

Competent patients can refuse treatment

Since the mid-1960s, state courts have increasingly taken up cases involving competent patients who sought to refuse life-sustaining treatment. The early cases involved Jehovah's Witnesses who refused blood transfusions. After reviewing a dozen significant court decisions, ethicist Robert Weir last year concluded that courts have increasingly acknowledged that patients may refuse medical treatment on the legal grounds of privacy, even if the refusal means they will die. "The right of privacy in such cases is not absolute. . . but its importance is evident in that *no appellate court in the past decade has overridden an autonomous patient's refusal of life-sustaining treatment* when the patient has laid claim to this very personal right outside the context of a prison," he wrote. The *Cruzan* case — in which five U.S. Supreme Court justices said a competent person had a right to refuse unwanted medical treatment — was further confirmation of this trend in judicial thinking.

And it wasn't just the courts that were coming to this conclusion. The President's Commission for the Study of Ethical Problems in Medicine and Biomedical and Behavioral Research stated in 1983 that "Health care professionals serve patients best by maintaining a presumption in favor of sustaining life, while recognizing that competent patients are entitled to choose to [forgo] any treatments, including those that sustain life." The American Hospital Association approved a statement along that line in 1985, and the American Medical Association's judicial council did so in 1986. "The social commitment of the physician is to sustain life and relieve suffering," the AMA council stated. "Where the performance of one duty conflicts with the other, the choice of the patient, or his family or legal representative if the patient is incompetent to act in his own behalf, should prevail."

Nevertheless, a patient's right to refuse medical treatment hasn't always been recognized in practice. "Historically," says George Annas of Boston University, "physicians ignored that [right] and thought that they knew best, and they would only follow the patient's wishes [if they] were consistent with their own judgment about what was best for the patient."

Take the case of Elizabeth Bouvia, a quadriplegic who suffered from severe cerebral palsy and was in constant pain. Against her wishes, a feeding tube was inserted through her nose, down her esophagus and into her stomach. The California woman, who had previously sought to starve herself to death, was eating voluntarily at the time, but her ability to take in sufficient nutrition by mouth had diminished and her weight had dropped below 70 pounds, so doctors decided to insert the feeding tube.

Bouvia sought a court order to have the feeding tube removed, but the trial court in February 1986 denied her request. The court said she had no right to refuse tube feeding because "in the opinion of the [hospital] medical staff . . . [her] refusal would to a reasonable medical certainty directly result in a life-threatening condition." A few months later, however, the California Court of Appeal overruled that decision, asserting that a patient has a right to refuse any medical treatment, even if the result is a life-threatening condition. "It is not a medical decision for her physicians to make," the appellate court stated. "[Rather, it] is a moral and philosophical decision that, being a competent adult, is hers alone."*

*Elizabeth Bouvia did not die as a result of having the feeding tube removed. A *Los Angeles Times* report on May 23, 1988, said her weight was up to about 90 pounds and that she ate at least one meal a day of "everyday food." The report said she had last tried starvation in January 1987, but gave it up when she found that it would take several weeks and that she could not stand the pain and the side-effects from

taking her various medications without food. The *Times* said she was trying to stay out of the public eye and to avoid doing anything that might cause members of the public to write, phone or seek to visit her.

As Congress' Office of Technology Assessment has noted, however, making such a decision and getting it carried out may be beyond the abilities of many patients. Because physicians and hospitals are strongly committed to curing disease and saving lives, "refusing treatment requires courage and personal force on the part of the patient — qualities that may be difficult for a critically or terminally ill or severely debilitated patient to muster."

In some cases, doctors may not be wrong to resist a patient's request to discontinue life-sustaining treatment. "Physicians who treat people who are seriously ill are familiar with the transitory depression such illness often causes," write Mark A. Hall and Ira Mark Ellman, professors of law at Arizona State University. Frequently, a temporarily depressed patient will want to give up fighting his illness. "Only to be grateful later that the physician kept treating despite the patient's indifference or resistance."

Nevertheless, it's the *patient's* views about life-sustaining treatment that have become more important in recent years. Physicians have been "slowly coming to recognize a [competent patient's] right to refuse medical treatment," Annas says. "I think the majority of physicians now at least would accept that the patient has the ultimate say here." And this change is not due only to philosophical considerations or legal decisions. "Unfortunately, what's driving this now is economics rather than ethics or the law," Annas says. "There's a lot of pressure not to do expensive things for people who are either terminally ill or unlikely to live very long."

Doctor's Authority

It's not always the patient or his family who wants to discontinue life-sustaining treatment. Sometimes it's the doctor. In recent years, many hospitals have required physicians to obtain the consent of the patient or family members before issuing so-called "do-not-resuscitate" orders, which direct that cardiopulmonary resuscitation not be attempted in the event the patient suffers a heart attack. Some ethicists and physicians, however, have begun to argue that when the procedure would clearly be "futile," doctors ought to be able to write do-not-resuscitate orders without having to get the consent of the patient or family members. For more information, see Tom Tomlinson and Howard Brody, "Futility and the Ethics of Resuscitation," *Journal of the American* *Medical Association,* Sept. 12, 1990, pp. 1276-1280, and "Family Consent to Orders Not to Resuscitate: Reconsidering Hospital Policy," *Journal of the American Medical Association,* Sept. 12, 1990

FOR FURTHER INQUIRY

SUGGESTED READINGS

• Ramsey, Paul. *Ethics at the Edges of Life.* New Haven: Yale University Press, 1978; Cantor, Norman.
• *Legal Frontiers of Death and Dying.* Bloomington, Indiana: Indiana University Press, 1987.
• Weir, Robert F., ed. *Ethical Issues in Death and Dying,* 2d ed. New York: Columbia University Press, 1986.
• Veatch, Robert M. *Death, Dying, and the Biological Revolution,* Revised Edition. New Haven,: Yale University Press, 1989.
• President's Commission for the Study of Ethical Problems in Medicine and Biomedical and Behavioral Research. *Deciding to Forgo Life-Sustaining Treatment: Ethical, Medical, and Legal Issues in Treatment Decisions.* Washington, D.C.: U.S. Government Printing Office, 1983.

ENDNOTES

1. Ramsey, Paul. *Ethics at the Edges of Life.* New Haven: Yale University Press, 1978; Cantor, Norman. *Legal Frontiers of Death and Dying.* Bloomington, Indiana: Indiana University Press, 1987. Weir, Robert F., ed. *Ethical Issues in Death and Dying,* 2d ed. New York: Columbia University Press, 1986. Veatch, Robert M. *Death, Dying, and the Biological Revolution,* Revised Edition. New Haven,: Yale University Press, 1989. President's Commission for the Study of Ethical Problems in Medicine and Biomedical and Behavioral Research. *Deciding to Forgo Life-Sustaining Treatment: Ethical, Medical, and Legal Issues in Treatment Decisions.* Washington, D.C.: U.S. Government Printing Office, 1983.

2. Sager, Mike. "City Seeks Court Order to End Life Support of Brain-Dead Boy." *Washington Post,* August 27, 1980, pp. A1, A12; Weiser, Benjamin. "Boy, 9, May Not be 'Brain Dead,' New Medical Examination Shows." *Washington Post,* Sect. B (September 5, 1980), p. 1; Sager, Mike. "Nine-Year-Old Dies after Four Months in Coma." *Washington Post,* Sect. B, Col 1 (September 17, 1980), p. 6.

3. Harvard Medical School. "A Definition of Irreversible Coma. Report of the Ad Hoc Committee of the Harvard Medical School to Examine the Definition of Brain Death." *Journal of the American Medical Association* 205 (1968):337-340.

4. President's Commission for the Study of Ethical Problems in Medicine and Biomedical and Behavioral Research. *Defining Death: Medical, Legal and Ethical Issues in the Definition of Death.* Washington, D.C.: U.S. Government Printing Office, 1981.

5. Kimura, Rihito. "Japan's Dilemma with the Definition of Death." *Kennedy Institute of Ethics Journal* 1 (1991):123-31.

6. Olick, Robert S. "Brain Death, Religious Freedom, and Public Policy." *Kennedy Institute of Ethics Journal* 1 (Dec. 1991):275-288; New Jersey Declaration of Death Act (1991). *New Jersey Statutes Annotated.* Title 26, 6A-1 to 6A-8

7. Brierley, J.B., J.A.H. Adam, D.I. Graham, and J.A. Simpson. "Neocortical Death after Cardiac Arrest." *Lancet* 2 (September 11, 1971):560-565.

8. Veatch, Robert M. "The Whole-Brain-Oriented Concept of Death: An Outmoded Philosophical Formulation." *Journal of Thanatology* 3 (1975):13-30; Green, Michael B., and Daniel Wikler. "Brain Death and Personal Identity." *Philosophy and Public Affairs* 9 (No.2, Winter 1980):105-133; Gervais, Karen Grandstand. *Redefining Death* New Haven: Yale University Press, 1986.

9. Bouvia v. County of Riverside, No. 159780 (Cal. Super. Ct. Dec. 16, 1983); Bouvia v. Superior Court of Los Angeles County. California Court of Appeal, Second District, 1986. 179 Cal. App. 3d 1127, 225 Cal. Rptr. 297, (Ct. App.), *review denied* (June 5, 1986).

10. Thomas Aquinas. *Summa Theologica.* Ed. by

Fathers of the English Dominican Province. London: R & T Washbourne, Ltd. 1915, 2a 2ae q.64a.

11. Hume, David. *On Suicide*. Edinburgh, Scotland, 1777.

12. Engelhardt, H. Tristram. *The Foundations of Bioethics*. New York: Oxford University Press, 1986.

13. Kant, Immanuel. *Groundwork of the Metaphysic of Morals*. Trans. by H.J. Paton. New York: Harper and Row, 1964.

14. American Medical Association. *Current Opinions of the Council on Ethical and Judicial Affairs of the American Medical Association: Including the Principles of Medical Ethics and Rules of the Council on Ethical and Judicial Affairs*. Chicago: American Medical Association, 1989.

15. Mansson, Helge Hilding. "Justifying the Final Solution." *Omega* 3:79-87.

16. Van der Maas, Paul J.; Van Delden, Johannes J. M.; Pijnenborg, Loes; and Looman, Casper W. N. "Euthanasia and Other Medical Decisions Concerned the End of Life." *The Lancet* 338 (September 14, 1991):669-74.

17. Pope Pius XII. "The Prolongation of Life: An Address of Pope Pius XII to an International Congress of Anesthesiologists." *The Pope Speaks* 4 (Spring 1958):393-398.

18. Meilaender, Gilbert. "On Removing Food and Water: Against the Stream." *The Hastings Center Report* 14 (No. 6, 1984):11-13.

19. Callahan, Daniel. "On Feeding the Dying." *The Hastings Center Report* 13 (No. 5, 1983):22.

20. Lynn, Joanne. *The Choice to Forgo Life-Sustaining Food and Water: Medical, Ethical, and Legal Considerations*. Bloomington, Indiana: Indiana University Press, 1986.

21. *In the Matter of Eichner vs. Dillon*. 426: NYS 2d 517; *Eichner vs. Dillon*, 52 N.Y. 2d 363, 438 N.Y.S. 2d 266.420 N.E. 2d 64 (1981).

22. Dresser, Rebecca S., and Robertson, John A. "Quality of Life and Non-Treatment Decisions for Incompetent Patients: A Critique of the Orthodox Approach." *Law, Medicine, & Health Care* 17 (1989):234-44.

23. Buchanan, Allen E., and Dan W. Brock. *Deciding for Others: The Ethics of Surrogate Decision-making*. Cambridge: Cambridge University Press, 1989.

24. The Catholic Health Association of the United States. "Christian Affirmation of Life: A Statement on Terminal Illness." St. Louis: The Catholic Health Association of the United States, 1982.

25. President's Commission for the Study of Ethical Problems in Medicine and Biomedical and Behavioral Research. *Deciding to Forgo Life-Sustaining Treatment: Ethical, Medical, and Legal Issues in Treatment Decisions*. Washington, D.C.: U.S. Government Printing Office, 1983, p. 153.

26. Veatch, Robert M. *Death, Dying, and the Biological Revolution*. New Haven, Connecticut: Yale University Press, 1976, p. 184-85.

27. *California "Natural Death" Act*. Ca. Stat. Chapter 1439, Code, Health and Safety, sections 7185-95.

28. Society for the Right to Die. *Refusal of Treatment Legislation: A State by State Compilation of Enacted and Model Statutes*. New York: Society for the Right to Die, 1991.

29. Superintendent of *Belchertown State School vs. Saikewicz*, 373 Mass. 728, 370 NE 2d 417 (1977).

30. Weinstein, Bruce, D., editor. *Ethics in the Hospital Setting: Proceedings of the West Virginia Conference on Hospital Ethics Committees*. Morgantown, WV: The West Virginia University Press, (1986); Cranford, Ronald E., and A. Edward Doudera, editors. *Institutional Ethics Committees and Health Care Decision-making*. Ann Arbor, MI: American Society of Law & Medicine, 1984.

31. Areen, Judith. "The Legal Status of Consent Obtained from Families of Adult Patients to Withhold or Withdraw Treatment." *Journal of the American Medical Association* 258 (No. 2, July 10, 1987):229-235.

32. Veatch, Robert M. "Limits of Guardian Treatment Refusal: A Reasonableness Standard." *American Journal of Law and Medicine* 9 (4, Winter 1984):427-68.

Chapter 8

Robert M. Veatch

BIOETHICS

"Had I been present at the creation, I would have given some useful hints for the better ordering of the universe."
— Alfonso The Wise (1221-1284)

"Claude Barnard ... is said to have announced that with a hundred years more of physiological knowledge we would be able to make the organic law ourselves — to manufacture human life, in competition with the Creator. We did not raise any objection ... but we do believe that at that particular stage of development the good Lord ... will say to humanity, just as they do at the Art Gallery at five o'clock, "Gentlemen, it's closing time."
— Edmond de Goncourt and Jules de Goncourt, *Journals,* April 7, 1869

"Whether or not we find what we are seeking is idle, biologically speaking."
— Edna St. Vincent Millay, *The Penitent*

Here, at the end of the 20th century, we are in the midst of one of the most radical projects in the history of the human species — what can be called the biological revolution. We now have the capacity to remove the human heart and keep someone alive entirely mechanically for days or even weeks and months. We are well into the amazing project of identifying every gene that makes up the human genetic code. We are starting to learn how to insert new genes hoping to cure gene-caused diseases. Someday soon we may begin to use the same technology to try to improve on the species, making people with different physical and psychological makeups. We have experimented on human subjects to overcome some feared diseases and, in the case of smallpox, actually to eliminate one of the worst diseases of humankind. New technologies permit us to use pills to control fertility, end

Robert Marlin Veatch, B.S. Purdue, M.S. California at San Francisco, B.D., M.A. and Ph.D. Harvard University, is director of the Kennedy Institute of Ethics at Georgetown University, Washington, D.C.

unwanted pregnancies, and snuff out lives that people no longer want to live. Now a woman who wants to become pregnant but does not want to carry the fetus can have egg cells removed so that they can be fertilized with her husband's sperm in a dish and then have the newly created life implanted in another woman – a surrogate – to carry the fetus to term. The same technology can be used to permit unmarried and lesbian couples to produce children with at least part of their natural genetic makeup.

In the process we may be changing the nature of the human species. It has been argued that the great mysteries of life are being replaced by *manufacturing* children, *inserting* spare body parts from left over "brain dead" corpses, and *redesigning* the nature of the human. Some are beginning to ask whether we have turned what once were deep religious mysteries into engineering projects.

Bioethics is the field of ethics that looks at these controversial uses of new biomedical technology. As a part of ethics it is closely related to the law, but not identical to it. Not everything that is legal is ethical; not everything ethical, legal. The law specifies what a particular state will enforce with public sanction; ethics deals with a more personal, but at the same time more overriding, standard of human conduct. It is not enforced by public sanction. It is more a matter of personal conscience, framed within religious communities or schools of philosophical thought.

This chapter focuses on bioethics, on the ethical implications of the biological revolution, and what it means for the individual and the family as we know them. It covers the issues that arise within the professional practice of medicine – what might be called *medical ethics*, but it also covers certain issues of the biological revolution that extend beyond the practice of medicine: ethical issues of biological research and genetics.

Certain of the issues usually covered in bioethics are taken up in other chapters in this volume including abortion, death and dying, and sexual ethics. But others, including informed consent for medical treatment, confidentiality, human subjects research, transplantation of organs, allocation of scarce medical resources, and genetic engineering, will be explored here.

Although it is too crude, all of bioethics can be reduced to three critical ethical questions. First, for any ethic we have to decide who is a member of the moral community to whom our ethical duties apply. For example, the ethical imperative not to kill is central to many ethical traditions, but it only applies to certain creatures. Many believe it does not apply to nonhuman animals, but others (some vegetarians and many members of nonwestern religions) extend it to at least some animals as well. Even when applied to humans, it is controversial. It is not always obvious to anyone exactly when a human is dead. Clearly we cannot be guilty of killing someone who is already dead, but it is not always obvious to anyone exactly when a human is dead. The definition of death debate, discussed in Chapter 7, is really nothing more than a debate over who is a member of the human moral community, who should be treated as having the same rights as other humans (including perhaps the right not to be killed). Likewise, the abortion debate (discussed in Chapter 6) is really a debate over whether certain fetuses are to be included in the community of humans who bear the moral and legal rights of other humans. Even the controversy over animal rights is in large part a debate over the moral standing of nonhuman creatures.

The first major issue in biomedical ethics is to determine *the moral standing of various creatures and exactly who is to be included when we make moral claims about rights and responsibilities.* Because these issues are taken up in other chapters of this volume, we will assume that one way or another we are dealing here with moral questions pertaining to humans who are bearers of human rights; that is, humans to whom certain duties are owed. The developments of the biological revolution force us as never before to determine exactly what those rights are and what duties are owed.

Two more major questions are raised by the biological revolution. The second question is *what should happen when someone believes that doing what will benefit someone conflicts with certain rights that that person possesses?* Classical medical ethics focuses on the individual patient. The single most well-known code of ethics in medicine is the Hippocratic Oath, a document written in ancient Greece probably dating from the fourth century B.C.[1] As summarized by its core ethical principle, it insists that the health professional should do what, according to the physician, is necessary to benefit the patient. That sounds platitudinous, but it can be surprisingly controversial. It has been interpreted to support treating patients against their will, failing to inform them of bad news, and breaking confidences when the physician believes it will benefit the patient to do so. After looking at the historical context of this debate, we will look at the conflict between patient benefit and patient's rights.

The third major question arising in bioethics *relates the interests and rights of the individual to those of others, other individuals or the society as a whole.* It asks what the relation of the individual should be to the society. We are beginning to discover that when the patient is the sole focus of medicine – whether the benefit of the patient or the rights of the patient – this can come at the expense of the interests of others. Doing research on human subjects, transplanting organs from one human to another, allocating scarce health resources and doing genetic engineering all raise these issues.

Consider a deceptively complicated case that arose in England several years ago. It became the focus of a major debate leading to a change in our medical ethic when the interests of the patient may conflict with the patient's rights as well as when they conflict with the interests of others in the society.

CASE 1:

Is The Pill Dangerous To Your Health?

A 16-year-old young English woman had reached the age at which she thought she needed counseling for birth control. She feared her family physician, Dr. Robert Browne, so she went to a clinic that provided contraceptive counseling.

After suitable history and physical examination, the clinic prescribed oral contraceptives for her. In the process, the clinic learned the name of the family physician and, believing that Dr. Browne should know of the medication in case of a side effect, it notified him. The young woman, perhaps not realizing the implications, agreed that her doctor could be informed.

One can imagine Dr. Browne receiving the unsolicited advice. After struggling with his options he took it upon himself to inform the young woman's father.

Charges of violating confidentiality were brought against Dr. Browne. When pressed he stated that he had two motives for disclosing. First, he was concerned about the physical hazards of the pill. Second, he was also concerned about the psychological hazards. He claimed that his interests were for the patient and for her alone. He wanted to do what was best for her. The review committee, after considering Dr. Browne's reasoning, concluded that it did not find Dr. Browne's action improper.[2]

While the question of keeping medical information confidential may seem old-fashioned or even trivial, cases like Dr. Browne's – as well as those involving AIDS patients–force us to deal with the classical ethic of medicine. Dr. Browne appealed to the ethic of Hippocrates, which states that the physician should not divulge that "which ought not to be spoken abroad." This, of course, implies that some information can be "spread abroad." Many like Dr. Browne, who work in the older, more paternalistic medical ethical framework, have claimed that we can tell what information can ethically be spread abroad by asking the physician what he or she believes will benefit the patient. There seems little doubt that Dr. Browne sincerely believed that telling the girl's father would benefit her. That many readers of the case disagree with Dr. Browne does not count in the old Hippocratic tradition; deciding to disclose was based on what *he* believed would benefit her. The case not only raises questions about whether Dr. Browne determined correctly what would be beneficial to his patient; it also raises questions about whether patients have rights, rights that the patient might invoke even in cases where the physician believes he is acting in a beneficial way.

Invoking the old Hippocratic, patient-benefiting principle to deal with questions of confidentiality also presents problems when others might need to know about a patient's medical condition. If a physician learns he or she is caring for an HIV-infected patient who remains sexually active, it is not necessarily the welfare of the patient that makes the physician consider disclosing; it is the welfare of others. The classical focus on patient benefit not only may violate the rights of patients, it also may jeopardize the interests and rights of others.

THE HISTORICAL CONTEXT

Dr. Browne's appeal to the Hippocratic Oath makes us ask why a 20th-century English physician would turn to this old medical ethical document.

The Hippocratic Oath. The Hippocratic Oath stems from one school of medical practice in ancient Greece.[3] It is part of a large group of writings associated with the physician, Hippocrates. He probably lived in the fifth century B.C. Almost certainly this person did not write all the documents, but they have been gathered together and have come to be identified with him. Some dealt with matters of medical science and notions of healing of the day. Others dealt with matters of ethics.

The Oath itself probably dates from the fourth century, perhaps from the Island of Cos where an enormous Aesclepion, a Greek healing temple, existed. The ruins are still present today. The thinking of the Hippocratic Oath has great similarities with Pythagoreanism, that strange school of Greek thought that grew out of a scientific-philosophical-religious cult – the same group that gave us the Pythagorean theorem in geometry.

The Oath appears to have been used to symbolize the adoption of the medical student into the family of the physician. It contains two major parts: the oath of initiation itself and a code of conduct.

The Oath of Initiation. The oath contains a pledge of loyalty to the teacher. It even requires the student to come to the financial aid of the teacher in times of need. It contains other elements alien to 20th century Western thinking, but compatible with the practice of a Greek cult of the day. Although it is strangely incompatible with our recent emphasis on making the patient a knowledgeable, educated consumer of health care, the Oath contains a pledge not to reveal medical secrets of the cult, a view seen elsewhere in Pythagorean thought. The Oath expresses the idea that knowledge can be dangerous when it is in the hands of the uninitiated layperson. The one taking the Oath swears by the Greek gods and goddesses, by Apollo, Aesclepius, Hygiea, and Panaceia.

The Hippocratic Code of Conduct. One reason we believe the Oath is Pythagorean is that, like Pythagoreanism, it divides medicine into three parts: diet, pharmaceuticals, and surgery. It includes some apparently religiously based prohibitions. The Hippocratic physician is expected not to give patients deadly drugs and not to provide abortions. Rather oddly, he or she is also forbidden from practicing surgery – all provisions compatible with the Pythagorean cult. The prohibition on surgery is not because they believed surgery to be too dangerous. Rather they seemed to believe that surgery would "contaminate" the physician. Many ancient cultures feared that contact with blood would make one impure. The Oath wants Hippocratic physicians to remain "pure and holy," leaving surgery to others more suited to the task.

The core principle of the Hippocratic Oath is the most important element carried forward into modern medicine. It requires the physician to pledge that he will "benefit the patient according to his ability and judgment and keep the patient from harm." This summarizes the commitment of the physician to benefit the patient, but paternalistically bases the benefit on the individual physician's own judgment.

Although many modern physicians might consider themselves as standing in the Judeo-Christian tradition, at least to some extent, the relation of the Hippocratic ethic to the major Western religions is controversial. We know that early Christianity was in conflict with Greek ideas. It wasn't until the fourth century A.D. that Christianity finally was accepted in the Greco-Roman world. It challenged the tradition of the Greek healing system. It is not clear why the Hippocratic Oath survived. Some claim it, of all Greek medical systems, was most compatible with Christian ethics,[4] but others see them as very different.[5] A Christian form of the oath from the middle ages shows significant changes including an abandonment of the secrecy requirement and the prohibition on surgery as well as the more obvious dropping of the reference to the Greek gods.[6] Given the radical changes in medical ethics in the past decade or two, a case can be made that Hippocratic ethics is in many ways different from that of the Jewish and Christian thought and the secular liberal philosophy that grew out of them.

MODERN PROFESSIONAL ETHICAL CODES

Thomas Percival's Medical Ethics. This ambiguity between Hippocratic and other forms of ethics has continued into modern times. Professional ethics of medicine in the Anglo-American world dates from a dispute at the Manchester Infirmary in England in the 1790s. An epidemic taxed the capacity of the infirmary and feuds erupted among the physicians, surgeons, and apothecaries over their responsibilities and relations among colleagues. Thomas Percival, a physician who because of a health problem had been forced to stop practicing medicine, was asked to mediate the dispute. He produced a "scheme of professional conduct" that eventually was published and became the basis for modern medical ethics in the United States.[7]

Percival's ethics is essentially Hippocratic. The main focus is on benefiting the patient, but it deals much more with institutional ethical questions of the hospital and takes into account the duties of the professional to society in a way that is totally absent in Hippocratic ethics.

The American Medical Association Code of 1847. In the 19th century American medicine was in a period of ferment with different schools of thought feuding over what should constitute proper practice. In 1847 the American Medical Association was founded. Among its purposes was to establish what we now think of as orthodox medical practitioners and separate them from other practitioners that they called quacks and charlatans. One of the ways that a profession can establish itself and gain credibility is to write a code of ethics. The AMA wrote such a code taking sections of Percival's writing verbatim.[8] It also was essentially Hippocratic, but included sections on the more social dimensions of medical ethics. That code has been revised many times, major changes coming in 1903, 1912, 1947, and 1957.

The World Medical Association's Declaration of Geneva. Meanwhile, the World Medical Association, the international association made up of the national physicians' organizations, was seeking a modern code of ethics for physicians. Convinced that the Hippocratic Oath remained the basis for the ethical duties of physicians, it set out to provide a modern revision. What emerged was the Declaration of Geneva.[9] First adopted in 1948 and revised in 1968, it follows closely the key moral commitments of the Oath, including the principle that "The health of my patient will be my first consideration."

COLLAPSE OF THE HIPPOCRATIC TRADITION – THE 1970S

The case of Dr. Browne was a key challenge to Hippocratic paternalistic commitment to the welfare of the patient. In that case people began to realize that there may be times when we really do not want physicians to do what they think will benefit the patient. One of those times may be when the patient prefers not being benefited. At the same time cases were beginning to emerge of patients being forced to undergo terribly painful efforts to prolong life when they were dying of advanced cancer. Physicians were claiming that the Hippocratic Oath required them to withhold the truth – about cancer diagnoses and many other medical problems – from patients if the physician believed disclosure would harm the patient by upsetting them or causing them to act irrationally.

In the United States the society had just come through a period of active, militant defense of individual rights: racial rights, women's rights, students' rights. Could patients' rights be far behind? The anti-war movement had led to a challenging of scientific and technological authority. Just as war was found to be too important to be left to the generals, so life–and–death medical decisions were beginning to be seen as too important to be left to people whose primary claim to expertise was technical. People began to challenge the Hippocratic ideal.

THREE CHALLENGES TO THE HIPPOCRATIC TRADITION

Problems with Assessing Benefits. The Hippocratic Oath was called into question in three ways. First, there are problems in the way benefits are assessed. Some versions of the Hippocratic principle commit the physician to *benefit* the patient in general while others, such as the Declaration of Geneva, commit the physician only to pursuing the patient's *health*. We began to realize that there were many ways that people could be benefited other than by promoting their health. We also pursue well-being in other spheres: the aesthetics, the family, our occupation, education, the law, and so forth. The physician cannot possibly be expected to be an expert in promoting all forms of welfare. It is unrealistic to expect the physician to make choices that will promote the total well-being of patients.

On the other hand, if they follow the Declaration of Geneva and pursue only the patient's health, there are equally serious problems. For one thing, health itself is a complex goal. It includes preserving life, curing disease, relieving suffering, and preserving and promoting health. Sometimes these conflict among themselves as when preserving life can only be done by inflicting terrible suffering in a cancer patient. There is no reason to expect the physician to be able to make these trade-offs in the way that will really promote the overall health of the patient without learning from the patient what mix of these health goals is appropriate.

Moreover, in a world of finite resources no one will be able to fully satisfy the goals of health and other spheres at the same time. In fact, sometimes we purposely fail to pursue our health in order to pursue some other aspects of our welfare. Those who smoke, eat a good steak, or spend time reading when they could be exercising understand this notion. Probably no rational person would want to totally maximize his or her health at the expense of these other goods. If this is so, then if the physician single-mindedly pursues the health of the patient, sometimes the patient's total well-being really won't be served as well as if some compromises were made.

Because the physician cannot be expected to know how to trade off health benefits with benefits in other spheres, the goal of expecting the physician to promote the well-being of the patient is unrealistic whether that goal is interpreted narrowly to refer only to health or more broadly to refer to total well-being. There are real problems with the apparently benign idea of physicians doing what they think is best for the patient.

Problems When Benefits Conflict with Other Moral Duties. That is not the only problem with the Hippocratic idea of benefiting the patient, however. Many ethical systems hold to the idea that sometimes we have duties other than simply maximizing good outcomes. Jewish ethics requires certain practices such as avoiding killing simply because killing is believed to be a violation of divine law. Hypothetically, patients might be so miserable that they would actually benefit from being killed. Jewish ethics holds that, even if that were true, it is still wrong to kill. Other ethics, such as Kantianism, hold that it is wrong to tell lies – even if the results are better when the lie is told. Kantians claim that it is wrong to break promises – even if the results are better if a promise were broken. These ethics all share in common the view that some behaviors can be morally wrong even if they produce the best consequences. Collectively, these positions are sometimes called *deontological ethics*. (See Chapter 3 for a fuller discussion of these views.)

Some of these deontological ethics may be quite sophisticated so that they avoid being applied rigidly and legalistically. In fact, some of them may be more flexible than some forms of ethics that focus exclusively on consequences. The key common feature, however, is that they all hold that sometimes something other than the consequences of an action can determine whether the action is morally right or wrong. A second major problem with the Hippocratic concentration on benefiting the patient is that in some ethics there are times when doing what will produce the most benefit or avoid the most harm may simply be morally wrong.

Problems of Conflict Between the Interest of the Individual Patient and Those of the Society. The third major problem with the ethic of benefiting the patient is that increasingly we are discovering that sometimes benefiting the patient either at the expense of the claims of others. Benefiting the HIV patient by keeping information confidential may do great harm to others. A physician who remains steadfastly loyal to one patient may, in the process, avoid helping other people who are in much greater need. While there are great risks in bringing the interests of the society into medical ethics, there are equally great dangers in avoiding all of the social ethical questions confronting medicine today. Many of the newer codes of medical ethics either address questions of the rights of patients that may conflict with having the physician do what he or she believes will be beneficial to the patient or questions of the conflict between the interests of the patient and those of the society.

CODES BREAKING WITH THE HIPPOCRATIC TRADITION
Several of the 20th century codes and oaths for ethics in medicine break with the Hippocratic tradition because of these problems.

The Nuremberg Code (1946). One of the most important problems with having the health professional focus exclusively on benefiting the individual patient is that, taken literally, no research using human subjects could ever be attempted (unless doing so could be justified by the potential benefits to the individual subject). The atrocities of the Nazi medical experiments in World War II led to a crisis in medicine. The Nazi physicians abandoned the portion of the Hippocratic ethic that required always focusing on the welfare of the individual patient. For example, they did studies designed to understand the effects of long exposures to freezing temperatures or high altitudes. Ignoring basic morality, they simply took concentration camp prisoners and exposed them to freezing water or high altitudes until they died.

At the trials at Nuremberg when these abuses were confronted, the international community had two options. They could have retreated to the Hippocratic ethic, insisting that every study done on humans be justified solely on the basis of benefit to the individual studied. That would, of course, have ended much important medical research. The other option was to figure out some way to permit the use of subjects without exposing them to these terrible abuses. The writers of the Nuremberg Code decided to renounce the Hippocratic answer, turning instead to a rule that subjects could be used in medical research provided that the subjects gave their *informed consent* and met other conditions. This is the first time that informed consent appears in any formal medical ethical document. That it comes not from within the medical profession but from a secular proceedings in international law is significant. Informed consent is alien to Hippocratic professional ethical thinking but easily understood within a framework of liberal political philosophy that focuses on self-determination and respect for the autonomy of the individual. In fact, legal cases in the United States had been acknowledging the patient's right to self-determination since 1914.

The American Hospital Association's Patients' Bill of Rights (1972). Another important event in the evolution of an ethic that replaces the Hippocratic ethic with one grounded in liberal philosophy and its focus on rights is the American Hospital Association's Patients' Bill of Rights. A group organized by the hospital association put forward a bill of rights for patients that included a limited right of patients to give their consent to treatment. It backtracked by providing an escape clause in cases in which the physician believed the patient would be harmed. With this proviso, however, it acknowledges a right of the patient to information, to considerate and respectful care, to refuse treatment, and a range of other rights.

The American Nurses' Association Code for Nurses (1976). Although the hospital association had referred to rights in the early 1970s, the first association of health professional to do so was the American Nurses' Association. In 1976 they revised their code of ethics, making it begin with a first principle referring to self-determination of clients. They explicitly acknowledged the moral and legal rights of all clients, a notion that signals the shift from the old Greek Hippocratic goal of benefiting patients and protecting them from harm to a more liberal notion of respecting them as self-determining beings. Later, that code also affirms the duty of the nurse to safeguard the client and to protect the public as well, leaving nurses struggling with cases in which one cannot do all of these at the same time. This was typical of the early days in this generation of health professional ethics in which we still felt the older commitments to promoting the welfare of the patient while simultaneously feeling the newer pull toward respecting the rights of patients and serving societal interests as well.

The AMA Principles of 1980. In 1980 a more dramatic shift away from the Hippocratic focus on benefit occurred when the American Medical Association once again revised its code. It spoke of the *rights* of patients, of colleagues, and other health professionals. Here was the clear confrontation between the older, more paternalistic concern with benefits and harms, and the newer concern with rights influenced not by the Hippocratic tradition but by secular liberal political philosophy and its tradition of human rights. This was the first time that the word *rights* had appeared in any formal code of ethics for physicians.

MEDICAL ETHICS FROM NON-PROFESSIONAL SOURCES

While the ethics written by health professional and hospital groups has always been historically important, it has never been the only source of medical ethics. Ethics is, after all, part of an overall cultural world view that has traditionally been expressed in religious as well as secular understandings of the world. Most religious traditions have in one form or another what could be called a medical ethic. They have a set of beliefs and value commitments that express the way physicians, other health professionals, and lay people ought to behave on medical matters. Talmudic ethics in Judaism provides such a framework governing not only dietary laws, but prohibiting abortion and mercy killing, severely limiting autopsy, and generally providing a framework for Jews to approach medical decisions.[10] Likewise, Roman Catholic moral theology has, since the 13th century, worked with a framework of "natural law" that distinguishes acceptable from unacceptable omissions of treatment. It proscribes active mercy killing, but permits killing in certain special cases. (See Chapter 7 for more details.) It has been interpreted as prohibiting intentional efforts to limit pregnancy using artificial means (including birth control pills, IUDs, condoms, and diaphragms). But it also presents an entire ethical system by which all decisions in medicine can be approached, even the most mundane ones. It provides an understanding of the goal or end of life, as well as a set of standards for shaping daily behavior.[11]

Protestant religious groups have a much less well-developed medical ethical system, but most denominations by now have adopted positions supporting the right to refuse medical treatment (sometimes referred to as the "right to die"). Sometimes they cautiously accept the legitimacy of abortion. But, once again, they also provide a basic system of beliefs and values upon which any medical decision might be based.[12]

Eastern religious groups also have medical ethical positions ranging from the ancient Caraca Samhita (a Hindu religious writing from the first century) and ancient Buddhist and Confucian writings to the 1981 Islamic Code of Medical Ethics prepared at a meeting in Kuwait by the International Organization of Islamic Medicine.[13]

Secular philosophical systems also provide a basis for addressing medical ethical questions. Liberal political philosophy, as we noted, is a major contributor, posing a significant challenge to the Hippocratic ethic. The United States Constitution's Bill of Rights provides a basis for addressing many ethical questions in medicine as does the United Nations Declaration of Human Rights. In some secular societies state documents have replaced, at least temporarily, professionally generated codes. The Soviet Oath for Physicians (1971) was written by the Soviet Government, not the medical profession.[14] It acknowledges "high responsibility . . . to my people and to the Soviet Government."

Any system of belief and value – religious or secular – ought to contain within it the seeds of an ethic for medical decision-making. There is no reason why they should be exactly the same as that contained in the Hippocratic ethic. On that basis, the Hippocratic ethic can be viewed as one system of belief and value about the ends and purposes of medicine. It might be seen as a kind of "quasi-religion" competing with other religious and philosophical systems for loyalty of health providers. When a provider is a member of one of the other traditions – when he or she is a Catholic or a Muslim, or a subscriber to the basic liberal beliefs of America's Founding Fathers – there is reason to suspect that these systems of belief and value may come into conflict from time to time. When the patient and the physician stand in different systems of belief and value, the conflicts may also arise. In this context, it is easy to see why it is increasingly controversial for physicians to hold to the Hippocratic principle that they should always work only to do what they believe will be for the benefit of the patient.

THE PATIENTS' RIGHTS MOVEMENT

As we have seen, one major conflict with the Hippocratic ethic has been with the view that sometimes there are duties to act in certain ways even if, hypothetically, doing so would not maximally benefit the patient. These duties are often expressed in rights-language. Rights are, after all, closely related to moral duties. If one person has a duty to act in a certain way, often someone else can be said to have a right to have the person act that way. Given the American propensity to express ethical claims in rights language, a major challenge to Hippocratism has come in the patients' rights movement that began in the 1970s.

Three major rights claims have received the most attention. Each represents a moral principle that is sometimes seen as standing against the duty simply to benefit the patient. These are the principles of veracity, autonomy, and fidelity, which give rise to the rights to the truth, informed consent, and the right to have promises kept.

THE PRINCIPLE OF VERACITY: THE RIGHT TO THE TRUTH

One of the first controversies that arose in the contemporary era of health care ethics was the debate over whether physicians owed the truth to their patients.

CASE 2:
Lying to the Woman with Cancer.

> Maria Martinez, a 54-year-old Puerto Rican born woman who had been living in New York for the past ten years, had been suffering severe pain in her abdomen. She also noticed a lump. A third-year-medical student, who was working closely with the patient, realized that she was very worried, fearing that it could be something serious. He tried to assure her.
>
> The physicians, concerned about the problem, scheduled exploratory surgery. The surgeon reported to the rest of the medical team, including the student, that they had found a stage IV cancer of the cervix, a condition with a less than 20% rate of five–year survival.
>
> The medical student, who knew the patient better than anyone else, favored telling her she had cancer and helping her prepare for her future. She had three adolescent children who would need attention.
>
> The attending physician reacted aggressively to the proposal saying, "We never use the word 'cancer' because they give up hope." He suggested using words like "tumor" and saying that, as far as they could see, they got it all out. Both he and the student knew that that was misleading. The student admitted that he had never "given a patient a death sentence before," but felt that she could handle it better if he were more honest. He also felt she had a right to know.[15]

Empirical Studies. As we have seen in the older Hippocratic ethic, physicians were told that they not only could, but should, withhold bad news when they believed it would harm their patients. In a study of physician attitudes, Donald Oken in 1962 found that 88 percent of physicians would tend to withhold a diagnosis of cancer.[16] In 1979, just 17 years later, Dennis Novak repeated essentially the same study and found that 98% of physicians would tend to disclose the cancer diagnosis.[17] What accounts for this dramatic shift?

THE MORAL REASONS FOR AND AGAINST TRUTH-TELLING

Hippocratic Therapeutic Privilege. Bernard C. Meyer, a New York psychiatrist writing in 1968, summarized the old view:

What is imparted to a patient about his illness should be planned with the same care and executed with the same skill that is demanded by any potentially therapeutic measure. Like the transfusion of blood, the dispensing of certain information must be distinctly indicated, the amount given consonant with the needs of the recipient, and the type chosen with the view of avoiding untoward reactions.[18]

Meyer's view was based on Hippocratic reasoning–that the physician is morally bound to do whatever will benefit the patient even if that means lying or withholding information. This is now sometimes referred to as the physician's "therapeutic privilege," the belief that the physician has the "privilege" of distorting the truth when he or she believes it will be beneficial to the patient.

Pro-truth Consequentialism. The ethic that requires the physician to benefit the patient–what can be called *patient-centered consequentialism*, of course, can also be used to defend disclosing the bad news to Mrs. Martinez. Joseph Fletcher, a medical ethicist at Episcopal Theological School in Cambridge, Massachusetts and then at the University of Virginia School of Medicine, until his death, was firmly committed to an ethic of maximizing good consequences. Yet he tended to believe that withholding a diagnosis from a patient would be more likely to do harm than to help.[19] He imagined patients like Mrs. Martinez, with unexplained painful growths agonizing as they imagine the worst. Added to that would be the further worry of feeling that people were hiding things from you. He believed that usually more harm than good would be done by following Bernard Meyer's strategy. He was a pro-truth consequentialist. Some people may have shifted into a pro-truth position because they have reassessed the consequences and come to the conclusion that telling is better for the patient. In a world of high-tech bureaucratic medicine, sometimes the private physician may not be able to control information completely. In the worst of cases, a patient learns of a terminal illness when a nurse or consulting physician lets the bad news slip out.

The Principle of Veracity. The major reason for the shift in favor of disclosing a cancer diagnosis may be something ethically quite different. We have seen that many in the liberal tradition of Western political philosophy simply believe that in order to respect persons, we owe them the truth. They cannot be treated as mature, responsible decision-makers able to consent or refuse consent to treatment unless they know what their condition is.

Some ethical theories hold that there is something inherently wrong with lying to patients regardless of the consequences. Immanuel Kant once wrote a remarkable essay entitled "On the Supposed Right to Tell Lies from Benevolent Motives." In it he claims:

The duty of being truthful ... is unconditional ... Although in telling a certain lie I do not actually do anyone a wrong, I formally but not materially violate the principle of right .... To be truthful (honest) in all declarations, therefore, is a sacred and absolutely commanding decree of reason, limited by no expediency.[20]

For Kant, deciding whether to tell Mrs. Martinez that she had cancer would not be a matter of calculating the consequences; it would be an unconditional duty. One major problem with Kantian ethics is that it is possible that two or more of these duties may come into conflict. Imagine, for instance, that you had promised Mrs. Martinez's relatives that you would lie to her. Kant held it was your unconditional duty to tell the truth, but that it was also your unconditional duty to keep promises. You would be in a bind. You couldn't do both simultaneously.

British philosopher W. D. Ross proposed a strategy of treating such duties as *prima facie*, that is as "binding other things being equal."[21] These would be one's duties if there were no competing considerations. When two of these duties came into conflict he believed one simply had to balance them. More recently, medical ethicist Baruch Brody has advocated using a "judgment" among what he calls "conflicting appeals."[22] One must simply exercise case-by-case judgment. But the conflict, according to Ross or Brody, cannot be settled simply by figuring out which course would produce the best consequences.

The American Medical Association was long committed to the Hippocratic notion of resolving such conflicts doing precisely this: seeing what would produce the best results for the patient. But in 1980 its members made a dramatic shift in the direction of Kantian, duty-based ethics. At that point they said simply that "a physician shall deal honestly with patients and colleagues ...."[23] They completely reversed their traditional consequence-oriented approach in favor of one committed to the right of the patient to the truthful diagnosis.

That the AMA is not completely firm in its conversion can be seen by the fine print that eventually emerged in the more detailed opinions of their Council on Ethical and Judicial Affairs, the group that is responsible for interpreting the Principles of Ethics adopted by their House of Delegates, their national legislative assembly. The Council saw fit to add a Hippocratic exception not in the House of Delegates' position. They added, "when risk-disclosure poses such a serious psychological threat of detriment to the patient as to be medically contraindicated," then the AMA physician need not inform the patient.[24]

Current bioethics is left with a controversy. The only important case is the one in which a physician might be tempted to invoke the therapeutic privilege and withhold potentially meaningful information on the grounds that he or she believes it will so upset the patient as to justify withholding it. Those who are committed to the patients' rights perspective tend to reject this exception added by the AMA Council. Those who remain Hippocratic and paternalistic are willing to consider it. Even they, however, must be satisfied that the patient is really better off not knowing.

INFORMED CONSENT AND THE PRINCIPLE OF AUTONOMY

One of the major problems with the therapeutic privilege position is that it makes truly informed consent impossible. Informed consent is the product of the transition to the ethic based on rights and duties to patients. It is totally absent from the traditional Hippocratic ethic. It emerged as a product of the ethical principle of autonomy, which, along with veracity, has become one of the centerpieces of the ethic of the tradition of liberal philosophy.

The Place of Autonomy in Medical Ethics. Autonomy can be understood as the notion of making choices according to individually chosen life plans. Autonomy is foreign to Hippocratic ethics. Likewise, autonomy played no role in early Judeo-Christian ethics. Judaism has little place for individuals making choices according to their life plans. Early Christianity didn't either, even if it did emphasize individual choice. Individuals were expected to convert to the new religion, leaving family, former religion, and community, if necessary, to do so. By the time of the Protestant Reformation in the 16th century, the individual was beginning to emerge as a more important figure. Precursors to Protestantism–such as the mystics, Wycliffe, Hus, and Tauler–expressed the notion of God speaking directly to individuals. Luther, Calvin, and especially the figures of the Left-Wing of the Protestant Reformation provided a context for questioning of authority and affirmation of individual choice. Many claim that these events were the precursors to the full-blown emergence of liberalism in the 18th century. Immanuel Kant, one of the principal advocates of the ethic of this tradition, and the philosophy of Locke, Hobbes, Rousseau, and the Founding Fathers of the American Constitutional system provided a foundation for elevating autonomy to a central place in ethics, a phenomenon not felt fully in medical ethics until the 1970s.

Other medical ethics are more like Hippocratism in down-playing autonomy. Marxism, Buddhism, Hinduism, Confucianism, and Islam all have no role for the choices of the individual based on self-selected life plans. This is a phenomenon primarily of the modern, liberal West. It is beginning to have impact in other cultures as well. For example, modern Japan, which traditionally gave no role to autonomy, has an active patient's rights movement influenced by physicians, lawyers, philosophers, and others who have interacted with Western thought and adapted portions of it that they believe fit their culture.

Informed Consent and the Principle of Autonomy. For bioethics, the most direct implication for bioethics of the principle of autonomy is in the doctrine of informed consent. Different ethics handle the notion of consenting to medical treatment very differently.

Consent in Hippocratic Ethics. A truly Hippocratic physician may, of course, from time to time tell patients about treatment alternatives and their risks and benefits. The physician may even give the patient a choice among the options, but only when, in the physician's opinion, it will serve to benefit the patient. Thus, the risk of driving will probably be mentioned when a drug may cause drowsiness. But if the physician believed that the patient might be irrationally persuaded not to accept the treatment if certain risks were mentioned, those risks would not be disclosed. The Hippocratic physician like Bernard Meyer would omit the consent when he believed consent would not benefit the patient and especially when he thought it would cause harm.

Consent with the Principle of Autonomy. If consent is grounded in the principle of autonomy in liberal political philosophy, it gets much greater weight. Information must be presented and consent must be obtained whenever it would be necessary to facilitate autonomous choice. Two legal cases show how autonomy has reshaped the consent doctrine in the past generation.

CASE 3:
Irma Natanson's Breast Cancer

In 1955 Irma Natanson suffered from breast cancer for which she had a radical left mastectomy performed. She also underwent cobalt radiation treatment performed by Dr. John R. Kline.

She claimed to suffer injury from the radiation and sued, charging Dr. Kline failed to warn her of the risks. Dr. Kline did not claim to have explained the risks; he simply used his medical judgment that the treatment was appropriate. The issue in the case was whether Dr. Kline should have explained the risks–including the possibility of radiation damage–so that she could consent (or refuse consent) for the treatment.

When the case finally reached the Kansas Supreme Court in 1960, the chief justice ruled that "Anglo-American law starts with the premise of a thoroughgoing self-determination. It follows that each man is considered to be master of his own body, and he may, if he be of sound mind, expressly prohibit the performance of life-saving surgery, or other medical treatment."

The question further arose as to exactly what the physician must say to the patient. On the subject the justice stated, "How the physician may best discharge his obligation to the patient in this difficult situation involves primarily a question of medical judgment. So long as the disclosure is sufficient to assure an informed consent, the physician's choice of plausible courses of action should not be called into question if it appears, all circumstances considered, that the physician was motivated by the patient's best therapeutic interests and he proceeded as competent medical men would have done in a similar situation."[25]

Here we see that by 1960 an explicit appeal to patient self-determination has entered the thinking of the judge in the court. The court reflects the rights-oriented liberal political philosophy of the American legal system. But simultaneously the judge still reflects Hippocratic elements in holding to a standard based on the commitment of the physician to the patient's best interest. He assesses this by an appeal to what competent physicians similarly situated would have done in a similar situation, assuming that they would be the authority. This is what has come to be called *the professional standard of consent*. Within the next decade this standard would change, as we can see in the next case.

CASE 4:
A Youth's Pain In His Back

In 1972 a case was heard in a United States Court of Appeals involving a 19-year-old youth named Canterbury. He had suffered severe back pain and had submitted to an operation performed by a neurosurgeon, one Dr. Spence. He was not informed of a risk of paralysis. He suffered a fall from his hospital bed the day after the surgery and was left paralyzed.

One of the critical questions in the case was whether Dr. Spence had to disclose risks such as paralysis in order to have an adequate consent for the surgery. Canterbury's lawyers challenged the professional standard that had been used in earlier cases.

The court ruled that some have measured disclosure by "good medical practice," others by what a reasonable practitioner would have bared under the circumstances, and still others by what medical custom in the community would demand." It went on to reject this approach as being inconsistent with the patient's right to decide, claiming, "Any definition of scope in terms purely of a professional standard is at odds with the patient's prerogative to decide on projected therapy himself. That prerogative, we have said, is at the very foundation of the duty to disclose, and both the patient's right to know and the physician's correlative obligation to tell him are diluted to the extent that its compass is dictated by the medical profession. In our view, the patient's right of self-decision shapes the boundaries of the duty to reveal."[26]

STANDARDS FOR DISCLOSURE

These cases force the question of exactly what must be disclosed in order for a consent to be informed. At first we might be tempted to say, "everything," that the consent should be "fully informed," but that turns out to be impossible. There are thousands of things that the physician could say about any given treatment, more than any reasonable physician would want to discuss and more than any reasonable patient would want to hear. It could take hours to cover all possible risks. Something short of "everything" will have to do.

These two cases make clear that with the evolution of the principle of autonomy, a new standard has emerged for answering the question of how much to disclose. The old Hippocratic approach, concentrating on benefit and harm, usually accepted less information.

The Professional Standard. The *professional standard* was often used by Hippocratic physicians: The patient must be told what a competent physician similarly situated would have disclosed. The idea was that it was a matter of "professional judgment"–not only whether the information was correct, but also whether its disclosure would do more good or harm. It simply should be a matter of professional judgment.

The Reasonable Person Standard. While that might work in a paternalistic era, it does not make much sense for someone trying to facilitate autonomy. It is quite possible that a patient would find a piece of information important to facilitate self-determination even though neither the physician nor his colleagues would disclose it. For example, consider the information that the physician knows that a colleague is more competent at performing the procedure. The patient might find that to be very interesting information, but it is not the sort of thing that physicians tend to discuss with patients. Even certain side effects of medication might be beyond what most physicians usually discuss with their patients, even though that information could be very important to the patient. Whether physicians tend to disclose does not seem very relevant to the question of whether the patient would want access to the information in making a treatment choice.

Critics of the old professional standard prefer what is now called the *reasonable person standard*. Under it, the physician must disclose what the reasonable person in the patient's situation would want to be told to make an informed choice. That does not mean telling everything, but it may mean considerably more than what was called for under the professional standard.

The Subjective Standard. Even the reasonable person standard may not perfectly satisfy the requirements of the principle of autonomy. Imagine a patient who is unreasonable, who wants more or less information than the hypothetical reasonable person. If this person wants less information about some subject, surely in the name of autonomy the patient should be able to decline further discussion of a topic. But, what if the patient wants more information about some topic than the reasonable person would?

Imagine a pianist who tells the physician that he was really worried about injuries to his fingers more than most people. If playing the piano is an important part of his life plan, then he would need to know more about the risks of injuries to his fingers than most ordinary reasonable people.

For such situations the *subjective standard* is now usually proposed. Under it the physician must tell what this particular patient would want to know, based on his or her subjective values and goals.

This presents a problem, though. How can the physician be expected to know all the special topics of interest to the patient? The answer has been that the physician must disclose only what the reasonable person would want to know plus anything the patient specifically signals an interest in and anything else that the physician should reasonably be expected to deduce would be of special interest to the patient, knowing what the physician knows about the patient. That may not give the patient exactly what he or she wants to know, but it is hard to imagine how the physician could do any more.

The legal implications are important. Under the professional standard, a physician accused of not getting an adequately informed consent would bring colleagues into the Courtroom to testify whether they would have acted the same way. Under the reasonable person standard, it will be up to a jury – a group selected to be reasonable typical citizens – to decide whether they would want the information. Under the subjective standard the jury would have to try to put themselves in the patient's shoes imagining what the patient would want to be told based on what the patient has revealed to the physician about the patient's special interests.

PROMISES, CONFIDENTIALITY, AND THE PRINCIPLE OF FIDELITY

In addition to truth-telling and autonomy, there is a third principle that raises a cluster of issues that challenge the idea that physicians should simply do what they believe will benefit the patient. It is sometimes referred to as the principle of fidelity or promise-keeping. The general idea is that if a commitment is made, other things being equal, it should be kept, even if the consequences might be better if it were not. According to those who hold this principle to be morally important, we can show respect for people not only by dealing honestly with them and respecting their autonomous choices, but also by showing fidelity to commitments made.

Fidelity: Contracts And Covenants. The general idea is that if a commitment is made it should be kept. This arises not only in specific commitments such as business contracts, but also in implied promises that are often conveyed when a patient/physician relation is established. When patients are asked what they dislike about relations with their physicians, they often point to what appear to be small things: that the physician doesn't listen and show his or her undivided attention, that the physician won't return phone calls and keeps them waiting for appointments. These episodes raise questions about the fidelity of the physician to the patient.

Sometimes the word *contract* is used to describe the patient/physician relation. It conveys that certain understandings are established, certain commitments made. In an earlier era the main focus was on the duties of the health professional to remain loyal to the patient. This was in part because it was assumed that only the health provider was an active decision-maker in the relationship. Increasingly, however, that view is being rejected. The contract is being interpreted as involving an active partnership with both parties playing an active role, each having obligations that ought to be fulfilled.[27] If the provider has the duty to give the patient his or her attention, to show respect, to keep appointments, to explain charges and bill accurately, and so forth, the patient also has a set of obligations: to show up on time, disclose potentially meaningful information, pay agreed–upon charges, and the like.

Among the duties of fidelity is the duty to keep the promise of confidentiality – to refrain from disclosing information revealed in the medical relationship without the permission of the patient. Correspondingly, the contract between the patient and the physician may imply that the patient has a duty to respect the integrity of the health professional's practice, possibly even refraining from discussing some information learned in the doctor's office. For example, a patient visiting an alcohol treatment clinic who sees a famous personality there may have some duty of confidentiality similar to that of the physician providing the treatment.

Some people bristle at the use of the term *contract* to describe these mutual promises and commitments. They see the term as too much of a business or legal notion. They object to the idea that the commitments made are binding and enforceable. They particularly resist the implication that the obligations of the physician and patient are limited to legalistically fulfilling the agreed-upon terms. These critics sometimes prefer to the use the term *covenant* to describe the commitments that establish the patient/physician relation.[28]

The defenders of the covenant language need to keep in mind, however, that sometimes in philosophy the term *contract* is used to describe fundamental social relations having nothing to do with legalistic business deals. The philosophers who influenced the founding of the United States – John Locke, Thomas Hobbes, and Jean Jacques Rousseau as well as Thomas Jefferson and the writers of the Constitution – spoke of a social compact or contract as the basic hypothetical agreement that establishes the fundamental moral bonds that link a people together.

Sometimes we speak of a marriage "contract" and mean by that something much deeper than a legally binding set of agreements. Some would argue that covenants have certain similarities with contracts, perhaps even should be thought of as a kind of contract. At least they share the notion of commitments of fidelity that generate obligations of loyalty. Holders of the principle of fidelity believe that the relation between health provider and patient involves such commitments – explicit and implied – that obligate the parties over and above any calculation of the consequences of keeping those commitments. Duties are created that are binding, at least if there are not overwhelming reasons to the contrary.

For example, when a physician makes an appointment, unless there are strong reasons to the contrary, it ought to be kept. The mere belief that seeing some other patient might do somewhat more good is not sufficient to release the physician from the obligation to keep the appointment. While some who support this principle of fidelity or promise-keeping might consider the duty exceptionless, not all holders of this view do. As we saw earlier, the duty might be one that is binding only *prima facie*, that is unless some other weighty obligation creates a conflict that is perceived as being overriding. It is a duty that is binding, other things being equal.

Thus, if someone else in the waiting room can only be helped by a modestly greater amount, that probably does not justify breaking the promise to the patient originally scheduled. However, if someone in the waiting room (or even on the street outside the physician's office) is having a heart attack, then the promise to the patient may have to give way. Ideally, the patient would release the physician from the promise of the appointment, at least for enough time to render emergency aid, but even if the patient were selfish enough to refuse to do so, the physician might well be justified in breaking the promise. Some believe that the fact that we could do overwhelmingly more good if we break the promise of the appointment would justify breaking it. Others believe that other ethical principles – the claims of justice or at least the claims of others to whom contradictory promises have been made – provide adequate justification.

Confidentiality: An Example Of Fidelity To Promises. The first case in this chapter, the case of the kindly old Dr. Browne who believed he could benefit his young patient by telling her father she was on the pill, poses the problem of why the physician has a duty to keep confidences and under what conditions disclosures can be made. It is important to realize that only under certain circumstances do we feel we have a duty not to disclose information we learn about other people. If we see some famous person on the street acting strangely, we do not feel obliged to keep the information secret; if it is a figure with public responsibilities, we may even feel obliged to call the newspaper or local radio station and report it. But in some cases we feel a duty exists to keep what we learn about others confidential.

This is particularly true in lay-professional relations in the physician's office or in conversations with lawyers or with priests. We expect these people to keep what is said confidential. One explanation of this is that we believe there is a promise made – implied or explicit – that what is disclosed will not be revealed to others. To the extent that a promise is made, then there is a duty (other things being equal) to keep it. Thus, when the American Medical Association announces that one of its principles of ethics includes the statement that the physician "shall safeguard patient confidences within the constraints of the law"[29] patients have a right to expect that they will be, at least if their physician is a member of the Association. It turns out, however, that not all physician codes of ethics make exactly the same promise.

Hippocratic Codes On Confidentiality. The Hippocratic Oath itself promises that the physician should not disclose "that which ought not to be spread abroad." That of course simply begs for the question of what ought to be spread abroad. Does it include the fact that a 16-year-old is on the pill when her physician believes being on it is bad for her?

The usual answer in the Hippocratic framework is that the physician should disclose only when he or she believes it will be for the benefit of the patient. The core Hippocratic principle provides a basis for determining what ought to be "spread abroad."

In Dr. Browne's case, which occurred in 1970, the British Medical Association's code seemed relevant. It held that exceptions can be made to the duty to keep confidences. "Always, however, the overriding consideration must be adoption of a line of conduct that will benefit the patient, or protect his interests." The American Medical Association at the time held essentially the same position. It said that confidences cannot be broken "unless it becomes necessary in order to protect the welfare of the individual or of the society." Both the BMA and the AMA seem to support Dr. Browne. On that basis he was acquitted of any violation of the duty of confidentiality.

Codes Prohibiting Disclosure. Partly as a result of this case, both the British and the American medical associations abandoned their Hippocratic paternalism in favor of a more rigorous promise of confidentiality. The British change stated: If in the opinion of the doctor, disclosure of confidential information to a third party seems to be in the best medical interest of the patient, it is the doctor's duty to make every effort to allow the information to be given to the third party, but where the patient refuses, that refusal must be respected.[30]

In 1980, the American association, as we have seen, switched from the Hippocratic paternalistic exception to confidentiality to a flat requirement of keeping confidences. Here they took a position similar to that of the World Medical Association's Declaration of Geneva, which provides a flat promise to "hold in confidence all that my patient confides in me."

The Problem Of Third Party Interests. While these anti-Hippocratic changes in the professional medical groups' views on confidentiality provide protection to patients like Dr. Browne's, they may actually be promises that are too inclusive. The all-inclusive promise of confidentiality covers not only cases in which the physician would like to disclose in order to protect what he or she believes is the interest of the patient, but also cases in which the physician believes the interests of others is at stake. Consider the following problem.

CASE 5:
Tatiana Tarasoff: The Patient's Threat To Kill His Girlfriend

In 1969 a college graduate student, Prosenjit Poddar, sought counseling from a school psychologist, Dr. Lawrence Moore. During the course of the treatment, he confessed is intention to murder his former girlfriend, Tatiana Tarasoff.

Dr. Moore was sufficiently convinced of his intentions that he reported the case to the campus police who detained Poddar briefly and then released him. In fact, when Tarasoff returned from a trip to Brazil Poddar killed her.

Her parents claimed that, even though it would mean breaching the confidentiality of the psychologist to his client, Dr. Moore had a duty to warn their daughter of the risk.

The World Medical Association's Declaration of Geneva makes what could be considered a blank-check promise of confidentiality: Whatever is disclosed will be kept confidential no matter what. But should a health professional make such a promise? The patient may be about to confess a plan to commit mass murder (or at least to commit a murder of one person like Tatiana Tarasoff).

Most physicians believe that the interests of third parties may sometimes require a limit on the confidentiality promise. Most lay people seem to agree. Hence, the courts in California ruled that there is a duty to warn in cases like Poddar's in which the provider has confidence that the patient will actually carry out the threat.

Both the British and the American Medical Associations have revised their codes of ethics to conform to this view. They first specify that confidences may be broken when required by law. This almost always applies to cases where there are serious threats to the interests of third parties. Laws require reporting gunshot wounds, venereal diseases, and infectious diseases all because of the concern for the risks to others. Now our society is debating whether reporting of HIV infection should also be reported in order to protect others. States have differed in their interpretation, perhaps because HIV is not an airborne disease easily transmitted to innocent third parties, but requires either sexual or blood contact for transmission. Still, some innocent parties–for example, spouses of infected people–may be at real risk if the diagnosis is not disclosed. The reporting of HIV is a test case of how we trade off the duty of confidentiality against the interests of protecting third parties from medical risk.

The American Medical Association's Council on Ethical and Judicial Affairs has gone beyond the general notion of making an exception to the confidentiality promise when disclosure is required by law. It says that, for its members:

"When a patient threatens to infli ct serious bodily harm to another person and there is a reasonable probability that the patient may carry out the threat, the physician should take reasonable precautions for the protection of the intended victim, including notification of law enforcement authorities."[31]

Of course, the fact that the AMA offers this promise does not automatically make it either what ethics or the law requires. But the AMA's view does appear to be emerging as a reasonable compromise between the rights of the patient to confidentiality and the interests of the society in protecting innocent third parties. Its position seems to conform with the requirement of the Tarasoff decision. The duty generated by a promise of confidentiality may be quite different when it is the serious interests of others that are at stake. The Hippocratic ethic focused on benefiting the patient (sometimes even when the patient wasn't interested in the benefit). Hippocratic ethics did not address breaking confidences to benefit others. Now, however, the paternalistic exception seems to have given way to an ethic that respects the right of people to have confidences kept. The controversial cases now are the ones in which the interests of others in the society conflict with the rights of the patient.

THE PATIENT VS. SOCIETAL INTEREST

This brings us to the third and overarching major issue in biomedical ethics: the relation of the individual patient to the interests of others in the society. While the major controversies of the 1970s and early 1980s in bioethics focused on the rights of the individual – to be told the truth, to consent or refuse consent to treatment, and to have confidential information kept secret – the biggest bioethical problems of the 1990s appear to be those posing conflicts between the individual and others in the society. Even if we can resolve the conflict between the rights of the individual and the physician's opinion of what will benefit the individual, we still will be left with cases in which doing what will serve the interests and rights of the individual will come at the expense of others. The most dramatic controversies at this level have involved the use of human subjects in medical research, the transplantation of organs, the allocation of medical resources, and genetic engineering.

SCIENTIFIC AND MEDICAL RESEARCH

Many physicians are shocked to realize that the Hippocratic ethic, taken literally, prohibits all medical research. We can define research as the effort to produce what can be called "generalizable knowledge," that is, knowledge for the purpose of general understanding to be applied to the world generally rather than for the benefit of a specific individual. The Hippocatic mandate to act only so as to benefit the individual patient makes all research unethical.

Distinguishing Research From Innovative Therapy. Since the time of Thomas Percival in the 18th century we have recognized that sometimes when a patient has a disease incurable with the available standard therapies, the physician is forced to try some innovation. While sometimes this is loosely called experimenting or research, it is actually just doing whatever the physician feels is best for the patient. The options available are not attractive, but sometimes it is rationally the best thing for the patient to try something out. This is not really research in the technical sense. It is not done to produce generalizable knowledge. In fact, researchers tell us that what is learned from such innovative trials cannot produce definitive knowledge. Real research needs more systematic design, carefully formulated hypotheses, careful statistical methods, and what is called *controlled trials*; that is, arrangements whereby some patients chosen randomly are given the experimental agent to be tested and others with the same condition are given some other treatment, either a placebo (a sugar pill) or a "standard" treatment that is not believed to be effective enough. In the best trials the assignment of the treatments is "double blind"; that is, both the patient and the investigator are kept ignorant of which treatment the individual subjects are receiving. That way any differences noted must really be differences resulting from the treatments rather than biases based on the expectations of the parties involved. Only when mathematical tests show that the difference could not likely have occurred by chance are investigators justified in concluding that a real difference exists.

The Historical Realization That Medicine Is Social. In the 18th and 19th centuries ethicists began to realize a medical ethic that focused exclusively on the welfare of the individual posed serious problems. For some situations even the notion of *disease* was called into question. By the end of the 18th century people were realizing that there was a social dimension to disease, that infection could be spread by contact with others. Medicine began challenging the notions that disease was strictly a problem of the individual and that the physician's duty could be thought of entirely in terms of the isolated patient.

By the middle of the 19th century Claude Bernard, often called the father of medical research, began articulating what were to become the basic methods and strategies of scientific medical investigation. He realized that the old patient-benefiting ethic was not going to be acceptable to the research enterprise, saying:, "Christian morals forbid only one thing, doing ill to one's neighbor. So, among the experiments that may be tried on man, those that can only harm are forbidden, those that are innocent are permissible, and those that may do good are obligatory."[32]

In this he surely went too far in saying if the experiment *may* do good, it is morally required. Many things in life may do good. They may do harm as well. And even if they may do only good, we are not necessarily required to engage in them. He probably also went wrong in his reading of what Christian morals require. Doing good is surely one element of that ethic, but some interpreters of that tradition recognize other moral limits as well. For example, many theological interpreters now accept the duties of telling the truth, respecting autonomy, and keeping promises as discussed in the previous section of this chapter. As we saw in the Nazi concentration camps, there may be other important moral issues in medical research beyond whether the experiments can do good. There may be issues of consent and fairness that should limit the researcher's right to try to do good.

We have seen that the events at Nuremberg were the watershed for the ethics of research on human subjects. Those sitting in judgment at Nuremberg could have retreated to the Hippocratic individualism and banned all research designed to benefit society. They did not. Instead, they specifically authorized research provided several conditions were met. One of those conditions was the social form of the ethic of producing benefits. It is variously called a social benefits ethic or the ethic of *utilitarianism*. The second principle of Nuremberg requires that for research to be ethical it must "be such as to yield fruitful results for the good of society, unprocurable by other methods or means of study, and not random and unnecessary in nature."[33] This is essentially the criterion of social utility – doing the greatest good possible, taking into account not only the welfare of the individual, but of all affected.

This ethic, utilitarianism, is one of the most powerful answers to the question of how we can make medical ethics social. It is one of the dominant ethical principles in contemporary social thought. It has been used to justify not only research on human subjects, but also cost-benefit analysis in allocating scarce medical resources, the allocation of scarce hearts for transplant, and the policies related to the new technologies of genetic engineering. But it is also controversial. It raises serious ethical problems not only of violating individual rights, but of fairness in social relations.

THE AMERICAN REVOLUTION IN RESEARCH ETHICS

Some people resist the Nazi comparison, claiming that such gross abuses could never happen in the United States or in other contemporary societies. The following case gives us pause:

CASE 6:

The Tuskegee Syphilis Study.

> In 1932 researchers wanted to understand the natural history of untreated syphilis. In order to do this, they recruited 400 black men with syphilis and another group of 200 to serve as controls. They followed them continually until 1972 when the study was stopped. During that time they offered no treatment, wanting to see what would happen if treatment were withheld. The men, many of them poorly educated, did not consent to be in the study and were not informed that treatments were available.
>
> In the early days the available treatments were not very effective. They included administration of arsenic and bismuth, but as early as the 1940s penicillin became available that was known to be effective in treating syphilis, and still the drug was withheld.[34]

No one can deny that syphilis was an important social medical problem. Conducting research to learn the long-term effects of untreated syphilis was something worth doing. A carefully controlled trial designed to eliminate the biases of subjects by keeping them ignorant might even be justified, if one appeals solely to the social benefits. Admittedly, a group of men would be at serious risk, but if the rest of the world could benefit (and the rest of humankind into endless future generations), then it could be argued that the total amount of good done by experimenting exceeded the harm done to this group of unfortunate men.

That, however, is reasoning strangely similar to the Nazi concentration camp experiments. Critics of a pure calculation of the total consequences for the future of humanity claim that even if the benefit/harm claims are true, there is still something ethically wrong with the Tuskegee experiment. They claim that the rights of the subjects were violated.

A similar conclusion was reached in the Nuremberg trial. Before acknowledging what we have called the utilitarian criterion (that there must be good envisioned, and unachievable by other means), the writers of the Nuremberg Code insisted that "the voluntary consent of the human subject is absolutely essential."[35]

Even if one can argue that this notion of consent was not part of the standard ethics of medicine in the 1930s when this study was begun, it surely was by the late 1940s, and the trial continued without the consent of the subjects until it was stopped. The Nuremberg consent principle was argued for by the American representatives at the trial.

It was not until about 1970 that the real conflict between the interests of the individual and those of the society became apparent in medical research. Slowly, a series of controversial medical experiments became known to the public. Live cancer cells were injected into human patients to study the development of cancer; whole-body radiation was administered to unconsenting subjects for research purposes; LSD was administered to military personnel to study the effects; placebos were given to a group of Mexican-American women in place of birth control pills to study the psychological effects of the pill. That last study produced at least seven undesired pregnancies. Distinguished Harvard pharmacologist Henry Beecher could stand it no longer. In 1966 he published an article in the prestigious *New England Journal of Medicine* summarizing the methods of some 22 medical studies, raising serious ethical questions of the sort mentioned here.[36] His expose' led to public outcry.

In December of 1971 the U.S. government's major research center, the National Institutes of Health, published a little yellow booklet on "Policy on Protection of Human Subjects."[37] It set out the first guidelines for protecting human subjects from medical research. It required the consent of the subjects to enter them into clinical trials, initial review of research protocols to see that the rights and welfare of subjects were adequately protected, and that the risks be justified by potential benefits.

Soon after the appearance of these initial guidelines, the Tuskegee story broke. Senator Edward Kennedy, outraged by the events, held Senate hearings that led to a law establishing a National Commission for the Protection of Human Subjects and eventually to a new set of federal regulations. The Commission issued what is called the Belmont Report,[38] the first federal document formally providing an ethical framework for assessing government activity. It called for federally funded research to conform to three ethical principles: not only maximizing benefit, but also respect for persons and for justice. Eventually federal regulations appeared in 1981 that now, in their revised form, structure all federally funded research involving human subjects. Almost all institutions conducting such research apply these same regulations to their work whether it is federally funded or not.

THE MORAL CONFLICT

These documents all apply what can be called the utilitarian ethic as the minimal condition for acceptable medical research. The benefit expected has to exceed the expected harms. But that is not the only moral principle that must be satisfied. There are also constraints that can be grouped under the general rubric of respect for the individual person: requirements for respecting autonomy, providing for adequate disclosure of relevant information, and keeping the promise of confidentiality. Much of the debate over the ethics of medical research today can be seen as focusing on the conflict between these rights of the individual and the interests of the society. One conclusion seems clear: Benefits to society alone, even major benefits, do not justify using human subjects in medical research unless additional moral criteria are met.

In addition to the criteria designed to respect the rights of individuals to consent, to be informed, and to have confidences kept, the Belmont Report introduced the moral principle of justice to the equation. *Justice* is an ethical principle concerned with giving people their due. It focuses on the distribution of benefits and harms, distributing both punishment and reward in a fair or equitable manner.

The principle of justice first was applied to the issue of subject selection. The subjects in the Tuskegee experiment do not seem to have been picked at random. They were largely black, poorly educated people with few alternative resources available. Likewise, the Mexican-American women given the fake birth control pills were low-income women who did not understand their alternatives. Similar questions have arisen about the use of prisoners, welfare patients in charity hospitals, and other subjects unable to defend their rights.

Now the formal criteria for approving research protocols require that there be equity in the selection of subjects and that the use of vulnerable populations such as children, the retarded, prisoners, and other confined groups be justified. Normally, using them in research is acceptable only if the study cannot be done on other populations.

This may just be the beginning in the use of the criterion of justice in assessing medical research. Some are suggesting that justice also has to be applied in the design and use of the research. In designing the research, some compromises may have to be made between the interests of the researchers in having ideally designed studies and the interests of the subjects. If the subjects are already among the worst off in the society because of severe illness, they should not be made even worse off by being asked to undergo extensive and marginal tests.

One research group was going to ask a group of subjects in a diabetes study to undergo an eye test that would require administering a drug that would likely make the subjects nauseous. The researchers wanted to do this every three months for 10 years. Because the knowledge gained from the test was marginal anyway, those pressing the criterion of justice argued that the test should be administered at the beginning of the study and then later only if special circumstances warranted. Justice requires allocating fairly the burdens as well as the benefits.

Justice also has emerged as a criterion in the use of the findings of the research. If, for example, subjects are put at significant risk or inconvenience, they should also have special claims to be the first to get access to the products of the research should it turn out to produce valuable results.

Transplantation Of Organs

Research involving human subjects is not the only controversy in medical ethics raising issues about the relation of the rights of the individual to the interests of the society. One of the major breakthroughs in biomedical technology of the past 20 years has been our new-found capacity to take organs from one human being and transplant them into another.

Thousands of people today are walking around, carrying on normal human functioning, with other people's hearts, livers, kidneys, lungs, and pancreases in them. We have even attempted to remove organs from other species – hearts from baboons and chimpanzees, and even livers from pigs – trying to get them to function as human substitutes.

These efforts have raised some questions related to the first major issue we identified as arising in bioethics. Some people have objected that moving organs from one human to another and from one species to another produces monstrosities, that it violates God's plan for human life. It raises questions about who is a member of the human moral community and whether there are some beings that we now have the capacity to create that we should not create.

For the most part, however, these basic religious and philosophical questions have been set aside. Most of the major religions clearly approve of the transplantation of organs. The real questions have focused on the matter of the reaction of the rights of the individual to the interests of society.

The Ethics Of Procuring Organs

The biotechnology of transplant has been so successful in saving life that today there is an enormous

demand for organs. Today more 30,000 people in the United States alone are on waiting lists for an organ, hoping to get one before they die. In the 1970s a debate began over the way organs would be procured and who should control the body parts of the deceased. The issue was whether society should consider valuable body parts to belong to the society, to be its for the taking when the organs can do enormous good for the living, or whether they should continue to be thought of as belonging to the individual so that they would have to be given as a gift before they could be used to help others.

Routine Salvaging. One group proposed what was called *routine salvaging* of organs.[39] The idea was that once a person dies, the body parts can no longer be of use to the individual. If the parts could help others, then society should be able simply to take them and use them as a public resource to save other lives. This method would have been efficient, cost-effective, and simple. However, it also raised critical moral questions about the relation of the individual to society. In the Western world the individual has been seen as having an autonomy over-against the society. The body has not been seen as belonging to the state. Critics of routine salvaging proposed the alternative of having the individual (or the next of kin) donate the organs provided that did not violate any deeply held personal beliefs and values.

Donation. In the United States and most other countries throughout the world the gift-model was endorsed. The United States developed a Uniform Anatomical Gift Act[40] that was passed in all states providing for the possibility of donating organs. An individual could express such a desire while alive or, if no wishes had been expressed while alive, the next of kin would have the right to do so. On this basis the family of deceased patients who are potential organ donors are asked whether they wish to donate and their wishes are respected. Legally, if the individual has executed a donor card (or marked a driver's license making a donation) the family has no legal authority to veto. Someday transplant surgeons may take such organs even against the wishes of the next-of-kin, but most today fear the wrath of the family even though they are clearly legally entitled to the organs. Some patients militantly favoring organ transplant are letting it be known that they believe surgeons have a moral duty to take such organs even if family members object. They claim the primary driving moral consideration must be respect for the wishes of the patient. The gift mode has prevailed in most countries, but we are increasingly realizing that it is not entirely successful. The waiting lists for organs are growing and many people who we know would be willing to donate simply have not taken the initiative to fill out the necessary donor card. Alternative strategies are beginning to be proposed.

Presumed Consent. Several people have begun advocating something called *presumed consent*.[41] Society would presume consent for organ procurement unless someone had executed a document to the contrary. This is sometimes called "opting out" as opposed to "opting in." It is rather like routine salvaging, especially when one realizes that most routine salvaging proposals permitted people to opt out. The one key difference may be conceptual. The language of presumed consent recognizes that Western culture feels very strongly about the sacredness of the individual and wants to hold onto something that looks like gift-giving rather than openly affirming that the body belongs to the state. Calling this opting-out strategy "presumed consent" makes it sound as if we are remaining in the donation mode while, in fact, there may be no reason to believe presumed consent would actually be obtained. We know that, depending on the community and the population group, there is about a 50% chance that an individual would be willing to donate organs. So, presuming consent once someone has died is somewhat of a fiction. There would be a 1 in 2 chance that the presumption would be wrong, hardly a sound basis for presuming agreement. Some have said that if we feel we really need the organs from people who have not explicitly donated, it would be better to simply say we are taking them.

Required Request. Another strategy that has been widely adopted has been to pass a law requiring that hospital personnel ask the relatives of all appropriate deceased patients whether they are willing to donate the organs for transplant.[42] Called *required request*, these laws simply increase the chance that the question will be asked. Whether they have increased the number of organs made available is controversial. One major problem with required request is that, rather than going to the individual himself or herself and relying on their personal decision, society is relying on a backup decision-maker whose views may not be in accord with those of the individual. The search goes on for other ways of getting donations directly from the one whose organs eventually would be used.

Markets In Organs And Rewarded Gifting. One well-tested capitalist method of motivating behavior is to pay people. Some have proposed a free-market in organs that would permit any willing buyer to sell his or her organs to any willing seller, either while the seller is alive (presumably limited to non-life-prolonging organs such as kidneys or, now, liver and lung lobes) or for procurement should the individual die in a way permitting procurement.[43]

The resistance to a market in organs has been strong. It is said to put coercive pressure on the poor and, in a pure market system, would deliver those organs obtained from the poor to those who could afford to pay. Straight markets in human organs are illegal in the U.S.[44] A variant on this scheme has emerged recently, however. Called *rewarded gifting*, it is a desperate effort to hold on to the idea of the gift mode. It would give some gift to individuals who donate in exchange for their donation. The gift could be a small life insurance policy, payment of funeral expenses, or some other gift that might serve as an incentive to donation. Critics have argued that this is little more than payment in disguise. For example, if $2,000 were given toward funeral expenses normally paid by the estate of the deceased, the estate would just be that much larger and the effect would be the same as paying the beneficiaries of the estate the $2,000.

Required Response. One final scheme has been called *required response*[45] or *mandated choice*. At some critical point, either upon admission to a hospital, during a routine physical exam, or upon renewal of a driver's license, all persons would be asked if they wish to donate organs and would be required to respond. They could answer either way, but they would have to answer.[46] This might increase the response from those willing to give while still retaining the donation model.

THE ETHICS OF ALLOCATING ORGANS

Once the organs are obtained, there is an equally controversial question of how they will be allocated to those waiting for the life-saving operation. While selling them to the highest bidder has been considered, the real debate is between those who believe they should go where the organs will do the most good and those who believe that justice requires that all people equally needy should have an equal shot regardless of the likelihood of success. These could be called the *efficiency* and *equity* views respectively. Consider the following problem.

CASE 7:
The UNOS Allocation Formula

> The United Network for Organ Sharing is the national quasi-governmental body responsible for allocating organs for transplant. Because there is much greater demand than supply, it must develop some basis for allocating.
>
> For kidneys, a point system has been devised that will take into account several factors thought relevant to claims on available kidneys. Points have been given for degree of tissue-matching, time on the waiting list, medical urgency, geographical proximity, and so forth. The critical moral question is how much each of these factors should count and why.
>
> One group favors maximizing the likelihood of benefit with the scarce supply of organs. They would give the points to those things, such as tissue-matching, that predict successful outcome. Others, concerned more about the fairness of the system, would give the points for reasons, such as time on the waiting list, that try to give people an equal chance of getting an organ.
>
> It gradually became apparent that not all people on the waiting list were equally easy to match with the pool of available kidneys. In particular, blacks and Hispanics were harder to match than Caucasians. To a lesser degree, males do somewhat better than females, younger people slightly better than older people, and middle-class patients better than lower-class ones. Now if we still want to get the best aggregate outcome, we would give the points for tissue-matching and these other factors that predict good outcome, while if we wanted to give all people an equal shot at an organ we would purposely downplay or exclude them. What percentage of the total points should go to factors that predict successful outcome, what percentage to those that try to make the allocation more equitable?

The UNOS Ethics Committee has an allocation subcommittee that dealt with this issue.[47] It realized it was divided between those wanting to emphasize good medical outcome and those who wanted to emphasize fairness. The committee consciously made a compromise and has proposed that in the future the formula give half its total points to measures of good outcome and half to factors included to try to make the allocation more equitable.

Underlying the entire debate about procuring and allocating organs is a larger question: Should the limited resources available for health care be spent on high-tech interventions such as transplants that, at considerable expense, will give a chance at life to a small number of people who are among the sickest and worst off in the society? Or should the resources be spent to provide benefits in a maximally efficient manner, targeting preventive and low-tech basic care that will produce greater aggregate benefit?

ALLOCATION OF SCARCE MEDICAL RESOURCES

This same problem—of choosing between arrangements that do the most good in aggregate and those that will likely benefit the worst–off arises not only in transplant, but in the full range of health-care allocation decisions. Each day in the United States more than $2-billion is spent on health care. Still, the health of Americans is not as great as it could be. Americans are far from the top in life expectancy at birth. Infant mortality is 70% greater than in Sweden. Even more dramatically, about 37-million Americans are without health insurance and another 10% of the population is under-insured. There are dreadful differences based on income, education, and race.

Rationing of scarce medical resources in one way or another is inevitable. Americans are spending upward of $2-billion per year on end-stage renal disease for about 8,000 people a year who come down with the disease, $6-billion for bypass surgery, another $1-billion for Caesarean sections, many of which may not even be needed. Dementias in the elderly cost as much as $50-billion a year, and addictions cost perhaps $60-billion. And that is without even considering obligations to those in other parts of the world. The costs of doing everything that patients would like done could easily exceed the entire gross national product. It is inevitable that some limits will have to be placed on health expenditures. The current debate over a national health plan will have to include some limits on access to some kinds of care. The ethical question is on what basis the rationing will be done. Consider the preliminary plan being developed in the state of Oregon.

CASE 8:
Rationing Medicaid In Oregon

Medicaid is a nationally funded plan for health care for the poor. Each state, however, runs its own program. Oregon was spending its entire Medicaid budget providing a rather extensive range of services for the poorest of the poor – those below 50% of the poverty level.

A Health Services Commission was established with a mandate to reassess the program and create a new arrangement that would fund everyone up to 100 of the poverty level by dividing all health services into a group of 709 diagnosis/treatment combinations.[48] Through a series of public meetings, and surveys of health professionals and lay people, officials attempted to rank these from highest to lowest priority.

They attempted to determine the amount of benefit per dollar of cost through an elaborate scheme that assessed the benefit in terms of the number of years of benefit each treatment would provide with the years adjusted according to the quality of the life after treatment.

The Commission used an elaborate scheme that tried to take into account how badly off people were that were being treated for various conditions as well as the likelihood of success from the treatment. For example, surgery for appendicitis and antibiotics for pneumonia ranked near the top while treating extremely low birth weight babies and uncomplicated hemorrhoids ranked near the bottom. Those things that produced dramatic results cheaply scored high, while both minor problems and serious ones where success was very unlikely did poorly.

Exercises such as this will become more and more common through the years. Each member of the Oregon Commission finally had to vote to rank the diseases in order, knowing that they would fund down the list only as far as the money would go. Imagine you were a member of the Oregon Health Commission. On what basis would you do your ranking?

MAXIMIZING THE AGGREGATE GOOD DONE

One criterion would be to maximize the total amount of good done for those in the program. That seems to have been the dominant instinct of the Commissioners. They were attracted to efficient, basic services that did a great deal of good for a low cost. There are real problems with that criterion, however.

First, we have already seen that there are enormous disputes over what counts as a good outcome. Should they have considered total good for the society, giving higher priority to those people who were more productive or to younger people who would get more years of benefit simply because they could be expected to live longer? If so, they would have to end up choosing between treatments for productive business people, housewives, or poets–just as the original group that tried to ration kidney machines did at the University of Washington in the early 1960s when that technology was new and scarce. Or should they have looked only at what can be called "medical benefit," focusing on changes in life expectancy and quality of life? If they were to limit their attention to the medical sphere, they would have to assign values to the various medical goods: saving life, curing disease, relieving suffering, and promoting health.

Distributing The Benefits Equitably. It is the nature of the project of trying to maximize the medical good that often those who are sickest are the hardest and least efficient to treat. If the goal is to get as much good as possible, whether the good is limited to the medical sphere or extended to all kinds of good, then directing the resources to those who are relatively well-off may be the more efficient approach. Targeting on those who are sickest may require more resources for each unit of benefit achieved. Critics say this is inequitable in rationing health care generally just as it is in allocating organs. Some mix between equity and efficiency seems inevitable, just as rationing itself is. There is no reason why we must choose to produce the greatest possible good. That is what utilitarians would pick, but not the choice of the egalitarians who give greater emphasis to equity. The choice will depend on what social ethic for health care is chosen and how the principle of justice gets played off against the principle of utility.

GENETIC ENGINEERING

One final example of the conflict between the more individual focus of the Hippocratic ethic and a newer, more social ethic is the rapidly emerging possibility of understanding and intervening to change the human genetic code. Patients with genetic diseases increasingly will have the opportunity to have their defective genetic material supplemented or replaced with genes that overcome problems that, until now, have often only meant a slow death.

Attempting the re-engineering of the human genetic code was the stuff of science fiction only a few years ago. Now such experiments have been attempted on several diseases and more will certainly follow rapidly. For example, a condition known as ADA deficiency results from a defective gene. It

causes a collapse of the body's immune system, making it impossible for it to fight infections. Infants born with ADA deficiency have been kept in a totally sterile environment, in a bubble completely cut off from direct human physical contact, for years. As long as they are not contaminated they thrive, but, once infected, they run a high risk of dying. Their life expectancy is short.

Recently the National Institutes of Health Recombinant DNA Advisory Committee approved the first experiment to insert the missing gene into such patients. It is, in this case, done by removing some bone marrow and exposing the marrow to a virus that has the capacity to insert the needed gene into the marrow cells. Then the marrow is re-injected into the patient.

Other gene therapy experiments are under way to deal with some forms of cancer. Still others are sure to be attempted soon. A multi-billion dollar project to map the entire human genetic code, the so-called human genome project, will make a rapid increase in such experiments possible.

But the ethical questions will remain. The first and most obvious are perhaps once again at the level of whether tampering with the genetic code is "playing God." Is it something that humans ought to refrain from? Does the desire to change the human species by producing entirely new kinds of beings make such efforts unethical? Or is it something that follows naturally from the human capacity to learn about and modify nature, attempting to improve on life as we know it. While some fear that, like the splitting of the atom, this is going too far, others are convinced that we finally have the beginnings of the capacity to truly cure diseases that up until now could only be treated symptomatically.

In addition to these fundamental questions about the nature of the species and our role in modifying our very existence, these genetic engineering projects pose serious questions about the relation of the individual to society. New genes are conveyed into patients–like those with ADA deficiency–by modified viruses called vectors. They supposedly have been modified so they cannot escape into the environment and accidentally infect other people, but things can go wrong. Skeptics fear that attempting these therapies will inevitably lead to mistakes exposing the entire species to some catastrophe. Once again, the entire future of the species could be hurt while the benefits will accrue to relatively small numbers. Still, in this case it is not only the patients on whom the experiments are initially tried who stand to benefit, but also all future sufferers from ADA deficiency and other diseases that can be changed genetically.

CONCLUSION

In these dramatic new technological possibilities in the world of biology and medicine, we have before us some of the most fundamental and crucial questions in philosophy. They cluster around the three overarching questions presented in this chapter: who is a member of the human moral community; what is the relationship between benefiting patients and protecting their rights; and, finally, what is the relationship between the rights of the individual and the interests of society? It is clear now, as never before, that what once may have sounded like abstract philosophical questions actually have immediate practical payoffs of enormous importance. It is also clear that different philosophical and religious views give significantly different answers to these questions.

FOR FURTHER INQUIRY

SUGGESTED READINGS

• Arras, John, and Nancy Rhoden. *Ethical Issues in Modern Medicine*, third edition. Mountain View, California: Mayfield Publishing Company, 1989.
• Beauchamp, Tom L., and James F. Childress, Editors. *Principles of Biomedical Ethics*. Third Edition. New York: Oxford University Press, 1989.
• Beauchamp, Tom L., and LeRoy Walters, editors. *Contemporary Issues in Bioethics*, third edition. Belmont, California: Wadsworth, 1989.
• President's Commission for the Study of Ethical Problems in Medicine and Biomedical and Behavioral Research. *Making Health Care Decisions: A Report on the Ethical and Legal Implications of Informed Consent in the Patient-Practitioner Relationship*, Vol. 1. Washington, D.C.: U.S. Government Printing Office, 1982.
• President's Commission for the Study of Ethical Problems in Medicine and Biomedical and Behavioral Research. *Securing Access to Health Care*, Vol. 1. Washington, D.C.: U.S. Government Printing Office, 1983.
• Veatch, Robert M., ed. *Medical Ethics*. Boston: Jones and Bartlett, 1989.

READING

SCIENTISTS MUST DEMONSTRATE TO WOULD-BE REGULATORS THAT THEY'RE CAPABLE OF RESPONSIBLE SELF-REGULATION
The Chronicle of Higher Education, May 10, 1989
Paul J. Friedman

The current controversies over the quality and integrity of research involve us all. Skeptical or uninformed faculty members and research scientists must become as concerned as is the public that reads sensationalized stories in the newspapers. While biomedical research has the worst record, other disciplines should also be concerned, for they too would suffer the consequences of regulations that could be imposed on a non-responsive research community.

As a member of the Institute of Medicine's Committee on the Responsible Conduct of Research, whose report was recently published (National Academy Press, February 1989), I have been sensitized to the need for a thoughtful, but active, response. As scientists, we say that integrity in research is immensely important — perhaps fundamental — to scientific progress.

But how much are we actually doing to insure the integrity of data, publications, or individuals? How many minor abuses have become so frequent as to be customary? How often are sloppy or sharp practices tolerated because it's not worth making a fuss? What steps must research institutions take to show would-be regulators that science is indeed capable of responsible self-regulation?

Maintaining the quality as well as the integrity of science requires more active questioning of what our associates are doing. Within each discipline, the standards of acceptable practice should be argued and defined, written down, disseminated, taught, and enforced. Mechanisms should be developed so that deviations from accepted practice can be questioned (without formal charges having to be filed) and discussed (without the questioner having to fear personal retaliation).

That means one or more people must be designated to accept confidential reports of all kinds, and then to exercise good judgment in providing counsel or pursuing more formal inquiries. Research scientists should be persuaded to change to more acceptable practices without threat to their position or reputation. Severe penalties might do more to deter the reporting of research malpractice than they would to eliminate the abusive practices.

How have we dealt with abuses of authorship, of intellectual property of trainees, or of the obligation to report results truthfully and completely? How often is hasty publication or uncollegial behavior impelled by the push for priority or by commercial considerations? What have we done to give credibility to the maxim that quality is more important than quantity?

These concerns require a twofold response. If it is true that pressure to publish is an important cause of abuses, then institutions must take steps to reduce this pressure. The first step is again to establish standards, in this case individual ones for the students and faculty members who have entered the academic competition. Communication of departmental or institutional expectations is an essential, but usually neglected, task.

The next step is to adopt standards that limit the number of publications that can be counted on for promotions or submitted to bolster grant applications. This change in the way we recognize quality is one whose time has come. If such limits were widely adopted by academic institutions as well as by grant-making agencies, they would contribute significantly toward alleviating the current unhealthy pressure to publish.

How well is the supervision of research trainees monitored at all levels? How many trainees find good role models for the practice of research by observing their mentors? How many have seen their chiefs in the laboratory? How many Ph.D. programs' curricula and supervisory practices are scrutinized as closely as their units' research output and grant support? Outside of Ph.D. programs, which are at least reviewed periodically, how many research laboratories are looked at with the quality of training in mind?

In several cases of research misconduct it became evident that the perpetrators had not been successfully indoctrinated with scientific norms, and that their early deviations in behavior had not been corrected by their supposed mentors. I have also heard at first hand how the questionable practices of lab chiefs have discouraged ethical trainees from pursuing research careers. Institutions need to address these problems by exercising their authority to review training programs. Again, standards for adequate supervision must first be articulated. They might include looking at the number of trainees who can be supervised in one laboratory, the actual availability of supervisors, and the curriculum for research training. In addition, thorough periodic review by a peer group is not too high a price to pay for improving the general level of laboratory practice.

High on the list of controversial issues right now are the standards for recording, retaining, and sharing original research data. Although some of the pressure for improvement comes from those concerned with fraud in research, others worry even more about the trend toward secrecy motivated by researchers' industrial ties or the commercial potential of discoveries. Often research scientists overestimate the restrictions necessary to protect their data and, as a result, avoid the collegial discussion of results so essential to good science.

As a first step in dealing with such concerns, institutional or discipline-specific standards for creating and preserving data must be developed, and they must be taught explicitly to all research trainees and made clear to young faculty members who never had the benefit of formal laboratory training.

The more complex problem of when data must be shared is next on the agenda; it will require wide discussion to achieve consensus. Institutions must help develop and disseminate patent policies that limit the restrictions placed on publication of research of potential commercial value. The University of Michigan's policy, for example, insists that companies that support university research specify in writing any information developed from the research that must be treated as proprietary.

Have we left room for ethical values in our competitive environment? How many research trainees learn early on that there are ethical choices to be made in research, and that there are standards to be followed? How many are taught that they have a personal responsibility to help correct poor or unethical research practices of which they become aware? How many have any idea of how to go about this without damaging their own careers? Just for a start, how many have read "Honor in Science," a pamphlet published by Sigma Xi, an honorary organization for students in science?

Good science must be ethical science. Cutting corners, cheating by mishandling statistics, biasing results by selection of data, failing to attribute previous work, making up conditions or data points, and even using old controls without acknowledgment are practices that are neither good nor ethical science.

Young scientists must learn to cope with the ethical issues that arise in research, not just concerning use of human and animal subjects, but also concerning the treatment of colleagues and trainees. Such issues include the art of deciding who should sign a publication, the scrupulousness with which problems and deviations are reported, the conscientiousness with which results are confirmed before they are reported, and the way to react to perceived misconduct in research.

Institutions must encourage their faculty members to teach ethics in research, just as most medical schools have developed programs to teach medical ethics to their students.

It is clearly possible to develop a stimulating and educational ethics course, such as Penny Gilmer's at Florida State University, or Michael Mullin's at the University of California at San Diego. It also is possible to develop teaching materials that provoke thought and teach by case study – such as the ethical-problem set written for the Council of Biology Editors.

It is probably not an exaggeration to say that the way the nation's scientists respond to all these issues will have much to do with the future of scientific research – its quality as well as its public support. If students are not trained in the best traditions of science, those traditions will be lost; the research establishment will look more and more like the defense industry – and it will be regulated accordingly.

ENDNOTES

1. Edelstein, Ludwig. "The Hippocratic Oath: Text, Translation and Interpretation." *Ancient Medicine: Selected Papers of Ludwig Edelstein*. Temkin, Owsei, and C. Lilian Temkin, editors. Baltimore, Maryland: The Johns Hopkins Press, 1967, pp. 3-64.
2. Based on General Medical Council: Disciplinary Committee." *British Medical Journal Supplement*, no. 3442, March 20, 1971, pp. 79-80.

3. Edelstein, pp. 3-64; Veatch, Robert M., ed. *Medical Ethics*. Boston: Jones and Bartlett, 1989, pp. 1-26.
4. Edelstein, p. 62.
5. Veatch, Robert M., and Carol G. Mason. "Hippocratic vs. Judeo-Christian Medical Ethics: Principles in Conflict." *The Journal of Religious Ethics* 15 (Spring 1987):86-105; see also Temkin, Oswei. *Hippocrates in a World of Pagans and Christians*. Baltimore:

Johns Hopkins University Press, 1991, for a complex account of the many tensions as well as some compatibilities between Christian and Hippocratic thought.

6. Jones, W. H. S. *The Doctor's Oath: An Essay In The History Of Medicine.* Cambridge: At The University Press, 1924.

7. Percival, Thomas. *Percival's Medical Ethics, 1803.* Reprint. Edited by Chauncey D. Leake. Baltimore: Williams and Wilkins, 1927.

8. American Medical Association. *Code of Medical Ethics: Adopted by the American Medical Association at Philadelphia, May, 1847, and by the New York Academy of Medicine in October, 1847.* New York: H. Ludwig and Company, 1848.

9. World Medical Association. "Declaration of Geneva." *World Medical Journal* 3 (1956), supplement, pp. 10-12. Reprinted in *Encyclopedia of Bioethics*, Vol. 4. Warren T. Reich, editor. New York: The Free Press, 1978, p. 1749.

10. Rosner, Fred, and J. David Bleich, editors. *Jewish Bioethics*. New York: Sanhedrin Press, 1979.

11. United States Catholic Conference, Department of Health Affairs. *Ethical and Religious Directives for Catholic Health Facilities.* Washington, D.C.: United States Catholic Conference, 1971.

12. Johnson, James T. "Protestantism: History of Protestant Medical Ethics." *Encyclopedia of Bioethics*. Edited by Warren T. Reich. New York: The Free Press, Vol. 4, 1978, pp. 1364-1373; International Organization of Islamic Medicine. *Islamic Code of Medical Ethics.* [Kuwait]: International Organization of Islamic Medicine, 1981.

13. For compendia of these medical ethical writings see the appendix in volume four of *Encyclopedia of Bioethics*. Edited by Warren T. Reich. New York: The Free Press, 1978; also International Organization of Islamic Medicine. *Islamic Code of Medical Ethics.* [Kuwait]: International Organization of Islamic Medicine, 1981.

14. "The Oath of Soviet Physicians." Zenonas Danilevicius, trans. *Journal of the American Medical Association* 217 (1971):834.

15. Based on "The Dying Cancer Patient," in Veatch, Robert M. *Case Studies in Medical Ethics.* Cambridge, Mass.: Harvard University Press, 1977, pp. 141-43.

16. Oken, Donald. "What to Tell Cancer Patients: A Study of Medical Attitudes." *Journal of the American Medical Association* 175 (April 1, 1961):1120-1128.

17. Novack, Dennis H., Robin Plumer, Raymond L. Smith, Herbert Ochitill, Gary R. Morrow, and John M. Bennett. "Changes in Physicians' Attitudes Toward Telling the Cancer Patient." *Journal of the American Medical Association* 241 (March 2, 1979):897-900.

18. Meyer, Bernard. "Truth and the Physician." *Ethical Issues in Medicine.* Edited by E. Fuller Torrey. Boston: Little Brown, 1968, p. 172 (159-177).

19. Fletcher, Joseph. *Morals and Medicine.* Boston: Beacon Press, 1954, pp. 34-64.

20. Kant, Immanuel. "On the Supposed Right to Tell Lies from Benevolent Motives." Translated by Thomas Kingsmill Abbott and reprinted in Kant's *Critique of Practical Reason and Other Works on the Theory of Ethics.* London: Longmans, 1909 [1797], pp. 361-365.

21. Ross, W.D. *The Right and the Good.* Oxford: Oxford University Press, 1939.

22. Brody, Baruch. *Life and Death Decision Making.* New York: Oxford University Press, 1988.

23. Their new principles were published the following year in American Medical Association. *Current Opinions of the Judicial Council of the American Medical Association.* Chicago: American Medical Association, 1981, p. ix.

24. Ibid., p. 25.

25. Natanson v. Kline 186 Kan. 393, 350 P. 2d 1093 (1960).

26. Canterbury v. Spence, 464 F. 2d 772 (D.C. Cir. 1972).

27. Veatch, Robert M. *The Patient as Partner—A Theory of Human-Experimentation Ethics.* Bloomington, Indiana: Indiana University Press, 1987; Veatch, Robert M. *The Patient-Physician Relation: The Patient as Partner, Part 2.* Bloomington, IN: Indiana University Press, 1991.

28. May, William F. "Code, Covenant, Contract, or Philanthropy?" *Hastings Center Report* 5 (December 1975):29-38.

29. American Medical Association. *Current Opin-*

ions of the Council on Ethical and Judicial Affairs of the American Medical Association: Including the Principles of Medical Ethics and Rules of the Council on Ethical and Judicial Affairs. Chicago: American Medical Association, 1989, p. ix.

30. "Central Ethical Committee." *British Medical Journal Supplement* (May 1, 1971), p. 30.

31. American Medical Association. *Current Opinions of the Council on Ethical and Judicial Affairs of the American Medical Association: Including the Principles of Medical Ethics and Rules of the Council on Ethical and Judicial Affairs*. Chicago: American Medical Association, 1989, p. 21.

32. Bernard, Claude. *An Introduction to the Study of Experimental Medicine*. Henry Copley Greene, A.M. (translator), New York: Dover Publications, Inc., 1957 [1865], p. 102.

33. "Nuremberg Code, 1946." In *Encyclopedia of Bioethics*, Vol. 4. Edited by Warren T. Reich. New York: The Free Press, 1978, pp. 1764-1765.

34. Levine, Robert J. *Ethics and Regulation of Clinical Research*, second edition. New Haven: Yale University Press, 1988, pp. 69-70.

35. Ibid.

36. Beecher, H.K. "Ethics and Clinical Research," *New England Journal of Medicine* 274 (1966):1353-1360.

37. U.S. Department of Health, Education, and Welfare. *The Institutional Guide to DHEW Policy on Protection of Human Subjects*. Washington, D.C.: U.S. Government Printing Office, 1971.

38. National Commission for the Protection of Human Subjects of Biomedical and Behavioral Research. *The Belmont Report: Ethical Principles and Guidelines for the Protection of Human Subjects of Research*. Washington, D.C.: U.S. Government Printing Office, 1978.

39. Dukeminier, Jesse, and David Sanders. "Organ Transplantation: A Proposal for Routine Salvaging of Cadaver Organs." *New England Journal of Medicine* 279 (1968):413-19.

40. Sadler, A. M., B. L. Sadler, and E. Blythe Stason. "The Uniform Anatomical Gift Act." *Journal of the American Medical Association* 206 (Dec. 9, 1968):2501-06.

41. Caplan, Arthur L. "Organ Transplants: The Costs of Success, An Argument for Presumed Consent and Oversight." *Hastings Center Report* 13 (December 1983):23-32; Matas, Arthur J., and Frank J. Veith. "Presumed Consent—A More Humane Approach to Cadaver Organ Donation. *Positive Approaches to Living with End-Stage Renal Disease: Psychosocial and Thanatological Aspects*. Edited by Mark A. Hardy, et al. New York: Praeger, 1986, pp. 37-51.

42. New York State Task Force on Life and the Law. *The Required Request Law: Recommendations of the New York State Task Force on Life and the Law*. March 1986.

43. Peters, David A. "Marketing Organs for Transplantation." *Dialysis & Transplantation* 13 (January 1984):40-41.

44. Public Law 98-507, October 19, 1984. *National Organ Transplant Act* 98 Stat. 2339.

45. Veatch, Robert M. *Death, Dying, and the Biological Revolution*, Revised Edition. New Haven, Connecticut: Yale University Press, 1989, p. 216.

46. They probably should be permitted to give an "I don't know" response in order to avoid pressuring them into refusing to donate. If they gave this response, then their next-of-kin would be asked for permission just as is presently the case.

47. Burdick, James F., Jeremiah G. Turcotte, and Robert M. Veatch. "General Principles for Allocating Human Organs and Tissues." *Transplantation Proceedings* 24 (October 1992, No. 5):2226-35.

48. Oregon Health Services Commission. *Prioritization of Health Services: A Report to the Governor and Legislature*. n.p.: Oregon Health Services Commission, 1991.

Chapter 9

Susan Neiburg Terkel

SEXUAL ETHICS

"The omnipresent process of sex, as it is woven into the whole texture of our man's or woman's body, is the pattern of all the process of our life."

– Havelock Ellis

"I consider promiscuity immoral. Not because sex is evil, but because sex is good and too important."

– Ayn Rand

"Sexuality is the lyricism of the masses."

– Charles Baudelaire

During autumn of 1992, the sexual morality of film director Woody Allen roared across media headlines when his former companion of 13 years, actress Mia Farrow, accused Allen of gross sexual misconduct. Besides other charges, Ms. Farrow railed against Allen for his sexual liaison with Soon-Yi, Farrow's 20-year-old adopted daughter from Vietnam. For Mr. Allen had not only taken nude photographs of Soon-Yi, a college sophomore, but had also admitted to being her first sexual partner and in the midst of a serious love affair with her.

Was Woody Allen guilty of sexual immorality? Was he right or wrong to date the daughter of a former lover? The sister of his three children? A virgin more than 30 years his junior and barely past the threshold of childhood? Should he have taken into account how much his conduct with Soon-Yi could invoke a public scandal?

It's easy to pass judgment on someone else's sexual behavior and character, especially that of a moody artist such as Woody Allen. But upholding our own sexual standards or finding suitable ones in the first place is a formidable challenge in our society.

Susan Neiburg Terkel, B.S. Cornell University, is author of 12 books on social and medical issues, including *Abortion: Facing The Issues, Should Drugs Be Legalized, Understanding Child Custody,* and *Ethics.*

Today, talk show guests reveal the most intimate details of their sex lives, while schools offer curriculums that would have made Sigmund Freud and Havelock Ellis blush. Sex scandals rock politicians from their roosts, and explicit scenes of sex entertain millions of movie voyeurs. In fact, few can escape the barrage of sexual messages in modern America.

Sex. Sex. Sex. Within marriage, sexual intercourse occurs on an average of one to three times a week.[1] But people are also having sex before marriage, outside marriage, and after their marriage ends. Today, the average American adult will have between five and 10 premarital partners, marry more than once, and at least half of them will have one or more extramarital affairs.[2] And nearly 2.8-million couples live together without getting married.[3] Many Americans routinely have sex with themselves, and some have sex with persons of their own gender.[4] Quite an alarming number of people have sex with children, clients, and people who don't want to have sex.

A few Americans are having sex with more than one person at a time, with people they hardly know, and with people they do not know and are never going to see again.[5] They are having sex in conventional and unconventional ways. Some are having sex in bars and public restrooms, and 12% of all Americans have lost their virginity in a car.[6]

Although it is illegal in many states, large numbers of people are having anal sex, oral sex, and paid sex. And when they aren't actually having sex, they are actively procuring sex – sometimes, any way they can. Via harassment. Voyeurism. Even bestiality. Indeed, the sexual landscape in the United States betrays a milieu of diversity and a hotbed of activity.

Yes, Virginia, there is a moral lesson here. Socrates advised that an unexamined life is not worth living. While many people might argue that an unexamined sex life can still bring enormous pleasure, taking stock of your moral standards can help place you in the moral driver's seat and give you control over an important area of your life.

In The Course Of History

Summing up the entire history of sexual ethics, one young man explained, "I guess sex was originally to produce another body; then I guess it was for love; nowadays it's just for feeling good."[7] Only he left it to philosophers to explain why.

The ancient Hebrews, who came up with some of the first moral rules on sexuality, perceived the issue as one of fecundity. Make lots of babies; make sure you know whose babies you are making; and don't stray from home to make them. A pretty clear recipe.

In contrast to Hebrew law, pagan worship encouraged nonmarital sex. Temple prostitutes served the gods by sexually serving the men who attended temple. And in Rome and Greece alike, though marital sex was the norm, both prostitution and homosexual sex were acceptable.

Classical Greek philosophers, in particular Plato, expounded on the subject of sexual ethics and took a more restrained view. Reasoning that body-and-sexuality have no connection to mind-and-reason, Plato concluded that mindful contemplation of life and love without sex (Platonic love) is superior to erotic love (with sex).

Drawing on both a cultural and a religious heritage, two monks, Augustine and Aquinas, born nearly a thousand years apart, shaped the unique sexual ethic of Roman Catholicism. Augustine (A.D. 344-430) taught that when Adam and Eve disobeyed instructions and ate of the Tree of Knowledge, the danger, uncontrollability, and sinfulness of sex were released for all humans to follow. As a result, for the devout Catholic, sex must be controlled, either through celibacy or by limiting it to procreation within marriage.

Taking a cue from the work of Plato's student, Aristotle, who observed animal behavior to determine what is natural and good, medieval monk Thomas Aquinas used his vast intellect to develop a rational theory of sexuality, based on what he called "natural law" (natural to animals and humans). A deeply pious man, Aquinas illuminated this natural law with Divine revelation and the Will of God.

In his observations, Aquinas could detect no masturbation among animals, and concluded, therefore, that such behavior is unnatural and immoral. In fact, for those who follow Aquinas, any sex act that does not deposit sperm inside a vagina is unnatural and sinful. This includes oral sex, anal sex, sex between homosexuals, and all erotic or pleasurable sex that is not for the primary purpose of procreation.

Moreover, according to Aquinas, parents should provide whatever is necessary to rear any offspring they do have. Both sex and childrearing, he concluded, are only moral in the context of monogamous marriage. Finally, observing man's active and woman's receptive roles in fertilization, Aquinas concluded that it is natural and therefore good for men to govern women.[4]

This "Thomistic" concept of sexual morality has strongly influenced Western culture, and continues to be the Vatican's official position.[8] Jewish and Protestant views on sexuality took a separate course. While Jewish scholars also emphasized fertility in marriage and the control of bodily passion, they interpreted the story of Adam and Eve quite differently. According to David Biale, author of an historic account of Jewish sexual ethics, *Eros and the Jews,* the rabbis interpreted the fall of Adam and Eve as punishment for their disobedience to God, and not for the discovery of sexuality itself.[9]

Furthermore, although humans act with a tendency toward sexual abandon at times, rabbinical thought stresses that sexual moderation and modesty can control such lack of restraint.

It is God's commandment and a blessing for every Jewish man to marry and have children, and the right of every Jewish woman to receive sexual pleasure from her husband, even when she is pregnant, menopausal, and otherwise infertile (although masturbation and sex during menstruation are violations of Orthodox Jewish law).

During the Age of Enlightenment, new Christian denominations, under the general umbrella of Protestantism, were formed that were apart from the Vatican. While many of these new churches clung to St. Augustine's theory of original sin, based on the fall in the Garden of Eden, other churches reinterpreted Biblical text and started their own theological dialectics, which produced even newer theories of sexual morality. Like Jewish sexual ethics, many of the Protestant theologians believed that the purpose of sex is not only procreative, but also unitive: It unites a husband and wife in emotional and spiritual bonds. Thus, in this view, even sex for pleasure (within the context of marriage) further sanctifies the holy state of matrimony and helps "the two become one flesh."

After the French and American Revolutions, when basic human rights became central to political morality, various philosophers, feminists, and humanists discovered the concept of women's equality in marriage and sex. Others lessened the emphasis on fertility and stressed the idea of eroticism and pleasure in sexuality. Valuing sexual freedom and sexual gratification, they remained out of sync with most societal views on sexuality until the 20th century.[11] The Victorians, with their propensity for sexual repression and restraint, saw to that.

Cupid in the Bedroom. One of the most significant influences on our sexual ethics, besides philosophy and religious teachings, is romantic love, [12] a universal behavior that, for Western civilization, began in the Middle Ages among nobility.[13] Knights and troubadours were allowed to "court" and love a married woman. Although our knight in shining armor was permitted to tuck "m'lady" into bed at nightfall, he was expected to bid adieu and leave her chaste by morning.[14]

Over several hundred years, the notion of sexual purity in romantic love changed to one of sex for love. By this time, our knight pursued a single lady, so that when he found his true love, and she found him, they married. In fact, the quest for true love reached nearly everyone, including members of the middle and working classes, who wholeheartedly embraced the notion.[15]

During the Industrial Revolution, the dominant pattern was that everyone married for love, and, ironically, during the 1960s, falling out of love became moral justification for scrambling out of a marriage.

By contemporary times, Cupid romped with Eros. Sex for love, unchaperoned dating, the automobile and the privacy it ensured – all these lured many couples into extramarital and premarital trysts, where they engaged in heavy petting and sexual activity. Ultimately they created a radical change in our sexual standards and sexual conduct, as well as loosening orthodox religion's grip on our sexual moral conscience.[16]

Sexual Revolution. During the 1800s, physicians started blaming sexual repression and sexual excess for certain disorders, including hysteria and depression.[17] Dr. John Harvey Kellogg, for example, created Kellogg's Corn Flakes to inhibit masturbation and control sexual desire through proper diet. And both the condom and the diaphragm were introduced after the invention of vulcanized rubber.

By the turn of the century, Freud began espousing his novel theories on childhood sexuality and the nature of our sex drive, while a few decades later Havelock Ellis researched and published volumes on the biology of sex and reproduction, including his more liberal viewpoints on sexual ethics.

In 1948 and 1953 respectively, Alfred Kinsey issued two landmark reports on the sexual behavior of American men and women, which documented the enormous gap between our sexual ideals and our actual behavior. From his reports, Americans learned that many of them masturbated regularly, had premarital coitus, committed adultery, and engaged in heavy petting.[18] And others reckoned that because many were behaving this way, maybe their behaving that way wasn't so abnormal or even immoral.

The National Organization of Women, founded in 1965, heralded a second wave of feminism, while the 1969 riot at Stonewall, a gay bar where homosexuals began the struggle for gay rights, marshaled many activists to a new quest for equality and sexual freedom.

By 1973, we had reliable birth control, medical cures for syphilis and gonorrhea, and legalized abortion. All these factors, together with a general social malaise, stemming in part from cynicism over the Vietnam War, inaugurated the most liberal sexual standards of any period in American history, and an unprecedented interest in sexual ethics.

Old stereotypes and myths were rapidly replaced by new ones: Sex and the single girl. The New Age man. Swinging singles. The joy of sex.

Albert Ellis's book, *Sex Without Guilt,* and Bertrand Russell's classic essay on trial marriage became incantations for "liberated" men and women. American society entered an intense period of self-analysis and search for personal fulfillment and a period of sexual experimentation and exploration. Through therapy and group encounters, men got in touch with their feelings and women discovered how to free themselves from male chauvinism. Masters and Johnson pioneered sexual research in the laboratory, documenting for the first time in scientific history, the nature of erections and orgasms. That research spawned a new field, sexual therapy, and many clamored for help with their own sexual performance and enjoyment.

Individuals and minority groups have long broken sexual taboos and trespassed on forbidden moral ground. The Mormons practicing polygamy and members of the Oneida community practicing free love in the 1840s predated hippiedom by more than a century.[19] According to sociologist Ira Reiss of the University of Minnesota, by the 1920s, one out of every two women and four out of every five men in America were breaking the taboo against premarital sex.[20] Only now, by the 1960s' Sexual Revolution, as the new era in sexual norms was dubbed, huge numbers of people – including teenagers, adult singles, and homosexuals – were crossing traditional barriers boldly, relentlessly, and apparently guiltlessly and fearlessly. Either that, or they were tearing them down altogether with an unabashed level of promiscuity, especially among the new homosexual neighborhoods in cities such as San Francisco and New York.[21]

The number of people openly engaging in premarital, nonmarital, and extramarital sexual intercourse soared and the number of people cohabitating skyrocketed. Abortions and teenage pregnancies rose dramatically, too.[22] Many people still played by the old rules. But they no longer dominated the playing field.

Perhaps the biggest contribution to the new sexual ethical terrain, however, was change itself. As soon as people got the message that "everyone is doing it," as the Egoism Exemplar suggests, many felt justified doing it themselves. And some people tried doing it all. Group sex, sex with strangers, and sex with apparatus. Yoko Ono and John Lennon bared their bodies on a record album cover and campus streakers bared their all with little restraint or concern for authority. "Mooning" was in; prudery was out.

With curfews and dormitory restrictions gone, sex became a vital part of campus social life (a female member of the State Board of Regents labeled the new mixed dorms "taxpayers' whorehouses"). Even the guru of child-rearing, septuagenarian Dr. Benjamin Spock, flaunted convention when he divorced his wife of some 30 years to marry his thirty-something nurse. In fact, Spock took much of the flak for the wave of permissiveness sweeping society.

Not everyone participated in the Sexual Revolution. Nor did everyone consider it social progress. As Lillian Rubin, author of the *Erotic Wars,* observes, "The revolution, which had freed women to say yes, also disabled them from saying no."[23]

By the discovery of AIDS in 1981, the Sexual Revolution was in high gear. And more than a decade later, according to many experts, there are few signs of its waning or of a rewinding of the clock of history.[24]

CHOOSING FROM THE MORAL MENU

The challenge facing anyone committed to sexual morality is how to determine which sexual standards are best and what is the right way to behave.

Because of its diversity, American society includes a wide range of sexual standards, from conservative to liberal. Philosophical reasoning – be it a utilitarian contract, Kant's Categorical

Imperative, the Golden Rule, or any of several other life-views – can be used to evaluate these standards and determine right conduct. Most people, however, do not apply such reasoning to their behavior (though perhaps they should). Instead, they inherit sexual guidelines from their parents, religions, peers, and what life itself teaches them.

In God We Trust. The most conservative moral standards are rooted in religious traditions, namely the theme that sex is a blessing intended by God within the context of marriage. Sex there is morally good, but only when it is channeled into responsible behavior,[25] which for most conventional religious denominations means heterosexual vaginal intercourse and foreplay leading up to it, and excludes nonconventional behavior such as homosexuality, and anal sex. And for the most traditional denominations, such as Roman Catholicism and Orthodox Judaism, it excludes masturbation as well.

Within such Divine Command life-views, sexual virginity for both bride and groom is a virtue; fidelity afterward an obligation. An essential purpose of sex is procreative, though for most denominations, it has the primary function of creating a spiritual union combining two personalities in one new expression – selfless, married love.

Not all theologians interpret religious law so strictly. Instead, with a more liberal outlook that stresses a person's right to sexual gratification and the loving, pleasurable purpose of sex, they allow modern methods of birth control and fertilization, abortion, and a variety of sexual behavior that includes oral sex and masturbation.[26]

Because of the restraints placed on sexuality among certain churches, sex and sin have a strong association that does not necessarily dissipate with a marriage license, and certainly causes a lot of guilt when a person fails to live up to the ideal. Moreover, people who marry late and must repress their sexual urges for many years sometimes experience difficulty overcoming their inhibitions when they do have sex. Being unable to use reliable birth control can, for members of certain denominations, cause anxiety about getting pregnant that may squelch sexual ardor. Finally, unless a person dates only within his or her social milieu, with strict chaperoning, sticking to such high standards represents a formidable challenge.

On the other hand, there are rewards for a conscience guided by this moral compass. These include moral certainty, because there is little to dispute or confuse about what is acceptable sexual conduct.[27] By saving sexual intimacy for marriage, people are protected against sexual jealousy, transmission of AIDS and a wide array of venereal disease, sexual scandal, and the like. According to Orthodox Rabbi Manis Freidman, author of *Doesn't Anyone Blush Anymore?*, conservative sexual behavior actually preserves and strengthens a person's sexuality and the marital bond two people share.[28] For some who believe in this moral compass, it can be a question of practicality. For most, trusting God's law is the only morally decent way to live.

'Boys Will Be Boys.' In this set of standards, men abide by a different set of moral rules than women. Basically, they are permitted to be more sexually active, more sexually assertive, and more sexually adventuresome than women.

Originally, the double-standard woman was a virgin when she married – or at least when she became engaged to be married – while men were allowed and even encouraged to acquire sexual experience long before marriage. Some men believed that later, it was all right to "have a little on the side" outside marriage, either by visiting prostitutes for the type of sex their wife would not consent to have, or via affairs with single women.

The historic rationalization for the double standard is twofold: first, to ensure paternity, and secondly, to reinforce the idea that men need to and can live by a freer set of rules. "Boys will be boys,"after all.

Sociologist Ira Reiss believes that such reasoning is based on erroneous assumptions that men cannot repress their sexual urges without dire consequences, and that woman have an inferior sex drive to men.[29] According to author and feminist Naomi Wolf, exploding the myth that women have inferior sex drives (or that women are entitled to less sexual fulfillment) is the crux of feminism and society's uneasiness with it. "The basic principle of social organization," explains Wolf, "is not just who gets power, but who gets pleasure."[30]

There are other problems with this particular moral compass. As Reiss observes, men are encouraged to exploit women and use them as a means to an end. Once they have "scored," they are prone to disrespect and even feel disgusted with their partner. Furthermore, double-standard men ("egoists" to the man?) show little empathy for women who are promiscuous, regardless of the myriad of social, economic, or emotional reasons why women become that way.

Besides exploiting women, Reiss contends the double standard encourages self-centered sexuality that is devoid of commitment and affection, an experience that hardly prepares men for the give-and-take an emotionally-rich, satisfying sexual relationship requires.

Trying to live a double standard has adverse effects on women, too. Those women who "fail" the test of sexual purity earn a reputation for being "easy" and are saddled with labels from men, such as "whore," "slut," and the like. To avoid a bad reputation and maintain their desirability as wives, many women become sexual teases or hide their true desire to initiate sex with a man. Compelled to send out only subtle cues about their sexual desires, they often send out unclear signals, which men easily misread.

Other women feign sexual innocence and lie about the sexual experience they do have. Putting up such facades may require painfully harboring secrets about infants given up for adoption, abortions, and sexual abuse or assault.

Finally, treating women as inferior, the way the double sexual standard does, encourages their devaluation in the rest of society, be it in the workplace, academia, home, or elsewhere. Worse, as Reiss also points out, in both *Journey into Sexuality* and *An End to Shame,* by holding women to an inferior status, while simultaneously validating machismo conquestial attitudes in men, "the double standard can actually contribute to the cause of rape."[31]

With Love And Affection. A legacy of women's demand for sexual freedom and equality, and men's respect for women, this secular liberal compass is undoubtedly popular, especially among college students.[32] Believing that sexual intimacy strengthens a couple's relationship and satisfies both their physical and emotional needs, and that men and women have equal sexual rights and responsibilities, this compass sanctions nonmarital sex.

Although sexual intimacy requires no wedding vows, people are expected to have affection toward their sexual partners, and to make an emotional investment in a relationship. How much emotional commitment is required varies, from the belief that two people should have a long-term commitment such as marriage or be in love, to the belief that they at least ought to mutually respect one another.

Within this broadly defined standard is also a wide spectrum of thought on monogamy and fidelity. Some people believe that all sexual relationships should be monogamous, if only for practical reasons, while others believe that as long as there is affection, openness, and mutual consent including fidelity and faithfulness to the relationship itself, then secondary sexual relationships are acceptable. Many famous people have lived and loved by this rule, including Jean Paul Sartre and Simone du Beavoir, French philosophers who laid the moral groundwork for other sexually liberated couples.

Many homosexual men have sex without love.[33] However, some of them – about one in four gay men and a much higher proportion of lesbians – subscribe to the idea that affection should be the basis for a sexual relationship.[34] (Paradoxically, they refer to themselves as "straight" gays.)

With this compass, most people put less emphasis on sexual coitus and more on the whole context of sexuality and feelings. Rather than a strict recipe for sexual conduct, traditional ethical principles are the yardstick for making decisions about sexual behavior: Do not harm, exploit, use, or deceive another person during or after sexual encounters. Among the sexually liberated, as long as you abide by these basic principles, then oral sex and increasingly unconventional sexual behavior between two consenting people are acceptable – and certainly are more widely practiced than among those with more conservative sexual standards.

Advocates of such a liberal standard argue that it is the emotionally healthiest preparation for marriage and the best way to live the single life. On the other hand, unless people take precautions, nonmarital pregnancy and sexually transmitted disease are a risk, as well as the emotional deception of people who profess to live by this moral compass but really don't. As the familiar adage goes, "Women give sex for love and men give love for sex."

No Strings Attached? This last moral compass is what Reiss calls "permissiveness without affection," because sex here is devoid of emotional commitment. "In" with this crowd are free-love, swinging singles, swinging couples, cruising and more. Ranging from recreational sex between two partners unready for any emotional commitment to totally anonymous sex among multiple strangers, this compass covers 360 degrees of sexual freedom to the max, although some of those who uses it may choose to impose occasional limitations.

Besides having sex without affection, some in this crowd will have sex with anyone, including bisexuals who like it both ways. A few individuals condone only conventional behavior,— say, heterosexual intercourse and oral sex – and refuse to do anything else. But in any case, those who lead the most nonconforming, adventuresome (and even reckless) sex lives subscribe to this compass.

Good sex. No strings attached. Whatever turns you on. Devoid of emotion or commitment .... Can such sex really be "good"?

While they may still adhere to such moral principles as refraining from harm, deceit or coercion, given the seemingly total freedom of this compass, it is tempting to selectively ignore such principles. Flight from responsibility, cynicism about relationships, and burnout over sex are other pitfalls. So is the empty or degenerate feeling one can get from having sex with hundreds or even thousands of sexual partners who care little or nothing about you afterward, or from sex that is degrading or painful. And what effect does such behavior have on children who are conceived during such casual, perhaps anonymous, encounters?

In addition to the emotional risks, and the danger of getting abused by strangers, disease lurks eerily behind the veneer of "safer sex." That sex can be dangerous at all, though, powers its very appeal to some people. Even the threat of dying cannot scare them into abandoning their sexually free, no-strings-attached lifestyle.

For many people, recreational sex is a temporary choice; they are *willing* to have just physical sex, but they *prefer* sex with affection. Or, exercising their own double standard, they are unable or unwilling to have affection for some of their partners, but quite willing to have it for others.

Critics of this compass claim that it has no morality at all – that by putting sex in the same category as "eating a good meal, listening to music, or getting a pleasant back rub," we deny its moral richness, and shortchange ourselves.[35]

Its proponents, on the other hand, believe that by isolating the physical context of sexuality from all its emotional layers, people can actually be more honest in their relationships and thereby avoid the game-playing and deception that go with other sexual standards. Their attitude might be characterized this way: Risky sex without affection or commitment is better than no sex at all.

On The Yellow Brick Road. "Be true to yourself and stick by your own moral compass" is a constant theme in moral education. Yet sex nearly always involves at least two people, often with different sexual moral standards. How can we be tolerant of a radically different moral viewpoint than our own? And when people whose respect we want pressure us to change, how can we maintain our own standards? Most of all, how can we make wise, informed choices about our sexual behavior?

"Selling out" on your sexual standards causes not only guilt, but also regret, according to Dr. Pam Bruboker, professor of sexual ethics at Cleveland State University. She observes that students who profess the most regrets about their sexual past are the ones who have changed their standards in order to accommodate themselves to someone else's expectations.[36]

Besides exposing your sexual standards to a thorough philosophical analysis, Bruboker suggests the "mirror approach": If you were to do what you have decided was right to do, could you still look yourself in the mirror and respect yourself?

"Do the right thing." But how does a person determine what is truly *right* sexual behavior? (It is the ultimate question all sexual ethicists and moralists ask.)

Reiss offers a litmus test, based on pluralism and the recognition that morality requires freedom of choice, a choice he suggests tempering with moral restraint. "Pluralism is not 'just say yes' or 'just say no'," explains Reiss, but rather "choosing wisely" and respecting the choices other people make. "If we oppose the prohibition of alcohol, that does not mean we favor drunkenness. A person can be sexually tolerant and still be discriminating," says Reiss.[37]

Reiss acknowledges the difficulty of developing our own moral judgment. "It takes careful self-examination and patience to work out one's own preferred sexual lifestyle."[38] According to Reiss, no matter what sexual lifestyle you choose, it should always be based on a concern for both the welfare of others and yourself. And this is possible only if "all sexual encounters are negotiated with an honest statement of your feelings, an equal treatment of the other person's feelings, and a responsibility for taking measures to avoid unwanted outcomes such as pregnancy or disease."[39]

CONSENT: ASK FIRST

"And yes, I said yes I will, yes" —James Joyce in *Ulysses.*

Let's consider a modern scenario:

> Dan arranges for a romantic evening with Angela dinner in a cozy restaurant, moonlit drive to the beach, bottle of wine, or even two. So far, Angela has not agreed to have sexual intercourse with Dan. "I'm just not ready for that kind of commitment," she always tells him.

"But I love you," he always says.

"Seduced" by the romance of the evening, and woozy from the two bottles of wine they share, Angela does have sexual intercourse with Dan – with regrets later.

Ill-prepared for the turn of events, Angela had used no birth control. And she is disappointed with both Dan and herself. She had not wanted to have sex, but Dan kept pushing for it, giving her his old line that if she loved him, she would want to have sexual intercourse with him. Sure, she wanted sex. Dan was right about that. But it didn't feel right to her, not yet. Why couldn't he take no for an answer and still keep loving her?

The other question that kept churning in her mind was whether or not it was fair to put all the blame on Dan for the episode, inasmuch as he hadn't *forced* her to drink an entire bottle of wine. Nor did she have to say yes when she meant no.

With all these issues churning in her mind, she couldn't decide if the incident was a lack of will power on her part,— or unfair persuasion, coercion, or date rape on his.

In the Driver's Seat. Ethics requires an ability to make rational decisions, an ability called moral agency. It also requires the free will to make them, which is called moral autonomy. In sexual ethics, both moral agency and autonomy are generally framed as consent: the obligation to ask for, not demand, sex; and the willingness to accept no for an answer. It also requires that you be true to yourself when you decide whether or not to consent to any sexual behavior.

Even the most libertarian view of sexual ethics recognizes that coercing persons into having any kind of sex against their will is *prima facie* wrong because it denies them autonomy over their own moral behavior. (Interestingly, denying people their free will also removes their moral responsibility for what occurs. Hence, a person who has been raped cannot be morally blamed for the rape.)

Often, though, despite the fact we haven't coerced a person into sex, we use subtle pressure on them that can take away some of their moral autonomy. A campus celebrity, such as a star quarterback, for example, may use his status to persuade a coed into having sex with him. Or like Dan, a person may "threaten" to withdraw his or her affection if a partner refuses to engage in sexual intercourse.

On the other hand, what responsibility does Angela have to keep her head clear enough to think rationally and maintain self-control?

In 1991, Naval pilots convened in Las Vegas for a weekend of fraternizing at their annual Tailhook Convention. Although the female pilots attending Tailhook knew of its reputation for hard partying and loose sex, many believed they were immune from harm – until they walked through a gauntlet of rowdy pilots who tore at their clothes, fondled, and sexually molested them. The full consequences of those acts and judgments still unfold at this writing, including psychological damage, military penalties, loss of reputation and loss of employment .

In an ideal world, we could trust everyone to respect our sexual rights. As long as society has members who fall short of the ideal, though, why volunteer for situations where forced sex is more likely to occur, or give away your right to choose by getting too drunk to resist sex or give an informed consent to it?

Ironically, many college women don't realize that their being forced into sex is rape, and many college men fail to realize that forcing a woman to have sex is rape. In a survey of college students sponsored by *Ms.* magazine in 1985, 15% of the coeds had experienced forced sex, while another 12% had resited it. Yet, three out of four women forced to have sex failed to label themselves as a rape victim, and nearly 9 out of 10 men who admitted to forced sex failed to understand they had committed rape.[40]

Many of the women thought that what had occurred to them was just part of a relationship, and somewhat their fault, while their male offenders stated that the women they had pressured into having sex had been ambivalent about what they wanted or had pretended not to want sex (or the men had misread their cues).

In his book, *An End to Shame*, sociologist Ira Reiss, says the fault for such misunderstandings, and for much of the date rape that is occurring, lies with our adversarial script for dating, which casts women in sexually reluctant roles, and men as persuaders. Such scripting works against honest communication. Women give unclear cues about their desires and men misread the cues. "Both men and women must stop playing this dangerous sexual guessing game," advises Reiss, "and sit down and tell each other how they feel about the relationship and about having sex with each other."[41]

For many reasons – they can range from mental disability to illness, depression, or insanity – some persons actually lack the ability to make a rational decision about their behavior. In 1989, a young woman with an IQ of only 64 and an "almost insatiable need to satisfy herself through sex" also gave satisfaction to four teenage boys in Glen Ridge, N.J. Despite her desire to please them, because she had a questionable ability to make a decision and rationally consent to sex, three of the teenagers were charged with rape.

Ethics is about choice choosing the best alternative. Some situations occur where people feel as though they face a Hobson's choice – they seem to lose either way. A woman at gunpoint may consent to being raped in order to save her life. A wife may consent to spousal rape, believing that giving in to her abusive husband's demands will spare herself and her children a worse fate. Or a young man may run away from a terrible homelife and resort to prostitution because he feels he has no better choice at the time. While these are extremely difficult moral dilemmas, they are, unfortunately, not uncommon ones.

Let's go back to our couple, Angela and Dan. Only now we'll give Angela a sexual history that includes promiscuity, multiple partners, and a great deal of sexual experimentation. Dan knows that this gal is one hot tamale. In fact, the entire campus knows it. What they don't know, however, is that as a teenager, Angela was repeatedly molested by her stepfather. She has little self-esteem and much craving for affection. As a result of her past, she allows herself to be used by Dan and any other fellow.

Given the high incidence of incest and sexual abuse in our society, Angela is not alone. Unfortunately, many people are victims of hardship, crime, and dysfunctional families. While these experiences may account for someone's behavior, do they morally excuse anyone from hurting or abusing others, or allowing themselves to be used for sex?

The Green Light. Many people erroneously believe that mutual consent is a moral green light, that anything two consenting adults do in the privacy of their home is right. But consent, however important, only completes part of the moral picture.

True, without consent, no sexual conduct can be moral. Yet two people can consent to behavior that is wrong. For instance, a professor can hold out high marks to students who consent to have sex with him or her. The consent is there, but for the wrong reason (assuming, perhaps self-righteously, that it is wrong to use sex to win other favors). Similarly, a psychiatrist who has sex with a patient and believes that the patient's consent puts a moral stamp of approval on the experience is rationalizing his or her behavior.

What about the kind of sexual activity two people consent to have? Is high-risk sex however consensual, morally right? Is consenting to use no birth control immoral when you know you need to avoid pregnancy? What reasons are anal sex, sadomasochistic sex, group sex, and the like, moral or immoral if they are consensual?

Let's turn to Angela and Dan one more time. Angela is 24 now, one of the few virgins left in her crowd. She and Dan have finished the bottle of wine, but before the night ever began, Angela had decided to make love to Dan. It is their wedding night, after all.

But, having practiced self-control for so many years, Angela is having difficulty finally saying yes. How much persuasion or coercion can Dan rightfully use to help her overcome her fears and inhibition?

For those of you who believe that Dan does have a right to at least persuade Angela to have sex on their wedding night, consider these other situations: Does he have any right to persuade her to have sex a month before their wedding? What about the night of their engagement? When he left to fight in the Gulf War? When they first fell in love? When they discovered their attraction for each other? When they had just met?

In all fairness to Dan, who is taking a lot of the rap here, does Angela have the right to seduce him? What if he is her coach and would prefer not to get involved with a student? What if he has broken up with her and no longer wants to be sexually involved with her? Is even asking for sex, when you are willing to accept no for an answer, ever wrong?

One of the legacies of the double standard was the game people learned to play about signals. Women coyly said "no" when they meant "maybe" or "yes." Some men learned never to take "no" for an answer. That sex requires consent in order to be moral is consistent with nearly all of our ethical exemplars. That we must choose our behavior is consistent with moral agency. But as we can see by the examples in this section (and by our laws against sex crimes), consent requires good communication skills. This means learning to be fair about the questions, and honest and wise about the answers.

AIN'T NOBODY'S BUSINESS IF I DO

The risk of acquiring HIV varies, depending on the population. Among intravenous drug users and other high-risk groups in the United States, one out of every four persons is infected. Among the general population, the risk drops to only one in 5,000 persons. But on college campuses, the risk increases again, to one in 500 students.[42] Moreover, each time a person has unprotected intercourse with anyone who is infected with the virus, that person has a one-in-500 chance of getting infected, too.[43]

For Allison Gertz of Manhattan, it was 100 percent. As a result of one romantic sexual encounter she had with a bisexual man, at the age of 16, Ms. Gertz contracted AIDS.

More than 1-million Americans are reportedly infected with HIV, and nearly 170,000 have died from AIDS, including both Gertz's infected boyfriend and Gertz herself.[44] Many of these people unknowingly or knowingly spread the infection to others, by failing to take precautions against spreading it to their partners, and keeping their condition a secret. Often, they have multiple partners to boot.[45]

Although they are not always life-threatening, other venereal diseases have also reached epidemic proportions. One in five Americans (56-million people) is infected with a sexually transmitted disease or bacterium. Each year, 12-million sexually transmitted infections will occur and be reported; many more cases will go undetected and untreated.[46] Because they often lead to pelvic infections that cause infertility, in 100,000 to 150,000 women a year, these diseases are especially threatening to women.

Whose responsibility is protection from pregnancy and disease? Are all women responsible for protecting themselves from pregnancy? Do their partners have any responsiblity, too? What responsibility does a person have to protect himself or herself from sexually transmitted diseases (STD), and to protect their partners as well?

Sixty percent of all American pregnancies (3.4-million out of 6-million annually) are unplanned and due to misuse of contraception, unreliable contraception, or no contraception at all.[48] While many of those pregnancies end in abortion or miscarriage, a considerable number will not and those women will give birth to beloved children. Too many "unwanted" babies, however, experience childhoods of neglect and abuse. Thousands of babies suffer physical and mental impairments as a result of parents who infected them with gonorrhea, syphilis, herpes, or caused them to become addicted to crack.

It is easy to believe that we are private citizens and that our sexuality is beyond and apart from the state; even from members of our immediate family. But then we realize that other people share the responsibility for our children, for educating them and footing their bills for housing, health, and other needs when we cannot or do not provide for them. What responsibility do we have to these family members and to the public at large for our sexual conduct? And what responsibility, in turn, do they have to us?

Used properly, condoms alone could prevent 98% of all unplanned pregnancies, and a significant number of sexually transmitted disease cases.[49] Despite a substantial increase in the use of condoms, according to a 1990 report by The Alan Guttmacher Institute of Planned Parenthood, 10% of all women at risk of pregnancy —nearly 4-million women —use no contraception,[50] and many more fail to use it consistently or properly. And from what we know of the epidemic number of sexually transmitted disease cases each year, both men and women fail to protect themselves with condoms or spermicides.

Now, many experts advocate abstinence as the only responsible protection against pregnancy and disease, and the only safe and moral behavior for single persons. Their argument has logic: If you don't have sex, you probably won't contract an STD. But, given the relative effectiveness of condoms and the strong desire of many for sexual relationships, is absence an effective option? As Reiss suggests, "Vows of abstinence break far more easily than do condoms."

Who is responsible for supplying condoms? Is it a private responsibility or should schools or public health clinics freely dispense condoms, Norplant, and other kinds of sexual protection? Do the news media have a responsibility to advertise and promote condom use? What responsiblity does the government have to fund research for new methods of birth control? The former U.S. Surgeon General, Dr. C. Everett Koop, believes that government is responsible in many of those areas. "We know that one person's behavior can be dangerous to another person's life and health," Koop told an audience in Minneapolis,"and that the ethics of the state can, in fact, intrude into the deepest corners of one's house."[52]

Others, especially from the conservative sectors of our society, disagree, claiming that the government has no moral authority to be involved in our personal sexual lives; that doing so undermines parents' right to impart their personal morals to their children.

But It's Against the Law. Besides laws against forced sex, it has been the public policy pattern in America to pass laws against other sexual behavior regarded as immoral and indecent. Adultery, homosexual relations, oral and anal sex, and fornication, for example, are illegal in many states. Prostitution is legal in Nevada, but only where there is a local ordinance allowing it. And a few states have recently enacted laws against marital rape and against knowingly transmitting veneral disease to an uninformed sexual partner.

In all states, masturbation is legal in private, but mutual masturbation is a crime in some states and masturbation in public in nearly all states is regarded as indecent exposure.[53] Certainly, sexual behavior that seriously harms people, such as rape, incest, and sexual harassment, belong within the sphere of the law. Might other behavior, though, particularly the private sexual behavior between two consenting adults, fall outside the public scope and beyond its legal parameters? Indeed, how much right does "big brother" have in our bedrooms?

At one time, sodomy was considered so "detestable and abominable (a) Vice ... committed by mankind or beast,"[54] that it was a felony punishable by death, no exceptions allowed. Even when our Bill of Rights was written and adopted, the death penalty for sodomy remained. Penal reform and the humanitarian effort to abolish cruel and unusual punishment ultimately eroded such harsh sentencing, until punishment for sodomy was limited to a few years in prison and/or a fine.

Because sodomy was considered such a degrading crime, its legal description was often vague language such as "crime against nature" or "buggery." Moreover, it contained a number of meanings, ranging from homosexual acts and oral and anal sex, to bestiality and necrophilia (acts with corpses). By 1961, all 50 states still outlawed sodomy and The Sexual Offenses Act of 1967 ensured that all homosexual acts sodomy, gross indecency, and procurement remain criminal.

Sodomy the Crime. Michael Hardwick is making love to a man in the bedroom of his home. A police officer enters his home and, through a partially open bedroom door, sees Hardwick having sex with another man. The officer arrests him on charges of sodomy. Hardwick now faces a minimum prison sentence of 20 years.

Hardwick challenges the constitutionality of his state's statute against sodomy. After losing his case in a federal district court, he appeals to a higher court. Eventually his case reaches the Supreme Court, as Bowers vs. Hardwick 478 U.S. 186, 194 (1986).

In a close (5-to-4) vote, Hardwick loses. Both Justice Byron R. White, who wrote the majority opinion, and Justice Lewis Powell, who cast the pivotal vote, reason that conduct which has been condemned for hundreds of years, as sodomy has been, cannot now become a fundamental right. As a result of their legal reasoning, it remains a crime, regardless of how many millions of Americans practice it and believe that it is right.

Nor is the homosexual community the only victim when the laws are stringently enforced. During his trial for allegedly raping his estranged wife, Jim Mosely admitted to engaging in oral sex with her on previous occasions. He was acquitted of the rape charges, but because oral sex is a crime in Georgia, Mosely was convicted of oral sex and given a five-year sentence, two of which he spent in jail before becoming eligible for parole. At various points in his confinement, Mosely was costing the taxpayers $11,000 a year.

Legal status, as we know from our civil rights past, does not automatically confer moral status on behavior. Nor, as we have learned from the front line of the abortion debate, can the judicial system adequately resolve certain moral debates. Yet, if laws do not reflect our society's ethical standards, what will ensure that we achieve a moral society – or that we at least aspire to be one?

When any game of sexual roulette risks pregnancy, childbirth, illness, broken promises, financial demands, and the like, our right to privacy competes with the moral claims of those who share responsibility for such consequences, including both the people who know us well and the public at large.

On the other hand, when we are in the position of accepting total responsibility for our behavior – when our sexual conduct is mutual and hurts no one – does that give us the right to keep the moral judgments of others, and the law as well, from intruding on our private lives? Of course, while mutual consent may be relatively easy to obtain, hurting absolutely *no one* may require a rare set of circumstances.

TO TELL THE TRUTH

Scenario I: Kevin and Christie had attended high school together and were close friends. One night, as Kevin was walking down the street where many college nightspots are located, he saw Scott, Christie's boyfriend, dressed in his unmistakable red jacket, come strolling out of a gay bar arm in arm with another man. Should Kevin tell Christie about the incident? Or should he "mind his own business" and keep it a secret?

To tell or not to tell vexes nearly each of us at some time or another. Harboring secrets such as incest or rape can interfere with our healing process. Secrets can also distance us from people with whom we are trying hardest to be close. On the other hand, candor and confessions, while cleansing your conscience, can be painful to the person whom you tell.

Scenario II: Two best friends, Heidi and Danielle make dinner for their boyfriends. When Heidi's boyfriend, Jason, plants a big sensual kiss on Danielle's mouth, whispers in her ear about how hot she is, and promises to stay interested in her, Danielle laughs off the incident. What a flirt, she thinks.

But a few nights later, Jason visits her in her apartment, where she is alone. Knowing she is doing something wrong, she nevertheless feels remarkably excited to walk on such a moral precipice. One thing leads to another, and before the night is over, she and Jason have had intercourse.

Afterward, overcome with guilt and remorse, Danielle asks Jason not to visit her again and certainly not to tell Heidi about their rendezvous. Yet what if Jason tells Heidi anyway? What if Jason never tells Heidi and marries her, as the two have already planned? Should Danielle warn her friend against marrying a man likely to cheat on her? On the other hand, if nothing is said of the incident, won't Heidi be spared the pain of betrayal? To tell the truth .. ..

Scenario III: Lynn's mother took the drug DES when she was pregnant with Lynn. As a result, Lynn had to have a complete hysterectomy when she was only 21. Is Lynn under any moral obligation to tell anyone who is interested in her romantically about her infertility? Does James, whose treatment for childhood cancer left him sterile, have any obligation to tell anyone he dates about his condition? If so, at what point does that obligation begin?

Does a woman have an obligation to tell someone she has had breast augmentation or reduction? Must a person reveal that they have a problem having orgasms? What about fetishes, cross-dressing, the need for dominance, excessive or underactive sex drives?

Scenario IV: Tom needs to borrow a blazer from his friend's room. In the ceiling of the closet, he notices a hook and rope dangling from the ceiling, raising the suspicion that his friend is engaging in a dangerous type of autoeroticism. What obligation to his friend does Tom have to confront him about the apparatus or to seek help for him by reporting it to someone else?

Sometimes the obligation to reveal a secret is obvious the dilemma is when and how.

Scenario V: Millions of Americans are infected with the herpes virus, for which there is limited treatment and no known cure. Debbie is one of those people. Although she feels obligated to tell any prospective sexual partner about her condition, her moral dilemma is when, how, and where to do it.

Should she tell about her herpes at the beginning of the relationship, thus giving a fellow the chance to end it before he gets too emotionally involved with her? Is it fair to her, though, to be judged so early, when he might work harder at overcoming a reluctance to have sex with her after he is emotionally committed to her?

Getting Even. "Against every claim to secrecy stands the awareness of its dangers," warns ethicist Sissela Bok, author of *Secrets.*[55] In the 1980s, a coed at a large university in Texas was talked into having intercourse and was secretly videotaped during it. When the tape was distributed all over campus, she experienced so much emotional trauma that she had to leave school over the incident. Did the students who plotted the scheme deserve the blame? After all, network television's "Candid Camera" got consent only after they filmed their unsuspecting guests? And did those who merely watched the tape have any responsibility for causing her pain?

What about telling a secret for the sole purpose of getting even? Can that ever be fair?

Scenario VI: Your companion has just decided to go on vacation without you and you are hurt. Does this give you the right to say, "Well, go ahead and have fun ... I can always have sex with your roommate ... which I already did the night you got drunk and passed out on me"? Sure, getting even feels good, at least temporarily. But are such truth serums really antidotes for problems? Are they fair? Are they good?

Sometimes though, while the telling of a secret may feel vindicatory to the person who has been snitched on, the person telling the secret in fact may have a legitimate moral claim. Consider the following situation in this light:

Scenario VII: When Joe was a child, he was raped by his drunken uncle. At the time he was too scared and embarrassed to tell anyone about it. As an adult, though, Joe sought help for the trauma. His uncle, now a grandfather, has been going to AA meetings for years and appears to have straightened himself out. Does Joe have any right or obligation to confront his uncle about the incident or tell any other family members about it?

A utilitarian might argue that the end justifies the means. But does it? Traditionally, the names of women who were sexually promiscuous or easily seduced (or who weren't, but someone wanted to say they were) were scrawled on the men's room walls, where the women had no way to refute the claims or clean up their reputations literally.

Now women on several campuses have begun to emulate the tradition. Only this time, the names of suspected or known campus rapists get top billing. Assuming that the fellows are guilty, does such vigilantism stand up to any of our moral exemplars? (From a deontological perspective, that the end doesn't justify the means, maybe not; utilitarians might argue otherwise.)

Keeping Secrets. According to Marty Klein, therapist and author of *Our Sexual Secrets,* most of us have sexual secrets we intend to keep forever, or at least from our current sexual partners. The most common of these secrets are sexual fantasies, fears, past sexual involvements, and the like.[56] Which of these secrets are we entitled to keep?

If we have fathered a child or given birth to a child out of wedlock who was placed in adoption, do we have the right to keep this information secret? Nearly half of all states have some kind of notification laws compelling pregnant women to inform their sexual partner (or those minors who are pregnant to inform their parents). Even in the absence of such laws, what prerogative does a pregnant woman have to keep her condition secret?

Scenario VIII: As a teenager, Joan ran away from home and resorted to prostitution to support her drug habit. That's all history, now, because Joan currently is working fulltime and enrolled in night school. What right does she have to guard her past? Does anyone who has been raped, molested or sexually harassed have the right to keep such incidents to themselves or at least keep their names from public view?

"Secrecy may be used to guard intimacy or invade," says Bok, "to nurture or consume it."[57] How much right do we have to remain silent about our fetishes, and sexual orientation? Do we have a right to keep silent about an STD that has been already cured or is under control? How much obligation do we have to let others keep their secrets? In fact, what questions do we even have the right to ask of them?

Keeping a secret can be difficult. How much right does someone have to expect you to keep that person's secret? For example, if a sibling tells you he or she is gay, do you have an obligation to guard the information from your parents or the rest of the family? What about a pregnancy, or merely having sex with someone of whom the family disapproves?

Do you have any duty to keep secret about someone's abortion, children out of wedlock, promiscuity, or sexual abuse, even when you think the information will help that person's partner understand him or her better?

What right do you have to reveal someone's bisexuality, transvestism, sexual inadequacy, homosexuality, fetishes, or sexual inadequacy? If a friend is having an affair with a married person, does she have the right to expect you to cover for her, or to keep the truth from someone else you both know?

Seeking The Truth. Sometimes, the moral responsiblity to ferret out the truth poses a moral dilemma. In a highly unusual, albeit provocative case, Trina Irene Kendry learned that the man she loved and had married might actually be her biological father who had abandoned her when she was only 3 years old.

After years of sexual abuse by her adopted stepfather, Trina left home for good at age 15. By her 18th birthday, she was pregnant and living in a maternity home when her brother showed up with a man 20 years her senior, a man with whom Trina fell in love and eventually married.

Only after their wedding did someone inform Trina that her husband could also be her father. In fact, on the strength of evidence in the case, the State of Florida annulled the marriage, convicted Jimmy Kendry of incest and incarcerated him for more than a year.

After his release, Jimmy and Trina resumed living together, though they were unable to remarry. The child she had from her previous liaison resided with them.

After a lifetime of unhappiness, Trina had finally found love and respect with a man whom she adored. And so, she refused to avail herself of the genetic blood work that could set to rest any doubts as to whether the man she loved was truly her father. Anything wrong with her decision?

Obviously, Trina's situation is rare. But having to make a decision whether or not to discover the truth is far more common. Unlike Trina, many adoptees search for their natural parents, wanting to know the truth about their conception and who their parents really are. Do these adoptees have any moral claim to know of the circumstances of their conception – whether it occurred during a rape, say, or a casual or paid sexual encounter? Whether it was with a blood relative of the natural mother, perhaps – her father, a brother, an uncle, or grandfather? Does a person have the right to know if he was conceived before his parents' betrothal? If he is the child of an adulterous liaison? If he was fathered by a sperm donor or mothered by a surrogate?

Carnal Knowledge. If you have had any sexual partners whom you now know have had multiple partners, casual sex, or dangerous sex, or were drug users, or if you were raped, is there any obligation to yourself and others you date to be tested for STD or HIV? Do you have any obligation to find out about *their* sexual history or go further in investigating them besides what they tell you?

On a lighter side, what right do you have to know about a lover's first sexual encounter or his or her entire sexual history? If you are dating a person whom one of your friends has dated, do you have the right to ask your friend to tell you how he or she performs in bed? And what kind of personal questions do you have the right to ask of an ex-lover?

Candor has an important place in sexual relationships. But according to both Klein and Bok, secrets have a rightful place, too. Whether or not to tell the truth has no easy answers. Sometimes we only know what is right after we have done the wrong thing! It helps to remember that those moral decisions that involve a great risk or sacrifice cause a lot of conflict. Also, a moral life requires accepting that we cannot always be certain of the truth; all that we can do is stay committed to the struggle to find it.

BROKEN PROMISES

"I promise to love, honor, cherish, and hold thee only unto me until death do us part." Most people marry and commit to monogamy. And despite the fact that 1-million couples divorce each year, twice that many will marry and attempt to share their lives in marital bliss. Okay, so it's not always blissful – is that any reason to go have an affair?[58]

Contemporary surveys reveal that adultery is widespread and spreading (women are catching up to men). Even the most conservative findings indicate that at least a third of all men and a fourth of all women admit to having an extra-marital sexual experience at least once.[59] Of course, most all moral exemplars declare statistics are no basis for morality.[60]

Philosopher Michael Wreen argues that adultery is wrong because it is so inconsistent with our basic definition of marriage – the agreement to make an emotional commitment to another person, have a sexual relationship with them, and have it be exclusive of anyone else. In his opinion, the very value of marriage makes monogamy a worthwhile sacrifice.[61]

According to both the law and our major religions, marriage, as Wreen suggests, is based on monogamy, and adultery is acceptable grounds for divorce. What about societies that are polygamous or polyandrous or where adultery, in the form of prostitution or mistresses, is encouraged? Do the values of those societies make the issue a morally relative one in ours?

Psychologists say that falling in love and desiring to have sex with someone else, even after a person has married, is natural. After all, consider how natural it is to love more than one child at a time. Neither because it is natural or desirous is why it may or may not be moral, though. Wanting to lie your way out of a sticky situation or cheat on an exam for which you are unprepared and destined to flunk is natural and desirable, but those reasons alone are insufficient arguments to make such lying or cheating right. In fact, only when we do acknowledge how natural it is to be sexually attracted or to fall in love can we set boundaries and have guidelines to help us guard against acting on those feelings when the patina of romance has worn away.

What if someone *needs* to fall in love or have sex, though? Does that make adultery less wrong? Is it reasonable to expect only one person to fulfill all your needs?

Christian theologian Stanley Grenz, author of *Sexual Ethics: A Biblical Perspective,* agrees that personal fulfillment may require outside influences. But instead of seeking it from an affair, he suggests that the morally appropriate place to augment your fulfillment is through religion and belief in God.[62] Even those who reject religious claims can find personal fulfillment through deep friendships, careers, creativity, charity, and leisure pursuits of an asexual nature.

Love And Commitment. What does love have to do with it anyway? If people choose to love only one person, does that preclude them from having extramarital sex with persons to whom they will not get emotionally attached, whether prostitutes, casual acquaintances, or an entire group that shares the same perspective? Indeed, can adultery ever be *right?*

Steinbock believes that if a person is in a loveless marriage, there is reason to turn elsewhere for affection and sex.[63] Is there, though? Aren't there better ways of solving a marital problem, such as counseling and therapy? Should such marriages be salvaged?

Some philosophers believe the issue pivots on consent. In this view, if two people consent to extramarital sex, or agree to tolerate it in their spouse, then it is not wrong.

In our society, open marriage is neither a new nor a rare concept. An estimated 5-15% of all couples consent to extramarital sex at least sometime in the course of their marriage. However, according to Lillian Rubin, who conducted a study on contemporary sexual behavior, and other experts, nearly two-thirds of all open marriages fail.[64]

Degree Of Guilt. The majority of Americans (including many who partake) believe that extramarital sex is wrong.[65] Just how wrong, though? Wreen suggests that in the scheme of things, adultery is worse than forgetting someone's birthday, though not as bad as killing them.[66] And on the list of sexual sins, Aquinas proposed that adultery was not as grievous a sin as masturbation.[67]

Is it worse to have a casual affair or commit to a long-term lover? Is there a difference between having casual sex or unrequited love? Does the gender or age of the third party in the triangle matter? (Some people claim they suffered more pain upon discovering the affair their spouse had was with a homosexual or a considerably younger person.)

How wrong is it to seek sexual gratification outside a marriage when your spouse fails to satisfy your sexual appetite, or to have an affair when your spouse is incarcerated or away for extended periods of time? Is it wrong to have an affair if your spouse has had one?

What about the single person who has an affair with a married person? If she mistakenly believed her lover was single, is it wrong to continue the affair after learning otherwise?

Richard Taylor, author of *Having Love Affairs,* puts a real twist on the whole issue, by suggesting that whether adultery is right or wrong, there is actually a "right" way to go about it that he claims can preserve a good marriage. [68]

Making The World Go Away. If adultery is so common and so natural, why is it viewed as so wrong? Peggy Vaughan, author of *The Monogamy Myth,* suggests that we ought to take adultery out of the moral realm altogether, and treat it as an amoral (morally neutral) issue entirely.

Writes Vaughan, whose marriage survived years of her husband's philandering: "We need to reject the Monogamy Myth, not to excuse those who have affairs, but to relieve the sense of shame and inadequacy felt by their mates." And she suggests that surviving the experience is best accomplished by dealing with the reality that adultery is natural, common, and often avoidable.[70]

Clearly, it is easy to dance circles around such a complicated moral issue. The reality test for most people – which admittedly skirts the moral issue, as Vaughan suggests we do – is that some marriages can survive adultery and a few may even be strengthened by having to deal with it; while many marriages, including the open ones, cannot.

HOLDING UP YOUR END OF THE DEAL

"Just say 'no'" may be the hallmark of sexual responsibility in the shadow of AIDS. How responsible, though, is saying no in the context of marriage or deeply committed relationships?

Scenario IX: Michael is relaxing in bed, watching television. No headache. No problems at work. No minor spats or serious marital discord. He is simply not in the mood for sex. And Maria, his wife of 10 years, is.

"Come on, honey," she tenderly says, kissing him and snuggling up to him. "Turn off the TV and make love to me."

Does Michael have any moral obligation to have sex with Maria? Many people would argue that he does not, that sex is something you do only when you are in the mood for it. Others disagree, and claim that for the sake of the relationship, Michael ought to have sex with Maria – not necessarily the kind of sex that gets scripted into passionate love scenes, just plain sex. Still others believe that in a healthy, loving relationship, Michael should let himself get aroused and really enjoy sex with Maria.

Relationships involve two people, each with the potential for a different sex drive, different attitudes toward sex, and a different set of sexual moral standards. How much right do we have to expect our partner to engage in lovemaking when that individual doesn't feel like having sex? We often prepare a meal, tend a sick mate, file the taxes, shop, put up with their friends, entertain their business associates, and make a host of other sacrifices for those whom we love. Is sex so exclusive from these other activities that it should stand alone and be reserved for only those times when the "mood" is right?

How much right do we have to expect more kissing, hand holding, massage, foreplay, or public displays of affection from our partners? What if one person is more sexually adventurous than the other? Which partner is obligated to appease the other? Does it depend on the type of sexual activity involved? Or, assuming there is no physical risk or harm involved, should a person be willing to experiment, if only once?

What about a diminished sex drive? Is a partner entitled to more sex than they get? Are they under any obligation to overcome an inhibition or change their moral perspective. (This is not to suggest that morality is relative, only that a person might remain open-minded in seeking a better, more truthful perspective on sexual morality.)

What rights does a person have when they are together with a person who is intentionally abstaining from sex, or who can't have sex? Although a person has a legal right to end an unconsummated marriage, do they have a moral right to maintain the marriage but seek sexual satisfaction outside the relationship?

Everyone has the right to ask for sex, but how often do they have that right? Over and over again or just occasionally? How much right do we have to turn down such requests and how much obligation do we have to accept them?

Ain't Gonna' Make Love No More. The place many start on this issue is abstinence (voluntarily refraining from sexual intercourse) and celibacy (refraining from all sexuality, including masturbation and even thinking about having sex).

Whether it is temporary or permanent, nearly one fifth of all marriages are celibate, and four percent of all men and 10% of all women have chosen to be celibate.[71]

Historically, and in most societies, celibacy, whose Latin root means single, is actually the expected norm for all unwed people. It was the price one was expected to pay for remaining single. But it wasn't always simply a case of doing without. In ancient Greece, for example, despite the Platonic ideal, celibacy was a crime. In Sparta, celibate men were barred from voting. On the other hand, throughout history, especially in religious life, chastity has long been regarded as virtuous moral behavior.[72]

For Mahatma Gandhi, father of India's struggle for independence, chastity was part of a spiritual quest. After more than three decades of marriage, Gandhi asked his wife Kasturba, who had married him when they were both only 13 years old, to take a vow of *brahmacharya* (Hindu vow of celibacy) in order for him to create peace within himself.

Ironically, temporary celibacy is often prescribed as an antidote for sexual problems. Other couples find themselves drifting into celibacy as sex becomes less frequent, more routine, and unimportant compared to other focuses in their lives. Others abruptly stop having sexual relations after a breech in the relationship, such as an affair, while fear of AIDS has caused still others to choose celibacy or abstention from intercourse.

Now, no one ever died from a lack of sex. But a lack of sexual interest from one's partner can diminish a person's self-esteem and destroy a relationship, as well as create a host of emotional problems in between. As one woman said of her husband's unwillingness to have sex with her, "It feels terrible ... I feel like I'm not beautiful enough, that I'm not attractive to him, that I don't turn him on ... it feels pretty bad."

Scenario X: Sherri and Jim have been married for 14 years and have two school-age children. During arguments, Jim remains quiet and withdrawn. She, in contrast, is quite vocal and extroverted – shouting, arguing, and often crying until an issue is resolved.

When Jim withdraws from Sherri and prevents her from confronting an issue directly, she, out of frustration and a fair amount of spite, withholds sex from Jim, often for weeks at a time, even though he is willing to have sex and the issue in dispute is long resolved. To Sherri, sex is power, power to make Jim suffer for his treatment of her.

Gabrielle Brown, therapist and author of the book, *The New Celibacy,* suggests that celibacy chosen for negative reasons – to punish, control, or withdraw love – does nothing to benefit a relationship, and in fact, only weakens it. Nor is celibacy beneficial that is initiated by only one partner. "Either both partners should decide to be sexual," advises Brown, "or both decide to be celibate in the service of love and positive commitment to their marriage."[73]

Obviously, if two people freely choose celibacy in their relationship –and some couples report great satisfaction with this choice even though they may be going against the norm – they are neither harming each other nor treating each other deceitfully or unfairly. When the hardware isn't working ...

For many people, abstention from intercourse is not a choice. Medications, injuries, medical conditions, hormonal changes, and physical disabilities can all contribute to a physical inability to enjoy or engage in coitus. Economic crises, death of a loved one, a sexual trauma, and the demands of parenthood can easily put sexual ardor on hold. Sometimes it is a matter of mismatched sex drives, inhibitions, fear of intimacy, or pain from sex that causes a person to avoid sex.[74]

Medical technology and improved sexual therapy have ushered in new choices for people. Do they have any duty to their partners or themselves to try one of them? Does a man have any obligation, for example, to get a medical implant device that would enable him to have an erection? Does a menopausal woman have any duty to her partner to take hormones in order to restore a waning sexual appetite?

Does a person have any moral obligation to use sexual apparatuses, dress provocatively or erotically, or view sexually explicit movies in order to help their partners achieve erections, sexual stimulation, or orgasms?

Many disabled people cannot experience a full range of sexual activity or even "normal" intercourse or masturbation. Yet they have learned to compensate in other ways that are sexually gratifying. And couples for whom intercourse is no longer possible also find other ways to remain sexually active. A kiss, a hug, a good massage is sexual and can bond people together.

Much of our sexuality (some would say most of it) occurs between our ears and in our hearts. Others have found much value in temporarily or permanently choosing to refrain from sexual contact. Like the issue of consent, holding up your end of the deal requires excellent communication and a mutual concern and empathy for others.

PRIVATE LIVES/PUBLIC PEOPLE

During a routine undercover operation on the evening of July 26, 1991, police entered an adult movie theater in Sarasota, Fla. and arrested four people, including a 38-year-old man, who had indecently exposed himself to masturbate twice while watching the porno movie *Catalina Tiger*. Paul Reubens, private citizen, dressed in shorts and a T-shirt and sporting a goatee, was unrecognizable from the clean-shaven comedian better known as Pee-wee Herman, star of the Emmy Award-winning children's television show, *Pee-wee's Playhouse*.

At the county detention facility, Reubens was charged, fingerprinted, and photographed. The next day, a reporter who recognized him from his mug shot quickly publicized the incident. Almost immediately, an ugly scandal erupted. Reuben's television show was canceled, and his once-prosperous career shattered, leaving him emotionally distraught and greatly embarrassed.

The private life of Reubens was altogether different from his public persona. In fact, aware that his proffered role as an "art photographer" in John Waters' 1990 movie, *Cry-Baby*, might strike a discordant note with his role as a children's host, he turned down the part.

Nor is Reuben's behavior an isolated incident. Sol Wachtler, a highly respected New York State Chief Judge, was charged in 1992 with an extortion plot connected to his former lover, a wealthy Republican fund-raiser. The same year, U.S. Senator Robert Packwood of Oregon was charged with sexually harassing a cadre of female employees after he had earned himself a reputation as a champion of women's right.

What private sexual standards of conduct should we expect our civil servants, teachers, clergy, and other role models and leaders to hold? Do we have any right to hold them to only the highest of moral standards or to conform to our own sexual moral compass?

Does their private life interfere with their duties to the public or the people they serve? What responsibility do they have to avoid scandal that may bring shame and ill-repute to their families or their profession? Is their private sexual behavior any of our business? And finally, what rights and obligations do writers and reporters have to expose those lives or shield them from our public view?

Missing The Mark. Some of the very people teaching us morality miss the moral mark themselves, shrinking from the ideals they are supposed to inspire in us. The rabbi of the largest reform Jewish temple in Cleveland, ignored one of the most basic commandments when he had an affair with someone else after his wife had delivered their second child. Only two years later, a Methodist minister, who had befriended the rabbi, committed the same sin. He, too, left a congregation whose members were stunned and now somewhat more cynical about foot soldiers of the Lord.

In fact, when Jimmy Swaggart and James Bakker, wealthy television evangelists who had mesmerized millions of followers with their family values and spiritual intonements, were literally caught with their pants down – Swaggart with a prostitute, Bakker with the seduction of former secretary Jessica Hahn – the public's respect for the clergy in general diminished significantly.[75]

Besides the sting of betrayal and hypocrisy, there is also a real threat. Don't people who have the trust of others have a duty to uphold that trust? Despite repeated reports of sexual abuse, homosexuality, and pedophilia among its members, officials of the Catholic church added another layer of wrongdoing by trying to cover up such scandals. Often an accused priest was simply transferred to another parish, with no attempt on the church's part to warn his new parishioners of his past.

Reading from a roster of notable presidents that includes George Washington, Thomas Jefferson, Franklin D. Roosevelt and John F. Kennedy, adultery and sexual dalliance are commonplace. In fact, as columnist Dennis Prager wryly notes, such ineffective and/or misguided leaders as Gerald Ford, Jimmy Carter and Richard Nixon left no trace of womanizing.[76] (You can, of course, find examples to illustrate just the reverse.)

When U.S. Senator Gary Hart, a Colorado Democrat, ran for the nation's highest office, he challenged reporters on the question of his marital fidelity. It was a challenge that felled Hart from his lofty plateau when they caught him spending the night with nubile model Donna Rice. Both Hart and Rice denied any sexual misconduct, but the political damage had already occurred. As Hart withdrew from the 1988 presidential race, he accused the media of unfair treatment, though when asked point-blank if he had ever committed adultery, he refused to answer.

The relevancy of a candidate's sexual conduct surfaced again when President Bill Clinton, then governor of Arkansas, was accused by one Gennifer Flowers of a 12-year liaison with her. Like Hart, Clinton evaded the question of whether or not he had committed adultery with Flowers. And like Hart, Clinton also failed to completely quell suspicions that he had ever committed adultery.

Americans care about such matters, as the intense media interest in both cases proves. Nearly 100-million viewers watched Clinton explain himself in a live interview on national television, while the story titillated the public for weeks. Still, Clinton was elected, if not by a landslide, at least by Americans who obviously overlooked his private affairs when casting their vote for him.

Do journalists have the right to inform us about our candidates' or leaders' private lives? And what right do we, the public, have to that information? In her book, *Secrets,* philosopher Sissela Bok argues that the right to tell and our right to know is a "patently inadequate rationale," and that while journalists can satisfy our curiosity, they must still "pay special attention to individual privacy."[77] But what if marital indiscretions interfere with leadership?

If politicians lie to a spouse, what real proof do we have that they will lie to their public? Actually, we have proof that regardless of what they tell or don't tell their spouses, they would lie anyway. The results of a 1988 *New York Times* survey indicated that on the average, adults admitted to lying 13 times a week.[78]

Moreover, the classic feminist argument – that men who cheat are contemptuous toward women and less likely to be sensitive to women's issues – was disproven by Senator Packwood, who sexually harassed women on his staff while fervently championing their rights in Congress.

Perhaps as Katha Pollitt, writing for *The Nation,* suggests, the entire argument is specious. "Call me cynical," she says, "but I'll bet almost no male politicians are monogamous and almost none of their wives think they are. If we are going to hold politicians to strict moral standards, why not demand that they read books and write their own speeches?"[79]

Out Of The Closet. An estimated 3- to 5-million homosexual men, and another 1-million lesbians, reside in America. Many gay activists believe these numbers are even higher, because most homosexuals choose, albeit painfully, to "stay in the closet" and keep their homosexual orientation a secret in order to protect themselves from job discrimination, social condemnation, social ostracism, gay bashing, and the like. (This remains a controversy as one recent study suggested homosexual practice may be as low as 1% of the U.S. population, or 2.5-million persons.) [1]

Allen Schindler, a 21-year old-sailor in the Navy who was suspected of being homosexual, was so brutally beaten to death that even his mother could not identify him had it not been for the tattoos she recognized on his arms.

After police raided the Stonewall, a gay bar in New York City's Greenwich Village, on June 28, 1969, many homosexual activists voluntarily "came out" and revealed their homosexual or bisexual orientation. Soon, though, homosexuals were being "outed" (their sexual orientation revealed) against their will, usually by other homosexuals.

Michalangelo Signorile, homosexual author of the now-defunct magazine *Outweek,* who began the practice of outing, claimed that by training the light of publicity on celebrities and politicians who were actually gay, he was providing role models for the gay community. Another rationale decried the hypocrisy of homosexuals who are "anti-gay" in public, but not in private.[82]

Following the particularly vocal and relentless bashes against liberalism, abortion, equal rights amendments, sex education and homosexuality at the 1992 Republican Convention in Houston, John Schlafly, 41-year-old son of Phyllis Schlafly, the doyenne of arch- conservative values, was outed. "I love my son," Phyllis Schlafly retorted, scoffing at accusations of hypocrisy. "I'm the most tolerant person in the world."[83] This was a view hardly supported by her unrelenting attacks on liberal lifestyles. But while there is little doubt about Schlafly's hypocrisy, was it fair to out her son, a private person?

According to Richard Mohr, professor of philosophy and author of *Gay Ideas: Outing and Other Controversies,* outing is both a permissible and an expected consequence of living morally, but not for the sake of providing role models, exposing political hypocrisy, or being vindictive. As Mohr explains, "Either being gay is okay or it isn't. To accept the closet is to have absorbed society's view of gays, to accept insult so that one avoids harm. Life in the closet is morally debased and morally debasing. It frequently requires lying, but it always requires much more ... Allowing homosexuality to take its place as a normal part of the human sexual spectrum requires ceasing to treat it as a dirty little secret."[84]

Most gays disagree, and believe that involuntary outing is wrong.[85] Writing for *The New Republic,* Andrew Sullivan stated his belief that people ought to be free to choose their own moments of self-disclosure.[86] When billionaire Malcolm Forbes, founder of *Forbes Magazine,* was outed posthumously, Fran Lebowitz, a columnist and friend of Forbes, condemned the outing as "despicable ... beneath contempt."[87]

If outing is fair, who has the right to do it – only a homosexual journalist, or any journalist? Some gay journalists believe that heterosexual journalists are wrong to out a homosexual, reasoning that a heterosexual can never understand what it is like to be gay in the first place.

Even though they may not have wanted it, some people are relieved to be outed. Case in point: Paul Monette, author of the award-winning autobiography, *Becoming a Man: Half a Life Story.* "I would not give up what the last 17 years of being out have meant to me," he wrote. "It has been a joyous experience and that even includes the decade of AIDS. I seem to be able to be as angry as I am and as despairing and still be a happy man, because I am now glad to be out."[88] But not everyone has had Monette's positive experience with outing.

Captain Dusty Pruitt may be pleased with her outing, but she clearly was displeased with the reception she received. After revealing her lesbianism in a newspaper interview, Pruitt, an ordained minister and 13-year veteran of the U.S. Army and Army Reserve, lost her military job. "It's sad," she said of the decision to discharge her from duty, "that the military wastes time bothering people about what they do in their private lives rather than what they do on duty."[89].

Mirror, Mirror On The Wall. When the virtuous images of our heroes and heroines fail to materialize, the public is often quick to strip them of their status. Whose gains or losses are such judgments?

Did young African-American girls lose a role model when Vanessa Williams, crowned the first black Miss America, had to give up the crown on the following day when nude magazine photographs of her emerged, shots taken long before her ascent to Miss America? Or did they gain a lesson in morality?

Was the public deprived of a good civil servant when Federal Judge Kimba Wood declined the nomination for U.S. Attorney General, in part out of concern that her one-week tenure as a London

Playboy bunny while studying in England would destroy public confidence in her ability to oversee the nation's legal structure?

Even heroes and heroines have feet of clay. From their public descents we can learn from their mistakes. When basketball star Magic Johnson admitted that he had acquired HIV after an exceedingly promiscuous sex life, he hardly looked worthy of being the role model he was. However, Magic influenced a number of people who gleaned a lesson from his mistakes. According to a Maryland clinic that was in the middle of a study of sexual behavior when the announcement was made, the number of people both engaging in casual sex and having multiple partners decreased substantially – from 1 in 3 to about 1 in 5 of those in the study.[90] On a final note, what responsibility does the public have to give its leaders, role models, and public servants a second chance?

ULTIMATE TEST: BEHAVIOR

This chapter opened with a look at director Woody Allen, antihero of the *avant garde*. We have concluded with basketball superstar Magic Johnson, hero to many. And we have looked at many private faces in between. The supreme test of sexual ethics, however, is not how we judge others, but how we judge ourselves. And even more essential is how we behave.

In a pluralistic society such as ours, during an era of such permissiveness, keeping your sexual standards or even knowing the right thing to do is often difficult. For many reasons, people do not follow their conscience when their sexual libido calls.

Nearly a third of all persons who describe themselves as having very religious standards commit adultery at least once in their life, while three out of four engage in premarital sex.[91] According to a 25-year study of Roman Catholic priests in the U.S., one out of every four admitted to homosexual activity, while six percent of the clerics reported they had had sex with a child or teenager.[92]

Among professionals, a picture of virtuosness also fails to emerge. Five percent of all physicians and health care workers, all of whom have a well-defined professional moral code, have intercourse with patients.[93] Toward the liberal side of the spectrum is irresponsibility where birth control and sexually transmittable diseases are concerned, not to mention using sex to get love and using love to get sex. And as we have learned earlier, much of the sexual violence in our society is a legacy of misbegotten values and archaic attitudes toward women and children.

In pursuit of love, intimacy, or just momentary companionship, many people simply compromise on their moral standards. Compromised too often, they find it impossible to regain their ideals.

Then there are the practitioners of situational ethics: people who have one set of sexual standards for sober times and another set of standards when drinking or on drugs; or one set for a person they respect and another for a person they hardly know. Still others trade a more conservative "home" compass for a looser, liberal one on vacations and business trips. Not much moral footing here.

There is no reason people cannot upgrade their moral compasses, learning from ethical inquiry and experience alike. Neither a lurid past nor an accumulation of sexual partners, a bad reputation or negative experience should stop people from improving their moral behavior or regaining their confidence in the moral compass they once had. People accustomed to being sexually exploited can regain their dignity, while people used to exploiting others for sex can learn respect and restraint. Sexual boundaries can be reset, and fear and inhibitions can be stripped away. And we can all improve our perspective on the sexual moral dilemmas and problems facing our society.

Such change isn't easy. But ethics is about living and learning. Depending on the seriousness of a mistake, it can be too late for second chance. Nor can we always undo a bad reputation, right a wrong, or move others and ourselves toward forgiveness. Nevertheless, we can learn from our past behavior and begin again to be the people we want to be.

FOR FURTHER INQUIRY

Suggested Readings
• Baker, Robert and Frederick Elliston, eds.; *Philosophy and Sex*, revised edition, Prometheus Books, Buffalo, New York, 1984.

• Reiss, Ira L., *An End to Shame*, Prometheus Books, Buffalo, New York, 1990.

• Scruton, Roger; *Sexual Desire: A Moral Philosophy of the Erotic*, The Free Press (Macmillan), New York, 1986.

• Soble, Alan, ed.; *The Philosophy of Sex*, Rowman & Littlefield Publishers, Inc., Savage, Maryland, 1991.

CASE STUDY 1
Ann and Steve have been dating for three years. Last year they were engaged to be married. They were sexually active with each other, though monogamous during the entire relationship. (In fact, both were virgins when they met, so they feel secure about each other's sexual history.)

Now that they are not going to get married, and are no longer emotionally committed to each other, is it right or wrong for Ann and Steve occasionally to have sexual intercourse with each other before either one of them settles into another relationship?

Does anything change if they were a divorcing couple instead?

CASE STUDY 2
Do parents have the right to have their child's genitals circumcised? For example, circumcision is routinely done on male babies; Jewish parents even hold a joyous celebration to mark the occasion. While there is a strong correlation between circumcision and protection from penile cancer, but conflicting evidence as to whether it affects a man's sexual performance or sensitivity, does a parent have the right to decide on such medically unnecessary surgery, for which the child cannot possibly give an informed consent?

The last known clitorectomy in the U.S. was performed in 1948, to control the masturbation of a young girl. This surgery remains popular throughout Third World nations. Do we have any obligation to try to stop such cultural practices?

CASE STUDY 3
In an effort to fight AIDS, city health officials closed down many commercial sex establishments. Despite the fear of AIDS, people are once again frequenting the clubs, where patrons pay an entrance fee to have sex in open areas and closed rooms.

Public health officials must balance public protection with civil liberties. To this end, public health laws prohibit sexual activities that pose a high risk of HIV transmission, such as anal intercourse, and compel the clubs to distribute condoms to all patrons.

Do people have the right to risk engaging in such casual sex? Do clubs have an obligation to distribute free condoms? Does the public have any right to close existing clubs and prohibit new ones from opening?

The purpose of schools' education: In New York City, the school board introduced the Rainbow Curriculum to teach tolerance and appreciation for ethnic and cultural diversity. One lesson, prepared by a teacher who is gay, is about tolerance for gay and lesbian parents, and on the recommended reading list for that lesson is the book, *Heather Has Two Mommies,* a story about a child with two lesbian mothers.

After strong parental protest about the lesson and the book, the school board agreed to revise it. What do you think about the issue?

QUESTIONS:

1. Beth's disease precludes her from having orgasms or genital sexual intercourse. Does the fact that she can no longer engage in traditional sexual activity – namely coitus – preclude her from any obligation to continue a sexual relationship with her spouse?

2. Is prostitution a victimless crime? Is there any logic to outlawing prostitution and licensing sex therapists who act as surrogates for their clients?

ENDNOTES

1. Samuel S. Janus and Cynthia L. Janus, *The Janus Report on Sexual Behavior*, John Wiley & Sons, New York, p. 25.

2. Ira L. Reiss, *An End to Shame: Shaping Our Next Sexual Revolution*, Prometheus Books, Buffalo, New York, 1990, p. 121.

3. Janus and Janus, *The Janus Report*, p. 176.

4. About 25% of adult men and 12% of adult women routinely masturbate, though the majority of adults have tried it. Janus and Janus, *The Janus Report,* pp. 30-31; Five to 10% of all Americans are gay or bisexual, Morton Hunt, *Gay,* Farrar, Straus, Giroux, New York, 1987, pp. 105-6.

5. In a 1988 national sample of 18 to 24-year-olds, 40% of the men and 15% of the women had 3 or more partners within the past 12 months; over 80% had at least one partner, Reiss, *An End to Shame*, p. 121.

6. Leslee Welch, *The Complete Book of Sexual Trivia*, Carol Publishing Group, New York, 1992, p. 76.

7. quoted in Lillian B. Rubin, *Erotic Wars,* Harper Collins, New York, 1990, p. 13.

8. For a brief discussion of Catholic sexual ethics, see James P. Hanigan, *What Are They Saying About Sexual Morality?*, Paulist Press, New York, 1982, pp. 18-20. For a discussion about Jewish sexual ethics, see David Biale, *Eros and the Jews*, Basic Books, New York, 1992. And for a source that briefly summarizes all religious veiwpoints on sexuality, see Geoffrey Parrinder, *Sex in the World's Religions*, Oxford University Press, New York, 1980.

9. Hanigan, *What Are They Saying?.*

10. Baile, *Eros and the Jews,* pp. 41-59.

11. For a very brief overview of the entire history of sexual ethics, see Robert Baker and Frederick Elliston, "Introduction," *Philosophy and Sex,* Robert Baker and Frederick Elliston, eds., Prometheus Books, Buffalo, New York, 1984, pp. 11-36.

12. Ira L. Reiss, *Premarital Sexual Standards in America,* The Free Press, New York, 1960, pp. 53-8.

13. Helen E. Fisher, *Anatomy of Love,* W.W. Norton and Co., New York, 1992, pp. 49-51.

14. Reiss, *Premarital Sexual Standards*, p. 56.

15. Ibid., p. 57.

16. An excellent account of religion and sexual behavior in the 19th century is in Peter Garella, *Innocent Ecstasy: How Christianity Gave Ameria an Ethics of Sexual Pleasure,* Oxford University Press, New York, 1985.

17. Garell, *Innocent Ecstasy;* and G.J. Barker-Benfield, *The Horrors of the Half-Known Life: Male Attitudes Toward Women and Sexuality in Nineteenth-Century America,* Harper & Row, New York, 1976.

18. Janus and Janus, *The Janus Report*, pp. 11-12.

19. Ibid., pp. 172-3.

20. Reiss, *An End to Shame*, p. 84.

21. Hunt, *Gay*, pp. 105-6.

22. Kristin Luker, *Abortion & the Politics of Motherhood,* University of California Press, Berkely, California, 1984, p. 94.

23. Rubin, *Erotic Wars*, p. 93.

24. People are more fearful about AIDS and a substantial number are using condoms as a result (80% among homosexual men having anal intercourse, for example). Still, fear of AIDS has not slowed down actual sexual activity in mainstream America, Janus, p. 18; Rubin, p. 79, personal conversation with Jean Burns, Ph.D., Kent State University, Department of Health Education, April 2, 1993, personal interview with Ira Reiss, Ph.D., University of Minnesota, Department of Sociology, April 2, 1993.

25. Hanigan, *What Are They Saying?*, p. 11.

26. Many contemporary theologians are rejecting traditional sexual ethics, including Charles E. Curran, James P. Hanigan, James B. Nelson, Carter Heyward, to name just a few of those prominent on the cutting edge of reform.

27. Findings from the *Girl Scouts Survey on the Beliefs and Moral Vaues of America's Children in 1989* indicate a significant correlation between religiosity and moral certainty and a reverse correlation among adolescents who are not religious.

28. Manis Friedman, *Doesn't Anyone Blush Anymore?* HarperCollins, San Francisco, 1990.

29. For two good discussions on the double standard, see Reiss, *Premarital Sex Standards in America,* pp. 107-116; Rubin, Erotic Wars, pp. 23-29; and Reiss, *An End to Shame,* pp. 151-168.

30. Naomi Wolf, "Feminist Fatale," *The New Republic*, March 26, 1992, p. 24.

31. Ira L. Reiss, *Journey into Sexuality*, Prentice-Hall, Englewood Cliffs, New Jersey, 1986, p. 190-193.

32. Albert D. Klassen, Colin J. Williams, and Eugene E. Levitt, *Sex and Morality in the U.S.*, Wesleyan University Press, Middletown, Connecticut, pp. 137-164; *Erotic Wars,* pp. 60-87.

33. Hunt, *Gay*, p. 195.

34. Hunt, *Gay,* see his chapter on "Straight Gays," pp. 187-220.

35. Richard Wasserstrom, "Is Adultery Immoral?" *Philosophy and Sex*, Robert Baker and Frederick Elliston, eds., Prometheus Books, Buffalo, New York, 1984, p. 97.

36. Personal interview, March 26, 1993.

37. Reiss, *An End to Shame,* pp. 218-19; personal interview with Reiss, April 2, 1993.

38. Reiss, *An End to Shame*, pp. 219-20.

39. Ibid., p. 219.

40. Ibid., pp. 157-8.

41. Ibid, p. 158-161.

42. Cited in Gabrielle Brown, *The New Celibacy,* McGraw-Hill, New York, 1989, p.10; and Norman Hearst and Steven Hully, Preventing the Heterosexual Spread of AIDS, cited in Reiss, *An End to Shame*, p. 124.

43. Reiss, *An End to Shame,* p. 124.)

44. Center for Disease Control Statistics, Atanta, Georgia, telephone interview, March 23, 1993.

45. *New England Journal of Medicine,* May 1990.

46. The Alan Guttmacher Institute Report, November 8, 1990. Available on request from the Institute. Some of the findings also reprinted in Felicity Barringer, "Report Finds 1 in 5 Infected by Viruses Spread Sexually," *New York Times,* April 1, 1993.

47. Ibid.

48. Ibid.

49. Reiss, *An End to Shame,* p. 116.

50. Guttmacher Report .

51. Reiss, *An End to Shame,* p. 125.

52. C. Everett Koop, M.D., "Public Health and Private Ethics," lecture, Minneapolis, October 17, 1986.

53. For a brief overview of medical, legal, ethical, and psychological facts on sexual behavior, see Neville Blakemore & Neville Blakemore, Jr., eds., *The Serious Sides of Sex,* The Nevbet Company, Louisville, Kentucky, 1991., p. 21.

54. For a good account of the history of sodomy laws in the U.S., see Wayne C. Bartee and Alice Fleetwood Bartee, *Litigating Morality,* Praeger, New York, 1992, pp. 31-55; and Richard D. Mohr, Gay Ideas, Beacon Press, Boston, 1992, pp. 54-86.

55. Sissela Bok, *Secrets: On the Ethics of Concealment and Revelation,* Vintage Books, New York, 1989, p. 25.

56. Marty Klein, *Your Sexual Secrets,* E.P. Dutton, New York, 1988, p. 56.

57. Bok, *Secrets,* p. 18.

58. U.S. Burearu of the Census, 1993.

59. Janus and Janus, *The Janus Report,* p. 169; Rubin, *Erotic Wars*, p. 179.

60. Flanigan, What Are They Saying about Sexual Morality?, p. 13.

61. Michael J. Wreen, "What's Really Wrong with Adultery," *The Philosophy of Sex,* 2nd Ed., Alan Soble, ed., Rowman & Littlefield Publishers, *Savage,* Maryland, 1991, pp. 179-186.

62. Stanley Grenz, *Sexual Ethics*, Word Publishing,

Dallas, 1990, p. 87.

63. Bonnie Steinbock, "Adultery," *The Philosophy of Sex,* pp. 191.

64. Rubin, pp. 182-183; Klassen, et. al. *Sex and Morality in the U.S.,* p. 391.

65. Janus and Janus, *The Janus Report,* p. 169.

66. Wreen, *"What's Really Wrong with Adultery?,"* p. 186.

67. Baker and Elliston, pp. 15-16.

68. That Richard Taylor finds a "just" way to conduct a love affair sounds light-hearted at first; his theory is published in a well-respected anthology of philosophical essays Richard Taylor, "The Ethics of Having Love Affairs," *Philosophy and Sex,* Robert Baker and Frederick Elliston, eds., pp. 71-92.

69. Ibid., p. 92.

70. Peggy Vaughan, *The Monogamy Myth,* Newmarket Press, New York, 1989, p. 7.

71. Brown, *The New Celibacy,* pp. 6-7. Among homosexuals, 10% may be celibate today.

72. For an overview of celibacy through history, see Brown, pp. 41-66.

73. Ibid., p. 152.

74. Joan Avan and Diana Walty, *Celibate Wives,* Contemporary Books, Chicago, 1992, pp. 12-13.

75. Gallup Poll, 1989.

76. Dennis Prager, "Faithful Unto Office," *National Review,* July 6, 1992, pp. 47.

77. Bok, Secrets, pp. 284, 287.

78. "Take an Honest Look," pamphlet (Columbus Commission on Ethics and Values, Columbus, Ohio, 1989, cited in Susan Terkel, *Ethics,* Lodestar, New York, 1992, p. 89.

79. Katha Politt, "Clinton's Affair?" *The Nation,* February 24, 1992, p. 221.

80. Hunt, *Gay,* pp. 12-13. Some gay activists claim that there are more than two to three times the number of gay people. Furthermore, more Americans have reported homosexual experience. In the Janus survey, respondents were asked whether they had at least one homosexual experience. 22% of the men and 17% of the women said yes, Janus Report, p. 53.

81. Estimates vary regarding the number of gays who keep their homosexuality a secret, but they usually vary between two-thirds to nine-tenths, according to Hunt, *Gay,* p. 90; For an excellent discussion of the ethics of outing, see Mohr, Gay Ideas, pp. 11-48.

82. Reported by Alexander Cockburn, "Beat the Devil: The Old In/Out," *The Nation,* August 26/Sept. 2, 1991, p. 220.

83. "Schlafly's Son: Out of the GOP Closet," *Newsweek*, Sept. 28, 1992, p. 18.

84. Mohr, *Gay Ideas,* p. 12

85. Ibid., p. 11.

86. Andrew Sullivan, "Washington Diarist: Sleeping with the Enemy," *The New Republic,* Sept. 9, 1991, p. 43.

87. Mohr, *Gay Ideas,* p. 12.

88. Paul Monette, "The Politics of Silence," *New York Times*, March 7, 1993, Op-Ed.

89. Quoted in Nancy Gibbs, "Marching Out of The Closet," *Time,* Aug. 9, 1991, p. 14.

90. *New York Times*, January 29, 1993, p. A7 (National).

91. Janus and Janus, p. 227.

92. Twenty-five year study by former priest, Richard Sipe.

93. Welch, *Sexual Trivia*, p. 71.

Chapter 10

Emily Baker

PORNOGRAPHY

"What is essential is invisible to the eye."
— Saint-Exupery, *The Little Prince*

"So far, about morality, I know only that what is moral is what you feel good after, and what is immoral is what you feel bad after."
— Ernest Hemingway

"Seven sins ... (The second is) pleasure without conscience."
— Mahatma Gandhi

Why discuss the subject of pornography? To some, all pornography is obscene and should be banned; to others, pornography is okay as long as it is available only to "consenting adults"; to still others, the only limitations should be those set by individuals governing their own conduct. Some find aspects of the subject too embarrassing even for open discussion; for a few the subject may open old wounds and be painful. Whatever your view, the subject has hounded society for many years. It has been central to a number of criminal cases, and the topic of two National commissions, numerous U.S. Supreme Court cases and congressional proposals. All this suggests it would be quite an omission not to discuss a subject so rich in public moral discourse.

Is pornography harmful or just distasteful? To some, pornography is harmless and should be protected by the First Amendment's "freedom of expression"; to others, it is both harmful and distasteful, degrading to women, and dangerous to society. What are your views about pornography? Is it wrong? Is it right? Should it be banned, censored, regulated or left alone?

Emily Baker, M.S. Criminal Justice, University of Southern Mississippi, and J.D. Mississippi College School of Law, is Instructor-in-Charge of the St. Petersburg Junior College Ethics Department and instructor of Applied Ethics.

Is it necessary to view pornography to discuss it? Certainly not. A person need not have gone to Vietnam to know it was a dubious war. We are able to study thousands of subjects without actually experiencing the presence of them. There is ample information in this chapter and all of the related readings to gain knowledge of pornography, and no one should infer from the existence of this chapter that use of pornography is suggested or implied as a necessary part of its study.

For some, if one is to give credence to studies such as that of Dr. James McGough from the University of California-Irvine, there is a danger of pornography users becoming addicted to pornography. This comes about, it is thought, because the body produces a chemical, epinephrine, which locks into the brain the experiences one has when one is sexually aroused; these remain and we continue to feed these experiences into the mind creating a need for additional activity. Users of pornography then move from casual use, to addiction, to acting out their fantasy through anti-social behavior. [1]

The study concludes that just as one does not know when the first drink is taken, if there is within oneself a predisposition to alcoholism leading to life as an alcoholic, so too does one not know if he is among those persons whose viewing of pornography will lead to addiction, unusual sexual behavior, perhaps even to sexual molestation. Sex is everywhere in today's society and pornography is sex in raw depiction. The U.S. Supreme Court recognized society's interest when it stated that sex is "a great and mysterious motive force in human life that has indisputably been a subject of absorbing interest to mankind throughout the ages; it is one of the vital problems of human interest and public concern." [2]

Here we will explain the history of pornography as it relates to freedom of expression, report results of studies (including those of two national commissions), consider the views of feminist and other groups, and ponder information both pro and con, so that you may use your critical thinking skills to reach your own moral/ethical decisions on this contemporary subject.

A note of caution: Words not normally used in polite society are workaday terms of the pornography industry and those who must deal with it. While they may not be terms you would wish to use in conversation, they reflect the content of pornography and the way it is described by law enforcement, the courts and medicine.

FREEDOM OF EXPRESSION

"Congress shall make no law ... abridging the freedom of speech or of the press ... "[3] These words, found in the First Amendment to our United States Constitution, create "freedom of expression" as one of the basic tenets of our democratic form of government.

Is this concept of "freedom of expression" an absolute? Is the phrase "Congress shall make no law" to be taken literally? Those who speak in defense of pornography often emphasize that they are defending First Amendment rights rather than pornographic content; therefore, the issue of "freedom of expression" must be examined in any meaningful discussion of pornography.

THE ORIGIN OF CENSORSHIP

Censorship – the official restriction of speech, writings or visual expression – comes into play when such forms of expression are thought to harm the public morals or public good. Its roots date back to ancient China and Egypt where official views were usually enforced in the name of politics and religion.

In the West, people have put great weight upon the authority of the written word. The British writer, Chaucer, said in 1380, "What people cannot know from experience, they assume on the basis of authority."[4] In Europe, books were costly, rare, and available primarily to the literate and wealthy. This exclusivity went hand in hand with considerable freedom of expression. However, in 15th century Europe, with the advent of the printing press, books became more readily available and this medium was used to exploit what aristocrats might call the baser side of life – the lower appetites of mankind.

As more people learned to read, both the Roman Church and the government began to be concerned about literary content and its effects on the new class of readers. As a result, there were often two publications of a writing – one an original uncut edition, expensive and available for the aristocrats, while the other was a more delicately worded, less expensive version for mass production.

To keep books "pure" for all of society became the rationale for censorship to be applied to "evil" and to "obscenity." The notion was to protect the minds of new readers from exposure to such evil. Several factors led to this concern for purity: The rise of evangelical forms of religion with strict beliefs, especially as to the role of women in the church; the Industrial Revolution, which brought men together in the workplace and left women alone in the home; and concern for the larger reading public who would be influenced by what they were to read. [5]

"Lord Campbell's Act," a bill passed by the British Parliament in 1857, allowed for warrants to be issued, followed by search for and seizure of obscene writings, pictures, drawings or obscene representations that were being held for either sale, distribution, or gain. [7] And so the move began to protect against obscenity in society and culture.

An English physician, Dr. Bowdler, began a crusade to protect readers from indelicate material by "purifying" literature – removing or changing words with sexual connotation. He said, "If any word or expression is of such a nature that the first impression which it excites is an impression of obscenity, that word ought not be spoke, or written, or printed; and if printed, it ought to be erased." [8]

The Bowdlers became so well known for their expurgation efforts on published works that a word – bowdlerized – was coined to describe their work. Even the *Holy Bible*, revered by many as the inspired word of God, written by saints and prophets, was not to escape. It was bowdlerized as passages referring to homosexuality and incest were deleted. [6]

For a time, America followed the expurgation idea. Because the U.S. did not have much in the way of notable literature, early efforts were aimed at dictionaries. In 1806, one of those responsible was the eminent Noah Webster, who said, "There is not a vocabulary of the English language so free from local, vulgar, and obscene words as mine."[9] Among the more notable works expurgated was the autobiography of Benjamin Franklin.

A United States Tariff Act was passed in 1842, which prohibited the importation from other countries of all art and literature considered indecent and obscene. Further, in 1865, the United States Congress prohibited the distribution of obscene material through the United States mail. Publishers during this period often took it upon themselves to keep their products "pure" and librarians strictly policed their shelves in order to ban all immoral books. Dr. Bowdler and his work impressed a young New Yorker named Anthony Comstock who, incensed that police were lax in enforcing existing laws, helped to found New York's Society for the Suppression of Vice and eventually became its director.

Comstock worked ardently to ban obscenity, stating: "Lust defiles the body, debauches the imagination, corrupts the will, destroys the memory, sears the conscience, hardens the heart, and damns the soul."[10] Comstock and his society joined with the YMCA in a successful effort to have federal laws enacted that allowed publishers and dealers of pornography to be prosecuted. Changes in the views of society led to promulgation of state laws restricting obscene expression. In addition, the Comstock Act was passed in 1873, strengthening restrictions as to the use of the mail for pornography and obscenity. Comstock was named as Special Agent for the postal department, with responsibility for policing the mails and bringing charges for all mail violations. He filed case after case and was extremely successful. Claiming to have destroyed some 4-million "obscene" pictures as well as some 50 tons of "obscene" books, he was to live to see attitudes begin to relax and his cause to lose its momentum. Comstock's work nevertheless led to his being recognized as "a benefactor and hero" for his work against obscenity by the *New York Times* upon his death in 1915. [11]

Even with increasing public acceptance of obscenity, restrictions on freedom of expression continue to this day. There are limitations on freedom of expression – limitations where speech might cause a "clear and present danger," as in the proverbial example of "yelling fire in a crowded theater" or breaching the national security, especially in time of war. So, too, do we see specific prohibitions in statutes concerning libel and slander, perjury, misrepresentation in advertising, conspiracy, and other words that provoke lawsuits. These are discussed in more detail in Chapter 18, while this chapter focuses on restrictions of the "obscene."

Just what is obscenity? What forms of expression resulted in censorship in Europe and the United States? How was and is obscenity defined? Can it be defined? How have the courts expanded or restricted the definitions as they apply to pornography? What interest groups have advanced their beliefs regarding pornography and why? Answering these questions charts our path through this chapter.

DEFINITIONS

"Pornography" – the depiction of erotic behavior *intended* to cause or causing sexual desire or excitement – derives from Greek words meaning "writing about whores." The *World Book Dictionary* defines pornography as "obscene writings, or pictures."[12] Obscenity has Latin roots meaning "offending modesty or decency; impure; filthy; vile."[13] Pornography has been present in society throughout recorded history. Drawings yet reflecting sexual activity were discovered on the excavated walls of the ancient city of Pompeii. Early Greek and Roman writings and art objects depicted then-current sexual practices including the use by adult males of young males for sexual pleasure. Oriental art was renowned for its sexually explicit depictions of the various positions of intercourse, particularly in pictures and delicate jade carvings.

Yet, to this day, pornography raises moral and ethical issues in society and continues to be a frequently litigated issue. Through the years the rulings of the United States Supreme Court have changed, though perhaps not as drastically as views in the general society.

Your own perspective may be colored by the way in which you were first introduced to pornography. *Was it presented as exciting – something adults got to see but children didn't, something "macho" to do, a movie viewed from an adult collection without its owner's knowledge? Was it presented as something lacking good taste, a terrible act of sin, causing you to feel uncomfortable and guilty?*

Each of us is a product of our own environment and experience which influence our perspective. We then are responsible for the moral environment we pass on to our children. *What will be that moral environment as it pertains to pornography? What perspective will pass on to them?*

Justice Potter Stewart once addressed perspectives when he said, "A book worthless to me may convey something of value to my neighbor, and so it is with pornography, for what is abhorrent to me may well be exciting to my neighbor." [14]

BRITISH LEGAL HISTORY – PORNOGRAPHY

Our own country has perspectives and roots deeply embedded in the British environment of our forefathers. The history of pornography in our own society can best be tracked through the manner in which the courts have acted. Because our law has its roots in English law, it is necessary to examine the background of pornography within the English system. Early cases were handled in the ecclesiastical (church) courts, because they were matters considered to be a violation of "Church law" and included cursing, performing obscene songs, poems or plays. Punishment often was excommunication from the Church of England.

There are two English cases that greatly affected pornography in the early days of our Country. The first (Curl) transferred pornography from the church to civil jurisdiction – indeed, the criminal court system. The second (Hicklin) set out the first "test" of obscenity for censorship.

In *Crown vs. Edmund Curl* (1727) [15], the judge established by common law (court-declared law rather than that set by statute) a "misdemeanor (lesser) offense" for the publication of obscene material and found the defendant Edmund Curl guilty for publishing an obscene book entitled *The Nun In Her Smock*. Curl was required to pay a fine and serve a period of time in the "pillory." The Lord Chief Justice said, If it (the obscene material) tends to disturb the civil order of society, I think it is a temporal (secular rather than religious) offense." [16]

Thus, pornography began its journey as a "criminal act" and this view was reinforced by Parliament with the passage of "Lord Campbell's Act" in 1857 which created a statutory violation for possession of pornography.[17]

THE HICKLIN TEST

Queen vs. Hicklin (1868) is the landmark English obscenity case. Henry Scott, a respectable citizen and member of the Protestant Electoral Union, an organization active in an attack upon the Jesuits, had seized from him 250 copies of a booklet. The booklets were ordered and destroyed by a local Justice as authorized under Lord Campbell's Act.[18] However, an appeal was taken and Benjamin Hicklin, the Recorder, directed the booklets be returned pending an opinion from the Queen's Bench, the high Court of England. Hicklin determined the booklet's purpose was not to "corrupt the morals of youth" but was instead an attack upon the Roman Catholic Church. The High Court disagreed with Hicklin and denied the appeal: "It is quite certain that it would suggest to the minds of the young of either sex, or even to persons of more advanced years, thoughts of impure and libidinous character ... the work itself is, in every sense of the term, an obscene publication, ... as the law of England does not allow for any obscene publication, such publication is indictable." [19]

The Hicklin Test was then set forth by the Queen's Bench: "The test of obscenity is this, whether the tendency of the matter charged as obscenity is to deprave and corrupt those whose minds are open to such immoral influences, and into whose hands a publication of this sort may fall." [20]

AMERICAN LEGAL HISTORY

The American colonies were not without their own restrictions even before Curl. There had been a ban on all obscene materials in Massachusetts since 1712. [21] The City of Boston was to become well known for its censorship efforts. After the Revolution, the Constitution separated Church and State (1788) and the Bill of Rights came into being with its First Amendment Protection (1791). The Curl obscenity offense became embodied in our common law and at the time of the American Revolution was recognized by the Commonwealth of Pennsylvania.

In the *Commonwealth of Pennsylvania vs. Jesse Sharpless* (1815), [22] Pennsylvania applied, for the first time, the common-law misdemeanor offense doctrine established in Curl. Sharpless, along with five others, was indicted for charging money while exhibiting one "certain lewd, wicked, scandalous, infamous, and obscene painting ... to the manifest corruption and subversion of youth and other citizens ... "

The case reflects only that the painting depicted a man "in an obscene, impudent and indecent posture with a woman." [23] The question before the court was whether or not this conduct was a violation of the common-law offense. Judge Yeates applied the doctrine, found the defendants guilty, and stated: "No man is permitted to corrupt the morals of the people. Secret poison cannot be thus disseminated." [24]

EROSION OF HICKLIN

Hicklin reflected a "class" distinction that was apparent when it was applied in the case of *United States vs. Clarke* (1889).[25] Dr. Clarke wrote a pamphlet allegedly covering "venereal, sexual, nervous, and special diseases." He was indicted and was brought before the court for sending this "scientific" treatise through the mail.

The judge gave the Hicklin test to the jury in his charge: "You must consider carefully the contents ... and then the effect that the reading of such contents would naturally have on the class of persons in to whose hands this publication might fall, whose thoughts, emotions, or desires are liable to be influenced or directed by reading matter such as the publication contained. There is to be found in every community a class of people ... so intelligent ... that their minds are not liable to be affected .... There is another large class to be found in every community – the young and immature, the ignorant, and those who are sensually inclined – those who are liable to be influenced to their harm .... " [26]

The jury using the Hicklin test found Dr. Clarke guilty, so justice was determined not using the general "average man" standard but on a standard set by "youth, immaturity and ignorance."

In the *United States vs. Kennerley* (1913) decision,[27] Judge Learned Hand challenged the "Hicklin Test," saying: "I scarcely think that they would forbid all which might corrupt the most corruptible, or that society is prepared to accept as its own limitations those which may perhaps be necessary to the weakest of its members." [28]

So began a pattern of erosion of the "Hicklin Test." *Halsey vs. New York Society for Suppression of Vice* (1922) [29] was an action filed before the court to ban the English translation of Theophile

Gautier's *Mademoiselle de Maupin* as obscene and indecent. The society had marked passages in the text to illustrate the portions they considered to be obscene and in violation of the law. Gautier was considered one of France's great writers of the 19th century, so the New York court admitted evidence bolstering his reputation and allowed literary experts to testify as to their opinions. The jury was instructed to consider the book as a whole, charging: "No work may be judged from a selection of such paragraphs alone ... The book ... must be considered *broadly as a whole*." [30] This represented a further erosion of the "Hicklin Test."

In *United States vs. One Book Called "Ulysses"*(1933),[31] James Joyce's *Ulysses* was brought before the United States District Court which found it not to be "obscene" within the meaning of the statute concerning the importation of obscenity from another nation.

District Judge Woolsey in reaching his decision used a new standard, that of someone with "average sex instincts," saying: "In many places it seems to me to be disgusting, but although it contains many words usually considered dirty, I have not found ... dirt for dirt's sake ... and ... where a book claims to be obscene it must first be determined whether the intent with which it was written was what is called, according to the usual phrase, pornographic; that is, written for the purpose of exploiting obscenity ... in Ulysses, in spite of its unusual frankness, I do not detect anywhere the leer of the sensualist. I hold, therefore, that it is not pornographic." [32]

The case was appealed, and the decision was upheld by a United States Circuit Court of Appeals. Circuit Judge Augustus Hand said "The book as a whole has a realism characteristic of the present age ... as a whole it is not pornographic, and, while in not a few spots it is coarse, blasphemous, and obscene, ... it does not, in our opinion, tend to promote lust ... (and) is so little erotic in its result that it does not fall within the forbidden class."[33] There were now two ways to reason: either the "class distinction" of Hicklin or else the "average sex instincts" test of Ulysses and the United States Courts were split in their choice of which standard to use.

THE ROTH TEST

In 1957 the Supreme Court had the opportunity to resolve the issue and establish its own "test" for obscenity in *Roth vs. United States* (1957) [34]. A certain Mr. Roth ran a publication and sales office in New York City using mail circulars to advertise and sell his products. Roth was convicted on four counts of a 26 count indictment for "mailing obscene literature." His conviction was affirmed by the United State Circuit Court of Appeals, and he then appealed directly to the United State Supreme Court.

The Constitutional question presented to the court was "Whether the Federal Obscenity Statute[35] violated the provision of the First Amendment ." Here, for the first time, the Supreme Court specifically held that *"Obscenity is not within the area of constitutionally protected speech."* [36] "Obscenity," then, seems to lie outside the protection of the First Amendment and is, therefore, an area where Congress or – through application of the Fourteenth Amendment – any of the states, can enforce regulations.

The new test established in Roth is stated as follows: "Whether to the average person, applying contemporary community standards, the dominant theme of the material, taken as a whole, appeals to the prurient (wanton) interest." [37] The material should continue to be *utterly without any redeeming social importance* in order to be excluded from First Amendment protection. Little did the court realize that pornographers would seize this phrase and include "moral" lessons, quotes from great literary works, or medical information in order to qualify as having "redeeming social importance."

The community standard was considered to be a "national" standard. The Supreme Court was fearful that unless a national standard was maintained, we would have in each state a separate interpretation of the First Amendment . However, not all Justices were pleased with the new test. Justice Harlan in writing a separate opinion in this case said, "the court merely assimilates the various tests into one indiscriminate potpourri."[38]

As the 1960s brought increased interest in civil rights and relaxation of many social mores, the court attempted to keep the "Roth" test, and not further define obscenity. In *Jacobelles vs. Ohio*, [39] a 1964 case, Justice Potter Stewart admitted, "I shall not today attempt to define the kind of material ... embraced ... but, I know it when I see it."

In *"Memoirs vs. Massachusetts"* (1965), [40] the Massachusetts Supreme Court found *Fanny Hill* obscene stating: "(That) this book has some minimal literary value does not mean it is of any social importance. We do not interpret ... (Roth) test as requiring that a book which appeals to prurient interest and is patently offensive must be unqualifiedly worthless before it can be obscene." [41]

The United States Supreme Court said "reversal is required because the lower court misinterpreted the social value" test. [42] It was clear in *Memoirs* that the Supreme Court intended for the "Roth Test" to be strictly followed. Yet, that same day the Supreme Court itself allowed some latitude in another pornography case.

In *Ginsberg vs. United States* (1966),[43] a lower Pennsylvania court had allowed the way in which publications were advertised to determine the publications' "appeal to the prurient interest." The High Court ruled: "We agree that the question of obscenity may include consideration of the setting in which the publications were presented as an aid to determining the question of obscenity ... there was abundant evidence to show that each of the accused publications was originated or sold as stock in trade of the sordid business of pandering – the business of purveying textual or graphic matter openly advertised to appeal to the erotic interest of their customers ... The 'leer of the sensualist' also permeates the advertising for the three publications." [44] Ginsberg's conviction seems to be based not so much on the obscene content of the publication but on the *manner in which he advertised* his product as obscene material.

In 1969, the court in *Redrup vs. New York* [45] recognized its inability to reach a viable definition of obscene and so ruled that when a majority of the court found material not to be obscene, such material would be protected by the First Amendment . Without clear definition the court found itself having more and more obscenity cases to "Redrup" (to decide under the Redrup guidelines).

Through the late 1960s, cases before the Supreme Court seemed to deal with the *public aspects* of pornography. What about a person's *private use* of pornography? Does an adult have a right to own and view pornography within the privacy of his/her own home? The court had the opportunity to address these issues in *Stanley vs. Georgia* (1969). [46] Stanley, a Georgia bookmaker whose home was being searched for gambling materials, was arrested after his private pornographic movies where found. Even though the reels where in his own home, he was charged with "possession of obscene films." He was convicted in the Georgia court and appealed to the United States Supreme Court which agreed with Stanley, saying: "Whatever may be the justification for other statues regulating obscenity, we do not think they reach into the privacy of one's own home ... a State has no business telling a man, sitting alone in his own house, what books he may read or what films he may watch."[47]

If, under the right to privacy, individuals have a right to possess pornography in their own homes, then where and how are they to obtain it? Does this right of possession expand into a right to advertise, sell, or produce pornography? Did Stanley, by raising these questions, add more ambiguity to the obscenity issue? How far will the Supreme Court take the Stanley view?

The Supreme Court under Chief Justice Earl Warren was reputed to be liberal in its views, to be concerned with extending basic fairness to all, and it was under this court that many of these decisions concerning obscenity had been rendered. The court itself was to undergo changes beginning with the appointment by President Nixon in 1969 of conservative Warren Burger as Chief Justice of the Supreme Court, the first of Nixon's four appointments. The makeup of the new court would result in a more conservative and restrictive view of pornography.

The "new" Supreme Court continued to struggle with obscenity cases and with their failure to arrive at a clear definition of obscenity. In 1981's *The Brethren* [48], authors Bob Woodward and Scott Armstrong noted that each Justice seemed to have his own view of material to be prohibited and his own definition of what was "obscene."

U.S. SUPREME COURT MEMBERS' VIEWS

Here are the individual views on pornography and obscenity of the then-members of the U.S. Supreme Court as reported in *The Brethren:*

> **Justice Black** – An absolutist who thought there should be no exception to the first amendment. Found it impossible to define.
> **Justice Blackmun** – Loathed it, found it distasteful and degrading to women
> **Justice Brennan** – Thought obscenity the one type of expression that should not be protected. Children and unwilling viewers should be protected. Was obscene if there were erections – penetration and oral sex were all right only if there no erections.
> **Justice Burger** – Loathed it, thought local standards should apply. Thought states could regulate obscene acts: normal or perverted sex acts (actual or simulated), masturbation, excretion, and display of genitals.
> **Justice Douglas** – Said it was impossible to define and should never have been declared an exception. Supported Stanley's privacy doctrine.
> **Justice Harlan** – Uncertain. During many of the cases, portrayed actions had to be described for his comments due to his sight problems.
> **Justice Marshall** – Thought it primarily a question of personal privacy. More amused than shocked.
> **Justice Powell** – Shocked at films, favored expansion of Stanley privacy doctrine.
> **Justice Rehnquist** – His opinion did not go so far as to say "any books without pictures could not be ruled obscene," although others seem to be willing to go that far.
> **Justice Stewart** – Could not define it but said he knew it when he saw it. Had his own "Casablanca" test. Thought only "hard core" should be defined obscene.
> **Justice White** – Should be able to define obscene acts so long as the acts were "hard core" and appealed to "prurient interest;" he allowed no erections, penetration, anal or oral sex.

In 1973, the court was scheduled to hear a number of pornography cases. Within the court there was a split in reasoning as to obscenity. Should the standard of "utterly without redeeming social value" remain? Should the absolutist (no laws) view prevail? Should there be *no* restrictions except for juvenile and unconsenting adults? Should the Stanley "right to privacy doctrine" be extended? [49]

Among the cases reflecting these different views was *Paris Adult Theater I* (1973) [50], in which the State of Georgia sought to prohibit the theater from showing two films, both allegedly obscene, where the entrance to the theater was inoffensive, and the sign stated "Mature Feature Films," with warnings as to "nudity" and "age" requirements.

The judge, at the time of trial in lower court, assumed "obscenity established," yet he dismissed the complaint.[51] The Georgia Supreme Court reversed the lower court's decision holding: "The films in this case leave little to the imagination. It is plain what they purport to depict, that is, conduct of the most salacious character. We hold that these films are also hard core pornography, and the showing of such films should have been enjoined since their exhibition is not protected by the First Amendment ." [52]

The United States Supreme Court in a 5-4 decision held that the Georgia Supreme Court properly reversed the original decision and Chief Justice Burger writing the majority opinion stated: "The States have the power to make a morally neutral judgment that public exhibition of obscene material ... has a tendency to injure the community as a whole, to endanger the public safety, or to jeopardize, ... the States' right ... to maintain a decent society ... To summarize, we have today reaffirmed that obscene material has no protection under the First Amendment ... We have directed our holdings, not at thoughts or speech, but at depiction and description of specifically defined sexual conduct that States may regulate within limits designed to prevent infringement of First Amendment rights. We have also reaffirmed ... that commerce in obscene material is unprotected by any constitutional doctrine of privacy ... In this case we hold that the States have a legitimate interest in regulating commerce in obscene material in places of public accommodation, including so-called "adult" theaters from which minors are excluded." [53]

In his dissenting opinion, Justice Douglas said: "I see no constitutional basis for fashioning a rule that makes a publisher, producer, bookseller, librarian, or movie house (operator) criminally responsible, when he or she fails to take affirmative steps to protect the consumer against literature or books offensive to those who temporarily occupy the seats of the mighty ... " [54]

Justice Earl Brennan, joined by Justice Potter Stewart and Justice Thurgood Marshall, also dissented, stating: "... At least in the absence of distribution to juveniles or obtrusive exposure to unconsenting adults, the First and Fourteenth Amendments prohibit the state and federal governments from attempting wholly to suppress sexually oriented materials on the basis of their allegedly 'obscene' contents ... " [55]

The landmark decision of *Miller vs. California* (1973), [56] another 5-4 decision, was handed down the very same day. Miller was convicted of violations of obscenity laws for mailing unsolicited and sexually explicit brochures, which included group pictures with two or more men and women (some with aroused genitalia), engaged in actual sex acts, all in order to advertise an adult film and adult books.

His conviction was affirmed by California's appellate court, and Chief Justice Warren Burger of the United States Supreme Court, in writing the majority opinion of the court announced: "Apart from the initial formulation in the Roth case ... no majority of the court has at any given time been able to agree on a standard to determine what constitutes obscene, pornographic material subject to regulation under the States' police power ... We have seen 'a variety of views among the members of the court unmatched in any other course of constitutional adjudication' ... This is not remarkable, for in the area of freedom of speech and press the courts must always remain sensitive to any infringement ... This much has been categorically settled by the court, that obscene material is unprotected by the First Amendment ... The First and Fourteenth Amendments have never been treated as absolutes." [57]

THE MILLER TEST

The court recognized the danger in regulating all expression and so limited regulations to those works that depicted and/or described sexual conduct. The new "Miller Test" is then set forth: "The basic guidelines for the trier of fact must be: (a) whether 'the average person, applying contemporary community standards,' would find that the work, taken as a whole, appeals to the prurient interest; (b) whether the work depicts or describes, in a patently offensive way, sexual conduct specifically defined by the applicable state law; and (c) whether the work, taken as a whole, lacks serious literary, artistic, political, or scientific value." [58]

The court would no longer consider the "utterly without redeeming social value" standard but did go on to give to the states guidelines for activity that could be regulated, including: (a) "Patently offensive representations or descriptions of ultimate sexual acts, normal or perverted, actual or simulated. (b) Patently offensive representations or descriptions of masturbation, excretory functions, and lewd exhibition of the genitals." [59] The court went on to say: "Sex and nudity may not be exploited without limit by films or pictures exhibited or sold in places of public accommodation any more than live sex and nudity .... " [60]

So we see Miller reflecting "Contemporary Community Standards" – local standards, rather than one national standard – and a "lack of serious literary, artistic, political or scientific" value used rather than the "utterly without redeeming social value" as put forth in *Memoirs*. The court changed the "Community Standards" stating: "People in different States vary in their tastes and attitudes, and this diversity is not to be strangled by the absolutism of imposed uniformity ... " [61]

Burger denounced the attitude of the dissenting justices: "The protection given speech and press was fashioned to assure unfettered interchange of ideas for bringing about the political and social changes designed by the people ... But the public portrayal of hard core sexual conduct for its own sake, and for the ensuing commercial gain, is a different matter." [62]

Justice Douglas in his dissenting opinion stated: "There are no constitutional guidelines for deciding what is and what is not 'obscene' ...." He added that "any regime of censorship should only be adopted by a constitutional amendment and not by court decisions ... "[63] Under Miller we see the court move from the early Hicklin test to the present contemporary test that gives more power to the States.

That the framers of our Constitution intended "freedom of expression" to exist in order to allow for exchange of ideas and even for political debate goes without question. However, at the time of the Constitution's framing, the camera had not been invented, much less the movie camera or home video. Not in their wildest dreams could those men have envisioned pornography as it is today, so the question remains: *Just how far should freedom of expression be extended? Should there be special protections for special classes of people?*

SPECIAL PROTECTION OF MINORS

By the late 1970s, states that continued to pass statutes regulating pornography were now following the Supreme Court Guidelines set forth in *Miller*. In their efforts to prevent pornography from reaching unconsenting adults and minors, many states, counties or cities passed "behind the counter laws," requiring stores to place "adult" publications in a location where they could not be viewed by minors and where they were not available for purchase without a specific request from an adult.

The court had the opportunity to review "obscenity" in a different medium, that of radio broadcasting and its relationship to minors as part of the listening audience when in 1978 it reviewed the case of *Federal Communications Commission (FCC) vs. Pacific Foundation* [64] where a New York radio station, as part of an afternoon program, broadcast a comedy routine entitled "Dirty Words" by George Carlin. A complaint filed by a listener brought an FCC ruling that the words used were "patently offensive," depicted sexual activities in an offensive manner, and included "indecent" language, all at a time in the afternoon when children were easily able to listen.

The Supreme Court ruled that the "FCC was warranted in concluding that indecent language was used ... " [65] The court took the position that the most limited First Amendment protection applied to broadcasting because radio invaded the privacy of the home where children had access to the broadcast and all that it contained. It was impossible, the court found, to completely avoid those programs that were patently offensive when the simple turn of a dial would place one within hearing of a broadcast already in progress.

This case illustrates the Supreme Court's continued concern about protecting minors from obscene materials. Yet today, FCC regulations have been relaxed and "indecent" materials may be broadcast from midnight to 6 a.m., times when children should have limited access.

The Supreme Court, for the first time, directly addressed the issue of child pornography in the case of *New York vs. Ferber* (1982).[66] Ferber, a New York bookstore owner, was convicted for selling films depicting male minors under the age of 16 masturbating, in violation of a law prohibiting "knowingly promoting a sexual performance by a child ... by distributing material which depicts such a performance." The New York Court of Appeals reversed the lower court decision based on the statute's failure to include a clear obscenity standard.

The Supreme Court held that the statute did not violate the First Amendment as applied to the States through the Fourteenth Amendment and recognized that *the exploitation of children through child pornography was a serious national problem*, and there was compelling interest to protect children, therefore states were entitled to more leeway in the regulation of child pornography.

The court stated: "The state's interest in 'safeguarding the physical and psychological well-being of a minor is compelling' ... (courts) have sustained legislation aimed at protecting the physical and emotional well-being of youth even when the laws have operated in the sensitive area of constitutionally protected rights ... virtually, all of the States and the United States have passed legislation proscribing the production of or otherwise combatting 'child pornography.'" [67] The court found that states could go further than *Miller* in order to protect children, saying: "Recognizing and classifying child pornography as a category of material outside the protection of the First Amendment is not incompatible with our earlier decision."[68]

The United States Supreme Court made clear in *Ferber* that children should be protected and gave states the power to do so. New technology brought a new avenue of pornography, and a new temptation to children – "Dial-A-Porn." In *Information Providers' Coalition vs. FCC*(1991), [69] a petition for review of a FCC order regulating access to "Dial-A-Porn" was filed. The petition was denied by the Ninth Court of Appeals where the Circuit Judge held that "an effective means of limiting minors' access to dial-a-porn services must be instituted," [70] and the Supreme Court denied the Petition for review, thereby adding additional protections for minors. One study of children ages 10-15 who were involved with dial-a-porn showed that the children, both male and female, became hooked on phone sex and continued calling until parents were finally made aware through large bills. Several cases reflected more than 300 calls and even though the study was conducted some 18 months to two years later, the children were still *ashamed, felt guilty and were able to recall the content* of the messages. The degree of harm to these children, if any, cannot be determined fully for some years.[71]

ADDITIONAL APPLICATIONS

Freedom of expression continues to be an issue. In the past few years, there have been attempts to close an exhibit of photographer Robert Mapplethorpe because it was "obscene"; and to challenge the National Endowment of the Arts for refusing grants to controversial artists such as Karen Finley (who, as part of her performance, spreads excrement over her body), claiming that such rejection violated NEA's guidelines and reflected a "political rather than artistic" basis for rejection. In addition, there have been efforts to secure labeling for musical lyrics (led, in part, by Tipper Gore, wife of Vice President Al Gore) in order for parents to monitor recordings available to children and to themselves ban obscene recordings.

Florida's Supreme Court declared as obscene the "2-Live Crew" recording, *As Nasty As they Wanna Be,* [72] and a store owner was convicted for selling the album. However, the finding of "obscene" was overturned by the United States Eleventh Circuit Court of Appeals, the circuit handling Florida appellate matters. It declared that the "Miller" test requirements had not been fulfilled in the lower court with respect to a finding of "no serious artistic value."

Cable TV has allowed more persons to view pornography – particularly children and adolescent viewers causing them to be exposed to all types of sexual attitudes, to actual or simulated sexual performances, and certainly to explicit sexual practices on television – sexual practices that they might otherwise never encounter. Many of these films are unrated and while many appear in late evening hours, they are being viewed by children. Special adult video stores, adult sections in regular video stores, adult sections of book stores, and adult movie houses can all be easily located. So, in spite of the long history of court cases, the pornography business flourishes.

How extensive is pornography? How harmful is pornography to society? Does the explicit sex shown on TV influence societal attitudes? Does the sexually explicit material desensitize a person's view of sexuality? Who, if anyone, benefits from pornography? What do studies about pornography reveal?

GOVERNMENTAL STUDIES

The United States Congress, concerned over the national problem of pornography, established in October 1967 *A Commission on Obscenity & Pornography* [73] charged with the responsibility to study the causal relationship between pornographic and obscene materials and antisocial behavior, including juvenile delinquency. The Commission, appointed by President Lyndon Johnson, was to report its findings and recommendations to Congress as to how the nation should deal with pornography.

After two years of intensive work, 80 studies, countless meetings, voluminous testimony, and endless review of research, at a cost of approximately $2-million, a multi-volume report was completed and forwarded to Congress in 1970. [74] L. Kupperstein and W.C. Wilson in their 1970 study, *Erotica and Antisocial Behavior: An analysis of Selected Social Indicator Statistics,* [77] reported that based on crime statistics, adult sex crimes did not, even though there was more sex-related materials available, increase any more than did other offences for the period from 1960-69. These conclusions were bolstered by the Denmark data which showed that sex crimes actually decreased after the Danes legalized pornography in the 1960s.[78]

The 1970 President's Commission rendered its findings: "In sum, empirical research designed to clarify the question has found no evidence to date that exposure to explicit sexual materials plays a significant role in the causation of delinquent or criminal behavior among youth or adults. The Commission cannot conclude that exposure to erotic materials is a factor in the causation of sex crimes or sex delinquency." [79]

The Commission recommended that "all federal, state and local laws prohibiting the sale of any erotic material to consenting adults be repealed" [80] since it found "no evidence" to link exposure to pornographic materials either to criminal behavior or to juvenile delinquency, [79] nor did it find that pornography would adversely affect the moral attitudes of our country even though there were findings that exposure to pornography was a strong prediction where sexual deviance was concerned.

The Commission reported that the majority of Americans resisted the idea of any restrictions on their freedom of expression rights, and that Americans felt strongly about the First Amendment. It did recommend more research and more public discourse concerning human sexuality.

The report was not well received in Congress. In fact, a Senate resolution was adopted, rejecting the Commission findings [81] and President Nixon declared the report to be "completely unsatisfactory" as it was out of line with Nixon's then hard-line "law and order" policies.

Among those recommendations the Congress *did act upon* was the one to restrict distribution of unsolicited sexually explicit materials through the mail [82] and one to strengthen the laws concerning distribution of sexually explicit materials to minors that included limitations on public displays of pornographic materials. These decisions, in part, were affected by the work of Dr. Victor Cline, clinical psychologist at the University of Utah, who had been involved in research and treatment of sex offenders and had determined that where there had been intensive exposure to "hard-core" pornography, he had been able to isolate a "near universal four-step pattern" in the effect pornography had on sex offenders.

Cline reported: "First, there is an *addictive* effect. The man gets hooked on obscene materials, which seem to provide him with a powerful and exciting aphrodisiac. So he keeps coming back for more to get his sexual "turn-ons." Second, there is an *escalation* in his need for rougher and more sexually shocking materials in order to get the same sexual stimulation as before. He prods his wife or partner into increasingly bizarre sexual activities. When the woman finally resists, the relationship crumbles. Third, there occurs over time a *desensitization* to the material's effect. What was at first gross, taboo, repulsive or immoral – though still sexually arousing – in time becomes acceptable, commonplace and, in a sense, legitimized. The person begins to believe that everyone does it. And fourth, there is an increased tendency to start acting out the sexual activities seen in the pornography. What was at first fantasy has become reality. [83]

Dissatisfaction prevailed as a result of the 1970 Commission report, and there was no clear national policy concerning pornography; therefore, a second commission was formally announced by Attorney General Edwin Meese III in May of 1985. Its mission was to "determine the nature, extent, and impact on society of pornography in the United States, and to make specific recommendations ... concerning more effective ways in which the spread of pornography could be contained, consistent with constitutional guarantees."[85]

This was a somewhat different charge from that of the earlier commission. The Attorney General's Commission was given far less time and money to do its investigation. The Commission's two-volume report was issued in July 1986, [86] wherein the Commission, after receiving testimony and reviewing research in the field, *reported a radical change in pornography* since the 1970 study. Pornography had not only become more violent, and more degrading; it now contained depictions of force and torture, and extreme violence including disfigurement, murder and, in addition, both its production and distribution were found to be dominated by "Organized Crime."

A total of 92 recommendations for curtailing pornography and its resulting harm were suggested in the report to the Attorney General. In the matter of the causal relationship between pornography and anti-social behavior, the Commission found it necessary to establish categories of pornography in order to better relate its findings:

> **Class 1) Sexually Violent Pornography:** That pornography featuring actual/simulated sexually explicit violence, some involving sadomasochistic themes, complete with whips, chains, *et cetera*; and rape and violent force, with the woman eventually begging for more; even extreme violence including disfigurement or murder, the "slasher" type used in snuff films. In this category the Commission found: "That the available evidence strongly supports the hypothesis that substantial exposure to sexually violent material as described here *bears a causal relationship* to antisocial acts of sexual violence and, ... possibly, to unlawful acts of sexual violence." [88]

> **Class 2) Non-Violent But With Degradation, Domination, Subordination Or Humiliation:** That which makes up a great amount of the available pornography. As to this type of pornography, the Commission points to women being shown as "sex objects" and concludes: "Substantial exposure to materials of this type bears some causal relationship to the level of sexual violence, sexual coercion, or unwanted sexual aggression." [89]

> **Class 3) Non-Violent And Non-Degrading,** a small amount of material, with the participants appearing to be equal and willing participants. The Commission concluded: "We are persuaded that material of this type does not bear a causal relationship to rape and other acts of sexual violence."[90]

Class 4) Nudity: The Commission addressed nudity and concluded: "By and large we do not find nudity that does not fit within any of the previous categories to be much cause for concern." [93]

Class 5) Child Pornography was defined as the sexual abuse of a child and as such violates state and federal laws. The great bulk of child pornography is produced by child abusers themselves in largely a "cottage industry" fashion. The Commission concluded: "Child pornography is extraordinarily harmful both to the children involved and to society ... dealing with child pornography in all of its forms ought to be treated as a governmental priority of the greatest urgency."[94]

The Commission noted that, while some laws could be strengthened, the problem did not seem to be "the law" or "the courts," but rather the "lack of enforcement " of the existing laws. The Commission recommended to the Attorney General that he appoint in the Department of Justice an obscenity task force that would be headed by a department official.

THE 1986 REPORT ALSO CRITICIZED

The Attorney General's Report also drew flak. It had not had as much time or money, so it did not have the 80-odd studies of the 1970 report. And it had gone deeper and wider into discussion of the subject. Its ideas found only limited acceptance in Congress. One of those notions accepted was the establishment of a task force, now known as the Child Exploitation and Obscenity Section (CEOS), which was created in 1986 as part of the Justice Department. The CEOS unit has been extremely active in the field of prosecution, especially of major producers and distributors of sexually oriented material, and also has provided assistance to local prosecuting attorneys on a case-by-case basis. It has prosecuted or assisted in more than 500 federal child pornography/child molestation cases and is reported never to have lost a single jury trial.

In 1992, as part of a plea-bargain, it obtained a guilty plea from Cal-Vista Direct, Ltd. for illegal distribution/transportation of obscene tapes. Cal-Vista agreed to "permanently" cease participation in the pornography business, forfeited all inventory and $100,000, all as part of the agreement. [95]

The CEOS is strongly opposed by many organizations, but especially by the American Civil Liberties Union, which argues that the Justice Department's actions are legally questionable, especially its "multiple prosecutions." Because of such tactics the ACLU claims that the CEOS has had a "chilling effect" on "art." The ACLU recommends that the CEOS be totally disbanded and its "war against the First Amendment " cease.[96]

THE TWO REPORTS COMPARED

The 1986 Report also bolstered some of the effects of the 1970 Commission as to Dr. Cline's earlier findings as the result of testimony of convicted Florida murderer Theodore Bundy, who was implicated in the deaths of as many as 28 females. [84] Bundy revealed that at about age 13, he discovered "girlie-magazines" and moved on to detective story pornography and then on to "hard-core" pornography, with violence displayed toward women. He continued to watch this violent pornography, and after two years began acting violently, beginning his killing spree.

In comparing the 1970 Presidential Commission Report with the 1986 Attorney General's Report, it is interesting to consider an attitude survey comparing approximately the same periods of time. [75] It was conducted through a national "person to person" survey concerning the general public's perceptions and attitudes about pornography. Notice the comparison between the 1970 findings and those of a 1985 Gallup-*Newsweek* poll as set forth in the 1986 Final Report of the Attorney General's Commission on Pornography and reflected below:

PERCEPTIONS OF EFFECTS OF PORNOGRAPHY

Percent Saying Statement "True"	1970	1985
Pornographic materials provide information about sex	61%	52%
They lead some to commit rape or sexual violence	49%	73%
They offer a safe outlet for those with sexual problems	27%	34%
They lead some people to lose respect for women	43%	76%
They can help improve sex lives of some couples	47%	47%
They provide entertainment	48%	61%
They lead to a breakdown of morals	56%	67%
(Base)	(2,485)	(1,020)

A DIVIDED FEMINIST VIEW

Many feminists have been concerned about the increase in pornography, especially the increase in violence toward women depicted in today's pornography. Feminists note the increasing number of rapes, especially "date rapes," and the fact that rapes are happening at ever younger ages.

Both Helen E. Longino [97] and Ann Gary [98] in their writings about pornography from the "feminist" point of view – a view which is endorsed by a number of male ethicists – add to their definitions of pornography: That "the role and status of women is degraded," and, further, that women are treated as "mere sex objects" to be "exploited and manipulated." Yet there are some feminists who object to any curtailment of freedom of expression, despite these overwhelming feminist concerns. That women feel strongly about pornography and its effects on them is certainly illustrated by this excerpt from the impassioned testimony of Andrea Dworkin, an attorney and author active for years in the fight against pornography, as given before the Attorney General's Commission:

> "In the country where I live as a citizen, there is a pornography of the humiliation of women where every single way of humiliating a human being is taken to be a form of sexual pleasure for the viewer and for the victim ... where women are murdered for the sexual pleasure of murdering women .... Pornography is used in rape – to plan it, to execute it, to choreograph it, to engender the excitement to commit the act .... When your rape is entertainment, your worthlessness is absolute. You have reached the nadir (the lowest point) of social worthlessness. The civil impact of pornography on women is staggering. It keeps us socially silent, it keeps us socially compliant, it keeps us afraid in neighborhoods; and it creates a vast hopelessness for women, a vast despair. One lives inside a nightmare of sexual abuse that is both actual and potential, and you have the great joy of knowing that your nightmare is someone else's freedom and someone else's fun... [99]

Lorenne M.G. Clark, another feminist, does not lash out as strongly as Dworkin. Nevertheless in excerpts below from *Liberalism and Pornography*, [100] she points out that pornography is "*hate literature*" and "relies on depicting women in ... degrading ... situations" and participating in such degradation "willingly." But she espouses a broader view by pointing out that the harmful effects of pornography apply to both men and women, and that the use of pornography will actually prevent equality between the sexes from becoming a reality.

"It is clear from a consideration of the issue of pornography that so far at least the ethic of liberalism has been unable to rethink its concept of harm in a way which is consistent with sexual equality ... *Hate literature* seeks to make one dislike and despise the people depicted, to *make those persons* seem inferior and *unworthy of our respect*. It seeks to set them apart and to show them as relevantly different from 'us' in a way which justifies 'us' in treating them differently, or it shows them as deserving to be treated badly because they have no respect for 'us' or 'our' values ... That there should be no laws prohibiting the manufacture, sale and distribution of pornography has traditionally and increasingly been defended as a freedom of speech .... The general principle underlying the liberal view is of course explained by Mill in 'On Liberty,' who argued against any form of censorship on the ground that it was only through the free flow of information that the true and the false could be separated ....

"Women must object to pornography because it both reflects and reinforces the patterns of socialization appropriate to a system based on the unequal status of the sexes, in which women are consistently regarded and treated as the inferiors, and the sexual property, of men ...."

"Thus *pornography is harmful, both to women and to men,* because it encourages men to combat feelings of inadequacy and low self-esteem by being aggressive and sadistic, and women to feel shamed and humiliated just for being women. It encourages just that radical difference between men and women which allows men to see women as deserving of treatment they would refrain from subjecting someone to whom they perceived to be like themselves. To the extent that it also encourages women to combat insecurity and low self-esteem by becoming passive and masochistic, it presents even clearer dangers to them than it does to men, since it creates the conditions for their own victimization, but the damage it does to men who do not identify themselves as aggressive and superior to women cannot be underestimated either ....

"While the liberal principle behind opposition to censorship is based on a recognition that desirable social change requires public access to information which challenges the beliefs and practices of the status quo, what it does not acknowledge is that information which supports the status quo through providing role models which advocate the use of threat or coercion as a technique of social control directed at an already identifiable group depicted as inferior, ... works against the interest both of desirable social changes and of the members of the sub-group .... Liberalism serves the interest of the dominant sex and the dominant class, though it contains within itself the potential for promoting greater equality and greater positive liberty for all. It can realize this potential, however, only by reconceptualizing harm in a way consistent with sex and class equality, and by recognizing that negative liberty must take second place to the promotion of equality, at least until we have achieved a framework of enforceable rules which guarantees equality within both the public and the private spheres." [101]

Philosophy professor Ann Gary, in her *Pornography and Respect for Women* ,[102] points out that the content of pornography generally treats women as sexual objects, as a "means to an end." By doing so, pornography violates the moral principles of Immanuel Kant and his "respect for persons." Gary goes on to raise questions about "censorship as a control mechanism" and the possibility of creating pornography that is both non-sexist and morally acceptable.

" ... I have been inclined to think that pornography is innocuous and to dismiss 'moral' arguments for censoring it because many rest on an assumption which I do not share – that sex is an evil to be controlled. At the same time I believe that it is wrong to exploit or degrade human beings, particularly women and others who are especially susceptible to it. So if pornography degrades human beings, then even if I would oppose its censorship, I surely cannot find it morally innocuous. In a study for the Presidential Commission, Donald Mosher conducted studies of the sex callousness of men towards women as reported in the Technical Report of the Commission on Obscenity and Pornography, Volume 8. He found that 'sexually arousing pornographic films did not trigger sexual behavior even in the (sex calloused) college males whose attitudes toward women were more conducive to sexual exploitation,' (Gary 12) (p. 306) and that sex-calloused attitudes toward women decreased after seeing pornographic films ...

"The content of pornography is what one objects to. It treats women as mere sex objects, to be exploited and manipulated, and degrades the role and status of women .... Pornography describes or shows women engaging in activities which are inappropriate for good women to engage in, or at least inappropriate for them to be seen by strangers engaging in it. If one sees these women as symbolic representatives of all women, then all women fall from grace with these women. This fall is possible, I believe, because the 'respect' men had for women was not genuine, wholehearted respect for full-fledged human beings, but halfhearted respect for lesser beings, some of whom they felt the need to glorify and purify. (Gary 23) ...

"Given the feminist's distinction, she has no difficulty at all saying that pornography treats women as sex objects, not as full-fledged people. She can object morally to pornography or anything else treating women as sex objects. "Because in our culture we connect sex with harm that men do to women and think of the female role in sex as that of harmed object, we can see that to treat a women as a sex object is automatically to treat her as less than fully human ...

"The sex-harm connection makes it clear why it is worse to treat women as sex objects than to treat men as sex objects, and why some men have had difficulty understanding women's anger about the matter .... The question is whether there is or could be any pornography with nonsexist, non-degrading content? .... Nonsexist pornography could show women and men in roles equally valued by society; sex equality would be more than having equally functional genitalia. Characters would customarily treat each other with respect and consideration. There would be no attempt to treat men or women brutally or thoughtlessly ....

"Of course, I could not deny that anyone who tries to change an institution from within will face serious difficulties. This is particularly evident when one is trying to change both pornography and a whole set of related attitudes, feelings, and institutions concerning sex and sex roles. But in conjunction with other attempts to change this set of attitudes, it seems preferable to try to change pornography instead of closing one's eyes in the hope that it will go away. For I suspect that pornography is here to stay.(Gary 35)

"Several 'final' points must be made. (i) I have not seriously considered censorship as an alternative course of action. Both Brownmiller and Sheehy are not averse to it. But as I suggested in note 5, other principles seem too valuable to sacrifice when we have other options available. In addition, before justifying censorship on moral grounds, one would want to compare pornography to other possibly offensive material: Advertising using sex and racial stereotypes, violence in TV and films, and so on. (ii) If my nonsexist pornography succeeded in having much 'educational value,' it might no longer be pornography in my definition. This possibility seems too remote to worry me, however. (iii) In talking about the audience for nonsexist pornography, I have focused on the male audience. But there is no reason why pornography could not educate and appeal to women as well." [103]

Gary's position is that even if pornography is immoral she is still not sure that censorship would be the correct way to handle regulation. What about her position that pornography is "here to stay?" Is it possible to change pornography? Would pornography as Gary envisioned it be a marketable item in today's society?

ANOTHER TACK ENTIRELY

Taking a totally different tack on pornography, feminist author Catherine MacKinnon [104] claims that pornography is in fact "sexual discrimination." MacKinnon has been active along with Andrea Dworkin (p. 329) in the drafting of pornography laws using a "civil rights" theory and attempting to hold "those who profit from and benefit from the injury accountable to those who are injured." These laws are not based on censorship, but rather on the theory that pornography can be legally defined as a form of sexual discrimination against women and would, therefore, be a violation of women's civil rights and, as a result, such laws would be enforceable under civil rights legislation and allow for damages.

An earlier ordinance, drawn for the City of Minneapolis was vetoed by its mayor. The idea, however, caught on and has now been used as a basis for laws in other areas of the country. A similar Indianapolis ordinance was challenged and declared "unconstitutional" by the Seventh Circuit of the United States Court of Appeals. [105] In this case the city admitted that it sought to restrict pornography that would not be "obscene" under the *Miller* test (p. 323), but insisted that they were not regulating speech but conduct – the "unacceptable subordination of women."

The court found that even though the ordinance was drafted as civil rights legislation, the very wording of the law illustrated that the city *was attempting to regulate speech*, including speech that went beyond that which would be considered legally obscene under the Miller test set out by the U.S. Supreme Court and thereby protected speech under the First Amendment. The ordinance was ruled unconstitutional.

So we see, then, many feminists objecting to pornography and supporting regulation under one theory or another, yet all women do not support the suppression of pornography, either under the aforementioned "freedom of expression" restrictions or as "civil rights violations." Betty Friedan, an ardent feminist has this to say.[106]

"I want to express my view, on behalf of a great many women in this country, feminists and believers in human rights, that this current move to introduce censorship in the United States in the guise of suppressing pornography is extremely dangerous to women. It is extremely dangerous to the rights of women as well as men to speak and think freely and to fight for our basic rights, to control our lives, or bodies, and have some degree of economic and political equality ... There is a dangerous attempt to use a feminist smokescreen and even to claim that this anti-pornography suppression legislation is a weapon against sex discrimination and a weapon to liberate women from the degradation of pornography. Now I speak as someone who has no particular liking for pornography ....

"You know, some pornography certainly does degrade women. It also degrades men and it degrades sex. The pornography that pushes violence is particularly deplorable. But the forces that want to suppress pornography are not in favor of suppressing guns. They are not in favor of legislation – they would undo legislation – protecting women and children from actual violence. What are they up to? ....

"Underneath the sideshow, *they are trying to excite the passions of the people against ideas –* sexually titillating or repulsive sexually – but *ideas, not actual deeds, not violence*, not the obscenity of poverty – to take our attention away while we are being manipulated in this country, being manipulated, and *our rights are being threatened ...*

"I deplore that even a very few feminists have been diverted by the issues of pornography from the basic protection of all our rights. Now, I urge all women to have their eyes opened to the dangers to our basic rights by the pushing of anti-pornography legislation." [107]

Then, there is the challenge to the sexual discrimination view by feminists Lisa Duggan, Nan Hunter and Carole Vance.[108] They express concern for the scope of materials that might be reached by legislation of this type, believing that far-right elements could use these ordinances to "enforce their sexually conservative world view." Their article points out that this type of legislation is more likely to "impede, rather than advance, feminist goals" and could indeed be a "useful tool in antifeminist moral crusades." They claim "the argument that pornography itself plays a major role in the general oppression of women contradicts the evidence of history." [109]

Feminists, then, while they dislike pornography and agree to its "degrading connotations" to women and may agree to its "immorality," differ in their view as to control. Among feminists who do believe in curtailment, there are differences in views as to how that control should be accomplished.

VICTIMS

A "Pornography Victims' Compensation Act" [110] was introduced in Congress in both the 1991 and 1992 sessions. The bill, an outgrowth of the work of MacKinnon and Dworkin, allows a victim to bring a civil action in either state or federal courts against "producers, distributors, exhibitors, renters or sellers of obscene material or child pornography" to recover actual damages as well as those for pain incurred as a result of a sex offense when the "exposure to such material" was actually a "substantial cause" of the offense.

Congress in its review of the proposed legislation found that while it was "tradition" in our system of justice for "victims to be made whole," our laws were "deficient" in this area because they omitted "victims of sex offenses."[111] The Senate bill failed to be reported out of committee both years, but with the current political climate it is expected to be reintroduced in further congressional sessions. The Bill is "a most troubling legislative initiate," according to Marjorie Heins, the Project Director of the Arts Censorship Project of the ACLU, [112] who said that if it were to become law, it could have the profoundly counterproductive effect of chilling discussion on a subject that urgently needs exposure: "The frightening reality of sexual violence in our society." [113]

CHILD PORNOGRAPHY

Child Pornography – the visual depiction of a child taking part in explicit sexual conduct – is, in essence, the picture of an ongoing crime and is prohibited by law, as is all sexual activity of adults with minors. State and federal laws have prohibited child pornography and the Supreme Court has upheld its prohibition and declared it to be outside the protection of the First Amendment , even *without* a finding of obscenity. (Ferber p. 324)

Commercial child pornography is not *openly* produced or sold in the U.S., although customs officials regularly confiscate such pornography being smuggled into the United States. Most child pornography today is produced by and/or for pedophiles, often with the very children they molest. Pedophiles, adults whose sexual preference is to have sex with children, place great value in their collections of child pornography. According to law enforcement authorities and court cases, they take their own pictures, save them, and swap them with other pedophiles. It is not unusual for some of their pictures to be traded about and eventually reach commercial producers in Europe, where they are added to publications, and then find their way back into America in a public form.

One American child, according to an Alabama customs agent, was able to be followed through foreign magazines for several years. Early editions reflected only her nudity, while later ones portrayed her in explicit sexual actions. Finally, in the last edition in which she was to be seen, she was pictured involved in an action depicted as unmistakably "hard-core" while her glassy-eyed expression seemed to indicate she was in a drugged state, unlike her appearance in the earlier editions.

Searches of future magazines failed to show any further trace of this child whose pictures seemed to span a time from approximately age 10 to age 15. The agent shared his frustrations at never being able to locate this child and his concerns over her failure to reappear.

What happens to these children? Can they ever hope to enter a "normal world," to lead a "normal life"? If they do get away from that life do they live in fear of being "found out"? What about "guilt feelings" and "embarrassment"? Can they ever trust or enjoy true love? What if this child was your daughter?

Child pornography is used to lower the inhibitions of children, to convince them that other children have engaged in this activity – and in doing so, had fun, thus encouraging children to cooperate with their molester. [114] "Regular" pornography as well as pornographic "comics" are also used to condition children, to arouse their curiosity, and to entice them to participate in sexual activity.

Many pedophiles apparently maintain an extensive picture library. Their pictures and tapes are often very carefully hidden in order to be used for their own personal satisfaction, especially when they are without child victims. Police report that pictures of children can also be used by the pedophile in blackmailing them not to tell, or to continue with the activity, and/or to coerce them to bring in other children to "play."

There are people who support the idea of sex with children, and these persons, including pedophiles, have a way of locating each other and of working together. The advent of the computer and of computer bulletin boards have made locating each other and keeping in touch easier. There are actual organizations that openly support sex between adults and children and who actively lobby to have "the age of consent" lowered so as to have more children legally available for sexual activity.

These organizations publish newsletters that are circulated among their memberships, covering stories referring to sexual activity with children and featuring pictures of young children. One such publication exploits what it calls "man/boy" love.

The Austin Pedophile Study Group II originally published a pamphlet entitled *How to Have Sex with Kids* and another, *Women Pedophiles?*. Other organizations that support and advocate child/adult consensual sexual activity include the Rene Guyon Society, the Child Sensuality Circle, the Pedo-Alert Network (PAN), and the National Diaper Pail Foundation.

That child pornography is of great importance to child molesters is illustrated by the testimony of Joe Henry, a pedophile, before the U.S. Senate on February 15, 1985,[115] testifying about the content of one of his letters to another pedophile: "If it were not for all the pictures ... I would think it was all just a fantastic dream. I will always be grateful to you for ... giving me a brief taste of heaven .... Pedophiles survive through explicit letters and the purchase and trading of child pornography, because live victims are not always available."

A 1986 study by Abel, as reported by the National Coalition Against Pornography,[116] showed that the 240 pedophiles studied averaged 30-60 victims *each* before even being caught, and on the average, *eventually* will abuse about 380 children.

Dr. Harry O'Reilly,[117] former supervisor of the New York City Sex Crimes Unit, once related the story of a New York City worker who volunteered at a local orphanage housing about 300 children. He would take the children in small groups on outings and to his home. He was well thought of for his devotion of time to the boys. Yet, when one child broke down and told of his sexual abuse, investigation revealed he had actually molested every child in the orphanage.

He used pornographic comics to entice the younger children by showing regular cartoons first and then slipping in a tape which contained "adult" comics including a version of "Jack and the Beanstalk." In it, Jack wanders into the Giant's home and finds the harp that, when played, causes various "bad" behavior in everyone from the turkey on the table to the Giant's wife. She then does all sorts of sex acts with Jack. The children, being curious, asked questions. This then gave the "volunteer" an opportunity to demonstrate to them just how these things happen.

Pornographic magazines were left about to excite the older boys. With the magazines and a few beers, the way was opened to involve them. Pictures were taken of these adolescents in sexual acts, which were then used to keep them involved and to secure their cooperation in order to bring in the other children. "The use of children as subjects of pornographic materials is harmful to the physiological, emotional, and mental health of a child," said the court in Ferber,[118] and molesting children, using them as sex objects, is equally devastating. Child sexual abuse robs a child of his/her innocence, of their trust in people – especially when the abuser is a known and trusted adult as are the majority of abusers.

Sexually abused children experience guilt and blame. If they are involved in the sex acts over a period of time they assume even more blame because they view themselves as having allowed it to continue; yet they are fearful, feel helpless and often are too ashamed to tell anyone of the abuse. Their self-esteem is low to non-existent, so these children generally possess poor social skills. Sociologists suggest the anger they carry within is directed not only at the abuser but at the adults who have allowed this to happen by failing to afford them protection. But most of all their anger is directed at themselves, which often results in emotional problems.

The 1970 Commission Report did not reflect any real focus on Child Pornography, but as sexual exploitation of children became more apparent, Congress in 1977 conducted its own investigation. The Senate Judiciary Committee in its report had this to say: "Child pornography and child prostitution have become highly organized, multimillion-dollar industries that operate on a nationwide scale." [120]

A permanent subcommittee dealing with the Investigation on Child Pornography and Pedophilia was established by Congress. It cited a 1986 Report of the Los Angeles Police Department, showing that of 700 child molesters, more than one-half had child pornography in their possession and 80 percent owned some type of pornography. [121]

Unfortunately, while laws restricting children being portrayed in pornography are on the books, child pornography continues to flourish in the United States. This occurs even though each depiction of child pornography is actually a crime in action.

PORNOGRAPHY AS BIG BUSINESS AND CRIME

The 1986 Attorney General's Commission found that the pornography industry had not only grown at an alarming rate but had reached out to *new* markets, and was now primarily a California-based industry of multibillion-dollar scope. [122] Performers themselves earn little in the overall scheme of pornography production. There are some 12-24 major companies. These producers, in addition to wholesalers and retailers, all receive sizeable profit, so much so that organized crime was attracted to the industry and now plays a substantial role in this deplorable business where the "gain far outreaches the risk." [123]

A 1978 FBI report stated: "Information received from sources of this Bureau indicates that pornography is (a major) income-maker for *La Cosa Nostra* (a major U.S. criminal organization sometimes, incorrectly, synonymous with 'the Mafia') in the United States behind gambling and narcotics. Although La Cosa Nostra does not physically oversee the day-to-day workings of the majority of pornography business in the United States, it is apparent they have 'agreements' with those involved in the pornography business, allowing these people to operate independently by paying off members of organized crime for the privilege of being allowed to operate in certain geographical areas." [124]

The 1986 Commission Report illustrated this involvement: "The Chicago Police Department has been involved in the investigation of organized crime families who are engaged in the distribution of pornography in the Midwest. Thomas Bohling of the Chicago Police Department Organized Crime Division, Vice Control Section reported that it is "the belief of state, federal, and local law enforcement that the pornography industry is controlled by organized crime families. If they do not own the business outright, they most certainly extract street tax from independent smut peddlers."

The overwhelming bulk of obscene and pornographic materials is produced in the Los Angeles area. Organized crime families from Chicago, New York, New Jersey and Florida are openly controlling and directing the major pornography operations in Los Angeles. According to then-Chief Daryl F. Gates of the Los Angeles Police Department, "organized crime" infiltrated the pornography industry in Los Angeles in 1969 due to its lucrative financial benefits. By 1975, organized crime controlled 80% of the industry and it is estimated that this figure is between 85 (and) 90% today. [125]

To illustrate the profit margin, consider one film, "Deep Throat." This was produced in Florida through the "Columbo organized crime family" at a cost of only $25,000. By the year 1982, it was estimated to have grossed an estimated $50-million, making its producers wealthy.[126]

Publishers of magazines and books fall into the "high-profit" category. The market for sexually explicit magazines has expanded, and represents some of the most widely distributed magazines in the country.[127] Adult theater profits have declined due to the now highly profitable home video market. Movies for cable television and "dial-a-porn" are recent additions to this profitable pornography industry.

With a moneymaking base totaling millions of dollars annually, those involved take a strong stand against any restrictions on freedom of expression. They are willing not only to fight court battles but to make large contributions to organizations that support First Amendment freedoms.

ORGANIZATIONAL STANDS

The American Civil Liberties Union (ACLU) founded in 1920 has been a longtime defender of pornography and takes a strong stand against any erosion of the First Amendment . The ACLU has made its presence known in recent fights to support absolute "freedom of expression" in the Arts. At the present time the ACLU is involved in an Arts Censorship Project to ensure such freedom.[128]

The ACLU is joined in its stand by other organizations including the National Coalition Against Censorship (NCAC), People for the American Way, and the Boston Coalition for Freedom of Expression. On the other side, there are organizations working diligently for the removal of obscenity and pornography. Reverend Donald Wildmon of the American Family Association recently attempted to block a documentary about censorship because of certain scenes in the television film, *Damned in the USA*.[129]

Two organizations, the National Coalition against Pornography and Focus on the Family, are organizations that have founded grass roots coalitions to halt the spread of pornography. The Religious Alliance Against Pornography holds an annual conference featuring well-known religious leaders as speakers, all as part of its battle-plan to restrict pornography.

Dr. C. Everett Koop, M.D. and former U.S. Surgeon General, called pornography a "crushing public health problem" posing a "clear and present danger to American public health." He issued a call to physicians to "stem the tide" of pornography adding "This material is blatantly anti-human. Its appeal is to a dark and anti-human impulse. We must oppose it as we oppose all violence and prejudice." [130]

SUMMARY

Pornography in all forms has been reviewed. Different views have been put forth. We have studied concerns for preserving our inherent right of freedom of expression; for preserving our First Amendment rights against all regulation of "freedom of speech"; for the need to limit that freedom due to the harm that pornography is said to cause, or because of the need to respect persons. We have heard arguments that autonomy would allow consenting adults to decide what they should see or read; listened to the concerns that because of the harm to *both* men and women, society would be best served by limitation; and heard the more paternalistic view that the state should protect its citizens. We have considered the view that pornography should be completely banned because it is immoral; the natural law concerns that the content of most pornography is unnatural and therefore wrong; and finally the view that pornography should be balanced against the right to privacy – which many think should extend beyond the home.

There have been questions posed throughout the chapter to stimulate your thoughts and reasoning about pornography. This examination would not be complete without two additional views on pornography.

The Pleasure Theory. Fred R. Berger, who supports pornography and the "pleasure" theory, says: "It seems to me, however, that we have yet to make the most important response .... The more important issue turns on the fact that a great many people like and enjoy pornography and want it as part of their lives .... For a society that accepts freedom and self-determination as centrally significant values cannot allow interferences with freedom on such grounds as these ....." [131]

The Divine Command Theory. The Vatican, in contrast and reflecting the Divine Command view, said in its pastoral response: [132] "While no one can consider himself or herself immune to the corrupting effects of pornography and violence or safe from injury at the hands of those acting under their influence, the young and the immature are especially vulnerable and the most likely to victimized. Pornography and sadistic violence debase sexuality, corrode human relationships, exploit individuals – especially women and young people – undermine marriage and family life, foster anti-social behavior and weaken the moral fibre of society itself ... " The Vatican added: "Thus, one of the clear effects of pornography is sin. Willing participation in the production or dissemination of these noxious products can only be judged a serious moral evil ... " [133]

CONCLUSION

What are your views now? Should pornography be restricted? If so, then to what degree? Under what method should it be restricted? Can you support your view with sound moral/ethical reasoning? Which approach best illustrates your own view?

READINGS
THE PORNOGRAPHIC SOCIETY
Edward J. Mishan
Pre-Attorney General's Commission

Familiar arguments, used to persuade us that the growth of sexual permissiveness has wholesome effects on the personality and increases the capacity for enjoyment, are, to say the least, inconclusive, while those attempting to persuade us that, no matter what the degree of depravity in a work, it cannot really harm anyone, are wholly unconvincing. It is time, therefore, to bring some thought to bear on the harmful consequences society may suffer if current trends toward increasing pornography continue.

I begin by acknowledging the fact that not all those favoring the abolition of censorship are equally comfortable at the turn of events. Some are prepared to admit that things have gone "too far," or far enough. Yet, as indicated, they continue for the most part to rest their hopes for containment, or improvement, on some eventual recoil from current excesses, or on some reassertion of an imagined natural law that is latent in liberal democracies, or, in the last resort, on the gradual onset of ennui. However, since there is no evidence at present of any slackening in the growth of the market in pornography, hard or soft, it is just possible that – unless the state takes action – our innocent Sex Lobbyists will be proved wrong by events. If so, the question of the consequences for Western societies of an unarrested trend toward increased public pornography becomes very pertinent. In addressing myself to so large a question, I admittedly enter the realm of speculation though without, I hope, forsaking the conventions of reasoned discourse.

In order to avoid tedious qualifications at every turn in the argument, let us project existing trends and think in terms of an emergent "Pornographic Society," one in which all existing restraints have vanished. There are no legal checks on any form of erotic experience, "natural" or "unnatural," and no limit with respect to place, time, scale, or medium, in the depiction of what today would be called the carnal and lascivious. Neither are there any limits placed on the facilities for auto-eroticism, or for participating in any activity, heterosexual, homosexual, bestial, or incestuous, sado-masochistic, fetishistic, or just plain cruel. Provided actors, audience, and participants are willing, provided there is a market for the "product," no objection is entertained.

Any who would accuse me of being an alarmist merely for proposing the concept as an aid to inquiry would surely be revealing also that, were such a society to come into being, there would indeed be grounds for alarm. Since, however, they would reject this possible outcome (in the absence of state action) it would be of some interest if they could be more articulate on the nature and strength of the forces they believe can be depended upon to stem the tide. It would be of further interest to know just how far they expect society to travel along the primrose path to all-out pornography. How far would they themselves wish to travel along this road or, to be more fastidious, what existing or possible features would they wish to admit or prohibit, extend or contract? In short, where would they wish to "draw the line," and having drawn it, on what principles would they defend it, and by what sanctions? Finally, if they could be persuaded that the forces they once relied upon to restore some

sort of equilibrium are too weak to operate, what measure would they favor now in order to stay the pace of movement toward the pornographic society?....

It is time to turn about in our minds some of the facets of the problem posed by the concept of the Pornographic Society; namely, whether such a society is compatible with the Good Life, *any* good life.

First, allowing that family life will continue in such a society, what are we to make of the effect on the child's psychology of his apprehension of a society obsessed with carnal indulgence? It has been alleged, occasionally, that children are immune to pornography; that, up to a certain age, it does not signify. Though this allegation cannot draw on any evidence – since they are not in fact exposed, when young, to sexual circuses – we need not pursue this controversial question here because, presumably, there does come an age when they begin to understand the significance of what is happening about them. It is appropriate, then, to question the effect on the child's emotional life, in particular his regard and feelings for his parents.

Is it not just possible that the child needs not only to love his parents but to esteem them? In his first gropings for order and security in a world of threatening impulse, does he not need to look up to beings who provide assurance, who appear to him as "good" and wise and just? Will such emotional needs not be thwarted in a society of uninhibited sexual device? I do not pretend to know the answers to these questions, but no one will gainsay their importance. In view of the possibly very grave consequences on our children's children, would it not be an act of culpable negligence to allow current trends toward an increasingly promiscuous society to continue without being in sight of the answers?

Consider next the quality of love in such a society. Three closely related questions arise.

Treated simply as a physical exploit with another body, and divorced from the intrusion of sentiment, is sexual fulfillment possible?[1] David Holbrook, for one, has doubts whether this is possible. Indeed, he concludes that the so-called sexual revolution is "placing limits on people's capacities to develop a rich enjoyment of sexual love by reducing it to sexuality."[2] Nor has Irving Kristol any brief for the more visible manifestations of the sexual revolution:

There are human sentiments ... involved in this animal activity. But when sex is public the viewer does not – cannot – see the sentiments.... He can only see the animal coupling. And that is why, when men and women make love, as we say, they prefer to be alone – because it is only when you are alone that you can make love, as distinct from merely copulating in an animal and casual way.

The second question that comes to mind in this connection is whether romantic love will become obsolete in a society of unfettered sexual recourse.

The "savage" in Aldous Huxley's brilliant satire, *Brave New World,* who commits suicide in despair, tried for romantic love but could obtain only instant sex. There might well continue to be sexual friendships, sexual rivalries, sexual jealousies. But the sublimation of sex, thought to be the well-spring of creative imagination and of romantic love, would be no more. One of the great sources of inspiration of poetry and song, of chivalry and dedication, throughout the ages would have dried up. To the denizens of the pornographic society the story of Abelard and Heloise or even the theories of Stendhal *On Love* would be implausible, if not incomprehensible.

The third related question is about the quality of love in general that can be expected to emerge along the road to such a society. One wonders if it would really be possible to love other people very much, or to care for them as persons very much in a world without opportunity for sublimation. Can such virtues as loyalty, honor, compassion, sacrifice, charity, or tenderness, flourish in an environment of uninhibited public exhibitionism and pornography?

Taking a wider perspective of the scene, one wonders whether it is possible to unite unchecked public sexual indulgence with the continued progress of any civilization – thinking of civilization in terms not merely of increasing scientific advance and technological innovation but in those, also, of a refinement of taste and sensibility. Let the reader ponder on the question at his leisure, bearing in mind the reflection that whereas the emergence in the past of a new civilization, or of a new age within the matrix of an existing civilization, has indeed always been associated with a rapid displacement of old conceptions, values, and purposes by new ones, it has never been associated with a mass movement toward unbridled sexual licentiousness. For, aside from the sexually neurotic elements at large in Western societies, there are in each of us – among "normal" people, that is – infantile and regressive elements that are for the most part dormant though deeply imbedded. "Emotional maturity" is a frail plant that can sustain itself only by clinging to an appropriate social structure. Familiar taboos that place a variety of constraints on freedom of sexual practices reflect a society's desire to guard against the activation of such elements. Until recently the laws of all Western societies sanctioned and reinforced taboos against an unlimited sexual freedom that, if actively sought, could be destructive of organized society.

Thus, a first experiment of this kind just might be the last experiment ever. Goaded on by the predatory forces of commercial opportunism, expectations of carnal gratification – aroused by increasingly salacious spectacles, and increasing facilities for new sexual perversions – would soar beyond the physical limits of attainments. In the unrelenting search for the uttermost in orgiastic experience, cruel passions might be unleashed, impelling humanity into regions beyond barbarism. One has only to recall the fantastic sadistic barbarities of the Nazi era – and to recall also that in 1941 the Nazis were within an ace of winning the War – to accept this conjecture as neither farfetched nor fanciful, and to recognize that civilization is indeed but skin-deep....

Such questions need not be regarded as merely rhetorical. They may be thought of as genuine questions. But unless the answers to them are quite other than what I suspect they are, there are clear and present dangers in the current drift toward increased sexual permissiveness.

Part III: The Individual and Ethical Issues

IS PORNOGRAPHY BENEFICIAL?

It is not sufficient, for the objectors' case, that they demonstrate that some harm has flowed from pornography. It would be extremely difficult to show that pornography had *never* had unfortunate consequences, but we should not make too much of this. Harm has flowed from religion, patriotism, alcohol and cigarettes without this fact impelling people to demand abolition. The harm, if established, has to be weighed against a variety of considerations before a decision can be reached as to the propriety of certain laws. Of the British Obscenity Laws the Arts Council Report comments[3] 'that the harm would need to be both indisputable and very dire indeed before it could be judged to outweigh the evils and anomalies inherent in the Acts we have been asked to examine.'

The onus therefore is upon the anti-pornographers to demonstrate not only that harm is caused by certain types of sexual material but that the harm is considerable: If the first is difficult the second is necessarily more so, and the attempts to date have not been impressive. It is even possible to argue that easily available pornography has a number of benefits. Many people will be familiar with the *catharsis* argument whereby pornography is said to cut down on delinquency by providing would-be criminals with substitute satisfactions. This is considered later but we mention it here to indicate that access to pornography may be socially beneficial in certain instances, and that where this is possible the requirement for anti-pornographers to *justify* their objections must be stressed.

The general conclusion[4] of the U.S. Commission was that no adequate proof had been provided that pornography was harmful to individual or society – 'if a case is to be made out against "pornography" (in 1970) it will have to be made on grounds other than demonstrated effects of a damaging personal or social nature.' ...

The heresy (to some ears) that pornography is harmless is compounded by the even greater impiety that it may be beneficial. Some of us are managing to adjust to the notion that pornography is unlikely to bring down the world in moral ruin, but the idea that it may actually do good is altogether another thing. When we read of Professor Emeritus E. T. Rasmussen, a pioneer of psychological studies in Denmark, and a government adviser, saying that there is a possibility 'that pornography can be beneficial,' many of us are likely to have *mixed* reactions, to say the least. In fact this thesis can be argued in a number of ways.

The simplest approach is to remark that people enjoy it. This can be seen to be true whether we rely on personal testimony or the most respectable index of all in capitalist society – 'preparedness to pay.' The appeal that pornography has for many people is hardly in dispute, and in a more sober social climate that would be justification enough. Today we are not quite puritan enough to deny that *pleasure* has a worthwhile place in human life: Not many of us object to our food being tasty or our clothes being attractive. It was not always like this. In sterner times it was *de riguer* to prepare food without spices and to wear the plainest clothes. The cult of puritanism reached its apotheosis in the most fanatical asceticism, where it was fashionable for holy men to wander off into a convenient desert and neglect the body to the point of cultivating its lice as 'pearls of God.' In such a bizarre philosophy pleasure was not only condemned in its sexual manifestations but in all areas where the body could conceivably take satisfaction. These days we are able to countenance pleasure in most fields but in many instances still the case for *sexual* pleasure has to be argued.

Pleasure is not of course its own justification. If it clearly leads to serious malaise, early death, or the *dis*pleasure of others, then there is something to be said against it. But the serious consequences have to be demonstrated: It is not enough to condemn certain forms of pleasurable experience on the grounds of *possible* ill effect. With such an approach *any* human activity could be censured and freedom would have no place. In short, if something is pleasurable and its bad effects are small or nonexistent then it is to be encouraged: Opposition to such a creed should be recognized as an unwholesome antipathy to human potential. Pleasure is good except where it is harmful (and where the harmfulness is *significant*) ....

That pornography is enjoyable to many people is the first of the arguments in its favor. In any other field this would be argument enough. It is certainly sufficient to justify many activities that have – unlike a taste for pornography – demonstrably harmful consequences. Only in a sexually neurotic society could a tool for heightening sexual enjoyment be regarded as reprehensible and such as to warrant suppression by law. The position is well summarized[5] in the *first* of the Arts Council's 12 reasons for advocating the repeal of the Obscenity Publications Acts: 'It is not for the State to prohibit private citizens from choosing what they may or may not enjoy in literature or art unless there were incontrovertible evidence that the result would be injurious to society. There is no such evidence.'

A further point is that availability of pornography may *aid*, rather than frustrate, normal sexual development. Thus in 1966, for example, the New Jersey Committee for a Right to Read presented the findings of a survey conducted among nearly a thousand psychiatrists and psychologists of that state. Amongst the various personal statements included was the view that 'sexually stimulating materials' might help particular people develop a normal sex drive.[6] In similar spirit, Dr. John Money writes[7] that pornography 'may encourage normal sexual development and broadmindedness,' a view that may not sound well to the anti-pornographers. And even in circumstances where possible dangers of pornography are pointed out, conceivable good effects are sometimes acknowledged. In a paper issued[8] by The Danish Forensic Medicine Council, it is pointed out that neurotic and sexually shy people may, by reading pornographic descriptions of normal sexual activity, be freed from some of their apprehension regarding sex and may thereby attain a freer and less frustrated attitude to the sexual side of life....

One argument in favor of pornography is that it can serve as a substitute for actual sexual activity involving another person or other people. This argument has two parts, relating as it does to (1) people who fantasize over *socially acceptable* modes of sexual involvement, and (2) people who fantasize over types of sexual activity that would be regarded as illegal or at least immoral. The first type relates to lonely and deprived people who for one reason or another have been unable to form 'normal' sexual contacts with other people; the second type (to) instances of the much-quoted *catharsis* argument.

One writer notes[9] that pornography can serve as a substitute for both the knowledge of which some people have been deprived and the pleasure in sexual experience which they have not enjoyed. One can well imagine men or women too inhibited to secure sexual satisfaction with other adults, and where explicit sexual material can alleviate some of their misery. It is facile to remark that such people should seek psychiatric assistance or even 'make an effort': The factors that prevent the forming of effective sexual liaisons are just as likely to inhibit any efforts to seek medical or other assistance. Pornography provides *sex by proxy,* and in such usage it can have a clear justification.

It is also possible to imagine circumstances in which men or women – for reasons of illness, travel or bereavement – are unable to seek sexual satisfaction with spouse or other loved one. Pornography can help here too. Again it is easy to suggest that a person abstain from sexual experience, or, if having *permanently* lost a spouse, seek out another partner. Needless to say such advice is often quite impractical – and the alternative to pornography may be prostitution or adultery. Montagu notes that pornography can serve the same purpose as 'dirty jokes,' allowing a person to discharge harmlessly repressed and unsatisfied sexual desires.

In this spirit, Mercier (1970) is quoted by the U.S. Commission:

Part III: The Individual and Ethical Issues

'... It is in periods of sexual deprivation – to which the young and the old are far more subject than those in their prime – that males, at any rate, are likely to reap psychological benefit from pornography.'

And also Kenneth Tynan (1970):

'For men on long journeys, geographically cut off from wives and mistresses, pornography can act as a portable memory, a welcome shortcut to remembered bliss, relieving tension without involving disloyalty.'

It is difficult to see how anyone could object to the use of pornography in such circumstances, other than on the grounds of a morbid anti-sexuality.

The *catharsis argument* has long been put forward to suggest that availability of pornography will neutralize 'aberrant' sexual tendencies and so reduce the incidence of sex crime or clearly immoral behavior in related fields. (Before evidence is put forward for this thesis it is worth remarking that it should not be necessary to demonstrate a *reduction* in sex crime to justify repeal of the Obscenity Laws. It should be quite sufficient to show that an *increase* in crime will not ensue following repeal. We may even argue that a small increase may be tolerable if other benefits from easy access to pornography could be shown: But it is no part of the present argument to put this latter contention.)

Many psychiatrists and psychologists have favored the catharsis argument. Chesser, for instance, sees[10] pornography as a form of voyeurism in which – as with sado-masochistic material – the desire to hurt is satisfied passively. If this is so and the analogy can be extended, we have only to look at the character of the voyeur – generally furtive and clandestine – to realize that we have little to fear from the pornography addict. Where consumers are preoccupied with fantasy there is little danger to the rest of us. Karpman (1959), quoted by the U.S. Commission, notes that people reading 'salacious literature' are less likely to become sexual offenders than those who do not since the reading often neutralizes 'aberrant sexual interests.' Similarly the Kronhausens have argued that

'these "unholy" instruments' may be a safety-valve for the sexual deviate and potential sex offender. And Cairns, Paul and Wishner (1962) have remarked that *obscene materials* provide a way of releasing strong sexual urges without doing harm to others.

It is easy to see the plausibility of this argument. The popularity of all forms of sexual literature – from the superficial, *sexless,* sentimentality of the popular women's magazine to the clearest 'hard-core' porn – has demonstrated over the ages the perennial appetite that people have for fantasy. To an extent, a great extent with many single people and frustrated married ones, the fantasy constitutes an important part of the sex-life. The experience may be vicarious and sterile, but it self-evidently fills a need for many individuals. If literature, as a *symbol* of reality, can so involve human sensitivies, it is highly likely that when the sensitivities are *distorted* for one reason or another, the same sublimatory function can occur: The 'perverted' or potentially criminal mentality can gain satisfaction, as does the lonely unfortunate, in sex *by proxy.* If we wanted to force the potential sex criminal on to the streets in search of a human victim, perhaps we would do well to deny him his sublimatory substitutes: Deny him fantasy and he will be forced to go after the real thing....

The importance of this possibility should be fully faced. If a causal connection *does* exist between availability of pornographic material and a *reduction* in the amount of sex crime – and the evidence is wholly consistent with this possibility rather than its converse – then people who deliberately restrict pornography by supporting repressive legislation are prime architects of sexual offenses against the individual. The anti-pornographers would do well to note that their anxieties may be driving them into a position the exact opposite of the one they explicitly maintain – their commitment to reduce the amount of sexual delinquency in society.

The most that anti-pornographers can argue is that at present the evidence is inconclusive – a point that would be taken by Kutschinsky *et al.* But if the inconclusive character of the data is once admitted, then the case for repressive legislation falls at once. For in a *free* society, or one supposedly aiming after freedom, social phenomena are, like individuals, innocent until proven guilty – and an activity will be permitted unless there is clear evidence of its harmful consequences. This point was well put – in the specific connection with pornography – by Bertrand Russell, talking[11] when he was well over 90 to Rupert Crawshay-Williams.

After noting how people beg the question of causation in instances such as the Moors murders (where the murders and the reading of de Sade *may* have a common cause), Russell ('Bertie') said that on the whole he disapproved of sadistic pornography being available. But when Crawshay-Williams put the catharsis view, that such material might provide a harmless release for individuals who otherwise may be dangerous, Russell said at once – 'Oh, well, if that's true, then I don't see that there is anything against sadistic pornography. In fact it should be encouraged....' When it was stressed that there was no preponderating evidence either way Russell argued that we should fall back on an overriding principle – 'in this case the principle of free speech.'

Thus in the absence of evidence of harm we should be permissive. Any other view is totalitarian....

If human enjoyment *per se* is not to be condemned then it is not too rash to say that we *know* pornography does good. We can easily produce our witnesses to testify to experiencing pleasure. If in the face of this – and no other favorable argument – we are unable to demonstrate a countervailing harm, then the case for easy availability of pornography is unassailable. If, in such circumstances, we find some people unconvinced, it is futile to seek out further empirical data. Once we commit ourselves to the notion that the evil nature of something is axiomatic, we tacitly concede that evidence is largely irrelevant to our position. If pornography never fails to fill us with predictable loathing then statistics on crime, or measured statements by careful specialists, will not be useful: Our reactions will stay the same. But in this event we would do well to reflect on what our emotions tell us of our own mentality....

FOR FURTHER INQUIRY

QUESTIONS
1. Explain the difference between pornography and obscenity.
2. What is the *Miller* test? Is all pornography restricted under *Miller*?
3. Experts disagree on the "causal connection" between pornography and anti-social behavior. Analyze your belief, the arguments, pro and con, then give an explanation.
4. What do you think the framers of the Constitution intended when they drafted the First Amendment ?
5. Do you believe that consenting adults should have the right to buy/see/read whatever they wish, including pornography, and why or why not?
6. What are the "feminist" views on pornography? With which do you agree? Why?
7. Using each of the approaches to moral reasoning covered in class, discuss whether or not pornography would be allowed and why or why not?
8. Using moral reasoning and sound argument, discuss: a) pornography is beneficial to society; b) pornography is harmful to society.
9. Discuss a) the laws governing child pornography, b) your opinion of them and c) the use of child pornography in today's society.
10. Do you believe that music and art should be censored? Why or why not?

11. Compare the findings of the 1970 President's Commission with those of the 1986 Attorney General's Commission.

12. Do you believe traditional family values are impacted negatively by pornography? Why or why not?

EXERCISE

The class could be broken into three groups in order to prepare and act out the following exercise:

Your city's ordinance on pornography has been declared unconstitutional by the court "for vagueness." The city council has decided to hold a public hearing to hear the community's views on pornography and in order to determine if a new ordinance should be drafted and, if so, just what should be covered.

Group 1. The City Manager and the City Council - The manager will moderate the hearing and the City Council will hear the testimony and reach a decision based on the arguments presented, outlining the rationale for their decisions.

Group 2. Citizens Against Pornography - "CAP" - A group of concerned citizens who want pornography banned. They represent groups, some of whom, wish to prohibit the sale of pornography books, magazines, *et cetera*; and some wish to prohibit the rental/sale of X-rated videos. Some are against topless clubs and their locations in the city.

Group 3. A group of interested citizens who wish to speak against any form of censorship or ban that limits any adult's freedom to visit clubs, to purchase or use films, books, *et cetera* of their choice. Included in the group are the owners of both a video store and a topless club. Each member of each group would draft two (2) arguments to support their view. Group 1 will do an argument pro and con as part of their preparation and to aid in asking questions of the group.

After hearing arguments from each side, moderated by the City Manager, the City Manager and Council will retire, discuss, and reach a decision. They will return to the class, announce their decision and explain the basis for their decision.

SUGGESTED READINGS

• ACLU Arts Censorship Project, "Above the Law; the Justice Department's War Against the First Amendment " New York: ACLU, 1991.

• Attorney General's Commission on Pornography, Final Report Vol. I and II. Washington, D.C.: Government Printing Office, 1986.

• Bender, David, Ed., *Censorship! Opposing Viewpoints.* St. Paul, Minn., Greenhaven Press, 1985.

• Berger, Fred R. "Pornography, Sex, and Censorship," Social Theory and Practice 4, 2 (1977).

• Burgess, Ann W., *Child Pornography and Sex Rings.* Lexington Mass., Lexington Books, D.C. Heath and Co., 1984.

• Final Report of the Attorney General's Commission on Pornography., with Introduction by Michael J. McManus. Nashville, Tenn: Rutledge Press, 1986.

• Finkelhor, David, *Sexually Victimized Children.* New York, N.Y.: The Free Press, Macmillan Publishing Co., 1979.

• Heins, Marjorie. "Crime & Punishment American Style," a paper distributed by The Arts Censorship

Project, ACLU, NY.

• "Pornography and Violence in the Communication Media," A Pastoral Response, Pontifical Council for Social Communication, Vatican City, Office for Publishing and Promotion Services, United States Catholic Conference, Washington, D.C., 1989.

Woodward, Bob and Scott Armstrong. *The Brethren.* New York: Avon Books, The Hearst Corporation, 1981.

ENDNOTES

1. Cline, Victor. The current status of research on pornography's effects on human behavior, *Pornogrophy: A Report.* American Family Association, Tupelo, Ms. 1989.

2. *Roth v. U.S.,* 354 U.S. 476 (1957).

3. United States Constitution, Amendment I.

4. Chaucer, Geoffrey (1380), quoted from The Bonfire of Liberties, Censorship of the Humanities, produced by Texas Humanities Resource Center, for a traveling exhibition sponsored by the Florida Center for the Book, 1992.

5. Perrin, Noel *Dr. Bowdler's Legacy, A History of Expurgated Books in England and America.* New York: Atheneum,1969.

6. Ibid., p. 115

7. Quoted in*Queen v. Hicklin,* (aka *Regina v. Hicklin*) L.R. 3 Q.B.
 (1868). Lord Campbell's Act, 20 + 21 Vict., c83.

8. Perrin, Ibid., p. 60

9. Ibid., p. 127

10. Ibid., p. 167

11. Hoyt, Olga G. and Edwin P. *Censorship in America.* New York: The Seabury Press, 1970, p. 25.

12. Barnhart, Clarence L. ed., *World Book Dictionary,* Field Enterprise Educational Corp., 1971.

13. Ibid.,

14. *Ginsburg v. U.S.,* 383 U.S. 463 (1966).

15. *Dominos Rex (Crown) v. Edmund Curl,* 2 Str. 788, 93 English Rept.
 849 (1727).

16. Ibid.

17. Lord Campbells Act, op.ct.

18. *Queen v. Hicklin,* (aka *Regina v. Hicklin*) L.R. 3 Q.B.
 (1868).

19. Ibid. p. 371

20. Ibid.

21. Acts and Laws of the Province of Massachusetts Bay Coloney, CV, § 8.

22. *Commonwealth of Penn. v. Jesse Sharpless,* 2 Serq and Rawle 91. (1815).

23. Ibid.

24. Ibid.

25. U.S. v. Clarke, 38 F. 732 (1889).

26. Ibid., p. 734

27. U.S. v. Kennerley. 209 F. 119 (1913).

28. Ibid., p. 121

29. *Halsey v. New York Society for Suppression of Vice* , 136 N.E. 219
 (1922).

30. Ibid.

31. U.S. v. One Book Entitled Ulysses, 5 F.Supp. 182, (SDNY, 1933), 72 F.2d 705 (1934).

32. Ibid.

33. Ibid.

34. *Roth,* opt. ct.

35. 18 USC § 1461.

36. *Roth,* opt. ct., p. 485

37. Ibid., p. 490

38. Ibid., p. 500

39. *Jacobellis v. Ohio,* 378 U.S. 184 (1964).

40. A Book Named *"John Cleland's Memoirs of a Woman of Pleasure", et. al. v. Attorney General of Massachusetts,* 383 U.S. 413 (1966).

41. Ibid., p. 419 (349 Mass. at 73).

42. Ibid.,

43. Ginsberg, op. ct.

44. Ibid., pp. 465-68

45. *Redrupt v. New York,* 386 U.S. 767 (1967).

46. *Stanley v. Georgia,* 394 U.S. 557 (1969).

47. Ibid., p. 565.

48. Woodward, Bob and Scott Armstrong. *The Brethren.* New York: Avon Books, The Hearst Corporation, 1981.

49. Ibid., pp. 290-300

50. *Paris Adult Theater I v. Salton,* D.A. et al., 413 U.S. 49 (1973).

51. Ibid., p. 53

52. Ibid., p. 53

53. Ibid., p. 69

54. Ibid., p. 72

55. Ibid., pp. 112-13

56. *Miller v. California,* 413 U.S. 15 (1973).

57. Ibid., pp. 22-23

58. Ibid., p. 24

59. Ibid., p. 25
60. Ibid., p. 25
61. Ibid., p. 33
62. Ibid., pp. 34-35
63. Ibid., p. 40
64. *Federal Communication Corporation v. Pacifica Foundation, et al.,* 438 U.S. 726 (1978).
65. Ibid., p. 727
66. *New York v. Ferber,* 458 U.S. 747 (1982).
67. Ibid., pp. 756-58
68. Ibid., p. 763
69. Information Providers Coalition for the Defense of the First Amendment et. al. v. F.C.C., 928 F. 2d 866 (9th, 1991).
70. Ibid.
71. Cline, op. ct.
72. *Luke Records Inc. v. Navarro* (1992) as reported in St. Petersburg Times, June 7, 1990.
73. *Public Law 90-100* (1967).
74. *Report of the Commission on Obscenity and Pornography,* New York: Bantam, 1970. (Here-in-after referred to as "Report").
75. Abelson, H., R. Cohen, E. Heaton, and C. Suder (1970), Technical Report of the Commission on Obscenity and Pornography, Vol. 6, Washington, D.C.: Govenment Printing Office, 1-255.
76. *Final Report of the Attorney General's Commission on Pornography.,* with Introduction by Michael J. McManus. Nashville, Tenn: Rutledge Press, 1986, p. 257. (Here-in-after referred to as "Final Report").
77. Ibid., pp. 311-324
78. Ibid., p. 259
79. Ibid., p. 223
80. Report, op. ct., p. 80
81. *Senate Resolution 477,* 91st Congress, 116 Cong. Rec. 36478 (1970).
82. 39 U.S.C. § 3008 et. sec.
83. Kirk, Jerry R. Dr., *The Power of the Picture: How Pornography Harms.* Pomona, Calif.: Focus on the Family, 1989.
84. Dobson, James and Gary L. Bauer, *Children at Risk, The Battle for the Hearts and Minds of Our Kids* . Dallas:Ward Publishing, 1990.
85. *Attorney General's Commission on Pornography, Final Report Vol. I and II.* Washington, D.C.: Government Printing Office, 1986.
86. Ibid.
87. Final Report, op. ct., p. 290
88. Ibid., pp. 38-40
89. Ibid., pp. 41-42
90. Ibid., pp. 43-45
91. Ibid., p. 40
92. Ibid., p. 42

93. Ibid., p. 47
94. Ibid., p. 70
95. *Standing Together.* Vol. 6:1, Feb.-March, 1992: Cincinnati, OH. The National Coalition Against Pornography.
96. *ACLU Arts Censorship Project, "Above the Law; the Justice Department's War Against the First Amendment".* New York: ACLU, 1991.
97. Longino, Helen E., "Pornography, Oppression, and Freedom: A Closer Look", in Marilyn Pearsall, ed. *Woman and Values.* Belmont, CA: Wadworth Publishing Co., 1986.
98. Gary, Ann, "Pornography & Respect for Women". *Social Theory and Practice.* Vol. 4:4. Tallahassee, FL: F.S.U., Dept. of Philosophy, 1978: pp. 395-421.
99. Dworkin, Andrea, testimony before the Attorney General's Commission on Pornography, New York, NY, Jan. 22, 1986 as reported in *Resources for Concerned Citizens* from the National Coalition Against Pornography, Cincinnati, Ohio.
100. Clark, Lorenne M.G."Liberalism and Pornography," *Pornography and Censorship,* ed. D.Copp and S. Wendell, Buffalo, N. Y.: Prometheus Book, 1983. rpt. in *Ethical Theory and Social Issues.* David Theo Goldberg. New York: Holt Reinhart and Winston, Inc., 1989. First published under the title "Sexual Equality and the Program of an Adequate Moral Theory, The Poverty of Liberalism", *Resources for Feminist Research*, Special Publication 5, Toronto: Ontario Institute for Studies in Education, 1979.
101. Ibid., pp. 302-306
102. Gary, op. ct.
103. Ibid., pp. 395-421
104. MacKinnon, Catherine. *Feminism Unmodified.* Cambridge, Mass.: Harvard Community Press, 1987. Reprinted as "Pornography, Civil Rights & Speech" in *Morality & Practice.* 3rd ed, James P. Sterba. Belmont, Ca.: Wadsworth Pub. Co.
105. *American Booksellers Association, Inc. v. William H. Hudnut III*, 598 F. Supp. 1316, 105 S.Ct. 1172 (1984).
106. Friedan, Betty speaking at a Public Information Briefing on the Attorney General's Commission on Pornography, the proceedings of a National Coalition Against Censorship, Jan. 16, 1986 and published in *The Meese Commission Exposed,* New York: NCAC, 1987.
107. Ibid., p. 24
108. Duggan, Lisa, Nan Hunter, and Carole Vance, "Feminist Antipornography Legislation" from *Women Against Censorship,* ed. Varda Bernstein, Ground-wood Books/Douglas & McIntyre, 1985 and reprinted in *Morality in Practice*, 3rd ed. James P. Sterba.

Belmont, Ca.: Wadsworth.

109. Ibid., p. 326

110. *Senate Bill 1521*, 102d Congress, 2d Session.

111. Ibid., Sec. 2 (1) ,(2) [Report No. 102-372]

112. Heins, Marjorie. "Crime & Punishment American Style", a paper distributed by The Arts Censorship Project, ACLU, NY.

113. Ibid.

114. Lanning, Kenneth V. *Child Molesters: A Behavioral Analysis for Law Enforcement Officers Investigating Cases of Child Sexual Exploitation.* National Center for Missing & Exploitation of Children. Washington, D.C., 1986.

115. Henry, Joe. Testimony of a Child Molestor, United States Senate:

15 February 1985. rptd. R. P. "Toby" Tyler, San Beradino County Sheriff's Department. San Bernadino, Calif.

116. *"Research on Pornography: The Evidence of Harm, Pornography's Relationship to Child Sexual Exploitation and Abuse."* National Coalition Against Pornography, Cincinnati, Ohio. 1989.

117. Child Abuse Conference. Pascagoula, MS.: March 13, 1985.

118. Ferber, op. ct., p. 758

119. Addis, Don. *St. Petersburg Times.* Jan. 7, 1993.

120. Senate Report 438, 95th Congress, 1st Session. 5(1977) as quoted in Report, op. ct., p. 132

121. Research, op. ct., (LAPD) p. 3

122. Final Report, op. ct., p. 341

123. Ibid.

124. Ibid., p. 293

125. Ibid., p. 294

126. Ibid., p. 295

127. *"Executive Summary: Images of Children, Crime and Violence. in Playboy, Penthouse, and Hustler Magazines"*, 1986, issued by the United States Department of Justice, National Center for Missing and Exploited Children, Washington, D.C., noted: pg. 3 , "Playboy reaches 15, 584,000 people per issue, Penthouse 7,673,000 and Hustler 4,303,000. This compares to Psychology Today with 4,704,000 readers, Sports Illustrated with 13,034,000, and Ms. with 1,635,000."

128. Heins, Marjorie, op. ct., p. 101

129. ACLU, op. ct.

130. American Medical News, October 10, 1986.

131. Berger, Fred R. "Pornography, Sex, and Censorship", *Social Theory and Practice.* Vol. 4:2, Tallahassee, FL: F. S. U. Dept. of Philosophy. 1977.

132. *"Pornography and Violence in the Communication Media"*, A Pastoral Response, Pontifical Council for Social Communication, Vatican City, Office for Publishing and Promotion Services, United States Catholic Conference, Washington, D.C., 1989.

133. Ibid., pp. 5-6

DEATH
PENALTY

Chapter 11

David I. Seiple

PUNISHMENT

"The broad effects which can be obtained by punishment in man and beast are the increase of fear, the sharpening of the sense of cunning, the mastery of the desires; so it is that punishment tames the man, but does not make him 'better.'"

–Frederick Wilhelm Nietzsche

"The generality of men are naturally apt to be swayed by fear rather than by reverence, and to refrain from evil rather because of the punishment that it brings, than because of its own foulness."

–Aristotle

Punishment is a philosophical problem. Should we punish someone for what they have done (or, as is often the case, for what we only *think* they have done)? What degree of punishment should we use? Or should we punish, ever? And how do we decide? As we approach these sorts of issues in this chapter, we will see that there is more than one broad position we could take on the matter of punishment, and that each possible viewpoint involves asking its own kind of questions and making its own use of relevant facts.

In the legal sense, "punishment" is a term linked with the idea of "crime." Crime is behavior that a society has judged to be intolerable and has devised codified sanction against. Punishment is that legal sanction against criminal behavior.

Obviously, one cannot be punished sensibly for something unless at least two conditions hold true: (1) the crime in question has been identified, and (2) the socially approved punishment has been determined. But aren't there other necessary conditions as well? For example, (3) it is widely (though

David I. Seiple, Ph.D. Columbia University, M.T.S. Drew University Theological School, is director of research, Workplace Literacy Foundation and Adjunct Assistant Professor of Humanities at New York University, S.C.E.

not universally[1]) supposed that it is unfair to punish someone *retroactively* – that is, by declaring an act to be a crime only *after* the defendant has committed the act. And similarly, (4) punishment is not commonly sanctioned (at least not in Western civilization) unless the defendants foresaw the likely consequences of what they did, or at least were aware of the legal status of their actions. If that sort of mental fact can be proven, then a court takes that as *proof of intent ion* on the part of the defendants. They knew what they were doing, legally speaking, when they did it, so they must have actually intended to break the law.

This last condition, however, can become the source of all kinds of complications. One of these concerns the question about how we really know what someone's mental state really is. No doubt people sometimes commit crimes when they are not, as the court later says, "mentally competent" – which means that they don't really "know" the difference between right and wrong. But when assessing the punishment to be imposed on a criminal, how can we reliably determine exactly what a person's mental state was when the crime was committed? What usually happens is that various psychiatric experts testify during the legal proceeding, and not all of them always agree.

Or take the case of driving while intoxicated. A guy is celebrating New Year's in a popular way and then drives home too soon after drinking too much alcohol. He loses control of his vehicle and kills a pedestrian. Clearly, he did not intend to kill the pedestrian. Why then should he be punished? One school might say the punishment should be inflicted to reflect the fact that society values life; another would say punishment is required because society values responsible persons and such irresponsibility or moral failure must not be sanctioned. This concerns the issue of what is called *derivative responsibility*. People often excuse themselves for something they find themselves doing, on the grounds that they can't now do anything else. And normally that seems perfectly acceptable: For how can I be blamed for something that somebody else *coerced* me into doing? To say that I was coerced into doing it means that I had no choice in the matter, I could not really have done otherwise, and so the responsibility is not really mine. But notice the limits to this appeal. If I have agreed to meet a friend at 1 p.m. but I am all the way across town at 12:59 p.m., then (I may like to think) I needn't trouble myself about it because, after all, I can't be expected to do the impossible, can I? I don't really have a choice in the matter, right? Because I have no choice at the current moment, does this mean that I had no choice anywhere along the way? (Let's say that I was stuck across town at the appointed hour because I just was not paying attention to the passing time all morning.) Maybe I should have planned my time better. In other words, *I am also responsible for foreseeing the consequences of what I do,* and managing my affairs so that my promises get kept.

Similarly, the drunk driver is held responsible for not foreseeing the increased risk of accidents under intoxication. What is his blameworthiness in this case? Not quite what it would be had he set out, well in advance, to target the pedestrian – that would probably be first-degree murder. And the likely charge in his case (manslaughter) reflects that difference, as does the lessened punishment that would probably be assigned by a court.

THE RELATION BETWEEN LAW AND MORALITY

Moral responsibility has much in common with legal responsibility. For one thing, similar issues having to do with intent surface in moral discussion as well. (We usually think it our duty *not* to give out wrong information to people, but suppose I give an incorrect answer I actually think is correct? It wasn't my actual intention to lie, after all.)

However, what is lawful is often a rather easy matter to determine: You simply look at the legal statutes. And even when a case in question falls into a legal gray area so that only the courts or further

This kind of abolitionist would foresee a sad pattern in the case of Jack. What is to be gained by placing him, as a young adult, back once again in the same kind of hostile environment that produced his anti-social behavior to begin with? Is incarceration alone, with no effort at rehabilitation, really effectual as a long-run social expedient? In the present system, we send an offender to jail, straight into the company of those who are likely to harden his attitudes and sharpen his criminal skills. If he stays there for a very long time, society must bear the very high cost of confinement. And then, whenever he is finally released, he returns (probably poor) to the street, a product of a society of prisoners who have very badly prepared him for ordinary life. If I were in circumstances like that, I'd probably think of a return to prison as an improvement. (At least I'd get three square meals and a roof overhead!) In that case imprisonment, which was supposed to serve as a deterrent, actually acts as a magnet instead.

RETENTIONIST ARGUMENTS

We have just seen that if your intuitions on this question of punishment lean toward abolitionism, there are two general kinds of approaches you can take. You can argue (as we saw in Chapter 3) that, for example, it is not morally *right* to punish someone if they are not responsible for their actions – or you might be struck by the idea that punishment causes suffering which it is *wrong* to make another human being endure. That is a deontological approach. On the other hand, you might be led to believe that punishment is not likely to improve the situation: Too many criminals are only embittered and alienated by a system that really ought to be treating them as dysfunctional human beings in need of psychological help. That would be a consequentialist approach.

But what if your intuitions lie in another direction entirely? In Chapter 3 we noticed that neither of these two bases for moral claims (the deontological and the consequentialist) always provides us with the same conclusions each time it is applied. An abolitionist might appeal to either strategy to support his position; but other philosophers, also arguing in either a deontological or consequentialist style, might arrive at very different conclusions from his.

For example: (1) Some philosophers have noted that rehabilitation looks only toward the interests of the individual offender, whereas other consequences might be every bit as compelling. For one thing, since rehabilitation occurs only after an offense is committed, the need to prevent the initial crime is left unaddressed. And here one needs to ask: Isn't Ferri being too quick to assume that the threat of punishment does not really prevent others from committing similar crimes? In other words, doesn't the rehabilitationist ignore the *general deterrence* achieved by the institution of punishment?

(2) Others, arguing along similar lines, would recommend an even more sophisticated view of the goal of punishment. Just as long as we think of punitive threats on a par with brute intimidation (they would say), we miss its important *educative* function. Respect for legal authority is more than just a response to coercive power. Legal authority is a vehicle and symbol of the cultural values that any society must convey to its members, and for that reason punishment has a ritualistic aspect. Here punishment is viewed as a means of expressing social disapproval, which not only purges lingering resentment but also reinforces norms, as the evil of the wrongdoer is dramatized through a publicly shared event.

So where are we at this point? Here we have examples of (a) *retentionist* arguments regarding punishment, which are (b} based on consequentialist assumptions. So we see that in addition to two main versions of abolitionism (the deontological and the consequentialist), we are also presented with two varieties of consequentialism (abolitionist and retentionist) which produce two very different conclusions – the one consequentialist insisting that punishment is socially regressive, the other insisting that punishment is socially indispensable. And it turns out that philosophers in this last group would agree with one general kind of statement made by an abolitionist like Ferri: When we ask whether or not punishment is justified, we need to look for the beneficial consequences of applying it. The difference with someone like Ferri lies with what kind of factual evidence is cited and how it is assessed.

A consequentialist, remember, is going to look at results, to see if the consequences are beneficial or not. But unfortunately this is not a simple, straightforward matter. Conflicting evidence seems to exist, in favor of each point of view. For Ferri, the evidence suggests that punishment is at best only a temporary preventative that "does not touch the causes, the roots, of evil." Others, such as Walter Berns, dispute the evidence on which this kind of claim is made.[5] Disagreements like this show how much more work is still needed in the social sciences.

PARADOX ISN'T POISON

In the meantime, however, we should not allow ourselves to be thrown off by the mere appearance of paradox. There are some strategies we can use for looking more closely at the nature of the evidence. One key here is to be alert to the limits of merely *anecdotal evidence*. "Anecdotes" are accounts of events that may give us a vivid picture of a circumstance, and provide us with a handy fix on our first intuitions about an issue. There is nothing wrong with considering anecdotes: Indeed, they typically provide us with our entry into the complexities of a problem. The description of Jack's situation toward the beginning of this chapter is an anecdote. But until we bear down on the complexities embedded in it – and so treat it as more than just an anecdote – we only glide along the surface of a problem, and we are left only with prior prejudice, or else with undispelled perplexity.

In other words, we need to concern ourselves with the appropriate *evidential assessment*. This comes into play early on in any dispute among consequentialists. For example, few if any abolitionists suppose that punitive measures never, ever have any appropriate application. Ferri himself admitted that "if a crime manifests itself, repression may be employed as one of the remedies of criminology"; his point simply was that "it should be the very last remedy, not the exclusively dominating one .... "[6] And, just so, consequentialist defenders of punishment have to admit that rehabilitation does sometimes work. So there is conflicting evidence that needs to be assessed, and the place to begin doing that is by identifying which piece of evidence should be treated as exceptional, and which should be treated as *paradigmatic*.

A *paradigm* is a related series of events described in a way that illustrates a general point we want to make. It can be used, as we did in Jack's case, to orient us toward a problem we want to discuss. But it can also be used to confirm an interpretation or theory we happen to favor. Let's say that whenever my grandfather wants to point out the truth of his favorite saying ("Spare the rod and spoil the child"), he always goes on to remind my mother of poor Jack down the block, who never had parents who disciplined him and who finally ended up in reform school. Here he's probably using that story as a paradigm in both ways. Certainly if I challenged his hallowed maxim, he would "prove" it by citing Jack. If he's on his toes, he'll tell me that the relationship between punishment and crime actually explains the fact that Jack is now charged with passing bad checks. That's why punishment shouldn't be abolished – the bad consequences of doing so.

I, on the other hand, might be a liberal sort who agrees with Ferri's abolitionism. I might not want to regard this story about Jack as paradigmatic in the least. Maybe Jack is some kind of exception. On the other hand, I'd have to admit, Jack's kind of case does actually happen, and it's not even all that uncommon. And if Granddad is on his toes, he'd quiz me about my beliefs, discover I'm one of those "soft-hearted abolitionists," and triumphantly mention Jack once again — as if Jack completely refutes my opposition to punishment. And here I'm in a bit of trouble if I can't respond. For I too have to be able to explain the exception my own way: After all, Jack is indeed about to appear in court for a serious crime, and why (I wonder) if not because of what Granddad believes? What can I say?

Let's say that gradually it occurs to me what I think the rule in society ought to be, generally speaking: that punishment only makes matters worse, and anti-social types ought to be helped by mental health experts or counselors or clergymen, so that they can deal with their deep personal problems. Sociologists tell us that such personal problems are brought on by an unfavorable environment. Well, this might get us somewhere. In fact, doesn't this begin to suggest how I might really stand up to Granddad's argument- by showing how this particular exception might actually *prove* my point? Now I think I see that it's not enough just to talk about the lack of discipline in Jack's past. I need to talk about the lack of love. Jack was never at dinner with his family. Maybe what drove him to reform school had more to do with the way he felt neglected. (What would I have done if I became convinced that no one ever loved *me,* I wonder?)

So I begin to develop a broader theory about this whole issue. Merely abolishing punishment is not nearly enough, then; you have to replace it with the kind of social interaction that nurtures a person's genuine sense of human dignity. And we need to explore treating disturbed people so that they can gain a sense of that. And if we do that well, then crime will be greatly diminished.

That, anyway, might be a plausible position to take, and arriving at it as we just have illustrates the use to be made of evidential cases that are taken as paradigmatic by one person and exceptional by another. This is what happens all the time in debates involving consequentialists.

But would that be the end of the discussion? For might Granddad not turn my attention to a different paradigm case? There was that kid on the television talk show who said he'd been tempted to pass a few bad checks, and had actually planned it all out, but then got scared by the news reports about Jack. In other words, doesn't punishment work as a general social deterrent, preventing others from making the same mistake? So I'm left to wonder whether Granddad might not have a point after all; maybe, for that kind of reason, punishment really needs to be retained as a social institution. And so on, the argument might go.

CONSEQUENTIALISM OR RETRIBUTIVISM?

So a consequentialist on this issue is going to approach a situation and look at what is likely to happen as a result of punishing someone. Is the offender going to be deterred from further crime? Are others going to be deterred by his example? Punishment, in other words, is evaluated in light of its causal influence. Here we need to take account of a whole complex of factors, including the offender's own assessment of the *likelihood* of a sentence actually being imposed and the *degree of its severity*. And this raises the issue of *determinate* sentencing. For some crimes, the judge or jury has wide latitude as to what sentence to prescribe for a guilty offender, whereas for other crimes (such as drunk driving, typically) there is far less leeway. The fact that all crimes are not treated as strictly as, say, drunken driving has been criticized by some, who claim that this leniency dilutes punishment's full deterrence. (This issue, as we'll see later in this chapter, has had a significant impact on recent legal developments concerning capital punishment.)

But here we might want to ask a very basic question. What really causes somebody to act morally rather than anti-socially? Might it not be the case that a good part of our capacity to act conscientiously is either innate or else so well fixed in character by an early age, that rehabilitating a badly deformed conscience is usually a hopeless enterprise? As we shall now see, this clears the way for a *deontological* strategy for the defense of punishment known as *retributivism*.

Retributivism is another name for deontological retentionism. All retentionists want to defend the moral value of retaining punishment as a social practice, but retributivists do not base their defense on considerations of beneficial results. Many retributivists, for example, tend to be rather skeptical about the deterrent value of punishment. They would remind us that deterrence clearly does not work (with some people, anyway). People drive the highways at unsafe speeds all the time, despite the obvious threat to their own and others' lives. And even in the case of many other ("more serious") crimes, ones that carry a more severe punitive threat than a speeding ticket, clever people probably realize that the chances of getting caught can be minimized with some careful planning.

So why don't more clever people rob banks or forge checks? If deterrence is going to work, it must have a preventive effect upon the motives that would otherwise cause a person to commit a crime. But what is it in humans that (on the one hand) causes them to act as they do – morally or immorally – and yet (on the other) seems impervious to such direct causal influence as punishment or treatment? One answer, the one favored by many deontologists, would be that people act morally from *conscience*. "Conscience" we generally take to be *the mental faculty that identifies our moral obligations.* We know from conscience that we are obliged to tell the truth in most cases, to keep our promises, to help others in need. And conscience is supposed to be the place we feel guilty when we don't do what we're supposed to. At such times we see we didn't meet our obligations, and we feel blame.

Now a consequentialist could admit the existence of "conscience" as well, but claim that our feeling of blame is really a socially induced phenomenon, like self-esteem. Other people, and the situations in which we experience them, cause us to feel blame. And the consequentialist is also likely to look at the occurrence of blame in terms of its social function: In many cases, it seems to induce individuals to obey the rules that civilized society requires. If everybody simply did what their impulses dictated, we'd have social anarchy, and if you are a politically conservative consequentialist, you might want to emphasize how punishment offers a deterrent against social anarchy.

Is this right? Some people think this is just a wrong-headed view about human nature, and a retributivist might want to argue that criminals suffer from irrevocable tendencies toward anti-social behavior. In that case, one's conscience is pretty well set, perhaps at birth or perhaps at a fairly early age. But even that kind of argument does not quite get at the heart of the retributivist position. Even if a person's conscience were shown to be as malleable as a lump of clay, that would not in the end affect a strict retributivist's view about punishment. A retributivist is going to insist that the feelings of blame a person has over some misdeed are altogether appropriate, regardless of the social consequences. Blame is the flip side of responsibility. To base a theory of punishment upon the fact that criminals are underprivileged, disturbed, or diseased (as the abolitionist does) is to turn the scope of blame away from the individual offender, and to place responsibility upon surrounding circumstances. And this is unacceptable because people really are responsible for what they do.

This sort of point, about the "truth" of holding someone morally responsible for his or her conduct, is often paired with a point about the appropriateness of the feelings of those who ascribe that responsibility. Blaming someone can be a form of retaliation for a committed offense: It is one form that social ostracism can take. In fact, it is often hard to make a clear distinction between the blame one allegedly deserves and the quality that social disapprobation takes, but certainly these two are not the same. A mother, for example, can kindly point out to a child that he has made a mistake and that he is responsible for making appropriate amends, but without at the same time making that child feel unloved. But some retributivists either fail to make this distinction at all, or else suppose that people who feel the effects of a committed offense are justified in exacting vengeance.

GEORGE WILL ON THURGOOD MARSHALL

Compare, for example, the consequentialist discussion above with a recent deontological justification of punishment by the *Newsweek* columnist George F. Will:

> In 1952 (U.S. Supreme Court) Justice Thurgood Marshall wrote that "punishment for the sake of retribution is not permissible under the Eighth Amendment." That is absurd. The element of retribution – vengeance, if you will – does not make punishment cruel and unusual. It makes punishment intelligible. It distinguishes punishment from therapy. Rehabilitation may be an ancillary result of punishment, but we punish to serve justice, by giving people what they deserve.[7]

Will's fundamental intuition is a deontological one, which does not essentially have to do with the actual consequences of taking one or the other moral point of view. As we saw in Chapter 3, a deontologist believes that a person enjoys basic rights that cannot normally be violated – even if doing so would bring a greater benefit to a greater number of people. Likewise, Will is suggesting here that a person might be said to *deserve* moral censure and even retaliation on account of some terrible deed he or she has committed; that this desert is not in itself affected by the actual results of society's imposing blame upon the offender.

For the retributivist, the issue of punishment proper enters right at this point. In some cases, what an offender actually deserves is not just blame: He is the proper recipient of the appropriately harsh social response. In those cases some institutionalized form of punishment would be the natural vehicle for that blame, so that the offender actually deserves punishment as well.

EMPIRICAL VS. VALUE STATEMENTS

What do these illustrations of different types of moral disagreements reveal about the process of moral deliberation? Here we find quite a difference in procedure between consequentialists and deontologists, one that is based on the possibility of distinguishing *empirical fact-statements* from *value-statements*.

Consequentialists tend to treat a value-statement as a *kind* of fact-statement. Let's regard "fact-statements" as statements that we can test out by checking our experience, especially ones that can be established by scientific observation. This means that not just any run-of-the-mill account of someone's experience will suffice. If, for example, someone claims that punishment makes offenders better human beings (because, perhaps, it "teaches them a lesson"), we need to ask what reliable evidence exists for such an opinion. And evidence is not scientifically "reliable" unless it is based on a fair sampling of cases. One or two anecdotes won't decide the matter for us.

Consequentialists, as we have seen here, believe that moral categories (like "person x deserves punishment") should be applied to people only if there are empirically observable benefits to doing so. The "value" of doing so, in other words, depends upon the likely "factual" consequences. Does holding people accountable for their actions by imposing punitive sanctions really make them better individuals? Does it benefit society as a whole? And do these two considerations ever conflict? Let's say Joe Smith was once a thief but now, after a stint in a very tough prison environment, goes to church regularly and has an honest job. Is a particular instance such as this paradigmatic or exceptional, and can we explain any exceptions in a way that allows us to keep to our own theory? A retentionist here could argue that Joe Smith is the typical case, whereas an abolitionist might bring in cases where strict prison life has not had any noticeable benefits, or additional facts about Joe's circumstance (yes, it was a tough environment, but there was also a strong counseling program for prisoners – and this, not punishment *per se*, is what explains the turn around in Joe's life).

Most consequentialists these days are *utilitarians*; and (as we saw in Chapter 3) utilitarians believe that basic moral questions can be decided by looking to see which moral decision is likely to improve the *general* human well-being – the greatest good for the greatest number of people. So current disputes among consequentialists typically take the form of a disagreement about which social course of action will bring about that benefit.

DISAGREEING DEONTOLOGISTS

For two disagreeing deontologists, on the other hand, matters are different. What separates them is a basic conflict of fundamental values that is not really open to arbitration by the observable facts. Does a criminal *deserve* humane treatment due to his stature as a member of the human race, or imposed suffering due to his standing as a moral reprobate? If we pose the question in those terms, the answer is not apparent just from looking at the facts. Different people, after all, may have different evaluative responses to identical facts. The facts about Jack, whose story opened up our discussion in this chapter, are likely to draw a different set of responses, depending upon what set of values govern a person's judgment. (And if you yourself are confused about what you really do think about Jack's case, that may be because you are sensitive to a range of conflicting values!)

If you are a deontologist, then, it becomes important to keep in mind a distinction between fact-statements and value-statements. Whether or not it's snowing outside, for example, can be determined by the observable facts – by looking out the window. And (though the process becomes more complicated and less certain) whether or not it is *likely* to snow tomorrow is still a matter of using observation as a basis for calculating the chances one way or the other. Any two people who follow the right procedures are almost certain to agree, so to that extent an empirical observation can be *shared*. (It's pretty clear what the correct procedures generally are, and even if we aren't trained meteorologists, we know that there are such procedures). But a deontologist is likely to insist that value-statements are different, because the way we back them up is not just a matter of shared observation. If someone asks us why we approach the issue of punishment the way we do, we can't claim to "observe" (in any straightforward sense) that people have very basic rights, responsibilities, and deserts. Nor do we "observe" that the way to determine a moral rule is to calculate the benefits of applying it in practice, or "observe" that people should treat each other according to the Golden Rule.

There are major difficulties with both the deontological and the consequentialist strategies. The problem with deontologism is rather apparent. There is no way of proving scientifically whether or not, in principle, an offender "deserves" to be punished. This is not to say that a court of law cannot determine one's guilt or innocence. That is a different matter – a legal, as opposed to a moral, question. The moral question here has to do with what society ought to do once guilt is already determined. *Should* an offender be punished? And if the fundamental question is a deontological matter, all we can do is appeal to each others' moral intuitions about right, wrong, blameworthiness, and so forth. And we have to wonder how intuition in this case differs from mere prejudice.

Now consequentialism is supposed to have the advantage of offering a scientific basis for assessing just this sort of question, so that our answers to it need not rest on personal intuition. A consequentialist appeals to the evidence, to predict what the effects of punishment are likely to be. But there are two different sorts of difficulties here. First, as we have begun to see, this is easier said than done. The consequentialist abolitionist position assumes, for example, that criminals *as a whole* (the average criminal) really can be rehabilitated, and admittedly there are cases where attempts at rehabilitation do appear to have succeeded. But the question remains: Should these successes be taken as paradigmatic, or should they be taken as exceptional? Once having turned to a life of crime, do all (or even most) persons really harbor the capacity for a wholesale transformation of character? Conceivably, those shining examples of reformed behavior might represent nothing more than a relatively few extraordinary exceptions, out of a criminal population that by and large remain intractably set in their ways. And even among the "rehabilitated" group, how many of them can we confidently predict will never revert (become *recidivists*)? Despite the fact that some people do get rehabilitated, shouldn't social policy balance long-run benefits against costs, rather than being set on the strength of a relatively small number of heroic anecdotes?

But there is always, once again, the other side of the issue. An abolitionist might question why recidivism occurs as it does. Is it really because most criminals are so hardened that no efforts to rehabilitate will have much effect? Or is it because enlightened treatment programs remain undeveloped or unimplemented? This sort of problem with consequentialism is a result of incomplete findings, and we might want to assume that careful social science will eventually decide the issue to our satisfaction.

But there is another kind of difficulty with consequentialism – especially in its utilitarian form – which does not have to do with the infancy of social research. The problem is that a utilitarian is concerned with the greatest good for the *greatest* number of people. Might that not mean punishing someone who is really innocent of a crime? For example: In the United States there has been much concern over the last two decades around the issue of due process. Courts have often held that a conviction obtained without regard to the rights of the accused should be overturned, and this has also raised the possibility that those guilty of crimes might end up being released on these grounds. Here a utilitarian might argue that an effective system of punishment is undercut by that kind of strict adherence to regulations protecting the rights of the accused. In other words, the institution of punishment cannot work as a deterrent if potential criminals begin to believe that a smart lawyer can win their release through a barrage of legal technicalities. And this is where deep questions about the utilitarian position loom. For a deontologist would respond here: Doesn't that mean that *anyone's* rights are in jeopardy, just as long as the government thinks that some greater good is forthcoming? Doesn't this come perilously close to arguing that the end justifies the means? At what point do we draw the line?

These are complicated issues, and it may be that the only way to handle them is to adopt a "mixed" (*integrative*) approach to punishment. It may be, for example, that rehabilitation is possible in some cases but not in others, and that it should be attempted only in promising circumstances. Or it may be that there are socially beneficial consequences to holding people blameworthy, in a deontological sense, and (at the same time) that they really are blameworthy in this sense as well. Remember the kind of counter-claim one might raise against consequentialist abolitionism, which attempts to base a theory of punishment upon the fact that criminals are underprivileged, disturbed, or diseased. You could point out, for example, that this would shift responsibility away from the individual offender, and onto surrounding circumstances, and (you might argue) this would have unacceptable consequences for society at large. (You might even argue that this same strategy has failed to deal very well with the welfare problem: If people think there is no reason for them to take responsibility for themselves, they just won't – and society is left with the burden of doing so.)

In any case, you will need to think these matters through carefully for yourself.

ULTIMATE APPLICATION
– CAPITAL PUNISHMENT

Few debates in recent years have evoked more public venom in the United States than debates over whether or not the death penalty is an acceptable form of punishment, and here some of the issues we have dealt with so far re-emerge. For example, does the death penalty really deter capital crimes? Once again, the evidence is not conclusive. For example, even though the murder rate in the U.S. doubled in the 14 years preceding 1974, does the fact that the number of executions declined to zero during that period prove their deterrent value? Even retentionists on this question are hesitant to make such a claim, because so many other factors might have come into play.[8]

Even if capital punishment does not deter, does it not at least restitute? Is there not , some would ask, a rather compelling appeal in the equation of "an eye for an eye"? Here there are even more complicated matters involved than in cases of ordinary punishment. One of these is the fact that death is irrevocable, and this puts into dramatic light the problem of mistaken sentences. Certainly if a person is only incarcerated over some years for a crime he did not commit, that part of his life has been irrevocably and unjustifiably lost to him; but at least he has some time left, and hopefully some chance to redeem meaning and value in what remains to him. But that is singularly impossible in the case of the death sentence, and it seems institutionally impossible to avoid some cases of mistaken executions. Some would say that even one innocent person legally executed invalidates the entire practice of capital punishment. They go on to say that we should impose mandatory life sentence rather than execution.

But then what about the case (had he lived long enough) of Lee Harvey Oswald? Do perpetrators of especially heinous crimes not deserve the natural consequences of justified public outrage? Consider here once again a claim by George Will: "Increasingly, a life sentence is seen as a fraud that mocks the dead and jeopardizes the living by trivializing the crime of murder and diluting the indignation society needs for self-defense."[9]

Legal History. The Eighth Amendment of the U.S. Constitution prohibits "cruel and unusual punishment," and the Fourteenth Amendment guarantees equal protection under the law. A number of U.S. Supreme Court decisions involving African-American defendants sentenced to death – most prominently, *Furman vs. Georgia* (1972) and *Gregg vs. Georgia (1976)* – have attempted to address the question as to how those Constitutional provisions affect that practice. Sometimes the issue has been dealt with broadly and unequivocally, as when Justice Thurgood Marshall declared, at the time of *Furman,* that the death penalty itself was "morally unacceptable" and did indeed fail the cruel-and-unusual test. But at the time, the majority of the court was not able to agree on such a sweeping determination and restricted the scope of the decision to invalidate only selected death-penalty statutes.[10]

Since then, the legal ground has shifted out from under the abolitionists, who had so welcomed the *Furman* result. Since the mid-1970s, attention has centered not so much upon the possibility of outright mistake in determining guilt, nor on the morality involved in sanctioning execution. The more pressing matter has seemed to be the issue of fairness. It is a matter of record, for example, that most juries do not sentence a guilty defendant to death, even when the crime is first-degree murder. Why is this, and what factors go into a jury's considerations? Are these factors always legally relevant?

In view of the history of racial inequity in the U.S., it is worth noting that, in the period 1930-1967, 50% of the inmates executed for murder were African-Americans, even though blacks comprised less than 20 % of the total population. And one study has indicated that offenders charged with killing a white person were 4.3 times more likely to be sentenced to death in Georgia as someone charged with killing a black person. This has led many to claim not just that capital punishment is "cruel," but that it is "unusual," in the sense of being too often applied capriciously.[11]

However, in the *Gregg* case, the court has held that the discriminatory aspect of death sentencing could be addressed if the wide latitude exercised by juries in Georgia and elsewhere was curtailed. This resulted in many states redrafting their statutes to call either for mandatory capital sentencing, or else for "guided" direction that spelled out sentencing parameters for aggravating and mitigating circumstances. Under Florida, law for example, trials of capital crimes have a bifurcated structure: The first is determination of guilt by the jury, while the second is a jury's option to recommend or not to recommend the death penalty. The judge may impose the jury's recommendation or is required to explain at length another sentence. If the jury fails to recommend the death penalty, the judge may still impose it with certain explanations.[12]

Eventually, the Supreme Court majority decided that a general pattern of unintentional discrimination is not sufficient to call into question the entire practice of capital punishment, and that defendants would have to show evidence of discrimination in their specific cases. In the *Furman* case, the court majority, even while lacking detailed empirical evidence, invalidated some existing state death-sentencing statutes on the ground that the laws were applied disproportionately to minorities. Yet, after exhaustive evidence was made available, the court determined that the actual "risk" of such discrimination was acceptably small.

Meanwhile, the prospect of "mandatory life sentences without parole" has become a campaign of some abolitionists who argue that the *certainty* of such a sentence would be a more likely deterrent on the one hand, and on the other would still pass the test of not being "cruel and unusual." Capital punishment advocates argue against the social costs of mandatory life sentences, but some admit the effect of certain imposition of any punishment as likely to increase deterrence of crime.

Included here are two excerpts, from authors who take two very different approaches to the question of capital punishment. As they speak for themselves, try to see what kind of arguments they are making, and what sort of responses you might be able to imagine in return.

READINGS

DEFENDING THE DEATH PENALTY

For Capital Punishment is, so far as I know, the first book-length defense of the death penalty written by someone other than a professional law enforcement officer. As its author, I expected to be denounced in the liberal press, and I was. The best I could have hoped for was that the book would not be reviewed in certain journals. Unfortunately, the *New York Times Review of Books* did review it, in a manner of speaking (the reviewer suggested that its author ought to be psychoanalyzed). Surprisingly, the *New York Times*, at least in its daily edition, gave it a good review, one I could have written myself; Garry Wills, on the other hand, devoted an entire column to the book, during the course of which he told several outright lies about me and the book. Then when I appeared on a live television show in Washington debating the death penalty with a man who has devoted his entire professional life to the effort to abolish it, my wife, at home, began to receive threatening telephone calls, many of them saying that her husband was the only person who deserved to be executed (or, as one persistent caller put it, "to sizzle"); these calls continued until we were forced to change our telephone number, which is now unlisted.

I recite these events only to make the point that capital punishment is a subject that arouses the angriest of passions. I suspect that opponents of the death penalty also receive threatening telephone calls, but somehow I doubt that theirs could match mine in nastiness. To the opponents of the death penalty, nothing can be said in its favor, and anyone who tries is a scoundrel or a fool. "Hang-hards" (Arthur Koestler's term) might defend it, the Ayatollah Khomeini might defend it, and police officers might be forgiven for defending it, but no rational person can defend it. That was Garry Wills's opinion, and that appears to be the opinion of the liberal world in general.

In one respect, at least, I have no quarrel with my hostile critics. The history of capital punishment is surely one that should give everyone pause: Too many fanatics, too much ruthlessness, and too many disgusting public spectacles. On the other hand, there is also a history of the argument concerning capital punishment, and that history reveals something that ought to give pause to its opponents and arouse some doubts regarding the opinion prevailing in today's intellectual circles. Long before the current debate, political philosophers addressed themselves to the question of justice and, therefore, of crime and punishment; none of them, with the qualified exception of Jeremy Bentham, opposed the death penalty. Opposition to capital punishment is in fact a modern phenomenon, a product of modern sentiment and modern thought. Except to unreconstructed progressives – I mean persons who believe that every area of thought is characterized by progress – this fact is one that ought to cause us at least to hesitate before, so to speak, picking up the telephone.

Do we really know more about crime and punishment than did the ancients? Are we better qualified to speak on these subjects than Sir Thomas More? Are we more concerned with human rights than were the founders of the school of human rights – say, John Locke? Than the founders of the first country – our own – established specifically to secure these rights? In matters of morality are we the superiors of Kant? Are we more humane than Tocqueville? Than John Stuart Mill? Thomas Jefferson? George Washington? Abraham Lincoln?

Or, alternatively, have we become so morally ambivalent, and in some cases so guilt ridden, that we cannot in good conscience punish anyone and certainly not to the extent of putting him to death? In this connection, it is relevant to point out that, contrary to the public statements of some modern churchmen, the Bible cannot be read to support the cause of abolition of capital punishment – not when its texts are read fairly. Furthermore, it is not insignificant that in the past, when the souls of men and women were shaped by the Bible and the regimes that ruled in the West were those that derived their principles from the Bible, death was a customary penalty. Some of these regimes were the most sanguinary known to history, which suggests that piety and harsh punishment go together.

I am not contending that there might not be moral objections to capital punishment (there certainly are when it cannot be imposed fairly, or in a non-discriminatory fashion), but only that neither political philosophy nor the Bible lends support to these objections. The abolition movement stems, instead, from what can fairly be described as an amoral, and surely an anti-religious, work: Cesare Beccaria's unusually influential *On Crimes and Punishments,* first published in 1764. Beccaria, whose teacher was Thomas Hobbes, set out to accomplish more than a few changes in the criminal codes of Western European countries: His revisions required the establishment of the modern liberal state, a state from which the Church's influence would be excluded. Like Hobbes, Beccaria argued that there is no morality outside the positive law. Here is the source of that moral ambivalence to which I referred and which has gradually come to characterize the so-called enlightened opinion respecting punishment; the public opinion lags behind somewhat. A Norwegian judge (quoted by the well-known criminologist Johannes Andenaes) remarked this when he said that "our grandfathers punished, and they did so with a clear conscience (and) we punish too, but we do it with a bad conscience."

Why, indeed, do we punish criminals? Some of us try to ease our uneasy consciences by saying that the purpose of punishment is the rehabilitation of the criminal. But we ought to know by now that we cannot in fact rehabilitate criminals. An occasional criminal, yes, but not criminals as a class or in significant numbers. We cannot rehabilitate them any more successfully than our penitentiaries can cause them to repent, or to become penitent. One reason for this is that too many of us, and especially those of us in the rehabilitation business, are of the opinion that criminals are not wicked. Who are we to ask them to repent when, essentially, we think they have nothing to repent of? How can we in good conscience ask them to be rehabilitated when, in effect, we deny that there is a moral order to which they should be restored? We look upon the criminal as disturbed, yes; sick, perhaps; underprivileged, surely; but wicked, no. Karl Menninger, a leading criminal psychologist, accused us in *The Crime of Punishment* of being criminals because we damn "some of our fellow citizens with the label 'criminal.'" We who do this are, he says, the only criminals. The others are sick and deserve to be treated, not punished. The immorality of this position, whose premise is that no one is responsible for his acts, requires no elaboration.

Or we punish criminals in order to deter others from becoming criminals. Punishment for this purpose is utilitarian, and, like Beccaria, we can justify something if it is truly useful. But again, to inflict pain on one person merely to affect the behavior of others is surely immoral, as our criminology texts have not hesitated to tell us.

Perhaps we can be persuaded of the necessity to punish criminals in order to incapacitate them, thereby preventing them from committing their crimes among us (but not, of course, against their fellow prisoners). I must point out, however, that unless we concede, as I do, that even incarcerated criminals are no less worthy of our concern than are law-abiding persons, this policy is also immoral.

What we have not been able to do (although there are signs here and there that this is changing) is to admit that we punish, in part at least, to pay back the criminal for what he has done to us, not as individuals but as a moral community. We exact retribution, and we do not like to admit this. Retribution smacks of harshness and moral indignation, and our Hobbesian-Beccarian principles forbid the public expression of moral indignation. In the 1972 death penalty cases, Justice Marshall went so far as to say that the Eighth Amendment forbidding cruel and unusual punishment, forbids "punishment for the sake of retribution." In the words of Marshall's closest colleague, Justice Brennan, to execute a person in order to exact retribution is to deprive him of his human dignity, and "even the vilest criminal (is) possessed of common human dignity."

In the past, when men reflected seriously on the differences between human and other beings, human dignity was understood to consist of the capacity to be a moral being, a being capable of choosing between right and wrong and, with this freedom, capable of governing himself. Unlike other animals, a human being was understood to be a responsible moral creature. The "vilest criminal" was not being deprived of his human dignity when he was punished, not even when he was punished by being put to death; he had lost his dignity when he freely chose to commit his vile crimes. Retribution means to pay back, or to give people what they deserve to get, and it implies that different people deserve to get different things. But if human dignity is the standard according to which we determine who deserves to get what, and if everyone, no matter what he does, possesses human dignity, as Brennan would have it, then no one deserves to be treated differently and, unless everyone deserves to be punished, no one deserves to be punished.

I agree that a world built on Brennan's idea of human dignity may not exact retribution. It has lost all confidence in its opinions of right and wrong, good and evil, righteous and wicked, deserving and undeserving, and human and inhuman. It is, as the most eloquent opponent of the death penalty put it – I refer to the late Albert Camus – a world without God. As he said so well in his brilliant novel, *L'Etranger,* this is a world of hypocrites affecting the language of justice, of moral outrage. Of course it is entitled to execute no one; such a world may punish no one. And that, he said, is our world. He did not act as if he believed it – he was a very brave enemy of both Hitler and Stalin – but he did most emphatically say it.

The issue of capital punishment can be said to turn on the kind of world we live in (or the world we want to live in); a moral world or a morally indifferent world.

Contrary to Justices Marshall and Brennan, we in the United States have always recognized the legitimacy of retribution. We have schedules of punishment in every criminal code according to which punishments are designed to fit the crime, and not simply to fit what social science tells us about deterrence and rehabilitation: The worse the crime, the more severe the punishment. Justice requires criminals (as well as the rest of us) to get what they (and we) deserve, and what criminals deserve depends on what they have done to us.

To pay back criminals is not only just but, as Andenaes allows us to see, useful as well. For years he has been speaking of what he calls "general prevention," by which he means the capacity of the criminal law to promise obedience to law, not by instilling fear of punishment (the way of deterrence), but by inculcating law-abiding habits. I think the criminal law has this capacity, although Andenaes has never been able to explain the mechanism by which it works. To do so requires me to adopt an old and by now familiar manner of speaking of the law.

The law, and especially the criminal law, works by praising as well as by blaming. It attaches blame to the act of murder, for example, by making it a crime and threatening to punish anyone convicted of having committed it. This function of the law is familiar to us. What is unfamiliar is the way in which the law, by punishing the guilty and thereby blaming them for deeds they commit, also praises those persons who do not commit those deeds. The mechanism involved here is the satisfaction of the law-abiding person's anger, the anger that person ought to feel at the sight of crime. This anger has to be controlled, of course, and we rightly condemn persons who, at the sight of crime, take it upon themselves to punish its perpetrators. But we ought not condemn the anger such persons feel; indeed, that anger is a condition of a decent community. When no one, whether out of indifference or out of cowardice, responds to a Kitty Genovese's screams and plaintive calls for help, we have reason really to be concerned. A *citizen* ought to be angry when witnessing a crime, and, of course, that

anger takes the form of wanting to hurt the cause of the anger – for example, whoever it was who mugged and murdered Kitty Genovese. The law must control or calm that anger, and one way it can do that is by promising to punish the criminal. When it punishes the criminal it satisfies that anger, and by doing so, it rewards the law-abiding persons who feel it. This is one purpose of punishment: To reward the law-abiding by satisfying the anger that they feel, or ought to feel, at the sight of crime. It rewards, and by rewarding praises, and therefore teaches, law-abidingness.

Anger, Aristotle teaches us, is the pain caused by him who is the object of anger. It is also the pleasure arising from the hope of revenge. It has to be controlled or tamed, but it is not in itself reprehensible; it can be selfish, but, contrary to Freud, it need not be selfish. In fact, it is one of the passions that reaches out to other persons – unlike greed, for example, which is purely selfish – and, in doing so, can serve to unite us with others, or strengthen the bonds that tie us to others. It can be an expression of our caring for others, and society needs people who care for each other – people who, as Aristotle puts it, share their pleasures and their pains, and do so for the sake of others. Anger, again unlike greed or jealousy, is a passion that can cause us to act for reasons having nothing to do with selfish or mean calculation; indeed, when tamed and educated, it can become a most generous passion, the passion that protects the community by demanding punishment for its enemies (and criminals are enemies). It is the stuff from which both heroes and law-abiding citizens are made; and when it is aroused for the right reasons (and it is the job of the law to define those reasons), it deserves to be rewarded.

Criminals are properly the object of anger, and the perpetrators of great crimes (James Earl Ray and Richard Speck, for example) are properly the objects of great anger. They have done more than inflict injury on isolated individuals (and this is especially evident in the case of Ray). They have violated the foundations of trust and friendship, the necessary elements of a moral community. A moral community, unlike a hive of bees or hill of ants, is one whose members (responsible moral creatures) are expected *freely* to obey the laws; and, unlike a tyranny, are *trusted* to obey the laws. The criminal has violated that trust, and in doing so, has injured not merely his immediate victim but also the community as such. It was for this reason that God said to the Jewish community, "Ye shall take no satisfaction (or ransom) for the life of a murderer, which is guilty of death; but he shall be surely put to death." The criminal has called into question the very possibility of that community by suggesting that human beings cannot be trusted freely to respect the property, the person, and the dignity of those with whom they are associated. Crime is an offense against the public, which is why the public prosecutes it.

If, then, persons are not angry when someone else is robbed, raped, or murdered, the implication is that there is no moral community because these persons do not care for anyone other than themselves. When they are angry, that is a sign of their caring; and that anger, that caring, should be rewarded. We reward it when we satisfy it, and we satisfy it when we punish its objects, criminals.

So the question becomes, how do we pay back those who are the objects of great anger because they have committed terrible crimes against us? We can derive some instruction in this subject from the book of Genesis, where we find an account of the first murder and of the first disagreement as to the appropriate punishment of a murderer. Cain killed Abel, and, we are told, God forbade anyone to kill Cain in turn: Vengeance, said the Lord, is mine, and he exacted that vengeance by banishing Cain "from the presence of the Lord." The appropriate punishment would appear to be death or banishment; in either case, the murderer is deprived of life in the community of moral persons. As Justice Frankfurter put it in a dissent in one of the expatriation cases, certain criminals are "unfit to remain in the communion of our citizens."

To elaborate this point, in my book I discussed two famous literary works dealing with murders: Shakespeare's *Macbeth* and Camus' *L'Etranger* (variously translated as *The Stranger* or *The Outsider*). I pointed out that in *Macbeth* the murderer was killed, and I argued that the dramatic necessity of that death derived from its moral necessity. That is how Shakespeare saw it.

As I indicated above, Camus' novel treats murder in an entirely different context. A moral community is not possible without anger and the moral

indignation that accompanies it; and it is for this reason that in this novel Camus shows us a world without anger. He denies the legitimacy of it, and specifically of an anger that is aimed at the criminal. Such an anger, he says, is nothing but hypocrisy. The hero – or antihero – of this novel is a stranger or outsider not because he is a murderer, not because he refuses to cry at his mother's funeral, not because he shows and feels no remorse for having murdered (and murdered for no reason whatsoever); he is a stranger because, in his unwillingness to express what he does not feel – remorse, sadness, regret – he alone is not a hypocrite. The universe, he says at the end of the novel, is "benignly indifferent" to how we live. Such a universe, or such a world, cannot justify the taking of a life – even the life of a murderer. Only a moral community may do that, and a moral community is impossible in our time; which means there is no basis for friendship or for the ties that bind us and make us responsible for each other and to each other. The only thing we share, Camus says in his essay on the death penalty, is our "solidarity against death," and an execution "unsets" that solidarity.

Strangely, when some of the abolitionists speak of the death penalty as a denial of human dignity, this is what they mean. Abe Fortas, writing after he left the Supreme Court, said that the "essential value," the value that constitutes the "basis of our civilization," is the "pervasive, *unqualified* respect for life." This is what passes for a moral argument for him (and I have no doubt that he speaks for many others). In contrast, Lincoln (who, incidentally, greatly admired Shakespeare's *Macbeth*), who respected life and grieved when it was taken, authorized the execution of 267 men. His respect for life was not "unqualified." He believed, as did the founders of our country, that there were some things for which people should be expected to give up their lives. For example, as he said at Gettysburg, Americans should be expected to give up their lives in order that this nation "shall have a new birth of freedom."

There are vast differences between Camus, a man of deep perception and elegance of expression, and Fortas, but they shared a single vision of our world. Camus, however, gave it a label appropriate to the vision: A world without dignity, without morality, and indifferent to how we treat each other. There are statutes in this world forbidding crimes, but there is no basis in the order of things for those statutes. It is a world that may not rightly impose the sentence of death on anyone – or for that matter punish anyone in any manner – or ask any patriot to risk his or her life for it.

Shakespeare's dramatic poetry serves to remind us of another world, of the majesty of the moral order and of the terrible consequences of breaching it through the act of murder (the worst offense against that order). Capital punishment, like banishment in other times and places, serves a similar purpose: It reminds us, or can remind us, of the reign of the moral order, and enhances, or can enhance, its dignity. The law must not be understood to be merely a statute that we enact or repeal at our pleasure and obey or disobey at our convenience, especially not the criminal law. Whenever law is regarded as *merely* statutory, by which I mean arbitrary or enacted out of no moral necessity or reflecting no law beyond itself, people will soon enough disobey it, and the clever ones will learn to do so with impunity. The purpose of the criminal law is not merely to control behavior – a tyrant can do that – but also to promote respect for that which should be respected, especially the lives, the moral integrity, and even the property of others. In a country whose principles forbid it to preach, the criminal law is one of the few available institutions through which it can make a moral statement and, thereby, hope to promote this respect. To be successful, what it says – and it makes this moral statement when it punishes – must be appropriate to the offense and, therefore, to what has been offended. If human life is to be held in awe, the law forbidding the taking of it must be held in awe; and the only way it can be made to be awful or awe-inspiring is to entitle it to inflict the penalty of death.

Death is the most awful punishment available to the law of our time and place. Banishment (even if it were still a legal punishment under the Constitution) is not dreaded, not in our time; in fact, to judge by some of the expatriated Vietnam war resisters I used to see in Toronto, it is not always regarded as punishment. And, despite the example of Gary Gilmore, the typical offender does not prefer death to imprisonment, even life imprisonment. In prison the offender still enjoys some of the pleasures available outside and some of the rights of citizens, and is not utterly outside the protection of the laws. Most of all, a prisoner has not been deprived of hope – hope of escape, of pardon, or of being able to do some of the things that can be done even by someone who has lost freedom of movement. A convicted murderer in prison (Ray) has retained more of life than has the victim (Martin Luther King). A maximum-security prison may be a brutal place, and the prospect of spending one's life there is surely dreadful, but the prospect of being executed is more dreadful. And for the worst of crimes, the punishment must be most dreadful and awful – not most painful (for the purpose of punishment is not simply to inflict pain on the guilty offender), but awful in the sense of "commanding profound respect or reverential fear."

Whether the United States, or any of them, should be permitted to carry out executions is a question that is not answered simply by what I have written here. The answer depends on our ability to restrict its use to the worst of our criminals and to impose it in a non-discriminatory fashion. We do not yet know whether that can be done.

THE FOLLY OF CAPITAL PUNISHMENT

The arguments in defense of capital punishment have remained essentially the same since Lord Ellenborough's days. In the recent Parliamentary debates the Home Secretary, Major Lloyd George, again patiently trotted out the three customary reasons why the Government opposed abolition: That the death penalty carried a unique deterrent value; that no satisfactory alternative punishment could be designed; and that public opinion was in favor of it.

The second and third points will be discussed in later chapters. At present I am only concerned with the first and main argument. To give it a fair hearing, we must set all humanitarian considerations and charitable feelings aside, and examine the effectiveness of the gallows as a deterrent to potential murderers from a coldly practical, purely utilitarian point of view. This is, of course, a somewhat artificial view, for in reality "effectiveness" can never be the only consideration; even if it were proved that death preceded by torture, or on the wheel, were more effective, we would refuse to act accordingly. However, it will be seen that the theory of hanging as the best deterrent can be refuted on its own purely utilitarian grounds, without calling ethics and charity to aid.

A deterrent must logically refer to a "deterree," if the reader will forgive me for adding a verbal barbarity to the barbarous subject. So the first question is: Who are the hypothetical deterrees, who will be prevented from committing murder by the threat of hanging, but not by the threat of long-term imprisonment? The fear of death is no doubt a powerful deterrent; but just how much more powerful is it than the fear of a life sentence?

The gallows obviously failed as a deterrent in all cases where a murder has actually been committed. It is certainly not a deterrent to murderers who commit suicide – and one-third of all murderers do. It is not a deterrent to the insane and mentally deranged; nor to those who have killed in a quarrel, in drunkenness, in a sudden surge of passion – and this type of murder amounts to 80% to 90% of all murders that are committed. It is not a deterrent to the type of person who commits murder because he desires to be hanged; and these cases are not infrequent. It is not a deterrent to the person who firmly believes in his own perfect method – by poison, acid bath, and so on – which, he thinks, will never be found out. Thus the range of hypothetical deterrees who can only be kept under control by the threat of death and nothing short of death, is narrowed down to the professional criminal class. But both the abolitionists and their opponents agree that "murder is not a crime of the criminal classes"; it is a crime of amateurs, not of professionals. None of the points I have mentioned so far is controversial; they are agreed on by both sides ...

Who, then, are the deterrees for whose sake this country must preserve capital punishment, as the only European democracy except Eire and France – which, from the judicial point of view, is not very enviable company? What type of criminal, to repeat the question in its precise form, can only be ruled by the threat of hanging, and nothing short of hanging? It is at this point that the issue between abolitionists and their opponents is really joined. The opponents' argument may be summed up as follows: As things stand, the professional criminal rarely commits murder; but if the threat of the gallows were abolished, he would take to murder, and the crime rate would go up.

This, of course, is an unproved assumption; a hypothesis whose truth could only be tested either (a) by experiment, or (b) by drawing on analogies from past experiences in Britain and abroad. The House of Commons in 1948 voted for the experiment. It said: Let us suspend executions for five years, and see what happens. The House of Lords rejected it after it was informed by the Lord Chief Justice that the 20 Judges of the King's Bench were unanimous in opposing the measure. His main argument against the five-year suspension was that the experiment would be too dangerous; his second argument, that if the dangerous experiment were tried, abolition would come to stay. He used both arguments in the same speech. So much for the experimental method.

Now for the second method: By analogy or precedent. Perhaps the oddest thing about this whole controversy is that the Judges, who live on bread and precedent, never quote a precedent in support of their thesis that abolition leads to an increase in crime. After all, the burden of proof for this assumption lies on them; and since there is a gold mine of precedent at their disposal of what happened after the abolition of capital punishment for some 220 different categories of crime, why do they never, never treat us to a single case? Why do we never hear: You want to repeal the capital statute for murder; look what happened after the repeal of statute 14 Geo. 2, c.6, s.1 (174)(burglary), 7 Will, 4 & 1 Vic.; c.89, s.2 (arson), 9 Geo. 4, c.31, s.16 (rape), 8 Geo. 1, c.22 (1921)(forgery)? Why is it that the reformers, these reckless destroyers of the bulwarks of tradition, always rely on history for support, whereas on this particular issue the keepers of tradition act as if the past did not exist?

Yet the present situation is fraught with precedents and echoes of the past. In the 10 years 1940-49 the number of murders known to the police in England and Wales amounted to 1,666 cases; the number of executions in the same period was 127. Expressed in annual averages, we have 170 murders but only 13 executions. That means that the law as it stands is only found applicable in practice in 7% of all cases; in Scotland even less: Only 1 in 35, that is, under 3% of all murderers are actually executed. The law says that murder shall be punished by death; but in about 95 out of 100 cases the law cannot be applied for a variety of reasons which will be discussed in detail later on. And that again means, as in all cases in the past when such glaring discrepancies occurred, that the law has outlived its time and has become an anachronism.

There are, as we saw before, two methods of remedying such a situation. The first is to bring the law up to date; the second, to put the clock of history back. The latter solution was advocated by the Lord Chief Justice in his evidence before the Royal Commission of 1948, when he suggested that fewer people ought to be reprieved and that it was perfectly proper to hang a person who is certified insane, but is not insane according to the M'Naghten Rules of 1843. We have discussed in sufficient detail the disastrous results to which such attempts to put the clock back have led in the course of the 18th and early 19th centuries.

The opposite method was tried from approximately 1920 onward. The basic reason why it was tried was the same which underlies the present inquiry: The law had become outdated, and therefore largely inapplicable and ineffective. In November 1830, the Jurors of London presented their remarkable petition to the Commons. It ran:

That in present state of the law, jurors feel extremely reluctant to convict where the penal consequences of the offense excite a conscientious horror in their minds, lest the rigorous performance of their duties as jurors should make them accessory to judicial murder. Hence, in Courts of Justice, a most necessary and painful struggle is occasioned by the conflict of the feelings of a just humanity with the sense of the obligation of an oath.

The deterrent of the gallows affected the jury more than the criminal; the juries went on strike, as it were. They made it a rule, when a theft of goods worth 40 shillings was a capital offense, to assess the value of the goods at 39 shillings; and when, in 1827, the capital offense was raised to five pounds, the juries raised their assessment to four pounds, 19 shillings. Present-day juries, as we shall see, bring in verdicts of "guilty, but insane" in cases where, according to medical evidence and the Judge's direction, the ac-

cused must be regarded as sane before the law. "It would be following strict precedent," says Mr. Gardiner in the *Law Quarterly*, "for the perversity of jurors to be the prelude to reform."

The perversity of the jurors reached such an extent that it led, in 1830, to the famous "Petition of Bankers from 214 cities and towns," urging Parliament to abolish the death penalty for forgery – not for any sentimental, humanitarian motives, but to protect themselves against the forgers to whom the gallows proved no deterrent. Here is the full text of the petition:

That your petitioners, as bankers, are deeply interested in the protection of property, from forgery, and in the infliction of punishment on persons guilty of that crime.

That your petitioners find, by experience, that the infliction of death, or even the possibility of the infliction of death, prevents the prosecution, conviction and punishment of the criminal and thus endangers the property which it is intended to protect.

That your petitioners, therefore, earnestly pray that your honorable House will not withhold from them that protection to their property which they would derive from a more lenient law.

Few of the bankers may have read Beccaria or Jeremy Bentham, and few would probably have subscribed to their philosophy. Yet for reasons of hardheaded expediency, they subscribed to the theory of the "minimum effective penalty. It took Parliament another six years to abolish capital punishment for forgery. The usual warnings were uttered that this measure would lead to the "destruction of trade and commerce" and, in Chief Justice Lord Mansfield's opinion, the answer to the predicament was that capital sentences for forgery ought always to be carried out. Yet when death for forgery was abolished, the number of commitments for that crime fell from 213 in the three years before repeal to 180 in the three subsequent years.

If the death penalty were a more effective deterrent than lesser penalties, then its abolition for a given category of crime should be followed by a noticeable increase in the volume of that crime, precisely as the hanging party says. But the fact tells a different story. After the great reform, the crime rate did not rise; it fell – as everybody except the oracles had expected. And yet the era of reform coincided with one of the most difficult periods in English social history. As if History herself had wanted to make the task of the abolitionists more difficult, the repeal of the death penalty for offenses against property during the 1830s was immediately followed by the "hungry forties." The great experiment of mitigating the rigor of the law could not have been carried out under more unfavorable circumstances. Yet halfway through the experiment, when the number of capital offenses had been reduced to 15, His Majesty's Commissioners on Criminal Law, 1836, summed up their report as follows:

It has not, in effect, been found that the repeal of Capital Punishment with regard to any particular class of offenses has been attended with an increase of the offenders. On the contrary, the evidence and statements to be found in our appendix go far to demonstrate that ... the absolute number of the offenders has diminished.

And at the conclusion of the most dangerous experiment in the history of English criminal law, Sir Joseph Pease was able to state in the House of Commons that "the continual mitigation of law and of sentences has been accomplished with property quite as secure, and human life quite as sacred."

"Deterrence" is an ugly and abstract word. It means, according to the *Oxford Dictionary*, "discouragement by fear." If the arguments in favor of the gallows as the supreme deterrent were true, then public executions would have the maximum discouraging effect on the criminal. Yet these public exhibitions, intended to prove that "crime does not pay," were known to be the occasion when pickpockets gathered their richest harvest among the crowd. A contemporary author explains why: "The thieves selected the moment when the strangled man was swinging above them as the happiest opportunity, because they knew that everybody's eyes were on that person and all were looking up."

Public executions not only failed to diminish the volume of crime; they often caused an immediate rise in their wake. The hanging of a criminal served less as a warning than as an incitement to imitate him. Fauntleroy confessed that the idea of committing forgery came to him while he watched a forger being hanged. A juryman, who found Dr. Dodd guilty of forgery, committed soon afterwards the same crime and was hanged from the same gallows. Cumming

was hanged in Edinburgh in 1854 for sexual assault, which immediately led to a wave of similar assaults in the region. In 1855, Heywood was hanged in Liverpool for cutting the throat of a woman; three weeks later, Ferguson was arrested in the same town for the same crime. The list could be continued indefinitely. The evidence was so overwhelming that a Select Committee of the House of Lords was appointed in 1856; it recommended that public executions should be abolished because they did not deter from crime. The Lords would not believe it, and did nothing. Ten years later, the Royal Commission of 1866 inquired into the same question, and came to the same result as the Select Committee. One of the most striking pieces of evidence before the Commissioners was a statement by the prison chaplain in Bristol, the Reverend W. Roberts, that out of 167 persons awaiting execution in that prison, 164 had previously witnessed at least one execution. What would the British Medical Association say of the value of a patent medicine for the prevention of polio, if it were found in 167 polio cases that 164 had been treated with that medicine?

Two years after the Royal Commission's reports, Parliament decided that executions should henceforth be private. However, if watching with one's own eyes the agony of a person being strangled on the gallows does not deter, it seems logical to assume that an unseen execution in a more gentlemanly manner would deter even less. One may further argue that if the penalty of hanging does not frighten even a pickpocket, it would not frighten a potential murderer, who acts either in momentary passion, or for incomparably higher stakes. Yet these were not the conclusions reached by the lawgivers. They assumed that while watching an execution from a few yards' distance did not act as a deterrent, reading a Home Office communiqué about it did.

The results of the abolition of the death penalty for crimes against property provide a powerful argument for abolishing it altogether. But in itself, the argument is not conclusive The fact that abolition of the death penalty did not increase the volume of cattle-stealing strongly suggests, but does not prove, that abolition of the death penalty would not increase the volume of murder. That proof can only be initiated by analogy with other crimes; it must be completed by actual precedents for the crime of murder itself.

Fortunately, these precedents are available through the experience of the 36 states which have abolished capital punishment in the course of the last hundred years.

The evidence has been studied by criminologists and Departments of Justice all over the world, and summarized with previously unequaled thoroughness by the British Parliamentary Select Committee of 1929-30 and the Royal Commission on Capital Punishment of 1948-53. The report and evidence of the first fills some 800 closely printed pages; the report of the second, plus its Minutes of Evidence, nearly 1400 pages of quarto and folio. The conclusion of the Select Committee is summed up as follows:

Our prolonged examination of the situation in foreign countries has increasingly confirmed us in the assurance that capital punishment may be abolished in this country without endangering life or property, or impairing the security of society.

The conclusions of the Royal Commission were essentially the same, although more cautiously expressed. Their terms of reference prevented them from considering the question whether capital punishment should be abolished or not; they were only allowed to make recommendations concerning changes in the existing capital law. Moreover, their report was unanimous, whereas the Select Committee report of 1930, as the previous Royal Commission report of 1866, was a majority report. The Commission's final conclusion regarding the expected consequences of abolition (which they managed to smuggle in, though the terms of reference excluded this question) was formulated thus:

There is no clear evidence of any lasting increase (in the murder rate following abolition) and there are many offenders on whom the deterrent effect is limited and may often be negligible. It is therefore important to view the question in a just perspective and not to base a penal policy in relation to murder on exaggerated estimates of the uniquely deterrent force of the death penalty.

They reached this conclusion by taking two types of evidence into account: On the one hand, the crime statistics of foreign countries; on the other, the opinion of the British Police Force, the prison services, and the judges.

Their findings are mainly based on comparisons between the homicide curves in closely related states in the U.S.A.; and between New Zealand and the Australian states:

If we take any of these groups we find that the fluctuations in the homicide rate of each of its component members exhibit a striking similarity. We agree with Professor Sellin that the only conclusion which can be drawn from the figures is that there is no clear evidence of any influence of the death penalty on the homicide rates of these States, and that, "whether the death penalty is used or not, and whether executions are frequent or not, both death penalty States and abolition States show rates which suggest that these rates are conditioned by other factors than the death penalty."

Once more the mountains labored and a mouse was born. The mountainous statistical survey of the Royal Commission of 1948 merely confirmed the findings of the Select Committee of 1930, which confirmed the findings of all abolitionist countries in the course of the last century for crimes against property: To wit, that abolition has not caused an increase in murder nor stopped the fall of the murder rate in any European country; and that in the non-European countries, the U.S.A., Australia, and New Zealand, the ups and downs of the murder rate show a striking similarity in states of similar social structure whether the death penalty is used or not.

The defenders of capital punishment are well aware that the statistical evidence is unanswerable. They do not contest it; they ignore it.

Now the evidence concerning abolition embraces 36 countries with vastly different populations, and in different periods of development; agricultural and industrial nations, old and new civilizations, countries rich and countries poor, Latin, Anglo-Saxon, and Germanic races, hot-tempered and placid people, countries which became abolitionist after a long period of peace and security, and others, like Germany and Italy, which have only just emerged from war, demoralized by defeat, brutalized by years of totalitarian terror. The convincingness of the proof rests precisely in the fact that, however different the countries and conditions, abolition was nowhere followed by an increase in the crime-rate, or any other noticeable ill effect.

The general reader who is new to this controversy would naturally assume that the opponents of abolition have their own arguments, figures, and evidence on the same reasoned and factual level as the abolitionists, and that it would require a good deal of expert knowledge to decide which party is right. This is not the case. The defenders of capital punishment have produced no evidence of their own; nor contested the correctness of the documentary material assembled by Royal Commissions, Select Committees, etc.; nor even tried to put a different interpretation on it. They simply ignore it; as they ignore the experience gained from mitigations of the law in this country's own past. When challenged, they invariably and uniformly trot out the same answers: There is no alternative to capital punishment; statistics don't prove anything; other nations can afford to abolish hanging, but not Britain, because the criminal Englishman (or Welshman or Scotsman) is different from any other criminal in the world; for foreigners prison may be a sufficient deterrent, the English criminal needs the gallows.

Since the Select Committee's report, the Royal Commission has vastly extended the scope of the former's inquiry, and arrived at the same results. The answer of the hang-hards remained the same. It seems hardly believable that in a nationwide controversy which has now been going on for some 25 years, one side should produce, with ant-like diligence, facts, figures, and historic precedent, mobilize the whole array of psychiatry and social science, borne out by impartial Royal Commissions – and the other side should content themselves with evasions, stonewalling, and the ever repeated nonsense about the unique and indispensable deterrent value of the death penalty. The legend about the hangman as the protector of society has been refuted and exposed to ridicule on every single past occasion, and yet it popped up again on the next.

This is perhaps the saddest aspect in this whole heart- and neck-breaking business. For it shows that an officially sponsored lie has a thousand lives and takes a thousand lives. It resembles one of the monster squids of deep-sea lore; it spurts ink into your face, while its tentacles strangle the victim in the interest of public welfare.

For Further Inquiry

• Stanley E. Grupp, ed., *Theories of Punishment* (Indiana University, 1971) has a brief, clear introduction that discusses the various theories of punishment, and provides a selection of readings that are written mostly by non-philosophers.
• For a much more philosophically sophisticated discussion covering similar ground, see the edited selections (together with the introduction) in Gertrude Ezorsky, *Philosophical Perspectives on Punishment* (SUNY Press, 1972).
• A reworking of this same territory but within a context involving related philosophical issues (especially freedom and determinism) occurs in Ted Honderich, *Punishment: The Supposed Justifications* (Harcourt, 1969).
• A detailed treatment of the issues from a deontological perspective occurs in Richard A. Wasserstrom, *Philosophy and Social Issues* (Notre Dame, 1980) and in Chapter 9 of John D. Hodgson, *The Ethics of Legal Coercion* (Reidel, 1983).
• For a series of essays that represent an abandonment of a retributivist position that the author once held himself, see Jeffrie G. Murphy, *Retributivism Reconsidered* (Kluwer, 1992).
• A discussion of the ritualistic/educative function of punishment occurs in Gordon Hawkins, "Punishment and Deterrence: The Educative, Moralizing, and Habituative Effects," in Grupp, *Theories of Punishment.*
• For an impressive scholarly treatment, including a detailed review of relevant literature, see R. A. Duff, *Trials and Punishments* (Cambridge, 1986).
• For a defense of capital punishment, see Walter Berns *For Capital Punishment: Crime and the Morality of the Death Penalty* (Basic Books, 1979).
• For an abolitionist perspective, see the writings of Hugo Adam Bedau, especially *Death is Different* (Northeastern University Press, 1987).

ENDNOTES

1. Scottish law, for example, does not recognize this as a firm legal principle. Under its provisions at least one shopkeeper has been prosecuted and imprisoned for supplying children with glue-sniffing equipment, even though there was no explicit legal provision against this at the time. The Constitution of the United States, on the other hand, specifically prohibits the passage of *ex post facto* ("after the fact") laws. See Article I, Section IX.

2. Sir Walter Moberly, *The Ethics of Punishment* (Hamden, Ct: Archon Books, 1968), p 38.

3. Richard Wasserstrom, "Why Punish the Guilty," in Gertrude Ezorsky. *Philosophical Perspectives on Punishment* (State University of New York, 1972), p. 330.

4. Enrico Ferri, "The Positive School of Criminology" in Stanley E. Grupp, ed., *Theories of Punishment* (Indiana University Press, 1971), p. 231.

5. Walter Berns, *For Capital Punishment* (Basic Books, 1979), pp. 83-152.

6. Ferri, "The Positive School of Criminology," p. 233.

7. George F. Will, "The Value of Punishment," *Newsweek* (May 24, 1982), p. 92.

8. See, for example, Walter Berns, *For Capital Punishment*, p. 87.

9. Will, "The Value of Punishment," p. 92.

10. Raymond Paternoster, *Capital Punishment in America* (Macmillan 1991), p. 156

11. D.C. Baldus, C. Pulaski, and G.G. Woolworth, *Equal Justice and the Death Penalty* (Boston: Northeastern University Press 1990).

12. *McCleskey vs. Kemp (1987).*

THE CONQUEROR

Chapter 12

Dorothy Kay Hall
Russell G. Wright

THE ENVIRONMENT

"To see the Earth as we now see it, small and blue and beautiful, in that eternal silence where it floats, is to see ourselves as riders on the Earth together... brothers who do not see they are truly brothers."
– Archibald MacLeish, after man's first landing on the moon

"Man has lost the capacity to foresee and to forestall. He will end by destroying the Earth."

– Albert Schweitzer

"When we try to pick out anything by itself, we find it hitched to everything else in the universe."

– John Muir, American naturalist

The Earth has undergone formidable changes since its formation about 4.5-billion years ago. The early Earth was a vastly different place from the Earth as we know it today. In the warmth of the primitive oceans, around 3.5-billion years ago, organic molecules became organized into the self-replicating forms we call life. Some of the early life forms utilized carbon dioxide, and gave off oxygen as a waste product. Over the millennia, oxygen became an important constituent of the atmosphere, permitting more advanced life forms to evolve.

Homo sapiens, the most advanced of these life forms, has developed the ability to adapt to and control some natural processes. Now, both natural and anthropogenic (human-impact) forces are constantly at work shaping the Earth. In this chapter, we will discuss anthropogenic changes and explore ethical questions raised by mankind's influence on the environment.

"When the prewar cohort was growing up, nature was the enemy, industrialization the ally," according to a 1989 article in *Newsweek.* "Nature spread disease and spoiled food, savaged the countryside with floods and dust bowls. Pesticides, pharmaceuticals, dams and similar interventions

Dorothy Kay Hall, Ph.D. Physical Geography, University of Maryland, is a scientist in the Laboratory for Hydrospheric Sciences at NASA/Goddard Space Flight Center. *Russell G. Wright,* B.S. and Ed.D. Science Education, University of Maryland, is director of the Event-based Science Project of the Montgomery County Schools, Rockville, Md.

held out the hope of a more civilized existence."[1] It was believed to be in the best interests of the civilized world to control natural processes as much as possible. Mankind has now developed the ability to control nature in many vital ways; in doing so, changes occur that were not anticipated.

Space-age monitoring techniques have demonstrated the extent to which the natural environment has changed. But it remains difficult to separate anthropogenic from natural change. And the question remains: Is all natural change desirable and anthropogenic change undesirable?

Rachel Carson, author of *Silent Spring*, is often credited with initiating the massive "ecology" movement. In 1962 she predicted dire consequences for life on Earth as a result of pesticide use: "As the tide of chemicals born of the Industrial Age has arisen to engulf our environment, a drastic change has come about in the nature of the most serious health problems...."[2]

Thirty years later, have Carson's predictions come true? Is the Earth – and are humans – resilient enough to rebound from the use of chemicals? For example, chlorofluorocarbons (CFCs) were developed in the late 1920s for refrigeration. Development of CFCs was a technological break-through, because CFCs are effective, non-polluting and non-toxic. Only later were CFCs shown to destroy the very fabric of our ozone layer – a layer of molecules that shield us from much of the harmful ultraviolet radiation emanating from the Sun. CFCs are especially dangerous because of their insidiousness. Their harmful effects were not confirmed until decades after their development, and after much damage to the ozone layer had already occurred. Were it not for the sustained efforts of key scientists, driven by an ethical desire to "save the world," we might still fail to understand the ozone-destroying power of CFCs and other, similar, man-made substances. CFCs are now being phased out of use, hopefully before any major damage has been done to life on Earth.

There are many important issues that face us today. Issues such as global warming, sea-level rise, deforestation, species extinction, ozone-layer depletion, air and water pollution, nuclear power generation, and solid-waste disposal are some of the major environmental issues. All of these issues are controversial.

In this chapter, we will see that often there may be more than simply two sides to an environmental issue. Many times the scientific issues are not fully understood. There often is also uncertainty about the extent to which human behavior contributed to a problem. In cases where the existence of a problem is clear, proposed solutions may be in direct conflict. The environmentally correct position is not always obvious, and the solution is almost always contentious. Political reality and environmental concern often require compromises that are seen as less than desirable to either side.

Is your moral obligation to protect the environment greater than your moral obligation to protect your job and therefore your own personal welfare? If you are like many students growing up in the 1970s and 1980s, you may think that your daily actions and choices move us incrementally closer to – or farther from – the brink of our own extinction. You recycle your newspapers. You return your car's motor oil to a designated recycling center. Before buying, you look for key words that indicate a product is safe for the environment. Words like "biodegradable," "recyclable," "ozone safe," and "organic" are found on many of the products you purchase. But, do you know for sure that the environmental positions you take are the "correct" ones?

For example, there is now a "biodegradable" plastic available. It contains up to 6% cornstarch scattered throughout the plastic. After as long as 20 years, the cornstarch degrades, leaving behind only small particles of plastic. Whatever the original shape of the object, it will be unrecognizable at the end of this degradational process. But the fact is *more* plastic will be left behind than if the object had been made of regular plastic in the first place because the cornstarch so weakens the "biodegradable" product that the plastic must be made thicker than its non-biodegradable cousin.[3] Given the difficult choice, if you had to choose which plastic to use, cost would probably be a factor in your decision.

Successful primitive civilizations were often in complete harmony with their environment. The Eskimo, before the arrival of white people, was an excellent example of such a successful civilization. Eskimos hunted and fished for survival, and wasted nothing; all parts of animals were utilized for food, clothing, tools or shelter. The drawback to a subsistence lifestyle is that it is all-consuming, leaving little time for anything but survival. Subsistence living necessitates a low population and large amounts of land. This would not be practical for most of the Earth today. Are we prepared to face the consequences of a consumption lifestyle?

GLOBAL CHANGE

GLOBAL WARMING

Scientific evidence suggests that the Earth is getting warmer, and many scientists believe that this warming is, at least in part, a result of human activities. It is well-known that the amount of carbon dioxide (CO_2) in the atmosphere has increased dramatically since the Industrial Revolution, which began about 1850. Beginning with the Industrial Revolution, CO_2 and other important trace gases were discarded in large quantities into the Earth's lower atmosphere as by-products of combustion. CO_2 and other trace gases absorb heat, trapping it close to the Earth's surface. But, even before the engines of the Industrial Revolution began to turn, the conversion of forests to agricultural fields, particularly in North America, released large amounts of CO_2 as trees were burned or left to decay. It is doubtful that people of that era considered the future impacts of their actions. Little was known then about trace gases in the atmosphere. Even if it had been considered, it is unlikely that anyone would have thought that releasing more gases into the atmosphere would be harmful on the global scale. People were interested in improving their own standard of living, and probably not particularly concerned with global, long-term, negative impacts of industrialization.

There is some evidence that global temperatures have been rising for about 100 years and that the average global temperature has increased between 0.5 and 0.7°C or more.[4] In fact, the decade of the 1980s is the warmest on record.[5]

Did the recent rise in global temperatures begin as a result of CO_2 being introduced into the atmosphere during the Industrial Revolution? Or, is the rise in global temperature part of a natural cycle of changing climate? These questions consume much scientific interest, but as yet have not been answered definitively.

The concentration of CO_2 in the atmosphere has increased by 25% since the beginning of industrialization.[6] In the 1950s Charles David Keeling, a young scientist with the Scripps Institute of Oceanography, along with others, began a measurement program to monitor the amount of CO_2 in the atmosphere on the assumption that the carbon resulting from human activities must be accumulating in the atmosphere, and may have long-term effects. Keeling began his measurement program atop Mauna Loa, a 13,678-feet-high volcano on the island of Hawaii. Interestingly, after two successful years of CO_2 measurements and much scientific interest in the results, the program was threatened with cancellation due to budgetary problems.[7] Fortunately, measurements continued, due to the efforts of Keeling and others, and monitoring stations were soon in operation in other parts of the world.

Startling increases in CO_2 were observed on what is now known as the "Keeling Curve." (Fig. 1). Keeling was hailed as a key figure in documenting and quantifying the global impacts of human activities. The profound disclosure – that huge amounts of CO_2 are being introduced into and retained in the atmosphere – has led to changes in the way many people think about their moral obligation to protect the environment. No longer can people claim ignorance when it comes to the impact of their actions on the environment. We are now convinced that actions we take may have an important effect on global weather and climate.

Sea-level rise, forest migration, drought, and agricultural shifts are all likely consequences of global-temperature increases. These outcomes of global warming are often cited as reasons that we must control our CO_2 emissions into the atmosphere. If we can reduce the emissions, we may be able to prevent some of the ill effects of global warming.

While it is not known with certainty that humans are causing global warming by the introduction of trace gases into the atmosphere, the effects of global warming are even less well-known. Many scientists and policymakers predict dire consequences if global warming occurs,[8] but others take a more moderate approach. A renowned professor of meteorology, the late Helmut Landsberg, wrote the following in 1984:

"As we have noted, the climate, both globally and locally, has not radically changed in the past few centuries. It is therefore not unreasonable to assume that it will stay within the range of the previously observed values and events. To the year 2000 this is a safe expectation. It is likely to hold also to 2025. Should a 0.5^OC global temperature rise occur (from CO_2 or any other cause), it is unlikely to cause ecological upsets. Similarly should it get globally 0.5^OC cooler it would be entirely within the realm of experiences of the not-too-distant past. Mankind has been able to cope with such variations. There is little doubt that technology can remedy any difficulties which may arise."[9]

CARBON DIOXIDE AND THE GREENHOUSE EFFECT

Carbon dioxide is a natural trace constituent of the air. Air is composed of 78% nitrogen and 21% oxygen. The remaining 1% contains argon, plus important but very small amounts of 'trace' gases such as CO_2. You might wonder why the addition of more CO_2 into the atmosphere could be bad. After all, atmospheric CO_2 is measured in parts per million (ppm)! (That is, for every 1-million air particles, there is only one CO_2 molecule.) The answer can be gleaned from the study of the atmosphere of the planet Venus.

Earth and Venus both retain the Sun's heat very efficiently due to the "greenhouse effect." The greenhouse effect is so-named because of the way heat is retained in a greenhouse. Radiation from the sun enters the greenhouse as light, and is transformed into heat as it is absorbed and re-emitted by the ground. The heat cannot escape through the glass and thus the air inside the greenhouse gets hotter and hotter. You have certainly noticed the greenhouse effect in your car as well. If you leave your windows closed on a sunny day your car will be much warmer than the air outside. This buildup of heat in your car when the windows are closed can be stifling! In the case of Venus, large amounts of atmospheric water vapor and CO_2 effectively absorb the sun's re-emitted energy; in fact, the greenhouse effect is so potent on Venus, the average surface temperature there is 455° C!

Without the greenhouse effect, life as we know it on Earth would not be possible. If it becomes too efficient, a climate like that of Venus can be envisioned in the extreme. Of the trace gases in our atmosphere, there are even more powerful heat absorbers than CO_2. Methane and CFCs are other gases that are many times more potent heat absorbers than is CO_2, although the quantity of methane and CFCs in the atmosphere is less than that of CO_2. Together, greenhouse gases act to retain the sun's heat near the Earth's surface.

One need only look at the results of ice-core studies to see that there is a strong relationship between the amount of CO_2 in the atmosphere and global temperature. Ice cores are samples of ice that are extracted from glaciers, such as from the Greenland Ice Sheet. Ice that formed thousands or hundreds of thousands of years ago remains intact in ice sheets that do not experience much melting. Air bubbles, formed at the same time as the ice, remain intact. Analysis of these ancient air bubbles can tell us what the composition of the air was at the time that the ice formed. What we do not know from these studies is whether CO_2 changes in the atmosphere caused the climate to change, or were caused by climate change. Because of the ice-core records we know that current levels of CO_2 are unprecedented for the past 200,000 years!

THE EARTH'S CLIMATE

There is no "normal" climate for Earth. However, there are conditions that are more or less favorable for human existence. There have been extended periods in the Earth's geologic history when the climate was much warmer than it is today. When the dinosaurs ruled the Earth some 65- to 220-million years ago, average global temperatures were 8-10°C warmer, on average, than they are today. Conversely, during the last major ice age when large glaciers or ice sheets covered much of North America and Europe, the Earth was an average of about 5-6°C colder than it is today. The cooling during the last ice age was not evenly distributed over the Earth, with some areas experiencing greater cooling than other areas. This uneven distribution of heat can, and historically has, wreaked havoc on human populations.

According to R. Gallant, author of *The Peopling of Planet Earth*, "The establishment of *Homo erectus* on the evolutionary landscape brings us to one of many times when glaciers crept overland and covered large areas of North America and Europe. In the process, dramatic changes in world climate patterns reshaped the lives and distribution of many species of animals and plants, as they had some 5 million-years before in Africa. The glaciers also served as geographical "barriers" that discouraged or made impossible the exploration of distant lands.

"The influence that climate and geological upheavals have had, and continue to have, on the evolution and distribution of plant and animal populations through time cannot be overemphasized. Geological events, such as the splitting apart of continents, are known to trigger major changes in climate, which in turn influence the spread and well-being of populations.

"The glaciation that gripped the Northern Hemisphere between 2- and 3-million years ago has continued off and on right up to the present. Several ice ages have come and gone over the past 1-million years alone. Over the past 700,000 years, according to climatologist Reid A. Bryson, seven ice ages have alternated with interglacial warmer periods. It seems that we in the Northern Hemisphere may be near the peak of such a warm, interglacial period now. If another ice age grips regions of the Northern Hemisphere again in a few thousand years and covers them with ice two miles thick, major global climate changes will occur and some major reshuffling of the population distribution of humans as well as of other species will be in store."[10]

SEA-LEVEL RISE

There is strong evidence that glaciers have generally been shrinking over the last century and this is caused by higher global-average temperatures. Sea level has risen 10-15 centimeters (4-6 inches) over the past century. If warmer global temperatures are sustained, sea level will continue to rise. This is at least partly because the glaciers of the world shrink and release water into the oceans as they melt.

Stephen P. Leatherman, a noted scientist who studies sea-level rise, states: "A global rise in sea level appears to be the most dramatic and certain effect of all potential consequences of human-induced climate change. In fact, sea level can be thought of as the 'dipstick' of climate change. Rising sea levels and growing coastal populations already place an increasing strain on the coastal zones of the world. Fortunately, societies can plan for the consequences of sea-level rise because at least we know the direction, if not the degree, of increase.

"The Chesapeake Bay region serves as an ideal laboratory to investigate the physical effects of accelerated SLR (sea-level rise) and explore the range of impacts and response strategies. This estuary, with over 3,200 kilometers (about 2,000 miles) of shore line, is subject to all SLR impacts: Erosion, inundation of low-lying lands and wetlands loss, salt-water intrusion into aquifers and surface waters, higher water tables, and increased flooding and storm damage."[11]

Millions of people live in coastal areas. Many are on the brink of survival. In 1987 and 1988, for example, Bangladesh was subjected to unusually severe floods. "The effects of the 1988 flood were devastating. It inundated more than 55,000 square miles of land area, affecting nearly half of the 110 million population, with 2,300 deaths. About 1.6 million tons of the standing monsoon rice crop was damaged. Many schools, houses, livestock, telecommunications, roads, railways and bridges were damaged or destroyed. Production in much of the country came to a standstill. Lines of communication were disrupted for over a month. Capital stock losses were well over $1-billion and GDP growth was set back severely."[12]

Sea-level rise is an inevitable result of global warming. Like the climate, there is no "normal" sea level. Sea level is constantly changing as a result of redistribution of water on the Earth's surface, from solid (ice) to liquid and vice versa.

GENERAL CIRCULATION MODELS

Some parts of the globe will undoubtedly benefit from warmer global temperatures because rainfall and presumably crop-growing potential will increase. Elaborate, computer-intensive mathematical formulations, or general circulation models, have been created to model the Earth's weather and climate and to study the effects of changing global temperature. These models, however, are not nearly as accurate as some scientists purport ,as pointed out by Landsberg: "neither the nature of the climate system nor its representation by numerical models has been fully grasped by some who have drawn far-reaching conclusions from some ongoing research studies and have suggested sweeping policy changes. One can only view these suggestions with skepticism in the face of very substantial uncertainties."[13]

Most general circulation models agree that if the CO_2 in the atmosphere doubles relative to the pre-industrialization level, there will be a 2-5°C increase in average global temperature.[14] While the accuracy of the global climate models is the subject of much controversy, one scenario shows that a significant increase in average global temperature could occur during the middle of the 21st century when human population is expected to swell from about 5.3-billion to 10-billion! Because of uneven warming, some areas will benefit, while other areas will become more arid and less able to support agriculture. Though the accuracy of general circulation models is not known, they represent the only tool we have to predict future climate trends. Populations may be forced to shift in the event of climate warming. Although disrupting and often devastating, human migration is not unprecedented.

CLIMATE CHANGE AND THE HUMAN CONDITION

"The littered ruins and barren landscapes left by dozens of former civilizations remind us that humans have been undercutting their own welfare for thousands of years," states Erik P. Eckholm, author of *Losing Ground.* "What is new today is the awesome scale and dizzying speed with which environmental destruction is occurring in many parts of the world. The basic arithmetic of world population growth reveals that the relationship between human beings and the environment is now entering an historically unique age of widespread danger. Whatever the root causes of suicidal land treatment and rapid population growth – and the causes of both are numerous and complex – in nearly every instance the rise in human numbers is the immediate catalyst of deteriorating food-production systems."[15]

Stories of drought and famine as well as flooding are ubiquitous in world-history books. A recent example of human suffering due to climate change is in Africa. During the 1960s, the Sahara Desert began creeping southward into the Sahel, a semi-arid region in which people rely on the annual summer monsoon rains for their existence. During much of the 1960s and the early 1970s, the monsoon rains did not come. Twenty-million people suffered a drought and at least 100,000 died. Rains that began to come again in 1973 and 1974 helped; however, much important topsoil had been lost. Vegetation that had held the topsoil shriveled, and the unprotected soil was blown or washed away when the rains returned.[16]

Millions of people in the world depend on the monsoons for their survival. India has a population of more than 600-million – three times the population of the United States in one-third of the space. Climate change that alters the monsoons could be devastating in India.

Drought is only one way in which climate change can adversely affect human settlements. In Iceland there are more than 1,000 years of records on climate. Some of the records are surrogate measures of temperature – for example, records of proximity of sea ice to the Iceland coasts. When Iceland was first settled between the years A.D. 870 and 930, until the 12th century, the climate of Iceland was relatively mild. Legend has it that the Vikings named this lush, green island "Iceland" to discourage invaders. Likewise, Greenland, an island almost totally covered by ice, was given its name by the Vikings to lure away the same potential invaders.

The economy of Iceland is based mainly on animal husbandry, and a good hay crop is necessary to provide food for livestock over the long winters. Records indicate that when the climate was "severe," as defined by the fact that sea ice reached the coasts of Iceland, epidemics occurred and hunger struck. A cold period during the 1780s was exacerbated by the eruption of the volcano, Lakagigar, in 1783.[17] Volcanic ash poisoned vegetation and livestock died. Nine thousand people, out of a population of 50,000, died in a famine.

"The Icelanders who have settled on the northern coasts are never safe from this most terrible visitor (ice). The ice is always to be found between Iceland and Greenland although sometimes it is absent from the shores of Iceland for many years at a time...."[18] Climate amelioration, such as has occurred during the 20th century, has permitted Iceland to flourish again.

Reliance on the growing of a single crop can have disastrous implications if weather patterns cause that crop to fail. "Until the mid-1700s, the Irish had grown and relied on cereals as their chief crop, but then they discovered the potato on importing it from America. So successful was it as a source of food that the Irish all but abandoned their cereal crops and became a one-crop nation, relying on the potato. Over the years to about 1840, the Irish became affluent and began to raise large families and marry at an earlier age than before. As their food source became plentiful and reliable, the Irish watched their population grow by leaps and bounds. But then in the 1840s a disastrous failure of the potato crop occurred for several successive years and widespread famine followed. Before the famine, Ireland's population had doubled to about 8-million. During and just after the famine the population dropped dramatically to 5-million. About 1-million had died, while another 2-million had left the country for Europe or North America. Stunned by the experience, the remaining 5-million did not overpopulate again and did not return to a single-crop system of agriculture."[19]

Clearly, changes in climate have had a major impact on human civilization since its inception. Well-documented examples, such as the few discussed above, show how closely human existence is tied to the vagaries of climate. Disaster, famine and human migration can occur as a result of natural climate change. Because of this, it is especially hard to separate natural from human-induced climate change. Do you think human-induced climate change would cause more serious problems than are known to be caused by Nature? Should we attempt to mitigate human-induced change, or focus our efforts on adapting to climate change?

"Many of the recent writings about climate are not really dealing with climate but with the impacts of climate on human activities, economics, and ecology. In fact, closer inspection reveals that these impacts are often produced by extreme weather events. These events are transitory but can be extremely damaging. Persistent weather aberrations, including lack or excess of precipitation, extremely high or low temperatures, sustained high winds, or lengthy periods of stagnation are, of course, the cause of many ills. They affect health and survival, cause failure of crops, damage or destroy property, fan fires, and cause air pollution episodes. The important climatic aspect is the frequency of such extreme events and any time-dependent changes in this frequency."[20]

The problems we are experiencing are not unique to the 20th century. "Vast forests have disappeared from mountains spurs and ridges; the vegetable earth accumulated beneath the trees by the decay of leaves and fallen trunks, the soil of the alpine pastures which skirted and indented the woods, and the mould of the upland fields, are washed away; meadows, once fertilized by irrigation, are waste and unproductive, because the cisterns and reservoirs that supplied the ancient canals are broken, or the springs that fed them dried up; rivers famous in history and song have shrunk to humble brooklets; the willows that ornamented and protected the banks of lesser watercourses are gone, and the rivulets have ceased to exist as perennial currents, because the little water that find its way into their old channels is evaporated by the droughts of summer, or absorbed by the parched earth, before it reaches the lowlands... "[21] George P. Marsh wrote this passage in 1864 in his book, *Man and Nature.*

We have shown that change has always been a natural part of Earth's climate, and that the consequences to human populations can be either negative or positive. However, within the past 50 years, scientists have begun to document the manner in which humans have been able to influence regional and global processes. This has been accomplished by ground-based monitoring systems such as the one on Hawaii's Mauna Loa, and by complex satellite sensors that are launched by the United States and other countries to develop an improved understanding of – and to monitor constituents of – Earth's atmosphere and biosphere. With the knowledge gained from the data collected by these sensors, we can assess some of the changes that are occurring to Earth's climate system. And this allows us to make better-informed decisions about environmental issues.

DEVELOPED VERSUS DEVELOPING COUNTRIES

Is it solely the responsibility of the industrialized countries to "correct" the problems they were primarily responsible for creating? Or can we feel morally absolved of guilt because, though we created some problems, we did not do so intentionally or with malevolence? Do we have a moral obligation to help developing countries so that they do not make the same "mistakes" we did? Should the developing countries be able to continue to exploit their resources to improve their futures? Is it not because of our exploitations that the United States is a relatively wealthy country today?

Since their inception, civilizations have inadvertently caused environmental change as a by-product of their survival, and environmental "damage" can be a by-product of a prosperous civilization. Today, industrialized nations are causing unprecedented changes – changes that are not always necessary for survival, but for increasing the comfort level of affluent people in the society. Meanwhile, in underdeveloped countries, some of the practices you will read about are perceived by the inhabitants to be necessary for survival. And unless other, more environmentally friendly practices can be introduced, the environment will continue to suffer great damage. As we will see, local environmental damage can have global consequences.

DEFORESTATION

"As a young forestry student in 1939, I spent three months at Olallie Guard Station on the Willamette National Forest in Oregon," wrote Stephen H. Spurr, a forest ecologist, in his book, *American Forest Policy in Development*, "Throughout this time I roamed the high country west of the Three Sisters, mingling with deer, elk, and bear, and never had a single other human being visit my domicile. The wilderness was encircling and perfect.

"Thirty-five years later I returned. It was only three months after open-heart surgery so I could not climb very much. Fortunately, a logging road had been pushed to a saddle 3-4 miles to the north, and my wife and I had an easy walk down the ridge and up a thousand feet to the old lookout. The logger had still not visited the area, but how it had changed! The mountain meadows, once the home of deer and elk, had seeded into thickets of young conifers, while the old fir were all too often lying dead on the ground."[22] Such is the saga of deforestation, both in temperate and tropical areas. Deforestation represents destruction of the forest; it produces a chain reaction of adverse ecological events including surface erosion, soil nutrient loss, increased flooding, water quality and quantity problems, and the devastation of irreplaceable plant and animal habitat.[23] In this chapter, we will address some of the impacts of deforestation, both its economic benefits and its ecological problems.

Some facts about deforestation: Over the past few centuries, global forest cover has declined by at least 15-20%.[24] Before A.D. 900, forests covered 90% of Europe, but by the year 1900, forests covered only 20%. Deforestation increases atmospheric CO_2 in two ways: indirectly by decreased removal of CO_2 by photosynthesis, and directly by burning. Thus deforestation is also a contributing factor in all global-warming scenarios. The act of planting more trees would surely have many benefits, including mitigating some of the effects of global warming, because trees absorb CO_2 and give off oxygen.

Many people think of deforestation as slash-and-burn "agriculture," where the tropical rain forests are burned to create room for agricultural fields. About 55% of Earth's rain forests have been cut for firewood or logging, or burned to produce agricultural land - and the area of the rain forests is being reduced by more than 62,000 square miles per year, or about 1% of the total cover.[25] Also implicated in climate-change scenarios is the deforestation that has been occurring over thousands of years as a direct result of other productive human activities. Species loss is another serious problem that is associated with deforestation. This issue will be discussed briefly in this section in the context of the needs of people versus the needs of the environment. Are they mutually exclusive?

In the United States, more than 60,000 acres of ancient forests are being cut per year, mostly for lumber. Most severely affected are the national forests of the Pacific Northwest, and The Tongass National Forest in Alaska, where up to 50% of the forest has been logged since 1950.[26] Is it morally responsible for the United States, a comparatively wealthy country, to advise developing countries that their destruction of old-growth forests should stop when we are doing the same thing, albeit on a smaller scale?

Tropical deforestation, that is, the cutting and/or burning of rainforests in tropical regions, is motivated by logging, shifting agriculture, and the demand for firewood. In shifting agriculture, subsistence farmers clear an area of forest by cutting and burning, cultivate it for 2-3 years, and then, after the soil has been depleted of nutrients, move on to another part of the forest. Because tropical forest soils are generally poor in nutrients, the length of time that agriculture can be supported on a given plot of land is very short.

Two Case Studies

In the next few paragraphs, in writings from Alan B. Nichols, we present two ways that people have managed their forest resources. You can mentally compare and contrast the methods.

Case Study 1. "Senegal, West Africa, is a good example of what can happen to the ecology and economy of a nation when trees are cleared indiscriminately. Over the last several decades, a great deal of deforestation has occurred in this coastal country resulting in the widespread loss of *Acacia albida*, a leguminous species that is well adapted to the dry, sandy soil. The acacia is a fast-growing, nitrogen-fixing tree, making it ideal for agriculture. By helping to hold moisture in the soil, it also is important to the hydrology of the country.

"Senegal's principal cash crop is peanuts. Recently, farmers have been under pressure from the government to expand production. Under a policy that was recently curtailed, the government paid to have acacia stands cleared for agriculture. This practice set in motion a vicious cycle: The loss of trees has resulted in erosion from wind and rain. Then to offset the lower per-hectare peanut yields, the farmers have destroyed more trees to expand cultivation. This cycle won't stop until the government shifts its policy to encourage natural regeneration of the acacia, according to Christopher Potter, a forest ecologist and a fellow in the joint American Association for the Advancement of Science/U.S Agency for International Development (AID) Fellowship Program, who has worked in the country.

"In addition to its program in biological nitrogen-fixation research, AID is sponsoring a reforestation project that includes reimbursing farmers to plant trees. A major feature of the project is educating farmers concerning the benefits of agroforestry, enhancing crop production by planting trees between crop rows. Unfortunately, says Potter, agroforestry has not caught on among local farmers as fast as planners had hoped.

"As to the water-quality effects of acacia destruction, Potter says that erosion and subsequent soil moisture loss has led to groundwater contamination in the coastal areas. After the trees are cut or damaged by burning and animal foraging, the soil dries out and the water table drops until eventually salt-water intrusion occurs. The mixing in some areas is so severe that salt deposits are crusting on the soil surface, says Potter, who adds that the government is slowly beginning to recognize the importance of the acacia to its economy and ecology."[27]

Case Study 2. "Sound land-use management in a cooperative effort between the government and local farmers produced a solution to needless poverty in the Chinese province of Jianxi.

"Much of the province lies in the watershed of the Yangtze River. The ecology is characterized by a tall, mixed forest. Good stands of *Cunninghamia* still cover the least accessible 10% of the province, which is bounded by rocky mountains. Another 25% of the slopes are heavily cut, secondary growth. The area has high rainfall. The vegetative cover has largely been destroyed by relentless harvesting of all woody growth and stripping of topsoil. The lower areas of the hill slopes are barren wasteland, shedding much of the 1,500 mm of annual rainfall as surface runoff.

"The provincial government agreed to build a dam if the farmers, whose incomes had declined precipitously, would restore the badly eroded watershed. Some 10,000 men, women, and children were recruited to dig contour ditches and plant trees including cedar, *Camellia sinensis* (tea), an edible nut species, and citrus undersown with a legume *(Lespedesa)*. The 12,355-acre watershed made a spectacular recovery in a short time, and within three years the reservoir was stocked with fish. By 1981, worker income had risen dramatically while the entire community enjoyed better food and housing."[28]

People who understand their environment can exploit its natural resources without damaging the environment or rendering it useless. Extensive planning and perhaps government intervention may be required in order to educate large numbers of people about the long-term benefits of certain environmental practices. Is governmental intervention necessary to cause large-scale change, or should we rely on the personal, ethical behavior of individuals to stop damaging practices and change their ways?

SPECIES DIVERSITY AND EXTINCTION

A species is a natural cluster of organisms that shares a common pool of genes. There are 5- to 10-million species that inhabit the Earth - the largest being the giant sequoia tree standing 300 feet tall and weighing about 5,593,469 kilograms (6,167 tons).[29] Man has been implicated in the extinctions of numerous species of animals. And now, with the disruption of habitats, e.g., following deforestation, many more species are threatened with extinction.

"Human activity has had a devastating effect on species diversity," according to Edward O. Wilson, a Harvard University entomologist, "and the rate of human-induced extinctions is accelerating. Fully one-half of the bird species of Polynesia have been eliminated through hunting and the destruction of native forests. In the 1800s most of the unique flora of trees and shrubs on St. Helena, a tiny island in the South Atlantic, was lost forever when the island was completely deforested."[30]

"Recent studies indicate that even with a limited knowledge of wild species and only a modest effort, more income can be extracted from sustained harvesting of natural forest products than from clear-cutting for timber and agriculture. The irony of cutting down tropical forests in order to grow crops or graze cattle is that after two or three years the nutrient-poor topsoil can no longer support the agricultural activity for which it was cleared in the first place."[31]

Because of the enormous species diversity in tropical rainforests, native peoples have learned to find uses for the abundant species, while at the same time, allowing species to survive. For example, the Chacobo Indians of Bolivia had uses for 76 species as food, building supplies, crafts or medicines. Similarly, the Ka'apor used 76 of 99 species of trees, and the Tembe Indians of Para, Brazil used 73 of 119 species.[32]

"To ensure a future for much of the Amazon rainforest that remains intact," wrote Ghillean Prance, an expert on biological diversity, "we must strike a balance between conservation and exploitation of biological diversity. Can we emulate the Indians and develop uses for many species? The very future of many rain forest species that we have already turned into industrial crops, such as rubber, cocoa, vanilla and quinine, may well depend on the conservation of the genetic material that resides in the wild relatives of those species.

"Biological diversity must be used and preserved. If we fail in the crucial task we will reduce the options of future generations to produce new medicines, foods, fibres, timbers and many other bounties of the rainforests."[33]

There is ample evidence for species extinction caused by ancient and modern man, as discussed by R. Gallant: "Some 11,000 years ago in Syria, hunter-gatherers had learned to slaughter entire herds of Persian gazelles by driving them into large enclosure traps, called kites, when the herds migrated northward in early summer. By 6,000 B.C. desert kites were common also in northern Jordan. Animal bones uncovered in the region show that from between 9,000 B.C. and 6,500 B.C., 80% of the bones were those of the Persian gazelle, and 10% were those of sheep and goats. The mass slaughters apparently reduced the number of gazelles severely, because after 6,500 B.C. only 20% of the bones were those of gazelles, and more than 60% were those of sheep and goats. Modern hunting in the region has caused the Persian gazelle to become extinct."[34]

While no one argues that the extinction of species is irreversible and final, there is controversy about the role of humans in the extinction of some species and the seriousness of species extinction. Since the beginning of time, animals and plants have been evolving; many, like the dinosaurs, have become extinct. There were at least five massive extinctions in geologic history, the most famous of which was during the Cretaceous period when all of the dinosaurs died. Prior to that, however, during the Permian period it is estimated that 77-96% of all marine animal species perished.[35] Species extinctions have occurred since life on Earth began. Is extinction an inevitable outcome of evolution?

We have learned that species extinction has occurred relentlessly since life began on Earth. Humans have caused the extinction of numerous species. However, many more species have become extinct from natural processes. Is there, in fact, any way to stop or reduce species extinction? What can an individual do to avoid partaking in species extinctions?

OZONE-LAYER DEPLETION

The depletion of Earth's delicate and vital ozone layer, which exists in the planet's upper atmosphere, is one of the most important environmental problems facing the world today. The ozone layer is found in Earth's upper atmosphere, the stratosphere, which is located at an altitude of about 6-25 miles. Ozone (O_3) is a form of oxygen (O) that is formed when energy from the Sun strikes an oxygen molecule (O_2) and breaks it apart into single O atoms; they recombine to form O_3 or ozone. Ozone is considered a pollutant when it is in Earth's lower atmosphere. (Ozone as a pollutant in the lower atmosphere will be discussed in the section on air pollution and acid rain.) But in the stratosphere, ozone plays a vital role. It shields Earth from much of the harmful ultraviolet radiation that emanates from the sun. The amount of ozone in the stratosphere is not great. If ozone were compressed to the pressure found at the Earth's surface it would consist of a layer only one-eighth of an inch thick.[36] Yet ozone is a powerful absorber of ultraviolet radiation.

Significant increases in the amount of ultraviolet radiation received at the Earth's surface could cause a range of health problems, such as an increase in skin cancers and cataracts, and possibly suppression of the human immune system. Decreased productivity of terrestrial and aquatic organisms, including some important crops, are also probable outcomes of the existence of greater ultraviolet radiation at the Earth's surface.[37] Additional effects of increased ultraviolet radiation at the Earth's surface are likely.

DEVELOPMENT AND USE OF CFCs

Safety was foremost in the minds of those who developed chlorofluorocarbons, or CFCs. CFCs were first developed in 1928 by a Du Pont Company chemist named Thomas Midgley Jr. following a major campaign to produce an efficient but safe refrigerant for home use that was non-polluting, non-poisonous, non-flammable and chemically inert. CFC use became widespread in the 1930s. CFCs have been of enormous importance; they are widely used as refrigerants, solvents, foam-blowing agents, and, in some countries, aerosol propellants. CFCs are also used in your automobile air conditioner, home refrigerator and freezer. CFCs seemed a welcome replacement for such chemicals as the ammonia and sulfur dioxide that had been used in refrigeration before the discovery of CFCs. The earlier refrigerants did not work very well and were toxic.

CFCs and other synthetic compounds like halons, however, have since been proven to have deleterious effects on the stratospheric ozone. In fact halon, a widely used fire extinguishing compound, is a more powerful ozone-destroying chemical than is CFC. Many facets of our society depend on the manufacture and use of CFCs and halons. Now most people agree they must be eliminated.

DISCOVERY OF THE PROBLEMS OF CFCs

In 1974, two scientists from the University of California at Irvine, F. Sherwood Rowland and Mario J. Molina, predicted the likelihood of ozone-layer destruction by CFCs. At the time of their discovery in 1974, Sherwood Rowland was a chemistry professor at the UC-Irvine and Molina was a postdoctoral student. In the book: *Ozone Crisis: the 15-Year Evolution of a Sudden Emergency*, Sharon Roan documents the discovery of the events that led to the ozone hole.

"It was Rowland's practice to offer his postdoctoral students a choice of problems to study. One of the problems was tracing the whereabouts of CFCs in the atmosphere, and Rowland was pleased when Molina selected the topic and set off happily to try to come up with some answers.

"We thought it would be a nice, interesting, academic exercise," Molina said later. "We both knew that these CFCs were rather stable so there was nothing obvious that would damage them soon after they would be released. But that's about as much as I knew at the time."[38]

In 1988 Carl Sagan wrote: "Who discovered that CFCs might endanger the ozone layer? Was it atmospheric chemists employed by the principal manufacturers, such as Du Pont, as a means of safety-testing their products? Was it some laboratory associated with the Environmental Protection Agency or the Department of Defense? (Discovering such a danger would unambiguously be defending us.) No, this danger was first pointed out by two university scientists pursuing pure, ivory-tower, abstract, 'impractical' science. Everybody else missed it."[39]

Because CFCs are inert and thus highly stable, they do not react with other natural substances. Rowland and Molina's theory, which later proved correct, was that because of their longevity and stability, CFCs eventually drift into the stratosphere from the Earth's lower atmosphere; it may take years for CFCs to find their way to the stratosphere. But once in the stratosphere, CFCs are broken apart by sunlight, freeing chlorine atoms to react with ozone molecules, thus destroying the ozone and producing oxygen.[40] One chlorine atom may destroy 100,000 or more ozone molecules.[41] In the extreme cold of the Antarctic stratosphere, polar stratospheric clouds contain ice particles that provide a surface on which chlorine molecules can more effectively convert to ozone-destroying molecules.

EVIDENCE FOR OZONE-LAYER DESTRUCTION

Concern about the ozone layer intensified in 1985 after a team of British scientists reported that ground-based measurements of ozone levels over Antarctica during October were decreasing each year. In 1986, NASA confirmed the existence of a "hole" in the ozone layer using satellite measurements. Scientific expeditions to Antarctica in 1987 provided the evidence needed to convince skeptics that synthetic compunds are responsible for ozone destruction.

Recently, detailed measurements from satellites and aircraft have proven that the synthetic CFCs are actively destroying ozone in the stratosphere and contributing to enlarged "holes" in the ozone layer over Antarctica and over the Arctic, as well as contributing to depletion of the ozone layer over more temperate areas. Concentrations of stratospheric ozone measured 9-20% below average in the middle and high latitudes of the Northern Hemisphere during December 1992 and January-February 1993. Though reduced, stratospheric ozone remained ample over the Northern Hemisphere during the 1992-1993 winter.[42,43]

Using the Total Ozone Measurement Spectrometer (TOMS) sensor on board a National Aeronautics and Space Administration satellite, scientists have measured and documented stratospheric-ozone depletion. In addition, ground-based studies in Antarctica have confirmed that ultraviolet radiation levels have increased at the surface, a direct result of ozone-layer depletion in the stratosphere.

CFCs have a lifetime of 50-100 years, while halons have a lifetime of 15-60 years. Even if we were to stop introducing ozone-depleting chemicals into the atmosphere today, the ozone destruction by CFCs and other chemical compounds like halons, that are currently in the stratosphere would continue for decades!

GOOD NEWS ABOUT THE OZONE HOLE

New evidence suggests that, as a result of successful efforts to curtail the world's use of ozone-depleting chemicals (see section on Legal History), scientists expect the peak of ozone depletion to occur in about the year 2000. At that time, maximum ozone losses over temperate zones will likely be about 6%. After 2000, the ozone layer should start to get thicker again, as ozone is a naturally-renewable resource.[44]

Because of the ozone hole over Antarctica, levels of ultraviolet radiation reaching the Antarctic region of the Earth's surface increase during a few weeks each year when the ozone depletion is greatest. The only other place where increased ultraviolet radiation, at ground level, has been shown to increase is at Barrow, Alaska. The cause of the increased depletion of the ozone layer above Barrow, however, may be a delayed result of the 1991 eruption of Mt. Pinatubo which injected naturally-formed, ozone-destroying chemicals into the stratosphere.[45]

In fact, according to *The Washington Post*, "Public debate over the possible effects of an eroding ozone layer often has been characterized by inflammatory claims and doomsday rhetoric. Vice President Albert Gore's popular book, *Earth in the Balance: Ecology and the Human Spirit,* says ozone depletion has become so bad that hunters in Patagonia are finding rabbits blinded by increased ultraviolet light. Anglers, Gore reports, are catching blind fish. Other accounts add that Patagonian sheep are going blind.

"The reports have gained credibility because Patagonia is at the tip of South America, not far from the Antarctic ozone hole. Yet, efforts to link the rabbit and fish claims to ozone depletion have failed. And the sheep, it turned out later, just had eye infections."[46]

The struggle for acceptance of the CFC-ozone theory. Rowland and Molina had an enormous struggle convincing people that the ozone layer was being destroyed by synthetic chemicals. In 1988 the *Los Angeles Times* reported that Sherwood Rowland did not sit by quietly waiting for the world to accept his theory: "Instead, shocked by the implications of his research, he took an unusual public stance - doggedly telling reporters, Congress, half a dozen state legislatures, and just about anyone who seemed interested that ozone loss could lead to skin cancer and catastrophic climatic change. And, again and again for more than a decade, he urged that CFCs be banned.

"In doing so, Rowland took on a \$28-billion-a-year industry whose products – ranging from home insulating materials to solvents for electronic equipment – have become an essential part of modern life."[47]

But Rowland and others persevered and finally scientists and politicians alike were convinced that action must be taken to curtail or eliminate the use of CFCs and other ozone-depleting substances. However, it was not until the 1985 discovery of reduced-ozone levels over Antarctica that Rowland and Molina's theory was generally accepted.

Part of the reluctance of people to accept Rowland and Molina's theory was that the CFC industry was responsible for many jobs. In 1974, profits from CFC production reached about \$500-million. The industry employed almost 600,000 persons with a payroll of \$6.7-billion; another 1.5-million workers were indirectly dependent on CFC production. In 1986, about 1-billion kilograms were used worldwide.[48]

Clearly, people whose jobs depend on the CFC industry were generally more skeptical, because they did not want to lose their jobs if the CFC industry were to decline. But the needed redesigns of cooling equipment to make use of non-CFC refrigerants will be a good opportunity to improve refrigeration technology to reduce energy consumption. The saved energy costs may even pay for the higher costs of CFC replacements.[49]

Everyone who is reading this chapter has reaped the benefits of CFCs. Not everyone will be equally adversely affected by the deleterious effects of CFCs should other holes develop in the future.

The moral dilemma of destroying and repairing the ozone layer. The motivation for developing CFCs was altruistic as well as practical. A safe, non-polluting refrigerant was needed. Other compounds, used previously, were not safe for home use. There was no perceived moral dilemma. CFCs were embraced as important chemicals that contributed to improved refrigeration and enhanced lifestyles. Halons are excellent for use in fire extinguishers. The moral dilemmas only became apparent after years of scientific research yielded critical information on the long-term effects of CFCs. For Sherwood Rowland, the struggle to convince the world that CFCs are dangerous chemicals was worth the result: A complete ban on CFCs is now planned. While he was pleased with a 1978 ban on aerosol-spray cans in the United States, he felt that such a ban was inadequate and that a complete phase-out was needed. For one thing, the United States accounts for only 30% of the world's CFC production.[50] This is a global problem.

It took years following the 1974 discovery to convince the world of the dangers of CFCs and other ozone-depleting chemicals. The amount of chlorine in the atmosphere is at least double what it was when Roland and Molina first made their dire prediction public in 1974.[51] It was a painful and slow process to convince, first, other scientists, and then the politicians and public that the ozone layer was being destroyed. Much of the world had to be convinced in order to eradicate CFC production effectively. This was a daunting task.

We now know that CFCs and other ozone-depleting substances are destructive to the ozone layer. What can the individual do to lessen the problem? Do we stop using our car's air conditioning? No, because CFCs will escape from the car anyway. Do we discard our refrigerator? No because eventually the CFCs will escape from the discarded refrigerator. How can we recover the CFCs that are already in our car or refrigerator before they reach the air and thus eventually end up in the stratosphere? What can we do until technological advances permit us to safely eliminate CFCs?

"Clearly, the problem will be solved if a cheaper and more effective CFC substitute can be found that does not injure us or the environment. But what if there is no such substitute? What if the substitute is more expensive? Who pays for the research, and who makes up the price difference - the consumer, the government or the chemical industry that got us into this mess?"[52]

CFCs and developing countries. Developing countries are truly in need of the benefits of CFCs. "In countries such as China and India that don't have much refrigeration, they, too, clearly want to benefit from the advances of refrigeration. Therefore, to reduce the amount of chlorine in the Earth's atmosphere is extremely difficult."[53] CFCs have become so useful in developed countries that the developing countries want to reap the benefits of CFC use. Refrigeration may be life-saving to many people. Without it, food preservation may either not be possible, or be much less efficient.

Is it morally justifiable for the developing countries to be deprived of the benefits of CFCs while the developed countries are primarily responsible for ozone-layer destruction? However, when substances that damage strato-

Reaching for the stars

spheric ozone are used anywhere in the world, the ozone is actively destroyed. We must ask ourselves, now that developing countries have the ability to manufacture and use CFCs, is there anything we can do to stop them? Can we convince them through education to reduce their use of CFCs? The problems associated with ozone-layer destruction do not seem important to people who are worried about whether or not they will be able to feed their families or if they will be able to get their next meal. To the vast majority of people in developing countries, ozone-layer depletion is probably not even considered as a problem because it does not seem to influence their daily existence. Fortunately, many of their governments understand the problem and are working to correct it through the international agreements that have been formulated (see section on Legal History).

Uneven distribution of effects of ozone-layer depletion. Some countries – Australia and South Africa, for instance, whose relative proximity to Antarctica makes for greater ozone-layer depletion

– may suffer graver consequences than mid-latitude countries. Ozone destruction may adversely affect parts of Earth unevenly. Thus the actions of people in mid-latitudes may have damaging effects on people in higher latitudes, and vice versa. Should the United States as a nation feel a moral responsibility toward higher-latitude countries that may experience more effects of ozone-layer depletion because of our actions?

Natural variability in stratospheric ozone. Ozone is continually being produced in the stratosphere as sunlight breaks apart oxygen molecules; they recombine to form ozone molecules. Because we have been studying changes in the ozone layer for a relatively short period of time, we do not know how large the natural variability in the amount of ozone is in the stratosphere. The ozone layer is constantly shifting, becoming thin in some places and thicker in others. The amount of ultraviolet light available to create ozone (by breaking apart oxygen molecules) is dependent upon the solar cycle to such an extent that in some years more ultraviolet light is produced than in others. Increases in ozone seem to occur during peak periods of solar activity occurring in 11-year cycles.[54]

Scientists began measuring ozone in the stratosphere in the 1930s and found a 7.5% increase in ozone during the 1960s.[55] We also know from satellite measurements that, even with greater CFC release there, the amount of ozone in the Northern Hemisphere is greater than that in the Southern Hemisphere. With the solar cycle contributing to the fluctuation of ozone, and other natural forces – including volcanic eruptions – contributing to ozone destruction, it remains difficult to sort out synthetic induced from natural ozone variability. In fact, recent decreases in ozone over the Northern Hemisphere may be attributable to the 1991 eruption of Mt. Pinatubo as mentioned previously.

Curtailment of CFC production and use. From 1974 to the present, major strides have been made in curtailing the uses of synthetic, ozone-depleting substances. Several international conferences have been held and numerous countries have agreed to phase out production of ozone-depleting chemicals. Action has been taken (see section on Legal History) and much progress has been made. In fact it is remarkable that so many people, world-wide, have been able to agree on anything, especially something that has little or no perceptible effect on daily living! The fact that its effects are insidious makes it even more significant that such world-wide concern has been engendered, and that serious action is being taken to curtail the use of ozone-depleting chemicals.

There were some years following the 1978 ban of aerosol-spray containers containing CFCs, that the ozone-depletion saga received little attention. But the discovery of an ozone hole over Antarctica in the mid-1980s provided the impetus for governments of many countries to enact strong measures to reduce synthetic, ozone-depleting chemicals.

Rowland never gave up attempting to convince the world that ozone-depleting chemicals should be banned. However important it was to discover the destruction of the ozone layer, it can only be considered a pyrrhic victory: After all, being right about their ozone theory meant confirmation of serious problems for inhabitants of the Earth for decades hence – unless, that is, our ethical behavior in deciding to curtail the use of ozone-depleting chemicals has been instituted in time to avoid serious problems.

AIR POLLUTION AND ACID RAIN

No one likes air pollution, but it is tolerated because it is associated with employment and with mobility. However, it is unarguable that some types of air pollution are a health hazard, and air pollution can be aesthetically unpleasing. More than 2-billion pounds of toxic air pollutants are emitted into the atmosphere each year. (Through wet or dry deposition, the pollution eventually falls to the Earth's surface.) Ozone, an important ultraviolet-light absorber in the stratosphere, is the most widely accepted indicator of bad air in Earth's lower atmosphere. Fumes from car exhaust, paint solvents, cleaning and even charcoal lighter fluids are turned into ozone by sunlight.

Ralph N. Perhac, a representative of the electric utility industry, writes: "Ozone is a health concern, and humans appear to be particularly sensitive to ozone exposure during exercise. The U.S. Office of Technology Assessment estimates that about 80,000 people are exposed to levels of ozone exceeding 0.12 parts per million, or ppm (the U.S. ambient standard), while doing heavy exercise, for an average of eight hours per person per year. The population exposed to concentrations exceeding the standard increases to 13-million when performing moderate exercise, for an average of about six hours per person per year, and 21-million are estimated to be exposed to levels exceeding the standard while performing low exercise, for an average of eight hours per person per year. Ozone reduction in nonattainment areas is a matter of high concern."[56]

Ozone is a major constituent of smog. Ozone can irritate the eyes, nose and throat and damage the lungs. Smog is formed by the action of sunlight on exhaust gases and, when trapped by a lack of wind or a thermal inversion, can build up to heavy concentrations and can cause illness and death. It can also destroy plant life and cause building materials to deteriorate. Carbon monoxide, another pollutant, is emitted by motor vehicles, some industries, and burning of coal and wood. Particulate matter, or small particles of smoke and dust, also come from the above sources.

What is acid rain and how does it form? The popular term, acid rain, refers to any type of precipitation (rain, snow, sleet or hail) that has been polluted by sulfuric or nitric acid. These acids are formed when water vapor in the air reacts with certain chemical compounds (primarily nitrogen oxides and sulfur dioxide) given off by automobiles, factories and other sources that burn such fuels as coal, gasoline and oil. Acidic gases and particles may fall to Earth even when it is not raining; the term "acid deposition" refers to both wet and dry acid pollution that falls to Earth.

The main sources of sulfur dioxide are coal-fired power stations and smelters, while the main sources of nitrogen oxides are automobiles. The oxides of nitrogen mix with other chemicals to produce poisonous and corrosive substances that either settle as dry fallout, or are flushed out by rain or snow as acid precipitation. On the east coast of the United States, the acidity of rain increased 100 to 1,000 times normal levels as a result of emissions mainly from electricity and industrial plants.[57]

Acid deposition occurs over widespread areas in eastern North America, northwestern and central Europe and parts of Asia. Effects of acid deposition are felt elsewhere as well.

There is wide disagreement about what can and should be done to mitigate the effects of acid rain. It is difficult to separate natural damage to ecosystems from human-induced damage because acid rain can fall hundreds of kilometers from the source of pollution. "Thus acid rain is a critical problem for international relations, and it rightly claims a high priority on the agenda of political debate both within and between countries," according to Chris C. Park of the University of Lancaster, England, "It is as much a question of ethics as of practice.... The acid rain debate is as much of a battle in politics as a struggle in science."[58]

Damage caused by acid rain. Changes in the acidity of rain and snow can lead to numerous environmental problems including acidification of lakes, rivers, soils, vegetation, trees and crops; in addition, acid rain can damage buildings.

Lake water that becomes too acid can kill fish populations, as has been the case in the Adirondack Mountains in New York and in other parts of eastern North America. The following excerpt from *The*

Washington Post illustrates a situation that is all-too common. "Harrisonburg, Va., April 6 – Acid snow has caused at least two fish kills in Virginia trout streams, and heavy rainfall is compounding pollution problems and hurting the state's fishery program.

"Last month's blizzard dumped about 20 inches of snow in the mountain ranges above the Shenandoah Valley. As that snow melted, the acidic water running into the streams killed rainbow trout that had been stocked for the opening of the fishing season, biologists said. The acid pollution primarily comes from coal-burning power plants west of Virginia and vehicle exhaust emissions from Northern Virginia ...."[59]

In Britain, as early as the 14th century, burning coal created serious air pollution. In the 19th century, much of Britain's air was smoky and acrid. For five days in December 1952, Britain had an air pollution event known as the "Great Smog" when sulfur dioxide gas combined with sooty emission from chimneys to form acid soot in the humid air. This was only one of many such events, but it was a particularly serious one. In the weeks and months that followed the Great Smog, there were about 4,000 additional deaths from lung and heart diseases.[60]

Acid rain is a major cause of damage to buildings made of stone and statues and other structures made of metal. "The problem is vividly illustrated in Krakow, Poland's major city, regarded as having one of the world's worst pollution problems, which receives acid deposition from upwind Katowice (a heavy industrial area); as a result Krakow is crumbling. The golden roof of the church had to be removed because it was dissolving. The faces of the statues are melting. Steeples are falling down, balconies disintegrating.... It is generally believed that air pollution has caused more deterioration of ancient statues in Rome since 1950 than had occurred in the previous 2,000 years."[61]

Health effects of air pollution. "It is estimated that air pollution contributes to the premature deaths of more than 50,000 people a year and costs the nation $10- to $25-billion in health bills."[62]

The effects of acid deposition on human health are difficult to identify. Obvious problems are eye, nose and throat irritation. There are also incidences of major pollution episodes during which and following, death rates from respiratory problems are much higher. London's "Great Smog" is one important example. In the United States there are many examples. For example, the town of Donora, near Pittsburgh, Pennsylvania experienced a severe air pollution episode in October 1948. A thermal inversion trapped air close to the surface and a fog shrouded the town. This meteorological condition lasted five days, during which time 20 people died and almost half of the town's population of 14,100 became ill, some seriously. The cause was sulphur pollution from the town's factories that became trapped near the ground by the meteorological conditions.

 A more recent example of an extreme air pollution event is the city of Kuwait following the Persian Gulf war when oil-well fires, set intentionally by the Iraqis, caused an environmental nightmare. A writer from *National Geographic* who was in Kuwait immediately following the war wrote: "In this dark and surrealistic landscape a drizzle of soot and oil flashes in our headlights and stains our protective gauze masks. The smoke cloud blocks the midmorning sun, and the fouled desert air is chill.

 "The oil fires in Kuwait, and the monstrous plume they exhaled, riveted the world's attention. Each day relentless flames devoured about 5-million barrels of oil, generating more than half a million tons of aerial pollutants, including sulfur dioxide, the key component of acid rain. Billowing two miles high, the sooty pall rode the winds to smudge far beyond Kuwait: black rains fell in Saudi Arabia and Iran; black snow greeted skiers in Kashmir more than 1,500 miles eastward."[63]

Respiratory ailments were rampant, and workers were worried about the long-term health effects of inhaling oil-laden air. The acts of "eco-terrorism"[64] caused by the Iraqis were initially thought to have little effect on global climate because the injection of soot into the atmosphere was at relatively low levels enabling the soot to be washed out or removed by dry deposition in an average of about 20 days. However, recent evidence indicates that some soot particles from the Kuwait oil-well fires were blown high into the Earth's stratosphere where global effects of the pollution are possible.[65]

Damage assessment of air pollution. Because acid rain is an invisible type of pollution (as compared, say, to smoke, which is highly visible), it has taken longer for it to be noticed and implicated in damage assessments. Assessment of human health effects is also very difficult unless there is a major air pollution event like London's "Great Smog" or the event in Donora. It is difficult to sort out causes of health problems when there are so many factors that can contribute.

We have discussed some extreme examples of air pollution events. But most air pollution is not so dramatic. In fact, air pollution may be unsightly, but may often not affect the average person noticeably on a daily basis. Health affects of low to moderate levels of air pollution are difficult or even impossible to assess. Long-term exposure to polluted air may be damaging, but the damage is very hard to quantify. Because health effects are generally not known, the task of cleaning the air is all-the-more difficult because it is very expensive and no one knows what the potential benefits will be.

Attempts to mitigate air pollution. In order to decrease local air pollution, tall stacks from factories were introduced in the United States in 1971 and in Great Britain in 1958. Tall stacks discharge pollutants up to 300 feet into the air where air currents pick up the pollutants and carry them downwind. The tall stacks did improve local air quality, but caused worse pollution downwind of the sources. Tall stacks contribute to acid rain problems because pollutants are dispersed in the atmosphere, enabling the plume of air to mix with surrounding clean air that carries oxidants which can change some primary pollutants into secondary pollutants.[66]

How are we ever to improve the quality of our air unless major compromises are made?. Will our energy-use patterns have to shift away from fossil fuels, the by-products of which are known to pollute the air? Are alternate, non-polluting energy sources safe? (See next section on nuclear energy.)

While pollution control may cost some offenders in the economy (and ultimately the consumer) money, innovative people can start businesses that help to mitigate the effects of air pollution. "In the U.S., the auto industry's increased outlays as it is forced to clean up tailpipe exhaust will flow directly into the pockets of corporations such as Allied-Signal and Corning Inc. The latter company, in Corning, N.Y., already is gearing up to produce more diesel filters and catalytic-converter parts. Corning is considering building a new plant to handle its share of an additional 200,000 to 600,000 orders a year for diesel truck filters that the legislation is expected to generate by 1994. And Corning says it expects "some very serious" business overseas as European nations follow the U.S. lead in enacting tighter requirements."[67] Clearly, some parts of the economy can benefit from tighter pollution controls.

The automobile is central to our society. It is now difficult to imagine a scenario whereby personal transportation is not used. Therefore, the use of cleaner alternative fuels for automobiles is another major potential industry that, if successful, could ultimately create many jobs, and could perhaps compensate for jobs lost elsewhere in the economy.

We can identify and measure various pollutants quite accurately, but can we convince people to act responsibly and thus help to control air pollution? Is it reasonable to expect people to drive less, and/or to carpool to work? Or do we depend solely on governmental control to reduce air pollution and acid rain?

Improvements in urban air quality. Because of controls on polluting, use of lower-sulfur fuels, and improved dispersion of pollutants, urban air quality has improved dramatically during the latter half of this century. This has been the case both in the United States and in Europe.

Smoke emissions in Britain have declined by more than 85% since 1958. Also, sulfur dioxide emissions have fallen by one-third to one-half since 1970 in some British cities including London. In fact, oak trees, which cannot tolerate smoke and industrial emissions, had almost disappeared from London after the Industrial Revolution because of the air pollution. But now, oak trees can again be planted and can survive.[68]

Part of the reason for improved urban air quality is the introduction of tall stacks that act to disperse local industrial air pollution. But, in addition, other measures – such as the requirement to use unleaded gasoline – have been legislated, at least in the United States, for the purpose of producing cleaner air. But the increased population in urban areas, and increased automobile use continues to thwart efforts to produce clean urban air.

NUCLEAR ENERGY

Before the early 1900s nothing was known of the awesome power contained in the atomic nucleus. A chain of important discoveries about matter and energy resulted in a splitting of the atom, and the first release of the energy that holds the nucleus together. In 1942, three years after the start of World War II, scientists at the University of Chicago succeeded in releasing that energy. Then in July 1945, the first atomic bomb was tested in a New Mexico desert, and in August, United States warplanes dropped atomic bombs on Hiroshima and Nagasaki, Japan.

Many peaceful uses of nuclear energy have been developed, but our lingering memory of the destruction caused by two relatively small nuclear weapons prevents many of us from accepting nuclear power as an energy source. Couple the potential destructive force with the issue of waste disposal, and a reluctance to accept a nuclear reactor into one's own neighborhood is understandable. Although about 20% of the electricity used in the United States comes from nuclear power, all new reactor orders since 1973 have been cancelled, and since 1978 no new orders have been placed. High construction costs, stagnant demand for electricity, regulatory problems, and the public controversy are the causes.[69] But before anyone rushes to join the anti-nuclear bandwagon, an examination of the facts is needed.

How nuclear energy is released and used. When nuclear energy is used to generate electricity, the reactor operates like a furnace. Fission (splitting the nucleus in two) of uranium-235 releases enormous amounts of heat. That heat in turn is used to boil water. Steam from the boiling water is used to power a turbine-driven generator. The fission of one metric ton of uranium releases as much heat as the burning of 3-million metric tons of coal or 13.3-million barrels of oil. And uranium does not release chemical or solid pollutants into the air. These are the advantages of nuclear over fossil fuels.

Disadvantages to the use of nuclear energy. Three main disadvantages to nuclear power exist: Nuclear plants cost more to build than fossil-fuel plants; public opposition to the use of nuclear energy is strong; and, nuclear waste emits dangerous radiation long after the fuel from which it came was used to generate electricity. Public opposition has been especially strong since the 1979 accident at the Three Mile Island nuclear plant in Pennsylvania.

CASE STUDY: THREE MILE ISLAND

In 1979, a combination of mechanical and human failure at the Three Mile Island nuclear power plant near Harrisburg, Pa. led to a breakdown of the reactor's cooling system that destroyed the core. A total core meltdown that would have released large amounts of radioactivity into the area surrounding the plant was prevented through the quick action of scientists and technicians. However, it took until the late 1980s to complete the cleanup.

The most controversial aspect of nuclear power is the waste left behind. Nuclear waste can remain dangerous for thousands of years. Paul and Anne Ehrlich write: "Until a means of safely disposing of these materials is found, the production of 'no risk' nuclear-generated electricity will be impossible."[70] A typical 1,000 megawatt commercial reactor produces about 20 tons of high-level waste (spent nuclear fuel) and 200-300 cubic meters of low-level waste annually.

The federal government is responsible for disposal of the highly radioactive, spent nuclear fuel. Under the Nuclear Waste Policy Act of 1982, the U.S. Department of Energy is studying the suitability of Yucca Mountain, Nev. for housing a deep underground repository for this and other high-level waste. The State of Nevada has fought DOE's efforts on the grounds that the site is unsafe. The state has identified the potential for volcanic activity, earthquakes, underground flooding, and the potential for future human activity at the site in order to extract fossil fuel and mineral deposits. Scientific evidence is currently on the side of the safety of deep burial as a disposal method. However, when specific sites are selected, the uncertainty that is inherent in predicting geologic behavior for the 10,000-year (or longer) period that nuclear waste must be isolated results in vocal public opposition. Because the Yucca Mountain site is not scheduled to open until 2010 at the earliest, there is plenty of time for its opponents to argue their case.

USES OF NUCLEAR WASTE

It is interesting to note that spent nuclear fuel should not be referred to as waste at all. It contains the heavy elements uranium and plutonium as well as some valuable high-level fission products. While the State of Nevada fights against the use of Yucca Mountain as a waste- disposal site, the city of Albuquerque, New Mexico plans to use radioactive cesium to sterilize its raw sewage. Other useful fission products include Americium, used to make smoke detectors, and others used to sterilize food and surgical dressings. Plutonium, which is popularly feared as the most lethal substance known, is in fact 80,000 times less toxic than the botulism toxin.[71]

Low-level nuclear wastes are also controversial. These wastes are generated by nuclear-power plants, medical institutions, industry, and research activities. Threats by South Carolina, Washington State, and Nevada to close the disposal trenches in their states led to a 1985 congressional authorization of regional compacts for low-level waste disposal. No new sites have been opened yet.[72] Some scientists believe the benefits of nuclear energy outweigh its drawbacks.

In order for an individual to choose the "environmentally correct" position, it is necessary to weigh advantages and disadvantages of both fossil fuel and nuclear fuel. For example, arsenic, beryllium, cadmium, chromium, and nickel are cancer-causing solid wastes released by burning coal. These wastes persist in the environment for thousands of years. What is the risk to human health from burning coal? When this calculation was made by Bernard L. Cohen, professor of physics at the

---

University of Pittsburgh, the following death estimates were obtained: For nuclear plants, deaths from high- and low-level wastes add up, over the next 1-million years, to 0.0184 deaths per year of plant operation; for coal-fired plants, deaths from air pollution, radon emissions, and residual cancer-causing chemicals, add up to 125 per year of plant operation, over the next 1-million years.[73]

Neither energy source provides a "no risk" solution. "One would have to be excessively naive to believe that those opposed to the potential benefits of nuclear power can be persuaded that their concerns are unfounded. Nuclear power, because of its emotional associations, is a useful rallying point for a number of disparate grievances."[74]

COST-EFFECTIVENESS OF NUCLEAR POWER

Residents of Sacramento voted in 1989 to shut down their nuclear power plant, and have survived quite well without it. Today the Sacramento Municipal Utility District (SMUD) is a showcase for the effectiveness of a duel approach of conservation and efficiency to power generation. Conservation includes a program of paying homeowners to replace inefficient refrigerators with new super-efficient ones. SMUD provides rebates for air conditioner replacement, pays for increased insulation, and has planted more than 28,000 shade trees. SMUD now buys replacement power from neighboring utility companies. Within a few years it will replace that borrowed capacity by adding highly efficient natural gas generating units to a mix that also includes solar power and wind. SMUD has been much more profitable since it closed its trouble-plagued nuclear reactor.[75]

The SMUD decision to shut down its reactor was a financial one. Many of the costs of running a nuclear reactor result from government regulations, including those requiring the purchase of liability insurance and participation in a liability pool. Although the Price-Anderson Act limits the liability of nuclear plant operators, it requires that every licensed commercial reactor must be covered by the maximum available private liability insurance. That maximum, currently $200-million, is called the "primary layer" of protection. If damages from a nuclear accident exceed the $200-million primary layer, the uninsured portion is divided equally among all 110 other commercial reactors, up to $63-million each. This secondary layer of coverage is payable at a rate of $10-million per year per reactor. The Price-Anderson Act thus limits liability to $7.1-billion for each nuclear accident.[76]

SOLID WASTE/RECYCLING

According to the U.S. Environmental Protection Agency, Americans generated 195-million tons of municipal solid waste in 1990.[77] This is not only more than any other country for which data are available; it represents per capita waste generation that is about twice that of Japan and other developed nations.[78]

What happens to our solid waste? There are four ways we deal with the solid waste that builds at a pace of about two kilograms per person per day. We dump it in a landfill, burn it, recycle it, or we attempt to reduce it at its source. Source reduction is inherently preferable. If we could eliminate all solid waste at its source there would be no need for further discussion. But that is not possible.

Source reduction. Source reduction is achieved through making products that last longer and are more easily repaired, re-used, or recycled; using less material to make the product; and, selecting alternative, lighter-weight and/or thinner materials for the fabrication of the product. An examination of automobile tires and food packaging reveals the tradeoffs inherent in this method of dealing with solid waste.

Because automobile tires are more durable and smaller than they used to be, tires' share of MSW (Municipal Solid Waste) has declined from 2% in 1975 to 0.9% in 1990, despite huge growth in the number of cars and number of vehicle-miles traveled. But the same development that made the tires more durable (the substitution of steel-belted radials for ordinary bias-ply tires) made car tires harder to retread or incinerate. As a result, tires pose a bigger disposal burden now than they did in the 1970s. The country is littered with an estimated 3-billion tires, many of them in huge piles that pose serious fire safety and environmental hazards.

"Food packaging provides a second example. The amount of food packaging has increased substantially in recent years as prepackaged, single-serving, and prepared food items capture a larger share of the food market. But the packaging may cause less food waste: According to EPA, food waste has declined from 13.9% of total MSW discards in 1960 to only 6.7% in 1990, at least in part due to better packaging. The amount of food waste (in tons) has barely increased during that period despite a 39% increase in population."[79]

The most common governmental approach to source reduction is public information that encourages voluntary efforts. Another approach is through economic incentives such as charging a variable rate for solid waste disposal, as was first tried by the City of Seattle. Under this system, items placed at curbside for recycling are collected free while there is a per bag or per can charge for waste placed out for disposal.

A third approach used by some states is to impose a ban on certain material. Yard waste for example, is no longer collected for landfill disposal in some communities; it must be composted or placed in special biodegradable brown paper bags for community composting. This alone reduces MSW by approximately 18% in some locales.

Landfills and incineration. No matter how effective source reduction programs are, there will always be waste that must be dealt with in one of the other ways. Currently, about two-thirds of our solid waste is disposed of in landfills, but the number of landfills is declining at a rate of 10% per year. Landfills not only close when they are full, they also are forced to close because they fail to meet increasingly- strict regulations intended to protect groundwater quality. The problem is that landfills are closing at a time when the amount of waste is increasing and the opening of new landfill sites has become increasingly difficult.

Incineration, or burning of solid waste, is the most commonly used alternative to landfills. Often called waste-to-energy facilities because they convert energy from the burning trash into steam or electricity, the use of incineration has grown rapidly over the past 40 years. However, growing concern over emissions and ash disposal have resulted in a slowing of growth that is reminiscent of early slowing in the nuclear-power industry. Heavy metals and organic contaminants, such as dioxin, are found in the ash from these incinerators. If the EPA and courts rule that incinerator ash should be treated as hazardous waste, that would increase the cost of disposal by as much as ten times. This will substantially alter the economics of incineration.[80]

Recycling. With increasing recognition of the problems facing landfills and incineration comes a growing interest in recycling. Once properly separated, every material in the waste stream (glass, plastic, metal, paper) can be recycled. If organic waste composting is included, estimates of recycling efficiency rise as high as 50%. The problem with recycling is that – as of the end of 1991 – 3,912 jurisdictions, with a combined population of more than 71-million now provide curbside collection of recyclable materials.[81] This has produced a scrap glut that has lowered prices paid for scrap and created a need for a mechanism to encourage the use of recycled material. All 50 states have preferential procurement programs for recycled products. These range from price preferences, which permit government to spend more for recycled products, to minimal content requirements for newsprint. While recycling can be regarded as "environmentally-correct" behavior, should our ability to recycle be used to justify conspicuous consumption?

Are our landfills composed mainly of discarded fast-food containers and disposable diapers? Dr. William Rathje, noted garbage archaeologist, has studied what happens to solid waste placed in a landfill. He and 750 students and colleagues have actually dug up over 14 tons since the Garbage Project began in 1973 at the University of Arizona. Their findings help refute commonly held myths, and therefore provide needed input before final judgments are appropriate on the question of solid waste and its disposal. The myth-and-fact combinations reported below are from an article by William Rathje and Cullen Murphy that appeared in *Smithsonian Magazine*.[82]

> **Myth**: Fast-food packaging, disposable diapers, and Styrofoam are major constituents of our garbage.
> **Fact**: These items constitute less than one-half of one percent of the material taken from landfills and approximately one-third of one percent of the volume.
> **Myth**: Plastic is a big problem in our landfills.
> **Fact**: Plastic represents 16% of landfill volume, according to the Garbage Project, and because it does not biodegrade it does not contribute to the ground-water contamination that has forced the closing of many old, unregulated landfills. Paper is actually a much greater problem. It has been estimated that a year of the *New York Times* has a volume equal to 18,660 crushed-aluminum cans.
> **Myth**: Paper and other organic materials biodegrade in a landfill.
> **Fact**: Modern landfill design discourages biodegradation. Rathje and colleagues have found that after some initial biodegradation of vegetable material and grass clippings, a landfill becomes a relatively stable place where all other contents are preserved.
> **Myth**: We are running out of safe places to put landfills.
> **Fact**: Although regional problems can be acute, there is plenty of room for the waste we generate. "Economist A. Clark Wiseman has calculated that at the current rate of waste generation, all of America's garbage for the next 1,000 years would fit into a single landfill space only 120 feet deep and 44 miles square - a patch of land about the size of three Oklahoma Citys."
> **Myth**: We are increasing the per capita rate of garbage production.
> **Fact**: Per capita solid waste generation over the past 30 years has been quite stable, with only minor fluctuations.
> So where should one stand with respect to the issues raised here? Should you use paper bags

or plastic at the grocery store? Should you support curbside recycling programs in your community? Would you rather have a landfill or an incinerator as a neighbor? Are you willing to pay the cost of shipping your community's waste?

WATER POLLUTION

With over 70% of its surface covered by water, Earth has been called the water planet. Clean, fresh water is necessary for life as we know it. Most (over 97%) of the water on Earth is salty and resides in the oceans; less than 3% of the total amount of water on the planet is fresh. Most of Earth's fresh water is stored (sometimes for thousands of years) as glacier ice. Of the liquid portion of the fresh water, nearly 99% is ground water, and about 1% is stored in lakes and as soil moisture, *etc.*[83] While water is plentiful on Earth, most of it is salty and therefore not available for personal consumption. When fresh water becomes contaminated with toxic substances the consequences can be dire.

U.S. Government action with respect to water quality has resulted in the Clean Water Act of 1948 and subsequent substantial amendments to it beginning in 1972. "The Act consists of two major parts: Regulatory provisions that impose progressively more stringent requirements on industries and cities in order to meet the statutory goal of zero discharge of pollutants, and provisions that authorize federal financial assistance for municipal wastewater treatment construction."[84]

Water pollution can be traced to either a single source or multiple sources. Single-source pollution is called point-source pollution and accounts for 40% of current violations of standards set in the Clean Water Act. Sixty percent of violations are nonpoint source in origin with 80% due to agricultural runoff.[85] In the case studies that follow, we deal with two examples of *point source* water pollution.

The *Exxon Valdez* oil spill is an example of a catastrophic contamination of surface water and the Charlestown leak an example of chronic ground water contamination. The former was spectacular, and therefore received abundant media attention. The latter was quiet, affected few people, and received only local attention. But ground water provides the drinking water for about one-half the U.S. population and nearly all the rural population; and because leaking old gasoline storage tanks are the major cause of contamination of ground water, it is an event similar to the Charlestown leak that has the greatest probability of affecting the most people.

CASE: THE *EXXON VALDEZ* OIL SPILL

At 12:07 a.m. on the morning of March 24, 1989, the 987-foot supertanker *Exxon Valdez* ran aground on Bligh Reef in Prince William Sound, Alaska. The impact tore open eight of the 11 cargo tanks, causing the largest oil spill in U.S. history. The approximately 11-million gallons of Alaskan-crude oil that spilled into the waters of the Sound killed and injured fish, birds, mammals, and a variety of other forms of marine life, habitats, and resources.

After the *Exxon Valdez* hit Bligh Reef, the response was far short of that called for in the contingency plan. Promised cleanup equipment was not available. The barge that was assigned to spill response had been damaged and was not loaded with the required equipment. Reloading the barge was made more difficult by the fact that one man had to run both a crane and forklift. Even locating the response equipment was made difficult by the covering of snow that obscured it. The result was that the loading and deployment took four times longer than called for in the contingency plan. Skimmers and booms did not arrive at the site until nearly 18 hours after the grounding. This was three times longer than called for in the plan. At 70 hours, a point at which the contingency plan stated that a spill of more than 200,000 barrels would be cleaned up, no more than 3,000 barrels had been recovered. Then the weather turned bad. The wind quickly spread the slick from one of eight-mile length to a 40-mile-long disaster for Prince William Sound – a disaster from which many experts predicted a very slow recovery.

The ecology and economy of Prince William Sound. Prince William Sound is located on the south-central Alaskan coast. It is part of a remote, pristine fjord/estuary-type ecosystem containing important natural resources. At least five species of threatened or endangered marine mammals frequent the area at certain times of the year. The Sound is one of the largest, undeveloped marine ecosystems in the United States, with a population of only about 6,000 people in scattered towns and villages.

The economy of the Prince William Sound area is based on utilization of its abundant natural resources, which include commercial fishing, recreation, subsistence or personal-use fishing and hunting, logging, and oil transportation. The Sound supports major commercial salmon and herring fisheries, as well as smaller fisheries for king crab, shrimp, and halibut. Port Valdez, located in the northeastern portion of Prince William Sound, is the southern terminus of the Trans-Alaska Pipeline.

On December 9, 1989, the state and federal governments signed an agreement with the Exxon Corporation to settle criminal charges and civil damage claims in exchange for a payment of $1.1025-billion.[86]

Some myths and facts about the oil spill. Although no one questions the fact that this oil spill created a disaster for life in Prince William Sound, there is controversy over the long-term severity of the problem, and myths about the Alaska spill persist.[87]

> **Myth**: Immediately after the spill, all of Prince William Sound was coated with oil.
> **Fact**: Less than 20% of the shoreline was oiled, and only 5% of the area was heavily oiled.
> **Myth**: The area is still heavily oiled.
> **Fact**: Today the shoreline of the Sound is essentially clear of oil.
> **Myth**: Entire populations of wildlife were destroyed.
> **Fact**: Although it is true that many animals lost their lives, there was no devastation of any species. Otters, seals, eagles, and sea birds are flourishing today.
> **Myth**: Fish were tainted and the fishing industry was destroyed.
> **Fact**: Herring and salmon catches set records in 1990, 1991, and 1992; and there is no evidence that commercial fisheries were damaged.

Cause of the oil spill. There is little controversy over the immediate cause of the grounding of the tanker. Captain Joseph Hazelwood had been in charge of loading his tanker during most of the day on March 23. This is a busy and tiring time for a tanker captain. At around 11:00 p.m. Captain Hazelwood and a pilot from Rocky Point, just north of Bligh Island, slowly edged the huge ship away from the floating dock at the Alyeska Oil Terminal. Several minutes later, after the Exxon Valdez was safely past the narrow entrance to Port Valdez, the pilot disembarked and turned over command to Captain Hazelwood. Almost immediately, Hazelwood began to encounter icebergs approaching from starboard. Icebergs calving off of Columbia Glacier were posing an immediate hazard, so Captain Hazelwood radioed the U.S. Coast Guard for permission to change course. He proposed that the Exxon Valdez be allowed to leave the outbound traffic lane and use the inbound lane instead.

Because there were no inbound vessels in the way, permission was granted and the maneuver was initiated. With the Exxon Valdez crossing out of its usual traffic lane, on a bearing aimed directly at Bligh Island, Captain Hazelwood turned over the helm to his third mate, Gregory Cousins. The Captain explained the maneuver. Mr. Cousins, a man not certified to command a ship in these waters, acknowledged that he understood the maneuver. The captain then retired to his cabin where he he admitted he had a drink or two. Minutes passed before the third mate realized that he had passed the turning point. The Exxon Valdez had passed through and beyond the inbound lane and, because it takes two miles to stop a supertanker, it was too late to do anything to prevent grounding the huge, oil filled tanker. So, at 12:07 a.m. on March 24, 1989, the Exxon Valdez struck Bligh Reef, just off the northwest coast of Bligh Island. (Bligh Reef and Island were named in 1778 by Captain James Cook for his good friend William Bligh, who would later captain the H.M.S. Bounty.)

Procedural changes as a result of the oil spill. It is interesting to note the procedural changes that have been instituted since this unfortunate accident. A careful look at those changes casts a degree of doubt on whether Captain Hazelwood was *solely* to blame or whether the cause was systemic.

The entrance from the Gulf of Alaska to Prince William Sound passes between Henchenbrook and Montague Islands. From that point to the entrance to Port Valdez is about 50 nautical miles. Before the oil spill, pilots boarded tankers near the entrance to Port Valdez, leaving and returning their mooring north of Bligh Island at Rocky Point. Current procedures require pilots to be in charge of all tankers beginning and ending south of Bligh Island. This procedural difference alone would probably have prevented the spill. Pilots are highly-trained individuals with a high level of familiarity with their assigned harbors. A pilot does not leave the helm under any circumstance.

Prior to the spill, oil-laden tankers were only escorted by tug through the narrows at the entrance to Port Valdez. They were unescorted as they navigated the narrow fjord of Port Valdez and passed through the more open Sound. Now, as a result of the oil spill, the U.S. Coast Guard requires two smaller vessels to accompany all laden tankers from the Henchenbrook entrance to the Alyeska Terminal. One of these escort vessels must be equipped for immediate oil spill response, carrying booms, skimmers, and absorbant material for use in the minutes immediately following a spill. Prompt containment of a spill can prevent much damage. Delay in the containment of the Exxon-Valdez spill was a major cause for the loss of wildlife.

Another procedural change can be seen in the radar room of the Coast Guard itself. Rather than the more casual monitoring of shipping traffic in the Sound that was common before the spill, current practice is much more cautious. A paper plot is now kept on all laden tankers transiting Prince William Sound. This requires more attentive monitoring than was required before the spill. In addition, permission to deviate from prescribed traffic lanes is no longer given routinely. Captain Hazelwood's request to crossover into the inbound-traffic lane would likely have been denied under current procedures. Instead, he would have been ordered to maintain his course and proceed more slowly through the icebergs in the outbound lane. All of these changes require closer and more frequent contact between the Coast Guard and tanker captains.

If the spill were entirely the fault of the captain, there would have been no need to make these changes in procedure. The procedural changes implicate the Alyeska Pipeline Company, Exxon (and other oil companies that use the terminal), the State of Alaska, and the U.S. Coast Guard. For these are the entities responsible for all aspects of the port operation.

On June 13, 1994, a federal court jury in Anchorage determined that Exxon Corp. acted recklessly before the spill, and that Captain Hazelwood was reckless and negligent. (Exxon already had acknowledged negligence on its part.) The same jury was expected to spend the summer establishing the amounts of compensation for thousands of Prince William Sound residents and businesses. Later punitive damages were to be determined.

Moral responsibility of the *Exxon Valdez* oil spill. What remains are not just questions about the adequacy of, and responsibility for cleanup efforts, but, prevention of similar spills. Further, are there questions of personal responsibility in the event of a catastrophe of this sort? Should you boycott Exxon? Should you buy gasoline from a company that uses only double-hulled tankers and hydrostatic loading? How would you even know what kind of tanker an oil company used? Or would the higher price of that company's gasoline turn you away? Do you support laws that would require all oil companies to use these and other practices to make spills less likely to occur? Would you support procedural changes to protect against the possibility of future "captain's errors?"

How about motor oil poured down storm drains and other small spills? The "far more numerous smaller spills that take place, unnoticed, every year probably do more cumulative damage to the oceans."[88] Would it be better to direct your energies to the creation of motor oil recycling programs in your community? Alternatively, because oil spills generally occur far from your home, perhaps it is of no concern and you need not worry about it. Which of these approaches to dealing with the oil spill would Kant have taken?

Some consequences of the cleanup effort. It is now recognized that the hot-water washing of heavily oiled shorelines that successfully removed visible signs of oil also destroyed marine life that survived the spill itself.[89] Furthermore, it cost $18-million for the rehabilitation of 357 sea otters. That works out to $50,420 per otter.[90] Was the money well spent? Is it humane to subject injured sea otters to the treatment required to "rehabilitate" them?

CASE: THE CHARLESTOWN LEAK

Charlestown is a small, rural town in Cecil County, Maryland. In October, 1986, two Charlestown residents began to complain of a bad taste in their well water. In response, the Cecil County Health Department tested the water and found it to be contaminated with benzene at a level of 15 parts per million (ppm). (The level considered safe is 5 parts per *billion*.) Benzene in ground water is an indicator of a gasoline leak.

Because the high level of gasoline contamination posed a health risk, the State of Maryland Department of the Environment offered free carbon filters – to remove gasoline from the water and make it drinkable – to all residents whose wells were affected. Some of the residents refused the filters, either because their water tasted okay or because they did not want the state telling them what to do.

The State Department of the Environment began its investigation of potential sources of the gasoline contamination in early November. Five potential sources were identified and reported as follows:

1. Trading Post, Bladen Street - two below-ground storage systems still in use
2. Market Street Cafe, Market Street - two below-ground storage systems removed three years before
3. Charlestown Marina, Water Street - five below-ground storage systems still in use
4. Charlestown Fire Department, Bladen and Market Street - one below-ground gasoline storage system in use
5. an individual homeowner, Bladen Street - one below-ground gasoline storage system that had been out of service approximately one year.[91]

Between December 8, and December 12, 1986, nine monitoring wells were drilled near potential sources. Tests of water taken from monitoring wells revealed that the source of the gasoline was the Trading Post, a three-generation, family-owned general store. The owner appeared to be unaware of the leak because of inadequate record keeping.

On December 26, the two below-ground storage systems were emptied, and on February 26, 1987, orders were issued to remove the tanks at the Trading Post. When the tanks were actually removed on March 6, perforations were found in one tank.

Even when a leaking tank is removed, the problem does not end for homeowners whose wells have become contaminated. State funds were used to remove as much gasoline from the ground water as possible. Although pumping contaminated water through special filtering units (at an initial cost of $17,733) removed 3,500 gallons of gasoline from the ground water, it left the water still contaminated far beyond acceptable levels.

When the Trading Post dug up its old tank and a small rusted hole was found, the owner claimed the hole was too small to have leaked the quantity of gasoline that was removed. He suggested that the nearby fire department or marina may have contributed to the problem. However, testing of water from the monitoring wells did not support his claim. Normally under such circumstances the owner of the tank would have to pay for the cleanup; but in this case, a few months after the investigation began the owner died, leaving no heirs. The state assumed responsibility for the cleanup while the estate was settled.

In early 1993, the gasoline pollution remained confined to a shallow, upper aquifer from which the residents of Charlestown draw their drinking water. A deeper, lower aquifer was found to be free of pollution. The type of rock in which both aquifers are located is unconsolidated sediment separated by an impermeable, confining layer. This may explain why deeper wells tested clean. But the faster water is pumped out, the faster the pollution spreads. If water is withdrawn from the deeper aquifer, its vulnerability to pollution is greatly increased.

Proposed actions included:

- Continue supplying free carbon filters to residents whose wells are contaminated.
- Initiate a public information campaign to inform local residents of the importance of carbon filtration and the health risk to homeowners and their families of not using the filters.
- Install a municipal water system fed by a newly dug deep well.
- Continue sampling the water to monitor the effectiveness of clean-up actions; and.
- Use either air stripping or bioremediation to remove enough of the contamination to restore the drinkability of the ground water.

Air stripping is a process in which water is converted to a mist, contaminants are released as gases, and clean water is returned to the ground. The cost is estimated to be about $250,000; it would take 2-5 years to clean up the water to acceptable levels. Bioremediation is a process of speeding the growth of bacteria (already in the water and soil) which break gasoline down into harmless compounds. This process will cost about $125,000 but would take at least 10 years before the water is cleaned to acceptable levels.

The total value of the estate of the owner of the Trading Post is not enough to clean up the ground water. Who should pay for the remaining cleanup process? Who will pay the medical expenses if health problems occur? Who will reimburse homeowners for the decrease in property values?

As of now, approximately 5,000 gallons of gasoline have been removed, and dispersed; a municipal well has been dug and clean water piped to the homes of Charlestown; and more than $1-million in costs have been passed on to the taxpayers of the State of Maryland. Records, it seems, are so inaccurate and/or incomplete that courts have ruled that ownership of the leaking tank is in doubt.[92]

What does this have to do with someone who lives in a community far removed from Charlestown, Maryland? The U.S. Environmental Protection Agency has reported estimates of between 5- and 7-million underground storage tanks. They also estimate that between 15 and 20% of those tanks are leaking. Many are leaking into the ground water and, in some cases, toward an unsuspecting community's drinking water supply.[93]

Gasoline is among the most toxic substances we are in contact with on a daily basis. Of the approximately 400 different compounds that make up gasoline, a few have been shown to cause cancer in laboratory animals, and one, benzene, is a human carcinogen. When ingested, gasoline causes such symptoms as anemia, nervous system disorders, kidney disease, cancer, and lead poisoning.[94]

If your community has underground gasoline storage tanks, are there laws in place that require accurate record keeping that might help to detect leaks early enough to prevent major contamination? Who monitors compliance with those laws? Whose job is it to insist upon enactment of such laws? Is your drinking water tested for contamination on a regular basis? How many substances are tested for?

Under current federal law, owners of underground storage systems must meet a range of requirements including a demonstration that they are financially capable of paying the costs of cleanup and damages resulting from leaks. This has forced the owners of the Trading Post to cease the sale of gasoline. Will such restrictions make gasoline less available in other rural areas?

LEGAL HISTORY

Governmental intervention and control of pollution has caused major improvements in the quality of our environment. However, caution must be exercised in passing and enforcing laws. According to the *New York Times,* "... what is now becoming apparent, some scientists and public health specialists say, is that some of these laws - written in reaction to popular concerns about toxic waste dumps or asbestos in the schools, as examples - were based on little if any sound research about the true nature of the threat. Since 1980, for instance, thousands of regulations were written to restrict compounds that had caused cancer in rats or mice, even though these animal studies often fail to predict how the compounds might affect humans."[95] Thus, it can be difficult for the individual to distinguish between serious concerns to health and insignificant concerns.

OZONE-LAYER DEPLETION CONTROL

Since 1977, the United Nations Environment Program (UNEP) has been coordinating, reporting and assessing the results of research by countries and international organizations through its Committee on the Ozone Layer. In 1985, 20 countries plus the European Economic Community agreed to hold a convention for the protection of the ozone layer. Meetings were held in December 1986, and February, April and September 1987 to discuss control measures for CFC use. An agreement was reached by 47 countries at the September 1987 meeting held in Montreal.

Known as the "Montreal Protocol on Substances that Deplete the Ozone Layer," it called for a freeze on consumption of specified CFCs at 1986 levels within a year. Thereafter, consumption would be reduced by 20% over a 3-year period and by an additional 30% by 1999. Developing countries were permitted to increase CFC usage for 10 years, but their total consumption was limited. The agreement took effect on January 1, 1989.[96]

Subsequent international meetings were held that made substantial changes to the Montreal Protocol. These new agreements tightened the regulations and introduced an accelerated phase-out of CFCs. In 1992 legislation, 100% phase out of CFCs was called for by 1996. Germany and Switzerland have since banned CFCs and other regulated substances by 1995. The United States ordered a phase out of CFCs by 1995, having already banned "nonessential" uses of CFCs – such as in aerosol-spray cans – in 1978.

Also in 1992, it was agreed to ban halons by 1994, and to end production of methyl chloroform – a dry-cleaning agent that was damaging to stratospheric ozone – by 1996. Industrialized nations decided to maintain a multilateral fund, financed by industrialized nations, to pay for ozone-friendly industrial development in developing nations. Ninety-two countries that produce and consume ozone-depleting substances have ratified the Montreal Protocol.[97] This represents a major step toward elimination of substances known to damage the ozone layer. However, it will take the atmosphere many decades to cleanse itself from the ozone-depleting chemicals that are already there, as well as those that will enter the atmosphere before the use of these substances is completely eliminated.[98]

AIR-POLLUTION CONTROL

In the United States, air pollution was first regulated locally, then its regulation became a state responsibility. In 1955, the federal government began to address air pollution with a focus on research and on financial and other support for state programs.[98]

The Clean Air Act was first enacted in 1970 at about the time the Environmental Protection Agency (EPA) was created. The EPA was authorized to carry out provisions to improve air quality and to enforce the Clean Air Act. It stressed a federal-state partnership to solve air pollution problems. Amendments in 1974 and 1977 allowed some delays in attainment of air-quality standards.

Under the Clean Air Act, the U.S. Environmental Protection Agency set standards for six air pollutants: Carbon monoxide, ozone, nitrogen dioxide, sulfur dioxide, particulate matter and lead. The Clean Air Act of 1977 initiated improvements in the previous Clean Air Acts. However, ozone (smog), carbon monoxide and particulate matter remained major problems in actual attainment of clean air in urban areas.

The Clean Air Act was again amended in 1990. The Clean Air Act of 1990 created a strategy for the country to control urban smog. It requires the federal government to reduce emissions from cars, trucks, buses and other sources.[99] The law also establishes an improved method of enforcement of the laws when geographical areas do not meet federal air pollution standards.

The new law promotes the use of clean, low-sulfur coal, and natural gas; it also creates a market for clean fuels derived from grain and natural gas, to reduce dependency on oil imports Further, the new law promotes energy conservation through a program that allows utilities flexibility in obtaining emission reductions through programs that encourage customers to conserve energy.

The Clean Air Act of 1990 establishes tighter pollution standards for emissions from automobiles and trucks. These standards will reduce tailpipe emissions and hydrocarbons, carbon monoxide and nitric oxides on a phased-in basis beginning in model year 1994. Auto manufacturers will also be required to reduce vehicle emissions resulting from evaporation of gas during refueling.

Because the Clean Air Act of 1977 did not result in substantial reduction of emission of toxic air pollutants – that is, pollutants that are carcinogens and mutagens – the Clean Air Act of 1990 includes a plan for achieving significant reductions in emissions of hazardous air pollutants. The new law includes a list of 189 toxic air pollutants for which emission must be reduced. [100]

The new law also addresses the sources of acid precipitation. (See section on Air Pollution.) Also, as a part of the new law, additional phase-out of the production of substances that deplete the ozone layer will be required. A complete phase-out of CFCs and halons is now mandated as discussed previously.

"The major air quality environmental concern over the past decade has been acid rain, (with) both sulfur dioxide (SO_2) and nitrogen oxides (NO_x) emissions playing an important role. Most attention, by far, has focused on SO_2. The importance of nitrogen oxides in the environment, however, should not be overlooked because they bear not only on the acid deposition issue but play an important role in another environmental concern: tropospheric ozone. Many metropolitan areas are in a state of nonattainment, hence the ozone issue is one of considerable concern to society and, particularly, to the electric utility industry. As recently as 1987, EPA designated 65 urban areas as nonattainment for ozone, and those 65 have an estimated population of nearly 130-million people."[101]

SUMMARY

It was the objective of this chapter to present scientific facts on several important environmental issues, and then to identify conflicting scientific and moral issues. If global warming is occurring, then sea level is likely to continue to rise, and changes in weather patterns are also likely to occur. Many scientists think that global change has already occurred due to anthropogenic forces. While it is not arguable that humans can exert global-scale influence on the planet, it is not known whether changes induced by humans are equal to or greater than (or complementary to) natural changes. Scientific research must continue in order to address these questions.

Change is a key component of climate. We have shown that human migrations due to climate change are not unprecedented in the Earth's history. But, are the changes that have been induced by humans causing such rapid changes that humans cannot adapt? Will the depletion of the ozone layer cause death to many species and disease for humans? Will desertification render large areas of arable land useless? The answers to these questions are controversial and probably lie somewhere between the extreme positions. While all the environmental problems discussed are real, the seriousness of the problems has not been quantified in many cases. Because of this, it is often unwise to institute expensive changes when the problems and consequences are uncertain. Alternatively, the wait-and-see approach can have disastrous consequences. Tougher laws seem necessary.

Further, what is the role of natural or human-induced disasters? Is the destroying-power of humanity equal to or greater than natural destruction? Natural disasters like volcanic eruptions can cause major and global-scale changes, and in a very short (measured in years) period of time.

Catastrophic acts of environmental terrorism, such as the oil-well fires following the Persian Gulf War, or accidents such as the *Exxon Valdez* oil spill cause considerable environmental damage. Though Earth is resilient, are there limits to its resiliency? More research is required.

Because the actions of humanity may have far-reaching effects, many environmental problems must be considered global in scope. The actions of mid-latitude people may affect people living in high latitudes and vice versa. Solutions to major problems (e.g., ozone-layer depletion) cannot be devised without attention to global concerns. People must work together on both a global and an individual level in order to solve many of the Earth's myriad environmental problems. The proposed solution to the ozone-layer depletion problem is an excellent example of an international effort to solve a global-scale problem.

Sometimes, the environmentally correct position is non-action. More energy can be expended – and damage done – by trying to "fix" some problems than by leaving them alone for nature to repair. But it is difficult to do nothing in the face of environmental disaster. There is much that an individual must consider in order to make informed decisions about environmental issues, especially in the context of incomplete scientific knowledge about many of the global environmental problems that face us today. Are you following a desirable course of action in light of your own moral judgment?

READINGS

SILENT SPRING
by Rachel Carson
Houghton Mifflin Co., Boston

THE OBLIGATION TO ENDURE

The history of life on earth has been a history of interaction between living things and their surroundings. To a large extent, the physical form and the habits of the earth's vegetation and its animal life have been molded by the environment. Considering the whole span of earthly time, the opposite effect, in which life actually modifies its surroundings, has been relatively slight. Only within the moment of time represented by the present century has one species - man - acquired significant power to alter the nature of his world.

During the past quarter century this power has not only increased to one of disturbing magnitude but it has changed in character. The most alarming of all man's assaults upon the environment is the contamination of air, earth, rivers and sea with dangerous and even lethal materials. This pollution is for the most part irrecoverable; the chain of evil it initiates not only in the world that must support life but in living tissues is for the most part irreversible. In this now universal contamination of the environment, chemicals are the sinister and little-recognized partners of radiation in changing the very nature of the world - the very nature of its life. Strontium 90, released through nuclear explosions into the air, comes to earth in rains or drifts down as fallout, lodges in soil, enters into the grass or corn or wheat grown there, and in time takes up its abode in the bones of a human being, there to remain until his death. Similarly, chemicals sprayed on croplands or forests or gardens lie long in soil, entering into living organisms, passing from one to another in a chain of poisoning and death. Or they pass mysteriously by underground streams until they emerge and, through the alchemy of air and sunlight, combine into new forms that kill vegetation, sicken cattle, and work unknown harm on those who drink from once pure wells. As Albert Schweitzer has said, "Man can hardly even recognize the evils of his own creation."

It took hundreds of millions of years to produce the life that now inhabits the earth - eons of time in which that developing and evolving and diversifying life reached a state of adjustment and balance with its surroundings. The environment, rigorously shaping and directing the life it supported, contained elements that were hostile as well as supporting. Certain rocks gave out dangerous radiation; even within the light of the sun, from which all life draws its energy, there were short-wave radiations with power to injure. Given time - time not in years but in millennia - life adjusts, and a balance has been reached. For time is the essential ingredient; but in the modern world there is no time.

The rapidity of change and the speed with which new situations are created follow the impetuous and heedless pace of man rather than the deliberate pace of nature. Radiation is no longer merely the background radiation of rocks, the bombardment of cosmic rays, the ultraviolet of the sun that have existed before there was any life on earth; radiation is now the unnatural creation of man's tampering with the atom. The chemicals to which life is asked to make its adjustment are no longer merely the calcium and silica and copper and all the rest of the minerals washed out of the rocks and carried in rivers to the sea; they are the synthetic creations of man's inventive mind, brewed in his laboratories, and having no counterparts in nature.

Among them are many that are used in man's war against nature. Since the mid-1940s over 200 basic chemicals have been created for use in killing insects, weeds, rodents, and other organisms described in the modern vernacular as "pests"; and they are sold under several thousand different brand names.

These sprays, dusts, and aerosols are now applied almost universally to farms, gardens, forests, and homes - nonselective chemicals that have the power to kill every insect, the "good" and the "bad," to still the song of birds and the leaping of fish in the streams, to coat the leaves with a deadly film, and to linger on in soil - all this though the intended target may be only a few weeds or insects. Can anyone believe it is possible to lay down such a barrage of poisons on the surface of the earth without making it unfit for all life? They should not be called "insecticides," but "biocides."

The whole process of spraying seems caught up in an endless spiral. Because DDT was released for civilian use, a process of escalation has been going on in which ever more toxic materials must be found. This has happened because insects, in a triumphant vindication of Darwin's principle of the survival of the fittest, have evolved super races immune to the particular insecticide used, hence a deadlier one has always to be developed - and then a deadlier one than that. It has happened also because, for reasons to be described later, destructive insects often undergo a "flareback," or resurgence, after spraying, in numbers greater than before. Thus the chemical war is never won, and all life is caught in its violent crossfire.

Along with the possibility of the extinction of mankind by nuclear war, the central problem of our age has therefore become the contamination of man's total environment with such substances of incredible potential for harm - substances that accumulate in the tissues of plants and animals and even penetrate the germ cells to shatter or alter the very material of heredity upon which the shape of our future depends.

Some would-be architects of our future look toward a time when it will be possible to alter the human germ plasm by design. But we may easily be doing so now by inadvertence, for many chemicals, like radiation, bring about gene mutatations. It is ironic to think that man might determine his own future by something so seemingly trivial as the choice of an insect spray.

All this has been risked - for what? Future historians may well be amazed by our distorted sense of proportion. How could intelligent beings seek to control a few unwanted species by a method that contaminated the entire environment and brought the threat of disease and death even to their own kind?

TOWARD A SUSTAINABLE WORLD
William D. Ruckelshaus
Scientific American, V.261, No.3

The difficulty of converting scientific findings into political action is a function of the uncertainty of the science and the pain generated by the action. Given the current uncertainties surrounding just one aspect of the global environmental crisis - the predicted rise in greenhouse gases - and the enormous technological and social effort that will be required to control that rise, it is fair to say that responding successfully to the multifaceted crisis will be a difficult political enterprise. It means trying to get a substantial proportion of the world's people to change their behavior in order to (possibly) avert threats that will otherwise (probably) affect a world most of them will not be alive to see.

The models that predict climatic change, for example, are subject to varying interpretations as to the timing, distribution and severity of the changes in store. Also, whereas models may convince scientists, who understand their assumptions and limitations, as a rule projections make poor politics. It is hard for people - hard even for the groups of people who contitute the governments - to change in response to dangers that may not arise for a long time or that just might not happen at all.

Can we move nations and people in the direction of sustainability? Such a move would be a modification of society to only two other changes: The agricultural revolution of the late Neolithic and the Industrial

Revolution of the past two centuries. Those revolutions were gradual, spontaneous and largely unconscious. This one will have to be a fully conscious operation, guided by the best foresight that scientists can provide - foresight pushed to its limit. If we actually do it, the undertaking will be absolutely unique in humanity's stay on the earth.

The shape of this undertaking cannot be clearly seen from where we now stand. The conventional image is that of a crossroads: A forced choice of one direction or another that determines the future for some appreciable period. But this does not at all capture the complexity of the current situation. A more appropriate image would be that of a canoeist shooting the rapids: Survival depends on continually responding to information by correct steering. In this case the information is supplied by science and economic events; the steering is the work of policy, both governmental and private.

Taking control of the future therefore means tightening the connection between science and policy. We need to understand where the rocks are in time to steer around them. Yet we will not devote the appropriate level of resources to science or accept the policies mandated by science unless we do something else. We have to understand that we are all in the same canoe and that steering toward sustainability is necessary.

Sustainability was the original economy of our species. Preindustrial peoples lived sustainably because they had to; if they did not, if they expanded their populations beyond the available resource base, then sooner or later they starved or had to migrate. The sustainability of their way of life was maintained by a particular consciousness regarding nature: The people were spiritually connected to the animals and plants on which they subsisted; they were part of the landscape, or of nature, not set apart as masters.

The era of this "original sustainability" eventually came to an end. The development of cities and the maintenance of urban populations called for intensive agriculture yielding a surplus. As a population grows, it requires an expansion of production, either by conquest or colonization or improved technique. A different consciousness, also embodied in a structure of myth, sustains this mode of life. The earth and its creatures are considered the property of humankind, a gift from the supernatural. Man stands outside of nature, which is a passive playing field that he dominates, controls and manipulates. Eventually, with industrialization, even the past is colonized: The forests of the Carboniferous are mined to support ever-expanding populations. Advanced technology gives impetus to the basic assumption that there is essentially no limit to humanity's power over nature.

This consciousness, this condition of "transitional unsustainability," is dominant today. It has two forms. In the underdeveloped, industrializing world, it is represented by the drive to develop at any environmental cost. It includes the wholesale destruction of forests, the replacement of sustainable agriculture by cash crops, the attendant exploitation of vulnerable lands by people such cash cropping forces off good land and the creation of industrial centers that are centers of environmental pollution.

In the industrialized world, unsustainable development has generated wealth and relative comfort for about one fifth of humankind, and among the populations of industrialized nations the consciousness supporting the unsustainable economy is nearly universal. With a few important exceptions, the environmental-protection movement in those nations, despite its major achievements in passing legislation and mandating pollution-control measures, has not had a substantial effect on the lives of most people. Environmentalism has been ameliorative and corrective - not a restructuring force. It is encompassed within the consciousness of unsustainability.

FOR FURTHER INQUIRY

EXERCISES:

1. For the following situations identify and discuss what approaches to moral reasoning the participants may have relied upon in making their decisions.

2. Choose one of the following situations and apply one of the exemplars studied in this course. As you do, (A) identify and apply to to the situation each step of the reasoning process inherent in that exemplar and (B) reach a conclusion reflecting that exemplar's reasoning process.

• The behavior of Sherwood Roland and Mario Molina after their research proved that Earth's ozone layer was being damaged by CFCs and other man-made chemicals.
• Exxon officials following the *Exxon Valdez* oil spill.
• Officials in the CFC industry upon being confronted by Rowland's theory.

ENDNOTES

1. Gregg Easterbrook, Cleaning up, *Newsweek*, July 24, 1989, p. 29.
2. Rachel Carson, *Silent Spring* (Houghton Mifflin Co., Boston), 1962, p. 187, 188.
3. William L. Rathje, Rubbish!, *The Atlantic Monthly* (V.264, No.6), 1989, p. 103.
4. James Hansen and Serjeg Lebedeff, Global trends of measured surface air temperature, *Journal of Geophysical Research* (V.92, No.D11), 1987, p. 13,345.
5. James Hansen and Serjeg Lebedeff, Global surface temperatures: update through 1987, *Geophysical Research Letters* (V.15, No.4), 1988, p. 323.
6. WMO, Land Management in Arid and Semi-Arid Areas (Technical Note No. 186), 1989, p. 5.
7. Mel Peterson, *NOAA's role in global change research, in: Global environmental change: The Role of Space in Understanding the Earth*, Richard G. Johnson (ed.), American Astronomical Society (Vol. 76), 1990, p. 39.
8. Albert Gore, *Earth in the Balance: Ecology and the Human Spirit* (The Penguin Group, New York), 1992.
9. Helmut E. Landsberg, Global climate trends, in *The Resourceful Earth*, Julian L. Simon and Herman Kahn (eds.), (Basil Blackwell, Oxford), 1984, p. 299.
10. Roy A. Gallant, *The Peopling of Planet Earth* (Macmillan Publishing Co., New York), 1990, p. 22.
11. Stephen P. Leatherman, Coastal land loss in the Chesapeake Bay region: An historical analog approach to global change analysis, Jurgen Schmandt and Judith Clarkson (eds.), *The Regions and Global Warming*, 1992 (Oxford University Press, N.Y.) p. 17.
12. Fasih U. Mahtab, The delta regions and global warming: Impact and response strategies for Bangladesch, Jurgen Schmandt and Judith Clarkson (eds.) *The Regions and Global Warming* 1992 (Oxford University Press, New York), p. 33.
13. Landsberg, p. 276.
14. D. Raynaud, J. Jouzel, J.M. Barnola, J. Chappellaz, R.J. Delmas and C. Lorius, The ice record of greenhouse gases, *Science* (V.259, No.5097), 1993, p. 926.
15. Erik P. Eckholm, *Losing Ground* (W.W. Norton & Company, New York), 1976, p. 18.
16. Reid A. Bryson and Thomas J. Murray, *Climates of Hunger*, 1977 (University of Wisconsin Press, Madison), p. 95.
17. Landsberg, p. 275.
18. A.E.J. Ogilvie, Documentary evidence for changes in the climate of Iceland, A.D. 1500-1800, in: *Climate Since A.D. 1500*, Raymond S. Bradley and Phillip D. Jones, 1992 (Routledge, London), p. 107.
19. Gallant, p. 96, 97.
20. Landsberg, p. 284.
21. Andrew Goudie, *The Human Impact on the Natural Environment* (The MIT Press, Cambridge, Massachusetts), 1986, p. 3.
22. Stephen H. Spurr, *American Forest Policy in Development*, (University of Washington Press, Seattle), 1976, p. 3.
23. Alan B. Nichols, Tropical deforestation triggers ecological chain reaction, *Water Environment and Technology*, October 1989, p. 321.
24. Fred B. Wood, Monitoring global climate change: The case of greenhouse warming, 1990, *Bulletin of the American Meteorology* (V.71, No.1), p. 42.
25. Edward O. Wilson, Threats to biodiversity, *Scientific American*, 1989 (V.261, No.3), p.111.
26. Wilson, p. 112.
27-28. Nichols, p. 327: p. 324.
29. Norman Myers and Marc Reisner, Vanishing genetic heritage, in *Life after '80: Environmental Choices we can Live With*, Kathleen Courrier (ed.) (Brickhouse Publishing Co., Andover, Massachusetts), 1980, p.72.
30-31. Wilson, p. 111; p 116.
32. Ghillean Prance, Fruits of the rainforest, *New Scientist*, 13 January 1990, p.44.
33. Prance, p. 45.
34. Gallant, p. 62.
35. Wilson, p. 111.
36. Sharon Roan, *Ozone Crisis* (John Wiley & Sons, Inc., New York), 1989, p. 8.
37. David E. Gushee, Stratospheric ozone depletion: regulatory issues, Congressional Research Service, 1993, IB89021, p. CRS-1.
38. Roan, p. 5.
39. Carl Sagan, A piece of the sky is missing, "Parade Magazine," a supplement to *The Washington Post*, September 11, 1988, p. 20.
40. Samual W. Matthews, Is our world warming?, *National Geographic*, October 1990, p. 94.
41. Roan, p. 8.
42. *Science News*, Northern Hemisphere Ozone Hits Record Low (V.143), March 20, 1993, p. 180.

43. Gushee, p. CRS-2.

44. Boyce Rensberger, After 2000, Outlook for the Ozone Layer Looks Good, *The Washington Post*, April 15, 1993 (No. 131), p. A1.

45. Rensberger, p. A2.

46. Rensberger, p. A19.

47. Lanie Jones, He sounded alarm, paid heavy price, *Los Angeles Times*, 14 July 1988, Front Page.

48. Roan, p. 51.

49. Rensberger, p. A19.

50. Sagan, p. 22.

51. Sagan, p. 21.

52. Sagan, p. 22.

53. Robert T. Watson, Status and issues in atmospheric sciences, *Global Environmental Change: The Role of Space in Understanding the Earth*, American Astronomical Society, 1990 (V.76), Richard G. Johnson (ed.), p. 77.

54. Roan, p. 68.

55. Roan, p. 68.

56. Ralph M. Perhac, Nitrogen oxides and ozone, James C. White (ed.), *Global Climate Change Linkages*, 1989, (Elsevier Science Publishing Co., New York), p. 219.

57. Chris C. Park, *Acid Rain Rhetoric: and Reality* (Methuen, London), 1987, p. 191.

58. Park, p. xiv (Preface).

59. Associated Press, Virginia fish kills attributed to acid snow, April 7, 1993 *The Washington Post*, p. B4.

60. Park, p. 10.

61. Park, p. 115.

62. Rose Gutfeld, For each dollar spent on clean air someone stands to make a buck, *Wall Street Journal*, October 29, 1990, p. A1.

63. Thomas Y. Canby, After the storm, *National Geographic* (V.180, No.2), 1991, p. 10.

64. National Geographic, Environmental Consequences of the Persian Gulf War 1990-1991, *National Geographic Research and Exploration*, V.7 (special issue), p. 11.

65. *Science News*, Debris from Kuwaiti fires travels far, March 7, 1992, p.159

66. Park, p. xxi (Preface).

67. Gutfield, p. A1.

68. Park, p. 11.

69. Nuclear Energy: Safety and Waste Issues, Congressional Research Service, IP 74N, p.1.

70. Ehrlich and Ehrlich, p.97.

71. Karl Cohen, Nuclear Power, in *The Resourceful Earth*, Julian L. Simon and Herman Kahn (eds.) (Oxford), 1984, p. 409.

72. Mark Holt, Civilian Nuclear Waste Disposal, Congressional Research Service, 1992, IB92059, p. CRS-2.

73. Cohen, p. 559.

74. Cohen, p. 410.

75. Thomas Lippmann, Sacramento Finds Nuclear-Free Power Saves Moner, Worry, *The Washington Post*, March 21, 1993, p. A3.

76. Mark Holt and Warren Donnelly, Nuclear Energy Policy, Congressional Research Service, 1993, IB88090, p. CRS-11.

77. Environmental Fact Sheet- Recycling Municipal Solid Waste: Facts and Figures, EPA/530-SW-91-024 July 1992 p. 1

78. McCarthy, p. 2.

79. McCarthy, p. 6.

80. McCarthy, p. 3.

81. McCarthy, p.4.

82. William Rathje and Cullen Murphy, Five major myths about garbage, and why they're wrong. *Smithsonian Magazine* (Vol. 23, No. 4), pp. 114-120.

83. Dorothy K. Hall and Jaraslov Martinec, Remote Sensing of Ice and Snow, 1985 (Chapman & Hall, London), p. 25.

84. Claudia Copeland, Water Quality: Implementing the Clean Water Act, January 11, 1993, CRS Issue Brief IB89102 p. CRS-2)

85. Copeland, p. 4.

86. Exxon Valdez OIl Spill Restoration, Volume II, 1992 Draft Work Plan, Exxon Valdez Oil Spill Trustees, Anchorage, AK, 1992, p. 1.

87. Ed Owens, Coastal Forum: Coastal Oil Spills: Myths and Reality, *Shore & Beach* (Vol. 60, No. 2), April, 1992, pp. 4-6.

88. Gore, p. 108.

89. *Science News,* Valdez spill leaves lasting impacts (Vol. 143), p. 102-103.

90. Janet Raloff, An Otter Tragedy, *Science News*, March 27, 1993 (Vol. 143), p. 201.

91. Maryland Department of Environment files

92. Barbara Brown, Maryland State Department of the Environment, Conversations, April 26, 1993.

93. U.S. EPA, *Here Lies the Problem... Leaking Underground Storage Systems*, 1990, p. 2.

94. U.S. EPA, 1990, p. 4.

95. Keith Schneider, New view calls environmental policy misguided, *New York Times*, March 21, 1993 (Vol. CXLll, No.49,277), p. 1.

96. Gushee, p. CRS-1.

97. *Science News* Ozone-protection treaty strengthened, December 12, 1992 (V. 141, No. 50), p. 415.

98. Susan Mayer, Air quality: implementing the Clean Air Act ammendments of 1990, Congressional Research Service; Issue Brief, p. CRS-2.

99. U.S. EPA, The Clean Air act Ammendment of 1990, summary materials, November 15, 1990, p. 3.

100. U.S. EPA, p. 4.

101. Perhac, p. 219.

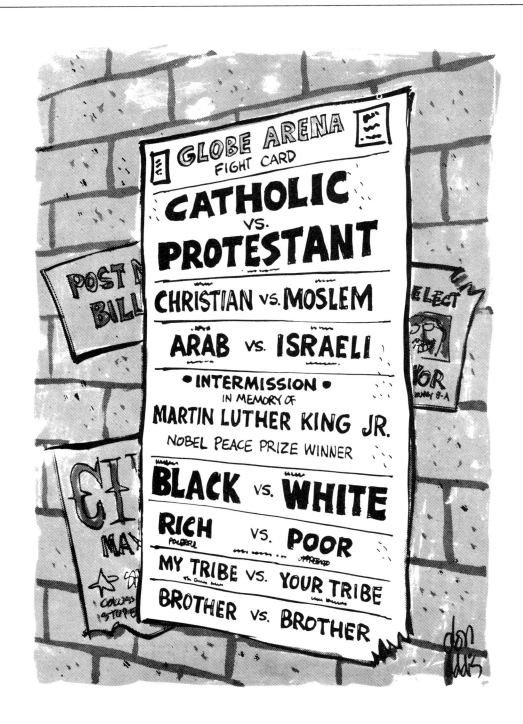

Chapter 13

David I. Seiple

WAR

"Older men declare war. But it is youth that must fight and die. And it
is youth who must inherit the tribulation, the sorrow, and the triumphs
that are the aftermath of war."
— Herbert Hoover, 1928 GOP National Convention

"War hath no fury like a non-combatant."
— Charles Edward Montague, *Disenchantment* 1922

When peoples go to war against one another, we might think of it in various ways: As a test of will for titanic personalities (George Bush vs. Saddam Hussein); as an indication of the strength or weakness of national character (Vietnam?); or as the culmination of centuries of ethnic rivalry (Serbs vs. Croats vs. Bosnian Muslims). But do we ever think of going to war as the failure or success of a clearly articulated and carefully pursued process of moral deliberation? The Gulf War, according to its proponents, was waged based on the principle of the sovereignty of nations – mainly to restore a small nation (Kuwait) from bullying and brutal annexation by its much larger neighbor, Iraq. (It may not have been that simple, as we shall see later). More often, war is the result of conflicting policy agendas between nations, which surely are formed out of some perception of national goals and circumstances. To what extent do those goals, and the strategies a government is willing to use to attain them, reflect morally acceptable principles? And should policy-makers care about this? (Should voting citizens in a democratic society care?)

David I. Seiple, Ph.D. Columbia University, M.T.S. Drew University Theological School, is director of research, workplace Literacy Foundation and Adjunct Assistant Professor of Humanities at New York University, S.C.E.

In this chapter we will be interested in looking at the relation between moral deliberation and war-making. We will discuss what "war" is, how war has often been glorified, and how some have refused to participate in war of any kind and why. We will explore the possibilities for formulating some restrictions on when war can be deemed morally acceptable ("just"). We will show how complex the issue has become in the nuclear age, and we will indicate how international law takes on a new importance as a result.

WAR AS A PHILOSOPHICAL TOPIC

"War," just as other terms we have been discussing, is a word used in various ways, and it will help us right off to see how differently it can be used. It is common to think of a "war" as an *officially* sanctioned state of affairs, *legally* declared by the parties involved (such as The Spanish-American War or World War II). That is the definition often given by military theorists. But what about Vietnam? That "war" was never officially declared. Do all conflicts that lack an explicit Congressional declaration necessarily lack the traits of warfare?

Take another example. The inhabitants of Los Angeles during the 1992 riots may have thought they were already living in a war zone. Millions of people saw Rodney King, a black man, beaten by white policemen over and over again on television news, and yet his assailants were acquitted (by a jury with no black members). Many felt that the U.S. court system had committed yet one more hostile act against the black community, and saw the vandalism as an expression of justifiable rage. Troops were called in after L.A. law-enforcers were unable to handle the insurrection, and some political groups on the other side claimed that "the people" were waging war on "the American system."

So let's think about whether actions taken to quell civil unrest in Los Angeles amount to "war." If they do, then wouldn't that cast those rioters in a special light? For in that case, doesn't the violence of the Los Angeles riots begin to look like the response of an oppressed community to an invading force? It's obviously an unequal struggle that the community could not realistically expect to win – not with the full force of the American military arrayed against it. So, in good American fashion, we might begin to feel some sympathy with the underdog here.

However, there are some strong reasons for resisting this way of looking at it. War is a state of affairs in which its participants are protected by international agreements. When captured in battle, for example, they have been required to reveal only name, rank, and serial number, and they are released through negotiation between captor and home country. Looters, on the other hand, can be convicted and sentenced purely at the behest of the captor's court system. That system holds *them* responsible (and not foreign leaders) for their acts of violence. So, in this important sense, could riots really be considered "wars"? Writers on military history have influenced standard usage by restricting the term "war" to a situation in which two organized, hostile parties enjoy, at least for a short time, some measure of military parity. The looters in Los Angeles obviously enjoyed no such status, and we'll be using the term "war" here in this restricted way.

But let's ask a more basic question at this point. Why does the term "war" have any philosophical interest for us in the first place? We are discussing ethical issues in this book, and ethics is the study of the moral standards we deem appropriate to guide our own conduct. Should we study war only from some different angle of interest instead – as military history, as the effect of economic dislocation, as a monumental event that heralds a sea-change in a nation's history – rather than as a moral question? If we decide that war is not a moral matter, then we will not be able to tackle the following sorts of ethical questions: Should we (as moral agents) ever sanction an act of war? And if so, under what conditions should we do so? What is our own moral responsibility when questions of war and peace are at stake? The changing face of society over the past several centuries has made these live questions. Can we afford to ignore them?

In the not-so-distant past, wars might have been waged at the behest of a feudal sovereign on behalf of his own very personal interest – to avenge a perceived insult, for example. This is probably how we think of King Arthur and the Knights of the Round Table. In those days armies were small professional units who owed allegiance to their lord and whose personal motives may not have reached far beyond the promise of glory and bounty. They undoubtedly thought very little about their responsibility as participants. But for us, participation in war is likely to raise deep questions. With the French Revolution in 1789, the constitution of armies began to change. Ordinary citizens were conscripted into a scene of combat they would much rather have avoided. With the expansion of voting rights, mothers and fathers and prospective inductees could all have some direct, democratic say in the governmental decisions that could bring that about.

Democracy carries with it a burden not borne by the citizens of other systems. In totalitarian societies such as Nazi Germany, voiced opposition to national military policy might qualify a person as a something of a popular, if dangerously marked, hero. How does this differ in a democracy? Democracy was originally founded on an historically revolutionary ideal – the notion that major governmental decisions should reflect the "will of the people." If asked today, many people in the Western democracies would still say that it's their own moral responsibility as citizens to become informed about the issues facing the country and to engage others in discussion about them, so that they can be informed voters. In that case, people who fail to participate as voting citizens become implicated in the responsibility for any morally questionable policy that gets enacted. So is it or is it not really important to talk seriously about the moral issues of war and peace? Are you an active participant in a democratic society?

So let's ask again: What is it about war that engages our moral interest? For one thing, isn't war, like punishment, an intrusion into the private sphere of the individual? Obviously, war is an act of orchestrated violence, undertaken as an arm of national policy that is bound to have severe consequences upon those it sweeps along. Wars, at the very minimum, seriously disrupt the everyday routines of persons who are otherwise engaged in the daily business of living ordinary, generally peaceable lives. Sometimes the disruption derives from the anxiety a war causes us after, say, catching a glimpse of a newspaper headline, but often it arises directly from the damage to life and limb that it visits on innocent bystanders. In other words, isn't war morally troublesome because it imposes such an unwelcome and undeserved suffering? What would we want to say about that kind of imposition? Doesn't it require a most convincing justification, long before it becomes a chosen option of a country's foreign policy?

Offensive Or defensive? So the central focus of our discussion here will concern the possible justification of war, and there are a number of specific questions worth keeping in mind. One, for example, trades on the purpose behind the waging. A war might be primarily offensive (as it was in the case of Germany's invasion of Poland in 1939, or the American invasion of Grenada), and in that case war is an instrument of a national policy that did not succeed, as anyone might naturally hope it would have, by diplomacy alone. On the other hand, a war can be undertaken in self-defense (as it was by the new French Republic after 1789, when it was threatened by invasion from royalist forces, or by the Americans against the Japanese after Pearl Harbor). To what extent then does this difference affect the strength of the justification behind the decision to conduct war?

Gravity of the consequences. A second issue worth considering here concerns the gravity of war's effects. All of us have lived for much of our lives under the threat of nuclear annihilation, and we need to consider what impact that possibility has upon the moral matters before us here.

And what about the idea that war is an organized *violent* intrusion upon the personal lives of human beings? We normally think of it as that. But one wonders about terrorism. Might that not be seen broadly as a kind of warfare? Palestinian airplane hijackers have claimed that. Or do we say the same thing about terrorism as we just have about armed rebellion against a government?

And, finally, think about the fact that in a democracy, despite the ideal of representing the will of the people, no one group has its way all the time. When the decision to go to war is made, there will be objectors. What is their status, morally speaking? Do they owe more than they are willing to give to their society? Or does society owe them more personal latitude than the majority, at such occasions of national stress, is typically eager to grant?

MILITARISM

War, as we all know, has been a part of human civilization for a very long time, and during much of that time the excitement and drama of war have appealed to many people – from the fans of John Wayne to the followers of Adolf Hitler. The value system that exalts these aspects of armed conflict (loyalty to country, defense of life and property, military efficiency, physical discipline and valor, hatred of the enemy) *at the expense of* other values (such as individual autonomy, humanitarian conduct toward others, or international cooperation) is called *militarism*. The full-fledged militarist, in other words, is one who glorifies the activity of war as humanity's highest calling.

The militarist mentality is a cultural descendant of an era when war could be conducted more or less in isolation from other aspects of society. Insulating innocents from war's effects was never perfectly achieved: We have only to think of the fall of Troy in Homer's *Iliad* to see that some innocents are always likely to suffer in war. But during much of human history it was sometimes possible even for thinking people to minimize this, because armies were often arrayed against each other in underpopulated areas – so that (for example) accounts of the Battle of Waterloo in 1815 (unlike, say, the military operations of the Vietnam conflict) do not include any high civilian casualty figures.

But World War I (1914-1918) put all this in a very different light. This saw the introduction of *total war* into human history. By that War's end, entire populations had been mobilized, more than 10-million Europeans had perished, and the economies of victor and vanquished alike were too enfeebled to enable restoration of prewar prosperity. And yet the exhausted armies persisted in a brutal war of attrition long after the glories of promised victory had faded from popular memory. What is so intriguing here is that wars of this kind could never be conducted unless the home population were actually willing to participate in all this.

You might well wonder why a population would ever support such a disastrous arrangement. There are complex reasons. Ancient border disputes flare. At other times, what drives a nation to battle might be a fierce sense of national pride. Trade battles break out over tariffs. Most frequently, wars erupt when a tyrannical leader uses fear of "enemies" and other inflammatory rhetoric to preserve national control and has some egomaniacal agenda to rule all or part of the world. His people harken to his ranting, to martial music and the flash of helmets. In "defense," the nation declares war with some palpable sense of grand purpose. Soon, however, the troops embark and the death notices begin to appear. Here's an account of the results of that process from World War I, according to *The Columbia History of the World*:

Governments did their best to whip up ever fresh enthusiasm for the killing, and in the process received ample help from the established classes. The chauvinistic cant that poured from press and pulpit was meant to rouse flagging spirits to new sacrifices. The techniques of propaganda, borrowed from prewar modes of advertising, became so important in the hands of governments that one English wit spoke of "propagandocracy" as the new type of rule. Wartime propaganda became ever cruder and uglier: It started with the theme "love your country and defend it" and gradually turned to "hate your enemy and kill him."[1]

So it is no secret why "militarism" has become such a term of disapproval among so many since then. For it was the susceptibility of entire populations to the appeals of militarism, it is argued, that allowed World War I to continue.

On the other hand, do we need to infer from this that qualities such as loyalty, discipline, courage, self-defense and efficiency have no legitimate place in human society, or that those who esteem them are necessarily "militarists"? Militarism is the value that places those qualities *above* others that most of us want preserved. The difficulty comes in attempting to reach a feasible balance.

PACIFISM

Some people, when confronted with the contrast between the requirements and purposes of military conduct, on the one hand, and the moral values of individual rights, human freedom and social cooperation, on the other, will insist that there is indeed a fundamental incompatibility. Those who refuse to sanction or participate in war, on the grounds of moral principle, are called *pacifists*.

Pacifism is more than just a concern for bringing about peace. By the end of the 19th century, many in Europe and the U.S. had joined peace advocacy groups, which were formed to give intellectual and political opposition to the prevailing militarist interests. But in World War I most peace advocates actually supported their own national war effort, in the hope that military victory would reshape the political landscape along more peaceable lines. That hope was perhaps the most heralded rationale for the American entry into the War.

And pacifism is not just the refusal to participate in war. In the days of the military draft, a young man might find serving in the military to be personally inconvenient or temperamentally distasteful, without necessarily adopting the stance of the pacifist. This is because those kinds of "self-regarding" considerations are probably not *moral* considerations. Likewise, someone might follow nonviolence as a kind of lifestyle choice, but insist that such views are only "true for him" and not to be imposed on others. Neither of these individuals is really a pacifist. A real pacifist is someone who declines to be involved in war because she thinks war is a morally wrong thing to be involved in. This is not just a choice of lifestyle; it is the declaration of what that person takes to be morally true for everyone, whether they know it or not. And a real pacifist refuses participation in war, even if doing so might provoke severe legal reprisal. A great many pacifists have been convinced in fact that merely avoiding active participation in war is not morally sufficient: War is seen as such an evil that they feel called upon not only to become *conscientious objectors*, but also to engage in *nonviolent resistance*. The personal consequences of that are likely to be highly unwelcome. During the Vietnam conflict, for example, an estimated 5,000 inductees made a public show of turning in their draft cards. In all, more than 200,000 men were accused of draft-related offenses. Most at the time must have been painfully aware of the social cost of doing so: 4,000 of them were eventually imprisoned and many more went into hiding.[2] For them, such a decision apparently was not motivated simply by personal convenience.

But all this is not to say that what they did was necessarily justified. For this, pacifists appeal to a wide range of considerations. Those with Christian commitments cite Biblical passages such as the Sermon on the Mount.[3] Others appeal to the teachings of the 20th-century Hindu sage Mahatma Gandhi, whose popular following made a successful political strategy out of nonviolent resistance to British rule over India. Others cite the moral arguments of the German philosopher Immanuel Kant,[4] whose Categorical Imperative directs us to avoid acting in any way we could not willingly universalize for others as well. In other words, what would the world be like if everyone were to resort to violence?

But then what about those cases of individual conduct? Is violence never, ever justified in one person's dealings with another? What about self-defense? Many people have admired saints such as Mahatma Gandhi, who can turn the other cheek if insulted or assaulted. But though this may be admirable, are we *morally required* to be saints? If you believe that there are certain circumstances when it is permissible for an individual to use violence, then it is only natural to consider seriously the possibility that there are circumstances when a nation as a whole is justified in using violence. And what about the possibility that the taking of some lives may be necessary for the saving of others? World War II is the classic example: It gradually became obvious that Hitler was pursuing a policy of genocide against the Jews, and that only military intervention could have saved them.

REALPOLITIK

But before we consider the ethical justification for using force as an instrument of national policy, we should consider whether ethics even has a place in this discussion. *Realpolitik* is the view that substantive moral principles simply cannot be applied to disputes between nations.

The idea that war *is* a moral topic is often based upon an analogy between individual persons and entire countries. For example, one factor we evaluate as moral agents is the intention that lies behind an act: If someone kills a person he instead meant to save, we don't regard him as morally responsible for murder. And in the case of nations, we could look at the national aims that inspire foreign conduct. We say that World War II, from the perspective of the Allies, was justified because its aim was to thwart German aggression. But proponents of *Realpolitik* hesitate to make this kind of moral assessment. One of the most prominent of these, Henry Kissinger (the U.S. Secretary of State during the later Vietnam era) is reported to have declined to speculate at all about the motives of the North Vietnamese ("I have too much difficulty understanding our own"[5]). But wouldn't this mean that a policy-maker is left with little moral basis for assessing his own policy options? For in a situation that involves more than one party, is it not necessary to accommodate more than just one's own particular point of view? Lacking either the will or the ability to understand the other side leaves only one's own aims and interests as motivating considerations.

Realpolitik attempts to be "realistic" (as its proponents would insist), by appealing for policy justification only to one's own national interests, at least as those policy-maker perceive them. Why would anyone think this? Here you might remark on the fact that different groups of people in different societies have different moral codes. Doesn't that make morality "culture-specific"? That would mean that moral disputes might be resolved rationally *within* a particular society but that conflicts *between* them cannot be morally decided. After all, if all morality is relative to some particular society, how can we try to assume a moral stance beyond our own restricted cultural perspective? Look, after all, at what some people say about white heterosexual males: Their morality is supposed to be limited by their sexist perspective. And why not think that everybody is limited in similar ways by perspectives of their own? Claims about moral principles then become nothing more than rhetorical exercises, designed to bowl people over into agreeing with one's own point of view. Moral "truth" becomes nothing but conversational power. (This reminds us of the Sophists we spoke about in Chapter 3.) *Realpolitik* could use this argument to bolster its claim that the only rational perspective a nation has is what looks good to that nation, from its own self-interested perspective.

Or we might want to put this same point in a slightly different way. Maybe the only universal moral code *just is* ethical egoism as applied to nations. Ethical egoism (see Chapter 3) is the view that says that people should care most about what only directly concerns themselves, and *Realpolitik* applies this to the conduct of nations. But this still seeks to deny the applicability of moral categories to the collective sphere, just as ethical egoism does to the personal. On this view, just as individuals ought to pursue their own self-interest, so too with nations. And this would mean that no nation, in war or in anything else, is constrained by any principle but the principle of self-interest.

This need not mean that other countries' interests are never accommodated. After all, any nation needs countries around it to be economically viable, to prevent the infection of political unrest from spreading. This puts certain constraints upon the conduct of war, doesn't it? Could any enlightened nation today so cripple the economy of its neighbor that it would put itself at an economic disadvantage? Of course not. It needs that neighbor as an export market. And that (so says *Realpolitik*) is just a rational, self-interested recognition of the need to maximize the benefits for oneself in whatever one does.

Of course, in the extreme case, as during the era of Western hegemony before the late 20th century, the competition for international position is heavily weighted toward one culture at the expense of another. At that point (some would argue) the need for the dominant power to have a neighborly export market turns into the need for a parasite to have a host; and this was the real basis for Western colonialism in the years before World War II. During those years, European powers established an economic base in foreign lands, for the cheap extraction of natural resources for use at home and, eventually, special rights for private industrialists to invest abroad. This was theoretically supported by the idea that other cultures were inferior to the European, so the fact that those natives lived in underprivileged conditions was seen to be partly a result of just their bad luck and partly the result of their laziness or stupidity.

Now what do the wars in the 20th century tell us about this? What, after all, is the logical result of ethical egoism? Wouldn't the logical result have to be that just any action, any at all, is permissible just as long as it suits one's own best interest? That would mean that if it seemed that an entire population had no value to the ascendant culture, that population would become expendable. And now we have the technology to do it. The Nazis used a sophisticated system of gas chambers to dispose of its unwanted humans.

This is trouble for *Realpolitik*. Almost no one who is not alienated from the entire international community is willing to justify the Nazis. And why not? Because (they would have to say) the Nazi conduct was morally wrong. It is plainly wrong to murder six-million Jews and many thousands of homosexuals and gypsies. But *Realpolitik* refuses to consider anything but perceived self-interest as a basis for foreign policy. Does *Realpolitik* actually provide an argument in favor of Nazism?

'JUST WAR' THEORY

Questions about war and peace are not idle items of academic interest: They are matters of deep concern to citizens of a democracy, who have the responsibility to play a role in determining national priorities. Unless we want to cede the political decision-making entirely to the specialists in the field, we need to have some basis for assessing our leaders and their policies. But doesn't this create a grave crisis for the democratic system? Notice how, at this point in history, culture has evolved to such a level of complexity that the factors to be considered are too diverse for the expertise of the average citizen. (What do *you* think really are the chances that Star Wars technology can be used, as its proponents claim, to protect American cities against a missile attack? On what basis could you possibly claim to know?) Unless subject to the sway of mere media appeal, the average voter is likely to be able to decide about certain complex issues only on moral grounds.

Do we have moral standards for our leaders? Of course, we do. And not just in matters of private conduct. Look at domestic policy. At present, could any U.S. President who systematically sought to place blacks in concentration camps avoid impeachment? So we really have to wonder: Is it true that there are no *international* moral standards for us to use in our moral assessment of the President's foreign policy? Think again about what *Realpolitik* claims. Is it true, as Henry Kissinger insists, that "The security of free peoples depend(s) on whether the United States could develop a concept of national interest that we would defend regardless of the guise that challenges to it might take"?[6] What if the "guise" were a moral principle against hoarding an unfair share of the world's industrial goods? Or a moral principle against harming innocents during a jungle bombing?

There are certainly international *standards*, and these have been encoded in the Geneva agreements and the United Nations Charter. Many countries recognize the authority of the 1950 European Convention on Human Rights, which mandates moral standards for the conduct of military trials. Wouldn't this mean that military conduct is not exempt from moral evaluation? And what is the significance of the harsh international war crimes judgment at Nuremberg, against Nazi conduct in World War II? Leading Nazis were sentenced to death for what they did during the War. So is any political leader really exempt from moral responsibility? There is general international agreement about the acceptable limits of conduct during wartime, and this has received refined philosophical expression in what is known as *the Just War Theory*.

1. Definition of "war." The Just War Theory was formulated to state the conditions of when and how to fight a "morally good" war. But, as we began to see earlier, we cannot determine what those conditions might be unless we can agree as to what a "war" is. We already saw that we should not assume just any kind of violence qualifies as "war," and whether acts of violence in situations besides war can be justified would be a separate question, not even addressed by the Just War Theory. During the 1960s, the radical group known as the Weathermen was engaged in a series of terrorist actions that at one point included blowing up New York police headquarters. But these were not acts of "war" – at least, not as defined by the Just War Theory. Today militant terrorists in Islam claim to be conducting a "holy war" (*jihad*) against the West by various bombings. Are these acts of war simply because the terrorists say so? Does it take a formal decision by an internationally recognized government to establish a legal war?

What is the advantage of such a narrow definition? First, we need a way of simplifying our discussion. Conceivably, there might be justification for some spontaneous uprisings, and we should not simply exclude the possibility that even terrorism might be justifiable under some conditions. But we would need to examine those issues separately – not as instances of "war." And secondly, prisoners of war are generally supposed to deserve treatment not awarded to outlaws or murderers. Soldiers, after all, are not responsible agents, in the way we often think of criminals as being responsible for their acts of violence. Soldiers are often conscripted against their will, and do most of what they do under orders from others. The distinction between these two groups would not be possible unless we understood how war differs from ordinary crime.

So we need at least a working definition. *War,* according to traditional proponents of the Just War Theory, is *a controlled use of force, undertaken by persons organized in a functioning chain of command under a competent authority, conducted against an opponent who enjoys some measure of military parity.*[7] Unfortunately, this is not as clear and adequate a definition as one might hope for. It excludes, as it should, marginal cases such as food riots and mass shootings by deranged people. But it also leaves unclear just how we determine what a "competent authority" is. (In a civil war, which side qualifies as the "competent authority"?) It also leaves unsettled how we should classify cases of armed insurrection, where the rebellion is effective against a government not out of military might, but owing to other factors. (Some people might, for example, think of the violent response of the Chinese government to the 1989 demonstrations by its own people in Tiananmen Square as an act of war.)

Nonetheless, it does open the discussion to those agreeing with St. Augustine (354-430), who held that (1) the use of violence on the part of private individuals is immoral, but that {2} there are occasions when governments have a right (and even perhaps an obligation) to go to war. In any case, at least some of the obvious instances – certain stages of World War II, the later stages of the Vietnam conflict, the invasion of Panama – are problems where this definition is not really an issue. Others, such as sending U.S. troops into Somalia on humanitarian grounds (to help distribute food in an impoverished nation that lacks political stability) might be considered "borderline cases."

2. Definition of "justice." At the moment we should probably be concerned less with the definition of "war" and more with the definition of "justice." On this theory (as its name implies) only *just* wars are morally permissible. So how do we decide what makes a war "just"? The traditional strategy on this has been to regard acts of war as one would regard actions of individual persons. Generally speaking, actions have intentions as well as consequences, both foreseen and unforeseen. And though consequences cannot always be foreseen with certainty, it is often possible to gauge which possible consequences are the more probable to occur. (If I send my unruly son to his room, is that really likely to change his behavior?) Likewise, actions can be seen as conforming (or not) to some given standard or rule. These sorts of considerations should be more or less familiar by now, because up to now we have been concerned with how a consequentialist or deontologist would use them over and over again in assessing the moral quality of a *person's* conduct (see Chapter 3). Traditionally, Just War Theory proposes to use similar considerations in assessing the moral quality of a *nation's* conduct.

2a. Right intention. This appeal to "right intention" is what we could call (following Chapter 3) "a deontological" tendency in Just War Theory: The "right" is defined in terms of accordance with a genuine moral standard ("helping others in need" or "coming to the defense of a friend"). These are general common-sense notions of the right and the good, which hardly anyone wants to deny. So if the Just War Theory could be plausibly grounded on the right-intention condition, it would provide a powerful (though very selective) defense of some wars.

So according to the traditional Just War Theory, war is unacceptable if the intention behind it is not morally right. To say that one's action proceeds from "a right intention" is to say one's motives are good, and it is easy to find accounts of bad motives that have brought war about – which would mean that those wars were unjustified. Historians usually cite Hitler's desire for domination of Europe as one major cause of World War II, and it is plausible to suppose that the war was prolonged due to the desire of the German command to spare themselves the punishment for their own genocide towards Jews, homosexuals, gypsies, et cetera. Even if pacifists are wrong, even if the general rule against killing and irreparably disrupting the lives of countless human beings can be overridden under certain extraordinary conditions, would a leader's desire for power, or for exemption from justifiable punishment, qualify as that sort of condition? Quite a few people will answer "no" to that last question.

But still, how do we really discover the motive behind national policy? This is a difficulty that does not face us as much when we are considering only the conduct of individual persons. We can imagine somebody acting for one single reason: I am going shopping only to buy food for dinner tonight. But how do we determine "the" motive behind the actions of an entire *nation*? Some ("radical left") groups opposing U.S. action during the Gulf War claimed that U.S. policy was nothing more than an instrument for securing a stable source for cheap oil imports. But surely the U.S. is now a multicultural land with many diverse and competing interests. For a nation to act cohesively, shouldn't many of those diverse interests be reflected in national policy? So even if oil interests played a part, wouldn't it be narrow to think of the American conduct of the Gulf War, for example, as *nothing but* the reflection of oil interests? (On the other hand, while oil is "only" one reason, the price of oil affects virtually everything done in America from the gasoline we buy to lights we turn on to the clothes we wear and the computers we use. So would it be morally naive to *ignore* forces that threaten such a sizeable component of a nation's economy?)

It may be difficult to imagine what it could mean for an entire *nation* to act out of right (or wrong) intention. As long as a multi-ethnic nation (such as the U.S.) is really democratic, its national policy is never a reflection of only one interest group: It would become politically fatal for a leader to push a policy as serious as war without many diverse groups recognizing crucial self-interested advantages of doing so. At those moments, there would need to be many *social* "intentions" that coalesce, for a time, into the harrowing national policy of war. There would be *individual* intentions as well, some of which may be morally "right" (helping others in need) or morally "wrong" (benefitting personally from the probable deaths of hundreds, maybe millions, of human beings). And, at the national level, who is even supposed to "have" that good intention, anyway? The President of the United States, who usually plays the role of proposing a war to the nation? The Congress of the United States, which, according to the Constitution, must declare war for the nation officially to be at war?

But even during times of the strongest Presidents and weakest voter interest in public affairs, are there not many people who have a substantial say in whether the President can do what he wants? These women and men do exist and could be of decisive influence. Members of Congress could declare war and if the President *vetoed* it, if they chose, they could override a President's veto. Influential members of the press corps can, if they choose, use airtime or news space to discuss the really important aspects of public policy. Civic and religious leaders can be the ones who go on the air. Look at Vietnam, when President Lyndon Johnson, starting with an impeccable political advantage as successor of the martyred Kennedy and victor over the "warmonger" Goldwater, was forced to abdicate the presidency; and after that his own successor (Nixon), despite having the strongest anti-Communist convictions, had to end the war by bailing out of South Vietnam. This would not have happened without the force of a great many different interests working through the vehicle of public opinion.

So at this point, how much reliance should the Just War Theorist really place on that "right intention" condition?

2b. Just Cause. We should probably recognize here two facts about *political* "intentions." The first is that a nation is comprised of a great many diverse, often competing intentions. The second is that intentions are normally rather concrete and practical in their scope. We have intentions about *doing* things, whether that means going to work on a menial job or going to work as President of the country. And these doings had better be concerned with *consequences*. You don't want to overspend your budget for too long, or keep your spouse forever disgruntled in your relationship. That sort of thing would have unpleasant consequences.

So we want to be clear about just what we are doing in any important situation. We become clear about that by asking ourselves what the facts are, what we value (and, perhaps, what we think the probable results of our conduct might be), and why we want to bring about any particular outcome. And those are the sorts of intentions we can evaluate morally. At the national level, where policy decisions are made, this means that a democratic nation would have to make clear the probable consequences of a proposed policy. Then it could be openly discussed, and different individual and group intentions would naturally come into play. And then the mechanism of the democratic process would do its work. A democratic nation, after all, is supposed to be one where a fair representation of different interest groups decides important issues. Interest-groups who define their concerns too narrowly, so as to exclude the essential well-being of others in the nation, will find that others are likely to deal with them in similar ways, and soon the democratic process begins to break down. At such times the public discussion degenerates into spectacular charges and countercharges concerning leveraged buy-outs or banking scandals – situations in which one interest group acts without any regard for those it opposes. (This would be "war" perhaps, but only in a metaphorical sense, so we don't need to be directly concerned about that here.)

But we do need to concern ourselves with the standards for deciding matters of public policy, such as the decision to conduct a war (always remembering that, conceivably, even the most plausible moral justification to wage war or rationalization to oppose its waging may not be good enough). And here we have an illustration of the value of studying applied ethics. As citizens, this view goes, we then are called on to exercise influence over the important affairs of the country, including (but not limited to) voting in a responsible manner. That means we need to see what the probable consequences of a proposed policy would be, and decide whether we could contribute our vote, no smaller than anyone else's, to that cause. This means we need to know how to think clearly on ethical matters and apply that thinking to the situation at hand.

Application: the American invasion of Panama. What would it mean to be able to apply moral considerations to the evaluation of war policy? In the planning stages, at least, it would involve deciding what the results of waging war, and its advantages or disadvantages, are likely to be. For the Panama invasion, American conduct even aspired to the stature of the morally justified act, with the Bush Administration calling it "Operation Just Cause." That is an invitation for any student of contemporary history to think about whether the conditions for correctly calling it that have really been fulfilled.

Sections of the Charter of the United Nations do not, except perhaps in the vaguest way, establish a criterion for what a "right" national policy would be. They talk instead about the kinds of things a nation should *not* do, which is summarized under a term such as "acts of aggression." However, though a nation should not act aggressively, it is permitted to respond in self-defense to aggression committed against it. And here the important point is that acts of aggression are defined *only* in terms of the unilateral, unprovoked, and threatening use of force against another country.

Was there any serious military threat to the United States from the armed forces of Panama? If not, one could argue that the invasion itself was a violation of international law. Of course, there might conceivably be other criteria for "justice" besides the very minimal one set forth by the U.N. In that case, we might want to look into the truth and the significance of the drug-smuggling charges against Panamanian strongman Manuel Noriega, and consider whether that kind of act could justify what the U.S. did.

First-Strike Theory. Other possible considerations need to be taken as well, besides the question of whether a war is launched in response to overt aggression. For example, can a nation justifiably go to war in *anticipation* of a hostile military threat – without, in other words, waiting for it to actually happen? That is what occurred in the weeks leading up to World War I, where millions of men throughout Europe were mobilized, as instruments of what has been called "gunboat" diplomacy. There the idea was: The louder the threat, the greater the chance your opponent will capitulate. Unfortunately, this was a strategy pursued with equal bravado on both sides, and it escalated out of hand when both sides decided they could not suddenly back down from the threats they had been broadcasting. This is exactly the kind of situation that the U.N. Charter was written to avert. The idea was that *if* no one went to war unless actually attacked, no one would ever be attacked. And of course that would be true.

But isn't that a rather big "if?" What if not all parties agree to that principle? In 1967 the state of Israel was actually faced with hostile Arab armies who did not recognize its very status as a nation, and at that point (some would argue) the legitimate state interest of self-preservation sanctioned the strategic first strike by the Israelis. Of course, this assumes that Israel really did enjoy statehood (and it was, after all, admitted to the United Nations, which only recognizes "legitimate" nations). A further question concerns the logical *implications* of such a justification. For even if adequate, does this justification of the Israeli action mean that the Arabs did not have legitimate interests, or that either side is blameless for the hostile conditions?

And what happens in the case when military intervention is recommended for clearly humanitarian purposes, such as distributing food in Somalia or saving the beleaguered Bosnian citizens of Sarajevo? These do not always start as "wars" – in Somalia, for example – but they might turn into wars if enough local opposition is drawn. The difficulties with deciding this kind of borderline case have often led involved parties to seek international consensus on the action to be taken. Thus, for example, starting in 1992, both the European Community and the United Nations began trying to negotiate a settlement in Bosnia. But this raises questions, too. Does the mere fact that an international body approves of an action in itself make the action morally just? The War in the Persian Gulf, conducted only after a favorable vote in the United Nations Security Council, has still been criticized by some on moral grounds, despite its international sanction.

And there is another complication with restricting a "just" war to include only the response to acts of overt aggression. What about a continuing violation of a nation's rights? Let's suppose a country's neighbor has exercised hostile control over that country's economy, perhaps by controlling the international market so that the disadvantaged country could not get the imports it needs for political stability. This is not an armed intervention. But isn't it an act of war ("by attrition")? That is the sort of charge that Saddam Hussein's government was making against Kuwait, as one pretext for the Iraqi invasion. Or what if a colonial power is exercising painful economic domination over its colonies?

That was the rationale offered by the Viet Cong against the Americans, by Indian nationalists joining Mahatma Gandhi against the British, and it was the same rationale as given by American revolutionaries at the time of the Boston Tea Party in 1773. We need to look very carefully, in each case, to assess the political rhetoric that attempts to portray a "just cause."

But what about the way that cause is actually pursued? This leads to another question: Even if the cause is just, does that always mean that the war is just?

2c. Just conduct. It would be hard to think of a national leader who would favor a policy he'd be willing to call "unjust"! The world is a very complicated place, with a long history of rights infringement, so it is relatively easy to find rather convincing grounds for war. The First World War (called "The Great War" only until the Second and greater one occurred) was described by the Americans as "The War to End All Wars," but its peace treaty foisted burdensome reparations on the defeated power (Germany) – and Germans knew full well that they were not alone responsible for the War's occurrence. Hitler used that to rally his people to the "justice" of the Nazi cause.

Most proponents of the Just War Theory will insist that a just cause does not always mean that a war is just, and this is because its actual conduct might not conform to a *rule of proportionality*. (A utilitarian – who evaluates conduct based on the greatest good/greatest number principle we discussed in Chapter 3 – would make use of this point.) In international matters, just as in the conduct of an individual's personal life, there are always trade-offs: Results of any extended endeavor always bring benefits and costs alike, and we need to weigh the one against the other in decisions of public policy, in order to decide if the proportion of good to bad consequences is acceptable. Think, after all, about what it may be costing you to receive your college degree! (Are the aims worth the human cost? Is the degree you finally get, after spending all those evenings in night school, really worth spending evenings away from your children?)

At the national level, any such assessment is a complicated matter, requiring the testimony of "experts" who may or may not be knowledgeable or reliable in their advice. (What, for example, does it take to stimulate economic investment in underclass neighborhoods? Should the government encourage "free enterprise zones" in the inner city?) In a democratic society these experts have a special obligation. And journalists have an obligation to present as many plausible points of view as possible, so that as many citizens as possible can have a say in the decision. And finally, whenever timeliness is a factor, especially when national debate on a decision cannot be fully completed, as when the Japanese attacked Pearl Harbor at the start of World War II, this just brings home how important it might be for the appropriate persons and legal procedures to be in place, so that the country does not embark on an ill-advised declaration of war.

But a war is never convincingly justified for very long in the abstract. If we talk of nothing *more* than a just cause, that's probably going to obscure the question of whether our actual military actions are justified. When, for example, it began to seem as if the Gulf War was going to be a lot less costly (from the standpoint of American lives lost) than people had feared, it became more politically feasible for American policy to continue on course, without having to be troubled by the pain of heavy casualties. All the American public had to consider then, it seemed, was whether or not Saddam Hussein was a "threat." And there was general agreement on that.

This, however, raises troubling questions indeed. First, is it moral to consider the factor of a potential or actual "body count" to evaluate whether a war is or may be just? Is it inherently dehumanizing to make such assessments as part of a justification for or argument against war? What sort of consideration should be paid to the lives lost on the *other* side? The Iraqis may have lost up to 243,000 people.[8] To what extent were those deaths really only a tragic moral necessity for achieving our own just military cause? This raises the whole question of *the collateral effects of war*. What weight do we pay to the destruction of nonmilitary property and the killing of innocent bystanders? Many proponents of the Just War Theory would reject the strategy of *total war* and recognize some commanding moral scruples against destruction that is purely arbitrary or vengeful.

This concern over collateral effects would probably invalidate Union General Sherman's "scorched-earth policy" during his Civil War march through Georgia, but that would still depend upon what sorts of action we take to be merely "vengeful." If a commander's aim is to prevent the current generation of inhabitants (the entire society) from ever again being in an economic position to wage war, then almost any conceivable property destruction would seem justified. But why would people think such drastic measures necessary? Do they reject the chances of securing a reliable agreement safeguarding the rights of all parties? When that sort of agreement exists, what remaining reason or enthusiasm for war could there be?

The need to preserve *noncombatant immunity* (the protection of innocent bystanders) would place a high moral burden on military commanders. Destruction, if it is not to be arbitrary or vengeful, must be limited to, or at least aimed at, military targets alone. Under this rule, commanders would need to discriminate between military and civilian targets and then make the heavy call on which targets are really necessary for the war aims. In 1940 and 1941, for example, the British kept only military objectives targeted, despite the indiscriminate German bombing of London. But it became clear that the German war effort remained intact as long as its heavily populated industrial base remained untouched. At that point British Prime Minister Winston Churchill shifted policy in favor of undercutting "the morale of the enemy population" by treating widespread civilian casualties as only a by-product of necessary military conduct. That would mean that the destruction of entire cities might not be classified as arbitrary or vengeful. And so, by 1944, terror raids on civilians had become Allied military policy, and by war's end Allied bombing probably killed as many as 593,000 German civilians.[9] During the Gulf War, on the other hand, it was stated American policy to avoid civilian targets. To find out whether or not that policy was actually implemented, of course, we would need to look carefully at reliable news reports.

Application: nuclear war. And this raises the impact of the claim of noncombatant immunity in the nuclear age. It took an immense effort on February 12, 1945, for the Allies to pull off the bombing of the German city of Dresden. Scores of planes were orchestrated to drop thousands of rather small bombs. But six months later, the nuclear bombing by a single American aircraft killed 100,000 people in Hiroshima and five times that in Nagasaki. How does this affect the argument?

For American President Harry Truman, the convincing military argument had been that more casualties might well have resulted if the Americans had been forced into a conventional invasion of the Japanese homeland. This was a utilitarian argument, one which many have questioned, and since the improvement of nuclear technology one wonders how strong this kind of justification can seem to us today. When the U.S. and the Soviet Union faced each other as two armed camps, with enough nuclear strength to destroy every living thing, and faced as well the likelihood of a cataclysmic escalation after any first strike, what could possibly justify the use of nuclear weapons?

Until very recently, however, it was U.S. policy to *threaten* the use of nuclear weapons, on the assumption (then called the theory of Mutual Assured Destruction) that neither side would be stupid enough to start a nuclear war under such conditions. That assumes the leadership on both sides would allow sane, rational considerations to direct military policy. But what if another Hitler came to power?

This nuclear policy also meant actually having the intention to use nuclear weapons if the other side *were* that stupid (or lost control of its own arsenal, by accident or through the unilateral action of rogue commanders). What can we say, morally, about that? The issue never received a full public discussion, so one could not claim that the policy was truly democratic. But that alone might not invalidate such a policy. For we have already admitted that there are cases such as Pearl Harbor, emergencies that make full consultation impossible. Would this be one of them?

The question really comes down to this: Would the American population ever agree, if asked, to regard itself as expendable? Perhaps. Maybe patriotism would make martyrs of them. On the other hand, maybe people really would rather be "Red than dead" (as the signs of early anti-war protesters used to say). In any case, imagine you are the President, or a Strategic Air Commander, and you don't have the time to find out. The moral burden is all yours. How do you decide? Do you surrender your sovereignty to the threat, or do you capitulate (for the sake of your people's very lives)?

Until the collapse of the Soviet Union – which makes nuclear holocaust seem much less likely, as long as a friendly Russian government retains power – the American leadership was in exactly this position. American plans were governed by what was called the *Countervailing Strategy*, under which even an ordinary, massive Soviet land attack, using only conventional, non-nuclear, weapons, would elicit an American nuclear strike, and this was because the Soviet conventional force was generally thought to be superior even to the strength of our allies in Europe combined under terms of the North Atlantic Treaty Organization (NATO). This bleak choice would be forced upon any American leader who loses confidence in the power of international agreements, agreements which would be secure only when all parties feel sufficiently protected by their provisions. At the desperate moment we are imagining here, as Soviet troops begin pouring into West Germany, such confidence might have worn pretty thin. What does this say about the wisdom of collectively securing the legitimate interests of all powerful potential adversaries?

The Countervailing Strategy was accepted by both sides during much of the Cold War. With the anti-ballistic missile (ABM) treaty in 1972, both agreed not to construct the anti-ballistic missile systems that would protect home cities, because if one side achieved that aim before the other, it might remove the main military impediment against a policy of first nuclear strike. But U. S. President Ronald Reagan proposed a drastic overhaul of military policy with his introduction of the Strategic Defense Initiative ("Star Wars"), which would do exactly what the ABM Treaty disavowed. American cities would be protected against Soviet missiles. And the reason the Soviets were so bitterly opposed to that was the fact that Americans could then launch a first nuclear strike, if they eventually chose not to share their technology, without fear of massive Soviet retaliation. This would mean that only American adherence to moral principle might stand in the way of millions of Soviet deaths. Would the moral caliber of the American leadership stand such a test? (The Soviets, at least, doubted that it would.) But, apparently, faced with a failed economic system that could not muster a continuing military juggernaut, the Soviets virtually capitulated to the United States as the strongest power in the world. Did Reagan's Star Wars Initiative speed that decision? Or was the decision taken in spite of any American initiative?

Obviously, the predominance of nuclear technology has presented the world with unappealing choices, and it puts traditional discussions about "just war" in a new light. But are these any longer serious matters for us? Isn't it obviously tempting to breathe more easily today, simply because there *is* no more Soviet Union? Tempting, yes. But it is also just as obvious that political realities are ever changing, and as long as there are nuclear weapons around, these questions will remain very much with us. By the beginning of 1993, for example, the political health of Russian President Boris Yeltsin was becoming increasingly precarious, and the possibility of some future change in Russian policy could no longer be ignored. So it is worth asking: When should national debate over these matters occur – when an immediate crisis is looming, or when we have enough cool distance to assess the alternatives calmly and thoughtfully? Consider what the alternatives fairly clearly seem to be:

1. On the one hand, as we have seen, the Countervailing Strategy targets massive retaliation against enemy arsenals, and gambles on the deterrent force of this kind of threat to prevent the enemy from ever launching an attack. But what about the chance of a tragic accidental launch? With perhaps insufficient time for the defenders to identify the accident as such, the intention of military policy would be to proceed with the nuclear option. And in the event of a ground attack upon our European allies, American intention was for a measured, tit-for-tat nuclear response against those forces – which would almost certainly obliterate thousands, maybe millions of people in the countries we are supposed to be protecting! Given the human costs of that, is it moral for any country's leadership to have such an intention?

2. The strategy of *Strategic Defense*, on the other hand, would seek to prevent those missiles from ever hitting their target, because technology would provide a nuclear shield of protection for the homeland. Yet the technology remains in its infancy, and there is no assurance as to how successful its development will turn out to be. What if it were 80% effective? A 20% failure rate is a pretty good return in some endeavors, but in this case it would still annihilate millions of people and jeopardize the ecological state of the entire planet. And because Strategic Defense would be enormously expensive as well, what social needs would have to be ignored in order to pay for it?

3. There is another option, however, which has been called *Finite Deterrence*. Unlike the Countervailing Strategy, under this view the use of nuclear weapons would not be treated as justified in any battlefield situation, and first use of any nuclear weapon would be strictly prohibited. But the military would retain a sufficient nuclear capability, stored in highly protected areas such as patrolling submarines, so that an eventual, searing second strike would surely be possible. And that, the theory insists, should be enough to deter an intentional enemy attack, while at the same time allowing the military to determine whether first-strike enemy missiles were mistakenly launched. This is akin to what actually happened in World War II when the U.S. responded, eventually, to the attack on Pearl Harbor by detonating atomic bombs on Nagasaki and Hiroshima bringing the war to an end. President Nixon would maintain that his controversial bombings of Haiphong brought the fierce North Vietnamese generals to the table to negotiate U.S. extrication from South Vietnam. But would deterrence really work today? Might the enemy leadership not decide that they could absorb a limited second-strike response, and that the costs of that, however terrible, would be outweighed by the benefits of total victory? (The Soviets, after all, suffered an estimated 20-million dead during World War II – but they helped stop Hitler!) And could even that second-strike response by "our" side ever be morally justified, in view of the terrible costs that it would inflict on millions of innocent human beings? Wouldn't this still amount to mass murder?

4. In the light of all this, many people continue to question whether a nuclear conflict can ever be a "just" war, and insist that the appropriate policy ought to be one of *Nuclear Disarmament*. Perhaps the prevailing pressures in favor of launching a first nuclear strike stem from the fear that the other side will do so. If one of the adversaries no longer possessed that capability, that motive would be eliminated. This is the central argument often presented by advocates of *unilateral* disarmament – the idea that we should abolish nuclear weapons without first gaining the assurance of similar action by

the other side. But the other side would no longer fear a crippling reprisal. So might this not instead increase the chance of attack? Not, of course, if we could be certain that its leadership took seriously its moral responsibilities, for surely there could be no moral justification for them to commit such an act. But can we be sure they would take these responsibilities seriously? (Most Americans, throughout the Cold War, were unwilling to trust the Kremlin on that.)

What unilateral nuclear disarmament might actually mean is that the chances of a *massive* nuclear attack would be lessened. For it may be a little hard to imagine even Joseph Stalin calling arbitrarily for the annihilation of an entire population. In any event we know that a massive nuclear holocaust, even if it did not directly touch the perpetrator's home base, would still have devastating ecological effects that no country on earth could avoid. But even so, how would unilateral disarmament affect the possibility of national self-determination? A healthy national life surely requires that important policy decisions not be held hostage to coercive stipulations by unfriendly forces, and wouldn't a nation that lacked a nuclear capacity find it difficult to withstand unscrupulous hostile demands of a foreign nuclear power (who could perhaps threaten to use a single nuclear device against, say, Miami)?

This leaves open the avenue of *bilateral* nuclear disarmament – a negotiated arrangement, with sufficient safeguards, where two adversaries agree to a gradual, eventual elimination of all nuclear weapons in their possession. Conceivably, this might be the actual result of the kind of arms control policy followed by both major powers after the Reagan-Gorbachev summit in 1987. But difficulties have persisted even under such favorable conditions. Without the *total* elimination of nuclear weaponry from both sides, the situation remains at best one of Finite Deterrence. How do we finally get down to zero on this? Isn't there a tremendous, self-interested advantage for either side to retain a few nuclear devices, fully hidden in some cave somewhere, as a threatening instrument of last resort?

SUMMARY

These questions about war are unresolved, perhaps, but nevertheless inescapable for each of us. They touch on many more issues than we can pursue here. One of the most important of these is the place of international arbitration. If disputes between nations could be settled under the framework of international law, would there be any further need for war of any kind? This in turn illustrates the need to ask why a nation would ever resort to the drastic expedient of war. Surely, only under the most dire circumstances would an entire people agree to the kind of sacrifice a prolonged conflict requires. What kind of circumstances would do that? In our culture, after all, we normally think that it is wrong to kill innocent people or to destroy others' property or to arbitrarily prevent them from attaining the quality of life we aspire to ourselves.

READINGS
YES TO WAR IN THE GULF
John C. Danforth, U. S. Senator, D-Missouri
Delivered to the United States Senate,
Washington, D.C., January 10, 1991

Madam President, like all my colleagues, I have been engaged in intensive soul–searching on how I will vote on the question now before the Senate, whether to support the President if he determines force is necessary to expel Iraq from Kuwait. Through-

out this soul–searching, two convictions have been foremost in my mind.

First, I am convinced beyond a doubt that the United States must not allow the status quo in Kuwait to stand. Some have argued that the President has not made a clear case for America's insistence that Iraq must withdraw from Kuwait, but for me the President's case is both crystal clear and overwhelmingly convincing.

This is the first major test of the post–cold–war world order. With the recent collapse of the Soviet Empire, the great threat we have feared since 1945 is no longer real. The likelihood is zero that the Soviet Union will precipitate war by invading Western Europe. But the events of August 2 have demonstrated to all that to be rid of one threat does not make the world safe. A growing list of countries now possess or soon will possess the instruments of mass destruction. One of those countries is Iraq. It is simply not sufficient to check the possibility of terrifying aggression at one of its sources. We must be prepared to check terrifying aggression at all of its sources.

In Kuwait, Iraq is the aggressor, and its actions cannot be tolerated. Nearly all of us agree on this point. Iraq attacked its neighbor, occupied its territory, and brutalized its people. It has fielded a massive army with chemical and biological warfare capability that it has no compunctions about using. It now controls 20% of the world's proven oil reserves, and if undeterred, it could control an additional 25% of the world reserves in Saudi Arabia by conquest or intimidation.

Some people have asked whether this conflict is not "just about" oil. To me, that is like asking whether it is not just about oxygen. Like it or not, our country, together with the rest of the world, is utterly dependent on oil. Our economy, our jobs, our ability to defend ourselves are dependent on our access to oil. To control the world's supply of oil is in a real sense to control the world. So what is involved in the Persian Gulf today is not only the preservation of the world order and the preservation of brutal aggression; it is the vital economic and security interests of the United States and the rest of the world as well.

For many years, commentators of various philosophical stripes, especially liberal commentators, have argued that the United States should not go it alone in the world. We should not take it upon ourselves to be the world's policeman. So the commentators have argued, with respect to Central America and elsewhere, that our country should not act unilaterally; we should work with other countries; we should address crises on a multilateral basis.

This is exactly what President Bush has done with respect to the present crisis. He has gone repeatedly to the United Nations Security Council for approval of concerted action. He and Secretary of State Baker have consulted incessantly with countries throughout the world. He has asked for and received the military and economic support of more than 20 nations. He has been widely acclaimed, especially by the liberals, for this multilateral approach.

It is argued that while many nations have done something, few nations have done enough. I suppose this point would always be made no matter what the degree of commitment by our partners. But what are we to make of such an argument? That multilateralism was a mistake after all? That no matter how assiduously pursued, it never really works?

The advocates of multilateralism cannot have it both ways. They cannot applaud it one day, and jeer at it the next. Would that there were more leaders from the free world, but the fact is that the United States is the leader. We are the one remaining world power. And if the United States now retreats from its commitment for a joint effort on the ground that others are not as strong or as firm as we are, all the efforts to seek Security Council resolutions and to consult with other governments will have been an exercise of futility, recognized as such throughout the world.

The captain cannot abandon the ship. Having gained the approval of so many other governments, some of which are on the very border of Iraq and in greater peril for their survival, it is unthinkable that our Government would now lose its will. Having urged the world to approve combined action, it is not an option for the Congress of the United States to disapprove what we for months have asked others to support.

This, then, is my first conviction: We cannot accept Iraq's occupation of Kuwait.

My second conviction is that war with Iraq would be a disaster we should do everything to avoid. I have believed and I do believe that the negative consequences of war far outweigh the positive. These negatives have totally consumed my thinking and I have expressed them to the President and to key members of his administration.

I foresee many casualties, the use of chemical weapons by Iraq, terrorist strikes, Israel's involvement, and long-lasting turmoil in the Middle East. Repeatedly, I asked myself the same question: When we win the war, then what happens? What happens to the balance of power in the Middle East? To the governance of Iraq? To the stability of friendly governments in Egypt and Saudi Arabia? Repeatedly I have come to the same answers. While the status quo is unacceptable, the alternative of war is even worse.

Because of this conclusion I have for some time believed that if I had to vote on the matter, I would vote against authorizing the President to use military force. I have taken comfort in the proposition that we will soon be voting on it here in the Senate. Let us give sanctions a chance to work.

But, Madam President, after consulting with the best advice I can find, I have concluded that there is no comfort to be found in that proposition. It is clear to me that sanctions alone cannot reverse the status quo. Sanctions alone will cause suffering to the civilian population of Iraq, but they will not force the Iraqi army from Kuwait. And causing suffering to a civilian population without military results should never be the objective of a civilized nation.

I refer the Senate, as others have today, to the public testimony of Director of Central Intelligence Webster before the House Armed Services Committee on December 5, 1990. I ask unanimous consent, as others have, Madam President, that a transcript of that testimony be printed in the Record at this point.

There being no objection, the material was ordered to be printed in the Record, as follows:

Sanctions in the Persian Gulf
Iraq – The Domestic Impact of Sanctions, December 4, 1990.

Thank you, Mr. Chairman. I appreciate the opportunity to address this committee on what the intelligence community believes the sanctions have already accomplished and what we believe the sanctions have already accomplished over time. Of course, sanctions are only one type of pressure being applied on Iraq, and their impact cannot be completely distinguished from the combined impact of military, diplomatic, and economic initiatives on Iraq.

At the technical level, economic sanctions and the embargo against Iraq have put Saddam Hussein on notice that he is isolated from the world community and have dealt a serious blow to the Iraqi economy. More than 100 countries are supporting the U.N. resolutions that impose economic sanctions on Iraq. Coupled with the U.S. Government's increased ability to detect and follow up on attempts to circumvent the blockade, the sanctions have all but shut off Iraq's exports and reduced imports to less than 10% of their pre-invasion level. All sectors of the Iraqi economy are feeling the pinch of sanctions and many industries have largely shut down. Most importantly, the blockade has eliminated any hope Baghdad had of cashing in on higher oil prices or its seizure of Kuwait oilfields.

Despite mounting disruptions and hardships resulting from sanctions, Saddam apparently believe that he can outlast international resolve to maintain sanctions. We see no indication that Saddam is concerned, at this point, that domestic discontent is growing to levels that may threaten his regime or that problems resulting from the sanctions are causing him to rethink his policy on Kuwait. The Iraqi people have experienced considerable deprivation in the past. Given the brutal nature of the Iraqi security services, the population is not likely to oppose Saddam openly. Our judgment has been, and continues to be, that there is no assurance or guarantee that economic hardships will compel Saddam to change his policies or lead to internal unrest that would threaten his regime.

Let me take a few minutes to review briefly with you some of the information that led us to these conclusions, as well as to present our assessment of the likely impact of sanctions over the coming months.

The blockade and embargo have worked more effectively than Saddam probably expected. More than 90% of imports and 97% of exports have been shut off. Although there is smuggling across Iraq's borders, it is extremely small relative to Iraq's pre-crisis trade. Iraqi efforts to break sanctions have thus far been largely unsuccessful. What little leakage that has occurred is due largely to a relatively small number of private firms acting independently. We believe most countries are actively enforcing the sanctions and plan to continue doing so.

Industry appears to be the hardest hit sector so far. Many firms are finding it difficult to cope, with the departure of foreign workers and with the cutoff of imported industrial inputs – which comprised nearly 60% of Iraq's total imports prior to the invasion. These shortages have either shut down or severely curtailed production by a variety of industries, including many light industrial and assembly plants as well as the country's only tire-manufacturing plant. Despite these shutdowns, the most vital industries – including electric power generation and refining – do not yet appear threatened. We believe they will be able to function for sometime because domestic consumption has been reduced, because Iraqi and Kuwaiti facilities have been cannibalized and because some stockpiles and surpluses already existed.

The cutoff of Iraq's oil exports and the success of sanctions also have been more effective and more complete than Saddam probably expected. In fact, we believe that a lack of foreign exchange will, in time, be Iraq's greatest economic difficulty. The embargo has deprived Baghdad of roughly $1.5-billion of foreign exchange earnings monthly. We have no evidence that Iraq has significantly augmented the limited foreign exchange reserves to which it still has access. As a result, Baghdad is working to conserve foreign exchange and to devise alternative methods to finance imports.

We believe Baghdad's actions to forestall shortages of food stocks – including rationing, encouraging smuggling, and promoting agricultural production – are adequate for the next several months. The fall harvest of fruits and vegetables is injecting new supplies into the market and will provide a psychological as well as tangible respite from mounting pressures. The Iraqi population, in general, has access to sufficient staple foods. Other foodstuffs – still not rationed – also remain available. However, the variety is diminishing and prices are sharply inflated. For example, sugar purchased on the open market at the official exchange rate went from $32 per 50 kilogram bag in August to $580 per bag last month. Baghdad remains concerned about its food stocks and, increasingly, (continues) to divert supplies to the military. In late November, Baghdad cut civilian rations for the second time since the rationing program began, while announcing increases in rations for military personnel and their families.

On balance, the embargo has increased the economic hardships facing the average Iraqi. In order to supplement their rations, Iraqis must turn to the black market, where most goods can be purchased but at highly inflated prices. They are forced to spend con-

siderable amounts of time searching for reasonably priced food or waiting in lines for bread and other rationed items. In addition, services ranging from medical care to sanitation have been curtailed. But these hardships are easier for (the Iraqi people to endure compared to the) high casualty rates, and repeated missile and air attacks that Iraqis lived with during the eight–year Iran–Iraq war. During this war, incidentally, there was not a single significant public disturbance even though casualties hit 2.3% of the total Iraqi population – about the same as the percentage of U.S. casualties during the Civil War.

Looking ahead, the economic picture changes somewhat. We expect Baghdad's foreign exchange reserves to become extremely tight, leaving it little cash left with which to entice potential sanctions-busters. At current rates of depletion, we estimate Iraq will have nearly depleted its available foreign exchange reserves by next spring. Able to obtain even fewer key imports, Iraq's economic problems will begin to multiply as Baghdad is forced to gradually shut down growing numbers of facilities in order to keep critical activities functioning as long as possible. Economic conditions will be noticeably worse, and Baghdad will find allocating scarce resources a significantly more difficult task.

Probably only energy-related and some military industries will still be fully functioning by next spring. This will almost certainly be the case by next summer. Baghdad will try to keep basic services such as electric power from deteriorating. The regime also will try to insulate critical military industries to reduce rations. Coupled with rapid inflation and little additional support from the Government, this will compound the economic pressures facing most Iraqis.

By next spring, Iraqis will have made major changes in their diets. Poultry, a staple of the Iraqi diet, will not be available. Unless Iraq receives humanitarian food aid or unless smuggling increases, some critical commodities such as sugar and edible oils will be in short supply. Distribution problems are likely to create localized shortages. But we expect that Baghdad will be able to maintain grain consumption – mainly wheat, barley, and rice – at about two-thirds of last year's level until the next harvest in May.

The spring grain and vegetable harvest will again augment food stocks, although only temporarily. To boost next year's food production, Baghdad has raised prices paid to farmers for their produce and decreed that farmers must cultivate all available land. Nonetheless, Iraq does not have the capability to become self-sufficient in food production by next year. Weather is the critical variable in grain production and even if it is good, Iraqis will be able to produce less than half the grain they need. In addition, Iraq's vegetable production next year may be less than normal because of its inability to obtain seed stock from abroad. Iraq had obtained seed from the United States, The Netherlands, and France.

Although sanctions are hurting Iraq's civilian economy, they are affecting the Iraqi military only at the margins. Iraq's fairly static defensive posture will reduce wear-and-tear on military equipment and, as a result, extend the life of its inventory of spare parts and maintenance items. Under now-combat conditions, Iraqi ground and air forces can probably maintain near-current levels of readiness for as long as nine months.

We expect the Iraqi Air Force to feel the effects of the sanctions more quickly and to a greater degree than the Iraqi ground forces because of its greater reliance on high technology and foreign equipment and technicians. Major repairs to sophisticated aircraft like the F-1 will be achieved with significant difficulty, if at all, because of the exodus of foreign technicians. Iraqi technicians, however should be able to maintain current levels of aircraft sorties for three to six months.

The Iraqi ground forces are more immune to sanctions. Before the invasion, Baghdad maintained large inventories of basic military supplies, such as ammunition, and supplies probably remain adequate. The embargo will eventually hurt Iraqi armor by preventing the replacement of old fire-control systems and creating shortages of additives for various critical lubricants. Shortages will also affect Iraqi cargo trucks over time.

While we can look ahead several months and predict the general deterioration of the Iraqi economy, it is more difficult to assess how or when these conditions will cause Saddam to modify his behavior. At present, Saddam almost certainly assumes that he is coping effectively with the sanctions. He appears confident in the ability of his security services to contain potential discontent, and we do not believe he is troubled by the hardship Iraqis will be forced to endure. Saddam's willingness to sit tight and try to outlast the sanctions or, in the alternative, to avoid

war by withdrawing from Kuwait will be determined by his total assessment of the political, economic, and military pressure arrayed against him.

The conclusion of Director Webster is that sanctions in themselves will not lead to the overthrow of Saddam Hussein, and that they will not lead him to change his policy toward Kuwait. The Director states that if Saddam Hussein decides to withdraw from Kuwait, that decision, and I quote, "will be determined by his total assessment of political, economic, and military pressure arrayed against him."

It is my privilege to serve on the Select Committee on Intelligence. I am precluded, of course from divulging classified information I have received in briefings in that committee. However, I am free to state my own conclusions on the basis of my total understanding. My conclusion is this: Standing by themselves and without the credible threat of military force, sanctions have no chance of expelling Iraq from Kuwait.

Some have argued that sanctions would, over time, weaken Iraq's military position and make an eventual conflict less costly to American forces. But this assumption is not borne out by the best available advice, including Director Webster's public testimony. The Director states that "under known combat conditions, Iraq ground and air forces can probably maintain near current levels of readiness for as long as 9 months." He further states that the Iraqi Air Force would feel the effects of sanctions to a greater degree than ground forces, which are more immune to sanctions, but it is ground forces that dug into Kuwait in massive numbers and it has been said that ground forces have never been defeated by air superiority alone.

Madam President, I know that there have been various interpretations offered in the Senate about exactly what Director Webster said in his testimony on December 5. It could be said that he testified that sanctions work, Madam President, if the meaning of "work" is to inflict pain on civilians; that the sanctions offer (a) possibility of removing Iraq from Kuwait in the foreseeable future.

I would like to quote just a few excerpts form the letter that Director Webster has written today to Chairman Aspin, of the House Armed Services Committee. These are the words of William Webster. First, characterizing his testimony of December 5, he said:

"I also testified that there was no evidence that sanctions would mandate a change in Saddam Hussein's behavior and that there was no evidence when or even if they would force him out of Kuwait."

And then the Director goes on and says this:

"The ability of the Iraqi ground forces to defend Kuwait and Southern Iraq is unlikely to be substantially eroded over the next 6 to 12 months even if effective sanctions can be maintained. This is especially true if Iraq does not believe a coalition attack is likely during this period. Iraq's infantry and artillery forces – the key elements of Iraq's initial defense – probably would not suffer significantly as a result of sanctions. Iraq could easily maintain the relatively simple Soviet-style weaponry of its infantry and artillery, (and) have additional opportunity to extend and reinforce their fortifications along the Saudi border, thereby increasing their defensive strength."

The Director then says:

"On balance, the marginal decline of combat power in Baghdad's armored units probably would be offset by the simultaneous improvement of its defensive fortifications.

"Iraq's air force and air defenses are more likely to be hit far more severely than its army, if effective sanctions are maintained for another 6 to 12 months. This degradation will diminish Iraq's ability to defend its strategic assets from air attack and reduce its ability to conduct similar attacks on its neighbors. It would have only a marginal impact on Saddam's ability to hold Kuwait and southern Iraq. The Iraqi Air Force is not likely to play a major role in any battle for Kuwait.

"Our judgment remains that even if sanctions continue to be enforced for an additional 6 to 12 months, economic hardship alone is unlikely to compel Saddam to retreat from Kuwait or cause regime-threatening, popular discontent in Iraq."

So is time on our side, Madam President, as I have long wanted to believe? I cannot persuade myself that this was any more than wishful thinking on my part.

What happens for the next 9 months, or a year, or more than a year, as we vainly wait for the Iraqis to leave their fortifications? Do we keep more than 400,000 troops in place through Ramadan, through the Hadj, through the summer? And if so, what happens to their readiness, their support by the American people, their acceptance by the Muslim masses? To ask these questions is to answer them.

To wait for sanctions to work is to wait while we get weaker and Iraq bides its time. The one and only chance to accomplish our objective without war is to maintain sanctions accompanied by a credible military threat. Without a credible military threat, our alternative is sanctions followed by nothing at all.

The key to peace is maintaining a credible military threat and this is precisely the point our pending votes will address. Those who would give sanctions a chance before military action is even possible would decouple the two components which must be kept linked, if we have any chance of getting Iraq out of Kuwait without a fight. They would foreclose any possibility of a just peace.

This is why I cannot vote for sanctions alone. This is why I cannot vote to deprive the President of the credible threat of force. It is indeed a supreme irony that it is only through the threat of force that a stable world can be maintained. But that is an irony we have recognized ever since World War II.

Madam President, I do believe that Saddam Hussein pays attention to what we do and say in the Senate. I do believe that the President's credibility is our best hope, if we are to preserve a stable world without war. We will soon vote to enhance that credibility or to undercut it. I will support the President with my votes and with my prayers.

NO TO WAR IN THE GULF
George J. Mitchell, D-Maine,
SENATE MAJORITY LEADER
Delivered to the United States Senate,
Washington, D.C., January 10, 1991

For two centuries Americans have debated the relative powers of the President and Congress. Often it has been an abstract argument. But today that debate is real. The men who wrote the Constitution had as a central purpose the prevention of tyranny in America. They had lived under a British king. They did not want there ever to be an American king. They were brilliantly successful. In our history there have been 41 presidents and no kings.

The writers of our Constitution succeeded by creating a government with separate institutions and divided powers. They correctly reasoned that if power were sufficiently dispersed, no institution or individual could gain total power.

Nowhere has their concept been more severely tested than in what they regard as one of the greatest powers of government – the power to make war.

The Constitution designates the President as Commander in Chief of the Armed Forces. With that designation comes the authority to direct the deployment of those forces.

But the Constitution also grants to the Congress the authority to raise and support armies and to declare war.

This division of authority was a decision consciously reached by the framers of the Constitution. The earliest draft of the Constitution would have empowered the Congress to "make war," a greater grant of power than to "declare war." It reflected the deep concern of the Founding Fathers about too great a concentration of power in a single pair of hands.

When it was argued that this wording might prevent the President from responding to an attack on this country, the Constitutional Convention agreed to share the power. After the Revolutionary War, the Founders knew that a legislative body could not direct the day-to-day operations of a war.

But they also knew that the decision to commit the nation to war should not be left in the hands of one man. The clear intent was to limit the authority of the President to initiate war.

Our subsequent history has borne out their wisdom. Acting in his capacity as Commander in Chief, President Bush has deployed a vast American military force to the Persian Gulf.

He was not required to seek the approval of Congress to order that deployment, and he did not do so.

But if he now decides to use those forces in what would plainly be war he is legally obligated to seek the prior approval of Congress.

The President has the authority to act in an emergency, and to authorize our forces to defend themselves if attacked. But, that's not what now is at issue.

Two days ago, the President in writing requested that Congress authorize him to implement the United Nations Resolution authorizing "all necessary means" to expel Iraq from Kuwait.

But yesterday the President said that, in his opinion, he needs no such authorization from the Congress. I believe the correct approach was the one taken by the President two days ago when he requested authorization. His request clearly acknowledged the need for Congressional approval.

The Constitution of the United States is not and cannot be subordinated to a United Nations resolution.

So today the Senate undertakes a solemn Constitutional responsibility; to decide whether to commit the nation to war. In this debate, we should focus on the fundamental question before us: What is the wisest course of action for our nation in the Persian Gulf crisis?

In its simplest form, the question is whether Congress will give the President an unlimited blank check to initiate war against Iraq, at some unspecified time in the future, under circumstances which are not now known and cannot be foreseen, or whether, while not ruling out the use of force if all other means fail, we will now urge continuation of the policy of concerted international economic and diplomatic pressure.

This is not a debate about whether force should ever be used. No one proposes to rule out the use of force. We cannot and should not rule it out. The question is, should war be truly a last resort when all other means fail? Or should we start with war, before other means have been fully and fairly exhausted?

This is not a debate about American objectives in the current crisis.

There is broad agreement in the Senate that Iraq must, fully and unconditionally, withdraw its forces from Kuwait.

The issue is how best to achieve that goal.

Most Americans and most Members of Congress, myself included, supported the President's initial decision to deploy American forces to Saudi Arabia to deter further Iraqi aggression.

We supported the President's effort in marshaling international diplomatic pressure and the most comprehensive economic embargo in history against Iraq.

I support that policy. I believe it remains the correct policy, even though the President abandoned his own policy before it had time to work.

The change began on November 8, when President Bush announced that he was doubling the number of American troops in the Persian Gulf to 430,000 in order to attain a "credible offensive option."

The President did not consult with Congress about that decision. He did not try to build support for it among the American people. He just did it.

In doing so, President Bush transformed the United States' role and its rank in the Persian Gulf crisis.

In effect, the President – overnight, with no consultation and no public debate – changed American policy from being part of a collective effort to enforce economic and diplomatic sanctions into a predominantly American effort relying upon the use of American military force. By definition, sanctions require many nations to participate and share the burden. War does not.

Despite the fact that his own policy of international economic sanctions was having a significant effect upon the Iraqi economy, the President, without explanation, abandoned that approach and instead adopted a policy based first and foremost upon the use of American military force.

As a result, this country has been placed on a course toward war.

This has upset the balance of the President's initial policy, the balance between resources and responsibilities, between interests and risks, and between patience and strength.

Opposition to aggression is not solely an American value. It is universal. If there is to be war in the Persian Gulf, it should not be a war in which Americans do the fighting and dying while those who benefit from our effort provide token help and urge us on. Yet, as things now stand, that's what it would be.

The armed forces in the region should reflect the worldwide concern about the problem. But they do not. Americans now make up more than three-fourths of the fighting forces in the effort. It should be an international effort in more than name only. Yet as things now stand, that's what it could be: An international effort in name only.

Iraq must leave Kuwait. There's no disagreement about that. Iraq must leave Kuwait. If necessary,

it must be expelled; if need be, by force of arms. There's no disagreement on that.

But in the event of war, why should it be an American war, made up largely of American troops, American casualties, and American deaths? We hope there is no war. But if there is, we hope and pray that it will not be prolonged with many casualties.

Certainly the United States has a high responsibility to lead the international community in opposing aggression.

But this should not require the U.S. to assume a greater burden and a greater responsibility than other nations with an equal or even greater stake in the resolution of the crisis. That's what's happening. And it's wrong.

It may become necessary to use force to expel Iraq from Kuwait.

But because war is such a grave undertaking, with such serious consequences, we must make certain that war is employed only as a last resort.

War carries with it great costs and high risk – an unknown number of casualties and deaths; billions of dollars spent; a greatly disrupted oil supply and oil price increases; a war possibly widened to include Israel, Turkey or other allies; a war possibly in the Persian Gulf region; long-lasting Arab enmity against the United States; a possible return to isolation at home.

The grave decision for war is being made prematurely. This is hard to understand.

The Administration has yet to explain why war is necessary now, when just a couple of months ago, the Administration itself said that sanctions and diplomacy were the proper course. There has been no clear rationale, no convincing explanation for shifting American policy from one of sanctions to one of war.

The policy of economic and diplomatic sanctions was the President's policy. He and other Administration officials repeatedly called it the best policy to pursue. They described positively the effect that the sanctions were having on Iraq.

President Bush told a joint session of Congress in September that "these sanctions are working, Iraq is feeling the heat ... Iraq's leader(s) ... are cut off from world trade, unable to sell their oil, and only a tiny fraction of goods get through."

Those were the President's words.

In October, Secretary of State Baker said sanctions must remain the focus of American efforts. He said: "We must exercise patience as the grip of sanctions tightens with increasing severity."

According to CIA Director William Webster, the policy of sanctions is dealing a serious blow to the Iraqi economy. In December, he testified that "all sectors of the Iraqi economy are feeling the pinch of sanctions, and many industries have largely shut down."

The President's initial policy against Iraq, to impose international sanctions and enforce them using all necessary means, is working – as CIA Director Webster detailed. He and others have noted that:

More than 90% of Iraq's imports and 97% of its exports have been stopped.

Industrial production in Iraq has declined by 40% since August.

Many industries, including Iraq's only tire manufacturer, have either closed or sharply reduced production due to the shortage of industrial imports.

The flow of spare parts and military supplies from the Soviet Union and France, Iraq's major suppliers, has stopped.

Iraq's foreign exchange reserves have diminished drastically, hindering its ability to purchase foreign goods from smugglers.

Food prices have skyrocketed. The Iraqi government has cut rations twice and has confiscated food on the open market.

Agricultural production has been weakened by the departure of foreign laborers.

Lines have appeared at government distribution points for natural gas.

Clearly, this policy is not failing. It is having a significant effect on Iraq.

Yet soon after the November 8 decision to deploy additional troops to the Persian Gulf, Administration officials suddenly began expressing skepticism about whether, with the sanctions on our side, the Iraqi military would be able to strengthen its position in Kuwait.

Not only are these arguments the opposite of what the same people were saying earlier, they are also not consistent with the assessment and projections of the Central Intelligence Agency. Director Webster told the Congress in December that continued sanctions will have an increasingly damaging effect not only on the Iraqi economy, but also on the

Iraqi military, weakening it over time.

The CIA estimated that continued sanctions will result in:

The virtual depletion of Iraq's foreign exchange reserves by spring.

Multiplying economic problems as Iraq transfers more resources to the military.

The shutdown of nearly all but energy-related and military industries by the summer.

Increasing inflation combined with reduced rations.

A severe reduction in basic commodities such as cooking oils and sugar.

A reduction in the grain supply by half.

These effects will certainly weaken the Iraqi regime and degrade Iraq's military capabilities:

A decrease in the Iraqi Air Force's ability to fly regular missions after three to six months, due to its dependence on foreign equipment and technicians.

A deterioration of the readiness of Iraq's ground and air forces after nine months.

A reduction in the Iraqi military transport and mobility capabilities, due to shortages of critical supplies.

Given these effects of continued sanctions against Iraq, it is clear that time is on the side of the international coalition.

But the anticipation of war has obscured a rational analysis of the initial policy set forth by the President.

It is significant that even the Administration cannot and does not say that the policy of sanctions has failed.

To this moment, neither the President nor any member of his Administration has said that sanctions have failed. In response to my direct question just a few days ago, both the Secretary of State and the Secretary of Defense acknowledged that sanctions have not failed. But, they say, they cannot guarantee that sanctions will get Iraq out of Kuwait by January 15. Of course, no one has ever asked for such a guarantee. Those who advocate continuing the policy of sanctions recognize that it does not guarantee success by January 15 or any other time certain. It involves a risk. The risk is that the international coalition will fall apart before Iraq leaves Kuwait.

But prematurely abandoning the sanctions and immediately going to war also involves risk. The risk there is foremost in human life. How many people will die? How many young Americans will die? That's a risk, a terrible risk.

Just this morning I heard it said that there may be "only" a few thousand American casualties.

But for the families of those few thousand – the fathers and mothers, husbands and wives, daughters and sons —— the word "only" will have no meaning.

And the truly haunting question, which no one will ever be able to answer, will be: Did they die unnecessarily? For if we go to war now, no one will ever know if sanctions would have worked if given a full fair chance.

The reality is that no course of action is free of risk. The prudent course now is to continue the President's initial policy of economic sanctions.

Time to fortify Iraq's defenses will do little good if some of its tanks can't move for lack of lubricants, if its infrastructure and ability to wage war (have) been weakened.

If it eventually becomes necessary for the United States to wage war, our troops will have benefited from the additional time given for sanctions to degrade Iraq's military capabilities.

The sanctions are being enforced. They are having an effect on Iraq. We should continue their enforcement and seek to enlarge their effect.

I believe the best course now for the President and the nation is to "stay the course," to continue the policy the President so clearly established at the outset of this crisis. It offers the best hope now for the achievement of our objectives at the lowest cost in lives and treasure. That is a goal we all share.

Two themes have recurred throughout this debate, from both sides. First, the Senate is unanimous in insisting that Iraq leave Kuwait. Iraq's invasion of Kuwait is brutal and illegal, should have been and was condemned, and must be reversed. It will be reversed.

This is not a debate about that objective.

In its simplest form, the question before us is whether Congress will give to the President an unlimited blank check to initiate war against Iraq, at some unspecified future time, under circumstances which are not now known and cannot be foreseen, or whether, while not ruling out the use of force if all other means fail, we will now urge continuation of the policy of concerted international economic and diplomatic pressure.

The arguments for and against sanctions have been made in detail.

I simply restate my firm conviction that the best course now for the President and the nation is to "stay the course," to continue the policy the President himself so clearly established at the outset of this crisis.

That policy is hurting Iraq's economy and reducing its military capability. It offers the best prospect for a peaceful solution, or, failing that, for weakening Iraq's military force.

In short the policy of continuing international diplomatic and economic pressure against Iraq offers the best hopes now for achieving our common objective at the lowest cost in lives and treasure.

The second recurring theme in this debate is that no Senator wants war. We all know that to be true. No Senator wants war. That is not the issue.

The issue is whether by our vote we authorize war immediately – war with its great cost, war with its high risk, was which could be avoided, war which may be unnecessary.

That's the issue.

Let no one be under any illusions about the differences between these two resolutions. They are fundamentally different.

One authorizes immediate war. The other does not.

That is the difference. That is the central issue we are voting on today.

Those Senators who vote for the second resolution are voting to authorize war immediately. That is the very title of the resolution. "Authorization for Use of Military Force Against Iraq."

I understand the argument of those who support that resolution – that they hope its passage prevents war.

But the reality is that if that hope is not realized, if immediate war does occur, passage of that resolution will have been an essential prerequisite for that war under our Constitution and our democratic system.

The essence of democracy is accountability and if immediate war occurs, that resolution, and those who voted for it, must share that accountability.

The President has submitted to the Congress a written request for authorization to use military force. That is the title of the resolution. In the current circumstances, clearly it would be of such a scope and intensity that can only be described as war. So the second resolution is, plainly, by its own words and by the circumstances which exist in the Persian Gulf, an authorization for war.

Of that there can be no doubt or dispute. That is what we will be voting for, or against, today.

I urge my colleagues to vote against authorizing an immediate war.

I have discussed two things we have heard a lot about. Let me close by discussing something we have heard little about.

It is this question: In the event of war, why should it be an American war, made up largely of American troops, American casualties, American deaths?

The first resolution, the Nunn Resolution, directly addresses this concern by supporting "efforts to increase the military and financial contributions made by allied nations."

The second resolution does not mention the subject.

Certainly the United States has a high responsibility to lead the international community in opposing aggression.

But this should not require the United States to assume a greater role and a greater responsibility than other nations with an equal or even greater stake in the resolution of this crisis. That's what's happening. And it is wrong.

It may become necessary to use force to expel Iraq from Kuwait.

But because war is such a grave undertaking, with such serious consequences, we should make certain that war is employed only as a last resort.

War carries with it great cost and high risk: The possibilities of spending billions of dollars; a greatly disrupted oil supply and oil price increase; a war widened to include Israel, Turkey, or other allies; the long-term American occupation of Iraq; increased instability in the Persian Gulf region; long-standing Arab enmity against the United States; a return to isolationism at home. All of these risks are there.

But the largest risk, the greatest risk, the most profound risk is that of the loss of human life. How many people will die? How many young Americans will die?

And for the families of those young Americans who die, for every one of us, the truly haunting question will be: Did they die unnecessarily?

No one will ever be able to answer that question. For if we go to war now. on one will ever know if sanctions would have worked if given a full and fair chance.

I urge my colleges to vote for continuing economic sanctions and diplomatic pressure. I urge my colleagues to vote against the second resolution, to vote against an authorization for immediate war.

FOR FURTHER INQUIRY

DISCUSSION

• What sorts of reasons would make *you* willing to support a war, see your spouse embark in uniform, fight in it yourself? What sorts of reasons do you think appealed to the North Vietnamese or the Iraqis? Would they be basically much different from yours? In other words, what would the nature of an international threat have to look like to a people who go to war? If war is to be a last resort, do we not need to turn our attention, as a global community, to diminishing those kinds of perceived threats?

• The evolution of an all-volunteer military, a Nixon stratagem, may have altered public support of recent military initiatives. How much of a difference does it make, in finding moral justification for war, if a nation's fighting forces are paid volunteers? Did it affect popular support for the Gulf War?

• It seems natural, from our discussion of nuclear war, to view war as a moral issue, and not simply a matter for the strategists of *Realpolitik*. The very possible consequences of war endanger life on this planet, and one could hardly hope for a better entry for moral theory. In any event, we do need some way of deciding on national policy – and in the Western democracies at this point, no one but the very marginalized seems willing to reject the idea of a fair ballot system for universal electoral participation. So it is useful to remind ourselves of the role of voters in a representative democracy.

Let's say that an American President decides that a brutally conducted series of air and ground strikes against an uncooperative country serves our own national interest. What should our response be? Does anyone really want to say that there are no moral standards for national leaders? And even if there were no "objective" moral standpoint for deciding international behavior (as some versions of *Realpolitik* might insist), does that mean that our leaders are not subject to the standards of morality espoused in our own culture?

SUGGESTED READINGS

• The classic treatment of the strategy and nature of war is Carl von Clausewitz, *On War* (Princeton, 1976), which was left unfinished at the author's death in 1831.

• The standard modern treatment of the Just War Theory is *The Just War: Force and Political Responsibility* (Scribners, 1968; University Press of America, 1983).

• One of the very best overall discussions of the philosophical issues involved is certainly Douglas P. Lackey, *The Ethics of War and Peace* (Prentice-Hall, 1989), and its extensive bibliography would be a valuable resource to anyone wanting to explore the details of the issue.

• For an even more detailed discussion, and a sustained defense of the idea that conventional and nuclear war are equally unacceptable morally, see Robert L. Holmes, *On War and Morality* (Princeton, 1989).

• Richard A. Wasserstrom devotes his last chapter of *Philosophy and Social Issues* (Notre Dame, 1980) to "Conduct and Responsibility in War." A good collection of essays, which include treatment of pacifism and the war crimes trial at Nuremberg, can be found in Wasserstrom, ed., *War and Morality* (Wadsworth, 1970).

• A Roman Catholic perspective is elaborated in W. L. LaCroix, S.J., *War and International Ethics: Tradition and Today* (University Press of America, 1988).

ENDNOTES

1. John A. Garraty and Peter Gay, ed., *The Columbia History of the World* (Harper & Row, 1972), p. 987-8.
2. Todd Gitlin, *The Sixties: Years of Hope, Days of Rage* (Bantam, 1987), p. 291.
3. In Matthew 5 we read: "Ye have heard it said, thou shalt love thy neighbor, and hate thine enemy. But I say unto you, Love your enemies, bless them that curse you, do good to them that hate you .... " Of course, in Matthew 10 the following saying of Jesus also appears: "Think not that I am come to send peace on earth; I came not to send peace, but a sword." (Obviously, the context of any authority figure's

remarks must be studied to gain full understanding of the statements.)
4. See Chapter 3.
5. Quoted by Lackey, *The Ethics of War and Peace*, p. 32.
6. Henry Kissinger, *Years of Upheaval* (Littel, Brown and Company, 1982), pp. 168.
7. This definition is suggested by the discussion in Douglas P. Lackey, *The Ethics of War and Peace*, pp. 29ff.
8. Douglas Kellner, *The Persian Gulf TV War* (Westview, 1992), pp 8-9 n2).
9. Lackey, *The Ethics of War and Peace*, pp 73-4.

Chapter 14

Ric S. Machuga

ECONOMIC JUSTICE

"To give aid to every poor man is far beyond the reach and power of every man ... Care of the poor is incumbent upon society as a whole."
— Benedict (Baruch) Spinoza, *Ethics* 1677

"It is preoccupation with possession, more than anything else, that prevents men from living freely and nobly."
— Bertrand Russell, *Principles of Social Reconstruction* 1916

We live in an affluent society. If all the money that people earned from wages, salaries, and investment dividends were thrown into one big pot and all people were allowed to take an equal share, each man, woman and child in the United States would have well over $14,000[1] per year on which to live. This means that every family of four would have over $56,000 per year in income. Yet, in a nation as rich as ours, many people go to sleep each night hungry and without a roof over their head. Is this fair?

Some would say that any government which allows some of its citizens to be malnourished and without even a simple home, while others are able to live a life of luxury without even having to work, is fundamentally unjust. Others would say that the only way a nation becomes as rich as ours is to provide economic incentives for hard work, brilliant inventions and entrepreneurial skill. If individuals were not allowed to keep the fruit of their labors, then the United States would not be nearly as rich as it is today. Thus, the only way a government can makes its citizens' income more equal is for it to make all its citizens poorer.

Ric S. Machuga, M.A. Philosophy, University of Oregon, M.A. History, California State University, teaches ethics, philosophy and history at Butte College in Oroville, Calif.

These are not new issues. The ancient Greek philosophers Plato and Aristotle addressed them in many of their works. In fact, it was Aristotle who first noticed that there are two fundamentally different meanings of the word "justice." On the one hand, there is the justice which fairly and appropriately punishes some prior wrongdoing. Aristotle called this *"retributive justice."* On the other hand, there is the justice which fairly and appropriately distributes everything from economic goods and services to public honors and awards. He called this *"distributive justice"* and it will be the kind of justice examined throughout this chapter.

While the issue of distributive justice is not new, many of the problems associated with it have been greatly exacerbated, or even created, by the Industrial Revolution of the 18th and 19th centuries. It is during these centuries that the idea of capitalism develops and the first great "Captains of Industry" – Carnegie, Rockefeller, Gould and others – become household names. It is also in these centuries that many people begin to refer to the super rich as "Robber Barons," and philosophers begin to speak of *socialism* as an alternative to *capitalism*. These economic theories and systems will be specially discussed in the second and third sections of this chapter.

The final issue that will be discussed is *world hunger*. While there have always been famines, up until quite recently there didn't seem to be much that could be done. Famine was a simple fact of nature, no more in humans' control than the weather. However, it now seems to many people that the situation is essentially different. Though we still cannot control the weather that is often a contributing cause of a famine, we now live in a world where food is always abundant *somewhere*. Furthermore, the means are readily available for transporting it to those parts of the world where it is desperately needed.

Do these two facts create new moral obligations? Are we who live in affluent societies morally obligated to help those who are starving to death in less developed countries? Some philosophers argue that from the moral point of view, letting someone starve to death when the means to save them are readily available is really no different than murder. Others argue that while there may be enough food to feed those who are currently malnourished, it is simply impossible for us to feed them indefinitely, especially because the countries in need are typically the countries which have the highest growth rates. The only choice, these people would say, is whether we let thousands starve now or millions starve later.

ENTITLEMENT THEORY

In his *Second Treatise on Government,* John Locke assumed that all people have a self-evident right to their own life and liberty. No person or government can *justly* deprive another person of life or liberty, unless that other person has committed some crime for which he deserves to be punished. More significantly for our purposes, Locke went on to argue that these first two rights logically imply a third fundamental right, namely, the right to private property.

Locke's defense of private property is simple and almost absolute. He begins by imagining a number of people living as a tribe of hunters and gatherers. The fact that these people are living without a formal government and written constitution does not, he thinks, mean that they are also living without the right to life and liberty. These are self-evident rights because they are rights guaranteed by nature.

Americans' right to trial by a jury of one's peers is guaranteed by the Constitution. This sort of right is often termed a *positive* right because its existence depends on a decision which is *explicitly laid down* by the legislative arm of the government. It is not self-evident that in a society of hunters and gatherers these same rights would also exist. However, *natural* rights are different. The right to life and liberty are bestowed by God and/or nature on every person who ever has or will have lived on this Earth. These rights do not depend upon any government's action or decision.

Now suppose, says Locke, that an individual in this tribe of hunters and gatherers goes out and collects a basket full of acorns. They become, so to speak, the fruit of his own labor. Because this person's labor flows from his liberty, it too is protected by a fundamental natural right. This means that any other person who forcefully or coercively takes this person's acorns from him violates his natural rights. Thus, according to Locke, the self-evident right to life and liberty naturally creates a right to private property over which no other person has a rightful say.

John Locke's theory of property has been articulated and championed by the contemporary Harvard philosopher, Robert Nozick, in an important book, *Anarchy, State and Utopia*. According to Nozick, the only legitimate role for any government is the protection of its citizens' free exercise of their rights to life, liberty and property. To do this, a government must tax individuals enough to provide for a police force to protect citizens from criminals within and a military force to protect them from enemies without. However, any other use of the government's power of taxation – for example, the taxation of the well-to-do to help the less fortunate – is a violation of fundamental rights because it deprives the well-to-do of money and property to which they are *entitled*.

In his defense of what is now termed the entitlement theory, Nozick says that an exhaustive understanding of all true principles of distributive justice follows straightaway from three simple definitions:

> 1) All people are entitled to that which they *acquire* justly.
> 2) All people are entitled to that which is justly *transferred* to them from someone else who justly acquired that which was transferred.
> 3) No person is entitled to anything except by (repeated) applications of (1) and (2).[2]

The crucial terms in the above definitions are "acquire justly" and "justly transfer." Much of Nozick's book is spent clarifying these notions. Not surprisingly, Nozick turns to Locke for help. Locke said that all land and its resources were originally held in common by all people. This meant that all people had an equal right to use or appropriate any land or resource that was not already being used or had already been appropriated by others.

He also believed that "the earth and all that is therein" are meant by nature to be used for the support and comfort of human beings. However, Locke did not believe that individuals had an absolute right to do with unappropriated land or resources anything they wished. While he believed that all people would consent to other people's *limited* use of unappropriated land and resources, no one would consent to their *unlimited* appropriation. More specifically, when people acquire property by appropriating previously unused land and resources, they must ensure (1) that "there is enough, and as good left in common for others" and (2) that they use what is appropriated before it spoils or is wasted. These two qualifications on the right to acquire property, Nozick calls the "Lockean proviso."[3]

The point of the first qualification is fairly evident. A person cannot, says Nozick, rightfully acquire, or purchase from someone who originally acquired, "all the drinkable water in the world" and then sell it to others for whatever the market will bear. This first aspect of the Lockean proviso is meant to ensure "that the situation of others is not worsened."[4]

THE NON-WASTE QUALIFICATION

The point of the non-waste qualification is less clear. Nozick suggests that it is necessary to stave off a problem that may arise with the limitation implicit in the qualification "that the situation of others is not worsened." Nozick writes:

> Consider the first person Z for whom there is not enough and no goods left to appropriate. The last person Y to appropriate left Z without his previous liberty to act on an object, and so worsened Z's situation. So Y's appropriation is not allowed under Locke's proviso. Therefore, the next to the last person X to appropriate left Y in a worse position, for X's appropriation wasn't permissible. But the appropriator two from last, W, ended permissible appropriation and so, because it worsened X's position, W's appropriation wasn't permissible. And so on back to the first person A to appropriate a permanent property right.[5]

Nozick then says that perhaps Locke "meant the non-waste condition to delay the end point from which the argument zips back."[6] Locke himself describes the deliberate waste of natural resources as a kind of "robbery" and a frustration of the Divine intent in creation which was "to give us all things richly to enjoy." Because that which is wasted isn't enjoyed by anyone, waste frustrates God's intention for his creation. But whatever Locke's own intentions were in the second qualification, it is clear that no person can justly acquire so much land, or so many natural resources, so as to make those who come after him *significantly* worse off.

How much can people justly acquire before they make the position of those who come after them significantly worse off? Obviously such a question cannot be answered with mathematical precision. Of course, very few important questions can be answered with such precision, so that in itself should not be construed as a criticism of the entitlement theory. Furthermore, Nozick believes the issue is not very pressing because "as an upper limit" no more than five percent of our nation's wealth is from "rental income representing the unimproved value of land, and the price of raw materials."[7]

Nozick's argument is this: If land and other natural resources constitute a great percentage of any community's wealth, then any appropriation of unheld land would significantly worsen the position of everyone else because they would no longer be able to appropriate a major source of wealth. However, if land and natural resources constitute only a small percentage of a community's wealth, then the appropriation of land would not significantly worsen the position of anyone else because the vast majority of potential earnings lie elsewhere.

In order to more fully understand how Nozick's appeal to the "facts of the matter" affects his understanding of the entitlement theory let us examine a situation in which there is clearly "enough and as good left." Suppose gold were as common as ordinary sand. In that case, the market value of gold jewelry would depend primarily on the skill, effort, and talent (in Nozick's words, "upon human actions") of the jeweler who formed, shaped and designed the objects in question. Now it has already been granted that people have rights and among them is the right to expend their time and effort in lawful pursuits. Because it is not unlawful to make jewelry, any individual has the right to do so. Let us also assume that all individuals have the right to engage in wholly voluntary contractual relations. This means that the jeweler in our example has the right to sell his jewelry for whatever other people are willing to pay. Moreover, because the value of the raw materials used to make the jewelry is, by hypothesis, negligible, there is no concern that the jeweler may have violated the "Lockean proviso." It follows that the jeweler has a right to the *full* market value of his product.

But what happens when gold is scarce? Most philosophers have little problem with Nozick's argument thus far. Difficulties begin to arise only when we consider a world in which gold is scarce.

Suppose a person, living in a world like our own in which gold is quite rare, purchased a piece of farm land, fully intending to farm it, but then discovered that his land sat on top of a rich and easy-to-mine vein of gold. With little effort, and no talent, this person could live a life of luxury and leisure. His neighbors, working long days in sweltering temperatures, might naturally be expected to feel a little jealous, and to mutter under their breath, "It isn't fair."

Nozick would dismiss these mutterings as no more than an expression of petty human jealousy. "After all," he might say to the mutterers, "your neighbor's good fortune in no way worsened your condition. He didn't become wealthy by taking something from you. How, then, can it be rightfully suggested that you have some claim on what he found?"

(In fact, it is possible that the neighbor's discovery of gold might actually *improve* the position of the rest of the farmers by increasing the money supply and thereby lowering the interest rates farmers must pay. During the 1890s, the discovery of gold in Alaska seems to have had this very effect for the American farmer.)

Yet not every complaint about the good fortune of others is the product of mere jealousy. Let us begin with the least problematic example.

Only the most callous among us would say that a person living in luxury has no obligation to help those who are living in absolute poverty. Nozick himself describes it as "an essential element" of Locke's theory that every person has (and now he quotes Locke) "title to so much out of others' plenty, as will keep him from extreme want, where he has no means to subsist otherwise."[8]

Real poverty vs. Nozick. To see how this admission might affect Nozick's argument, let us imagine a whole community living in "extreme want"; let this include inadequate clothing and housing, malnutrition and a total lack of medical care. Now suppose several members of this community, solely as the result of good fortune, strike it rich. If these people kept all of their newly found wealth to themselves, or even if they resisted efforts by the rest of the community to tax their riches for the benefit of others, Locke and Nozick would both agree that it is more than petty jealousy for those in "extreme want" to mutter, "It isn't fair." And note: Those who struck it rich cannot be said to have violated the Lockean proviso and thus to be without clear title to their possessions. They have not worsened the material condition of others. The only thing they could possibly have worsened would be the *relative* position of those in extreme want.

"Extreme want" is admittedly a slippery notion. It becomes even more slippery when we introduce the social scientist's distinction between absolute poverty and relative poverty. Sometimes social scientists say an individual or group is living in poverty even when they are not malnourished, not lacking in shelter, not without medical care. Their poverty, it is said, is due only to the disparity between their station in life and that of others in their community. If 95% of your community drove Mercedes Benzes and lived in million-dollar houses while you drove a 1980 Ford Pinto and lived in an one-room apartment, there would undoubtedly be times when you felt like you lived in "extreme want." Is this feeling justified, or again, is it really another instance of petty jealousy?

Certainly few of us would feel much sympathy with the plight of the five percent who drove Pintos and live in apartments if we ourselves had *no* car and lived under a bridge on a local interstate highway. But suppose that within the community in question everyone owned at least a Pinto and a two-room apartment. Would we then feel more sympathy for the plight of the bottom five percent? Perhaps. But even if we did, what would that tell us about the justice of the situation? Suppose the 95% who drove a Mercedes and lived in million-dollar houses gained their wealth purely by good fortune and did so in a way that involved no great skill, talent, or effort on their part. Could those at the bottom claim that their "extreme want" entitled them to a portion of the good fortune of the 95%?

Some people might feel that it does, but personal idiosyncrasies, says Nozick, don't establish individual rights. Even if they did, Nozick would argue that the sort of hypothetical example we just considered is totally unrealistic because, as a matter of fact, "95% of the income and wealth of Americans is not solely the result of 'good fortune.' Instead, it is based upon individual effort, talent and skill, and clearly one has earned, and thus has the right to keep, that which is so based."

We have now summarized Locke's and Nozick's theory of just acquisition. The rest of the entitlement theory follows fairly simply. We have already alluded to the idea of "just transfers." By this Nozick only means that if a person is justly entitled to a basket of acorns because he gathers them himself while leaving plenty for other people, then he is free to transfer that basket of acorns to another person either as a free gift or as an exchange for something in return, for example, a pair of sandals.

Distributive justice: Part 3. The third part of Nozick's definition of distributive justice simply says that there is no other way to justly acquire some other than that specified by the first two principles. The point of the third principle is to exclude principles of need, equality or utility from consideration in determining a just distribution of economic goods and services.

Nozick's primary concern here is to make it clear that according to the entitlement theory, no government has the right to use its power of taxation and coercion to *re*distribute its citizens' income and wealth in accordance with some *pattern* of need, equality or utility that it deems to be more fair or just. Some philosophers have thought it is blatantly unfair or intrinsically harmful that some people live in luxury while others live in poverty. Plato, for example, argued in *The Laws* that no government should allow any of its citizens to become more than four times as wealthy as its poor citizens.[9] We will discuss more fully Plato's reason later on in this section, but for now, let us take Plato's proposal as a prime example of a patterned principle of redistribution.

The problem with Plato's proposal, and all other government plans for redistribution of income, according to the entitlement theory, is that they necessarily violate a person's natural right to liberty. Nozick attempts to show that this is the case in his widely discussed "Wilt Chamberlain example."

Suppose you are made "Dictator for the Day" so that you have the freedom and power to impose upon a nation what you deem to be the most just pattern for the redistribution of all income and wealth. Let's suppose, just for the sake of the argument, that you favor Plato's proposal. Therefore, you change Shaquille O'Neal's contract with the Magic so that during the next year they will pay him no more than five times as much as the average full-time employee at McDonald's earns in a year. As "Dictator for the Day" you have that power.

But now suppose O'Neal and a few other star players get together during the off season, rent a gymnasium with their own money, and begin playing games. Word gets out, and soon people want to come watch Jordan and other NBA stars practice. O'Neal and the others have no objection, but they do ask all who come to drop a dollar bill in the box before they enter to help pay the cost of renting the gym. Pretty soon so many of McDonald's employees are taking every opportunity to watch O'Neal play basketball, that now he and the other NBA stars have far more than five times the income as the average McDonald's employee.

Thus, what by hypothesis *began* as a just pattern of distribution is soon turned into something else so long as O'Neal's freedom is not violated. As Nozick says, "Any distributional pattern with any egalitarian component is overturnable by the voluntary actions of individual persons over time."[10]

The alternative to all patterned principles of distribution is a *historical* principle that looks not at the current pattern of distribution but, instead, considers only how the currently existing pattern of distribution arose. If it arose solely in accordance with the principles of just acquisition and just transfers, then no matter how unequal the present distribution, it is nonetheless a *just* distribution and any government that used its coercive powers to change it would necessarily be violating individuals' natural rights.

Finally, while the entitlement theory has strict requirements as far as justice is concerned, and while these requirements may permit some to live in luxury when others are living in poverty, it says nothing about what well-to-do individuals might *voluntarily* decide to do to help their less well-off neighbors. There is, in other words, a strict distinction between matters of justice and matters of charity, according to the entitlement theory. In fact, entitlement theorists are free to argue that principles of morality should *encourage* the rich to help the poor whenever possible. All the entitlement theory forbids is that laws be framed that allow governments to use their power of coercion to *require* the rich to help the poor.

EGALITARIANISM

Another Harvard philosopher, John Rawls, wrote a book in 1971, *A Theory of Justice,* which may well turn out to be one of the most important philosophical books written in the 20th century. In it Rawls develops in great detail and defends with powerful arguments a much more egalitarian theory than the entitlement theory. According to Rawls, justice *does* require that a certain pattern of distribution be maintained.

Rawls recognizes the debt his theory owes to the social contract theories of Rousseau and Immanuel Kant. But in this case, Rawls' own development of what he calls "justice as fairness" is so clear and powerful that we won't bother to discuss its historical antecedents. The fundamental assumption of Rawls' theory is that for any economic system to be just it must allocate both burdens and benefits *fairly*. The bulk of his book is an attempt to flesh out in some detail what constitutes a fair distribution of social goods such as jobs, income, and wealth.

Often we rely on the judgment of impartial observers to establish a fair distribution of burdens and benefits. However, there are two problems with such a solution when applied to fundamental questions. First, there are no impartial judges of such fundamental issues as which principles a society is going to adopt for distribution of jobs, income and wealth. Any decision the judge makes is necessarily *interested*, i.e., all possible decisions will affect the judge's own job, income and wealth. Second, even if we could find a wholly altruistic judge without the slightest tendency to make a judgment benefiting his own situation, it is unlikely that everyone else would willingly abide by his decision, especially if it appeared that *their* interests were adversely affected.

Rawls circumvents these problems by relying, as much as possible, on a purely *procedural* understanding of justice. Here is an example of a purely procedural solution to a problem: You are hosting a birthday party for 6-year-olds and two of them have been arguing with each other from the start. It is time to cut the birthday cake, and it is obvious that no matter how carefully it is cut, one of the boys will surely complain that he received the smaller piece. A purely procedural solution would be to have one of the boys cut the cake while the other boy is given the first choice. That way, no matter how the cake was actually distributed, neither boy would have a rational complaint. While Rawls does not pretend to have discovered so neat a solution to all the complex issues surrounding distributive justice, he does believe there is a procedural solution to many of the enduring problems.

The guiding idea behind Rawls' conception of justice as fairness is that the fundamental principles regulating social and economic intercourse ought to be principles to which free and rational persons would all consent if they were starting from a position of initial equality. To determine what these principles would be, Rawls performs a kind of "thought experiment," which he refers to as the "original position." Suppose, he said, that we imagine all members of society (or representative members from all classes) coming together in a kind of constitutional convention where the fundamental principles of justice are to be decided. If the outcome is to be fair, it is essential that the people making these crucial decisions start from a position of initial equality. So, to insure fairness, Rawls says we must imagine that all agreements are made from behind a *veil of ignorance.*"

OF SAINTS AND SINNERS

The reason for the veil of ignorance is clear. People born with physical strength would be tempted to formulate principles that would reward the physically strong; those born with mental gifts would be tempted to formulate principles that would favor the intellectually gifted; and those born with musical talent would be tempted to favor a society whose fundamental principles richly rewarded great musicians, *et cetera.* Only a community of saints could reach an agreement with such temptations.

Because very few, if any, of us are really saints, Rawls says we must imagine that the parties in the original position do not know their "fortune in the distribution of natural assets and abilities, intelligence, strength, and the like." Thus, Rawls concludes that this veil of ignorance "ensures that no one is advantaged or disadvantaged in the choice of principle by the outcome of natural chance or the contingency of social circumstance. Because all are similarly situated and no one is able to design principles to favor his particular condition, the principles of justice are the result of a fair agreement or bargain."[11]

Before we examine the principles of justice that Rawls thinks people would adopt in such a situation, a couple of assumptions and implications about the original position should be made clear. First, Rawls assumes that while parties to the original position are not saints, they are nonetheless *rational* sinners. And by "rational" he means no more than "taking the most effective means to given ends." Now because all people, says Rawls, want certain primary goods such as liberty, political and economic opportunities, secure and adequate income, wealth, and self-respect, a rational person can be defined as a person whose decisions maximize the acquisition of these primary goods.

Second, Rawls' theory implies that justice ought to nullify "the accidents of natural endowment and the contingencies of social circumstance as counters in the quest for political and economic advantage."[12] Because no one *deserves* the genes they are born with, and because no one *chooses* the family, community and nation into which he or she is born, Rawls thinks that it will be simply obvious to any person willing to take a moral point of view that no just society would reward or punish people for factors that are completely outside their control. (While there is much to be said for Rawls' point of view, it should be noted that a philosopher like Nozick would not be willing to make such assumptions. For Nozick, the only morally relevant issue is a person's rights, and while a handsome person does not deserve his good looks, he nonetheless has a right not to unjustly be deprived of his good looks.)

And what are the fundamental principles of justice that Rawls believes would be adopted by those in the original position behind a veil of ignorance?

> • First: Each person is to have an equal right to the most extensive basic liberty compatible with a similar liberty for others.

- Second: Social and economic inequalities are to be arranged so that they are both (a) reasonably expected to be to everyone's advantage, and (b) attached to positions and offices open to all.[13]

The meaning and justification of the first principle is fairly obvious. Because liberty is assumed to be a primary good that all people desire, it follows that all people would argue for social and economic institutions that would maximize their own freedom. However, because no one knows, for example, whether she will be born physically strong or weak, she would not be willing to formulate laws that would permit a person the freedom to punch another person in the nose whenever she wanted. Thus, the liberty they would choose would be a "liberty compatible with a similar liberty for others."

Rawls' second fundamental principle is often referred to as the "difference principle." It can best be understood and justified if we picture the total economic output of a society as composing a single pie that is then cut into different-size pieces for distribution to each member of the society. Suppose 10 persons work together in a simple society. In this society work is looked upon as a burden that is only freely chosen if it is rewarded with a pay check. If the economic pie is divided equally among all 10 members of society, it would undoubtedly be smaller than it would be if the more productive members were given a larger share of the pie. With these assumptions, consider the following table:

	Total GDP	Lowest 1/5	Middle 3/5	Top 1/5
A	30	3	3	3
B	60	4	6	8
C	120	2.5	10	27.5
D	150	1	6	56

Table 14.1

In society A, the economic pie is divided equally and each member of society receives 3 PUs (pie units). In society B, the economic pie is not divided equally. The two poorest members receive only 4 PUs each, while the two richest members receive 8 PUs each. In societies C and D there is even more economic inequality, and, given our assumptions, greater rewards for skill, talent, and effort bring forth even greater total productivity.

Now, according to Rawls, no rational person would choose to live in society A if given a choice between A and B. This is because all people want to maximize their primary goods (for the sake of simplicity we are here ignoring primary goods other than income). Even if they end up being the poorest members of society B, they are better off than if they end up being the richest member of society A. In this case, though there are inequalities in society B, they are justifiable according to the difference principle because they work to the *advantage* of the least favored members of society.

The choice between B and either C or D is not as simple. If a party in the original position opts for either C or D then that party is making a big gamble. Whether he wins big will only be known after the veil of ignorance is removed. Would rational people be willing to make such a gamble? Rawls thinks not. His reasons are twofold. First, he emphasizes the fact that the choices made in the original position are absolutely binding for all of one's own life and perhaps even for one's posterity. Given the importance of a steady and secure income, Rawls thinks it is unlikely that one would gamble about such fundamental issues. This is especially true if it turned out, as it very well may, that the 1 PU the two poorest members of society D receive is not even enough on which to survive.

CAKECUTTING REVISITED

If this first argument leaves one unconvinced, Rawls strengthens the procedural element in the theory. In our original example of a purely procedural solution to a problem, we imagined that the boy who cut the cake was forced to select his own piece last. This insures that he will cut the cake fairly by exercising the greatest possible care in cutting *equal*-size pieces. Likewise, Rawls' second argument requires that all parties to the original position assume that it is their own worst enemy who will assign them at birth their actual talents, skills, and educational opportunities. Given this stronger procedural assumption, it seems clear that all rational people would agree to the difference principle when selecting the fundamental principles by which their society was going to be ordered.

All that remains to discuss is Rawls' method for implementing his reform. Though Rawls lays down no specific political requirements for a just society, he does say that the first and second principles of justice are *lexically* ordered. That is, one can't move on to the second principle until the first principle is fully satisfied. In other words, Rawls doesn't believe that people in the original position would be willing to sacrifice their political freedoms for improved economic conditions, except in the most severe situations. If a group of people are literally starving to death, then they may be willing to trade in their right to vote for improved economic conditions. Short of that, however, Rawls believes that people's sense of self-worth as expressed by their participation in self-government is more important to them than mere economic advantages such as driving a late-model car or taking a vacation in Europe. Though Rawls provides few specific details about the actual political organization of a just society, it is clear that it will be democratic in the broadest sense.

CLASSICAL REPUBLICANISM

Classical Republicanism embodies a theory of justice which began with the attempts of Plato and Aristotle to make philosophical sense of the Greek city-state and to determine its ideal form. It was carried on and refined by Thomas Aquinas in the Middle Ages and has been picked up by such modern philosophers as Alasdair MacIntyre, Charles Taylor and Michael Sandel. The core of this conception of justice is a theory of human nature which emphasizes the fact that all people are rational, social animals.

By speaking of a "theory of human nature" Classical Republicans mean to deny the now prevalent view that people *are* what they choose to be. Conventional wisdom emphasizes the variety of goods that different people choose to pursue. Some people enjoy intricate intellectual problems; other people enjoy physical and athletic challenges; still other people enjoy social interaction, the pursuit of political power, or simply helping other people in distress. There are probably even a few people who, as Rawls says, would enjoy nothing more than "to count blades of grass in various geometrically shaped areas such as park squares and well-trimmed lawns."[14]

Which of these pursuits is better or more worthy of people's essential natures? According to both of the previous philosophies we have examined, these questions have no answer. Thus, a just state must be neutral with respect to various conceptions of the "good life" and allow its citizens maximum freedom to choose the life they prefer. The only limit a state may properly impose on its citizens' free choice is that they cannot impinge upon the freedom of other people to act as *they* choose to act. This conception of freedom is captured well by the cliche: "The freedom to move one's fist ends at everyone else's nose." Because both Nozick and Rawls heartily endorse this conception of freedom, both the Entitlement theory and the Egalitarian theory are correctly called *liberal* theories of justice.

CONTRASTING ENTITLEMENT AND EGALITARIAN THEORIES

There is, of course, an important difference in these two liberal views of freedom. The Entitlement theory emphasizes *negative* freedom – freedom *from* all forms of restraint, especially restraint from the coercive arm of the state and its taxes. The Egalitarian theory emphasizes *positive* freedom, i.e., the freedom *to* act as one chooses.

The difference between these two forms of freedom is clear if we imagine a person shipwrecked on an uninhabited desert island. Such a person would have complete negative freedom because there are absolutely no restraints on his actions. But obviously, such a person is not in an enviable position because he lacks the means to satisfy many of his desires. Without these enabling means (e.g., access to food and water) a person's negative freedom isn't worth much. Because in most modern societies the most important enabling means is money, egalitarians are willing to permit the state to use its powers of taxation to equalize the positive freedom of its citizens.

While Classical Republicans acknowledge the value of both negative and positive freedom, their conception of a just and well-ordered society requires an additional kind of freedom. A contemporary Aristotelian, Mortimer Adler, calls it *moral* freedom and he describes it this way:

> Moral freedom consists in our having a will that is habitually disposed by virtue to will as it ought. Virtue ... is the habitual disposition to desire aright, which means choosing what one needs – the real goods one ought to desire. The obstacles or impediments to right desire stem from appetites or wants that tempt or solicit us to make the wrong rather than the right choices.[15]

According to Classical Republicans, a just society – and, hence, a just system of distributive justice – is defined as one that maximizes the moral freedom of its citizens. Classical Republicanism stands or falls on the distinction between wants and needs. If all there is are individual wants, desires and preferences, then it makes no sense to speak of virtuous citizens whose "habitual disposition (is) to desire aright." The notion of a *right* desire presupposes that not all desires are equally worthy. Thus, Classical Republicans must deny the prevalent conception of human nature as being infinitely malleable and constituted wholly by the equally worthy choices individuals make. Some choices naturally lead to a full and flourishing life, while other choices lead to a life buffeted and burdened by conflicting and insatiable desires.

According to Classical Republicans, human nature is not infinitely malleable, but instead, is such that humans are *by nature* rational, social animals. It therefore follows that those desires which are in accordance with one's nature are more worthy than those which reflect desires which are in fundamental opposition to human nature. In other words, the more worthy desires are in accordance with real needs, whereas the less worthy desires only reflect individual preferences.

Though it is impossible to fully flesh out a picture of humans' essential nature as conceived by Classical Republicans in this chapter, we must at least draw a quick sketch. We will do this by focusing on the three essential elements of human nature: Rationality, sociability, and membership in the animal kingdom.

The fact that humans are rational animals means that they are born with capabilities and potentialities which other members of the animal kingdom lack. Perhaps the most important of these is the ability to communicate with other members of their species using an infinitely complex set of symbols. This ability to use language gives humans an ability to learn, and in turn teach, an incredible variety of important survival skills. It also gives humans the ability to formulate abstractions which allows them to ask not only technical questions about how things work, but also, philosophical questions about *why* they work as they do.

For example, people have not only figured out *how* to raise crops by determining the spring and fall equinoxes of the sun, but they also want to know *why* the sun and stars move the way they do. Human rationality entails infinite curiosity. As Aristotle says in the opening lines of the *Metaphysics,* "All men by nature desire to have knowledge." And that which we desire *by nature* constitutes a real need.

THE SOCIAL HUMAN

Humans' social nature is a natural outgrowth of their rationality and their use of language. Hermits have no use for language. And the converse is also true: Those who have a use for language must live in societies with other members of their species. But beyond the fact that humans' social nature is implied by their rationality, we need only to look around at others and at ourselves to observe that humans derive much enjoyment from social relations. Aristotle devoted a fifth of his *Nicomachean Ethics* to a discussion of friendship. So again, the fact that we are social *by nature* means that the desire for friendships and other forms of social interaction constitute a real need.

One of those other forms of social interactions which is important to contemporary Aristotelians is participation in the political process. All societies require some form of government. Because a society's political organization affects all other social interactions, this means that all people have an interest in their societies' form of government. Thus, all people have a real need to have some say in the laws that govern their social relations.

Finally, Classical Republicans do not ignore the fact that humans are all members of the animal kingdom. This simple fact means that in addition to the real needs of knowledge, friendship, and some form of political freedom, all human beings have real needs of a purely material nature, e.g., food, drink, shelter, medical attention, *etc.*

Earlier we said Classical Republicans define a just society as one which maximizes the moral freedom of all its citizens. We can now understand their justification for such a definition. If these philosophers are correct, people can only flourish if their real needs are being met, and people's real needs can only be met if they live in a society which distinguishes between wants and needs. Furthermore, a just society will insist on meeting all its citizens' needs *before* attempting to satisfy individual wants. Only then will the *common good* of all its citizens be met.

Classical Republicans have no particular formula for distributing economic goods and services. What is best in one time and situation may not be best in another time and situation. However, for the modern societies of the West, there are certain safe generalizations that most Classical Republicans are willing to make. First, no society can be considered just that does not meet the fundamental material needs of *all* its citizens. This entails a certain minimum standard of living for everyone.

And where is that line to be drawn? Again, it is impossible to say with mathematical precision. As Aristotle noted long ago, one of the marks of an educated person is that a person "searches for that degree of precision in each kind of study which the nature of the subject at hand admits."[16]

Nonetheless, this much can be said without fear of contradiction: The limits of justifiable inequalities in any society lie somewhere in between the 4-to-1 ratio permitted in Plato's *Laws* and the 93-to-1 ratio that currently exists in the United States.[17] And only those who are blinded by greed would argue that our current practice is closer to the truth than Plato's legislation.

Classical Republicans are not only concerned with how much an economy produces and how it is distributed, they are also concerned with *what* an economy produces. A society that richly provided for all its citizens' material needs, yet ignored their need for knowledge and friendship, may be a *fair* society, but it would not be a *good* society. Thus, Classical Republicans would insist that a society's economy makes ample provision for the education of all its citizens, and, of course, education is not conceived of as mere training that allows its citizens to compete better on the world market. Instead, it is conceived of as a liberal education which leads to a flourishing of *all* the human arts and sciences, irrespective of their economic value.

THE 'JUST SYSTEM' MEETS THE PEOPLE

Finally, a just economic system does not ignore the social and even spiritual values of its citizens when making economic decisions. Such a society, for example, willingly forgoes economic advantages in order to make ample provision for its citizens to gather together and enjoy each other's fellowship. This may include everything from parks to "blue laws" which provide for a common day of rest.

Having sketched in outline the principles of a just economy as conceived of by Classical Republicans, it is necessary to say something about its implementation in today's society. Contemporary philosophers who favor such a theory of justice are usually called communitarians. They are fully aware that their position is a radical departure from modern liberalism. Liberals inevitably ask: "Who makes all these crucial decisions? And how can one person, or group of people, decide what is best for someone else?"

Such questions cannot be adequately answered without considering the Aristotelian system of ethics in its entirety (see also Chapter 3). All that can be said here is that all totalitarian or dictatorial regimes are categorically rejected because they are inconsistent with humans' social nature, which requires political freedom. Thus, according to communitarians, all social and economic change must begin by changing the conventional wisdom of the age and convincing people of the truth of this conception of justice.

Of course, it is no small task to form a new consensus on such fundamental ethical issues. But in response to the liberal cliche – "Who's going to decide?" – communitarians offer another cliche: "We'll do it one step at a time." Robert Bellah, a sociologist at the University of California, says: "That happiness is to be attained through the limitless material acquisition is denied by every religion and philosophy known to man, but is preached incessantly by every American television set."[18]

However, even when there is widespread agreement, the liberal's conception of individual rights as a card that trumps all other concerns makes it virtually impossible for us to act for the common good of society. Thus, a necessary second step, according to communitarians, is to persuade people of the truth of Article 15 of the Virginia Bill of Rights:

> No free government, or the blessing of liberty, can be preserved to any people, but a firm adherence to justice, moderation, temptation, frugality and virtue and by frequent recurrence to fundamental principles.

A liberal conception of individual rights, even when there is such widespread agreement, makes it virtually impossible for us to *act* as a society on such a truth because a person's rights are viewed as a card that trumps all other concerns. Communitarians argue that this absolutist conception of individual rights will slowly, but surely, lead to our own self-destruction.

COMPARISON AND CONTRAST

These three theories of distributive justice are distinct, yet they each share some common characteristics. Entitlement and Egalitarian theories both emphasize individual rights. Though they are usually founded on a Kantian conception of the dignity of each individual, sometimes they are founded on a utilitarian concern to maximize the general welfare. Only free people are happy, say utilitarians. As John Stuart Mill writes in *On Liberty,* "The only freedom which deserves the name is that of pursuing our own good in our own way, so long as we do not attempt to deprive others of theirs, or impede their efforts to obtain it."

Nonetheless, according to both these theories, whether based on a Kantian or utilitarian theory of ethics, all people have a right to as much freedom as is consistent with equal freedom to others. And though the Entitlement theory emphasizes negative freedom while Egalitarianism emphasizes positive freedom, both understand freedom in terms of persons doing what they *want* to do.

Classical Republicans and contemporary communitarians emphasize the common good. While a person's *needs* are never inconsistent with the good of the whole society, a person's *wants* often are. When this occurs, both these philosophies subordinate individual preferences to the good of the larger whole. But in doing so, they argue that they are not restricting freedom, properly conceived, but only restricting license. Of course, none of this makes sense apart from an Aristotelian conception of human nature and the whole ethical system that grows out of it.

The Entitlement theory and Egalitarianism are both based on a "thin" conception of the good and thus can tolerate a society in which citizens have widely varying conceptions of what is good. Classical Republicanism and contemporary communitarianism are based on a "thick" theory of the good which presupposes that on certain fundamental issues a shared conception of the good is possible. Such a theory of justice cannot tolerate widespread viciousness in its citizens and, thus, presupposes that all just governments must actively encourage the development of virtuous citizens.

Modern liberalism, of which the Entitlement theory and Egalitarianism are two different versions, leads to an atomistic conception of persons. That is, liberalism conceives of people as essentially autonomous and independent agents. Classical Republicanism and contemporary communitarianism lead to a more social conception of person that emphasizes both socially shared responsibilities and individual privileges.

Thus, the Entitlement theory favors a minimalist state; Egalitarianism favors an interventionist state; Classical Republicans and contemporary communitarians favor an activist state.

ECONOMIC SYSTEMS

CAPITALISM

The seminal work of modern capitalism is *The Wealth of Nations*. It was written in 1776 by the English philosopher, Adam Smith. In this long book (over 700 pages) Smith argues against the current mercantilist definition of a nation's wealth.

According to mercantilism, a nation's wealth consists solely of the sum total of its gold and silver bullion. This meant that for a nation like England, which has no gold or silver mines of its own, the only way to become wealthy was to maintain a positive balance of trade. If a nation consistently sold more abroad than it purchased, then it would increase its stores of bullion and would, according to the mercantilist's definition, be wealthy. Because all nations want to become wealthy, the standard practice of governments was to actively regulate their nation's economy with a large number of laws designed to encourage exports and discourage imports. For example, it might pass a law that allowed only a certain number of cobblers to purchase leather from other nations, and forbid all shopkeepers to purchase cheap wine from another country.

Smith argued that the mercantilist's understanding of wealth was fundamentally misguided. The true measure of a nation's wealth was the sum total of the market value of all the goods and services that its people produced. A nation of manufacturers and merchants like England, according to Smith, would inevitably become wealthy if government would simply allow its citizens the economic freedom to do as they pleased. Cobblers who were good at making shoes should be free to purchase raw materials from wherever they pleased and to make as many shoes as they could. Furthermore, they should be free to sell them for as much as they could get on the free market. Similarly, shopkeepers who were good at buying cheaply from other countries should be free to do so and they should also be free to sell their merchandise for as much as they could.

To many people, this seemed to entail certain fundamental problems: If cobblers were free to sell shoes for as much as they liked and if shopkeepers were free to sell their goods as dearly as they could, then what is to stop them from selling shoes at an *unfair* price or making an *unfair* profit on the exchange of goods? That is, what is to prevent some particular individual from becoming rich at the expense of the nation as a whole? Smith's great insight was that a free and unregulated market is guided by an "invisible hand" that would ensure no cobbler or shopkeeper was making an unfair profit. If governments stopped issuing licenses that determined who could be a cobbler and where shopkeepers could purchase goods, then all cobblers and shopkeepers would *automatically* have to sell their goods for a fair price.

For example, if cobblers started selling shoes for too high a price, then shopkeepers would start making and selling shoes and that would drive down the cost of shoes. Conversely, if shopkeepers began to make unfair profits on imported wines, then cobblers would stop making shoes and start keeping shop. All this would work without a hitch just as long as government did not pass laws regulating who could make shoes and sell wine. By individuals actively and rationally pursuing their own respective self-interests, Smith argued, the nation as a whole would prosper because it would have the most efficient system of production and distribution.

Adam Smith was not only the great defender of free markets, he also sang the praises of the Industrial Revolution, which was just beginning in England. The heart of industrialization is the division of labor. It takes a considerable amount of skill and training to turn untanned leather, glue and thread into a good-fitting and handsome pair of shoes. However, if the manufacturing of shoes is broken down into its individual operations so that one person tans the leather, another person cuts out the sole, a third person attaches the heel, *et cetera*, then a collection of relatively *unskilled* laborers can produce goods that would require a large amount of skill if a single individual were to make the entire shoe by himself. Furthermore, by dividing the manufacturing of goods into relatively simple and mundane procedures, it is possible to house a large number of workers in a single factory and take advantage of water or steam powered machines.

BUT WHO CONTROLS PRODUCTION?

A natural question then arises: Who should organize and control these new factories – private individuals or the government? Once again, Smith argued that government ought to keep clear of a nation's economy. While the actual work of making a pair of shoes can be broken down into individual operations that require no particular skill, knowing how to most efficiently organize workers – and to ensure that the whole operation runs smoothly – is a job that requires a great deal of skill.

It also requires a good deal of capital, i.e., saved up resources that allow a person to purchase the land, buildings and machines which go into making a modern factory. Rather than having government determine who has such skills and capital, it is more efficient to allow anyone the freedom to raise the capital, build the factory, purchase the machinery and organize the workers in any way they choose. If government adopts such a *laissez faire* position, all these complex decisions will be made in accordance with the highest degree of efficiency by the invisible hand of the market. However, it should be noted that, unlike his followers, Smith never said *laissez-faire* economics was in *all* ways superior to government intervention.

In sum, capitalism can be defined as an economic system where *all* property (including factories and other "means of production") is privately owned and operated for individual profit as determined by a free market. The principal advantage of capitalism is economic efficiency and the fact that it preserves individual freedom.

SOCIALISM

The great theorist of socialism is Karl Marx. Marx produced his major work on economics almost a century after Smith. In that three-volume work called simply *Capital,* Marx did not argue that Smith was wrong about the virtues of the free market, the division of labor and industrialization. His fundamental objection was that Smith's picture of industrial capitalism was incomplete. The final stage of economic development had yet to be reached.

Marx himself believed that a socialist economy is only possible *after* an economy has obtained a high degree of industrialization. Socialism presupposes capitalism, according to Marx. Only given a highly developed industrial base is it possible for a nation's economy to produce the wealth of goods necessary to supply *all* its citizens' needs. It is therefore a mistake to view Marx as a totally unsympathetic critic of capitalism.

According to Marx, capitalists tend to view industrialization as nothing more than the most efficient means of production. Again, Marx was not blind to these efficiencies. However, he argued that they carried with them great social costs. A single skilled cobbler making shoes in pre-industrial Europe may not be able to produce as many shoes as unskilled laborers in large 19th century factories, but the shoes that he did produce were *his*. And this is true not only in the sense that whatever profit he could make selling them was his, but also in the sense that he could take pride in his own creation and the craftsmanship it reflected. In pre-industrial economies, work carried with it its own *intrinsic* rewards.

In an industrialized economy, the worker owns nothing except his own labor. Everything a factory worker produces is owned by someone else. But even more important, the way it is produced requires little skill on the worker's part. This leads to a state of *alienation* between the worker and his work, according to Marx. A person's work is no longer significantly connected to her own creative abilities. Work in a factory is nothing but an economic necessity that no person would freely endure were it not for the wages it paid. Rather than being a natural and joyful expression of a person's own skill and talent, factory work becomes an activity whose only reward is wages, often extremely meager.

The second social cost of industrial capitalism is the *exploitation* of the worker. Marx's theory is based on the "Labor Theory of Value." On this theory the value of everything is determined by the amount of labor it takes to produce the good in question. Of course, the work of a doctor is more valuable than the work of a garbage collector. However, that is only because it takes a tremendous amount of labor to train a doctor, whereas it takes very little labor to train a garbage collector. Though skilled labor is more costly than unskilled labor, all labor is nonetheless a commodity and its value is the cost of producing a single unskilled laborer.

And what is that cost? Defenders of the labor theory of value said that the cost of producing an unskilled laborer is nothing other than a subsistence wage. Pay laborers less than a subsistence wage and they will not be able to reproduce themselves. And if unskilled laborers are not able to reproduce themselves then there are not enough workers. This will in turn cause individual factory owners to have to increase their wages. If they don't, then they won't be able to attract workers to enable them to keep their mills and furnaces operating.

Of course, this all sounds very condescending and cruel to the unskilled laborer. But we must remember that at this time, the extreme poverty of the masses and harshness of factory work seemed to fit well with such a theory of value.

Profit As Surplus Value

All this leads Marx to ask an interesting theoretical question: If the value of everything is the amount of labor it takes to produce the item in question, and if all items sell for their true value in a free market, then how can factory owners ever make a profit? As Adam Smith demonstrated, factory owners must pay laborers their actual value and sell their products for actual value. So whence the profit?

Marx's answer is found in his notion of *surplus value*. Though the laws of the free market demand that workers be paid their true value (i.e., subsistence wages), factory owners are free to work their employees 12-14 hours a day, even if it takes only six hours' work to produce a subsistence wage. This six- to eight-hour-a-day difference is what creates the profit for the capitalist. Surplus value, which is the source of all profit, is thus a result of the exploitation of workers.

But how is such exploitation possible in a free market? After all, in a capitalist economy, no person has the right to *force* another person to work for them. Marx found the answer in the fact that the worker needs the wages of the factory owner more than the factory owner needs the labor of the worker. This inequality of needs is created by the fact that in capitalist economies there exists, in Marx's term, an "Industrial Reserve Army," or in modern terms, unemployment. If an individual laborer chooses not to work in a factory, the factory owner can typically find some other worker who is willing to take his place. However, the laborer cannot typically find another factory that is willing to pay his wages.

A final problem with free market capitalism according to Marx is its inherent instability. For reasons that we won't lay out in detail here, Marx predicted that as capitalist economies developed, there would be a natural tendency for the number of individual firms to decrease while their size increased. However, this trend toward a few, very large companies will not come about in a gradual and orderly manner. Instead, it will be characterized by fits of rapid expansion followed by a collapse, which will then start another cycle. Though many economists disagree with the explanation that Marx gave for these business cycles, Marx's prediction that they would arise clearly came true. And while government intervention in the economy has made these cycles much less severe than they used to be, they still remain as a source of significant social problems.

Modern socialists distance themselves from Marx's revolutionary politics and a number of his specific economic explanations of the interworkings of capitalism. However, they typically begin with Marx's analysis of capitalism, and define socialism as an economic system in which all the means of production are socially owned and operated for the good of the public as a whole.

Now it is important to understand that neither Marx nor modern socialists want to eliminate all private property. Houses, automobiles, boats, *et cetera*, are still going to be bought and sold on the free market and owned by private individuals. The only forms of private property that socialists wish to eliminate are those forms of property that allow individuals to profit from the work of *other* people. For example, socialists do not wish to eliminate the family farm where a husband and wife grow food to sell on the free market. They do, however, wish to eliminate the corporately owned farm where laborers work for wages while the owners receive all the profit.

Secondly, to say that large-scale means of production are socially owned and operated is not inconsistent with democracy. In fact, one philosopher has said, "Socialism is democracy extended to the world of work and money."[19] Social ownership of the means of production simply means that all people, or at least all the people who work in a particular factory, have an equal say in how the factory is going to be organized and run.

Finally, to say that all means of production will be run for the good of the whole public simply means that issues of alienation, exploitation and instability will be addressed like all other political issues. For example, if the majority of a nation's citizens or their elected representatives decide that closing a large automobile plant in Detroit would cause too much social dislocation, then it would not be closed, even if a purely *economic* analysis showed that the plant was not profitable. And the reason is simple: According to socialists, economic efficiency is not the only goal of a just economy. Worker satisfaction, fairness of wages, and reasonable job security are all factors that a just economic system will take into consideration when allocating goods and resources.

ARGUMENTS PRO AND CON

Having defined two alternative economic systems, let us examine, in a fairly cursory manner, seven arguments for and against capitalism and socialism. (Specific details and examples will be discussed in the next section.)

1. Personal Freedom

Capitalism: It maximizes individual freedom. Only under a capitalist system are people fully free to employ their specific skills, talents and efforts in any lawful manner that they see fit.

Socialism: While individual freedom from governmental coercion is valuable, such negative freedom is only a single element in any adequate understanding of freedom. True freedom includes not only being unconstrained by laws and regulations, but it also includes the enabling means to carry out one's wishes. Without a job or some other source of income, a person will not be able (i.e., free) to purchase food for his family even if there is no law forbidding such a purchase.

2. Production/Efficiency

Capitalism: By providing material incentives, the free enterprise system produces far more than competing economic systems. There is no better motivation to work both hard and efficiently than personal profit.

Socialism: It is not obvious that the free enterprise system is economically the most efficient. Such countries as Sweden, Germany and Japan all have governments that take an active role in regulating their economies, and these countries all have economies that are doing as well as or better than that of the U.S. But even if a free enterprise system were shown to be the most efficient, that would not make it a *just* system.

3. Private Property

Capitalism: The bottom line of all socialist systems is the "Robin Hood" principle of robbing the rich to help the poor. And just as Robin Hood violated the rights of the rich, all socialist systems that tax the rich to support the poor violate the rights of the rich, even if those taxes are written into a country's legal system.

Socialism: As Thomas Aquinas said, "It is not theft, properly speaking, to take secretly and use another's property in cases of extreme need; because that which he takes for the support of his life becomes his own property by reason of the need."[20]

4. Poverty

Capitalism: Except in cases of absolute poverty, the "Robin Hood" principle violates individual's natural rights.

Socialism: Material goods and services have not historically been distributed solely, or even primarily, by a system of free markets and uncoerced contracts. Fraud and brute force have historically been of much greater significance than free and fair trade. Furthermore, the politically powerful have always had the ability to get laws passed that promote their own interests, e.g., hat manufacturers who get a high tariff passed on imported hats or large farm corporations that get governments to build huge dams and then "sell" the water back to them at a highly subsidized rate. Therefore, for a government to suddenly insist that all economic exchanges will take place according to the dictates of free markets only institutionalizes and freezes in place past injustices.

5. Taxation

Capitalism: All people have a natural right to the fruit of their own labor. For government to tax individuals for any reason other than providing for the common defense (against criminals from within or aggressors from without) is no different than a system of forced labor.

Socialism: Luck, nature's bounty, and the existing social order contribute at least as much to any individual's productivity as does her own talent and effort. As R. H. Tawney wrote, "Few tricks of the unsophisticated intellect are more curious than the naive psychology of the businessman, who ascribes his achievements to his own unaided efforts, in bland unconsciousness of a social order without whose continuous support and vigilant protection he would be as a lamb bleating in the desert."[21]

6. Redistribution

Capitalism: People who work hard and save their resources ought to be rewarded for their effort and their willingness to delay gratification of their own desires.

Socialism: Perhaps this is true for the actual generation that did the work and saved the capital. However, no such effort is expended by the next generation. That is, the first generation of Rockefellers and DuPonts may in some sense have earned their wealth, but this is not true of succeeding generations of Rockefellers and DuPonts. They receive large incomes from their inheritances without any effort on their own part.

7. Experience

Capitalism: We know from recent experience that socialism doesn't work — just look at Eastern Europe and the former Soviet Union.

Socialism: The socialist ideal was no more real in countries such as East Germany and the Soviet Union than the capitalist ideal was in such countries as Peron's Chile and Marcos's Philippines. To judge the virtues of socialism by looking at the former countries is to set up a straw man.

MIXED SYSTEMS

Thus far we have been treating capitalism and socialism as if they were two distinct economic systems. In fact, the vast majority of actually existing economic systems are combinations of both systems. We defined capitalism as a system where *all* the means of production are privately owned, and socialism as the system where *none* of the means of production is privately owned. A mixed economic system is one where *some* of the means of production are privately owned while others are publicly owned. The United States, for example, clearly has a mixed system. Here automobile factories, steel mills, and resort hotels are all privately owned; the postal system, air traffic control system, and all large water projects are publicly owned.

The principal advantage of a mixed system is its ability to balance competing values in a manner politically acceptable to the majority of its citizens. In the United States, as in most modern industrial countries, *both* economic efficiency and social justice are believed to be of significant value. Thus, when these two values conflict, there is no need in a mixed system to choose one or the other. Instead, a workable political compromise is sought.

COMPATIBILITY OF THEORIES AND ECONOMIC SYSTEMS

The entitlement theory requires a capitalist system because only in a free market system are free and enforceable contracts the *sole* method for distributing economic goods and services. Egalitarian theories tend to favor a socialist system because socialism gives the largest consideration to economic equality. However, because a system like Rawls' also has an important place for considerations of personal freedom, such a theory is also compatible with some mixed systems.

Finally, Classical Republicanism tends to prefer a mixed system, though it is conceivable that in a very simple agrarian society, it might favor a capitalist system, and in a highly developed industrial system, it might favor socialism. The important point to note is that Aristotle and Aquinas made it clear in all their political writings that the best way to achieve a just society will vary from place-to-place and from age-to-age.

DOMESTIC PERSPECTIVES

THREE STANDARDS FOR DETERMINING INCOME

Philosophers and economists are not the only people who ask questions about distributive justice. Almost everyone – politicians, taxpayers, soon-to-be politicians and soon-to-be taxpayers – has asked whether their taxes are too high or whether their employer is paying them as much as they deserve. Serious thought about either of these questions involves important issues of distributive justice.

When ordinary people ask whether they or a friend are being paid what they are really worth for their work, they almost always have one or more of the following standards in mind:

1. need/equality
2. contribution/productivity
3. moral worth/effort

An obvious criterion for determining what constitutes a just wage is need. If a young widow is working two jobs just to support her three pre-teenage children and her combined take-home pay is insufficient to provide her family with a modest apartment, simple clothes and nutritious meals, then almost all would agree that she should be paid more.

Now it is important to understand that by invoking need as a criterion we are implicitly assuming equality of moral worth. We believe that such a person ought to be paid a living wage because we believe that *all* people who work hard are equally worthy of a living wage. Thus "equality of personhood" is the presupposition that supports our conviction that this young widow deserves better treatment.

A second common standard is productivity or contribution. If two people are performing the sort of work where it is fairly easy to determine their productivity – say, foresters planting trees or maids cleaning hotel rooms – and one person is doing twice as much as the other, then it seems reasonable to suppose that the first should get paid twice as much.

When we start thinking about many other kinds of work it is often more difficult to measure productivity, but we nonetheless make the same sorts of judgments. If one person is making important purchasing decisions for a large company and another person is doing janitorial work for the same company, it is difficult to directly compare their "productivity." Instead, we typically think in terms of comparative contribution. The person making important purchasing decisions usually makes a larger contribution to the profitability of the company than does the janitor. And one of the reasons we say this is that it is typically more difficult to replace a purchasing agent than it is a janitor. Many people can perform janitorial work; only specially trained and talented people can perform well the tasks of purchasing agents. In short, while it is often impossible to make a direct comparison between two very different kinds of work, we do make judgments about their relative "difficulty" and then equate the more difficult with the more productive.

The final standard is moral worth or effort. This standard is really more of a judgment about the person than the work. Students, for example, will sometimes approach their instructor after receiving a grade and say something like this: "I know this paper isn't especially good, but I really put a lot of time and effort into writing it so I would really appreciate it if you gave me a 'B.'" Though it doesn't happen all that often, some instructors will sometimes honor the student's request, and oftentimes they do so for good reasons. But in saying that there were good reasons, we do not mean to imply that a "C" paper magically turns into a "B," or even that the instructor was wrong about her original judgment. Essays are graded on what is written, not how long it took to write them or how many drops of sweat dripped from the brow of the author. Yet, rewarding effort is sometimes justifiable. It often motivates a student to continue trying to improve her writing skills which, in the end, usually has the desired results.

Thus, while most of us believe that effort should not be the sole criterion of an essay's worth, it is *one* of the relevant factors. Furthermore, this principle seems to apply just as well to some jobs as it does to some graded essays. It seems not only fair but also useful in some situations to reward the employee who is obviously trying harder than one who is not even trying to work up to his full potential.

How Much Inequality Actually Exists?

How can these standards be applied in the United States? When we consider the standard of equality, it is natural to begin by asking how much equality or inequality actually exists. How many young widows *really* are working two jobs and are still not able to adequately support their families? While no one knows how many people meeting this description actually exist in the United States today, some useful conclusions can be drawn from what we do know about income distributions. The most widely used measure of equality/inequality is in terms of quintiles, i.e., dividing people into five categories from richest to poorest and then comparing the top and bottom fifths.

The most recent figures (1990) show the top fifth earning 43.5% of the GDP while the bottom fifth earned only 5.1%.[22] (These figures include all welfare payments to the poor and subtract all taxes paid by the rich.) And while all figures show that inequality increased during the 1980s, it has nonetheless remained relatively constant throughout this century. A historical view of personal income in the United States between 1910 and 1970 shows this:

- The top fifth received between 40 and 45% of all family income
- The middle fifth received between 15 and 18%
- The bottom fifth received between 4 and 6%.

Thus, we can say with a high degree of confidence that in the United States over the long run, the average person in the top fifth earns between six to 10 times as much as the average person in the bottom fifth.[23]

Comparing actual incomes of the top and bottom fifths has one advantage and one disadvantage. The advantage is that income figures are relatively easy to come by and their accuracy is quite high.[24] The disadvantage is that they tend to strongly *understate* the inequalities that actually exist. The reason is simple: The poor's total wealth is almost completely based on current income, whereas the rich's wealth is typically based to a large degree on what they *own*, not what they earn. A poor person cannot by definition have either a large income or a large estate; but many rich people have very large estates without having a very large income.

Government estimates of the distribution of wealth in the United States in 1972 show that the top fifth owned 76% of the total wealth, the middle three-fifths 23%, while the bottom fifth owned only 0.2%. More recently, it was estimated by the Joint Economic Committee of Congress that the top one-half of one percent of the United States households owned 26.9% of the nation's total wealth.[25] While these figures are only estimates, they cannot be ignored. And even if they are a little inaccurate, it is clear that the inequality of wealth is skewed far more in favor of the rich than the inequality of income.

So how many people in the United States are unable to afford modest housing, simple clothes and nourishing food? To get an accurate picture about these matters we need to look at poverty rates in the United States. In 1990 the official poverty income for a family of four was $13,359.[26] This is hardly a liberal amount with which to house, clothe and nourish a family of four when one considers that rents for modest housing for such a family in metropolitan areas of the United States average between $800 and $1,000 per month (or between $9,600 to $12,000 per year).

And exactly how many Americans are living below these modest standards? In 1990 more than 33-million persons, or 13.5% of the population, lived at or below the official poverty level. Even more troublesome is the fact that one in five Americans 18 years old or under is living in poverty.[27] One of the reasons this is so troublesome is that it is hard to say that these 12-million Americans somehow *deserve* their plight. While we will never know how many industrious and hardworking young widows can't support their families, we do know that a sizable number of Americans are living with essential needs unmet through no fault of their own.

THREE KINDS OF TAXES

While most Americans – Republican, Democrat or Independent – will agree that this sort of inequality presents a serious problem, there is no agreed-upon solution. But one thing is clear: Whether a person favors "enterprise zones," a cut in the capital gains tax to create new jobs, or fully funding "Head Start" and other government programs to help the poor, all of these ultimately require government spending. And there are only two sources of revenue for government spending: Taxes and borrowing. Because borrowing is really no more than a tax on future generations, we need to consider only taxes here.

With respect to issues of distributive justice, all taxes fall into one of three categories:

A *proportional tax* or "flat tax" is one that taxes each unit of income, wealth or expenditure at the same percentage rate. Most states, for example, have sales taxes that meet this definition.

A *progressive tax* is one that taxes additional units of income, wealth, or expenditure at an increased rate. The federal income tax is an example of a tax that is (at least) designed to be minimally progressive. Up to $27,300 is taxed at 15% ; from $27,301 to $70,450, the rate of taxation is around 28% ; and all income above that is taxed at 31%.

A *regressive tax* is one that taxes additional units of income, wealth or expenditure at a decreasing rate. The Federal Social Security tax is regressive in this sense. All people pay a flat rate (i.e., proportional) on the first $50,000 of income, while additional income is not taxed at all.

Entitlement theorists, Libertarians, and conservative Republicans view all taxes as at best a necessary evil. If these people had their way, there would be no taxes except those necessary to provide for the common defense against criminals at home and aggressors from abroad. Taxes for any other purpose, according to Nozick, are no better than "involuntary servitude."

However, in the real world of political give-and-take it is extremely unlikely that these ideals ever could be fully implemented. Most people believe that money spent for schools, roads, and even some kinds of welfare are legitimate expenditures for a government. Moreover, it is often difficult to separate defense from non-defense expenditures. Is the money spent on street lights a form of defense spending because it makes it easier for police to capture criminals? Is the money spent by publicly supported colleges and universities to train engineers a form of defense spending because without qualified engineers we couldn't sustain our defense industries? Was the National Defense Highway Fund, which paid for our interstate highway system in the 1950s and '60s, really a military expenditure?

Given these political realities it seems likely that government expenditures for such purposes will continue for the foreseeable future. The most conservatives can reasonably expect to accomplish is to restrict the *kind* of taxes imposed. Though they believe all taxes for non-defense expenditures are wrong, a "flat" or proportional tax is the least evil. First, it doesn't place an unequal and additional burden on the rich, and second, it doesn't create a *disincentive* for the hard-working and creative businessperson.

Contemporary communitarians, socialists and liberal Democrats take a different position. They often harken back to the idea of *noblesse oblige*, i.e., wealth brings with it not only privileges but also obligations. These people therefore favor some form of progressive taxation. And in doing so, they implicitly deny the claim that a progressive tax places an unequal burden on the rich. While it is true that progressive taxes require an additional monetary contribution from the wealthy, the justification for doing this is to equalize the *real* burden. The widow's mite proportionally costs her much more than the same amount from the rich man. Therefore, because the rich can afford to pay more, the idea of "equal burden" favors a progressive tax system.

The second argument against a progressive tax is that it creates a disincentive to hard work and creativity. If this is in fact true, then even an egalitarian like Rawls would argue against such a tax. Suppose a progressive tax reduces the total productivity of a nation to such a degree that even though the poor are receiving a larger percentage of the national product as a result of government transfer payments, in actual dollar totals they are receiving less because there is so much less to distribute. If this ever happens, then the difference principle has been violated, and Rawls would say that the tax structure should be made *less* progressive (See system "A" in table 14-1).

It is extremely difficult to determine exactly how much less productive a progressive tax system makes an economy. Some people have argued that European countries (e.g., Germany) have more progressive tax structures yet are just as productive. Others argue that the large tax cut on upper incomes in the early 1980s produced a growth in the economy that improved everyone's position. Though the economy certainly expanded, it is less clear that it produced a tide that lifted all boats. What in the '80s was proudly termed "supply side" economics is now derisively referred to as "trickle-down" economics.

Whichever of these is a more accurate description of our recent past, there has been some interesting work done on the relation of taxation and productivity by contemporary philosophers and economists which combines both liberal and conservative points of view.

FLAT-TAX DANGERS

Let us grant the conservative's contention that a tax on income is an incentive not to work and a tax on wealth is an incentive not to save. Because both work and saving are important elements of economic prosperity, progressive taxation of either work or saving is *prima facie* a mistake, from at least an economic point of view. The only other source of revenue is a tax on consumption. However, the traditional sales tax, even though it is in name "flat" or strictly proportional, in fact turns out to be quite regressive. The poor must spend almost all of their income to live while the rich only spend a fraction of their income. This causes the poor to pay a much higher percentage of their income in taxes than the rich which, from the liberal point of view, is morally objectionable.

A proposed solution to this dilemma is to use the existing tax system to determine, first, people's taxable income and, second, their actual savings or capital investments. By subtracting the latter from the former, a person's *consumption* would be determined. Once this figure is determined, tax tables on consumption could be made as progressive as is politically desirable. The first $15,000 of consumption, for example, might be tax free for a family of four; the next $15,000 of consumption might be taxed at a 20% rate; the next $15,000 at a 30% rate, *et cetera*. The advantage of such a taxing system is that it would equalize real burdens on families without creating a disincentive to work – and in fact creating an incentive to save and invest.

ARE PEOPLE PAID ACCORDING TO THEIR CONTRIBUTION?

When we turn from the ideal world of philosophers and economists to the muddled world in which we all live and work, it is natural to wonder how much correlation there is between theory and actual practice. One area in which this has become especially acute in recent years concerns the salaries of top executives. These have become so large, many people are beginning to wonder whether something has gone wrong with the system.

In 1960, the average chief executive officer (CEO) in a major corporation was making 41 times as much as the average factory worker. In 1988, it was up to 93 times as much. As recently as 1980 the average of the two top executives in the top 354 corporations was a little more than $600,000 per year. By 1988 it had risen to more than $2-million per year.[28] It is hard to believe that their productivity more than tripled in these eight years. Workers, on the other hand, increased their productivity 13% during these years, yet in real terms, their income only increased seven percent. With figures like these it seems understandable that *Business Week* (May 1, 1989) would conclude that workers are not getting rewarded in proportion to their contribution and that top management is "skimming" profits off the top.

How are we to evaluate such a charge? First, it is worth noting that these sorts of complaints are not new. As early as the end of the 19th century, such social critics as Edward Bellamy were arguing that there is no particular correlation between a person's output and his earnings:

> All that a man produces today (over and above) his cave-dwelling ancestor, he produces by virtue of the accumulated achievements, inventions, and improvements of the intervening generations, together with the social and industrial machinery which is their legacy... Nine hundred and ninety-nine parts out of the thousand of every man's produce are the result of his social inheritance and environment. The remaining part would probably be a liberal estimate of what by "sacred justice" could be allotted him as "his product, his entire product, and nothing but his product."[29]

George C. Lodge has recently argued that "labor increasingly means skill, knowledge, education and organization."[30] He goes on to conclude that this makes Lockean individualist thought obsolete because these factors are intangible and not obviously owned by individuals the way a person "owns" his body and its labor.

Classical economists and entitlement theorists tend to reject these claims. They argue that in a free market all people, from the farmer laborer to the CEO, are paid according to their "marginal product." It is both impossible and unnecessary to consider here the intricacies of marginal product theory. In essence it is no more than a sophisticated working out of the implications (in an ideal world) of the intuitively plausible notion that we hinted at earlier: The reason purchasing agents earn more than janitors is that if both the purchasing agent and janitor quit their jobs, it is easier to find another janitor than it is to find another purchasing agent. Therefore purchasing agents are paid more than janitors. How much more? According to marginal product theory, companies will pay both their purchasing agents and janitors *just* enough to keep them from quitting.

It is important to note that according to this theory, both workers and employers are continually making decisions on the basis of *subjunctive conditionals,* i.e., judgments about what *would* happen if something else happened. Workers don't usually quit their jobs and employers don't usually cut workers' pay without first asking, "What *would* happen if...? And while workers' and employers' judgments are sometimes tested by the real world, when people are acting rationally, this happens only *after* a judgment is made on the subjunctive.

Now subjunctive conditionals are philosophical and extremely tricky. It is undoubtedly true that if Mother Teresa had the power of a king, then she would decree that no person be deprived of simple food and shelter as long as others were living in luxury. But how is the truth of such a statement to be verified? Contemporary epistemologists who make it their business to understand such statements are far from agreement about how even the simplest subjunctives are verified. That in itself should give marginal product theorists reason to pause. But even if such problems are overcome, there is a much more mundane problem with using the notion of marginal product to measure *actual* contribution.

Suppose two entrepreneurs, Smith and Jones, both have the managerial skill to double an investment in five years. Now suppose that Smith and Jones are given, respectively, $1-million and $10-million with which to work and they both work up to their full potential. By our original supposition, Smith's investments will be worth $2-million in five years while Jones's will be worth $20-million. How much do Smith and Jones deserve to be paid for their skill, work and effort?

If this is all we know, then according to marginal product theory, all we can say is that Smith and Jones will be paid the same because, by supposition, that are equally skilled and both worked equally hard. We can't determine the absolute value of their contributions until we know what the *next* most skilled and efficient entrepreneur *would* have done with an equal investment. So let us suppose that this next most efficient manager is Miller and that Miller only has the skill to turn a $10-million investment into $18-million at the end of five years. Then the difference between what Jones *in fact* did and what Miller *would have done* is $2-million. It seems to follow that Jones' marginal product is $2-million.

WORKING THE PUZZLE

However, this creates a puzzle: Because both Jones and Smith are equally skilled and hard-working entrepreneurs, they should be paid equally. But in this case, that would mean that Smith should also be paid $2-million. Yet where does this money come from? Smith turned a $1-million dollar investment into $2-million. Moreover, if he gets paid $2-million, then the people who invested $1-million with Smith lose their entire investment. Of course, this can't be correct.

While Smith's contribution *would* have been worth $2-million *if* he had been working with a $10-million investment, he will only be paid $2-million if he is actually working with a $10-million investment. While the worth of a person's skills, talents and efforts is determined by what the next most efficient person could do, a person's actual *pay* is not determined by what he *could* do, only by what he in fact does. In short, a person's worth and pay will only correspond if all people have equal opportunity to utilize all their skills to their full potential.

When we turn and consider the real world, which is more important – the rational calculations of consumers and producers based on an infinite series of subjunctive conditions, or being lucky enough to have friends with $10-million to invest? Many people have argued that recent history suggests there is much less rationality in the real world than in the ideal world of marginal product theory. Their primary evidence is that there is no particular correlation in the real world between the economic worth of CEOs to their company and their pay.

These critics point to studies by *The Wall Street Journal* (April 18, 1990) and *Business Week* (May 7, 1990), two relatively conservative publications, which strongly suggest that there is little actual connection between executives' total compensation and the profitability of their companies. While the corporate profits for the top 325 companies *fell* by 4.2% in 1989, the pay of CEOs increased by 8.0%. Looking at the performance of individual CEOs reveals similar discrepancies between marginal product *theory* and the *real world*. Between the years 1987 and 1989, Lee Iacocca, chairman of Chrysler Corporation, earned more than $25-million even though the return on investment by Chrysler's owners went down 10%. During those same years, Albert Ueltschi was paid a little over $700,000 by Flight Safety International. But their owners received more than a 200% return on their investment!

What accounts for such a wide discrepancy between theory and actuality? Many critics have argued that the problem ultimately stems from the separation between the ownership of a corporation (the stockholders) and the control of a corporation (the management).

On paper the way a modern corporation works is like this: Top management is hired and controlled by the board of directors and the directors are elected by the shareholders. Thus, the owners of the company have theoretical control over their investment. But in point of fact, boards of directors have neither the time nor access to the information necessary to exercise effective review of managements' actions, and thus boards are typically no more than a rubber stamp of management's decisions.

The problem is exacerbated by the fact that most shareholders in all modern corporations are *not* individual investors carefully choosing the best directors to watch over their investment. Instead, most stock in a large corporation is controlled by groups of investors (mutual funds) or insurance companies, and this removes management from ownership by yet another step.

When one considers that 80% of all employment in the United States is in corporations with 20 or more employees, the discrepancy between contribution and compensation that seems to exist in corporate America is certainly of more than academic interest.

IS WELFARE A RIGHT OR A PRIVILEGE?

Welfare is another place where questions of distributive justice touch real people. Those receiving public assistance are touched directly; those paying taxes are touched indirectly.

And how *hard* are these respective groups touched? Many people believe that welfare payments make up a significant portion of the federal budget and, thus, that taxpayers would be significantly affected by any reduction of these payments. While nearly half of the federal budget is spent on transfer payments *from* the federal government to individuals or corporations, only 15% of those payments are made to the poor. Most of the rest is spent on non-needy seniors, both retirees and Medicare claimants.[31] Thus, any changes made in transfer payments to the poor are going to directly affect them much more than they will indirectly affect taxpayers.

One way to get at philosophically important issues in this case is by asking: Is welfare a right or a privilege? If it is a "right," then it can be nothing other than a person's need which has created that right. A person does not lose his right to a fair trial if he is lazy or unwilling to work up to his full potential. Likewise, if a certain minimal income is everyone's right, then it cannot legitimately be withheld because a person is deemed morally unworthy.

However, if welfare is a privilege or a form of charity, then the moral worth and behavior of the person on welfare becomes a legitimate criterion for withholding welfare payments. Is the person making a reasonable effort to support herself and her family? And does the person make good use of the funds she receives? If so, then public assistance seems a legitimate use of public funds; if not, then it is not a legitimate use of such funds.

If the history of American jurisprudence on this issue is any indication of public opinion, then our view of welfare has evolved over the last century, but it has yet to reach a stage of clarity and coherence.

At the beginning of this century, any attempt by legislators to pass laws protecting the health and welfare of even the working poor was looked on by the courts as a violation of property rights and the "due process" clause of the Fourteenth Amendment. In 1905, for example, the U.S. Supreme Court considered legislation passed by the State of New York designed to protect the health and safety of employees by limiting the number of hours (in this case, to 60) they could be obligated to work by contract. Lochner, a bakery owner, filed suit charging that the law had infringed upon the freedom of individuals to freely make and enter enforceable contracts. The majority in *Lochner vs. New York* agreed and struck down the New York law, writing: "The general right to make a contract in relation to his business is part of the liberty of the individual protected by the 14th Amendment to the Federal Constitution." In one of his famous dissenting opinions, Justice Holmes retorted that "the Constitution is not intended to embody a particular economic theory, whether of paternalism and the organic relation of the citizen to the state or of *laissez faire*."

THE SUPREME COURT'S ATTITUDE SHIFT

By the 1970s, the court's and public's attitude had changed considerably. Not only had laws protecting the health and welfare of the working poor become generally accepted, but largely as a result of President Roosevelt's "New Deal" and President Johnson's "Great Society," government-funded programs to help the non-working poor became common.

In 1970 the Supreme Court once again considered a New York case. The issue this time was whether the state could terminate Aid to Families with Dependent Children (AFDC) payments without a full legal hearing. The administrators of New York's program argued that they could because welfare was a privilege, not a right.

The Supreme Court disagreed with New York, saying that welfare payments were entitlements more like "property than a gratuity" and therefore protected by the "due process" clause of the 14th Amendment. Furthermore, the court argued on sociological grounds that "we have come to recognize that forces not within the control of the poor contribute to their poverty" and on moral grounds that "public assistance, then, is not mere charity, but a means to 'promote the general Welfare, and secure the Blessing of Liberty to ourselves and our Posterity.'"[32]

However, in less than a year, the court muddied the clarity of the Goldberg decision. In *Wyman vs. James* still another New York law was under scrutiny. This time it was a piece of legislation that required a social worker to periodically visit the home of all welfare recipients, presumably to make a judgment about their use of funds. When one of these recipients, Ms. James, refused to allow a social worker into her house, the state terminated her AFDC payments. She then filed suit to reverse the decision. Her lawyers argued that there was no reason to suspect that she had violated any law and hence her 4th Amendment rights protecting her home against unlawful searches were being violated by the New York law.

Once again, the state responded that welfare payments are a privilege, and not a right, and thus they can be lawfully terminated if a person's (lawful) behavior is deemed inappropriate. This time, the majority on the high court agreed with the State of New York. They wrote, "One who dispenses purely private charity naturally has an interest in and expects to know how his charitable funds are utilized and put to work. The public, when it is the provider, rightly expects the same."[33]

Given the court's indecision on this question, it is not surprising that the public at large has been unclear about the nature of welfare. Is it a right created by the need of the recipient or a privilege which the charity of the well-to-do dispense to the needy?

INTERNATIONAL PERSPECTIVES

Though poverty is clearly a problem in the United States, only a *tiny* percentage of Americans are living in absolute poverty, i.e., poverty that constitutes an immediate and direct threat to a person's life. However, when considering the problem of poverty in lesser developed countries, those percentages change significantly. Every year throughout the past decade 18-20 million people died as a direct result of insufficient food and lack of clean water. That is more than twice the number of persons who died in all of World War II. As one person put it, "This death toll is equivalent to the number killed instantly by a Hiroshima bomb every two days."[34]

Of course, the fact that many people die from malnutrition does not by *itself* constitute a moral problem. A large number of people die each year from cancer and other untreatable diseases. But cancer deaths (as a whole) constitute a scientific problem, not a moral problem, because most forms of cancer are neither preventable nor treatable. However, given the huge surplus of grain around the world, not to mention the millions of Americans who are suffering from *"over*nutrition," the death of millions from malnutrition does seem to be preventable and, hence, a fit topic to be *morally* explored.

THE NEO-MALTHUSIAN ARGUMENT

Yet, appearances are sometimes deceptive. Shortly after Adam Smith sang the praises of industrial capitalism in the *Wealth of Nations,* Thomas Malthus (1766-1834) played a dirge in his *Essay on Population.* In that book, Malthus argued that no matter how productive and efficient an economy became, there would always be a significant number of deaths from starvation and malnutrition given the lack of sexual restraint by the lower classes.

The problem, said Malthus, is that agricultural output at best increases at an arithmetic ratio, but population tends naturally to double after each generation and, hence, increases at a geometric ratio.

"Taking the population of the world at any number... the human species would increase in the ratio of 1, 2, 4, 8, 16, 32, 64, 128, 256, 512, *etc.* and subsistence as 1, 2, 3, 4, 5, 6, 7, 8, 9, 10, *etc.* In two centuries and a quarter the population would be to the means of subsistence as 512 to 10; in three centuries as 4,096 to 13, and in 2,000 years the difference would be incalculable."[35]

Malthus concluded: "The power of population is so superior to the power of the Earth to provide subsistence, that premature death must in some shape or other visit the human race." Maybe those deaths would be caused by war or maybe by disease. But if we should ever succeed in eliminating these, then "gigantic inevitable famine stalks in the rear, and with one mighty blow, levels the population with the food of the world."[36]

Malthus's perspective on population and world hunger has been adopted and defended by contemporary thinkers. One of the most clearly identifiable neo-Malthusians is Garrett Hardin. Trained as a biologist, Hardin has argued both in the popular press and in more scholarly essays and books that the unchecked growth human population constitutes a serious threat to the Earth's fragile ecosystem.

Many people have likened the Earth to a giant spaceship. Because we all live on the same Earth, unless we take care of it and all its passengers, all of us will inevitably suffer the consequences. Hardin argues that this metaphor is quite misleading and even dangerous. Spaceships have a captain with coercive powers to insure that all aboard the spaceship act in a responsible fashion. The Earth has no such captain.

Rather than being like a spaceship, Hardin says, the Earth is more like a lifeboat – both have a limited carrying capacity. It is self-defeating to let more people on board a lifeboat than it can safely carry. To allow 110 to climb aboard a boat that is made for 100 persons is *not* being generous to the last 10 persons. Now, all aboard are likely to die. Similarly, it is self-defeating for affluent countries to continue to send food to nations that are chronically suffering from hunger. There is nothing generous, says Hardin, about affluent countries shipping food relief to countries with chronic food shortages. Such charity and foreign aid only encourages these countries to continue their irresponsible population growth. Sooner or later, population will exceed Earth's carrying capacity and the empirical evidence, says Hardin, demonstrates that we are fast approaching that point.

The problem with foreign aid and private famine relief is that it ends in "the tragedy of the commons." "A farmer," Hardin writes, "will allow no more cattle in a pasture than its carrying capacity justifies. If he overloads it, erosion sets in, weeds take over, and he loses the use of the pasture. If a pasture becomes a commons open to all, the right of each to use it may not be matched by a corresponding responsibility to protect it."[37] To treat the agricultural resources of the affluent nations as resources to be shared equally by all people will inevitability lead to tragedy. Once the ecological balance of the Earth is destroyed by the scourge of overpopulation, we will all perish.

The only solution, according to Hardin and other neo-Malthusians, is to adopt a "triage policy." Those countries which will survive without our aid don't need it; those countries that are *perennially* poverty stricken should be allowed to perish – to provide aid will only prolong their suffering or destroy the whole Earth. Only those countries suffering the *temporary* effects of some natural disaster should receive our charity or foreign aid.

UNJUST DISTRIBUTION AS THE PROBLEM

Neo-Malthusians emphasize overpopulation as the primary cause of world hunger. Their critics are often called developmentalists. According to developmentalists, the primary cause of world hunger is injustice. While Hardin says that the empirical data show that the Earth is fast approaching its "carrying capacity," developmentalists like Lappe and Collins dispute such data. They write:

> The world today produces enough grain alone to provide every human being on the planet with 3,600 calories a day. That's enough to make most people fat! And this estimate does not even count the many other commonly eaten foods – vegetables, beans, nuts, root crops, fruits, grass-fed meats, and fish. *Abundance, not scarcity, best describes the supply of food in the world today.* Rarely has the world seen such a glut of food looking for buyers. Increases in food production during the past 25 years have outstripped the world's unprecedented population growth by about 16%. Indeed, mountains of unsold grain on world markets have pushed prices downward over the past three decades.[38]

The reason people are dying of malnutrition, say developmentalists, is the gross inequality in the distribution of food produced by our planet. In 1989 the world had 157 billionaires, perhaps 2-million millionaires, and 100-million homeless. Moreover, the inequality has been increasing during the past decade. World Bank figures suggest that the global poverty rate declined steadily up to 1980 when it reached its low point of 22.3% of the global population. That trend was reversed in the mid-80s and has now climbed up to 23.4%.[39]

Developmentalists are also quick to point out that the industrialized countries of the West are not nearly as generous and self-sufficient as we like to believe. The United States, for example, allocates a mere fifth of one percent of its gross development product (GDP) to developmental assistance. Furthermore, the vast majority of that money is distributed for wholly political reasons. Less than five percent of all bilateral economic assistance in fiscal year 1985 went to the world's two poorest countries.[40] And during the past three decades the industrialized countries of the West have consistently *imported* more food from the less-developed countries than it has exported to them.[41]

Though there are no longer any colonial empires, developmentalists argue that the West has continued to exploit the resources of the Third World with little concern for the well-being of the people living there. The island of Mindanao in the Philippines constitutes a single case in point. Prior to the mid-1960s, small farms produced a large variety of crops on the island for consumption by the local farmers. That changed radically when Del Monte, Dole, and other multinational corporations began offering contracts to the area's largest landowners to grow bananas for export to Japan. The Japanese are now able to purchase cheap produce, the large corporations have improved their earnings ratio, and those who labor in the fields earn less than a dollar a day and are regularly exposed to pesticides.[42]

WHAT CAN BE DONE?

Even though neo-Malthusians and Developmentalists approach the problem of world hunger from quite different perspectives, they nonetheless agree on a couple of points. First, they both support increased developmental assistance to help underdeveloped countries raise capital and improve agricultural techniques because both appreciate the truth of the Chinese proverb: Give a man a fish and you'll feed him for a day; teach him to fish and you'll feed him for a lifetime. Furthermore, both understand the care with which such aid needs to be distributed. Too often in the past it ended up in the hands of corrupt governments and the ruling oligarchy instead of helping to alleviate hunger.

Second, neo-Malthusians and Developmentalists both agree on the appropriateness of *emergency* famine or disaster relief to help less-developed countries meet a particular problem. The fundamental disagreement concerns the *chronically* malnourished countries. Neo-Malthusians argue that foreign aid should be withheld unless coercive measures are introduced to bring about reduced population growth. Aid for such countries only makes the problem worse and will in fact increase suffering in the long run.

Developmentalists resist coercive measures. Instead, they argue that history demonstrates that as food supplies increase and become more secure, population growth naturally decreases. When Western countries industrialized there was a "demographic transition" during which birth rates fell sharply without any coercive restraints being imposed. The reasons are manifold. In a pre-industrial farm economy even young children are an economic asset because they produce more than they consume. Children are also the only support parents have in their old age. Finally, a "lottery mentality" is associated with poverty everywhere. No matter how long the odds, the hope is that the next child will be the one who is clever and bright enough to get an education, land a job in the city, and be able to support the entire family.

WHAT ARE WE OBLIGATED TO DO?

While everyone thus agrees that there is much that *can* be done, there remains a further question: What are we in the West *morally required* to do? In recent years, this question has been addressed from both a utilitarian and Kantian point of view.

Peter Singer, a contemporary defender of utilitarianism, has summarized his argument like this:

- First premise: If we can prevent something bad without sacrificing anything of comparable moral significance, we ought to do it.
- Second premise: Absolute poverty is bad.
- Third premise: There is some absolute poverty we can prevent without sacrificing anything of comparable moral significance.[43]
- Conclusion: We ought to prevent some absolute poverty.

The justification of the first premise is implicit, says Singer, in the following sort of example: Suppose I am walking to class in a new pair of wingtip shoes. Along the path I see a small child face down in the middle of a two-foot deep pond struggling to catch a breath. It would be easy for me to walk out and save the child's life, yet it would undoubtedly ruin my new shoes. However, only the most morally corrupt would contend that I am not obligated to sacrifice my shoes to save the child's life.

The second premise Singer takes to be virtually self-evident.

Some people might object to the third premise on the ground that there will always be poor people and thus it is impossible to eliminate poverty. However, the third premise doesn't require that absolute poverty be totally eliminated. It only requires that as long as *some* absolute poverty is preventable without sacrificing something else of comparable moral significance, then our obligation to help the poor remains.

Given these premises, the conclusion is logically inescapable. However, a neo-Malthusian objection remains. Hardin, for example, would argue that in many cases helping those in absolute poverty *does* cost something of comparable moral significance, namely, the future death of even more people. Such an objection clearly presupposes a utilitarian ethical theory, and Singer is happy to meet it on those grounds. All calculations of the consequences of action necessarily concern probabilities. Says Singer: "Better one certain unit of benefit than a 10% chance of 5 units; but better a 50% chance of 3 units than a single certain unit. The same principle applies when we are trying to avoid evils."

The slow and painful death by famine and disease of millions this year is a certain evil if we do nothing. But the future growth of populations a generation from now to an absolutely unmanageable size is based on forecasts that are notoriously fallible. In the early 1970s, for example, the population of mainland China was 830-million. Population experts were then predicting that by 1990 it would top 1.3-billion. In fact, it only reached 1.1-billion.[44] That's an error of 57% in less than 20 years. For reasons like these, and because Singer believes there is strong evidence to support the "demographic transition" theory mentioned above, he believes that Hardin's prediction of worldwide disaster in the future is at best uncertain. Therefore, it is argued, a 10% chance of future disaster ought not to deter us from acting to prevent the certain death of millions this year.

Henry Shue argues from an essentially Kantian perspective that we all have a fundamental moral obligation to alleviate world hunger. Shue defines a *basic right* as any right that would be self-defeating to sacrifice for the enjoyment of some other right. For example, if a soldier is caught behind enemy lines during a war, he may willingly forego a desire to sing "The Battle Hymn of the Republic." His basic right to physical security is obviously more important than his right to free speech. Furthermore, it would be no violation of anyone else's right if one soldier forcefully prevented another soldier from exercising his right to free speech in similar situations. Without physical security, no other rights are of any value.

Thus, the right to physical security is more basic than the right to free speech because the right to free speech *requires* physical security. It makes no sense to sacrifice physical security to obtain a right to free speech. If a person's right to physical security is not guaranteed, then everyone else is free to shoot him the moment he chooses to exercise his right to free speech. Obviously, placing free speech before physical security on any list of rights is self-defeating.

Shue then argues that "the same considerations that support the conclusion that physical security is a basic right support the conclusion that subsistence (minimal economic security) is a basic right."[45] If a person is so emaciated from lack of food that he hasn't the strength to speak, then his right to free speech is defeated. Therefore, if there are *any* rights, then there must be the basic right to minimal economic security.

Finally, Shue argues that all rights attach to human beings *as* humans, and not to members of a particular racial group or national state. This means that if *any* person has a right, then *all* persons have the same right. Combining these two conditional statements, Shue concludes that if any person has any rights, then all people have a basic right to minimal economic security. Because every right carries with it a corresponding duty for others not to infringe upon that right, Shue believes we all have an obligation to

> 1) *avoid* depriving the poor of the means of obtaining subsistence through structural injustices;
> 2) *protect* the poor from others who would deprive people of the only available means of subsistence, and
> 3) *aid* those who are unable to provide for their own subsistence.[46]

A Broad Versus A Narrow View Of Human Rights

There is nothing in the United States Constitution or Bill of Rights which guarantees basic rights as Shue conceives of them. "The United Nations Universal Declaration of Human Rights" is much broader. When it was adopted by the General Assembly of the United Nations in 1948, it called upon all Member countries to publicize the rest of the Declaration and "to cause it to be disseminated, displayed, read and expounded principally in schools and other educational institutions." It thus seems appropriate to close with selections from this document:

ARTICLE 23

1. Everyone has the right to work, to free choice of employment, to just and favorable conditions of work and to protection against unemployment...

3. Everyone who works has the right to just and favorable remuneration ensuring for himself and his family an existence worthy of human dignity....

ARTICLE 25

1. Everyone has the right to a standard of living adequate for the health and well-being of himself and of his family, including food, clothing, housing and medical care and necessary social services....

FOR FURTHER INQUIRY

CASE 1

During WW II Smith and Jones fought side-by-side. After the war they both took their small savings and bought adjoining parcels of cheap farm land in California. The land wasn't very good, but they worked hard and were able to earn a modest living for their families. Though they were forced to do without many of the new products which were becoming readily available after the war – televisions, stereos, second cars, *et al* – their families did enjoy each other's company, and were even able to take a yearly camping trip together.

In the mid-1950s, their circumstances began to change. As a result of the "National Defense Highway Act," a new interstate highway was built which passed through the eastern portion of Jones's land. While laws of eminent domain gave him few choices, Jones was well compensated for the three acres of land the state took as a right of way for the new highway. In fact, the Joneses' condition improved a little. With the money from the state, Jones was able to purchase some new equipment that allowed him to farm his remaining land more intensively. Their income increased significantly. They were now able to afford a second car and a trip to San Francisco for their vacation; the Smiths weren't able to go.

A couple of years later, a major oil company offered the Joneses what seemed to them a huge amount of money for a half-acre of their land next to the interstate upon which it was going to build a gas station. This was an offer the Joneses could not refuse. For the first time in his life, Jones was able to hire help during the planting and harvesting sessions. Furthermore, he now had enough capital and equipment to get a loan from a bank to purchase some more land. His income continued to increase significantly each year.

Within a few years, it became apparent that the Joneses' good fortune was a mixed blessing. The increased money and vacation time were certainly appreciated by all the Joneses. But as their income increased, their "happiness" didn't seem to keep pace. While they were always busy doing something, there never seemed to be time for their old friends. The Smiths simply didn't have the income to "keep up with the Joneses."

Questions for discussion:

1. Were the Joneses *entitled* to their higher standard of living? What would Nozick say?
2. Does the fact that Jones' farm was more productive than Smith's farm mean that Jones was either a harder worker or a more skilled and efficient worker than Smith? Is there a way to square your answer with marginal product theory?
3. Should the money the oil company paid Jones for a half-acre of land be taxed at a higher, lower, or same rate of tax as Jones's other income?
4. Should the Joneses offer to pay the Smiths' way on their next vacation? Should the Smiths accept

such a "charitable" offer if it is made? Are there any issues of *justice* in such questions?

5. Suppose the Smiths' daughter develops a liver disease that requires a costly organ transplant if she is to live. The Smiths were never able to afford an insurance plan that would cover the cost of such a procedure, yet they would not be eligible for Medicare unless they sold their farm and used the money to help pay for the operation. Should the Joneses voluntarily accept a significant reduction in their standard of living in order to be able to help the Smiths? Is there an issue of *justice* for either our government or the Joneses in such a question? Are there any *other* moral issues involved?

Case 2

The year is 2003. India has been facing a significant famine for the past three years. This year a million Indians will die if the countries in the West don't offer significant contributions in food and foreign aid.

It wasn't always like this. Prior to the drought, India was agriculturally self-sufficient. In fact, India was even able to export some grain. But it wasn't just the drought that caused India's troubles. For the past decade the cost of oil had been rising dramatically. This in turn led to a huge increase in the cost of nitrogen fertilizer. And then there was the most recent presidential election in the United States. Three years ago the winning candidate ran on the platform of "putting Americans first" and holding down increasing fuel costs. One of her first acts as President was to ban the export of any petroleum-based products, including fertilizers. Prior to the drought, this didn't seem like a particularly controversial move. But now, many Americans have said her policies were responsible for the deaths of thousands.

Partly in response to demonstrations at home, and partly out of her own moral convictions, the President promised to increase American foreign aid from .2% to the .7% recommended by the United Nations – but only if the other "G-7" countries would do likewise. This began a series of long and drawn-out negotiations in Europe and Japan.

However, while members of the "G-7" were trading proposals, thousands of Indians were dying each day. India's Prime Minister was herself facing tremendous pressure to do something to save her people. During one of her sleepless nights she recalled the Thomistic principle she had learned while studying in England: "It is not theft, properly speaking, to take secretly and use another's property in cases of extreme need." Though she could hardly "take secretly" from the grain elevators of the "G-7," she did have at her control several nuclear weapons. Harkening back to a scenario that was discussed in the 1970s, she took action: She ordered her military leaders to ship four nuclear bombs in unmarked containers rigged with remote control detonators to major ports in four different countries. After they arrived, she made the following demand: "Either the G-7 negotiators come to an agreement in the next 12 hours, or I will order one bomb to be exploded for each day you delay."

Needless to say, the Prime Minister's plan is not without risks. There is no way she can prevent the threatened nations from launching their own pre-emptive strike, killing her and millions of other Indians. Of course, such a strike is itself extremely risky because it would do nothing to save the cities of the "G-7" either.

Questions for discussion:

1. Has the Prime Minister of India correctly applied Thomas's principle?

2. Irrespective of the political wisdom of the Prime Minister's action, can it be justified *morally*?

3. In a press conference after her announcement, the Prime Minister justifies her threat to kill millions of *individually* innocent people by arguing that because they had been the recipients of *corporate or national* economic advantages all their lives, it is only just that they share the corporate or national "burdens" as well. Is she correct?

4. To bomb the cities of another nation is universally acknowledged to be an act of war. Is it an act of war for one nation to withhold essential exports for another nation's survival?

CASE 3

The economic pressure on York International was great. Foreign imports had significantly reduced their share of the domestic automobile market to the point where York's survival as a corporation depended on the success of the newly designed Jupiter. The normal three years it took from the initial concept to the finished product had been squeezed to 18 months. Market tests indicated that the Jupiter had successfully anticipated new consumer preferences, and York International was eight months to a year ahead of its foreign competitors. In fact, production had already begun and the first Jupiters would be in the showrooms in a couple of months.

It was under these circumstances that the CEO of York and a handful of top executives were faced with an agonizing decision: A memo from the chief design engineer of the Jupiter revealed that a design flaw would cause the air bags to fail in approximately one out of every 250 head-on crashes. The mistake could be corrected, but it would cost millions to retool and would delay sales for at least six months.

After the top legal and marketing executives were consulted, the options were quickly reduced to two: First, continue production, re-establish market share and the profitability of the company, and then pay generous settlements if (when?) suits are brought against the company. Second, recall the Jupiter, discontinue production during retooling and almost certainly face the demise of York International. The CEO of York chose the former.

Three years later, after York had re-established itself as a viable company, the CEO of York read the following statement at a news conference prior to beginning his five- to 10-year sentence at the federal penitentiary:

"While I have broken the law, my conscience is clear. The livelihood of thousands of employees was on the line three years ago. Life is tragic. Either option was sure to cause great pain. My critics will retort: Human life is priceless; no purely economic advantage will ever outweigh the loss of even a single life. But that is simply not true. First, there is no such thing as a *purely economic* advantage. When 10,000 employees lose their jobs, it is statistically certain that there will be one or two suicides, hundreds of divorces, and the neglect or abuse of thousands of children. Second, our economic system continually engages in cost-benefit analysis. We trade tobacco subsidies for cancer deaths; the reduction of air traffic controllers for airline accidents; and political expediency for the lives of famine-stricken children in foreign countries when their governments vote against us in the United Nations. My decision was no more immoral than any of these and the countless others that all politicians and business executives make at least once in their lives."

Questions for discussion:

1. Was the CEO of York International correct when he said that there is no such thing as a *purely economic* advantage? Is he correct to suggest that all major economic decisions inevitably involve matters of life and death?
2. The CEO's second argument seems to be open to the objection that "two wrongs don't make a right." But if we make such an objection, does moral consistency demand that we also become *actively* involved in correcting the other abuses of economic power mentioned above?
3. If the CEO of York were a conscientious utilitarian, how might he have acted? A conscientious Kantian? A conscientious communitarian?

ENDNOTES

1. U.S. Bureau of the Census, *Statistical Abstract of the United States: 1992* (112th edition). Washington, DC, 1992. p. 454.

2. Robert Nozick, *Anarchy, State and Utopia.* (New York: Basic Books), 1974. p. 151.

3. Nozick, p. 175-176.

4. Nozick, p. 179, 178.

5. Nozick, p. 176.

6. Nozick, p. 176.

7. Nozick, p. 177.

8. Nozick, p. 288.

9. Plato, *Laws* (Bk. 5). Penguin Classics, 1970. p. 215.

10. Nozick, p. 164.

11. John Rawls, *A Theory of Justice.* (Cambridge: Harvard University Press), 1971. p. 12.

12. Rawls, p. 15.

13. Rawls, p. 60.

14. Rawls, p. 432.

15. Mortimer J. Adler, *Six Great Ideas.* (New York: Macmillan), 1981. p. 141.

16. Aristotle, *Nicomachean Ethics* (Book 1, sec. 3. line 1094b 23-27.) Martin Ostwald, translator. Library of Liberal Arts, (New York: Bobbs-Merrill), 1962. p. 5.

17. For Plato, cf. note 9; for current figures cf. *Business Week* (May 1, 1989), p. 146.

18. Robert N. Bellah, *The Broken Covenant.* (New York: Seabury Press), 1975. p. 134.

19. Carl Cohen, *Four Systems.* (New York: Random House), 1982. p. 42.

20. Thomas Aquinas, *Summa Theologica.* (II-II, Question 66, Art. 7)

21. R. H. Tawney, *Religion and the Rise of Capitalism.* (New York: Penguin), 1947. p. 221.

22. *Statistical Abstract*, p. 462. Before welfare and taxes the numbers are: 1.1% for the bottom fifth and 50.7% for the top fifth.

23. Milton Fisk, *Ethics and Society.* (New York: New York University Press), 1980. p. 224-225.

24. Another advantage is that this method facilitates international comparisons. In Japan and West Germany the bottom fifth earned 9% and 8% respectively, while the top fifth earned 37% and 40% (Lester R. Brown, *State of the World 1990* p. 138). Thus, two of our chief economic competitors have equity ratios of between 4 and 5, while we have an (after taxes) equity ratio of 8.5.

25. Kevin Phillips, *The Politics of Rich and Poor.* (New York: Random House), 1990. Appendix B.

26. *Statistical Abstract*, p. 427.

27. *Statistical Abstract*, p. 458.

28. *Business Week* (May 1, 1989) p. 146.

29. Joseph Dorfman, *The Economic Mind in American Civilization: 1895-1981* vol. 3. (New York: Viking Press), 1949. p. 151-152.

30. George C. Lodge, *The New American Ideology* (New York: New York University Press), 1986. p. 204.

31. *U. S. News and World Report* (Oct. 31, 1988) p. 55.

32. *Goldberg vs. Kelly* United States Supreme Court. 397 U.S. 254 (1970).

33. *Wyman vs. James* United States Supreme Court. 400 U.S. 309 (1971).

34. Frances M. Lappe and Joseph Collins, *World Hunger: Twelve Myths.* (New York: Grove Press), 1986. p. 3.

35. Thomas Robert Malthus, *Population: The First Essay* (Ann Arbor: University of Michigan Press), 1959. p. 9 (chap. 2).

36. Malthus, p. 49 (chap. 7)

37. Garrett Hardin, "Lifeboat Ethics: The Case Against Helping the Poor." *Psychology Today* (1974) vol. 8.

38. Lappe, p. 9.

39. Alan B. Durning, "Ending Poverty." *State of the World: 1990*, Lester R. Brown, *et. al.* p. 135, 139.

40. Lappe, p. 106.

41. Ronald J. Sider, *Rich Christians in an Age of Hunger.* (Downers Grove: Inter-Varsity Press), 1984. p. 145. Cf. Lappe, p. 86ff.

42. Lappe, p. 89.

43. Peter Singer, *Practical Ethics.* (New York: Cambridge University Press), 1979. p. 169-170.

44. Susan Greenhalgh, "Socialism and Fertility in China" *The Annals of the American Academy of Political and Social Science.* vol. 510, July 1990. p. 74.

45. Henry Shue, *Basic Rights: Subsistence, Affluence, and U.S. Foreign Policy.* (Princeton: Princeton University Press), 1980. p. 24.

46. Shue, p. 60.

Part IV

Ethics
Applied

McGraw-Hill

'The Business Of America ...'

BIG MONEY   LITTLE CITIZEN   BIG BUREAU

12-19

Chapter 15

William F. Edmonson

BUSINESS AND PROFESSIONAL RESPONSIBILITY

"The business of America is business."

President Calvin Coolidge
to American Society of Newspaper Editors, 1925

"You can tell the ideals of a nation by its advertisements."
— Norman Douglas

"The foundation of morality is to have done, once and for all, with lying."
— T. H. Huxley

"*Carpe diem* ... Seize today, and put as little trust as you can in tomorrow."
— Horace

In a general sense ethics involves human beings determining proper goals and legitimate actions. Business ethics, therefore, is the application of ethical concepts related to business. The argument that business and ethics conflict may have stemmed from the theory that profit is the ultimate business goal and that the special regulations and goals of the business climate make unnecessary ethical standards for decision. However, business is an institution established on a moral base. The free market system is an outgrowth of concern about the production and fair distribution of goods and services for societal use. Making a profit allows the business to exist, but it is not a pursuit void of moral standards. In the profit-making process, many would argue, business also needs to contribute to the good of society without losing touch with its moral foundation.[1]

Today, society's lack of confidence in the ethics of business seems to be growing. In fact, business's values and morals may have reached a crisis level which may be reflected, in part, by the spawning

William Fred Edmonson, M.B.A. University of Southern MS., Ed.D. University of Mississippi, dean of instructional affairs at Itawamba Community College in Fulton, MS is president of Panola College in Carthage, Tex.

of business organizations formulating conduct codes and value statements (and, in part, may be further reflected by this textbook's allocation of an entire chapter to "Codes of Ethics"; cf. Chapter 21). Some executives, as well, have become more concerned about ethics and have begun to pursue ways to establish ethical standards for their companies.[2]

The ethical values of society as well as business are determined by the values of the individuals who make up the society and organizations. Some say we now live in a society dominated by greed and selfishness, resulting in lower ethical standards. To stop this decline and return to the foundational values of a nation's moral ethics, corporate leaders would have to address the issue.[3]

Media report that U.S ethical standards have reached an all-time low. This has caused business leaders to bring the ethics issue to the table. As yet, it seems hard to find significant improvement in our ethical and moral standards, but business leaders at least are willing to discuss them.[4] As we examine business ethics, we see that personal, corporate and national values are at the very center of any ethical position. We as humans identify and adopt our values, then our actions are built around them. As employees identify their own ethics, they influence the ethics of the organization they work for, either positively or negatively. *Positive ethics* calls for sound judgment, persistence and leadership by executives who are in a position to improve the ethical climate of their organization.[5]

PARAMETERS OF ETHICAL BEHAVIOR

Three levels of ethical behavior affect people: Codified laws, organizational policies, and ethical posture. Within these levels, individuals define what is permissible and what is not as they relate to personal behavior. Policies or guidelines exist in every organization, institution, or corporation. For example, families verbalize expected behaviors; colleges and universities write policies and procedures on academic and behavioral discipline; a nation's military forces have strict procedures describing what can be done while in uniform; corporations have adopted policies and procedures relative to every facet of their operation. For business, policies and procedures are critical to efficient operation, but they alone are insufficient if high ethical standards are to be maintained.[6]

Employees will assume an ethical/moral posture when making decisions on subjects or issues that are not well defined by the organization's policies and procedures. Early teachings from families, teachers and religious organizations affect this behavior. If employees have not had moral ethical teaching early in their lives, is it too late to seek to assimilate ethics and values after they become adults?[7] Our society requires that we live civil lives if we are to exist and to prosper. So schools and corporations have a responsibility to their communities – and individuals have a responsibility to their neighbors – to help them acquire an understanding of ethical and moral values that will uplift and strengthen them and their communities; then all individuals can enjoy the highest quality of life they are able to attain.[8] Inevitably, it would seem from this argument, we become our brothers' and sisters' keepers.

"If a business behaves unethically, the company derives only short-term advantage from its actions, and, over the long term, skimping on quality or service doesn't pay. It is not good business.[9] Each level of the corporation or business faces difficult decisions regarding ethical behavior. And, the decision-making effort doesn't always pay immediate dividends. Nevertheless, by ensuring that the organization's ethical posture is protected, the fiscal integrity and thus the financial capital of the firm also are protected. This constitutes the best way an organization can serve its customers, employees, the community, board of directors and stockholders.[10]

In an attempt to answer the question of whether there is an ethical crisis within the U.S. business community, Touche-Ross, a national accounting firm, conducted a 1988 survey entitled "Ethics In

American Business, A Special Report." The survey concluded that between 95 and 99% of the business college deans and corporate executives interviewed agreed that the nation's business community as a whole is troubled by ethical problems. Sixty-eight percent of them agreed that the issue of business ethics is not overblown.[11] Sixty-three percent of executives thought that high ethical standards strengthened rather than weakened a firm's competitive position.

Attention to this concept is certainly not a recent phenomenon. An ancient Chinese proverb says: "The effects of our actions may be postponed, but they are never lost. There is an inevitable reward for good deeds and an inescapable punishment for bad. Meditate this truth and seek always to earn good wages from Destiny."[12] During the past 15 years, business ethics has been recognized as a legitimate course to be taught in schools of business. In fact, it has developed into a growth industry with new courses, books, and new magazine articles appearing in many business-related publications. A bibliography for 1976-1980 listed more than 2,000 published works on ethics. The 1981-85 edition of that same publication listed nearly 5,000.

Surprisingly, however, prior to 1978, a textbook on business ethics did not exist. Perhaps Harvard University's president Derek Bok initiated an academic interest in the subject when he asked that the "Harvard Business School curriculum be reviewed and redesigned to recognize the new social and ethical requirements for business leaders." Bok concluded that many executives spend up to one-half their time on the job dealing with government, regulatory and community affairs. Despite this responsibility of executives, most business curricula have paid little attention to these matters.[13]

APPROACHING ETHICAL ISSUES

1. Business – Webster defines a business entity as "a commercial or mercantile activity customarily engaged in as a means of livelihood and typically involving some independence of judgment and power of decision."[14]

2. Corporation – Webster also defines the corporation as "a legal entity, consisting usually of a group of people who have a charter granting it perpetual life, that is invested with many of the legal powers to govern individuals; a corporation may enter into contracts, buy and sell property, etc. Any of the political and economic bodies forming a corporative state, each being composed of the employers and employees in a certain industry profession."[15]

3. Ethics – According to *Webster's New Collegiate Dictionary,* ethics is "the discipline dealing with what is good and bad and with moral duty and obligation."[16] Ethics has become a term we make reference to in situations which create some sense that something right or wrong has occurred or is about to occur. When managers ask for a definition of ethics, they present different descriptions of this term, such as:

- "Ethics consists of eternal verities of right and wrong."
- "They (ethics) are really rules — rules of behavior."
- "Integrity is what it means; it has to start from within (the individual)."[17]

Perhaps the most realistic meaning of "ethical," in the business context, is conforming to the standards of a given profession or group so the standards of that given profession or group are upheld. So, any group can set its own ethical standards and then live by them or not."[18]

These statements represent the four categories of personal definitions offered by Webster and Toffler: " ... basic truths, rules of behavior, the integrated unity of an individual's character, and institutional (or cultural) codes." There is a common link among these definitions.[19] "Ethical" has to do with "right and wrong, good and evil, virtue and vice." "Moral" has to do with "duty and responsibility as an individual functions within society and a business organization."[20]

"Ethical" comes from the Greek word "ethos," meaning "character" and "sentiment of the community" – what we might call culture. Peter Drucker's book *Management: Tasks, Responsibilities, Practices* explains business ethics in a critical light; however, he also is concerned with the idea of responsibility.[21] He argues that business professionals are no different than other professionals in that they should adhere to the "principle of non-maleficence." Simply put, this principle holds that a chief obligation of professionals is to "do no harm." Drucker claims that such a principle needs to be followed more closely and cites instances where he feels it has not been.[22]

Managers are challenged to recognize they not only have an obligation to their organization to do what is ethically correct but also to feel an obligation to their employees who look to them for leadership.[23] Those responsible for ethics training may find that regular use of a little tool known as the "Ethics Check" can guide executives and employees:[24]

> • **Is it legal?** Will I be violating either civil law or company policy?
> • **Is it balanced?** Is it fair to all concerned in the short term as well as the long term? Does it promote win-win relationships?
> • **How will it make me feel about myself?** Will it make me proud? Would I feel good if my decision was published in the newspaper? Would I feel good if my family knew about it?[25]

4. The Professions – Webster defines a profession as "a calling requiring specialized knowledge and often long and intensive preparation including instruction in skills and methods as well as in the scientific, historical, or scholarly principles underlying such skills and methods, maintaining by force of organization or concerted opinion high standards of achievement and conduct, and committing its members to continued study and to a kind of work which has for its prime purpose the rendering of a public service."[26]

PROFESSIONAL OBLIGATIONS

The first responsibility of a professional was well defined some 2,400 years ago in the Hippocratic oath of a Greek physician: "*primum non nocere* – above all, not knowingly to do harm." (Is this not a prime example of Kant's Categorical Imperative? See Chapter 3.) No one who claims to be a professional – including doctors, lawyers, teachers, or managers – can promise that they will always do good for their patients or clients. All that they can honestly do is to *try* to do good. However, they can promise not knowingly to do harm, which is consistent with the original Greek oath. Under the terms of the implied social construct, the patients or clients, in turn, should trust the professionals to act accordingly. Professionals need to have sufficient autonomy to do their jobs. In other words, professionals' actions are not supposed to be subject to undue political or ideological influence. At the same time, however, the welfare of the professionals' patients or clients establishes limits and conveys obligations on the professionals' actions and words.[27]

If professional integrity "comes from within the individual," as suggested earlier, consider what those inner resources might be. For example, Dr. Deborah Hyde-Rowan, one of only two black female neurosurgeons in the United States, was honored by *Esquire* magazine as one of the "best of the new generation – those who exemplify in their professional lives the qualities of courage, originality, ingenuity, vision and selfless service." In an interview in Sayre, Pa. she stated:

"I believe that divine intervention has guided my journey through life. I am not implying predestination, for I do not believe that one's fate is predestined. Rather, opportunities present themselves; how one deals with those opportunities determines one's fate. I prefer to call my life a series of divine accidents! I was initially discouraged from entering a field that was clearly man's domain. Academic achievements (including special honors in the General Surgery Clerkship and election to the Alpha Omega Honorary Medical Society), as well as support from the neurological staff, opened the door for me to become the first woman and first black to be accepted into the neurosurgical training program at the University Hospitals of Cleveland, Ohio ... I thank God for giving me the ability to do my job. I give thanks for continued strength, compassion, humility, and sensitivity. I accept my responsibility. My work is fulfilling and makes me feel that my contribution to the health of mankind will be my legacy. I feel an obligation to serve as a role model for minorities, in particular blacks and women. But I hope I can be a role model for anyone interested in neurosurgery. It is physically and emotionally demanding, but tremendously rewarding."

A poem by Will Allen Dromgoole is cited by Dr. Hyde-Rowan as representative of her philosophy of service:

The Bridge Builder

An old man going a lone highway
came in the evening cold and gray
to a chasm vast and deep and wide.
The old man crossed in the twilight dim,
the sullen stream had no fears for him,
but he stopped when safe on the other side
and built a bridge to span the tide.
"Old man," said a fellow pilgrim near,
"You are wasting your strength with building here;
Your journey will end with the ending day,
You never again will pass this way,
You've crossed the chasm deep and wide,
Why build you this bridge at evening tide?"

The builder lifted his old gray head,
"Good friend, in the path I have come," he said,
"There followeth after me today
A youth whose feet must pass this way,
This chasm which has been as naught to me
To that fair-haired youth might a pitfall be;
He, too, must cross in the twilight dim,
Good friend, I am building the bridge for him."[28]

"I hope I am a 'bridge builder,' Rowan stated. "I would like to feel that my influence will guide other people into the field of neurosurgery or medicine in general. I would like to feel that I can influence some young person to pursue a higher education in any chosen occupation. I have been influenced by wonderful bridge builders throughout my life who have guided me, instilled confidence , instilled racial and personal pride, and provided me with strength and perseverance. If I can accomplish this to some degree, then I, too, will have built a bridge to span the tide."[29]

A PROFESSIONAL'S IMPACT ON A BUSINESS

For most individuals employed in large corporations, because of bureaucratic structure, initiative at the periphery is not encouraged. There is one exception to this rule. The "professional" is a type of expert who provides services required because of increasing complexity in the social and legal climate. Professionals' expertise makes them special in the corporate world.[30] Only they are qualified to direct the work of the nature of their profession. Professionals, unlike other employees in a bureaucratic organization, must comply with two sets of standards – the policies and procedures of the organization and the standards of their profession. Professionals experience a conflict most acutely when they must play the role of an organizational administrator. The closer professionals come to the power center of the organization, the more conflict they experience.[31]

Modern-day corporations have created new professions that do not necessarily adhere to a traditional, professional "service" philosophy such as is found in medicine, law, or teaching. Because these new professionals – such as the data systems analyst, the marketing specialist, the labor negotiator, etc. – often are not seen as service-oriented in the historically recognized sense, unique problems associated with ethical responsibility develop.[32]

As the influence of professionals increases in corporations, the need for moral reinforcement through an individual's profession also increases. Henry Ford said he made every major decision about automobile design and production when the first mass-produced car came on the scene. The Ford Model T was Henry Ford's brainchild. Today, however, the automobiles rolling off the assembly line of a Ford plant have been developed by technocrats (i.e. production experts and design engineers).[33]

DRUCKER'S DOCTRINE

In 1970, Peter Drucker returned to General Motors following a study he had completed some 20 years earlier. He complained that GM had failed to solve a fundamental problem. That was the balancing of GM's needs with "concern for its environment and compassion for its community." Drucker concluded that much of the blame for this condition is the responsibility of the new professional. "General Motor's financial success is clearly the success of the technocrat," he stated, "but so is General Motors' failure."[34]

Underlying any business or profession must be a recognized body of knowledge accepted by and considered essential to the society. For example, the subject matter of accounting meets this criterion. A widely publicized and accepted statement describing the accounting profession is "Horizons for a Profession" by Robert H. Roy and James H. MacNeill (New York: American Institute of Certified Public Accountants, 1967). This statement refers to the myriad accounting reports and filings required by agencies of municipal, state and federal governments as well as the Securities and Exchange Commission, which requires financial reports filed with it to be certified by an independent public accountant. Of no small consequence, is the widespread demand for college graduates with training in accounting.[35]

The structure of a profession may be seen as analogous to the framework erected on a building foundation. Three elements comprise this framework: 1) an educational process to acquire and maintain the body of knowledge, 2) an examination and licensing procedure to determine whether individuals have a firm knowledge and understanding of the subject matter, and 3) a sense of responsibility to society relative to the use of this knowledge. All three of these tenets are essential.[36]

But just as the walls and roof of a building must be attached to the frame, so the professional structure must have some additions for it to be complete. Three elements in particular are needed by professionals: 1) professional associations, 2) codes of ethics, and 3) technical standards.[37] If a practicing professional falls short of the standards that have been established, Mark Brimer and Michael Moran ask, "What can be done to establish and maintain an ongoing philosophy of ethical and moral behavior?"[38]

Barry Posner and Warren Schmidt suggest the following response: "Commitment to building an effective organization based on the highest standards of ethical and moral behavior should be the primary goal of those in management positions."[39] As a member of the management team, one must continually reinforce and reward behaviors that are important to the profession and to the organization. There are seven critical areas upon which to focus the building of a staff committed to the highest of ethical and moral standards. These are:

1. Recruit, select and promote the "right" people.
2. Train others in ethical decision-making.
3. Identify and communicate high standards.
4. Maintain open channels of communication.
5. Review policies and procedures on a regular basis.
6. Remain visible.
7. Exhibit model ethical behavior.[40]

An organization that is efficient, and has high morale and a good reputation is exemplary of management identifying the best ways to keep employees satisfied on the job while providing high quality productivity.[41] A leader possesses values that are consistent, clear, and based upon sound ethical and moral principles. As executives, those who focus their best efforts toward creating an ethical climate in which employees can work are more likely to gain the support of their colleagues and peers.[42]

POLICING THE PROFESSIONS

Consumers' attitudes toward the professions of law and medicine have been a mixture of trust and suspicion. We want to trust doctors and lawyers with our health and financial resources, and because we do, we want to believe they are highly ethical and moral. The general public, however, has limited competence to judge the ethics or morality of doctors and lawyers. Consequently, these professionals are not held as accountable for their actions as are ordinary entrepreneurs.[43]

Many of the doctors and lawyers support the current system of regulating their professions through peer review. They argue that only their peers have the expertise needed to judge fairly their conduct and performance, particularly as it relates to protecting the public from the incompetent and/or negligent practitioner.[44] Critics, on the other hand, argue that peers are least capable of effectively protecting the best interest of the public, because they can't be objective in judging their colleagues' unethical or immoral behavior. They argue that a lawyer who is unethical "is generally somebody's friend who is basically a good guy who has gone bad temporarily," says California State Bar Governor Richard Annotico. "And who," he argues, "enjoys being an executioner?"[45]

Those who defend the current system of peer review say the primary reason for it is the protection of the public from charlatans (i.e., those practicing a profession without a legitimate license). They argue that doctors and lawyers should be held responsible for higher ethical standards than the average entrepreneur, and the only way to ensure that these professionals adhere to these higher standards is through peer review.[46]

HOW SELF-POLICING (PEER REVIEW) WORKS

In "Policing the Professions" (Editorial Research Reports 1989, p.290-291), Sarah Glazer summarizes: "Lawyers are regulated by lawyers acting through their state board associations or through the courts. The American Bar Association's Model Rules of Professional Conduct serve as the model code for the state disciplinary systems. It is up to each state disciplinary body, whether it be a state board association or an independent body, to draft and adopt the state ethical code, usually a variation on the ABA's Model Rules. Separate procedural rules set out the obligation of each state to have a procedure by which violation of its ethical code will be investigated and penalized. In 1986, the ABA issued model standards for imposing lawyer sanctions, noting that the sanctions for the same violation vary widely from state to state. Licensed lawyers have a legal obligation to follow the ethical code of the state in which the license was issued."[47]

"Doctors are regulated by state medical boards. The boards derive their power from state laws giving them the right to grant and revoke licenses. Individual state laws lay out the boards' powers, the types of violations for which they may punish incompetent or miscreant doctors, and the types of penalties they may impose. The American Medical Association and its affiliated state medical societies also issue ethical codes to be followed by their members but which have no legal force."[48]

A supporter of this position is Michael Josephson, a former professor of law at Loyola University in Los Angeles and now president of the Josephson Institute for the Advancement of Ethics, a nonprofit organization in Marina Del Rey, Cal. "Professionals are trying to do more than just 'maximize profits,'" says Josephson. "They're trying to help people, which creates a fiduciary relationship between the professional and his client that's different from other occupations."[49]

"That's a lovely fiction," counters Kay A Ostberg, deputy director of HALT, a national consumer group based in Washington, D.C., that advocates legal reform. "The fact is that lawyering is a business. Anyone who works in a law firm for 10 minutes can tell you that."[50]

These conflicts in the interpretation of professionalism are illustrated by two modern U.S. Supreme Court decisions. Until 1975, federal law supported the position that doctors and lawyers could not be considered "commerce" under the definition of the Sherman Antitrust Act. After that year the Supreme Court, in *Goldfarb vs. Virginia State Bar*, brought the profession of law within reach of the federal antitrust laws. The high court ruled that lawyers and bar associations violate federal antitrust laws against price-fixing when they require lawyers to adhere to minimum-fee schedules in charging for their services.[51] In 1975 the Federal Trade Commission filed a complaint against the American Medical Association and two affiliates. It charged them with conspiring to restrain trade through their ethical codes. The FTC argued, and the Supreme Court agreed, that the AMA codes of ethics banning solicitation of patients through such means as advertising was in restraint of trade and should be removed from the code.[52]

ECONOMICS AND THE MOVE TOWARD SELF-POLICING

The early history of the U.S. indicates that until the late 19th century doctors and lawyers struggled to achieve recognition for the professional training they had received. But by 1898, all states and territories of the U.S. except Alaska had passed laws requiring medical doctors to obtain a license before they could practice their profession. State Medical Boards were given the power to grant licenses. This practice remains in place today throughout the U.S.[53] The legal profession also established itself as a profession when powerful bar associations were formed in the 1870s, first in the states and then on the national level. An association's initial purpose was to limit the number of lawyers and to regulate itself.[54] The professional license today has come to be recognized as a desirable credential for practically every organized occupation.[55]

More than 30 occupational groups are licensed in California alone. Other states license dozens of different groups. One state licenses private detectives, egg graders, electricians, elevator inspectors, guide-dog trainers, horse shoers, librarians, manicurists, masseurs, milk certifiers, mine inspectors, motor vehicle dealers, oculists, pest controllers, plumbers, shorthand reporters, social workers, watchmakers, well drillers and yacht brokers. The list likely will lengthen as groups perceive the benefits that having a license brings.[56]

COMMERCIALIZATION: NEW THREAT OR OLD REALITY?

"Professions are becoming indistinguishable from any other moneymaking trade," says former law professor Michael Josephson, adding: "But outside regulation is not necessarily the solution because professionals tend to view it with hostility." He believes that "the key is to retrain professionals to think of their mission as distinct in character from that of the average businessman."[57] Critics of the professions, such as Robert C. Fellmeth, argue that medicine and law are inherently different from commercial enterprises because they have a unique capacity to impose "irreparable harm" on their clients. He says: "Because you're in this position, we have a right to demand a bit more of you."[58]

Josephson, urging professionals to adopt a professional ethic on their own, doubts that it will be enforceable without outside assistance. He has learned that each occupation group believes it is more ethical than any other group. "That's universal," he reports. "All that means to me is that when it comes to issues of propriety and ethics, we all have such heavy filters that they effectively blind us to issues that outsiders can see."[59] (See also Chapter 21.)

BUSINESS OBLIGATIONS

Throughout America's history, the major responsibility of business has been to produce goods and services and to sell them for a profit. This perception of business's role has been a cornerstone of society's belief in the free enterprise system. Recently, however, business started to be required to obey a multitude of laws, and also to go beyond the demands of the law – to exercise moral judgments in making its decisions. What are the reasons for this change in the perception of business's social responsibility?[60] The traditional ideology portrayed businesses as pieces of private property, existing primarily to make money for their owners. Milton Friedman, one of the most vocal supporters of the traditional ideology, states that "the social responsibility of business is to increase its profits."[61] But the business – the corporation, in particular – is evolving away from the traditional enterprise Friedman prescribes.

George Cabot Lodge describes a new ideology, called communitarianism, that is already reflected in the policies and procedures of many corporations. This notion suggests ethical business actions are those that serve the best interests of a community. Supporting the communitarian philosophy are such writers as Christopher Stone, Anthony Buono and Lawrence Nichols, Keith Davis and Thomas Donaldson – all of whom argue that corporations are no longer merely economic institutions but sociological institutions as well.[62]

Christopher Stone states: "There seems to be no firm basis for the claim that management's only obligation is to produce a profit ... To be sure, managers may have this obligation, but that does not relieve them of all other responsibilities. There are obligations more fundamental ... an obligation not to sell products that are dangerous to consumers, for example — such as the Ford Pinto — even if by doing so it will make a profit." Thomas Donaldson supports this idea, arguing that because society recognizes corporations as legal entities with special status under the law and permits them to use natural resources and hire employees, society should be permitted to demand at least that the benefits of corporate behavior outweigh the liabilities. If Donaldson is correct, the corporation is a social entity from the moment it is legally recognized. And, the legitimacy of corporate activity lies in the successful exercise of social responsibility.[63]

STOCKHOLDERS AND STAKEHOLDERS

How, indeed, should corporations be received by society? Two opposing ideologies are known as the "stockholder model" and the "stakeholder model." Adherents of the stockholder model, such as Friedman, believe the sole purpose of the corporation is to make a profit for its shareholders. Adherents of the stakeholder model believe the corporation has many purposes. That is, it should be operated not merely for the benefit of shareholders, but for all "stakeholders" – all those who contribute to the success of the firm? Supporters of this model believe that long-term self interest and ethical duty require its adoption [64].

Support for the stakeholder model is evidence of a high degree of public cynicism about corporate ethics and a strong willingness to take action to change company behavior. Corporations now are being held responsible for their actions by consumer groups, shareholders and activists, in ways that thrust corporate accountability into the spotlight.[65] For example, toxic materials disposed of 30 years ago were dumped before people knew of their carcinogenic side effects. Most of the managers who dumped them retired long ago. Nevertheless, the firms – DuPont, Allied Chemical, Monsanto, Dow Chemical and Union Carbide – now acknowledge that they have a responsibility for these dumpings. They have gone so far as to set up their own cleanup operations. The companies made ethical judgments with the knowledge that when they first dumped those chemicals, they made larger profits because safely disposing of the chemicals would have been more costly. Those chemicals that now are leaking into the water supplies are "their" chemicals, and these corporations have voluntarily assumed some of the responsibility for cleanup. This position, which they call "product stewardship," results from ethical sensitivity along with public pressure and fear of liability.[66]

Justice, jobs, efficiencies, long-term consequences – these are all factors in discovering the ethical resolution of external responsibility of the business entity. A *utilitarian* ethical norm would calculate the "greatest good for the greatest number." (See Chapter 3.) This calculation also would take into account future generations. When we consider the many short- and long-term benefits of saving resources, even though it will demand some losses and short-term sacrifice, some corporations seem to occupy theoretical high ground. Continuing to enforce high automobile gasoline efficiency standards, for example, does not prevent auto firms from taking other means to bolster return on investments. At the same time, continuing those standards will contribute to the freedom of customers. Less threatened by the danger of high gasoline prices and not forced to submit to anonymous market forces, domestic and foreign consumers will benefit in the long run.[67]

Historically business has been concerned strictly with its economic role in society. Recently, however, business has had to deal with a great many social issues that have profoundly affected the conduct of business and other institutions. These guidelines are collectively referred to as the "social responsibility" mode.[68] The major themes of this notion, according to Keith Davis in *Business Horizons* (June 1975), include the following:

Social responsibility involves minority employment and environmental pollution. If business is to act responsibly in these areas, business must consider the social consequences of its actions.[69] Business decisions no longer can be made solely for economic reasons. Today's business must become concerned with the total effect of its actions on society. Any business that ignores this responsibility will find its social power threatened. Society has entrusted to business large amounts of resources. Therefore, in addition to its economic role, business has a new role as trustee of society's resources.[70] Heretofore, business has operated under conditions that did not allow for two-way communication between society and the executive suite. Social responsibility demands that business must know what society needs and wants in order to respond effectively.[71]

THE CORPORATE SOCIAL AUDIT

The social responsibility model proposes a policy of full disclosure about products and social impact information relative to a firm's activities. A "social audit" is proposed to accomplish this. (For further discussion of the social audit, see Raymond A. Bauer and Dan H. Fenn Jr., *The Corporate Social Audit.* New York: The Russell Sage Foundation, 1972; and John J. Corson and George A. Steiner, *Measuring Business's Social Performance: The Corporate Social Audit.* New York: Committee for Economic Development, 1975.)[72] The idea is that this audit would serve the same purpose in social areas that an accounting audit serves in economic areas. It would measure whether a corporation has been using its assets in a responsible manner. It would show where progress has been made and where additional work must be done. It could be a guide to improving corporate performance, a check on management or mismanagement of resources relative to social benefit, and an encouragement to "operation in the sunshine" relative to social performance.[73]

The social audit model is, of course, an ideal, and presently not likely to be operational. In fact, decades may pass before it is refined to the degree that would match an accounting audit. The social audit, however, is justifiable in that most agree it will cause a much-needed improvement in communication between a corporation and its affected parties, from stockholders to government to consumers and other communities of interest.[74] Another proposition of this approach is that social costs be calculated and considered in order for a corporation to decide whether to proceed with the production of a product or service. In the past, business has been required to consider technical feasibility and economic profitability. If favorable, the activity was undertaken. Under the social-audit model, business would have the third basic factor to measure: The social effect of the activity. Only if all factors are favorable would it be acceptable to proceed.[75]

For example, major business projects, such as doubling a plant's capacity and employment in a suburban area, would have a significant impact on the economy, community, environment, and other factors affecting the public's best interest.[76] Environmental impact statements would be of great benefit. Opponents to this concept argue that what is being threatened is the business decision-making process itself. However, business is expected to make responsible decisions based on a thorough examination of costs, benefits, and social impact, and to proceed only after groups affected have had the opportunity to be heard and their interests considered.[77]

If corporations refuse to undertake procedures to ensure responsible decision-making, then the so-called Iron Law of Responsibility will be imposed by others – i.e., by rule-making powers of government and the influence of representatives of affected interest groups. Another basic proposition would require that social costs be included in the price that the consumer pays for the "effects of his consumption on society." This idea proposes that an equitable consumer price for a product or service is one that includes all costs of production including social costs. Historically, however, society had to bear the social costs while the consumer benefited from product prices that did not include social costs.[78]

In the case of the environment, for the most part, it has been considered a free economic resource that a corporation could use. It has been considered a resource in the public domain available to all without charge. The strip miner could mine coal without restoring the topsoil. The steelmaker could use oxygen from the air for the company's blast furnaces without paying society for polluting air with its waste. And, companies could draw water from rivers and lakes, then discharge waste into them, without paying for this privilege.[79] Society placed no economic value on these resources in the public domain. They were considered free goods. This practice was not a serious problem as long as the cost to society was light, but when it became heavy, society discovered that the burden of paying for cleaning up was a burden too heavy to bear.

The philosophy that the user pays is a good general guide. However, there are exceptions. For example, technology is not available for the complete removal of pollutants from the air, so some are allowed to remain at no cost to the consumer or user of products that contribute to pollution. Thus, the consumer buys electricity, for example, more cheaply than could be bought if the total removal of pollutants were technologically feasible.

Another approach would be for the government to underwrite part of the costs of the removal of pollutants from the environment in the name of the public interest. The costs of these actions, no doubt, would be absorbed in the price of goods produced or in higher taxes to offset such costs.

A final proposition would require business actions to solve social problems on the same basis that private citizens are expected to volunteer for free community service. Because business is a major social institution, it should bear the same kind of citizenship costs as any other citizen. When society benefits, the business will benefit. Therefore, business, which is a "citizen of society," has a responsibility to help identify social problems and contribute its talents and abilities to the solution of the problems.[80]

SUMMARY: EXTERNAL RESPONSIBILITIES

The primary premise of these propositions has been that business, just as any citizen, needs to act responsibly relative to the consequences of its actions. Furthermore, the "social quality of life" should be considered worth protecting and improving by all of society's citizens including business.[81] The "social responsibility model" would include the following applications:

1. It should apply to all organizations and individuals alike. All citizens should be held accountable for the consequences of their actions.
2. This concept should not be a fad but a fundamental change in social direction. Social responsibility will not disappear and business probably has contributed significantly to its

rise because it has done its economic job so well that it freed people from economic want, providing time for them to pursue new social goals.

3. Social responsibility exhibited by business will increase economic costs. It is not a "free ride." For example, the reduction of pollution will take large amounts of economic resources. Consequently, individuals in society should expect to see higher prices as these costs reflect the prices of[82] the goods and services business provides.

If corporations did behave in this way, how might it affect the concerns of "economic justice" considered in Chapter 14?

CORPORATE CULTURE

People are the chief resource of business managers; they are to be viewed as the primary raw material with which managers work. Consequently, it is important for the manager to understand why people behave as they do.[83] Formal organizations that assign duties and specify relationships provide only one set of motivations to which people respond – e.g., the American Bar Association. An organization's structure that carries "official" approval is a strong influence, but there are many other pressures, and a wise manager will try to design the organization so that these other influences support, rather than detract from, desired results.[84] Another important set of influences arises from a simple and obvious characteristic of human behavior: People live and work together. Their relationships soon result in patterns of behavior and belief. Social scientists call such patterns "cultures." Every enterprise develops, within the broader national culture, its own "subculture"; that is, the beliefs and patterns of conduct that are associated with living and working together in an organization. [85]

Management executives within businesses – and corporations in particular – adopt policies, procedures, and guidelines, to ensure that the organization operates in a manner that will achieve the goals and objectives identified as necessary for a thriving, successful and productive business entity. An outgrowth of such activity is a "culture" unique to each business entity. This culture has a major impact upon the ethics of the business. Jay Lorsch suggests that a corporate culture is "a shared set of beliefs top managers have in a company about how they should manage themselves and other employees, and how they should conduct their business(es); ... These beliefs are often invisible to the top managers but have a major impact on their thoughts and actions."[86] Stanley M. Davis suggests that "culture is the pattern of shared values and beliefs that give members of an institution meaning and provide them with rules for behavior in their organization."[87]

Finally, W. Brook Tunstall, Assistant Vice President and Director of Corporate Planning of American Telephone and Telegraph Company, describes corporate culture as "a general constellation of beliefs, mores, customs, value systems, behavioral norms, and ways of doing business that are unique to each corporation, that set a pattern for corporate activities and actions, and that describe the implicit and emergent patterns of behavior and emotions characterizing life in the organization."[88] Tunstall believes these definitions include ideas that are crucial to the development of an ethical management system and effective set of internal responsibilities:

> 1. Customs, habits, and ways of working together develop informally in a growing enterprise. These customs, which grow up around normal company activities, elaborate and extend – or perhaps modify – formal organization.
> 2. The informal social groups among employees strongly influence their attitudes, beliefs, and behavior. These informal groups often (though not necessarily) center on personal interest and objectives not directly related to the company's product.

Although social traditions and informal relationships can be annoying to an executive, they are also essential for getting a day's work accomplished smoothly. Like fire, the force is destructive when improperly handled; but once a person understands a force and how to work with it, he or she can employ it for constructive purposes. Managers cannot manipulate social behavior any way they please, but they can attempt to design work structures so that social pressures and formal organization tend to support each other. It is this melding of these two phenomena that the effective manager must understand in order to establish effective internal working relationships.

Emphasis on behavior based on experience should be a warning to anyone who thinks of managing purely through formal organization and written plans. Before formal instructions become customary behavior, they have to be accepted in actual use. What an employee considers to be acceptable is determined by a variety of factors, such as favorable reaction of other employees, approval by his immediate supervisor, contribution to company goals, and personal satisfaction from doing the work.

For example, if an immediate supervisor does not insist that workers follow official plans, then other considerations are likely to determine the particular work pattern that becomes customary (i.e., if employees can disregard a no-smoking rule without serious consequences, they are liable to adopt smoking on the job as customary conduct). Formal plans can have their full impact only when they become an integral part of custom.

Ideally, the job description that stems from formal organization and the other sets of expectations should merge into a single, consistent concept of a job. But this concept can be formalized only if 1) the job description is realistic in terms of both the technological and human resources available, 2) there is full communication and agreement by everyone concerned on what a person in the job is expected to do, and 3) the person actually on the job performs as anticipated. It is when these three conditions are fulfilled that a formal organization becomes a living reality .[89] Many effective managers seek to harmonize social groups and the formal organization by implementing the following practices:

1. Adopting group practice. Many times, people in a company envision new ways of doing things that are not only more satisfying to their group but also enhance company efficiency. The manager's first step in dealing with informal group actions that don't "fit" the formal structure should be at least to entertain the hypothesis that the group standards and behavior are good. The manager need not accept the group behavior, of course. But after investigation, he or she may decide that the informal action must be changed to meet company requirements; however, the manager should always be alert for the possibility that behavior which develops informally serves the company well and should be incorporated into the formal structure.

2. Forming integrated task teams. A second possibility of harmonizing small group practice with formal organization lies in the structure itself. Formal organization – that is, how workers are grouped together and what the specified relationships are – provides the setting for many informal groups. The manager should investigate whether a formal organization can be designed so as to encourage social groups to conform to it rather than conflict with it and the aims of the enterprise. Three guides for organization-design help foster informal groups sympathetic to company goals and encourage effective internal working relationships. The three are these:

   a. Assign work in terms of "meaningful" end products.
   b. Place people with all skills necessary to complete the assigned task as close as possible to the point of action.

c. Supply each task team with full facts on its work. Members of the team, because they have personal contact with what is happening, know whether all phases of the operation are proceeding as planned.

Armed with such information, the team itself regulates its efforts to achieve desired end results. This kind of self-control affects a social group in two ways: It can base its beliefs, at least those related to work, on fact, not fiction. Secondly, having prompt knowledge of its progress, (coupled with full delegation) will encourage the group to concern itself with results rather than to spar with a supervisor.

If a manager or executive looks at an organization as a social unit rather than as a work-producing machine, three important conclusions can emerge: *First,* the social relationships in an organization are not based on crisp decisions that remain static once they are made but on a series of continuing personal actions and reactions over a long period. Defining relationships in an organization manual may be useful, but even sharp definitions take on their full meaning only as people learn to work together.

In a business firm, as in a local parent-teacher association or National Guard unit, people gather knowledge and information from organizational charts, definition of duties, and other formal statements of how an enterprise is expected to work. Nevertheless, to get full "feel" of an organization, a manager also needs to know which members have the most influence on accepted beliefs, what the prevailing attitude is toward the role of the various officers and executives, what small groups there are and what their influence is, and whether strong cliques are at work.

Second, the manager should view the behavior of people in the organization objectively. When a motor won't run or a fuse blows out, the employee tries to find the cause and correct it, then proceed with business. But when the manager deals with human behavior, his or her response is much more emotional. If an employee fails to do what the organization policy specifies, emotions may flare. Having designed a beautiful organization plan, managers often think everyone should behave according to the plan.

Finally, if a manager understands the social forces at work, he or she can be more skillful in planning, leading and controlling an organization. Emphasis on social behavior simply indicates that organizing is a more delicate task than it appears when our attention is focused only on the work to be done. When a manager includes social dimensions in the total picture, this may call for modifying the organizational design. Perhaps task teams or some other arrangement that recognizes social behavior in groups can be introduced; or while thinking about changes in assigned duties, the manager may give attention to the tugs and pulls in learning new social relationships. In shaping the organization, the manager should consider not only social behavior but also the personal needs of individuals.[90] For any manager, ethics and leadership go hand-in-hand. An ethical environment contributes to effective leadership.

RISING OR FALLING ON LEADERSHIP

Ethics[91] and leadership function as both cause and effect. Beginning the chain of causal relations is the role of the manager because the manager is the person who influences others within the organization. This is done in a number of ways: Through a manager's ability to acquire power and use it to achieve worthwhile ends; through vision and the ability to transform it into action; and through enthusiasm and ability to empower others.

Rather than say that an effective manager is one who casts a shadow on the organization, it is more realistic to say that an effective manager is one who casts light on it. This light helps establish the organizational climate for ethical conduct. The organization's climate refers to "how we do things around here" – the ground rules that determine proper and improper conduct on the part of the organization's members.

The ground rules may or may not exist in written form; nevertheless, they do exist and are communicated through words, actions, and impression. The manager of an organization is the principal agent in establishing a climate and determining whether it promotes or inhibits ethical conduct on the part of the other[92] executives and employees. Assuming that leadership is conducive to an organizational climate promoting ethical conduct, then the direct effect is the building of trust. And, astute observers of organization behavior view trust as the "miracle ingredient," the bond that holds an organization together. Without this bond, the organization becomes an assemblage of diverse individuals going their separate ways and promoting their own interests. When executives and employees have established a bond of trust between them, the organizational whole is greater than the sum of its parts, its individual membership.[93]

This bonding leads to the final link in the chain: Long-term success as an outgrowth of trust. An organization's long-term success can be defined in terms of its productivity, financial performance, satisfaction of stakeholders – or, simply, the achievement of its stated mission. This long-term success is influenced greatly by trust among the organization's members and all other stakeholders (i.e. those parties having an interest in the success of the organization).

Trust alone will not guarantee success. However, everything else being equal, those organizations that generate trust among executives and employees are much more likely to achieve long-term success than those organizations that fail to generate trust. Trust must be established and maintained over time if it is to have any long-lasting impact. It is most important that leader-managers be aware of their considerable influence on the ethical conduct of their employees. To this end, leader-managers are advised to do three things: 1) achieve an understanding of ethics; 2) serve as role models in making ethical decisions; and 3) develop and implement a plan of action for promoting ethical conduct on the part of their staffs.[94]

MANAGING ACCOUNTABILITY IN THE CORPORATION

The first problem in restoring individual accountability lies within the very structure of corporate bureaucracy. Those individuals nearer the bottom of the corporate ladder are affected the most. Impersonal rules created to solve immediate authority relationships often lead to a deterioration in morale.[95] There are two possible solutions to this problem. In considering them, we will see notions that give rise to a contrast between an adaptation of authoritarian (deontological?) approaches and those of a social contract (cf. Locke) and utilitarian thinking.

First, corporations might be encouraged to reinstate direct-authority relationships, thereby dispensing with impersonal rules. This inveighs an image, say, of Lee Iacocca having to approve any changes in any aspect of a Chrysler Corporation car. Second, corporate organizations might try a more democratic form of accountability that allows more participation in the management of the organization by employees. This suggests themes that are attributed to Japanese automakers. These two alternative solutions are similar to Dorothy Emmet's definition of mechanistic and organic organizations. "Mechanistic" refers to organizations that have a chain of command originating from a central location. "Organic" refers to organizations with lateral lines of communication that permit participatory management.[96] The first model closely resembles the classical, pyramid-shaped organization. A return to this form of management would probably make matters worse. The second, though ideal in theory, will require acceptance on the part of executives and employees if it is to survive. [97]

The philosopher Paul Kurtz believes that the only way bureaucratic organizations can be held accountable is by adopting the participatory model. "We need," he says, "an organization bill of rights, an emancipation proclamation by means of which we can build a plurality of democratic institutions."[98] Although it is not clear what form this emancipation might take in the corporation, employees would participate in the decision-making process to some extent. Even though bureaucratic control would remain in the form of impersonal rules, the corporation would be held accountable for the application of those rules.[99] Participatory management has its advantages and disadvantages. Reversing the tradition of centralized, hierarchal decision-making puts the employee on the same level with management. Conversely, participation does not allow employees to separate themselves from their work. Some do not want to give up their privacy and individualism in order to become part of management. As many persons who have been involved in totally democratic institutions realize, democracy can be messy. At the same time, bureaucratic structures do not always blend well with democratic values.[100]

There is evidence that increased worker participation in the design of work conditions yields greater productivity, but the evidence is slight and must be weighed in terms of the "Hawthorne Effect"[101] (Richard Sennette, "The Boss's New Clothes," The New York Review of Books, February 22, 1979, p. 44). (The Hawthorne experiment showed that production tends to increase whenever management alters work conditions, regardless of the nature of the change.)

Nevertheless, the ultimate moral justification for attempting to solve accountability problems by introducing participatory mechanisms may not be greater productivity. The justification could be that our moral ideals require accountability whenever our actions affect the well-being of large numbers of people. (Again, consider this analysis in the light of the "exemplars" studied in Chapter 3.) And corporations do affect large numbers of people (Donaldson p. 120).[102] For comparison, in Japan, each work-section of a Japanese company is three-layered, consisting of young on-the-job trainees (a status that often lasts for several years); mature, experienced workers who carry most of the burden; and older employees whose productivity has fallen off due to their age. Direct, specific orders do not set well with the members of these work-sections. Such orders leave them with the impression they are not trusted and that management has no respect for them.[103] (Boye De Mente, *Japanese Etiquette & Ethics in Business.* Lincolnwood,Ill: Passport Books, 1987, p. 74.)

Even the lowest clerk or delivery boy in a company is sensitive about being treated with respect. In the case of the Japanese, they say they prefer general "ambiguous" instructions. All that work-groups want from management "are goals and direction."[104] (Boye De Mente, p. 74.) Because human relations are given precedence in the Japanese management system, great importance is attached to the "unity of employees" within each of these groups. The primary responsibility of senior managers in a group is not to direct the people in their work but to make "adjustments" among them in order to maintain harmonious relations within the group.[105] (Boye De Mente, p. 74.) What is required of ideal managers, say the Japanese, is that they know how to adjust human relations rather than be knowledgeable about the operation of their department or the overall function of the company. In fact, persons who are independently competent and work very hard are not likely to be popular with other members of their group and as a result do not make good managers."[106] (Boye De Mente, p. 74.) Besides "appearing somewhat incompetent" as far as work is concerned, while being skilled at preventing inter-employee friction, ideal Japanese managers have one other important trait: They are willing to shoulder all the responsibility for any mistakes or failings of their subordinates – hoping, of course, there will be no loss of face.[107] (Boye De Mente, p. 74.)

The efficient operation of this group system is naturally based on personal obligations and trust between the manager and the staff. Managers must make the staff obligated to them in order to maintain cooperation and in order to ensure that none of the staff will deliberately do anything or leave anything undone that would cause managers embarrassment. Whatever knowledge and experience are required for the group to be productive is found among subordinates if the manager is weak in this area.[108] (Boye De Mente, p. 75.)

DEVELOPING CORPORATE CULTURE

"Every family, every college, every corporation, every institution needs tribal storytellers," writes Max DePree, retired CEO and current chairman of the board of Herman Miller, Inc., in his book *Leadership Is an Art.* "The penalty for failing to listen is to lose one's history, one's historical context, one's binding values." He adds: "Without a folklore, a stock of core values that is passed along formally and informally among people and generations, any group of people will begin to forget who they are.

"In a time when individual productivity is at an all-time low and there is a growing mistrust between management and workers, we can't afford to lose that folklore. It is adherence to a set of values that gives focus to our lives, and it is adherence to a set of values that drives us to perform. The question is, what values?"

David Lankford approached the subject of business ethics by first helping students identify certain values that form the basis for decision-making. The values include honesty, generosity, helpfulness, self-reliance, and kindness. He then encouraged the students to examine the sources of their basic beliefs, sources such as home, church, synagogue, mosque, school and peers.[109] People today, especially young people, "are forced to make tough decisions without the tools to do it," says Linda McKay of St. Louis.[110] Lankford and McKay have presented workshops at seven St. Louis high schools. These workshops have been so successful, they prompted William Kanaga, chairman of the advisory board of Arthur Young and Co., a leading accounting and consulting firm, and the immediate past board chairman of the U.S. Chamber of Commerce, to say: "If (McKay and Lankford) can set up a model program, then replicate it across the country, I applaud them. This is an area that has been neglected too long." [111]

In *The Power of Ethical Management.* , Blanchard and Peale have proposed five principles of ethical power for individuals. They suggest that leaders of a socially conscious corporation consider them as motivational elements for any employee productivity program, indeed for goals of the corporation itself. The principles are these:

> 1. Purpose: I see myself as being an ethically sound person. I let my conscience be my guide. No matter what happens, I am always able to face the mirror, look myself straight in the eye, and feel good about myself.
> 2. Pride: I feel good about myself. I don't need the acceptance of other people to feel important. A balanced self- esteem keeps my ego and my desire to be accepted from influencing my decisions.
> 3. Patience: I believe that things will eventually work out well. I don't need everything to happen right now. I am at peace with what comes my way!

4. Persistence: I stick to my purpose, especially when it seems inconvenient to do so! My behavior is consistent with my intentions. As Churchill said, "Never! Never! Never! Never give up!"

5. Perspective: I take time to enter each day quietly in a mood of reflection. This reflection helps me to get myself focused and allows me to listen to my inner self and to see things more clearly.[112] (Kenneth Blanchard and Norman Vincent Peale, *The Power of Ethical Management.* New York: Wm. Morrow & Co., 1988. p. 80.)

In the final section of this chapter are several sets of corporate values included in case histories. They form a body of thought that can be critiqued for its ethical efficacy or as a guide for anyone seeking to develop benchmarks of a corporate culture.

CASE HISTORIES

Consider the two strategies cited under "Managing Accountability In The Corporation" above and suggest what their philosophical roots might be by comparing them to the "exemplars" found in Chapter 3.

Consider the case histories below and analyze their philosophical foundations. Compare and contrast these "corporate cultures."

Cummins Engine Company

When Cummins Engine was founded in 1919, the company explicitly highlighted individual worth and ingenuity as the core of its values, but over the years these were gradually forgotten. As the company grew, they hired managers from Detroit's large automotive firms instead of developing managers from within. These new supervisors, who were not steeped in Cummins' values, neglected the many talents the line workers had to offer; instead they operated by a management system developed at the height of the Industrial Revolution, when the assembly line had been broken down into simple tasks that the under-educated, mostly immigrant workers of that day could understand.

As a result, by the time James Henderson joined Cummins, the company had had seven strikes within a three-year period. "Accountants and production managers loved that old management system," says Henderson, now Cummins' president, "because they could easily count bolts and widgets as they came along the line." That became the measure of produc-

tivity, and it created an ever-widening chasm between the worker and management. It was time for Cummins to return to the basics.[113] The first step was to develop a set of core values that employees could use to measure their own performance and be measured by. The Cummins team created a list that focused on people:

- Trust, respect, and equity for workers.
- Commitment to the workers' full potential.
- Training as a keystone for attaining organization excellence.
- Worker participation in decision making.

Cummins decided to test its new approach in a new plant in South Carolina, and the model worked better than Henderson and his associates dared hope. Quality rose, and so did the workers' sense of commitment. For example, two women began drawing a rose on each engine they assembled. Although the artwork was hidden when the engine was painted, the rose was the women's unique statement of their commitment to quality. In the model plant, jobs were no longer broken down into narrowly defined tasks. This took some getting use to, as Henderson learned the day he called the plant manager's office several times and no one answered. When he finally reached the manager at his home later in the evening, Henderson learned that the manager, his secretary, the receptionist, and every other available person in the building had been down on the assembly line all day filling a rush order.[114]

Eckerd's Corporate Values

The Eckerd Corporation (a large drugstore chain) developed a list of six core values "which we believe will make a difference in the productivity and morale of any enterprise," according to Max DePree in *Leadership Is An Art*. They are: "(1) The Value of the Worker – As Martin Luther said, every job is to glorify God, and every worker is infinitely significant. All who labor, no matter how menial their task, must be treated with respect and dignity. That means corporate leaders need to enlist the help of every employee in solving workplace problems. It's the right thing to do — and it's good business. (2) Walking and Talking in the Trenches – How do you get those values out to the people doing the work? How do you find out what values the worker needs? Ivory-tower management doesn't work; managers need to lead their forces by going to the front lines themselves. (3) Responsibility and the Pursuit of Excellence – No work that is less than our best can be personally meaningful or rewarding. And no work that is less than our best can be truly profitable. When we encourage excellence, we undercut the corrosive ethic of entitlement. (4) The Value of Training – Developing the skills of employees is not only good for the individual, increasing loyalty and sense of self-worth; it also makes them more valuable to the organization. (5) Dollars and Sense – This is the profit motive. We're not so other worldly as to think that multi-million-dollar corporations ought to exist just for the general good, or that people work hard just because they like to. For most, the greatest motivation comes from incentive pay and healthy competition. (6) Working to Serve – Effective leadership includes enabling others to meet goals. No one said it better than Jesus: He who would lead, let him serve. Incorporating these six principles into the workplace will not only give workers a sense of the dignity and goodness of work, it will improve productivity and profitability as well. But don't take our word for it. Look at those who have embraced these principles. Their successes speak for themselves."[115]

Alcoa Example

Fred Fetterolf, Alcoa's president, knows every side of the aluminum industry, having worked his way up through the ranks of Alcoa over many years. "I've worked for Alcoa all my life," said Fetterolf, "but we had really never articulated a vision for the company or a set of values that we wore on our foreheads and could be judged by." Led by Fetterolf and Paul O'Neill, Alcoa's chairman (who had distinguished himself as assistant budget director for the federal government), the company spent millions of dollars and thousands of work hours to define and instill six core values into its 60,000 workers, managers, and executives: 1) integrity, 2) safety and health, 3) quality of work, 4) treatment of people, 5) accountability, and 6) profitability.

Once the values were set, O'Neill and Fetterolf faced the task of convincing the workers they were sincere. Since such moral principles as truthfulness, compassion, and accountability formed the cornerstone of the six values, O'Neill and Fetterolf began talking openly about their own strong personal beliefs, which provided the resolve it took to see new values put to work in the company. Fetterolf said he "used to duck" the issue of his personal religious faith "by talking generally about faith and ethics." "Now with our new set of values, I felt compelled to get up-front about my (personal) convictions. Everyone may not agree, but I believe there is respect for those who declare themselves."

For some time, those new values were against basic, bottom-line business instincts, as Fetterolf discovered when he and a vice president visited one of the company's most remote sites, a bauxite mine in Suriname. After landing on the single airstrip cut into a lush tropical hillside, the two executives were escorted by the plant manager to the mining site. There they watched an earth mover claw through the rock into the ore. As the operator backed away to position the vehicle for a new approach, two other workers almost stumbled into its path because its safety lights and siren weren't working. The vice president asked the plant manager why the safety equipment wasn't working and how long it would take to fix it. "Ordinarily, repairs are made at night after the mine shuts down," the manager said. "It could take a couple of hours or more."

"Shut down the mine until that vehicle is repaired,"

the vice president said firmly. The news spread fast. Alcoa's managers were actually practicing what they preached, placing worker safety above production! Of course it takes more than one decision to convince workers that a company is serious about new values. Employees wondered if this was just another management whim that would pass when the economy turned sour. They soon learned that the changes were real. And it has made a difference. The company recently reported that, companywide, work days lost to injuries declined significantly over the past several years.[116]

The Employee As Partner

A set of corporately held values and goals is the soul of an organization, and the first of those, the heart of any enterprise, should be the value placed on individual workers. Jack Eckerd learned this early on. He remembers well the summer of 1959 when he sat nervously outside the office of the president of one of Tampa's largest banks. Jack's weathered briefcase bulged with the financial reports he hoped would prove his young chain of five self-service drugstores was worthy of the bank's support. He was convinced the figures spoke for themselves. So was George Jenkins, the founder of Publix Supermarkets. Jenkins had just offered Jack the opportunity to open Eckerd Drugstores in five new Publix centers around Tampa Bay – and also the right of first refusal each time the successful grocer opened one of the hundreds of strip centers springing up throughout Florida.[117] All Jack needed was a bank loan.

"But his banker thought differently, as Jack discovered once he got inside the man's office. "You're trying to grow too fast, Jack," said the bank president. "Two Publix locations instead of five." Jack couldn't do that – the deal he'd been offered was double or nothing. He needed funds for five new stores, and he needed them fast. So he scooped up his spreadsheets and calculations, thanked the banker and headed across the street to talk to the bank's fiercest competitor. Once again he explained his plan as hard as he knew how. "These numbers and projections are real," Jack said. "I can double my size and profits in two years. The economies of scale will increase each store's purchasing power and decrease its advertising

costs." "Yes, I can see how you could say that," the banker said dryly as he stared out the window overlooking Tampa Bay, avoiding Jack's gaze. "He's going to turn me down," Jack thought. Figuring he had little to lose at this point, he played his last card. Leaning across the bank president's desk, he pointed to the balance sheet. "You bankers look at my projections, my balance sheet, and my 35% annual growth from this new type of drugstore," Jack said insistently. "But you're missing the biggest asset I have. My people. They are the best. You won't find that on any spread sheet, but believe me, it's true."

Jack left the bank with a $750,000 loan. His belief in his people had turned the tide. "Over the succeeding years, those employees did indeed help make the difference. And when he was finally in a position to do so, and for the rest of his business career, Jack rewarded his employees' efforts many times over for their part in the success of Eckerd Drugs. Eckerd's doubled its size and profits on schedule, and large amounts of capital were needed again. Jack's financial advisers convinced him that converting Eckerd Drugs from a privately held to a publicly traded company was the best way to get the capital to continue growing. Within weeks of going public the stock price almost doubled. "Well Jack, you're a wealthy man," said his attorney, referring to the proceeds from newly issued shares of Eckerd stock. "Only on paper," Jack quipped. "And besides, it's not all mine." "What do you mean? It was your company and you only sold a small part of it." "Yes, but some of the rest belongs to my employees. They deserve to be cut in on the action. They also worked hard to build this company." "You mean you want to sell them some of the stock at a reduced rate?" "No," Jack said, " I want to give them some stock! – on some sort of equitable basis. Maybe length of time with the company and the degree of individual responsibility." The lawyer protested: "The IRS will give us problems. They'll want to charge you a gift tax." "Well, that's your job," Jack said. "Work it out."

The attorney worked it out. Those Eckerd employees who held onto the stock saw their personal fortunes grow right along with the company's. But his employees were not the only people Jack cared for. The day he took the company public, he made a silent pledge never to make a business decision unless it looked good for his customers, his stockholders, and Eckerd Drug employees. Eckerd also responded to his customers' needs and concerns, not just their buying power. In 1971 a concerned grandmother wrote complaining about the risque books sold on Eckerd's book racks. She did not like a paperback her 14-year-old grandson had purchased at Eckerd's. She sent Jack a copy in which she had underlined the steamy and provocative passages. Jack was shocked. Within 48 hours the books came off the shelves, along with *Playboy* and *Hustler* magazines. "Mr. Eckerd, we'll lose $3-million in sales by eliminating those books from the racks," one of his vice presidents told him. "I don't think we'll lose anything," Jack replied, "because our customers trust us to do the right thing. After all, we do advertise as 'America's Family Drug Stores.'" Sales the next year increased 43%.[118]

Brock Candy

Frank Brock, of the Brock Candy Company and now president of Covenant College in Lookout Mountain, Tenn., provides a compassionate and concrete example of how respect for individual workers helped him turn his business around. Frank Brock has always had the loose gait and "gee whiz" manner of a boy from Tennessee; at 29 years of age, he looked 19. Straight out of a hitch with the Air Force and with his Harvard Business School diploma in hand, he felt less than confident about taking over the family business. He had the right last name to become the executive vice president of the Brock Candy Company, but little else. Still, he was determined to run the business. It was in his blood. Initially Frank spent 90% of his time at the plant just learning the ropes. Often he felt he was on the ropes himself. Brock's market share was plummeting, and he had to find out why. It was then that the young executive remembered the advice his Air Force commanding officer had given him: "A general can't fight a battle from the War Room. He's got to get to the troops." So Frank assembled his troops, the men and women on the line – bakers, candy boilers, and assembly operators. "You folks know more about candy making than I'll ever know," the soft-spoken Brock told them. "Some of you have

been at it longer than I've been alive. So tell me, what's wrong?"

The workers shifted nervously. Sensing their anxiety and the reason for it, Frank reassured them. "People, trust me when I tell you that what you say in this room will stay with me. No manager is going to hassle you because of it." Evelyn, the chief baker who had been with Brock for almost 20 years, looked up at Frank and sighed heavily. "If you want to know what's wrong with the candy, Mr. Brock, just ask one of my kids. They'll tell you there's more scrap in the bag than there is whole candy."

Referring to Brock's autocratic and immensely unpopular predecessor, Evelyn added: "That crazy German ordered us to throw some of the crushed candy scraps into every bag to get the weight up." "If you want to know why Brock candy ain't sellin', that's it – or at least part of it," observed Delmer, a key operator on the assembly line. "That will be changed. Today!" Frank declared. "Now what else do I need to know?" Gradually the workers opened up, telling him ways they thought quality and production could be improved. Some were helpful, others were not. But the young manufacturer learned his first important lesson: People want to work, and they want to take pride in the products they produce. And the workers learned something, too: Their boss would listen, and he cared about them as people, not just as cogs in a machine.

After the meeting, Evelyn held back until the others had left. "Mr. Brock, there's something else you may want to know about. You know Delmer, the operator in assembly?" Frank nodded. "Well, Mr. Brock, he hasn't got any water in his house. Maybe someone could look into it." Then she scurried from the room, afraid she had said too much. A few days later Frank drove up into the foothills surrounding Chattanooga, around treacherous curves and through cuts in the rugged mountain, to the small town where Delmer lived. There he found that Delmer not only had no running water, but that his wife, Mildred, was bedridden. Deeply moved by their plight, Frank began to look for some solutions. A water line, he discovered, ran along the main road that led to the rural home. It wouldn't take much to dig a line a quarter of a mile up the the hollow to the house. Evelyn agreed to recruit a couple of men from the plant to help, and Frank provided the materials. Before long, Delmer and Mildred had "runnin' water." At the next meeting of Frank's new Employee Task Force, Evelyn said: "Mr. Brock, we all know what you did for Delmer, and we want you to know that we all appreciate it. We just want to say thanks." Then, following the meeting, she walked right up and addressed her boss confidently: "Mr. Brock, you know we've got no windows in this plant?" The following year the workers at Brock Candy Company moved into their new, sunlit facility.

Frank's eyes still sparkle when he remembers those early days and the wellspring of wisdom he found in his employees. His deeply held belief that each individual is valuable enabled him to lead effectively, make better business decisions, and encourage greater productivity from his employees.[119] It is unrealistic to suggest that managers can become personally involved in the lives of each and every worker. But a sense of intimacy and mutual trust can be instilled in the workplace when managers show genuine concern for the individual employees.

READINGS

IN THE EYE OF THE BEHOLDER
James M. Kouzes and Barry Z. Posner

What you have heard about leadership is only half the story. Leadership is not only about leaders, it is also about followers. Leadership is a reciprocal process. It occurs between people. It is not done by one person to another.

Successful leadership depends far more upon the follower's perception of the leader than upon the leader's abilities. Followers determine when someone possesses the qualities of leadership, not the leader. Leadership is in the eye of the follower.

Unfortunately, writings, old and new, about leadership ignore the follower. We know what Lee Iacocca, Harold Geneen, Robert Townsend and other executives say about leadership. But what do their subordinates say about them? Those might make even more insightful and entertaining books.

Over the past five years we (with Warren Schmidt) have been investigating the perceptions followers have of leaders. We have asked more than 3,400 managers nationwide from a wide range of private and public organizations to tell us what it is they look for or admire in their leaders.

The results from these surveys have been striking in their regularity. It would seem there are several essential tests a leader must pass before we are willing to grant him or her the title of "Leader."

Most of those characteristics are never taught in leadership classes or found in textbooks. However, if we look closely, we will see that traits are shared by all great leaders. What are those characteristics? According to our research true leaders are honest, competent, forward-looking, inspiring and, ultimately, credible. Surprised?

In every survey we conducted, honesty was selected more often than any other leadership characteristic. When you think about it, honesty is a reasonable requirement. After all, if we are to willingly follow someone, whether it be into battle or into the boardroom, we first want to assure ourselves that the person is worthy of our trust. Is that person truthful? Of high integrity? Have character? Ethical? Is he or she principled?

That is not a simple question to answer. How do followers measure such subjective characteristics? In our discussions with respondents we found that it was the leader's behavior that provided the evidence. In other words, whatever leaders say about their integrity, followers wait to be shown.

Leaders are considered honest by followers if they do what they say they are going to do. Agreements not followed through, false promises, coverups, inconsistency between word and deed are all indicators that an ostensible leader is not honest. On the other hand, if a leader behaves in ways consistent with his or her stated values and beliefs, then we can entrust to that person our careers, our security, even our lives.

This element of trustworthiness is supported in another study we conducted of leadership practices. In that study we found that of all behaviors describing leadership, the most important single item was the leader's display of trust of others. Irwin Federman, President and CEO of microchipmaker Monolithic Memories, says it best: "Trust is a risk game. The leader must ante up first."

Sam Walton, founder and chairman of Wal-Mart Stores Inc., provides an excellent example of honesty in leadership: In 1983 Walton – rated by Forbes to be the richest man in the country – made a wager. Concerned the company might have a disappointing year, he bet Wal-Mart employees that if they achieved a greater profit than in previous years he would put on a hula skirt and hula down Wall Street. They did; and he did.

Sam kept his word. He did what he said he was going to do. He showed he had integrity, even if it meant public embarrassment. But imagine what would have happened had Sam not kept his word. Would his employees then have anted-up for the next bet?

The attribute chosen next most frequently for leaders is competence. To enlist in another's cause, we must believe that person knows what she or he is doing. We must see the person as capable and effective. If we doubt the leader's abilities, we are unlikely to enlist in the crusade.

Leadership competence does not necessarily refer to the leader's technical abilities. Rather, the competence followers look for varies with the leader's position and the condition of the company.

For example, the higher the rank of the leader, the more people demand to see demonstration of abilities in strategic planning and policy-making. If a company desperately needs to clarify its corporate strategy, a CEO with savvy in competitive marketing may be seen as a fine leader. But, at the-line functional level, where subordinates expect guidance in technical areas, these same managerial abilities will not be enough.

We have come to refer to the kind of competence needed by leaders as value-added competence. Func-

tional competence may be necessary, but it is insufficient. The leader must bring some added value to the position.

Tom Melohn, President of North American Tool and Die in San Leandro, Cal., is a case in point. Tom, along with a partner, bought NATD seven years ago. A former consumer products executive, Tom knows nothing about how to run a drill press or a stamping machine. He claims he can't even screw the license plates on his car. Yet, in the seven years since he bought the company, NATD has excelled in every possible measure in its industry.

If Tom brings no industry, company or technical expertise to NATD, what has enabled him to lead the firm to its astounding results? Our answer: Tom added to the firm what it most needed at the time – the abilities to motivate and to sell. Tom entrusted the skilled employees with the work they knew well, and for his part, he applied the selling skills he had learned from a quarter-century in marketing consumer products. He also rewarded and recognized the NATD "gang" for their accomplishments, increasing their financial and emotional sense of ownership in the firm.

Over half of our respondents selected "forward-looking" as their third most sought-after leadership trait. We expect our leaders to have a sense of direction and a concern for the future of the company. Some use the word "vision." Others, the word "dream." Still others refer to this sense of direction as a "calling," "a personal agenda." Whatever the word, the message is clear: True leaders must know where they are going.

Surprisingly, even executives at the top, where one would think it a prerequisite, are wanting in this area. A study we conducted of 284 senior executives found "developing a strategic planning and forecasting capability" as the most critical concern. These same senior managers, when asked to select the most important characteristics in a CEO, cited "a leadership style of honesty and integrity" first, followed by "a long-term vision and direction for the company."

It is important to note that by forward-looking we do not mean the magical power of a prescient visionary. The reality is far more down-to-earth: It is the ability to set or select a desirable destination toward which the organization should head. The vision of a leader is the compass that sets the course of the company. A leader's "vision" is, in this way, simple to an architect's model of a new building or an engineer's prototype of a new product.

Think of it another way. Suppose you wanted to take a trip to a place to which you had never been before – say, Nairobi, Kenya. What would you do over the next few days if you knew you were going to go to Nairobi in six months? Probably get a map, for one thing. Read a book on the city. Look at pictures. Talk to someone who has been there. Find out what sites to see. What the weather is like. What to wear. Where to eat. Where to shop. Where to stay ....

Followers ask nothing more from a leader than a similar kind of orientation. Just what will the company look like, feel like, be like when it arrives at its goal six months or six years from now? Describe it to us. Tell us in rich detail so that we will know when we have arrived and so we can select the proper route to take getting there.

We expect our leaders to be enthusiastic, energetic and positive about the future. A bit of a cheerleader, as a matter of fact.

It is not enough for a leader to have a dream about the future. He or she must be able to communicate the vision in ways that encourage us to sign on for the duration. As Apple Computer manager Dave Patterson puts it, "The leader is the evangelist of the dream."

In his book *Working,* Studs Terkel quotes Nora Watson, an editor: "I think most of us are looking for a calling, not a job. Most of us, like the assembly line worker, have jobs that are too small for our spirit. Jobs are not big enough for people."

Her words underscore how important it is to find some greater sense of purpose and worth in our day-to-day working life. While the enthusiasm, energy and positive attitude of a good leader may not change the nature of work on the assembly line, they surely can make that work more enjoyable.

Some people react with discomfort to the idea that "inspiring" is an essential leadership quality. One chief executive officer of a large corporation even told us, "I don't trust people who are inspiring" – no doubt in response to past crusaders who led their followers to death or destruction. Other executives are skeptical of their ability to inspire others.

Both are making a terrible mistake. In the final analysis, it is essential that leaders inspire our confidence in the validity of the goal. Enthusiasm and excitement signal the leader's personal conviction to pursuing that dream. If a leader displays no passion for a cause, why should others?

Honest. Competent. Forward-looking. Inspiring. This may not be an altogether surprising list of leadership attributes – except, perhaps, for honesty. Put together, these four characteristics comprise what communications experts refer to as "credibility."

What we have found, quite unexpectedly, in our investigation of admired leadership qualities is that more than anything, we want leaders who are credible.

Ask yourself: Do you talk about your boss when he or she isn't around? Of course, you say. We all do. But what do you say? Do you say, "You've got to be careful around him," or, "You can't always believe what she says"? Or do you say, "If she says it's so, you can count on it," or, "He's a man of his word"? The confidence we privately express in the credibility of our leaders is what ultimately determines whether we will allow that person to lead us.

Why? It's a matter of security.

When we believe a leader is credible; when we believe he or she is honest, competent, has a sense of the future and a personal conviction about the path, then we somehow feel more secure around that leader. This sense of security enables us to let go of our reservations and release enormous personal energy on behalf of the common vision.

Credibility is extremely fragile. It takes years to earn it, an instant to lose it. Credibility grows minute by minute, hour by hour, day by day, through persistent, consistent, patient exhibition of the four leadership traits. It is lost with one false step, one thoughtless remark, one inconsistent act, one broken agreement, one lie, one coverup. It may not seem right to be judged so harshly or measured so toughly. But followers perceive leadership in their own terms, and those terms aren't always fair.

The astute commentator Edward R. Murrow put it so concisely when he said, *"To be persuasive we must be believable; to be believable, we must be credible; to be credible we must be truthful."*

Leadership is a relationship. A unique and special trust between leader and follower. The development of this relationship requires our full attention as potential leaders. We have found five prerequisites to building this trust.

1. Know your followers. Building any relationship begins with getting to know those we desire to lead. Get to know their hopes, their fears, their values, their biases, their dreams, their nightmares, their aspirations and their disappointments. Find out what is important to your followers. Come to know what they seek. Only in this way can you show them how their interests can be served by aligning with yours.

Michael McCall and Michael Lombardo of the Center for Creative Leadership, in reporting on their study of executives who were derailed during their careers, point out: *"Ability – or inability – to understand other people's perspectives was the most glaring difference between arrivers and the derailed."* Richard Hagberg of Knowdell, Martin, Hagberg Inc., reports similar results of a study of terminated executives. He found these individuals to be socially unskilled, unable to trust others and having a history of poor relationships.

2. Stand up for your beliefs. In our culture we appreciate people who take a stand. We resolutely refuse to follow people who lack confidence in their own values and decisions. Confusion among your followers over your stand creates stress; not knowing what you believe leads to conflict, indecision and political rivalry.

There is, however, a danger in always standing on principle. It can make one rigid and insensitive, precisely the attributes that lead to derailment and termination. The key to escaping rigidity is to remain open to others. Listen. Understand. Empathize.

We respect a leader who can listen to and understand our point of view, yet believe in his or her heart that other viewpoints are superior. If your beliefs are strongly held, ethical and based on sound thinking, followers will find ways to align themselves with you.

3. Speak with passion. Managers constantly talk about motivating their people, of lighting a fire under them. But if the leader is a wet match, there will be no spark to ignite passion in others. Enthusiasm, energy and commitment begin with the leader. To gain the commitment of others you must communicate your excitement about the dream.

Donald Kennedy, president of Stanford University, identifies one way to effectively communicate with others: *"The essence of leadership is to energetically reflect back to the institution how it best thinks of itself."*

People need to know how they are when they are at their best, not at their worst. The leader has a responsibility to help followers see a positive image of themselves. A negative image depresses performance.

Effective leadership means delivering the message in a way that lives and breathes. Napoleon is reported to have said, "If you want to lead the people, you must first speak to their eyes." Paint word pictures. Tell stories. Relate anecdotes. Weave metaphors. Enable others to see, hear, taste, smell, feel what you experience. When the dream lives inside others, it lives forever.

Being expressive does not require you to preach. It might help to be a bit of an evangelist, but it certainly isn't necessary. Faith sits in the pews as well as stands in the pulpit. To inspire literally means to "breathe life into." Share your dreams, your hopes, your aspirations with others.

4. Lead by example. Leaders are role models. We look to them for clues on how we should behave. We believe their actions over their words, every time.

We will never forget the story told to us by a young supervisor, John Shultz, about his days as a high school football player:

"When I played high school football, I had three coaches. The first two were exactly alike. Each said, 'Men while you are training I don't want you to smoke, drink, stay up late or fool around with girls. Got that?'

"Then we would watch our coaches during the season. They would smoke, drink, stay up late and fool around with women. So what do you suppose we did? Boys will be boys, after all.

"My third coach was the best I ever had. At the beginning of the season we had the same locker room sermon as with the other coaches. Except this coach just said, 'I have only one rule. You can do anything I do. If I smoke, drink, stay up late or fool around with women, then I would expect you to do the same. But if I don't, you better not! '"

If leaders ask followers to observe certain standards, then the leaders need to live by the same rules. That is exactly what we were told many times by exemplary leaders. You can only lead by example.

Leadership is not a spectator sport. Leaders don't sit in the stands and watch. But hero myths aside, neither are leaders in the game substituting for the players. Leaders coach. They show others how to behave on and off the field. They demonstrate what is important by how they spend their time, by the priorities on their agenda, by the questions they ask, by the people they see and the places they go.

Every step a leader takes, every move he or she makes is watched. Leaders are always on stage. They are always being tested. And it is the followers who decide whether to leave quietly at intermission or stay through the final act and loudly applaud the performance.

5. Conquer yourself. Jim Whittaker is the first American to reach the summit of Mt. Everest. He is also the first to lead an American team to the summit of K2, the second highest mountain in the world. One of the many things Jim says he has learned from his mountain climbing experience is that "you never conquer a mountain . Mountains can't be conquered. You conquer yourself – your hopes, your fears."

It might brighten our heroic image of leaders to believe that they conquer organizations, communities, states, nations, the world. It might make good cinema to picture the leader riding into town on a white horse and single-handedly destroying the villains. But this Lone Ranger portrait of great leaders only perpetuates a falsehood.

The real struggle of leadership is internal. Do you understand what is going on in the company and the world in which it operates? Are you prepared to handle the problems the company is facing? Did you make the right decision? Did you do the right thing? Where do you think the company should be headed? Are you the right one to lead others there? These and more are the everyday struggle of leadership.

This inner leadership struggle places enormous stress upon the leader. Followers do not want to see that their leaders lack self-confidence. Sure, they like to know their leaders are human, that they can laugh and cry and have a good time. But followers will not place their confidence in someone who appears weak, uncertain or lacking in resolve. Followers need to sense that the leader's internal struggle has been fought and won.

What Is a Leader To Do?

The self-confidence required to lead has in its core two sources: knowledge and integrity.

Warren Bennis and Burt Nanus, in their book *Leaders: The Strategies for Taking Charge,* observe that "Leaders are perpetual learners ... Learning is the essential fuel for the leader, the source of high-octane energy that keeps up the momentum by continually sparking new understanding, new ideas, and new challenges."

Conquering yourself means learning about yourself – skills, inadequacies, beliefs, prejudices, talents and shortcomings. Self-confidence develops as one builds on strengths and overcomes weaknesses.

Self-confidence also comes with worldliness. The leader, being in the forefront, is usually the first to encounter the world outside the boundaries of the organization. The more the leader knows about that world, the easier it is to approach it with assurance. Thus, he or she should seek to learn as much as possible about the forces that affect organizations, be they political, economical, social, moral or artistic.

With knowledge of the inner and outer worlds comes an awareness of the competing value systems, of the many different ways to run a business. The internal resolution of these competing beliefs is what leads to personal integrity. A leader with integrity has one self, at home and at work. The same one with family and with colleagues.

However, a person with integrity is not one-dimensional. He or she may have numerous pursuits and interests – arts and literature, science and technology, entertainment and sports, politics and law.

Holding these parts together is a fundamental set of values and beliefs. The late industrialist, John Studebaker, stated it most clearly:

"To have integrity the individual cannot merely be a weathervane turning briskly with every doctrinal wind that blows. He must possess key loyalties and key convictions which can serve as a basis of judgment and a standard of action."

Conquering yourself begins with those key convictions, with determining your value system. Strongly held beliefs compel you to take a stand.

There is no well-cut path to the future, only wilderness. If you as a prospective leader are to have the self-confidence needed to step out into the unknown you might begin each day by looking in the mirror and asking, "Just what do I stand for?"

(Excerpted from *Vision/Action*, March 1986, by James M. Kouzes and Barry Z. Posner.)

ETHICS AND THE INVESTMENT INDUSTRY
Thomas C. Widner

About three-dozen business men and women, educators, church people and lawyers came together for three days in early November at the University of Notre Dame to find out if ethics has any relevance to the investment industry. They were brought there by John W. Houck and Frank K. Reilly, both professors in the Notre Dame College of Business, and Oliver F. Williams, C.S.C., the university's associate provost and co-director with Professor Houck of the Notre Dame Center for Ethics and Religious Values in Business, which convened the conference.

In the keynote address John W. Phelan Jr., chairman of the board of the New York Stock Exchange, described three temptations to resist in business ethics. The first is the temptation to think one can set "crystal clear" rules for the industry; the second, to equate business ethics with the law; and the third, to look down on commerce and ignore it as an unworthy endeavor. Mr. Phelan called for strict accountability in the business world. Its goal, he said, is to produce products and services and provide employment opportunities for all "so they find their part in the American dream. It is to raise the standard of living for people so they find a better quality of life."

Mr. Phelan noted that the Exchange had spent three years studying and identifying its own values – integrity, excellence, respect for people and sensitivity to customers. Its employees are now questioning themselves about the meaning of these values – a difficult task, Phelan admitted, since leaders in an organization have to be living them constantly. They have to do more than just make the company more efficient. "It is only by businessmen setting up and adhering to the highest principles and making sure that everyone who comes under their authority adheres and subscribes to them that we can ever begin to make an impact on all the ethical problems that we see in our industry. A truly ethical person observes a stricter set of standards than merely the legal ones."

Though Phelan's address was the keynoter, it was not the starting point of the conference. That role was taken by Gregg A. Jarrell, former chief economist of the Securities and Exchange Commission, who said the surge of insider trading scandals "is supporting the impression that the business of Wall Street is fundamentally unethical." Mr. Jarrell believes that "there is nothing inherently unethical about the business conducted by the investment bankers, corporate lawyers and institutional traders." Indeed, Jarrell regards the heavy mergers and acquisitions activity of the past few years as "a beneficial process of change that is absolutely vital to the efficient allocation of corporate assets among competing management teams." Moreover, he sees this process as "unavoidable and essential if America is to prosper in the face of growing global competition."

Richard DeGeorge, professor of philosophy at the University of Kansas, told participants there are two ethical principles that apply to market competition – fairness, and the benefit of society in general. To those who demand that business schools be required to graduate ethical students, DeGeorge responds that such schools "tend to produce the kinds of people business wants." These he described as the kind of "savvy, skilled, aggressive, imaginative people who are able to increase the profits of the companies for which they will work."

Two Notre Dame law professors addressed the legal problems of the insider trading scandals. G. Robert Blakey and Patricia O'Hara quoted R. Foster Winans, the former *Wall Street Journal* reporter whose conviction along with two others on mail and wire fraud charges was upheld recently by the U.S. Supreme Court. Mr. Winans said he knew "it was unethical to have an undisclosed interest in the subjects I write about." Nevertheless, "I couldn't see what laws I had broken."

According to Professors Blakey and O'Hara, this attitude is too often the bottom line in any of the public discussions about insider trading. They claim that laws on insider trading do not coincide with the people's perception of the ethics of such conduct. "Stripped to its barest essentials, use of material, non-public information is conversion (unlawful appropriation and use of another's property) or theft." The trader uses his information – intended only for corporate purposes – for his personal benefit. The law's difficulty is that the corporation may not be damaged by the wrong, while the persons on the other side of the defendant's trades may not always be able to establish a causal link between the defendant's conduct and their alleged injury. So the difference between what is ethical and what is legal is not always clear, and the public, in its inability to recognize the significance of such a distinction, remains confused.

What is unjust about insider trading? Donald W. Shriver Jr., president of Union Theological Seminary in New York City, suggested that "it expands and capitalizes on unjust distributions of power already in place in society." It corrupts by inducing those in power to impose their will on the least powerful; it undercuts majorities by putting their interests second to the interests of a secretive minority; it misappropriates information, and it attempts to subvert and bypass legal controls that express something of the ethical wisdom of political democracy.

Few of the delegates to the conference left completely reassured they could work in an investment industry flawless in its ethical stance. Yet the fact that many had come together seeking answers was significant. The program was supported by some major corporation – General Electric, Dean Witter, Hershey Foods. The Notre Dame Center for Ethics and Religious Values in Business will publish the papers presented at the conference. They will be an important reference for future participants in the international business community.

(Reprinted from *America*, December 12, 1987, by Thomas C. Widner.)

ENDNOTES

1. Michael W. Hoffman and Jennifer Mills Moore, *Business Ethics*, McGraw-Hill, N.Y., 1990, pp. 1-3.
2. "Corporate Ethics: A Prime Business Asset," *The Business Roundtable*, February, 1988, p. 4.
3. Thomas G. Labrecque, "Good Ethics is Good Business," *USA Today*, May, 1990, pp. 20-21.
4-10. Labrecque, p. 20-21.
11. Paul O. Sand, "Business Ethics: A Trend Toward Ethical Cynicism," *Vital Speeches of the Day*, Nov. 15, 1988, pp. 85-86.
12. Sand, p. 86.
13. Daniel E. Maltby, "The One-Minute Ethicist," *Christianity Today*, Feb. 19, 1988, pp. 26-29.
14. *Webster's Third New International Dictionary*, G. & C. Merriam, Springfield, Mass., 1981, p. 302.
15. *Webster's New World Dictionary of American English*, 3rd. ed., Simon & Schuster, New York, 1988, p. 311.
16. *Webster's New Collegiate Dictionary*, G. & C. Merriam, Springfield, Mass., 1975, p. 392.
17. Barbara Lay Toffler, *Tough Choices: Managers Talk Ethics*, Wiley and Sons, New York, 1986, pp. 10.
18-21. Toffler, p. 10.
22. Peter Madsen and Jay M. Shafritz, eds., *Essentials of Business Ethics*, New American Library, New York, 1990, p. 11.
23. Kenneth Blanchard and Norman Vincent Peale, *The Power of Ethical Management*, William Morrow, New York, 1988, pp. 27-28.
24-25. Ibid.
26. *Webster's Third New International Dictionary*, p. 1811.
27. Madsen and Shafritz, p. 30.
28. Phillip L. Berman, *Courage of Conviction*, Dodd, Mead, Inc., New York, 1985, pp. 109-110.
29. Berman, p. 111.
30. Thomas Donaldson, *Case Studies in Business Ethics*, Prentice-Hall, Englewood Cliffs, N. J., 1984, p. 111.
31-32. Donaldson, p. 112-113.
33. Thomas Donaldson, *Corporations and Morality*, PrenticeHall, Englewood Cliffs, N. J., 1982, pp. 114-115.
34. Peter Drucker, *Concept of the Corporation*, rev. ed., JohnDay, Inc., New York, 1972, p. 88.
35. Floyd W. Windal and Robert N. Corley, *The Accounting Professional: Ethics, Responsibility, and Liability*, Prentice-Hall, Englewood Cliffs, N. J., 1980, p. 8.
36. Windal and Corley, p. 8.
37. Windal and Corley, p. 10.
38. Mark Brimer and Michael Moran, "Building Ethical Organizations - The Role of Management," *Physical Therapy Forum*, May 22, 1992, p. 4.
39. Barry Posner and Warren Schmidt "Values and the American Manager: An Up-Date," *California Management Review*, Spring, 1984, pp. 202-215.
40-42. Brimer and Moran, p. 6.
43. Sarah Glazer, "Policing the Professions," *Editorial Research Reports*, May 26, 1989, p. 290. 44.

Glazer, p. 290.

45-59. Glazer, p. 291, 295, 302

60-64. Hoffman and Moore, pp. 1-3, 129, 130,133.

65. "How Business Should Act Under Fire," *Business Week*,May 29, 1989, p. 122.

66. Gerald F. Cavanagh and Phillip J. Chmielewski, "Ethics and the Free Market," *America*, Jan. 31, 1987, pp. 79-82.67. Cavanagh and Chmielewski, p. 82.

68. Keith Davis, "Five Propositions for Social Responsibility," *Business Horizons*, June, 1975, pp. 19-24.

69-82. Davis, p. 22-24.

83. William H. Newman, Charles E. Summer, and E. Kirby Warren, *The Process of Management*, Prentice-Hall, Englewood Cliffs, N. J., 1967, p. 173.

84. Newman, Summer, and Warren, p. 173.

85. Newman, Summer, and Warren, p. 173.

86. Jay W. Lorsch, "Managing Culture: The Invisible Barrier to Strategic Change," *California Management Review,* Winter, 1986, pp. 95-109.

87. Stanley M. Davis, quoted by Alyse Lynn Booth, "Who Are We?" *Public Relations Journal,* July, 1985, pp. 14-44.

88. W. Brooke Tunstall, "Cultural Transition at AT & T," *Sloan Management Review*, Fall, 1983, pp. 15-26.

89. Newman, Summer, and Warren, p. 178.

90. Newman, Summer, and Warren, pp. 188-189.

91. William D. Hitt, *Ethics and Leadership: Putting Theory Into Practice*, Battelle Press, Columbus, Ohio, 1990, p. 1.

92-94. Hitt, p. 2-3.

95. Donaldson, p. 118.

96. Dorothy Emmet, *Rules, Roles and Relations*, St. Martin's Press, New York, 1967, p. 118-215.

97. Donaldson, p. 119.

98. Paul Kurtz, ed., "The Individual, the Organization, and Participatory Democracy," *Problems in Contemporary Society*, Prentice-Hall, Englewood Cliffs, N. J., p. 193.

99-100. Donaldson, p. 119-120.

101. Richard Sennette, "The Boss's New Clothes," *The New York Review of Books,* Feb. 22, 1979, p. 44.

102. Donaldson, p. 120.

103. Boye De Mente, *Japanese Etiquette & Ethics in Business*,Passport Books, Lincolnwood, Ill., 1987, p. 74.

104-108. De Mente, p. 74.

109-111. Thompson, p. 39.

112. Blanchard and Peale, p. 80.

113. Chuck Colson and Jack Eckerd, *Why America Doesn't Work*, Word Publishing Co., Dallas, Texas, 1991, p. 127.

114-119.Colson and Eckerd, p. 127-138.

120. Preston Townley, "Business Ethics," *Vital Speeches of the Day,* Nov. 3, 1991, pp. 208-211.

121. Thomas C. Widner, "Ethics and the Investment Industry," *America*, Dec. 12, 1987, pp. 444-445.

122. James E. Perralla, "The Right Way," *Vital Speeches of the Day*, Apr. 1, 1989, pp. 375-376.

123. Myron Magnet, "The Decline & Fall of Business Ethics," *Fortune*, Dec. 8, 1986, pp. 65-72.

124. Thomas McCarroll, "Who's Counting?" *Time*, Apr. 13, 1992, pp. 48-50.

125. Thomas McCarroll, "Trading on the Inside Edge," *Time,* June 15, 1992, pp. 47-49.

126. Jacques Attali, "Finance and Ethics," *Vital Speeches of the Day*, May 1, 1992, pp. 433-437.

127. Sarah Glazer, "Policing the Professions," *Editorial Research Reports*, May 26, 1989, pp. 290-302.

FOR FURTHER INQUIRY

SUGGESTED READINGS

• Jacques Attali, "Finance and Ethics," *Vital Speeches of the Day*, May 1, 1992, Vol. 58, no. 14
• Sarah Glazer, "Policing the Professions," *Editorial Research Reports,* Congressional Quarterly, 1989
• Moskowitz, Daniel B. and John A. Byrne. "Where Business Goes to Stock Up on Ethics." *Business Week,* 3 June 1991.
• Perrella, James E. "The Right Way: A Matter of Principle." *Vital Speeches of the Day* 1 April 1989.

Chapter 16

William F. Edmonson

SOCIAL IMPLICATIONS IN BUSINESS

"We demand that big business give the people a square deal; in return we must insist that when any one engaged in big business honestly endeavors to do right he shall himself be given a square deal."

— **Theodore Roosevelt**

"Without some dissimulation, no business can be carried on at all."

— **Philip Dormer Stanhope, the Earl of Chesterfield**

"Here are all sorts of employers wanting all sorts of servants, and all sorts of servants wanting all kinds of employers, and they never seem to come together."

— **Charles Dickens, in *Martin Chuzzlewit***

An anonymous sage paraphrased philosopher Jean Jacques Rousseau to describe the modern employee: "Man is born free, but everywhere he is in organizations." Rousseau said humanity was "everywhere in chains." Those who slave for insensitive corporations see little difference.

Life in large, modern corporations too often involves succumbing to the pressures of evolution and experiencing problems typical in bureaucracies. Their troubles carry direct implications for the issue of corporate responsibility, because the extent to which people are submerged in and controlled by bureaucracies is the extent to which ordinary individual responsibility is threatened. The clerk who

William Fred Edmonson, M.B.A. University of Southern Mississippi, Ed.D. University of Mississippi, former dean of instructional affairs at Itawamba Community College in Fulton, Miss., is president of Panola College in Carthage, Tex.

works for a multibillion-dollar corporation behaves in accordance with a system of rules, but he does not make the rules, and he is not directly accountable for their consequences. In order to attain the status of moral agency, can a corporation use a decision-making process that is immoral? Hardly. So a principal aim of this chapter is to unravel the problems for developing such a process despite the complexities of modern bureaucracies.[1] Another objective is the discussion of other issues facing employers and their various obligations inside and outside the organization.

As organizations become larger, they become more bureaucratic. "The same share of manufacturing assets that was controlled by the largest 1,000 corporations in 1946 was controlled by the largest 200 corporations in 1973." More important, changes in basic structure are occurring; modern corporations look less like the traditional model, with clearly defined authority and accountability structures, and are becoming more complicated and impersonal.

The demands of technology have blurred the traditional demarcations of authority and responsibility. The resulting problems of moral responsibility are logical as well as empirical. (See also Chapter 3.) There are difficulties in assigning responsibility to corporations that deny any moral responsibility other than to make profits. The increasing bureaucratization of the corporation has threatened meaningful corporate responsibility. Three specific tendencies constitute the overall movement toward bureaucratization: 1) the increase of impersonal rules, 2) the move toward centralized decision-making, and 3) the isolation of various employees grouped by function in the corporation hierarchy. Each will be examined separately.[2]

The subjugation of the individual by the organization is an old problem. Only two centuries ago, employers openly coerced their employees into carrying out company directives with little or no question. Today, modern methods of generating conformity have an equally effective, though more subtle impact.

Of special importance is the ongoing deterioration of systems of direct supervision in favor of elaborate systems of impersonal rules and regulations. Although rule-bound work relieves people from the watchful eyes of their superiors, it causes special problems in morale and accountability.[3] Organizational theorists agree that increasing bureaucratization of the corporation results in an increase in impersonal rules.

One theorist, Max Weber, maintains that the evolution toward large-scale organizations is unrelenting, and he identifies an increase in rules as a necessary feature of that evolution. In order to achieve increasing efficiency, expertise, rationality and predictability, organizations must not only develop effective control structures, but must specify spheres of competence and increase the number and the impact of rules. In an efficient organization, individual people must be replaceable without provoking crisis. Decision-making, then, must depend on rules, not people. Other forces also prompt systems of impersonal rules. The subordination of one individual to another creates a predictable tension (especially in societies in which the ideal of individual freedom is strong) and these tensions can be alleviated by management imposing impersonal bureaucratic standards. But a vicious cycle develops. Impersonal rules perpetuate the tensions that generated them: Such rules reinforce low motivation, which in turn creates a need for close supervision.[4]

The immediate consequence of the emergence of impersonal rules is that responsibility becomes submerged in rules. A special advantage of rule structures is that they are more permanent than people; they relieve the organization from a dependence on particular individuals. From the standpoint of moral responsibility, this advantage becomes a disadvantage in that rule-bound individuals refuse accountability for their own actions. "I only follow the rules," is the typical, threadbare, bureaucratic response. If the antagonisms between worker and manager are severe, the curious phenomenon of ritualism may develop. We all know of the stubborn clerk who makes a point of following the regulations to the letter, even when doing so involves ignoring realities and frustrating the goals of the organizations. Members of a labor union, in a similar manner, may defy management by "working to rule," that is, working up only to the level explicitly stated in the union contract, even when exceeding that level is easier.[5] If, in a bureaucracy, responsibility is submerged in rules, then it follows that ultimate responsibility should attach to those who make the rules. Though this implication is logical, it neither simplifies nor resolves the problem. Rules outlive their makers, and it is often impossible to hold a single person accountable for a bad rule.

Furthermore, individuals in a bureaucracy seldom make rules alone Committees or informal groups usually make them, and those groups become the logical focus of accountability. This is problematic, however, because the committee or group is at a distance from the clerk or employee who follows its directives, and because such groups can account for their activities only when they are in session.[6] In addition to impersonal rules, corporate bureaucracies generate centralized authority. As Paul Kurtz remarks, "The logic of the organization is essentially conservative. Thus, there is a standardization and consistency of behavior. Increasingly, there is a tendency for individual responsibility to give way to corporate responsibility, and the individual denies he is responsible for what the corporation does."

The elimination of discretionary personal power in lower corporate ranks pushes that power up the ranks. Commands then flow from the pinnacle of the bureaucracy to its base, and when the bureaucracy is large, the lines of accountability become over-extended. John Lachs characterizes the resulting problem as one of "psychic distance." When the Japanese General Yamashita was tried (and eventually executed) for war crimes following World War II, he protested that the atrocities his soldiers committed in the Pacific Islands were so distant from the center of his organization that they occurred despite his good intentions.

Lachs observes that the centralization inherent in large bureaucracies demands that responsibility be assigned to the center; but this assignment is weakened because the psychic distance between center and periphery is often so great that effective control vanishes.[7] Closely connected to the problem of impersonal rules and centralization is the problem of the isolation of different managerial levels in the corporate hierarchy.

When authority is converted into impersonal rules, and when ultimate power is transferred to the center of the corporation, the result is a separation of authority in the hierarchy. Impersonal rules require the need for face-to-face relationships, and this in turn means a separation of subordinate and superordinate structures. One always obeys the rules, but it no longer is necessary to submit to the whims of individual people. If there is no need to yield to higher authority, the importance of peer pressures increases. Nevertheless, either by accident or design, the peer pressures to which people submit are not ones that assume moral responsibility for the actions of the organization. Peer pressures and impersonal rules eliminate day-to-day decision-making in a corporate bureaucracy, but neither promotes genuine moral responsibility.[8]

Because of the isolation of the various strata, it often happens that the center of the organization, i.e., its decision-making nucleus, is isolated from the peripheral areas at which the organization has its direct contact with the public. Here the problem of isolation of strata overlaps with that of centralization. Executives at the center of a corporation often find it difficult to respond effectively to, and be responsible for, actions at the periphery. In his classical analysis of General Motors in 1946, Peter Drucker identifies one of that company's greatest problems as the isolation of its top executives from the sentiments of the general public, and he pointed out that it was an isolation which resulted in *poor communication of ideas from the public to the executives.* [9]

So we will now address the various obligations of an employer, beginning with that most important constituency, the customer.

OBLIGATIONS TO CUSTOMERS

History reveals marked differences in the ways that cultures treat business obligations to consumers. The "Code of Hammurabi," almost 4,000 years old, holds merchants to certain standards of fair dealing and product safety. 17th century France under the rule of Louis XIV maintained a complex set of regulations and procedures governing product quality. Yet with the dawn of the Industrial Revolution and the influence of laissez-faire economic theorists such as Adam Smith, there came a dramatic loosening of government restraints. Smith and others argued that efficiency is significantly impaired when government tries to guarantee consumer satisfaction and safety; in turn the doctrine of *caveat emptor* ("buyer beware") dominated the economic scene during the early history of the United States. Since the mid-19th century, however, there has occurred a gradual shift in product liability law away from *caveat emptor* in favor of *caveat venditor,* or "seller beware."

In 1850, U.S. law decreed that only those who could prove fraud or breach of warranty could collect damages even though they were harmed by a defective product. Not only did consumers find it extremely difficult to satisfy the courts' strict concepts of "fraud" and "breach of contract," but they were also required to sue only those with whom they entered into a relationship of "privity." "Privity" referred to a direct commercial relationship. So, a consumer who purchased a toxic bottle of aspirin from a drugstore could sue only the owner of the drugstore (with whom he or she had privity) and not the maker of the aspirin.[10]

This inability to litigate was true even when it was the maker of the aspirin who through negligence had mislabeled the toxic substance.[11] By the turn of the century, courts had struck down the doctrine of privity in these types of cases (privity still applies in other types of cases) and were forcing companies to compensate injured consumers in a variety of instances. By the mid-20th century courts were holding corporations liable according to a doctrine of "strict liability," a doctrine under which consumers can collect damages even when it is impossible to prove corporate negligence. This doctrine means that so long as the product is defective and causes damage, the producer is liable for damages even when the producer took all safety precautions in the production of the product. For example, if a can of hair spray explodes in a consumer's hands, the manufacturer of the spray is liable regardless of safety precautions taken.[12]

Courts have justified strict liability using some of the following rationale: The burden for consumer damage is best shouldered by corporations, who have more substantial financial reserves than do individual consumers. Because producers will necessarily raise prices somewhat to cover most of the anticipated liability, it will be consumers, not corporations, who will shoulder the ultimate financial burden for liability protection. But it is more efficient to protect the general public in this way than to rely on individual consumers to purchase a complex package of individual insurance for hair spray liability, jet engine liability, cosmetics liability, *et cetera.*

Producers hold themselves to be "experts" and hence offer an "implied warranty" that their products will perform their intended function without damaging the user. That is to say, few of us could be expected to know about the combination of steel and stress in the design of a lawnmower; yet we assume that the manufacturer does, and that the lawnmower will mow grass without throwing its blade dangerously from underneath the mower. If and when it throws its blade, then we can claim the violation of an implied warranty, and we can claim it even when unable to prove that the manufacturer was, in fact, negligent.[13]

Finally, a policy of strict liability is seen as a deterrent to dangerous practices. If a manufacturer knows that any attempt to hide behind excuses will fail in court, then the manufacturer may well be prompted to take special precautions to insure that nothing goes wrong.[14] Individuals must clearly distinguish between legal liability from either criminal or moral responsibility. Legal liability, for example, can occur when there is no criminal or moral responsibility. If a small child throws a rock through a neighbor's window, the parents may be legally liable; that is, they may be required to compensate the injured party financially. And yet the parents may not be morally or criminally responsible at all. Similarly, a corporation may be found financially liable for compensating an injured consumer without criminal or moral blame being attached.[15]

For example, the Ford Motor Company, in a long series of trials, was found financially liable time after time in Ford Pinto cases. The company was required by the courts to compensate the victims and relatives of victims of the Pinto's exploding gas tank. In a short time the issue of whether Ford was liable was settled. The Pinto was less safe than comparable cars, the company knew it, and it knew how to bring the car up to standard for less than $12 per car, but it refused to do so until required by the federal government in 1978.[16]

OBLIGATIONS TO THE CORPORATE BOARD OF DIRECTORS

All modern state corporate statutes describe a common image of corporate governance, an image in pyramid form. At the base of the pyramid are the shareholders or owners of the corporation. Their ownership gives them the right to elect representatives to direct the corporation and to approve fundamental corporate actions such as mergers or by-laws amendments. The intermediate level is held by the members of the board of directors, who are required by a provision common to nearly every state corporation law "to manage the business and affairs of the corporation."[17] On behalf of the shareholders, the directors are expected to select and dismiss corporate officers, to approve important financial decisions, to distribute profits, and to see that accurate periodic reports are forwarded to the shareholders. Finally, at the apex of the pyramid are the corporate officers. In the eyes of the law, the officers are the employees of the shareholder owners. Thus, the directors limit the executive officers' responsibilites.[18]

In reality, this legal image is virtually a myth. In nearly every large American business corporation, management autocracy exists. This autocrat is usually titled the President, or the Chairman of the Board, or the Chief Executive Officer – or a small group of executives rules the corporation. Far from being chosen by the directors to run the corporation, this chief executive or executive clique chooses the board of directors and, with the approval of the board, controls the corporation.[19] A common theme of many instances of mismanagement is a failure to restrain the power of these senior executives. A corporate chief executive's decisions to expand, merge, or even violate the law can often be made without accountability to outside scrutiny.[20] At Gulf Oil Corporation, three successive chief executive officers were able to pay out over $12.6-million in foreign and domestic bribes over a 15-year period without the knowledge of "outside" or non-employee directors on the board.

At Northrop Corporation, without the knowledge of the board or, apparently, other senior executives, Chairman Thomas V. Jones and Vice President James Allen were able to create and fund the Economic and Development Corporation, a separate Swiss company, and pay $750,000 to Dr. Herbert Weisbrod, a Swiss attorney, to stimulate West German jet sales. At the 3M corporation,

Chairman Bert Cross and Financial Vice President Irwin Hansen ordered the company insurance department to pay out $509,000 for imaginary insurance, and the bookkeeper to fraudulently record the payments as a "necessary and proper" business expense for tax purposes. Ashland Oil Corporations's chief executive officer, Orwin E. Atkins, involved at least eight executives in illegally generating and distributing $801,165 in domestic political contributions; also without question.[21] The legal method used for such a consolidation of power in the hands of the corporations's chief executive is the proxy election. Annually the shareholders of each publicly held corporation are given the opportunity of either attending a meeting to nominate and elect directors or returning proxy cards to management or its challengers, signing over their right to vote.

Few shareholders personally attend meetings. Sylvan Silver, a Reuters correspondent, covers more than 100 annual meetings in Wilmington, Del., each year. He described representative 1974 meetings in an interview. At Cities Service Company, the 77th largest industrial corporation with some 135,000 shareholders, 25 shareholders actually attended the meeting; El Paso Natural Gas with 125,000 shareholders had 50 shareholders; at Coca Cola, the 69th largest corporation with 70,000 shareholders, 25 shareholders attended the annual meeting; at Bristol Myers with 60,000 shareholders, 25 shareholders appeared. Even "Campaign GM," the most publicized shareholder challenge of the past two decades, drew no more than 3,000 of General Motors' 1,400,000 shareholders, or roughly two-tenths of one percent.[22]

Corporate directors almost invariably are chosen by written proxies. Yet management usually dominates the proxy machinery, and a ballot usually lists only one slate of candidates. Although federal and state laws require the annual performance of an elaborate series of rituals pretending there is "corporate democracy," in 1973, ninety-nine percent of the directorial elections in our largest corporations were uncontested.[23] The key to management's monopoly in electing board members is money. Effectively, only incumbent management can nominate directors, because it has a nearly unlimited power to use corporate funds to win board elections while opponents must prepare separate proxies and campaign literature entirely at their own expense.[24]

There is, first, management's power to print and mail written communications to shareholders. In a typical proxy contest, management will "follow up" its initial proxy solicitation with a bombardment of 5-10 subsequent mailings. Attorneys Edward Aranow and Herb Einhorn explain in their treatise, "Proxy Contests for Corporate Control": Perhaps the most important aspect of the follow-up letter is its role in the all-important efforts of a soliciting group to secure the latest-dated proxy from a stockholder. It is characteristic of every proxy contest that a large number of stockholders will sign and return proxies to one faction and then change their minds and want to have their stock used for the opposing faction.[25]

The techniques of the Northern States Power Company in 1973 are illustrative. At that time, Northern States Power Company voluntarily employed cumulative voting, which meant that only 7.2% of outstanding shares was necessary to elect one director to Northern's 14-person board. Troubled by Northern's record on environmental and consumer issues, a broadly based coalition of public interest groups called the Citizens' Advocate for Public Utility Responsibility nominated Ms. Alpha Snaby, a former Minnesota state legislator, to run for director. These groups then successfully solicited the votes of more than 14% of all shareholders, or more than twice the votes necessary to elect her to the board. Northern States then bought back the election. By soliciting proxies a second time, and then a third, the power company was able to persuade the shareholders of 71% of the 2.8-million shares cast for Ms. Snaby to change their votes.[26]

Larger, more experienced corporations are usually less heavyhanded. Typically, they will begin a proxy campaign with a series of "buildup" letters preliminary to the first proxy solicitation. In "Campaign GM," General Motors elevated this strategy to a new plateau by encasing the "Project on Corporate Responsibility's" single 100-word proxy solicitation within a 21-page booklet specifically to refute each of the Project's charges. The Project, of course, never could afford to respond to GM's campaign. The postage costs of soliciting GM's 1.4-million shareholders alone would have exceeded $100,000.

The cost of printing a document comparable to GM's 21-page booklet, mailing it out, accompanied by a proxy statement, a proxy card, and a stamped return envelope to each shareholder might have run as high as $500,000.[27] Nor is it likely that the Project or any other outside shareholder could match GM's ability to hire "professional" proxy solicitors such as Georgeson & Company, which can deploy up to 100 solicitors throughout the country to personally contact shareholders, give them a campaign speech, and urge them to return their proxies. By daily tabulation of returned proxies, professional solicitors are able to identify on a day-by-day basis the largest blocks of stock outstanding which have yet to return a favorable vote.[28]

REVAMPING A BOARD

Like a rival branch of government, the board's function must be defined as separate from operating management. Rather than pretending directors can "manage" the corporation, the board's role as disciplinarian clearly should be described. Specifically, the board of directors can:

- establish and monitor procedures to assure that operating executives are informed of and obey applicable federal, state, and local laws;
- approve or veto all important executive management business proposals such as corporate by-laws, mergers, or dividend decisions;
- hire and dismiss the chief executive officer and be able to disapprove the hiring and firing of the principal executives of the corporation; and
- report to the public and the shareholders how well the corporation has obeyed the law, protected the shareholders' investment and operated profitably or unprofitably.[29]

To reform the corporation, a federal chartering law also could specify the manner in which the board performs its primary duties. First, to insure that the corporation obeys federal and state laws, the board should designate executives responsible for compliance with these laws and require periodic signed reports describing the effectiveness of compliance procedures.[30] Second, the board should actively review important executive business proposals to determine their full compliance with the law, to preclude conflicts of interest, and to assure that executive decisions are rational and informed of all foreseeable risks and costs.[31] Only with respect to two types of business decisions should the board exceed this limited review role.

First the awarding of salaries and fringe benefits inherently possesses such obvious conflicts of interest for executives that only the board should make these decisions.[32] Second, because the location or relocation of principal manufacturing facilities tends to have a greater effect on local communities than any other type of business decision, the board should require management to prepare a "community impact statement." This public report would be similar to the environmental impact statements currently required by the National Environmental Policy Act. It would require the corporation to state the purpose of a relocation decision, to compare feasible alternative means, to quantify the costs to the local community, and to consider methods to mitigate these costs. Although it would not prevent a corporation from making a profit-maximizing decision, it would require the corporation to minimize the costs of relocation decisions to local communities.[33]

PROPOSED REFORMS

Restructuring the board is hardly likely to succeed if boards remain as homogeneously white, male, and narrowly oriented as they are today. Echoing John Locke's principle that no authority is legitimate except that granted "the consent of the governed," it argues that employees and other groups substantially affected by corporate operations should have a say in its governance.[34]

Professor Dahl holds a similar view. "Why should people who own shares be given the privileges of citizenship in the government of the firm when citizenship is denied to other people who also make vital contributions to the firm?" he asks. "The people I have in mind are, of course, employees and customers, without whom the firm could not exist, and the general public, without whose support for the myriad protections and services of the state the firm would instantly disappear ... "Yet Dahl finds proposals for interest group representation less desirable than those for worker self-management. He also suggests consideration of co-determination statutes such as those enacted by West Germany and 10 other European and South American countries, under which shareholders and employees separately elect designated portions of the board.[35]

From a different perspective, Professor Stone has recommended that a federal agency could appoint "general public directors" to serve on the boards of all the largest industrial and financial firms. In certain extreme cases in which a corporation repeatedly violates the law, Stone recommends that the federal courts could appoint "special public directors" to prevent further delinquency.[36] There are substantial problems with each of these proposals. Nonetheless, the essence of the arguments is well taken. The boards of directors of most major corporations are, as CBS's Dan Rather criticized the original Nixon cabinet, too much like "12 grey-haired guys named George." This tradition and the problems it has created have resulted in important public – and, for that matter, shareholder – concerns being ignored.[37]

At least part of the solution is structural. To end the boards' homogeneity, do this: In addition to the general duty each director has to see that the corporation is profitably administered, give each a separate oversight responsibility, a separate expertise, and a separate constituency so that every important public concern would be guaranteed by at least one informed representative on the board.

There might be nine corporate directors elected from both inside and outside the corporation, each of whom is elected to a board position with one of the following oversight responsibilities:

1. Employee welfare
2. Consumer protection
3. Environmental protection and community relations
4. Shareholder rights
5. Compliance with law
6. Finances
7. Purchasing and marketing
8. Management efficiency
9. Planning and research [38]

By requiring each director to balance responsibility for representing a particular social concern against responsibility for the overall health of the enterprise, the problem of isolated "public" directors could be avoided. No executive, attorney, representative, or agent of a corporation would be allowed to serve simultaneously as a director of that same corporation. Directorial and executive loyalty could be furthered by an absolute prohibition of interlocks. No director, executive, general counsel, or company agent would be allowed to serve more than one corporation, subject to the Federal Corporate Chartering Act. [39]

Corporate campaign rules could be redesigned to emphasize qualifications, allowing shareholder voters to make rational decisions based on information clearly presented to them. It is also a fair assumption that shareholders, given an actual choice and role in corporate governance, might want to elect the men and women most likely to safeguard their investments.[40] In fact, if the reins on our imagination are loosened, America has a large, rich, and diverse pool of possible directorial talent from academics to public administrators, from community leaders to corporate and public interest lawyers. But any directors become stale after a time so reformers suggest they should be limited to four two-year terms. Six weeks prior to the shareholders' meeting to elect directors, each shareholder could receive a ballot and a written statement on which each candidate for the board sets forth his or her qualifications to hold office and purposes for seeking office. (Candidates may not necessarily own stock in the corporation.) All campaign costs could be borne by the corporations. These strict campaign and funding rules would assure that all nominees will have an equal opportunity to be judged by the shareholders. By preventing directorates from being bought, these provisions would require board elections to be conducted solely on the merit of the candidates.[41]

A New Role For Shareholders

These reforms are not without their flaws. For example, who would police the elected board members? Without a full-time body to discipline the board, it would be easy for the board of directors and executive management to become friends. Active vigilance could become awkward in an uncritical partnership. The same board theoretically elected to protect shareholder equity and internalize law might instead become management's lobbyist.[42] Relying on shareholders to discipline directors may strike many as an ineffective approach. Historically, the record of shareholder participation in corporate governance has been a poor one. The monumental indifference of most shareholders is a well known fact. But taken together, the earlier proposal for an outside, full-time board, nominated by rival shareholder groups and voted on by beneficial owners, will increase involvement by shareholders. And cumulative voting insures that an aroused minority of shareholders, even one as small as 9-10% of all shareholders, could have the opportunity to elect at least one member of the board.[43]

To keep directors responsive to law and legitimate public concerns requires surer and more immediate mechanisms. It requires arming the victims of corporate abuses with the powers to swiftly respond to them. For only those employees, consumers, racial or sex minorities, and local communities harmed by corporate depravations can be depended upon to complain. By allowing any victim to become a shareholder and by permitting any shareholder to have an effective voice, there will be the greatest likelihood of continuing scrutiny of the corporation's directorate.[44]

For example, when a federally chartered corporation engages in production or distribution of nuclear fuels or the emission of toxic air, water or solid-waste pollutants, citizens whose health is endangered should not be left, at best, with receiving money damages after a time-consuming trial to compensate them for damaged property, impaired health, even death. Instead, upon finding of a public health hazard by three members of the board of directors or three percent of the shareholders, a corporate referendum should be held in the political jurisdiction affected by the health hazard. The referendum would be drafted by the unit triggering it, either the three board members or a designate of the shareholders. The affected citizens by majority vote should then decide whether the hazardous practice shall be allowed to continue. This form of direct democracy is similar to the initiative and referendum procedures familiar to many states, except that the election will be paid for by a business corporation and will not necessarily occur at a regular election.[45]

This type of election procedure gives enduring meaning to the democratic concept of "consent of the governed." To be sure, this proposal goes beyond the traditional assumption that the only affected or relevant constituents of the corporation are the shareholders. No longer can we tolerate corporate destruction of local health and property and expect the public to absorb the cost. In an equitable system of governance, the perpetrators should answer to their victims.[46]

Any changes made in a corporation to improve moral and ethical practices must avoid violating the rights of stockholders. The property rights of stockholders, on the other hand, do not permit the freedom to do anything at all to trespass on the rights of consumers, employees, or other citizens. In a society that respects property rights, stockholders have definite prerogatives. For example, if changes are made in management structure affecting the investment value of the stock, the stockholder must be informed. He or she may not desire such changes, having invested in the stock exclusively for the purpose of making money, and stockholders' desires as *de facto* owners of the corporation must be considered in corporate decision-making.[47] Early in the 20th century, a U.S. president could proclaim, "The business of America is business," as Calvin Coolidge did, and feel assured that everyone listening to him would understand the reference. The underlying belief was that what was good for such economic bastions as General Motors was good for the country.[48]

It was virtually inconceivable that anyone who was not somehow "misguided" would question a system that had been so successful in providing so much in the way of goods, income, and wealth for[49] so many people. Today, most people would agree that business is still the dominant social institution in our country. It is becoming increasingly difficult, however, to reach consensus on the specific mission of the corporate sector. Indeed, despite many of the historic achievements of our business system, U.S. corporations and their leaders have suffered severe losses of public support and confidence.[50,51,52] Over the past two decades, business organizations and their management have faced many new demands that are based on changing societal expectations about the appropriate role of the corporation in the larger society. Current attitudes toward IBM, which was generally viewed as the new bastion of U.S. economic power, exemplify much of this tension and uneasiness.[53]

DEMONS OR DOMINANT FORCES

IBM is described in such extremes as a "major resource," and "singlehandedly ... defending America's trade imbalance" and even a "malevolent force because of its stranglehold on the computer industry."[54] Perhaps we should ask, "What is the proper role of business today?" One way of clarifying our understanding of the tensions underlying business's social role is to assess relationships between corporations and their different social groups that are affected by the corporations' operation: Stockholders, employees, unions, customers, suppliers, local communities, public and special interest groups, government agencies, and so forth. The exact nature of the bond between corporations and these groups, as one might expect, is quite variable in intensity, duration, and significance. This has given rise to two opposed perspectives on business's role – the stockholder and stakeholder models of corporate activity.[55]

We remember from Chapter 15 that throughout most of our history, the *stockholder* model has been the norm. Based on this traditional business concept, a corporation essentially has been viewed as a piece of private property owned by those who hold its stock. These individuals elect a board of directors whose responsibility is to serve the best interest of the owners. This model assumes that the interactions between business organizations and the different groups affected by their operations (employees, consumers, suppliers) are most effectively structured as buyer/seller relationships. The forces of supply and demand and the pressures of a competitive market will ensure the best use of business and its economic resources. In essence, the board of directors and its appointed managers are fiduciary agents or trustees for the owners. The directors and managers fulfill their social obligations when they operate in the best financial interests of the stockholders. In other words, when they act to maximize profits.[56]

In contrast to the stockholder view, a new perspective, referred to as the *stakeholder* model, suggests that corporations are servants of the larger society. This approach acknowledges that there are expanding demands being placed on business organizations which include a wider variety of groups not traditionally defined as part of the corporation's immediate self-interest. In a narrow sense, stakeholders are those identifiable groups or individuals on which an organization depends for its survival, sometimes referred to as primary stakeholders, stockholders, employees, customers, suppliers, and key government agencies.

On a broader level, however, a stakeholder is any identifiable group or individual who can affect, or is affected by, organizational performance in terms of its products, policies, and work processes. In this sense, public interest groups, protest groups, local communities, government agencies, trade associations, competitors, unions, and the press also are organizational stakeholders.[57,58] Stockholders continue to occupy a place of prominence, but profit goals are to be pursued within the broader context of the public interest. Businesses are socially responsible when they consider and act on the needs and demands of these different stakeholders. In addition to the tension created by the stockholder and stakeholder models of corporate performance, arguments about business's social role inevitably include questioning motive: Should business operate in its own self interest or should it consider broader social or moral duties? A number of prominent economists, Milton Friedman for one, argue that the pursuit of profit is and must always remain the most fundamental social responsibility of any business, provided that such activity occurs within accepted moral and legal rules.[59]

The corporation is a highly specialized social instrument, designed for the explicit purpose of creating wealth. Business, therefore, must operate in its own self-interest. Proponents of the social or moral view rebut these arguments by underscoring the idea of a social contract for business, the corporation's character as servant of the larger society. Because businesses are socially created, they have greater responsibilities to the good of the larger society.[60] Although arguments over the appropriate role of business and its relationship to the larger society always have existed, today's debate is urgent and widespread. Corporate horror stories seem to unfold in the news media on a daily basis. A *New York Times*/CBS News poll found that 55% of those interviewed think that most corporate executives are dishonest in their business dealings. Moreover, two-thirds of the sample felt that government was not doing enough to catch these individuals and that for those who were caught, punishment was too lenient.[61,62] For example, Michael Milken, a New York stockbroker, pleaded guilty to six felony counts for violating federal securities laws. He made $550-million in one year and, even after paying the government a $600-million fine, is said to be worth about $2.5-billion. Federal Judge Kimba Wood, who sentenced Milken to 10 years in prison, reduced Milken's sentence to 24 months for cooperating with the government. The prosecutors have replied that most of the information Milken has given them has "limited value" and that they "do not believe that Milken has completely disclosed all wrongdoing of which he is aware."[63]

COMPARING MODELS

To come to some conclusion about the proper role of business may be essential for the survival of both business and society. The well-being of business and society requires the adoption of a stakeholder model. This need not mean that business must abandon its interest in profits or adopt an exclusively "ethical idealist" position. The stakeholder model also leaves room for a progressivist stance. Concern for the stakeholders and interest in profits are not mutually exclusive. Its proponents advocate that the stakeholder model is preferable to the stockholder model for several reasons:

> 1. The stockholder model has not dealt adequately with contemporary societal problems and the complexities of economic transactions and interactions.
> 2. It is in the long-term interest of business to take a broader view of its responsibilities. If business does not become accountable for its actions on its own, growing stakeholder pressures will ensure government-imposed accountability.
> 3. Understanding and satisfying the needs of stakeholders is important to the well-being of the firm. Being aware of the multiple forces that influence events allows individuals to be in a better position to make corporate decisions. In today's highly competitive economic and social environment, no important stakeholder should be ignored.
> 4. The stakeholder model is in keeping with our notions of fairness. Employees, consumers, communities, etc., are not just instruments for enriching stockholders. They have legitimate goals and interests of their own. Business has an obligation to treat its stakeholders with a sense of fairness and justice, and to acknowledge their fundamental rights, not simply because it will be in its own vested interest in the long term, but because it is the ethical thing to do as well.[64]

OBLIGATIONS TO THE COMMUNITY

Tracing the development of business ethics as a field in its own right will help to understand what factors have been responsible for the evolution of technical concerns as they relate to social responsibility and the community at large. While the subject of business ethics received some attention prior to the 1960s, it was with the rise of the social-responsibility debate that ethical concerns became of major importance to business organizations.[65]

From 1960 to 1970, sweeping social change affected business organizations and the management of those organizations. The concern about civil rights for minorities, equal rights for women, protection of the physical environment, safety and health in the workplace, and a broad array of consumer issues has had far-reaching and long-lasting impacts on business organizations. The long-term effect of this social change has been dramatic change in the "rules of the game" by which business is expected to operate.[66]

Given this kind of social revolution, it is not surprising that the social environment of business was given increasing attention during the 1960s and 1970s by business corporations and by schools of business and management. The concept of social responsibility came into its own as a response to the changing social values of society. Business executives began to talk about the social responsibilities of business and to develop specific social programs in response to problems of a social, rather than economic, nature. Schools of business and management implemented new courses in business ethics or in the social responsibility of business.[67] In general, social responsibility means that a private corporation has responsibilities to society that go beyond the production of goods and services for a profit; that a corporation has a broader constituency to serve than stockholders alone. Corporations relate to society through more than just marketplace transactions and serve a wider range of values than the traditional economic ones that are prevalent in the marketplace. Corporations are more than economic institutions and have a responsibility to devote some of their resources to helping to solve some of the most pressing social problems, many of which corporations helped to cause.[8]

The concept of social responsibility was referred to as a change in "the terms of the contract" between business and society that reflected changing expectations regarding the social performance of business.[69] The old contract between business and society was based on the view that economic growth was the source of all progress, social as well as economic. The engine providing this growth was considered to be the drive for profits by competitive private enterprise. The basic mission of business was thus to produce goods and services at a profit, and in so doing, business was making its maximum contribution to society and, in fact, being socially responsible.[70]

The pursuit of economic growth did not necessarily lead automatically to social progress. In many instances it led instead to a deteriorating physical environment, unsafe workplaces, needless exposure to toxic substances on the part of workers and consumers, discrimination against certain groups in society, urban decay and other social problems. This new contract between business and society involved reducing these social costs of business by impressing upon business the idea that it has an obligation to work for social as well as economic betterment. This new contract did not invalidate the old contract; it simply added new terms or additional clauses to that contract.[71] Today it is clear that the terms of the contract between society and business are, in fact, changing in substantial and important ways. Business is being asked by society to assume broader responsibilities than ever before and to serve a wide range of human values. Business enterprises, in effect, are expected to contribute more to the quality of American life than just supply quantities of goods and services.[72]

The concept of social responsibility is fundamentally an ethical concept. It involves changing notions of human welfare and emphasizes a concern with the social dimensions of business activity that have to do with improving the quality of life in society. It has provided a way for business to concern itself with these dimensions and pay some attention to its social impacts. Responsibility implies some kind of obligation – which business organizations are believed to have to the society within which they function – to deal with relevant social problems.[73] The debate about social responsibility reflects many of these ethical or moral dimensions. Proponents of the concept argue as follows.

For Social Responsibility

1) Business must accommodate itself to social change if it expects to survive.
2) Business must take a long-run or enlightened view of self-interest and help solve social problems in order to create a better environment for itself.
3) Business could gain a better public image by being socially responsible.
4) Government regulation could be avoided or at least reduced if business meets the changing social expectations of society before the issues become politicized.
5) Business has enormous resources that could be useful in solving social problems.
6) Social problems could be turned into profitable business opportunities.
7) Business has a moral obligation to help solve social problems that it has created or at least perpetuated.[74]

The opponents of social responsibility have equally formidable arguments. These arguments are as follows.

Against Social Responsibility

1) The social responsibility concept provides no mechanism for accountability as to the use of corporate resources.
2) Managers are legally and ethically bound to earn the highest possible rate of return on the stockholder's investment in the companies they manage.
3) Social responsibility poses a threat to the pluralistic nature of our society.
4) Business executives have little experience and incentive to solve social problems.
5) Social responsibility is fundamentally a subversive doctrine that would undermine the foundations of a free-enterprise system if taken seriously.[75]

After more than four decades of discussion on this issue it became obvious to many proponents and opponents of corporate social responsibility that there were several key issues in the debate that had not, and perhaps could not, be settled. One key issue concerned the operational definition of social responsibility. How shall a corporation's resources be allocated to help solve social problems? With what specific problems shall a given corporation concern itself? What priorities shall be established? Does social responsibility refer to company action taken to comply with government regulations or only to those voluntary actions that go beyond legal requirements? What goals or standards of performance shall be established? What measures shall be employed to determine if a corporation is socially responsible or socially irresponsible?[76]

The traditional marketplace provided little or no information to the manager that would be useful in making decisions about solving social problems. But the concept of social responsibility in itself did not make up for this lack and provided no clearer guidelines for managerial behavior. Given this lack of precision, corporate executives who wanted to be socially responsible were left to follow their own values and interests or some rather vague generalizations about changing social values and public expectations. What this meant in practice, however, was often difficult to determine.[77] Another key problem with the concept of social responsibility was that the concept did not take into account the competitive environment in which corporations functioned. Many advocates of social responsibility treated the corporation as an isolated entity that had almost unlimited ability to engage in unilateral social action. Eventually society came to recognize that corporations are severely limited in their ability to respond to social problems. If a firm unilaterally engages in social action that increases its costs and prices, it will place itself at a competitive disadvantage relative to other firms in the industry that may not be as concerned about being socially responsible.[78]

The debate about social responsibility never took this institutional context of corporations seriously. Concerted action to solve social problems is not feasible in a competitive system unless all competitors pursue roughly the same policy on these problems. Since collusion among competitors is illegal, however, the only way such concerted action can occur is when some other institution, such as government, makes all competitors engage in the same activity and pursue the same policy.[79] While the debate about social responsibility continued and corporate executives were asking for a definition of their social responsibilities, government was requiring the rules under which all

---

corporations operated in society by developing a vast amount of legislation and regulation pertaining to the physical environment, occupational safety and health, equal opportunity, and consumer concerns.[80] The last issue that remained unresolved in the debate about social responsibility concerned moral underpinnings. The term "responsibility" is fundamentally a moral one that implies an obligation to someone or something. It is clear to most people that business has an economic responsibility to produce goods and services efficiently and to performed other economic functions for society. These economic responsibilities constitute the reason for having something like a business organization. But why does business have social responsibilities? What are the moral foundations for a concern with social impacts?[81]

The proponents of social responsibility produced no clear or generally accepted moral principle that would impose upon business an obligation to work for social betterment.[82] Ascribing social responsibility to corporations does not necessarily imply that they are moral agents that are then responsible for their social impacts. However, various moral strictures were used to try to impose this obligation on business, and various arguments were made to try to link moral behavior to business performance. Little was accomplished, however, by way of developing solid and acceptable moral support for the notion of social responsibility. So, the debate about social responsibility was moralistic in many of its aspects, a debate that often generated a good deal of heat but little light in most instances.[83]

The intractability of these issues, according to one scholar, "posed the dreadful possibilities that the debate over corporate social responsibility would continue indefinitely with little prospect of final resolution or that it would simply exhaust itself and collapse as a viable legitimate question."[84] But beginning in the 1970s, theoretical and conceptual reorientation began to take place regarding the corporation's response to the social environment. This new approach was labeled corporate social responsiveness, and while initially it appeared that only semantics was involved, it gradually became clear that the shift from responsibility to responsiveness was much more substantive.

The shift represented an attempt to escape the unresolved dilemmas that emerged from the social-responsibility debate. Frederick defines this new concept of social responsiveness as: "The capacity of a corporation to respond to social pressures; the literal act of responding, or of achieving a generally responsive posture to society is the focus of corporate social responsiveness ... one searches the organization for mechanisms, procedures, arrangements, and behavioral patterns that, taken collectively, would make the organization as more capable of responding to social pressures. It then becomes evident that organizational design and managerial competence play important roles in how extensively and how well a company responds to social demands and needs."[85]

As a result, attention shifted from debate about a moral notion, social responsibility, to a more technical or at least morally neutral term, social responsiveness.[86] In the mid-1970s academics and business managers began to realize that a fundamental change was taking place in the political environment of business – that government was engaged in shaping business behavior and making business respond to a wide array of social problems by passing an unprecedented amount of legislation and writing new regulations pertaining to these problems.

The political system responded to the social revolution of the 1960s and 1970s by enacting over a hundred new laws regulating business activity. Many new governmental regulatory agencies were created, and new responsibilities were assigned to old agencies. These agencies issued thousands of new rules, and procedural requirements that affected business decisions and operations.[87] This regulatory role of government continued to expand until the 1980 election of the Ronald Reagan administration. The new type of social regulation, as it came to be called, affected virtually every department or functional area within the corporation and every level of management. The growth of this new type of regulation was referred to as a second managerial revolution, involving a shift of decision-making power and control over the corporation from the managers of corporations to a vast cadre of government regulators, who were influencing, and in many cases, controlling managerial decisions in the typical business corporation.[88] Decisions becoming increasingly subject to government influence and control were basic operational decisions such as what line of business to go into, where products could be made, how they could be marketed, and what products could be produced.[89]

Government regulations created a serious concern with public policy as a new dimension of management. Many business leaders recognized the importance of public policy to business and advocated that business managers become more active in the political process and work more closely with government and other groups to help shape public policy. The motivation for this concern with public policy is clear. If the rules of the game for business are being rewritten through the public-policy process and business is being forced to respond to social values through complying with laws and regulations, then business has a significant interest to learn more about the public-policy process and become involved in helping to write the rules by which it is going to have to live.[90] Business since has come to adopt a more sophisticated approach to public policy, an approach that has been called the proactive stance. This term means that rather than fighting change, which often has proved to be a losing battle, or simply accommodating itself to change, business attempts to influence change by becoming involved in the public-policy process. Business can attempt to influence public opinion with regard to social issues of concern to society, and it can attempt to influence the legislative and regulatory process with regard to specific laws and regulations.[91]

THE ROLE OF GOVERNMENT REGULATION

Obviously, the public-policy approach treats business in its institutional context and advocates that managers learn more about government and the public policy process so that they can appropriately influence the process. Government is recognized as the appropriate body to formalize and formulate public policy for the society as a whole. Some form of response by government to most social issues is believed to be inevitable, and no amount of corporate reform along the lines of corporate social responsibility or corporate social responsiveness is going to eliminate some form of government involvement. Government has a legitimate right to formulate public policy for corporations in response to changing public expectations.[92] Society can choose to allocate its resources any way it wants and on the basis of a criteria it deems relevant. If society wants to enhance the quality of air and water, it can choose to allocate resources for the production of these goods and put constraints on business in the form of standards. These non-market decisions are made by those who participate in the public policy process and represent their views of what is best for themselves and society as a whole. It is up to the body politic to determine which market outcomes are and are not appropriate. If market outcomes are not to be taken as normative, a form of regulation which requires public participation is the only alternative. And then, the social responsibility of business becomes inoperative and certainly not to be trusted.

When business acts contrary to the normal pressures of the marketplace, it remains for public policy and official regulation to replace the dictates of the market.[93] There is also, at least on the surface, no need for a moral underpinning for a business obligation to produce social betterment. Society makes decisions about the allocations of resources through the public-policy process based on its notions about social betterment. The result is legislation and regulation that impinge on business behavior.

Business, then, as a good citizen, obviously has an obligation to obey the law. Failure to do so subjects business and executives to all sorts of penalties. The social responsibility of business is to follow the directives of society at large as expressed in and through the public policy process.[94] Beyond social costs business institutions, like citizens, have responsibilities for social involvement in areas of their competence where major social needs exist. Business actions are only indirectly related to certain social problems: Nevertheless, business often is obliged to help solve them.[95]

Business is a major social institution that should bear the same kinds of citizenship costs for society that an individual citizen bears. Business will benefit from a better society just as any citizen will benefit; therefore, business has a responsibility to recognize social problems and actively contribute its talents to help solve them.[96] Business will not have primary responsibility for solving problems, but it should provide significant assistance. For example, business did not directly cause educational problems, but it does stand to gain some benefit from their solutions; therefore, it has some responsibility to help develop and apply solutions.[97] The thrust of the foregoing proposition is that business, like any individual, needs to act responsibly regarding the consequences of its actions. The socially responsible organization behaves in such a way that it protects and improves the social quality of life along with its own quality of life. In essence, quality of life refers to the degree to which people live in harmony with their inner spirit, their fellow man, and nature's physical environment. Business has a significant effect on each of these, particularly the last two. It can support harmony among people as well as in the environment if it will take the larger role's view.[98]

> **❝Beyond social costs business institutions, like citizens, have responsibilities for social involvement in areas of their competence where major social needs exist.❞**

Although quality of life embraces harmony, it is not a static concept that seeks to preserve a utopian status quo. Rather, it is a dynamic concept in which people live harmoniously with the changes occurring in nature and in themselves. It is, however, a utopian concept in the sense that most people use it as an ultimate goal that they realize will never be obtained absolutely.

It is essentially a set of criteria by which judgments may be made about social progress. The social responsibility model seeks to improve the quality of life through its five propositions. Certain observations can be made concerning the implementation of the social responsibility model.[99] First, it applies to all organizations. Although this discussion has been presented in the context of business, the social responsibility / responsiveness model does not single out business for special treatment. All organizations have equal responsibilities for the consequences of their actions. Similarly, social responsibility/responsiveness applies to all persons in all of their life's roles, whether, employer, employee, home owner, home renter, or bus driver. An individual who tosses his rubbish along a road side is just as irresponsible as a business that pours pollutants into a river. The individual may argue that his offense is less in magnitude, but when his rubbish is added to all the rest, it becomes a massive offense against the public interest.[100]

As a matter of fact, quality of life will be improved less than people expect if only business is socially responsible and responsive. Substantial improvement will be achieved only when most organizations and persons act in socially responsible ways.[101] Second, the movement toward greater social responsibility is not a fad but a fundamental change in social directions. Business executives will do their organizations grievous damage if they assume social responsibility is merely something to be assigned to a third assistant with action to be taken only when absolutely necessary and when the organization is backed into a corner. [102]

Social responsibility is here to stay despite its intangibles and imponderables. Business's actions probably have been a significant cause of the rise of social responsibility and responsiveness ideas because business did its economic job so well that it released people from economic want, freeing them to pursue new social goals. Third, social response by business will increase business's economic costs. Social responsibility/responsiveness is not a free ride or a matter of simple goodwill. Actions such as the reduction of pollution take large amounts of economic resources. It is true that some of the costs are transferred from other segments of society, so society as a whole may not bear higher costs for some actions; however, these costs are brought into the business system and, in most instances, will flow through in the form of higher prices.[103]

This situation is likely to put further strain on business-consumer relations. It may lead to consumer demands for less social involvement in the short run, but the long-run secular trend toward more social involvement seems likely to remain. [104]

OBLIGATIONS TO EMPLOYEES

How can large, bureaucratic corporations escape the problems that threaten meaningful responsibility? If corporations are to become accountable, the actions of corporations that contribute to more bureaucratization must be limited. One of the most devastating effects of this action is the suffocation of individual moral accountability by imposing an ever-increasing load of procedures and rules upon *employees*. For example, the clerk is caught in a web of rules and forgets about a deeper sense of accountability to the customer. The clerk, the mechanic, or the safety inspector often excuse themselves from the normal obligations of morality by simply saying "I only follow the rules."[105]

According to some writers, the most reliable way to relieve the bureaucratic forces threatening individual accountability and to extricate the employees caught up in the corporate bureaucracy is to formally recognize and protect employees' rights. The expression "employee rights" has gained considerable respectability in the past decade and is now applied to a variety of actions aimed at recognizing the central role and worth of the employee. Among the "employee rights" presented and defended are:

> • the right of an employee to complain about dangerous products or practices without being penalized;
> • the right of an employee to participate in political activities outside the workplace without being penalize;
> • the right of an employee to refuse lie-detector tests without being penalized;
> • the right of an employee to a hearing before being fired; and
> • the right of an employee to refuse immoral orders without being penalized.

Such a list is incomplete (other proposed rights will be mentioned in the next chapter) but it indicates the character of moral reforms urged by defenders of employee rights. Such rights are meant to apply not only to employees in corporations but to those in private and government organizations as well. The last 200 years have brought revolutionary changes in the way employers treat employees. Once forbidden even to organize into unions under the threat of "conspiracy" laws, most employees now possess the legal right to unionize, a right protected by sweeping federal legislation such as the Taft-

Hartley Act. Once treated with the personal domination typical of highly structured family life, employees now may sue their employers for a variety of misbehavior. Today one would never see a sign posted in the workplace like that in a 1878 New York carriage shop, reading:

"It is expected that each employee shall participate in the activities of the church and contribute liberally to the Lord's work ... All employees are expected to be in bed by 10 p.m. Except: Each male employee may be given one evening a week for courting purposes ...."[106]

Still, today's employers have enormous prerogatives. David Ewing, perhaps the foremost defender of employee rights, argues that the rights of U.S. citizens possessed through the U.S. Constitution are "left at the door" when employees enter their places of employment. There is a constitutional right to free speech, but Ewing points out that employees who complain about dangerous products can be fired for expressing their personal concerns. For example: [107]

CASE 1:

George Geary, an employee at a large steel corporation, complained that tubular steel casing being sold by the company was faulty and dangerous. None of his superiors would listen and they responded curtly that the casing had been tested adequately. When he finally went to the vice president, he was fired, and the Supreme Court of Pennsylvania said no to his attempt at reinstatement.

CASE 2:

Shirley Zinman, a secretary at a small corporation, refused her boss's demand to tape telephone calls with clients. She would not record such calls, she said, unless the clients were informed. For this, she was forced to resign. Although legal authorities granted her the right to qualify for unemployment insurance, they refused to acknowledge any right to retain her job.[108]

Reports like these have resulted in serious criticism heaped upon corporate executives and have brought critics to recommend an employees' "Bill of Rights." A formal policy with enough force behind it to require management compliance is the only response that can effectively counteract any abusive actions of management toward employees. Labor unions have been effective in increasing wages and fringe benefits; however, they are not perceived by most scholars and practitioners as the solution to employee rights because traditionally, at least they concentrate more on wages.

Even if unions could be persuaded to take rights seriously, critics say, the overall changes they could bring would be negligible, for the vast majority of U.S. workers are not unionized. In 1992, only one in five workers belong to a union. In most instances, employers have the legal power to fire employees at will. As the legal theorist Lawrence Blades puts it, "Employers may dismiss their employees at will ... for good cause, for no cause, or even for cause morally wrong, without thereby being guilty of legal wrong."[109] Employees complain about their lack of rights. The absence of employee rights is felt more acutely, many agree, because in modern society work itself is in many cases dehumanizing. Employee rights are needed to counter the dehumanizing tendencies of mechanized routine and boredom brought on by technology and economic necessities.

If work in corporate America is dehumanizing, then the reason for it should be investigated. Two reasons have been proposed by academicians: 1) certain jobs are dehumanizing because of features of the workplace; and 2) managerial behavior causes employees to perceive their work to be dehumanizing. If the former is the only reason, then the introduction of employee rights will not relieve the problem, however, if the latter is true, then there is hope that changes in management's behavior and the introduction of employee rights will bring to the worker a ˌ ˌling of autonomy and self-respect. In turn, the problem of dehumanization will be lessened.[110]

The introduction of employee rights may be simply a codification of the evolution that brought improved working conditions and higher pay for employees. But some theorists believe it is an extension of the natural evolutionary process which brought legal and constitutional rights to citizens in the political arena. Just an autocracy stepped aside for democracy, so corporate leaders must give into more worker-centered organizational structures which protect employees and provide for their participation in the managerial process.[111] A review of the law affecting employees in the U.S. from the 1950s until today shows that, from the time of its introduction, employers had few legal restraints placed upon their management styles relative to treatment of employees.

Sections 383 and 385 of the Restatement of Agency (revised in 1958), declare that as an "agent" the employee has a duty to obey all "reasonable" directions of the principal (employer). Although this implies that an employee can refuse illegal, unethical, or immoral acts, it actually only means that the employee has the right to terminate his employment. The employer also has the right to fire the employee for failure to carry out a directive. That is, he has no inherent right to keep his job. Section 387 also reinforces the right of the employer by noting that in the agent-principal relationship, the agent "is under a duty not to speak or act disloyally."[112]

EXCEPTIONS TO THE RIGHT TO FIRE

Today, the legal right of employers to fire for good reason, bad reason, or for no reason continues to exist, but exceptions are now recognized. In the case of *National Labor Relations Board vs. Jones and Laughlin Steel Co.*, the court reasserted the employer's "normal" right to discharge employees, but insisted that employees had a right to unionize, a right that could not be blocked through employers' arbitrarily discharging pro-union employees.[113]

During the 1970s, additional laws were adopted to prevent dangerous corporate practices and increase restrictions on employers actions. 1) The Coal Mine Safety Act was passed in 1974. It specifies that no employee can be penalized for reporting violations of the Act; 2) the Occupational Safety and Health Act (OSHA) also prevents the penalizing of employees who complain about health and safety violations; and 3) the Water Pollution Control Act blocks the penalizing of employees who complain about water pollution violations.[114] By the end of the 1970s, legislation or administrative directives were in place to protect employees' rights to free speech. Most of the legislation, however, was narrow in scope and related to the enforcement of specific regulatory acts.[115]

Employers anticipate employee concerns: Generally speaking, employees want to do well at their assignments, to get along with their peers, and to have their contributions to the organization recognized. Their job tasks, working conditions, wages, and the possibility for promotion occupy their day-to-day thoughts. [116]

More than 9 out of 10 members of the workforce are employees working for another person or a corporation. A high proportion of them finds such dependence less than satisfactory. This is true for it contradicts fundamentals of the American myth binding workers to groups rather than allowing independent work, requiring them to merge their efforts with those of others in joint activities. The Harris polls found that a majority of those interviewed in recent years agreed that business did not allow "people to use their full creative abilities." A survey conducted by the Public Agenda

Foundation of New York in 1983 showed that many workers distinguished between agreeable jobs and jobs that motivate them. They would work harder, they said, if there were potential for advancement, a chance to develop abilities and were given a challenging job. Most workers reported, however, that employers had little knowledge of how to motivate workers, and less than a quarter of those surveyed said they were performing on the job to full capacity.[117]

Employees' dissatisfaction with their condition at work may lie at the heart of a nation's lagging economic performance. Andrew C. Sigler, chairman of Champion International Inc., warns that managers are going to have to learn more sophisticated ways of increasing productivity than the traditional solution of cutting costs alone, which he points out can all too easily be "stupid arbitrary judgments." More important than new robots, more computerized machines, or automated plants, industry needs systems that get management and labor on the same side.[118] Ford Motor Company has pulled ahead of General Motors in recent years, primarily because it has included its workers and their unions in every step of its changed operations.

The new, unprecedented cooperation on joint, not just managerial goals, has probably been more important than the massive capital investments Ford has made. Companies that have delegated authority down the line report excellent results. At two of Champion International's smoothest-running plants, workers, called "members," belong to teams that do their own hiring and firing. This is a remarkable, startling innovation for a major manufacturing firm. Also TRW has experimented with pushing production responsibility down, rather than maintaining it at the top. Small groups of employees at a few plants now possess responsibility for maintaining their equipment and interacting with customers. The increase in productivity and quality has been tremendous, according to local managers. However, such experimentation is still rare in industry.[119]

With the education level of the U.S. workforce continually rising, it is surprising that managers have held on to old modes of supervision and worker control. One out of every four workers is now a college graduate, compared with one of five only 23 years ago. An additional 20% have had some college training, up from 16% a decade ago.[120] Moreover, the fastest growing employment is in high technology. Between 1978 and 1987, manufacturing employment fell by almost seven percent, but high tech employment increased by almost a third.[121] These reasons and more bode well for management to identify how to create working environments and conditions that are conducive to high worker productivity. When seeking solutions to problems, information and involvement from the individuals who are affected most directly usually yield answers. In this approach, the workers should be the problem solvers. In recent years, the term "employee rights" define what workers perceive will improve their working conditions.

LEGAL OBLIGATIONS

People are fired for many reasons. A common one is an economic recession, which forces a firm to cut back on production and so decrease the number of employees. But there are other reasons as well. Inefficiency, immorality on the job, chronic lateness or absenteeism, and lack of ability to perform at the level expected are all common reasons, and are also examples of reasonable cause. Other reasons are less clearly justifiable, such as incompatibility with management or other workers, lack of respect or deference to superiors, poor attitude toward work, voicing of dissent, or an employer's belief that someone can be found who can do the job better. In some instances an employer fires an employee simply because the employer dislikes the employee for personal reasons, or because the employee refuses the sexual advances of the employer, or because the employee knows of an irregularity in the firm and cannot be trusted not to expose it.[122]

Fairness requires that workers not be fired arbitrarily. Arbitrary firing violates the ordinary expectations assumed by workers when they accept employment. They expect to be treated as persons deserving of respect. They are not objects to be discarded or replaced at the whim of an employer. But exactly what rules should govern the termination of employment is a controversial issue. Two general principles are often applied. One states that the longer a person has been employed by a firm, the greater the obligation of the firm not to fire, except for just cause. A beginning employee may be required to work on probation.

Although even a beginner should not be terminated on a whim, the reason for termination can be less substantive if the term of employment is short. The reason given in favor of that principle rests on what a probation period means and how it is defined. Another consideration is that, unless a firm is allowed to fire beginning people whom, for one reason or another it does not want, it becomes chained to employees simply by virtue of having initially hired them. Even civil service regulations allow for probation periods; and academic tenure is not usually awarded except a fixed number of years (three to six, at most institutions) of full-time teaching.[123]

A second principle states that the employer should inform the employee of the reason for the termination of employment. This principle is derived from the obligation to treat persons with respect.[124] The extent to which an employee has a right to "due process" in the case of firing is still being debated. But there is ample precedent in the areas of civil service, union contracts, and tenure systems to show that due process is practicable in cases of firing. There are laws that preclude the firing of whistle blowers in government positions, and many have suggested that such laws be extended to cover the private sector as well.[125]

FREEDOM OF SPEECH

Here we find two distinct types of employee rights. These are rights concerning speech about 1) affairs of the organization and 2) affairs not directly related to the organization. The first typically concerns whistle-blowing while the second concerns political activities outside working hours, such as an employee's campaigning for a political candidate. It is possible to endorse number 1 without number 2 or vice versa.[126]

A storm of controversy about employee rights developed in 1975 when the Kennedy hearings for Senate Bill 1210 revealed instances of potential rights abuses by government agencies. One man, working for the Office of Economic Opportunity, was fired when he blew the whistle about arbitrary expenditures of day-care funds. Two women working for The Indian Health Service were fired when they mailed a letter to President Nixon showing how patients were mistreated at an Indian hospital. Another woman, working for the Department of Health, Education and Welfare, was penalized for raising questions about possible discrimination in the hiring practices of HEW.[127]

Critics insist that these cases never should have occurred and that they prove the need for formal adoption of employee rights regulations. Some business executives, of course, do not agree. They emphasize that the potential for employee rights regulations to decrease productivity, refutes the need of employees to participate in whistle blowing.[128] Recent legislation has favored the defenders of employee rights. Some states have adopted statutes making it unlawful for companies to fire employees who participate in political activities outside the workplace. In the past, it was legal for a corporation to fire all employees who refused to vote for a particular candidate and some companies did.[129]

Today, threats of this kind are illegal in states such as California, Wisconsin, Missouri, and Minnesota.[130] This trend gained momentum in the late 1960s when the U.S. Supreme Court reached its landmark Pickering decision, which reinstated a high school teacher fired for criticizing school policies. The teacher, Pickering, had complained that athletics were emphasized at the expense of academic quality and said so in a letter to the local newspaper. In its decision the court emphasized the fact that Pickering's remarks concerned matters of general public interest and that the right to discuss such matters was protected by the first Amendment to the U.S. Constitution.[131] Management can support the concept of employee freedom of speech but deny that every instance of free speech should be protected. In his textbook on business ethics, Professor Thomas Garrett argues that free speech should be protected but remarks that "If a vice-president belongs to the American Nazi Party, the situation is different since people may not want to deal with him or with a company that has such a man in a key position." [132]

If allowing workers certain rights of free speech tends to spark an increase in organizational friction and disharmony, then are the rights themselves unjustified? Possibly not, because disharmony and friction sometimes yield positive results. In the political arena we allow freedom of speech even in circumstances in which denying it might reduce friction. We allow Marxists, critics of U.S. foreign policy, and even proponents of racism to express their views, although many agree doing so takes its toll on the peace and harmony of society. A bit of friction, it is said, is the price of meaningful freedom. Without such friction, prevailing ideas would be immune to criticism and hence immune to the improvement which follows on the heels of criticism.[133]

> **❝Management can support the concept of employee freedom of speech but deny that every instance of free speech should be protected.❞**

The same, perhaps, is true in the workplace: Without criticism, corporations would plow ahead, blind to their worst faults, firing and penalizing the very employees who might cure their blindness. The real question is how much criticism to allow, and when.[134] For those defending the right of employee free speech, a crucial issue is how to formulate the right itself. Formulating free speech is complex, and limits must be imposed. We can't, for example, allow a trickster to yell "fire" in a crowded theatre. A reasonable statement for companies might be: "Employees are free to criticize dangerous or unjust activities, and to participate in political activities of their choosing off the job, without being penalized."[135]

PRIVACY

Only recently has a right to "privacy" been considered an employee right. Recently critics of managerial arbitrary actions have identified four violations of employee privacy. These are: 1) managers' eavesdropping on employees' private phone calls; 2).unauthorized searches of employees' desks; 3) termination or penalizing employees who refuse polygraph tests; and 4).refusing employees access to information in their personnel files.

Of the four, the polygraph or lie-detector test imposed upon job applicants or employees is the most troublesome. Businesses cite several reasons for using the polygraph to detect lying. *First,* the polygraph is a fast and economical way to verify the information provided by a job applicant. Lying on resumes frequently occurs among applicants. The cost of running background checks on applicants can be prohibitive. In contrast, for $80 to $100 the polygraph supposedly can give employers all the answers they need about the applicant. A *second* reason for using the polygraph relates to the staggering annual losses companies suffer through in-house theft. The polygraph, say its supporters, allows employers to identify dishonest employees or likely ones.

Third, companies argue that in certain decentralized retail operations, like small chain groceries, the use of the polygraphs permits business to abolish audits and oppressive controls. They say the use of polygraphs actually increases workers' freedom. *Fourth,* employers say the polygraph is a good way to screen candidates for employment: It can help reveal personal philosophy, behavioral patterns, and character traits incompatible with the organizations' purpose, function, and image.[136]

To date, in the U.S., no court of law has permitted polygraph test information to be admitted as evidence without the expressed permission of the accused, and most courts refuse to allow such information even with permission. The rationale presumably is that the lie detector is a fallible instrument and may mislead the judge or jury.[137] Less explosive, but equally troublesome, are issues concerning collection and retention of information about employees. Since 1975, many states have introduced legislation establishing standards for corporate behavior, but the legislation varies from state to state in its character and impact. Various defenders of employee rights have suggested that corporations establish internal ethical principles regarding such matters which would apply whether supported by law or not. Among the principles suggested are:

No performance evaluations older than four years should be retained in an employee's files. Employees should have access to most material in their files and should know what type of information is kept there. No search of an absent employee's desk may be undertaken without his or her permission or written authorization from a specified member of upper management. Employee phone calls should not be monitored without the employee's knowledge. Access to personal files should be limited to a specifically designated few corporate employees. Employees should be notified when and if information from their files is given to outside agencies or individuals.[138]

'QUALITY OF LIFE' ISSUES

For some firms "quality of work life" may mean providing workers with less supervision and more autonomy. For others it may mean providing work opportunities to develop and refine skills. Still other firms may try to provide workers with greater participation in the conception, design, and execution of their work, that is, with greater responsibility and a deeper sense of achievement. Perhaps all companies ought to examine the impact of technology on job satisfaction. While typically increasing the efficiency of operations and eliminating the physical drudgery that plagued yesterday's workers, today's technology sometimes results in repetitive and boring tasks that, in the long run, may diminish productivity and destroy job satisfaction.[139]

One purpose of the "quality of work life" programs is to thaw the antagonistic worker-boss climate that exists in many plants and hurts production. But the prime purpose is to improve workers' performance in the production process by seeking their ideas. Accordingly, these programs are known by various names: "Worker participation", "labor-management teams" and "industrial democracy."[140] One promising response to the need for "quality of work life" programs is quality control circles, which two American personnel consultants introduced to Japanese industries about twenty-five years ago. Now widely used in Japan, the "circles" are committees of workers and supervisors who meet to discuss quality improvement. Some U.S. companies are now rediscovering the concept. Westinghouse, Inc., has established about 150 quality circles at 50 locations. According to reports from Westinghouse personnel, these circles have suggested changes that have saved the company more than $1-million in two years.[141] The only way management can implement such programs is with the full cooperation of workers and their representatives. Investigators believe that the success of "quality of work life" programs and other workplace reform efforts depends on the ability of the organization to reinforce and sustain high levels of trust. To the extent that it does so, the organizational performance can improve.[142]

Today, the trend toward a softer and more sympathetic view toward employee rights in general is evident. Considered from a practical perspective, employee rights pose problems of implementation, even though corporations are more receptive to the concept. Two means of implementing them are available: 1) from the outside through the courts or government agencies, or 2) from the inside, relying on voluntary corporate initiative and self-regulation. Giant steps have been taken by the courts in recent years to protect employee rights, especially in companies with government affiliations. But the second means of implementation is preferable. Moral suasion, most people agree, is preferable to government coercion. But can rights programs be implemented voluntarily by corporations? The answer depends upon the moral posture of individual corporations and the corporate community – the quality of their relationships with customers, regulators, stockholders and the communities they serve.[143]

Jacqueline Dunckel presents a pragmatic approach to implementing an ethics program within a business organization and cites the Ford Motor Company as an example of a corporation which has implemented a program which she advocates: "Ford Motor Company is a worldwide leader in automotive and automotive-related products and services as well as in newer industries such as aerospace, communications and financial services. The company's mission is to continually improve products and services to meet customers' needs, allowing the company to prosper as a business, and to provide a reasonable return for the stockholders, the owners of the business."[144]

Dunckel begins the description of her program with a description of basic values: "How a company accomplishes its mission is as important as the mission itself. Fundamental to its success are these basic values:

Dunckel's Basic Values

PEOPLE: The people, executives and employees, are the sources of the company's strength. They provide the corporate intelligence and determine the company's reputation and vitality. Involvement and teamwork are its core human values.

PRODUCTS: It's products are the end result of company efforts and as its products are viewed, so the company is viewed.

PROFITS: Profits are the ultimate measure of how efficiently the company provides its customers with the best products for their needs. Profits are required to survive and grow within the U.S. economic system.[145]

"Quality comes first: To achieve customer satisfaction, the quality of the company's products and services must be its number one priority. Customers are the focus of everything the company does: It's work must be done with the customers in mind, providing better products and services than its competition. Employee involvement should be a way of life for the company: The employees and executive should be viewed as a team. They should be expected to treat each other with trust and respect. Dealers and suppliers are the company's partners: The company must maintain mutually beneficial relationships with dealers, suppliers, and other business associates. Integrity should never be compromised: The conduct of the company worldwide must be pursued in a manner that is socially responsible and commands respect for its integrity and for its positive contributions to society. Its doors should be open to men and women alike without discrimination and without regard to ethnic origin or personal beliefs."[146] Consumers lost faith when Ford Motor Company dragged its feet on accepting the problems of its Pinto model in the 1970s. They felt the company had not acted in a socially responsible manner when Ford didn't react until court action prompted it to recall the cars in which several people died.

The lessons learned from big business are not just in how companies deal with their customers, but also in how they treat employees and suppliers. In 1989, Leona Helmsley, President of Helmsley Hotels, was accused of evading federal taxes by diverting $4-million of business property to personal acquisition.[147] She was accused of abuse and humiliation of her staff, compromising suppliers, and refusing to pay contractors for work completed and approved. When she refused to pay a meat supplier's bill of $8,500 because she disliked a cornedbeef sandwich and $353,191 to her renovator, both parties complained, first to the press, then to the grand jury. Suppliers also testified that she extorted money, liquor, and television sets from them in order to get her hotel contracts. It was this testimony that proved damaging to Helmsley personally and to her company. [148] One big business that sets good examples and reports consistently high profits is Lanier/Harris/3M, a multi-national marketing, sales, and service company for copiers and facsimile equipment, a highly competitive industry. Lanier makes three basic guarantees to its customers: 1) 98% guaranteed up-time or the customer's money back for the time the equipment is down; 2) a free loaner of a copier if one is out of service for more than 8 hours; and 3) an after-hours, toll-free help line to assist the customer with minor emergencies.

This service has paid off. Lanier has enjoyed a 20% revenue growth rate in each of the past three years, 100% revenue growth rate in each of the past three years, 100% increase in facsimile sales over 1988, and product marketing arrangements with 102 countries.[149] A second company which has set a good example is the Chubb Corporation, a long-established company not just interested in "the bottom line."

Hendon Chubb stated, "While an insurance policy is a legal contract that expresses our minimum responsibility, there are many occasions when equity demands that we recognize a moral obligation beyond the strictly legal terms, and this is always a consideration in our settlements."[150] Today, the company's philosophy of looking past profits to people and community is stated in the company brochures: "The Chubb group has a very simple business philosophy. It believes in strict standards of business conduct and high standards of performance. Chubb recognizes its responsibility to each of its clients as well as to its employees and its appointed agents and brokers. Chubb also recognizes its responsibility to society, as manifest by its "matching fits" program, community outreach efforts, and vigorous support of public broadcasting."Fortunately, this philosophy does not just appear on paper; it is the credo by which the company has governed itself for over 100 years.

THE LESSONS LEARNED
Jacqueline Dunckel in her study of successful businesses discovered the following lessons are learned in the process of pursuing ethical standards:

> 1. If a company sets ethical standards for itself, the company, and its employees, all must live by them.

2. It must have a way to monitor the ethical standards to ensure that they are being met.

3. It must have a means to react if the standards are not adhered to.

4. It must take the initiative to see that the standards are being followed, monitored and action is taken if there is deviation.

5. Most important, the president or chief executive officer must set the example for all other employees. If he or she loses their good reputation, all is lost relative to the ethics program.

6. Although the company is in business to make money, if it becomes greedy its reputation will be compromised and it may be tempted to yield to unethical practices.[151]

READINGS

AN ETHICS PLANNING PROGRAM
Jacqueline Dunckel

The following is a suggested agenda, based on Dunckel's experience, for developing an ethics program. Evaluate it in light of the various ethical life-views described in Chapter 3:

1. Commitment and leadership by the president, chief executive officer and company managers is essential to a successful program.

2. Involvement and commitment by employees is essential from the very outset of the program.

3. The company should be structured to encourage ethical decision-making at all levels.

4. If the company does not have a mission statement, it must determine its purpose for being in business.

5. Guidelines must be included for making ethical decisions, the means of reporting unethical behavior, and how enforcement will take place. The code of ethics must be in a form that can be used by all employees.

6. The company should establish an ethics committee, ombudsman, hotline and judiciary board.

7. The ethics program must be introduced to all employees initially. Communication must be ongoing about it and information about how it works should be promoted regularly. Procedures for reporting unethical behavior must be established and all new employees must be educated relative to the program and its importance to the company.

8. Management and employees should be trained in ethical decision making based on the company code of ethics. Training may be generated internally or led by outside trainers. New employees must be trained and employees who have problems in ethical decision making re-trained.

9. The company must set a definite date to begin the program. A strong commitment must be voiced by the president or chief executive officer. It will be his or her example that will directly affect the success of the program.

10. Identify, monitor, measure, report, and evaluate the effects of the program. Keep records of numbers, not names of reports and questions. Results should be reported to all involved: Managers, employees, and stockholders. Good news will motivate employees.

11. Provision must be made for an annual review to evaluate, add, or adjust the code itself as well as the report and enforcement procedures.

12. The company's business ethics program must not be perceived as tactics of spying or punishment. The ethics program must be positive; a source of strength and pride. Rewards should be all encompassing, a tribute to all employees for their loyalty, dedication, and ethical behavior.

13. There must be consistency in the decision-making process and the enforcement of policy. Any approved deviation from the code will negate its purpose.[152]

WRITING THE MISSION STATEMENT AND CODE OF ETHICS

The Company Mission Statement should be limited to one or two sentences if possible. It should state the company's purpose and singular goal for being in business. In writing its mission statement, the company should make determinations from the following factors.

1. Who will be involved in writing the mission statement and code of ethics? (Preferably, representatives from all levels within the organization will have the opportunity to participate including: Top management, middle management, employees, support staff, maintenance staff, grounds staff, etc.)
2. Who will chair the proceedings?
3. When and how often will the group or committee meet?
4. Where will the meeting(s) occur?
5. What is the deadline for completion of the mission statement and code of ethics?
6. Do any group or committee members need release time/overtime in order to participate?

The Company Code of Ethics: What does the company need to say about its products? Services? Employees? Customers? suppliers? Safety? Environment? Community? Shareholders? Others?

Here are some questions to critique a code of ethics:

1. Does any one feature of the code affect or contradict another?
2. Will there be any confusion if all the features are practiced at the same time?
3. Are the results for non-compliance clearly stated?
4. Is the company enforcement procedure fair and just to all?
5. Have strong guidelines been included for decision making?
6. Has an environment for ethical behavior throughout the organization been created?
7. Are all business systems — personnel, technical, financial — included in the code of ethics and their activities based on ethical practices?
8. Has the company allowed for open, ongoing communication at all levels?
9. Does the code reflect a positive attitude to ethical business behavior as opposed to a judgmental attitude? (See also Chapter 21.)[153]

Providing training for all is crucial to success of such programs. Within the training, the company should:

1. Explain why the company needs an ethics program.
2. Explain what needs to be taught.
3. Explain who needs the training, (from the chief executive officer to the last support staff person hired).
4. Explain who will teach all the employees about the program.
5. Implement measures to ensure that training on ethics is being used in every day practice.
6. Identify how often the training should occur.
7. Identify and explain how the company will work ethics training into the ongoing business goals and objectives.

ENFORCEMENT

(One or a combination of the following methods of enforcing the code should be considered.)

1. Enforcement through an Ethics Committee or Board:
a. Who will serve?
b. How many will serve?
c. How will the chairperson be appointed or selected?
d. To whom will the ethics committee or board report?
e. In what form will the committee receive its information regarding unethical behavior? (oral, written, both?)
f. Who will be responsible for seeing that the decisions of the committee are carried out?
g. Does the code of ethics state clearly what is considered unethical behavior?
h. What authority does the ethics committee or board have if the code has been breached?
i. What action will result from a reprimand, fine or firing?
j. How can a decision of the committee or board be appealed?
2. Enforcement through the Ombudsman
a. Will an ombudsman be appointed and if so, will he or she be employed full-time or serve as ombudsman while performing other duties.
b. What is the educational and work experience criteria required to hold the position?
c. Who will make the selection of the ombudsman?
d. How will confidentiality of information be ensured and maintained?
e. How long is the ombudsman appointment for?
f. To whom will the ombudsman report?
g. In what form does the ombudsman receive information regarding unethical behavior?
h. How will the decisions of the ombudsman be carried out?
i. How does the code of ethics provide the ombudsman with a clear measurement for making and

enforcing decisions?

j. How can the decision of the ombudsman be appealed?

In establishing a company hotline, a company would ask:

1. Who will answer the hotline?
2. Where does the information go?
3. Who follows through on the hotline information?
4. Can the caller be assured of anonymity?
5. How will confidentiality be maintained?
6. How much detail concerning persons, date, time, place must the caller provide?
7. What are the safety checks to follow so that no one will be falsely accused?

MEASURING SUCCESS

The management and employees of the organization will know the ethics program is working when the following statements accurately describe the positive feelings of all:

PURPOSE: The mission of the organization is communicated from the top. The top management team is committed to the ethics' program. Each person's individual behavior sets an example for others within the organization.

PRIDE: The employees exhibit pride in themselves, their work, and their organization. They do nothing which would jeopardize the reputation of the organization or that of their fellow employees.

TIME: What the employees do today will ultimately affect the organization in the future. Personnel do not look for short- term gain at the risk of long-term pain. Management and employees care not only about profit, but how the profit is achieved. Sufficient time is taken by management and employees alike to consider all aspects before making a decision.

COMMITMENT: The management and employees of the organization not only believe in the company purpose, they are committed to it. They make sure all of their actions and decisions are in accordance with their commitment to their code of ethics.

EVALUATION: The management and employees take sufficient time to evaluate the ethics program, discuss changes, set new goals and determine how to reach them.

COMMUNICATION: All personnel know they have open communication between management and employees and between employees and other employees. What is communicated is honest.

FAIRNESS: All personnel know that a deviation from the code of ethics will have a fair hearing and will be dealt with without prejudice or bias.

TRUST: Personnel believe that procedures have been adopted to ensure trust of those who make decisions concerning unethical behavior.

LOYALTY: Personnel have a strong sense of loyalty to the organization for they believe it has made a commitment to them and considers each individual to be a valuable asset. [154]

FOR FURTHER INQUIRY

SUGGESTED READINGS

• "Paul Hawken Replies" Editorial. *INC.*, July, 1992, pp. 41-42.(See copy enclosed)
• Frank K. Sonnenberg and Beverly Goldberg, "Business Integrity: an [142] Oxymoron?", *Industry Week*, April 6, 1992, pp. 53-55.(See copy enclosed)
• Karin Ireland, "The Ethics Game," *Personnel Journal,* March, 1991, [143] pp. 73-75. (See copy enclosed)
• Anthony Bianco and Sana Siwolop, "The Drexel Debacle's 'Teflon [144] Guy'", *Business Week,* June 8, 1992, pp. 92-94.(See copy enclosed)
• Paul Hawken, "The Ecology of Commerce", *INC.*, April, 1992, pp. [145] 93-100. (See copy enclosed)
• Paul O. Sand, "business Ethics - A Trend Toward Ethical Cynicism", Vital Speeches of the day, November 15, 1988, pp.85-87.
• Gerald F. Cavanagh and Philip J. Chmielewski, "Ethics and the Free Market", *America,* January 31, 1987, pp. 79-82.

• Robert Benne, "Ethics, Economics and the Corporate Life", *The Christian Century,* January 23, 1991, pp. 77-85.; "Events and People", *The Christian Century,* March 11, 1992, p. 270.

• Daniel E. Maltby, "the One-Minute Ethicist", *Christianity Today*, February 19, 1988, pp. 26-29.

• Daniel B. Moskowitz, "Where business Goes to Stock Up on Ethics", *Business Week,* October 14, 1985, pp. 63-64.

• M. Euel Wade, Jr., "The Lantern of Ethics", *Vital Speeches of the Day,* March 15, 1988, pp. 340-343.

• John A. Byrne, "Businesses are Signing Up for Ethics 101", Business Week, February 15, 1988, pp. 56-57.

• John A. Byrne, "Can Ethics be Taught? Harvard Gives It the Old College Try", *Business Week,* April 6, 1992, p. 34.

• "The Right Time to Teach Ethics", Editorial, *Business Week,* October 21, 1985, p. 148

• "Business Ethics of the Rich and Famous?" The Week, *Time,* June 15, 1992, p. 24.

• John A. Byrne, "The Best-Laid Ethics Program ... " *Business Week*, March 9, 1992, pp. 67-69.

• Edwin Whenmouth, "A Matter of Ethics-Why Japan is not like the U.S.", *Industry Week,* March 16, 1992, pp. 57-62.

• "Who Cares Who Wins", Editorial, *The Economist*, May 16, 1992, pp. 19-20.

• Todd Barrett, "Business Ethics for Sale", *Newsweek,* May 9, 1988, p. 56.

ENDNOTES

1. Thomas Donaldson, *Corporations and Morality.* Prentice-Hall, Inc., Englewood Cliffs, N.J., 1982, p. 109.

2-15. Donaldson, p. 110-113, 146-147.

16. DeGeorge, p. 193.

17. Excerpt from Ralph Nader, Mark Green, and JoelSeligman, *Taming the Giant Corporation,* New York: W. W. Norton, 1976. Copyright 1976 by Ralph Nader;

18. appearing in Michael W. Hoffman and Jennifer Moore, *Business Ethics*, McGraw-Hill, Inc., New York, 1989, p. 210.

19-46. Hoffman and Moore, p. 210-219.

47. Donaldson, p. 174.

48. A. F. Buono and L. T. Nichols, *Corporate Policy, Values and Social Responsibility*, Praeger, Inc., New York, 1985, p. 1.

49. G. F. Cavanagh, *American Business Values*, Prentice-Hall, Inc., Englewood Cliffs, N.J. 1984, p. 1.

50. F. W. Steckmest, *Corporate Performance: The Key to Public Trust*, McGraw-Hill, Inc., New York, 1982, p. 5.

51. D. O. Frederichs, "The Legitimacy Crisis in the United States: A Conceptual Analysis," *Social Problems, Vol. 27*:5, 1980, pp. 540-555.

52. R. B. Reich, "On the Brink of an Anti-Business Era," *The New York Times*, April 12, 1987, p. F-3.

53. Original Essay, Copyright 1990 by A. Buono, Department of Management, Bentley College, and Lawrence T. Nichols, Department of Sociology and Anthropology, University of West Virginia, appearing in Hoffman and Moore, p. 171.

54. "Is IBM Good for America?" *Business and Society Review,* no. 56, Winter, 1986, pp. 4-16.

55. Hoffman and Moore, p. 171.

56. Hoffman and Moore, p. 171.

57. R. E. Freeman, *Strategic Management: A Stakeholder Approach,* Pitman, Inc., Boston, 1984, p. 88.

58. R. E. Freeman and D. L. Reed, "Stockholders and Stakeholders: A New Perspective on Corporate Governance," *California Management Review,* vol. 25, Spring, 1983, pp. 88-106.

59. Hoffman and Moore, p. 172.

60. Keith Davis, "Five Propositions for Social Responsibility," *Business Horizons,* June, 1975, pp. 19-24.

61. A. Clymer, "Low Marks for Executive Honesty," *The New York Times*, June 9, 1985, pp. F-1, F-6.

62. Ralph Nader, "White Collar Fraud: America's Crime Without Criminals," *The New York Times*, May 19, 1985, p. F-3.

63. Jeanie Kasindorf, "The Chutzpah Defense," *The New York Magazine*, November 11, 1991, p. 39.

64. Hoffman and Moore, p. 175.

65. Richard T. DeGeorge, "The Status of Business Ethics: Past and Future," *Business Ethics Research Workshop*, Stanford University, August 14-15, 1985, p. 1.

66. Madsen and Shafritz, p. 299.

67. Madsen and Shafritz, p. 299.

68. Madsen and Shafritz, p. 299

69. Melvin Ashen, *Managing the Socially Responsible Corporation*, MacMillan Co., New York, 1974, p. 5.

70. Milton Friedman, "The Social Responsibility of Business Is to Increase Its Profits," *The New York Times Sunday Magazine,* September 13, 1970, pp. 122-126.

71. Madsen and Shafritz, p. 300.

72. Committee for *Economic Development, Social Responsibilities of Business Corporations*, CED, New York, 1971, pp. 29030.

73-81. Madsen and Shafritz, p. 301-303.

82. William C. Frederick, "From CSR1 to CSR2: The Maturing of Business and Society Thought," Graduate School of Business, University of Pittsburgh, 1978, *work paper no. 279,* p. 5.

83. Madsen and Shafritz, p. 303.

84. Frederick, p. 5.

85. Frederick, p. 6.

86. Madsen and Shafritz, p. 305.

87. Madsen and Shafritz, p. 306

88. Murray L. Weidenbaum, *Business, Government and the Public*, Prentice-Hall, Inc., Englewood Cliffs, N.J., 1977, p. 285.

89. Murray L. Weidenbaum, *The Future of Business Regulation,* New York: AMACOM, 1979, p. 1.

90. Madsen and Shafritz, p. 307.

91. Madsen and Shafritz, p. 308.

92. Madsen and Shafritz, p. 308.

93. Rogene A. Buchholz, "An Alternative to Social responsibility," Michigan State University *Business Topics* - 25 no. 3, Summer, 1977, pp. 12 and 16.

94. Madsen and Shafritz, p. 309.

95-104. Hoffman and Moore, p. 169-170.

105. Donaldson, p. 129.

106. David Ewing, *Freedom Inside the Organization,* McGraw- Hill, Inc., New York, 1977, p. 120.

107. Ewing, p. 99.

108. David Ewing, "Sunlight in the Salt Mines," *Harvard Law School Bulletin*, Fall, 1977, p. 133.

109. Lawrence E. Blades, "Employment at *Will vs. Individual Freedom*: On Limiting the Abusive Exercise of Employer Power," *Columbia Law Review*, no. 67, 1967, p. 1405.

110. Donaldson, p. 131-132.

111. Donaldson, p. 132.

112. Donaldson, p. 133.

113. Ewing, p. 32.

114. Donaldson, p. 133.

115. Donaldson, p. 133

116. William H. Shaw, *Business Ethics*, MacMillan Co., Inc., Belmont, CA., 1991, p. 194.

117. Clarence C. Walton, ed., *Enriching Business Ethics,* Plenus Press, Inc., New York, 1990, pp. 172-173.

118. Walton, p. 173.

119. Claudia H. Deutsch, "U.S. Industry's Unfinished Struggle," *The New York Times*, February 21, 1988, p. F-8.

120. "Educational Level of U.S. Workforce Rises, Report Shows," *The Wall Street Journal*, August 30, 1988, p. B-12.

121. Ibid., p. B-12.

122. Richard T. DeGeorge, *Business Ethics,* MacMillan Publishing Co., New York, 1990, p. 332-333.

123. DeGeorge, pp. 334-335.

124. DeGeorge, p. 335.

125. DeGeorge, p. 335.

126. Donaldson, p. 146.

127. Ewing, pp. 77-78.

128. Donaldson, p. 147.

129. Ralph Nader and Mark Green, "Owing Your Soul to the Company Store," *Ethical Issues in Business*, Thomas Donaldson and Patricia Werhane, eds., Prentice-Hall, Inc., Englewood Cliffs, N.J., 1979, pp. 197-202.

130. Donaldson, p. 123.

131. Donaldson, p. 147

132. Thomas Garrett, *Business,* Prentice hall, Inc., Englewood Cliffs, N.J., 1966, p. 68.

133. Donaldson, pp. 147-148.

134. Donaldson, p. 148.

135. Donaldson, p. 148.

136. Keith L. Davis and Robert L. Blomstrom, *Business and Society*, McGraw-Hill, Inc., New York, 1975, p. 319.

137. Donaldson, p. 150.

138. Ewing, pp. 133-138.

139. William H. Shaw, *Business Ethics,* Wadsworth Publishing Co., Belmont, CA, 1991, p. 244.

140. Shaw, pp. 244-245.

141. Shaw, p. 245.

142. Thomas A. Kochan, Harry C. Katz, and Robert B. McKersie, *The Transformation of American Industrial Relations*, Basic Books, Inc., New York, 1986, p. 175-176.

143. Donaldson, p. 156.

144. Jacqueline Dunckel, *Good Ethics, Good Business: Our Plan for Success*, Self Counsel Press, North Vancouver, B.C., 1989, p. 12.

145-154. Dunckel, p. 12-16, 85-86,89-92,96-97.

Chapter 17

William F. Edmonson

EMPLOYEE ISSUES AND OBLIGATIONS

> "Measure not the work until the day's out and the labor's done."
> – Elizabeth Barrett Browning, *Aurora Leigh*

> "The world works only for today, as the world worked twelve thousand years ago, and our children's children will still have to toil and slave for the bare necessities of life."
> – Richard Jefferies, 1883

> "'A fair day's-wages for a fair day's-work': it is as just a demand as governed men ever made of governing. It is the everlasting right of man."
> – Thomas Carlyle, 1843

S tudying the rights of employees in the workplace has stirred ethicists as a primary issue for many years. The record of abuses of employees in the workplace and violation of basic human rights has been a long one, even in the not too distant past. The practice of requiring employees to perform their duties in sweatshops and factories was common at the turn of the 20th century. Uncaring owners forced men, women and children to work 14- to 16-hour days. Exploitation was prevalent throughout industrialized America.[1]

This inhumane treatment of America's workforce brought about formation of labor unions as employees joined together to fight against exploitation in the workplace. This deplorable treatment also brought about numerous pieces of legislation to make these sweatshops illegal. Labor unions also worked to bring the law down on sweatshops. Labor unions have worked to bring dignity, personal safety, better working conditions and better salaries to the workplace. The political effectiveness of labor unions has been decreasing in recent years; nevertheless, the American workforce has derived significant benefits from lobbying efforts and collective bargaining which otherwise would not have been possible.[2]

William Fred Edmonson, M.B.A. University of Southern Mississippi, Ed.D. University of Mississippi, former dean of instructional affairs at Itawamba Community College in Fulton, Miss., is president of Panola College in Carthage, Tex.

Below is a guide to terms used in this chapter's discussions.

Working Terms

1. **Nepotism** – Showing favoritism to relatives or close friends in employment.

2. **Due Process** – Specific and systematic procedures allowed workers for appealing disciplinary and discharge action by employers.

3. **Conflict of Interest** – When employees or members of their immediate family receive an unearned, personal benefit as a result of the employee's job or position.

4. **Proprietary Information** – Information and trade secrets of the employer, his customers and suppliers.

5. **Foreign Corrupt Practices Act** – A law that prohibits employees from paying (bribing) a foreign government official to award business to their employers.

6. **U.S. Antitrust Laws** – Laws designed to ensure that Americans enjoy the benefits that flow from a free-market economy, unrestrained by anti-competitive practices such as price fixing, market allocation or bid rigging.

7. **Whistle-blowing** – Publicly spotlighting neglectful or abusive practices by an employer that threaten the public interest.

8. **Bribe** – Anything of value, usually cash, given to induce behavior, especially illegal actions.

9. **Kickback** – The return of part of a payment to the payor, under the table, not as an official part of a transaction or contract – often in exchange for special information or services provided to the payee.

10. **Gift** – Freely given item or cash, often as a "reward" for services or actions considered favorable.

11. **Insider trading** – Sale (or purchase) of a company's stock by insiders in the company who possess special information about the company not known to the trading world – usually referring to windfall profits made as a result of such trading.

As employees have gained additional rights either through union activity or from enlightened managers, they also have had to assume additional responsibilities for their behavior and performance.

Employees should increasingly police themselves to ensure that their behavior brings credit to their employers. They should strive to refrain from using alcoholic beverages or illegal drugs on the job, maintain the confidentiality of company information, and discourage discrimination against their fellow employees.

INSIDER TRADING: TEXAS GULF SULPHUR CASE

It's easy to understand how the term "insider trading" was coined when you consider the case of Texas Gulf Sulphur (1963). The facts of the case were these: Texas Gas Company performed some test drilling at one of its sites and found a body of rich ore. Some officials of the company, in pondering just how to describe this discovery to the media, decided to minimize its importance in the initial press release. They blandly described the drilling site as a "prospect." This was on April 12. On April 16, a second press release emerged that was much more accurate. It described the drilling site as a "major discovery."

Bad enough that the officials had used the media and misled the public in such a fashion. But between April 12 and April 16, insider investors – including Texas Gas Co. directors, officers and employees – purchased stock in the company as they were withholding the real information about the drilling discovery. Their ploy, of course, kept the stock at a lower price during the four-day interim. When the facts came to light, the Securities and Exchange Commission charged these insiders with violation of disclosure rules.

The court held that the first press release was misleading to other potential investors. The insiders were ordered to pay back all the profits they had made by acting on their insider information, plus all the profits made by *outsiders* whom the insiders had tipped.

PRIVACY IN THE WORKPLACE

Accusations of arbitrary behavior against employers now require that employees examine issues from the employer's point of view. For example, the random use of drug testing of workers is considered arbitrary, unethical treatment of employees. However, management argues that drug testing is necessary in fulfilling corporate responsibilities. Organizations claim they have an obligation to insure that the workplace is free from hazards; that customers of their products and services have a moral and ethical right to believe that the goods they purchase and the services they buy are safe and reliable. In fact, since the safety and reliability of products and services are so important – because so many might be affected by poor-quality workmanship or by workers who are impaired on the job – it is argued that the rights of workers to privacy must yield to the rights and responsibilities of corporations and their customers. Hence, drug testing is justified as a means toward desirable ends.[3]

Furthermore, this question of employee drug testing is not only an essential issue about the ethics of privacy rights in the workplace and the ethical treatment of workers, it is also a question surrounded by much legal argument brought to the courts in a number of lawsuits over the past few years. In fact, in March 1989 the U. S. Supreme Court ruled that, in certain safety-sensitive jobs (such as those of flight controllers), the federal government has the right to screen its employees for drug use. Legal scholars conjecture that when the Supreme Court hears a drug-testing case from the private sector, it will use the same reasoning and conclude that private employers also have a right to test employees engaged in safety-sensitive jobs. And it will be even more interesting to see the Supreme Court's ruling on testing those whose positions are not defined as safety-sensitive.[4]

If the 1989 ruling appeared as a setback for the cause of privacy in the workplace, proponents could take heart in the recently passed Employee Polygraph Protection Act. With this legislation Congress greatly reduced the legal use of polygraph testing in private business. Also restricted is the use of other mechanical devices, such as voice-stress analyzers and psychological-stress evaluators, which had been used increasingly as personnel tools. Not prohibited by the act, though, are paper-and-pencil honesty and dishonesty tests. Yet employee-rights advocates looked upon the passage of this act as a major victory in the battle for employee privacy.

These critics of business, however, see other problems in the ethical treatment of employees over and above those that deal with employee screening tests. They point to the lack of freedom workers have at their places of employment and the few rights that are granted them in the workplace. David Ewing, a past editor of the *Harvard Business Review,* has remarked that most employees in this country surrender their basic constitutional rights when they arrive at work in the morning and that those rights remain suspended until they leave in the evening. Freedom of speech, the right to due process, the right to equality of treatment, the freedom to dissent – all of these rights,[5] which American have come to take for granted, are abridged daily in the workplace, according to the most vocal business critics.[6]

In recognition of the workers' rights problem, Patricia Werhane, business ethicist at Loyola University in Chicago, has proposed a "Bill of Rights for Employees and Employers." She suggests the minimum rights of employees and employers in the context of 12 workplace issues, such as discrimination, equal pay for equal work, firings, due process and job security. Her program of workplace rights is unique in that it recognizes that employers as well as employees may lay claim to fundamental rights in the workplace. The rights have as their goal a more ethical organizational environment for labor and management.[7] Whether or not such programs of reform will substantially change the workplace remains to be seen.

Business would argue that such changes, giving workers special new rights, will have an expensive price tag that might put many businesses, especially smaller ones, in jeopardy. Business might also argue that the cost of such changes would have to be passed along to the consumer, thereby driving up the price of goods and services.[8] In any case, there will be business resistance to any reforms in the area of workers' rights. For critics, this resistance is not surprising, for it has its source in what they would say is a questionable attitude on the part of business – namely, the attitude of seeing human labor solely as another cost of doing business. When the skills, talents, and abilities of human beings are equated with raw materials, energy and machinery; when human labor is seen as just another operating expense necessary to conduct business; then, critics charge, exploitation of "human resources" will be the norm, and humans will be reduced to an item on an accountant's ledger. Many argue that until this fundamental attitude is overcome, there will always be tension between management and labor.[9]

WHAT ARE SOME EMPLOYEE RESPONSIBILITIES?

Contrasting with Werhane's list of employee rights (which are described more fully later in this chapter), and reflecting some of the issues she raises, here are some areas of employee responsibility. They are enumerated for discussion purposes, and are not ranked by any values:

1. Employees should provide accurate personal information at the time of employment. Falsification of an employment application should be grounds for dismissal.
2. Employees should never be found guilty of discriminating against a fellow employee or behaving in a discriminatory manner against his or her employer.
3. Employees should give their best effort in the performance of their job. If they are unable to perform their job, they should ask for additional training or ask to be transferred to another position which they can perform satisfactorily and equitably.
4. Employees should refrain from drinking alcoholic beverages on the job, taking drugs that will interfere with satisfactory performance of duties, committing a crime against the company which employs them, or otherwise behaving illegally while on the job.
5. Employees should behave so as to bring credit to the company or agency employing them.
6. Employees should not slander the company or agency which employs them.
7. Employees should keep confidential all information the employer requires under an agreement of privacy.
8. Employees should agree to evaluation of (their) work as a means of improving their individual performance and that of the company or agency as a whole.
9. Employees should refrain from securing a second job with an employer who is a direct competitor of the first employer.
10. Employees should perform the duties assigned to them unless these conflict with commonly accepted moral standards or (unless) the duties create a real and present danger to the employee or employer.

EMPLOYEE INVOLVEMENT IN DECISION-MAKING

Increasingly, employees are seen as participants in company decision-making processes. For example, the trends toward "participatory management" and employee-owned companies suggest a redefinition of the traditional adversarial relationship between labor and management. In the service industry the emphasis is now on employee involvement rather than employee alienation. And in a number of American factories one can observe experiments based upon the success of Japanese management with "quality circles," which give labor a chance to voice their suggestions directly to their companies' decision-makers and to become more of a part of the productive process. This is a norm, and these trends represent change from the devaluing attitude of American management toward labor to a more ethical treatment of employees.[10]

FAIRNESS IN PERSONNEL MATTERS

William H. Shaw presents these as contemporary issues facing employees in today's workplace. Some very successful companies have taken the lead in respecting employees' rights and human dignity. They have found that corporate profits and efficient management are compatible with a fair workplace environment. Fairness in personnel matters requires, at least, that policies, standards, and decisions affecting workers are directly job-related and are applied equally. Incomplete job descriptions can injure candidates by denying them information they need to reach informed occupational decisions. Ordinarily, questions of sex, age, race, national origin and religion are not job-related and thus should not enter into personnel decisions. Educational requirements also may not be job-related or fair – as when, for example, employers require more formal education than a job demands or summarily disqualify a candidate for being "overqualified."

A **job test** is valid if it measures precisely what it is designed to determine and is reliable when it provides reasonably consistent results. Tests that lack either validity or reliability are unfair. Tests also may be unfair if they are culturally biased or if the performance they measure does not relate directly to job performance. Most moral concerns in **interviewing** relate to how the interview is conducted. Interviewers should focus on the humanity of the candidate and should avoid allowing their personal biases to color their evaluations. A key issue in **promotions** is whether job qualification alone should determine who gets promoted. Seniority, or longevity on the job, is not necessarily a measure of either competency or loyalty. The challenge for management is to accommodate its twin responsibilities of promoting on the basis of qualifications and recognizing long-term contributions to the firm. Inbreeding, or promoting exclusively from within the organization, presents challenges similar to those presented by seniority.

Nepotism, showing favoritism to relatives or close friends, is not always objectionable. However, it may result in keeping more highly qualified applicants from being employed and also may result in unfair treatment of other employees when promotions are awarded. Employers should be aware that employees are sensitive to any activity, real or perceived, that they believe shows partiality to one or more employees and discriminates against one or more other employees.

Most moral issues in employee discipline and discharge concern how management carries out these unpleasant tasks. Due process and just cause must operate if treatment is to be fair. *"Due process"* refers to specific and systematic means allowed workers for appealing discipline and discharge. To ease the trauma associated with discharge, employers should provide sufficient warning, severance pay, and perhaps displacement counseling. The factors that bear on the fairness of wages include the law, the prevailing wage in the industry, the community wage level, the nature of the job, the security of the job, the company's financial capabilities, and the wages it is paying other employees for comparable work.

Especially important is the manner in which the wage is established. Fairness requires a legitimate work contract, one arrived at through free and fair negotiation. Unions attempt to protect workers from abuse and give them a voice in matters that affect their lives. Critics charge that forcing workers to join unions infringes on autonomy and the right of association. They allege that union workers receive discriminatory and unlawful favoritism. A direct strike is justified, argue some moral theorists, when there is just cause and proper authorization and when it is called as a last resort. Sympathetic strikes support other workers who have grievances with companies. When the companies involved are in different industries, questions arise concerning possible injury and injustice to innocent employers, consumers and workers. Primary boycotts – refusing to patronize companies experiencing a strike – seem morally comparable to direct strikes. Secondary boycotts – refusing to patronize companies handling products of struck companies – are morally analogous to sympathetic strikes. In corporate campaigns, unions enlist the cooperation of a company's creditors to pressure the company to permit unionization or to comply with union demands.[11]

The following statements of employees' obligations to their employer are extracts from a model code of ethics published by the United Technologies Corporation:

CONFLICT OF INTEREST – Employees must deal with suppliers, customers and others doing business with the firm. The employee is responsible for avoiding even the appearance of conflict between his or her personal interests and those of the business or corporation. This requirement applies equally to business relationships and personal activities relative to the employees conduct in the areas of:

* direct or indirect financial or stock ownership interest in suppliers, customers or competitors;

* seeking or accepting gifts or any form of compensation from suppliers, customers or others doing business, or seeking to do business with the firm; directorships, employment with or voluntary service rendered to another company or organization; or

* the use of confidential or non-public information that may be acquired in the course of employment related activities.

ANTI-TRUST COMPLIANCE – Businesses and corporations must comply with the antitrust laws of every jurisdiction in which the firm does business, both within and outside the United States. Every employee, no matter what position he or she holds in the firm, is responsible for compliance with the applicable anti-trust laws.

U.S. GOVERNMENT PROCUREMENTS – A corporation expects all employees and any consultants used by the business or corporation to comply with the laws and regulations regarding government procurements. Special care must be taken to comply with the unique and special rules of the U.S. Government procurement process and to ensure the accuracy of all data submitted to the Government.

PRODUCT QUALITY AND SAFETY – All operating employees of the business or corporation have the responsibility to design, manufacture and deliver quality products and services. All required inspection and testing operations should be properly completed by employees. Likewise, all products must be designed, produced and delivered with the safety and health of customers and product users as a primary consideration.

MARKETING AND SELLING – The employee has the responsibility to understand customer requirements and to seek to satisfy those requirements by offering quality products and services at competitive prices and terms. Employees must offer to sell products and services honestly, based upon their merits, and will not pursue any sale that requires the firm to act unlawfully or in violation of company policy just to win a sale.

PROTECTION OF PROPRIETARY INFORMATION – Employees must respect the proprietary information and trade secrets of the customers and suppliers of a firm. New employees are not to divulge the proprietary information of their former employers. And, employees of the firm will not disclose any proprietary information of customers or suppliers unless the release or disclosure is properly authorized by the individual or firm owning the information.

SUPPLIERS, VENDORS AND SUBCONTRACTORS – Employees of a firm should follow policy relative to the purchase of all equipment, supplies and services on the basis of merit. Suppliers, vendors and subcontractors must be treated with fairness and integrity and without discrimination.

ERROR RECONCILIATION – Firm policy should be followed to advise customers and suppliers of any clerical or accounting errors, and promptly to effect correction of the error through credits, refunds or other mutually acceptable means.

DRUG AND ALCOHOL ABUSE – The firm expects all employees to abide by applicable laws and regulations relative to the possession or use of alcohol and drugs. Employees should abide by policies which prohibit the illegal use, sale, purchase, transfer, possession or presence in one's system of drugs, other than medically prescribed drugs, while on company premises. Similarly, employees are expected to abide by policy which prohibits the use, sale, purchase, transfer or possession of alcoholic beverages by employees while on company premises, except as authorized by the firm.

PROTECTION OF ASSETS – Every employee of the firm is responsible for the proper use, conservation and protection of corporate assets, including its property, plants and equipment.

INTELLECTUAL PROPERTY – The firm's employees frequently have access to the intellectual property of the business, such as inventions, sensitive business information, and sensitive technical information, including computer programs, product designs, and manufacturing expertise. All employees are charged with the responsibility to use and protect these assets in accordance with the firm's guidelines.

ACCURACY OF COMPANY RECORDS – Firm business transactions must be properly authorized and be completely and accurately recorded on the firm's books and records in accordance with generally accepted accounting practice and established firm financial policy. Budget proposals and economic evaluations must fairly represent all information relevant to the decision being requested or recommended. No secret or unrecorded cash funds or other assets will be established or maintained for any purpose. The retention or proper disposal of company records shall be in accordance with established firm financial policies and applicable statutory requirements.

EMPLOYEE INVOLVEMENT IN THE POLITICAL PROCESS – The firm encourages all employees to be informed voters and to be involved in the political process. Personal participation, including contributions of time or financial support, shall be entirely voluntary. Employees, representatives, consultants or agents who are designated to represent the firm or its entities must comply fully with all applicable laws and corporate policy relevant to participation in political and public affairs.

FOREIGN CORRUPT PRACTICES ACT – Employees involved directly or indirectly in non-U.S. operations must abide by the provisions of the Foreign Corrupt Practice Act of 1977. Business transactions outside the U.S. will be governed by the company's policies regarding payments to foreign representatives and foreign payments reviews.

COMMUNITY SUPPORT – As a good corporate citizen, firm policy is to support the organizations and activities of the communities in which the firm resides. Employees are urged to participate personally in civic affairs.

ANTITRUST LAWS – Firm employees never must exchange information with competitors regarding prices, market share, or any other data that could be in violation of U.S. Antitrust law or comparable competition laws that apply to firm operations outside the U.S.

COMPETITIVE INFORMATION – In the highly competitive global marketplace, information about competitors is a necessary element of business. Such information should be accepted by employees only when there is a reasonable belief that both receipt and use of the information is lawful.

MARKETING, SELLING AND ADVERTISING – Firm competition in the global marketplace is on the basis of the merits of firm products and services. Legal and ethical considerations dictate that marketing activities be conducted fairly and honestly. Marketing and selling practices by employees should be based on the superiority of the firm's product offerings. In making comparisons to competitors, care must be taken to avoid disparaging a competitor through inaccurate statements.

COMPLIANCE WITH THE FIRM'S STANDARDS OF CONDUCT – The employee is responsible for complying with the standards of conduct adopted by the firm and implementing policies. Failure to comply with the standards and the associated policies will result in appropriate employee sanctions, to be determined by the cognizant operating manager in conjunction with the business practices office. As with all disciplinary matters, principles of fairness and equity will apply.

REPORTING VIOLATIONS – (All employees have) personal responsibility to bring violations or suspected violations of the standards of conduct to the attention of their supervisor, the legal department of the firm, or to the company ombudsman, as appropriate. Firm policy prohibits any retribution against employees for making such reports.

The following examples of issues that arise from such codes are taken from the United Technologies Corporation's "Questions and Answers About the UTC Code of Ethics."

1. A conflict of interest exists when an employee, or a member of his or her immediate family, receives an unearned, personal benefit as a result of the employee's job or position with the company.

2. Multi-national corporations doing world-wide business must comply with the Foreign Corrupt Practices Act which prohibits employees from paying (bribing) a foreign government official to award business to the firm. How does the law apply if the firm uses a third party, or "agent," to deal with the foreign government? The use of an intermediary, such as an agent or representative, does not relieve the firm from the requirement to comply with the Foreign Corrupt Practices Act. It is the employee's responsibility to prevent improper payments, whether made directly or indirectly.

3. Many codes talk about possible antitrust problems in dealing with customers as well as competitors. What is the reason behind Antitrust Laws? The U.S. economic system encourages as many companies as wish the freedom to compete for consumer acceptance. The success of this process depends on free and fair competition among suppliers. If the competition is not free and fair, then consumers and the American economy may be subjected to higher prices and inferior goods. The purpose of the U.S. Antitrust Laws is simply to ensure that American consumers enjoy the benefits that flow from a free market economy, unrestrained by anti-competitive practices such as price fixing, market allocation or bid rigging.[12]

EMPLOYEE RIGHTS AND OBLIGATIONS

In her book *Persons, Rights and Corporations* (1985), ethicist Patricia Werhane argues that one can modify the relationship between corporations and their employees in such a way that justice can be done to both; so that employees can exercise their rights as human beings and corporations can still reap the benefits of the free enterprise system. Her program for reform entails a recognition of the importance of moral rights in the workplace, which serve as the basis for this mutual relationship. Reprinted here is her list of the kinds of moral rights she believes are necessary for both employees and employers, if workplace injustice is to be eradicated.[13]

Employee Rights

1. Every person has an equal right to a job and a right to equal consideration at the job. Employees may not be discriminated against on the basis of religion, sex, ethnic origin, race, color, or economic background.
2. Every person has the right to equal pay for work, where "equal work" is defined by the job description and title.
3. Every employee has rights to his or her job. After a probation period of 3-10 years every employee has the right to his or her job. An employee can be dismissed only under the following conditions:
   a. He or she is not performing satisfactorily the job for which he or she was hired.
   b. He or she is involved in criminal activity either within or outside the corporation.
   c. He or she is drunk or takes drugs on the job.
   d. He or she actively disrupts corporate business activity without a valid reason.
   e. He or she becomes physically or mentally incapacitated or reaches mandatory retirement age.
   f. The employer has publicly verifiable economic reasons for dismissing the employee, e.g., transfer of the company, loss of sales, bankruptcy, et cetera.
   g. Under no circumstances can an employee be dismissed or laid off without the institution of fair due process procedure.
4. Every employee has the right to due process in the workplace. He or she has the right to peer review, to a hearing, and if necessary, to outside arbitration before being demoted or fired.
5. Every employee has the right to free expression in the workplace. This includes the right to object to corporate acts that he or she finds illegal or immoral without retaliation or penalty. The objection may take the form of free speech, whistle-blowing, or conscientious objection. However, any criticism must be documented or proven.
6. The Privacy Act, which protects the privacy and confidentiality of public employees, should be extended to all employees.
7. The polygraph should be outlawed.
8. Employees have the right to engage in outside activities of their choice.
9. Every employee has the right to a safe workplace, including the right to safety information and participation in improving work hazards. Every employee has the right to legal protection that guards against preventable job risks.
10. Every employee has the right to as much information as possible about the corporation, about his or her job, work hazards, possibilities for future employment, and any other information necessary for job enrichment and development.
11. Every employee has the right to participate in the decision-making processes entailed in his or her job, department, or in the corporation as a whole, where appropriate.
12. Every public and private employee has the right to strike when the foregoing demands are not met in the workplace.

Employee Obligations

1A. Any employee found discriminating against another employee or operating in a discriminatory manner against his or her employer is subject to employer reprimand, demotion, or firing.

2A. Any employee not deserving equal pay because of inefficiency should be shifted to another job.

3A. No employee who functions inefficiently, who drinks or takes drugs on the job, commits felonies or acts in ways that prevent carrying out work duties has a right to a job.

4A. Any employee found guilty under a due process procedure should be reprimanded (e.g., demoted or dismissed), and, if appropriate, brought before the law.

5A. No employer must retain employees who slander the corporation or other corporate constituents.

6A. The privacy of employers is as important as the privacy of employees. By written agreement employees may be required not to disclose confidential corporate information or trade secrets unless not doing so is clearly against public interest.

7A. Employers may engage in surveillance of employees at work (but only at work) with their foreknowledge and consent.

8A. No employee may engage in activities that literally harm the employer, nor may an employee have a second job whose business competes with the business of the first employer.

9A. Employees shall be expected to carry out job assignments for which they are hired unless these conflict with common moral standards or unless the employee was not fully informed about these assignments or their dangers before accepting employment. Employers themselves should become fully informed about work dangers.

10A. Employers have rights to personal information about employees or prospective employees adequate to make sound hiring and promotion judgments so long as the employer preserves the confidentiality of such information.

11A. Employers as well as employees have rights. Therefore the right to participation is a correlative obligation on the part of both parties to respect mutual rights. Employers, then, have the right to demand efficiency and productivity from their employees in return for the employee right to participation in the workplace.

12A. Employees who strike for no reason are subject to dismissal. Any employee or employer who feels he or she has been unduly penalized under a bill of rights may appeal to an outside arbitrator.[14] In the public sector, government employees have special ethical obligations.

Much progress has been made in improving the rights of employees; however, those who criticize business still contend that more needs to be done to establish fair employment practices in America's workplace. Modern spokespersons of the employee-rights movement critique business on issues such as workplace privacy, job security, employee screening tests, lie-detector tests, workers' right to know of hazardous materials in the workplace, equal employment opportunity and affirmative action, comparable worth, and freedom of speech and dissent in the workplace.[15]

In the past the obligations between a business organization and its employees could be summarized as "A fair wage for an honest day's work." Business's primary obligation to its employees was to pay a decent wage. In return, employees were expected to work efficiently and to demonstrate loyalty and obedience to their employer. Obviously, this model of employer-employee relations is too simple and fails to come to terms not just with the dilemmas facing corporations today but also with many other major moral issues that arise in today's workplace.[16]

GOVERNMENT EMPLOYEE ETHICS

A news release dated December 9, 1992 from the office of President-elect Bill Clinton cited a statement written by Warren Christopher on the Clinton administration's ethics "pledges." He stated: "During his presidential campaign, Governor Clinton promised the American people that he would seek to 'stop the revolving door' by requiring his top appointees to refrain from lobbying their agencies for five years. Today, we are announcing rules that keep that promise to the American people. Top officials will be required to sign a pledge agreeing to these new standards. These rules seek to change the climate in Washington, and usher in a new era of public service."

OBLIGATIONS TO THE CUSTOMER AND COMMUNITY

"**Whistle-blowing**" is a new label used to describe some ethical conflicts encountered at work. Whistle-blowers spotlight neglect or abuses that threaten the public interest. In such cases, they may choose to inform appropriate parties outside the firm. Moral conflicts on several levels confront anyone who is wondering whether to speak out about abuses, risks, or serious neglect. (At the very least, the whistle-blower invites labels of "tattletale," "rat fink" or worse.) In the first place, the employee must decide whether, other things being equal, speaking out is in the public interest. The whistle-blower must consider who is responsible for the abuse or neglect, how great the threat is, and whether speaking out will bring about change. In the second place, a would-be whistle-blower must weigh his/her responsibility to serve the public interest against the responsibility owed to colleagues and the institution in which he/she works. While the professional ethic requires collegial loyalty, the codes of ethics often stress responsibility to the public over and above duties to colleagues and clients. Thus, the United States Code of Ethics for Government Servants asks them to "expose corruption wherever uncovered" and to "put loyalty to the highest moral principles and to country above loyalty to persons, party, or government." (Code of Ethics for Government Service passed by the U.S. House of Representatives in the 85th Congress, 1958 and applying to all government employees and office holders.)

Similarly, the largest professional engineering association requires members to speak out against abuses threatening the safety, health and welfare of the public (Code of Ethics of the Institute of Ethical and Electronics Engineers, Article IV). A third conflict for would-be whistle-blowers is personal in nature and cuts across the first two: Even in cases where they have concluded that the facts warrant speaking out, and that their duty to do so overrides loyalties to colleagues and institutions, they often have reason to fear the results of carrying out such a duty. However strong this duty may seem in theory, they know that, in practice, retaliation is likely. As a result, their careers and their ability to support themselves and their families may be impaired unjustly.[17]

We can assume that when one blows the whistle, it is not with the consent of the firm, but against its wishes. It is, then, often perceived as a form of disloyalty and of disobedience to the business. Whistle-blowing, some would assume, does injury to a firm.[18] It results in either adverse publicity or in an investigation of some sort, or both. If we adopt the principle that one ought not to do harm without sufficient reason, then, if the act of whistle-blowing is to be morally permissible, some good must be achieved to outweigh the harm that will be done.[19] DeGeorge cites five conditions that, if satisfied, change the moral status of whistle-blowing. If the first three are satisfied, the act of whistle-blowing will be morally justifiable and permissible. If the additional two are satisfied, the act of whistle-blowing will be morally obligatory.

According to DeGeorge, whistle-blowing would be *morally permissible* if the following obtain: (1) The firm, through its product or policy, will do serious and considerable harm to the public, whether in the person of the user of its product, an innocent bystander, or the general public. (2) Employees identify a serious threat to the user of a product or to the general public, report it to their immediate supervisor, and make their moral concern known. (Unless they do so, the act of whistle-blowing is not clearly justifiable.) (3). The employees' immediate superior does nothing effective about the concern or complaint, and the employees then exhaust the internal procedures and possibilities within the firm. (This usually will involve taking the matter up the managerial ladder, and, if necessary—and possible—to the board of directors.)

Whistle-blowing is *morally required* in DeGeorge's view if, additionally, the following two conditions are met: (1) The whistle-blower has, or has accessible, documented evidence that would convince a reasonable, impartial observer that one's view of the situation is correct, and that the company's product or practice poses a serious and likely danger to the public or to the user of the product. (2) The employee has good reasons to believe that by going public the necessary changes will be brought about. The chance of being successful must be worth the risk one takes and the danger to which one is exposed.[20] It is more important to change the legal and corporate structures that make whistle-blowing necessary than to convince people to be moral. Because it is easier to change the law than to change the practice of all corporations, it should be illegal for any employer to fire an employee, or to take any punitive measures, at the time or later, against an employee who satisfies the first three aforementioned conditions and blows the whistle on the company. Because satisfying those conditions makes the action morally justifiable, the law should protect employees when acting in accordance with what their conscience demands.

COMPANY RESPONSES TO WHISTLE-BLOWING

If the whistle is appropriately blown, the company should suffer the consequences of its actions being made public. But to protect a whistle-blower by passing such a law is no easy matter. Employers can make life difficult for whistle-blowers without firing them. For instance, there are many ways of passing over an employee. Employers can find reasons not to promote or to award a raise. In all cases, because whistle-blowing involves disloyalty or disobedience at some level, it should be justified, rather than assuming it needs no justification. If the action needs no justification, it is probably not an instance of whistle-blowing. To distinguish the various kinds of whistle-blowing, listing conditions that make it morally permissible and those that make it morally required is useful as a guide. In personal whistle blowing, there are many instances in which it is permitted but not obligatory. Many people may prefer to change employers rather than blow the whistle, and this may be justifiable. In all cases, one must weigh the harm done to individuals against the good to be achieved and their rights to be protected.

Whistle-blowing is a relatively recent phenomenon in the workplace. It is one more indication of the falsity of the myth of amoral business. Whistle-blowing also should alert corporations to what can and should be done if they wish to be both moral and excellent. When corporate structures preclude the need for whistle-blowing, they protect both workers' rights and the public's good.[21]

EXTRA SERVICE BY EMPLOYEES

Today's corporate leaders recognize that identifying customers' needs and developing products and services to meet those needs make the difference between corporate survival and demise. From power plant suppliers to packaged goods producers, companies are revamping the way they sell to serve their customers better. They are reorganizing sales forces around clients, encouraging sales to collaborate with other arms of the company, or uniting salespeople into customer-focused teams. Richard Slember, president of the U.S. Power Plant subsidiary of Asea Brown Boveri Inc., a $29-billion-a-year manufacturing business, says, "If you want to be a customer-driven company you have to design the sales organization from the outside in, around individual buyers rather than around your products.[22] "A company, to be successful, must encourage coordination, especially between sales and other departments. Procter and Gamble has been most innovative in this regard. In the late 1980s, the Cincinnati powerhouse combined some of its U.S. sales forces in order to reduce the excessive number of people calling on retailers. To overcome P & G's reputation for being arrogant and dictatorial with customers, management assigned employees from other areas of the company (marketing, finance, distribution, operations) to coordinate with sales and work with key buyers to help them solve problems.[23]

Doing more for customers is crucial, particularly in a difficult, super-competitive era. The hot-shot sales representative of this decade will be a facilitator, not a pitch man – an expert on the customer's industry who coordinates with colleagues to make buying easy and efficient.[24] Harry L. M. Artinian, vice president for corporate quality, Colgate-Palmolive Co., recently stated in a speech delivered to a Marketing Institute Conference on sales force quality initiatives: "We (American businesses) have largely been operating on a three-step basis: 1) designers design, 2) producers produce, and 3) salespeople sell. What seems to have become lost in this equation is a fourth step: 'The customers consume.'"[25] It is, in fact, the customer who buys products, whose needs have to be understood and whose expectations have to be met or exceeded. It is the customer, not the company, who needs to be the focal point of company efforts, and the final and best judge of company performance.[26]

> **"Doing more for customers is crucial, particularly in a difficult, super-competitive era."**

The search is on for new and better ways to serve the customer. Michael P. Cronin reports that Enterprise Builders Inc. initiated a program in which each employee was given written instructions instructing them to consider themselves "Customers" of one another. Each employee went around to 13 others one at a time and asked them to list their 10 greatest needs as a customer. They then agreed on an action plan to meet each need. Later, employees looked at all the responses they had gathered, identified those needs mentioned most frequently, and made them immediate goals. They also agreed to meet a month later to discuss progress on the problems.[27] The exercise sanctioned workers to identify what didn't work and to fix it instead of excusing it as "the way things are done." During the exercise, the senior project manager of the company heard about the high degree of frustration with the job-cost reporting system. He worked with six users to develop a better model, then brought it to the accounting department. Together, the employees improved the system and put it into practice.[28]

Paul Berg, company president, states: "In our business, there are so many levels of customers – the subcontractors, the architects, the owners. I wanted our people to understand service in a living and personal way, so we started on the inside, and we'll work our way out to every layer of customers.[29]

More recently, the icons of customer service – 800 numbers, guarantees, suggestion cards, and surveys – have become recognized as necessary to compete in today's fast paced economy. However, even these customer services no longer provide a competitive advantage. Identifying how to satisfy customers must become a successful company's obsession. Perhaps one of the most unique approaches to satisfying customers is the "mystery shopper questionnaire." Au Bon Pain Company's mystery shoppers are part of an ongoing, extensive program to measure whether the company's quality and service standards are being met. The program's emphasis is on improving performance by rewarding employees for excellence.[30]

Anonymous non-company-affiliated customers buy a meal and fill out a questionnaire about the restaurant, the food, and the service. Bonuses for everyone from line employees to vice presidents are based in large part on how well they treat the average customer, i.e., the mystery shopper. An average of 20 people from the 69 company-owned restaurants and fast food units receive rave reviews each week. For these plaudits they receive a healthy bonus and companywide recognition. Overall site performance scores have risen from an average of 72% to 80%.[31]

Individual workers (the servers) get points if they score 100% in six areas of customer interaction, from an overall willingness to serve, to greeting the shopper within three seconds. Indeed, recognition for treating a mystery shopper well is a culmination of the constant reinforcement employees receive for good customer service. Winners' names are posted on each store's bulletin board next to a list of the judging criteria, and all winners get letters of congratulations from the company president and the vice president of operations. Notices reminding employees about the service priorities also are periodically included in paychecks. Shoppers are expected to fill out the forms surreptitiously, so the employees won't give them special treatment; length of time to be served, for example is supposed to be noted subtly and at a later time. But the employees look out for the mystery shoppers. "We encourage our people to wonder," says the president, "It's a good motivator."[32]

Businesses' survival in the economy and employees' survival in the workplace are dependent upon satisfying the customer so that he or she continues to purchase goods and services, thus making the businesses and jobs necessary. Businesses who do not "keep the customer first" are doomed. Long-term success is surely dependent upon customer satisfaction through identification of their needs and constant attention to their demands for goods and services. The old adage, "The customer is king," is as true today as it was the day it was penned.

EMPLOYEES' OBLIGATIONS TO COWORKERS

William Shaw's *Business Ethics* presents a compelling inquiry into employees' obligations to third parties:

- A worker knows that a fellow worker occasionally snorts cocaine on the job. Should she inform the boss?
- A chef knows that his restaurant typically reheats 3– or 4-day-old food and serves it as fresh. When he informs the manager, he is told to forget it. What should the chef do?
- A consulting engineer discovers a defect in a structure that is about to be sold. If the owner will not disclose the defect to the potential purchaser, should the engineer do so?
- An accountant learns of the illegal activities of a client, including deliberate violations of

building codes. What should she do about it?

• On a regular basis, a secretary is asked by her boss to lie to his wife about his whereabouts. "If my wife calls, "the boss tells her, "don't forget to confirm that I'm on a business trip." In fact, as the secretary well knows, the boss is having an affair with another woman. What should the secretary do?[33]

Such cases are not unusual, but they are different because they involve workers caught in the crossfire of conflicting obligations. On the one hand, workers have obligations to the employer or organization; on the other, they have obligations to third parties: to fellow employees, to customers and other outside individuals affected by the organization; to government, and to society in general.

Conflicts between a worker's obligation to the firm and to others are at the heart of many moral decisions. A way to resolve the workers' conflicts is needed, but that in turn requires identifying what obligations workers have to third parties. Employees have three basic obligations to third parties as a matter of ordinary morality: truthfulness, non-injury, and fairness. In some instances the application of these obligations to outside parties is relatively straightforward. For example, in engineering, obligations to third parties are fundamental, and the obligation of non-injury predominates because almost all architectural and engineering projects have a potential for injuring people. Whether the design is an automobile, an airplane, building, bridge, electric power system, sewer system, or nuclear power plant, a faulty design clearly can result in injury to others.

Similarly, those commercially serving alcoholic beverages have a non-injury obligation to monitor the amount of alcohol they serve customers, despite the U.S. Supreme Court's 1979 ruling ending liability for overseeing intoxicated customers. For accountants, it is not the obligation of non-injury that dominates the relationship to third parties but the obligations of truthfulness and justice. Most of the injury that accountants cause others results from deceit, carelessness or unfairness. Accordingly, auditors certify that financial statements present data fairly, as determined by generally accepted accounting principles. An untruthful audit can cause others to make unwise investments. Likewise failure to be truthful and fair in preparing an income-tax statement cheats government and society.

OBLIGATIONS, IDEALS, AND EFFECTS

Any moral decision should take account of the relevant obligations, ideals, and effects, according to modern philosopher Vincent Ryan Ruggiero. As indicated, the specific responsibilities that one assumes in a given business or professional role affects the strength of one's *obligations* to third parties. When an engineer or an accounting auditor, for example, suspects some "irregularity," he or she may have a stronger obligation to get to the bottom of the matter than would an ordinary employee who has a hunch that something is not in order in another department. How far must an employee go to uncover or remedy possible violations of those obligations by others? It is unlikely that any moral theory can give a general answer to this question that can be applicable in all cases.

Third parties are always the "public" at large. They often are friends, co-workers and family members. Sometimes these obligations have to be balanced against obligations to the business and obligations arising from the business, professional, or organizational roles the employee has assumed.

The impact of our action on significant moral *ideals* is another consideration, according to Ruggiero. Moral decisions must take into account not only distinct ethical obligations but also the various ideals advanced or respected, ignored or hindered, by the alternative actions open to us. In addition, our moral choices often are influenced strongly by the personal weight we place on the different values that may be at stake in a specific situation. Sometimes these values can point in different directions, as when our simultaneous commitment to professional excellence, personal integrity, and loyalty to friends pulls us in three different ways. We also, says Ruggiero, must examine the *effects* of the different courses of action and the likely results of our actions as they relate to individuals' moral assessment. We have a duty to promote human well being. In addition, considerations of consequences can help us determine the exact strength of our different obligations in a given situation. We must first identify the relevant obligations, ideals, and effects and then try to decide where the emphasis should lie.

There is nothing mechanical about this process, but when we as employees weigh moral decisions, two simple things can help keep our deliberations free from the various rationalizations to which we are all prone. First, we can ask ourselves whether we would be willing to read an account of our actions in the newspaper.[34] That is, when we must have made our decisions, are the contemplated actions ones that we would be willing to defend publicly? Second, discussing a moral dilemma or ethical problem with a friend can often help us avoid bias and gain a better perspective. People by themselves, and especially when emotionally involved in a situation, sometimes focus unduly on one or two points, ignoring other relevant factors. Advice from others can keep us from overlooking pertinent considerations, thus helping us make a better, more objective moral judgment.

Employees frequently know about the illegal or immoral actions of a supervisor or firm. When an employee tries to correct the situation within institutional channels and is thwarted, a central moral question emerges: Should the employee go public with the information? Should a worker who is ordered to do something illegal or immoral, or who knows of the illegal or immoral behavior of a supervisor or organization, inform the public?

PRIVACY: THE EMPLOYEE'S PERSPECTIVE

Employee privacy previously was discussed as an issue between employees and employers in Chapter 16. This is an issue that poses an ethical dilemma for employers. On the one hand, they have the responsibility to ensure that the workplace is drug-free or free from dishonest workers who might steal. Yet some degree of worker privacy may be abridged (or even completely sacrificed) to achieve this. With few legal precedents to serve as guidelines, finding a middle ground between an employer's myriad responsibilities and an employee's right to privacy is no easy task. Many companies engage in activities that civil libertarians find questionable; for example, random urine tests to discover drug use, computer surveillance of employee activities, telephone monitoring, breaches of the confidentiality of persons with AIDS, and the use of advanced technology to test worker suitability by means of genetic screening. Some perceive these kinds of employer tactics (ostensibly to promote the common good in the workplace) as unacceptable infringements on a worker's rights. Note that the legislation mentioned in the article regulating the use of lie detectors by private industry has been passed as part of the Polygraph Protection Act of 1988; most companies are now prohibited from using the device to screen prospective and current employees.[35]

THE COURTS AND PRIVACY

The right to privacy, U. S. Supreme Court Justice Louis D. Brandeis wrote in 1928, is "the right to be let alone, the most comprehensive of rights and the right most valued by civilized men." Brandeis was referring to the Fourth Amendment's guarantee against "illegal searches and seizures' by government. Today, Americans are asserting the "right to be let alone" by a different adversary: their employers. A nationwide controversy is erupting as companies probe deeper into workers' habits and health.[36] Unlike past labor uprisings, workers aren't mounting strikes over the privacy issue. Today's combat involves lawsuits, huge jury awards, and demands for leave-me-alone legislation. Individual employees and unions are filling court dockets with challenges to random drug testing. AIDS patients are suing employers for breach of confidentiality when co-workers learn about their condition. Employee advocates are demanding limits on electronic and telephone eavesdropping. And concern is growing over the potential for employers to delve into electronic data bases that collect the tiniest pieces of an employee's lifestyle under one neat label – the Social Security number.[37] The protests are being heard.

Both the U.S. House and the Senate in late 1992 passed bills restricting lie detector tests by private companies. Declares Paul Saffo, an expert on information technologies at the Institute for the Future: "After health care, privacy in the workplace may be the most important issue in the 1990s."[38] It's not that most companies are idly snooping into their employees' lives. Behind the erosion of privacy lie pressing corporate problems. Drug use costs American industry nearly $50-billion a year in absenteeism and turnover. When employer groups opposed the lie detector bills, they cited employee theft, which is estimated at up to $10-billion annually. Moreover, in the litigious 1980s, failing to ensure a safe and drug-free workplace can subject an employer to millions in liability claims when and if people are injured by an errant employee or faulty products.[39]

The difficulty is maintaining a proper balance between the common good and personal freedom. It may be laudable for companies to hold down soaring medical costs by giving employees checkups and offering exercise programs. But what keeps helpful advice on high blood pressure from becoming an ominous decision on an employee's promotion potential? There are few standards to help answer such questions.

"It is an era of legal uncertainty," says Robert B. Fitzpatrick, a Washington lawyer who represents both companies and employees. "In a lot of states the law is in flux, and it is unclear what the rules are any longer." What is clear is that employers face a complex challenge. For years, American workers seemed to lack the body-and-soul dedication of their Japanese counterparts. Now, U. S. companies are beginning to gain the commitment of workers, who often build their private lives around the job and the pension and health plans linked to it. But as this happens, employees also bring their off-the-job values and demands to work. Increasingly, says Alan F. Westin, a Columbia University professor who has studied individual rights in the corporation since the 1950s, "Americans are coming to believe that the rights we attach to citizenship in the society – free expression, privacy, equality, and due process – ought to have their echo in the workplace."[40]

"Privacy today matters to employees at all levels, from shop-floor workers to presidents. "I don't think politicians and corporate executives realize how strongly Americans feel about it," says Cliff Palefsky, a San Francisco lawyer who handles employees lawsuits. "It's not a liberal or a conservative issue, and the fear of abuse doesn't emanate from personnel policies. It's coming out of the larger, impersonal notion that workers are expendable items."[41]

Huge jury awards in recent privacy cases reflect these concerns: A supervisor for Georgia-Pacific Corporation in Oregon fired a man based on an anonymous letter stating that the worker had been drunk in public. Then the supervisor repeated the allegation at a meeting of 100 employees. Concluding that such wide dissemination damaged the worker's reputation, a state appeals court upheld a $350,000 defamation award.[42] A drugstore employee refused to take a lie detector test during an investigation of stock shortages at Rite-Aid of Maryland Inc. Though the company violated a state law in ordering the test, it forced the woman to resign. A state appeals court affirmed a $1.3-million award for corporate behavior that "amounted to a complete denial of (her) dignity as a person."[43]

These aren't isolated stories. A survey by Ira Michael Shepard and Robert L. Duston, members of a management law firm in Washington, turned up 97 jury verdicts against employers in privacy cases from 1985 to mid-1987. Damage awards averaged $316,000. Before 1980 employees suits for invasion of privacy rarely reached a jury.[44] They do now largely because a decade of litigation and legislation involving employees' rights has laid the groundwork. This movement has led to laws that give employees the right to know about hazardous workplace chemicals, that protect whistle-blowers, and that give workers access to medical and personnel records. Complaints of discrimination by age, race, and sex are also increasing fast.

Meanwhile, nonunion workers, aided by state courts, are successfully challenging the once-undisputed employment-at-will doctrine. This gave private companies the right to dismiss employees without cause.[45] The erosion of the at-will concept clears the way for workers to sue employers over privacy issues. Otherwise, such cases are often difficult to file. State laws that regulate polygraph testing, for example, provide for prosecution of corporate violators but give no redress to wronged employees. But using precedents from employment-at-will cases, workers can often prove unfair dismissal and win big awards.[46]

All these trends are creating chaos in the rules that govern the workplace. And the changes this will bring in the employer-employee relationship could be as far-reaching as those that followed the breakthrough of industrial unionism in the 1930s. The difference is that today the courts and Congress may do much more quickly what unions would take decades to achieve. "The idea that the employment relationship cannot be regulated will never be with us again," says William B. Gould, a labor law professor at Stanford University. "In some form or another, we're going to have regulation."[47]

The tension over privacy, in fact, marks a turning point in the cycle of management-labor relations. Starting in the early 19th century and for decades after, employers exercised wide dominion over employees' lives. Companies built and ran company towns. In 1914, Henry Ford's workers were promised a $5-a-day wage only after Ford's "sociologists" visited their homes and deemed them morally qualified. The growth of unions, the improved education of the workforce, and the civil-rights and civil-liberties movements of the 1960s seemed to kill off these Big Brother policies. In the 1980s, however, the cycle is reversed – as the controversy over these major issues indicates.[48] Employees with AIDS, as of spring 1993, are protected by federal and state laws that guarantee job rights for the handicapped. Nonetheless, some people with AIDS have been fired and in several instances not reinstated before they died.[49] Most companies have neither a policy nor an educational program on AIDS. Emerson Electric Co. in St. Louis has had "a couple" of employees with AIDS, says John C. Rohrbaugh, vice president for corporate communications. Those who have the disease became known "because other employees didn't want to share phones or work in the same offices," Rohrbaugh adds. Typically, "We didn't take any type of action, and eventually the employee became more and more debilitated until he was too sick to work, and frankly, he died."[50]

OBLIGATIONS TO FORMER EMPLOYEES

Employees often sue when a former employer gives damaging information to a prospective employer. Because companies sometimes need to compare notes on hiring, their communications are considered "privileged." But they can lose this protection if they give information to too many people or hand out false information maliciously. The fear of defamation suits has caused many companies, probably the majority, to refuse to say anything about a former employee except "name, rank, and serial number." But this practice is having an adverse effect on screening job applicants, which sometimes causes companies to hire people with unsavory backgrounds. Their unlawful conduct can lead to a negligent-hiring suit and enormous damages. For example, in 1985 a car rental agency had to pay $750,000 in damages to atone for an employee who repeatedly hit a customer with "judo chops." In that case, a court found, the employer had ignored evidence of the worker's irascibility.[51] Considerable private information about workers exists in computer data bases kept by practically every business and government agency – and it's available to a surprisingly wide range of snoops. A crazy quilt of state and federal laws, as well as court rulings, regulates employer access to such information. Some areas, such as medical data, are highly protected. But others aren't.[52] Credit bureaus, for instance, sell information on employees' bank accounts, outstanding bills, and tax liens or bankruptcies, although all negative records must be purged after seven years. Only recently, TRW Inc., the largest supplier of consumer credit information, began selling such data to employers. "It didn't sound like the kind of thing we wanted to be involved in," says Edward F. Freeman, vice president and general manager of TRW's information services division. But "it's what our customers wanted, and all our competitors were doing it." [53]

Certain employers, such as banks and nuclear power plants, can get criminal histories of prospective employees from the Federal Bureau of Investigation's Identification Division data base on more than 20-million people. In some states, other employers can get FBI information, too. Now the Bureau is considering lifting a major restriction on its criminal history data base: It may delete a rule requiring that information on people who are arrested but not convicted can't be disseminated after one year. Critics say this would add to the volume of potentially false information that employers can collect. Many large employers have guidelines requiring managers to prove a specific business purpose before gaining access to sensitive information. But many don't. And the American Civil Liberties Union fears that voluntary guidelines won't work if the political climate changes. "What happens if society's pendulum shifts to be less concerned about personal liberty?" asks Jerry Berman, director of the ACLU's project on information technology and civil liberties. [54]

SECRET MONITORING OF WORKERS' PERFORMANCE

Over the past decade, practically every major employer has gained the ability to monitor workers' performance through the computers and phones they use. This practice is already prevalent in service-oriented businesses such as insurance and telecommunications. And unless it's done carefully, workers resent it. "I don't think people mind having their work checked," says Morton Bahr, president of the Communications Workers of America (CWA). "It's the secretiveness of it. It's like being wired to a machine." The CWA is pushing a bill in Congress that would prohibit secret monitoring in all industries and require regular beeps when a supervisor is listening.[55]

Worker-advocates in Massachusetts are carrying the fight further in a bill that has raised strong objections by industry groups. In addition to requiring beeps, the proposal would limit the amount of monitoring and require employers to explain in writing the purpose and results of monitoring. [56] The most pernicious use of technology to invade privacy may be yet to come. Scientists already can identify genetic traits that indicate a predisposition to such diseases as heart disease and cancer. In 1980, Du Pont Company came under fire for testing black employees and applicants for sickle cell anemia. The tests were given as a "service to employees," and the results were not used in hiring or career decisions, says Dr. Bruce W. Karrh, a Du Pont vice president. But because of the controversy, the company now does testing only at workers' request.[57] Genetic testing might be used legitimately to ensure that employees susceptible to certain occupational diseases aren't put in the wrong work environments.

And as far as can be reasonably determined, no companies now use the tests to deny employment. But Mark A. Rothstein, director of the University of Houston's Health Law Institute, believes employers eventually will try that, if only to help hold down health care costs. "Unless we have some clear indication that employers aren't going to be engaged in screening, legislation may be necessary," he says.[58] A preview of this issue may come as companies mount more aggressive "wellness" programs that try to push employees toward healthier lifestyles. So far these programs seem aimed at helping employees live longer and improving their productivity. But the logical next step is mandating off-the-job behavior. "I think employers are going to get deeper and deeper into the wellness business," says Columbia's Westin. "This is going to throw up a series of profound ethical and legal dilemmas about how they should do it and what we don't want them to do."

Most workplace privacy issues pose these kinds of difficult questions. They pit the needs of the company against the worker's feelings of dignity and worth. To sacrifice much of the latter would make work life untenable. So the U. S. must decide which rights of a citizen in society should extend to an employee in the corporation – and in what form. If employers don't voluntarily start this process, the courts or legislatures will do it for them.[59]

DRUG ABUSE

On October 29, 1987, Eastern Air Lines,Inc. apparently received an anonymous tip that some of its baggage handlers at Miami International Airport used drugs. Security guards rounded up 10 workers in the plane-loading area. Then, in full view of other employees and passengers, the workers were marched down a guard-lined path to waiting vans – "like terrorists," as a lawsuit filed by the workers describes it. After questioning the men, supervisors put them aboard a bus, once again in front of onlookers, and took them to a hospital. Then came an ultimatum: Either take a urine test or be fired on the spot.[60] All 10 employees, members of the International Association of Machinists, tested negative. Later they filed suit in federal court, seeking at least $30,000 each on charges of invasion of privacy, defamation, and intentional infliction of emotional distress. Eastern refuses to discuss the incident. In its motion to dismiss the case, Eastern contends that the complaint should be resolved in a union grievance procedure.[61] Wherever this case winds up, it's a gripping example of the quintessential and growing American concern about privacy.

When guards conducted an early morning drug sweep of the Albuquerque Publishing Co. (in January 1985), company officials said it was for good reason: an estimated 20% of the firm's employees had "an abuse problem," said company president Thompson Lang – and of all the job applicants who'd taken drug tests in recent months, "no one ... passed." Few companies face problems quite so dramatic, but drug use does take a serious toll: The U. S. Chamber of Commerce estimates that drug and alcohol abuse among workers costs employers $60-billion a year – the total tab for lost productivity, accidents, higher medical claims, increased absenteeism and theft of company property (the means by which many workers finance their drug habits).

Relatively few companies seem to be tackling alcohol abuse with as much conviction, but concern about drugs is plainly growing, and it has spread well beyond the private workplace. In June 1986 Boston's police commissioner called for mandatory drug testing of all officers. [62] To root out drug abusers among applicants or employees, meanwhile, companies such as Michigan-based Consumers Power Company, Westinghouse Electric Corporation, Du Pont,. and Albuquerque Publishing have turned to relatively inexpensive urine tests, such as EMIT (Enzyme Multiplied Immunoassay Test), manufactured by Syva Company, a subsidiary of Syntex Corporation of Palo Alto, California. But whether use of these tests does much to control drug abuse is a matter of fierce debate.

A major flaw of the most widely used tests is that they don't measure an employee's degree of impairment or level of job performance at the time of the test but show only traces of drugs in the urine. Cocaine may show up as much as three days after consumption; marijuana may be present from five days to three weeks afterward. A drug test, then, may nab even drug users who don't use them at the workplace. "What someone does outside the job isn't a concern for the employer unless it affects what they do on the job," argues Erwin Chemerensky, professor of constitutional law at the University of Southern California (USC). [63] An even bigger problem is that the tests aren't always accurate. Results can vary widely with the skills of the individuals carrying out the tests or the laboratories analyzing the results. Over-the-counter drugs such as Advil and Nuprin have shown up as illegal drugs on some tests, notes Kerry Shannon, marketing director of Bio-Analytical Technologies, a Chicago lab that conducts urinalysis tests. The most widely used tests claim a 95-99% accuracy rate; in companies where blanket testing is carried out, this means that, on average, 1-5 of every 100 tests will produce inaccurate results.

A recent Northwestern University study suggests an even worse record. It found that 25% of all EMIT tests that came up positive were really "false positives." And James Woodford, a forensic chemist in Atlanta and a consultant to the U. S. Public Health Service, contends that urinalysis tests may be racially biased. The reason: Test results may be skewed by blacks' higher concentrations of the pigment melanin, which has an ion identical to THC, the active ingredient in marijuana – and which may also soak up body substances similar to THC. [64] Manufacturers of urine tests acknowledge some of their deficiencies. Michelle Klaich, a spokeswoman for Syntex, stresses that a positive reading on one test shouldn't by itself be a ground for firing; she says Syntex recommends follow-up tests and other measures to verify the results.

To improve accuracy, meanwhile, some companies are at work on the next generation of testing devices. National Patent Analytical Systems Inc. of Roslyn Heights, N.Y., is awaiting results of clinical tests of its Veritas 100 Analyzer, which uses computer hardware and software to analyze the electrical stimuli given off by the brain in the presence of certain drugs. Company president Joseph Boccuzi says the device measures only the presence of drugs at the time of the test and cuts the false-positive rate to less than 5%. [65] But Ira Glasser, executive director of the ACLU, worries that the growing testing industry will become its own reason for being, propounding the use of testing to justify its existence. He recommends "an unused method for detecting (drug abuse) – it's called 'two eyes.'"

Most employees who are drug abusers reveal telltale signs of their problem, such as erratic behavior or inability to concentrate. A watchful supervisor, says Glasser, should be able to spot drug use and help an employee into a drug-rehabilitation program, an approach that ultimately may be most helpful in eliminating drug abuse. [66] Despite a growing number of lawsuits, courts so far have generally upheld the legality of drug testing. But some state and local legislatures are moving to restrict and regulate it. California Assemblyman Johan Klehs has proposed a bill that would require a company's testing policy to be in writing; test results would be kept confidential, and all labs that analyze tests of employees and job applicants would be licensed.

The Civil Liberties Union of Massachusetts is drafting a bill that would allow testing of only those employees whose performance had a bearing on public safety – nuclear plant operators, school-bus drivers and the like – and who show some signs of impairment. Similarly, in San Francisco, a new ordinance prohibits drug testing by private employers unless there is a high degree of what's known as individualized suspicion – that the employees to be tested are not only impaired but also pose a "clear and present danger" to themselves or others.

Only through such measures will companies be barred from "rummaging through another person's biology," says San Francisco supervisor Maher, unless testing is absolutely necessary.[67] At Enserch Corp., a diversified energy company based in Dallas, officials were horrified: Last summer the *maitre d'hotel* of the executive dining room was discovered to have AIDS. When the company summarily ordered mandatory AIDS tests for its other food-service workers, another was discovered to have the AIDS antibody. Both employees were suspended with full pay and medical benefits and escorted from the premises. [68]

The consternation that followed among gay-rights groups and civil libertarians pointed up the controversy around a growing area of testing: monitoring employees' health. Examining blood or tissue samples for signs of disease or certain genetic traits could protect employees and the public from health risks – while sparing employers higher medical insurance costs and reduced productivity.

But as tests get increasingly sophisticated, they could also provide a powerful tool for discrimination against homosexuals, women, anyone predisposed to certain diseases, or other groups of employees.[69] Testing for AIDS is especially problematic. Most of the tests offered have high rates of both false positives and "false negatives" (incorrect negative results) – traumatic enough in drug testing but particularly so with AIDS. Nor is it clear just what AIDS testing accomplishes, given most experts' belief that the disease isn't spread through the casual contact typical of the workplace but through sexual relations or contact with AIDS-contaminated blood. Yet as of 1986, only California had acted to prohibit AIDS testing as a condition of employment. [70] Looming on the horizon is genetic testing.

Each year 390,000 workers contract occupational illnesses including lung, bladder and other cancers; about 100,000 die. The belief that some workers possessed genetic "hyper-susceptibility" to some of these conditions that could be triggered by exposure to toxins in the workplace led companies like Du Pont and Dow Chemical to conduct tests on workers beginning in the 1970s. But "after a number of years we were not seeing what we thought we might find," says Dr. John Venable, medical director of Dow. Negative publicity about the tests – particularly Du Pont's testing of workers for sickle-cell trait, which leads to a condition that affects many blacks – further dampened corporate enthusiasm for testing. By the time a 1983 report by the Office of Technology Assessment determined that existing genetic tests couldn't predict what happen on the job, most companies had quit the field. [71]

Recently, however, biologists have discovered genetic "markers" for a number of genetic diseases such as cystic fibrosis and are now searching for others for more commonplace conditions such as Alzheimer's disease and breast cancer. "We're still many years away" from the time when genetic tests for such conditions could come into widespread use, asserts Alexander Morgan Capron, professor of law and medicine at USC. But because so many people may be prone to these diseases, there is the distant prospect that companies could one day undertake genetic screening – declining to hire employees who seem likely to become sick on the job, use up expensive medical benefits or die young. [72] As the technology of testing advances, say the experts, so must the public's attention to the range of economic, ethical and legal issues it raises. Columbia's Westin is confident that such awareness will increase; as a consequence, he predicts, within 10 years a "latticework of legislation" will be in place to balance employers' aims with employees' rights. Society has much to gain from careful and sophisticated testing – a potentially more productive corps of workers whose skills more closely match the requirements of their jobs. But the preeminent challenge for on-the-job testing will be whether it can avoid unwarranted encroachment on the rights and freedoms Americans hold dear.[73]

For many companies, such *ad hoc* handling of the situation may be a costly mistake, says David Herold, Director of the Center for Work Performance Problems at the Georgia Institute of Technology. In a survey conducted for the Center last year, 35% of 2,000 workers said they didn't believe that AIDS can be transmitted only by sexual contact or blood contamination. The same percentage of workers said they would be "concerned" about using the same bathroom as people with AIDS. Herold believes the costs of caring for AIDS sufferers could pale by comparison with the productivity losses if healthy employees refuse to work alongside them. And he disparages the policy of many companies to treat AIDS "like any other illness." Adds Herold: "If that's what they mean by policy, that's nonsense, because other employees will not treat it like any other illness." Some 30 of the nation's largest employers agree. IBM, AT&T, and Johnson & Johnson, among others, have endorsed a 10-point bill of rights on AIDS issues. It calls for education to dispel fears, urges that medical records be kept confidential and pledges not to test for the AIDS virus in hiring.

READINGS

TRUST CANNOT BE LEGISLATED
Vital Speeches of the Day
September 1, 1990
Richard G. Capen Jr.
Publisher, *Miami Herald*

"Americans are drifting away from spiritual values as they become richer ... We look to America, and we expect from you a spiritual richness to meet the aspirations of the 20th century."

– Lech Walesa, Poland 1990

It's a sad commentary on the state of our nation's ethical and spiritual values that we need a blunt lecture from a powerful figure who struggled so long behind the Iron Curtain. For Lech Walesa, human dignity and freedom were ultimate values, but here in America, these values seem to be casually and carelessly taken for granted.

Historic events in Eastern Europe remind us of the power and significance of the moral and ethical principles upon which our country was founded. Many believe these dramatic changes in Europe reflect a resurgence of spiritual faith. Whatever the motivation, our friends in Poland, Czechoslovakia, Hungary, Rumania, East Germany and elsewhere are turning to us – more than ever – for encouragement, for example and for inspiration.

America is still viewed as the land of opportunity. We're seen as the model of democracy and human dignity, and yet, I wonder if we really deserve that compliment, that vote of confidence.

Politicians cheat on their constituents. Brokers rip off their clients. S&L executives drive their institutions into the ground and leave taxpayers footing the bill. Preachers and would-be presidents cheat on their wives. Kids cheat on exams, and millions destroy themselves and others though the ravages of drugs and crime.

More than ever, there's a need to restore ethics and integrity in all that we do: ethics in business, ethics in the language we use, ethics in dealing with each other, ethics in professional life, ethics in public life.

Television commentator Ted Koppel once urged that, above all, we need a new moral compass. "There's harmony and inner peace," Koppel said in a college commencement speech, "to be found in following a moral compass that points in the same direction regardless of fashion or trend."

We desperately need ethical standards in all aspects of our lives, and that's why I believe we must be willing to speak out forcefully for the values we hold sacred. The widespread debate on ethics and integrity is encouraging. Through it, I believe we can redefine the priorities of our own lives.

Greed within a rootless society makes it far too easy to confuse right from wrong and dozens of convicted public officials, businessmen and even preachers can attest to that reality.

Are we truly a nation of integrity, of fairness, of ethical standards worth emulating? Have we earned that reputation as freedom's moral compass? I suspect most of you think not, and that's why you are here – to help pre-define ethical performance in a changing world.

The foundation of trust and ethics has been seriously eroded by today's mobility, materialism and by lust for power. It has also been devastated by a shocking collapse of family life. The family unit, as we once knew it, has all but disappeared. Today, it doesn't even exist in the inner city.

Fifty percent of all marriages end in divorce. Twenty-two percent of all children born today are born out of wedlock, and one-third of all children will live with step-parents before they are 18. Clearly, the disintegration of family is massive.

If you assume that the molding of values starts at home – early in life – then the reasons for a breakdown in ethics are obvious.

I will not lecture on ethics because I do not believe ethics can be taught in a classroom or at a professional seminar. Defining acceptable ethical standards is a process, a dialog, a choice among conflicting, sometimes unclear alternatives.

Ultimately, discussion and debate will help reestablish the parameters of our own values. Then, we will be better equipped to define who we really are. That's why I'm encouraged that ethics is high on the public agenda these days.

It's very tough to set moral absolutes in today's divided world. There's hurt and need everywhere: drugs, divorce, crime, unemployment, and massive personal displacement caused by dramatic change around us.

In such a cauldron, we face hard choices. We simply cannot be all things to all people. Clear, well articulated values are important to any individual or organization. As a newspaper publishing executive, I frequently faced tough moral and ethical issues, many of which led to controversy and criticism. It is often in such circumstances, however, that personal growth can occur – as I think it did for me.

I live in a truly international community where there is no majority. Miami is now one-third Catholic, one-third Protestant and one-third Jewish. Our home county is 50% Hispanic, 33% anglo, and 18% black.

In many respects, Miami is a city of the future: multi-lingual, multi-ethnic and sometimes hopelessly divided. And yet, we somehow get along because, in the end, we have no other choice. The incredible diversity is not just Miami's reality, it's a fact of life in most cities in America today.

Like many others in leadership positions (public service or private sector), I struggle to balance personal ethics with public responsibility to a diverse, pluralistic people, some of whom reflect far different values than I.

South Florida is a world of Christians and Jews, blacks and whites, Asians and Hispanics, cynics and doubters, believers and non-believers – and thousands of those who simply drift through life with no spiritual anchor at all.

In this diverse environment, there often is a clash of cultures and issues. What is expected in one group, is irrelevant in another. Where there is little concern about the rights of others, almost anything goes. And, sometimes no one cares. A few news stories in my own newspaper illustrate the point:

– Local politicians buy expensive suits from a suspicious downtown apartment. The best labels, low prices, no sales tax. Sure they knew that the goods were stolen. Sure they knew sales taxes should be collected, but so what?

– A powerful CEO builds a teak dock for his $6 million yacht. He decorates his home with a multi-million dollar art collection and charges it all to his bank. Before the binge is over, he's run up a $16 million tab, and it will cost taxpayers $3 billion to bail out the Miami bank driven into bankruptcy by grossly unethical performance.

– A surgeon, lawyer and insurance agent conspire to prescribe unneeded back surgery for auto accident victims. The bills are padded, the patient suffers incredible pain for unneeded surgery – and the perpetrators of the crime walk off with millions. Worse yet, the professional groups involved do nothing.

In crises, we quickly learn who we are and where we're willing to draw the line. In the end, our personal reputation is at stake. Who are we anyway? How do you want to be remembered? How will your grandchildren describe who you are – in a single sentence? What are the headlines of your life?

In the late 1930s, Jews in Europe had very little to pass along, other than personal values. Hitler was on the rise, prejudice and hatred against Jews was rampant. In that atmosphere of oppression, Jews feared for their lives – and with good cause.

While Jews then had no material wealth, they had something far more precious: a lifetime of tradition and values. Sensing doom, they reduced those values to writing and shared them with their children – as ethical wills. What a powerful tradition.

Wouldn't it be an inspiring, personal testimony if each of you took the time to write an ethical will? Could you describe concisely who you are and how you want to be remembered? How do you define trust? What are your values? Your ethics? Your traditions? Your priorities? Do you reflect to the world who you really are?

In the end, we must ask ourselves if we will be remembered as a generation that worked together, that lived by ethical standards. Or, will we be nothing more than a brief chapter describing chaos, friction and corruption?

Setting standards of integrity and trust is a straightforward, every day proposition. Reverend Robert Fulghum, author of *All I Ever Really Need To Know I Learned in Kindergarten,* put ethics into a language anyone could follow:

> Share everything.
> Play fair.
> Don't hit people.
> Put things back where you found them.
> Clean up your own mess.
> Say you're sorry when you hurt somebody.
> When you go out into the world, watch out for traffic, hold hands and stick together.

Trust cannot be legislated, nor can it be mandated by the courts. Solid ethical performance is based on what's right, not just what's legal. Long gone is the time when we worried simply about perceptions of performance, rather than allowing our conduct to teeter on the outer edge of legality.

Shortly after Soviet author Alexander Solzhenitzyn arrived in the U.S. in 1978, he experienced shock at the decline in American values. "A society which is based on the letter of the law, and never reaches any higher, is taking very scarce advantage of the high level of human possibilities."

We should strive toward that high level of human possibility. But I do not see that objective as an abstract, academic platitude – something to be sought but never quite attained.

So, let me be practical by dealing with four specific tasks I consider essential ingredients to ethical performance: building trust, reflecting optimism, being an encourager and leading by personal example. To me, these are key *ethical values.*

1. Build Trust

Getting along in today's pluralistic world starts with trust. Trust is an ultimate value that protects an orderly, civilized society from chaos and anarchy. Trust in marriage. Trust at work. Trust among friends. Trust in public life.

If we can't trust our husbands or wives, if we can't trust our children, if we can't trust our boss, or our preacher, or our senator, what in the world is left upon which to build a stable way of life???

Banks delay clearing checks because they don't trust their customers. Hospital emergency rooms turn away patients because they fear they won't be paid. We install burglar alarms, carry guns, insist on pre-nuptial agreements and employment contracts because no one trusts anyone anymore. It's a sad commentary.

Trust is not some abstract, idealistic goal we can never quite achieve. Trust is embedded in every action we take, and it has practical, day-to-day ramifications in all that we do.

Trust binds relationships. It defines respect for others. It becomes the fabric that holds together our entire society.

It starts at home – by trusting our spouses and children. It extends to the office, around our neighborhood, on the playing field, in our schools.

Trust is never guaranteed. It must be constructed carefully, nurtured vigorously and reinforced daily.

2. Be Optimistic

Attitude in the process of serving others is important. Often what happens in our lives comes down to the way we look at life.

If we believe it will be a lousy day, it will be. If we believe there is no hope, the chances are there will be no hope. If we are convinced we will fail, we most certainly will fail.

On the other hand, if we believe we can win, the chances are we will. If we think we can make a difference in life, we will. The difference between such success – and future – is usually a matter of attitude.

I call them good signs of life. they can often be power fortifiers.

3. Be an Encourager

Each week, dozens cross our paths crying out for help, for love, for encouragement. For them, it's a challenging, lonely world, and such people desperately need our love.

In my business, I'm surrounded by special opportunities – big and small – to be a thoughtful listener, an enthusiastic encourager, a caring advisor, a special friend.

The odds are overwhelming that there are people nearby in your life who are suffering from broken relationships, from alienation, from physical or spiritual hurt. Many have no place to turn.

In seven years as Miami Herald publisher, I wrote more than 200 Sunday columns. Through my column, I was blessed with special opportunities to salute dozens of those who are striving to build goodness into their lives. Many were unsung heroes. Such special people who take on thankless, mundane acts of kindness are everywhere.

I often think about the times in my life when I have passed by those begging for help around me. They have wanted love, and they have begged for understanding. Above all, they needed a helping hand, a word of optimism, a caring friend.

A simple word of encouragement can do amazing things to lift a person's spirit, to temper a blow to his ego, or to help shake him off a terrible setback.

4. Lead by Personal Example

The final ethical value is the need to lead by personal example.

Business leaders must articulate clearly their vision of corporate values. In my organization, we call it the Knight-Ridder promise. "We seek to be "one of the world's leading publishing and information companies," and we see our enterprise as "both a business and public trust, built on the highest standards of ethics and integrity."

Our Knight-Ridder values statement also underscores "our moral obligation ... to excel in all that we do" and to see to it that "the name of Knight-Ridder shall be forever synonymous with the best."

To be the best, leaders must be truthful and candid. They must be decisive and courageous. They must keep promises and be loyal to their family, friends, employees, clients and country.

They must respect human dignity, they must pursue excellence and they must be compassionate. They especially must celebrate the goodness in others.

In every decision, we must consider the moral implications. We must set a personal example, because personal example is a far more powerful statement of ethics than any direct order, or corporate regulation.

Finally, I firmly believe there must be a spiritual component to moral and ethical performance. Our country was founded on religious faith, but we've gone so far to protect rights that we have lost sight of that ultimate value.

I respect the rights of others to believe differently, or to not believe at all. However, those who do differ have an equal responsibility to respect where I'm coming from. Religious faith defines my values, it sets my moral compass, and it's central to my ethical will.

Equally as important is the integrity of family. I lean heavily on the strength of a very close family. We believe in each other, we care about each other, and yes, we pray for each other.

These ethical values are keys in the lives of many leaders, and, as we discuss ultimate ethics, we owe it to ourselves to keep that reality in focus.

In conclusion, we have enormous challenges ahead. The task will not be easy. Yet, it is a noble cause for any business or profession.

If we are to succeed, I suggest that we must build trust, reflect optimism, be an encourager, lead by personal example.

In the end, no enterprise will reflect institutional integrity unless its leaders reflect personal integrity, and that starts by setting a moral and ethical example at the top.

THE LAST WORD: CUSTOMER SERVICE
John Case
Inc., April 1991

Suppose your company could *really* satisfy its customers. Suppose you could provide a product or service that was better than they expected, for less money than anybody else charged. Suppose that every time you brought out something new it was just what buyers wanted. Suppose your after-sale service was so good that customers with problems went away feeling better than before.

What would happen? Easy – you'd own your marketplace. People would buy from you over and over again, would relish the experience, would never even dream about doing business with anybody else. They would proselytize on your behalf, telling their friends and associates to buy from you. You'd hardly need salespeople.

Impossible, you say. Farfetched. Then again, you haven't met Scott Cook, and you probably don't know much about his company, Intuit Inc. All those statements apply to Intuit. Better yet, Cook has figured out how to build that kind of customer orientation into the organizational bricks and mortar of his company.

"Operating without a safety net," the 38-year-old president calls it. Or "the Toyota approach." Or simply "getting it right." Whatever – it's partly a matter of management techniques, partly a matter of fundamental philosophy. And it's what sets Cook's company way, way apart from the competition.

Intuit makes microcomputer software. Its flagship product is Quicken, a program that allows consumers and small businesses to write checks and keep track of their finances on a personal computer. Owning the marketplace? Quicken is probably the most successful personal-finance program ever written, holding a market share estimated at 60%. "It has become the brand-name product in what would otherwise be a commodity business," says Jeffrey Tarter, editor of the industry publication *Softletter*. "It's the Kleenex or Xerox of its market." Intuit, accordingly, has been exploding. It ranked #15 on the 1990 *Inc.* 500. Revenues last year hit $33 million, up from $19 million the year before. After tax earnings were into double digits.

Granted, the software industry has always been populated by hotshot fast-growth companies. But Intuit doesn't fit the conventional mold. Unlike, say Lotus, it started without venture capital or other early advantages. Unlike VisiCorp or Wordstar, it has dominated its marketplace through several generations of software, beating back waves of would-be competitors. Consumers yank Quicken off the shelves virtually unbidden. Intuit sold close to a million units in 1990. Its product is carried by retailers all over the country, by Target stores and Wal-Marts as well as computer chains. Yet the company's sales force numbers exactly two.

So what moves the goods? Asked that question, founder and president Scott Cook peers mock-earnestly through his thick glasses, allowing only the hint of a grin to cross his face. "Really," he says innocently, "we have hundreds of thousands of salespeople. They're our customers." Suddenly missionary-sober, he adds that he wants his customers to be "apostles" for Quicken. Intuit's mission is to "make the customer feel so good about the product they'll go and tell five friends to buy it."

And as to what would make a customer feel that good, which is to say better than most customers feel about *any* product or service – well, the only way to understand it may be to watch Cook and his company at work.

The year is 1984; the place Palo Alto, Calif., not far from Intuit's current hometown of Menlo Park. Cook and three colleagues are in a room with a bunch of computers and several well-dressed women. The women – members of the Palo Alto Junior League – are not what you'd call computer nuts; some have never even touched one of the machines before. But today, after croissants and orange juice, they are sitting at the keyboards, trying to use the computers to write checks. Cook and his colleagues watch but don't help.

Cook – a Harvard M.B.A., a Procter & Gamble-trained marketer – is a bit on edge. In a way, his fledgling company depends on what he learns here.

His epiphany, a year or so earlier, was simplicity itself. More and more consumers and small businesses were buying PCs. All those computer buyers wrote checks and kept financial records. Outfitted with the right software, a computer should be able to automate such tasks. The only rub: a few dozen check-writing programs were already on the market, and Cook had no money to elbow them aside. If he wanted to start a software company – and he did – he would have to offer customers something his competitors didn't.

Wondering what that something might be, he and a newly hired assistant began placing telephone calls to middle- and upper-middle-income households. They didn't stop until the calls numbered in the hundreds – and until they began hearing the same responses over and over.

The vast majority of respondents said they did financial work every month, they didn't like spending so much time on it, and they would consider using a computer to do the work. But they couldn't be bothered with learning a complex program, and they certainly didn't want to spend more time on the chore than they were spending now. Curious, Cook assembled a panel of computer buffs to test the most popular programs then available, writing checks and keeping records first by computer and then by hand. Sure enough – in every case, the computer was slower.

Conclusion: there was a market out there, already big and undoubtedly growing bigger, a market capable of appealing to Cook's P&G-honed aspirations. But if he wanted to reach that potential mass market, his program had better be fast, cheap, hassle free, and above all easy to use, so easy that anyone could sit down at the computer and start writing checks.

So, now he's watching very intently as the Junior Leaguers stare at the unfamiliar keys. He and his chief programmer, a recent Stanford graduate named Tom Proulx (rhymes with *true*), have developed a prototype, and today's trial is one of many to see how well they've done. If the women flunk, so does the program.

For a while the test goes swimmingly. The women hunt and peck, but they don't have much trouble selecting "write checks" from a menu on the screen. The outline of a check appears, and the cursor jumps neatly from date to payee to amount. Anyone who has ever written a paper check, they discover, can write one with this new software. And the computer's check register looks just like an ordinary checkbook.

Then, alas, they go to print the checks they've written. Cook and the others have loaded up the printers with specially prepared checks, and the testers find "print checks" on the menu. But the first check prints too high, or maybe too low.

Cook cringes. So does Proulx; so does Tom LeFevre, another colleague present at the creation.

"We knew one thing," recalls Proulx, now the company's vice-president of product development. "If people had that much trouble the first time they used the program, they'd never use it again."

"Scott looked at Tom and me," adds LeFevre, also a vice-president. "He said, 'You guys figure out a way to solve that problem.' His tone said, And don't come back until you do."

Jump cut: 1990. Proulx and LeFevre have long since resolved the alignment problem, developing a fancy bit of programming (patented and still unique in the industry) that makes the computer line the checks up automatically. And Quicken has long since been released, upgraded, and released again. It has climbed to the top of the best-seller charts; it has won industry awards. Intuit is making a lot of money selling not only the programs but upgrades, special checks, and other supplies.

Yet now Alex Young, a product development manager for the next release of Quicken, is sitting in the home of a man he doesn't know, watching him open a shrink-wrapped box.

Maybe it was the P&G training, maybe the lesson of the Junior Leaguers, maybe just the impact of the original market research. Whatever the reason, figuring out how to satisfy customers has become Cook's, and Intuit's, obsession. The company runs an annual customer survey, asking which of Quicken's features buyers use and don't use, like and don't like. It polls dealers anonymously, asking what personal-finance programs they recommend and why. It compiles data from customers who call in with problems or write in with suggestions. It runs focus groups, usually consisting of people who aren't Quicken customers but (according to Intuit) ought to be. Information from all those sources flows directly to product-development teams (working on the next version of Quicken), to the documentation department (which regularly updates the manual), and to marketing.

The company also tests its programs relentlessly. And not just the so-called alpha and beta testing commonly practiced by most software companies – tests that are designed primarily to locate bugs in the programming – but tests at a much earlier stage of product development. Get in some experienced Quicken users – see if this new version is going to confuse them in any way. Get in some Junior League-style novices. What's their reaction to a certain screen? "You watch their eyebrows, where they hesitate, where they have a quizzical look," says Cook. "Every glitch, every momentary hesitation is our fault."

Enough, you might think. That'll do it, you might think. Not that all the research costs so much – only the big sample surveys represent much of a cash outlay, in the neighborhood of $150,000 a year. But surely Intuit has been finding out all it possibly can about its customers' experiences with the product?

Nope. "There's still a group of people we were missing," says product manager Mari Latterell. "People just setting the program up. In fact, we didn't really know how easy it was to get started with Quicken. When you survey customers, they've been using it for six months or a year and won't remember. When you bring in testers, you have them in an artificial situation. They aren't entering their own data in their own homes."

Which is why Latterell, imbued with Cook's market-research mission, proposed the Follow-Me-Home program, in which Quicken buyers from local stores are asked to let an Intuit representative observe them when they first use Quicken. And why Alex Young, who volunteered to participate, is now watching his new acquaintance unwrap the shrink-wrapped Quicken box.

Today Young will spend five hours with his subject, longer than any of the dozens or so other employees who have so far followed customers home. Sitting behind the customer, he watches and listens. Customer confronts the program's main menu. (Confusion, notes Young: he thinks the word *register*, meaning the check register, has something to do with the product-registration card.) Customer begins to enter data from his checkbook. (Problem: he tries to enter a balance manually. You can't do that; once the opening balance is entered, the program calculates the balances automatically.) Customer tries to print checks. (He prints more samples than he needs to.) Finally, the day is done, and the customer is happy. As part of the deal, Young is now allowed to offer a little help and advice.

Young and Intuit, for their part, have their payoff: a thick sheaf of notes on the myriad ways that the next incarnation of Quicken, already the most popular program on the market , might be made just a tiny bit easier for first-time users.

"If people don't use the product," observes Tom LeFevre, "they won't tell their friends to use it, either."

Suna Kneisley, senior customer support specialist, can't quite believe the fax. A customer she has just spoken with wants to know how to put his various records onto Quicken and has just faxed her nine pages worth of data. It's a Friday; no way she can go through it all today. Oh, well! She calls the customer and leaves a message; she'll take it home with her over the weekend and get back to him Monday. Monday she has the answers he wants.

Technical-support reps such as Kneisley are Intuit's front-line employees, like waiters in a restaurant or reservation clerks at an airline. There are 40 of them, almost a quarter of the company's 175-person work force. You've just bought a new printer and you can't get it to work with Quicken? Call tech support. You've damaged a disk and lost some data? Call tech support. The response you get, of course, will define your attitude toward Quicken and Intuit, probably forever.

So ask yourself: How much is it worth to the company when a customer gets a response like Kneisley's – not only that she'll answer a request going well beyond the ordinary, but that she'll take it home and work on it *over the weekend?*

Kneisley, 24 has been at Intuit only five months when this particular request comes in. No matter – she has already absorbed the messages that Cook has somehow built into the very structure of his company: *Intuit stands or falls with what happens in tech support. Do whatever you need to do to satisfy the customer.* The messages are hammered home in several different ways:

Thank-you letters from customers are read aloud, circulated throughout the company, and then framed and posted on the wall. Kneisley's colleague Debbie Peak gets a letter because she faxed a customer some printer information, then thought to call the next day to make sure it had arrived safely. Kneisley herself gets one from a woman who damaged four years' worth of data; working at home with a special data-recovery program, Kneisley salvaged it.

Virtually everyone in the company, from Cook on down, spends a few hours each month working the customer service lines, underscoring by example the importance of what the department does. "I was hired in September," recalls Victor Gee, who started as a rep and is now a supervisor in tech support. "That same month Scott came by and started taking calls, too. I thought, What other company would have the president do the same thing I'm doing?" Every few months, moreover, each employee is taken to lunch by a top manager. Lunch with a Dork, employees have christened the program – but its message is not lost. "My last one was with Scott," says customer support specialist Dwight Joseph. "He had his notebook with him and he writes down what you say, any ideas you might have. It's pretty gratifying."

A torrent of statistics – daily write-ups, weekly summaries, hand-lettered charts covering a whole quarter – tracks the tech-support department's performance for all to see. How many callers have to wait longer than 60 seconds? How many give up? At the company's Monday morning meetings, says Cook, "the first four numbers we go through have to do with customer service. Even before we get to revenues. It creates real peer pressure to improve service – people see how we're doing each week."

At a lot of companies, pressure to improve customer service creates a white-collar sweatshop: harried managers browbeat supervisors; supervisors keep an iron grip on employees. Intuit, by contrast, is structured to encourage cooperation and to make improvements through innovation rather than through tighter controls. Greg Ceniceroz, recently promoted from tech-support rep to product specialist, is assigned the job of figuring out how to cut down on the average time spent with each customer. His first step toward a solution: a big loose-leaf reference binder containing answers to customers' most frequent questions, for every rep's desk. He encourages reps to submit questions and answers for inclusion in the binder and makes sure those who do get a public thank-you.

Kneisley, meanwhile, notices that management is looking for a volunteer to chair a group dubbed the Innovative Ideas Committee, which has been charged with collating and following up on every product-improvement idea emanating from the tech-support department and from Quicken users. She writes a four-page proposal about what she thinks the group ought to do, and gets the job. "We worked with her to set the committee's objectives," says Tom LeFevre, "because she had been here only a few months. But she was *very* interested. And the more interested someone is, the better job they'll do."

Involvement of that sort, of course, translates into a sense of ownership more valuable and more productive than any amount of iron-grip supervision. "Most of us work at least 50 hours a week," says Kneisley. "We don't get any extra compensation. But we do have a profit-sharing plan, and if Intuit does well, we will, too."

Scott Cook is showing me Intuit's latest ad campaign. I'm a little incredulous, but there it is: Send for a copy of Quicken. Pay only an $8 shipping-and-handling charge. If you don't think you're doing useful work within a few minutes, don't pay for the product. No, not "send it back for a refund" *Keep it.* Just don't pay for it.

Why would a company do this?

"It's like the Japanese," Cook says.

"Oh," I answer, trying to think of the last time a Japanese company offered me something virtually free. Fortunately, Cook elaborates.

"It's like the Japanese assembly lines, where they have only two hours' worth of inventory. There's no margin for error – they have to have superreliability from their suppliers." Cook goes to his bookshelf, pulling out a copy of *The Machine That Changed the World,* the new book about Toyota's "lean production" system. "What we're doing is the Toyota approach. We take away the safety net. If you do that you have to get it right."

The more Cook talks, the more the scenes I have observed at Intuit begin to fall into place.

Tech support, for example. Here are 40 people answering all kinds of crazy questions – for free. Here is a $500,000 state-of-the-art telephone system, installed in late 1989 just so callers won't have to wait so long. This isn't normal: nearly all of Intuit's competitors put a limit on tech support, some charging for it and some curtailing it so many months after purchase. And nearly every company with an after-sale call-in line doesn't mind keeping customers waiting for a few minutes.

But then, those companies have a safety net. "Most software companies would go broke if they didn't charge for tech support," argues Cook. "We said, We're not going to charge. If our customers have problems, we pay. That makes us get the product right the first time."

Take the product itself. For $50 or less – sometimes as low as $20 on store-sponsored special sales – you can buy a copy of Quicken. In its latest form, you get a program capable not only of writing checks but of tracking investments, generating profit-and-loss statements, and doing a dozen other chores a small-business owner or financially sophisticated consumer might want to do on a computer. You also get a 460-page manual, the right to regular upgrades at modest costs, and access to unlimited help. Once again: abnormal. Quicken's chief competitor lists for three and a half times as much as Quicken, and Quicken's price could probably double before Intuit noticed much of a sales decline.

But that would be a safety net. "We sell an inexpensive product, and we offer free customer support," says Alex Young. "We have to make sure it's right when it goes out the door." Suddenly, refinements like the Follow-Me-Home program make perfect sense.

And finally, look at Intuit's marketing. The no-pay ad, for example. "We heard from our focus groups that people really didn't believe the product could be so easy to use," recalls Mari Latterell. "After all, software never is. So we did this big advertising campaign – 'You'll be using Quicken in six minutes or it's free.' The goal was to put our money where our mouth is." Even the company's tiny sales force – two people – begins to seem comprehensible. Outside salespeople could maybe push more product into stores. But depending on pull-through marketing means the company can't survive without satisfying its customers. "When someone comes in and thanks a clerk for selling him Quicken," says marketing vice-president John Monson, "there's nothing a salesperson could do that would come close to being as powerful a recommendation."

Funny that Monson should conjure up that image. When I return from my visit to Intuit, I call up the manager of the local Egghead Discount Software store and ask him about the product. "People love it," he says. "Someone actually came in here and thanked me for selling it to him. That doesn't happen too often."

By some reckonings, Intuit's approach to customer satisfaction is costly.

Technical support and other departments that have customer contact (the one taking orders for checks, for example) cost the company about 10% of revenues, or upwards of $3-million a year. The testing, surveys, fancy telephone systems, focus groups, and other stay-close-to-the-customer expenses add another $1-million to $2-million. Imagine yourself a corporate raider concerned only with the next quarter's earnings: you'd buy up Intuit, cut back on all such expenditures, and boost profits anywhere from 50% to 100%.

"That," says Scott Cook, "is the advantage of owning the company. When you own the company, you take the long view."

In that long view, the payoff of the Intuit approach is far higher than the immediate cost. Quicken is likely to continue its utter domination of the market. Other products introduced by Intuit will be launched with a running start. Even now, fully one-third of Quicken customers say they bought the product because it was recommended by a friend. As they say in the trade, that's advertising money can't buy.

So is this: As I am working on this article, my friend Bruce stops by. "I hear you're writing about Intuit," he says. "I just bought its program, Quicken."

Bruce doesn't buy much software. A copy of Lotus 1-2-3 given to him by his sister-in-law sits on the shelf unopened. He uses his computer mostly for writing. But he bought Quicken because two different people urged him to. "You've got to get this program," they told him.

Now he has become an apostle himself. The reason: one day, while working on some financial records, he left the room. His two-and-a-half-year-old daughter, Emma, waltzed in and cheerfully turned off the computer. In a panic, Bruce turned it back on and booted up Quicken. "Don't worry!" the screen cheerfully informed him. Quicken had saved all but the last little bits of data.

Somewhere, at some point, Scott Cook's engineers had put that capability and its comforting message into the program. Intuit, they knew, was depending on its customers to sell the product.

And customers, they knew, don't really want money-back guarantees or complaint forms or even 800 numbers. What they want is the product to be right.

FOR FURTHER INQUIRY

EXERCISES

1. Explain the moral issues surrounding each of the following:

   a. Nepotism.
   b. Whistle-blowing.
   c. Secret monitoring of workers' performance.
   d. Drug abuse while on the job.
   e. Drug testing of all employees.

2. Identify the moral issue(s) and describe how a "Kantian:" would resolve the following: An employee learns that a fellow employee is stealing company property. What action should he take?

3. Identify the moral issue(s) and describe how an "egoist" would resolve the following: A sales representative learns that one of his fellow salesmen is bribing a foreign vendor to do business with their company. What should he do?

4. Identify the moral issue(s) and describe how a "consequentialist" would resolve the following: An accountant learns of the failure of a client to report income to the Internal Revenue Service amounting to over $10,000. What action should he take?

5. Identify the moral issue(s) and describe how a "contractarianist" would resolve the following: An employee learns that one of his fellow employees has been submitting falsified receipts for reimbursement of personal expenses to his company. What action should she take?

SUGGESTED READINGS

• Ellyn E. Spragins, "T or F? Honesty Tests Really Work," INC., February, 1992, p. 104.
• Andrew S. Grove, "What's the Right Thing" Everyday Ethical Dilemmas," Working Woman, June, 1990, pp. 16-18.
• Harry L. M. Artinian, "Don't Change the rules: Change the Game," Vital Speeches of the Day, May 1, 1992, pp. 445-448.
• Laurel Touby, "How to Hire Employees Your Customers will Love,"Working Woman, December, 1989, pp. 40-41.
• Ronald B. Taylor, "Making Waves: Whistle-Blower Keeps Heat on Navy in Revealing Waste of Dollars," Los Angeles Times, June 26, 1984.
• Norman C. Miller, "U.S. Business Overseas: Back to Bribery?" Wall Street Journal, April 30, 1981, p. 22.
• David Johnston, "Boning Up on New Ethics of Procurement," New York Times, May 24, 1989, p. A-16.
• Alan F. Westin, "Michigan's Law to Protect the Whistle Blowers, "Wall Street Journal, April 13, 1981, p. 18.
• Richard T. DeGeorge, *Business Ethics*, New York: MacMillan Publishing Co., Inc., 1990, pp. 200-216.
• Tom L. Beauchamp and Norman E. Bowie, *Ethical Theory and Business* , Englewood Cliffs, N.J.: Prentice-Hall, Inc., 1988, pp. 204-213.

EndNotes

1. Peter Madsen and Jay M. Shafritz, eds., *Essentials of Business Ethics*, New American Library, New York, 1990, p. 79.

2-10. Madsen and Shafritz, p. 79-83.

11. Shaw, pp. 215-216.

12. W. F. Edmonson, *A Code of Ethics: Do Corporate Executives and Employees Need* It? Itawamba Community College Press, Fulton, MS., 1990, pp. 58-77.

13. Patricia H. Werhane, *Persons, Rights and Corporations,* Prentice-Hall, Inc., Englewood Cliffs, N.J., 1985, pp. 168-170.

14. Werhane, P. 170.

15. Madsen and Shafritz, pp. 79-80.

16. William H. Shaw, *Business Ethics*, Wadsworth Publishing Co., Belmont, CA, 1991, p. 193.

17. Rosemary Chalk and Frank von Hippel, "Due Process for Dissenting Whistle-Blowers," *Technology Review,* no. 81, June-July, 1979, pp. 48-55.

18. Richard T. DeGeorge, *Business Ethics,* MacMillan Publishing Co., New York, 1990, p. 208.

19. DeGeorge, p. 208.

20. DeGeorge, pp. 215-216.

21, DeGeorge, p. 216.

22. Patricia Sellers, "How to Remake Your Sales Force," *Fortune,* May 4, 1992, p. 98.

23. Sellers, p. 100.

24. Sellers, p. 103.

25. Harry L. M. Artinian, "Don't Change the Rules: Change the Game," *Vital Speeches of the Day,* May 1, 1992, p. 447.

26. Artinian, p. 447.

27. Michael P. Cronin, "In-House Customer Service," *INC.,* March, 1992, p. 97.

28. Cronin, p. 97.

29. Cronin, p. 97.

30. Leslie Brokaw, "The Mystery-Shopper Questionnaire," *INC.*, June, 1991, p. 94.

31. Brokaw, p. 94.

32. Brokaw, p. 97.

33. Shaw, pp. 269-271.

34. Richard G. Capen, Jr., "Ethical Values-Trust Cannot be Legislated," *Vital Speeches of the Day*, September 1, 1990, pp. 685-687a.

35-73. Madsen and Shafritz, p. 84-93, 102-104, 106-108.

Chapter 18

Garland Thompson

DISCRIMINATION
IN THE WORKPLACE

"No people were ever found who were better than their laws, though many have been known to be worse."
    – William Goodell, 19th-century Abolitionist[1]

"While statutes usually speak falsely as to actual behavior, they afford probably the best single means of ascertaining what a society thinks behavior ought to be; they sweep up the felt necessities of the day and indirectly expound the social norm of the legislators."
    – Winthrop D. Jordan, *White Over Black*[2]

Discrimination, whether on the basis of race, ethnic background or sex, has as its prime purpose the isolation of the victim from normal relations with the people and institutions of society. Such a course of behavior may offer to its perpetrators an artificially heightened sense of personal worth: I may not amount to much, but I am still better than *you*.

Because it is built on an imaginary foundation, such an exaggerated view of individual and collective self-worth is bound to shatter in a confrontation with reality. A few examples:

Jesse Owens in the 1933 Munich Olympics. He was competing not only against the world's best athletes but also against Adolf Hitler's claims of Aryan "supremacy" and American images of blacks as a lazy, somehow less "human" race. Owens made hash of such pretensions, winning multiple Gold Medals and embarrassing the German dictator.

Heavyweight boxing champion Joe Louis. If anyone missed the lesson of Jesse Owens in those years of economic Depression, social malaise and a fearful march to world war, Louis repeated it in the ring

Garland Thompson, J.D. Temple University School of Law, is a member of the Editorial Board of the *Baltimore Sun,* executive editor of *The Crisis,* official publication of the National Association for the Advancement of Colored People, and a Freedom Forum Fellow teaching at the University of Kansas.

against Max Schmeling, a man Hitler had called a racial "superman." The "Brown Bomber," who had lost to the accomplished German in an earlier bout, demolished Schmeling the second time around, sparking wild celebrations in black communities all over the world.

Super Bowl MVP Doug Williams. A more recent demonstration of stereotypes tumbling down came in 1988, when Doug Williams led Washington's professional football team to a Super Bowl championship and was named the game's Most Valuable Player. Williams had been electrifying while playing for Grambling State University, but a myth persisted that African-Americans lacked the intellect to be big-league quarterbacks. Williams, who would not have started but for an injury to the No. 1 signal caller, was all but ignored in the pre-game hoopla by broadcasters and sportswriters extolling the abilities of Denver's John Elway.

AFFIRMATIVE ACTION AT ITS BEST

One irony of Williams' MVP performance, noted by the author in a 1988 *Baltimore Sun* column,[3] is that Washington was last among all National Football League teams to hire African-American athletes. The team's then-owner, George Preston Marshall, had sparked protests over his racial bias in 1957. Marshall was then negotiating to have the U.S. Congress fund a new stadium in the District, but Interior Secretary Stewart L. Udall, whose department had to build it, refused to cross NAACP and Congress of Racial Equality picket lines to attend games at the old Griffith Stadium. "We carry the rifle," one sign read. "Why can't we carry the ball?"

Udall, himself under heavy pressure, pushed Marshall to hire blacks as the new D.C. Stadium prepared to open in 1961. Then, 26 years after the team was forced to sign its first African-American player, a black Washington quarterback won the Super Bowl.

It was not just in sports that the stereotypes were knocked apart. In art, Henry Ossawa Tanner helped redefine American painting after the turn of the century, although he did spend many years in Europe, far from the less favorable social climate of his hometown of Philadelphia. In science and technology, Garrett Morgan invented a gas mask that saved lives at fire scenes, in the mining industry, on construction sites and later in World War I. His company was forced to use white salesmen, because white municipal authorities would not buy its lifesaving products from a black man.

Today, many Americans acknowledge the wrongs of racial discrimination. Stories of people who achieved despite the obstacles of prejudice evoke shame and remorse even from whites who had no part in their unfair treatment. What is not so often acknowledged is that discrimination imposed terrible costs on the nation as a whole and on individuals, institutions and companies far from the scene of the discriminatory acts. As we shall see, although the ideal of individual fairness is compelling, the cost to society – to individuals, families, institutions and companies – remains the ultimate justification for legal remedies against discrimination.

REAL COSTS OF DISCRIMINATION HURT EVERYONE

One has only to look at the life of the great contralto Marian Anderson, who died in April 1993, to see how heavy a price bias can exact. Ms. Anderson's nephew, Portland, Ore,, conductor James DePriest, found old passports that put her birth date in 1897, showing she was older than earlier accounts claimed. That meant Ms. Anderson was 28 years old in 1925 when she won the competition for young aspirants to perform with the New York Philharmonic Orchestra. In 1935, when she gave a performance that caused the world-famous Arturo Toscaninni to exclaim, "Yours is a voice such as one hears once in a hundred years,"[4] Marian Anderson was already 38 years old.

She became a symbol of resistance to discrimination in 1939, when a major controversy erupted over the Daughters of the American Revolution's refusal to let her sing at Washington's Constitution Hall. Her dramatic concert before 75,000 people at the Lincoln Memorial created an image that followed her the rest of her life. In 1955, Ms. Anderson became the first black American to sing with New York's Metropolitan Opera Company. Wild applause greeted her performance, but observers noted that, at 58, she was well past her prime.

Ms. Anderson, widely praised for her dignity in the face of appalling bigotry, later disclosed that she wished she could have made such appearances in her youth.

"If only I could give what I had to offer then," she said. "But they wouldn't accept it, or me. Other Negroes will have the career I dreamed of."[5]

Another example of the social cost of bias arose during the Civil War. As white Americans were fighting to determine the future of the United States, free blacks were fighting political skirmishes over the privilege of joining the contest. Eventually, more than 178,000 blacks fought for the Union in 166 regiments and provided enough Navy crewmen to suffer a third of the Navy's casualties.[6]

As documentary filmmaker Ken Burns' great PBS TV series *The Civil War* revealed, however, that only came after strenuous protests by blacks and their Abolitionist friends, well after the war began. By that time, many thousands of white Americans had been killed or wounded in battle.

Glory, the 1991 Hollywood movie about a black Massachusetts volunteer regiment, veered off the record in many places. The soldiers who led that brave if futile attack on a Confederate coastal fort were free black tradesmen, not shoeless ex-slaves, and the top sergeant was none other than Frederick Douglass' son. *Glory,* based on its white colonel's diary, did reacquaint many Americans with the fact that blacks fought with distinction in the war which guaranteed their freedom, however. Other Civil War accounts had overlooked blacks' role entirely.

Discrimination has many faces. Not only did Civil War historians ignore the contributions of blacks to the Union cause, so did many ordinary citizens and military officers. Thus, by the time World War II began, black groups found themselves once again fighting for the right of blacks to serve equally with whites.

An oral history book by Paul Stillwell, to be published by the U.S. Naval Institute, traces the lives of 13 black World War II veterans who were the first black Navy officers. Stillwell's background piece on that effort, reproduced in part here, is accompanied by excerpted recollections of retired Illinois Appellate Court Justice William S. White, one of the "Golden Thirteen."[7]

WHEN THIRTEEN TURNED GOLDEN
by Paul Stillwell
U.S. Naval Institute *Proceedings*
February 1993

At a time when the United States was fighting a global war to free the persecuted, its naval officer corps was, ironically, as white as it had been a century earlier, before the Civil War. Some 100,000 African-American enlisted men were in the Navy at the midpoint of U.S. involvement in World War II, so its leaders timidly, reluctantly set about to commission a few black officers as well. To be sure, the step was a political one, taken in response to growing pressure from U.S. civil rights organizations. The national consciousness was slowly beginning to realize that the elimination of injustice abroad could hardly be served by a military force that perpetuated injustice at home.

In January 1944, 16 black enlisted men gathered at the Great Lakes Naval Training Station in Illinois to begin a crash course that would turn them into the first African-American naval officers on active duty. Although the Navy had to be compelled to take this step, it chose the officer candidates well. All had demonstrated top-notch leadership as enlisted men. The pace was demanding and forced the 16 men to band together so that all could succeed. Their common perception was that they would set back the course of racial justice if they failed. All 16 passed the course, but not all became officers. Twelve received commissions as ensigns; the 13th made warrant officer. The three who did not fit within the quota returned to enlisted duty.

Years later the pioneer officers came to be known as the Golden Thirteen. In 1944, however, Navy leadership treated them more as pariahs than pioneers. In many instances they were denied the privileges and respect routinely accorded to white naval officers. Once commissioned, their assignments were usually menial and not worthy of their abilities and training. They were token blacks. But they had at least opened the door for all those who would follow. In the years since 1944, the Navy has kept pace with the nation in racial awareness and integration. In some cases it has made even greater strides. The Golden Thirteen were there at the outset.

For a variety of reasons, only one of the 13 made a career of the Navy, and he was instrumental in opening still more doors for those to come after. Other members of the group made their marks in civilian life. Their achievements provide a measure of their talents and their determination to deal with a society that was too often reluctant to deal with them.

Their number included a professional engineer, a justice of a state appellate court, the first black member of the council of the National Collegiate Athletic Association, a respected social worker, a successful attorney, a teacher and coach who inspired a generation of students, an official of the Urban League, a professional model, and the first black department head in the city government of Dayton, Ohio.

The only record likely to survive and perpetuate the achievements of the Golden Thirteen is this collection of their own oral recollections. Memory is admittedly an imperfect tool, but it can convey a great deal of authentic human experience.

Graham Martin, for example, remembers the 1930s when boxer Joe Louis and sprinter Jesse Owens stunned the world with their athletic achievements. He found it difficult to reconcile their success with the oft-repeated notion that black people were inherently inferior. James Hair, the son of a slave, broke down in tears during one interview as he recalled the lynching of a brother-in-law whom he had idolized. George Cooper told of going out of his way to convince white enlisted men that he was a fellow human being, not "a black son of a bitch wearing officer shoulder boards."

Jesse Arbor told of shaming a white senior officer who referred to a "g—d—— nigger in the woodpile" after he lost a game of poker. Sam Barnes recalled that white people in the South preferred to address a black man by his first name rather than according him the respect that went with the term, "Mister Barnes." John Reagan, given only menial duties in World War II, had the satisfaction of being recalled to active duty shortly before the Korean War and eventually becoming executive officer of a fleet unit.

Frank Sublett looked back on his naval experience as the highlight of his entire life. Justice William Sylvester White suggested that the Navy could have come up with many more capable black officers than just 13 when it finally decided to integrate its officer corps.

Following is an excerpt from White's recollection.

Justice William S. White Recalls:
My father was a chemist and a pharmacist, a graduate of Fisk University and the University of Illinois. My mother was a public school teacher, a graduate of Fisk University and the University of Chicago. During the Depression, they sacrificed and sent their only child to college and law school.

I knew that the opportunity to go to school was a precious opportunity which should not be wasted. Civil servants and small business people don't live so high on the hog that they can afford to waste a chance for their son to go to school. My father used to tell me that his mother told him that almost anything you get, the white folks can take away from you, except learning.

Few professional fields were open to blacks when I was going to school. The choices were essentially law, medicine, religion, and education. Early on I found that law depended more on the powers of reasoning rather than memorization, so I preferred it to medicine, where you call a certain bone the tibia simply because that is its name .....

In 1939 a friend of mine who had gone both to Hyde Park High School and to the University of Chicago asked me how I would like to be an assistant United States attorney. I said, "I'd like it very much. I'd like to be a United States senator. I'd like to be President of the United States. What else is new?"

He said, "No, no kidding." It developed that he had worked with a man who was about to be appointed the United States attorney, and he was going to clean the office and put in new people. He asked this friend of mine, Charles Browning, to suggest who should be the token black. Almost everything good that has happened to me since then has happened as the result of that chance conversation I had with Charles Browning ....

As the draft board looked at me with more and more interest, I turned to Lewis Reginald Williams, a friend who was in the Navy .... He was in the selection office at Great Lakes Naval Training Station, so he said, "You ought to do well on the tests that they give you, and that ought to give you the preferment of getting into the service school of your choice." So I enlisted in October 1943 and went to boot training.

The experience to some extent followed the pattern of the outside world, in that blacks did play on the Great Lakes football team, because in those days there were a few blacks playing on college football teams. It sounds ridiculous now, but blacks could not play on the Great Lakes basketball team. You wonder now how they could get 10 white guys who knew how to play basketball, don't you? But they did. Imagine, blacks played football but not basketball. Prejudice is not a logical thing. So why was it all right for them to play football? I guess because they had more clothes on. I don't know.

I had intended to go to quartermaster school. A quartermaster deals with navigation and is in one of the most intellectual of the Navy's enlisted ratings.

But the officer school came up so quickly that I never got a chance to be a quartermaster. I recall being summoned to Camp Lawrence, which was one of the Negro camps, and told that I was wanted on the main side ....

One part of the interview I well remember is that one of them said, "Now, the policy of the Navy regarding the utilization of Negro personnel is being attacked by some Negroes. The Negro newspapers have been particularly vigorous in their attacks upon the Navy's policy. If the Navy makes decisions regarding the utilization of Negroes and that decision comes under attack by Negro leaders and Negro writers in the press, would you be able, still, to carry out the Navy policy?"

I said, "Well, we are at war and men are dying in following orders. And if men can die to follow orders, I guess I can follow orders." That's about all I remember. I don't know whether my being chosen for the program depended on my answer to that question. It was a question I was not prepared for, but, mind you, this was 1943. I was very conscious of the fact that this is still a democracy. I lauded the efforts of the black newspapers to change the policy through mass pressure. But I thought my duty on the inside was to follow orders, so, although I wasn't prepared for the question, my answer was forthcoming.

Going through that officer training was kind of like fighting in the dark. It was demanding, I thought. I thought they worked us pretty hard. I thought they didn't know what they were going to do with us. It seemed to me that they were trying hard to make us prepare for any eventuality. I didn't really desire to go to sea at that point. If they had started me down a different path, yes, I would have. But I was totally unequipped I had had this officer training thing, but I didn't feel I knew enough. If they had let me go to quartermaster school, I would have wanted to go. But I didn't think I had learned enough signaling and navigation to put me aboard a ship. Maybe I did. I just wouldn't know, because that was never an option ....

Of our group undergoing the training, Reginald Goodwin had been in the Navy longest and had the ear of those in power. He was probably closest to the principal Annapolis graduate associated with the Negro program, Commander Daniel Armstrong. I spoke at Goodwin's funeral. I said then that he played a difficult role. I believe that the white power structure would make known their desires to him, believing that he would transmit those desires to us. And we did the same thing in the other direction. He also carried information back and forth. His role was one that really I didn't appreciate too much while he was performing it, because it smacked of being an Uncle Tom. From the vantage point of more than 40 years, I can say what he did was useful for both sides. He did it in a way that he held our respect because he was smart, and his information and assistance were accurate.

Looking back over those years, I can tell you now I resented it some, but I never resented it so much that I would say, "Goody, I don't like what you're doing." Just down deep, I guess my resentment was part of not liking the position I was in, where having such a courier and such an emissary was necessary.

I remember Armstrong as being Southern, aristocratic, egotistical, and sincerely interested in advancing the status of Negroes in the Navy – according to his viewpoint. I think he was sincere when he told us that we were officers, but we should remember we were colored officers and not do all the things that white officers do. In particular we were not supposed to go to the officers' club. He thought by that course we would ensure the success of the program. We hated it, but I'm sure he thought it best. I guess, in a sense, it was rather like Branch Rickey in talking with Jackie Robinson, the first black player in major league baseball. Robinson was feisty by nature, so Rickey told him, "Don't let that show. You're a pioneer, and that might hamper others coming along."

There was one sad aspect to the program. The man who urged me to get into the Navy, Mummy Williams, was also selected as an officer candidate. He went through the training with us, and then at the very end, although he had passing grades, he was not commissioned. I don't know why, but he wasn't. Three people did not get commissioned, and my friend was one of the three, and he was crushed.

After the other 13 of us were commissioned, I was made a public relations officer at Great Lakes. The Navy at that time wanted to service the Negro press, so my staff and I ground out press releases. There was also a CBS radio show called "Men of War, brought to you by the men of the Negro regiments of Great Lakes." Then they eliminated the Negro regiments, so we proudly went on with our radio show "brought to you by the men of the Negro companies at Great Lakes." Then pretty soon you had no more Negro companies as the integration went on, and we had no radio show either ....

The newspapers were receptive to our efforts; we got linage in the black press. It was not equal to the amount of space given the Army. Of course not, because the Army had generals and whatnot that were black, and the Navy only had us. I remember a paper in New York. In a political cartoon that characterized the Navy, it showed the Navy a proud ship going through the waves, and a towline out pulling a little rowboat. It had, under the big ship, "The Navy," and it had under the rowboat, "Negro programs." So 99% of the blacks coming through the selection process would pick the Army. They did not want the Navy, because the Navy had a history of mistreating blacks. I don't know that the Navy is yet the preferred service.

After the war I left the service and returned to the U.S. attorney's office. After working there for a number of years, I received an appointment from Otto Kerner, who had been my boss when he was U.S. attorney. When he became governor of Illinois in 1961, he asked me to join him in the cabinet. I was Director of the Department of Registration and Education, and in that, I was the licensing officer of the state. I also directed the state's research in the fields of water and oil and natural history. I was also chairman of the board of the state museum. I did all that for $15,000, but I enjoyed it very much.

Then I was elevated to the bench in 1964. I spent some time as a judge in juvenile court. In that job I was amazed at the number of people who are conscientiously interested in trying to do something for kids. The people trying to do something are not always on the right track, but, by golly, they're really trying – often when nobody else cares ....

In 1980, I was appointed to the Illinois Appellate Court, where I sat until retirement as a presiding judge of the Third Division. A few years after my appointment, I was the judge who was author of the opinion that settled legally and judicially the fact that Harold

Washington's forces were in control of the city council. Washington was Chicago's first black mayor and had established a very sound principle that majority rules. Isn't that profound? I took about 20 pages to say it, but it boiled down to that.

In looking at the group that came to be known as the Golden Thirteen, I've always said that we were lucky. The Navy reached down into a group of over 100,000 black enlisted men and picked up 13 of us to be trained as officers. They could easily have dipped this hand into that pool and come up with 13 more and 13 more and 13 more. We were not unique. There was a lot of talent to choose from.

As the years passed and the original black officers got together again, some people suggested that a ship might be named for us. Nothing ever came of it. I think that I'm one of those who came up with the idea that, "Since we can't get a ship named after us, why not a building?" Some other people came up with that idea, too, but I know that I advanced it. In June 1987 the in-processing center at the Great Lakes Naval Training Center was named for the Golden Thirteen. I think it's appropriate, because most of us were not on ships, and this will reach a whole lot more people than a ship would.

The admiral at Great Lakes then was a woman named Roberta Hazard. As one of the Navy's early woman admirals, she explained to us, "I, too, am a pioneer. And I want to be part of the celebration, where we're celebrating your pioneering efforts." She did a great job with that dedication. It's ironic that we are now revered, because back in 1944 we were reviled. There were articles in the newspapers and *Life* magazine. People intelligent enough to read *Life* decried the fact that the Navy was lowering its standards to admitting blacks to the officer ranks.

Much progress has been made since 1944. Sam Gravely was commissioned shortly after we were and eventually became a vice admiral in the 1970s. Certainly a vice admiral is the equivalent of a president of a corporation. I don't think General Motors or United States Steel has made the progress that the Navy has .... I still think, on the whole, that the Navy is more democratic than the country it serves.

THE PROBLEMS CONTINUE

If it seems unusual that a college graduate (and accomplished lawyer and assistant federal prosecutor as well) should have trouble winning a commission to help fight his country's greatest war, that is only from the perspective of the late 20th century. In the days of Justice White's youth, it was not at all uncommon for blacks, whatever their qualifications, to see those qualifications disregarded and their accomplishments ignored.

The bitter, racially demeaning attitudes Justice White met in the workplace and in uniform during the late 1930s and early 1940s are less openly expressed today, but sadly, still are quietly held by too many adults who, it seems, would know the law. Otherwise, the Equal Employment Opportunity Commission would not be seeing complaints of bias in hiring and promotions still going up, rather than down.[8] Yet, in 1992, 50 years after the Golden Thirteen made waves, federal discrimination complaints reached their second-highest yearly total, more than 70,000 complaints, since the 1964 Civil Rights Act was passed. This article from the *Los Angeles Times* in 1992 summarizes recent complaint trends under the Civil Rights Act:

EEOC Complaints Rise

Job-related discrimination complaints reached their second-highest annual total since the 1964 Civil Rights Act became law, the Equal Employment Opportunity Commission said Tuesday.

The EEOC said for fiscal year 1992 ending Sept. 30, there were 70,339 complaints filed – including, for the first time, filings based on the new Americans with Disabilities Act.

That law, which took effect in June, expanded existing laws to prohibit discrimination against those with physical handicaps. There were 774 complaints based on this new law, a figure that represented 1.1% of the total.

However, EEOC Chairman Evan J. Kemp Jr. noted in a statement that the ADA was in effect for just two months of fiscal year 1992, and later statistics show significant increases in ADA charges filed.

"These are really a lot of charges," department spokeswoman Janice Hearty said. "We average around 60,000 per year."

The all-time record was set in fiscal 1988, when 70,749 complaints were filed.

Complaints based on race continue to be the most frequently cited cause for filing, accounting for 40.8% of all charges filed. However, that figure represents a decline of 3% from the previous year.

Sex-based charges rose by 2.2%, to 29.8%, and the EEOC attributed this increase to a vastly higher number of alleged incidents of sexual harassment.

Nearly half of the complaints, 49.8%, came only after the person filing the charge had been fired, the EEOC said.

Settlements totaling $65.6-million were recovered in 1992, said EEOC General Counsel Donald R. Livingston, who added that that total is the second highest ever.

A record portion of that total, $50.7-million, came in settlements of age discrimination suits, Livingston said.

The EEOC enforces Title VII of the Civil Rights Act of 1964, which prohibits discrimination on the basis of race, color, religion, sex or national origin. The agency also enforces laws banning discrimination on the basis of age or physical disabilities.

(*Los Angeles Times*, December 2, 1992)

It is also worth noting that the yearly *average* of bias complaints the agency had received for the several years before 1992 stood at 60,000.[9] Of course, not every complaint can fairly be believed to have prevailed. Still, that continued high incidence of complaints of job bias, the biggest number focused on race bias, shows how far we have yet to go toward a discrimination-free workplace.

This ignoring of qualifications, and the accompanying under use and mistreatment of minorities in the workplace, eventually caused the passage of "affirmative action" laws. Later, many of their provisions were strengthened to provide protection for women as well.

LEGISLATING A MORE OPEN WORKPLACE

"In the field of fair employment law, it is necessary to be aware of the multiple and overlapping federal, state and municipal enactments, and their almost never-ending amendment or modification. (We focus here on federal law, because it is more generally applicable.) However, it is necessary to recognize the growing importance of non-federal regulation, which may provide more expansive coverage or protection,[†] or afford a greater remedy."[10]

THE CIVIL RIGHTS ACT OF 1866

Several current federal laws, passed after extensive debate in the U.S. Congress, forbid discrimination in hiring, promotions and pay. The grandfather of such laws is the Civil Rights Act of 1866.

Race discrimination in the employment "contract" is proscribed by the 1866 Civil Rights Act. Enacted immediately after the Civil War, this statute was designed to grant to newly freed slaves basic civil rights, such as the right to contract and the right to purchase, hold, and sell property. The portion of the Act now codified at 42 U.S.C.A. §1981 provides that "all persons ... shall have the same right ... to make and enforce contracts ... as is enjoyed by white citizens .... " While this prohibition overlaps with Title VII (of the Civil Rights Act of 1964), the 1866 Act has broader coverage, allows more extensive monetary remedies, and is enforced through private judicial remedies without the administrative prerequisites imposed on Title VII plaintiffs.

The 1866 Act was recodified in the 1870s soon after ratification of the Fourteenth Amendment, which granted against state action the rights of due process and equal protection of the laws. For nearly 100 years it was assumed that this codification made Section 1981 applicable only to governmental actions. By the 1970s, well after the effective date of Title VII, the Supreme Court held that §1981 was enacted pursuant to power granted by the Thirteenth Amendment, which abolished slavery, and was thus applicable to private refusals to contract; "state action" was not required to assert a claim under the 1866 Act. *Runyon vs. McCrary* (S.Ct.1976).[11]

Congress has rejected proposals to repeal or limit the application of §1981 or to make Title VII the exclusive remedy in employment discrimination cases. However, a Supreme Court decision holding that §1981 did not apply to "post formation" discrimination, such as racial harassment, prompted legislative reform in the 1991 Civil Rights Act. This amendment makes the Act applicable not only to the "making" of contracts but also to "the performance, modification, termination, and the enjoyment of all benefits, privileges, terms and conditions of the contractual relationship."[12]

Later law: Title VII of the Civil Rights Act of 1964 – One of the biggest legislative battles of the 20th century came over passage of the 1964 Civil Rights Act, 42 U.S.C.A. §2000e et seq., an "omnibus"[13] bill whose titles were separate proposals, each with its own very different legislative history. Title VII of that law prohibits discrimination because of race, color, religion, sex and national origin. It covers employers, labor unions and employment agencies. In 1972, Congress rewrote and clarified Title VII, to change the time frame to file actions and to sharpen the Act's focus on religious discrimination. Congress also gave the Equal Employment Opportunity Commission (EEOC) power to enforce the law by bringing court actions. In 1978, Congress amended Title VII to include "pregnancy and childbirth" within the definition of "sex."

The Age Discrimination in Employment Act of 1967 – The Age Discrimination in Employment Act, 29 U.S.C.A. §621 et seq., forbids job discrimination against people over age 40. It covers groups similarly to Title VII's provisions, but provides different enforcement tools. It also allows successful plaintiffs to recover "liquidated damages," which means cash awards.

During the intense debate over the Civil Rights Act of 1964, proponents were unable to include protection against age discrimination in Title VII. They did carry through a resolution to direct the Secretary of Labor to propose a new law to fight age discrimination, however, and the Labor Department's 1965 report became the basis of the Age Discrimination Act. Originally, the Labor Secretary had power to enforce the Age Discrimination in Employment Act, but in 1978 the EEOC took over.

The Act now covers governmental employers as well as private ones and now expressly proscribes mandatory retirement of workers. Several 1980s amendments reconcile the Act's requirements for employee benefit programs with the obligations imposed on employers under Medicare and Medicaid. Later amendments required age-based differences in benefits to be cost-justified and set standards for employees' severance as part of early retirement offers.

Getting into the act: the Americans With Disabilities Act of 1990 (ADA); The Rehabilitation Act of 1973 – These two laws bar discrimination against people with physical or mental disabilities. The Rehabilitation Act, written in 1973, covers government agencies, organizations receiving federal financial assistance and federal contractors. The ADA provided a similar package of protection against bias, but it was written to cover all employers that would be subject to Title VII of the 1964 Civil Rights Act.

In 1978, Congress rewrote the Rehabilitation Act to spell out more clearly what the protections were against job bias. A decade later, as it moved to reverse the Supreme Court's restrictive interpretation of discrimination law in the *Grove City College* ruling, Congress extended the reach of this law as well as of other statutes covering entire programs.

The Civil Rights Restoration Act of 1987, PL 100-259, strengthened the Rehabilitation Act and the Civil Rights Act's Title VI as well as Title IX of the Education Act, redefining "program or activity" covered to mean not only specific programs receiving federal funds, but the institutions, corporations or organizations to which such programs belong. The Civil Rights Restoration Act also knocked out the immunity from lawsuits that had been enjoyed by state governments under the Eleventh Amendment. The Americans With Disabilities Act of 1990 (ADA) covers employment, public services, public accommodations and telecommunications. Under its Title I, it prohibits job discrimination against disabled persons by employers covered by Title VII of the Civil Rights Act. It adopts the procedures and remedies of Title VII to give force to its provisions. As one legal analyst has noted:

> While the ADA utilizes more extensive language in defining the scope of protection and the extent of required accommodation of disabilities than does the Rehabilitation Act, the legislative history of the ADA indicates that the purpose of this language was to mirror Title VII and to adopt judicial constructions given the more general language of the earlier Rehabilitation Act. The Rehabilitation Act was not repealed by the ADA.[14]

The ADA's job bias provisions carried a two-stage phase-in. The law went into effect July 26, 1992 and full coverage is to be extended in mid-1994.

Protecting the newcomers: The Immigration Reform and Control Act of 1986 – Job discrimination against American citizens and defined "intending citizens" on the basis of citizenship or national origin by employers not covered by Title VII is prohibited by the Immigration Reform and Control Act. The Act covers all employers with more than three workers and is enforced by a Justice Department special counsel, using administrative fact-finding procedures that differ greatly from the procedures used under Title VII and the Age Discrimination in Employment Act.

The 1980s saw a dramatic increase in illegal immigration to the United States. Large numbers of the illegal aliens were from Mexico, Caribbean islands and Central America, although many also came from geographic regions farther away. A long and involved debate arose about how to stem this unplanned cross-border flow as lawmakers sought to make it illegal to hire foreigners not authorized to work in the United States. Civil rights groups were afraid that sanctions against employers would be counter-productive: Punish the employers for hiring *illegal* aliens and they might refuse to hire *any* aliens, even those here legally.

Title VII of the Civil Rights Act bars national-origin discrimination, but the civil rights advocates feared an over-reaction against persons with non-English names, "foreign" accents or a "different" appearance. Thus, the Immigration Reform Act makes it a prohibited "immigration related practice" to discriminate against job applicants on the basis of "national origin" or on the basis of "citizenship" for people who already are citizens or are "intending citizens" of the United States.

Sex discrimination: the Equal Pay Act of 1963 (EPA) – Inspired by the "equal pay" practices of the World War II War Labor Board, Congress enacted the Equal Pay Act as an amendment to the Fair Labor Standards Act. In effect, it wrote into law the first 20th century anti-job bias statute, as Congress amended a law that had regulated minimum wages, overtime and child labor.

EPA provisions require employers to provide "equal pay" for men and women who perform "equal work" in the workplace unless any pay differential can be shown to be based on a seniority or merit system or other "factor other than sex." For would-be plaintiffs, the Equal Pay Act offers a different basis than Title VII for protection against sex-based bias in compensation. One major difference from Title VII is that the EPA also provides statutory liquidated damages. It also may be enforced by private action, irrespective of administrative requirements, unlike Title VII of the Civil Rights Act.

The original statue called for enforcement by the secretary of Labor, but in 1978 an executive reorganization shifted the enforcement responsibilities to the EEOC.

Affirmative action: an executive push (Presidential Executive Order 11246) – Since World War II, presidents have required government contractors to take "affirmative action" to open up opportunities for minorities and women.[15] These orders were nine-tenths exhortation in the eyes of social critics, such as the legendary A. Philip Randolph, but they were on the books. During the administration of President Lyndon Baines Johnson, however, affirmative action began to carry new force in a sweeping new presidential mandate, Executive Order 11246.

During the early 1970s, Arthur Fletcher, assistant Labor secretary in the Nixon administration, began pushing to sharpen affirmative action's focus on strategies for change. Secretary Fletcher's "Philadelphia Plan" for building contractors opened doors long closed in the construction industry and became a pattern for ambitious redress of longstanding grievances of minorities who had been excluded from jobs and business opportunities for generations.

What began as quiet urging in 1935 became public policy – enforced policy – under presidential order. The Labor Department implements such Executive Orders with regulations, and during the early 1970s its regulations for the first time defined "affirmative action" as imposing a duty on business to hire and promote minorities and women and to seek subcontracting partners from racial minorities and women, formerly disadvantaged groups.[16] Executive Order 11246 covers those who sell services, fill supply contracts or who engage in federally financed construction contracts. Thus, the effects of Secretary Fletcher's experiments were deep and wide: The affected businesses were employing about a quarter of America's workers.

In addition to barring discrimination by reason of race, national origin and sex, which is already barred by Title VII, the Executive Order requires contractors to develop a "utilization analysis" to explore the extent to which qualified minorities and women are under-represented in various job categories in comparison to their percentages available in the relevant labor market. Further, it requires employer-contractors to adopt written plans to correct any imbalances found. Such plans must include reasonable numerical goals and timetables of reaching them. The plans also involve commitments by the contractors to use hiring ratios that take race, sex or national origin into account to help reach the stated goals.

That puts employers who do business with the government under contract to reach affirmative action goals. Contracted obligations can be enforced in court, and obligations incurred under Executive Order 11246 can be and are enforced by lawsuits by the contracting agencies. In some cases, an employer may even be brought before an administrative panel from the Department of Labor and debarred from doing further federal contract work.

This order, coming by authority of the president of the United States, is not itself a law. It provides no private legal remedies for violation. Violations must be brought to the attention of the Labor Department through administrative complaints. And an Office of Federal Contract Compliance oversees covered businesses' performance in women and minority hiring, promotion and contracting.

While not a law *per se*, Executive Order 11246 has been upheld on challenge in the courts. In *Contractors Ass'n of Eastern Pa. vs. Secretary of Labor* (3d Cir. 1971),[17] the court found that it was within the power of the Executive Branch to determine the terms and conditions under which it would do business.[18]

President Ronald Reagan, a longtime opponent of "quotas," appeared prepared to revoke Executive Order 11246 during the mid-1980s, but a major outcry persuaded him not to do so. Among other reasons, many federal contractors rushed to complain that the established regime under the Executive Order made for a more stable, more predictable environment. With the employment targets known and with specified grievance procedures, it worked well for employers as well as providing better access for minorities and women to careers that would otherwise be closed to them. And having affirmative action goals and timetables in the contract means that even non-minority workers know that affirmative action is part of the job itself.

REBUFFING THE HIGH COURT: THE CIVIL RIGHTS ACT OF 1991

In evaluating the development of labor law, John J. Ross offered this summation:

> The 1988-89 Supreme Court term provided a number of decisions that involved restrictive statutory interpretations of various civil rights statutes. These decisions produced an immediate and orchestrated criticism. This in turn generated an immediate legislative response. This reaction was predictable, as these decisions were viewed as disasters by the civil rights community and involved statutory construction.
>
> The immediate legislative result, the Civil Rights Act of 1990, a dramatic and far-reaching retort to the Supreme Court, was vetoed by President George Bush on Oct. 23, 1990. The Senate failed by one vote to override the veto.
>
> On the first day of the next Congress, in January of 1991, the legislative battle began again and culminated in the Civil Rights Act of 1991, which was signed by President Bush on November 21, 1991.[24]

Thus, at that time – after two years of debate, negotiations and struggle – a major restructuring of the nation's civil rights laws relating to employment was enacted. This Act reverses or modifies eight Supreme Court decisions and amends seven statutes. The law expands protections against race and ethnic discrimination; provides for compensatory and punitive damages, plus the right to jury trial for intentional discrimination under Title VII and ADA (Americans with Disabilities Act of 1990); permits the inclusion of expert's fees in attorney's fees awarded a prevailing party in employment discrimination litigation; codifies and restructures the rules of "disparate impact"[19] litigation; restructures "mixed motive"[20] litigation; under Title VII prohibits "race norming"[21] in testing; limits the right of non-parties to challenge actions taken under litigated or consent decrees;[22] applies Title VII and the Americans with Disabilities Act extraterritorially (to U.S. firms doing business overseas);[23] lengthens the limitation period under Title VII to challenge adoption of a seniority system for a discriminatory purpose; extends the period under Title VII for government employees to commence suit and permits the award of interest against the United States; and conforms the procedure and time for filing suit under ADEA (Age Discrimination in Employment Act of 1967) to that of Title VII.[24]

(In addition, by adding a new subsection to § 1981, the 1991 Act restored the reach of the 1866 Civil Rights Act. With its decision in *Patterson vs. McLean Credit Union*,[25] the high court had restricted § 1981's coverage to the "formation" or "enforcement" aspects of an employment agreement. Congress, deciding that unduly curtailed the intent of the law, provided protections against workplace harassment and other discriminatory actions after the individual began working on the job.)

Immediately upon enactment, arguments developed concerning a number of points. The President was accused of caving in, and both sides claimed they had prevailed. Perhaps the best assessment of the legislative outcome was that of Stuart Taylor, whose perceptive analysis concluded that this was a "classic," convoluted legislative deal. The White House won more than it lost on the restructuring of "disparate impact" litigation. But it did cave in on the "lawyers' bonanza" – jury trials and damage awards.[26]

DOWN TO CASES: THE BACKDROP TO THE BATTLES IN COURT

As we survey legislative and judicial doctrines, it will be difficult to isolate one and only one factor as the sole explanation for the legislated, adjudicated, and upheld racial deprivation that gained the official approval of the American legal establishment (during most of the life of this country). As in most things, the causal factors were multifaceted. On some occasions the economic concerns seemed the dominating influence, while in other instances a moral or religious aspect appeared to be more significant. But however tightly woven into the history of their country is the legalization of black suppression, many Americans still find it too traumatic to study the true story of racism as it has existed under their "rule of law." For many, the primary conclusion of the National Commission on Civil Disorders is still too painful to hear:

> What white Americans have never fully understood – but what the Negro can never forget – is that white society is deeply implicated in the ghetto. White institutions created it, white institutions maintain it, and white society condones it."[27]

'THREE REALITIES'

"Three Realities: Minority Life in the United States," a report by the Business-Higher Education Forum, lays bare the results of that study:[28]

• While many minority families are making it out of the nation's poorest communities, far too many are not. About 30% of the nation's minority population, and roughly one-fourth of the working-age population, fall in the underclass.

• There is even an "underclass" within the poverty population. Although it is most readily apparent in the cities, the underclass extends into isolated, rural areas.

• Despite the piecemeal strategies developed since the 1960s, the underclass has endured for two generations. Indeed, the population living in areas of extreme poverty within the five largest cities increased by 161% between 1970 and 1980.

• In the inner cities, the collapse of the two-parent family and a 30-year rise in out-of-wedlock births to young women are painful trends that "defeat most hopes for upward mobility." By 1985, births to unmarried mothers accounted for 60% of all births to black women.

The report noted hopeful trends as well. One happy result of the efforts of many people over the decades, and the push of minorities for more education, is that "a significant number of minority group members are succeeding in the American society, economy and culture." A growing middle class – black and Hispanic – is repeating the successes of ethnic immigrants, the report said, and doing it in much the same way. That is, the new successes are coming as minorities insist that they be accorded the equal treatment that is every American's due and, by diligence, seizing on opportunities and sacrificing today for their children's tomorrow's.

"Three Realities" found that more than a third of all blacks are now middle class, and that singling out working-age blacks 22 to 65 boosts the total to more than 40%. Nearly half of all blacks own their own homes as well. On the labor front, 1.5-million blacks work as managers, business executives and professionals. The number of black elected officials has grown between from 1970 and 1990 to nearly 7,000, including more than 300 black mayors. In 1987, the report said, 36% of all black families had incomes of $25,000 or more.

Among Hispanics, 40% of families were in the $25,000-and-up income bracket and 40% also owned their homes. Hispanics holding elected offices totaled more than 3,700, including 128 state legislators and 10 members of Congress.

The study found more than 200,000 Hispanic-owned firms in six states – California, Texas, Florida, New York, New Mexico and Arizona. These businesses had gross sales of more than $12-billion in 1982, the last year for which state-by-state data were available.

Detailed analysis of Hispanic demographics in California shows that integration for Mexican-Americans and their children is similar to that of European immigrants. Newcomers struggle to establish themselves and the generations coming after them move rapidly into the mainstream. The process is working "better now than 20 years ago," according to another study. More than half of all Mexican-born immigrants have an eighth-grade education or less, the study says, but by the second generation, more than 40% have some education beyond high school.

That translates into occupational gains. More than half of all Mexican-Americans without high-school diplomas work as farm laborers, "Three Realities" said. Conversely, more than half of those with diplomas work in crafts, sales, managerial, professional and technical jobs.

But at bottom, the report found too much still undone for Hispanics or blacks to be considered truly integrated into the mainstream. It noted that Hispanic unemployment is about 20% higher than that of white, Anglo Americans. It repeated analyses of 17-year-olds' educational attainment which showed that the average proficiency of black and Hispanic students approximates that of white 13-year-olds.

That may have fearful implications for minorities in a workplace scheduled to shift even further away from high-paying, low-skilled factory jobs by the end of this decade. All jobs are moving up in skill requirements,[29] but the populations feeding the largest groups of new entrants into the labor force – inner-city minorities – are being left behind in critical educational areas.

The situation of women, especially non-minority women, is different. Another report, by Massachusetts Institute of Technology economics professor Paul R. Kaufman, in the magazine *U.S. News and World Report,* noted, "Women have made slow progress," but that compared to racial minorities, their advances are undeniable.[30] While women's earnings remained stable at 60% of men's wages during the 1970s, this was partially accounted for by a rapid rise in women entering the labor force: From

1965's 37% female labor force participation, the 1980 figure had jumped to 51%. Most of these new entrants were inexperienced, the magazine said, and their income was also squeezed by the competition in fields traditionally dominated by women.

Since 1980, Kaufman said, opportunities for women "have widened and there is a modest spurt in relative earnings. Over the past decade, women's wages have jumped from 64% to 72% of men's earnings. Big differences remain – especially among male and female executives. Women now hold 38% of all managerial positions in America, but these female supervisors are paid only 64% as much as their male counterparts."

The "Three Realities" report found four common elements affecting America's minorities, no matter how well they are living:

Racism. All the progress aside, racism is still deeply and subtly embedded in the fabric of the nation. Almost 40% of American blacks see racism hindering their access to quality education. The majority of African-Americans believe they face discrimination on the job in terms of wages and access to skilled and managerial positions. Most whites, looking from another perspective, believe blacks are treated equally despite the continuing complaints of discrimination and have little understanding of minorities' tenuous connection to the larger institutions of American life.

Poor educational attainment. While every major analysis shows links between educational attainment and moving into the economic mainstream, 28% of Hispanic youth and more than 15% of black youths reported in 1985 that they had dropped out of high school. Those who do graduate, the report found, are less inclined to enroll in colleges and universities today than in 1975.

The stranglehold of the inner city. America's cities were once launching pads for the ethnic poor, the report says, but today inner-city neighborhoods "effect a stranglehold on youth, who grow up in a culture characterized by welfare dependency, rejection of education as the route to personal advancement, and the collapse of the two-parent family." Conventional approaches to these problems, the report says, "both the generous-spirited and the hard-nosed," have failed.

Participation in the nation's economic life. "Three Realities" called for new approaches to improve the participation of minorities in the overall economic life of the nation. It noted that affirmative action among federal contractors had an important impact, but said that was too limited. It demanded greater efforts to spur entrepreneurial development in black and Hispanic communities, noting that although blacks and Hispanics make up nearly 20% of the population, they own less than five percent of the small businesses. "Many of these minority-owned companies, in fact, are painfully small," it said. In 1982, it showed, there were 340,000 black-owned businesses, which together had gross receipts of $12.4-billion. But nearly half of these businesses had annual receipts of less than $5,000.

Clearly, many important leaders of corporate America are sounding a battle call with this and other reports. Clearly, they are saying, "Our companies can and must do more, even as we urge the society to do more."

Among the recommendations in the "Three Realities" report, the proposals for corporations stand out: In hiring and promotions, continue and expand recruitment of minorities for entry-level and middle management jobs and for positions among top management and on boards of directors. "Among the strategies that can be particularly helpful," it said, "are *affirmative action*[31] policies, formal partnerships with traditionally black colleges and universities, multicultural work environments and family-oriented policies that help employees meet their child-care needs."[32]

In capital development, examine the "viable, existing community models and help replicate them." Such strategies could include developing partnerships with local banks and community development groups to bring business back to the inner cities. Corporations could also deposit small fractions of their corporate assets in banks that form the cornerstone of these ventures, to provide pools of money for mortgage and business loans and investing for profit in venture-capital efforts for community developments.

It also recommended banding together with other corporations, chambers of commerce and industry-affiliated groups to set up formal service-delivery mechanisms to supply counseling and technical assistance to minorities who have the potential to succeed in the marketplace and to subcontract with and purchase from minority-owned firms.

"Three Realities" also recommended that corporate chiefs re-examine their policies governing franchises, to find ways of boosting minority ownership by including targets for minority ownership, intensive training for potential owners and liberalized financing and capitalization.

Such proposals, when backed up by concrete action, can go a long way toward moving minorities into the economic mainstream. There are, however, costs to be paid and not everyone agrees that the weight should fall on their shoulders. One affirmative action effort, by the Kaiser Corporation, produced just such a reaction from one of its white workers: "Why me? Why here and why now?" Those questions were asked by Brian Weber, whose case is described by *Los Angeles Times* writers Barry Bearnak and David Lauter:

AFFIRMATIVE ACTION: THE PARADOX OF EQUALITY
Barry Bearak and David Lauter
Los Angeles Times, November 4, 1991

GRAMERCY, LA. – America's debt of conscience had become Brian Weber's account to settle. He was no racist. And to his mind, neither was his company. But suddenly blacks were being lifted over him on the seniority list.

He was furious. The year was 1974, and Weber did not so much blame his employer, Kaiser Aluminum & Chemical Corp., as that familiar old meddler Uncle Sam. The government was pushing affirmative action as a sort of racial amends.

Weber believed in equality for blacks, but to him that meant they deserved to get in line with everyone else. Instead, the line was being rearranged by some hand that seemed to reach out for retribution across the generations.

He sued. And over the next five years, his anger would echo all the way to the U.S. Supreme Court, along the way picking up a shorthand moniker that was the grumble of a million white males: reverse discrimination.

Like Weber, the nation's laws against bias in the workplace were in a quandary. Was the goal simply to treat all people, black and white, the same? Or was it to end the long legacy of racism by giving blacks a boost up? If the latter, could that be accomplished without discriminating against whites?

Nearly two decades later, the answers remain an elaborate twine of conflict. They involve some of the knottiest trade-offs in a century of social change. And while politicians have preferred not to discuss such matters head on, they have been at the center of the debate between Congress and the White House over a new civil rights bill.

Since it passed a landmark law in 1964, Congress has forfeited the crucial choices in the nation's anti-discrimination efforts to others. Federal regulators – and sometimes employers themselves – have made up the fateful rules as they went along, then waited for the courts to sort out the legalities.

At Kaiser's plant here in Gramercy, 25 miles up the Mississippi River from New Orleans, the decisions carried stakes as real as the pile in any poker game. Kernell Goudia, a black, would soon be earning $25,000 a year as a skilled craftsman. Weber wanted that job. He made only $17,000 a year as a lab technician.

The two men were friends. One of their conversations repeated itself so often it carried the unvarying cadences of a ritual chant.

Weber: "It's not just integration now. You're taking our jobs."

Goudia: "That's because of all the discrimination in the past."

Weber: "I didn't do the discriminating."

Goudia: "Your father did and his father did."

Weber: "But that's no reason to do it to me."

Brian F. Weber was a near perfect soldier for this battle. Son of a grocer, he had grown up not far from here in Reserve, LA. Railroad tracks separated the white part of town from the black. Racism hovered as naturally in the air as the mosquitoes in the bayou.

But Weber was somehow spared the germ, or so say the blacks he worked with. They believe his lawsuit was based entirely on principle. Plain and simple, Weber felt he was getting cheated.

He had been a good student in high school. He won a statewide math contest that awarded him a scholarship to Louisiana State University. But he had plans for a more romantic nature. He was getting married. What he needed was a job.

It was 1964, and times along the river were flush. The delta had proven a lodestone for refineries and chemical plants. Weber traded up from one job to another; then he heard they were hiring at Kaiser.

The aluminum plant was an enormous boast of rust-colored smokestacks and horizontal pipes. One part of it was a chlorine-making operation, purging the chemicals from the great salt domes in the Louisiana soil. Another operation produced sugary granules of alumina powder from tons of Jamaican bauxite.

Weber and Goudia began work there in 1968, the same memorable year that Richard M. Nixon won the presidency. America was suffering a fit of domestic convulsions then, Nixon inheriting the stubborn dyspepsia of Vietnam.

There were other, less conspicuous ailments as well, including one that was upsetting businessmen and confusing bureaucrats.

It had a high-sounding name: affirmative action.

That alliterative coupling – affirmative action – was coined in the fine print of a section on unfair labor practices in the 1935 Wagner Act. The words carried a graceful, progressive lilt, but they were empty of definition.

The lawyerly aides of President John F. Kennedy resurrected the phrase in 1961. And then, in 1965, Kennedy's successor, Lyndon B. Johnson, used it once more in a far-reaching executive order that forbade discrimination by private companies with federal contracts.

The words again went unaccompanied by explanation, which was an important omission. More than 25% of the American labor force worked for companies that were federal contractors. For decades, the government had been commanding these businesses to end bias in hiring. But there had been little in the way of change.

Brian Weber and his white coworkers had "claimed to be victims of disparate treatment discrimination because the union and employer's policy considered race in making selection decisions. To support their claim, the plaintiffs relied upon Section 703(j) of the Civil Rights Act of 1964, which, in pertinent part, provides that nothing in Title VII 'shall be interpreted to require any employer ... to grant preferential treatment to any group because of race, color, religion, sex, or national origin' because of an imbalance between members of these groups in the employer's workforce and the relevant labor market from which the employer draws its applicants and employees. In a 6-3 decision, the Supreme Court upheld the affirmative action plan. Justice Brennan, writing for the majority, relied on a construction of Title VII that supported the disparate impact theory and its underlying goal of remedying the effects of societal discrimination. He wrote:

> "The (Title VII) prohibition against racial discrimination ... must therefore be read against the background of the legislative history ... and the historical context from which the Act arose .... Congress' primary concern in enacting the prohibition against racial discrimination in Title VII ... was with 'the plight of the Negro in our economy.'

> " ... It would be ironic indeed if a law triggered by a Nation's concern over centuries of racial injustice and intended to improve the lot of those who had 'been excluded from the American dream for so long' ... constituted the first legislative prohibition of all voluntary, private, race-conscious efforts to abolish traditional patterns of racial segregation and hierarchy."[34]

It also would have been unreasonable to assume that the shift away from patterns of discrimination established over centuries could be accomplished without pain to those who once could count on receiving a lion's share of the benefits. One of the earliest demonstrations of that point for American workers came in 1944, when racial segregation was still the law of the land.

FAIR DEALING IN LABOR GROUPS

In *Steele vs. Louisville & Nashville Railroad Company et al.*,[35] an African-American named Bester William Steele sued to block discriminatory firings. The majority of the company's firemen were white and represented by the Brotherhood of Locomotive Firemen and Enginemen in collective bargaining. The petitioner, Steele, was a member of a substantial minority of black firemen, who worked for the railroad but were excluded from the union. Because the Railway Labor Act required that all members of a labor group be represented by a union if the majority selected it as their bargaining representative, for the purposes of the Act the blacks were represented by the union, too, even if they could not join it. In its ruling, the court's summarization read in part as follows:

> On March 28, 1940, the Brotherhood, purporting to act as representative of the entire craft of firemen, without informing the Negro firemen or giving them opportunity to be heard, served a notice on respondent Railroad and on twenty other railroads operating principally in the southeastern part of the United States. The notice announced the Brotherhood's desire to amend the existing collective bargaining agreement in such manner as ultimately to exclude all Negro firemen from the service. By established practice on the several railroads ... , only white firemen can be promoted to serve as engineers, and the notice proposed that only "promotable," i.e., white, men should be employed as firemen or assigned to new runs or jobs or permanent vacancies in established runs or jobs.

> On February 18, 1941, the railroads and the Brotherhood, as representative of the craft, entered into a new agreement which provided that not more than 50% of the firemen in each class of service in each seniority district should be Negroes; that until such percentage should be reached all new runs and all vacancies should be filled by white men; and that the agreement did not sanction the employment of Negroes in any seniority district in which they were not working. The agreement reserved the right of the Brotherhood to negotiate for further restrictions on the employment of Negro firemen on the individual railroads. On May 12, 1941, the Brotherhood entered into a supplemental agreement with respondent railroad further controlling the seniority rights of Negro firemen and restricting their

employment. The Negro firemen were not given notice or the opportunity to be heard with respect to either of these agreements, which were put into effect before their existence was disclosed to the Negro firemen.[36]

Bester Steele had been a fireman on passenger trains, one of the more desirable jobs in terms of wages, hours and other benefits. After a reduction in the mileage covered by his "passenger pool," in which one white fireman and five blacks had worked, all jobs in the pool were declared vacant April 1, 1941.

The Brotherhood and the Railroad, acting under the agreement, disqualified all the Negro firemen and replaced them with four white men, members of the Brotherhood, all junior in seniority to (Steele) and no more competent or worthy. As a consequence petitioner was deprived of employment for 16 days and then was assigned to more arduous, longer and less remunerative work in local freight service. In conformity to the agreement, he was later replaced by a Brotherhood member junior to him, and assigned work on a switch engine, which was still harder and less remunerative, until January 3, 1942. On that date, after the bill of complaint in the present suit had been filed, he was reassigned to passenger service.

Protests and appeals of petitioner and his fellow Negro firemen, addressed to the Railroad and the Brotherhood, in an effort to secure relief and redress, have been ignored. Respondents have expressed their intention to enforce the agreement of February 18, 1941, and its subsequent modifications. The Brotherhood has acted and asserts the right to act as exclusive bargaining representative of the firemen's craft. It is alleged that in that capacity it is under an obligation and duty imposed by the Act to represent the Negro firemen impartially and in good faith; but instead, in its notice to and contracts with the railroads, it has been hostile and disloyal to the Negro firemen, has deliberately discriminated against them, and has sought to deprive them of their seniority rights and to drive them out of employment in their craft, all in order to create a monopoly of employment for Brotherhood members .... [37]

Steele and his fellow black petitioners were represented by the redoubtable Charles Hamilton Houston, former dean of Howard University Law School and mentor of Thurgood Marshall.[38] Their lawsuit, a major attack on workplace discrimination, won a ruling, per Chief Justice Stone, that "(w)e think that Congress, in enacting the Railway Labor Act and authorizing a labor union, chosen by a majority of the craft, did not intend to confer plenary power upon the union to sacrifice, for the benefit of its members, rights of the minority of the craft, without imposing upon it any duty to protect the minority .... [39]

... Here the discriminations based on race alone are obviously irrelevant and invidious. Congress plainly did not undertake to authorize the bargaining representative to make such discriminations ....

The representative which thus discriminates may be enjoined from so doing, and its members may be enjoined from taking the benefit of such discriminatory action. No more is the Railroad bound by or entitled to take the benefit of a contract which the bargaining representative is prohibited by statute from making .... [40]

Another lawsuit, *Local Union No. 12, United Rubber, Cork, Linoleum & Plastic Workers vs. NLRB,*[41] was decided by the Fifth Circuit in 1966. Here the court confronted segregation in representation, in a Gadsden, Ala. Goodyear plant.

Local 12 had represented plant workers since 1943 and, "As a matter of custom during this period, Negro employees with greater seniority had no rights over white employees with less seniority, and vice versa, with respect to promotions, transfers, layoffs, and recalls."[42]

A man named Buckner was one of eight complainants who had been laid off in 1960 and recalled to work a year later. Notified in October 1961 that he'd be laid off again, Buckner asked why a white worker with less seniority could stay at work. The plant's assistant labor manager told Buckner the posted job was a "white job." So Buckner and the other complainants, all to be laid off, filed affidavits that during the time they were last laid off, new workers had been hired in violation of seniority rules.

The affidavits went to Local 12's president, with a request that the local investigate and take action. The union's grievance committee met in December 1961, and heard a more complete "Statement of Complaint" which charged:

> 1. that the original layoff and recall had violated the contract-stated seniority and that the complainants demanded reinstatement with back wages;
> 2. that upon recall the complainants wanted all transfer privileges set forth in the contract;
> 3. that the complainants demanded the right to all plant privileges without color barriers.

The grievance committee concluded that "no contract violation exists, therefore, the Union has no ground on which to base a complaint against the company." Appeals to the union executive board and the full membership were also denied. Next, in March 1962, Buckner and company appealed to the union's international president, who decided the refusal to process the grievance should be reversed.

The local still refused to press the grievance, but its representatives met with Goodyear officials and a representative of the President's Committee on Equal Employment Opportunity, established by Executive Order in March 1961. What resulted was a verbal agreement to discontinue any application of the bargaining contract that confined blacks and whites to particular jobs and restricted opportunities for upgrading, recall and transfer. Buckner and the other complainants were reinstated, but Local 12 continued to refuse to process their grievances on back pay or those concerning segregated plant lunchrooms, showers and restrooms. Finally, the complainants went to the NLRB, which filed unfair labor practices charges against the local.

A trial examiner found for the union, but the labor board reversed the decision, saying the union local, by refusing to process the grievances, had:

> 1. restrained or coerced complainants in their statutory right to be represented without invidious discrimination;
> 2. caused or attempted to cause Goodyear to discriminate against them;
> 3. and refused to bargain on their behalf, violating the National Labor Relations Act.

The Appeals Court, citing *Steele,*[43] and noting the similarities between the labor relations act and the Railway Labor Act, upheld the NLRB. It also examined Title VII, which had been passed three years after the alleged violations occurred, and concluded it was inapplicable. "Nevertheless," it said, "it is equally clear that had these claims arisen after July 2, 1965, the complainants under our holding today would be at liberty to seek redress under ... Title VII or to assert unfair labor practice charges before the Board .... The mere fact ... that Congress has seen fit to provide specific protection to employees from union and employer discrimination in the area of civil rights in no way detracts from the legal and practical bases of our determination that a breach of the union's duty of fair representation constitutes a violation (of the labor laws)."[44]

This duty of fair representation, imposed on unions by federal labor laws, is a recurring theme. In *National Labor Relations Board vs. Local No. 106, Glass Bottle Blowers Association,*[45] the Sixth Circuit Court of Appeals found that "a labor union with a bargaining relationship in a plant commits an unfair labor practice by maintaining two different locals on the basis of sex and by segregated processing of grievances."

From 1949 on, the Glass Blowers Association had represented production and maintenance workers at Owens-Illinois' Columbus, Ohio, plant. From the outset, the union maintained two locals: 106 for men and Local 245 for women. The plant had about 800 male employees and 370 women.

By early 1969, the company and union had agreed to merge employee seniority lists and to eliminate previous inequities on job availability based on sex. "Men's jobs" or "women's jobs" designations ended and all jobs were open to bidding by all employees. But the union continued to segregate membership in its locals and its grievance processing by sex.

While neither the collective bargaining agreement nor the constitution and bylaws of the international union contained provisions for sex discrimination, the locals continued to process grievances separately. An NLRB administrative law judge had found that male and female employees received separate but equal treatment and, therefore, no violation of labor law had occurred.

The NLRB disagreed, in a divided opinion, and required merger of the two locals. The Board, noting that some women had actually asked to join the men's local and been rebuffed and that some men had asked to attend meetings of the women's local, ruled: "Separate but equal treatment on the basis of sex is as self-contradictory as separate but equal on the basis of race ... In both areas, separation in and of itself connotes and creates inequalities. Not only can separating females from males solely because of sex generate a feeling of inferiority among the females as to their work status, because the policy of separation is usually interpreted as reflecting the inferiority of the females, but also it can ... adversely affect the working conditions of both groups solely because of the differences in sex."[46] The Appeals court agreed with the Board.

RACIST ORGANIZATIONS

A Virginia man managed to get himself dismissed from a department-store job because of visible participation in a racist organization, however. *Bellamy vs. Mason's Stores, Inc.*,[47] details the complaint of John F. Bellamy Jr., who claimed he had been fired because he was a member of the United Klans of America.

Bellamy went to work for Mason's Stores, the defendant, in February 1972. Five months later, he was fired, and said he was told by a Mason's Stores area supervisor that he was being discharged because he was a member of United Klans. Bellamy sued, interestingly enough, under the Civil Rights Act of 1964. The U.S. District Court ,which heard his complaint per Judge Merhige, noted:

> "Plaintiff asserts that because his dismissal was based upon membership in an organization which he contends is racially exclusive in composition and ideology and dedicated to anti-Semitism, he falls within the protection afforded by § 2000e. (But) Accepting the exclusivity asserted, there is no indication in the complaint that either the plaintiff or any other person was discharged by the defendants because of race. Nor is there any indication that defendants have discriminated in any way against members of the Caucasian race. Furthermore, the proclaimed racist and anti-Semitic ideology of the organization to which Bellamy belongs takes on, as advanced by that organization, a narrow, temporal and political character inconsistent with the meaning of 'religion' as used in § 2000e. Thus, plaintiff's claim ... fails to allege facts which indicate discrimination on a basis prohibited by the act, and that claim is, in the court's view, without merit." [48]

PRE-EMPLOYMENT TESTING

Griggs vs. Duke Power Co.,[49] resolved in 1971, has since provided the basis for much of the discussion of equal-opportunity law. Griggs was a class action by black employees charging that a North Carolina utility's requirements of high school diplomas or passing a standardized general education test for jobs violated Title VII.

The District Court found that, before passage of Title VII, Duke Power had an egregious history:

> (T)he Company openly discriminated on the basis of race in the hiring and assigning of employees at its Dan River plant. The plant was organized into five operating departments: (1) Labor, (2) Coal Handling, (3) Operations, (4) Maintenance, and (5) Laboratory and Test. Negroes were employed only in the Labor Department where the highest paying jobs paid less than the lowest paying jobs in the other four "operating" departments in which only whites were employed. Promotions were normally made within each department on the basis of job seniority. Transferees into a department usually began in the lowest position.
>
> In 1955 the Company instituted a policy of requiring a high school education for initial assignment to any department except Labor, and for transfer from the Coal Handling to any "inside" department (Operations, Maintenance, or Laboratory). When the Company abandoned its policy of restricting Negroes to the Labor Department in 1965, completion of high school was also made a prerequisite to transfer from Labor to any other department. From the time the high school requirement was instituted to the time of trial, however, white employees hired before the time of the high school education requirement continued to perform satisfactorily and achieve promotions in the "operating" departments ...
>
> The Company added a further requirement for new employees on July 2, 1965, the date on which Title VII became effective. To qualify for placement in any but the Labor Department it became necessary to register satisfactorily scores on two professionally prepared aptitude tests, as well as to have a high school education. Completion of high school alone continued to render employees able to transfer to the four desirable departments from which Negroes had been excluded if the incumbent had been employed prior to the time of the new requirement .... (Of two tests used alternatively to high school completion to qualify for transfers from Labor or Coal Handling to "inside" jobs) neither was directed or intended to measure the ability to learn or to perform a particular job or category of jobs .... [50]

The District Court had found that Duke Power had discriminated in the past, but that after the Act was passed, this had ceased. It held that Title VII was intended to be prospective only, so the effect of prior inequities was beyond its reach.

The Court of Appeals reversed that holding in part, rejecting the notion that discrimination left over from prior employment practices could not be corrected. It also agreed, however, with the lower court's finding of no showing of racial purpose or invidious intent in the company's high-school diploma requirement or general intelligence testing and that those standards had been applied fairly to whites and blacks alike.

The Appeals Court rejected the claim that because the two requirements disqualified a "markedly" disproportionate number of blacks, they violated Title VII unless they could be shown to be job-related. Here, the Supreme Court, per Chief Justice Burger, disagreed:

> The objective of Congress in the enactment of Title VII is plain from the language of the statute. It was to achieve equality of employment opportunities and remove barriers that have operated in the past

to favor an identifiable group of white employees over other employees. Under the Act, practices, procedures, or tests neutral upon their face, and even neutral in terms of intent, cannot be maintained if they operate to "freeze" the status quo of prior discriminatory employment practices.

The Court of Appeals' opinion ... agreed that, on the record in the present case, "whites register far better on the Company's alternative requirements" than Negroes. 420 F.2d 1225, 1239 n. 6. This consequence would appear to be directly traceable to race. Basic intelligence must have the means of articulation to manifest itself fairly in a testing process. Because they are Negroes, petitioners have long received inferior education in segregated schools and this Court expressly recognized these differences in *Gaston County vs. United States,* 895 U.S. 285, 89 S.Ct. 1720, 23 L.Ed.2d 309 (1969). There, because of the inferior education received by Negroes in North Carolina, this Court barred the institution of a literacy test for voter registration on the ground that the test would abridge the right to vote indirectly on account of race. Congress did not intend by Title VII, however, to guarantee a job to every person regardless of qualifications. In short, the Act does not command that any person be hired simply because he was formerly the subject of discrimination, or because he is a member of a minority group .... What is required by Congress is the removal of artificial, arbitrary, and unnecessary barriers to employment when the barriers operate invidiously to discriminate on the basis of racial or other impermissible classification.[51]

Thus, "on the record before us," the high court concluded, "neither the high school requirement nor the general intelligence test is shown to bear a demonstrable relationship to successful performance on the jobs for which it was used .... "

"Nothing in the Act precludes the use of testing or measuring procedures; obviously they are useful. What Congress has forbidden is giving those devices and mechanisms controlling force unless they are demonstrably a reasonable measure of job performance .... Far from disparaging job qualifications as such, Congress has made such qualifications the controlling factor, so that race, religion, nationality, and sex become irrelevant. What Congress has commanded is that any test used must measure the person for the job and not the person in the abstract."[52]

In *Boston Chapter, NAACP, Inc. vs. Beecher,*[53] the First Circuit Court of Appeals considered a decision on actions by the NAACP and the U.S. Justice Department against pre-employment tests found to be discriminatory against black and Hispanic applicants for Massachusetts firefighter jobs.

The first lawsuit against Boston, its fire commissioner and Massachusetts civil service officials was filed in 1972 by the NAACP's Boston chapter and by black and Spanish-surnamed individuals under the Civil Rights Act of 1866, 42 U.S.C. §§ 1981, 1983 and the Fourteenth Amendment. The plaintiffs claimed that standards and procedures for recruiting and hiring firefighters "had the forseeable effect of discouraging minority employment."[54] A multiple-choice pre-employment test, which had disqualified many black and Hispanic applicants over the years, was challenged, as was a swim requirement and the disqualification of those with felony records.

The U.S. Attorney General brought the second suit in 1973 under Title VII of the Civil Rights Act of 1964, 42 U.S.C. § 2000e *et seq.* as amended by the Equal Employment Opportunity Act of 1972. Both suits sought to stop the challenged practices and also affirmative action – remedial hiring of enough minority firefighters to offset past discrimination.

The lower court's hearing produced evidence of discriminatory hiring practices and the disproportionate racial impact of the test. It ordered a halt to the test in its current form and required the Boston fire commissioner to begin additional hiring to remove the effects of past discrimination.

Noting that in *Castro vs. Beecher,* 459 F.2d 725, 732 (1st Cir. 1972), it had upheld use of a high-school diploma requirement for police officers despite its "racially disparate impact" on black and Spanish-surnamed applicants, the Appeals Court affirmed the District Court's judgment: "In *Castro* ... we thought a high school education was a 'bare minimum for successful performance of the policeman's responsibilities.' *Castro, supra.* But we disapproved a paper-and-pencil test which also bore more heavily on blacks and Spanish than others because it was not proven 'convincingly' that there was a 'fit between the qualification and the job.' *Id.* at 732."

DISCRIMINATORY HIRING

The 1977 lawsuit heard in *International Brotherhood of Teamsters vs. United States*[55] detailed complaints by blacks and Hispanics that their employer, a nationwide motor freight company, and their union discriminated against them in hiring and promotions.

Here the high court, per Justice Stewart, found that the employer, TIME-DC Inc., had 6,472 employees at the time the lawsuit began in 1971.

> "Of these, 314 (5%) were Negroes and 257 (4%) were Spanish-surnamed Americans. Of the 1,828 line drivers (over-the-road, long-distance drivers), however, there were only 8 (0.4%) Negroes and 5 (0.3%) Spanish-surnamed persons, and all of the Negroes had been hired after the litigation had commenced. With one exception – a man who worked as a line driver at the Chicago terminal from 1950 to 1959 – the company and its predecessors *did not employ a Negro on a regular basis as a line driver until 1969.*[56] And, as the Government showed, even in 1971 there were terminals in areas of substantial Negro population where all of the company's line drivers were white.[57] A great majority of the Negroes (83%) and Spanish-surnamed Americans (78%) who did work for the company held the lower paying city operations and serviceman jobs, whereas only 39% of the nonminority employees held jobs in those categories.[58] (Emphasis added.)

Government witnesses also testified to more than 40 specific instances of discrimination by the company. The trial court, accordingly, found that "(n)umerous qualified black and Spanish-surnamed American applicants who sought line-driving jobs at the company over the years, either had their request ignored, were given false or misleading information about requirements, opportunities, and application procedures, or were not considered and hired on the same basis that whites were considered and hired." Minorities already working for TIME-DC Inc. who tried to transfer to line-driver jobs met with similar difficulties, the Supreme Court said.

In its defense, the company attacked the government's statistics. It conceded it had no nonwhite line drivers in July of 1965, when Title VII went into effect, but said its business had fallen off, requiring a smaller workforce. It contended that low turnover, not discrimination, caused its continuing statistical disparities in minority hiring. Moreover, it had hired substantial numbers of minorities after 1971.

Justice Stewart thought little of these arguments.

> The argument would be a forceful one it this were an employer who, at the time of suit, had done virtually no new hiring because the effective date of Title VII. But it is not. although the company's total number of employees dropped somewhat during the late 1960s, the record shows that many line drivers continued to be hired throughout this period, and that almost all of them were white.[59]

> ... (T)he District Court and the Court of Appeals found upon substantial evidence that the company had engaged in a course of discrimination that continued well after the effective date of Title VII. The

company's later changes in its hiring and promotion policies could be of little comfort to the victims of the earlier post-Act discrimination .... [60]

The District Court and the Court of Appeals also found that the seniority system contained in the collective bargaining agreements between the company and the union operated to violate Title VII of the Act. It "locked" minority workers into inferior jobs and perpetuated prior discrimination by discouraging transfers to jobs as line drivers. While the disincentive applied to all workers, including whites, it was Negroes and Spanish-surnamed persons who, those courts found, suffered the most because many of them had been denied the equal opportunity to become line drivers when they were initially hired.[61]

In the end, the Supreme Court upheld the seniority system, but the point was made yet again: Sleight-of-hand in collective bargaining cannot hide discrimination.

SEXUAL DISCRIMINATION

What do you do when the boss is attracted to one of your coworkers, or even to you? Two scandals from the executive suite, widely reported in public media and debated in living rooms across the country, illustrate the problem: the 1991 confirmation of Clarence Thomas to the U.S. Supreme Court, and the 1980 debacle that forced Mary Cunningham from a high-level job at Bendix Corp.

In October 1991, former Equal Employment Opportunity Commission chief Clarence Thomas appeared headed for easy confirmation when law professor Anita Hill's accusations of sexual harassment stunned the country. Hill, a former EEOC lawyer now teaching at the University of Oklahoma, had been a reluctant witness. Senate staff investigators had heard rumors that Thomas had pursued the woman while she worked for him. Office gossip had it that the episode was very embarrassing. Professor Thomas spoke to the probers, and later to the FBI, on condition that her name would be kept from the public.

As *The New York Times* (Oct. 8, 1991) reported her statement to a packed press conference in Oklahoma: "The control and timing of this information, and the release of this information, has never been with me. I have never had any control about when this information would be released. I spoke with the Judiciary Committee about it early in September (1991), and through a number of discussions it was not until the 20th of September that an FBI investigation was suggested to me .... Senator Biden's office (Joseph R. Biden Jr., D-Del., Judiciary Committee chair) than arranged for the investigation, and statements were taken from me ... and a statement was taken from Clarence Thomas ...."

A "leak" to National Public Radio of the story she told the probers proved to be sensational news: Hill had worked for Thomas at the Education Department's Office of Civil Rights and, she said, had become the object of Thomas's sexual desires. He allegedly had pursued her with overt sexual comments, invitations, and discussion of X-rated movies he had enjoyed. The behavior allegedly had continued and even worsened when the two moved to the Equal Employment Opportunity Commission, an agency charged with protecting women from such unwanted attention on the job.

That burst like a bombshell in the male-dominated halls of the U.S. Senate, prompting an intense debate over the truthfulness of then-Judge Thomas, Professor Hill and a cast of supporting and dissenting witnesses, many of them Yale Law School graduates. One woman, now a newspaper editor, testified that Thomas had pursued her in ways similar to the alleged pursuit of Anita Hill. Another, later described as a person Hill did not know, claimed Hill had been pursuing Thomas.

Thomas, for his part, denied the allegations. He won his confirmation, but not before he stood before the cameras and called the whole affair "a high-tech lynching."

The way the Senate handled the allegations, and the visible disbelief of several senators on the all-white/all-male Judiciary panel, itself became a subject of national debate. A national *New York Times/CBS News* poll of that October 11 suggested "that sexual harassment, even if largely unreported, is a pervasive problem in the workplace. Five out of 10 men said that at some point while on the job, they had said something that could have been construed by a female colleague as harassment."

Interestingly, both men and women poll respondents agreed that sexual harassment need not involve physical contact. Some 81 percent of the women and 75 percent of the men felt that harassment could "just involve unwanted sexual conversations." Nearly two-thirds of the survey respondents said that if the Senate had contained more female members, Professor Hill's complaint would have been treated more seriously. After Thomas's confirmation by a badly divided Senate, that became a rallying cry for women in politics.

The following election year (1992), strong protests by women in Pennsylvania nearly unseated Senator Arlen Spector, a ranking Republican who had harshly grilled Professor Hill in the hearings. In Illinois, a loudly criticized Judiciary Committee performance by Alan Dixon, a ranking Democrat, helped get him driven from office. Former Cook County Recorder of Deeds Carol Mosely Braun became the country's first-ever black female senator. With new female senators elected from California as well, and with new and vocal female members of the House of Representatives moving into office during the '92 elections, the issue is far from settled.

GOSSIP EMPTIES EXECUTIVE SUITES

Harassment is but one kind of difficulty that can arise from expressions of sexual interest on the job. Sometimes the alleged object of the attentions of the person in power is not troubled at all, but coworkers may be. The scandal that drove Mary Cunningham from her post at Bendix Corporation, and which followed her even after her marriage to former Bendix Chairman William Agee, is a case in point.

Cunningham, described in a recent *Chicago Tribune* (Feb. 23, 1993) business story as "a vertical blur" at Southfield, Michigan-based Bendix, was a Harvard Business School graduate described by many persons as an extremely bright woman. She had been recruited by the company in 1979, at age 28, after a Harvard professor recommended her as having the best chance of becoming the school's first woman graduate to reach the top at a non-cosmetics company.

Fifteen months after walking onto the job as Agee's assistant, Cunningham was named vice president of strategic planning. It usually takes years to win such a promotion, even for a person with great recommendations and obvious talent. Thus, many Bendix employees gossiped about a suspected romantic link between the corporate chairman and his female assistant, both of whom were married to other people. It didn't take long for Agee to notice the gossip, or to acknowledge it at a staff meeting, in which he said his friendship with Cunningham had nothing to do with her rapid promotion. Cunningham, for her part, as the *Tribune* reported it, still says she was "a loyal employee, not a lover."

Intense rivalries often develop in the competition for top jobs. When fellow employees suspect promotions are being made for reasons having less to do with performance on the job than with romantic connections, the fallout can spread far beyond the office. The rumors at Bendix quickly reached the news media, growing into No. 1 business story of the early '80s.

In 1981, with her face on the covers of national news magazines and speculation filling the pages of major newspapers, Cunningham resigned. She "holed up" at New York's Waldorf Astoria Hotel, depressed and losing weight. Agee, struggling to quiet the gossip and working even harder to complete a hostile takeover of Martin Marietta Corporation, found himself transformed from a corporate darling to the butt of bad jokes. Here was a man who, at the age of 31, had risen to chief financial officer at Boise Cascade Corporation; who had helped invent a new way to manage companies; who had begun to speak of the "reindustrialization of America" from the top post at Bendix. But he left the company when its takeover bid failed. Bendix itself was taken over, by Allied Signal Corporation and Agee now heads the Morris Knudsen Corporation, another industrial giant, located in Boise.

The marriages of Cunningham and Agee were annulled. The two then began a new marriage, in June 1982. They live in Idaho and in Pebble Beach, Calif. Mrs. Agee now runs a non-profit organization known as the Nurturing Network, which helps professional women with "crisis pregnancies" and offers alternatives to abortion.

The Cunningham-Agee story continues to be revisited by news organizations profiling the way romantic relationships can affect business decisions. And in 1991, a similar case erupted as Standley H. Hoch resigned as the top officer at General Public Utilities, an electric power company operating in New Jersey and Pennsylvania. Hoch, married with four sons, admitted an affair with the company's vice president of corporate affairs, Susan Schepman. As the New York Times reported (June 13, 1991), a few months after he resigned, she, too, left the company.

Plainly, the perceptions, feelings and fears of coworkers about the relationship between a boss and a subordinate can have devastasting effects on morale in the office, and, eventually, on the effectiveness of the person in charge. As a consequence, numerous sexual harassment lawsuits have been filed, new laws proposed, and "awareness" seminars and workshops held, while a new sensitivity to favoritism, discrimination and harassment based on sex is demanded in the workplace.

LEGAL ISSUES IN SEXUAL DISCRIMINATION

Sex discrimination on the job raises some of the thorniest of legal issues, especially when it is coupled with claims of sexual liaisons between workers and supervisors. *King vs. Palmer,* 778 F.2d 878 (1985), presents such a situation. Mabel King, a forensic/clinical nurse at the District of Columbia Jail, filed a Title VII action because another woman, Norma Jean Grant, was promoted to supervisor over her. She alleged that Ms. Grant was "engaged in an intimate relationship with Dr. Francis Smith, the Chief Medical Officer at the Jail."[62] Moreover, she said, she had been the victim of a discriminatory work environment and that she had met reprisals for filing a complaint with the Equal Employment Opportunity Commission.

The trial court had found that Ms. King had "demonstrated that the sexual relationship between Ms. Grant and Dr. Smith had been a substantial factor in the promotion decision. (It) held that the defendants' attempt to explain the selection of Ms. Grant was *clearly pretextual,*"[63] but decided she had not proven consummation of the relationship.

The D.C. Circuit Court of Appeals reversed that decision, saying this: "When, as here, the plaintiff successfully makes out a *prima facie* case and discredits the defendants' purported explanation, she has carried her ultimate burden .... Moreover, as the District Court found, there was clearly some direct evidence of sexual conduct between Ms. Grant and Dr. Smith that provided sufficient grounds for Ms. King's allegation that sex was a substantial factor in Ms. Grant's promotion; further proof (in the form of actual evidence of a fully consummated relationship) was unnecessary .... [64]

UNFAIR REFUSALS TO PROMOTE

One of the more notorious discrimination lawsuits decided in the 1980s was that of Ann B. Hopkins, a candidate for partnership at the Price Waterhouse national accounting firm.[65] Hopkins had been a senior manager and officer at Price Waterhouse when she was proposed for partnership in 1982. Her superiors tabled her candidacy for reconsideration the following year. The partners in her office then refused to repropose her for the promotion, and she sued under Title VII.

Hopkins had worked for the company for five years when the dispute began. At the time of her candidacy, there were seven female partners of the company's 662. Of 88 people proposed for elevation, she was the only woman. The court found that 47 of those candidates became partners, 21 were turned down and 20, including Ms. Hopkins, were "held" for reconsideration. Thirteen of the 32 partners who offered written comments on her bid supported her. Three wanted her put on hold, eight said they didn't know enough about her and eight wanted to deny her partnership, the court said.

Ann Hopkins' performance had been exemplary. Partners in her office showed she had won, after a two-year campaign, a $25-million State Department contract. They said she had carried it out "virtually at the partner level." The trial court concurred, noting that "none of the other partnership candidates at Price Waterhouse that year had a comparable record in terms of successfully securing major contracts for the partnership."[66]

The plaintiff "had no difficulty dealing with clients and her clients appear to have been very pleased with her work" and she "was generally viewed as a highly competent project leader who worked long hours, pushed vigorously to meet deadlines and demanded much from the multidisciplinary staffs with which she worked," the trial court found. But, as the Supreme Court noted:

> On too many occasions, however, Hopkins' aggressiveness apparently spilled over into abrasiveness. Staff members seem to have borne the brunt of Hopkins' brusqueness. Long before her bid for partnership, partners evaluating her work had counseled her to improve her relations with staff members. Although later evaluations indicate an improvement, Hopkins' perceived shortcomings in this important area eventually doomed her bid for partnership. Virtually all of the partners' negative remarks about Hopkins – even those of partners supporting her – had to do with her "interpersonal skills .... "[67]

> There were clear signs, though, that some of the partners reacted negatively to Hopkins' personality because she was a woman. One partner described her as "macho" ... another suggested that she "overcompensated for being a woman" ... a third advised her to take "a course at charm school" .... Several partners criticized her use of profanity; in response, one partner suggested that those partners objected to her swearing only "because it's a lady using foul language .... "[68] But it was the man who, as Judge Gessell found, bore responsibility for explaining to Hopkins the reasons for the Policy Board's decision to place her candidacy on hold who delivered the coup de grace: In order to improve her chances for partnership, Thomas Beyer advised, Hopkins should "walk more femininely talk more femininely, wear make-up, have her hair styled, and wear jewelry."

Dr. Susan Fiske, a social psychologist from Carnegie-Mellon University, testified convincingly that the partner selection process had likely been influenced by sex stereotyping. She considered not only the overt, sex-related comments, but also those considered gender-neutral, noting that partners who knew Hopkins only slightly were intensely critical of her.

That stereotyping lost the argument for Price Waterhouse. Its claim of other, valid reasons (i.e., poor interpersonal skills in dealing with staff) for not promoting her fell on deaf ears when it was shown to have used sex-role stereotyping in its decision.

SUMMATION: FAIR DEALING ON THE JOB

It isn't necessary to bend over backward to give preference to people who clearly are not prepared for the job at hand, or to promote people who clearly have not earned the recognition. What should be apparent from these selected cases is that a large body of federal law, supplemented by state and local enactments, mandates an end to discrimination. The way things once were done is no longer valid. Is it an excuse to say that "things have always been this way," or that a newly color-blind, sex-blind society can overnight eradicate the residue of centuries of discrimination without major efforts?

Brian Weber does not seem at all the kind of person who would have held Justice White back from the benefits his education and experience should have won for him. Yet Weber, losing out in the competition for promotions, did his level best to destroy a program his company put together to remedy its own past discrimination. Someone always loses in a competition in which someone else wins, but the fact that Weber lost out to minorities seeking redress of longstanding grievances became a kind of *cause celebre*.

Ann Hopkins was not seen as an acceptable partner on her job, mainly because those above her resented her aggressive, take-no-prisoners style, an approach often celebrated in men. Change in our society means many people in new jobs will behave in ways observers will find out of the expected paths, but this does not translate into grounds for denying benefits the newcomers have earned.

The essence of affirmative action, despite mythology in the public debate, is that qualified people get their fair turn at bat in the American workplace. As the story of Justice White shows, without a sincere, sustained effort, real change cannot take place. Too much societal inertia dooms it.

READINGS

DISCRIMINATION NOW
Paul R. Krugman
Professor of Economics, the Massachusetts Institute of Technology

WOMEN HAVE MADE SLOW PROGRESS. The national furor over Clarence Thomas, Anita Hill and sexual harassment has forced Americans to re-examine the roles of gender and race in the workplace. The institution that Thomas once headed, the Equal Employment Opportunity Commission, was created to narrow the economic gaps between men and women and whites and nonwhites. When the Civil Rights Act of 1964 was passed, overt racial discrimination in hiring was still widespread and prejudice against women was almost universal. These biases were accompanied by sharp economic inequality: Black households earned only about 60% as much as white households, and female workers earned only about 60% as much as male workers. What has a generation of antidiscrimination efforts achieved? The answer is somewhat disturbing. American women have made measurable progress toward economic

equality, especially over the past decade. Their progress has been slow – many would say inadequate – but there is no question that women have improved their relative position. Blacks, on the other hand, have made little if any relative economic progress over the past 20 years.

The earnings of women stagnated during the 1970s, remaining stable at about 60% of men's wages. To some extent, this may have been due to the rapid increase in the number of women working. The female labor-force participation rate jumped from 37% in 1965 to 51% in 1980. This temporarily depressed women's earnings for two reasons: Women who entered the labor force were often inexperienced and the relative wages paid for traditional women's jobs were squeezed by competition. Since 1980, the opportunities for women have widened and there has been a modest spurt in relative earnings. Over the past decade, women's wages have jumped from 64% to 72% of men's earnings. Big differences remain – especially among male and female executives. Women now hold 38% of all managerial positions in America, but these female supervisors are paid only 64% as much as their male counterparts.

BLACKS ARE STILL STRUGGLING. The dismal experience of blacks stands in contrast to the qualified success recently enjoyed by women. While some blacks have achieved success, the overall figures are grim. In 1970, the median income of black families was 60% of white family income; by 1990, the ratio had actually fallen to 58%. Over the past 20 years, unemployment among blacks has risen higher in each successive recession and fallen less with each recovery. In 1970, black unemployment was 8.2%; by 1990, it had reached 11.3%. Black impoverishment hasn't fallen either. In 1990, almost 32% of blacks lived in poverty, up from about 30% in 1974. And black men who work full time earn 30% less than white male counterparts, a gap that has grown since the 1970s. Working women are an exception. Black women who hold full-time jobs earn just 10% less than white women.

Discrimination remains a real issue for both blacks and women in the workplace. But to explain the limited progress of women and the actual decline of blacks, one must analyze a complex social environment in which the shared interests of these two groups are less obvious. For women, the key issues have become the problems of reconciling the demands of children and family with those of the workplace. For blacks, the problems are far more painful. Racism is still a key factor in their economic woes. Yet few observers would attribute the growth in poverty to an actual increase in racism over the past generation. It is virtually impossible to look at the economic state of blacks today without turning to issues of family and social cohesion – and it is next to impossible to raise those issues without touching raw nerves. And, with 45% of black children living in poverty and 62% born out of wedlock, these problems are likely to get worse.

INCREASING POLITICAL TENSION. Given these vastly different experiences, it has become increasingly difficult for blacks and women to form a common economic front. And this growing schism may have contributed to the heightened political tension of the past few weeks.

UNEQUAL PAY
Earnings ratio in percent

	Black-to-white	Female-to-male
1970	61.3 pct.	62.3 pct.
1971	60.3 pct.	61.7 pct.
1972	59.4 pct.	63.1 pct.
1973	57.7 pct.	61.7 pct.
1974	59.7 pct.	60.8 pct.
1975	61.5 pct.	62.0 pct.
1976	59.5 pct.	62.2 pct.
1977	57.1 pct.	61.9 pct.
1978	59.2 pct.	61.3 pct.
1979	56.6 pct.	62.5 pct.
1980	57.9 pct.	64.4 pct.
1981	56.4 pct.	64.6 pct.
1982	55.3 pct.	65.4 pct.
1983	52.6 pct.	66.7 pct.
1984	52.9 pct.	67.8 pct.
1985	54.5 pct.	68.2 pct.
1986	54.5 pct.	69.2 pct.
1987	55.9 pct.	70.0 pct.
1988	57.0 pct.	70.2 pct.
1989	56.2 pct.	70.1 pct.
1990	58.0 pct.	71.8 pct.

Women are slowly closing the wage gap with men, but black family incomes have fallen further behind those of white families.

DEEP-ROOTED POVERTY

Percentage of persons below the poverty line 1990

White	10.7 %
Black	31.9 %
Black children	44.8%

Nearly one third of blacks and almost one half of black children live below the poverty line.

USN&WR – Basic data: U.S. Depts. of Commerce and Labor
GRAPHIC: Charts: Unequal pay; Chronic unemployment; Deep-rooted poverty
(USN&WR – Basic data: U.S. Depts. of Commerce and Labor)
From U.S. News & World Report, Nov. 4, 1991

FOR FURTHER INQUIRY

QUESTIONS:

1. Suppose you had to hire a young man like Illinois Justice White – well educated, polite-spoken and cleanly dressed, but you knew many or even most of the people who would work with him would object to his race. What would you do?

    a. Hire him regardless, and let the chips fall where they may?

    b. Delay hiring someone like him, until you could persuade the other workers to accept "his kind"?

    c. Hire him and plan meetings with your other workers, to prepare them and to acquaint them with the state of the law and the practical reasons why they should recognize that he represents less of a threat than a welcome change?

2. Suppose you were confronted with sex-stereotyping on the job; let's say you were a man on a job thought to be for "women only." How would it make you feel if most of the people you met at work commented on your unexpected role and many even refused to work with you?

3. It is not unusual for people who work together to form strong impressions of each other's competence, character or even attractiveness. How would you feel if:

    a. You were a young man your boss found very attractive, but you did not feel very attracted to her?

    b. You were a co-worker with the above pair and watched a romance bloom and afterward, watched the young man win rapid promotions?

    c. You were an attractive woman in the work group, who found herself criticized by the boss whenever your duties put you in proximity to the first young man?

4. What would you do if you had worked your way through junior college while raising a family and continuing on a full-time job, only to find that employers rejected you for better jobs because they thought your family's health-care needs would be too expensive for their benefit plans?

5. What would you do if, having won the job, you watched several newcomers get promotions you had earned, without putting in the same time you did, while your employer waited for "the right time" to move you up?

Such situations have led to lawsuits all over the country. The law as written by the Congress of the United States and signed by presidents mandates a level of ethics that transcends personal preferences and looks to performance on the job. Examine the court battles we have described above closely. Try to put yourself mentally into some of the situations hypothesized.

An aggressive type of fairness, driven by a plan rather than a mere feeling of wanting to do "the right thing" at the proper time, can prevent many of the kind of battles these lawsuits became. That kind of fairness can keep many individuals and managers and their companies or agencies from getting into court and becoming examples of what to avoid in dealing with ethical issues in the workplace.

ENDNOTES

1. William Goodell, *The American Slave Code in theory and Practice* (1853; reprint ed., New York: New American Library, 1969), p. 17.

2. Winthrop Jordan, White Over Black (Chapel Hill: University of North Carolina Press, 1968), p. 588.

3. Garland L. Thompson, "Exploding Old Myths," *The Baltimore Sun,* Feb. 4, 1988.

4. Stephen Wigler, "Marian Anderson: Pioneer of Music, Civil Rights and the Human Spirit," *The Baltimore Sun,* April 9, 1993.

5. Richard Green, the Associated Press, "Singer Marian Anderson Dies; Contralto had fought racial bias throughout her entire brilliant career," *The Kansas City Star,* April 9, 1993, p. E-5.

6. Garland L. Thompson, "A Reaffirmation of Old Themes," *The Baltimore Sun,* March 8, 1991.

7. Paul Stillwell and William S. White, "When Thirteen turned Golden," *Proceedings* of the U.S. Naval Institute, Annapolis, Md., February 1993, pp.26-30.

8. "Complaints of Bias Climbed in '92, EEOC Says; Workplace: The 70,339 Filings were the Highest Since 1988. Race Was the No. 1 Concern, While Claims of Handicapped Discrimination Jumped," by the Associated Press; *The Los Angeles Times,* Dec. 2, 1992, p. D-3.

9. *Los Angeles Times,* Dec. 2, 1992, supra.

10. John J. Ross, "The Employment-Law Year in Review (1991-1992)" *21st Annual Institute on Employment Law* (New York: Practising Law Institute, 1992), p. 11. In two endnotes, the author pointed out that,

†(note 4.) The District of Columbia, for example, is the only jurisdiction that prohibits discrimination based on "family responsibilities." *See Simpson vs. District of Columbia Office of Human Rights,* No. 90-49 (D.C. App. Oct. 1, 1991), *reported in* Current Developments, 1991 DLR 197:A-1 (Suggesting this protection may require an employer to accommodate a flexible schedule so an employee is able to care for her father); *see also Doe vs. Boeing Co.,* 923 P.2d 1159 (Wash. App. 1992) (Transsexualism is a protected handicap under state's anti-bias law, whereas it is specifically excluded under the federal Americans with Disabilities Act).

††(note 5.) In *Rendine vs. Pantzer,* No. L-37088-89 (N.J.Super. Mar. 24, 1992) *reported* in 1992 DLR

64:A-1, a jury awarded two women $935,000 in compensatory and punitive damages for pregnancy discrimination, which even under Title VII, as amended, substantially exceeds the cap set by the Civil Rights Act of 1991.

11. *Runyon vs. McCrary,* 427 U.S. 160, 96 S.Ct. 2586, 49 L.Ed.2d 415 (1976).

12. Mack A. Player, *Federal Law of Employment Discrimination in a Nutshell, 3rd Ed.,* West Publishing Co., St. Paul, Minn., 1992, pp. 18-19.

13. Player, *Employment Discrimination in a Nutshell,* Ibid., p.12.

14. Mack A. Player, *Employment Discrimination in a Nutshell,* supra, pp. 16-17

15. The phrase "affirmative action" actually appeared in a section on unfair labor practices in the 1935 Wagner Act. With no legal definition, however, it was lacking in force. According to the Los Angeles Times, "The lawyerly aides of President John F. Kennedy resurrected the phrase in 1961. And then, in 1965, Kennedy's successor, Lyndon B. Johnson, used it once more in a far-reaching executive order that forbade discrimination by private companies with federal contracts.

"The words again went unaccompanied by explanation, which was an important omission. More than 25% of the American labor force worked for companies that were federal contractors. For decades, the government had been commanding these businesses to end bias in hiring. But there had been little in the way of change .... " Barry Bearnak and David Lauter, "U.S. Anti-Bias Regulations Disrupt Lives, Workplaces ... " *The Los Angeles Times,* Los Angeles, Calif., Novs. 4, 1991, p.A-1.

16. 41 CFR Parts 60-1 and 60-2.

17. *Contractors Ass'n of Eastern Pa. vs. Secretary of Labor,* 442 F.2d 159 (3rd Cir. 1971).

18. *Contractors Ass'n of Eastern Pa. vs. Secretary of Labor,* supra. Since Asst. Labor Secretary Arthur Fletcher began his thrust toward affirmative action with the "Philadelphia Plan" for construction contracting, it was fairly predictable that a challenge would arise from among Philadelphia-area contracting companies.

19. Established under *Griggs vs. Duke Power Co.,* 401 U.S. 424, 91 S.Ct. 849, 28 L.Ed.2d 158 (1971),

the "disparate impact" theory was described by Robert Belton in the *Yale Law & Policy Review* as "a results-oriented conception of workplace equality in which race and sex can be taken into account to remedy societal discrimination. Under this theory, employment practices that do not intentionally discriminate but still have an adverse effect on minorities and women can violate Title VII. *Griggs* soon became the focus of an intense national debate about whether (this) results-oriented conception (should) coexist with the color- and sex-blind conception of equality embodied in the disparate *treatment**theory.

"Eighteen years after *Griggs,* the Supreme Court revisited the question and reached an opposite conclusion. In *Wards Cove vs. Atonio,* the court held that the goal of Title VII is to remedy only intentional discrimination .... "— Robert Belton, "The Dismantling of the *Griggs* Disparate Impact Theory and the Future of Title VII: The Need for a Third Reconstruction," 8 *Yale Law & Policy Review* 223. (* my emphasis – G.T.)

20. *Price Waterhouse vs. Hopkins,* 490 U.S. 228, 109 S.Ct. 1775 (1989), under which the Supreme Court barred damages recovery under Title VII for adverse actions by an employer motivated by both discriminatory and legitimate, non-discriminatory reasons, if the employer could show he would have made the "same decision" even without discrimination.

A Congressional Research Service report, *Civil Rights,* by Charles Dale, coordinator of the American Law Division, noted that "the new law modifies the 'same decision' rule applied in Price Waterhouse to 'mixed motive' Title VII cases to provide for declaratory and injunctive relief, together with attorney's fees and costs, for victims of an unlawful employment practice motivated by both discriminatory and non-discriminatory factors. It specifically denies damages or affirmative hiring relief in such situations, however .... *Congressional Research Service, the Library of Congress,* No. IB90027, Updated Dec. 4, 1991 (Archived), p. CRS-5.

21. Under "race norming," the performance of job candidates on pre-employment tests was not compared with test results of all candidates, but only against a "norm" established for whatever racial or ethnic group they fit in. Critics claimed this meant better-qualified white candidates could lose out to poorer-performing minority job applicants, but offi-cials at state employment offices and many employers said it worked well in practice.

22. In its decision in *Martin vs. Wilks,* 490 U.S. 755, 109 S.Ct. 2180 (1989), the Supreme Court had ruled that the doctrine of "impermissible collateral attack" should not bar employees who were not parties to a civil-rights lawsuit from challenging as "reverse discrimination" any affirmative action plan coming out of the suit.

The Civil Rights Act of 1991 sharply limited such post-litigation challenges to those non-party employees who:

   – had no notice of the proposed order;
   – did not have a reasonable opportunity to object; and
   – whose interests were not represented by another who had previously presented the same legal objections to the order.

23. In *EEOC vs. Aramco Oil Co.,* 111 S.Ct. 1227, 113 L.Ed.2d 274 (1991), the Supreme Court had ruled that Title VII protections did not extend to persons employed abroad by domestic companies.

24. John J. Ross, "the Employment-Law Year in Review (1991-1992)" *21st Annual Institute on Employment Law, Volume One* (New York: Practising Law Institute, 1992), pp. 11-13.

25. *Patterson vs. McLean Credit Union,* 491 U.S. 164, 109 S.Ct. 2363, 105 L.Ed.2d 132 (1989).

26. John J. Ross, "the Employment-Law Year in Review (1991-1992)" *21st Annual Institute on Employment Law, Volume One* (New York: Practising Law Institute, 1992), pp. 11-13.

28. *Three Realities: Minority Life in the United States* (Washington, D.C.: The Business-Higher Education Forum, 1990). Don M. Blandin, Director, explained in a letter accompanying the report's re-release in the wake of the recent Los Angeles riots that "the Forum, affiliated with the American Council on Education, is a membership organization of 100 chief executives of major American corporations. The centerpiece of the Three Realities report was a new analysis of the complicated reality of minority life in America. The document took a focused look at the plight of the urban minority poor, particularly African Americans and Hispanics, but it also pointed to two other realities that are often ignored and provide some grounds for cautious optimism: The patient efforts of millions of

working minority people barely on the economic margins of American life, and the success of a large, and growing, minority middle class "making it" in this society.

"The report concluded with an action agenda for government, business and higher education, and included two dozen profiles of exemplary efforts .... "

29. Consider, as example, a *New York Times* report on the impact of automation on service-sector employment. Between April 1989 and April 1993, the city lost 350,000 jobs, nearly one in 10. Economists attributed much of that loss to the national recession, but that ended officially in March 1991.

What is happening here reflects something happening throughout the country. Companies that provide service – from banks and insurers to accounting and law firms to phone companies, airlines, retailers and hotels – are following the lead of manufacturers in making great strides in getting work done with fewer employees, mainly because of advances in technology .... (Steven Prokesch, "Service Jobs Fall As Business Gains," *The New York Times,* Vol. CXLII .... No. 49,305) pp. 1-22.

... The city's economy appears to be creating fewer, though better-paying, full-time jobs. From 1987 through 1991, clerical jobs in the city plummeted by 80,000 or 12%. That is an ominous development for a city with more than 1-million people receiving public assistance.

"What we may be moving toward is a tale of two cities: Growth in higher-paying jobs and a shrinking in lower-paying jobs," said City Comptroller Elizabeth Holtzman. A failure to create lower-skilled jobs "will create turmoil – more social dislocation, more crime, more poverty," she warned. *New York Times,* April 18, supra, p.22.

30. Paul R. Krugman, "The painful cost of workplace discrimination," *U.S. News and World Report,* Vol 111, No. 19, Business Outlook section, Novs. 4, 1991, p. 63.

31. My emphasis – this is a telling recommendation, coming from business leaders who might be presumed to be against goal-directed employment actions which disturb longstanding hiring and promotional practices and generate disquiet among non-protected white workers –G.T.

32. "Three Realities," supra.

33. Barry Bearnak and David Lauter, "U.S. Anti-Bias Regulations Disrupt Lives, Workplaces; Race Relations: Attempts to End Job Discrimination have Created Confusion and a White Backlash," *Los Angeles Times,* Los Angeles, Calif., November 4, 1991, p. 1.

34. *United Steelworkers of America, AFL-CIO-CLC vs. Weber,* 443 U.S. 193, 99 S.Ct. 2721, 61 L.Ed.2d 480 (1979), quoted in Robert Belton, "Overview: Civil Rights in the 1990s – Title VII and Employment Discrimination," *The Dismantling of the Griggs Disparate Impact Theory and the Future of Title VII: The Need for and Third Reconstruction,* 8 *Yale Law & Policy Review* 223. (Footnotes omitted)

35. 323 U.S. 192, 65 S.Ct. 226 (1944)

36. *Steele vs. Louisville & N. R. CO.,* 323 U.S. 192, at pp. 195-196.

37. *Steele vs. Louisville & N. R. CO.,* Ibid, at 196-197.

38. In "The Moses of that Journey," *Constitution,* vol. 5 No. 1, Winter 1993, pp. 29-35, Harvard Law professor Randall Kennedy cited Houston as "*the* pioneering civil rights attorney who marked the path down which Marshall and others marched toward their landmark triumph over *de jure* segregation in *Brown vs. Board of Education.*" Professor Kennedy noted that in addition to building a cadre of attorneys to spearhead the litigation campaign against Jim Crow, Houston "helped forge a new role for attorneys as professional social reformers. As the first special counsel for the NAACP, Houston created a type of legal practitioner – the public interest lawyer: An attorney who shapes litigation into a vehicle of sustained social protest, choosing cases to argue not only on the basis of an individual's need but also on the basis of the needs of a cause .... "

39. 323 U.S. 197, at 199.

40. *Steele vs. Louisville & N. R. CO.,* supra, at 203, 204.

41. *Local Union No. 12, United Rubber, Cork, Linoleum & Plastic Workers of America, AFL-CIO vs. National Labor Relations Board,* 368 F.2d 12 (1966).

42. *Local Union No. 12, United Rubber Workers vs. NLRB,* supra, at 14.

43. *Steele vs. Louisville & N. R. Co.,* supra.

44. 368 F.2d, at 24.

45. *N.L.R.B. vs. Local No. 106, Glass Bottle Blowers Ass'n, AFL-CIO,* 520 F.2d 693 (1975)

46. (NLRB's footnote 4) Cf. *Brown vs. Board of Education,* 347 U.S. 483, 74 S.Ct. 686, 98 L.Ed. 873, in which the Supreme Court held that segregation of

children in public schools solely on the basis of race was "inherently unequal."

47. *Bellamy vs. Mason's Stores, Inc., et al,* 368 F.Supp. 1025 (1973)

48. 368 F.Supp., at 1026.

49. *Griggs vs. Duke Power Co.,* 401 U.S. 424, 91 S.Ct. 849 (1971)

50. 401 U.S., at 427, 428.

51. *Griggs,* 401 U.S., at 430, 431. Footnotes omitted.

52. Griggs, 401 U.S., at 436.

53. *Boston Chapter, N.A.A.C.P., INC., et al, vs. Nancy vs. Beecher,* 504 F.2d 1017 (1974).

54. 504 F.2d, at 1018.

55. *International Brotherhood of Teamsters vs. United States et al,* 431 U.S. 324, 97 S.Ct. 1843, 52 L.Ed.2d 396 (1977)

56. 431 U.S., at 338, 97 S.Ct., at 1855. Court's emphasis – G.T.

57. *Teamsters vs. U.S., Ibid. (Court's note 17.:)* In Atlanta, for instance, Negroes composed 22.35% of the population in the surrounding metropolitan area and 51.3% of the population in the city proper. The company's Atlanta terminal employed 57 line drivers. All were white. In Los Angeles, 10.84% of the greater metropolitan population and 17.88% of the city population were Negro. But at the company's two Los Angeles terminals there was not a single Negro among the 374 line drivers. The proof showed similar disparities in San Francisco, Denver, Nash-ville, Chicago, Dallas, and at several other terminals.

58. *Teamsters vs. U.S., supra,* 97 S.Ct., at 1856.

59. (Court's note 21.) Between July 2, 1965, and January 1, 1969, hundreds of line drivers were hired system-wide, either from the outside or from the ranks of employees filling other jobs within the company. None was a Negro. Government Exhibit 204.

In note 22, Stewart added that, "in 1971 the company hired 116 new line drivers, of whom 16 were Negro or Spanish-surnamed Americans. Minority employees composed 7.1% of the company's systemwide work force in 1967 and 10.5% in 1972 and 1973, presumably due at least in part to the existence of the consent decree (settling part of the claim). See 517 F.2d, at 316 n. 31."

60. *Teamsters vs. U.S.,* 431 U.S. at 341, 342. 97 S.Ct., at 1857, 1858.

61. *Teamsters vs. U.S., supra.*

62. *Mabel A. King, Appellant, vs. James F. Palmer, Director, D.C. Department of Corrections, et al.,* 778 F.2d 878, 879.

63. 778 F.2d, at 879. (Court's emphasis – G.T.)

64. *Ibid.* (Court's emphasis)

65. *Price Waterhouse vs. Hopkins,* 490 U.S. 228, 109 S.Ct. 1775 (1989).

66. 109 S.Ct., at 1782.

67. *Ibid,* at 1782.

68. *Ibid.*

INTERPRETER

© 1989 Creators Syndicate, Inc.

Chapter 19

Joanna DiCarlo Wragg

COMMUNICATIONS
IN COMMERCE

"The trouble with lying and deceiving is that their efficiency depends
entirely upon a clear notion of the truth that the liar and deceiver wish
to hide. In this sense, truth, even if it does not prevail in public, possesses
an ineradicable primacy over all falsehoods."
— Hannah Arendt, "Lying in Politics," *Crises of the Republic*

"Euphemisms, like fashions, have their day and pass, perhaps to return
at another time. Like the guests at a masquerade ball, they enjoy social
approval only so long as they retain the capacity for deception."
— Freda Adler, *Sisters in Crime*

Everyone in the world of work communicates at least to some degree – the delivery person,
receptionist, bookkeeper, secretary, supervisor. They all move in a world of sending and
receiving communications. The clarity of those messages sent and received often spell profit or loss;
occasionally, that clarity – or the lack of it – can mean promotion or termination.

Fawn Hall, assistant to Marine Lt. Col. Oliver North, found herself on the front pages of newspapers
across America as part of the Iran-Contra scandal, because she had been involved in the destruction
of communications, as instructed by her boss. Was she merely doing her duty and ignoring a higher
value (the prohibition against destruction of certain public records) ? Should she have been aware how
sensitive the documents were that she was destroying? Was it her ethical duty to know the difference?

When the communications take on written form, their significance changes – under law, under ethical
codes, under professional standards, under the weight of those printed words. The 19th century poet

Joanna DiCarlo Wragg, B.A. Florida State University, a Pulitzer Prize-winning editorial writer and former associate editor of the
Miami Herald, is vice president of Wragg & Casas Public Relations, a communications and public relations firm in Miami.

Edward Fitzgerald, in his "The Rubaiyat of Omar Khayyam," put it this way: "The Moving Finger writes; and, having writ, moves on: Nor all your Piety nor Wit shall lure it back to cancel half a line, nor all your Tears wash out a Word of it."

Sometimes what you write can lead you to success, sometimes to shame; to the head of the class or to the front of the courtroom. And communication as a business activity takes on another dimension when it is institutional, or "official," communication. At that point it typically is the province of professional communicators – those persons designated with the responsibility of speaking for a business or institution. They may work in advertising and public relations. Sometimes they are vice presidents, sometimes designated spokespersons; often they are lawyers or former journalists, even physicians and accountants. They may practice separate professions and may subscribe to different codes of professional ethics. Nevertheless, they share the attribute of shouldering the responsibility for conveying messages that may not be primarily of their own choosing. All of these sometimes fit the definition of professional communicator.

They and those who assist them know that there are ethical communications and there are unethical ones. For the rest of us, those distinctions are not always clear. Learning how the professionals know the difference is one of our goals here. We will examine herein some of their ethical choices and conflicts.

The nature of the communicators' work is to be interme-diaries – messengers. As such, they live a professional life on the fault line of potential conflict between the interests of the people who *send* the message and the interests of the people who *receive* it. Those groups' interests may be in serious opposition as buyers or sellers, as readers or public figures, as editors or adver-tisers, as executives or employees.

Conflict is the norm in the communicator's environ-ment. Communicators have obligations to their employ-ers, and those duties may conflict with the interest of the client or, in the case of a journalist, with the interests of the readers. As a citizen, the communicator also has obligations to the community at large and to other practitioners of the profession.

The pen may or may not be mightier than the sword, but it certainly shares the sword's capacity to be double-edged and therefore dangerous to user and target alike. In order to remain sane and effective, the communicator needs a clear sense of ethical balance as a guide for making the myriad decisions that present themselves in every working day.

As they use this chapter, students may be tempted to give up the exercise of pursuing ethical communications as an impossible task. If they succumb, they will be joining the legions of burnt-out, embittered cynics and "hacks" (a pejorative term used by writing professionals to describe those souls who write neither artfully nor ethically). These types already wreak much havoc in the communica-tion professions. They are the thoughtless or cruel (or plain lazy) practitioners who have given rise to such ridicule as journalism's hack and "mad dog reporter," public relations' "flack" (a term of derision for those who work in "PR"), and advertising's "Madison Avenue" – all synonyms for untruthfulness.

The real-life versions of those cliches exist, certainly. So do the professional outlaws who believe and practice a doctrine that "anything goes" if it serves their purposes. For these individuals, there are no rules except the rule of not getting caught. (You may have met some of their cronies in Chapter 3 among the Egoists.)

Happily, this type is more prevalent in fiction than in the mainstream world of successful journalists and commercial communicators. The practical fact is that communicators who shade the truth put their employer or client *at risk* – of lawsuits, of damage to their credibility, or of disrepute among their peers. Consequently, communicators who gain a reputation for sleaziness tend to be systematically weeded out of their various trades. In other words, their shortcuts may get them a job but they rarely provide them a career.

The professionals who stick are those who deal in truthfulness and trust. In the hardball realm of political campaigns, inevitably we meet the "spin doctor" – a creative wordsmith who can make bad news sound promising by spinning a yarn of a different context. Even these souls must maintain the trust of the candidate. No campaign rhetorician operates for long outside the boundaries that mark the comfort zone of the candidate. Campaign communicators who go too far inevitably go all the way – out the door and off the payroll – because they made their candidate look bad.

Voters rightly hold candidates responsible for the tone of their campaign literature and rhetoric. Dirty or racist campaigns, for example, reflect the principles of candidates who choose the campaign operatives that specialize in such appeals. The professional communicators in such campaigns are not operating as free agents; they can't write whatever they alone think. It must truly reflect their candidate's mind on the matter. The truly renegade political operative, like the rebel reporter, publicist, or ad writer, doesn't last long.

When professional communicators gather, whether they are journalists or other business communicators, they discuss this outlaw phenomenon and the danger that young, entry-level professionals might glamorize and imitate it. The experienced practitioners make reference to "kids who believe what they see in the movies," or who "watch too much television."

Knowing the damage that a no-holds-barred attitude can do when paired with immature judgment, supervisors and editors watch carefully for telltale signs – a cavalier attitude toward the facts, for example; or a cynical view that "everybody lies." Everybody does not lie, but people who make that claim usually do. Mainstream executives in journalism, advertising and public relations know that dishonesty is the fundamental problem in communications.

The goal of this chapter, then, is to help and encourage today's students to avoid those pitfalls, to think through the issues, to reach their own conclusions about the value of ethical communications, and thus to become part of the solution.

LEGAL HISTORY

The history of professional communication in the United States is itself a history of tension between two inherently conflicting ideals. One is common-law and statutory prohibition against hurting other people through falsehood in the form of fraud (the outright misrepresentation of a claim) and libel (the maliciously published falsehood impugning someone's character). The other is the First Amendment to the Constitution, which guarantees the rights of free speech and freedom of the press. As a result of these two ideals, Americans are free to say or publish what they wish, without prior restraint by government censors. But they also are responsible for what they say or write. They can be sued in civil court or prosecuted in criminal court, if their communication is damaging or deceitful.

(The exception to First Amendment rights is National Security, and the debate over what restrictions are legitimate in order to protect the nation's security is a robust one. That debate is not covered here because it is far removed from most business communications and arises rarely even for journalists. This chapter attempts to focus on ethical choices that confront communicators regularly.)

The frequent battleground is over personal privacy. What right does anyone have to communicate publicly about matters that are essentially private? The courts are still deciding. Some tabloid newspapers believe "anything about anyone" goes. And some of those newspapers have found themselves on the losing end of libel suits. The line that separates personal privacy from press freedom is a constant theater of struggle and one mined with real conflicts as well as widespread misunderstanding. For example, television viewers who are offended by an interview taped in the home of a tearful crime victim may not realize that the victim's consent was required for the reporter and camera crew to enter the home. Likewise, photographs and broadcasts of funeral services often are criticized in ignorance of the fact that families and churches can and do bar cameras when they wish. The First Amendment does not give reporters a license to trespass on private property.

But many strongly disagree among themselves about the gray area of sidewalk interviews and reporting on lifestyles. Let's join the discussion:

> 1. Do the media have a right to photograph people in public places who don't want to have their picture taken, such as a crime victim on the street? A crime suspect on the courthouse steps? A nursing mother on a bus? A child in a park swing?
> 2. Do they have a right to investigate the private behavior of a presidential candidate? A high school coach? An insurance company bookkeeper? A simple housekeeper?

LIBEL LAW IN HISTORY

Libel is the area of law most important to journalists. Libel essentially is the publication of a false and damaging report. If the report is false but not damaging, as in a parody that no one takes seriously, then there is no libel.

Modern American press behavior has been influenced greatly by the 1964 Supreme Court decision in *Times vs. Sullivan.* Traditionally, people who sued news media for libel tried to prove that the published report was false and had damaged their reputation. Truth was the press's usual defense. This case, involving the *New York Times*, set a new standard for *public* figures, including public officials.

Under *Sullivan,* such persons can no longer win a libel suit merely because the published report was false. The Sullivan decision said that a public figure also must prove that the false report was the result of "actual malice" on the part of the news organization. What actual malice means is that the journalists knew they were publishing a false report, or that they published the false story "with reckless disregard of whether it was false or not." The title of the movie *Absence of Malice*, starring Sally Field as a reporter and Paul Newman as a controversial businessman, turns on the Supreme Court's phrase.

In the three decades since Sullivan, however, the decision has turned out to be more complex than most news people had thought. The notion of malice, after all, refers to a state of mind. If an injured celebrity is required to prove malice in order to win libel suits, then clearly the lawyers for those celebrities are bound to inquire about the attitudes of reporters and editors. In the 1979 case of *Herbert vs. Lando*, the Supreme Court ruled that plaintiffs in libel cases indeed have the right to seek testimony about how the writers and editors did their jobs, and what their attitudes were.

The First Amendment says: *Congress shall make no law respecting an establishment of religion, or prohibiting the free exercise thereof; or abridging the freedom of speech, or of the press; or the right of the people peaceably to assemble; and to petition the Government for a redress of grievances.*

The First Amendment does not single out major media corporations for special protection. There were none in colonial America. Indeed, it does not even mention newspapers, and for good reason: The general circulation newspaper that is an institution in America today did not begin to gain prevalence until a couple of generations after the adoption of the Bill of Rights. The "press" of the First Amendment consisted primarily of pamphlets full of essays advocating the opinion of the editor, who usually was the man who owned or rented the local printing press.

Thus, the "new" concept of "advertorials" – space purchased to advocate a company's positions rather than sell its product – has deep historical roots. The business press in Florida, for example, was surprised in 1992 when United States Sugar Corporation purchased a months-long series of multi-page spaces in *Florida Trend* magazine to explain its position on the controversy over allegations that agribusiness was harming the Everglades. But the Founding Fathers would not have batted an eye.

While there is little dispute about the right of a business to publish its opinion on public issues, there is considerable debate over restraints on "commercial speech" in the form of spoken or written language that is part of a sales message. In other words, can a product we'll call "Bestub" claim it removes "all the germs" from your bathtub? Without supporting documentation? Without tests involving humans and at least one dog named Spot? And what if "Bestub" does all that it claims but also damages the environment after its chemicals go down the drain? Do these factors affect what *Bestub*'s makers can communicate about their products? Yes, is the primary answer. But there remains debate over such issues because while the Constitution does allow for the regulation of commerce, it protects speech and the words of the press. Such issues arise every morning on Madison Avenue and in various media offices: "We can't say that ... Yes, we can ... Well, we shouldn't!"

Fraud is a crime. Intrinsically, it also is an act of speech or print – an act of communication. Thus the notions of free speech and regulation of commerce have been on a collision course since the birth of the republic. This historic tension surfaces regularly in debates over certain kinds of advertising, such as for tobacco or unconventional medical treatments, abortion clinics or crude entertainment. It also is involved in debates over "political correctness" and other controversial political expressions such as bigotry, anti-democratic theories or the defense of either communism or unfettered capitalism.

CONTEMPORARY ISSUES

Those are large social issues. Sometimes more troubling are the more narrow and local conflicts that the typical communicator faces every day, and some of these will be discussed later. However, the first question for the communicator – as for any other person in business or the professions – is this: *Is it ever ethical to do things in your role as a businessperson/professional that would be unethical/ immoral in your personal life?* If your answer is Yes, then other questions demand answers:

> 1. Which of your usual rules can you break at the office? Misleading someone? Lying? Cheating? Stealing? Intimidation? Physical violence?
> 2. What office goals are sufficient to justify breaking your personal code? Getting a raise? Winning a Pulitzer Prize? Saving your business from bankruptcy? Satisfying your client? Easing public hysteria? Avoiding an unjust tax burden? Contributing to community harmony? Beating an unscrupulous competitor? Serving the public's "right to know"?

In other words, does the end justify the means? If so, which ends justify which means?

If your answer is No, then life may be simpler because you will need only one ethical formula. However, that formula will have to be complete enough to cover every eventuality.

JOURNALISM

The notion of a special license to break the normal rules arises subtly throughout business and the professions, but it is overt in journalism. Professional and otherwise law-abiding news people routinely engage in serious discussion over whether to break the law.

Professor Philip Meyer's analysis of the 1982 ethics survey of the American Society of Newspaper Editors (ASNE) is quite telling. Meyer notes that journalists uniformly reject the idea of any right to violate laws or rules in order to pursue personal gain.[1] The ASNE Code of Ethics is specific on this point.[2] However, when they are acting in their role as journalist, many take a different view.

From the ASNE data, Meyer identifies approximately 20% of the U.S. newspaper industry as "First Amendment fundamentalists" who will violate norms, such as an individual's privacy or the secrecy of a Grand Jury, if the material at issue is "newsworthy." Another 57% adopt a "situation ethics" approach and will violate rules selectively; for example, if they believe "the importance of the material revealed outweighs the damage to the system from the breaching of its security."[3]

Modern technology is stretching the issue of means and ends even further. The 1992 case of *NBC News* and General Motors illustrates the point. In order to illustrate a report that claimed GM trucks were more likely than other makes to catch fire on impact, *NBC News* attached fireworks to a GM truck being portrayed as an example in order to make the fire sufficiently eye-catching. GM sued. At first the network defended its action as merely cosmetic, but subsequently retracted the position, apologized, and fired several producers and reporters. Not long thereafter, the president of *NBC News* changed jobs, too. The NBC doctoring of the visual image "for effect" has echoes of the 1981 incident involving *Washington Post* reporter Janet Cooke. Writing about the real horror of drugs in the inner city, Cooke won a Pulitzer Prize for her gripping story about "Jimmy," an 8-year-old heroin addict. Only in the glare of publicity about the Pulitzer was it discovered that Jimmy was not a real child at all, but a sensationalized composite of many ghetto residents. The *Post* fired Cooke and returned the Pulitzer Prize.

HIGH TECHNOS, LOW ETHOS

That hardly settles the issue, however. While Cooke was a classic liar who deceived her own editors, and *NBC News* applied its "cosmetics" the old fashioned way, with actual explosives, new technology is posing new challenges. NBC could have achieved exactly the same effect with *computer imaging*. The same techniques that allow the crime-stopper programs to artificially "age" a missing child or a fugitive can produce footage of nearly anyone doing nearly anything. How can these technologies be used ethically? If a viewer doesn't know what the medium they are seeing really is, can the communication involved be ethical?

The new generation of professional communicators will face the challenge: Just when does an "enhanced" image stop being a factual representation and become a work of fictionalized computer art? At what point is the communicator obliged to disclose the doctoring of the image, and to whom?

Likewise, traditional copyright law is being tested by the ease of copying computer software, and the concept of "public records" is expanding to include the Electronic-Mail (usually called "E-Mail") of public employees. No doubt libel lawyers soon will discover the computer billboard and push the courts to rule that a notice on such an electronic device constitutes "publishing." Computer-hacking (the invasion of various parties' databases for fun or profit) clearly presses the definitions of trespass, privacy, and property rights. Today's students will need clear ethical standards that they can apply to the rapidly changing communications technology.

COMPUTER ETHICS

Did *you* know? Unauthorized copying of software is illegal. Copyright law protects software authors and publishers, just as patent law protects inventors. Unlawfully copying software can wreck a professional's business and reputation. Illegal copying and use of software deprives publishers and developers of a fair return for their work, increases prices, reduces the level of future support and enhancements, and can inhibit the development of new software products. Here's the law:

PUBLIC LAW 102-561—OCT. 28, 1992 106 STAT. 4233

102d Congress

An Act

To amend title 18, United State Code, with respect to the criminal penalties for copyright infringement. Oct. 28, 1992 (S. 893)

Be it enacted by the Senate and House of Representatives of the United States of America in Congress assembled,

SECTION 1. CRIMINAL PENALTIES FOR COPYRIGHT INFRINGEMENT.

Section 2319(b) of title 18, United States Code, is amended to read as follows:

"(1) shall be imprisoned not more than 5 years, or fined in the amount set forth in this title, or both, if the offense consists of the reproduction or distribution, during any 180-day period, of at least 10 copies or phonorecords, of 1 or more copyrighted works, with a retail value of more than $2,500;

"(2) shall be imprisoned not more than 10 years, or fined in the amount set forth in this title, or both, if the offense is a second or subsequent offense under paragraph (1); and

"(3) shall be imprisoned not more than 1 year, or fined in the amount set forth in this title, or both, in any other case."

EDUCOM is a consortium formed to get this message delivered. It urges "respect for the intellectual work of others." This respect traditionally has been essential to most professions. Just as professions do not tolerate plagiarism, ethical computer users do not condone the unauthorized copying of software, including programs, applications, data bases and code. Here are excerpts from the EDUCOM Code:

Software and Intellectual Rights

Respect for intellectual labor and creativity is vital to academic discourse and enterprise. This principle applies to works of all authors and publishers in all media. It encompasses respect for the right to acknowledgement, right to privacy, and right to determine the form, manner, and terms of publication and distribution.

Because electronic information is volatile and easily reproduced, respect for the work and personal expression of others is especially critical in computer environments. Violations of authorial integrity, including plagiarism, invasion of privacy, unauthorized access, and trade secret and copyright violations, may be grounds for sanctions against members of the academic community.

EDUCOM's Educational Uses of Information Technology (EUIT) Program encourages the broadest possible adoption of this statement of principle. The EDUCOM code is intended for adaptation and use by individuals and educational institutions at all levels.

Classification of Software

In terms of copyright, there are four broad classifications of software, i.e., Commercial, Shareware, Freeware, and Public Domain. The restrictions and limitations regarding each classification are different.

COMMERCIAL software represents the majority of software purchased from software publishers, commercial computer stores, etc. When you buy software, you are actually acquiring a license to use it, not own it. You acquire the license from the company that owns the copyright. The conditions and restrictions of the license agreement vary from program to program and should be read carefully. In general, commercial software licenses stipulate that (1) the software is covered by copyright, (2) although one archival copy of the software can be made, the backup copy cannot be used except when the original package fails or is destroyed, (3) modifications to the software are not allowed, (4) decompiling (i.e., reverse engineering) of the program code is not allowed without the permission of the copyright holder, and (5) development of new works built upon the package (derivative works) is not allowed without the permission of the copyright holder.

SHAREWARE software is covered by copyright, as well. When you acquire software under a shareware arrangement, you are actually acquiring a license to use it, not own it. You acquire the license from the individual or company that owns the copyright. The conditions and restrictions of the license agreement vary from program to program and should be read carefully. The copyright holders for SHAREWARE allow purchasers to make and distribute copies of the software, but demand that if, after testing the software, you adopt it for use, you must pay for it. In general, SHAREWARE software licenses stipulate that (1) the software is covered by copyright, (2) although one archival copy of the software can be made, the backup copy cannot be used except when the original package fails or is destroyed, (3) modifications to the software are not allowed, (4) decompiling (i.e., reverse engineering) of the program code is not allowed without the permission of the copyright holder, and (5) development of new works built upon the package (derivative works) is not allowed without the permission of the copyright holder. Selling software as SHAREWARE is a marketing decision; it does not change the legal requirements with respect to copyright. That means that you can make a single archival copy, but you are obliged to pay for all copies adopted for use.

FREEWARE also is covered by copyright and subject to the conditions defined by the holder of the copyright. The conditions for FREEWARE are in direct opposition to normal copyright restrictions. In general, FREEWARE software licenses stipulate that (1) the software is covered by copyright, (2) copies of the software can be made for both archival and distribution purposes, but that distribution cannot be for profit, (3) modifications to the software are allowed and encouraged, (4) decompiling (i.e., reverse engineering) of the program code is allowed without the explicit permission of the copyright holder, and (5) development of new works built upon the package (derivative works) is allowed and encouraged with the condition that derivative works must also be designated as FREEWARE. That means that you cannot take FREEWARE, modify or extend it, and then sell it as COMMERCIAL or SHAREWARE software.

PUBLIC DOMAIN software comes into being when the original copyright holder explicitly relinquishes all rights to the software. Since under current copyright law, all intellectual works (including software) are protected as soon as they are committed to a medium, for something to be

PUBLIC DOMAIN it must be clearly marked as such. Before March 1, 1989, it was assumed that intellectual works were NOT covered by copyright unless the copyright symbol and declaration appeared on the work. With the U.S. adherence to the Berne Convention this presumption has been reversed. Now all works assume copyright protection unless the PUBLIC DOMAIN notification is stated. This means that for PUBLIC DOMAIN software (1) copyright rights have been relinquished, (2) software copies can be made for both archival and distribution purposes with no restrictions as to distribution, (3) modifications to the software are allowed, (4) decompiling (i.e., reverse engineering) of the program code is allowed, and (5) development of new works built upon the package (derivative works) is allowed without conditions on the distribution or use of the derivative work.

QUESTIONS YOU MAY HAVE ABOUT USING SOFTWARE

1. What do I need to know about software and the U.S. Copyright Act? It's really very simple. The Copyright Law recognizes that all intellectual works (programs, data, pictures, articles, books, etc.) are automatically covered by copyright unless it is explicitly noted to the contrary. That means that the owner of a copyright holds the exclusive right to reproduce and distribute his or her work. For software this means it is illegal to copy or distribute software, or its documentation, without the permission of the copyright holder.

If you have a legal copy of software, you are allowed to make a single archival copy of the software for backup purposes. However, the copy can only be used if the original software is destroyed or fails to work. When the original is given away, the backup copy must also be given with the original or destroyed.

2. If software is not copy-protected, do I have the right to copy it? Lack of copy-protection does NOT constitute permission to copy software without authorization of the software copyright owner. "Non-copy-protected" software enables you to make a backup copy. In offering non-copy-protected software to you, the developer or publisher has demonstrated significant trust in your integrity.

3. May I copy software that is available through facilities on my campus, so that I can use it more conveniently in my own office or room? Software acquired by colleges and universities is usually covered by licenses. The licenses should clearly state how and where the software may be legally used by members of the relevant campus communities (faculty, staff, and students). Such licenses cover software whether installed on stand-alone or networked systems, whether in private offices and rooms, or in public clusters and laboratories. Some institutional licenses permit copying for certain purposes. The license may limit copying, as well.

4. May I loan software? The 1990 modification to the Copyright Law makes it illegal to "loan, lease or rent software" for purposes of direct or indirect commercial advantage without the specific permission of the copyright holder. Non-profit educational institutions are exempted from the 1990 modification, so institutional software may be loaned. Some licenses may even restrict the use of a copy to a specific machine, even if you own more than one system. In general, licenses usually do NOT allow the software to be installed or resident on more than a single machine, or to run the software simultaneously on two or more machines.

5. Isn't it legally "fair use" to copy software if the purpose in sharing it is purely educational? Historically, the Copyright Law was modified to permit certain educational uses of copyrighted materials without the usual copyright restrictions. However, "fair use" of computer software is still a cloudy issue. The "fair use" amendments to the Copyright Law are intended to allow educational use of legally protected products, but it is limited (for paper-based products) to small portions of full works. For most software it is clearly illegal to make and distribute unauthorized, fully functional copies to class members for their individual use. Making copies of a small section of code from a program in order to illustrate a programming technique might not be a violation. The best alternative is to clear any such use with the copyright owner or consult the appropriate authorities at the college.

Alternatives to Explore
Software can be expensive. You may think that you cannot afford to purchase certain programs that you need. Site-licensed and bulk-purchased software are legal alternatives that make multiple copies of software more affordable. Many educational institutions negotiate special prices for software used and purchased by faculty, staff and students. Consult your campus computing office for information. As with other software, site-licensed or bulk-purchased software is still covered by copyright, although the price per copy may be significantly lower than the normal commercial price. A usual condition of site-licensing or bulk-purchasing is that copying and distribution of the software is limited to a central office which must maintain inventories of who received it. When you leave the college by graduation, retirement, or resignation you may no longer be covered by the institutional agreement and may be required to return or destroy your copies of the software licensed to the institution.

Many colleges sell software through a campus store at "educational discounts." If you purchase software for yourself through such an outlet, the software is yours and need not be destroyed or surrendered when you leave the institution. It is, however, still covered by normal copyright protection and covered by the specific conditions of the licensing agreement.

A Final Note
Restrictions on the use of software are far from uniform. You should check carefully each piece of software and the accompanying documentation yourself. In general, you do not have the right to:

•Receive and use unauthorized copies of software, or
•Make unauthorized copies of software for others.

If you have questions not answered by this brochure about the proper use and distribution of a software product, seek help from your computing office, the software developer or publisher, or other appropriate authorities at your institution.

This brochure has been produced as a service to the academic community by the Educational Uses of Information Technology Program (EUIT) of EDUCOM and the Information Technology Association of America (ITAA). EDUCOM is a non-profit consortium of colleges and universities committed to the use and management of information technology in higher education. ITAA is an industry association providing issues management and advocacy, public affairs, business-to-business networking, education and other member services to companies which create and market products and services associated with computers, communications and data.

(Although this brochure is copyrighted, you are authorized and encouraged to make and distribute copies of it, in whole or in part, providing the source is acknowledged.)

PUBLIC RELATIONS
Unlike Meyer's survey in the newspaper industry, there is no comparably comprehensive survey of the attitudes of public relations professionals, in part because this relatively young industry lacks the organizational structure of the news business. While the general circulation newspaper in the U.S. dates from the 19th century, public relations as a profession is an outgrowth of the rapid social changes of post-World War II America. Those changes include urbanization, increases in mobility and a multiplication of the media of mass communication.

While more than 200,000 persons in the United States identify themselves as "public relations professionals," only 14,000 are members of the Public Relations Society of America (PRSA), the largest organization in the field. As with journalists, there is no licensing mechanism and no disciplinary body. The First Amendment umbrella prevents government from licensing communicators the way it regulates lawyers, physicians and accountants.

The best survey of practitioner ethics, then, is Cornelius Pratt's 1991 compilation of the existing data on public relations ethics. Perhaps the most important finding in Pratt's study for the purposes of this chapter is the correlation between age and ethical standards in public relations, with older practitioners reporting stronger moral values in their business conduct.[4] Indeed, the sum of the surveys of the successful seasoned professionals who make up the membership of PRSA is an emphasis on the importance of ethics education. These practitioners ranked the need for more and better ethics study as their top priority.

This survey supports the observation earlier in this chapter that young professionals frequently underestimate the importance of sound ethics within their chosen profession. Students thus may be encouraged that the exercise in which they are engaged here is not an idle or a futile one. The ability to recognize ethical problems and to discuss them intelligently is an important value to in-house corporate communicators and to the owners and executives of most of the nation's best known and most profitable public relations firms. There is wide acceptance within the field of the view that "the success of public relations in the 1990s and beyond will depend to a large degree on how the field responds to the issue of ethical conduct."[5]

On the specific question of whether the practitioner possesses a license to suspend his personal morality in pursuit of his profession, there is no parallel in mainstream public relations to the extreme First Amendment fundamentalist of the newspaper world. There is, however, considerable overlap with journalism's situation ethics and subjectivism as a major tendency within public relations.[6] There are disagreements among practitioners about what is ethical and what is not.

It is important to note, however, that "responsibility to society was perceived as more important than the practitioner's responsibility to an employer or client."[7] The PRSA Code of Ethics flatly asserts: "A member shall conduct his or her professional life in accord with the public interest."[8] Thus, there is no widely accepted theory within the profession, as there is in journalism, that permits practitioners to view themselves as above the rules of ordinary society.

Seasoned public relations professionals know that even clients may not understand the practitioner's role. It is common, in an early interview with a new public relations counselor, for the client to say something like, "This situation is making our company look terrible. What are you going to do to improve our image?"

The professional's answer may be, "We'll get to the image later. First, let's find out what the reality is. Let's start at the beginning. We have to see clearly what caused this situation that is making you look bad and what you can do to correct it. When we have those answers, then we can develop a message for your employees, customers and stockholders."

Discussion: After the above conversation, the client of the agency or the boss of the in-house public relations specialist says, "Never mind what we train our salespeople to tell customers. That's not your concern. You just go out there and make the media stop calling us swindlers." How should the communicator respond?

ADVERTISING

Advertising consists of paid-for space or air time, and is the most "commercial" of the communications disciplines; also the one least protected by the First Amendment. Commercial speech does not enjoy the same protection as political speech or even general business speech. The Federal Trade Commission Act and other specific laws attempt to define what is "fair" or "deceptive" in the field of advertising. States commonly provide penalties for "bait-and-switch" advertising (in which the bargain item is used as bait and stocked in small quantities, if at all, in a planned effort to "switch" the buyer to a higher- priced product.) States even govern the manner in which the prices of individual items may be displayed in a store or outside a gas station.

While people in business may make reference to the old *caveat emptor* ("let the buyer beware") attitude as a justification for blatantly deceptive practices, American courts have rendered that position largely moot. The 1993 federal fraud convictions of several former executives of Miami-based General Development Corporation strongly reinforced the responsibility of advertisers and promoters to represent their products honestly. *Miami Herald* Business Columnist James Russell saw in those convictions a lesson that the *caveat emptor* theory does not excuse "fraud and deception."[9] As a consequence of this long and growing body of law, advertising seems even further removed than public relations from any theory of immunity from ordinary morality such as the one that many journalists claim.

TRUTHFULNESS IS THE PIVOTAL IDEA

Once the issue of special professional privilege has been settled, the communicator faces the basic demand of her role, which is how, and how much, to serve Truth. Issues of accuracy, completeness, disclosure and good faith punctuate all the ethical case studies involving professional communications. It is inherent in the concept of communicating that listeners and readers expect not to be lied to.

Distortions and sensationalizing will instill a sense of betrayal whether or not the practitioner intended to betray. A professional communicator, after all, cannot hide behind the excuse, "I didn't mean it that way." If she didn't mean it the way it was taken, then she is incompetent as a communicator. Granted, incompetence is a defense of sorts against the charge of unethical or immoral behavior, but it is a poor argument for keeping one's job or professional reputation. Communicators are hired precisely because they are supposed to be better than most people at getting the message across the way it's intended it should be received. That skill imposes a serious burden that business and news organizations alike tend to recognize. It is that the communicator assumes some responsibility for the content of the message and for the policy implications inherent in the message. The ethical complexity of that role can hardly be exaggerated.

THE COMMUNICATOR AS CONSCIENCE

Take, for example, the issue of advertising standards set by publications. Publishers devote considerable attention to standards by which advertising will be judged as to suitability for their publications. Advertising standards rarely attract public attention, and when they do it typically is because a major product is pushing conventional boundaries in its new ad campaign. This is most likely to happen when sexier-than-usual images are injected into ads for consumer items, such as perfume or blue jeans. When the public learns that a major magazine, for example, has rejected a new perfume ad, the reader can be sure that the advertiser expects to benefit from the resulting notoriety. Controversy itself can be an effective means of communicating a message of unconventionality.

Most discussions of ad standards, however, take place within the organization. Newspapers, magazines, television stations and networks all have guidelines that set limits on what they choose to convey as paid advertising. Most reject hard profanity, for example, even though they have a legal right to publish it. Many also refuse advertising for pornographic movies or books, or severely restrict the content of ads for those products.

Though the public may not be aware of them, such rules actually are quite common. For many years, the *Los Angeles Times* refused ads for "triple-X" movies or liquor. The *St. Petersburg Times* and its sister publication, the *Evening Independent,* refused liquor ads during the lifetime of their legendary publisher, Nelson Poynter. Later executives relaxed those rules at all three papers. The *Miami Herald* and other newspapers still require evidence in support of claims made by candidates in political ads in the paper.

Scenario for discussion : A common battleground for communicators is the desire of tobacco companies to advertise their products to the widest possible audience. The issue provides an excellent short course in the ethical issues of communications. A few questions for discussion:

1. Should a newspaper accept cigarette advertising when it editorially condemns cigarettes?
2. When that newspaper holds a monopoly on print advertising in the community, does it violate the First Amendment when it denies a platform to the advertising of a legal product?
3. Should that same newspaper invest its pension funds in the stocks of tobacco companies?
4. Should advertising copywriters who oppose smoking develop an ad campaign for cigarettes?
5. Should a public relations specialist who opposes smoking help a cigarette company executive improve his image in the community through generous charitable contributions?
6. Substitute guns, condoms, liquor or other controversial products for cigarettes in the first five questions. Does your position change? If so, justify the inconsistency.

These are questions that professional communicators face regularly. Because of the go-between role between the institution and the public at large, the communicator typically is the conscience of the organization.[10] Those who work only inside the organization may escape the impact of their message on others. Example: People who make cigarettes may not consider the possibility that children will use them. Likewise, those who are outside an institution may eschew understanding of what went into the institution's message or of the impact of their own reaction to the message. Example: Customers protesting a price hike may not realize that a policy of fair wages and humane health insurance forced the company to choose between the price hike or bankruptcy.

The communicator does not have the luxury of not knowing. Communication is an inherently values-laden activity. It consists of a series of myriad choices, comparisons and omissions. It selects a particular tone, rests on specific assumptions, draws conclusions and defines balance according to its own directives. The act of communicating forces the communicator to look at both sides of the sender/recipient relationship.

That is not always a comfortable position.

CASE STUDY 1: THE LINGERIE CAPER

An editor, back in the newsroom, may insist that the reporter bring her a detailed story about the bank teller who embezzled $50,000 to spend on his girlfriend and on drugs. That editor does not see the embezzler's children, who are devastated by the arrest and will be impacted greatly by printed descriptions of their father's illicit love nest. Contrarily, the reporter may want to use all the facts he has garnered, while the editor may feel an obligation to exercise restraint.

There is little dispute over the news media's duty to report the arrest of the embezzler. There is considerable debate, however, over the ethics of including colorful details, such as descriptions of the sexy lingerie the bank teller bought for the girlfriend. While those journalists whom Meyer identifies as First Amendment fundamentalists would not hesitate to publish every detail they could get, an even greater number feel an obligation to consider the entire situation before deciding.

ASKING THE HARD QUESTIONS

Consider and evaluate the ethical implications of your answers to these questions:

1. Does an alleged criminal have any right to privacy from media scrutiny? A convicted criminal?
2. The reporter and editor will make hundreds of decisions in the course of framing the stories about this embezzlement case. Is it ethical for them to be influenced by the potential impact of their decisions on innocent parties, such as the children or spouse?
3. Is it ethical to make decisions that will affect other persons without considering the impact on them?
4. How far is the journalist obliged to go in informing his superiors about any negative impacts he foresees from the news story?

- Just far enough to raise the subject?
- Far enough to annoy them?
- Far enough to be get disciplined?
- Far enough to be fired or quit?
- Or, should he conceal the entire story so the problem won't arise?

Question 3 raises the crucial issue of the communicator's responsibility to his employer. The respective obligations of employers and employees was discussed in Chapters 16 and 17 and will not be discussed at length here. However, the professional Codes of Ethics make clear that the obligation to an employer or client is taken very seriously.

For the communicator, the question often is *whether* to communicate:

- Whether to inform the employer, and how forcefully to inform her, of the reasons not to issue the communication that the employer has indicated.
- Whether, as a business information officer, to inform an inquiring reporter of information he didn't know to request.
- Whether, as an editor, to inform the public that your reporter lied or trespassed in order to get some of the information in the story.

The case study above involves a journalist, but professionals in advertising and public relations face similar problems daily in their relations with employers or clients.

CASE STUDY 2: LEROY AND THE MAGIC POTION

LeRoy, advertising account executive, has spent months developing a $6-million ad campaign for a major pharmaceutical company. His agency's fee on the campaign will be $900,000, and his bonus for the work could add $10,000 to his own salary. If the campaign succeeds, the contract could be multiplied several times.

The ads are designed to introduce a new product, Breathe Free, an antihistamine for allergy sufferers that relieves the nasal congestion from pollen, dust, etc. Breathe Free is to be marketed as a general remedy for the entire family, with dosages for children assigned by body weight.

A "Family Album" is the visual centerpiece of the ads. It portrays family members of various ages, from pre-schoolers to great-grandparents, enjoying wholesome activities together. The product is in a moderate price range intended to undercut the leading over-the-counter remedies. Many of the families pictured are minorities. The message is that Breathe Free keeps you in the flow and doesn't let allergies put you on the sidelines.

Two weeks before the campaign is to launch, the client calls the account executive to an emergency meeting. A few of the photos have to be dropped, he says. They want to remove the pictures of old people because the latest testing shows some unexpected risks to people with high blood pressure. The fine print on the bottle now will warn that people with high blood pressure should not use the product without consulting a physician.

There is time to drop those pictures, but not time to redo the campaign without a very costly delay. The company president is proud of his responsible action in avoiding the appeal to older people, who are more likely to have high blood pressure. After all, the campaign is perfectly legal; he is taking a voluntary step in the public interest by reducing the risk to the elderly. He is enthusiastic about the Breathe Free campaign and has high praise for the ad executive who devised it.

Back at the ad agency, LeRoy is worried. He has pitched this campaign to minorities, especially African-Americans. He knows that hypertension – high blood pressure – is at epidemic proportion in the United States among blacks. From his earlier work on an unrelated public health campaign, he is aware that many thousands of middle-aged and even teen-aged African-Americans do not know that they are suffering from the disease that is called "the silent killer."

QUESTIONS:

What are LeRoy's obligations to the public? To his employer? To his client? Let's also consider *the competition*. There are many similar products on the market that also pose risks to people with high blood pressure, including Breathe Free's leading competitors. Minorities already buy those products. Given these facts, consider again:

> 1. Should LeRoy try to stop the campaign? Why (or why not)? Whom should he talk to first, his employer or his client? Why?
> 2. Does it matter that LeRoy's boss is ill and the agency needs the $900,000 fee to stay afloat? That LeRoy's own father died recently and he is counting on the bonus to move his widowed mother to a secure new home? That the pharmaceutical company is suffering from severe competitive pressures from abroad?

Now, consider *the consequences*. LeRoy decided to say nothing about his concerns. Breathe Free is launched on schedule as a budget anti-allergy remedy and is an instant economic success. It sells especially well in low-income minority neighborhoods. LeRoy's client and his employer are both happy, and he is looking forward to collecting his bonus at the end of the year.

However, six months after the launch, with the campaign in its second phase, *Newsweek* reports that black public health officials are becoming concerned about the Breathe Free campaign. They see all those black faces in the ads along with the appeal to tight budgets. They fear that many black Americans who are both poor and suffering from high blood pressure will fail to read the fine print and will risk serious harm by using Breathe Free.

Civil rights leaders note the *Newsweek* article. They are reminded of the time when some cigarette and beer companies tried to market brands specifically for blacks and were hounded out of the market for cynically singling out blacks for an unhealthful product.

These leaders attack the Breathe Free campaign as racist. Noting that the company also sells prescription drugs for high blood pressure, they accuse corporate executives of racist disregard for the health of black consumers. The company's entire line of products is subjected to a national boycott. Revenues plunge 30% and the price of the company's stock plummets to a fraction of its previous level.

At the next meeting of the drug company and the ad agency, the president of the drug company pounds the table.

"Why didn't anybody warn me about this?" he demands to know. "We're ruined. How could you let this happen? Why didn't you tell me?"

What does LeRoy say now?

CLARITY IS A MAJOR CONSIDERATION

Truthfulness is a matter of intentions, while clarity is a measure of competence. Yet, the two ideas often are inextricably linked. Take, for example, the matter of "weasel words." These are the words – such as "virtually, ordinarily, probably, likely, reportedly" – that provide an escape hatch for the writer when the reader becomes angry over being misled. They are the equivalent of fine print that a writer may use to observe the letter of the law while skirting its spirit.

Or not. An oddity of weasel words – qualifiers – is that sometimes they aren't misleading at all, but are required for clarity and accuracy. The impact of their use depends on the context, on how the rest of the piece of writing is structured. For example, a writer might say, "The middle-aged person who exercises regularly is likely to have more energy and enjoy better general health than those who are sedentary." The statement is true, but it would not be without the qualifier "likely," as exercise does not *guarantee* better health.

For contrasting use of a qualifier, take this paragraph: "The Slither Corporation has developed an astounding new remedy for the wrinkles associated with aging. Nothing like it has ever been available in the USA before. Women who use Youth Scrub are likely to be mistaken for the sisters of their own children! It must be experienced to be believed."

As with so many aspects of communication, context and emphasis are extremely important. It is the writer's job to ensure that the message the reader receives is the message the writer intended to send. Failure to get the message across is the writer's failure, not the reader's. Any ambiguity, accidental error, insensitivity or carelessness is the fault of the writers because clarity and accuracy are their responsibility.

Would-be communicators who think this burden is the same as a recipe for weak or pandering messages should think again. The message may be strong or challenging and may provoke controversy. The point is that heated responses should not come as a surprise. They should be predictable because the communicator understood the likely impact of the communication and made a conscious decision rather than an accidental blunder. The professional communicator's responsibility fits into the antebellum Code of the Carolina Gentleman. In an era of duels over honor, when the lords of the various manors constituted an aristocracy in the classic sense, it was said, "A Carolina gentleman never gives offense inadvertently."

THE ISSUE OF PROFITS

In discussions such as those above, some students may find themselves criticizing a course of action on the ground that its only purpose is to achieve or increase profitability, that it serves no broad social purpose or value. This tension is hardly confined to classrooms. On the contrary, it colors much of the activity of professional communicators at every level. It is therefore useful to consider at this point whether profitability in itself has ethical value for communicators, whether profits are inherently worthy or inherently unworthy as motives for behavior. The answer matters a great deal. A communicator who harbors a basic suspicion of the morality of the profit motive is likely to react very differently than one who sees profitability as a basic responsibility of management.

© 1988 Creators Syndicate, Inc.

Among journalists, the Meyer analysis of the 1982 ASNE study is again instructive. By cross matching editors' answers to seemingly unrelated questions, Meyer concludes that some two-thirds of editors and staff embrace an unspoken rule that "If it involves money, it is probably bad." Meyer describes this attitude as business-averse or anti-money, and concludes that its origin lies partly in the fear of improper influence by advertisers over news reporting. He also suspect that it derives from the traditional view of journalists that they are underpaid.[11] The attitude that money as a motive is inherently suspicious has major implications for reporters, especially those covering business or any public issues in which businesses or wealthy persons are involved.

Ronald M. Green poses another basis for attitudes toward the legitimacy of profit as a motive: religion. In an article that offers Catholic, Protestant and Jewish perspectives on business ethics, Green notes: "Classical Jewish teaching has always had a positive view of commercial activity ... unlike Christianity in some of its moods, Judaism was never greatly attracted to asceticism. As a result, private enterprise, the everyday business of buying and selling for profit, was always regarded as normal and perfectly acceptable behavior."[12]

Green's characterization of the traditional Jewish view contrasts with Louke Van Wensveen Siker's description in the same article of the Protestant view as including "a wide variety of attitudes toward business – anything from radical rejection of business as a realm of sin to uncritical acceptance of business as a realm reflecting God's providential rule." Donahue, in the Catholic section of the article, describes the Catholic tradition as "somewhat suspicious of the unfettered economic marketplace" and given to "modified communitarianism."[13]

Given these differences in traditional religious attitudes, it is wholly predictable that the diverse population of America's newsrooms, ad agencies and public relations departments would reflect ambivalent attitudes about profits. There is no American consensus on how much profit is enough, or on what emphasis the pursuit of material gains should have in an individual's priorities.

In discussing ethics for practitioners, however, it is important to avoid the snare that these underlying attitudes might set. If a communicator steers clear of conflicts, makes all appropriate disclosures, and performs competently, he should not be criticized on ethical grounds solely because his efforts produce – or fail to produce – high financial rewards.

The morality of profits is a legitimate subject for discussion, and attitudes toward money, charity and allied values should be discussed openly. However, given the unspoken anti-money bias that Meyer discovered in two-thirds of all American journalists, it is crucial that students guard against letting biases about money taint their assessment of communication ethics. A communication principle that is moral should be equally ethical whether it is employed on behalf of a nonprofit venture or to enhance the profits of a lucrative business.

FINDING SOUL IN COMMUNICATIONS

Any one of the many approaches to formal ethics may be applied to the practice of communications in commerce. Whether the approach is through Utilitarianism or Kant, Natural Law or Contractarianism, problems in communications ethics are accessible to the student of formal ethics. If the student by this time in his course of study has chosen a favorite ethical approach, he would do well to reread this chapter from that point of view, testing his approach against these real-life questions.

As he does so, the student is likely to confront the centrality of the idea of Truth in his chosen philosophy of ethics, for communication problems invariably touch that question. Whether to tell the truth, whether to tell the whole truth, and whether to tell anything that is not the truth – all these are inescapable issues for the professional communicator.

That fact should come as no surprise, for the assumption of honesty is the basis for all communication, whether personal or professional. No society could function unless people could assume that most others tell the truth most of the time. Whether asking directions from a stranger, inquiring about merchandise in a store or chatting idly with a neighbor, we tend to assume that we are being told the truth and will take offense if we discover otherwise. Honesty thus is a central issue in any discussion of ethics. As the issue of truth is explored, the notion of passive and active deception arises: Is there a moral difference between speaking an untruth and merely standing mute in the knowledge that the person in front of you believes an untruth?

The next question is likely to be that of differing levels of obligation: Is the requirement of truth-telling or disclosure always the same, or does it vary depending on the nature of the relationship in whose context the communication occurs? Are we required to tell our bosses everything that we would tell our mothers? And vice versa? If the requirements are variable, then by what principles do we apply them to different situations? How do we decide when it is all right just to keep quiet when we know something that others don't? Conversely, how do we decide when an obligation of confidence to someone else requires us to keep quiet?

These are not simple questions, but neither are they impossible ones for the student to answer. To the contrary, the issues of communication ethics are no more – and no less – complex than the ordinary issues of family life and general citizenship. If you are certain that it is always wrong to lie to your parent or spouse, many other decisions fall into place automatically.

Likewise, if you are certain that it is permissible always to lie to them, other decisions are clarified. It is uncertainty about the morality of an action or about the strength of the obligation involved that makes ethics – and life – complex.

There are many models for decision-making to be found in schools of management, and most of those models can be adapted for communicators. However, the unique fact is that communication intrinsically involves a relationship based on some level of trust. That fact suggests the need for a model tailored for professional communications.

In the quotation at the beginning of this chapter, Hannah Arendt identifies the starting point of any model for ethical communicating. Because truthfulness is the central issue, the communicator must first identify the facts of the matter. Decisions about which facts to use and how to characterize them must come second. The communicator's first obligation is to learn What Is.

Next comes the need to define the purpose of the communication.

Is it to inform? Whom? Why?

To persuade? Whom? Why?

To entertain? Whom? Why?

To deceive? Whom? Why?

Once these questions are expressed in plain language, the ethical requirements of the situation should be clear. If not, there is one final test that may be useful: Is there any person I admire whom I would not want to learn about my actions and motives here? If there is, then either the admiration is misplaced or the action is unjustifiable. The communicator who answers that question has resolved the ethical dilemma.

Uncertainty can be reduced only by thinking through the issues and making certain decisions *in advance* of the situation that requires them. Thus, when students confront an ethical question in their workplace, they will have sound reasons and techniques to guide them to a quick decision instead of wallowing in moral crisis.

A MODEL FOR ETHICAL COMMUNICATING

Consider these principles of public communications:
1. Learn the facts. What is the actual situation?

2. Define the purposes. What goals am I trying to accomplish?

3. Assess the obligations. Who are the parties that have legitimate claim on my loyalty here?

4. Weigh the impact of disclosure. Would I be willing to expose my actions and motives here to people who trust me and whom I admire?

In another context, Shakespeare observed, "Cowards die many times before their death; the valiant only taste of death but once." A similar efficiency accrues to successful students of ethics: Once they reach a decision about a basic principle of ethical behavior, they will not have to worry much about it in the future. In a complex world that demands constant relearning and readjusting, that steady moral compass provides a benefit that is as practical as it is admirable.

READINGS
SOME ARGUE WITH DISPOSITION OF GDC CASE

James Russell
Miami Herald Financial Editor
Feb. 25, 1993

Unless an appeals court intervenes, the former top executives of General Development Corp. will be in jail in a few months. Not in one of those minimum-security country club facilities, either. Robert Ehrling, who was president of the big Florida lot and home sales company, and David Brown, the former chairman, have been assigned to prison camps with security fences and armed guards.

It sounds like harsh treatment for two men who lived the good life of corporate executives and enjoyed respected positions in the Miami community for years. Two real estate experts who testified for the defense in the executives' long fraud trial in federal court in Miami think the GDC officials got a raw deal.

"Innocent until proved guilty?" asked Paul Black, of AREEA, a real estate consulting firm. "Don't you believe it."

Black and another consultant, Lewis Goodkin, offered their impressions of the trial in talks before the Economic Society of South Florida the other day. A main point dealt with how real estate is valued.

"The lesson is this case is: Let the seller beware," Black said. "The government can come after you if you don't tell the buyer he can get it cheaper elsewhere." The thousands of home and lot buyers who said they were defrauded by GDC discovered much too late that their property was worth far less than they paid for it. The prosecution depicted them as trusting souls who were conned.

Black and Goodkin thought otherwise. The buyers were not unsophisticated, as the prosecution claimed, they said. The judge, Lenore Nesbitt, would not allow testimony about differences between short- and long-term investing. GDC's spending of millions of dollars on "amenities and infrastructure" in its developments was virtually ignored.

"The judge was the second prosecutor," Goodkin complained.

"The fact is that the judge wanted those men in jail," Black said.

The Economic Society said that it invited Nesbitt to appear on the program but that she declined because the case is under appeal. So the audience heard a one-sided story.

But the other side was clearly stated in her summation before she sentenced Ehrling and Brown. The case, she said, was not about failure to disclose that lower-priced property was available elsewhere in areas where the homes and lots were sold.

"The indictment alleged and the evidence showed that GDC ... induced its customers to purchase these houses by using intentionally misleading advertising and marketing programs, and by employing a sales force who were encouraged to misrepresent the nature of the product," Nesbitt said.

Does the GDC case imperil aggressive salesmanship in general? The judge said it does not.

"The verdict ... is not a threat to the American way of doing business nor to a free market," she said. It is "a reiteration of a very simple fact that the free-market system does not condone a fraud."

She quoted the late Supreme Court Justice Hugo Black, who said:

"The best element of business has long since decided that honesty should govern competitive enterprise and that the rule of caveat emptor (let the buyer beware) should not be relied on to reward fraud and deception."

It's hard to argue with that conclusion. Whether it applies to the GDC case, which is on appeal, is still questionable. But a final decision may come too late to keep Ehrling and Brown out of jail.

CODE OF PROFESSIONAL STANDARDS
FOR THE PRACTICE OF PUBLIC RELATIONS
Public Relations Society of America

This code was adopted by the PRSA Assembly in 1988. It replaces a Code of Ethics in Force since 1950.

Declaration of Principles

Members of the Public Relations Society of America base their professional principles on the fundamental values and dignity of the individual, holding that the free exercise of human rights, especially freedom of speech, freedom of assembly, and freedom of the press, is essential to the practice of public relations.

In serving the interests of clients and employers, we dedicate ourselves to the goals of better communication, understanding, and cooperation among the diverse individuals, groups and institutions of society, and of equal opportunity of employment in the public relations profession.

We pledge:

To conduct ourselves professionally, with truth, accuracy, fairness, and responsibility to the public;

To improve our individual competence and advance to knowledge and proficiency of the profession through continuing research and education;

And to adhere to the articles of the Code of Professional Standards for the Practice of Public Relations as adopted by the governing Assembly of the Society.

Code of Professional Standards for the Practice of Public Relations

These articles have been adopted by the Public Relations Society of America to promote and maintain high standards of public service and ethical conduct among its members.

1. A member shall conduct his or her professional life in accord with the public interest.

2. A member shall exemplify high standards of honesty and integrity while carrying out dual obligations to a client or employer and to the democratic process.

3. A member shall deal fairly with the public, with past or present clients or employers, and with fellow practitioners, giving due respect to the ideal of free inquiry and to the opinions of others.

4. A member shall adhere to the highest standards of accuracy and truth, avoiding extravagant claims or unfair comparisons and giving credit for ideas and words borrowed from others.

5. A member shall not knowingly disseminate false or misleading information and shall act promptly to correct erroneous communications for which he or she is responsible.

6. A member shall not engage in any practice which has the purpose of corrupting the integrity of channels of communications or the processes of government.

7. A member shall be prepared to identify publicly the name of the client or employer on whose behalf any public communication is made.

8. A member shall not use any individual or organization professing to serve or represent an announced cause, or professing to be independent or unbiased, but actually serving another or undisclosed interest.

9. A member shall not guarantee the achievement of specified results beyond the member's direct control.

10. A member shall not represent conflicting or competing interests without the express consent of those concerned, given after a full disclosure of the facts.

11. A member shall not place himself or herself in a position where the member's personal interest is or may be in conflict with an obligation to an employer or client, or others, without full disclosure of such interests to all involved.

12. A member shall not accept fees, commissions, gifts or any other consideration from anyone except clients or employers for whom services are performed without their express consent, given after full disclosure of the facts.

13. A member shall scrupulously safeguard the confidence and privacy rights of present, former, and prospective clients or employers.

14. A member shall not intentionally damage the professional reputation or practice of another practitioner.

15. If a member has evidence that another mem-

ber has been guilty of unethical, illegal or unfair practices, including those in violation of this Code, the member is obligated to present the information promptly to the proper authorities of the Society for action in accordance with the procedure set forth in Article XII of the bylaws.

16. A member called as a witness in a proceeding for enforcement of this Code is obligated to appear, unless excused for sufficient reason by the judicial panel.

17. A member shall, as soon as possible, sever relations with any organization or individual if such relationship requires conduct contrary to the articles of this Code.

OFFICIAL INTERPRETATIONS OF THE CODE
Interpretation of the Code Paragraph 1, which reads, "A member shall conduct his or her professional life in accord with the public interests."

The public interest is here defined primarily as comprising respect for and enforcement of the rights guaranteed by the Constitution of the United States of America.

Interpretation of Code Paragraph 6, which reads, "A member shall not engage in any practice which has the purpose of corrupting the integrity of channels of communication or the processes of government."

1. Among the practices prohibited by this paragraph are those that tend to place representatives of media or government under any obligation to the member, or the member's employer or client, which is in conflict with their obligations to media or government, such as:

a. the giving of gifts of more than nominal value;

b. any form of payment or compensation to a member of the media in order to obtain preferential or guaranteed news or editorial coverage in the medium;

c. any retainer or fee to a media employee or use of such employee if retained by a client or employer, where the circumstances are not fully disclosed to and accepted by the media employer;

d. providing trips, for media representatives, that are unrelated to legitimate news interest;

e. the use by a member of an investment or loan or advertising commitment made by the member, or the member's client, or guaranteed coverage in the medium.

FOR FURTHER INQUIRY

SUGGESTED READINGS
- Meyer, Philip, *Ethical Journalism*. (New York: Longman), 1987. pp. 247-254.
- American Society of Newspaper Editors. *Statement of Principles*. Reston, Va. 1975.

ENDNOTES

1. Meyer, Philip, *Ethical Journalism*. (New York: Longman), 1987. pp. 247-254.
2. American Society of Newspaper Editors. *Statement of Principles*. Reston, Va. 1975.
3. Meyer, p. 27.
4. Pratt, Cornelius B. "Public Relations: The Empirical Research on Practitioner Ethics," *Journal of Business Ethics*, March, 1991, p 230.
5. Pratt, p.230.
6. Pratt, p. 230.
7. Pratt, p. 230.
8. Public Relations Society of America. Code of Professional Standards. New York, NY. 1988.
9. Russell, James. *Some Argue With Disposition of GDC Case*. Miami Herald, Miami, Fla. Feb. 25, 1993.
10. Pratt, p. 231.
11. Meyer, p. 32-33.
12. Siker, Louke Van Wensveen, Donahue, James A. and Green, Ronald M. *Does Your Religion Make a Difference in Your Business Ethics?* "The Case of Consolidated Foods." *Journal of Business Ethics,* November, 1991. p 828.
13. Siker et al., pp. 820-827.

Part V

Institutional Responses
To Ethical Conflict

THE ADVISER   THE LEADER   THE CRITIC

Chapter 20

Donald Pride
Michael Richardson

ETHICAL DECISION-MAKING IN PUBLIC OFFICE

"My basic principle is that you don't make decisions because they are easy, you don't make them because they are cheap, you don't make them because they are popular; you make them because they are right. Not distinguishing between rightness and wrongness is where administrators get into trouble."
– Father Theodore Hesburgh, former president,
University of Notre Dame

"That's why we hold our political leaders to such a high standard – not because we expect them to be perfect, but because we know there has to be an image projected, an expectation aroused, a standard raised."
– William Moyers, journalist,
former press secretary to President Johnson

"Always do right. This will gratify some people, and astonish the rest."
– Mark Twain

Reality Check: You're a candidate for governor of Florida. You have just completed taping a television program in Miami. You step into a restroom at the station. A man approaches you with a brown paper bag, holds it out and says: "Take it. All we want is to be heard when you're elected." You look inside the bag; it's filled with cash, thousands of dollars. What do you do?

That situation happened. The candidate declined the cash, telling the person that the alcohol industry did not need to deliver money illegally to a candidate in order to have a chance to be "heard" in the Florida governor's office. Not every politician responds with such integrity. This was an ethical

Donald Pride, former press secretary for Florida Governor and U.S. Senate candidate Reubin Askew, is director of investigations for the Chief Inspector General, Office of the Governor, State of Florida. *Michael Richardson,* former editor of editorials in St. Petersburg, Fla., author, and past president of National Conference of Editorial Writers Foundation, is executive assistant to the president of St. Petersburg Junior College.

decision *on the way* to public office. It also, however, may have been a test of the moral fiber of one Reubin Askew, who in his second term as governor of Florida was recognized as one of the nation's 10 most outstanding governors of the entire 20th century.[1]

Public service in American political life once was considered a "high calling," in the classical sense of a noble profession uplifting all persons. "Public service is a sacred trust," were words heard as the American democratic experiment was being launched. Parents encouraged children to think of it as a career of high purpose serving humanity, equated with such service professions as the clergy, medicine, and the law. Becoming president of the United States was a plausible childhood goal.

In the nation's second hundred years, families cited the inspiring example of Abraham Lincoln, who never won an election until his first try for President. Holding public office commanded respect with the stations of university faculty, judgeships, medical doctors. By the 1990s the image of those professions also had been tarnished as the robes of secrecy and privilege had been lifted to reveal incidents of scandal, ethical lapse, abuse of trust, and moral failure. But perhaps no other American profession's image has fallen as fast and as far as that of the public servant, both elected and appointed. American opinion surveys in recent years show the public holds members of Congress, for example, at the bottom of any listing of professions; dogcatchers fare better in the perceptions of ordinary citizens.

It has been argued that the modern technology-driven information explosion, scandal-seeking media and the human bent for juicy gossip distort the perception of public service. "I am not a crook," an American president felt compelled to disclaim in the spring of 1975. Within weeks, Richard Nixon became the first American president to resign from office, driven by the catastrophic moral failures uncovered by the Watergate affair of 1974-75. Nixon in 1972 had received an overwhelming vote of the American people for re-election – a modern record plebiscite. Historians suggested his quest for power, his desire to wreak retribution on an "enemies list," and his unrelenting attempt to "cover up" the breaches of public trust and the law within his Committee To Re-Elect the President (CREEP) were vain abuses of power. Indeed, CREEP had gone so far as to plot a campaign of "dirty tricks" to embarrass, discredit and taint supporters of Democratic presidential candidate George McGovern.

Nixon had extricated the nation from the divisive and demoralizing Vietnam War, but his personal and political tactics prevented him from retaining the power he so zealously had won. By August 1975 he was gone from the White House, and the nation groped for its moral foundations. It was not mere public cynicism that drove him out. A cadre of young persons involved in his campaign, directed by their political elders (all Nixon cronies), had lied, violated criminal laws, abandoned virtually any sense of ethical standard, and operated not by the *Golden Rule* but a perverse corollary: Do unto others before they do unto you.

Not only presidents stumbled. In those same '70s, Wilbur Mills, who was one of the powerful Americans of his time as chairman of the U.S. House Ways and Means Committee – the man who decided whether you could deduct your donations to the Red Cross or the United Way – fell from power. His downfall was not over some of the special tax breaks he had given industries who had favored him with cash for his campaigns; rather it was fueled by his escapades with Fanne Foxe, a female Washington dancer who engaged in alcohol-laced soirees with Mills and others. Over the ensuing years, his career drew sad parallels: U.S. Senator John Tower of Texas, a brilliant defense policymaker and presidential adviser, retired due to his lack of control of alcohol. U.S. Senator Gary Hart abandoned a dynamic campaign for president because his marital fidelity, or lack thereof, became an ongoing campaign topic. Americans, hypocritically perhaps, embraced soap operas laden with moral failure where ethical factors never prevailed over hormonal impulse, and then scoffed at politicians whose soap-opera values propelled them into the spotlight. Meanwhile, in Europe America's political antecedents wondered why the U.S. took such matters so seriously. Europe's social critics, however, had to admit that from the British Profumo scandal in the 1950s to more recent events, public officials did lose their jobs and their influence as a result of immoral behavior.

A NEW GENERATION

But the "70s also saw American resilience in ethical public service emerge. Across the nation, especially in the South perhaps, there arose a new breed of politicians. Socially conservative, family-centered individuals became governors and U.S. senators from states such as Arkansas, Georgia, Tennessee, North Carolina, Texas and Florida. Among them were Dale Bumpers of Arkansas, Reubin Askew of Florida, Terry Sanford of North Carolina and Jimmy Carter of Georgia. Indeed, with his fellow governors' help, Carter's politics of hope – of restoring public confidence in government, of repudiating the corruption within the Washington beltway – made him the nation's first president from the so-called Deep South. (Of course, less than two decades later, one Bill Clinton, a governor of Arkansas, mustering some of the legacy of these New-South leaders, fulfilled a youthful dream of becoming President of the United States.)

In this chapter we will consider the ethical decision-making principles and processes of a range of public officials. In public service, is it enough for officials merely to obey the law, or does the oath of office demand a higher standard, one of avoiding the appearance as well as the actuality of unethical behavior? Taking a closer look at Florida government and particularly the career of Reubin Askew will help serve as a vehicle to walk through some of those decisions as examples of the dilemmas faced by public officials. It was Askew who acted within his sphere of influence to try to restore the portrait of public service in his state and beyond – as he became U.S. Trade Representative in the Carter Administration, a candidate for the U.S. Senate and a candidate for President. The authors, who often witnessed these events or were part of the public discourse about them (and in Donald Pride's case, actually participated in some of the decisions), will share some of the experiences from their vantage points at the time.

ACCOUNTABILITY

If public officials are to be accountable to the people they serve, they must be willing to let the people see and judge their actions. As Thomas Jefferson once said, "When a man assumes a public trust, he should consider himself as public property." Of course, all candidates for public office say they want to serve the people. On the campaign trail, they're ready and willing to be held accountable. But some begin acting as if they own the office once they achieve it. From City Hall to the White House, American politics is rife with examples of politicians who not only forgot they were public property, but assumed that the *public's* property – or money – was their own.

> **66 A public office is a public trust. The people shall have the right to secure and sustain that trust against abuse. 99**
>
> – Sunshine Amendment,
> Florida Constitution, 1976

One Florida governor bluntly expressed that attitude in 1966, as an era of rural and often secretive control of state government neared its end. A reporter for the *St. Petersburg Times* had discovered the State Road Department was paying the costly upkeep on a 17-passenger executive airplane provided by one of the South's largest grocery chains for the political and other travels of Governor Haydon Burns. When confronted with this finding, Burns accused the reporter of prying into his personal business "and that of my friends."

The governor angrily threatened to deny the reporter access to state government news. "As governor," he growled, "I don't have to account to you or anybody else." Given the nature of Florida politics at the time, the governor's arrogance was understandable, if inexcusable.[2]

THE END OF THE 'PORK CHOP' ERA

Florida politics had been dominated for years by a brazen band of state senators elected from the largely rural northern half of the state. The *Tampa Tribune* dubbed these senators the "Pork Chop Gang," a term that reflected both their rural orientation and their habit of taking home the best cut of the pig (state appropriations for roads, prisons and other projects). The Senate's rural clique retained control through an alliance with banking, insurance, phosphate, pulpwood, trucking, grocery, liquor and other powerful private interests. Its members benefited not only from the interests' financial support at election time but also from personal loans, retainers and other lucrative business ties. The special interests, in turn, thrived under a state policy of taxing people instead of land and business.

The partnership between the pork-choppers and the vested interests largely ignored growing needs for new and better schools, highways and other improvements in the more urban regions of Central and South Florida. For years, members of the Senate's ruling bloc and their rural-based counterparts in the House of Representatives fought off every effort to reapportion the Legislature's seats according to population. As the decade of the 1960s opened, barely 12% of the state's citizens could elect a majority of the Senate. Fewer than 15% could elect a majority of the House. Big Dade County, embracing booming Miami and home to 935,047 people, had only one senator – the same as tiny Jefferson, a northern Florida county with fine roads and only 9,543 residents, including Senator S. Dilworth Clarke.

A wealthy Monticello banker and former Senate president, Dil Clarke had long since sealed friendships with his fellow lawmakers by extending them thousands of dollars of personal loans. Not surprisingly, his Senate pals rarely crossed him, even after he had stepped down from the presidency. The aging Clarke could still get his way by slowly rising out of his big leather chair on the Senate floor and solemnly declaring: "This is a good bill. Vote for it." Or, on rarer occasions: "This is a bad bill. Kill it."

Most legislation opposed by the Gang, or by the business lobbyists, never reached the floor for debate. Senator Bart Knight, representing a rural Panhandle district, once headed a judiciary panel widely recognized as the Senate's "killer committee." Once, when reporters sought the status of a reform bill, Knight declared it dead. "I just had a meeting walking down the hall," he smiled, referring to the proxy votes in his pocket.

Lobbyists wrote many of the laws that were enacted and flaunted their influence in the halls and meeting rooms of the old Capitol. Senator Philip Beall, a Pensacola lawyer whose clients included a major utility situated 650 miles away in Miami, chaired the committee that oversaw the pulpwood industry. When he couldn't make a meeting one day, the pulpwood interests' lobbyist sat in Beall's chair, banged the gavel, and declared the committee adjourned.

The Pork Chop Gang regularly held secret meetings at a fish camp on the Aucilla River, owned by a lobbyist for small-loan companies. Or they sipped bourbon over friendly hands of nickel-limit knock poker at an Ocala National Forest retreat owned by an influential electric company lobbyist. Not only the cards, but legislative deals were cut at these hideaways, unwitnessed by the senators' constituents back home or the capital press corps in Tallahassee.

INTEGRITY IS THE ISSUE

Despite the Supreme Court's "one man, one vote" decision in 1964, rural lawmakers resisted reapportionment and clung to fading power in the state capital when Haydon Burns took the oath as governor in January 1965. Burns brought to Tallahassee a reputation for getting things done in his Northeast Florida home town of Jacksonville. Though larger than many of its sister cities to the south, Jacksonville, home to big banking, insurance, railroad, shipping and grocery chain interests, was known for its conservative views. Its political makeup was more akin to the towns and hamlets that stretched from the city's boundaries to sleepy Tallahassee and all the way to Pensacola at the western end of the Panhandle. In five terms as the city's mayor, Burns had built urban expressways, lured new industry and revitalized the downtown riverfront. He had also routinely doled out city business to political supporters, presided over secret meetings of the City Council, and improperly enlisted the help of police officers and others on the city payroll in his election campaigns.

If the Supreme Court's reapportionment rulings were about to create a power vacuum in Tallahassee, Haydon Burns seemed poised to fill it. A Democrat who had campaigned against the national Civil Rights Act, he was elected in November 1964 to serve a special, two-year term as governor. The bobtailed term, created to separate Florida's statewide races from the party's more liberal national tickets, left Burns eligible for re-election to a full four-year term in 1966. But his claims on the spoils of government did not play well in the downstate newspapers. Editorialists cried foul when hundreds of thousands of dollars in state contracts and purchases went to the governor's business cronies. His plan for a $300-million road bond issue, bulging with pork for every section of the state, was emphatically rejected by the voters. When Burns himself faced the voters again, the governor learned that he indeed was accountable, and beatable, in a bitter Democratic primary.

Robert King High, the mayor of Miami, won the 1966 Democratic nomination for governor by opposing the special interests and "hogpen morality" in Tallahassee. But his campaign theme of "Integrity is the Issue" – so effective against Burns in the spring primary – could not overcome, in November, Florida's traditional conservatism and volatile feelings about race. During the primary runoff, Burns had indelibly branded High a racial liberal. The divisive primary enabled the relatively unknown Republican nominee, Claude Roy Kirk Jr., to become Florida's first GOP governor since Reconstruction. Charming, debonair and flamboyant, Kirk was no racist. He was, however, an opportunist. With High already wounded, Kirk, in the general election, merely invoked code phrases such as "law and order" and "a man's home is his castle." The voters understood.

Kirk's four-year term, from January 1967 to January 1971, was marked by major advancements in state government: Reapportionment, sweeping out the remnants of the Pork Chop Gang; a new Constitution, finally replacing the cluttered 1885 state charter; reorganization, consolidating state agencies into a more effective work force; environmental concern, recognizing for the first time that the state's natural wonders needed protection. In addition, the Legislature enacted a model open-meetings law in 1967, after four reporters one day refused to leave an "executive" meeting of the Senate and had to be physically ejected. Kirk, of course, couldn't claim full credit for any of these advancements. But he undoubtedly helped awaken Florida's capital city from its long nap. No one could dispute that the light-hearted, unpredictable governor was a catalyst for change.

And, yet, the Kirk years raised ethical and accountability questions every bit as serious as those of the Pork Chop and Haydon Burns periods:

• Shunning the idea that politicians are public property, Kirk, as a candidate, steadfastly rejected questions about his financial affairs and, once elected, hid them from public view in a blind trust.
• An influential St. Augustine banker confirmed that he and a small group of bankers and business leaders had secretly paid off a $75,000 bank loan for Kirk after the 1966 campaign.
• Kirk formed a private $500-per-member "Governor's Club" to support his jet-set lifestyle. He also sought donations for a private "War on Crime" and other controversial ventures, raising upward of $3-million from various interests during his four years in Tallahassee. After the Florida Supreme Court forced open the membership rolls of the Governor's Club, the press and Legislature discovered that nearly $48-million in state consulting, road-building and other contracts had gone to Kirk's contributors.
• The Commerce Department, responsible for promoting tourism and luring industry to the Sunshine State, became the unofficial campaign headquarters for Kirk's inflated political ambitions. State tax dollars, including $90,000 a year for a New York publicist, were squandered on the governor's vain quest for a spot on the 1968 national GOP ticket.[3]

Whereas Haydon Burns had reacted to bad press by denouncing the reporters as "illegitimate," the irrepressible Kirk shrugged off negative newspaper stories. When the *New York Times* called him an "overweight ladies' man," the governor allowed that he liked skinny ladies, too. When the *St. Petersburg Times* and *Miami Herald* revealed that Kirk and his bride had flown to a European honeymoon at state expense, the governor called a news conference to thank the reporters for uncovering a "clerical error."

If two years of Burns had been enough for Florida voters, four years of Claude Kirk were more than enough. Integrity indeed was the issue. The tenures of both men, lacking a moral compass, opened the door to an entirely different kind of politician in the governor's mansion.

A Defeat For Florida's Shadow Government

Reubin Askew, a Democrat who overwhelmed Kirk in the 1970 gubernatorial election, once said this of his own political ambition: "Running for office was something I knew I had to do. I have never tried to hide that desire. I feel God has plans for the world and men: If I had any talent, I had to use it for public service."

A non-cussing, non-smoking, non-drinking Presbyterian elder from Pensacola, Askew was virtually unknown statewide despite 12 years of service in the Legislature, where he had unseated Pork Chop Senator Beal after serving two terms in the House. For a lawmaker from the conservative Panhandle, he had taken some unusual stands. In 1959, when he first came to the House at age 30, he sided with then-Governor LeRoy Collins against "last resort" legislation that would have closed the state's schools rather than desegregate them. Then, initially as a floor leader for Collins and continuing through the mid-1960s, he stood up against the Pork Chop Gang in favor of giving South Florida its fair share of legislative seats.[4]

Announcing his candidacy for governor in February 1970, Askew said: "I intend to fight the system that seems to thrive on the raising and spending of millions of dollars in campaigns and undisclosed thousands of dollars in donations after assuming office. It's a system that, more frequently than not, robs an officeholder of his freedom to act in the best interest of the people." As the campaign developed, Askew surprised and angered influential lobbyists and business leaders by handing back contributions he felt came with strings attached. The special interests, tagged the "shadow government" for their clout in Tallahassee, took their support elsewhere.

(One of Askew's Senate colleagues, Lawton Chiles, waged a different kind of campaign against the moneyed interests that same year – reaching average Floridians by walking the length of the state in his successful bid for a U.S. Senate seat. Both men became staunch advocates of campaign finance reform and open government on the state and national levels.)

Askew's gubernatorial candidacy made little headway against more prominent candidates for the Democratic nomination until he enlisted Florida's elected Secretary of State, Tom Adams, as his running mate, then focused their campaign on the need to reform the state's regressive tax structure. Advocating any tax was risky, even one that would shift part of the burden from people to big business. But Askew's straight talk and sincere manner persuaded the voters that, contrary to the claims of the large business interests, an income tax on large corporations wouldn't simply be passed onto consumers.

Askew not only won his party's nomination and then unseated Kirk but also went on to win both legislative and voter approval of his "fair share" tax package in his first year as governor. He took on virtually every special interest in the state, spearheading a constitutional amendment for the corporate income tax, a severance tax on phosphate, and real tax relief for homeowners, renters, and consumers of household utilities. "The voters say they want tax reform," he told an audience of hostile lobbyists. "They mean shifting a substantial portion of Florida's tax burden from those who can least afford it to those who have been best at avoiding it."[5]

When the voters adopted the corporate tax amendment on November 2, 1971, the governor met reporters with his wife, Donna Lou, at his side. He pulled from his pocket a crumpled note that had arrived during the heat of the campaign. From the same grocery chain interests that had furnished Haydon Burns' airplane, the note suggested that Askew spell his name with a double "s."[6]

"We have brought the shadow government into the sunshine," Askew said, "and it may have blinded their eyes." Later, in an interview with *New York Times* reporter Jon Nordheimer, Askew elaborated: "This shadow government has never been challenged frontally before, but now the public got a good close look at them and I don't believe the public will ever let them run loose again. I think there's a lesson for the rest of the country in what has happened in Florida. It just wasn't luck or an accident. I think we've shown that the office can be responsive to the people. I was told over and over again – you can't be honest with the people. I was sure you could."

'DOING THE RIGHT THING'

Askew served the limit of two full terms, or eight years, as Florida's governor. He took up where Claude Kirk left off on the environment, working with House Speaker Richard Pettigrew, Senator Bob Graham and other concerned lawmakers to enact new protections for endangered lands, coastal marshes and water supply areas. When he couldn't persuade the Legislature to enact a law requiring public officials to publicly disclose their personal finances, Askew took the issue directly to the voters and won the "Sunshine Amendment" to the Florida Constitution. With Senator Dempsey Barron, Representative Talbot "Sandy" D'Alemberte, and a young D'Alemberte aide named Janet Reno, the governor also spearheaded an overhaul of the state's outmoded court system. He appointed the South's first black state Supreme Court justice since Reconstruction, Florida's first woman Cabinet member and first black Cabinet member in 100 years. And, when the state attorney in populous Dade County resigned in 1978, Askew named Janet Reno to the chief prosecutor post that 15 years later would lead to her appointment by President Bill Clinton as the first female Attorney General of the United States.

The governor risked his own political future by defending controversial school busing as a necessary means of desegregating Florida's schools. But why? The public schools were about to open for the 1971 fall term, and Alabama Governor George Wallace, eyeing Florida's 1972 presidential primary, was fanning anti-busing fever in the Sunshine State. Popular political wisdom suggested Askew should merely stay out of a referendum in his state that would have national implications. He recognized the issue as a moral dilemma, not merely a political choice. Failing to desegregate public schools would mean harm to the state's minorities. Failing to lead in a time of such moral significance would have violated his own conscience. He chose to confront the matter head-on. Addressing a summer graduating class at the University of Florida in Gainesville, Askew urged Floridians to remain calm.

He didn't stop there. Urging the graduates to help "seek the broad community desegregation and cooperation which ultimately will make busing unnecessary," Askew called busing "an artificial and inadequate instrument of change" and added: "Nobody really wants it – not you, not me, not the people, not the school boards, not even the courts. Yet the law demands, and rightly so, that we put an end to segregation in our society."

The rhetoric soon became legislation. Wallace backers persuaded the Legislature to include on the 1972 presidential preference primary ballot a straw vote against busing for desegregation. Askew again could have turned away from the issue. Instead, he constructed a second straw-ballot question, this one in favor of providing equal educational opportunity for all. Both proposals received majority votes, but Askew's version and his vision of the future of education in his state prevailed.

For all his achievements and moral courage, Askew also presided over state government during a period of unprecedented political scandals in the executive and judicial branches. Three state Cabinet members, elected independently of the governor under Florida's unique Cabinet system, were forced out of office for misconduct. Two Supreme Court justices resigned under threat of impeachment. And, most embarrassing to Askew, his own lieutenant governor, Tom Adams, was censured by the House for using a state employee to run Adams' private farm.

We will explore some of these issues on the following pages. The important point to be made here is that the citizens of Florida never lost their confidence in Askew. Ordinarily, governors, presidents or other elected chief executives suffer the voters' wrath when something goes wrong on their watch, regardless of whether they had anything to do with it, or any control over it. And, ordinarily, politicians will go to any length to avoid sticking their necks out on issues such as race, for fear of angering voters. Yet, from a conservative Panhandle district that disagreed with him on race and reapportionment, Askew was elected to the Legislature four times. He was overwhelmingly re-elected governor in 1974, despite his unpopular stand on busing and the ethical lapses of some of those around him. A statewide survey conducted in the final months of his tenure in Tallahassee showed that 68% of the voters rated the governor's performance as good or excellent, an unusually high rating for any politician after eight years in office.

"He helped restore the people's faith in government during an era when politicians in general were considered slightly less reprehensible than purse snatchers," John Van Gieson, a veteran capital reporter, wrote in the *Miami Herald*.

How did Askew earn such trust? How do you explain such durable popularity? What are the lessons for those who may wish to pursue a career in the public sector? Consider the words of one who applied the lessons well over the intervening years. Upon becoming U.S. attorney general in early 1993, Janet Reno instructed the Justice Department's 92,000 lawyers, investigators, agents and marshals: "While I'm attorney general, we will address each issue with one question: What's the right thing to do?"

Askew himself, in an interview during his governorship, explained his own decision-making this way: "There must be a sense of right and wrong. All legislation, to be effective, to be lasting, must have moral content to it."

But Askew recognized that more than individual conscience is needed to ensure good, honest, open government. He also realized that the standards of criminal law and the voters' ability to throw the rascals out are not, by themselves, enough. He believed the law also must contain appropriate guidelines for ethical conduct and public decision-making and disclosure by those who would be entrusted with the public's business.

In an address to the national Council on Governmental Ethics Laws three years after stepping down as Florida's governor, Askew said: " ... The important work of our democracy must be conducted in an atmosphere in which people have confidence that those in positions of power within the government perceive the public interest as paramount and are committed to keeping the public trust.

"There is no single or simple way to create such an atmosphere of confidence. But whatever else it may take to inspire the confidence we need, surely an indispensable prerequisite is an ethical framework for government. For how the people view public officials, how they perceive their priorities, and how they discern their values is intimately and inevitable related to governmental ethics ... Ethics laws alone obviously are not and will not be enough. But they are essential."[7]

In the pages ahead we will examine some of these laws and see how they have worked, or not worked, on both the state and national level. First, we'll look at laws governing the election of public officials. Then we'll examine attempts to regulate conduct in public office itself, with a focus on Florida's pioneer "Government in the Sunshine" laws.

CAMPAIGN FINANCE

A federal case. In 1992 the Washington bureau for the Knight-Ridder newspapers examined an exclusive group of campaign supporters known inside the Bush White House as the "Team of 100." The team's wealthy business leaders, real-estate developers, financiers, ranchers and racetrack owners – actually some 250 in all – had each contributed $100,000 through the Republican Party to George Bush's 1988 election. (Funneling huge corporate and large individual contributions, or so-called soft money, through state party organizations circumvents federal restrictions on contributions made directly to the candidates. This scheme has been utilized by both Democrats and Republicans in recent presidential elections.) The Knight-Ridder reporters found that Team 100 members had received a variety of special benefits, appointments and favorable policy decisions during Bush's four-year term.

Case in point: Cable television executive Bill Daniels was a $100,000 contributor. In 1990 he became alarmed over proposals to curb soaring cable TV rates and wrote to the President urging that the administration "take a strong stand now against re-regulation." The White House did.

A Florida case. When the president of the Florida Senate decided to seek an elective state Cabinet seat in 1988, he wanted his friends to be the first to know. So he summoned the special-interest lobbyists to his Capitol office to break the news. Then, with the Legislature about to decide the state budget and other key issues, more than 100 lobbyists with a huge stake in those decisions attended a fund-raising reception to hand-deliver their contributions to the senator's campaign.[8]

Although he lost his bid for state insurance commissioner, he was hardly the first to engage in what the Common Cause public interest lobby calls "legalized extortion." Powerful state and federal officials are constantly putting the arm on special interests and their political action committees (PACs) to help finance increasingly costly campaigns for re-election or higher office.

Is there anything wrong with any of this? Isn't a candidate's fund-raising ability one sign of his or her ability to build the support needed to govern? Is the money not needed to reach today's busy voters via costly television advertisements? Don't wealthy contributors, or powerful special interests, have a right to be heard – just like everyone else? Isn't this the American way?

The trouble is, Common Cause and other critics say, this increasingly *is* the American way. In Florida, despite new limits on the size of campaign contributions, about $16-million was raised or spent on behalf of the winning candidates in the 1992 state legislative elections. Across the nation, $678-million was raised and spent by candidates for the U.S. Senate and House. On average, it cost $410,000 to win a House seat in 1990, compared to just $87,200 in 1976. A Senate seat cost $3.3-million, up from $609,100 in '76. Senator Phil Gramm, R-Texas, raised more than $11.6-million in the two years prior to his 1990 re-election, an average of almost $112,000 per week. According to campaign finance authority Herbert Alexander, total spending on all elections in the United States rose from $540-million in 1976 to $3-billion in 1992.

Closer examination of campaign finance reports reveals that incumbent lawmakers, in Washington, Tallahassee and other capitals, collect most of their campaign money from special interests, PACs or lobbyists. The greater the incumbent's clout, the easier the money flows. U.S. House Speaker Thomas Foley, D-Washington, and Majority Whip David Bonior, D-Michigan, each received 72% of their total contributions from PACs during the 1991-92 election cycle.

Certainly, special interests have a right to be heard. But does the voice of the average citizen get lost in the din? Undue influence by special interests, whether perceived or real, contributes to public cynicism and distrust. Political competition is discouraged, by both the soaring cost of campaigns and the propensity of the vested interests and PACs to support incumbent officeholders. And the incumbents find themselves spending more time raising money for the next election than they devote to the legitimate concerns of their constituents.

Public disgust with all of this created a new wave of campaign finance reform efforts in the states and the nation's capital during the 1990s. The outcome was by no means clear. Because they benefit from the status quo, members of the Congress and state Legislatures have been slow over the years to correct abuses of the American political system. But scandals, from time to time, have virtually forced reluctant lawmakers to enact election reforms – sometimes with unintended consequences. A look at past and recent efforts follows.

CAMPAIGN FINANCE REFORM

The Watergate scandals precipitated a spate of campaign finance reforms at federal and state levels during the 1970s. In all, 21 corporations and/or their executives were indicted in 1973 and 1974 for secretly and illegally contributing millions of dollars to Richard Nixon and other candidates. Congress, alarmed by the abuses, expanded campaign finance laws first enacted in 1971, requiring uniform disclosure of campaign receipts and expenditures and offering future presidential candidates public funds in exchange for limits on private contributions and overall spending. But the Supreme Court, in its 1976 *Buckley vs. Valeo* decision, struck down other parts of these reforms, invalidating overall expenditure ceilings not tied to public financing and limitations on independent expenditures and candidate expenditures from personal funds. The court's landmark finding that such restrictions violated freedom of speech effectively erased spending caps in state as well as federal campaigns.[9]

Ironically, the reforms of the 1970s, coupled with the Buckley ruling, led to a proliferation of special-interest expenditures that critics say are "independent" of candidate campaign organizations in name only. And they've encouraged even greater reliance on political action committees, known as PACs, as a means of funneling corporate, union and other special-interest money into political campaigns.

Moreover, the reforms left several loopholes through which individuals may raise and spend money to influence elections in ways unintended by Congress. The law allows, for example, separate campaign contributions to be "bundled" for a particular candidate by a lobbyist or other intermediate, thus raising money from interest groups far in excess of what its individual members could contribute. And, as mentioned above, it permits candidates and their political parties to skirt federal restrictions by channeling unlimited amounts of "soft money" into state and local party organizations for spending on the candidates' campaigns. In 1992, more than $60-million in soft money was raised by the two major parties, circumventing the spending limits that Bill Clinton and George Bush had accepted in exchange for $46-million each in public funds.

On becoming President in 1993, Clinton began work on new reform proposals expected to include measures designed to restrict soft money donations, reduce from $5,000 to perhaps $1,000 the limit on individual PAC contributions, and provide additional ways to voluntarily limit overall campaign spending.

WHO GAVE IT, WHO GOT IT

Among the 50 states and the federal government, Florida pioneered the development of laws to publicly disclose the giving and spending of campaign money. Its original "Who Gave It, Who Got It" disclosure law was enacted in 1951, three years after three rich power brokers had secretly put up $450,000 to elect Fuller Warren governor.

The law has been improved over the years in the wake of periodic newspaper revelations on how various candidates disguised the real source of their campaign money (for example, listing among contributors people who happened to be dead). A *St. Petersburg Times* examination of Governor Burns' $1.4-million re-election fund in 1966 revealed that not only did the money largely come from interests benefiting from state contracts but much of it did *not* come from average citizens listed as $1,000 contributors on the governor's campaign reports. "There must be some mistake," said one young man on the list who had just had been graduated from college and turned out to be the son-in-law of Burns' campaign coordinator.[10]

New state limits on overall expenditures and Reubin Askew's abhorrence of large, special-interest contributions temporarily halted the rise in gubernatorial campaign spending through most of the 1970s, only to give way to a spiraling increase after the Supreme Court's *Buckley vs. Valeo* decision and the end of the Askew era in 1978. Democrat Bob Graham raised $2.8-million that year to defeat Republican millionaire Jack Eckerd, whose $3-million war chest consisted mostly of his own money. Then, with the limit on individual contributions hiked from $1,000 to $3,000 per election, Democrat Steve Pajcic spent almost $9-million in losing the 1986 race to Republican Bob Martinez, who spent more than $7.2-million.

In order to avoid even the appearance of undue influence, Askew and veteran U.S. Senator Lawton Chiles each adopted voluntary limits of $100 on campaign contributions in their successful re-election bids. Chiles again invoked the $100 cap in unseating Governor Martinez in 1990. As refreshing as these campaigns were, most political observers believe that such limits wouldn't work for unknown challengers in large, media-market states such as Florida.

Askew, who eventually turned to university teaching, continued his advocacy of campaign finance reform after unsuccessfully seeking the Democratic presidential nomination in 1984 and abruptly abandoning a race for the U.S. Senate in 1988 (a decision based largely on his distaste for constant fund-raising). As governor, Lawton Chiles in 1991 persuaded the Legislature to reduce the state's $3,000-per-election limit on individual contributions to candidates to $500, one of the lowest limits in the nation. In 1993 he tried unsuccessfully to impose limits on the aggregate amount that candidates could accept from PACs and a ban on lawmakers accepting contributions from lobbyists during legislative sessions. The House effectively killed the governor's reform proposals by amending onto them an unacceptable repeal of a statutory promise of public financing for statewide races. The '93 Legislature also did nothing to reform its own "soft money" loophole, allowing use of the state political parties as conduits for channeling contributions exceeding the $500 cap into legislative campaigns selected by legislative leaders.

In many state capitals and in Washington, efforts to curb special-interest influence in elective politics continue, with no easy or lasting fixes in sight, although President Clinton announced proposed reforms in May 1993 that targeted the "soft money" issue.

'PEOPLE OF VIRTUE'

"Public leaders face a crisis of confidence," U.S. Rep. Lee H. Hamilton, D-Indiana, wrote in 1988. "There are significant social costs when the public trust is violated. Opinion polls indicate that a lack of confidence in the integrity of elected officials is a major reason for the low voter turnout in recent elections. Without trust, democratic government just does not work."[11]

Hamilton, who chaired the House hearings on the Iran-Contra affair, recalled the testimony of witnesses who claimed that the ends justified the means and that lying to Congress and the American people was an acceptable practice. "So often during the hearings I was reminded of President

Jefferson's statement: 'The whole art of government consists in the art of being honest,'" Hamilton continued. "Our Founding Fathers recognized that no matter how well-structured government is, it will not work unless its offices are held by people of virtue."

The question, of course, is this: How do you ensure that the occupants of public office indeed are "people of virtue?" Many have argued that morality cannot be legislated, and their assertions have proved at least partly correct. Recurring scandals have afflicted every level of government, regardless of the laws enacted to prevent them. In the case at hand, for example, the flurry of reform legislation that followed the Watergate coverup didn't deter the Reagan administration from illegally funding the Nicaraguan Contras with profits from a secret arms sale to Iran.

But if campaign finance reforms and formal ethics codes and rules are no cure-all, they nevertheless can provide a helpful framework and guideline for cleaner politics and government. The 1978 Ethics in Government Act, part of Watergate's legacy, required financial disclosures by officials in the federal executive and judicial branches, restrained the "revolving door" between public and private sector employment, and created an independent counsel to investigate wrong-doing in the executive branch. Many of the states have enacted or strengthened their own codes of ethics to guard against conflicts of interest and other abuses, restricted gifts, required greater disclosure by officials and lobbyists, and created ethics commissions and elections commissions to enforce the higher standards.[12]

Ethics and elections codes are always subject to adjustment and improvement. Some officeholders may not like them, but it's difficult to argue that the public would be better off without them. It's even more difficult to make a case against requirements for open meetings, public records and financial disclosure. For, while public disclosure is no guarantee of virtuous behavior in public office, it provides constituents with the information they need to judge official behavior. Another look at the Florida experience is instructive.

SUNSHINE GOVERNMENT

In their 1976 book, *The Transformation of Southern Politics*, Jack Bass and Walter de Vries wrote: "No state matches Florida in experience with openness in government, and political leaders there understand that secrecy breeds suspicion and that public confidence derives from trust. The sunshine law is considered by Governor Askew to have had 'the single biggest good effect upon government since I have been in politics.'" [13]

The state already had a strong public records law on its books when in early 1967 four reporters balked at leaving the Senate chamber so the senators could meet in secret, ostensibly to discuss executive appointments or suspensions. Reapportionment was the hot issue of the day, and the press had become increasingly skeptical when the Senate kept closing its doors on the public.

Although the reporters' sit-in was brief, the adverse publicity over their forcible removal had an impact. Within a few months, the Legislature enacted legislation stipulating that all meetings of public officials must be open. The Sunshine Law has been strengthened over the years by attorney general opinions, far-reaching court rulings and, finally in the 1990s, constitutional amendments clarifying that requirements for open meetings and records apply to state legislators as well as to members of the executive branch and local governments.

WHAT IS 'OPEN'?

Florida's courts have concluded, understandably, that it is not only the *final decisions* that the people have a right to know, but *how* and *why* their elected officials reach those decisions. "Every thought, as well as every affirmative act, of a public official as it relates to and is within the scope of his official duties, is a matter of public concern," the Second District Court of Appeal ruled in *Times Publishing Company vs. Williams* in 1969; "and it is the entire decision-making process that the Legislature intended to affect by the enactment of the statute before us. This act is a declaration of public policy, the frustration of which constitutes irreparable injury to the public interest. Every step in the decision-making process, including the decision itself, is a necessary preliminary to formal action. It follows that each such step constitutes an 'official act,' an indispensable requisite to 'formal action,' within the meaning of the act."[14]

Reubin Askew believed the people's right to know went beyond the official actions and records of their representatives in government. He believed the people had a right to know the sources of their representatives' income, and whether their representatives profit from public service. Beginning with his initial gubernatorial bid in 1970, he voluntarily filed annual statements revealing his personal finances to the public. In the eight years of his governorship, his net worth increased from $72,700 to $126,066, largely due to the normal increase in the value of his life insurance and a home he purchased for his mother in Pensacola.

If a few of Askew's executive branch colleagues had followed his example and handled their own finances scrupulously and openly, they might have spared themselves and their state the embarrassments that plagued Florida in the mid-1970s. Instead, the state's elected education commissioner, insurance commissioner and comptroller were each indicted on unrelated charges involving financial matters. Across from the Capitol in the Florida Supreme Court, two justices were forced to resign for other forms of ethical misconduct.[15]

Askew's only role in any of these cases was to assign a special prosecutor, when and where the circumstances warranted such action. The governor wasted no time doing his duty. He appointed Duval County State Attorney Ed Austin to investigate in 1974, even when the target was Education Commissioner Floyd Christian, a state Cabinet ally toward whom Askew felt great empathy. When Christian one day sought the governor's advice, Askew's sincere response was: "Pray." Christian later admitted in effect that he took $29,000 in kickbacks from a longtime friend doing business with the Department of Education, and committed perjury in lying about it. He paid $43,000 in fines and restitution, and served several months in prison for federal income tax evasion.

Scandal had hit closer to the governor's office a year earlier when the *Fort Lauderdale News* and Tampa television station *WTVT* revealed that Lieutenant Governor Tom Adams, whom Askew had assigned to run the Department of Commerce, was using a state employee to work, while on state time, on a cattle farm that Adams had quietly leased in Gadsden County west of Tallahassee. Askew ordered the state personnel director to investigate, uncovering other improper work that Adams had assigned to the employee. Adams was fired as commerce secretary, dropped from Askew's 1974 re-election ticket and forced to repay the state $1,736 for the employee's time and travel expenses. "I cannot condone the practices followed in this situation," Askew told a news conference.[16]

In the wake of the Adams and Cabinet scandals, Askew tried to persuade the Legislature to require full financial disclosure from major officeholders in the state and local governments. When the Legislature balked, Askew led Florida's first successful petition campaign to place the issue on the November 1976 general election ballot. The voters overwhelmingly adopted Askew's "Sunshine Amendment," writing both personal financial disclosure and campaign finance disclosure into the Florida Constitution.[17]

In addition to its disclosure requirements, the Amendment prohibits members of the Legislature and statewide officials from lobbying their former government body or agency for two years after leaving office, prohibits incumbent legislators from representing clients before any state agency, and makes public officials and employees financially liable to the state for breaches of the public trust.

DECISION MODELS

Reviewing these cases brings into focus some of the decisions public officials must make. As each of the potential scandals came to Askew, he faced essentially the same moral dilemma. He could: (1) act promptly on the serious information before him and call upon the appropriate investigators and prosecutorial authorities to act immediately; (2) delay his decision, buying time for himself to consider every ramification but also providing helpful time for the parties involved; or (3) ignore the information as incomplete and not sufficient to warrant his action. Askew's pattern was to choose the first course without hesitation. (And political scientists might ask: Was this period in Florida political history especially scandalous or was it that the people knew a governor was in office who would investigate behavior that previously had been ignored?)

APPROACHING DECISIONS

As public officials approach decision-making, they are faced with an array of competing values and interests. Fundamentally, they are sworn to uphold respectively the Constitution of the United States and, where applicable, the Constitution of their state. Next they are sworn to uphold the *laws* of the land. Pursuant to the laws are official *regulations* that detail how and when certain actions may be taken.

Then there are suggested *guidelines* within the regulations, and then a board or agency has *precedents and procedures* for conducting the public's business that must be followed – not the least of which is a maze of requirements subject to *audit* by other branches of the government. Overarching all those responsibilities is an awareness that both federal and state governments have "inspectors general" who may investigate operations of a given agency at any time.

That's not all. Specific *codes of ethics* exist for federal employees and most state and local officials, and the provisions of these codes have the force of law. Then there are prevailing *court rulings* of the U.S. Supreme Court or the federal appeals court in their region of the nation. Sometimes transcending this multitude of requirements in public decision-making are moral concerns, commonly held beliefs, and values of the public officials involved. These become part of a governing *culture* – the dominant values around which most decisions are made in any particular office or agency of government. Not surprisingly, as all these competing laws, codes, cultures, personal values and procedures intersect and compete, public officials often find themselves in a quagmire from which it seems difficult simply to "do the right thing."

APPLYING VALUES

Peter Madsen and Robert Mertzman of the Center for the Advancement of Applied Ethics at Carnegie-Mellon University suggest that public officials, as they approach decisions, first must distinguish between "management mischief" and "moral mazes." This is not unlike the notion of "cardinal" and "venal" sins in Roman Catholic tradition. The attempt is to recognize that some decisions have greater moral stakes and more significant impact on society than others. "Management mischief" at the national level might include the use of official aircraft for personal and-or partisan use by the White

House Chief. A "moral maze" surely was involved in the decision to enter the Persian Gulf War with its competing and conflicting vales.[18]

It should be noted, for example, that under the conception of management mischief a public employee's home use of an office computer to produce personal work is not morally less deficient than a White House official using federal airplanes for personal or political use. Money isn't the standard; morality is. In like thinking, the Josephson Institute of Ethics emphasizes that the amount of money involved does not determine the morality or immorality of a decision.For 30 pieces of silver, it may be remembered, Judas Iscariot betrayed a 33-year-old Jewish teacher whose subsequent death gave rise to an entirely new religion. For less than $10,000 Americans have sold national secrets involving billions of dollars worth of defense materiel and thousands of lives to avowed enemies of the U.S. In this view, then, the amount of money, though a seeming preoccupation of many in the 1980s in the U.S., does not establish the moral value of a decision.

THE VCR STYLE

Madsen and Mertzman offer three phases of official decision-making, which they shorten to "VCR." The first is the "V" stage, wherein "Values and Virtues" of the decision-maker are brought into focus. These include the person's own "core" values, those "shared" values held jointly with co-workers – such as courage, temperance, strength of character and justice. These may include a keen awareness of "character, conscience and community" – and they lead to the application of "virtues," which are defined as "developed dispositions to do the right thing in certain recurrent situations." Many official decisions never seem to have begun at this stage, and these often are the decisions citizens oppose after they assess according to their own values and virtues.

The second is the "C" stage, wherein the decision-maker weighs "contingencies and consequences." (Compare this with the consequentialist and teleological exemplars in Chapter 3.) Madsen and Mertzman ask: "Has the (official) acted in such a way that good consequences are produced or ... that produced evil or harm?" If this is the point from which many official actions emanate – a mere analysis and assessment of the positive and negative aspects of a decision – what is missing?

The third is the "R" stage, where officials evaluate the "rights and responsibilities" of all the parties involved. (Compare this with the deontological and Kantian exemplars of Chapter 3.) Duties, obligations and responsibilities to obey various prescriptions – official and unofficial – provide the *dominant* motivations for the decision-maker. [19]

THE JOSEPHSON MODEL

In developing a decision-making model that avoids the shortcomings of each traditional theory and that can be practically applied to common problems, the Josephson Institute has combined features of each and added the stakeholder concept. Josephson terms its theory "Golden Kantian Consequentialism" – a combination of the Golden Rule, Kant's categorical imperative and a healthy dose of consequentialist doctrine. There are three steps:

I. All decisions must take into account and reflect a concern for the interest and well being of all stakeholders.

II. Ethical values and principles *always* take precedence over nonethical ones.

III. It is ethically proper to violate an ethical principle only when it is *clearly necessary* to advance another *true ethical principle* which, according to the decision maker's conscience, will produce the greatest balance of good *in the long run.*

FIVE STEPS TO PRINCIPLED REASONING

1. CLARIFY – Determine precisely what must be decided. Formulate and devise the full range of alternatives (i.e., things you could do). Eliminate patently impractical, illegal and improper alternatives. Force yourself to develop at least three ethically justifiable options. Examine each option to determine which ethical principles and values are involved.

2. EVALUATE – If any of the options require the sacrifice of any ethical principle, evaluate the facts and assumptions carefully. Distinguish solid facts from beliefs, desires, theories, suppositions, unsupported conclusions, and opinions which might generate rationalizations. Take into account the credibility of the sources of information and the fact that self-interest, bias, and ideological commitments tend to obscure objectivity and affect perceptions about what is true. With regard to each alternative, carefully consider the benefits, burdens and risks to each stakeholder.

3. DECIDE – After evaluating the information available, make a judgment about what is or is not true, and about what consequences are most likely to occur. If there is not an ethical dilemma, evaluate the viable alternatives according to personal conscience, prioritize the values so that you can choose which values to advance and which to subordinate, and determine who will be helped the most and harmed least. It is sometimes helpful to consider the *worst case scenario* – what is the worst outcome possible if things go wrong. In addition, consider whether ethically questionable conduct can be avoided by modifying goals or methods or by consulting with affected people to get their input or consent. Finally, you may want to resort to three *"ethics warning systems."*

> A) **Golden Rule** – Are you treating others as you would want to be treated?
> B) **Publicity** – Would you be comfortable if your reasoning and decision were to be publicized (i.e., how would it look on the front page of tomorrow's papers?).
> C) **Kid-On-Your-Shoulder** – Would you be comfortable if your children were observing you? Are you setting the example you preach?

4. IMPLEMENT – Once a decision is made on *what* to do, develop a plan of *how* to implement the decision in a way that maximizes the benefits and minimizes the costs and risks. Remember, any decision or act – no matter how intrinsically ethical – that is accompanied by a sanctimonious, pious, judgmental or self-righteous attitude, is bound to be less effective, if not counterproductive.

5. MONITOR AND MODIFY – An ethical decision-maker should monitor the effects of decisions and be prepared and willing to revise a plan, or take a different course of action, based on new information. Since most decisions are based on imperfect information and the "best efforts" predictions, it is inevitable that some of them will be wrong. Those decisions will either fail to produce the consequences anticipated or they will produce unintended and/or unforeseen consequences. The ethical decision-maker is willing to adjust to new information.[20]

Source: The Josephson Institute

SEEKING OFFICIAL MORAL ARCHITECTURE

Searching to establish sets of values as a base for official decisions can be a useful but frustrating exercise. Consensus on official values seems a rare commodity at first glance. Consider some of these summations of what constitute the most important official virtues, as researched by Kathryn G. Denhardt in *Ethical Frontiers In Public Management* (Jossey-Bass, 1991, p.101):

- Charles Goodsell (1989) says: "One can argue persuasively that government must be based not only on democratic responsiveness but also on the moral foundations provided by natural law, the Judeo-Christian ethic, or the founding fathers. Values such as equality, justice, honesty, fairness, and the protection of individual rights must prevail, despite election returns, the wording of statutes or the orders of elected officials."

- Worthley and Grumet (1983) cite the roots of public service as being "the rule of law, accountability, efficiency, responsiveness, competence, objectivity, and fairness." Frederickson and Hart advocate a "patriotism of benevolence" that comprises "a combination of patriotism (the love of regime values) with benevolence (the love of others)."

- Terry Cooper (1987) asserts that justice is the main "internal good" (an Alasdair MacIntyre distinction), and Cooper speaks of just practice as being accompanied by popular sovereignty, accountability, due process and the enhancement of excellence. His keys for achieving these goals include benevolence, courage, rationality, fairmindedness, prudence, respect for law, honesty, self-discipline, civility, trustworthiness, respect for colleagues, responsibility for the practices and independence.

- York Wilbern (1984) proposes "six types, or levels, of morality for public officials." These are "basic honesty and conformity to law, conflict of interest, service orientation and procedural fairness, an ethics of democratic responsibility, an ethics of public policy determination and an ethics of compromise and social integration.

- Stephen Bailey (1965) says such basic virtues as honesty and loyalty are relevant for public service but should be presumed and not require explanation. But he adds that a useful list of moral qualities in public servants "begins beyond the obvious and ends where essentiality ends," including "optimism, courage and fairness tempered by charity."[21]

THE DENHARDT DESIGN

Studying these and other paradigms of public service virtue, Kathryn Denhardt arrived at her own triad of values: *honor, benevolence, justice.* Her treatise serves as an excellent synthesis of the values that have been the foundation for the vast majority of public service in American history.

UNEARTHING THE MORAL FOUNDATION OF PUBLIC ADMINISTRATION: HONOR, BENEVOLENCE, AND JUSTICE
Kathryn Denhardt[22]

Honor. Honor is adherence to the highest standards of responsibility, integrity, and principle. It is a term often used to mean being held in public esteem or being well thought of—in other words, a desirable by-product of virtue (MacIntyre, 1966, p.60). But as interpreted here, rather than being a by-product of virtue, honor is the preeminent virtue in that it is understood as magnanimity or greatmindedness, presupposing excellence in all of the virtues (McNamee, 1960, pp.1-7). Honor denotes a quality of character in which the individual exhibits a high sense of duty, pursuing good deeds as ends in themselves, not because of the deeds. It is these high standards of personal integrity and this commitment to principled and responsible conduct that characterize the ideal of public service. Public service is often described as an honor, a privilege, even a calling. In recent times these words have been used most often to involve a revival of this view of public service after years marked by scandal and widespread criticism of public servants. But public service as an honorable calling has remained the ideal, even during difficult times. It challenges public servants to exhibit honor as a most fundamental dimension of that calling.

Why are virtues, or qualities of character, associated with honor so essential to the moral foundations of public administration? For societies to function adequately, social interaction must be based on an assumption of honesty, truth, and the keeping of promises or commitments. This is particularly true of the relationship between members of society and their powerful institutions (especially government but also other institutions and professions). Therefore, the highest standards of honesty and integrity must be the cornerstone of any ethics of public service. Stephen Bailey (1965) argues that honesty is so obviously fundamental that it needs no explanation. Sissela Bok (1978) discusses honesty in detail in *Lying*. It is the basis on which public confidence rests. Without a fundamental commitment to honesty, public administration will have no legitimacy in the eyes of the public and will find its capacity to serve that public severely restricted.

But basic honesty does not sufficiently define what the public administration profession stands for. Beyond honesty, the highest standards of integrity, sincerity, and principle are demanded of us. To be *honorable* is to be known for exhibiting those high standards consistently. It is to put principle before self-interest. It is a standard to which few others are held, certainly a higher standard than usually expected of business executives. But it nevertheless defines in part the moral foundation of public administration.

Honor involves truth telling, avoidance of deception, acknowledging the decisions and actions to which one was a partner, the fulfillment of duty, and holding oneself to a standard higher than self-interest. It requires a commitment to something beyond oneself.

In the case of public administration this commitment is to the public interest, to the principles of democratic governance, and to the moral principles that define the commitments of our social contract.

Honor is a broadly encompassing tenet. It calls public servants to exhibit excellence in virtue. It is the failure to be honorable that raises the "character question" in the eyes of the public. The frequency with which the question of character has arisen in recent years (most often among elected officials and high-level appointees) testifies to the powerful presence of honor as a defining characteristic of the public service ideal. This ideal applies no less to career public servants. And while it might be claimed that it is an impossibly high standard, it nevertheless helps define the moral foundation on which the *ideal* of public service has been built.

Benevolence. In benevolence is found the other-regarding essence of public service. It is the disposition to do good and to promote the welfare of others. The very foundation of public administration is commitment to service (both to the public and the elected representatives of that public). But service is itself but an expression of the more fundamental moral principle of benevolence. Based on the Latin words *bene* (well) and *volens* (wishing), benevolence implies not only *actions* that promote good and the welfare of others but also *motivation* to pursue those ends. This point is important. Beneficence (performing acts of kindness and charity) is a somewhat lower standard in that the acts need only be kind and charitable, but no such motivation or concern is demanded of the individual responsible for the act. Benevolence, in contrast, requires not just doing good but also a driving motivation to do good *for the sake of others.*

It seems clear that in terms of acting on behalf of the welfare of others, public officials are held to a higher standard than those in private life. Private sector managers are expected by many to adhere to a standard of beneficence – expected to act in a socially responsible manner, doing things that provide some benefit to (or at least do not harm) the society. But few would argue that social responsibility should be the primary purpose or motivation for businesses. It is generally accepted that the socially responsible actions of businesses will be motivated by the value placed on good public relations or profit maximization rather than benevolence, but from those in the public sector more is expected.

A recent Hasting Center report discusses the "public duties" of professions, counting public administration among those professions with an explicit public service orientation. Public duties, or "the obligations and responsibilities owed in service to the public as a whole" (Jennings, Callahan, and Wolf, 1987, p.3), encompass an orientation toward both the *common good* ("that which constitutes the well-being of the community") and the *public interest* ("the aggregation of the private interests of individuals") (Jennings, Callahan, and Wolf, 1987, p. 6).

Benevolence is a moral principle that encompasses the public duties of the profession and also prescribes the motivation that should guide the pursuit of these public duties. Benevolence implies both sympathy and enthusiasm (regard for others and purposeful intent to help) – characteristics that Thompson (1975) suggests the public demands of bureaucracies but cannot get. Clearly it is a standard to which not all public officials adhere, but it nevertheless defines the moral foundation on which the profession rests and on the basis of which the public determines its level of trust in the profession.

Codes of ethics directed towards public administrators regularly invoke these notions of the public interest and the common good, describing a public service ideal dedicated to these public duties. The codes of ethics for the American Society for Public Administration and the International City Management Association both make references to the public interest, the good of all, and regard for the interests of others being more important than personal interests (Chandler, 1989). These aspects of the codes are often seen as cautions to avoid conflict-of-interest situations. However, it is important to understand that the fundamental moral principle reflected in these codes is benevolence as a moral imperative. Benevolence clearly requires avoidance of conflicts of interest, but more important, it enjoins public servants to act affirmatively on behalf of others, holding the public in highest regard.

Benevolence, then, encompasses the service organization and the other-regardingness, of public administration and as a moral standard will help administrators recognize and balance obligations to various (and sometimes competing) groups. For example, benevolence requires that public administrators act as advocates on behalf of certain policies and proposals, not merely a technician carrying out the instructions of elected officials.

But "service" in public administration also means to serve the particular administration in which one finds oneself, and a moral standard of benevolence provides support of that kind of service as well. By grounding a service orientation on the standard of benevolence rather than on institutional obligations to particular officials, however, the profession will be better able to discern the appropriate course of action on those occasions when service obligations to various groups come into conflict with one another. When serving the interests of a particular elected official coincides with acting benevolently to pursue the public interest, no conflict exists. But when service to the elected official comes in conflict with the interests of the public, the moral standard of benevolence should provide some guidance for the administrator in discerning the acceptable limits to serving either group.

Justice. Justice signifies fairness and regard for the rights of others. The rights of others include, most fundamentally, respect for the dignity and worth of each individual. This is the foundation of democratic morality as Redford (1969) has described it, but it is also the foundation of Kant's "categorical imperative" and Rawls's (1971) theory of justice.

Attendant to basic respect for the dignity and worth of individuals is a commitment to developing and preserving rights for individuals that will ensure that their dignity and worth will not be violated by others in the society. Such rights are essential to a just society. As Aristotle argues, "Political justice is manifested between persons who share a common way of life which has for its object a state of affairs in which they will have all they need for an independent existence as free and equal members of the society," and, "Justice can exist only among those whose relations to one another are governed by law" (1953, p.156).

For public administration, then , a commitment to justice demands that public servants be committed to respecting the dignity and worth of every member of the society, to promoting a government of laws that protects the rights of those free and equal members of the society. Even though the role of the public administrator is not to make laws or to define rights for individuals, even applying and implementing the law properly are possible only for someone committed to the principle of justice.

Because justice can only be ensured through the virtuous acts of public servants *and* through a set of laws and other institutions that protect the rights of individuals, one can see the strong connection between the moral foundations of public administration and the institutions of democratic governance. Democracy, the Constitution, laws, and "regime values," then, are institutional means of achieving justice and are thus to be respected and upheld. But it is important to recognize that these institutions are means and not ends in themselves. *Justice* is a fundamental moral principle helping form the moral foundation of public administration. It is because they rest on this principle of justice that the law and regime values are to be respected and upheld. Only by putting justice first, followed by laws and regime values, will public administrators be able to identify and oppose unjust laws, interpretations of regime values that are unfair or inequitable, and other forms of injustice that are inevitable in any society. In contrast, if obedience to the law is identified as the primary moral imperative, then it is implied that even unjust laws are to be actively upheld by public administrators.

In the fundamental moral principle of justice we find the foundation needed to support public administration's commitment to democracy, individual rights, regime values, laws and the constitutional order. Justice requires that public administrators permit and promote informed participation in the governing process. It requires commitment to equality and fairness as rights that individuals can claim. It requires that administrators act to improve the decision-making process in their area of responsibility, giving full consideration to how current policies affect future structure of rights and legitimacy of institutions (Moore, 1981).

An argument for identifying justice as an essential element of the *ethos* of public administration is not new. For example, justice was the cornerstone of the ethics advanced by the new public administration (Hart, 1974; Henry, 1975). Where the argument of this chapter differs from earlier arguments is that justice is seen as one of three fundamental values – neither the single most important moral imperative nor only one of a long list of principles and virtues.

Honor, benevolence, and justice together delineate the moral foundations of public administration ethics. They offer the essence of the many ideals that characterize public service ethics and do so in a way that permits a ready answer to the question: What does public administration really stand for? Few of us could identify many of the components of commonly referred to codes of ethics because the codes are relatively long and detailed. Honor, benevolence, and justice capture the essence of these longer codes, but with the advantage of providing a more easily articulated identity and moral focus to the enterprise of public administration.

Identifying a core of fundamental values (as opposed to a single most important principle) creates a situation whereby excessive zeal for any one of the moral principles will be tempered by the other two. As Aristotle argues, "It is the nature of moral qualities that they can be destroyed by deficiency on the one hand and excess on the other" (1953, p.58). Thus defining the essence of public administration ethics as justice, or equality, or any other single moral principle opens up the possibility that the unbridled pursuit of that single moral good will result in unacceptable excesses that would then erode the very foundation on which public administration ethics rests.

A definition of the moral foundations of public administration that balances the complementary and competing values of honor, benevolence, and justice will lead to striking the mean in each. For example, benevolence in excess implies paternalism. Justice, in contrast, demands self-determination. Any tendency toward paternalism, therefore, could be "checked" by the principle of justice. Because justice tends to focus on individual rights, taken to the extreme it might stand in the way of working toward the common good. Benevolence, as it is oriented toward doing good for others, could be a check on excessive individualism. Whereas honesty associated with honor would appear to require telling the truth regardless of any harm that might result (as in some national security areas), both benevolence and justice would permit otherwise. Where benevolence requires extraordinary efforts to help others, justice offers a mitigating influence, as it compels consideration of the burden borne by those who must pay for the helping services (that is, taxpayers). Finally, while benevolence and justice articulate moral principles, it is honor that defines the virtue, or quality of character, necessary to put principle into action.

Conclusion

All three imperatives – honor, benevolence, and justice – make up the moral foundation of public administration, and this foundation should have a central place in the education of students of public affairs and administration. Teaching these moral imperatives is not moral indoctrination. It is instead the obligation and prerogative of a profession to impart its values to those seeking to enter the profession. Articulating, studying, and internalizing these moral commitments are essential steps in becoming a true professional.

Students of public administration can develop an awareness of these guiding principles and can be assisted in cultivating these principles and virtues in their own lives and actions. The education process can help students equip themselves with the skills needed to act virtuously. For example, Stephen K. Bailey suggested that there are three essential mental attitudes: "(1) a recognition of the moral ambiguity of all men and of all public policies, (2) a recognition of the contextual forces which condition moral priorities in the public service, and (3) a recognition of the paradoxes of procedures" (1965, p.285). By helping students to develop these and other awarenesses and attitudes, educators help them to act in a principled and virtuous manner without being rigid, absolutist, or dogmatic.

For practitioners, the identification of the moral foundations of public administration ethics would help restore a meaningful identity to a discipline that has experienced an identity crisis during the past three decades. A strong foundation provides an anchor for resisting unreasonable demands felt during shifting political winds. It also helps practitioners readily articulate the meaning of public service, thus serving both as an essential guide to action and as a defense of the legitimacy of public administration when questioned by other entities.

A case has been made for honor, benevolence, and justice as the moral foundations of public administration ethics. Perhaps this can serve as a springboard to the next step of engaging in dialogue about these moral foundations, a dialogue involving critique, elaboration, and adjustment. Research in the discipline has already begun to examine the role of virtue in public administration ethics, and the continuation of this line of research will illuminate the meaning of honor in public service. Justice, as a central principle of public administration ethics, has been explored in some detail over the past 20 years, but the principle of benevolence has not. Discouraged about the possibility of defining "the public interest," scholars have generally abandoned the effort. By recasting the public interest question in terms of benevolence, perhaps the line of research could be resurrected – not in terms of defining the specific content of the public interest but in terms of the duty and motivation to be other-regarding – and could *pursue* the public interest and the common good. Finally, research on the *interaction among and balancing of* multiple public service values might prove very fruitful. Arguments for any single moral principle serving as the focus of public administration ethics will be met with numerous examples of potential abuses. A response to this problem might be finding a combination of core principles with the potential of creating an equilibrium.

NOTE

McNamee (1960) explores the changing concept of honor over the centuries. He describes a shift from the exaggerated individualism of the concept of honor among ancient Greeks to periods of exaggerated statism. He also describes "an attempt on the part of Christianity to check, elevate, and transform both exaggerations with the new virtues of humility and charity" (1960, p. 181). It is this latter concept of honor – one characterized by humility and charity – that influenced 19th century liberalism and the birth of public administration as a profession.[23]

COMPARING ETHICAL SYSTEMS

Now when you see a public official making a decision, you might ask which of the above sets of values were dominant in the decision. Further, you can evaluate these decision models according to the dominant "ethical system" in each, as propounded by William Hitt in *Ethics and Leadership* (Battelle Press, Columbus, Ohio, pp.66-67):

> **END-RESULT ETHICS – John Stuart Mill (1806-1873) – The moral rightness of an action is determined by considering its consequences.** "I would make the decision on the basis of *expected results*, what would give us the greatest return on investment."
>
> **RULE ETHICS – Immanuel Kant (1724-1804) – The moral rightness of an action is determined by laws and standards.** "I would make the decision on the basis of *what the law says*, on the legality of the matter."
>
> **SOCIAL CONTRACT ETHICS – Jean Jacques Rousseau (1712- 1778) – The moral rightness of an action is determined by the customs and norms of a particular community.** "I would make the decision on the basis of the *strategy and values* of my organization."
>
> **PERSONALISTIC ETHICS – Martin Buber (1878-1965) – The moral rightness of an action is determined by one's conscience.** "I would make the decision on the basis of my *personal convictions* and what my conscience told me to do." [24]

For the *elected* official, there apparently is a significant difference between the kinds of decision-dilemmas faced as a candidate and those faced as a politician in office. Walter Lippman, longtime Washington-based journalist and political critic, said: "The role of the leader would be easier to define if it were agreed to give separate meanings to two very common words ... 'politician' and 'statesman.'"

For Lippman, the politician says: "I will give you what you want." But the statesman says: "What you think you want is this. What it is possible for you to get is that. What you really want, therefore, is the following ... " Lippman concludes: "The politician stirs up a following; the statesman leads it."

Further contrasting the two roles, Lippman adds: "The politician, in brief, accepts unregenerate desire at its face value and either fulfills it or perpetrates a fraud; the statesman reeducates desire by confronting it with the reality, and so makes possible an enduring adjustment of interests within the community."

Where can such leadership be found? "It requires courage, which is possible only in a mind that is detached from the agitations of the moment," Lippman postulates. "It requires insight, which comes only from an objective and discerning knowledge of the facts, and a high and imperturbable disinterestedness."[25]

CONFLICTS OF INTEREST

A focus of ethical concern that seems to be perpetually challenging includes conflicts of interest, real and apparent. Discussed broadly among professions, business and government in Chapter 1, the discussion here focuses on actual cases wherein conflicts of interest officially were ruled upon by the

Florida Commission on Ethics. In reviewing these case rulings, identify the ethical dilemmas and the various conflicting interests. In public acts, obviously, the democratic society itself is one interest, the public official another, and then various other interests of a personal, professional or agency nature compete for the official's primary allegiance.

> **Case 1:** No prohibited conflict of interest would exist were a circuit court clerk to attend an annual conference for the Florida Association of Court Clerks where some of the meals and activities are sponsored by entities doing business with county governments. The purpose of the conference is to provide continuing education and training for the clerks attending. As stated in earlier Commission opinions, the Code of Ethics does not absolutely prohibit a public officer from accepting a gift or other thing of value from a business entity which may be doing business with his agency, and it does not prohibit a public officer from accepting hospitality within reasonable limits. Rather, whether an official may accept such a gift depends on the intent of the donor and on the circumstances under which it is given. Here, the fact that some meals and social hours are sponsored by entities doing business with county governments does not create a prohibited conflict of interest.[26]

The commission raises the notion that a public official should consider "the intent of the donor" and "the circumstances" under which the gift is given. The official will rely heavily on documents related to the event to substantiate claims of sufficient disinterest by the giver and the official.

> **Case 2:** Section 112.313(2)(a), F.S. 1975, prohibiting a public officer or employee from accepting any gift which would cause a reasonably prudent person to be influenced in the discharge of his public duty, was declared to be unconstitutionally vague by the Florida Supreme Court. Anderson vs. D'Alemberte, S.Ct. Case No. 49,851. Paragraph (b) prohibits a public employee from accepting a gift that is based upon any understanding that the official action or judgment of the employee would be influenced thereby. In the absence of any such understanding, the provision would not be violated were employees of a municipal building department to accept a box of candy from a general contractor or were an official of the department to accept a magnum of whiskey from an aluminum contractor.
>
> However, s. 112.313(4) further prohibits a public employee from accepting anything of value which the employee knows, or with the exercise of reasonable care should know, was given to influence his official action. This provision similarly requires knowledge on the part of the public employee, or circumstances which strongly suggest, that a particular gift is being given with the intent that the employee's future official action will be influenced. In the absence of any testimony to this effect, we can only offer the language of the provision for guidance. Also, please note that a person required to file financial disclosure by s. 112.3145. F.S., must disclose gifts of $100 in value received during the disclosure period.[27]

This case, among other things, demonstrates the public official's burden of trying to interpret vaguely drawn laws and how something as seemingly insignificant as a box of candy can spell ethical trouble.

> **Case 3:** A prohibited conflict of interest is created where a city councilwoman owns a material interest in a wrecker business which accepts wrecker rotation list calls from the police department for the towing of impounded vehicles, at city expense, as a public officer is prohibited from acting in a probate capacity to sell services to any agency of his political subdivision, Fla. Stat. s. 112.313(3)(1975). Although Florida Statues s. 112.316 provides that it is not the intention of the Code of Ethics to preclude private pursuits which do not interfere with the discharge of public duty, this provision is inapplicable in the instant case, as the rotation list does not contain the names of all licensed wreckers in the city. Rather, the chief of police has the authority to establish requirements for wrecker services appearing on the list. Inasmuch as the police chief is employed by and is subject to the supervision of

the city council, the potential for interference with public duty is not precluded. However, calls may be accepted for the towing of disabled vehicles for which service the vehicle owner pays.[28]

Some cases are easier than others. When a public official's authority can affect a decision that directly benefits a business interest of that public official, no Socratic debate is needed: Conflict of interest.

> **Case 4:** Section 112.313(7)(a), Florida Statues , prohibits a public officer from having any employment or contractual relationship with a business entity which is doing business with his agency. CEO's 74-82, 78-55, 84-112, 82-28, 88-19, and 81-76 are referenced.[29]

An even less subtle conflict surfaces when a public official fails to recognize the conflict of interest in serving for compensation with two entities who enter into a contractual relationship.

> **Case 5:** An alternate member of the city board of adjustment is prohibited by Section 112.3143, Florida Statutes, from voting on variance petitions of persons who are clients of his surveying and engineering firm at the time of the vote and from voting on variance petitions where the client is expected to require further surveying or engineering work as a result of the decision on the variance. CEO's 78-59 and 84-1 are referenced.[30]

How easy it is, in selecting an "alternate" appointed official, to name "someone who really knows this business" – someone actually *in* that business. How easy, and how clearly creating a conflict of interest. (At the end of this chapter consider five other case rulings.)

SUMMARY

This lone chapter barely scratches the surface of the complexities of official decision-making within an ethical context. But we have seen that (1) public officials do have ethical and moral responsibilities beyond merely obeying the law, (2) there are core values that contribute to effective and honorable public service, (3) processes and systems exist for ethical official decision-making, and (4) there, indeed, are individuals who have taken seriously the "calling" of public service and have performed honorably. Meanwhile, voters still need a healthy skepticism of a campaigner's promises and a well-founded respect for the checks and balances of the three branches of government and for the role the media play in uncovering dishonorable public service.

It is highly unlikely any single law or code will guarantee ethical public service, but reformers hope that the raising of standards and the discussion of new laws, modified codes and ethical decision-making processes ultimately will contribute to government in which the people's trust can be more justifiably placed.

READINGS
DANGERS OF THE 'QUICK FIX' ETHICS LEGISLATION

Bonnie J. Williams
Executive Director
Florida Commission On Ethics[31]

As evidenced by the Council on Governmental Ethics Laws' own experience in developing model laws, the drafting of ethics legislation is a complex undertaking. Reaching a consensus on issues highly subjective in nature requires a great deal of skill and cooperation, as does the drafting of language sufficiently clear to put affected officials on notice of the standards to which their behavior is expected to conform. Among the many conflicting considerations are the preservation of public trust vs. officials' rights to a degree of privacy in their personal lives; whether particular issues are best addressed by public disclosure or outright prohibition; and the degree to which the public's right to know unreasonably interferes with the efficient administration of governmental functions.

Deliberations generally are long and torturous, often giving rise to heated arguments. In the legislative arena, these intrinsic difficulties are exacerbated by legislators' personal stake in ethics legislation; i.e., the fear that they are constructing traps into which they themselves risk becoming ensnared. In Florida, and I suspect in most other states, this self-protective instinct is so strong as to render legislators unwilling and virtually incapable of addressing ethics reform absent an unusually strong push from the outside.

That push most often comes from the media. The Ethics Commission, Common Cause, League of Women Voters, and others can make impassioned pleas for ethics reform, but seldom is there any meaningful response by the Legislature until the media become involved. Moreover, the more intense and long-running a story, and the closer it hits home, the more likely and the more quickly the issue is to be addressed by the Legislature. Paradoxically, this can be detrimental, as the rush to respond to media pressure undercuts the very elements necessary for the development of meaningful, articulate ethics laws, and the resulting "cure" may be as bad as or worse than the malaise itself.

Florida's new gift law, touted by persons unfamiliar with its intricacies as one of the strongest in the nation, is illustrative of the dangers inherent in quickfix ethics legislation. Battered by media stories of legislators' numerous trips at the expense of lobbyists, the Florida Legislature convened in special session in the fall of 1990 to quell the rising tide of indignation through the introduction and passage of what was promised to be a comprehensive bill relating to gifts. A joint committee, working within a very limited time frame, made a pretense of taking public testimony. It became apparent, however, that the bill's conceptual framework had been preconceived by the leadership and that this groundwork had been laid without the input of any agency or organization with experience in the administration of ethics laws.

Among the preconceptions was that the gift law should apply to persons who file financial disclosure, which includes approximately 40,000 public officers (elected and appointed) and employees statewide, at both the state and local government levels. Of questionable logic to begin with, this decision proved to be profoundly unwise as the substantive provisions of the bill unfolded, creating ethical quagmires, if not outright traps, for thousands upon thousands of public servants throughout the state.

Taking its cue from press reports, the joint committee quickly focused on gifts from "lobbyists," defining a lobbyist essentially as one who for compensation seeks, or within the past 12 months sought, to influence governmental decision-making of a "reporting individual," i.e., any one of the 40,000 or so persons subject to disclosure. Persons who attempt to influence "governmental decision-making," of course, include many not generally perceived as "lobbyists" in the common understanding of that term. Vendors of goods and services, for example, come within the law's purview. The already significant problem of an official's being aware of every person trying to influence decisions within his agency is further magnified by the law's prohibition against the acceptance, directly or indirectly, of gifts valued at over $100 not only from agency lobbyists, but also from the partners, firms, employers, or principals of such lobbyists. (Although the statute stipulates that such prohibited gifts would have to be accepted "knowingly" in order to constitute a violation, affected officials find cold comfort in the language as it shifts the burden of proof to the recipient of a gift, who would have to demonstrate in a complaint proceeding that he was not aware that the donor was among the classes of persons prohibited from providing the gift.)

Apparently in recognition of this problem of identifying prohibited donors, and in a striking display of myopia, legislators included an alternative: If an agency has established a lobbyist registration system, the term "lobbyist" includes only those persons registered with that system. In other words, the impact of the law presumably can be narrowed through the adoption of a rule or ordinance which contains a more restrictive definition of "lobbyist," and, again presumably, every city, county, state department, and special district can adopt its own unique definition. It is noteworthy that the Florida Legislature already has a lobbyist registration system which identifies both lobbyists and their principals, affording legislators immediate access to a list of persons from whom they cannot solicit or accept gifts. As virtually none of Florida's 67 counties or 396 municipalities had at the time the law was passed, or to my knowledge have today, a lobbyist registration system, local officials are handicapped in terms of knowing or learning who may have endeavored to influence decision-making within their agencies, much less know who those persons' partners, firms, employers, or principals may be.

SELF-SERVICE

Even more blatantly self-serving on the part of the Legislature is a section of the law which affords a legislator the right to receive within 10 days a legal opinion about the law's applicability from the general counsel of the house of which he is a member, upon which opinion the legislator "may reasonably rely." This opportunity is in addition to that afforded all public officers and employees to receive legally binding opinions from the Commission on Ethics. No such provision for quick and friendly service (not to mention defense from prosecution) was made on behalf of other statewide elected officers, local elected officers, appointed officers state and local, or the thousands of state and local employees covered by the law. It goes without saying that the existence of three separate bodies of legal opinion (issued by the Commission on Ethics, the Senate, and the House of Representatives) has created some confusion and uncertainty about how the law is to be interpreted.

It is difficult to believe that these and other short-sighted aspects of the (new) law would have withstood scrutiny had there been time to scrutinize. Even had there been more time, though, it is unlikely that many of the loopholes and ambiguities would have been discovered by those following the bill's progress simply as a result of it being so difficult to comprehend. Sections are arranged illogically, definitions defy common sense, and the underlying rationale for many provisions is unclear. Even after a year and a half of working with the law, virtually no one is comfortable discussing any aspect of it without first reviewing the statute itself at the very least, and often rules and opinions interpreting it as well.

The word "gift," for example, is defined as "that which is accepted by a donee or by another on the donee's behalf, or that which is paid or given to another for or on behalf of a donee, directly, indirectly, or in trust for his benefit or by any other means, for which equal or greater consideration is not given," followed by a long list of examples. The list, which is comprehensive, ends with "(a)ny other similar service or thing having an attributable value not already provided for in this section." Curiously, though, one of the examples is "(f)ood or beverage, other than that consumed at a single sitting or event." This exception

is hammered home in the next subsection, which lists what "gift" does *not* include, one of seven examples of which is "(f)ood or beverage consumed at a single sitting or event," thus ensuring beyond any doubt the continuance of a longstanding perquisite of legislative service.

Equally enigmatic is an exception for "(s)alary, benefits, services, fees, commissions, *gifts*, or expenses associated primarily with the donee's employment or business" from the definition of "gift." (Emphasis supplied.) That there may be instances in which a gift is not a gift is perplexing. Even more discomfiting is the notion that a public employee who is provided a gift associated with that employment has not received a "gift" under the gift law, the exception thus subsuming the rule. (This was not the intended effect, but another example of the Legislature's egocentrism. The Legislature apparently overlooked or disregarded the fact that the law applies to public employees as well as to public officers and that "employment" therefore could be interpreted to mean public employment as well as employment outside of government.)

Having defined "gift" and having determined that gifts from lobbyists and their principals (as well as certain political committees) valued at over $100 should be prohibited, the joint committee fleshed out the new gifts law largely in response to "what abouts" and "what ifs." It was determined that gifts otherwise prohibited can be accepted on behalf of a governmental entity or charitable organization; from state government entities, counties, municipalities, school boards, and airport authorities if a public purpose can be shown for the gift; and, obscurely, from a direct-support organization for a governmental entity if the recipient is an officer or employee of that entity. Based on the examples of a House member who is married to a lobbyist and another who is engaged to a lobbyist, the joint committee struggled with how to handle gifts from family and intimate friends. Ultimately, the bill draft declared in its opening subsection (probably the last place one would look for an exemption to the law) that the provisions of the gift law do not apply to gifts solicited or accepted by a reporting individual from a relative. Then "relative" was defined to include, in addition to the usual blood and step kin, "(a) person who is engaged to be married to the public officer or employee or who otherwise holds himself or herself out as or is generally known as the person whom the public officer or employee intends to form a household, or any other natural person having the same legal residence as the public officer or employee."

A second major section of the bill, dealing with honoraria, applies to the same group of public officers and employees, deals with the same types of donors, and suffers from some of the same infirmities as the gift section. But it has the added distinction of seeking to regulate activity which never has been an issue here in Florida. In a nutshell, honoraria related to public position may not be solicited or accepted from lobbyists or their principals. However, "the payment or provision of actual and reasonable transportation, lodging, and food and beverage expenses related to (an) honorarium event" is acceptable for both the reporting individual and spouse, provided such expenses are disclosed.

And the law does provide for disclosure. Gifts promised or received before January 1, 1991 are reportable under the old law as part of the annual financial disclosure statement. Gifts valued at over $100 (other than those otherwise prohibited, those from relatives, or those associated primarily with the recipient's employment or business; gifts from certain governmental entities; honorarium-related expenses; or the use of a public facility or public property, made available by a governmental agency, for a public purpose) received after January 1, 1991 are reportable quarterly. Gifts received from governmental entities and direct support organizations are reportable annually by July 1, as are reports of honorarium-related expenses. Additionally, donors (lobbyists, their principals, etc.) must report gifts between $25 and $100 to reporting individuals on a quarterly basis and must notify the intended recipient at the time a reportable gift is made that the gift will be disclosed. Governmental entities and direct support organizations must report gifts to reporting individuals by March 1 of each year for the preceding calendar year, and lobbyists who pay official expenses related to an honorarium event must provide the recipient a report of the expenses within 60 days of the honorarium event.

BEWILDERING AND BYZANTINE

The plethora of players, prohibitions, exceptions, and disclosures is bewildering. While the adoption of rules by the Commission on Ethics has added a measure of consistency to interpretation of the law by the Commission, its staff, and a handful of persons with the tenacity to follow through on the legislation, most claim that the rules simply have added another layer of complexity to an already inscrutable law. They have thrown up their hands in exasperation, despairing of ever coming to grips with it.

I want to make it clear, if perhaps somewhat belatedly, that I do not ascribe bad motives to the Florida Legislature in its passage of this law. Self-protection is among the most basic of human instincts, and ambiguity is central to the philosophy of ethics. Given these two conditions, it is my proposition that no area of the law requires a greater commitment of time and reliance on expertise in its drafting than do ethics laws. Ideally, legislatures would acknowledge the political climate that demands ethics reform, would assign their best and brightest to the task, and would commit the time and resources necessary to garner expertise, conduct research, and propose articulate legislation supported by meaningful data. There is too much at risk to do otherwise. Poorly conceived and poorly written ethics laws not only create traps which can wreck political careers. they also trivialize and discredit the entire area of governmental ethics and erode respect for both the makers of the law and its administrators.

FOR FURTHER INQUIRY

SUGGESTED READINGS

• James S. Bowman, Editor, *Ethical Frontiers In Public Management,* Jossey-Bass Inc., Publishers, San Francisco, Calif. 1991
• Michael Josephson, *Making Ethical Decisions,* The Josephson Institute of Ethics, Marina del rey, Calif. 1991
• William D. Hitt, *Ethics andLeadership,* Battelle Press, Columbus, Ohio
• Walter Lippmannm, *A Preface To Morals,* pp. 279-81,83, Transaction Publishers, Brunswick, N.J. 1982

EXERCISES:

Following are five rulings of the Florida Commission on Ethics as to conflicts of interests involving public officials. Consider each case and answer these questions:

1. What are the conflicting interests?

2. Using one of the "decision models" described in the chapter, identify the stage of the decision-making process where the conflict should have been identified and determine upon what basis a decision should have been made to avoid the conflict.

Case A: An attorney for the Florida Real Estate Commission is prohibited by s. 112.313(7), F. S. 1975, from holding outside employment as a real estate salesman or broker, as he would be employed by a business entity subject to the regulation of his public agency, the Real Estate Commission, and would hold employment which creates a continuing conflict between his private interests and the performance of his public duties and potentially would interfere with the full and faithful discharge of his public duties. His public responsibility is to advise and interpret state laws pertaining to real estate licensing, to prepare rules, and to prosecute or defend matters as directed by the Commission. Such duties would not necessarily coincide with his private real estate interests. The Ethics Commission is unable to advise whether or not conflicts might exist in such attorney engaging in the private practice of law, as opinions must be issued within a particular factual context [see s. 112.322(3)(a)] rather than offering general guidelines.[32]

Case B: A prohibited conflict of interest is created where an elected mayor of a municipality is employed within that city as the designated fire and rescue employee. Although said employee is compensated by the county pursuant to an interlocal agreement, he would be subject to the supervision of the municipal fire chief administrative officer of the city. He therefore would hold employment with an agency in violation of s. 112.313(7)(a), F.S. 1975.[33]

Case C: A prohibited conflict of interest exists where a state wildlife officer accepts outside employment involving security patrol and wildlife law enforcement for a private landowner within the area to which he is assigned as an officer, and where the land is used for hunting by the landowner, his guests or associates. Employment of this type would present a continuing or frequently recurring conflict with the wildlife officer's public duties to check for compliance with the game laws and to arrest for violations. CEO's 78-29, 78-82, 79-23, and 81-67 are referenced. A prohibited conflict of interest exists where a wildlife biologist with the Commission is employed with a private hunting club to perform consulting work relating to deer populations on the club's land. As the employee's duties include advising landowners and hunting clubs regarding deer management and analyzing permits necessary to manage deer herds, this type of outside employment would impede the full and faithful discharge of his public duties in violation of Section 112.313(7), Florida Statutes. A prohibited conflict of interest would be created were a fisheries biologist supervisor with the Commission, whose position requires that he be involved in restoration of public lakes, to accept outside employment involving native aquatic plant transplanting on public lakes for riparian owners. However, the employee may accept outside employment involving restoration, management, and native aquatic plant transplanting on private lakes, as his public duties do not involve private lakes.[34]

Case D: No prohibited conflict of interest under the Code of Ethics would be created were a state employee to do consulting work with the federal Department of Health, Education and Welfare relative to programs being developed in other states in his field of expertise. There is no violation of Fla. Stat. s. 112.313(7)(1975), for the state exercises no regulatory authority over a department of the federal government; nor is "business" transacted between the two. Florida Statues s. 112.313(8) is not breached, because the employee's expertise would not be utilized by another state agency or by any political subdivision of the state which would be bound by or directly related to state standards and regulations. Only where outside employment interferes or conflicts with one's public duty is it to be discouraged on an ethical basis. See Fla. Stat. s. 112.316(1975). The Commission on Ethics exercises no jurisdiction, however, over ethics regulations unique to particular agencies of state government so long as the state code is not contradicted.

Case E: A prohibited conflict of interest exists where a secretary in a city attorney's office is employed part-time as the administrator of the city's police pension trust fund and where the city and the pension board have been and in the future may be in litigation. Because of the secretary's access to confidential information in the city attorney's office, her employment as administrator of the pension board would present a continuing or frequently recurring conflict of interest prohibited by Section 112.313(7)(a), Florida Statutes.

Whether a public employee should be precluded from outside employment on the basis of the amount of time required by the outside employment is a matter for the discretion of the public employer and is not addressed by the Code of Ethics. Whether a public employee's outside employment will result in a conflict of interest will turn on the nature of the interests of both employers, not whether the employee has adequate time to properly perform the responsibilities of both jobs.

ENDNOTES

1. Michael Richardson, personal interview with Reubin Askew, 1970.
2. Donald Pride, personal experience or interview with Reubin Askew.
3. Frank Trippett, *The States: United They Fell,* World Publishing Company ,Cleveland, Ohio. 1967.
4-8. Ibid.
9. Congressional Research Service, Jan. 29, 1993, *CRS Issue Brief on Campaign Financing*
10. Pride, personal interview.
11. Neal R. Peirce, *The Megastates of America,* W.W. Norton & Co., New York, N.Y. 1972
12. Anne Marie Donahue, editor, *Ethics in Politics and Government*, H. W. Wilson Co. 1989
13. Jack Bass and Walter De Vries, *The Transformation of Southern Politics*, 1976, Basic Books.
14. Office of Attorney General of Florida, *Government in the Sunshine Manual,* 1993, First Amendment Foundation
15. Pride, personal interview.
16-17. Ibid.
18. Robert Mertzman and Peter Madsen, *Ethical Issues in Professional Life: A Multimedia Course* (unpublished), Carnegie-Mellon University, Pittsburgh, Penn. Copyright 1992.
19. Ibid.
20. Michael Josephson, *Making Ethical Decisions,* pp. 20-26. The Josephson Institute of Ethics, Marina Del Rey, Calif. 1991.
21. James S. Bowman, Editor, *Ethical Frontiers In Public Management,* Jossey-Bass Inc., Publishers, San Francisco, Calif. 1991.
22. Kathryn Denhardt, "Unearthing the Moral Foundations of Public Administration: Honor, Benevolence, Justice," *Ethical Frontiers In Public Management,* pp. 101-111, Jossey-Bass. 1991.
23. Ibid.
24. William D. Hitt, *Ethics and Leadership*, pp. 98, 100-101. Battelle Press, Columbus, Ohio, 1974.
25. Walter Lippmannm, *A Preface To Morals,* pp. 279-81,83, Transaction Publishers, Brunswick, N.J., 1982.
26. Florida Commission on Ethics, CEO 86-73 – September 17, 1986.
27. Ibid. CEO 77-96 – July 21, 1977.
28. Ibid. CEO 76-148A – October 25,1976, (CEO 76-148 revoked).
29. Ibid. CEO 88-25 – April 28, 1988.
30. Ibid. CEO 86-9 – February 20, 1986.
31. Bonnie Williams, executive director, Florida Commission On Ethics, an unpublished speech.
32. Florida Commission on Ethics. CEO 76-207 – December 16, 1976.
33. Ibid. CEO 77-11 – February 1, 1977.
34. Ibid. CEO 85-1 – January 24, 1985.
35. Ibid. CEO 76-28 – February 13, 1976.
36. Ibid. CEO 75-185 – October 1, 1975.

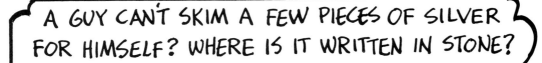

Chapter 21

Keith Goree

CODES OF ETHICS

"The last temptation is the greatest treason: To do the right deed for the wrong reason."

– T.S. Eliott

"Seven sins: Wealth without work. Pleasure without conscience. Knowledge without character. Commerce without morality. Science without humility. Worship without sacrifice. Politics without principle."

– Mahatma Gandhi

"The Japanese recognize that there are really only two demands of leadership: One is to accept that rank does not confer privileges, it entails responsibilities. The other is to acknowledge that leaders in an organization need to impose on themselves that congruence between deeds and actions, between behavior and professed beliefs and values, that we call 'personal integrity'."

– Peter Drucker

A young accountant in New York City is offered an "incentive bonus" of 15% of the amount he saves a corporation on its state and federal taxes this year. Should he accept the deal? In Dallas, a buyer for a major department store chain opens his mail one morning to find a rather expensive gift from a supplier with a note thanking him for placing such a large order. Should he keep it? A California state senator is told by a lobbyist for a powerful special interest group that strings can be pulled to get the politician's underachieving son into a prestigious Ivy League university if the senator will vote against an upcoming bill. Should she do so?

What do these scenarios have in common? Of course, they represent situations requiring ethical decisions. More than that, they are examples of dilemmas in which individuals are not simply left alone to wrestle with their own consciences and principles, hoping that their decision will be able to

---

Keith Goree, B.A. Harding University, M.A. Abilene Christian University, is associate professor of Applied Ethics and Honors Applied Ethics at St. Petersburg Junior College.

withstand the scrutiny of peers or superiors. In each of these cases, the person in question has an additional form of guidance; a corporate, professional, or governmental code of ethics.

What is a code of ethics?

A code of ethics is a written set of principles and rules intended to serve as a guideline for determining appropriate ethical behavior for those individuals under its authority. It is "a formal statement of good intentions"[1] from a corporation or profession. An ethics code delineates in behavioral terms "a system of value-based principles or practices and a definition of right and wrong."[2] It represents a bridge spanning the chasm between the idealistic and ethereal principles of moral philosophy and the cold, hard realities of business. However, a code of ethics is not the same as a moral code. A moral code is a definitive statement of right and wrong.[3] As Richard DeGeorge states, "No individual or group can make actions moral or immoral by fiat. Every code, therefore, can and should appropriately be evaluated from a moral point of view." In other words, while a typical code of ethics contains rules and principles of behavior based on moral principles, these are not moral principles in themselves, and should not be treated as such. To do so invites the dangerous practice of "code worship" – i.e., assuming that anything the code allows must be moral and anything it forbids must be immoral. A profession or corporation that falls into this trap will be unlikely to be able to make the kinds of genuine changes and adaptations in the code that are necessary to keep it relevant and useful.

Are Codes Necessary?

Why not just pass laws? Indeed, some states and the federal government have enacted laws embodying codes of ethics. Both codes of ethics and laws are frequently based on ethical principles. But, as Christopher Stone points out, there are limits to what a law can do[4]. While laws often are only passed and enforced after the damage has been done (e.g., environmental protection statutes, airline safety regulations, *etc.*), codes of ethics tend to be more preventative in nature. Also, because the politicians who write the laws cannot possibly have expertise in all the complexities of business, industry, and the professions, formulating appropriate laws and designing effective regulations are difficult. In addition, basing all corporate and professional behavior on the letter of the law invites a "loophole mentality," in which individuals seem to expend more energy in trying to get around the law than in obeying it.

Because taking legal action against corporations is so expensive and these cases can spend so many years tied up in litigation, it seems wiser to find another approach. William Shaw says, "Stone's argument is not intended to show that regulation of business is hopeless. Rather, what he wants to stress is that the law cannot do it alone. We do not want a system in which business people believe that their only obligation is to obey the law and that it is morally permissible for them to do anything not (yet) illegal. With that attitude, disaster is just around the corner."[5]

George Reiger, in an article protesting the over-regulation of other areas of American life, makes a similar point. He states: "The reason most people confuse ethics with law is that most have been taught in schools that emphasize rules over consensus opinion. A society that nurtures its conscience is more likely to maintain a high level of sportsmanship than one preoccupied with legal loopholes."[6] Is this not just as true of corporations and professions who aspire to be ethical?

How Do Codes Of Ethics Vary?

Business and professional codes of ethics can vary widely in several important ways. First, the *purposes* of the codes are not all the same. Some corporate codes are written primarily to give administrators a tool for controlling employees, or even as an excuse for firing them. Some professional codes are purely ceremonial. They are read at initiations or graduations with great pomp, but the principles are antiquated and irrelevant to modern issues in the field. Other codes are constructed with the central goal of improving public relations. The words are comforting, the principles reassuring, but the code does not seem to have much impact on the behavior of those who are supposed to be following it. On the other hand, there are also many effective codes of ethics. Their purposes are to create and maintain a sense of professionalism, to offer some guidance to those facing thorny ethical dilemmas, and to give the public a standard to which it can hold a corporation or profession.

Codes also vary according to *authorship*. Corporate codes are often written at a management or administrative level and, unfortunately, sometimes with little contribution from the employees who are to follow it. Therefore, these codes can seem authoritarian and heavy-handed, geared more toward increasing company profits than fulfilling social responsibilities. In contrast, codes of professional organizations are often constructed at the peer level because many of the individuals in the professions are self-employed (or at least are granted more autonomy than corporate employees). For instance, the American Dental Association code of ethics was written by dentists, the American Bar Association code by lawyers, and the American Institute of Certified Public Accountants code by accountants. There are strengths and weaknesses in peer-level codes which will be discussed later in this chapter, but one important step in critiquing any code is considering the identity and motives of who wrote it.

Finally, codes can vary in their *ethical level* – the degree of ethical behavior to which they call their subjects. Some codes seem to be little more than a collection of lofty ideals to which everyone should aspire, but which no one is realistically expected to practice consistently. These codes sound nice but are unenforceable, and thus have little effect on people's behavior. They come across as shallow and insincere. At the opposite end of the spectrum are the minimum standard codes. These consist of little more than lengthy lists of rules that must be followed to keep one's job or license to practice. Each rule has a corresponding penalty for its violation, and ethical behavior is generally seen as not violating the letter of the code. This approach spawns searches for loopholes, as mentioned above, and, ironically, may actually lower the ethical level of behavior of some individuals who might otherwise have followed higher personal principles. The most relevant and useful codes of ethics, whether for corporations or professions, have their roots somewhere between these extremes. They are the blended codes; combining the noble principles of lofty ideals with clearly stated, enforceable rules that can be monitored for compliance.

For purposes of this study, codes of ethics are divided into three main categories: corporate codes, professional codes, and governmental/public service codes. This is not the only possible approach to such a study, and there will be instances where a code may overlap categories, but this approach can effectively demonstrate how the factors of purpose, authorship, and ethical level can impact the ability of a code of ethics to uplift the ethical behavior of its subjects.

CORPORATE CODES OF ETHICS

The year was 1982. The headlines were terrifying. Someone had been taking Tylenol capsules off the shelves of stores, removing the acetaminophen inside, and replacing it with poison. Four people had died already and the public did not know whether they could tell the good capsules from the poisoned ones. Tylenol's manufacturer, Johnson & Johnson Corporation, was deluged with panicked callers from all over the nation. Lives were in danger, but so was the future of a company that was itself a victim. How should the manufacturer respond? The most extreme alternative considered was an unprecedented nationwide recall, removing all of the Tylenol boxes from every store shelf. The customers would then be protected from any capsules that had been poisoned, and the company could change the packaging to make tampering more difficult. The cost? Over $100-million. Who would have to pay it? The Johnson & Johnson stockholders. Did the company have a higher obligation to consumers or to stockholders? In such a situation, when the welfare of two groups to which a company has important responsibilities is in conflict, how does the corporation decide what to do?

Johnson & Johnson's leaders turned to their code of ethics, which they refer to as "Our Credo." Its first sentence states, "We believe our first responsibility is to the doctors, nurses, and patients, to mothers and all others who use our products and services."[7] They chose to pull the product off the shelves. In referring to the role played by the code of ethics in this decision, James Burke, the corporation's chairman, said, "This document spells out our responsibilities to all our constituencies: consumers, employees, community, and stockholders. It served to guide all of us during the crisis, when hard decisions had to be made in what were often excruciatingly brief periods of time. All of our employees worldwide were able to watch the process of the Tylenol withdrawal and subsequent reintroduction in tamper-resistant packaging, confident of the way in which the decisions would be made. There was a great sense of shared pride in the knowledge that the Credo was being tested ... and it worked!"[8]

The premise that a corporate code of ethics can make a significant impact on the behavior of individuals within the company is not universally accepted. As will be seen further in the chapter, a few critics have even argued that such codes can never amount to more than publicity ploys, capable only of making a corporation *appear* ethical to a gullible public. On the other hand, there are many more voices in the business arena who argue that, while we must be realistic about the scope of what a code should be expected to accomplish, it can indeed make a substantive difference in the ethical behavior of the people within a company.

HOW PERVASIVE ARE CORPORATE CODES OF ETHICS?

Surveys have not reported identical findings, but there does seem to be an overall consensus that many American businesses have constructed such codes and rely on them for guidance. Raiborn and Payne write of one recent study of 300 major companies by the Conference Board showing that more than 75% of the corporations responding had adopted written codes of conduct for their employees.[9] Catherine Fredman found that in the period between 1984 and 1987, the number of American companies among the Fortune 500 who had a stated code of ethics increased by 12%.[10] Patrick Murphy reports that approximately 90% of the Fortune 500 firms and almost half of all companies in America currently have codes of ethics in place.[11]

One of the most ambitious studies to date on corporate codes of ethics was done by the Ethics Resource Center in Washington, D. C. This 1987 survey of 2,000 American companies found, among other things, that 85% of the corporations responding said that they had "a code, policy statement, or other written guidelines on ethics."[12] This figure varied widely, however, with different types and sizes of corporations. Bigger corporations were more likely to have developed codes than smaller ones. The practice of distributing the code to all company employees ranged from 72% among defense contractors, and 71% in the finance/insurance industry, to only 36% in construction, and only 30% of retail sales firms. But it is interesting to note that only 2% of defense contractors, 4% of finance/insurance industry firms, and only 3% of very large firms (more than 50,000 employees) said that they had no code and no plans to implement one. Also revealing is that fact that these codes are not just gathering dust on a shelf. But 76% of firms with a written code were currently revising it or had done so within the previous five years. Only 15% of firms who had a code reported that theirs had never been revised.

Why would a corporation want to develop a code of ethics? There are many reasons why companies see the development and maintenance of a code as a worthwhile endeavor. Of course, it is in the corporation's best interests to be perceived as ethical by the public. In a survey by Touche Ross, most of the respondents believed that businesses actually strengthen their competitive positions by maintaining high ethical standards.[13] Codes can help a firm to do that. In the same study, 39% of those responding cited adoption of a code of ethics as the best way to inspire ethical behavior in a corporation. The industries rated by the respondents as having the best reputations for ethical behavior were commercial banking, utilities, pharmaceuticals, and cosmetics. The main reason given for their prestige was the existence of strong industry standards, which would be directly related to the development of strong codes of ethics.

Another reason for developing a corporate ethical code stems from the great pressure upon employees to increase profits for the company, tempting them to act unethically to do so. Wartzman reports a survey from the early 1980s that found more than 70% of the executives interviewed felt the pressure to conform to organizational standards and often had to compromise personal principles.[14] Obviously, unethical employees are often more expensive for the company due to more frequent litigation, damage to the corporation's public image, decreased morale, employee theft, abuse of sick time, and so forth. Shaw states, "If those inside the corporation are to behave morally, they need clearly stated and communicated ethical standards that are equitable and enforced."[15] He adds that codes "encourage members to take moral responsibilities seriously." Raiborn and Payne note, "Companies want to communicate management's concern for high-level ethical standards of behavior and corporate social responsibility."[16] These corporations suggest that it would not be fair to hold employees to a standard of ethical conduct that had not been clearly spelled out to them in advance.

Richard DeGeorge lists six reasons why a corporation would want to develop, implement and maintain a company code of ethics:[17]

> 1. The exercise is in itself worthwhile. The company receives inherent benefits simply from discussing these ethical issues.
> 2. Once adopted, the code generates continuing, open discussion of ethical issues.
> 3. The code helps instill proper ethical attitudes in employees at all levels.
> 4. The code provides employees with a reference when asked to do something contrary to the code.
> 5. The code helps reassure customers and the public; giving them a "touchstone" for measuring the corporation.
> 6. The code gives workers and managers a way to evaluate in moral terms the goals and practices of the firm to ensure that the corporation as a whole is acting in accordance with the code.

Jack Behrman adds a different light. He states, "Regardless of why codes of ethics are being established, one of the major benefits of establishing (such codes) is the process of discovery and harmonization of interests that occurs from the participation of many different managers in the formulation of the code."[18]

What kinds of behaviors are included in corporate codes? Obviously, because codes of ethics are written for a variety of different purposes, the content of the codes will vary widely as well. Each company will develop a code tailored to meet its own specific needs. For instance, a corporation that has had a problem with sexual harassment is likely to put a rule prohibiting such acts in its code of ethics. Since each company's history and value system is different, each code will be unique.

There are, however, some common threads among corporate codes. In the Ethics Resource Center study previously cited, an attempt was made to determine which ethical issues were addressed the most often. Companies were asked (1) to rank the ethical issues they considered to be the most important, (2) to report issues covered by their own code of ethics, and (3) to further report issues also covered in employee ethics training sessions.

A cursory analysis of these results produces some interesting conclusions. It is obvious that many of the ethical issues that corporate leaders consider to be important are not reflected as such in company codes of ethics or employee training. Therefore, many companies are probably failing to communicate the importance of those issues to their employees. Drug and alcohol abuse is ranked as the most important issue facing American businesses, yet only 64% of the companies that have written codes of ethics include anything about substance abuse. Only 36% of the corporations responding include drug and alcohol abuse as part of employee training. Are corporate leaders effectively communicating their values to the employees? How are those employees to understand that this issue is considered crucial to the well-being of the company? Is it fair to discipline a worker harshly for actions for which he has been given little guidance by the company? William Shaw warns, "If management does not make explicit the values and behaviors it desires, the culture will typically develop its own norms, usually based on the types of behavior that lead to success within the organization."[19]

Are codes of ethics effective? Do they upgrade the behavior of employees? Not always. There are several factors that may make codes less likely to be effective. First, they will obviously not achieve much when written "just for show." "Codes of conduct continue to be criticized as ... serving purely as public relations ploys, or being designed strictly to avoid legal problems."[20] If anything, such codes might actually work to lower the ethical behavior of employees. Because the corporation itself appears insincere or intellectually dishonest, the employees may tend to treat the codes lightly.

Codes of ethics also lose effectiveness when the expectations of the code are unrealistically high. Kenneth Arrow, in his award-winning business essay states, "One must not expect miraculous transformations in human behavior. Ethical codes, if they are to be viable, should be limited in their scope."[21]

Most business ethicists maintain that a code of ethics is doomed to failure if its principles appear to be inconsistent with the actual corporate culture. The *corporate culture* is something akin to Jean-Jacques Rousseau's "social contract" – that mutual understanding of expected values and behaviors among the members of a society. The corporate culture represents the real attitudes of the company; the understood expectations of how individuals within the company should act. It is "the pattern of shared values and beliefs that give members of an institution meaning and provide them with rules for behavior in their organization."[22] For instance, an automotive repair company could put dozens of rules in its code of ethics concerning the importance of "treating the customer right" and "upholding honesty and integrity." But if that same company pays its mechanics commissions or bonuses based on the amount that customers end up paying for their repair work, which would tend to encourage them to do unnecessary repairs, then the code loses its integrity and relevance.

There is a principle of interpersonal communications which says that if there is a "mixed message" between what a person says (verbally) and how that person acts (non-verbally), then others will tend to disregard the verbal message and believe the non-verbal one to be the truth. For example, when a person's eyes and facial expressions have an angry look, others will assume he feels that way, even if he denies having those emotions. A code of ethics can be seen as a verbal message to the public and the employees from the top management of a corporation. But it is only one of many different types of messages the company sends. Employees, for example, may read company policies, contracts, job descriptions, corporate guidelines and memos. Where does the company's code of ethics fit into this hierarchy? If an employee notices discrepancies between the code and memos from his boss, which should take priority?

A corporate code of ethics will only be accepted, believed, and effective, when the actions and expectations of those administrators are consistent with the message of the code. For example, one study found, in studying corporate codes of ethics, that "codes give more attention to unethical conduct likely to decrease the firm's profits than to conduct that might increase profits."[23] This assertion is supported by the findings of the Ethics Resource Center study. Protecting the company's proprietary information was ranked third among issues addressed in company policies, while ethical policies regarding gathering that same information from competitors was ranked last. When these kinds of inconsistencies exist between what a corporation says it believes and what it actually emphasizes in daily operation, then the code's effectiveness in upgrading the ethical behavior of the employees is weakened.

One final criticism of the effectiveness of codes of ethics should be noted. La Rue Hosmer, among others, argues that these codes, in general, cannot be particularly effective because they have an inherent defect related to the diverse groups to whom corporations have obligations. "The problem is that it is not possible to state the norms and beliefs of an organization relative to the various constituent groups (employees, customers, suppliers, distributors, stockholders, and the general public) clearly and explicitly, without offending at least one of those groups ... The basic difficulty ... is that they do not establish priorities (among those groups). The code does not tell us how to choose between our distributors, our customers, and ourselves."[24] Hosmer cites the Johnson & Johnson Credo as an example of the problem, noting that it contains an inherent contradiction. The first sentence states, "We believe our first responsibility is to the doctors, nurses and patients, to mothers and all others who use our products and services." This is the principle that the company claimed guided it through the Tylenol-tampering crisis. But Hosmer points out that there are other competing statements, such as, "We are responsible to our employees, the men and women who work with us throughout the world," and, "Our final responsibility is to our stockholders." Which one of these groups should take priority? Does the code of ethics offer more guidance or confusion? Hosmer concludes, "I think that we can agree that the employees of Johnson & Johnson should be proud of the response of their firm, which put consumer safety ahead of company profits, but we also have to agree that that response, and that priority ranking, is not unequivocally indicated in the Credo of the company."[25]

> " A corporate code of ethics will only be accepted, believed, and effective, when the actions and expectations of those administrators are consistent with the message of the code. "

While there is some honest disagreement as to how effective codes of ethics can be, there is relative consensus regarding the conditions necessary for increasing their effectiveness. This consensus holds that a code with the capacity to have a substantive impact on the behavior of the members of a corporation will have the following characteristics:

QUALITY CODES OF ETHICS

1. **Its expectations are clearly communicated and specific.**[26] There is a place for value statements and principles, but employees need specific guidelines to follow when facing difficult decisions. Is it forbidden to accept any gifts at all from clients, or just gifts worth more than a nominal sum of, say, $25?

2. **It is comprehensive, covering virtually all conduct associated with the workplace.**[27] How fair is it to discipline an employee for using unethical methods of gathering information from a competitor if your firm is one of the 72% of the companies that has a codes of ethics, but does not offer any guidance in that area?

3. **It is direct, even blunt and realistic about violations and their consequences.**[28] If there is to be any deterrent effect, it will be because individuals see that unethical behavior has negative consequences.

4. **It is widely accepted.**[29] Employee involvement is essential. If a code is simply handed down to workers from above without their input or participation, then it is not likely to win their allegiance. On the other hand, if the employees can be meaningfully involved in the process of developing a code, then they are more likely to take personal ownership of the code; to think of it and act on it as something important belonging to them.

5. **It is understood to benefit everyone.** Kenneth Arrow states, " ... above all it must be clearly perceived that the acceptance of these ethical obligations by everybody does involve mutual gain. Ethical codes that lack the latter property are unlikely to be viable."[30]

6. **It is a public document, as opposed to a tool used only for internal employee control.**[31] If the employees believe that the administrators and managers who produced the code are less interested in ethical behavior than in employee control, and especially if the employees believe that those administrators and managers are not acting ethically themselves, the code becomes meaningless and subject to ridicule.

7. **It is written at an appropriate ethical level.** In evaluating codes of ethics, Raiborn and Payne have created a hierarchy of ethical behavior based on the types of standards used in cost accounting.[32] Their four levels of ethical behavior are as follows:

The theoretical level represents the ethical ideal. This level is virtually impossible to consistently attain, but represents "the highest potential towards which society should continually strive." For example, the hypothetical Lincoln Construction Company wants to develop a reputation in the community for dealing with its clients honestly. To do so, it could develop a code of ethics requiring absolute honesty and integrity. The company might even begin to advertise that "all of our employees are as honest as ol' Abe ever was"; or "we would walk two miles to return your penny."

The practical level represents behavior which can be achieved the majority of the time through diligent effort. In its early days, the J. C. Penney Corporation was known across America as the "Golden Rule Company." The company's foundational principle was that its employees would treat customers like the employees themselves would wish to be treated. Such a policy represents an admirable goal, and it can be argued that most people could conceivably meet this standard most of the time if they tried earnestly.

The currently attainable level represents the behavior normally exhibited by individuals. This behavior is socially acceptable, but not particularly praiseworthy, since reaching it does not require much effort. For example, an air conditioner repair company could develop and advertise policies such as, "We will not cheat our customers," "Employees shall not curse at the customers," and "Employees will be expected to work forty hours per week."

The basic level represents behavior within the letter of the law. At this level there is no concerted effort to comply with the spirit of the law, thus producing the "loophole mentality," in which the person is more concerned with getting around the rules than in doing the right thing. An example might be a code of ethics for a chemical company stating that its employees will not dump any more than the legal limit of a dangerous pesticide into a nearby river.

This process of analyzing a code of ethics to determine its ethical level is more than just an academic exercise. The level of ethical behavior required by a code impacts the actions of the employees who are to follow it, especially if the corporate ethical climate is consistent with the provisions in the code. Codes written at the higher levels should motivate the employees to maintain higher ethical standards than would codes written at the basic level. (See Figures 1-5, next page.)

SPEAKING OF CODES OF ETHICS

 Ethics is a binary problem; either you is or isn't.
– U.S. Representative Newt Gingrich, D-Ga.

No individual or group can make actions moral or immoral by fiat. Every code, therefore, can and should appropriately be evaluated from a moral point of view.
– Richard DeGeorge

The reason most people confuse ethics with law is that most have been taught in schools that emphasize rules over consensus opinion.
– George Reiger

If management does not make explicit the values and behaviors it desires, the culture will typically develop its own norms, usually based on the types of behavior that lead to success within the organization.
–William Shaw

Notice that in **Figure 1**, demonstrating a corporation with no code of ethics, the expected ethical behavior of employees varies widely but is concentrated on the unethical end of the spectrum. This expectation is based on the principle voiced by William Shaw earlier in this chapter. It is important enough that it bears repeating. "If management does not make explicit the values and behaviors it desires, the culture will typically develop its own norms, usually based on the the types of behaviors that lead to success within the corporation."[19] What kinds of behaviors typically lead to success within a corporation that has no clearly stated ethical standards for its employees? Commission earnings? Sales? Revenue generated for the company? While these represent the healthy goals of many companies, notice that they are goals or ends, and the means used to accomplish them may more often be unethical if employees are not given ethical guidance.

Figure 2 represents the anticipated employee behavior of a corporation with a basic level code. Notice that the code requirements are relatively low, since they are based on the minimal letter of the law. Most behavior is concentrated around the level called for in the code, which is to be expected. Notice that while there are a few employees maintaining higher personal conduct, the presence of a minimal code has actually *lowered* the behavior of others. In a company with lower-level ethical expectations, acting on a higher level may go unrewarded or even be actively discouraged. Many highly principled individuals have been demoted or fired for blowing the whistle on unethical corporate policies and practices.

Figure 3 represents expected employee behavior under a code of ethics written at the currently attainable level, or the level normally exhibited by most individuals. As you see, the code requirements have risen somewhat and the behaviors have risen with them. Notice also that as the ethical expectations rise, the number of individuals failing to meet that standard increase.

Figure 4 demonstrates the ethical behaviors anticipated under a practical level code of ethics. This is the standard which could be achieved the majority of the time through diligent effort. Again, the behavior level should rise to meet the requirements of the code, and more individuals would be expected to fail to meet this higher standard. Such individuals might be dealt with less harshly than at the lower levels since it would be unreasonable to expect people to be able to maintain such lofty behavior all of the time.

Finally, **Figure 5** represents expected employee behavior under a theoretical level code of ethics, or one based on ethical ideals. On the surface this would seem to be the superior type of code, but the lofty nature of its principles presents some practical problems. Only a few individuals would be able to consistently meet these requirements; the failure rate would be much higher. Such a system could tend to produce a certain cynicism toward the code, since no one seems to be expected to achieve it very often. It would seem unfair to punish violators very harshly, thus making enforcement difficult, if not impossible.

Raiborn and Payne argue that codes of ethics should be written *at least* at the currently attainable level, with incentives for reaching toward higher levels. If the code is written at the theoretical level, then enforcement is impossible because only rarely will individuals reach it. If the code is written at the practical level, then the company is accepting the responsibility of requiring additional efforts of its employees to do the right thing. On the other hand, if the code is written at the currently attainable or basic levels, the punishments for deviations from the code should be harsh, because these are minimal standards. Snoeyenbos and Jewell concur, adding that a code "should not be window dressing, or so general as to be useless. It should set reasonable goals and subgoals, with an eye toward blunting unethical pressures on subordinates."[33]

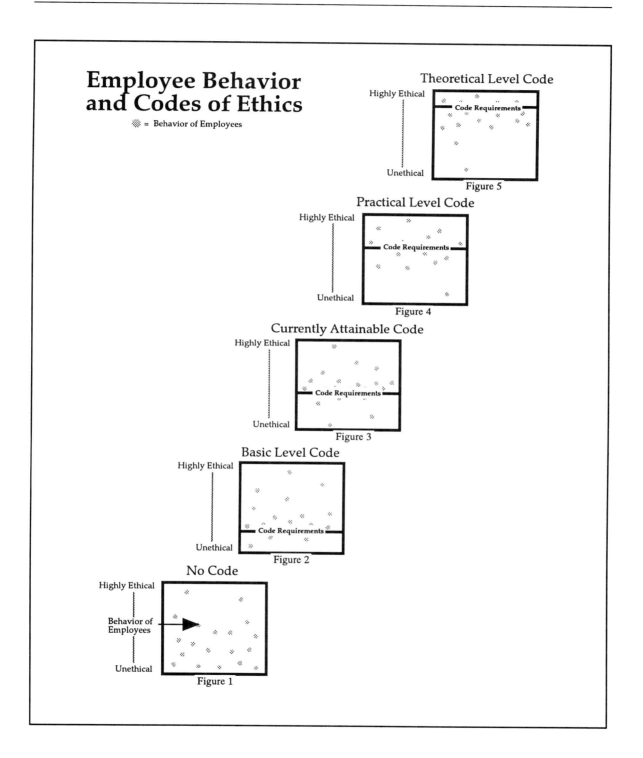

Employee Behavior
and Codes of Ethics

※ = Behavior of Employees

Theoretical Level Code

Highly Ethical

Code Requirements

Unethical

Figure 5

Practical Level Code

Highly Ethical

Code Requirements

Unethical

Figure 4

Currently Attainable Code

Highly Ethical

Code Requirements

Unethical

Figure 3

Basic Level Code

Highly Ethical

Code Requirements

Unethical

Figure 2

No Code

Highly Ethical

Behavior of
Employees

Unethical

Figure 1

8. It is monitored and enforced. Even for companies who have spent considerable time and effort developing a viable code, enforcement is often a problem. The Ethics Resource Center (ERC) study found that while 46% of the corporations responding to their survey reported allegations of misconduct occuring at a rate of less than 1 per 1000 employees per year, 27% indicated that their companies had no way to determine even an approximate number of allegations.[34] Nearly 50% were unable to estimate what percentage of allegations in the previous year turned out to be valid. Obviously, if a code of ethics cannot be enforced, then its usefulness is limited.

The ERC study also noted that the highest ratings on the effectiveness of monitoring and enforcement of the code of ethics were among corporations who shared these important characteristics:

a. The firms distributed the code of ethics to all employees of the corporation.
b. The firms had developed ethics training for all employees.
c. The companies frequently used videotapes, articles, posters and speakers as methods of communicating ethics policies.
d. The firms demonstrated the greatest range of company departments used by employees as sources of advice on applying ethics policies.
e. The companies had corporate ethics committees at the board of director level, where policy decisions are made.
f. The firms used "hot lines" to allow employees to report unethical behavior without risking retaliation by other employees.
g. These companies often established a separate corporate ethics office to monitor and enforce compliance with the code.

9. It is revised periodically.[35] A company's needs, values, and concerns are constantly changing. A code of ethics that is never revised and updated becomes stagnant and irrelevant.

10. It is supported by management and employee ethics training. This may be the area in which businesses need the most improvement. The Ethics Resource Center study found that only 28% of their respondent companies provided employee training on ethical issues in business.[36] Ethics training was the least common in retail and wholesale industries (19%) and most common among defense contractors, who are subject to much more stringent federal ethics laws (52%). This absence of training is puzzling. Perhaps managers believe that giving out the code of ethics will be sufficient in itself. Perhaps the company is writing the code more for the public relations value than for its employees to follow. Perhaps it is related to the common misconception that ethics cannot be taught to adults (in which case, why have a code at all?).

Whatever the reason, a reasonable conclusion is that codes of ethics, in themselves, are inadequate to effect change in the behavior of the members of a corporation, even when written well. The corporate climate, and the factors which go along with it (management/employee communication, commonality of goals and values, sincerity of purpose in the development and implementation of the code, *etc.*), are often the decisive factors in how effectively or ineffectively a code of ethics will be in motivating and enabling members of the company to act ethically.

There is an old joke that asks how many psychologists it takes to change a light bulb. The answer is, "Just one, but the bulb really has to want to be changed." One of the primary purposes of a code of ethics is to change people's behavior; an outcome that humans tend to vigorously resist. Writing, developing, and implementing a code is a difficult process, fraught with political obstacles and interpersonal landmines. Even if a company's management is committed to the importance of a code, the feat of getting one implemented is daunting.

Raiborn and Payne point out several problems that typically arise in the process of designing and implementing a corporate code of ethics.[37] First, it sometimes gives employees the implication that the administration believes someone is doing something wrong. This may or may not be the case, but an atmosphere of distrust and suspicion can result, making communication about the code even more difficult. Second, if the top managers themselves are the ones acting unethically, and the code is only intended for image-building, then trying to communicate the value of ethics to all employees will be virtually impossible. As stated previously, it is the unethical (non-verbal) behavior that will be seen as more accurately representing the actual beliefs of those leaders. Third, there are problems inherent in determining who has violated a code. How much credibility should be given to the information provided by whistle-blowers? How much protection should they be given? When it boils down to one person's word against another's (in sexual harassment cases, for instance), who should be believed? Fourth, determining the level of specificity in a code can be problemmatic. At which ethical behavior level should it be written? Theoretical? Practical? Currently attainable? Basic? How can general principles and specific rules be combined? Finally, Raiborn and Payne point out that a challenge also exists in keeping the tone of the code positive, rather than negative. If the code is too negative, with every other sentence beginning with "Thou shalt not ... ," then the suspicions of the workers that they are distrusted will be magnified, morale impaired, and the code's effectiveness limited.

But effective codes of ethics exist and more are being written. While the obstacles are formidable, there are company-wide benefits that result from the process of creating and implementing an ethics code. The most valuable goals often involve the biggest challenges. Robert E. Sweeney[38] has suggested five steps that he believes are necessary in the development of a viable corporate code of ethics:

Develop the code. It must be assembled by a company's ownership and top management. It is, after all, the statement of their values, principles, and priorities. The code should provide guidelines for conduct, aid in resolving conflicts, and spell out disciplinary action for violations of the code. To avoid pitfalls already mentioned, it should consist of broad guidelines supported by detail.

Gain approval. For the code to be effective, everyone needs to buy into it. This can be accomplished by continually seeking workers' input into its content, keeping its tone positive, and pointing out to employees that they will also benefit from having a code of ethics. Unfortunately, many companies do not seem to understand the criticality of employee support in this process. For example, according to the Ethics Resource Center survey, only 50% of the responding companies having codes of ethics in place had guidelines in their codes regarding employee right to privacy.[39] Only 46% of the codes stated support for employees' volunteer community activities, and only 29% contained information concerning administrative policies on plant closings and layoffs. While the ultimate goal of a company's code of ethics should be to maintain high levels of ethical behavior by its employees, getting workers to accept and value the code will be easier if they can see that it has been constructed with their interests in mind.

Implement the code. There are a variety of methods that can be used, but management must fix responsibility for getting the code in place and operative. Some corporations have found it worthwhile to set up a separate ethics office to oversee the process. Others have delegated the task to one administrator. How this is done does not seem to be as important as that it is done. Simply passing out copies of the code will not be sufficient.

Communicate the ethical message. Each employee should have a copy of the code, but the company must add training sessions including the use of videotapes, seminars with speakers and consultants from outside the firm, and indoctrination workshops for new employees or promotees. Discussions regarding relevant ethical issues should become a regular part of meetings involving management and employees. At one community college in Florida, time is set aside at every meeting of the president's cabinet for some discussion of ethical issues facing the college. This is an important step in developing the *ethical climate* discussed earlier on this chapter. In addition, ethics "hot lines" should be installed for reporting violations of the code. Without them, and the inherent protection which they give to whistle-blowers, monitoring compliance to the code is much more difficult. Also the code should be communicated externally to the public/community. While public relations should not be the solitary goal of developing a code of ethics, publicizing the code gives members of the community an important standard to which they can hold the company's behavior. If the corporation lives up to the good intentions expressed in the code, then there should be a substantially positive public relations effect.

Administer the code. Compliance to the tenets of the code must be diligently monitored. Disciplinary procedures for violations of the code should be established and consistently followed. Provisions need to be made for whistle-blowing and the investigation of reported violations. The code itself must be revised periodically to keep it current and relevant to the needs of the company.

In summary, when analyzing corporate codes of ethics, consider these questions:

1. How well do these codes effectively communicate the most important ethical issues facing businesses? Are there important issues which are not included?
2. How well do these codes provide employees with appropriate guidance in making difficult decisions?
3. Are enforcement policies explained adequately?
4. At what ethical level is each code written? (See Figure 1)
5. What are the strengths and weaknesses of each? How do you think each could be improved?

THE *CHALLENGER* CASE AND ETHICAL DECISION-MAKING

Codes of ethics are important and necessary tools for businesses and corporations. That is not to say that all American workers are incapable of relying on personal conscience and reasoning in making ethical decisions, but maintaining integrity in the chaos of the marketplace is difficult. The dilemmas faced are complex, but decisions must often be made very quickly. The potential consequences of making the wrong choices can destroy individuals and damage corporations.

On a bitterly cold morning in January of 1986, the NASA space shuttle *Challenger* exploded only 73 seconds into its mission. Millions of American school children watched in confusion, and then horror as it became clear that school teacher Christa McAuliffe and six of her comrades were dead. The nation was traumatized. As the official investigation into the disaster proceeded it turned up serious deficiencies in NASA's decision-making policies. Engineers at NASA and Morton Thiokol, the company that made the booster rockets used for launching the shuttles, had been aware for eight years of design flaws in the O-ring seals that made launching in cold weather extremely dangerous, and had vigorously warned the company's management that a serious explosion was possible.[44] Their warnings were ignored, and none of the engineers went to the press or to higher government officials with the information. Morton Thiokol's recommendation not to launch was overruled by NASA officials, who demanded that the company agree to the early morning launch. The shuttle program was already far behind schedule and NASA was under heavy pressure from Washington to avoid any further delays. Future funding was at stake. Morton Thiokol complied and agreed to recommend the launch. The astronauts were not informed of the additional risk. The engineers held their breath as the launch commenced. The O-rings cracked as predicted. The shuttle blew up.

Of course, no one had known with certainty that the spacecraft would explode. It would be oversimplistic and unfair to argue that the administrators who made the decision to launch were choosing to sacrifice innocent human life for money. Nevertheless, those odds were unacceptable according to NASA's own launching guidelines, and those guidelines had been intentionally bypassed. Engineers who "blew the whistle" and made public the truth about how the decision was made were fired or demoted, producing further complaints about a possible coverup.

In hindsight it is easy to see that the negative consequences far outweighed any possible benefits that NASA could have expected to receive by keeping the shuttle program on schedule. The agency was forced to temporarily halt all shuttle flights. Claiming negligence, the families of the astronauts successfully sued the companies involved for millions of dollars. Eventually, the agency's top administrator was fired. No one is stating that if NASA had had a better code of ethics, the *Challenger* disaster would not have occured. The point is that in the high-pressure environment in which administrators, managers, engineers, and employees must work, crucial decisions must often be made very quickly and without enough accurate information. The consequences can at times involve life and death. A code of ethics is not a guarantee that all future decisions will be right, or that employees will always do the right thing. It does offer a set of guidelines, based on a clear philosophy of business, which can be invaluable when those tough choices must be made.

U. S. Representative Newt Gingrich of Georgia has been quoted as stating that ethics is "a binary problem; either you is or you isn't".[45] To be sure, there are people at both ends of that spectrum in every company. There are those who would act with integrity and honor with no outside guidance and those who will act unethically regardless of what preventative steps are taken. Corporate codes of ethics are most effective for the majority of employees in the middle who need a little help and encouragement to do the right thing.

PROFESSIONAL CODES OF ETHICS

Should a doctor accept "kickbacks" from pharmaceutical companies in exchange for writing more prescriptions for their drugs than for those of their competitors? Should an engineer obey the insistent demands of his client to disregard minor, or even major, safety violations? Should a psychologist break her promise of confidentiality if she believes doing so would help her client in the long run? Should a dentist refuse to treat any individuals she suspects of being infected with the HIV virus? What if she receives letters from her other patients insisting that she do so or they will find another dentist?

What distinguishes these cases from those mentioned earlier is that the individuals facing these dilemmas do not work for a corporation, and therefore are not subject to any corporate codes of ethics. People identified as "professionals" in our society are often, though not always, self-employed. Thus, they do not have managers or administrators peering over their shoulders. They have much more autonomy and independence than do corporate employees. Yet, professionals face just as many thorny ethical dilemmas, and probably bear even more personal responsibility for their choices. We have already seen that the law, all by itself, is limited in its ability to resolve many of these kinds of dilemmas. What, beyond the law, guides the behavior of these professionals?

William Shaw states, "Somewhere between etiquette and the law lie professional codes of ethics. Generally speaking, the members of a profession are understood to have agreed to abide by those rules as a condition of their engaging in that profession. Violations of the professional code may result in the disapproval of one's peers and, in serious cases, loss of one's license to practice that profession."[46]

What is a "profession"? According to the *American Heritage Dictionary* (2nd edition), a profession is "an occupation or vocation requiring training in the liberal arts or the sciences and advanced study in a specialized field."[47] This brings to mind individuals such as doctors, lawyers, dentists, psychiatrists, and engineers. Thus, for many people, the term "professional" has come to be associated with high salaries, social prestige, and independence. As a result, the boundaries surrounding the concept of a "profession" have been blurred in recent years. Attempts have been made, with mixed success, to upgrade many occupations to the status of "profession" which traditionally have not fit the technical definition. These fields include, to name but a few, pest control, journalism, acupuncture, counseling, advertising, physical therapy, teaching, interior decorating, and law enforcement.

This raises some interesting questions. Is journalism, for instance, a profession? Does it require "advanced study in a specialized field"? What about education? Does teaching at the college/ university level fit the technical definition of being a profession? Does doing so at the elementary or high school level? Are there justifiable distinctions? In addition, there are questions of semantics. We speak of "professional athletes," yet understand that they must meet few, if any, educational requirements.

We are left, therefore, with more than a little confusion. Today, the traditional definitions do not always lend themselves to clear distinctions among trades, crafts, and professions. Interestingly, however, many persons in various occupational fields wish to be considered as professionals. Their motivations seem to be increased prestige, income, and especially autonomy. Richard DeGeorge states, "Typically, professions have been self-governing, and society has allowed them a large amount of autonomy ... Members of a profession set their own standards, regulate entry into the profession, discipline their own members, and function with fewer restraints than others."[48] Can the practice of giving a group this much power over its own affairs be justified?

The answer is a cautious yes. DeGeorge adds, "In return for such increased autonomy, however, they are properly expected to serve the public good, to set higher standards of conduct for their members than those required of others, and to enforce a higher discipline than others do ... More is expected of them because of their roles, not less. The argument in favor of allowing a profession to govern itself is based on two claims. The first is that the knowledge that the members of a profession have mastered is specialized, useful to society, and not easily mastered by the layman. The second is that the members of the profession set higher standards for themselves than society requires of its citizens, of unskilled workers, and of those in the business world."[49]

In the medical profession, for example, it is accepted that doctors have mastered a body of knowledge that fits these criteria. It is highly specialized, extremely useful to society (Can you imagine our trying to survive without it?), and beyond the understanding of average members of society. It is also assumed, but not as widely accepted anymore, that doctors will understand that they have additional responsibilities to the community to use these abilities for the common good. In return, society allows the medical profession to determine, through its medical schools, how many new doctors will be admitted into the field. The profession is allowed to determine what are considered good medical practices and to discipline its own members when they fail to meet those standards.

As long as the members of a profession fulfill these obligations and voluntarily maintain this higher level of ethical behavior, then it is unnecessary for society to burden them with additional regulations. Interestingly, one of the first actions taken by an occupational field to demonstrate that it is capable of meeting this level of responsibility is to develop its own code of ethics.

How are professional codes of ethics different from corporate codes? Professional codes are written, monitored, and enforced on a peer level, while corporate codes are generally handed down from top management to employees. Therefore, members of a profession tend to have more individual input into the rules and principles contained in the code, have more of a personal stake in making the code successful, and find more peer support for complying with the code.

Also, professional codes tend to exhibit more variety than corporate codes. For instance, they vary widely in purpose. Some are written simply to declare that a group wishes to be thought of as a profession (exterminators, respiratory therapists, *etc.*). Other codes have been developed (or revised at a lower level) as a substitute for the higher personal moral standards which their members were once expected to maintain. DeGeorge illustrates by pointing out that doctors were once expected to treat patients whether they could pay or not, to keep inconvenient office hours, to make house calls when necessary, and to keep both their personal and professional conduct above reproach.[50] Today's society has less lofty expectations and the American Medical Association code of ethics reflects those changes.

Shaw adds that professional codes vary according to the kinds of behaviors allowed and disallowed, whether those behaviors are defined in vague generalities or minute detail, the level of enforcement (if any), and the relevance of the code to the daily operations of those individuals covered.[51] So, while corporate codes of ethics vary in terms of the content of the rules and principles included in them, professional codes are even more diverse. Some are simply ceremonial documents, others are idealistically worded public relations gestures. Some are disciplinary tools, others do not even attempt enforcement.

What makes professional codes effective? DeGeorge has detailed four characteristics of a viable professional code.[52] He states that, first and foremost, it should be *regulative*. Ideals and principles are appropriate, but "unless a code actually regulates the conduct of the members of a profession, the profession has no public statement to which it can be held by the public."

Second, it should be *protective* of the public interest and the interests of the individuals who are served by that profession. In other words, the code should not exist simply to serve the needs of the profession. Surprisingly, there are codes (or at least parts of codes) which exist to serve the profession at the expense of the public's interests. For instance, there could be regulations unduly restricting the number of new practitioners allowed into the profession. By keeping demand (and therefore salaries) artificially high, costs to the public are inflated. Some professions have tried to restrict advertising by their members, making it more difficult for new members to establish a practice. DeGeorge specifically points out the American Medical Association and the American Bar Association as examples of groups who have been criticized for using their codes of ethics in self-serving manners.

Third, the code should be *specific and honest*. As stated previously, any good code must be more than "window-dressing." DeGeorge adds, "If a code is honest, it deals with those aspects of the profession that pose particular and specialized temptations to its members ... Unless these are being addressed, the profession is not truly regulating itself."

Finally, the code must be *enforceable and actually policed.* While the code as a whole is more than just a composite of minimum standards, it is essential that some of those minimum standards be present, be monitored, and be diligently enforced. Professional codes, by the nature of the autonomy the profession has been granted by society, should encourage their members to go above and beyond the bare requirements of the law. In corporate codes this is preferred; in professional codes it is mandatory. When a profession has the appearance of giving lip service to ethics but is not attempting to pull its members up to this higher plane, it runs the risk of losing the social trust which it has been granted. Then it will lose the autonomy it cherished and even lose its identity as a profession.

What are the limitations of professional codes? Some limitations already have been indirectly discussed. Some codes are too self-serving to a particular profession, at times even at the expense of those the profession is supposed to be serving. Others are mere collections of "lofty ideals," written primarily with public relations in mind, and thus can seem so vague and general as to be useless. Some codes, and public service codes may be the best example, rely almost exclusively on already established laws for their rules. If a group is going to be respected as a profession, and granted the autonomy discussed earlier, then it must call its members to a standard of behavior higher than the mere letter of the law.

There are some other important limitations. There are situations in which following the precepts of one's professional code of ethics can mean violating other moral principles. For instance, what should a defense attorney do if a client charged with the murder of a child admits, in confidence, that he did indeed commit the crime and reveals the location of the body? Should the confidence be broken and the police informed? Should the grieving family be told of the new information, even if doing so would aid the prosecutors in convicting the client? Assuming that all of the other evidence is circumstantial in nature, should the attorney continue trying to get a "not guilty" verdict? Our society – and that includes members of the Bar Association itself – believes in the principle of justice. Yet the code implies that protecting attorney-client confidentiality has an inherent value as high as, perhaps even higher than, justice itself. Does the attorney follow his or her conscience or the code? Shaw comments, "Adherence to a professional code does not exempt your conduct from scrutiny from the broader perspective of morality."[53] And DeGeorge concurs, adding, "Members of a profession are people first and members of a profession second. Hence, there is no special ethics that allows people in a profession to do as professionals what it is immoral for others to do."[54]

DeGeorge also notes that sometimes professional codes can produce conflicts in obligations to the client or patient, the employer, the public, and the profession. He gives a hypothetical example of a company doctor who knows about hazardous working conditions but is instructed not to say anything. This physician may be subject to a corporate code of ethics requiring her to keep such proprietary information confidential, and a professional code which insists that she do whatever is necessary to protect the health and safety of the workers. Which code takes priority? What happens when it boils down to a judgment call?

A final limitation, as DeGeorge also mentions, is that professional codes give little guidance of what actions should be taken when the profession as a whole acts inappropriately. Some fields, such as architecture and engineering, have been criticized for allowing too much "word of mouth" advertising of employment opportunities. This practice can lead to a "good ol' boy" environment in which only people who know someone at the firm have a fair shot at getting a job there. The criticism is that, as a result of this tradition, women and minority members have not had equal access to these professional fields. If these charges are true, is it reasonable to expect that a code of ethics written at a peer level by some of the very individuals who have been participating in this practice could effectively deter the discrimination? Does it not seem more likely that the legislature or courts would have to step in and insist that fair practices by set in place? As stated previously, the autonomy granted to a profession by society could eventually be revoked if the profession does not live up to that expected higher plane of ethical behavior. On the other hand, it is difficult to find an example of a profession that has had that autonomy taken away. It is possible, therefore, that the professions do not consider this to be a serious threat to their welfare.

How can professional codes of ethics be analyzed? The process of evaluating a professional code is very similar to that of evaluating a corporate code. The first thing to note is *content*. What does the code say? Which principles and rules are spelled out? Are the statements vague and fuzzy, or concrete and clear? The nursing code of ethics, for example, seems to focus primarily on patients' rights and the responsibility of nurses to protect those rights. The American Institute of Certified Public Accounting's code of ethics deals more with avoiding situations that could produce a conflict of interest, or even the appearance of one. The Accreditation Board for Engineering and Technology code of ethics has rules concerning conflicts of interest, but adds important principles regarding public safety. In other words, the code of ethics for a profession can reveal the kinds of issues that individuals within that profession must face. There are some principles, such as avoiding conflicts of interest, that are present in many different professional codes because they are relevant to many occupational areas, but each code has its own unique combination of these rules.

Professional codes can also be evaluated in terms of their *ethical level*. Remember Raiborn and Payne's four ethical levels? Consider whether the code is written at (1) the theoretical level, representing an almost unreachable ethical ideal; (2) the practical level, or behavior which can be achieved the majority of the time through diligent effort; (3) the currently attainable level, representing behavior considered normal for most individuals; or (4) the basic level, or the letter of the law. Since these are professional codes, and one of the qualifications for being considered a profession was that the group would agree to hold itself to higher ethical standards than are expected of society in general, the ethical level should be higher than for corporate codes. Because enforcement is very difficult at the theoretical level, it would seem that most of the rules and principles should be written at the practical level.

Finally, a professional code should be evaluated in terms of its *monitoring and enforcement* procedures. If a code contains no provisions for enforcement, then it is safe to assume that it was written for public relations value and that the members are not likely to take it seriously. Punishments for violations of a code may range from admonishment or censure, to fines, to suspension of one's license, or even expulsion from the profession or group. Keep in mind that some professions are limited in their abilities to monitor compliance of the code, enforce the rules, and punish offenders because they lack the kind of powerful national organization that makes this possible. For instance, the American Medical Association would seem to have the power and resources to carefully monitor how well its members follow their code. The American Association of College and University Professors currently does not. And even in the professions generally recognized as having the most elaborate enforcement systems, the effectiveness of those processes continues to be controversial. Can a system designed so that doctors or lawyers decide when fellow doctors or lawyers have erred function objectively? In the words of California State Bar Governor Richard Annotico, a lawyer who violates the code "is generally somebody's friend who is basically a good guy who has 'gone bad' temporarily. And who in hell enjoys being an executioner?"[55]

Society grants special status to the professions based, in part, on the assumtion that higher standards will be self-imposed, monitored for compliance and enforced. Yet, skepticism is mounting regarding how well this arrangement is working. Robert Fellmeth states that, in California, 97% of seemingly valid complaints against doctors are never even investigated. He adds: "The attitude of those making these decisions (the disciplinary boards) is openly solicitous of the physician."[56] In a 1987 report of the California state bar's discipline system, Fellmeth called attention to an apparent conflict of interest. He noted that a committee dominated by a majority of practicing attorneys was "making a final decision based on a record given to them by another practicing attorney about the discipline of a third practicing attorney."[57] These self-governing professions defend their ability to maintain high ethical standards among their membership and are resistant to governmental interference. But remember that if a profession is not able to adequately maintain a higher level of behavior among its members than is present in society at large, then it risks losing the status of being considered a profession at all. After all, providing enforcement resources is a test of a profession's commitment to ethical behavior, is it not?

GOVERNMENT/PUBLIC SERVICE CODES

A mayor for a city of 100,000 residents has recently signed an agreement in principle with a large corporation to locate one of their factories in her town. Assuming that the arrangement has not yet been made public, would it be wrong for the mayor to buy stock in the company as a sign of good faith? Across the city, the owner of the local paint store is married to the woman who oversees the purchasing office for the local school system. Should he be able to bid on painting contracts for the schools? Would it be all right as long as the bids are sealed? A secretary in the office that handles building permits discovers that several of her superiors have been accepting illegal gifts from contractors and developers in exchange for speeding up the permit process. Should she blow the whistle, even if it means placing her own job in jeopardy?

Our final category of codes of ethics are the codes for public officials; those individuals who work for the government at the federal, state, or local level, and whose salaries are paid by tax dollars.

How are government/public service codes of ethics different? First, these codes frequently look like corporate codes of ethics in style and function, but are written, and often enforced, at the peer level like professional codes. The government represents an employer and yet the legislators consider themselves to be a part of the profession of public service. The legislators who write the rules of these codes are themselves subject to those rules, and do not necessarily function as managers or bosses to the employees at lower levels of government service, as would normally be seen in a corporate code written by top administrators. The prohibitions and principles contained in these codes are similar to the type found in the corporate codes already examined; however, an important distinction must be understood. Because of the unique nature of these government/public service codes of ethics, once adopted as part of the code, the rules become laws.

Thus, the guidelines given in these government/public service codes are, by definition, based on the minimum requirements of the law. This has been referred to as the *basic* level, or the lowest possible ethical level at which a code can be written. Writing a code of ethics at this level was not preferred in corporate codes because it can lead to the "loophole mentality" discussed previously, and because doing so implies that anything not illegal must be ethical. Such codes were strongly discouraged in the professions, because they hinder the ability a group might have to lift up the behavior of its members to the higher ethical plane required to gain social prestige and autonomy. It is no small coincidence that, with these comparatively weak codes of ethics, American legislators and government workers in recent years have found themselves with declining social prestige and less autonomy than at almost any time in recent history.

A final idiosyncrasy of these government codes of ethics is that they tend to be much more limited in scope than corporate or professional codes. For example, the Florida Code of Ethics for Public Officers and Employees deals almost exclusively with the concept of conflicts of interest, and primarily financial ones at that[58]. There is certainly nothing wrong with attempting to prevent conflicts of interest, for they indeed present strong temptations to our elected and appointed government officials. However, limiting the scope of a code of ethics to conflicts of interest alone implies there are no other serious ethical issues that are relevant. What about campaign issues? Should candidates be able to use negative campaign tactics that verge on slander and libel? What if these personal attacks come, not directly from an opposing candidate, but from a third party, as did the "Willie Horton" advertisements which were used effectively against Democratic presidential candidate Michael Dukakis in 1988?

There are other important ethical issues that fall through the cracks of current ethics codes. The system at times appears to discourage higher-level ethical behavior. For example, a candidate who refuses to accept any large contributions from special interest groups as a matter of principle, may find it difficult to compete with other candidates who feel bound only by the letter of the law. In many states, a judicial candidate is allowed to solicit campaign contributions from the very lawyers who will make arguments before her bench. What implications are present for attorneys who choose not to contribute?

What about the issue of partisanship? Is it an ethical issue if the Republicans and Democrats alike are working harder to promote the interests of their respective parties than the interests of the citizens who elected them? Clearly, there are other issues at stake than avoiding financial conflicts of interest. The absence of these and other important issues in most government service codes of ethics weakens the codes themselves and the public's perception of the credibility of the officials who are subject to them.

What are the strengths of government/public service codes? Government codes of ethics serve several important functions. They give the citizenry a public statement of ethical conduct to which public servants can be held. Thus, officials who are found to be in violation of the rules of the code have more difficulty arguing that the issue is just a matter of perception. Also, these codes do at least call public officials to a minimal level of ethical conduct. Compared to governments in other parts of the world, where open corruption, bribery, and even violence seem to be the norm, this would have to be seen as a step in the right direction. From the point of view of the public servants themselves, the codes give them some guidance in regards to what is considered appropriate and inappropriate conduct. In the confusing world of politics, where conflicting values and obligations are almost a daily given, these guidelines are helpful.

What are the weaknesses of government/public service codes? Some have already been noted. Because they are usually written at the *basic* ethical level, which is based on the minimal requirements of the letter of the law, they invite the abuse of "searching for loopholes." Because the provisions of these codes automatically become laws upon their adoption, it could be argued that they are not technically codes of ethics at all, but simply compilations of laws about ethics. Calling such a collection a "code of ethics" probably leads people to further confuse the legal standard with the very different standard of ethics. Thus, it could be argued that those government "codes of ethics" which are simply listings of laws might be doing as much harm as good.

Second, these public service codes do not typically require of government officials any higher standards than are required of citizens at large. In the earlier section on professional codes of ethics it was noted that it is important for a profession to call its members to a higher ethical plane if it wanted to maintain the respect and admiration of the community. Raiborn and Payne maintain that "a code of ethics should be based at the highest possible moral level in order to have an ultimate standard towards which to strive."[59] A code written at the basic level would not have this effect; in fact, it might act to pull the ethical behavior of some officials down to the letter of the law in order that they might remain competitive with other candidates for office. A possible solution to this problem would be for public officials to organize themselves into an actual profession. If there existed a non-partisan organization named the American Association of Ethical Public Officials, or something similar, the group could write its own code of ethics on a higher level than is allowed by law. Only individuals agreeing to maintain this higher level of ethical behavior would be admitted into fellowship in the group. Compliance with the provisions of the code could be monitored and enforced from within the association. While membership in the organization could not be a requisite for holding elected or appointed office, voters would almost certainly support candidates who represented higher ethical standards than mandated by law.

Another weakness in government/public service codes of ethics is that, because of the political factors involved in their development, at times the inconsistencies in their rules and principles are indefensible. For example, according to the Florida Code referred to earlier, it is permissible for a legislator to accept a gift, but not a gift intended to influence his or her judgment. But are not all of these gifts intended to influence? Why else would anyone give a legislator a gift? And why would it be ethically acceptable for an appreciative constituent to give a $500 watch to a legislator, but a travesty of justice if an appreciative plaintiff gave a similar gift to a judge? Does it make sense that an attempt to influence the judgment of the person *interpreting* the law is worse than an attempt to influence the judgment of the person *enacting* the law?

In a similar vein, consider the laws regarding "revolving door" lobbying. Should a government official who leaves office be permitted to immediately return as a paid lobbyist, attempting to influence the decisions of his or her ex-colleagues? Most public service codes of ethics include restrictions on such behavior, often mandating a period of time which must elapse before the individual may begin lobbying where he or she used to work. The Florida code, for example, requires a two-year waiting period applicable to all elected officials, appointed officials, and most bureaucrats. In Washington, D. C., however, an interesting inconsistency exists. Employees in the executive branch of the federal government are required to wait at least one year from the date they leave government service before they may return as a paid lobbyist. This wise law, written by Congress, is designed to prevent the misuse of their influence with those with which they used to work. However, these rules do not apply to legislative members and their staffs, who are permitted to begin lobbying their ex-colleagues for money the day after they leave office. Can a behavior be judged wrong if conducted by a member of the executive branch working in the White House, but judged right if performed by a staff member on Capital Hill? Is there some different ethical issue at stake?

Finally, there are problems in implementing these government/public office codes. The provisions of the codes vary widely and change every year. It can be difficult for public officials to know with certainty whether an action is acceptable or not. In Florida, for example, officials are encouraged to seek advisory opinions from the state Ethics Commission. Adapting and updating a code of ethics regularly helps to keep it viable and relevant, but if the changes are motivated by something other than a sincere desire to improve the ethical climate, they may not always be for the better.

In the areas of monitoring and enforcement, whistle-blowing has not been dealt with adequately in most public service codes. What are an official's obligations when he or she becomes aware of illegal or unethical actions by others within government? When is going public with that information justified? In one of the best-known cases of whistle-blowing by a government employee, A. Ernest Fitzgerald, a former high-level manager in the U.S. Air Force and CEO of Lockheed, told Congress and the press about a systematic practice of unethical bidding conducted by Lockheed and the Air Force in the 1960s.[60] Lockheed would intentionally underbid to ensure that it received a contract, as it did for the C-5A cargo plane, and then bill the Air Force for cost overruns on the projects. Fitzgerald went public with the truth and was fired for his efforts. He fought for 13 years to be reinstated and eventually was, in 1982, at full rank. Nevertheless, his case underscores the lack of protection typically afforded individuals who choose to follow the dictates of conscience. Even codes of ethics that do make provisions for protecting whistle-blowers from retaliation often have loopholes that undercut their effectiveness. Former Morton Thiokol engineer and whistle-blower, Roger Boisjoly, voiced the feelings of many when he said of his decision to inform the public of the shuttle O-ring design flaws, "I stepped into quicksand ... It was the total destruction of my career."[61]

CONCLUSION

There often appears to be an inverse relationship between competition and ethical behavior. As competition grows more intense, people become more tempted to bend the rules. The areas of life we have considered in this chapter – corporate America, the professions, and government service – are each fiercely competitive. Too often the path to success is not defined in terms of excellence, but of vanquishing an opponent. It is as if the old cliche had been updated to say, "All's fair in love, war, business, and politics." And yet we know inside that "all isn't fair." We understand that the end of success does not justify all possible means. We realize that fairness and integrity are important, if for no other reason, because that is how we wish to be dealt with by others. And often the most tenacious proponents of this "no holds barred" approach are those who complain the loudest when they perceive that they have been cheated or mistreated.

The appeal for business and professional ethics is a call to make the playing field level and fair. Corporate and professional codes of ethics represent voluntary attempts to do that. However, developing, writing, and distributing a code of ethics is not enough. There must be a solid connection between the rules and principles of the code and the universal ethical principles discussed earlier in this book. Further, the individuals subject to the code must understand that connection. Participating in a conflict of interest is not wrong because the chief executive officer of the company says so, and it is not wrong because a committee of accountants votes that it is; it is wrong because it violates important ethical principles. DeGeorge explains:

"A code should appropriately and helpfully refer to the principles from which the code flows, to principles of justice and fairness ... An objection might be that this is asking too much of a code. It cannot and should not provide general moral principles because these are assumed to be held by everyone ... But unless the code is understood in terms of moral principles, it will tend simply to be the expression of rules learned in rote – or even worse, of ideals never to be obtained. If the members of a profession are to internalize the rules of their profession, or if workers are to internalize the rules of their firm, they must understand how the rules are derived, and how they implement moral principles ... Ideally, each member who is covered by a code should understand its moral principles, as well as the nature of his or her profession or firm. Rather than memorizing a code, each could then derive the same code by thinking clearly and objectively about the moral issues typically faced by those covered by the code." [62]

FOR FURTHER INQUIRY

In the Appendix are examples of all three kinds of codes of ethics. As you read them, use the information that you have read to help you analyze their effectiveness. These questions may be useful:

1. What types of actions are allowed and disallowed? Are the rules consistent and fair?
2. Are there important ethical issues that have been omitted or avoided?
3. At what ethical level is each code written? Is that level appropriate?
4. What are the strengths of the codes? What changes do you think should be made? Why?

ENDNOTES

1. Catherine Fredman, "Nationwide Examination of Corporate Consciences," *Working Woman* (December 1991), p. 39.
2. Cecily A. Raiborn and Dinah Payne, "Corporate Codes of Conduct: A Collective Conscience and Continuum," in *Taking Sides: Clashing Views on Controversial Issues in Business Ethics and Society, 2nd edition*, Lisa H. Newton and Maureen M. Ford (eds.), The Dushkin Publishing Group, Inc., Guilford, Connecticut, 1992, p. 18.
3. Richard T. DeGeorge, *Business Ethics, 3rd Edition*, Macmillan Publishing Company, New York, 1990, p. 389.
4. Christopher D. Stone, *Where the Law Ends*, Harper and Row, New York, 1975. (Quoted in William H. Shaw, *Business Ethics*, Wadsworth Publishing Company, Belmont, CA, 1991, p. 172.)
5. William H. Shaw, Ibid, p. 173.
6. George Reiger, "A Question of Ethics," *Field and Stream*, January, 1992, p. 14-15.
7. Johnson & Johnson Corporate "Credo," Company Annual Report for 1982, p. 5. (Published in Lisa H. Newton and Maureen M. Ford (eds), *Taking Sides: Clashing Views on controversial Issues in Business and Society*, The Dushkin Publishing Company, Guilford, CT, 1992, p. 29.)
8. Quoted by LaRue T. Hosmer in "Ethical Codes," in Newton and Ford, Ibid, p. 30.
9. Raiborn and Payne, Ibid, p. 20.
10. Fredman, Ibid, p. 39.
11. Patrick E. Murphy, "Implementing Business Ethics," *Annual Editions: Business Ethics, 1991-2*, John E. Richardson (ed), The Dushkin Publishing Group, Inc., 1991, p. 101.
12. *Ethics Policies and Programs in American Business: Report of a Landmark Survey of U. S. Corporations*, Ethics Resource Center and Behavioral Research Center, Washington, D. C., 1987, p. 6.
13. *Ethics in American Business: A Special Report*; Touche Ross and Company, 1988, p. 7.
14. Rick Wartzman, "Nature or Nurture? Study Blames Ethical Lapses on Corporate Goals." *The Wall Street Journal*, (October 9, 1987), p. 21.
15. Shaw, Ibid, p. 174.
16. Raiborn and Payne, Ibid, p. 21.
17. DeGeorge, Ibid, p. 391-392.
18. Jack N. Behrman, *Essays on Ethics in Business and the Professions*, Prentice Hall, Englewood Cliffs, NJ, 1988, p. 156. (Quoted by Raiborn and Payne, Ibid, p. 21.)
19. Shaw, Ibid, p. 175.
20. Murphy, Ibid.
21. Kenneth Arrow, "Social Responsibility and Economic Efficiency," *Public Policy* (21), Summer 1973. (Republished in William Shaw and Vincent Barry, *Moral Issues in Business, 4th Edition*, Wadsworth Publishing Company, Belmont, CA, p. 217.)
22. Alyse Lynn Booth, "Who Are We?," *Public Relations Journal*, July, 1985. (Quoted in Shaw, Ibid, p. 174.)
23. Donald R. Cressy and Charles A. Moore, "Managerial Values and Corporate Codes of Ethics," *California Management Review*, (Summer, 1983), p. 53-57. (Quoted by Murphy, Ibid, p. 101-102)
24. Hosmer, Ibid, p. 27.
25. Hosmer, Ibid, p. 30.
26. Arrow, Ibid.
27. Raiborn and Payne, Ibid, p. 23.

28. Murphy, Ibid, p. 102.
29. Arrow, Ibid.
30. Arrow, Ibid.
31. Murphy, Ibid, p. 102.
32. Raiborn and Payne, Ibid, p. 23-24.
33. Milton Snoeyenbos and Donald Jewell, "Morals, Management and Codes," in Milton Snoeyenbos, Robert Ameder and James Humber (eds), Business Ethics, Promethius Books, Buffalo, NY, 1983, p. 107. (Quoted in Shaw and Barry, p. 196.)
34. Ethics Resource Center, Ibid, p. 11.
35. Murphy, Ibid, p. 102.
36. Ethics Resource Center, Ibid, p. 8.
37. Raiborn and Payne, Ibid, p. 22.
38. Robert E. Sweeney, holder of the Thompson-Hill Chair of Excellence in Accountancy at Memphis State University, in a speech entitled, "Developing an Ethical Climate Within Business" at the University of South Florida, March 9, 1992.
39. Ethics Resource Center, Ibid, p. 25.
40. The Ethics Code at Johnson & Johnson, "Our Credo," (Published in *Taking Sides: Clashing Views on Controversial Issues in Business Ethics and Society*, The Dushkin Publishing Company, Guilford, CT, 1992, p. 29)
41. Mary Kay Cosmetics, Inc. - Code of Ethics
42. GTE - Our Code of Business Ethics
43. Merrill Lynch - Guidelines For Business Conduct
44. Lindorff, Dave, "Engineers' Duty To Speak Out," *The Nation*, June 28, 1986. (Republished in William Shaw and Vincent Barry, *Moral Issues in Business*, 4th Edition, Wadsworth Publishing Co., Belmont, CA, 1989, p. 508-511.)
45. Sweeney, Ibid.
46. Shaw, Ibid, p. 10-11.
47. *The American Heritage Dictionary (2nd College Edition)*, Houghton Mifflin Company, Boston, 1985.
48. DeGeorge, Ibid, p. 381.
49. DeGeorge, Ibid.
50. DeGeorge, Ibid, p. 385.
51. Shaw, Ibid, p. 11.
52. DeGeorge, Ibid, p. 387.
53. Shaw, Ibid, p. 11.
54. DeGeorge, Ibid, p. 382.
55. Annotico, Richard. Quoted by Sarah Glazer in "Policing the Professions," *Editorial Research Reports*, May 26, 1989, p. 291.
56. Fellmeth, Robert C., Quoted by Sarah Glazer, Ibid, p. 294.
57. Fellmeth, Ibid, p. 300.
58. Florida Commission on Ethics, *Guide to the Sunshine Amendment and Code of Ethics for Public Officers and Employees, 1992*.
59. Raiborn and Payne, Ibid, p. 24.
60. Nielsen, Richard P., "Changing Unethical Organizational Behavior," *Executive*, May 1989, p. 123-130. (Republished in *Annual Editions: Business Ethics, 1991-92*, John E. Richardson (ed), The Dushkin Publishing Group, Inc. 1991, p. 91.)
61. Boisjoly, Roger, in a speech at the University of Tampa, September 23, 1991.
62. DeGeorge, Ibid, p. 390-391.

Appendix

Glossary

Index

APPENDIX

LETTER FROM THE BIRMINGHAM JAIL

Why We Can't Wait
Martin Luther King Jr.
Harper Collins Publishers, Inc. 1963, 1964

We know through painful experience that freedom is never voluntarily given by the oppressor; it must be demanded by the oppressed. Frankly, I have yet to engage in a direct-action campaign that was "well timed" in the view of those who have not suffered unduly from the disease of segregation. For years now I have heard the word "Wait!" It rings in the ear of every Negro with piercing familiarity. This "Wait" has almost always meant "Never." We must come to see, with one of our distinguished jurists, that "justice too long delayed is justice denied."

We have waited for more than 340 years for our constitutional and God-given rights. The nations of Asia and Africa are moving with jetlike speed toward gaining political independence, but we still creep at horse-and-buggy pace toward gaining a cup of coffee at a lunch counter. Perhaps it is easy for those who have never felt the stinging darts of segregation to say, "Wait." But when you have seen vicious mobs lynch your mothers and fathers at will and drown your sisters and brothers at whim; when you have seen hate-filled policemen curse, kick, and even kill your black brothers and sisters; when you see the vast majority of your twenty million Negro brothers smothering in an airtight cage of poverty in the midst of an affluent society; when you suddenly find your tongue twisted and your speech stammering as you seek to explain to your six-year-old daughter why she can't go to the public amusement park that has just been advertised on television, and see tears welling up in her eyes when she is told that Funtown is closed to colored children, and see ominous clouds of inferiority beginning to form in her little mental sky, and see her beginning to distort her personality by developing an unconscious bitterness toward white people; when you have to concoct an answer for a five-year-old son who is asking, "Daddy, why do white people treat colored people so mean?"; when you take a cross-country drive and find it necessary to sleep night after night in the uncomfortable corners of your automobile because no motel will accept you; when you are humiliated day in and day out by nagging signs reading "white" and "colored"; when your first name becomes "nigger," your middle name becomes "boy" (however old you are) and your last name becomes "John," and your wife and mother are never given the respected title "Mrs."; when you are harried by day and haunted by night by the fact that you are a Negro, living constantly at tiptoe stance, never quite knowing what to expect next, and are plagued with inner fears and outer resentments; when you are forever fighting a degenerating sense of "nobodiness" – then you will understand why we find it difficult to wait. There comes a time when the cup of endurance runs over, and men are no longer willing to be plunged into the abyss of despair. I hope, sirs, you can understand our legitimate and unavoidable impatience.

You express a great deal of anxiety over our willingness to break laws. This is certainly a legitimate concern. Because we so diligently urge people to obey the Supreme Court's decision of 1954 outlawing segregation in the public schools, at first glance it may seem rather paradoxical for us consciously to break laws. One may well ask: "How can you advocate breaking some laws and obeying others?" The answer lies in the fact that there are two types of laws: just and unjust. I would be the first to advocate obeying just laws. One has not only a legal but a moral responsibility to obey just laws. Conversely, one has a moral responsibility to disobey unjust laws. I would agree with St. Augustine that "an unjust law is no law at all."

Now, what is the difference between the two? How does one determine whether a law is just or unjust? A just law is a man-made code that squares with the moral law or the law of God. An unjust law is a code that is out of harmony with the moral law. To put it in the terms of St. Thomas Aquinas: An unjust law is a human law that is not rooted in eternal law and natural law. Any law that uplifts human personality is just. Any law that degrades human personality is unjust. All segregation statutes are unjust because segregation distorts the soul and damages the personality. It gives the segregator a false sense of superiority and the segregated a false sense of inferiority. Segregation, to use the terminology of the Jewish philosopher Martin Buber, substitutes an "I-it" relationship for an "I-thou" relationship and ends up relegating persons to the status of things. Hence segregation is not only politically, economically, and sociologically unsound, it is morally wrong and sinful. Paul Tillich has said that sin is separation. Is not segregation an existential expression of man's tragic separation, his awful estrangement, his terrible sinfulness? Thus it is that I can urge men to obey the 1954 decision of the Supreme Court, for it is morally right; and I can urge them to disobey segregation ordinances, for they are morally wrong.

Let us consider a more concrete example of just and unjust laws. An unjust law is a code that a numerical or power majority group compels a minority group to obey but does not make binding on itself. This is difference made legal. By the same token, a just law is a code that a majority compels a minority to follow and that it is willing to follow itself. This is sameness made legal.

Let me give another explanation. A law is unjust if it is inflicted on a minority that, as a result of being denied the right to vote, had no part in enacting or devising the law. Who can say that the legislature of Alabama which set up that state's segregation laws was democratically elected? Throughout Alabama all sorts of devious methods are used to prevent Negroes from becoming registered voters, and there are some counties in which, even though Negroes constitute a majority of the population, not a single Negro is registered. Can any law enacted under such circumstances be considered democratically structured?

Sometimes a law is just on its face and unjust in its application. For instance, I have been arrested on a charge of parading without a permit. Now, there is nothing wrong in having an ordinance which requires a permit for a parade. But such an ordinance becomes unjust when it is used to maintain segregation and to deny citizens the First-Amendment privilege of peaceful assembly and protest.

I hope you are able to see the distinction I am trying to point out. In no sense do I advocate evading or defying the law, as would the rabid segregationist. That would lead to anarchy. One who breaks an unjust law must do so openly, lovingly, and with a willingness to accept the penalty. I submit that an individual who breaks a law that conscience tells him is unjust, and who willingly accepts the penalty of imprisonment in order to arouse the conscience of the community over its injustice, is in reality expressing the highest respect for law.

Of course, there is nothing new about this kind of civil disobedience. It was evidenced sublimely in the refusal of Shadrach, Meshach and Abednego to obey the laws of Nebuchadnezzar, on the ground that a higher moral law was at stake. It was practiced superbly by the early Christians, who were willing to face hungry lions and the excruciating pain of chopping blocks rather than submit to certain unjust laws of the Roman Empire. To a degree, academic freedom is a reality today because Socrates practiced civil disobedience. In our own nation, the Boston Tea Party represented a massive act of civil disobedience.

We should never forget that everything Adolf Hitler did in Germany was "legal" and everything the Hungarian freedom fighters did in Hungary was "illegal." It was "illegal" to aid and comfort a Jew in Hitler's Germany. Even so, I am sure that, had I lived in Germany at the time, I would have aided and comforted my Jewish brothers. If today I lived in a Communist country where certain principles dear to the Christian faith are suppressed, I would openly advocate disobeying that country's anti-religious laws.

I must make two honest confessions to you, my Christian and Jewish brothers. First, I must confess that over the past few years I have been gravely disappointed with the white moderate. I have almost reached the regrettable conclusion that the Negro's great stumbling block in his stride toward freedom is not the White Citizen's Counciler or the Ku Klux Klanner, but the white moderate, who is more devoted to "order" than to justice; who prefers a negative peace which is the absence of tension to a positive peace which is the presence of justice; who constantly says, "I agree with you in the goal you seek, but I cannot agree with your methods of direct action"; who paternalistically believes he can set the timetable for another man's freedom; who lives by a mythical concept of time and who constantly advises the Negro to wait for a "more convenient season." Shallow understanding from people of good will is more frustrating than absolute misunderstanding from people of ill will. Lukewarm acceptance is much more bewildering than outright rejection.

I had hoped that the white moderate would understand that law and order exist for the purpose of establishing justice and that when they fail in this purpose they become the dangerously structured dams that block the flow of social progress. I had hoped that the white moderate would understand that the present tension in the South is a necessary phase of the transition from an obnoxious negative peace, in which the Negro passively accepted his unjust plight, to a substantive and positive peace, in which all men will respect the dignity and worth of human personality. Actually, we who engage in nonviolent direct action are not the creators of tension. We merely bring to the surface the hidden tension that is already alive. We bring it out in the open, where it can be seen and dealt with. Such as a boil that can never be cured so long as it is covered up but must be opened with all its ugliness to the natural medicines of air and light, injustice must be exposed, with all the tension its exposure creates, to the light of human conscience and the air of national opinion, before it can be cured.

SAMPLE CODES OF ETHICS

CORPORATE CODES:
CORPORATE CODE 1
THE ETHICS CODE AT JOHNSON AND JOHNSON - "OUR CREDO"[1]

We believe our first responsibility is to the doctors, nurses and patients, to mothers and all others who use our products and services.

In meeting their needs everything we do must be of high quality

We must constantly strive to reduce our costs In order to maintain reasonable prices.

Customers' orders must be serviced promptly and accurately.

Our suppliers and distributors must have an opportunity to make a fair profit.

We are responsible to our employees, the men and women who work with us throughout the world.

Everyone must be considered as an individual.

We must respect their dignity and recognized their merit.

They must have a sense of security in their jobs.

Compensation must be fair and adequate, and working conditions clean, orderly and safe.

We must be mindful of ways to help our employees fulfill their family responsibilities.

Employees must feel free to make suggestions and complaints.

These must be equal opportunity for employment, development and advancement for those qualified.

We must provide competent management, and their actions must be just and ethical.

We are responsible to the communities in which we live and work and to the world community as well.

We must be good citizens—support good works and charities and bear our fair share of taxes.

We must encourage civic improvements and better health and education.

We must maintain In good order the property we are privileged to use, protecting the environment and natural resources.

Our final responsibility is to our stockholders.

Business must make a sound profit.

We must experiment with new ideas.

Research must be carried on, innovative programs developed and mistakes paid for.

New equipment must be purchased, new facilities provided and new products launched.

Reserves must be created to provide for adverse times.

When we operate according to these principles, the stockholders should realize a fair return.

CORPORATE CODE 2
MARY KAY COSMENTICS INC. - CODE OF ETHICS [2]

You will want to uphold the highest standards. in your dealings with customers and sister Consultants, as set forth in the Mary Kay Beauty Consultant's Code of Ethics.

1. The golden rule and the true go-give spirit are practiced in all facets of the Mary Kay business.

2. Using Company-supplied literature, the *Perfect Start Workbook* and the *Consultant's Guide* as references, the Mary Kay skin care program, other Mary Kay products, and all facts concerning a Mary Kay career will be presented to customers and to prospective Consultants in a truthful, sincere and honest manner.

3. When serving any customer of Mary Kay, the Mary Kay Independent Beauty Consultant always keeps in mind the customer's needs. The personal and professional approach to serving customers is what sets the Mary Kay Beauty Consultant apart from someone who just sells cosmetics.

4. Every Mary Kay Beauty Consultant reflects the highest professional standards of integrity, honesty and responsibility in dealings with customers or fellow Consultants and the Company.

Mary Kay Cosmetics, Inc. is a member of the Direct Selling Association and endorses all private and governmental efforts which seek to promote high ethical standards in selling. DSA Member.

CORPORATE CODE 4
MERRILL LYNCH - GUIDELINES FOR BUSINESS CONDUCT [3]

Integrity, honesty, and dedication to the highest ethical standards are but a few of the attributes that set Merrill Lynch apart from many other organizations.

The attached brochure explains in some detail the basic tenets of Merrill Lynch's commitment to the highest standards of business conduct. The brochure is important. Every employee must know the commitment, believe in it, and work actively to keep it. That is why we provide each new employee with the brochure.

The brochure describes basic standards of conduct involving:
- Use of confidential information
- Conflicts of interest
- Regard for Merrill Lynch s assets

By signing this document, you agree to read Guidelines for Business Conduct, ensure that you understand it, and accept the obligation to follow the Guidelines. If you have any questions, you should consult with your manager.

Signature

Date

Introduction

Merrill Lynch has built its reputation as a leader in the financial services industry through its commitment to the standards of ethical business conduct. This document is a reminder to all Merrill Lynch employees of the seriousness of that commitment. It is also designed to offer them guidance in their continuing efforts to help the Firm enhance its position of achievement and respect in this regard.

Success in our business requires trust – the trust of our clients, our stockholders, and the general public. The first step toward earning that trust is, of course, our observance of the law. To this end, Merrill Lynch has established detailed policies and procedures, many of which are far more exacting than those set by others. These policies, some of which are mentioned in this booklet, are set forth in detail in the Policy Manual, which should be consulted for the authoritative statement of Management of Merrill Lynch policy.

Severe penalties and consequences flow from certain kinds of conduct that are illegal. But beyond acting legally, Merrill Lynch's commitment requires that we act ethically. By adhering to high ethical standards, we avoid the possibility of violating the law and enhance our own, and the Firm's reputation. Ethical business is good business.

Strict policies and procedures alone, however, cannot produce integrity and the high standards of ethical behavior for which we strive. Even these guidelines do not establish hard and fast rules of right and wrong that, if observed, will ensure ethical behavior in a particular situation. They will, however, establish an awareness and an understanding of ethical responsibilities and a sensitivity to ethical concerns. This will enable each Merrill Lynch employee, regardless of his or her position and role in the Firm, not only to recognize the existence of ethical concerns but to react honestly, intelligently, and professionally, with the utmost regard for both his or her own personal moral precepts and Merrill Lynch's commitment to the highest standards of business ethics.

Conflicts of Interest

Merrill Lynch expects that every employee will avoid any activity, interest, or association that might interfere or even appear to interfere with the independent exercise of his or her judgment in the best interests of the Firm, its stockholders, and the public.

Merrill Lynch policy identities and addresses many of the more obvious specific conflict situations that are likely to occur in the context of our Firm's business. In some cases, conduct is proscribed for more than ethical considerations; it is illegal.

Our Clients' Interests Come First

Serving client's effectively is, in a sense, our most important goal. Information gathered by Merrill Lynch is intended for the use of clients, and no employee is permitted to gain personal benefit from the advance knowledge of such information.

For example, many employees are engaged in corporate activities that may provide them with advance knowledge of securities information or market trends. Employees must not only refrain from using this information to their own advantage, but they must not disclose it to others, be it a spouse, relative, friend, or select customer, before it is generally available to the public. At times this may mean that employees are at an actual disadvantage in the marketplace, and, because of their constant possession of nonpublic information, some employees may never be able to trade in their areas of specialization. Similarly. in the case of an offering of publicly traded securities by Merrill Lynch, all clients orders must be filled before any employee will be allowed to participate.

Although it is most commonly identified in that context, the concept of inside information is not unique to the area of securities. Employees in the many other areas of Merrill Lynch's business, such as real estate or insurance, must exercise the same care in not using improperly nonpublic corporate information or their position with Merrill Lynch for their own financial benefit.

Outside Business Connections

Employees are prohibited from engaging in any outside business activities that might give rise to conflicts of interest or jeopardize the Firm's integrity or reputation. Many employees are engaged in outside business activities. Such activity may involve a financial interest as a partner or stockholder in another business, an officer position in a family-owned corporation, or an outside directorship in another company. The concern here is one of divided loyalty. The relevant considerations are many; the nature and extent of your outside interest; the relationship between Merrill Lynch and the other concern; the duties of your position with Merrill Lynch and the other business *etc.* In addition New York Stock Exchange and NASD rules impose requirements relating to outside employment and directorships.

In an effort to avoid even the appearance of a divided loyalty Merrill Lynch requires that all outside business connections be reported so that they can be scrutinized for potential conflicts by the General Counsel. More specifically Merrill Lynch policy prohibits service as a director of a publicly traded corporation and requires that service as a director, officer, or employee of any other corporation or business be expressly authorized.

Public Office

Merrill Lynch policy permits employees to run for and serve in a local elective office of a civic nature, provided that such activity including campaigning for the office occurs outside normal business hours, is carried on solely in the individual's capacity as a private citizen and not as a representative of Merrill Lynch and involves no conflict of interest. In this regard, employees must take care that the duties of office do not involve matters, such as money management or investment activities, that are related to their responsibilities and duties as a Merrill Lynch employee, for the likelihood of a conflict of interest in such cases is greatly increased. To assure that conflicts are avoided, employees must receive the approval of the General Counsel's office prior to making any commitment for candidacy.

Employees may also support others in their campaign for public office provided that the time spent on such activity is outside normal business hours and no use is made of Merrill Lynch's name, facilities, or corporate funds.

Gifts and Gratuities

Employees (including members of their immediate families) may not, directly or indirectly, take, accept, or receive bonuses, fees, commissions, gifts, gratuities, excessive entertainment, or any other similar form of consideration, of other than nominal value, from any person, firm, corporation, or association with which Merrill Lynch does or seeks to do business. Conversely, it is generally against corporate policy to give gifts or gratuities absent specific approval by the General Counsel or his designee.

The foregoing are just a few examples of the potential conflicts that may arise. It is virtually impossible to envision, much less enumerate, every potential conflict situation. Being aware that conflicts of interest can and do exist greatly increases the likelihood that they will be recognized in a particular situation and, if they cannot be avoided, faced in an ethical, responsible manner.

In those cases where it is difficult to distinguish between proper and improper behavior, employees are encouraged to be guided by their own sense of ethical responsibility, assisted by the guidelines for using your own judgment set forth in the final section of this booklet— and, if appropriate, to seek advice.

Use of Information

Information is received by Merrill Lynch and its employees in many ways. Much of that information is of a nonpublic nature. It is essential for Merrill Lynch to maintain the inteqrity of confidential information (whether relating to Merrill Lynch or to a client) and to ensure that it is used only for the purpose for which it is intended. Information may be sensitive for a variety of reasons such as market impact, effect on negotiations, strategic positioning, relationships with competitors and vendors, and potential embarrassment. Merrill Lynch's basic policy is clear. Confidential information cannot be misused. The securities laws specifically prohibit any trading in a security by a person in possession of material nonpublic information. They further prohibit disclosure of the information to others. Merrill Lynch has adopted stringent policies limiting disclosure of confidential information to those with a need to know. It is essential that employees strictly adhere to these policies. Similarly employees should refrain from acting on information concerning publicly traded securities even if it is received in their individual capacities when the employee has reason to believe the information is derived from nonpublic sources.

Merrill Lynch is proud of the internal procedures it initiated long before the recent emphasis on insider trading violations, but the Firm is even more proud of the attitudes and ethics of its people. The Firm's image with the public and the regulatory community is unequaled in the financial services industry. Its reputation is its single most precious asset and depends on the actions of its people. Every employee shares in the responsibility to protect the Firm's reputation.

Even greater emphasis has been placed on maintaining proper restrictions on the use of nonpublic information as a result of the enactment of the Federal Insider Trading and Securities Fraud Enforcement Act of 1988. This law requires the establishment maintenance and enforcement of policies and procedures governing the use of material nonpublic information and imposes very stringent new sanctions against violators.

For guidance on particular issues employees should consult with legal counsel for their business unit.

Regard for Merrill Lynch Assets

Merrill Lynch is committed to the use of a strong effective system of internal controls designed to safeguard and preserve the Firm's assets. Each company in the Merrill Lynch organization is responsible for maintaining and enforcing a system of internal administrative and accounting controls. These systems of control, which are mandated by law, are designed to ensure that all business transactions are properly authorized at the appropriate management level, are executed in accordance with such authorization, and are properly reflected on the Firm's books and records.

The cooperation of each and every employee is necessary for this system to be effective in enabling Merrill Lynch to document transactions and dispositions of its assets accurately. Where employees are responsible for the acquisition or disposition of assets for the Firm, or are authorized to incur liabilities on the Firm's behalf, they must he careful not to exceed the authority vested in them. Every employee is involved, if not in the authorization or execution of business transactions, at least in reporting of some kind, if only expenses for travel and entertainment or hours worked on a time card. It is important that it be done honestly and accurately and that employees cooperate fully with both internal and independent audits.

Merrill Lynch's assets include more than its capital—there are its premises, equipment, information, business plans, ideas for new products and services, client lists, and most importantly, in a very real sense, its people. It is expected that employees will use these assets only for the purposes intended and not for their personal benefit unless they have been approved for general employee or public use. This even extends to business opportunities that come to employees as a result of their employment—they are the proprietary opportunities of Merrill Lynch.

Relationships with Clients

As previously mentioned, it has long been Merrill Lynch's policy that its clients' interests come first. It is this philosophy that has gained for Merrill Lynch the investor confidence that has enabled us to grow into the diversified financial services company we are today.

Merrill Lynch's continued growth and success depends, to a large extent, on the ability of its employees to increase that level of investor confidence. This means competing vigorously in the marketplace for business, but competing fairly and honestly. It means giving each client the time and attention needed to find the products and services most suitable for his or her needs. It means providing timely and accurate information that is not in any way misleading. We can be proud of the diversity and quality of the products and services Merrill Lynch, as an industry leader, has to offer. Employees must nevertheless be careful not to exaggerate their characteristics or make disparaging comparisons with the products and services of competitors.

Our clients trust us not only with their money but with a lot of confidential personal information. Merrill Lynch respects the privacy of client records, and access to personal information should be restricted to a business need-to-know basis. Absent the client's consent, disclosure of personal information is prohibited, except to the extent required by law. Client information may not be discussed with, or provided to, any person other than the client without the prior approval of counsel.

Relationships with Competitors

The two principal ways in which Merrill Lynch deals with other financial services organizations are through competition and cooperation. Each involves serious legal as well as ethical considerations. Competing too vigorously or unfairly and cooperating too closely or collusively are not only unethical but may be illegal.

Free and open competition in the business environment is healthy and desirable. Being competitive necessitates keeping an eye on competitors, gathering public information on their activities, products and services, and attempting to be as good or better. Competition however must always be fair; unfair competition is in fact anticompetitive. Hiring competitors employees to get trade secrets or other proprietary information for example may be improper. Sales can be increased by offering better quality products and services or by disparaging those offered by others. The latter is unfair competition.

It is entirely appropriate and desirable under certain circumstances to cooperate with our competitors. In the case of a public offering of securities, for example, Merrill Lynch often participates with other securities firms as a member of a syndicate. In the context of an industry association, members of competing firms often work together toward the solution to a common problem or the achievement of a common goal. What must be avoided in this or any other context is the discussion of such things as proprietary or confidential information, business plans, and pricing or sales policies, which might be viewed as an attempt to conspire. Extreme caution should be exercised to avoid any conduct that might violate antitrust laws; violation may carry criminal sanctions. If such a discussion is initialed by a competitor or a third party, it is a Merrill Lynch employees responsibility to object and, if the discussion does not stop, to leave the meeting and report the incident to legal counsel.

Relationships with Governmental Authorities

In recent years there has been much public concern with corporate payments and political contributions, both in the United Slates and abroad. Federal legislation, imposing substantial criminal as well as civil penalties, prohibits the making of certain types of improper payments abroad.

Payments

Merrill Lynch policy forbids payments of any kind by the Firm its subsidiaries, affiliates, officers or employees, to any person. government official, corporation or other entity, within the United States or abroad, for the purpose of obtaining or retaining business, or for the purpose of influencing favorable consideration of applications for a business activity or other matter. This policy covers all types of payments—including bribes and payoffs to minor government officials, which may or may not be considered legal under the circumstances.

Political Contributions

It is similarly contrary to Merrill Lynch policy, and indeed in many instances illegal, to make corporate contributions to political parties or candidates for public office within the United States unless approved by, or under a procedure adopted by, the Merrill Lynch & Co., Inc. Executive Committee. The approval process includes a review of each contribution to confirm its legality. This is not to say that individuals are not free, as private citizens, to endorse or contribute to political parties or candidates of their choice. Employees may do so on their own or through the Merrill Lynch Political Action Committee. In either case, however, Merrill Lynch will not directly or indirectly reimburse employees for their individual political contributions or in any way pressure an employee in his or her choice as to whom and in what amount a political contribution is to be made.

Under special circumstances, political contributions by subsidiaries or affiliates doing business outside the United States may be permitted. In such cases, the proposed contribution must be not only lawful, but sufficiently recognized and widely accepted as to be considered appropriate. Moreover, the contribution must be authorized by the Executive Committee.

Relationships with Employees

Just as important as our relationships with outsiders are our internal relationships with fellow employees. Accordingly, Merrill Lynch demands that we observe among ourselves the same high standards of integrity and ethical responsibility required in our dealings with the public. In addition, the Firm recognizes its responsibility to promote this type of behavior by providing a healthy and supportive work environment that enhances the physical and emotional well-being of its employees.

In hiring, developing, promoting, and compensating employees, Merrill Lynch strictly adheres to a policy of equal employment, without discrimination on the basis of race, religion, color, national origin, age, sex, or disability unrelated to job performance. Its compensation program is designed to be competitive and reward employee performance. Personal advancment in terms of education and the upgrading of skills is encouraged through various in-house training programs as well as tuition assistance programs for outside job-related educational opportunities. Promotions are based on qualification and merit.

Merrill Lynch recognizes and respects the privacy and confidentiality of employee records. Personnel, medical, benefits, and other employee records are afforded the same confidentiality given to client records. Information is collected, utilized, and disclosed only on a business need-to-know basis, except as may otherwise be required by law.

Using Your Own Judgment

In all of the foregoing we have tried to establish guidelines for conduct in some of the general areas that pose ethical concerns. It is impossible to define or even envision every conceivable situation in which employees will be confronted with an ethical dilemma. This booklet will, however, have established an awareness and alertness to ethical responsibilities that will cause you to stop before taking action in a particular situation and to make an evaluation of the ethical concerns involved. In making a final decision an individual will then often have to be guided by his or her own personal ethical standards.

You may find it helpful to ask yourself the following questions:
• Does the action enhance the Firms reputation?
• Is it legal?
• Does it conform to Merrill Lynch policy?
• Would you like to see it become a general industry or public practice?
• Would you lose customers if this action were generally known to them?
• Does it endanger anyone's financial stability, life, health, or safety?

• Would you be embarrassed if all the details were known by your manager, your peers, your subordinates, your family, or your friends?
• Could it in any way be interpreted as or have the appearance of an inappropriate act or manner of behavior?
• What would you think of your manager, peers, or subordinates who acted in a similar fashion?
• How would your conduct be viewed by the public if reported in the news media?
• Are you compromising your own personal ethics in any way? Does it make you feel uncomfortable?

Merrill Lynch asks and requires that every employee make a personal commitment to the observation of the highest ethical standards and exercise of proper judgment in all aspects of his or her business dealings. If we all make and honor this commitment we can be sure that honesty and trust will continue to be a way of life at Merrill Lynch.

Your Obligation to Report Misconduct

Protecting the Firm's reputation is a collective effort. Employees should be diligent in questioning situations that they believe violate Merrill Lynch's high ethical standards. Improprieties should be reported to whatever level of Management necessary to properly address the situation.

To report unethical behavior on a confidential basis, the General Counsel's Office has established a HOTLINE; the telephone numbers are (212) 449-9590 (New York) and (800) 338-8954 (outside New York).

PROFESSIONAL CODES:
STANDARDS OF PRACTICE AMERICAN ASSOCIATION OF ADVERTISING AGENCIES[4]

We hold that a responsibility of advertising agencies is to be a constructive force in business.

We hold that, to discharge this responsibility, advertising agencies must recognize an obligation, not only to their clients, but to the public, the media they employ and to each other. As a business, the advertising agency must operate within the framework of competition. It is recognized that keen and vigorous competition, honestly conducted, is necessary to the growth and the health of American business. However, unethical competitive practices in the advertising agency business lead to financial waste, dilution of service, diversion of manpower, loss of prestige, and tend to weaken public confidence both in advertisements and in the institution of advertising.

We hold that the advertising agency should compete on merit and not by attempts at discrediting or disparaging a competitor agency, or its work, directly or by inference, or by circulating harmful rumors about another agency, or by making unwarranted claims of particular skill in judging or prejudging advertising copy.

To these ends, the American Association of Advertising Agencies has adopted the following *Creative Code* as being in the best interests of the public, the advertisers, the media, and the agencies themselves. The A.A.A.A. believes the Code's provisions serve as a guide to the kind of agency conduct that experience has shown to be wise, foresighted, and constructive. In accepting membership, an agency agrees to follow it.

Creative Code

We, the members of the American Association of Advertising Agencies, in addition to supporting and obeying the laws and legal regulations pertaining to advertising, undertake to extend and broaden the application of high ethical standards. Specifically, we will not knowingly produce advertising which contains:

a. False or misleading statements or exaggerations, visual or verbal.

b. Testimonials which do not reflect the real opinion of the individual(s) involved.

c. Price claims which are misleading.

d. Claims insufficiently supported, or that distort the true meaning or practicable application of statements made by professional or scientific authority.

e. Statements, suggestions or pictures offensive to public decency or minority segments of the population.

We recognize that there are areas that are subject to honestly different interpretations and judgment. Nevertheless, we agree not to recommend to an advertiser, and to discourage the use of, advertising that is in poor or questionable taste or that is deliberately irritating through aural or visual content or presentation.

Comparative advertising shall be governed by the same standards of truthfulness, claim substantiation, tastefulness, etc., as apply to other types of advertising.

These Standards of Practice of the American Association of Advertising Agencies come from the belief that sound and ethical practice is good business. Confidence and respect are indispensable to success in a business embracing the many intangibles of agency service and involving relationships so dependent upon good faith.

Clear and willful violations of these Standards of Practice may be referred to the Board of Directors of the American Association of Advertising Agencies for appropriate action, including possible annulment of membership as provided by Article IV, Section 5, of the Constitution and By-Laws * * *.

ASSOCIATION CODE FOR NURSES - AMERICAN NURSES [5]

Preamble

The *Code for Nurses is* based on belief about the nature of individuals, nursing, health, and society. Recipients and providers of nursing services are viewed as individuals and groups who possess basic rights and responsibilities, and whose values and circumstances command respect at all times. Nursing encompasses the promotion and restoration of health, the prevention of illness, and the alleviation of suffering. The statements of the *Code* and their interpretation provide guidance for conduct and relationships in carrying out nursing responsibilities consistent with the ethical obligations of the profession and quality in nursing care.

Code for Nurses

1. The nurse provides services with respect for human dignity and the uniqueness of the client unrestricted by considerations of social or economic status, personal attributes, or the nature of health problems.

2. The nurse safeguards the client's right to privacy by judiciously protecting information of a confidential nature.

3. The nurse acts to safeguard the client and the public when health care and safety are affected by the incompetent, unethical, or illegal practice of any person.

4. The nurse assumes responsibility and accountability for individual nursing judgments and actions.

5. The nurse maintains competence in nursing.

6. The nurse exercises informed judgment and uses individual competence and qualifications as criteria in seeking consultation, accepting responsibilities, and delegating nursing activities to others.

7. The nurse participates in activities that contribute to the ongoing development of the profession's body of knowledge.

8. The nurse participates in the profession's efforts to implement and improve standards of nursing.

9. The nurse participates in the profession's efforts to establish and maintain conditions of employment conducive to high quality nursing care.

10. The nurse participates in the profession's effort to protect the public from misinformation and misrepresentation and to maintain the integrity of nursing.

11. The nurse collaborates with members of the health professions and other citizens in promoting community and national efforts to meet the health needs of the public.

CODE OF ETHICS OF ENGINEERS [6]

THE FUNDAMENTAL PRINCIPLES

Engineers uphold and advance the integrity, honor and dignity of the engineering profession by:
I. using their knowledge and skill for the enhancement of human welfare;
II. being honest and impartial, and serving with fidelity the public, their employers and clients;
III. striving to increase the competence and prestige of the engineering profession; and
IV. supporting the professional and technical societies of their disciplines.

THE FUNDAMENTAL CANONS

1. Engineers shall hold paramount the safety, health, and welfare of the public in the performance of their professional duties.

2. Engineers shall perform services only in the areas of their competence.

3. Engineers shall issue public statements only in an objective and truthful manner.

4. Engineers shall act in professional matters for each employer or client as faithful agents or trustees and shall avoid conflicts of interest.

5. Engineers shall build their professional reputation on the merit of their services and shall not compete unfairly with others.

6. Engineers shall act in such a manner as to uphold and enhance the honor integrity and dignity of the profession.

7. Engineers shall continue their professional development throughout their careers and shall provide opportunities for the professional development of those engineers under their supervision.

ABET, 345 East 47th Street New York, NY 10017
*Formerly Engineers' Council for Professional Development. (Approved by the ECPD Board of Directors, October 5, 1977)

SOCIETY OF PROFESSIONAL JOURNALISTS - CODE OF ETHICS [7]

The SOCIETY of Professional Journalists, believes the duty of journalists is to serve the truth.

We BELIEVE the agencies of mass communication are carriers of public discussion and information, acting on their Constitutional mandate and freedom to learn and report the facts.

We BELIEVE in public enlightenment as the forerunner of justice, and in our Constitutional role to seek the with as part of the public's right to know the truth.

We BELIEVE those responsibilities carry obligations that require journalists to perform with intelligence, objectivity, accuracy, and fairness.

To these ends, we declare acceptance of the standards of Practice here set forth:

I. RESPONSIBILITY

The public's right to know of events of public importance and interest is the overriding mission of the mass media. The purpose of distributing news and enlightened opinion is to serve the general welfare. Journalists who use their professional status as representatives of the public for selfish or other unworthy motives violate a high trust.

II. FREEDOM OF THE PRESS

Freedom of the press is to be guarded as an inalienable right of people in a free society. It carries with it the freedom and the responsibility to discuss, question, and challenge actions and utterances of our government and of our public and private institutions. Journalists uphold the right to speak unpopular opinions and the privilege to agree with the majority.

III. ETHICS

Journalists must be free of obligation to any interest other than the public's right to know the truth.

1. Gifts, favors, free travel, special treatment or privileges can compromise the integrity of journalists and their employers. Nothing of value should be accepted.

2 Secondary employment, political involvement, holding public office, and service in community organizations should be avoided if it compromises the integrity of journalists and their employers. Journalists and their employers should conduct their personal lives in a manner that protects them from conflict of interest, real or apparent. Their responsibilities to the public are paramount. That is the nature of their profession.

3. So-called news communications from private

sources should not be published or broadcast without substantiation of their claims to news values.

4. Journalists will seek news that serves the public interest, despite the obstacles. They will make constant efforts to assure that the public's business is conducted in public and that public records are open to public inspection.

5. Journalists acknowledge the newsman's ethic of protecting confidential sources of information.

6. Plagiarism is dishonest and unacceptable.

IV. ACCURACY AND OBJECTIVITY

Good faith with the public is the foundation of all worthy journalism.

1. Truth is our ultimate goal.

2. Objectivity in reporting the news is another goal that serves as the mark of experienced professional. It is a standard of perforrnance toward which we strive. We honor those who achieve it.

3. There is no excuse for inaccuracies or lack of thoroughness.

4. Newspaper headlines should be fully warranted by the contents of the articles they accompany. Photographs and telecasts should give an accurate picture of an event and not highlight an incident out of context.

5. Sound practice makes clear distinction between news reports and expressions of opinion. News reports should be free of opinion or bias and represent all sides of an issue.

6. Partisanship in editorial comment that knowingly departs from the truth violates, the spirit of American journalism.

7. Journalists recognize their responsibility for offering informed analysis, comment, and editorial opinion on public events and issues. They accept the obligation to present such material by individuals whose competence, experience, and Judgment qualify them for it.

8. Special articles or presentations devoted to advocacy or the writer's own conclusions and interpretations should be labeled as such.

V. FAIR PLAY

Journalists at all times will show respect for the dignity, privacy, rights, and well being of people encountered in the course of gathering and presenting the news.

1. The news media should not cornmunicate unofficial charges affecting reputation or moral character without giving the accused a chance to reply.

2. The news media must guard against invading a person's right to privacy.

3. The media should not pander to morbid curiosity about details of vice and crime.

4. It is the duty of news media to make prompt and complete correction of their errors.

5. Journalists should be accountable to the public for their reports and the public should be encouraged to voice its grievances against the media. Open dialogue with our readers, viewers, and listeners should be fostered.

VI. MUTUAL TRUST

Adherence to this code is intended to preserve and strengthen the bond of mutual trust and respect between American journalists and the American people.

The Society shall—by programs of education and other means—encourage individual journalists to adhere to these tenets, and shall encourage journalistic publications and broadcasters to recognize their responsibility to frame codes of ethics in concert with their employees to serve as guidelines in furthering these goals.

GOVERNMENT CODES

FLORIDA COMMISSION ON ETHICS GUIDE TO THE SUNSHINE AMENDMENT and CODE OF ETHICS for PUBLIC OFFICERS and EMPLOYEES (1992) [8]

I. HISTORY OF FLORIDA'S ETHICS LAWS

Florida has been a leader among the states in establishing ethics standards for public officials and recognizing the right of her people to protect the public trust against abuse. Our state constitution was revised in 1968 to require that a code of ethics for all state employees and non-judicial officers prohibiting conflict between public duty and private interests be prescribed by law.

Florida's first successful constitutional initiative resulted in the adoption of the "Sunshine Amendment" in 1976, providing additional constitutional guarantees concerning ethics in government. In the area of enforcement, the Sunshine Amendment requires that there be an independent commission (the Commission on Ethics) to investigate complaints concerning breaches of public trust by public officers and employees other than judges.

The "Code of Ethics for Public Officers and Employees" adopted by the Legislature is found in Chapter 112 (Part 111) of the Florida Statutes. Foremost among the goals of the Code is to promote the public interest and maintain the respect of the people in their government. The Code is also intended to ensure that public officials conduct themselves independently and impartially, not using their offices for private gain other than compensation provided by law. While seeking to protect the integrity of government, the Code also seeks to avoid the creation of unnecessary barriers to public service.

Criminal penalties which initially applied to violations of the Code were eliminated in 1974 in favor of administrative enforcement. The Legislature created the Commission on Ethics that year "to serve as guardian of the standards of conduct" for public officials, state and local. Five of the Commission's nine members are appointed by the Governor, and two each are appointed by the President of the Senate and Speaker of the House of Representatives. No more than five Commission members may be members of the same political party, and none may hold any public employment during their two-year terms of office. A chairman is selected from among the members to serve a one-year term and may not succeed himself.

II. ROLE OF THE COMMISSION ON ETHICS

In addition to its constitutional duties regarding the investigation of complaints, the Commission:
• Renders advisory opinions to public officials;
• Prescribes forms for financial disclosure;
• Prepares mailing lists of public officials subject to disclosure laws for use by Supervisors of Elections and the Secretary of State in distributing forms and notifying delinquent filers;
• Makes recommendations to disciplinary officials when appropriate for violations of ethics and disclosure laws, because it does not impose penalties;
• Administers the Executive Branch Lobbyist Registration Law;
• May file suit to void contracts.

III. THE ETHICS LAWS

The ethics laws generally consist of two types of provisions, those prohibiting certain actions or conduct and those requiring that certain disclosures be made to the public. The following descriptions of these laws are simplified to put people on notice of their requirements. However, we also suggest that you review the wording of the actual law. Citations to the appropriate laws are contained in brackets. The laws summarized below apply generally to all public officers and employees, state and local, including members of advisory bodies. The principal exception to this broad coverage is the exclusion of judges, as they fall within the jurisdiction of the Judicial Qualifications Commission. The laws also do not apply to independent contractors with governmental agencies.

A. PROHIBITED ACTIONS OR CONDUCT

1. Solicitation or Acceptance of Gifts

Public officers, employees, and candidates are prohibited from soliciting or accepting anything of value, such as a gift, loan, reward, promise of future employment, favor, or service, that is based on an understanding that their vote, official action, or judgment would be influenced by such gift. (Sec. 112.313(2), Fla. Stat.)

Persons required to file financial disclosure FORM 1 or FORM 6 (see part 111 F of this brochure), as well as procurement employees for the State, are prohibited from *soliciting* any gift, food, or beverage from a political committee, committee of continuous existence, lobbyist who has lobbied their agency within the past 12 months, or the partner, firm, employer, or principal of such a lobbyist. (Section 112.3148, Fla. Stat., as amended by Ch. 90-502 and Ch. 91-292, Laws of Fla.)

Persons required to file FORM 1 or FORM 6, as well as State procurement employees, are prohibited from directly or indirectly *accepting* a gift worth over $100 from such a lobbyist, from a partner, firm, employer, or principal of the lobbyist, or from a political committee or committee of continuous existence. (Section 112.3148, Fla. Stat., as amended by Ch. 90-502, Laws of Fla., and as further amended by Ch. 91-292, Laws of Fla.)

2. Unauthorized Compensation

Public officers or employees and their spouses and minor children are prohibited from accepting any compensation, payment, or thing of value when they know, or with the exercise of reasonable care should know, that it is given to influence their vote or official action. (Sec. 112.313(4), Fla. Stat.)

3. Misuse of Public Position

Public officers and employees are prohibited from corruptly using or attempting to use their official positions to obtain a special privilege for themselves or others. (Sec. 112.313(6), Fla. Stat.)

4. Disclosure or Use of Certain Information

Public officers and employees are prohibited from disclosing or using information not available to the public and obtained by reason of their public positions for the personal benefit of themselves or others. (Sec. 112.313(8), Fla. Stat.)

5. Solicitation or Acceptance of Honoraria

Persons required to file financial disclosure FORM 1 or FORM 6 (see part 111 F of this brochure), as well as procurement employees for the State, are prohibited from *soliciting* an honorarium which is related to their public office or duties. (Section 112.3149, Fla. Stat., as created by Ch. 90-502, Laws of Fla.)

Persons required to file FORM 1 or FORM 6, as well as State procurement employees, are prohibited from knowingly *accepting* an honorarium from a political committee, committee of continuous existence, lobbyist who has lobbied their agency within the past 12 months, or the partner, firm, employer, or principal of such a lobbyist. However, they may accept the payment of expenses related to an honorarium event from such persons or entities, provided that the expenses are disclosed. See part 111 F of this brochure. (Section 112.3149, Fla. Stat., as created by Ch. 90-502, Laws of Fla.)

Lobbyists and their partners, firms, employers, and principals, as well as political committees and committees of continuous existence, are prohibited from *giving an honorarium* to persons required to file FORM 1 or FORM 6 and to State procurement employees. Violations of this law may result in fines of up to $5,000 and prohibitions against lobbying for up to two years. (Section 112.3149, Fla. Stat., as created by Ch. 90-502, Laws of Fla.)

B. PROHIBITED EMPLOYMENT AND BUSINESS RELATIONSHIPS

1. Doing Business With One's Agency

(a) Public employees acting as purchasing agents, or public officers acting in their official capacity, are prohibited from purchasing, renting, or leasing any realty, goods, or services for their agency from a business entity in which they, their spouse, or child own more than a 5% interest. Sec. 112.313(3), Fla. Stat.)

(b) Public officers and employees, acting in a private capacity, also are prohibited from renting, leasing, or selling any realty, goods, or services to their own agency if they are state officers or employees, or, if they are officers or employees of a political subdivision, to that subdivision or any of its agencies. (Sec. 112.313(3), Fla. Stat.)

2. Conflicting Employment or Contractual Relationship

(a) Public officers and employees are prohibited from holding any employment or contract with any business entity or agency regulated by or doing business with their agency. (Sec. 112.313(7), Fla. Stat.)

(b) Public officers and employees also are prohibited from holding any employment or having a contractual relationship which will pose a frequently recurring conflict between their private interests and public duties or which will impede the full and faithful discharge of their public duties. (Sec. 112.313(7), Fla. Stat.)

3. Exemptions—The prohibitions against doing business with one's agency and having conflicting employment may not apply:

(a) When the business is rotated among all qualified suppliers in a city or county.

(b) When the business is awarded by sealed, competitive bidding and the official, his spouse, or child have not attempted to persuade agency personnel to enter the contract. NOTE: Disclosure of the interest of the official, spouse, or child and the nature of the business must be filed on Commission FORM 3A with the Secretary of State or Supervisor of Elections, depending on whether the official serves at the state or local level.

(c) When the purchase or sale is for legal advertising, utilities service, or for passage on a common carrier.

(d) When an emergency purchase must be made to protect the public health, safety, or welfare.

(e) When the business entity is the only source of supply within the political subdivision and there is full disclosure of the official's interest to the governing body on Commission FORM 4A.

(f) When the aggregate of any such transactions does not exceed $500 in a calendar year.

(g) When the business transacted is the deposit of agency funds in a bank of which a county, city, or district official is an officer, director, or stockholder, so long as agency records show that the governing body has determined that the member did not favor his bank over other qualified banks.

(h) When the prohibitions are waived in the case of ADVISORY BOARD MEMBERS by the appointing person or by a two-thirds vote of the appointing body (after disclosure on Commission FORM 4A).

(i) When the public officer or employee purchases in a private capacity goods or services, at a price and upon terms available to similarly situated members of the general public, from a business entity which is doing business with his agency.

(j) When the public officer or employee in a private capacity purchases goods or services from a business entity which is subject to the regulation of his agency where the price and terms of the transaction are available to similarly situated members of the general public and the officer or employee makes full disclosure of the relationship to the agency head or governing body prior to the transaction. (Sec. 112.313(12), Fla. Stat.)

4. Additional Exemption

No elected public officer is in violation of the conflicting employment prohibition when employed by a tax exempt organization contracting with his agency so long as the officer is not directly or indirectly compensated as a result of the contract, does not participate in any way in the decision to enter into the contract, abstains from voting on any matter involving the employer, and makes certain disclosures. (Sec. 112.313(14), Fla. Stat.)

5. Lobbying State Agencies By Legislators

A member of the Legislature is prohibited from representing another person or entity for compensation during his term of office before any state agency other than judicial tribunals. (Art. 11, Sec. 8(e), Fla. Const. and Sec. 112.313(9), Fla. Stat., as amended by Ch. 91-85, Laws of Fla.)

6. Employees Holding Office

A public employee is prohibited from being a member of the governing body which serves as his employer while simultaneously continuing as an employee of that body. (Sec. 112.313(10), Fla. Stat.)

7. Professional and Occupational Licensing Board Members

An officer, director, or administrator of a state, county, or regional professional or occupational organization or association, while holding such position, may not serve as a member of a state examining or licensing board for the profession or occupation. (Sec. 112.313(11), Fla. Stat.)

8. Contractual Services: Prohibited Employment

A state employee of the executive or judicial branches who participates in the decision-making process involving a purchase request, who influences the content of any specification or procurement standard, or who renders advice, investigation, or auditing, regarding his agency's contract for services, is prohibited from being employed with a person holding such a contract with his agency. (Sec. 112.3185(2), Fla. Stat.)

C. RESTRICTIONS ON APPOINTING, EMPLOYING, AND CONTRACTING WITH RELATIVES

A public official is prohibited from seeking for a relative any appointment, employment, promotion or advancement in the agency in which he is serving or over which he exercises jurisdiction or control. No person may be appointed, employed, promoted, or advanced in or to a position in an agency if such action has been advocated by a related public official who is serving in or exercising jurisdiction or control over the agency. NOTE: This prohibition does not apply to school districts, community colleges, and state universities. Also, the approval of budgets does not constitute "jurisdiction or control" for the purposes of this prohibition. (Sec. 112.3135, Fla. Stat.)

A state employee of the executive or judicial branches is prohibited from directly or indirectly procuring contractual services for his agency from a business entity of which a relative is an officer, partner, director, or proprietor, or in which he, his spouse, and children own more than a 5% interest. (Sec. 112.3185(6), Fla. Stat.)

D. POST OFFICE HOLDING AND EMPLOYMENT (REVOLVING DOOR) RESTRICTIONS

1. Lobbying By Former Legislators Or State wide Elected Officers

A member of the Legislature or a state wide elected official is prohibited for two years following vacation of office from representing another person or entity for compensation before the government body or agency of which the individual was an officer or member. (Art. 11, Sec. 8(e), Fla. Const. and Sec. 112.313(9), Fla. Stat., as amended by Ch. 91-85, Laws of Fla.)

2. Lobbying By Former State Employees

Certain employees of the executive and legislative branches of state government are prohibited from personally representing another person or entity for compensation before the agency with which they were employed for a period of two years after leaving their positions, unless employed by another agency of state government. (Sec. 112.313(9), Fla. Stat., as amended by Ch. 91-85, Laws of Fla.) These employees include the following:

(a) Executive branch employees serving in the SENIOR MANAGEMENT SERVICE and SELECTED EXEMPT SERVICE, as well as any person employed by the DEPARTMENT OF THE LOTTERY having authority over policy or procurement.

(b) Employees serving in the following position classifications: the Auditor General; the Sergeant at Arms and Secretary of the Senate; the Sergeant at Arms and Clerk of the House of Representatives; the executive director of the Advisory Council on Intergovernmental Relations and the executive director and deputy executive director of the Commission on Ethics; an executive director, staff director, or deputy staff director of each joint committee, standing committee, or select committee of the Legislature; an executive director, staff director, executive assistant, legislative analyst, or attorney serving in the Office of the President of the Senate, the Office of the Speaker of the House of Representatives, the Senate Majority Party Office, the Senate Minority Party Office, the House Majority Party Office, the House Minority Party Office; any person, hired on a contractual basis and having the power normally conferred upon such persons, by whatever title; and any person having the power normally conferred upon the above positions.

Employees who were employed prior to July 1, 1989, or who reached normal retirement age and retired from State employment by July 1, 1989, are exempt from these lobbying prohibitions.

PENALTIES: Persons found in violation of this section are subject to the penalties contained in the Code (see PENALTIES, Part V) as well as a civil penalty in an amount equal to the compensation which the person receives for the prohibited conduct. (Sec. 112.313(9)(a)5., Fla. Stat., as amended by Ch. 91-85, Laws of Fla.)

3. Additional Restrictions on Former State Employees

A former executive or judicial branch employee is prohibited from having employment or a contractual relationship, at any time after retirement or termination of employment, with any business entity (other than a public agency) in connection with a contract in which the employee participated personally and substantially by recommendation or decision while a public employee. (Sec. 112.3185(3), Fla. Stat.)

A former executive or judicial branch state employee who has retired or terminated employment is prohibited from having any employment or contractual relationship for two years with any business entity (other than a public agency) in connection with a contract for services which was within his responsibility while serving as a state employee. (Sec. 112.3185(4), Fla. Stat.)

Unless waived by the agency head, a former executive or judicial branch state employee may not be paid more for contractual services provided by him to his former agency during the first year after leaving the agency than his annual salary before leaving. (Sec. 112.3185(5), Fla. Stat.)

E. VOTING CONFLICTS OF INTEREST

NO STATE PUBLIC OFFICIAL IS PROHIBITED FROM VOTING IN HIS OFFICIAL CAPACITY ON ANY MATTER COMING BEFORE HIM. However, a STATE PUBLIC OFFICER who votes on a measure which inures to his special private gain, or which he knows would inure to the special private gain of any PRINCIPAL by whom he is retained, of the PARENT ORGANIZATION or ELECTED CONSTITUTIONAL OFFICERS, OTHER STATE OFFICERS, and SPECIFIED STATE EMPLOYEES who must file annually FORMS 1, 6, 7 or 10 will be sent these forms by mail from the Department of State by JUNE 1 of each year. Newly elected and appointed officers and employees should contact the heads of their agencies or the Department of State for copies of the forms.

Any person needing one or more of the other forms (FORMS 2, 3A, 4A, 8A, 8B, 9,30, and 50) described herein may obtain them upon request from a Supervisor of Elections or from the Department of State, Division of Elections, Room 1801, The Capitol, Tallahassee, Florida 32399.

V. PENALTIES

A. Non-criminal Penalties for Violation of the Sunshine Amendment and the Code of Ethics

There are no criminal penalties for violation of the Sunshine Amendment and the Code of Ethics. Penalties for violation of those laws may include: impeachment, removal from office or employment, suspension, public censure, reprimand, demotion, reduction in salary level, forfeiture of no more than one-third salary per month for no more than twelve months, a civil penalty not to exceed $5,000, and restitution of any pecuniary benefits received.

B. Penalties for Candidates

CANDIDATES for public office who are found in violation of the Sunshine Amendment or the Code of Ethics may be subject to one or more of the following penalties: disqualification from being on the ballot, public censure, reprimand, or a civil penalty not to exceed $5,000.

C. Penalties for Former Officers and Employees

FORMER PUBLIC OFFICERS or EMPLOYEES who are found in violation of a provision applicable to former officers or employees or whose violation occurred prior to such officer's or employee's leaving public office or employment may be subject to one or more of the following penalties: public censure and reprimand, a civil penalty not to exceed $5,000, and restitution of any pecuniary benefits received. (Sec. 112.317, Fla. Stat., as amended by Ch. 91-85, Laws of Fla.)

D. Penalties for Lobbyists and Others

An executive branch lobbyist who has failed to comply with the Executive Branch Lobbying Registration law (see Part VlII) may be reprimanded, censured, or prohibited from lobbying executive branch agencies for up to 2 years.

Lobbyists, their employers, principals, partners, and firms, and political committees and committees of continuous existence who give a prohibited gift or honorarium or fail to comply with the gift reporting requirements for gifts worth between $25 and $100 may be penalized by a fine of not more than $5,000 and a prohibition on lobbying, or employing a lobbyist to lobby, before the agency of the public officer or employee to whom the gift was given for up to 2 years.

E. Felony Convictions: Forfeiture of Retirement Benefits

Public officers and employees must forfeit all rights and benefits under the retirement system to which they belong if convicted of certain offenses prior to their retirement. These offenses include embezzlement or theft of public funds; bribery; felonies specified in Chapter 838, Florida Statutes; impeachable offenses; and felonies committed with intent to defraud the public or their public agency. (Sec. 112.3173, Fla. Stat.)

VI. ADVISORY OPINIONS

Conflicts of interest may be avoided by greater awareness of the ethics laws on the part of public officials and employees through advisory assistance from the Commission on Ethics.

A. Who Can Request An Opinion

Any public officer, candidate for public office, or public employee in Florida who is in doubt about the applicability of the standards of conduct or disclosure laws to himself, or anyone who has the power to hire or terminate another public employee, may seek an advisory opinion from the Commission about himself or that employee.

B. How To Request An Opinion

Opinions may be requested by letter presenting a question based on a real situation and including a detailed description of the situation. Opinions are issued by the Commission and are binding on the conduct of the person who is the subject of the opinion, unless material facts were omitted or misstated in the request for the opinion. A published opinion will not bear the name of the persons involved unless they consent to the use of their name.

C. How To Obtain Published Opinions

Published opinions of the Commission on Ethics are available for purchase at prices below their actual cost. The opinions are printed in looseleaf volumes containing a subject-matter index and a citator to all Florida Statutes and State constitutional provisions construed or relied upon by the Commission. Every agency of government should have a set of opinions for ready reference when the need arises.

The Commission also publishes a Digest of its advisory opinions which is available to anyone upon request. The Digest is published quarterly and is sent free of charge. The order form at the end of this booklet may be used to request copies of the Commission's published opinions and its Digest of Opinions.

VII. COMPLAINTS

A. A Citizen's Responsibility

The Commission on Ethics cannot conduct investigations of alleged violations of the Sunshine Amendment or the Code of Ethics unless a person files a sworn complaint with the Commission alleging such violation has occurred.

It is your responsibility as a citizen, when having knowledge that a person in government has violated the standards of conduct or disclosure laws described above or has committed some other breach of the public trust, to report these violations to the Commission. Otherwise, the Commission is unable to take action, even after learning of such misdeeds through newspaper reports and phone calls.

Should you desire assistance in obtaining or completing a complaint form (FORM 50), you may receive either by contacting the Commission office at the address or phone number shown on the inside front cover of this booklet.

B. Confidentiality

The complaint, as well as all proceedings and records relating to the complaint, are confidential until the accused requests that such records be made public or until the complaint reaches a stage in the Commission's proceedings where it becomes public. This means that unless the Commission receives a written waiver of confidentiality from the accused, the Commission is not free to release any documents or to comment on a complaint to members of the public or press, so long as the complaint remains in a confidential stage.

IN NO EVENT MAY A COMPLAINT BE FILED OR DISCLOSED WITH RESPECT TO A CANDIDATE FOR ELECTION WITHIN 5 DAYS PRECEDING THE ELECTION DATE.

C. How the Complaint Process Works

The Commission staff must forward a copy of the original sworn complaint to the accused within five days of its receipt. Any subsequent sworn amendments to the complaint also are transmitted within five days of their receipt.

Once a complaint is filed, there are three procedural stages which it goes through under the Commission's rules. The first stage is a determination of whether the allegations of the complaint are legally sufficient, that is, whether they indicate a possible violation of any law over which the Commission has jurisdiction. If the complaint is found not to be legally sufficient, the Commission will order that the complaint be dismissed without investigation, and all records relating to the complaint will become public at that time.

If the complaint is found to be legally sufficient, a preliminary investigation will be undertaken by the investigative staff of the Commission. The second stage of the Commission's proceedings involves this preliminary investigation and a decision by the Commission of whether there is probable cause to believe that there has been a violation of any of the ethics laws. If the Commission finds no probable cause to believe there has been a violation of the ethics laws, the complaint will be dismissed and will become a matter of public record. If the Commission finds probable cause to believe there has been a violation of the ethics laws, the complaint becomes public and usually enters the third stage of proceedings. This stage requires the Commission to decide whether the law was actually violated and, if so, whether a penalty should be recommended. At this stage, the accused has the right to request a public hearing (trial) at which evidence is presented or the Commission may order that such a hearing be held. Public hearings usually are held in or near the area where the alleged violation occurred.

When the Commission concludes that a violation has been committed, it may recommend one or more penalties to the appropriate disciplinary body or official and issues a public report of its findings.

When the Commission determines that a person has filed a complaint with malicious intent and the complaint further is found to be frivolous and without basis in law or fact, the complainant will be liable for costs plus reasonable attorney's fees incurred by the person complained against. The Department of Legal Affairs may bring a civil action to recover such costs, if they are not paid willingly.

D. Dismissal of Complaints At Any Stage of Disposition

The Commission may, at its discretion, dismiss any complaint at any stage of disposition should it determine that the public interest would not be served by proceeding further, in which case the Commission will issue a public report stating with particularity its reasons for the dismissal. (Sec. 112.324(10), Fla. Stat., as created by Ch. 91-85, Laws of Fla.)

E. Statute of Limitations

Beginning October 1, 1993, all sworn complaints alleging a violation of the Sunshine Amendment or the Code of Ethics will have to be filed with the Commission within 5 years of the alleged violation or other breach of the public trust. Time starts to run on the day AFTER the violation or breach of public trust is committed. The statute of limitations is tolled on the day a sworn complaint is filed with the Commission. If a complaint is filed and the statute of limitations has run, the complaint will be dismissed and the complaint and related materials will remain confidential. (Sec. 112.3231, Fla. Stat., as created by Ch. 91-85, Laws of Fla.)

VIII. EXECUTIVE BRANCH LOBBYING

As of October 1, 1989, any person who, for compensation and on behalf of another, lobbies an agency of the executive branch of state government with respect to a decision in the area of policy or procurement may be required to register as an executive branch lobbyist with the Commission on Ethics. Registration is required before lobbying an agency and is renewable annually on or before January 1 of each year. In addition, expenditure reports must be filed semi-annually. Persons who lobby in behalf of governmental agencies need not register.

Beginning October 1, 1991, the fee structure for registering to lobby executive branch agencies in calendar year 1992 will change from $10 per LOBBYIST annually to $20 per PRINCIPAL registered annually. (Sec. 112.3215, Fla. Stat., as amended by Ch. 91-292, Laws of Fla.)

Additional information may be obtained by contacting the Lobbyist Registrar at the following address:

Executive Branch Lobbyist Registration
Room 2105, The Capitol
Tallahassee, FL 32399-1450

IX. WHISTLE-BLOWER'S ACT

In 1986, the Legislature enacted a "Whistle-blower's Act" to protect employees of agencies and government contractors from adverse personnel actions in retaliation for disclosing information in a sworn complaint alleging certain types of improper activities on the part of an agency contractor, or for participating in an investigation or hearing conducted by an agency.

In 1991, the Legislature revised this law to afford greater protection to these employees by allowing a WRITTEN and SIGNED complaint rather than a sworn complaint. Further changes provide that the reporting of a public employer's gross waste of funds is an employee protected action. The most significant revision to the law is the shift to the employer of the burden of proof that an adverse personnel action was not taken in retaliation for the disclosure by an employee of any information pursuant to the "Whistle-blower's Act."

This law also creates a private sector "Whistleblower's Act" which will prohibit a private employer who employs more than 10 people from discharging, suspending, demoting, or taking any other adverse personnel action against an employee in retaliation for disclosing, or refusing to participate in, an illegal activity or practice of an employer. As created, the new law provides private employee and employer protections, specifies the mechanism by which an employer's violation of law may be reported, and describes remedies that can be imposed by the courts.

Employees who are subject to adverse actions as a result of reporting improper activities or disclosing information under this Act may, after exhausting all contractual or administrative remedies, bring a civil action against their employer in the appropriate court of law. (Sec. 112.3187 and Sec. 112.3188, Fla. Stat., as amended by Ch. 91285, Laws of Fla.)

While this language is contained within the Code of Ethics, the Commission has no jurisdiction or authority to proceed against persons who violate this Act in behalf of a person who is being retaliated against. Therefore, a person who has disclosed information alleging improper conduct as described above and who may suffer adverse consequences as a result should consult an attorney for information about his legal rights.

X. ADDITIONAL INFORMATION

As mentioned above, we suggest that you review the language used in each law for a more detailed understanding of Florida's ethics laws. The "Sunshine Amendment" is Article 11, Section 8, of the Florida Constitution. The Code of Ethics for Public Officers and Employees is contained in Part 111 of Chapter 112, Florida Statutes.

Additional information about the Commission's functions and interpretations of these laws may be found in Chapter 34 of the Florida Administrative Code, where the Commission's rules are published, and in *The Florida Administrative Law Reports,* which publishes many of the Commission's final orders.

If you are a public officer or employee concerned about your obligations under these laws, you may wish to contact an attorney who represents your agency or a private attorney for advice. The staff of the Commission will be happy to respond to oral and written inquiries by providing information about the law, the Commission's interpretations of the law, and the Commission's procedures.

ENDNOTES TO CODES

1. The Ethics Code at Johnson & Johnson, "Our Credo," (Published in *Taking Sides: Clashing Views on Controversial Issues in Business Ethics and Society*, The Dushkin Publishing Company, Guilford, CT, 1992, p. 29)
2. Mary Kay Cosmetics, Inc. - Code of Ethics
3. Merrill Lynch - Guidelines For Business Conduct
4. Standards of Practice - American Association of Advertising Agencies. (Published in Gorlin, Rena A., *Codes of Professional Responsibility*, 2nd Edition, The Bureau of National Affairs, Inc., Washington, D. C., 1990, p. 17-18.)
5. Association Code for Nurses - American Nurses. (Published in Gorlin, Ibid., p. 259-266.)
6. Code of Ethics of Engineers, Accreditation Board of Engineering and Technology, 345 East 47th Street, New York, NY, 1977.
7. Society of Professional Journalists - Code of Ethics. (Published in Gorlin, Ibid., p. 141-142.)
8. Florida Commission on Ethics, Ibid.

THE PROBLEM OF ETHICS
Vital Speeches of the Day
Charles W. Colson
Harvard University
April 4, 1991

I THINK HARVARD well deserves the reputation that it enjoys of being a very liberal university, liberal in the best sense of that word because you would have as a lecturer in the university today someone who is an ex-convict. But that maybe is not so inappropriate after all, as you look at what is happening on Wall Street in the business community. Perhaps in the business courses here at the business school they should take a little bit of attention to what is happening in prisons. I just spent three hours last week with one of your distinguished alumni, who is headed off for four years of free room and board, courtesy of the United States Government, as I did. I must also say that Harvard deserves the reputation for being a liberal university in the best sense of the word for inviting me to speak, because for the last three or four years I have written articles that here in Harvard could be considered quite impertinent, in which I have described my views at least on why it is impossible to teach ethics at Harvard. I may touch on that briefly today and I hope you will all accept it in good spirit, and I will be prepared for your questions.

I'm no longer in politics. I've done my time, literally and figuratively, but it's awfully hard not to watch what is happening in the political scene with a certain sense of dismay when we see the Keating 5, as you've read about, 5 United States Senators tried in effect by their own tribunal. Just before that another Senator, who happens to be a good friend of mine, Dave Durenberger, who was censured by the Senate. I spent some time recently with Mayor Barry, the former mayor of the District of Columbia, who was of course arrested for drug use. You look at South Carolina and Arizona and you see scams going on in the legislatures that have been now exposed by Federal prosecutors and I saw a press release in which the Department of Justice boasted last year that they had prosecuted and convicted 1,150 public officials, the highest number in the history of the republic. They were boasting about it and I read it with a certain sadness because it seems that that kind of corruption has become epidemic in American politics. We see Congressmen one after another, Coehlo, Wright, Frank, Lukens, both sides of the aisle, either being censured or forced out of office. We see, probably the most cynical of all, was the HUD scandal, where people were ripping off money from the public treasury that was designed to help the poor. And then we've seen more spy scandals in the past 5 years than in all previous 195 years of American history combined – people selling their national honor for sexual favors or for money. Business is not immune. The savings and loan scandals are bad enough on the face of them, but the fact that they're so wide spread, almost a looter's mentality. Mr. Milken, Mr. Boesky, who spoke at UCLA Business School five years ago and said, "Greed is a good thing," and ended up spending 3 years in a Federal prison. Just last week one of the major pharmaceutical firms fined $10-million for covering up, acting, violating criminal statutes. It affects athletics – if you picked up a newspaper this week, you saw that Sugar Ray Leonard was just admitted for drug use. He's been a role model for lots of kids on the street. Pete Rose spent time in prison for gambling. Academia. I don't know how many of you saw Stanford University President Kennedy charged with spending $7,000 to buy a pair of sheets – they must be awfully nice bedsheets, bedlinens – and charging it to the government improperly on government contracts. A Nobel Prize winner one day was exposed for presenting a fraudulent paper and the very next day a professor at Georgetown University was charged with filing a fraudulent application for a grant from the Federal Government, from the National Institutes of Health – this all in the matter of the past two weeks. And probably saddest of all, at least from my perspective, religious leaders. Jim Bakker, whom I've also visited in prison, Jimmy Swaggart prosecuted for violating what should be the most sacred trust of all, to speak for God and to minister to people in their spiritual needs.

Well, the first question that comes to mind is whether this is simply an example of people – rotten apples, or maybe better prosecution, or maybe you can dismiss this by simply saying, well, this is simply the nature of humanity. I think it was Bishop Fulton Sheen in quoting G.K. Chesterton or paraphrasing G.K. Chesterton, who once said that the doctrine of original sin is the only philosophy empirically validated by 3,500 years of human history. And so maybe you sort of dismiss this and say well, this is just the way people are. Or is there something of a pattern here is the question that I would pose to you today.

Time magazine, doing a cover story on ethics,

recently said what's wrong: Hypocrisy, betrayal and greed unsettle a nation's soul. *The Washington Post* said that the problem has reached the point where common decency can no longer be described as common. And *The New Republic* magazine said there is a destructive sense that nothing is true and everything is permitted. Now I would submit to you that when *The Washington Post* and *The New Republic* magazine and *Time* magazine, which have never been known as bastions of conservative, biblical morality, begin to talk about some sort of ethical malaise, that a line has been crossed and that this isn't simply isolated instances, but rather there is a pattern emerging in American life. No institution has been more sensitive to that than Harvard. President Bok has given some quite extraordinary speeches talking about, decrying the loss of ethics in the American business community, and business school students, I think maybe some of you have seen the recent polls, business school students across America by 2 to 1 believe that businesses are generally unethical. It's a very fragile consensus that holds together trust in our institutions, and when 2 to 1 business school students believe there aren't any unethical operations, you begin to have to wonder if something isn't affecting us a lot more broadly than simply isolated instances of misbehavior that have been exposed. In my view I believe we are experiencing in our country today what I choose to call crisis of character, a loss of what traditionally through Western civilization had been considered those inner restraints and inner virtues that prevent us from pandering to our own darker instincts. If you look back through the history of Harvard, you'll see that President Elliott was as concerned about the development of character as he was about education, and classically education. Plato once said if you asked why we should educate someone, we educate them so that they become a good person because good persons behave nobly. And so I come to a place today where we should be deeply concerned about the loss of what Edmund Burke might have called the traditional values of republican citizenship – words that will almost sound quaint when uttered in these surroundings, words such as valor, honor, duty, responsibility, compassion, civility – words which have almost fallen into disuse.

Well, why has this happened? I'm sure many of you studied philosophy in your undergraduate courses and if so, you are well aware that through 23 centuries of Western civilization, we were guided by a consensus, a shared set of assumptions that there was a transcendent value system, not always the Judeo-Christian value system, though I think the Judeo-Christian values were, as Christopher Dawson, the eminent historian, wrote, "sort of the heart and soul of Western civilization." But it goes back to the Greeks. It goes back to Plato saying that if there were no God, there could be no concord and justice and harmony in a society. And there is a strain all through the 23 centuries of the civilization, the history of the West, a strain of belief in a transcendent value system, whether it was the unknown god of the Greeks, whether it was the Christ of the Scriptures revealed to the Christian, whether it was the Yahweh of the Old Testament revealed to the Jews or whether it was as enlightenment thinkers chose to call it, natural law, which I believe to be not inconsistent with Judeo-Christian revelation. Nonetheless that guided our conduct for 23 centuries until a great cultural revolution began in America. A great cultural revolution took place in our country in the 1960s. Some think it goes back further. When I met a historian, Paul Johnson, who happens to be one of my favorites, Paul Johnson wrote the history of Christianity, the history of the Jews, he wrote a classic book called *Modern Times.* If you're not too busy with your business school studies, it's a wonderful history of the 20th century. Paul Johnson said all of this began in 1919 when Einstein's discovery of relativity in the field of physical sciences was confused with the notion of relativism in the field of ideas, and that gradually through the '20s and '30s people began to challenge what had been fixed assumptions by which people lived, a set of fixed and shared common values. In the '60s it exploded. If any of you here were on campuses in the '60s, you will well remember that the writings of Camus and Sartre invaded American campuses and basically what they said was exactly what Camus said when he came to America and spoke at Columbia University in 1947 and to the student body assembled said, "There is nothing." The idea was introduced that there is no God, God is dead, it was on the cover of *Time* magazine. There is no transcendent value; life is utterly meaningless and the only way that we can derive meaning out of life is if we overcome the nothingness of life with heroic individualism and the goal of life is to overcome that nothingness and to find personal peace and meaning through your own autonomous efforts. And most of the people of my generation dismissed what was happening on the campuses as a passing fad, protest, in the '60s. It was *not.* The only people who behaved logically in the

'60s were the flower children. They did exactly what they were taught. If there was no other object in life than to overcome the nothingness, then go out and sniff coke or smoke pot and make love and enjoy personal peace.

Then America came through the great convulsion of Watergate and Vietnam, a dark era, and into the '70s, and we thought we shook off those protest movements of the '60s. We did not, we simply embraced them into the mainstream of American culture. That's what gave rise to the "me" decade. That's why if you look at the bestsellers of the '70s, it's very revealing. The bestselling books of the '70s were *Winning Through Intimidation, Look Out For Number One, I'm Okay, You're Okay*, which is saying, "Don't worry about we." And we emerged into a decade that Tom Wolfe, the social critic, called "the decade of Me." And very logically that graduated into the '80s into what some have cynically called "the golden age of greed." There's a professor at the University of California by the name of Robert Bellah, who wrote a book, a take-off on the title from Tocqueville's classic work on American life entitled, *Habits of the Heart,* and Robert Bellah took a couple hundred of average middle-class Americans and tried to examine really what their values were. He came to the conclusion that the reigning ethos in American life in the '80s was what he called "otological individualism," radical individualism – the idea that the individual is supreme and autonomous, lives for himself or herself. And he found that Americans had two overriding goals: vivid personal feelings and personal success. He tried to find out what people expected from the institutions of society. From business they expected personal advancement. Okay. That's fair enough. From marriage personal development. No wonder marriages are in trouble. And from church personal fulfillment! But the personal became the dominant consideration. Now I would simply say to you today and I'll try to be as brief with this as I possibly can, I would simply say to you that this self-obsession destroys character, it *has* to! All those quaint-sounding virtues I talked about that historically have been considered the elements of character are no match for a society in which the exaltation and gratification of self becomes the overriding goal of life. *Rolling Stone* magazine did a survey of the baby boom generation of which many of you in this room are baby boomers, emerging leaders. Forty percent said there was no cause for which they would fight for

their country. If there's nothing worth dying for, there's nothing worth living for. Literally the social contract unravels when that happens and there can be no ethics. How can you have ethical behavior? The crisis of character is totally understandable when there are no absolute values. The word "Ethics" derives from the Greek word "ethos," and "ethos'" literally meant "a cave," a hiding place. It was the one place you could go and find security. There could be rest, there could be something there that you could depend upon, it was unmovable. "Morals" derives from the word "mores," which is "always changing." "Ethics" or "ethos" is the normative, that is what ought to be. "Morals" is what is, and unfortunately in American life today we are totally guided by moral determinations. So we're not even looking at ethical standards. Ethical standards don't change. It's the cave, it's the ethos, it's the environment in which we live. Morals change all the time, and so with shifting morals, if 90% of the people say that it's perfectly all right to do this, well, then, that must be perfectly all right to do it because 90% of the people say it. It's a very democratic notion. Ethics is not, *cannot be*, democratic. Ethics by its very definition is authoritarian, and that's a very nasty word to utter on any campus in America, particularly at Harvard where Arthur Schlesinger has written a magnificently argued assault on the perils of absolutism, and I'll refer to that in just a moment.

In a relativistic environment ethics deteriorates to nothing more than utilitarian or pragmatic considerations, and if you're really honest with yourselves and you look at the ethical questions that you're asked to wrestle with in your courses here at Harvard, you will see that what you are being taught is how you can arrive at certain conclusions yourself and make certain judgments yourself that ultimately are going to be good for the business, and that's fine. You should do that. That's a prudential decision that has to be made and that's being a responsible business leader. It just isn't ethics and shouldn't be confused with ethics. Ethics is the what *ought* to be, not what is or even is prudential. There was a brilliant professor at Duke, Stanley Hauerwas, who writes that moral life cannot be found by each person pursuing his or her options. In relativism all you have then are a set of options. The only way moral life can be produced is by the formation of virtuous people by tradition-formed communities, and that was the accepted wisdom of 23 centuries of Western civilization until the cultural revolution of the '60s with which we are still plagued.

Well, what is the answer? I'd like to address two points today. First, how each of us individually might view our own ethical framework and then why some set of transcendent values – we live in a pluralistic environment, pluralistic society, I happen to be a Baptist, I believe *strongly* in a pluralistic environment and that I should be able to contend for my values as you should be able to contend for your values, and out of that contention comes some consensus that we can all agree to live by. That's the beauty of pluralism. It doesn't mean extinguishing all ideas; it means contending for them and finding truth out of that consensus. Out of that battle comes some consensus by which people live, but I would argue that there must be some values and I would take the liberty of arguing for my belief in a certain set of historic values being absolutely essential to the survival of society. But first, let me just go to the question of how we find it ourselves, and I know if you studied on your philosophy courses as an undergraduate, you read about Immanuel Kant and the Categorical Imperative, you read about rationalism, you read about the ways in which people can find their own ethical framework. I guess the only thing I can tell you, having tried that, is that in my life, and I can't speak for anyone else, it didn't work.

I grew up in America during the Great Depression and thought that the great goal of life was success and material gain and power and influence. That's why I went into politics, I believed I could gain power and influence how people lived and that if I earned a law degree as I did at night, and if I had academic honors and awards that would enable me to find success and power and fulfillment and meaning in life. I had a great respect for the law. When I went through law school I had a love for the law. I learned really the history of jurisprudence and the philosophy underlying it. I studied Locke and the Enlightenment, social contract theories as an undergraduate at Brown, I had a great respect for the political process. I also had a well-above-average I.Q. and some academic honors. I also became very self-righteous. When I went to the White House I gave up a law practice that was making almost $200,000 a year and that was back in 1969, which wasn't bad in those days. It's kind of ordinary now for graduates of Harvard Business School, but then it was a lot of money. I had accumulated a little bit of money and took a job in the White House at $40,000 a year and so I took everything I had and I stuck it in a blind trust at the Bank of Boston. Now let me tell you, if you want to lose money, that's the surest way to do it! After 3-1/2 years when I saw what the Bank of Boston had done to my blind trust, I realized I was a lot poorer when I came out of the government than I was when I went *in* to the government. But there was one thing about it. I was absolutely certain that no one could corrupt me. *Positive!* And if anybody ever gave me a present at Christmas time, it went right to the driver of my limousine. They used to send in bottles of whiskey and boxes of candy and all sorts of things. Right to the driver of my automobile. I wouldn't accept a thing. Patty and I were taken out on someone's boat one day. I discovered it was a chartered boat, ended up paying for half of it because I didn't want to give the appearance of impropriety. Imagine me worried about things such as that! Tom Phillips, my blessed friend who is with me today, had been counsel for Raytheon before going to the White House, so I wouldn't see anybody from Raytheon.

I ended up going to prison. So much for the Categorical Imperative. Categorical Imperative says that with our own rational process we will arrive at that judgment which if everyone did it would be prudential, would be the best decision for everyone. In other words, that which we would do, we would do only if we could will it to be a universal choice for everybody. I really thought that way and I never once in my life thought I was breaking the law. I would have been *terrified* to do it because I would jeopardize the law degree I had worked four years at night and worked my way onto the Law Review and Order of Croif and Moot Court and all the things that lawyers do and I had graduated in the top of my class. I wouldn't put that in jeopardy for anything in the world! I was so sure, but you see there's two problems. Every human being has an infinite capacity for self-rationalization and self-delusion. You get caught up in a situation where you are absolutely convinced that the fate of the republic *rests* on the reelection of, in my case, Richard Nixon and I'm sure next year people will think the same thing about George Bush. And there's an *enormous* amount of peer pressure and you don't take time to stop and think, "Wait a minute. Is this *right* by some absolute standard or does this seem right in the circumstances, is it okay?" I was taught to think clearly and carefully. As a lawyer that's what you do – you briefcase it, you spend four years in law school and you go like a monkey. You're briefing cases, briefing cases. We used the case method as you use the case method here in business and the case method in law school. However, it is a little bit different because you always have a fixed conclusion, so at least I knew there was a fixed law that you would arrive at. I had all the mental capacity to do that. I was capable of infinite self-delusion. But secondly, and even more importantly, and this goes to the heart of the ethical dilemma in America today, even if I had known I was doing wrong, would I have the *will* to do what is right? It isn't hindsight. I have to tell you the answer to that is no. The greatest myth of the 20th century is that people are good. We aren't. We're not morally neutral. My great friend, Professor Samenow, happens to be an orthodox Jew. I asked him one day, I said, "Stan, if people were put in a room and no one could see what they were doing or no one knew what they were doing, would they do the right thing half the time and the wrong thing half the time? Would they do the wrong thing all the time, or would they do the right thing all the time?" He said they would *always* do the wrong thing. We aren't morally neutral. I know that's a terribly unpopular thing to say in America today, but it happens to be true. And the fundamental problem with learning how to reason through ethical solutions is it doesn't give you a mechanism whereby your natural tendency to do what is wrong is overridden. There's nothing that makes your will, this is what C.S. Lewis whose writings had such a profound influence on my life. Tom Phillips gave me the book, *Mere Christianity*, when I came to him in the summer of 1973 at a moment of great anguish in my life because I wasn't so worried about what was going on in the Watergate, but I knew what was going on in my heart I didn't like, and so I went to see him and visited him one evening. Something different about him. I went and that was the evening that, if you've read it, any of you know my story, that an ex-Marine captain, White House tough guy, the Nixon hatchet man and all kinds of things you can't write about in print or wouldn't say in polite company that I was called in those days, much of it justifiably, I found myself when I left his home that night after he had told me of his experience with Jesus Christ, I found myself unable to drive the automobile out of the driveway. I was crying too hard, and I took that little book he had given me, *Mere Christianity,* and began to read that and study it as I studied for a case. I'd take my yellow sheets. I still use them.

Yellow legal pad. Get down with all the arguments, both sides, and I was confronted with the most powerful mind that I had been exposed to, I saw the arguments for the truth of Jesus Christ and I surrendered my life 18 years ago. My life has not been the same because, and can never be the same again. But I discovered something, that Christ coming into your life changes that will. It gives you that will to do what you know is right where even if you know what is right, and most of the time you won't, you don't have the *will* to do it. It's what C.S. Lewis wrote in that tremendous little book, *Abolition of Man.* I'd love you to read *Mere Christianity,* but if you had to read just *Mere Christianity* or *Abolition of Man* for today's cultural environment, read *Abolition of Man.* Wonderful book. I don't know how to say this in language that is inclusive, but he wrote a marvelous essay called "Men Without Chests." I can't say "men and women without chests," I can say "persons without chests," I guess. But it's a wonderful article about the will and he said the passions of the stomach can't control — the intellect can't control the passions of the stomach except by means of the will, which is the chest. And that we make geldings and then bid them to multiply. We mock honor and then we are alarmed when there are traitors in our midst. He was talking about the loss of character and he was talking about it in 1947 and 1948, long before we have seen the results of what the loss of character means in American life today.

Well, so much for the individual. What about society as a whole? Margaret Thatcher gave what I consider to be one of those remarkable speeches. You'll only find it reprinted in *The Wall Street Journal.* One of the most remarkable speeches that has been given in modern times was given 2-1/2 years ago before the Church of Scotland, and what Margaret Thatcher said basically is, and I'll paraphrase what was marvelous, eloquent speech. What Margaret Thatcher said is that the truths of the Judeo-Christian tradition is infinitely precious, not only because she said I believe it to be true, and she professed her own faith, but she said it provides the moral impulse that causes people to rise above themselves and do something greater than themselves without which a democracy cannot survive, and she goes on to make the case I think quite convincingly that without Judeo-Christian values at the root of society, society simply can't exist. Our founders believed this. All of our founders said this. We were not formed as a totally tolerant, neutral, egalitarian democracy. We were formed as a republic with a certain sense of republican virtue built into the citizenry without which limited government simply couldn't survive. No one said it better than John Adams. But there were four ways in which that moral impulse works. Someone sent me a letter with a suggested topic for this speech, and the speech was "Why Good People Do Bad Things." I didn't have time to write back and say I really think that it would be a more appropriate thing to say "Why Bad People Do Good Things" because that's a more difficult question. Why do we do good things? I mean if we live in an age of otological individualism, if radical individualism is the pervasive ethos of the day, if we simply live for the gratification of our senses, of our personal success and vivid personal feelings, why do anything good? Who cares? It won't make a particle of difference unless it's important to your balance sheet, but that's pragmatism. That isn't doing good things. That's pure utilitarianism. We do good things because there is something in us that calls us to something greater than ourselves. I work in a ministry in prisons, not a very glamorous place to be. I was just in prison this weekend, in three prisons. I was so moved in one prison because there were 600 inmates that came out and saw their lives change. Now those were people who were lost, forgotten, and I also saw the 50 volunteers who go in there regularly. One man stood up and he said, "Ten years ago I was in this prison and one of your volunteers came in, Mr. Colson, and they befriended me, this couple from Akron, Ohio," and he said, "You know, they've been visiting me every month and writing to me ever because for 10 years," and he said, "I get out of prison in September and they've invited me to live in their home." He said, "I'm going to make it." Why do people do that? Why do they go to the AIDS wards? One of my friends goes into the AIDS wards all of the time in prison and people die in his arms. I mean do we do it because we have some good instinct? No! It's a moral impulse. Why did William Wilberforce stand up on the floor of the Parliament in the House of Commons and denounce the slave trade? Because he said it was barbaric and he cost himself the prime ministership of England when he did it! But he said, my conscience is held captive to the revelation of God. I have no choice as a Christian! And he spent the next 20 years battling the slave trade and brought to an end the slave trade in England because of his Christian conscience.

What informs our conscience? What is it that makes us as otherwise self-centered people disposed if my friend Stan Samenow and the history of the 20th century and the history of civilization is correct, if we're disposed to evil, what is it that makes us do good?

Secondly, I don't believe. I think Margaret Thatcher's absolutely right. I do not believe that a society can survive, and I tell you this as one who sat next to the President of the United States and saw the moral consensus which kind of holds our country together during Vietnam, just fragile. We were really — we did some excessive things, and we were wrong, but we did it in a feeling that if we didn't, the whole country was going to fall apart and it was like a Banana Republic having the 82nd Airborne down in the basement of the White House. My car one night was firebombed on the way. They had 250,000 protesters in the streets and the smell of tear gas and busses and you almost wondered if the White House was going to be overrun. The moral consensus which holds the country together was in great peril during that era and during the entire Watergate aftermath of Vietnam. A free society can't exist without it. Now what gives it to us? Aquinas wrote that without consensus, without moral consensus, there can be no law. Chairman Mao gave the other side of that. Chairman Mao said morality begins at the muzzle of a gun, and every society has two choices, and that is whether it wants to be ruled by an authoritarian ruler or whether there can be a set of shared values, whether people can say there are certain things we hold in common and we hold dear and they give us the philosophical underpinnings of our value system in our life. I submit to you that without that, call it natural law if you wish, call it Judeo-Christian revelation, call it the accumulated wisdom of 23 centuries of Western civilization, but without that I don't believe a society can exist. The reason we have the most terrible crime problem in the world in America today is a simple reason. We've lost our moral consensus. We're people living for themselves. You know, we have doubled the prison population in America in the 1980s. We are today number 1 in the rate of incarceration per capita in the world. When I started in this ministry 15 years ago, we were number 3. We trailed the Soviet Union and South Africa. Today we're number 1! The more prisons we build and the more people we put in, the recidivism rate remains constant at 75% . Those people come right back in. And the answer to it is very simple. There are kids being raised today from broken families who are not being given – remember what I said Stanley Hauerwas said the way you treat ethics is from tradition-formed communities – they're not being given values in the home, they're not being given values in the school, they're watching the television set for 7 hours and 36 minutes a day, and what they're seeing is you only go around this way once, so grab for all the gusto while you can. Now if that's the creed by which you live, then at 12 years old they're out on the streets sniffing coke. We arrest them and put them in jail. They think we're crazy. So do I. Until you have some desire in the society to live by a different set of values, we'll be building prisons in America until, as is the case today, 25% of the black inner-city population in America is either in prison or on probation or parole. Can't make it without that moral consensus. It will cost us dearly if we can't find a way to restore it. Professor James Wilson at the Harvard Law School wrote one of the most telling pieces I've ever read and I refer to it in one of my books, *Kingdoms in Conflict*, if you care to look at it and find the resource for it. He wrote a little primer while he was here at Harvard – he's no longer at Harvard – about the relationship between spiritual values and crime. It was really interesting. Crime – the prevailing myth is – that it goes up during periods of poverty. Actually it went down in the '30s. And he found during periods of industrialization it went up as what he called Victorian values began to fade, and when there was a resurgence of spiritual values, crime went down. He saw a direct correlation. Crime was going up whenever spiritual values were declining; whenever spiritual values were going up, crime was going down. It's a lack of a moral consensus.

Third, so often I think we miss the basis of sound policy because we have become so secularized in our views in America, so afraid to look at biblical revelation. We're terrified of it. When Ted Koppel gave that speech at Duke's commencement a few years ago in which he said the 10 Commandments weren't the 10 Suggestions. God handed commandments to Moses at Mt. Sinai. And you know what the press did to him. It was horrible. A fellow such as Ted Koppel couldn't possibly say something like this. So we blind ourselves to what can often be truth.

I have spoken to over half of the state legislators in America. Just met with the Governor of Ohio last Friday, the Lieutenant Governor of Ohio. Talked with the Governor of Ohio on many occasions. And with many of the political leaders around this country and I always make the same argument to them about our prisons. We have way too many people in prison. Half the prison population are in for non-violent offenses. Which to me is ludicrous, they should be put to work. People should not be sitting in a cell at a cost of $20,000 a year to us taxpayers while doing absolutely nothing and their victims getting no recompense. That offender ought to be put in a work program paying back their victims. Whenever I speak about that it's amazing the response I get from political officials. It really is. Any legislator, the same thing happened in Texas. I gave that talk and they all applauded. Afterwards the speaker of the house said, "Mr. Colson, wait here. I'm sure some of the members would like to talk to you." They came flooding in afterwards. They all said that restitution is a wonderful idea – where did that come from? I said you got a Bible at home. They say, have I got a Bible at home? Well, you go home and dust it off and you'll see that's exactly what God told Moses on Mt. Sinai. That's biblical truth. That's the lesson of Jesus and Zaccheus. But we blind ourselves to it because we think there's something wrong with that in today's tolerant society. In a pluralistic society that ought not to be wrong. We ought to be seeking that out if we can find wisdom, find it. So often we find wisdom in the teachings of the Holy Scripture.

And fourth, no society exists in a vacuum. Vacuums don't remain vacuums, they get filled. In a vacuum a tyrant will often emerge. You've just seen 70 years of that crumbling in the east. But isn't it interesting that when it crumbles, it so often crumbles because people have an allegiance to a power above the power of that earthly potentate. I remember when the Pope said that he would return to Poland if the Soviets invaded. And Stalin said, "Hah, The Pope! How many divisions does he have?" Well, as a result of the solidarity movement we saw how many divisions he had – a whole lot more than the Soviets. I remember getting on a plane coming up to Boston to see our first grandson when he was born and so therefore I can date it, back in 1981. A man got up in the aisle of the plane and he was all excited to see me. He said, "Chuck Colson!" He was blocking the people coming behind me, so I finally got him into his seat. He looked Oriental, I didn't know his background. He was talking so fast, I couldn't understand him. To make a long story short, he introduced himself as Benigno Aquino. Aquino told me that when he was in jail for 7 years and 7 months, a political prisoner of Marcos, he had read my book *Born Again*. He was in a prison cell and had gotten down on his knees and surrendered his life to Jesus Christ. He said after that his entire experience in prison changed. Well, Nino and I became pretty good friends. We did some television programs together and we visited frequently. He called me up one day and said "I'm going back to the Philippines." I said, "Nino, do you think that's wise?" He said, "I have to, I'm going back because my conscience will not let me do otherwise." He was safe here in America, he had a fellowship here at Harvard, he could lecture anywhere he wanted, lived here with his wife in Newton, they had everything they could possibly want. But he knew he had to go back to the Philippines. "My conscience will not let me do otherwise." He said if I go to jail, it'll be okay, I'll be president of Prison Fellowship in the Philippines. He said if there are free elections I'll be elected president, I know I can beat Marcos. And if I'm killed I know where I'll be with Jesus Christ. He went back in total freedom. He never got off the plane, as you know, he was shot and killed.

But an extraordinary thing happened. What's known as people power. People went out in the streets. The tanks stopped. People went up and put flowers down the muzzles of guns and a tyrant was overthrown. And a free government was reasserted. Because people believed in a power above themselves.

I was in the Soviet Union last year, visited five prisons, four of which had never been visited by anyone from the West. I met with Soviet officials. It was really interesting. I met with Vadim (Russian name), the minister of foreign officials, who has since been sacked because he was too liberal, and when talking about the enormous crime problem in the Soviet Union he said to me, "What are we going to do about it?" I said Mr. (Pekadin?) your problem is exactly the one that Feodor Dostoyevsky, your great novelist, diagnosed. When in *Brothers Karamazov* he had, you remember if you read it, that wonderful debate between the older brother who is unregenerate and the younger brother Alexis, who is the priest, over the soul of the middle brother, Ivan. At one point Ivan yells out and he says, "Ah, if there is no God, everything is permissible, crime becomes inevitable." I said your problem in the Soviet Union is 70 years of atheism. He said, "You're right. We need what you've got. How do we get it back in the Soviet Union?" All

I could think was how foolish in America that we're squandering our heritage. And in a country where they are seeing the collapse because as the king of greater power that they've ignored for 70 years, they're losing it all.

I can only leave you with a very simple message. I know in my own life as someone who had thought he had it all together and got to a position of great power. I never thought I'd be one of the half dozen men sitting around the desk of the President of the United States, with all that power and influence, I discovered that there was no restraint on the evil in me. In my self-righteousness I was never more dangerous. I discovered what Solzhenitsyn wrote so brilliantly from a prison. That the line between good and evil passes not between principalities and powers but it oscillates within the human heart. Even the most rational approach to ethics is defenseless if there isn't the will to do what is right. On my own, and I can only speak for myself, I do not have that will. That which I want to do, I do not do; that which I do, I do not want to do. It's only when I can turn to the One who this past weekend we celebrated, was raised from the dead, that I can find the will to do what is right as best that I'm able to discern it. It's only when that value and that sense of righteousness pervade a society that there can be a moral consensus and I would hope I might leave with you as future business leaders the thought that a society in which we are a part and which you should have a great sense of responsibility and stewardship desperately today, desperately needs these kind of values. And if I might say so, each one of us do as well.

Thank you.

GLOSSARY

A

abolitionist — a person who supported the legal abolishment of slavery; today, one who seeks abolishment of capital punishment.

abortion — permanently halting the development of a fetus or baby in the womb of its mother, usually by expulsion from the womb.

accountability — the moral relationship whereby a person reports deeds and attitudes, usually to another person or authority; e.g., a student has accountability for class performance to an instructor; a taxpayer has accountability for paying taxes to the Internal Revenue Service; a family member has accountability for actions and attitudes to that family. See Chapter 4.

act-utilitarianism — A subset of utilitarianism in which the moral quality of an action is assessed only upon the total happiness produced at a single time and place among a single set of persons and circumstances; e.g., an act might be good only in one context and wrong in others.

ad hominem — see fallacies, Chapter 5.

affirmative action — in American law, the notion of taking assertive action to redress past discrimination patterns in the workplace by providing opportunities for the aggrieved class.

air pollution — unnatural degradation of the air and its atmospheric gases.

ambiguity — vagueness; see fallacies, Chapter 5.

amphiboly — see fallacies, Chapter 5.

a priori **reasoning** — from cause to effect; making determinations based on what is understood to be universally true.

a posteriori reasoning — from effect to cause; making decisions based on the gathering of knowledge gained from experience.

applied ethics — actual use in decision-making of moral standards of behavior.

approach to moral reasoning — the manner in which one chooses to resolve human problems by applying a body of moral standards; see exemplar.

B

bad — a moral judgment; not good, nor as it should be; contradictory to one's moral philosophy; usually referring to acts but also to persons and things.

bestiality — human sexual relations with non-human species, or beasts.

beneficence — quality of kindness and honorable treatment of others including generosity, favor and liberality; the quality of "doing good" and often including the results of so doing.

bioethics — the discipline of assessing the rightness or wrongness of acts performed within the life sciences.

bisexual — referring to a person who has sexual relations with persons of both sexes.

bribe — anything presented to induce illegal activity or favorable treatment that would not otherwise have been provided.

business ethics — standards related to what is good and bad including moral duty and obligation, values and beliefs used in critical thinking about behavior in the marketplace. (In 1959 the Ford Foundation and Carnegie Corporation sponsored a study, "The Education of American Businessmen," that urged training for managers to develop "a personal philosophy or ethical foundation.") It includes such issues as whether to pay bribes, take outside compensation, insider trading and disclosing publicly improper company behavior.

C

capitalism — the economic system in which the means for producing and distributing goods is privately owned and controlled; a prominent capitalist thinker was Adam Smith.

care — as a noun in ethical context, it is the quality of giving acts of value to a person or situation; help, improvement of condition; see Gilligan, Chapter 4.

capital punishment — state-sanctioned taking of life to punish a person for being convicted of a capital crime, usually murder or treason; see Chapter 11.

cardinal virtues — from Christian tradition, those qualities of life to be revered including wisdom, prudence, justice, temperance and fortitude.

carnal knowledge — a term referring to sexual experience with another person, usually including intercourse.

categorical imperative — a concept put forth by Immanuel Kant (1724-1803) declaring that a person has a moral obligation to perform "duty for duty's sake," as a universally applicable obligation. Therefore, one does not kill or lie or steal, for example, out of respect for a moral duty.

censorship — the act of prohibiting certain statements, ideas or depictions from general usage as a result of the value judgment of a few.

character — in human personality, the unconscious doing of right, consistently making honorable decisions according to high moral standards.

cheating — the act of deceiving by any maneuver or trick to gain temporary or permanent advantage over others.

CFC (chlorofluorocarbon) — an inert gas developed by man that has the capacity to destroy ozone.

Christianity — one of the world's primary religions based on the life and teachings of Jesus of Nazareth, found in Protestant and Catholic denominations and emphasizing one true God, the Holy Bible as its sacred scriptures for faith and practice, prayer and acts of love and kindness as evidenced by Jesus Christ.

civil disobedience — the conscious breaking by deed of an enactment, statute or ordinance adopted by a government; e.g., Rosa Parks refused to sit in the "Negro section" reserved by local ordinance at the back of a bus in Montgomery, Ala. See Martin Luther King's "Letter from the Birmingham Jail."

civil rights — fundamental benefits, freedoms and responsibilities afforded to an individual or group by a state.

clarity — in journalism, the fundamental standard for writing; that statements made are expressed plainly for the understanding of the reader.

codes of ethics — a collection of statements of moral principles for guiding behavior of persons sharing a common interest; see Chapter 21.

communism — the economic system in which the means for producing and distributing goods is owned and controlled by the state; the pre-eminent advocate of world communism was Karl Marx (1818-1883).

competence — fitness, the ability to act according to a set of standards; see Chapter 7.

computer ethics — an embryonic discipline in which moral standards are applied to the use of computers; involving all ethical questions of the rightness or wrongness of "using," "borrowing," or "stealing" software and shareware, as well as the use of computers for moral or immoral purposes — such as the collection of information on persons by big business or government to impose certain behavior on those persons; see also Chapter 19.

conclusion — a statement that can be made as a result of reasoning the effects of propositions and variables and inferences upon each other; see Chapter 5.

conflict of interest — the predicament arising when a person confronts two actions that cannot be ethically reconciled; competing loyalties and concerns with others, self-dealing, outside compensation; divided loyalties among, for example, public and-or professional duties and private and-or personal affairs.

consent — expressed or implied agreement with or support for a certain course of action.

conscience — an internal awareness of right and wrong, otherwise explained by various disciplines such as religion and philosophy; the conscience usually communicates a desire to do right.

consequentialism — a moral philosophy where the moral quality of an action is based on assessing the likely outcomes resulting from that action.

copyright — a right vested by law to an individual or corporation prohibiting the copying of one's "work" product by others without permission of the copyright-holder; thus enforceable in a court of law.

corporate culture — the atmosphere or environment of an entity as to the values and beliefs that guide its decision-making.

corporate social audit — an accounting of a corporation's assets testing whether they are used in a responsible manner for the benefit of society.

D
death — the cessation of human, physical life; as medically determined, it may be marked by the cessation of the heart or brain or both, and the loss of certain other bodily functions.

decision-maker — a person who makes choices when confronted by sets of circumstances and conflicting or competing interests; ethical decision-makers are those who have applied moral values (a philosophical life-view — see exemplars) to reach a conclusion as to the most beneficent way of solving human problems.

defeasibility — the potential for overriding one moral prescription when other commanding considerations intersect with that philosophy.

deforestation — wholesale cutting and clearing of a forest that erases its normal growth, thus removing the natural effects of the presence of trees, including their absorption of carbon dioxide and their emission of oxygen.

deontologism — a moral philosophy in which acts are based on a self-determined, inner sense of moral "duty." Someone who adopts the exemplar of the Divine Command theory, for example, adopts the Will of God as "the inner sense of duty." But a deontologist may choose any set of values as the basis for this innate comprehension of duty.

disclosure — a revealing; in ethical terms, especially the making public of information about oneself that "puts all the cards on the table" before the fact of a decision; usually referring to real or perceived conflicts of interest and mainly involving knowledge about personal financial dealings affecting a pending decision.

discrimination — an act or pattern of acts that *irrationally* deny opportunities or benefits to persons solely based, for example, on their race, religion or sex; denying a person due rights and opportunities without considering the person's abilities or character.

disinterest — that quality of being or attitude of self-detachment regarding a situation; without bias; sometimes termed disinterestedness; to act with disinterest is to assist without seeking gain for oneself; e.g., the Good Samaritan acted with disinterest. It is not lack of interest.

Divine Command — a moral philosophy in which good acts are based on conforming to an understanding of the Will of God, as may be determined from prayer and Holy Scriptures (Bible, Talmud, Koran, *et al.*) and as declared by those speaking for God — ministers, priests, prophets, sages, clerics, mullahs, rabbis; see Kant, Aquinas, Butler, Hobbes *et al.*. and Chapter 3.

'doing the right thing' — the phrase used in decision-making whereby the intent is to pursue both a decision and an outcome that is moral, ethical and beneficent; most agree it is easier said than done.

due process — specific and systematic procedures allowed workers for appealing disciplinary and discharge action by employers.

duty — any action required by one's position or by moral or legal consideration; often contrasted with personal inclination or pleasure.

E

economic justice — the notion that equality of human condition can be attained by the fair distribution of goods and wealth.

egalitarianism — the theory of full political and social equality for all people.

egoism — a moral philosophy in which persons are required always to act in their own best, long-term interest even if the act might harm others.

empirical, empiricism — referring to gathering of information to verify statements.

employment — performing work for another for compensation.

environment — all the conditions surrounding and affecting the development of an organism, usually referring to those conditions of the Earth.

entitlement theory — advanced by John Locke, the notion that all persons have a self-evident right to their own life and liberty that no government can justly deprive them of unless they have committed some crime deserving punishment.

equality — a condition in which there is a perceivable identity of value, status, quantity or function among persons or things.

equivocation — not deciding; also see fallacies, Chapter 5.

ethics — a discipline related to what is good and bad including moral duty and obligation, values and beliefs used in critical thinking about human problems.

ethics construct — any method of approaching human problems that applies ethical standards to reach conclusions.

ethical level — a way of assessing the practicality and effect upon human behavior of codes of ethics, as applied to persons covered by such codes. See Chapter 21.

ethical decision-making — see decision-makers.

eudaimonia — a Greek word for which no single English equivalent exists; a state of satisfaction or fulfillment or happiness as to one's condition in life; life-goal espoused by early philosophers; see Socrates, Plato, Aristotle and Chapter 3.

euthanasia — from Greek "good death," whereby persons — whose lives seem to be irreversibly ending without continued use of extraordinary means of life support — choose immediate death or authorize death in anticipation of such an eventuality; see Chapter 7; see also right to die.

exemplar — an ideal model or pattern; any of several philosophical life-views and their approaches to moral reasoning to solve human problems; e.g., egoism, Divine Command, utilitarianism, *et al.*.; see Chapter 3.

expedience — acting on the basis of what is temporarily useful or resolving, not necessarily on the basis of what is right or wrong; classically seen in the decision of Pontius Pilate to let a crowd decide the fates of the thief Barabbas and Jesus Christ.

F

fallacies — from Latin, "to deceive;" statements made contrary to logic; formal fallacies are due to the form of the argument or statement; informal fallacies are due to the wording of the statement or argument.

faulty causation — see fallacies, Chapter 5.

false appeal to authority — see fallacies, Chapter 5.

fetus — the developing human being in the mother's womb, used here to include all the stages of development such as zygote, conceptus and embryo.

fidelity — loyalty, faithfulness, trustworthiness, especially to one's own moral standards.

First Amendment — the First Amendment to the U.S. Constitution declaring: "Congress shall make no law respecting an establishment of religion, or prohibiting the free exercise thereof; or abridging the freedom of speech, or of the press; or the right of the people peaceably to assemble; and to petition the Government for a redress of grievances."

first-strike theory — the notion, in defense of a nation, that the most effective means of protecting a nation against war is to be first to launch an attack against potential aggressors.

flack — a person working in the public relations field whose work seems lacking in ethical and professional norms.

free will — a concept in philosophy and law whereby an individual has self-inherent authority and moral agency to choose without coercion.

G

gay — homosexual.

gene — a unit in a chromosome whereby hereditary traits are passed from one generation to the next.

general moral principle — issuing from a moral philosophy, it is a statement of what should always be done in a certain situation; e.g., the Golden Rule; see Chapter 3.

genetic engineering — changing the makeup of a gene, presumably to improve or enhance the mental or physical health of the being in which it resides.

genetic defects — abnormalities in the nature or structure of genes.

genetic fallacy — see fallacies, Chapter 5.

gifts — anything given freely with no intent to induce behavior, often in connection with favorable treatment; in some ethics codes, these must be reported by employees who receive them if the value of the item given is of a specified dollar value.

global warming — a phenomenon on the Earth in which atmospheric temperatures are rising.

Golden Rule — Attributed to Jesus Christ, the saying: "Do unto others as you would have them do unto you." A similar statement emphasizing the negative (do not do unto others as you would not want them to do unto you) is attributed to the Chinese philosopher Hsuntzu. See Chapter 2.

good — not bad; not evil; positive, helpful to oneself and-or to others; valuable, honorable, benevolent, just; expressed in personal or societal situations — usually referring to acts but also to people and things.

Good Samaritan — character in a parable told by Jesus Christ who stops his travel in order to help an injured person.

greenhouse effect — the phenomenon in which heat, rather than circulating in and out of a structure; is retained in that structure or system, usually referring to a place where plant growth is fostered and more recently referring to heat being retained in the Earth's atmosphere rather than being in circulation.

guilt — the human emotion related to feeling responsible for the fact that one's moral values have been violated.

H

hack — a person working in the communications field whose work evidences compromise and unethical behavior.

happiness — from Greek *eudaimonia* (which see), literally, "goodly demon;" Aristotle called this the *goal* of life, fulfillment, complete life satisfaction. In utilitarianism, however, the *degree* of happiness is measured. The U.S. Declaration of Independence asserts that among an American's inalienable rights is the pursuit of this quality of life.

hasty conclusion — see fallacies, Chapter 5.

heterosexual — referring to a person who has sexual relations only with persons of the opposite sex.

Hippocratic Oath — attributed to a Greek physician, Hippocrates (c. 460 - 377 B.C.), this pledge by physicians has as its essential tenet to "do no harm." It has been subsequently revised. See discussion in Chapter 7.

Holy Bible — Most widely published book in history, it is a compendium of 66 books or letters considered sacred scriptures and relied upon primarily by Christians for faith and practice, although most of its authors are Jewish and most of its topics related to Jewish history.

homo sapiens — humans; the most advanced life form on Earth, which has the capacity to adapt and to control other life forms.

homosexual — referring to a person who has sexual relations only with persons of the same sex.

honesty — from Latin *honor*, "a mark of respect," essentially referring to truth-telling and including self-disclosure.

human rights — morally authorized claims applying to all people solely on the basis of their being human individuals.

hypocrisy — pretending to possess qualities which, in fact, are not objectively apparent; e.g., those who preach love and abuse their families are hypocrites.

I
illegal — in violation of a statement of behavior adopted as law by a state or nation's legislative body, and subject to enforcement by that state or nation.

incest — sexual relations with a member of one's own family other than one's spouse.

inconsistency — the quality of not maintaining the same conduct in same circumstances; also see fallacies, Chapter 5.

inductive reasoning — thinking or reasoning from within and applying the conclusion generally, usually based on intuitively measuring the probability of its application.

inference — statements that can be drawn from combining propositions and variables; contrasted with "implication," which is the intended suggestion of the maker of the statement; see Chapter 5.

informal logic — intuitive human processes of critical thinking including the acts of observing, analyzing, developing potential solutions, verbalizing them and evaluating them. See Chapters 2 and 5.

informed consent — a legal term referring to a person who, upon having suitable information , grants authority to someone else to take actions affecting that person.

insider trading — purchase or sale of stocks by officers or employees of a company based on information that only certain employees of that company could possess, usually for profit; a violation of law.

intuition — the ability of the mind to perceive data, receive impressions, and make judgments without formally submitting these factors to a conscious, rational decision-making process.

invincible ignorance — see fallacies, Chapter 5.

Islam — a prominent world religion based on the teaching of the prophet Mohammed and relying upon the Koran as its sacred scriptures and Mecca as its holy city and Allah as its God; adherents are Moslems (also Muslims).

J
Judaism — the monotheistic religion of most Jews, based on the teachings of Moses and various prophets as recorded primarily in the Talmud (some of which are books of the Old Testament of the Holy Bible) and relying upon one God, known by many names but most often referred to as Jehovah or Elohim; its holy city is Jerusalem. See Talmud.

justice — the quality of fairness among persons or societies or acts including: administration of justice (as in fair procedures and due process), distributive justice (as in apportioning advantages and rewards), retributive justice (as in punishing the wrong conduct of wrongdoers) and remedial justice (as in setting right of wrongs).

'just war' theory — the notion that war may be justified by certain moral conditions having been met — such as the war is a last resort, formally authorized by civil authority; its motive is just, including the vindication of justice; it has a reasonable probability of success; good consequences can be expected to outweigh the evils; only the force necessary to prevail is exercised; targets are only those under arms.

K

kickbacks — giving back part of money received as payment, usually based on favorable treatment

Koran — sacred scriptures for faith and practice of Moslem adherents; see also Islam.

L

legal — behavior that conforms to a law enacted by a state or nation's legislative body and having behind it the enforcement power of that state or nation.

lesbian — a female who has sexual relations only with other females.

Letter from the Birmingham Jail — a classic letter conveying the doctrine of civil disobedience, portraying the conflict between morality and ethics as against civil laws, written by Dr. Martin Luther King Jr. See Chapters 2 and 4 and Appendix.

libel — the tort in law whereby a person's reputation is maliciously damaged by printed or recorded statements in permanent form; while the U.S. Supreme Court in *Times vs. Sullivan* virtually set aside this right to sue as it applies to essentially public persons, it remains a right for most Americans.

logic — a system of evaluating statements or arguments.

lobbyist — a person who represents an interest in seeking to affect legislation pending before a legislature or Congress; derived from meetings between such persons and those legislators in a lobby near the seat of decision.

lying — not telling the truth, including verbal and non-verbal expressions; one of the acts forbidden by most religious traditions and by every Western court of law.

M

masturbation — from Latin literally meaning "one who defiles himself," it is sexual self-stimulation to climax.

metaethics — a system of assessing moral philosophy emphasizing the meaning of the language used;

e.g., what is "love" to one person may not be to another, so the definitional context of the language used becomes the basis for determining the ethical value of the act.

militarism — a philosophy of governing in which a nation relies upon aggressive military power, including war, as its chief instrument of foreign policy.

moral — capable of distinguishing right from wrong with a predilection for right; as an adjective, it describes a person or act or thing that conforms to agreed-upon standards of conduct; as a noun, it is a summation of truth from an incident or parable.

moral development — human growth in awareness of rightness and wrongness of actions, often accompanying maturity but not necessarily; see Kohlberg, Gilligan in Chapter 4.

morality — the inherent right or wrong nature of an action or conduct.

moral judgment — a personal conclusion about the rightness or wrongness of an action in a particular set of circumstances based on general moral principle(s).

moral reasoning — any process that applies general moral principle(s) to a situation or human problem and reaches a conclusion or decision; see exemplar; see also Chapter 5.

motive — the basis, reasoned or irrational, for the way a person acts; see Kohlberg, Chapter 4.

N

naturalism — a moral philosophy emphasizing the intrinsic good of natural desires and actions; a prime advocate was John Dewey, who held that there is no final and unchanging good of the moral life and that morality flows from the use of science, respect for the judgment of others, and democracy as the preferred social order.

natural law — a moral philosophy based on the perceived order inherent in the universe; acts that seem to conform to this order are considered good, those not conforming are considered bad.

nuclear war — any war in which strategic nuclear weapons of mass destruction are used

neo-Malthusian argument — the economic proposition that contends the primary cause of world hunger is overpopulation and unjust social policy; see Chapter 14.

nepotism — formerly, this concept applied only to relatives; now it often refers to favoritism in the workplace toward relatives or close friends.

Nicomachean Ethics — A treatise by Thomas Aquinas, especially glorifying the value of human endeavor (work) as ordained by God as valuable and uplifting.

nuclear energy — power derived from the collision and interaction of the nuclei of atoms.

nuclear waste — the residue from the creation of nuclear energy, in the form of substances.

O
obligations — duties or debts to others; constraints on behavior because of a favor granted or received from another.

obscenity — filthy or foul language or depiction characterized by immodesty and indecency; compare with rulings of the U.S. Supreme Court noted in Chapter 10.

ozone layer — a condition of the upper atmosphere (stratosphere) in which there is present large amounts of ozone, which is developed when the sun's rays strike an oxygen molecule.

P
pacifism — a moral principle renouncing war; a philosophy of governing in which a nation rejects the use of military power as its chief instrument of foreign policy, relying exclusively on negotiation.

person — a human being who is a subject of moral concern and who possesses a right to life and certain medically described abilities such as (but not limited to) consciousness, reasoning, and communication; theoretically, medical science could deem a being of a non-human species also as a person. See also definitions in Chapter 7.

personal freedom — individual liberty enabling moral agency in making choices; see Chapter 14.

philosophy — the study of principles that underlie human conduct and order in the universe; see Chapter 3.

photosynthesis — the natural process whereby plant life absorbs carbon dioxide and emits oxygen.

plagiarism — the action whereby one appropriates another's writings or works or art and makes use of them as one's own; implied is the notion that by so doing one is "stealing" original work produced by another.

pleasure theory — a moral theory in which acts are deemed good if they bring pleasure.

pornography — from a Greek term meaning "writing about whores;" defining it has stumped modern courts and societies; the visible depiction of erotic behavior, often including acts of sexual activity in violation of law; see Chapter 10.

post hoc — from Latin, literally, "after this." See fallacies; Chapter 5.

poverty — the condition of being poor due to the lack of possession of certain living standards such as quality housing, goods or money.

prima facie — from Latin, "at first sight;" obvious meaning adequate to establish fact unless refuted.

private property — goods, land, structures owned by private individuals or corporations.

profession — a vocation that has codified its values and strives to enforce them among those who participate in that vocation.

professional ethics — the standards or codes of conduct adopted formally by a group of persons practicing the same vocation.

production — the process of making things by human action in industry or art; see Chapter 14.

proposition — a basic thought; see Chapter 5.

proprietary information — information and trade secrets belonging to a person or corporation.

punishment — from the Latin, *poine*, meaning "penalty;" the intended infliction of non-pleasurable feelings or activity upon a person, by an appropriate authority, sometimes including acts of pain, the denial of liberty and even the taking of life (capital punishment) — as a result of a the peron violating a law, code or other set of standards.

R

realpolitik — referring to the view that substantive moral principles cannot be applied to disputes between nations.

red herring — see fallacies, Chapter 5.

redistribution — a system for reallocating wealth among members of a society.

recycling — the notion of reusing materials and substances so as not to deplete naturally occurring resources that produce those materials and substances.

republicanism — the theory that denies that people are only what they choose to be; see Chapter 14.

retentionist — a person who opposes abolition of capital punishment; also one who supported slavery; see also abolitionist.

retribution — the act of imposing a penalty upon someone convicted of immoral behavior

right — correct moral judgment producing actions that are deemed consistent with a moral philosophy .

right to die — the notion that persons have state-sanctioned authority to make choices affecting the length of their life.

right of privacy — the notion, explicit in some state constitutions, that each individual has a legal right prohibiting invasion of a person's home or personal life.

rule-utilitarianism — a subset of utilitarianism in which the guiding principle is the value of a determining rule and whether that rule works *only* if it is *generally* applied; i.e., does it *always* produce happiness for *all* parties?

rules — established guidelines and procedures for guiding human conduct.

S

self-realization — a moral philosophy in which the goal is acting in ways to develop one's own human potential.

sex — the essential maleness or femaleness of a human being; also, commonly used to refer to sexual intercourse and even to acts of petting and foreplay in anticipation of intercourse.

sexism — discrimination based on whether a person is a male or female.

sexual harassment — acts or pattern of acts discriminating against an individual on the basis of sex.

sin — the violation of a Divine Command, an evil or wicked wrongdoing

situational ethics — determining what is right or good solely on the basis of the momentary context; implying that what is right or good today in this situation may not be right tomorrow in another set of circumstances.

slippery slope — see fallacies, Chapter 5.

socialism — the economic system in which the means for producing and distributing goods is owned by society, all of whom share in its operation.

sodomy — performing oral and-or anal sex with another person.

suicide — death brought about by one's own premeditated action.

Sunshine Amendment — an amendment to the Florida Constitution causing public officials to disclose personal finances, declaring public meetings and records open to the public, prohibiting certain actions by former officials; when adopted it codified the notion of "open government" in the state.

surrogate — a substitute, usually referring to those who stand in for actions that need to be taken by a member.

syllogism — two statements followed by a third that is conclusionary.

T

Talmud — foremost among sacred scriptures of Judaism, a body of religious laws including the Mishnah and Gemara, relied upon by Jewish adherents for faith and practice.

taxation — fees or charges levied by a government upon residents of a state or nation.

teleological ethics — the notion that moral decisions are constituted by actions aimed at pleasure, self-realization and happiness.

terrorism — planned violent acts against persons that evoke fear, usually causing death.

Times vs. Sullivan — a landmark U.S. Supreme Court ruling involving libel law, which essentially holds that legal protections against libel do not apply to the lives of public officials; see libel..

truth — objectively accurate statements, always applicable.

U

utilitarianism — a subset of consequentialism in which the guiding principle is to always act in order to produce the most pleasure-fulfillment-happiness for the greatest number of people; prime advocates include Jeremy Bentham and John Stuart Mill; see Chapter 3.

V

variable — a modification to a proposition; see Chapter 5.

veil of ignorance — a philosophical concept assuming that persons can operate morally without understanding all the implications of their actions.

virginity — the quality of human sexuality prior to ever having sexual intercourse.

virtue — from Latin *virtus*, literally lionizing "manhood," a single term conveying all the qualities comprising excellence in human beings.

W

war — a formal declaration of armed conflict by a sovereign nation against another nation; also, a condition of aggression between populations in which disputed claims, usually of territory, are pursued by systematic and violent means.

water pollution — the unnatural degradation of water on the Earth.

whistle-blowing — bringing into public view the neglectful or abusive practices of an employer that threaten the public interest.

INDEX

Platonic ethics, 73
   sexual ethic, 282
   on violence, 427
Authority, fallacious appeal to, 156
Autobiography, 48-49, 52
Autonomy, 81-82, 119
   incompetent patient treatment decisions, 231
   patients' rights, 223-224, 252, 256-259
   sexual ethics, 290
Ayer, A. J., 94

Bait-and-switch, 634
Bakker, James, 303
Basic rights, 481
Bearak, Barry, 602-604
Beccaria, C., 366
Bellah, Robert, 461
Bellamy vs. Mason's Stores, Inc., 607
Belmont Report, 266
Bendix Corporation, 612-613
Benevolence, 83, 354, 665-666
Bentham, Jeremy, 57, 88-91, 366
Berger, Fred, 338
Bernard, Claude, 264
Berns, Walter, 365-370
Bible, 79
Biomedical ethics, 245-247
   abortion, *See* Abortion
   challenges to Hippocratic tradition, 250-251
   confidentiality, 247-248, 261-263
   conflicts of interest, 251
   consent and, *See* Informed consent
   disclosure standards, 258-259
   fidelity principle, 259-261
   genetic engineering, 272-274
   Hippocratic ethics, *See* Hippocratic Oath
   innovative therapy, 264
   life and death decisions, *See* Death and dying,
   medical treatment issues
   modern ethical codes, 249-250, 251-252
   non-professional traditions, 252-253
   Nuremberg code, 264-265
   organ transplantation, 267-271
   patient autonomy, 223-224, 256-259. *See also*
   Patients' rights
   patient competence, *See* Incompetent patients
   physician decision-making authority, 236, 241-242
   professional standard of consent, 258
   research, 251-252, 263-267. *See also* Research ethics
   resource allocation, 270-272
   utilitarianism, 265, 266
   veracity principle, 254-256
   See also Professional ethics
Birth control, 247, 265, 286, 293
Black war veterans, 587
Blackmun, Harry A., 175
Blame, 360
Blanchard, Kenneth, 506-507
Board of directors, 525-530
Bouvia, Elizabeth, 219, 221, 241

Bowdlers, 315
"Boys will be boys" standard, 286-287
Brain, and definitions of death, 217-219
Bribery, 21, 23, 525
   definition, 554
   Russian government corruption, 27
British legal history, pornography, 317
British Medical Association code of ethics, 261-262, 263
Brock Candy Company, 510-511
Brutus, Marcus Junius, 145
Buber, Martin, 669
Buckley vs. Valeo, 657, 658
Buddhism, 107
Bundy, Theodore, 328
Bureaucratization, and moral responsibility, 521-524
Burns, Haydon, 651
Business, defined, 491
Business cycles, 466
Business ethics, 489-491, 575-578
   accountability, 495-497, 504-506
   board of directors and, 525-530
   case histories, 507-511
   codes for, 681-692. *See also* Ethics codes
   communications, *See* Communications issues
   conflicts of interest, 670-671
   consistency standards, 54-55
   corporate culture, 501-507, 684
   definitions, 491-492
   "Ethics check", 492
   ethics planning program, 547-549
   insider trading, 554-555
   leadership, 503-504, 511-516
   levels of ethical behavior, 490
   motivational principles, 506-507
   nepotism, 554, 557
   pollution, 398
   profit vs., 639-640
   self-interested motivations, 59
   senior management, 525-530
   sexual relationships, 612-613
   shareholder roles, 529-530
   social audit, 499-500
   social responsibility, 532-538. *See also* Corporate
     responsibilities
   stockholder/stakeholder models, 498
   structural considerations, 494-495, 502-503
   See also Employee issues; Professional ethics
Butler, Joseph, 82-83, 91

Cable TV, 325
Caesar, Julius, 145
Callicles, 70
Camp, Josef, 215-216
Campaign finance, 655-661, 699
Camus, Albert, 367, 369
Capen, Richard G., Jr., 575-578
Capitalism, 463-468
   arguments for and against, 466-468
   defined, 464
   Marx on, 464-466

freedom of speech, 539, 542-543
government workers, 535-536, 563, 661,
698-701. *See also* Public office
insider trading, 554-555
model code of ethics, 558-560
participatory management, 504-505, 557
personnel decisions, 557-558
privacy, 543-544, 568-572
quality of life, 544-545
rights, 538-541, 556, 558-562, 567-568
sexual relationships, 612-613
surveillance, 543, 571-572
termination, 540-542, 570
testing and evaluation, 557, 608-610
whistle-blowing, *See* Whistle-blowing
Employment testing, 608-610
Engineers, ethics code for, 714
Entitlements, 475-477
Entitlement theory, 451-455, 459, 462
compatibility with economic systems, 468
Lockean proviso, 451-452
poverty in, 453-454
Environmental impact statement, 499, 527
Environmental issues, 379-381
acid rain, 396-397
air pollution, 391-399, 410-411
CFCs (chlorofluorocarbons), 380, 391-395
Charlestown leak, 407-409
civilizational relationships, 385-386
corporate obligations, 498-500
deforestation, 387-389
developed vs. developing countries, 386-387
Exxon Valdez oil spill, 404-407
global warming, 381-384
legal history, 409-411
nuclear energy, 399-401
ozone layer depletion, 390-395, 409-410
pesticides, 380, 412-413
solid waste and recycling, 401-403
species diversity and extinction, 389-390
sustainability, 413-414
water pollution, 403-409, 540
whistle-blowing safeguards, 540. *See also*
Whistle-blowing
Environmental Protection Agency (EPA), 410
Equal Employment and Opportunity Commission
(EEOC), 593-594
Equal Pay Act of 1963, 596-597
Equivocation, 154
Essay on Population (Malthus), 477
Ethical egoism, *See* Egoism
Ethical naturalism, 95-96
Ethics:
benefits of, 61-62
defined, 491
law and, 60, 680
levels of, 490
meta-ethics, 93-94
sources of, 5-7
Ethics Check, 492

Ethics codes:
advertising agencies, 712-713
Alcoa, 508
AMA, 249, 252, 256, 261-263, 496, 695
American Bar Association, 496
American Nurses' Association, 252, 716
behavioral context, 684
British Medical Association, 261-262, 263
Clinton proposed code, 25
corporate codes, 681-682
corporate culture and, 684
Cummins Engine Company, 507-508
Declaration of Geneva, 249-250, 262
defined, 680
design and implementation of, 691-692
Dunckel program for development of, 547-549
Eckerd Corporation, 508
effective characteristics of, 686-687
effectiveness of, 684-685, 695-696
enforcement, 548, 690, 696-698
engineers, 714
ethical levels of, 681, 686-689, 697
evaluation of, 697
Florida law, 718-724. *See also* Florida Commission
on Ethics
government and public service, 26, 563, 661, 698-701
Hippocratic, *See* Hippocratic Oath
Islamic Code of Medical Ethics, 253
Johnson & Johnson, 682, 707
laws vs., 680
management support for, 690
Mary Kay Cosmetics, 707-708
Merrill Lynch, 708-711
Nuremberg Code, 251-252, 266
pervasiveness of, 683
professional codes, 693-698
public relations, 643-644
reasons for creating, 683
United Technologies Corporation,, 558-560
variability of, 680-681
whistle-blowing in, 701
Ethics history, 67-83. *See also* Exemplars;
particular philosophers and philosophies
Ethics in Government Act of 1978, 659
Eudaimonia, 74
Euthanasia, *See* Mercy killing
Euthanasia Educational Council, 232-233
Euthyphro dialogue (Plato), 71-73
Evidence, 358, 361
Ewing, David, 555
Exemplars:
consequentialism, 88
in critical thinking, 49-53
deontology, 86
Divine Command theory, 78
Egoism, 69
natural law, 76
self-realization, 71
See also specific moral philosophies
Existentialism, 96

Intuit Inc., 579-583
Intuition, 87, 94
Investment industry, 516-517
Invincible ignorance, 156-157
Iran-Contra scandal, 623
Islam, 80-81
    medical ethics, 216, 253
Islamic Code of Medical Ethics, 253

Jacobelles vs. Ohio, 320
Japan, 24, 26
    definitions of death, 217
    organizational culture, 505-506
    patients' rights movement, 257
Jefferson, Thomas, 59, 117
Jesus Christ, 60, 77, 79, 93
Jewish ethics:
    business ethics, 639
    exemplars, 51
    medical ethics, 251-253
    sexuality, 282, 283, 286
Job descriptions, 502, 557
Job discrimination, *See* Discrimination
Job testing, 557, 608-610
Johnson, Earvin "Magic", 306
Johnson & Johnson Corporation, 681-682, 707
Josephson, Michael, 497
Josephson Institute, 662-663
Journalism:
    code of ethics, 714-718
    ethical communications, 628
    libel law, 625
    See also Communications issues; News media
Joyce, James, 319
Justice:
    Aristotle on, 450
    and care, 130-131, 137
    Classical Republicanism, 458-462
    Kohlberg model, 124-130
    law and, 59
    moral development, 124-131, 137-138
    public administration ethics, 666-667
    Rawls' theory, 455-458
    research ethics, 266-267
    stages of, 119
    See also Distributive justice
Just wages, 469
Just war theory, 426-432

Kant, Immanuel, 56, 86-87, 100-106, 669
    a priori reasoning, 150
    on good, 87, 100, 103-104
    on truth, 255
    on violence, 221, 424
Kantianism:
    Golden Kantian Consequentialism, 662
    Hippocratic tradition vs., 251
    world hunger alleviation, 481

See also Deontological ethics
Keating, Charles, 15, 19
Keating Five, 15
Keeling, Charles D., 381
Kennedy, John F., 22
Kevorkian, Jack, 220, 227
Kickbacks, 554
Kidney dialysis machines, 272
Kidney transplants, 270
Kierkegaard, Soren, 141-142
Killing, medical ethics of, 220-225, 229-230, 233.
    See also Abortion; Capital punishment
Kilpatrick, William, 6
King, Martin Luther, Jr., 11, 58, 127, 129, 137
    on law, 353
    Letter From The Birmingham Jail, 129, 705-707
King, Rodney, 420
King vs. Palmer, 613
Kinsey reports, 284
Kirk, Claude Roy, Jr., 651-652
Kissinger, Henry, 426
Knowledge, 44
Koestler, Arthur, 370-375
Kohlberg, Lawrence, moral development theory of, 120, 126-130
    conventional stage, 120-122, 124
    "Heinz" story, 123, 132
    postconventional stage, 120-122, 125-126
    preconventional stage, 120-124
Koop, C. Everett, 337
Koran, 80-81
Kouzes, James M., 511-515
Krugman, Paul R., 615-616
Kuwait War, 397-398, 430, 431, 435-445

Labor Theory of Value, 465
Labor unions, 539, 604-607, 610-611
Laissez-faire, 464, 524
Landers, Robert K., 239-242
Language, 84
    ambiguity, 154-155
    human problems in, 37-38
    meta-ethics, 93
    meta-language, 110
    Sophists and, 68-70
Lauter, David, 602-604
Lavoisier, Antoine, 42
Law, 58-60
    ethics codes vs., 680
    Greek philosophy, 69
    Kohlberg moral development model, 124-125
    morality and, 352-353
Lawyers:
    attorney-client confidentiality, 19, 696
    peer review, 495-496
    See also Professional ethics
Leadership, 503-504, 511-515
Learning, 42-43
Lesbian lifestyles, 288, 308
Letter From The Birmingham Jail (King), 129, 705-707
Liability, product warranties and, 524-525

faulty reasoning processes, 149-151, 154-162. *See also* Fallacies

Josephson five-step model, 663

logic, 148-149, 154-162

validity test, 153

See also Critical thinking

Moral virtue, *See* Virtue

Morton Thiokol, 692-693, 701

Motivation, ethical principles for, 506-507

Motives, 115-116, 121

Multinational corporations, 560

Mutual assured destruction, 432

Mystery shoppers, 566

NAACP, 609

Natanson, Irma, 257

National Association for the Advancement of Colored People (NAACP), 609

National Coalition Against Censorship (NCAC), 337

National Endowment of the Arts (NEA), 325

National interest, 424-425

National Organization of Women (NOW), 284

Naturalistic fallacy, 95

Natural law, 76, 78

medical ethics, 253

sexual ethics, 283

suicide and, 221

Natural rights, 450-451

NBC News, 628

Negation, 148

Neo-Malthusianism, 477-479

Nepotism, 13-14, 554, 557, 721

News media:

conflicts of interest, 9-10, 16-18

plagiarism, 17-18

privacy rights vs., 9-10

Nicomachean Ethics (Aristotle), 74, 76, 99-100, 460

Nietzsche, Frederick Wilhelm, 351

Nixon, Richard, 657

Noncognitivism, 94, 95, 96

Nonviolent resistance, 423

Noonan, John, 179, 198-202

Normative ethics, 93, 96

North, Oliver, 623

Northrop Corporation, 525

Nozick, Robert, 451-454456

Nuclear disarmament, 434-435

Nuclear energy, 399-401

Nuclear war, 432-435

Nuclear waste, 400

Nun In Her Smock, The (Curl), 317

Nuremberg Code, 251-252, 264-265

Nurses, ethics code for, 252, 716

Obedience, 120, 123

Obscenity, defined, 316. *See also* Pornography

Odyssey (Homer), 107

Official values, 664-668

Oil spills, 404-407

Oil well fires, 397-398

Open marriage, 299

Operation Just Cause, 429-430

Oregon, Medicaid rationing in, 271-272

Organic organizations, 504-505

Organizational culture, *See* Corporate culture

Organized crime, 336-337

Organ transplantation, 267-271

allocation, 270-271

procurement, 268-270

Original sin, 80

Osgood, Donald, 143

Outing, 304-305

Overpopulation, 477-481

Ozone, as pollutant, 395-396, 411

Ozone hole, 392

Ozone layer depletion, 390-395, 409-410

Pacifica Foundation, 323

Pacifism, 423-424

Packwood, Robert, 303, 304

PACs, 21, 656

Pain:

medical treatment ethics, 224-225. *See also* Death and dying, medical treatment issues

and moral development, 113

utilitarian model, 57

Panama, U.S. invasion of, 429-430

Paradigm, 358

Parental consent, to abortion, 197

Paris Adult Theater, 322

Participatory management, 504-505, 557

Partnership agreements, 54-55

Patients' rights, 250

autonomy, 223-224, 231, 252, 256-259

Bill of rights, 252

confidentiality, 261-263

consent, 256-258. *See also* Informed consent

fidelity principle, 259-261

incompetent patients, 231

veracity principle, 254-256

Peale, Norman Vincent, 506-507

Peer review, 495-496

Pee-wee Herman, 302-303

Percival, Thomas, 264

Perry, William, 142-143

Persian Gulf War, 397-398, 430, 431, 435-445

Persistent vegetative state, 218, 232, 237

Personal development, *See* Moral development

Personhood:

bioethical questions, 246

in death definitions, 218

definition of, 177-181

fetal status, 175-181, 198-202

liberal conception of, 462

Pesticides, 380, 412-413

Phelan, John W., Jr., 516

Piaget, Jean, 119

Pickering decision, 543

Placebos, 266

Plagiarism, 7, 17-18

decision models, 661-669
ethical systems, 669
ethics codes, 698-701
Florida ethics law, 29-32, 653, 659-661
Florida state politics, 649-655, 659-660
gifts laws, 672-674
influence from former positions, 24-25
integrity issues, 651-652, 658-659, 665
lobbyists and, 2, 25, 700, 721
Merrill Lynch ethics code, 711
"moral mazes" and "management mischief", 661-662
official values, 664-668
standard of conduct (1986), 26
Public relations, 633-634, 643-644
Publix Supermarkets, 509
Punishment, 351-352
    abolitionist arguments, 354-357
    consequentialist views, 356-363
    death penalty, 364-375. *See also* Capital punishment
    deontological views, 355-357, 360-363
    deterrence effects, 357, 359, 360, 364, 370-375
    educational function, 359
    mandatory life sentences, 364, 365
    mental illness and, 356
    retentionist arguments, 357-363
    retributivism, 360-361
    retroactive, 352
    sentencing inconsistencies, 364-365
Pythagoreanism, 248

Quality circles, 544-545,
Quality of life, 537, 544-546
Quinlan, Karen, 230-231, 232

Race norming, 598
Racism, 87
    capital punishment and, 364-365
    personhood definitions and, 177
    "Three Realities" report, 601
    See also Discrimination
Racist organizations, 607
Rainbow Curriculum, 308
Rainforests, 389-390
Ramsey, Paul, 240
Rape, 185, 290-291, 329
Raspberry, William, 7
Rationalism, 77-78
Rationality, 459-460
Rawls, John, 50, 92-93, 149, 151, 455-458
Realpolitik, 424-425
Reason, 71, 73, 101
    Kant on, 101, 105-106
Reasonable person standard, 259
Recombinant DNA, 273
Record keeping, 559
Recycling, 402-403
Red herring fallacy, 157
Redeeming social value, 319-320, 323
Reflective experience, 38
Regressive taxes, 471

Rehabilitation Act of 1973, 595-596
Reiss, Ira, 287, 291
Religious ethics, *See* Christian ethics; Divine
    Command theory; Jewish ethics; Roman Catholic
    ethics
Reno, Janet, 653
Required request, 269
Required response, 270
Research, defined, 263
Research ethics, 252-253
    Nuremberg Code, 251-252
    Tuskegee syphilis study, 265
Resuscitation, 228, 240, 241-242
Retribution, 367, 368, 450
Retributivism, 360-361
Retroactive punishment, 352
Reubens, Paul, 302-303
Reverse discrimination, 602-604, 615
Rewarded gifting, 269
Right action, 86
Rights:
    basic, 481
    decision-making models, 661
    to die, *See* Death and dying, medical treatment issues
    of employees, 556, 558-562, 567-568
    fetus vs. mother, 182-186
    human rights, 91-92, 253, 481-482
    natural, 450-451
    UN Universal Declaration, 253, 481-482
    utilitarianism and, 91-92
Roe vs. Wade, 176, 195-196
Role models, 305-306
Roman Catholic ethics:
    business ethics, 639-640
    medical ethics, 226, 233, 239-240, 253
    pornography, 338
    sexual ethics, 282-283, 286, 303
    See also Aquinas, St. Thomas; Augustine, Saint;
    Christian ethics
Ross, W. D., 94, 255
Roth vs. United States, 319
Rousseau, Jean Jacques, 669
RU 486, 198
Ruckelshaus, William D., 413-414
Rule-based ethics, 60-61, 81
Rule-utilitarianism, 89-90
Russell, Bertrand, 148
Russia, 27

Sacramento Municipal Utility District (SMUD), 40
Safety, 50
    drug testing and, 573
    employee obligations, 558
    whistle-blowing, 539
Sales tax, 473
Sartre, Jean-Paul, 96, 153
Savings and loan scandal, 12, 15, 19
Schafly, Phyllis, 305
Schmidt, Warren, 495
Scientific research, *See* Research ethics

Scientific testing, 38
Sea-level rise, 383-384
Secularism, 97
Secularization, 83-84
Segregation, 87
Self-consciousness, 177
Self-defense, 429-430
Self-interest:
    Hobbes on, 82-83
    and moral development, 118
    See also Egoism
Self-love, 82-83
Self-realization, 68, 71, 73-74, 78-79
Senior management:
    corporate responsibility and, 525-530
    income for, 473-474
Seniority rules, 606-607, 611
Sentience, 177-178, 180
Sex crimes, 326-327, 329
Sex discrimination, 596-597, 611-616
    pornography as, 332
    separate but equal treatment, 607
    See also Discrimination
Sex selection, 191-195
Sex therapy, 285
Sexual ethics, 281-282
    celibacy, 301-302
    and children, 324-325, 333-336, 341
    consent, 289-292
    critical thinking example, 46-47
    disease risks, 292-293, 296
    extramarital affairs, 89, 90, 282, 298-300, 306
    gender double standards, 286-287
    history of, 282-285
    legal aspects, 294
    love, 284, 287-288, 299, 341
    media sex and violence, 38-39
    modern religious morality, 286
    non-affectionate relationships, 288-289, 341
    obligations within relationships, 300-302
    pregnancy risks, 293
    professional relationships, 8-9, 291, 306
    public/private behavior, 281
    utilitarian moral reasoning, 89, 90
    workplace relationships, 612-613
    See also Pornography
Sexual harassment, 116-117, 290, 303, 594, 611-612
Sexually transmitted diseases, 265-266, 292-293. *See also*
    AIDS
Sexual Offenses Act of 1967, 294
Sexual revolution, 39, 284-285
Shareholders, 526, 529, 530
Shareware, 630
Sharpless, Jesse, 318
Shaw, William, 566-567
Sherman Antitrust Act, 496
Sherwood Rowland, F., 391, 393
Shue, Henry, 481
Sickle cell testing, 571
Silent Spring (Carson), 380, 412-413

Simons, L., 341-344
Sin, 80
Singer, Peter, 480
Site-licensing, 632
Situational ethics, 9, 150-151, 306
Slavery, 117
Slavin, Robert J., 168-169
Slippery slope, 155, 203
Small groups, 502-503
Smith, Adam, 56, 69, 463, 524
Smog, 396
Sociability, 459-461
Social audit, 499-500
Social contract, see Contracts
Socialist systems, 464-468
Social responsibility, 498-499
    alleviation of hunger, 480-481
    of business, 532-538. *See also* Corporate
        responsibilities
Social responsiveness, 535
Social Security number, 569
Socioeconomic status, 28, 599-602, 615-616.
        See also Poverty
Sociopathic personality, 116
Socrates, 68-73
Sodomy, legal status of, 294
Software, 29-30, 628-632
Solid waste, 401-403
Solomon, 138
Sophists, 68-70, 94
Soul, 97
South Carolina legislature, 21
Soviet Oath for Physicians, 253
Species diversity, 389-390
Speciesism, 177
Spiritual development, 62
Spock, Benjamin, 285
Stakeholder model, 498, 530-532
Standard argument forms, 159-161
Stanley vs. Georgia, 320-321
Star Wars program, 432-433
Statistical correlation, fallacious use of, 156
Steele vs. Louisville & Nashville Railroad
    Company et al, 604
Stereotypes, 158
Stevenson, Charles, 94
Stilwell, Paul, 589-590
Stockholder model, 498, 530-532
Stoicism, 76, 78, 148
Stories, 48-49, 118
Straight gays, 288
Strategic Defense Initiative (SDI), 432-433
Straw man fallacy, 157
Subjunctive conditionals, 474
Substituted judgement, 232
Suicide, 150, 221
    arguments against, 221
    doctor-assisted, 220-221
Sumner, Wayne, 180
Sunshine Amendment, 653, 659-661, 715-722

Supreme Court, *See* United States Supreme Court decisions
Surplus value, 465
Surrogate mothers, 246
Surveillance, 543, 571-572
Sustainability, 413-414
Swaggart, Jimmy, 303
Syllogism, 159
Syphilis research, 265-266

Tailhook scandal, 290
Taoism, 60
Task teams, 502-503
Taxation, 471-473
    capitalist and socialist principles, 467
    egalitarian theory, 459
    entitlement theory, 451, 454
    reform, 653
Teleologism, 88
Telephone surveillance, 543, 571
Temptation to dishonor, 14
Ten Commandments, 84
Teresa, Mother, 11, 137
Testing, 608-610
Texas Gulf Sulphur, 554-555
Theory of Justice, A (Rawls), 455-458
Therapeutic privilege, 254-255
Thomas, Clarence, 611-612, 615
Thomson, Judith Jarvis, 183-186, 202-211
Three Mile Island nuclear accident, 400
"Three Realities" report, 599-602
Times vs. Sullivan, 626
Tobacco advertising, 635
Tower, John, 648
Training, employee ethics, 690
Transplantation of organs, 267-271
Truth:
    ethical communications, 634, 640-641
    Kant on, 86-87, 104, 255
    medical ethics, 254-256
    utilitarian approach, 95
TRW Inc., 541, 571
Tylenol tampering incident, 681-682, 685

Ulysses (Joyce), 319
Understanding, in critical thinking model, 44-45
Unemployment, 465-466
Uniform anatomical gift Act, 268-269
Unions, 539, 604-607, 610-611
United Nations Universal Declaration of Human Rights,
    253, 481-482
United States Agency for International Development
    (AID), 388
United States Supreme Court decisions:
    abortion, 175, 176, 195-198
    affirmative action, 604
    campaign finance reform, 657
    capital punishment, 364
    commercial status of professionals, 496
    drug testing, 555
    employee free speech, 543

    job testing, 608-609
    libel, 626
    pornography, 319-325
    privacy rights, 468
    sex discrimination, 614
United Technologies Corporation,, 558-560
Unplanned pregnancies, 293
Urine tests, *See* Drug testing
Ury, William, 46
Utilitarianism, 57, 88-90, 362
    consequentialist exemplar, 88
    contractarian interpretation, 92-93
    distributive justice theory, 462
    human rights in, 91-92
    medical research ethics, 265, 266
    poverty alleviation, 480
    virtue theory, 97
Utility Principle, 88, 89, 91, 95-96

Validity, 153, 159-161, 164-166
Value:
    Labor Theory of, 465
    statements, 361-362
    surplus, 465
Values, 36
    corporate culture development, 506
    cultural relativism, 150
    decision-making models, 661
    ethical naturalism, 95
    expression of, 38
    integration of, 51-52
    official, 664-668
Vance, Carole, 333
Variables, 148
VCR model, 662
Vegetative state, 218, 232, 237
Veil of ignorance, 50, 149, 151, 456
Vengeance, 361
Veracity principle, 254-256
Virtue:
    Aquinas on, 79
    Greek philosophy, 68, 73, 74-75
    intellectual, 75
    intelligence as, 98
    modern theories, 96-98

Wachtler, Sol, 303
Wages, 558
Walesa, Lech, 575
Wallace, George, 654
Walton, Sam, 512
War, 419-420
    civilian casualties, 422, 432
    crimes, 523
    definitions, 420, 426-427
    first-strike theory, 430-431
    Gulf War arguments, 435-445
    international standards, 426
    "just war" theory, 426-432
    militarism, 422-423